3-95

GW00702904

Longman Pocket Companion Series

Pocket Companion

English Dictionary

Longman

Longman Group Limited,
Longman House, Burnt Mill, Harlow,
Essex CM20 2JE, England
and Associated Companies throughout the world.

© Merriam-Webster Inc. and Longman Group Limited 1983
All rights reserved ; no part of this publication
may be reproduced, stored in a retrieval system,
or transmitted in any form or by any means, electronic,
mechanical, photocopying, recording, or otherwise,
without the prior written permission of the Publishers.

First published 1983
ISBN 0 582 55690 2

British Library Cataloguing in Publication Data

English dictionary.—(Longman pocket companion series)
   1.   English language—Dictionaries
   423   PE1625

   ISBN 0-582-55690-2

Set in 6/6½pt. Times

Printed in Great Britain
by Wm. Clowes Ltd
Beccles & London

Introduction

Here is a dictionary which is an ideal pocket-sized companion for all those who like to have a ready guide to the rich and ever-changing English language.

The material has been carefully selected from Longman's extensive dictionary database, and then revised and updated to tailor it to suit this popular Pocket Companion Series.

Definitions are written clearly and concisely, and the International Phonetic Alphabet (IPA) is used to represent the pronunciation of every main entry in the dictionary. The form of British speech (accent) that is represented is called 'Received Pronunciation' and is the kind of English which is common among educated speakers in England.

Certain conventions have been adopted in the writing of this dictionary, and these are explained below.

1. Order of Entries
Main entries (headwords) are printed in bold type and arranged in alphabetical order, whether they are single words, hyphenated words, or compounds consisting of two or more individual words.

2. Undefined Entries
Words whose meaning can easily be guessed from their related headword are not given in definitions. They follow the main entry and are shown in the following ways:

a Where the undefined word is the same as the main entry (but has a different part of speech) it appears at the end of the definition followed by its part of speech.

b Where the main entry forms a stem to which an ending is added to form the undefined word, the stem is represented by a ∼ followed by the ending:

eg **content** *adj* ... ∼ **ment** *n*

c Where any part of the main entry forms the stem of an undefined entry, the unchanged part is represented by a –.

eg **indifferent** *adj* ... **–ence** *n*

Occasionally no shortening of the undefined entry is possible and it is thereafter given in full.

3. Form of Entries
Information about the entry is set out after the headword in the following manner:

3.1 Variants
If a headword has an alternative spelling, this is shown following the headword. If the variant is an infrequent one, it is preceded by the word *also*.

3.2 Pronunciation

IPA pronunciation symbols follow the headword and are enclosed within slash marks / /. The symbols used are as follows:

Consonants			*Vowels*	
symbol	key word		symbol	key word
b	*b*ack		æ	b*a*d
d	*d*ay		ɑː	p*a*lm
ð	*th*en		ɒ	p*o*t
ʤ	*j*ump		aɪ	b*i*te
f	*f*ew		aʊ	n*ow*
g	*g*ay		aɪə	t*ire*
h	*h*ot		aʊə	t*ow*er
j	*y*et		ɔː	c*augh*t
k	*k*ey		ɔɪ	b*oy*
l	*l*ed		ɔɪə	empl*oyer*
m	su*m*		e	b*e*d
n	su*n*		eə	th*ere*
ŋ	su*ng*		eɪ	m*a*ke
p	*p*en		eɪə	pl*ayer*
r	*r*ed		ə	*a*bout
s	*s*oon		əʊ	n*o*te
ʃ	fi*sh*ing		əʊə	l*ow*er
t	*t*ea		ɜː	b*ir*d
tʃ	*ch*eer		i	prett*y*
θ	*th*ing		iː	sh*ee*p
v	*v*iew		ɪ	sh*i*p
w	*w*et		ɪə	h*ere*
z	*z*ero		uː	b*oo*t
ʒ	plea*s*ure		ʊ	p*u*t
			ʊe	p*oor*
			ʌ	c*u*t

Certain additional special signs are also used:

/ˈ/	shows main stress
/ˌ/	shows secondary stress
/r/	at the end of a word means that /r/ is pronounced when the next word begins with a vowel sound
/ɪ̯/	means that either /ɪ/ or /ə/ may be used
/ə/	means that /ə/ may or may not be used.

3.3 Part of Speech

The part of speech of the headword is shown in the following way:

adjective	*adj*
adverb	*adv*
conjunction	*conj*
interjection	*interj*
noun	*n*
preposition	*prep*
pronoun	*pron*
verb	*v*

Headwords that the editors have reason to believe constitute trademarks have been described as such. However, neither the presence nor absence of such description should be regarded as affecting the legal status of any trademark.

3.4 Other Information
Various other kinds of information are given following the part of speech. These include irregular inflections or plurals, feminine forms, whether the word is sometimes capitalized, whether the word belongs to a specific variety of English, or whether it is obsolete. Where such information refers only to a particular sense of a word, it follows the sense number (see 2.5).

3.5 Sense Division
The main senses of a headword are numbered (1, 2, 3, etc.) where there is more than one sense. Subdivisions of the senses are distinguished by lower-case letters, and further subdivisions by bracketed numerals.

Those senses that would be understood anywhere in the English-speaking world are shown first, in their historical order: the older senses before the newer. After these come the meanings whose usage is restricted in some way (eg because they are used in only one area, or have gone out of current use).

3.6 Notes on Usage
Notes on usage usually follow the definition, separated by a – . These show levels of usage, eg slang, vulgar, formal, etc.

When such a note applies to all or several meanings of a word, it follows the last definition, and is introduced by the word *USE*.

Abbreviations

The following abbreviations are used in this dictionary:

abbr abbreviation	**naut** nautical
AD Anno Domini	**neg** negative
adj adjective	**neut** neuter
adv adverb	**NZ** New Zealand
apprec appreciative	**obs** obsolete
approx approximate/ly	**orig** original/ly
arch archaic	**part** participle
attrib attributive	**pass** passive
BC before Christ	**perf** perfect
Br British	**pers** person
c century	**phr** phrase
C Celsius, centigrade	**pl** plural
cap capital/ized	**pp** past participle
cm centimetre	**prep** preposition
compar comparative	**pres** present
conj conjunction	**pron** pronoun
constr construction	**pron** pronunciation
derog derogatory	**prp** present participle
dial dialect	**refl** reflexive
E East/ern	**rel** relative
eg for example	**S** south/ern
Eng English, England	**sby** somebody
esp especially	**Scot** Scotland, Scottish
etc etcetera	**sing** singular
euph euphemistic	**specif** specifically
F Fahrenheit	**sthg** something
fem feminine	**subj** subjunctive
ie that is	**substand** substandard
imper imperative	**superl** superlative
indef indefinite	**tech** technical
indic indicative	**UK** United Kingdom
infin infinitive	**US** United States
infml informal	**USA** United States of
interj interjection	America
interrog interrogative	**usu** usually
irreg irregular/ly	**v** verb
journ journalistic	**var** variant
lat latitude	**vulg** vulgar
long longitude	**W** West/ern
n noun	**WWI** World War 1
N north/ern	**WWII** World War 2

A

a /eɪ/ *n, pl* **a's, as** *often cap* **1a** (a graphic representation of or device for reproducing) the 1st letter of the English alphabet **b** a speech counterpart of written *a* **2** one designated *a*, esp as the 1st in order or class **3** a grade rating a student's work as superior

a *indefinite article* **1** one – used before singular nouns when the referent is unspecified (e g *a* sheep) and before number collectives and some numbers (e g *a* great many) **2** the same (e g birds of *a* feather) **3a**(1) any (e g *a* bike has 2 wheels) (2) one single (e g can't see *a* thing) **b** one particular (e g health is *a* good thing) **c** – used before the gerund or infinitive of a verb to denote a period or occurrence of the activity concerned (e g *a* good cry) **4** – used before a proper name to denote (1) membership of a class (e g born *a* Romanov) (2) resemblance (e g *a* little Hitler) (3) one named but not otherwise known (e g *a* Dr Smith) **5** – used before a pair of items to be considered as a unit (e g *a* collar and tie) *USE* used before words or letter sequences with an initial consonant sound

a *prep* **1** per **2** *chiefly dial* on, in, at *USE* used before words or letter sequences with an initial consonant sound

A /eɪ/ *n or adj* (a film that is) certified in Britain as suitable for all ages but requiring parental guidance for children under 14

A1 *adj* **1** *of a ship* having the highest possible classification of seaworthiness for insurance purposes **2** of the finest quality; first-rate

abandon /ə'bændən/ *v* **1** to give up completely, esp with the intention of never resuming or reclaiming **2** to leave, often in the face of danger **3** to forsake or desert (e g a responsibility) **4** to give (oneself) over *to* an emotion or activity – ~ment *n*

abbey /'æbi/ *n* **1a** a religious community governed by an abbot or abbess **2** the buildings, esp the church, of a (former) monastery

abbreviate /ə'briːvieɪt/ *v* to reduce to a shorter form – **-ation** *n*

abdicate /'æbdɪkeɪt/ *v* **1** to relinquish (e g sovereign power) formally **2** to renounce a throne, dignity, etc – **-cation** *n*

abdomen /-'æbdəmən, æb'dəʊ-/ *n* **1** (the cavity of) the part of the body between the thorax and the pelvis that contains the liver, gut, etc **2** the rear part of the body behind the thorax in an insect, spider, etc – **-dominal** *adj*

ability /ə'bɪlɪti/ *n* **1a** being able; esp physical, mental, or legal power to perform **b** natural or acquired competence in doing; skill **2** a natural talent; aptitude – usu pl

able /'eɪbl/ *adj* **1** having sufficient power, skill, resources, or qualifications *to* **2** marked by intelligence, knowledge, skill, or competence

aboard /ə'bɔːd/ *adv or prep* **1** on, onto, or within (a ship, aircraft, train, or road vehicle) **2** alongside

abolish /ə'bɒlɪʃ/ *v* to do away with (e g a law or custom) wholly; annul – **-ition** *n*

abort /ə'bɔːt/ *v* **1** to expel a premature foetus **2** to fail to develop completely; shrink away **3** to induce the abortion of (a foetus) **4** to end prematurely – ~ion *n* – ~ionist *n*

¹about /ə'baʊt/ *adv* **1** round **2** in succession or rotation; alternately **3** approximately **4** almost **5** in the vicinity

²about *prep* **1** on every side of; surrounding **2a** in the vicinity of **b** on or near the person of **c** in the make-up of **d** at the command of **3a** engaged in **b** on the verge of – + *to* **4a** with regard to, concerning **b** intimately concerned with **5** over or in different parts of **6** *chiefly NAm* – used with the negative to express intention or determination

³about *adj* **1** moving from place to place; *specif* out of bed **2** in existence, evidence, or circulation

¹above /ə'bʌv/ *adv* **1a** in the sky overhead **b** in or to heaven **2a** in or to a higher place **b** higher on the same or an earlier page **c** upstairs **3** in or to a higher rank or number **4** upstage

²above *prep* **1** higher than the level of **2** over **3** beyond, transcending **4a** superior to (e g in rank) **b** too proud or honourable to stoop to **5** upstream from

³above *n, pl* **above 1a** sthg (written) above **b** a person whose name is written above **2a** a higher authority **b** heaven

⁴above *adj* written higher on the same, or on a preceding, page

abreast /ə'brest/ *adv or adj* **1** side by side and facing in the same direction **2** up-to-date in attainment or information

abroad /ə'brɔːd/ *adv or adj* **1** over a wide area; widely **2** away from one's home; out of doors **3** beyond the boundaries of one's country **4** in wide circulation; about

abrupt /ə'brʌpt/ *adj* **1** ending as if sharply cut off; truncated **2a** occurring without warning; unexpected **b** unceremoniously curt **c** marked by sudden changes in subject matter **3** rising or dropping sharply; steep – ~ly *adv* – ~ness *n*

absence /'æbsəns/ *n* **1** being absent **2** the period of time that one is absent **3** a lack

¹absent /'æbsənt/ *adj* **1** not present or attending; missing **2** not existing; lacking **3** preoccupied – ~ly *adv*

²absent /əb'sent, æb-/ *v* to take or keep (oneself) away – usu + *from*

absolutely /'æbsəluːtli, ˌæbsə'luːtli/

adv totally, completely – often used to express emphatic agreement

absorb /əb'sɔːb, əb'zɔːb/ *v* **1** to take in and make part of an existing whole; incorporate **2a** to suck up or take up **b** to assimilate; take in **3** to engage or occupy wholly – ~**ent** *adj*

¹**absurd** /əb'sɜːd, -'zɜːd/ *adj* **1** ridiculously unreasonable or incongruous; silly **2** lacking order or value; meaningless – ~**ly** *adv* – ~**ity** *n*

²**absurd** *n* the state or condition in which human beings exist in an irrational and meaningless universe, and in which their life has no meaning outside their own existence

abundant /ə'bʌndənt/ *adj* **1a** marked by great plenty (e g of resources) **b** amply supplied *with*; abounding in **2** occurring in abundance – ~**ly** *adv*

¹**abuse** /ə'bjuːz/ *v* **1** to attack in words; revile **2** to put to a wrong or improper use **3** to use so as to injure or damage; maltreat – ~**ive** *adj*

²**abuse** /ə'bjuːs/ *n* **1** a corrupt practice or custom **2** improper use or treatment; misuse **3** vehemently expressed condemnation or disapproval **4** physical maltreatment

¹**academic** /ˌækə'demɪk/ *also* **academical** *adj* **1a** of an institution of higher learning **b** scholarly **c** very learned but inexperienced in practical matters **2** conventional, formal **3** theoretical with no practical or useful bearing

²**academic** *n* a member (of the teaching staff) of an institution of higher learning

accelerate /ək'seləreɪt/ *v* **1** to bring about at an earlier time **2** to increase the speed of **3** to hasten the progress, development, or growth of **4** to move faster; gain speed **5** to increase more rapidly

¹**accent** /'æksənt/ *n* **1** a distinctive pattern in inflection, tone, or choice of words, esp as characteristic of a regional or national area **2a** prominence given to 1 syllable over others by stress or a change in pitch **b** greater stress given to 1 musical note **c** rhythmically significant stress on the syllables of a verse **3a accent, accent mark** a mark added to a letter (e g in à, ñ, ç) to indicate how it should be pronounced **b** a symbol used to indicate musical stress **4** special concern or attention; emphasis

²**accent** /ək'sent/ *v* **1** to pronounce (a vowel, syllable, or word) with accent; stress **2** to make more prominent; emphasize

accept /ək'sept/ *v* **1a** to agree to receive; *also* to agree to **b** to be able or designed to take or hold (sthg applied or inserted) **2** to give admittance or approval to **3a** to endure without protest; accommodate oneself to **b** to regard as proper, normal, or inevitable **c** to recognize as true, factual, or adequate **4** to undertake the responsibility of **5** to receive favourably sthg offered

accident /'æksɪdənt/ *n* **1a** an event occurring by chance or arising from

unknown causes **b** lack of intention or necessity; chance **2** an unexpected happening causing loss or injury **3** a nonessential property or condition of sthg

¹**accidental** /ˌæksɪ'dentl/ *adj* **1** arising incidentally; nonessential **2a** occurring unexpectedly or by chance **b** happening without intent or through carelessness and often with unfortunate results – ~**ly** *adv*

²**accidental** *n* **1** a nonessential property or condition **2** (a sign indicating) a note altered to sharp, flat, or natural and foreign to a key indicated by a key signature

accommodation /əˌkɒmə'deɪʃən/ *n* **1a** lodging, housing **b** space, premises **2a** sthg needed or desired for convenience; a facility **b** an adaptation, adjustment **c** a settlement, agreement **d** the (range of) automatic adjustment of the eye, esp by changes in the amount by which the lens bends light, for seeing at different distances

accompany /ə'kʌmpəni/ *v* **1** to go with as an escort or companion **2** to perform an accompaniment (to or for) **3a** to make an addition to; supplement *with* **b** of a thing to happen, exist, or be found with

accomplish /ə'kʌmplɪʃ/ *v* **1** to bring to a successful conclusion; achieve **2** to complete, cover (a measure of time or distance)

¹**accord** /ə'kɔːd/ *v* **1** to grant, concede **2** to give, award **3** to be consistent *with*

²**accord** *n* **1a** accordance **b** a formal treaty of agreement **2** balanced relationship (e g of colours or sounds); harmony

accordance /ə'kɔːdəns/ *n* **1** agreement, conformity **2** the act of granting

account /ə'kaʊnt/ *n* **1** a record of debits and credits relating to a particular item, person, or concern **2** a list of items of expenditure to be balanced against income – usu pl **3a** a periodically rendered calculation listing purchases and credits **b** business, patronage **4** a business arrangement whereby money is deposited in, and may be withdrawn from, a bank, building society, etc **5** a commission to carry out a particular business operation (e g an advertising campaign) given by one company to another **6** value, importance **7** profit, advantage **8** careful thought; consideration **9a** a statement explaining one's conduct **b** a statement of facts or events; a relation **10** hearsay, report – usu pl **11** a version, rendering

accumulate /ə'kjuːmjʊleɪt/ *v* **1** to collect together gradually; amass **2** to increase in quantity or number

accurate /'ækjərət/ *adj* **1** free from error, esp as the result of care **2** conforming precisely to truth or a measurable standard; exact – ~**acy** *n* – ~**ly** *adv*

accuse /ə'kjuːz/ *v* to charge with a fault or crime; blame – ~**sation** *n* – ~**singly** *adv*

accustom /ə'kʌstəm/ *v* to make used

to through use or experience; habituate

¹ace /eɪs/ *n* 1 a die face, playing card, or domino marked with 1 spot or pip; *also* the single spot or pip on any of these 2 (a point scored by) a shot, esp a service in tennis, that an opponent fails to touch 3 a combat pilot who has brought down at least 5 enemy aircraft 4 an expert or leading performer in a specified field

²ace *v* to score an ace against (an opponent)

³ace *adj* great, excellent – *infml*

¹ache /eɪk/ *v* 1a to suffer a usu dull persistent pain b to feel anguish or distress 2 to yearn, long

²ache *n* a usu dull persistent pain

achieve /əˈtʃiːv/ *v* 1 to carry out successfully; accomplish 2 to obtain by effort; win – **achievable** *adj*

achievement /əˈtʃiːvmənt/ *n* 1 successful completion; accomplishment 2 sthg accomplished by resolve, persistence, or courage; a feat 3 performance in a test or academic course

¹acid /ˈæsɪd/ *adj* 1a sour or sharp to the taste b sharp, biting, or sour in speech, manner, or disposition; caustic 2 of, like, containing, or being an acid; *specif* having a pH of less than 7

²acid *n* 1 a sour substance; *specif* any of various typically water-soluble and sour compounds having a pH of less than 7 that are capable of giving up a hydrogen ion to or accepting an unshared pair of electrons from a base to form a salt 2 LSD – *infml*

acknowledge /əkˈnɒlɪdʒ/ *v* 1 to admit knowledge of; concede to be true or valid 2 to recognize the status or claims of 3a to express gratitude or obligation for b to show recognition of (e g by smiling or nodding) c to confirm receipt of – **-gment** *n*

acorn /ˈeɪkɔːn/ *n* the nut of the oak, usu seated in a hard woody cup

acquaintance /əˈkweɪntəns/ *n* 1 personal knowledge; familiarity 2a *sing* or *pl in constr* the people with whom one is acquainted b a person whom one knows but who is not a particularly close friend

acquire /əˈkwaɪə^r/ *v* 1 to gain or come into possession of, often by unspecified means; *also* to steal – *euph* 2 to gain as a new characteristic or ability, esp as a result of skill or hard work

acquit /əˈkwɪt/ *v* 1 to free from responsibility or obligation; *specif* to declare not guilty 2 to conduct (oneself) in a specified, usu favourable, manner

acre /ˈeɪkə^r/ *n* 1 *pl* lands, fields 2 a unit of area equal to 4840yd² (4046.86m²) 3 *pl* great quantities – *infml*

acrobat /ˈækrəbæt/ *n* one who performs gymnastic feats requiring skilful control of the body – ~ **ic** *adj* – ~ **ically** *adv*

¹across /əˈkrɒs/ *adv* 1 from one side to the other crosswise 2 to or on the opposite side 3 so as to be understandable, acceptable, or successful

²across *prep* 1a from one side to the other of b on the opposite side of 2 so

as to intersect at an angle 3 into transitory contact with

¹act /ækt/ *n* 1 a thing done; a deed 2 a statute; *also* a decree, edict 3 the process of doing 4 *often cap* a formal record of sthg done or transacted 5a any of the principal divisions of a play or opera b any of the successive parts or performances in an entertainment (e g a circus) 6 a display of affected behaviour; a pretence

²act *v* 1 to represent by action, esp on the stage 2 to feign, simulate 3 to play the part of (as if) in a play 4 to behave in a manner suitable to 5 to perform on the stage; engage in acting 6 to behave insincerely 7 to function or behave in a specified manner 8 to perform a specified function; serve as 9 to be a substitute or representative for 10 to produce an effect

action /ˈækʃən/ *n* 1 a civil legal proceeding 2 the process of acting or working, esp to produce alteration by force or through a natural agency 3 the mode of movement of the body 4 a voluntary act; a deed 5a the state of functioning actively b practical, often militant, activity, often directed towards a political end c energetic activity; enterprise 6a combat (e g in a war) b (the unfolding of) the events in a play or work of fiction 7 an operating mechanism (e g of a gun or piano); *also* the manner in which it operates 8 (the most) lively or productive activity – *infml*

¹active /ˈæktɪv/ *adj* 1 characterized by practical action rather than by contemplation or speculation 2 quick in physical movement; lively 3a marked by or requiring vigorous activity b full of activity; busy 4 having practical operation or results; effective 5 of a volcano liable to erupt; not extinct 6 of a verb form or voice having as the subject the person or thing doing the action 7 of, in, or being full-time service, esp in the armed forces 8 capable of acting or reacting; activated – ~ **ly** *adv*

²active *n* 1 an active verb form 2 the active voice of a language

activity /ækˈtɪvɪti/ *n* 1 the quality or state of being active 2 vigorous or energetic action; liveliness 3 a pursuit in which a person is active – usu *pl*

actor /ˈæktə^r/, *fem* **actress** *n* one who represents a character in a dramatic production; *esp* one whose profession is acting

actual /ˈæktʃʊəl/ *adj* 1 existing in fact or reality; real 2 existing or occurring at the time; current

actually /ˈæktʃʊəli, -tʃəli/ *adv* 1 really; in fact 2 at the present moment 3 strange as it may seem; even

adapt /əˈdæpt/ *v* to make or become fit, often by modification

add /æd/ *v* 1 to join so as to bring about an increase or improvement 2 to say or write further 3 to combine (numbers) into a single number – often + *up* 4a to perform addition b to come together or unite by addition 5 to make or serve as an addition *to*

add

¹**addict** /ə'dɪkt/ v 1 to devote or surrender (oneself) to sthg habitually or obsessively – usu pass 2 to cause (an animal or human) to become physiologically dependent upon a habit-forming drug

²**addict** /'ædɪkt/ n 1 one who is addicted to a drug 2 a devotee, fan – ~**ive** adj

addition /ə'dɪʃən/ n 1 sthg or sby added, esp as an improvement 2 the act or process of adding, esp adding numbers

¹**address** /ə'dres/ v 1 to direct the efforts or attention of (oneself) 2a to communicate directly b to speak or write directly to; esp to deliver a formal speech to 3 to mark directions for delivery on 4 to greet by a prescribed form 5 to take one's stance and adjust the club before hitting (a golf ball)

²**address** n 1 a formal communication; esp a prepared speech delivered to an audience 2 a place of residence (where a person or organization may be communicated with); also a detailed description of its location (e g on an envelope)

adequate /'ædɪkwɪt/ adj (badly) sufficient for a specific requirement – ~**ly** adv – -**quacy** n

adjective n a word that modifies a noun or pronoun by describing a particular characteristic of it – -**tival** adj – -**tivally** adv

adjourn /ə'dʒɜːn/ v to suspend (a session) until a later stated time – ~**ment** n

adjust /ə'dʒʌst/ v 1 to bring to a more satisfactory or conformable state by minor change or adaptation; regulate, correct, or modify 2 to determine the amount to be paid under an insurance policy in settlement of (a loss) 3 to adapt or conform oneself (e g to climate) – ~**able** adj – ~**ment** n

administer /əd'mɪnɪstə'/ v 1 to manage, supervise 2a to mete out; dispense b to give or perform ritually 3 to perform the office of administrator; manage affairs – -**tration** n

admirable /'ædmərəbəl/ adj deserving the highest respect; excellent – -**bly** adv

admiration /ˌædmɪ'reɪʃən/ n a feeling of delighted or astonished approval

admire /əd'maɪə'/ v to think highly of; express admiration for – sometimes sarcastically

admission /əd'mɪʃən/ n 1 acknowledgment that a fact or allegation is true 2a allowing or being allowed to enter sthg (e g a secret society) b a fee paid at or for admission

admit /əd'mɪt/ v 1a to allow scope for; permit b to concede as true or valid 2 to allow to enter sthg (e g a place or fellowship) 1 to give entrance or access 2a to allow, permit – often + of b to make acknowledgment – + to

ado /ə'duː/ n fussy bustling excitement, esp over trivia; to-do

adolescent /ˌædə'lesənt/ n sby in the period of life between puberty and maturity – ~**cence** n

adopt /ə'dɒpt/ v 1 to take by choice into a new relationship; specif to bring up voluntarily (a child of other parents) as one's own child 2 to take up and practise; take to oneself 3 to vote to accept 4 of a constituency to nominate as a Parliamentary candidate 5 Br, of a local authority to assume responsibility for the maintenance of (e g a road) – ~**ion** n

adore /ə'dɔː'/ v 1 to worship or honour as a deity 2 to regard with reverent admiration and devotion 3 to like very much – infml – **adoration** n

adorn /ə'dɔːn/ v 1 to decorate, esp with ornaments 2 to add to the pleasantness or attractiveness of – ~**ment** n

¹**adult** /'ædʌlt, ə'dʌlt/ adj 1 fully developed and mature; grown-up 2 of or befitting adults 3 suitable only for adults; broadly salacious, pornographic

²**adult** n a grown-up person or creature; esp a human being after an age specified by law (in Britain, 18)

¹**advance** /əd'vɑːns/ v 1 to bring or move forwards in position or time 2 to accelerate the growth or progress of; further 3 to raise in rank; promote 4 to supply (money or goods) ahead of time or as a loan 5 to bring (an opinion or argument) forward for notice; propose 6 to go forwards; proceed 7 to make progress 8 to rise in rank, position, or importance

²**advance** n 1a a moving forward b (a signal for) forward movement (of troops) 2a progress in development; an improvement b advancement; promotion 3 a friendly or esp an amorous approach – usu pl 4 (a provision of) money or goods supplied before a return is received

³**advance** adj 1 made, sent, or provided ahead of time 2 going or situated ahead of others

advantage /əd'vɑːntɪdʒ/ n 1 superiority of position or condition – often + of or over 2 a benefit, gain; esp one resulting from some course of action 3 (the score of) the first point won in tennis after deuce

¹**adventure** /əd'ventʃə'/ n 1 an undertaking involving danger, risks, uncertainty of outcome, or excitement 2 an enterprise involving financial risk – ~**rous** adj

²**adventure** v 1 to hazard oneself; dare to go or enter 2 to take a risk

adverb /'ædvɜːb/ n a word that modifies a verb, an adjective, another adverb, a preposition, a phrase, a clause, or a sentence, and that answers such questions as how?, when?, where?, etc – ~**ial** n, adj – ~**ially** adv

advertise /'ædvətaɪz/ v 1 to make publicly and generally known 2 to announce (e g an article for sale or a vacancy) publicly, esp in the press 3 to encourage sales or patronage (of), esp by emphasizing desirable qualities, or by description in the mass media 4 to seek *for* by means of advertising – ~ r *n*

advertisement /əd'vɜ:tɪsmənt/ *n* a notice published, broadcast, or displayed publicly to advertise a product, service, etc

advice /əd'vaɪs/ *n* **1** recommendation regarding a decision or course of conduct **2** communication, esp from a distance; intelligence – usu pl **3** an official notice concerning a business transaction

advise /əd'vaɪz/ *v* **1a** to give advice (to) **b** to caution, warn **2** to give information or notice to; inform

¹**aerial** /'eəriəl/ *adj* **1a** of or occurring in the air or atmosphere **b** consisting of air **c** growing in the air rather than in the ground or water **d** operating overhead on elevated cables or rails **2** lacking substance; thin – ~ly *adv*

²**aerial** *n* a conductor (e g a wire) or arrangement of conductors designed to radiate or receive radio waves

aeroplane /'eərəpleɪn/ *n, chiefly Br* an aircraft that is heavier than air, has nonrotating wings from which it derives its lift, and is mechanically propelled (e g by a propeller or jet engine)

aerosol /'eərəsɒl/ *n* (a container of) a substance dispersed from a pressurized container as a suspension of fine solid or liquid particles in gas – **aerosol** *adj*

affair /ə'feə/ *n* **1a** *pl* commercial, professional, or public business or matters **b** a particular or personal concern **2a** a procedure, action, object, or occasion only vaguely specified **b** a social event; a party **3** *also* **affaire, affaire de coeur** a romantic or passionate attachment between 2 people who are not married to each other **4** a matter causing public anxiety, controversy, or scandal

¹**affect** /ə'fekt/ *n* the conscious subjective aspect of an emotion considered apart from bodily changes

²**affect** /ə'fekt/ *v* **1** to be given to **2** to put on a pretence of (being); feign

³**affect** /ə'fekt/ *v* **1** to have a material effect on or produce an alteration in **2** to act on (e g a person or his/her mind or feelings) so as to effect a response

affection /ə'fekʃən/ *n* **1** emotion as compared with reason – often *pl* with sing. meaning **2** tender and lasting attachment; fondness

afflict /ə'flɪkt/ *v* **1** to distress so severely as to cause persistent suffering **2** to trouble

affluent /'æfluənt/ *adj* **1** flowing in abundance **2** having a generously sufficient supply of material possessions; wealthy – ~ence *n*

afford /ə'fɔ:d/ *v* **1a** to be able to do or to bear without serious harm – esp + *can* **b** to be able to bear the cost of **2** to provide, supply

afloat /ə'fləʊt/ *adj or adv* **1a** borne (as if) on the water or air **b** at sea or on ship **2** free of debt **3** circulating about; rumoured **4** flooded with or submerged under water

afraid /ə'freɪd/ *adj* **1** filled with fear or apprehension **2** regretfully of the opinion – in apology for an utterance

¹**after** /'ɑ:ftə/ *adv* **1** behind **2** afterwards

²**after** *prep* **1** behind in place or order – used in yielding precedence or in asking for the next turn (e g *after* you with the map) **2a** following in time; later than **b** continuously succeeding **c** in view or in spite of (sthg preceding) **3** – used to indicate the goal or purpose of an action (e g go *after* trout) **4** so as to resemble: e g **a** in accordance with **b** in allusion to the name of **c** in the characteristic manner of **d** in imitation of **5** about, concerning

³**after** *conj* later than the time when

⁴**after** *adj* later, subsequent

afternoon /ɑ:ftə'nu:n/ *n* the time between noon and sunset

afterwards /'ɑ:ftəwədz/ *adv* after that; subsequently, thereafter

again /ə'gen, ə'geɪn/ *adv* **1** so as to be as before **2** another time; once more **3** on the other hand **4** further; in addition

¹**against** /ə'genst, ə'geɪnst/ *prep* **1a** in opposition or hostility to **b** unfavourable to **c** as a defence or protection from **2** compared or contrasted with **3a** in preparation or provision for **b** with respect to; towards **4** (in the direction of and) in contact with **5** in a direction opposite to the motion or course of; counter to **6** in exchange for

²**against** *adj* **1** opposed to a motion or measure **2** unfavourable to a specified degree; *esp* unfavourable to a win

¹**age** /eɪdʒ/ *n* **1a** the length of time a person has lived or a thing existed **b** the time of life at which some particular qualification, power, or capacity arises **c** a stage of life **2** a generation **3** a period of time dominated by a central figure or prominent feature **4** a division of geological time, usu shorter than an epoch **5** a long time – usu pl with sing. meaning; infml

²**age** *v* **aging, ageing** **1** to become old; show the effects of increasing age **2** to become mellow or mature; ripen **3** to cause to seem old, esp prematurely **4** to bring to a state fit for use or to maturity

agenda /ə'dʒendə/ *n* **1** a list of items to be discussed or business to be transacted (e g at a meeting) **2** a plan of procedure; a programme

agent /'eɪdʒənt/ *n* **1** sthg or sby that produces an effect or that acts or exerts power **2** a person who acts for or in the place of another by authority from him/her: e g **a** a business representative **b** one employed by or controlling an agency **3a** a representative of a government **b** a spy

aggravate /'ægrəveɪt/ *v* **1** to make worse or more severe **2** to annoy, irritate – **-tion** *n*

aggressive /ə'gresɪv/ *adj* **1a** tending towards or practising aggression **b** ready to attack **2** forceful, dynamic – ~ly *adv* – ~ness *n*

agile /'ædʒaɪl/ *adj* **1** quick, easy, and

graceful in movement **2** mentally quick and resourceful – ~**ly** *adv* – **-ility** *n*

agitate /'ædʒɪteɪt/ *v* **1** to move, shake **2** to excite and often trouble the mind or feelings of; disturb **3** to work to arouse public feeling for or against a cause – **-tation** *n*

ago /ə'gəʊ/ *adj or adv* earlier than now

agony /'ægənɪ/ *n* **1** intense and often prolonged pain or suffering of mind or body; anguish **2** the struggle that precedes death – **-nize** *v*, – **-nized** *adj*, – **-nizing** *adj*

agree /ə'griː/ *v* **1** to admit, concede – usu + a clause **2** to bring into harmony **3** *chiefly Br* to come to terms on, usu after discussion; accept by mutual consent **4** to give assent; accede – often + *to* **5a** to be of one mind – often + *with* **b** to decide together **6a** to correspond **b** to be consistent **7** to suit the health – + *with*

agreeable /ə'griːəbəl/ *adj* **1** to one's liking; pleasing **2** willing to agree or consent

agreement /ə'griːmənt/ *n* **1a** harmony of opinion or feeling **b** correspondence **2a** an arrangement laying down terms, conditions, etc **b** a treaty **3** (the language or document embodying) a legally binding contract

agriculture /'ægrɪˌkʌltʃə'/ *n* the theory and practice of cultivating and producing crops from the soil and of raising livestock – **-tural** *adv* – **-tur(al)ist** *n*

ahead /ə'hed/ *adv or adj* **1a** in a forward direction **b** in front **2** in, into, or for the future **3** in or towards a better position

¹**aid** /eɪd/ *v* **1** to give assistance to; help **2** to bring about the accomplishment of; facilitate

²**aid** *n* **1** help; assistance; *specif* tangible means of assistance (e g money or supplies) **2a** a helper **b** sthg that helps or supports ; *specif* a hearing aid

¹**aim** /eɪm/ *v* **1** to direct a course; *specif* to point a weapon at an object **2** to channel one's efforts; aspire **3** to have the intention; mean **4** to direct or point (e g a weapon) at a target **5** to direct at or towards a specified goal; intend

²**aim** *n* **1a** the pointing of a weapon at a mark **b** the ability to hit a target **c** a weapon's accuracy or effectiveness **2** a clear intention or purpose – ~**less** *adj*

¹**air** /eə'/ *n* **1a** the mixture of invisible odourless tasteless gases, containing esp nitrogen and oxygen, that surrounds the earth **b** a light breeze **2a** empty unconfined space **b** nothingness **3a**(1) aircraft (2) aviation **b** the supposed medium of transmission of radio waves; *also* radio, television **4a** the appearance or bearing of a person; demeanour **b** *pl* an artificial or affected manner; haughtiness **c** outward appearance of a thing **d** a surrounding or pervading influence; an atmosphere **5** a tune, melody

²**air** *v* **1** to expose to the air for drying, freshening, etc; ventilate **2** to expose to public view or bring to public notice

aircraft /'eəkrɑːft/ *n, pl* **aircraft** a weight-carrying structure that can travel through the air and is supported either by its own buoyancy or by the dynamic action of the air against its surfaces

airport /'eəpɔːt/ *n* a fully-equipped airfield that is used as a base for the transport of passengers and cargo by air

ajar /ə'dʒɑː'/ *adj or adv, esp of a door* slightly open

¹**alarm** /ə'lɑːm/ *n* **1** a signal (e g a loud noise or flashing light) that warns or alerts; *also* an automatic device that alerts or rouses **2** the fear resulting from the sudden sensing of danger

²**alarm** *v* **1** to give warning to **2** to strike with fear

album /'ælbəm/ *n* **1** a book with blank pages used for making a collection (e g of stamps or photographs) **2** a recording or collection of recordings issued on 1 or more long-playing gramophone records or cassettes

alcohol /'ælkəhɒl/ *n* **1** a colourless volatile inflammable liquid that is the intoxicating agent in fermented and distilled drinks and is used also as a solvent **2** any of various organic compounds, specif derived from hydrocarbons, containing the hydroxyl group **3** (intoxicating drink containing alcohol; *esp* spirits

¹**alert** /ə'lɜːt/ *adj* **1** watchful, aware **2** active, brisk – ~**ly** *adv* – ~**ness** *n*

²**alert** *n* **1** an alarm or other signal that warns of danger (e g from hostile aircraft) **2** the danger period during which an alert is in effect

³**alert** *v* **1** to call to a state of readiness; warn **2** to cause to be aware (e g of a need or responsibility)

algebra /'ældʒɪbrə/ *n* a branch of mathematics in which letters, symbols, etc representing various entities are combined according to special rules of operation – ~**ic(al)** *adj* – ~**ically** *adv*

alibi /'ælɪbaɪ/ *n* **1** (evidence supporting) the plea of having been elsewhere when a crime was committed **2** a plausible excuse, usu intended to avert blame or punishment

¹**alight** /ə'laɪt/ *v* **alighted** *also* **alit** **1** to come down from sthg: e g **a** to dismount **b** to disembark **2** to descend from the air and settle; land

²**alight** *adj* **1** animated, alive **2** *chiefly Br* on fire; ignited

¹**alike** /ə'laɪk/ *adj* showing close resemblance without being identical

²**alike** *adv* in the same manner, form, or degree; equally

alive /ə'laɪv/ *adj* **1** having life **2** still in existence, force, or operation; active **3** realizing the existence of sthg; aware of sthg **4** marked by alertness **5** showing much activity or animation; swarming **6** of all those living – used as an intensive following the noun

alkali /'ælkəlaɪ/ *n, pl* **alkalies, alkalis** any of various chemical bases, esp a hydroxide or carbonate of an alkali metal – ~**ne** *adj*

¹**all** /ɔːl/ *adj* **1a** the whole amount or

quantity of (e g awake *all* night) **b** as much as possible (e g say in *all* honesty) **2** every one of (more than 2) **3** the whole number or sum of (e g *all* cats like milk) **4** every (e g *all* kinds of fish) **5** any whatever (e g beyond *all* hope) **6a** given to or displaying only (e g was *all* attention) **b** having or seeming to have (some physical feature) conspicuously or excessively (e g *all* thumbs)

¹all *adv* **1** wholly, altogether (e g sitting *all* alone) **2** to a supreme degree – usu in combination (e g *all*-powerful) **3** for each side (e g a score of 3 *all*)

²all *pron, pl* **all** **1** the whole number, quantity, or amount (e g it was *all* we could afford) **2** everybody, everything (e g give up *all* for love)

³all *n* one's total resources (e g gave his *all* for the cause)

allergy /'æləd͡ʒi/ *n* **1** exaggerated reaction by sneezing, itching, skin rashes, etc to substances that have no such effect on the average individual **2** a feeling of antipathy or aversion – infml – **-ic** *adj*

¹alley /'æli/ *n* **1** a bowling alley **2** a narrow back street or passageway between buildings

²alley *n* a playing marble (of superior quality)

alliance /ə'laɪəns/ *n* **1** a union of families by marriage **2** a uniting of nations by formal treaty **3** a tie, connection

allow /ə'laʊ/ *v* **1a(1)** to assign as a share or suitable amount (e g of time or money) **(2)** to grant as an allowance **b** to reckon as a deduction or an addition **2a** to admit as true or valid; acknowledge **b** to admit the possibility (of) **3a** to make it possible for; enable **b** to feel it proper to; permit **c** to prevent; let **4** to make allowance for

allowance /ə'laʊəns/ *n* **1a** a (limited) share or portion allotted or granted; a ration **b** a sum granted as a reimbursement or bounty or for expenses **2** a handicap (e g in a race) **3a** permission, sanction **b** acknowledgment **4** the taking into account of mitigating circumstances – often pl with sing. meaning

¹alloy /'ælɔɪ/ *n* **1** a solid substance composed of a mixture of metals or a metal and a nonmetal thoroughly intermixed **2** a metal mixed with a more valuable metal **3** an addition that impairs or debases

²alloy *v* **1** to reduce the purity or value of by adding sthg **2** to mix so as to form an alloy **3a** to impair or debase by addition **b** to temper, moderate

¹all right *adv* **1** well enough **2** beyond doubt; certainly

²all right *adj* **1** satisfactory, acceptable **2** safe, well **3** agreeable, pleasing – used as a generalized term of approval

³all right *interj* **1** – used for giving assent **2** – used in indignant or menacing response

¹ally /ə'laɪ/ *v* **1** to join, unite *with/to* **2** to relate *to* by resemblance or common properties to form or enter into an alliance *with*

²ally /'ælaɪ/ *n* **1** a sovereign or state associated with another by treaty or league **2** a helper, auxiliary

¹almighty /ɔːl'maɪti/ *adj* **1** *often cap* having absolute power over all **2** having relatively unlimited power **3** great in extent, seriousness, force, etc – infml

²almighty *adv* to a great degree; mighty – infml

Almighty *n* God – + *the*

almost /'ɔːlməʊst/ *adv* very nearly but not exactly or entirely

alone /ə'ləʊn/ *adj or adv* **1** considered without reference to any other; *esp* unassisted **2** separated from others; isolated **3** exclusive of other factors **4** free from interference

¹along /ə'lɒŋ/ *prep* **1** in a line parallel with the length or direction of **2** in the course of (a route or journey) **3** in accordance with

²along *adv* **1** forward, on (e g move *along*) **2** as a necessary or pleasant addition; with one (e g bring the picnic *along*) **3** in company and simultaneously *with* (e g caught flu *along* with the others) **4** on hand, there (e g I'll be *along* soon) **5** also; in addition

aloud /ə'laʊd/ *adv* with the speaking voice

alphabet /'ælfəbet/ *n* a set of characters, esp letters, used to represent 1 or more languages, esp when arranged in a conventional order; *also* a system of signs and signals that can be used in place of letters – **~ical** *adj* – **~ically** *adv*

already /ɔːl'redi/ *adv* **1** no later than now or then; even by this or that time **2** before, previously

also /'ɔːlsəʊ/ *adv* as an additional circumstance; besides

alter /'ɔːltə/ *v* **1** to make different without changing into sthg else **2** to become different – **~able** *adj* – **~ation** *n*

¹alternative /ɔːl'tɜːnətɪv/ *adj* **1** affording a choice, esp between 2 mutually exclusive options **2** constituting an alternative – **~ly** *adv*

²alternative *n* **1** an opportunity or need for deciding between 2 or more possibilities **2** either of 2 possibilities between which a choice is to be made; *also* any of more than 2 such possibilities

although /ɔːl'ðəʊ/ *conj* in spite of the fact or possibility that; though

¹altogether /ˌɔːltə'geðə/ *adv* **1** wholly, thoroughly **2** all told **3** in the main; on the whole **4** in every way

²altogether /ˌɔːltə'geðə/ *n* the nude – infml

aluminium /ˌæljʊ'mɪnɪəm, ˌælə-/ *n* a bluish silver-white malleable light metallic element with good electrical and thermal conductivity and resistance to oxidation

always /'ɔːlwɪz, -weɪz/ *adv* **1a** at all times **b** in all cases **2** on every occasion; repeatedly **3** forever, perpetually **4** as a last resort; at any rate

am /m, əm; *strong* æm/ *pres 1 sing of* be

AM *adj* of or being a broadcasting or receiving system using amplitude modulation

amateur /'æmətə', -tʃʊə', -tʃə', ˌæmə'tɜː'/ *n* **1** one who engages in a pursuit as a pastime rather than as a profession; *esp* a sportsman who has never competed for money **2** one who practises an art or science unskilfully; a dabbler – **amateur** *adj*

amaze /ə'meɪz/ *v* to fill with wonder; astound – ~ **ment** *n*

amazing /ə'meɪzɪŋ/ *adj* – used as a generalized term of approval – ~ **ly** *adv*

ambassador /æm'bæsədə'/ *n* **1** a top-ranking diplomat accredited to a foreign government or sovereign as a temporary or resident representative **2** a representative, messenger – ~ **ship** *n* – ~ **ial** *adj*

ambiguous /æm'bɪgjʊəs/ *adj* **1** vague, indistinct, or difficult to classify **2** capable of 2 or more interpretations – **guity** *n* – ~ **ly** *adv* – ~ **ness** *n*

ambition /æm'bɪʃən/ *n* **1a** a strong desire for status, wealth, or power **b** a desire to achieve a particular end **2** an object of ambition

ambitious /æm'bɪʃəs/ *adj* **1a** having, resulting from, or showing ambition **b** desirous of, aspiring **2** elaborate – ~ **ly** *adv* – ~ **ness** *n*

ambulance /'æmbjʊləns/ *n* a vehicle equipped to transport the injured or ill

¹ambush /'æmbʊʃ/ *v* to attack from an ambush; waylay

²ambush *n* the concealment of soldiers, police, etc in order to carry out a surprise attack from a hidden position

amen /ɑː'men, eɪ-/ *interj* – used to express solemn confirmation (e g of an expression of faith) or hearty approval (e g of an assertion)

amendment /ə'mendmənt/ *n* **1** the act of amending, esp for the better **2** an alteration proposed or effected by amending

amends /ə'mendz/ *n pl but sing or pl in constr* compensation for a loss or injury; recompense

amiable /'eɪmiəbəl/ *adj* **1** (seeming) agreeable and well-intentioned; inoffensive **2** friendly, congenial – **bility** *n* – **bly** *adv*

amid /ə'mɪd/ *prep* in or to the middle of – poetic

ammunition /ˌæmjʊ'nɪʃən/ *n* **1** the projectiles, together with their propelling charges, used in the firing of guns; *also* bombs, grenades, etc containing explosives **2** material used to defend or attack a point of view

among /ə'mʌŋ/ *prep* **1** in or through the midst of; surrounded by **2** by or through the whole group of **3** in the number or class of **4** between – used for more than 2 (e g fight *among* themselves)

¹amount /ə'maʊnt/ *v* to be equal in number, quantity, or significance *to*

²amount *n* **1** the total quantity **2** the

quantity at hand or under consideration

amphibious /æm'fɪbiəs/ *adj* **1** able to live both on land and in water **2a** relating to or adapted for both land and water **b** involving or trained for coordinated action of land, sea, and air forces organized for invasion

ample /'æmpəl/ *adj* **1** generous in size, scope, or capacity **2** abundant, plentiful – **ply** *adv*

amputate /'æmpjʊteɪt/ *v* to cut or lop off; *esp* to cut (e g a damaged or diseased limb) from the body – **-tation** *n*

amuse /ə'mjuːz/ *v* **1** to entertain or occupy in a light or pleasant manner **2** to appeal to the sense of humour of

amusement /ə'mjuːzmənt/ *n* a means of entertaining or occupying; a pleasurable diversion

¹an /ən; *strong* æn/ *indefinite article* **a** – used (1) before words with an initial vowel sound (2) frequently, esp formerly or in the USA, before words whose initial /h/ sound is often lost before the **an**

²an, an' *conj* and – *infml*

³an *prep* **a** – used under the same conditions an ¹

anaesthetic /ˌænɪs'θetɪk/ *n* a substance that produces anaesthesia, e g so that surgery can be carried out painlessly – **anaesthetic** *adj*

analyse /'ænəlaɪz/ *v* **1** to subject to analysis **2** to determine by analysis the constitution or structure of **3** to psychoanalyse

anarchy /'ænəki/ *n* **1a** absence of government **b** lawlessness; (political) disorder **c** a utopian society with complete freedom and no government **2** anarchism – **-chic, -chical** *adj* – **-chically** *adv*

anatomy /ə'nætəmi/ *n* **1** dissection **2** structural make-up, esp of (a part of) an organism **3** an analysis **4** the human body – **-ist** *n* – **-ical** *adj* – **-ically** *adv*

ancestor /'ænsəstə', -ses-/, *fem* **ancestress** *n* **1a** one from whom a person is descended, usu more distant than a grandparent **b** a forefather **2a** a progenitor of a more recent (species) of organism – **-tral** *adj*

¹anchor /'æŋkə'/ *n* **1a** a usu metal device dropped to the bottom from a ship or boat to hold it in a particular place **2** sby or sthg providing support and security; a mainstay **3** sthg that serves to hold an object firmly

²anchor *v* **1** to hold in place in the water by an anchor **2** to secure firmly; fix **3** to become fixed; settle

¹ancient /'eɪnʃənt/ *adj* **1** having existed for many years **2** of (those living in) a remote period, specif that from the earliest known civilizations to the fall of the western Roman Empire in AD 476 **3** old-fashioned, antique

²ancient *n* **1** sby who lived in ancient times **2** *pl* the members of a civilized, esp a classical, nation of antiquity

and /ənd, ən; *strong* ænd/ *conj* **1** – used to join coordinate sentence elements of the same class or function expressing addition or combination (e g cold *and* tired) **2** – used, esp in Br speech, before the numbers 1–99 after the number 100; used also orig between tens and units **3** plus **4** – used to introduce a second clause expressing temporal sequence , consequence , contrast, or supplementary explanation **5** – used to join repeated words expressing continuation or progression (e g for miles *and* miles) **6** – used to join words expressing contrast of type or quality (e g fair, fat *and* forty) **7** – used instead of *to* to introduce an infinitive after *come, go, run, try, stop* (e g go *and* look)

angel /'eɪndʒəl/ *n* **1** a spiritual being, usu depicted as being winged, serving as God's intermediary or acting as a heavenly worshipper **2** an attendant spirit or guardian **3** a messenger, harbinger **4** a very kind or loving person, esp a woman or girl **5** a financial backer of a theatrical venture or other enterprise – chiefly infml – ~ic *adj* – ~ically *adv*

¹**anger** /'æŋgə/ *n* a strong feeling of displeasure and usu antagonism

²**anger** *v* to make or become angry

¹**angle** /'æŋgəl/ *n* **1** a corner **2a** the figure formed by 2 lines extending from the same point or by 2 surfaces diverging from the same line **b** a measure of the amount of turning necessary to bring one line of an angle to coincide with the other at all points **3a** a precise viewpoint; an aspect **b** a special approach or technique for accomplishing an objective **4** a divergent course or position; a slant – esp in *at an angle*

²**angle** *v* **angling 1** to place, move, or direct obliquely **2** to present (e g a news story) from a particular or prejudiced point of view; slant **3** to turn or proceed at an angle

³**angle** *v* to use artful means to attain an objective

Angle *n* a member of a Germanic people who invaded England along with the Saxons and Jutes in the 5th c AD

angling /'æŋglɪŋ/ *n* (the sport of) fishing with hook and line – -**gler** *n*

angry /'æŋgri/ *adj* **1** feeling or showing anger **2** seeming to show or typify anger **3** painfully inflamed – **angrily** *adv*

anguish /'æŋgwɪʃ/ *n* extreme physical pain or mental distress – ~**ed** *adj*

¹**animal** /'ænɪməl/ *n* **1** any of a kingdom of living things typically differing from plants in their capacity for spontaneous movement, esp in response to stimulation **2a** any of the lower animals as distinguished from human beings **b** a mammal – not in technical use **3** a person considered as a purely physical being; a creature

²**animal** *adj* **1** of or derived from animals **2** of the body as opposed to the mind or spirit – chiefly derog

ankle /'æŋkəl/ *n* the (region of the) joint between the foot and the leg; the tarsus

anniversary /ˌænɪ'vɜːsəri/ *n* (the celebration of) a day marking the annual recurrence of the date of a notable event

announce /ə'naʊns/ *v* **1** to make known publicly; proclaim **2a** to give notice of the arrival, presence, or readiness of **b** to indicate in advance; foretell **3** to give evidence of; indicate by action or appearance – ~**r** *n* – ~**ment** *n*

annoy /ə'nɔɪ/ *v* **1** to disturb or irritate, esp by repeated acts; vex – often pass + *with* or *at* **2** to harass **3** to be a source of annoyance – ~**ance** *n*

¹**annual** /'ænjʊəl/ *adj* **1** covering or lasting for the period of a year **2** occurring or performed once a year; yearly **3** *of a plant* completing the life cycle in 1 growing season – ~**ly** *adv*

²**annual** *n* **1** a publication appearing yearly **2** sthg lasting 1 year or season; *specif* an annual plant

anonymous /ə'nɒnɪ̯məs/ *adj* **1** having or giving no name **2** of unknown or unnamed origin or authorship **3** nondescript – -**mity** *n* – ~**ly** *adv*

¹**another** /ə'nʌðə/ *adj* **1** being a different or distinct one **2** some other **3** being one additional (e g *another* baby) **4** patterned after (e g *another* Picasso)

²**another** *pron, pl* **others 1** an additional one; one more **2** a different one

¹**answer** /'ɑːnsə/ *n* **1** a spoken or written reply to a question, remark, etc **2** an esp correct solution to a problem **3** a response or reaction **4** sby or sthg intended to be a close equivalent or rival of another

²**answer** *v* **1** to speak, write, or act in reply (to) **2a** to be responsible or accountable for **b** to make amends; atone for **3** to correspond *to* **4** to reply to in justification or explanation **5** to act in response to (a sound or other signal) **6** to offer a solution for; *esp* to solve

ant /ænt/ *n* any of a family of insects that live in large social groups having a complex organization and hierarchy

antarctic /æn'tɑːktɪk/ *adj, often cap* of the South Pole or surrounding region

anthology /æn'θɒlədʒi/ *n* a collection of selected (literary) passages or works

anticipate /æn'tɪsɪ̯peɪt/ *v* **1** to give advance thought, discussion, or treatment to **2** to foresee and deal with in advance; forestall **3** to act before (another) often so as to thwart **4** to look forward to as certain; expect **5** to speak or write in knowledge or expectation of sthg due to happen – -**pation** *n*

anticlimax /ˌæntɪ'klaɪmæks/ *n* **1** (an instance of) the usu sudden and ludicrous descent in writing or speaking from a significant to a trivial idea **2** an event (e g at the end of a series) that is strikingly less important or exciting than expected

anticlockwise /ˌæntɪ'klɒkwaɪz/ *adj or adv* in a direction opposite to that in which the hands of a clock rotate when viewed from the front

¹**antique** /æn'tiːk/ *adj* **1** belonging to or surviving from earlier, esp classical, times; ancient **2** old-fashioned **3** made in an earlier period and therefore valu-

able; *also* suggesting the style of an earlier period

²antique *n* **1** *the* ancient Greek or Roman style in art **2** a relic or object of ancient times **3** a work of art, piece of furniture, or decorative object made at an earlier period and sought by collectors

¹antiseptic /ˌæntɪˈsɛptɪk/ *adj* **1a** opposing sepsis (in living tissue), specif by arresting the growth of microorganisms, esp bacteria **b** of, acting or protecting like, or using an antiseptic **2a** scrupulously clean **b** extremely neat or orderly, esp to the point of being bare or uninteresting **3** impersonal, detached

²antiseptic *n* an antiseptic substance; *also* a germicide

anxiety /æŋˈzaɪəti/ *n* **1a** apprehensive uneasiness of mind, usu over an impending or anticipated ill **b** a cause of anxiety **2** an abnormal overwhelming sense of apprehension and fear, often with doubt about one's capacity to cope with the threat

anxious /ˈæŋkʃəs/ *adj* **1** troubled, worried **2** causing anxiety; worrying **3** ardently or earnestly wishing *to* – ~ **ly** *adv*

¹any /ˈeni/ *adj* **1** one or some indiscriminately; whichever is chosen **2** one, some, or all; whatever: e g **a** of whatever number or quantity; being even the smallest number or quantity of (e g there's never *any* salt) **b** no matter how great (e g make *any* sacrifice) **c** no matter how ordinary or inadequate (e g *any* old card will do) **3** being an appreciable number, part, or amount of – not in positive statements (e g not for *any* length of time)

²any *pron, pl* **any 1** any person; anybody **2a** any thing **b** any part, quantity, or number

³any *adv* to any extent or degree; at all

anybody /ˈeni,bɒdi, ˈenibədi/ *pron* any person

anyhow /ˈenihaʊ/ *adv* **1** in a haphazard manner **2** anyway

¹anything /ˈeniθɪŋ/ *pron* any thing whatever

²anything *adv* in any degree; at all

anyway /ˈeniweɪ/ *adv* **1** in any case, inevitably **2** – used when resuming a narrative (e g *anyway,* the moment we arrived ...)

¹anywhere /ˈeniweəʳ/ *adv* **1** in, at, or to any place **2** to any extent; at all **3** – used to indicate limits of variation (e g *anywhere* between here and London)

²anywhere *n* any place

apart /əˈpɑːt/ *adv* **1a** at a distance (from one another in space or time) **b** at a distance in character or opinions **2** so as to separate one from another **3** excluded from consideration **4** in or into **2** or more parts

apathy /ˈæpəθi/ *n* **1** lack of feeling or emotion; impassiveness **2** lack of interest or concern; indifference

¹ape /eɪp/ *n* **1** a chimpanzee, gorilla, or any similar primate **2a** a mimic **b** a large uncouth person

²ape *v* to imitate closely but often clumsily and ineptly

apologize, -ise *v* to make an apology

apology /əˈpɒlədʒi/ *n* **1** a excuse **2** an admission of error or discourtesy accompanied by an expression of regret **3** a poor substitute *for*

appal /əˈpɔːl/ *v* **-ll-** to overcome with consternation, horror, or dismay

apparatus /ˌæpəˈreɪtəs/ *n, pl* **apparatuses, apparatus 1** (a piece of) equipment designed for a particular use, esp for a scientific operation **2** the administrative bureaucracy of an organization, esp a political party

apparent /əˈpærənt/ *adj* **1** easily seen or understood; plain, evident **2** seemingly real but not necessarily so **3** having an absolute right to succeed to a title or estate – ~ **ly** *adv*

¹appeal /əˈpiːl/ *n* **1** a legal proceeding by which a case is brought to a higher court for review **2a(1)** an application (e g to a recognized authority) for corroboration, vindication, or decision **(2)** a call by members of the fielding side in cricket, esp by the bowler, for the umpire to decide whether a batsman is out **b** an earnest plea for aid or mercy; an entreaty **3** the power of arousing a sympathetic response; attraction

²appeal *v* **1** to take (a case) to a higher court **2a** to call on another for corroboration, vindication, or decision **b** to make an appeal in cricket **3** to make an earnest plea or request **4** to arouse a sympathetic response *USE* often + *to*

appear /əˈpɪəʳ/ *v* **1a** to be or become visible **b** to arrive **2** to come formally before an authoritative body **3** to give the impression of being; seem **4** to come into public view

appearance /əˈpɪərəns/ *n* **1** the coming into court of a party in an action or his/her lawyer **2** a visit or attendance that is seen or noticed by others **3a** an outward aspect; a look **b** an external show; a semblance **c** *pl* an outward or superficial indication that hides the real situation

appendix /əˈpendɪks/ *n, pl* **appendixes, appendices 1** a supplement (e g containing explanatory or statistical material), usu attached at the end of a piece of writing **2** the vermiform appendix or similar bodily outgrowth

appetite /ˈæpɪtaɪt/ *n* **1** a desire to satisfy an internal bodily need; *esp* an (eager) desire to eat **2** a strong desire demanding satisfaction; an inclination

applaud /əˈplɔːd/ *v* to express approval (of), esp by clapping the hands

applause /əˈplɔːz/ *n* **1** approval publicly expressed (e g by clapping the hands) **2** praise

apple /ˈæpəl/ *n* **1** (the fleshy, edible, usu rounded, red, yellow, or green fruit of) a tree of the rose family **2** a fruit or other plant structure resembling an apple

appliance /əˈplaɪəns/ *n* an instrument or device designed for a particular use; *esp* a domestic machine or device powered by gas or electricity (e g a food mixer, vacuum cleaner, or cooker)

application /ˌæpliˈkeɪʃən/ n **1a** an act of applying **b** a use to which sthg is put **c** close attention; diligence **2** a request, petition **3** a lotion **4** capacity for practical use; relevance

apply /əˈplaɪ/ v **1a** to bring to bear; put to use, esp for some practical purpose **b** to lay or spread on **2** to devote (e g oneself) with close attention or diligence – usu + to **3** to have relevance – usu + to **4** to make a request, esp in writing

appoint /əˈpɔɪnt/ v **1** to fix or name officially **2** to select for an office or position **3** to declare the disposition of (an estate) to sby

appointment /əˈpɔɪntmənt/ n **1** an act of appointing; a designation **2** an office or position held by sby who has been appointed to it rather than voted into it **3** an arrangement for a meeting **4** pl equipment, furnishings

appreciate /əˈpriːʃieɪt/ v **1a** to understand the nature, worth, quality, or significance of **b** to recognize with gratitude; value or admire highly **2** to increase in value

appreciation /əˌpriːʃiˈeɪʃən/ n **1a** sensitive awareness; esp recognition of aesthetic values **b** a judgment, evaluation; esp a favourable critical estimate **c** an expression of admiration, approval, or gratitude **2** an increase in value

¹apprentice /əˈprentɪs/ n **1** one who is learning an art or trade **2** an inexperienced person; a novice

²apprentice v to set at work as an apprentice

¹approach /əˈprəʊtʃ/ v **1a** to draw closer (to) **b** to come very near to in quality, character, etc **2a** to make advances to, esp in order to create a desired result **b** to begin to consider or deal with

²approach n **1a** an act or instance of approaching **b** an approximation **2** a manner or method of doing sthg, esp for the first time **3** a means of access **4a** a golf shot from the fairway towards the green **b** (the steps taken on) the part of a tenpin bowling alley from which a bowler must deliver the ball **5** the final part of an aircraft flight before landing **6** an advance made to establish personal or business relations – usu pl

¹appropriate /əˈprəʊprieɪt/ v **1** to take exclusive possession of **2** to set apart (specif money) for a particular purpose or use **3** to take or make use of without authority or right

²appropriate /əˈprəʊpriɪt/ adj especially suitable or compatible; fitting – ~ly adv – ~ness n

approval /əˈpruːvəl/ n **1** a favourable opinion or judgment **2** formal or official permission

approve /əˈpruːv/ v **1** to have or express a favourable opinion (of) **2a** to accept as satisfactory **b** to give formal or official sanction to; ratify – approvingly adv

¹approximate /əˈprɒksimɪt/ adj nearly correct or exact – ~ly adv

²approximate /əˈprɒksimeɪt/ v **1** to bring or come near or close – often + to **2** to come near to; approach, esp in quality or number

April /ˈeɪprɪl/ n the 4th month of the Gregorian calendar

apt /æpt/ adj **1** ordinarily disposed; likely – usu + to **2** suited to a purpose; relevant – ~ly adv – ~ness n

aptitude /ˈæptɪtjuːd/ n **1** a natural ability; a talent, esp for learning **2** general fitness or suitability – usu + for

aquarium /əˈkweəriəm/ n, pl **aquariums, aquaria** **1** a glass tank, artificial pond, etc in which living aquatic animals or plants are kept **2** an establishment where collections of living aquatic organisms are exhibited

arbitrary /ˈɑːbɪtrəri/ adj **1** depending on choice or discretion **2a** arising from unrestrained exercise of the will **b** selected at random and without reason – rily adv – riness n

¹arch /ɑːtʃ/ n **1** a typically curved structural member spanning an opening and resisting lateral or vertical pressure (e g of a wall) **2** sthg (e g the vaulted bony structure of the foot) resembling an arch in form or function **3** an archway

²arch v **1** to span or provide with an arch **2** to form or bend into an arch **3** to form an arch

³arch adj **1** principal, chief **2a** cleverly sly and alert **b** playfully saucy – ~ly adv

archaeology /ˌɑːkiˈɒlədʒi/ n the scientific study of material remains (e g tools or dwellings) of past human life and activities – **gical** adj – **gically** adv – **gist** n

archaic /ɑːˈkeɪɪk/ adj **1** (characteristic) of an earlier or more primitive time; antiquated **2** no longer used in ordinary speech or writing – ~ally adv

architect /ˈɑːkɪtekt/ n **1** sby who designs buildings and superintends their construction **2** sby who devises, plans, and achieves a specified objective

architecture /ˈɑːkɪtektʃə/ n **1** the art, practice, or profession of designing and erecting buildings; also a method or style of building **2** product or work of architecture – **tural** adj – **turally** adv

arctic /ˈɑːktɪk/ adj **1** often cap of the N Pole or the surrounding region **2a** extremely cold; frigid **b** cold in temper or mood

arduous /ˈɑːdjuəs/ adj **1** hard to accomplish or achieve; difficult, strenuous **2** hard to climb; steep – ~ly adv – ~ness n

are /ə; strong ɑː/ pres 2 sing or pres pl of be

area /ˈeəriə/ n **1** a level piece of ground **2** a particular extent of space or surface, or one serving a special function **3** the extent, range, or scope of a concept, operation, or activity; a field

arena /əˈriːnə/ n **1** (a building containing) an enclosed area used for public entertainment **2** a sphere of interest or activity; a scene

argue /'ɑːgjuː/ *v* **1** to give reasons for or against (sthg); reason, discuss **2** to contend or disagree in words **3** to give evidence of; indicate **4** to (try to) prove by giving reasons; maintain

argument /'ɑːgjʊmənt/ *n* **1** a reason given in proof or rebuttal **2a** the act or process of arguing; debate **b** a coherent series of reasons offered **c** a quarrel, disagreement **3** an abstract or summary, esp of a literary work

arise /ə'raɪz/ *v* **arose, arisen 1a** to originate from a source – often + *from* **b** to come into being or to attention **2** to get up, rise – chiefly fml

aristocracy /ˌærɪ'stɒkrəsi/ *n* **1** (a state with) a government in which power is vested in a small privileged usu hereditary noble class **2** *sing or pl in constr* a (governing) usu hereditary nobility **3** *sing or pl in constr* the whole group of those believed to be superior (e g in wealth, rank, or intellect)

aristocrat /'ærɪstəkræt, ə'rɪ-/ *n* **1** a member of an aristocracy; *esp* a noble **2** one who has the bearing and viewpoint typical of the aristocracy – ~**ic** *adj* – ~**ically** *adv*

arithmetic /ə'rɪθmətɪk/ *n* a branch of mathematics that deals with real numbers and calculations with them **2** computation, calculation – ~**al** *adj* – ~**ally** *adv*

¹**arm** /ɑːm/ *n* **1** (the part between the shoulder and the wrist of) the human upper limb **2** sthg like or corresponding to an arm: e g **a** the forelimb of a vertebrate animal **b** a limb of an invertebrate animal **3** an inlet of water (e g from the sea) **4** might, authority **5** a support (e g on a chair) for the elbow and forearm **6** a sleeve **7** a functional division of a group or activity – ~**less** *adj*

²**arm** *v* **1** to supply or equip with weapons **2** to provide with sthg that strengthens or protects **3** to equip for action or operation **4** to prepare oneself for struggle or resistance – ~**ed** *adj*

³**arm** *n* **1a** a weapon; *esp* a firearm – usu pl **b** a combat branch (e g of an army) **2** pl the heraldic insignia of a group or body (e g a family or government) **3** pl **a** active hostilities **b** military service or profession

¹**armchair** /'ɑːmtʃeə'/ *n* a chair with armrests

²**armchair** *adj* **1** remote from direct dealing with practical problems **2** sharing vicariously in another's experiences

armour /'ɑːmə'/ *n* **1a** a defensive covering for the body; *esp* a covering (e g of metal) worn in combat **b** a usu metallic protective covering (e g for a ship, fort, aircraft, or car) **2** armoured forces and vehicles (e g tanks)

army /'ɑːmi/ *n* **1a** a large organized force for war on land **b** *often cap* the complete military organization of a nation for land warfare **2** a great multi-

tude **3** a body of people organized to advance a cause

arose /ə'rəʊz/ *past of* **arise**

¹**around** /ə'raʊnd/ *adv, prep* **1** round **2** about

²**around** *adj* **1** about **2** in existence, evidence, or circulation

arrange /ə'reɪndʒ/ *v* **1** to put in order or into sequence or relationship **2** to make preparations (for); plan **3** to bring about an agreement concerning; settle **4** to adapt (a musical composition) by scoring for different voices or instruments

arrangement /ə'reɪndʒmənt/ *n* **1a** a preliminary measure; a preparation **b** an adaptation of a musical composition for different voices or instruments **c** an informal agreement or settlement, esp on personal, social, or political matters **2** sthg made by arranging constituents or things together

¹**arrest** /ə'rest/ *v* **1a** to bring to a stop **b** to make inactive **2** to seize, capture; *specif* to take or keep in custody by authority of law **3** to catch and fix or hold

²**arrest** *n* **1** the act of stopping **2** the taking or detaining of sby in custody by authority of law **3** a device for arresting motion

arrival /ə'raɪvəl/ *n* **1** the attainment of an end or state **2** sby or sthg that has arrived

arrive /ə'raɪv/ *v* **1** to reach a destination **2** to come **3** to achieve success

arrogant /'ærəgənt/ *adj* aggressively conceited

¹**arrow** /'ærəʊ/ *n* **1** a projectile shot from a bow, usu having a slender shaft, a pointed head, and feathers at the end **2** sthg shaped like an arrow; *esp* a mark to indicate direction

²**arrow** *v* to indicate with an arrow

arson /'ɑːsən/ *n* the criminal act of setting fire to property in order to cause destruction – ~**ist** *n*

¹**art** /ɑːt/ *archaic pres 2 sing of* be

²**art** *n* **1** a skill acquired by experience, study, or observation **2** pl the humanities as contrasted with science **3a** the conscious use of skill and creative imagination, esp in the production of aesthetic objects; *also* works so produced **b** (any of the) fine arts or graphic arts

³**art** *adj* **1** composed, designed, or created with conscious artistry **2** designed for decorative purposes

artery /'ɑːtəri/ *n* **1** any of the branching elastic-walled blood vessels that carry blood from the heart to the lungs and through the body **2** an esp main channel (e g a river or road) of transport or communication

¹**article** /'ɑːtɪkəl/ *n* **1a(1)** a separate clause, item, provision, or point in a document **(2)** pl a written agreement specifying conditions of apprenticeship **b** a piece of nonfictional prose, usu forming an independent part of a magazine, newspaper, etc **2** an item of business; a matter **3** a word or affix (e g *a, an,* and *the*) used with nouns to give

indefiniteness or definiteness **4a** a particular or separate object or thing, esp viewed as a member of a class of things **b** a thing of a particular and distinctive kind

²**article** v to bind by articles (e g of apprenticeship)

artificial /ˌɑːtɪˈfɪʃəl/ adj **1** made by human skill and labour, often to a natural model; man-made **2a** lacking in natural quality; affected **b** imitation, sham – ~**ly** adv – ~**ity** n

artillery /ɑːˈtɪləri/ n **1** large-calibre mounted firearms (e g guns, howitzers, missile launchers, etc) **2** sing or pl in constr a branch of an army armed with artillery

artist /ˈɑːtɪst/ n **1a** one who professes and practises an imaginative art **b** a person skilled in a fine art **2** a skilled performer; specif an artiste **3** one who is proficient in a specified and usu dubious activity; an expert – infml

artistic /ɑːˈtɪstɪk/ adj **1** concerning or characteristic of art or artists **2** showing imaginative skill in arrangement or execution – ~**ally** adv

¹**as** /əz; strong æz/ adv **1** to the same degree or amount; equally **2** when considered in a specified form or relation – usu used before a preposition or participle (e g blind as opposed to stupid)

²**as** conj **1a** to the same degree that – usu used as a correlative after as or so to introduce a comparison or as a result **b** – used after same or such to introduce an example or comparison **c** – used after so to introduce the idea of purpose (e g hid so as to escape) in the way that –used before so to introduce a parallel **3** in accordance with what (e g late as usual) **4** while, when **5** regardless of the fact that; though (e g late as it was, I phoned her) **6** for the reason that; seeing (e g as it's wet, we'll stay at home)

³**as** pron **1** a fact that; and this (e g which, as history relates, was a bad king) **2** which also; and so (e g he's a doctor, as was his mother)

⁴**as** prep **1** like **2** in the capacity, character, role, or state of (e g works as an actor)

ascend /əˈsend/ v **1** to move or slope gradually upwards; rise **2a** to rise from a lower level or degree **b** to go back in time or in order of genealogical succession **3** to go or move up **4** to succeed to; begin to occupy – esp in ascend the throne – ~**ancy** n – ~**ant** adj

¹**ash** /æʃ/ n (the tough elastic wood of) any of a genus of tall trees of the olive family

²**ash** n **1a** the solid residue left when material is thoroughly burned or oxidized **b** fine particles of mineral matter from a volcano **2** pl the remains of sthg destroyed by fire **3** pl the remains of a dead body after cremation or disintegration

ashamed /əˈʃeɪmd/ adj **1** feeling shame, guilt, or disgrace **2** restrained by fear of shame – ~**ly** adv

ashore /əˈʃɔː/ adv on or to the shore

¹**aside** /əˈsaɪd/ adv or adj **1** to or towards the side **2** out of the way **3** apart; in reserve **4** apart

²**aside** n **1** an utterance meant to be inaudible; esp an actor's speech supposedly not heard by other characters on stage **2** a digression

ask /ɑːsk/ v **1a** to call on for an answer **b** to put a question about **c** to put or frame (a question) **2** to make a request of or for **3** to behave in such a way as to provoke (an unpleasant response) **4** to set as a price **5** to invite **6** to seek information

asleep /əˈsliːp/ adj **1** in a state of sleep **2** dead – euph **3** lacking sensation; numb

aspire /əˈspaɪə/ v to seek to attain or accomplish a particular goal – usu + to

aspirin /ˈæsprɪn/ n, pl **-rin, -rins** (a tablet containing) a derivative of salicylic acid used for relief of pain and fever

¹**ass** /æs/ n **1** the donkey or a similar long-eared hardy gregarious mammal related to and smaller than the horse **2** a stupid, obstinate, or perverse person or thing

²**ass** n, chiefly NAm the arse

assassin /əˈsæsɪn/ n **1** cap any of a secret order of Muslims who at the time of the Crusades committed secret murders **2** a murderer; esp one who murders a politically important person, for money or from fanatical motives

assassinate /əˈsæsɪneɪt/ v to murder suddenly or secretly, usu for political reasons – **-ation** n

¹**assault** /əˈsɔːlt/ n **1** a violent physical or verbal attack **2a** an attempt to do or immediate threat of doing unlawful personal violence **b** rape **3** an attempt to attack a fortification by a sudden rush

²**assault** v to make an (indecent) assault on **2** to rape

assemble /əˈsembəl/ v **1** to bring together (e g in a particular place or for a particular purpose) **2** to fit together the parts of **3** to gather together; convene

assembly /əˈsembli/ n **1** a company of people gathered for deliberation and legislation, entertainment, or worship **2** cap a legislative body **3a** an assemblage **b** assembling or being assembled **4** a bugle, drum, etc signal for troops to assemble or fall in **5** (a collection of parts assembled by) the fitting together of manufactured parts into a complete machine, structure, etc

assert /əˈsɜːt/ v **1** to state or declare positively and often forcefully **2** to demonstrate the existence of

assess /əˈses/ v **1a** to determine the rate or amount of (e g a tax) **b** to impose (e g a tax) according to an established rate **2** to make an official valuation of (property) for the purposes of taxation **3** to determine the importance, size, or value of – ~**ment** n

asset /ˈæset, ˈæsɪt/ n **1a** pl the total property of a person, company, or institution; esp that part which can be used to pay debts **b** a single item of property **2** an advantage, resource **3** *pl* the items on a balance sheet showing the book value of property owned

assist /ə'sɪst/ *v* **1** to give support or aid **2** to be present as a spectator **3** to give support or aid to – ~**ance** *n*

association /ə,səʊsi'eɪʃən, ə,səʊʃi-/ *n* **1** an organization of people having a common interest; a society, league **2** sthg linked in memory, thought, or imagination with a thing or person **3** the formation of mental connections between sensations, ideas, memories, etc

assorted /ə'sɔːtᵻd/ *adj* **1** consisting of various kinds **2** suited by nature, character, or design; matched

assortment /ə'sɔːtmənt/ *n* a collection of assorted things or people

assume /ə'sjuːm/ *v* **1a** to take to or upon oneself; undertake **b** to invest oneself formally with (an office or its symbols) **2** to seize, usurp **3** to pretend to have or be; feign **4** to take as granted or true; suppose – often + *that*

assurance /ə'ʃʊərəns/ *n* **1a** a pledge, guarantee **b** *chiefly Br* (life) insurance **2a** the quality or state of being sure or certain; freedom from doubt **b** confidence of mind or manner; *also* excessive self-confidence; brashness **3** sthg that inspires or tends to inspire confidence

assure /ə'ʃʊə/ *v* **1** to make safe; insure (esp life or safety) **2** to give confidence to; reassure **3** to inform positively **4** to guarantee the happening or attainment of; ensure

astonish /ə'stɒnɪʃ/ *v* to strike with sudden wonder or surprise – ~**ment** *n*

astrology /ə'strɒlədʒi/ *n* the art or practice of determining the supposed influences of the planets on human affairs – **-ger** *n* – **-gical** *adj* – **-gically** *adv*

astronomy /ə'strɒnəmi/ *n* a branch of science dealing with the celestial bodies – **-er** *n*

at /ət; *strong* æt/ *prep* **1** – used to indicate presence or occurrence in, on, or near a place imagined as a point (e g *sick at heart*) **2** – used to indicate the goal or direction of an action or motion (e g *aim at the goal*) **3a** – used to indicate occupation or employment (e g *at tea*) **b** when it comes to (an occupation or employment) (e g *an expert at chess*) **4** – used to indicate situation or condition (e g *at risk*) **5** in response to (e g *shudder at the thought*) **6** – used to indicate position on a scale (e g of cost, speed, or age) (e g *at 80 mph*) **7** – used to indicate position in time (e g *at midday*)

ate /et, eɪt/ *past of* eat

athlete /'æθliːt/ *n* sby who is trained in, skilled in, or takes part in exercises, sports, etc that require physical strength, agility, or stamina

athletics /æθ'letɪks, əθ-/ *n pl but sing or pl in constr*, *Br* competitive walking, running, throwing, and jumping sports collectively

atlas /'ætləs/ *n* **1** *cap* one who bears a heavy burden **2** a bound collection of maps, charts, or tables **3** the first vertebra of the neck

atmosphere /'ætməsfɪə/ *n* **1** a mass of gas enveloping a celestial body (e g a planet); *esp* all the air surrounding the earth **2** the air of a locality **3** a surrounding influence or environment **4** a dominant aesthetic or emotional effect or appeal

atom /'ætəm/ *n* **1** any of the minute indivisible particles of which according to ancient materialism the universe is composed **2** a tiny particle; a bit **3** the smallest particle of an element that can exist either alone or in combination, consisting of various numbers of electrons, protons, and neutrons **4** nuclear power

atom bomb *n* a bomb whose violent explosive power is due to the sudden release of atomic energy derived from the splitting of the nuclei of plutonium, uranium, etc by neutrons in a very rapid chain reaction; *also* a hydrogen bomb

atomic /ə'tɒmɪk/ *adj* **1** of or concerned with atoms, atom bombs, or atomic energy **2** *of a chemical element* existing as separate atoms – ~**ally** *adv*

atomic energy *n* energy liberated in an atom bomb, nuclear reactor, etc by changes in the nucleus of an atom

atrocious /ə'trəʊʃəs/ *adj* **1** extremely wicked or cruel; barbaric **2** of very poor quality – ~**ity** *n*

attach /ə'tætʃ/ *v* **1** to seize by legal authority **2** to bring (oneself) into an association **3** to appoint to serve with an organization for special duties or for a temporary period **4** to fasten **5** to ascribe, attribute **6** to become attached; stick *USE* often + *to*

¹**attack** /ə'tæk/ *v* **1** to set upon forcefully in order to damage, injure, or destroy **2** to take the initiative against in a game or contest **3** to assail with unfriendly or bitter words **4** to set to work on, esp vigorously **5** to make an attack

²**attack** *n* **1** the act of attacking; an assault **2** a belligerent or antagonistic action or verbal assault – often + *on* **3** the beginning of destructive action (e g by a chemical agent) **4** the setting to work on some undertaking **5** a fit of sickness or (recurrent) disease **6a** an attempt to score or to gain ground in a game **b** *sing or pl in constr* the attacking players in a team or the positions occupied by them; *specif* the bowlers in a cricket team

¹**attempt** /ə'tempt/ *v* to make an effort to do, accomplish, solve, or effect, esp without success

²**attempt** *n* **1** the act or an instance of attempting; *esp* an unsuccessful effort **2** an attack, assault – often + *on*

attend /ə'tend/ *v* **1** to take charge of; look after **2** to go or stay with as a companion, nurse, or servant **3** to be present with; accompany, escort **4** to be present at **5** to deal with **6** to apply the mind or pay attention; heed *USE* – often + *to*

attendance /ə'tendəns/ *n* **1** the number of people attending **2** the number of times a person attends, usu out of a possible maximum

attention /ə'tenʃən/ *n* **1** attending, esp through application of the mind to an object of sense or thought **2** consideration with a view to action **3a** an act of civility or courtesy, esp in courtship – usu pl **b** sympathetic consideration of the needs and wants of others **4** a formal position of readiness assumed by a soldier – usu as a command

attentive /ə'tentɪv/ *adj* **1** mindful, observant **2** solicitous **3** paying attentions (as if) in the role of a suitor – ~ ly *adv* – ~ ness *n*

attitude /'ætɪtjuːd/ *n* **1** the arrangement of the parts of a body or figure; a posture **2** a feeling, emotion, or mental position with regard to a fact or state **3** a manner assumed for a specific purpose **4** a ballet position in which one leg is raised at the back and bent at the knee

attract /ə'trækt/ *v* **1** to pull to or towards oneself or itself **2** to draw by appeal to interest, emotion, or aesthetic sense **3** to possess or exercise the power of attracting sthg or sby – ~ ive *adj*

attraction /ə'trækʃən/ *n* **1** a characteristic that elicits interest or admiration – usu pl **2** the action or power of drawing forth a response (e g interest or affection); an attractive quality **3** a force between unlike electric charges, unlike magnetic poles, etc, resisting separation **4** sthg that attracts or is intended to attract people by appealing to their desires and tastes

audience /'ɔːdɪəns/ *n* **1a** a formal hearing or interview **b** an opportunity of being heard **2** *sing or pl in constr* a group of listeners or spectators

august /ɔː'gʌst/ *adj* marked by majestic dignity or grandeur – ~ ly *adv*

August /'ɔːgəst/ *n* the 8th month of the Gregorian calendar

aunt /ɑːnt/ *n* **1a** the sister of one's father or mother **b** the wife of one's uncle **2** – often used as a term of affection for a woman who is a close friend of a young child or its parents

authentic /ɔː'θentɪk/ *adj* **1** worthy of belief as conforming to fact or reality; trustworthy **2** not imaginary, false, or imitation; genuine – ~ ally *adv* – ~ ity *n*

author /'ɔːθə'/, *fem* **authoress** *n* **1a** the writer of a literary work **b** (the books written by) sby whose profession is writing **2** sby or sthg that originates or gives existence; a source

authority /ɔː'θɒrɪ̣ti, ə-/ *n* **1a** a book, quotation, etc referred to for justification of one's opinions or actions **b** a conclusive statement or set of statements **c** an individual cited or appealed to as an expert **2a** power to require and receive submission; the right to expect obedience **b** power to influence or command **c** a right granted by sby in authority; authorization **3a** *pl* the people in command **b** persons in command; *specif* government **c** *often cap* a

governmental administrative body **4a** grounds, warrant **b** convincing force; weight

autobiography /ˌɔːtəbaɪ'ɒgrəfi/ *n* the biography of a person written by him-/herself; *also* such writing considered as a genre

¹**autograph** /'ɔːtəgrɑːf/ *n* an identifying mark, specif a person's signature, made by the individual him-/herself

²**autograph** *v* to write one's signature in or on

¹**automatic** /ˌɔːtə'mætɪk/ *adj* **1a** acting or done spontaneously or unconsciously **b** resembling an automaton; mechanical **2** having a self-acting or self-regulating mechanism **3** *of a firearm* repeatedly ejecting the empty cartridge shell, introducing a new cartridge, and firing it – ~ ally *adv*

²**automatic** *n* an automatic machine or apparatus; *esp* an automatic firearm or vehicle

autumn /'ɔːtəm/ *n* **1** the season between summer and winter, extending, in the northern hemisphere, from the September equinox to the December solstice **2** a period of maturity or the early stages of decline – ~ al *adj* – ~ ally *adv*

available /ə'veɪləbəl/ *adj* **1** present or ready for immediate use **2** accessible, obtainable **3** qualified or willing to do sthg or to assume a responsibility – -ability *n* – -ably *adv*

avenue /'ævɪ̣njuː/ *n* **1** a line of approach **2** a broad passageway bordered by trees **3** an often broad street or road

¹**average** /'ævərɪdʒ/ *n* **1** a single value representative of a set of other values; *esp* an arithmetic mean **2** a level (e g of intelligence) typical of a group, class, or series **3** a ratio expressing the average performance of a sports team or sportsman as a fraction of the number of opportunities for successful performance

²**average** *adj* **1** equalling an arithmetic mean **2a** about midway between extremes **b** not out of the ordinary; common

³**average** *v* **1** to be or come to an average **2** to do, get, or have on average or as an average sum or quantity **3** to find the arithmetic mean of **4** to bring towards the average **5** to have an average value of

aviation /ˌeɪvɪ'eɪʃən/ *n* **1** the operation of heavier-than-air aircraft **2** aircraft manufacture, development, and design

avoid /ə'vɔɪd/ *v* **1a** to keep away from; shun **b** to prevent the occurrence or effectiveness of **c** to refrain from **2** to make legally void – ~ able *adj* – ~ ance *n*

await /ə'weɪt/ *v* **1** to wait for **2** to be in store for

¹**awake** /ə'weɪk/ *v* **awoke** *also* **awaked**; **awoken** **1** to emerge or arouse from sleep or a sleeplike state **2** to become conscious or aware of sthg – usu + *to* **3** to make active; stir up

²awake *adj* **1** roused (as if) from sleep **2** fully conscious; aware – usu + *to*

¹award /ə'wɔːd/ *v* **1** to give by judicial decree **2** to confer or bestow as being deserved or needed

²award *n* **1** a final decision; *esp* the decision of arbitrators in a case submitted to them **2** sthg that is conferred or bestowed, esp on the basis of merit or need

aware /ə'weə'/ *adj* having or showing realization, perception, or knowledge; conscious – often + *of* – ~**ness** *n*

¹away /ə'weɪ/ *adv* **1** on the way; along (e g get *away* early) **2** from here or there; hence, thence **3a** in a secure place or manner (e g locked *away*) **b** in another direction; aside (e g looked *away*) **4** out of existence; to an end (e g laze *away* an afternoon) **5** from one's possession (e g gave the car *away*) **6** on, uninterruptedly (e g chatted *away*)

²away *adj* **1** absent from a place; gone **2** distant (e g a town some way *away*) **3** played on an opponent's grounds

¹awful /'ɔːfəl/ *adj* **1** extremely disagreeable or objectionable **2** exceedingly great – used as an intensive; chiefly infml – ~**ly** *adv*

²awful *adv* very, extremely – nonstandard

awkward /'ɔːkwəd/ *adj* **1** lacking dexterity or skill, esp in the use of hands; clumsy **2** lacking ease or grace (e g of movement or expression) **3a** lacking social grace and assurance **b** causing embarrassment **4** poorly adapted for use or handling **5** requiring caution **6** deliberately thwarting or obstructive – ~**ly** *adv* – ~**ness** *n*

¹axe /æks/ *n* **1** a tool that has a cutting edge parallel to the handle and is used esp for felling trees and chopping and splitting wood **2** drastic reduction or removal (e g of personnel)

²axe *v* **1a** to hew, shape, dress, or trim with an axe **b** to chop, split, or sever with an axe **2** to remove abruptly (e g from employment or from a budget)

axle /'æksəl/ *n* **1** a shaft on or with which a wheel revolves **2** a rod connecting a pair of wheels of a vehicle

B

¹baby /'beɪbi/ *n* **1a(1)** an extremely young child; *esp* an infant **(2)** an unborn child **(3)** an extremely young animal **b** the youngest of a group **2** an infantile person **3** a person or thing for which one feels special responsibility or pride **4** a person; *esp* a girl, woman – slang; usu as a noun of address

²baby *adj* very small

³baby *v* to tend or indulge with often excessive or inappropriate care

baby-sit *v* to care for a child, usu for a short period while the parents are out – ~**ter** *n*

bachelor /'bætʃələ'/ *n* **1** a recipient of what is usu the lowest degree conferred by a college or university **2** an unmarried man **3** a male animal (e g a fur seal) without a mate during breeding season – ~**hood** *n*

¹back /bæk/ *n* **1a** the rear part of the human body, esp from the neck to the end of the spine **b** the corresponding part of a quadruped or other lower animal **2a** the side or surface behind the front or face; the rear part; *also* the farther or reverse side **b** sthg at or on the back for support **3** (the position of) a primarily defensive player in some games (e g soccer)

²back *adv* **1a(1)** to, towards, or at the rear **(2)** away (e g from the speaker) **b** in or into the past or nearer the beginning; ago **c** in or into a reclining position **d** in or into a delayed or retarded condition **2a** to, towards, or in a place from which sby or sthg came **b** to or towards a former state **c** in return or reply

³back *adj* **1** at or in the back **b** distant from a central or main area; remote **2** being behindhand or in arrears **3** not current

⁴back *v* **1a** to support by material or moral assistance – often + *up* **b** to substantiate – often + *up* **c(1)** to countersign, endorse **(2)** to assume financial responsibility for **2** to cause to go back or in reverse **3a** to provide with a back **b** to be at the back of **4** to place a bet on (e g a horse) **5** to move backwards **6** *of the wind* to shift anticlockwise **7** to have the back in the direction of sthg

background /'bækgraʊnd/ *n* **1a** the scenery or ground behind sthg **b** the part of a painting or photograph that depicts what lies behind objects in the foreground **2** an inconspicuous position **3a** the conditions that form the setting within which sthg is experienced **b** information essential to the understanding of a problem or situation **c** the total of a person's experience, knowledge, and education

backing /'bækɪŋ/ *n* **1** sthg forming a back **2a** support, aid **b** endorsement

backlash /'bæklæʃ/ *n* **1** a sudden violent backward movement or reaction **2** a strong adverse reaction

backward /'bækwəd/ *adj* **1a** directed or turned backwards **b** done or executed backwards **2** retarded in development **3** of or occupying a fielding position in cricket behind the batsman's wicket – ~**ly** *adv* – ~**ness** *n*

backwards /'bækwədz/ *adv* **1** towards the back **2** with the back foremost **3** in a reverse direction; towards the beginning **4** perfectly; by heart **5** towards the past **6** towards a worse state

bacon /'beɪkən/ *n* (the meat cut from) the cured and often smoked side of a pig

bacterium /bæk'tɪəriəm/ *n, pl* **bacteria** a small, often disease-causing microorganism – **-rial** *adj*

¹bad /bæd/ *adj* **worse; worst 1a** failing to

reach an acceptable standard; poor, inadequate **b** unfavourable **c** no longer acceptable, because of decay or disrepair **2a** morally objectionable **b** mischievous, disobedient **3** unskilful, incompetent – often + *at* **4** disagreeable, unpleasant **5a** injurious, harmful **b** worse than usual; severe **6** incorrect, faulty **7a** suffering pain or distress; unwell **b** unhealthy, diseased **8** sorry, unhappy **9** invalid, worthless **10** *of a debt* not recoverable – ~ness *n* – ~ly *adv*

²bad *n* an evil or unhappy state

badge /bædʒ/ *n* **1** a device or token, esp of membership in a society or group **2** a characteristic mark **3** an emblem awarded for a particular accomplishment

¹badger /'bædʒə'/ *n* (the pelt or fur of) any of several sturdy burrowing nocturnal mammals widely distributed in the northern hemisphere

²badger *v* to harass or annoy persistently

baffle /'bæfl/ *v* to throw into puzzled confusion; perplex – **-ing** *adj* – **-ingly** *adv* – ~**ment** *n*

²baffle *n* a structure that reduces the exchange of sound waves between the front and back of a loudspeaker

¹bag /bæg/ *n* **1a** a usu flexible container for holding, storing, or carrying sthg **b** a handbag or shoulder bag **2** sthg resembling a bag; *esp* a sagging in cloth **3** spoils, loot **4** *pl chiefly Br* lots, masses **5** *infml* **5** a slovenly unattractive woman – *slang* **6** a way of life – *slang*

²bag *v* **1** to swell out; bulge **2** to hang loosely **3** to cause to swell **4** to put into a bag **5a** to take (animals) as game **b** to get possession of, seize; *also* to steal

baggage /'bægɪdʒ/ *n* **1** portable equipment, esp of a military force **2** superfluous or useless things, ideas, or practices **3** luggage, esp for travel by sea or air **4** a good-for-nothing woman; a pert girl – *infml*

¹bait /beɪt/ *v* **1** to provoke, tease, or exasperate with unjust, nagging, or persistent remarks **2** to harass (e g a chained animal) with dogs, usu for sport **3** to provide with bait

²bait *n* **1a** sthg used in luring, esp to a hook or trap **b** a poisonous material placed where it will be eaten by pests **2** a lure, temptation

bake /beɪk/ *v* **1** to dry or harden by subjecting to heat **2** to cook (food) by baking **3** to become baked **4** to become extremely hot – ~**r** *n*

¹balance /'bæləns/ *n* **1** an instrument for weighing **2** a counterbalancing weight, force, or influence **3** stability produced by even distribution of weight on each side of a vertical axis **4a** equilibrium between contrasting, opposing, or interacting elements **b** equality between the totals of the 2 sides of an account **5** an aesthetically pleasing integration of elements **6** the ability to retain one's physical equilibrium **7** the weight or force of one side in excess of

another **8a** (a statement of) the difference between credits and debits in an account **b** sthg left over; a remainder **c** an amount in excess, esp on the credit side of an account **9** mental and emotional steadiness

²balance *v* **1a(1)** to compute the difference between the debits and credits of (an account) **(2)** to pay the amount due on **b** to arrange so that one set of elements exactly equals another **2a** to counterbalance, offset **b** to equal or equalize in weight, number, or proportion **3** to compare the relative importance, value, force, or weight of; ponder **4** to bring to a state or position of balance **5** to become balanced or established in balance **6** to be an equal counterweight – often + *with*

balcony /'bælkənɪ/ *n* **1** a platform built out from the wall of a building and enclosed by a railing or low wall **2** a gallery inside a building (e g a theatre)

bald /bɔːld/ *adj* **1a** lacking a natural or usual covering (e g of hair, vegetation, or nap) **b** having little or no tread **2** unadorned, undisguised **3** *of an animal* marked with white, esp on the head or face – ~**ness** *n*

¹ball /bɔːl/ *n* **1** a round or roundish body or mass: **a** a solid or hollow spherical or egg-shaped body used in a game or sport **b** a spherical or conical projectile; *also* projectiles used in firearms **c** the rounded slightly raised fleshy area at the base of a thumb or big toe **2** a delivery or play of the ball in cricket, baseball, etc **3** a game in which a ball is thrown, kicked, or struck; *specif, NAm* baseball **4a** a testis – usu *pl*; *vulg* **b** *pl* nonsense – often used interjectionally; *vulg*

²ball *v* **1** to form or gather into a ball **2** to have sexual intercourse (with) – *vulg*

³ball *n* **1** a large formal gathering for social dancing **2** a very pleasant experience; a good time – *infml*

ballet /'bæleɪ/ *n* **1** (a group that performs) artistic dancing in which the graceful flowing movements are based on conventional positions and steps **2** a theatrical art form using ballet dancing, music, and scenery to convey a story, theme, or atmosphere

¹balloon /bə'luːn/ *n* **1** an envelope filled with hot air or a gas lighter than air so as to rise and float in the atmosphere **2** an inflatable usu brightly coloured rubber bag used as a toy **3** a line enclosing words spoken or thought by a character, esp in a cartoon

²balloon *v* **1** to inflate, distend **2** to ascend or travel in a balloon **3** to swell or puff out; expand – often + *out* **4** to increase rapidly

³balloon *adj* relating to, resembling, or suggesting a balloon

¹ballot /'bælət/ *n* **1** (a sheet of paper, or orig a small ball, used in) secret voting **2** the right to vote **3** the number of votes cast

bal

²ballot v **1** to vote by ballot **2** to ask for a vote from

ballpoint /'bɔːlpɔɪnt/ n a pen having as the writing point a small rotating metal ball that inks itself by contact with an inner magazine

bamboo /ˌbæm'buː/ n any of various chiefly tropical giant grasses including some with strong hollow stems used for building, furniture, or utensils

¹ban /bæn/ v to prohibit, esp by legal means or social pressure

²ban n **1** an ecclesiastical curse; excommunication **2** a legal or social prohibition

banana /bə'nɑːnə/ n (a tropical tree that bears) an elongated usu tapering fruit with soft pulpy flesh enclosed in a soft usu yellow rind that grows in bunches

¹band /bænd/ n **1** a strip or belt serving to join or hold things together **2** a ring of elastic **3** a more or less well-defined range of wavelengths, frequencies, or energies of light waves, radio waves, sound waves, etc **4** a narrow strip serving chiefly as decoration: e g **a** a narrow strip of material applied as trimming to an article of dress **b** pl **2** cloth strips sometimes worn at the front of the neck as part of clerical, legal, or academic dress **5** a strip distinguishable in some way (e g by colour, texture, or composition) **6** Br a group of pupils assessed as being of broadly similar ability

²band v **1** to fasten a band to or tie up with a band **2** Br to divide (pupils) into bands **3** to unite for a common purpose; confederate – often + together

³band n sing or pl in constr a group of people, animals, or things; esp a group of musicians organized for ensemble playing and using chiefly woodwind, brass, and percussion instruments

bandage /'bændɪdʒ/ n a strip of fabric used esp to dress and bind up wounds

bandit /'bændɪt/ n, pl **bandits** also **banditti 1** an outlaw; esp a member of a band of marauders **2** a political terrorist – ~**ry** n

¹bang /bæŋ/ v **1** to strike sharply; bump **2** to knock, beat, or strike hard, often with a sharp noise **3** to have sexual intercourse with – vulg **4** to strike with a sharp noise or thump **5** to produce a sharp often explosive noise or noises

²bang n **1** a resounding blow; a thump **2** a sudden loud noise – often used interjectionally **3** an act of sexual intercourse – vulg

³bang adv **1** right, directly **2** exactly USE infml

⁴bang n a short squarely-cut fringe of hair – usu pl with sing. meaning

banger /'bæŋə'/ n, Br **1** a firework that explodes with a loud bang **2** a sausage **3** an old usu dilapidated car USE (2&3) infml

banish /'bænɪʃ/ v **1** to require by authority to leave a place, esp a country **2** to dispel – ~**ment** n

banister /'bænɪstə'/ also **bannister** n a handrail with its upright supports

guarding the edge of a staircase – often pl with sing. meaning

¹bank /bæŋk/ n **1a** a mound, pile, or ridge (e g of earth or snow) **b** a piled up mass of cloud or fog **c** an undersea elevation rising esp from the continental shelf **2** the rising ground bordering a lake or river or forming the edge of a cut or hollow **3** the lateral inward tilt of a surface along a curve or of a vehicle when following a curved path

²bank v **1** to surround with a bank **2** to keep up to ensure slow burning **3** to build (a road or railway) with the outer edge of a curve higher than the inner **4** to rise in or form a bank – often + up **5** to incline an aircraft sideways when turning **6** to follow a curve or incline, specif in racing

³bank n **1** a bench for the rowers of a galley

⁴bank n **1** an establishment for the custody, loan, exchange, or issue of money and for the transmission of funds **2** a person conducting a gambling house or game; specif the banker in a game of cards **3** a supply of sthg held in reserve: e g **a** the money, chips, etc held by the bank or banker for use in a gambling game **b** the pool of pieces belonging to a game (e g dominoes) from which the players draw **4** a place where data, human organs, etc are held available for use when needed

⁵bank 1 to deposit (money) or have an account in a bank **2** to rely on; count on

bankbook /'bæŋkbʊk/ n the depositor's book in which a bank enters a record of his/her account

¹bankrupt /'bæŋkrʌpt/ n **1** an insolvent person whose estate is administered under the bankruptcy laws for the benefit of his/her creditors **2** one who is destitute of a usu specified quality or thing

²bankrupt v **1** to reduce to bankruptcy **2** to impoverish

³bankrupt adj **1** reduced to a state of financial ruin; specif legally declared a bankrupt **2a** broken, ruined **b** destitute – + of or in – ~**cy** n

banner /'bænə'/ n **1** a usu square flag bearing heraldic arms; broadly a flag **2** a headline in large type running across a newspaper page **3** a strip of cloth on which a sign is painted **4** a name, slogan, or goal associated with a particular group or ideology – often + under

banquet /'bæŋkwɪt/ n, v (to provide with or partake of) an elaborate ceremonial meal for numerous people often in honour of a person; (to have) a feast

baptism /'bæptɪzəm/ n **1** the ritual use of water for purification, esp in the Christian sacrament of admission to the church **2** an act, experience, or ordeal by which one is purified, sanctified, initiated, or named – ~**al** adj – **tize** v

¹bar /bɑː'/ n **1** a straight piece (e g of wood or metal), that is longer than it is wide and has any of various uses (e g as a lever, support, barrier, or fastening) **2a** the extinction of a claim in law **b** an intangible or nonphysical impediment **c** a submerged or partly submerged bank (e g of sand) along a shore or in a river, often obstructing navigation **3a** the dock in a law court; *also* the railing that encloses the dock **b** *often cap* (1) *sing or pl in constr* the whole body of barristers (2) the profession of barrister **4a** a stripe or chevron **b** a strip of metal attached to a military medal to indicate an additional award of the medal **5a**(1) a counter at which food or esp alcoholic drinks are served (2) a room or establishment whose main feature is a bar for the serving of alcoholic drinks **b** a place where goods, esp a specified commodity, are sold or served across a counter **6** (a group of musical notes and rests that add up to a prescribed time value, bounded on each side on the staff by) a bar line **7** a small loop or crosspiece of oversewn threads used, esp on garments, as a fastening (e g for a hook), for joining, or for strengthening sthg

²**bar** *v* **1a** to fasten with a bar **b** to place bars across to prevent movement in, out, or through **2** to mark with stripes **3a** to shut in or out (as if) by bars **b** to set aside the possibility of; rule out **4a** to interpose legal objection to **b** to prevent, forbid

³**bar** *prep* except

⁴**bar** *adv, of odds in betting* being offered for all the unnamed competitors

barbarous /'baːbərəs/ *adj* **1** uncivilized **2** lacking culture or refinement **3** mercilessly harsh or cruel – ~ly *adv*

barber /'baːbəʳ/ *n* sby, esp a man, whose occupation is cutting and dressing men's hair and shaving

¹**bare** /beəʳ/ *adj* **1** lacking a natural, usual, or appropriate covering, esp clothing **2** open to view; exposed – often in *lay bare* **3a** unfurnished, empty **b** destitute of **4a** having nothing left over or added; scant, mere **b** undisguised, unadorned – ~ness *n*

²**bare** *v* to make or lay bare; uncover, reveal

barely /'beəli/ *adv* **1** scarcely, hardly **2** in a meagre manner; scantily

¹**bargain** /'baːgɪn/ *n* **1** an agreement between parties concerning the terms of a transaction between them or the course of action each pursues in respect to the other **2** an advantageous purchase

²**bargain** *v* **1** to negotiate over the terms of a purchase, agreement, or contract **2** to come to terms; agree **3** to be prepared *for*

¹**barge** /baːdʒ/ *n* **1a** a flat-bottomed boat used chiefly for the transport of goods on inland waterways or between ships and the shore **b** a flat-bottomed coastal sailing vessel with leeboards instead of a keel **2a** a large naval motorboat used by flag officers **b** an ornate carved vessel used on ceremonial occasions

²**barge** *v* **1** to move in a headlong or clumsy fashion **2** to intrude *in* or *into*

¹**bark** /baːk/ *v* **1** to make (a sound similar to) the short loud cry characteristic of a dog **2** to speak or utter in a curt, loud, and usu angry tone; snap

²**bark** *n* **1** (a sound similar to) the sound made by a barking dog **2** a short sharp peremptory utterance

³**bark** *n* the tough exterior covering of a woody root or stem

⁴**bark** *v* to abrade the skin of

⁵**bark** *n* a boat – poetic

barley /'baːli/ *n* a widely cultivated cereal grass whose seed is used to make malt and in foods and stock feeds

barn /baːn/ *n* **1** a usu large farm building for storage, esp of feed, cereal products, etc **2** an unusually large and usu bare building

¹**barrack** /'bærək/ *n* **1** (a set or area of) buildings for lodging soldiers in garrison – often *pl* with *sing.* meaning but *sing.* or *pl in constr* **2** a large building characterized by extreme plainness or dreary uniformity with others – usu *pl* with *sing.* meaning or *pl in constr*

²**barrack** *v* to lodge in barracks

³**barrack** *v chiefly Br* to jeer, scoff (a)

barrel /'bærəl/ *n* **1** an approximately cylindrical vessel with bulging sides and flat ends constructed from wooden staves bound together with hoops; *also* any similar vessel **2a** a drum or cylindrical part: e g **a** the discharging tube of a gun **b** the part of a fountain pen or pencil containing the ink or lead

barren /'bærən/ *adj* **1a** *of a female or mating* incapable of producing offspring **b** habitually failing to fruit **2** not productive; *esp* producing inferior or scanty vegetation **3** lacking, devoid *of* **4** lacking interest, information, or charm – ~ness *n*

barrier /'bæriəʳ/ *n* **1** a material object (e g a stockade, fortress, or railing) or set of objects that separates, demarcates, or serves as a barricade **2** sthg immaterial that impedes or separates **3** a factor that tends to restrict the free movement, mingling, or interbreeding of individuals or populations

¹**base** /beɪs/ *n* **1a** the bottom of sthg; a foundation **b** the lower part of a wall, pier, or column considered as a separate architectural feature **c** that part of an organ by which it is attached to another structure nearer the centre of a living organism **2** a main ingredient **3** the fundamental part of sthg; a basis **4a** a centre from which a start is made in an activity or from which operations proceed **b** a line in a survey which serves as the origin for computations **c** the locality or installations on which a military force relies for supplies or from which it starts operations **d** the basis from which a word is derived **5a** the starting place or goal in various games **b** any of the stations at each of the 4 corners of the inner part of a baseball field to which a batter must run in turn in order to score a run **6** any of various

typically water-soluble and acrid or brackish tasting chemical compounds that are capable of taking up a hydrogen ion from or donating an unshared pair of electrons to an acid to form a salt

²**base** v 1 to make, form, or serve as a base for 2 to use as a base or basis for; establish, found – usu + *on* or *upon* – ~ **ly** *adv* – ~**ness** n

³**base** *adj* constituting or serving as a base

⁴**base** *adj* 1 *of a metal* of comparatively low value and having relatively inferior properties (e g resistance to corrosion) 2 lacking higher values; degrading 3 of relatively little value

baseball /'beisbɔ:l/ n (the ball used in) a game played with a bat and ball between 2 teams of 9 players each on a large field centring on 4 bases arranged in a square that mark the course a batter must run to score

basement /'beismənt/ n the part of a building that is wholly or partly below ground level

¹**basic** /'beisik, -zik/ *adj* 1 of or forming the base or essence; fundamental 2 constituting or serving as the minimum basis or starting point 3 of, containing, or having the character of a chemical base

²**basic** n sthg basic; a fundamental

BASIC n a high-level computer language for programming and interacting with a computer in a wide variety of applications

basin /'beisən/ n 1a a round open usu metal or ceramic vessel with a greater width than depth and sides that slope or curve inwards to the base, used typically for holding water for washing b a bowl with a greater depth than width esp for holding, mixing, or cooking food c the contents of a basin 2a a dock built in a tidal river or harbour b a (partly) enclosed water area, esp for ships 3a a depression in the surface of the land or ocean floor b the region drained by a river and its tributaries

basket /'bɑ:skɪt/ n 1a a rigid or semi-rigid receptacle made of interwoven material (e g osiers, cane, wood, or metal) b any of various lightweight usu wood containers c the contents of a basket 2 sthg that resembles a basket, esp in shape or use 3 a net open at the bottom and suspended from a metal ring that constitutes the goal in basketball 4 a collection, group

basketball /'bɑ:skɪtbɔ:l/ n (the ball used in) an indoor court game between 2 teams of 5 players each who score by tossing a large ball through a raised basket

¹**bastard** /'bæstəd, bɑ:-/ n 1 an illegitimate child 2 sthg spurious, irregular, inferior, or of questionable origin 3a an offensive or disagreeable person b a fellow of a usu specified type – infml

²**bastard** *adj* 1 illegitimate 2 of an inferior or less typical type, stock, or form 3 lacking genuineness or authority; false – ~**ize** v

¹**bat** /bæt/ n 1 a stout solid stick; a club

2 a sharp blow; a stroke 3 a (wooden) implement used for hitting the ball in cricket, baseball, table tennis, etc 4a a batsman b a turn at batting in cricket, baseball, etc

²**bat** v 1 to strike or hit (as if) with a bat 2 to strike a ball with a bat 3 to take one's turn at batting, esp in cricket – **batter** n

³**bat** n any of an order of nocturnal flying mammals with forelimbs modified to form wings

⁴**bat** v to blink, esp in surprise or emotion

batch /bætʃ/ n 1 the quantity baked at 1 time 2 the quantity of material produced at 1 operation or for use at 1 time 3 a group of people or things; a lot

¹**bath** /bɑ:θ/ n 1 a washing or soaking (e g in water or steam) of all or part of the body 2a water used for bathing b a vessel for bathing in; *esp* one that is permanently fixed in a bathroom c (a vat, tank, etc holding) a specified type of liquid used for a special purpose (e g to keep samples at a constant temperature) 3a a building containing an apartment or a series of rooms designed for bathing b a swimming pool – usu pl with sing. meaning but sing. or pl in constr c a spa USE (3a&3c) usu pl with sing. meaning

²**bath** v, Br 1 to give a bath to 2 to take a bath

¹**bathe** /beið/ v 1 to wash or soak in a liquid (e g water) 2 to moisten 3 to apply water or a liquid medicament to 4 to suffuse, esp with light 5 to take a bath 6 to swim (e g in the sea or a river) for pleasure 7 to become immersed or absorbed

²**bathe** n, Br an act of bathing, esp in the sea

¹**batter** /'bætə'/ v 1 to beat persistently or hard so as to bruise, shatter, or demolish 2 to wear or damage by hard usage or blows 3 to strike heavily and repeatedly; beat

²**batter** n a mixture that consists essentially of flour, egg, and milk or water and is thin enough to pour or drop from a spoon; *also* batter mixture when cooked

battery /'bætəri/ n 1a the act of battering b the unlawful application of any degree of force to a person without his/her consent 2 *sing or pl in constr* a tactical and administrative army artillery unit equivalent to an infantry company 3 one or more cells connected together to provide an electric current 4a a number of similar articles, items, or devices arranged, connected, or used together; a set, series b(1) a large number of small cages in which egg-laying hens are kept (2) a series of cages or compartments for raising or fattening animals, esp poultry 4a an impressive or imposing group; an array 5 the position of readiness of a gun for firing

¹**battle** /'bætl/ n 1 a general hostile encounter between armies, warships, aircraft, etc 2 a combat between 2

people **3** an extended contest, struggle, or controversy

²**battle** /v/ **1** to engage in battle; fight against **2** to contend with full strength, craft, or resources; struggle **3** to force (e g one's way) by battling

bazaar /bəˈzɑːʳ/ n **1** an (Oriental) market consisting of rows of shops or stalls selling miscellaneous goods **2** a fair for the sale of miscellaneous articles, esp for charitable purposes

be /biː; *strong* biː/ *v, pres 1 sing* **am**; *2 sing* **are**; *3 sing* **is**; *pl* **are**; *pres subjunctive* **be**; *pres part* **being**; *past 1&3 sing* **was**; *2 sing* **were**; *pl* **were**; *past subjunctive* **were**; *past part* **been 1a** to equal in meaning; have the same connotation as (e g Venus *is* the evening star) **b** to represent, symbolize **c** to have identity with **d** to belong to the class of **e** to occupy a specified position in space (e g Dundee *is* in Scotland) **f** to take place at a specified time; occur (e g that concert *was* yesterday) **g** to have a specified qualification, destination, origin, occupation, function or purpose, cost or value, or standpoint **2** to have reality or actuality; exist **3** – used with the past participle of transitive verbs as a passive-voice auxiliary **4** – used as the auxiliary of the present participle in progressive tenses expressing continuous action or arrangement in advance **5** – used with *to* and an infinitive to express destiny, arrangement in advance, obligation or necessity, or possibility *USE (1)* used regularly as the linking verb of simple predication; used in the past subjunctive or often in the indicative to express unreal conditions; often in British English used of groups in the plural form

¹**beach** /biːtʃ/ n a (gently sloping) seashore or lakeshore usu covered by sand or pebbles; *esp* the part of this between the high and low water marks

²**beach** /v/ to run or drive ashore

¹**bead** /biːd/ n **1** a small ball (e g of wood or glass) pierced for threading on a string or wire **2** *pl* (a series of prayers and meditations made with) a rosary **3** a small ball-shaped body: e g **a** a drop of liquid **b** a small metal knob on a firearm used as a front sight **4** a projecting rim, band, or moulding

²**bead** /v/ **1** to adorn or cover with beads or beading **2** to string together like beads **3** to form into a bead

beak /biːk/ n **1** the bill of a bird; *also* any similar structure on another creature **2a** the pouring spout of a vessel **b** a projection suggesting the beak of a bird **3** the human nose – *infml* **4** *chiefly Br* **a** a magistrate – *slang* **b** a schoolmaster – *slang*

¹**beam** /biːm/ n **1a** a long piece of heavy often squared timber suitable for use in construction **b** the bar of a balance from which scales hang **c** any of the principal horizontal supporting members of a building or across a ship **d** the width of a ship at its widest part **2a** a ray or shaft of radiation, esp light **b** (the course indicated by) a radio signal transmitted continuously in one direction as an aircraft navigation aid **3** the width of the buttocks – *infml*

²**beam** /v/ **1** to emit in beams or as a beam, esp of light **2** to aim (a broadcast) by directional aerials **3** to smile with joy

bean /biːn/ n **1a** (the often edible seed of) any of various erect or climbing leguminous plants **b** a bean pod used when immature as a vegetable **c** (a plant producing) any of various seeds or fruits that resemble beans or bean pods **2a** a valueless item **b** the smallest possible amount of money *USE (2) infml*

¹**bear** /beəʳ/ n **1** any of a family of large heavy mammals that have long shaggy hair and a short tail and feed largely on fruit and insects as well as on flesh **2** a surly, uncouth, or shambling person **3** one who sells securities or commodities in expectation of a fall in price

²**bear** /v/ **bore; borne** *also* **born 1a** to carry, transport – often in combination **b** to entertain mentally **c** to behave, conduct **d** to have or show as a feature **e** to give as testimony **2a** to give birth to **b** to produce as yield **c** to contain – often in combination **3a** to support the weight of **b** to accept the presence of; tolerate; *also* show patience *with* **c** to sustain, incur **d** to admit of; allow **4a** to become directed **b** to go or extend in a usu specified direction **5** to apply, have relevance **6** to support weight or strain

¹**beard** /bɪəd/ n **1** the hair that grows on the lower part of a man's face, usu excluding the moustache **2** a hairy or bristly appendage or tuft (e g on a goat's chin)

²**beard** /v/ to confront and oppose with boldness, resolution, and often effrontery; defy

beast /biːst/ n **1a** an animal as distinguished from a plant **b** a 4-legged mammal as distinguished from human beings, lower vertebrates, and invertebrates **2** a contemptible person

¹**beastly** /ˈbiːstli/ adj **1** bestial **2** abominable, disagreeable – **-liness** n

²**beastly** adv very – *infml*

¹**beat** /biːt/ v **beat; beaten; beat 1** to strike repeatedly: **a** to hit repeatedly so as to inflict pain – often + *up* **b** to strike directly against (sthg) forcefully and repeatedly **c** to flap or thrash (at) vigorously **d** to strike at or range over (as if) in order to rouse game **e** to mix (esp food) by stirring; whip **f** to strike repeatedly in order to produce music or a signal **2a** to drive or force by blows **b** to pound into a powder, paste, or pulp **c** to make by repeated treading or driving over **d** to shape by beating; *esp* to flatten thin by blows **3** to overcome, defeat; *also* to surpass **4** to leave dispirited, irresolute, or hopeless **5** to act ahead of, usu so as to forestall – *chiefly in beat someone to it* **6** to bewilder, baffle – *infml* **7** to glare or strike with oppressive intensity **8a** to pulsate, throb **b** to sound on being struck **9** to progress with much difficulty; *specif, of a sailing vessel* to make way at sea

against the wind by a series of alternate tacks across the wind

²**beat** n **1a** a single stroke or blow, esp in a series; *also* a pulsation, throb **b** a sound produced (as if) by beating **2a** (the rhythmic effect of) a metrical or rhythmic stress in poetry or music **b** the tempo indicated to a musical performer **3** an area or route regularly patrolled, esp by a policeman **4** a deadbeat – *infml*

³**beat** adj **1** of or being beatniks **2** exhausted – *infml*

⁴**beat** n a beatnik

beautiful /'bju:tɪ̩fəl/ adj **1** having qualities of beauty; exciting aesthetic pleasure or keenly delighting the senses **2** generally pleasing; excellent – ~**ly** adv

beauty /'bju:ti/ n **1** the qualities in a person or thing that give pleasure to the senses or pleasurably exalt the mind or spirit; loveliness **2** a beautiful person or thing; *esp* a beautiful woman **3** a brilliant, extreme, or conspicuous example or instance **4** a particularly advantageous or excellent quality

¹**beaver** /'bi:və'/ n **1a** a large semiaquatic rodent mammal that has webbed hind feet, a broad flat tail, and builds dams and underwater lodges **b** the fur or pelt of the beaver **2** a heavy fabric of felted wool napped on both sides **3** an energetic hard-working person

²**beaver** v to work energetically

³**beaver** n **1** a piece of armour protecting the lower part of the face **2** a helmet visor

because /bɪ'kɒz, bɪ'kəz/ conj **1** for the reason that; since **2** and the proof is that

beckon /'bekən/ v **1** to summon or signal, typically with a wave or nod **2** to appear inviting

become /bɪ'kʌm/ v **became; become 1** to come into existence **2** to come to be **3** to suit or be suitable to **4** to happen to – usu + of

¹**bed** /bed/ n **1a** a piece of furniture on or in which one may lie and sleep and which usu includes bedstead, mattress, and bedding **b** a place of sexual relations; *also* lovemaking **c** a place for sleeping or resting **d** sleep; *also* a time for sleeping **2** a flat or level surface: e g **a** (plants grown in) a plot of ground, esp in a garden, prepared for plants **b** the bottom of a body of water; *also* an area of sea or lake bottom supporting a heavy growth of a specified organism **3** a supporting surface or structure; *esp* the foundation that supports a road or railway **4** a stratum or layer of rock **5** a mass or heap resembling a bed; *esp* a heap on which sthg else is laid

²**bed** v **1a** to provide with a bed or bedding; settle in sleeping quarters **b** to go to bed with, usu for sexual intercourse **2a** to embed **b** to plant or arrange (garden plants, vegetable plants, etc) in beds – often + out **c** to base, establish **3** to lay flat or in a layer **4** to find or make sleeping accommodation **5** to form a layer

¹**bedroom** /'bedrʊm, -ru:m/ n a room furnished with a bed and intended primarily for sleeping

²**bedroom** adj dealing with, suggestive of, or inviting sexual relations

bee /bi:/ n **1** a social 4-winged insect often kept in hives for the honey that it produces **2** a gathering of people for a usu specified purpose

beech /bi:tʃ/ n (the wood of) any of a genus of hardwood deciduous trees with smooth grey bark and small edible triangular nuts

¹**beef** /bi:f/ n **1** the flesh of a bullock, cow, or other adult domestic bovine animal **2** an ox, cow, or bull in a (nearly) full-grown state; *esp* a bullock or cow fattened for food **3** muscular flesh; brawn **4** a complaint – *infml*

²**beef** v **1** to add weight, strength, or power to – usu + up **2** to complain – *infml*

been /bi:n, bɪn/ past part of be; *specif* paid a visit

beer /bɪə'/ n **1** an alcoholic drink brewed from fermented malt flavoured with hops **2** a carbonated nonalcoholic or fermented slightly alcoholic drink flavoured with roots or other plant parts

¹**beetle** /'bi:tl/ n **1** any of an order of insects that have 4 wings of which the front pair are modified into stiff coverings that protect the back pair at rest **2** a game in which the players attempt to be the first to complete a stylized drawing of a beetle in accordance with the throwing of a dice

²**beetle** v Br to move swiftly – *infml*

³**beetle** n a heavy wooden tool for hammering or ramming

beetroot /'bi:tru:t BrE/ n, pl **beetroot, beetroots** *chiefly Br* a cultivated beet with a red edible root that is a common salad vegetable

¹**before** /bɪ'fɔ:'/ adv **1** so as to be in advance of others; ahead **2** earlier in time; previously

²**before** prep **1a** in front of **b** under the jurisdiction or consideration of **2** preceding in time; earlier than **3** in a higher or more important position than **4** under the onslaught of

³**before** conj **1** earlier than the time when **2** rather than

beg /beg/ v **1** to ask for alms or charity **2** to ask earnestly (for); entreat **3a** to evade, sidestep **b** to assume as established or proved without justification **4** to ask permission – usu + an infinitive

¹**beggar** /'begə'/ n **1** one who lives by asking for gifts **2** a pauper **3** a person; *esp* a fellow – *infml*

²**beggar** v **1** to reduce to beggary **2** to exceed the resources or abilities of

begin /bɪ'gɪn/ v **began; begun 1a** to do the first part of an action; start **b** to undergo initial steps **2a** to come into existence; arise **b** to have a starting point **3** to call into being; found **4** to come first in

behalf /bɪ'ha:f/ n representative interest – usu in on someone's behalf

behave /bɪ'heɪv/ v **1** to conduct (oneself) in a specified way **2** to conduct (oneself) properly

behaviour /bɪ'heɪvɪə/ n **1a** anything that an organism does involving action and response to stimulation **b** the response of an individual, group, or species to its environment **2** the way in which sthg (e g a machine) functions – ~ **al** adj

¹**behind** /bɪ'haɪnd/ adv **1a** in the place, situation, or time that is being or has been departed from **b** in, to, or towards the back **2a** in a secondary or inferior position **b** unpaid, overdue slow

²**behind** prep **1a**(1) at or to the back or rear of (2) remaining after (sthg who has departed) **b** obscured by **2** – used to indicate backwardness, delay, or deficiency (e g he's always a long way behind the rest) **3a** in the background of **b** in a supporting position at the back of

³**behind** n the buttocks – slang

being /'biːɪŋ/ n **1a** the quality or state of having existence **b** conscious existence; life **2** the qualities that constitute an existent thing; the essence; esp personality **3** a living thing; esp a person

belief /bɪ'liːf/ n **1** trust or confidence in sby or sthg **2** sthg believed; specif a tenet or body of tenets held by a group **3** conviction of the truth of some statement or the reality of some being, thing, or phenomenon, esp when based on examination of evidence

believe /bɪ'liːv/ v **1a** to have a firm religious faith **b** to accept sthg trustfully and on faith **2** to have a firm conviction as to the reality or goodness of sthg **3** to consider to be true or honest **4** to hold as an opinion; think – **believable** adj – **believably** adv – ~ **r** n

¹**bell** /bel/ n **1** a hollow metallic device that vibrates and gives forth a ringing sound when struck **2** the sound of a bell as a signal; specif one to mark the start of the last lap in a running or cycling race or the start or end of a round in boxing, wrestling, etc **3a** a bell rung to tell the hour **b** a half-hour subdivision of a watch on shipboard indicated by the strokes of a bell bell-shaped: e g **4** sthg bell-shaped **a** the corolla of any of many flowers **b** the flared end of a wind instrument

²**bell** v **1** to provide with a bell **2** to make or take the form of a bell; flare

³**bell** v, of a stag or hound to make a resonant bellowing or baying sound

bellow /'beləʊ/ v **1** to make the loud deep hollow sound characteristic of a bull **2** to shout in a deep voice – **bellow** n

¹**belly** /'beli/ n **1a** the undersurface of an animal's body **b** a cut of pork consisting of this part of the body **c** the stomach and associated organs **2** an internal cavity; the interior **3** a surface or object curved or rounded like a human belly

²**belly** v to swell, fill

belong /bɪ'lɒŋ/ v **1** to be in a proper situation (e g according to ability or social qualification), position, or place **2** to be attached or bound to by birth, allegiance, dependency, or membership **3** to be an attribute, part, or function of a person or thing **4** to be properly classified

¹**below** /bɪ'ləʊ/ adv **1** in, on, or to a lower place, floor, or deck; specif on earth or in or to Hades or hell **2** under **3** under the surface of the water or earth

²**below** prep **1** in or to a lower place than; under **2** inferior to (e g in rank) **3** not suitable to the rank of; beneath **4** covered by; underneath **5** downstream from **6** under

³**below** n the thing or matter written or discussed lower on the same page or on a following page

¹**belt** /belt/ n **1** a strip of material worn round the waist or hips or over the shoulder for decoration or to hold sthg (e g clothing or a weapon) **2** an endless band of tough flexible material for transmitting motion and power or conveying materials **3** an area characterized by some distinctive feature (e g of culture, geology, or life forms); esp one suited to a specified crop

²**belt** v **1a** to encircle or fasten with a belt **b** to strap on **2a** to beat (as if) with a belt; thrash **b** to strike, hit – infml **3** to sing in a forceful manner or style – usu + out; infml **4** to move or act in a vigorous or violent manner – infml

³**belt** n a jarring blow; a whack – infml

bench /bentʃ/ n **1a** a long usu backless seat (e g of wood or stone) for 2 or more people **b** a thwart in a boat **2** often cap **a** a judge's seat in court **b** the office of judge or magistrate **3** any of the long seats on which members sit in Parliament **4** a long worktable

¹**bend** /bend/ n any of various knots for fastening one rope to another or to an object

²**bend** v bent **1** to force into or out of a curve or angle **2** to make submissive; subdue **3a** to cause to turn from a course; deflect **b** to guide or turn towards sthg; direct **4** to direct strenuously or with interest; apply **5** to alter or modify to make more acceptable, esp to oneself **6** to move or curve out of a straight line or position **7** to incline the body, esp in submission; bow **8** to yield, compromise

³**bend** n **1** bending or being bent **2** a curved part, esp of a road or stream **3** pl but sing or pl in constr pain or paralysis caused by the release of gas bubbles in body tissue occurring typically when a diver returns to the surface too quickly

¹**beneath** /bɪ'niːθ/ adv **1** in or to a lower position; below **2** directly under; underneath

²**beneath** prep **1a** in or to a lower position than; below **b** directly under, esp so as to be close or touching **2** not suitable to; unworthy of **3** under the control, pressure, or influence of

¹**benefit** /'benɪfɪt/ n **1a** an advantage **b** good, welfare **2a** financial help in time of need (e g sickness, old age, or unem-

ployment) **b** a payment or service provided for under an annuity, pension scheme, or insurance policy **3** an entertainment, game, or social event to raise funds for a person or cause

²**benefit** v **1** to be useful or profitable to **2** to receive benefit

¹**berry** /'beri/ n **1** a small, pulpy, and usu edible fruit (e g a strawberry or raspberry) **2** an egg of a fish or lobster

beside /bɪ'saɪd/ prep **1a** by the side of **b** in comparison with **c** on a par with **2** besides

¹**besides** /bɪ'saɪdz/ adv **1** as an additional factor or circumstance **2** moreover, furthermore

²**besides** prep **1** other than; unless we are to mention **2** as an additional circumstance to

¹**best** /best/ adj, superlative of **good 1** excelling all others (e g in ability, quality, integrity, or usefulness) **2** most productive of good **3** most, largest **4** reserved for special occasions

²**best** adv, superlative of **well 1** in the best manner; to the best extent or degree **2** better

³**best** n, pl best **1** the best state or part **2** sby or sthg that is best **3** the greatest degree of good or excellence **4** one's maximum effort **5** best clothes **6** a winning majority

¹**bet** /bet/ n **1a** the act of risking a sum of money or other stake on the forecast outcome of a future event (e g a race or contest), esp in competition with a second party **b** a stake so risked **2** an opinion, belief **3** a plan of action; course – usu in best bet; infml

²**bet** v bet also betted **1** to stake as a bet – usu + on or against **2** to make a bet with (sby) **3** to be convinced that – infml

betray /bɪ'treɪ/ v **1** to deceive, lead astray **2** to deliver to an enemy by treachery **3** to disappoint the hopes, expectation, or confidence of **4a** to be a sign of (sthg one would like to hide) **b** to disclose, deliberately or unintentionally, in violation of confidence – ~ er n – ~ al n

¹**better** /'betə/ adj, comparative of **good** or of **well 1** improved in health; recovered **2** of greater quality, ability, integrity, usefulness, etc

²**better** adv, comparative of **well 1** in a better manner; to a better extent or degree **2a** to a higher or greater degree **b** more wisely or usefully

³**better** n **1** sthg better **b** one's superior, esp in merit or rank – usu pl **2** the advantage, victory

⁴**better** v **1** to make better: e g **a** to make more tolerable or acceptable **b** to make more complete or perfect **2** to surpass in excellence; excel – ~ ment n

¹**between** /bɪ'twiːn/ prep **1a** through the common action of; jointly engaging **b** in shares to each of **2a** in or into the time, space, or interval that separates **b** in intermediate relation to **3a** from one to the other of **b** serving to connect or separate **4** in point of comparison of **5**

taking together the total effect of; what with

²**between** adv in or into an intermediate space or interval

beverage /'bevərɪdʒ/ n a liquid for drinking; esp one that is not water

beware /bɪ'weə/ v to be wary (of) – usu in imper and infin

bewilder /bɪ'wɪldə/ v to perplex or confuse – ~ ment n

¹**beyond** /bɪ'jɒnd/ adv **1** on or to the farther side; farther **2** as an additional amount; besides

²**beyond** prep **1** on or to the farther side of; at a greater distance than **2a** out of the reach or sphere of **b** in a degree or amount surpassing **3** besides **4** later than; past

³**beyond** n **1** sthg that lies beyond **2** sthg that lies outside the scope of ordinary experience; specif the hereafter

bias /'baɪəs/ n **1** a line diagonal to the grain of a fabric, often used in the cutting of garments for smoother fit – usu + the **2a** a personal prejudice **b** a bent, tendency **3** (the property of shape or weight causing) the tendency in bowls for a bowl to take a curved path when rolled

²**bias** v **1** to give a prejudiced outlook to **2** to influence unfairly

bible /'baɪbl/ n **1a** cap the sacred book of Christians comprising the Old Testament and the New Testament **b** any book containing the sacred writings of a religion **2** an authoritative book – -lical adj

bicycle /'baɪsɪkl/ v or n (to ride) a **2** wheeled pedal-driven vehicle with handlebars and a saddle – **bicyclist** n

¹**bid** /bɪd/ v bade, bid, (3) bid; bidden, bid also bade **1a** to issue an order to; tell **b** to invite to come **2** to give expression to **3a** to offer (a price) for payment or acceptance (e g at an auction) **b** to make a bid of or in (a card at cards) – ~ der n

²**bid** n **1a** the act of one who bids **b** a statement of what one will give or take for sthg; esp an offer of a price **2** an opportunity to bid **3** (an announcement of) the amount of tricks to be won, suit to be played in, etc in a card game **4** an attempt to win or achieve sthg

¹**big** /bɪg/ adj **1** of great force **2a** large in bulk or extent, number or amount **b** large-scale **c** important in influence, standing, or wealth **3a** advanced in pregnancy **b** full to bursting; swelling **4** of the voice loud and resonant **5** older, grown-up **6** of great importance or significance **7a** pretentious, boastful **b** magnanimous, generous **8** popular – infml – ~ ness n

²**big** adv **1a** outstandingly **b** on a grand scale **2** pretentiously USE infml

bigot /'bɪgət/ n one who is obstinately or intolerantly devoted to his/her own religion, opinion, etc – ~ ed adj – ~ edly adv – ~ ry n

¹**bill** /bɪl/ n **1** (a mouthpart resembling) the jaws of a bird together with variously shaped and coloured horny cover-

ings 2 a projection of land like a beak

²**bill** v to caress affectionately – chiefly in *bill and coo*

³**bill** n 1 a long staff with a hook-shaped blade used as a weapon up to the 18th c 2 a billhook

⁴**bill** n 1 a draft of a law presented to a legislature 2 (an itemized account of) charges due for goods or services 3a a written or printed notice advertising an event of interest to the public (e g a theatrical entertainment) b an item (e g a film or play) in a programme entertainment

⁵**bill** v 1 to submit a bill of charges to 2 to advertise, esp by posters or placards b to arrange for the presentation of as part of a programme

billion /'bɪljən/ n 1 Br a million millions (10^{12}) 2 NAm a thousand millions (10^9) 3 an indefinitely large number – often pl with sing. meaning – ~ **th** adj, n, pron, adv

bin /bɪn/ n 1 a container used for storage (e g of flour, grain, bread, or coal) 2 a partitioned case or stand for storing and aging bottles of wine 3 Br a wastepaper basket, dustbin, or similar container for rubbish 4 Br a mental hospital – infml

¹**bind** /baɪnd/ v bound 1a to make secure by tying (e g with cord) or tying together b to put under a (legal) obligation 2 to wrap round with sthg (e g cloth) so as to enclose or cover 3 to encircle, gird 4 to cause to stick together 5 to cause to be attached (e g by gratitude or affection) 6 to form a cohesive mass 7 to jam 8 to complain – infml

²**bind** n a nuisance, bore – infml

¹**bingo** /'bɪŋgəʊ/ interj 1 – used to express the suddenness or unexpectedness of an event – used as an exclamation to show that one has won a game of bingo

²**bingo** n a game of chance played with cards having numbered squares corresponding to numbers drawn at random and won by covering or marking off all or a predetermined number of such squares

binoculars /bɪ'nɒkjʊləz, baɪ-/ n pl, field glasses or opera glasses

biography /baɪ'ɒgrəfɪ/ n 1 a usu written account of a person's life 2 biographical writing as a literary genre – **-phic, -phical** adj – **-phically** adv – **-pher** n

biology /baɪ'ɒlədʒɪ/ n a science that deals with the structure, function, development, distribution, and life processes of living organisms – **-gical** adj – **-gically** adv – **-gist** n

¹**birch** /bɜːtʃ/ n 1 (the hard pale close-grained wood of) any of a genus of deciduous usu short-lived trees or shrubs typically having a layered outer bark that peels readily 2 a birch rod or bundle of twigs for flogging

²**birch** vt to whip (as if) with a birch

bird /bɜːd/ n 1 any of a class of warm-blooded vertebrates with the body more or less completely covered with feathers and the forelimbs modified as wings 2a a (peculiar) fellow – chiefly infml b chiefly Br a girl – infml 3 a hissing or jeering expressive of disapproval or derision – chiefly in *give somebody the bird/get the bird*; infml 4 Br a spell of imprisonment – slang

Biro /'baɪərəʊ/ trademark – used for a ballpoint pen

birth /bɜːθ/ n 1 the act or process of bringing forth young from within the body 2 being born, esp at a particular time or place 3 (noble) lineage or extraction 4 a beginning, start

birthday /'bɜːθdeɪ/ n 1a the day of a person's birth b a day of origin 2 an anniversary of a birth

biscuit /'bɪskɪt/ n 1 earthenware or porcelain after the first firing and before glazing 2 a light yellowish brown colour 3 Br any of several variously-shaped small usu unleavened thin dry crisp bakery products that may be sweet or savoury 4 NAm a soft cake or bread (e g a scone) made without yeast

bishop /'bɪʃəp/ n 1 a clergyman ranking above a priest, having authority to ordain and confirm, and typically governing a diocese 2 either of 2 chess pieces of each colour allowed to move diagonally across any number of consecutive unoccupied squares

¹**bit** /bɪt/ n 1 a bar of metal or occas rubber attached to the bridle and inserted in the mouth of a horse 2 the biting, boring, or cutting edge or part of a tool

²**bit** n 1a a small piece or quantity of anything (e g food) b(1) a usu specified small coin (2) a money unit worth ⅛ of a US dollar c a part, section 2 sthg small or unimportant of its kind: e g a a brief period; a while b an indefinite usu small degree, extent, or amount 3 all the items, situations, or activities appropriate to a given style, role, etc 4 a young woman – slang

³**bit** n a unit of computer information equivalent to the result of a choice between 2 alternatives (e g *on* or *off*)

¹**bitch** /bɪtʃ/ n 1 the female of the dog or similar flesh-eating animals 2 a malicious, spiteful, and domineering woman

²**bitch** v to complain – infml

¹**bite** /baɪt/ v bit; bitten also bit 1a to seize or sever with teeth or jaws b to sting with a fang or other specialized part 2 of a weapon or tool to cut, pierce 3 to cause sharp pain or stinging discomfort 4 to take strong hold of; grip 5 of fish to take a bait

²**bite** n 1 the amount of food taken with 1 bite; also a snack 2 a wound made by biting 3 the hold or grip by which friction is created or purchase is obtained 4 a sharp incisive quality or effect

¹**bitter** /'bɪtər/ adj 1a being or inducing an acrid, astringent, or disagreeable taste similar to that of quinine that is one of the 4 basic taste sensations b distressing, galling 2a intense, severe b

very cold **c** cynical; full of ill-will
– ~ **ly** *adv* – ~ **ness** *n*

²**bitter** *n* **1** *pl but sing or pl in constr* a
usu alcoholic solution of bitter and
often aromatic plant products used esp
in preparing mixed drinks or as a mild
tonic **2** *Br* a very dry beer heavily
flavoured with hops

¹**black** /blæk/ *adj* **1a** of the colour black
b very dark in colour **2** *often cap* a
having dark pigmentation; *esp* of the
Negro race **b** of black people or culture
3 having or reflecting little or no light **4**
of coffee served without milk or cream
5 thoroughly sinister or evil **6** very
dismal or disastrous **7** characterized by
grim, distorted, or grotesque humour **8**
bought, sold, or operating illegally and
esp in violation of official economic
regulations – ~ **ness** *n*

²**black** *n* **1** the colour of least lightness
that belongs to objects that neither
reflect or transmit light **2** sthg black;
esp black clothing **3** one who belongs
wholly or partly to a dark-skinned race;
esp a Negro **4** (the player playing) the
dark-coloured pieces in a board game
(e g chess) for 2 players **5** the condition
of being financially in credit or solvent
or of making a profit – usu + *in the*

³**black** *v chiefly Br* to declare (e g a
business or industry) subject to boycott
by trade-union members

blackberry /ˈblækbəri/ *n* (the usu
black seedy edible fruit of) any of various prickly shrubs of the rose family

blackbird /ˈblækbɜːd/ *n* a common Old
World thrush the male of which is black
with an orange beak and eye rim

blackboard /ˈblækbɔːd/ *n* a hard
smooth usu dark surface for writing or
drawing on with chalk

blackmail /ˈblækmeɪl/ *v* to extort or
obtain money by threats, esp of exposure of secrets that would lead to loss of
reputation, prosecution, etc
– **blackmail** *n* – ~ **er** *n*

blacksmith /ˈblæk,smɪθ/ *n* one who
works iron, esp at a forge

bladder /ˈblædə/ *n* **1a** a membranous
sac in animals that serves as the receptacle of a liquid or contains gas; *esp* the
urinary bladder **2** a bag filled with a
liquid or gas (e g the air-filled rubber
one inside a football)

blade /bleɪd/ *n* **1** (the flat expanded
part, as distinguished from the stalk, of)
a leaf, esp of a grass, cereal, etc **2a** the
broad flattened part of an oar, paddle,
bat, etc **b** an arm of a screw propeller,
electric fan, steam turbine, etc **c** the
broad flat or concave part of a machine
(e g a bulldozer) that comes into contact
with material to be moved **3a** the cutting part of a knife, razor, etc **b** the
runner of an ice skate **4** *archaic* a dashing lively man – now usu *humor*

¹**blame** /bleɪm/ *v* **1** to find fault with;
hold responsible for **2** to place responsibility for (sthg reprehensible) – + *on*

²**blame** *n* **1** an expression of disapproval
or reproach **2** responsibility for sthg
reprehensible – ~ **worthy** *adj*
– ~ **worthiness** *n*

¹**blank** /blæŋk/ *adj* **1a** dazed; taken
aback **b** expressionless **2a** lacking
interest, variety, or change **b** free from
writing; not filled in **3** absolute,
unqualified **4** having a plain or
unbroken surface where an opening is
usual – ~ **ly** *adv* – ~ **ness** *n*

²**blank** *n* **1** an empty space **2a** a void **b**
a vacant or uneventful period **3** a piece
of material prepared to be made into
sthg (e g a key or coin) by a further
operation **4** a cartridge loaded with
powder but no bullet

³**blank** *v* **1** to make blank – usu + *out* **2**
to block – usu + *off*

¹**blanket** /ˈblæŋkɪt/ *n* **1** a large thick
usu rectangular piece of fabric (e g
woven from wool or acrylic yarn) used
esp as a bed covering or a similar piece
of fabric used as a body covering (e g for
a horse) **2** a thick covering or layer

²**blanket** *adj* applicable in all instances
or to all members of a group or class

blare /bleə/ *v* **1** to emit loud and harsh
sound **2** to proclaim loudly or sensationally

¹**blast** /blɑːst/ *n* **1** a violent gust of wind
2 the sound produced by air blown
through a wind instrument or whistle **3**
a stream of air or gas forced through a
hole **4** (a violent wave of increased
atmospheric pressure followed by a
wave of decreased atmospheric pressure
produced in the vicinity of) an explosion
or violent detonation **5** the utterance of
the word *blast* as a curse

²**blast** *v* **1** to injure (as if) by the action
of wind; blight **2** to shatter, remove, or
open (as if) with an explosive **3** to apply
a forced draught to **4** to denounce vigorously **5** to curse, damn **6** to hit vigorously and effectively – **ed** *adj*

³**blast** *interj, Br* – used to express annoyance; *slang*

¹**blaze** /bleɪz/ *n* **1a** an intensely burning
flame or sudden fire **b** intense direct
light, often accompanied by heat **2** a
sudden outburst **3** *pl* hell – usu as an
interjection or as a generalized term of
abuse – **zing** *adj*

²**blaze** *v* **1a** to burn intensely **b** to flare
up **2** to be conspicuously brilliant or
resplendent **3** to shoot rapidly and
repeatedly

³**blaze** *n* **1** a broad white mark on the
face of an animal, esp a horse **2** a trail
marker; *esp* a mark made on a tree by
cutting off a piece of the bark

⁴**blaze** *v* to lead or pioneer in (some
direction or activity) – chiefly in *blaze
the trail*

blazer /ˈbleɪzə/ *n* a jacket, esp with
patch pockets, that is for casual wear or
is part of a school uniform

¹**bleach** /bliːtʃ/ *v* **1** to remove colour or
stains from **2** to make whiter or lighter,
esp by physical or chemical removal of
colour

²**bleach** *n* a chemical preparation used in
bleaching

bleak /bliːk/ *adj* **1** barren and windswept **2** cold, raw **3a** lacking in
warmth or kindness **b** not hopeful or

encouraging **c** severely simple or austere

bleat /bli:t/ *v* 1 to make (a sound like) the cry characteristic of a sheep or goat 2 to talk complainingly or with a whine

bleed /bli:d/ *v* **bled** 1 to emit or lose blood 2 to feel anguish, pain, or sympathy 3 to lose some constituent (e g sap or dye) by exuding it or by diffusion 4 to extort money from 5 to extract or drain the vitality or lifeblood from

¹**blend** /blend/ *v* **blended** *also* **blent** 1 to mix; *esp* to combine or associate so that the separate constituents cannot be distinguished 2 to produce a harmonious effect

²**blend** *n* 1 an act or product of blending 2 a word (e g *brunch*) produced by combining other words or parts of words

bless /bles/ *v* **blessed** *also* **blest** 1 to hallow or consecrate, esp by making the sign of the cross 2 to invoke divine care for 3a to praise, glorify **b** to speak gratefully of 4 to confer prosperity or happiness on 5 – used in exclamations chiefly to express mild or good-humoured surprise

blessing /'blesɪŋ/ *n* 1a the invocation of God's favour upon a person **b** approval 2 sthg conducive to happiness or welfare

blew /blu:/ *past of* **blow**

¹**blind** /blaɪnd/ *adj* 1 unable to see; sightless 2a unable or unwilling to discern or judge **b** not based on reason, evidence, or knowledge 3 without sight or knowledge of anything that could serve for guidance beforehand 4 performed solely by the use of instruments within an aircraft 5 hidden from sight; concealed 6 having only 1 opening or outlet – ~ly *adv* – ~ness *n*

²**blind** *v* 1 to make blind 2 to rob of judgment or discernment 3 to dazzle

³**blind** *n* 1 sthg to keep out light: e g **a** *chiefly Br* an awning **b** a flexible screen (e g a strip of cloth) usu mounted on a roller for covering a window 2 a cover, subterfuge

⁴**blind** *adv* 1 to the point of insensibility – usu in **blind drunk** 2 without seeing outside an aircraft

¹**blink** /blɪŋk/ *v* 1 to close and open the eyes involuntarily 2 to shine intermittently 3a to wink **b** to look with surprise or dismay *at*

²**blink** *n* 1 a glimmer, sparkle 2 a usu involuntary shutting and opening of the eye

blister /'blɪstə/ *n* 1 a raised part of the outer skin containing watery liquid 2 an enclosed raised spot (e g in paint) resembling a blister 3 a disease of plants marked by large swollen patches on the leaves

blitz /blɪts/ *v or n* 1 (to make) an intensive aerial bombardment 2 (to mount) an intensive nonmilitary campaign – chiefly *journ*

blizzard /'blɪzəd/ *n* 1 a long severe snowstorm 2 an intensely strong cold

wind filled with fine snow 3 an overwhelming rush or deluge

blob /blɒb/ *n* 1 a small drop of liquid or of sthg viscous or thick 2 sthg ill-defined or amorphous

¹**block** /blɒk/ *n* 1 a mould or form on which articles are shaped or displayed 2 a rectangular building unit that is larger than a brick 3 a wooden or plastic building toy that is usu provided in sets 4 the metal casting that contains the cylinders of an internal-combustion engine 5 a head – *slang* 6 an obstacle 7 a wooden or metal case enclosing 1 or more pulleys 8 (a ballet shoe with) a solid toe on which a dancer can stand on points 9 a part of a building or set of buildings devoted to a particular use 10 *chiefly NAm* (the distance along 1 side of) a usu rectangular space (e g in a town) enclosed by streets and usu occupied by buildings 11 a piece of engraved or etched material (e g wood or metal) from which impressions are printed

²**block** *v* **1a** to hinder the passage, progress, or accomplishment of (as if) by interposing an obstruction **b** to shut off from view **c** to obstruct or interfere usu legitimately with (e g an opponent) in various games or sports **d** to prevent normal functioning of 2 to arrange (e g a school timetable) in long continuous periods – ~ **age** *n*

bloke /bləʊk/ *n, chiefly Br* a man – *infml*

blond /blɒnd/ *adj* **1a** (having hair) of a flaxen, golden, light auburn, or pale yellowish brown colour **b** of a pale white or rosy white colour 2 of a light colour

¹**blood** /blʌd/ *n* **1a** the usu red fluid that circulates in the heart, arteries, capillaries, and veins of a vertebrate animal, carrying nourishment and oxygen to, and bringing away waste products from, all parts of the body **b** a comparable fluid of an invertebrate animal **2a** human lineage; *esp* the royal lineage **b** kinship 3 temper, passion 4 *archaic* a dashing lively esp young man; a rake – now usu *humor*

²**blood** *v* 1 to stain or wet with blood; *esp* to mark the face of (an inexperienced fox hunter) with the blood of the fox 2 to give an initiating experience to (sby new to a particular field of activity)

bloody /'blʌdɪ/ *adj* 1 smeared, stained with, or containing blood 2 accompanied by or involving bloodshed **3a** murderous, bloodthirsty **b** merciless, cruel 4 – used as an intensive; *slang* – **bloodily** *adv* – **bloodiness** *n*

¹**bloom** /blu:m/ *n* **1a** a flower **b** the flowering state 2 a time of beauty, freshness, and vigour **3a** a delicate powdery coating on some fruits and leaves **b** cloudiness on a film of varnish or lacquer 4 a rosy or healthy appearance

²**bloom** *v* 1 to produce or yield flowers **2a** to flourish **b** to reach maturity; blossom

¹**blossom** /'blɒsəm/ *n* **1a** the flower of a plant **b** the mass of bloom on a single

blo

plant **2** a high point or stage of development

²blossom *vi* **1** to bloom **2** to come into one's own; develop

¹blot /blɒt/ *n* **1** a soiling or disfiguring mark; a spot **2** a mark of reproach; a blemish

²blot *v* **1** to spot, stain, or spatter with a discolouring substance **2** to dry or remove with an absorbing agent (e g blotting paper)

blotting paper *n* a spongy unsized paper used to absorb ink

blouse /blaʊz/ *n* a usu loose-fitting woman's upper garment that resembles a shirt or smock

¹blow /bləʊ/ *v* blew; blown **1** *of air* to move with speed or force **2** to act on with a current of gas or vapour **3** to make a sound by blowing **4a** to pant **b** *of a whale* to eject moisture-laden air from the lungs through the blowhole **5** *of an electric fuse* to melt when overloaded **6a** to shatter, burst, or destroy by explosion **b** *of a tyre* to lose the contained air through a spontaneous puncture – usu + *out* **7** to produce or shape by the action of blown or injected air **8** to damn, disregard – *infml* **9** to squander (money or an advantage) – *slang* **10** to leave hurriedly – *slang*

²blow *n* **1** an instance of (the wind) blowing **2** a walk or other outing in the fresh air – *infml*

³blow *v* blew; blown to cause (e g flowers or blossom) to open out, usu just before dropping

⁴blow *n* **1** a hard stroke delivered with a part of the body or with an instrument **2** *pl* a hostile or aggressive state – esp in *come to blows* **3** a shock or misfortune

blowup /'bləʊ-ʌp/ *n* **1** an outburst of temper **2** a photographic enlargement

blow up *v* **1** to explode or be exploded **2** to build up or exaggerate to an unreasonable extent **3** to fill up with a gas, esp air **4** to make a photographic enlargement of **5** to become violently angry **6** to come into being; arise

¹blue /bluː/ *adj* **1** of the colour blue **2** discoloured through cold, anger, bruising, or fear **3** low in spirits **4** *Conservative* **5a** obscene, pornographic **b** off-colour, risqué – ~ness *n* – bluish *adj*

²blue *n* **1** a colour whose hue is that of the clear sky and lies between green and violet in the spectrum **2** a blue preparation used to whiten clothes in laundering **3a** the sky **b** the far distance **4** any of numerous small chiefly blue butterflies **5** *often cap, Br* a usu national award given to sby who has played in a sporting contest between Oxford and Cambridge universities; *also* sby who has been given such an award

³blue *v Br* to spend lavishly and wastefully – *infml*

¹bluff /blʌf/ *adj* **1** rising steeply with a broad, flat, or rounded front **2** good-naturedly frank and outspoken – ~ly *adv* – ~ness *n*

²bluff *v* to deceive by pretence or an outward appearance of strength, confidence, etc

¹blunder /'blʌndəʳ/ *v* **1** to move unsteadily or confusedly **2** to make a blunder – ~er *n*

²blunder *n* a gross error or mistake resulting from stupidity, ignorance, or carelessness

¹blunt /blʌnt/ *adj* **1** having an edge or point that is not sharp **2a** aggressively outspoken **b** direct, straightforward – ~ness *n* – ~ly *adv*

²blunt *v* to make less sharp or definite

¹blush /blʌʃ/ *v* to become red in the face, esp from shame, modesty, or embarrassment – ~ingly *adv*

²blush *n* **1** a reddening of the face, from shame, embarrassment, etc **2** a red or rosy tint

¹board /bɔːd/ *n* **1a** a usu long thin narrow piece of sawn timber **b** *pl the stage* **2** daily meals, esp when provided in return for payment **3** *sing or pl in constr* **a** a group of people having managerial, supervisory, or investigatory powers **b** an official body **4** a flat usu rectangular piece of material designed or marked for a special purpose (e g for playing chess, ludo, backgammon, etc or for use as a blackboard or surfboard) **5** any of various wood pulps or composition materials formed into stiff flat rectangular sheets (e g cardboard)

²board *v* **1** to come up against or alongside (a ship), usu to attack **2** to go aboard (e g a ship, train, aircraft, or bus) **3** to cover with boards – + *over* or *up* **4** to take one's meals, usu as a paying customer

boarder /'bɔːdəʳ/ *n* **1** a lodger **2** a resident pupil at a boarding school

boast /bəʊst/ *v* **1** to praise oneself **2** to speak of or assert with excessive pride – ~ *n* – ~ful *adj*

¹boat /bəʊt/ *n* **1** a usu small ship **2** a boat-shaped utensil or dish

²boat *v* to use a boat, esp for recreation

¹bob /bɒb/ *v* **1** to move down and up briefly or repeatedly **2** to curtsy briefly **3** to try to seize a suspended or floating object with the teeth

²bob *n* **1** a short quick down-and-up motion **2** (a method of bell ringing using) a modification of the order in change ringing

³bob *n* **1a** a knot or twist (e g of ribbons or hair) **b** a haircut for a woman or girl in which the hair hangs loose just above the shoulders **2** a float **3** *pl* a small insignificant item – in *bits and bobs*

⁴bob *v* to cut (hair) shorter; crop

⁵bob *n, pl* bob *Br* a shilling; *also* the sum of 5 new pence – *infml*

body /'bɒdi/ *n* **1a(1)** the organized physical substance of a living animal or plant **(2)** a corpse **b** a human being; a person **2** the main, central, or principal part: e g **a** the main part of a plant or animal body, esp as distinguished from limbs and head **b** the part of a vehicle on or in which the load is placed **3** the part of a garment covering the body or trunk **4a** a mass of matter distinct from other masses **b** sthg that embodies or gives concrete reality to a thing; *specif* a material object in physical space **5** *sing or pl in constr* a group of people or things: e g **a** a fighting unit **b** a group of individuals organized for some purpose **6a** compactness or firmness of texture **b** comparative richness of flavour in wine – **bodily** *adj*

bog /bog/ *n* **1** (an area of) wet spongy poorly-drained ground **2** *Br* a toilet – *slang* – ~**gy** *adj*

boil /boil/ *n* a localized pus-filled swelling of the skin resulting from infection in a skin gland

boil *v* **1a** *of a fluid* to change into (bubbles of) a vapour when heated **b** to come to the boiling point **2** to bubble or foam violently; churn **3** to be excited or stirred **4** to subject to the action of a boiling liquid (e g in cooking)

boil *n* the boiling point

boiler /'boila⁽r⁾/ *n* **1** a vessel used for boiling **2** the part of a steam generator in which water is converted into steam under pressure **3** a tank in which water is heated or hot water is stored

bold /bəʊld/ *adj* **1** showing or requiring a fearless adventurous spirit **2** impudent, presumptuous **3** standing out prominently; conspicuous – ~**ly** *adv* – ~**ness** *n*

bold *n* boldface

bolt /bəʊlt/ *n* **1a** a short stout usu blunt-headed arrow shot from a crossbow **b** a thunderbolt **2a** a sliding bar or rod used to fasten a door **b** the part of a lock that is shot or withdrawn by the key **3** a roll of cloth or wallpaper of a standard length **4a** a metal rod or pin for fastening objects together **b** a screw-bolt with a head suitable for turning with a spanner **5** a rod or bar that closes the breech of a breech-loading firearm

bolt *v* **1** to move rapidly; dash **2a** to dart off or away; flee **b** to break away from control **3** to produce seed prematurely **4** to swallow (e g food) hastily or without chewing

bolt *adv* in a rigidly erect position

bolt *n* a dash, run

bolt *v* to sift (e g flour)

bomb /bom/ *n* **1a** any of several explosive or incendiary devices usu dropped from aircraft and detonated by impact **b** nuclear weapons – + *the* **3** *Br* a large sum of money – *infml* **4** *NAm* a failure, flop – *infml*

bomb *v* **1** to attack with bombs; bombard **2** to fail; fall flat – *infml*

bond /bond/ *n* **1** sthg (e g a fetter) that binds or restrains **2** a binding agreement **3** an adhesive or cementing material **4** sthg that unites or binds **5a** a legally enforceable agreement to pay **b** a certificate of intention to pay the holder a specified sum, with or without other interest, on a specified date **6** the system of overlapping bricks in a wall **7** the state of imported goods retained by customs authorities until duties are paid

8 a strong durable paper, now used esp for writing and typing

²bond *v* **1** to overlap (e g bricks) for solidity of construction **2** to put (goods) in bond until duties and taxes are paid **3** to cause to stick firmly

¹bone /bəʊn/ *n* **1a** (the material that makes up) any of the hard body structures of which the adult skeleton of most vertebrate animals is chiefly composed **b** (a structure made of) ivory or another hard substance resembling bone **2** *the* essential or basic part or level; *the* core **3** *pl* the core of one's being **4** a subject or matter of dispute **5a** *pl* thin bars of bone, ivory, or wood held in pairs between the fingers and used to produce musical rhythms **b** a strip of whalebone or steel used to stiffen a corset or dress **c** *pl* dice – ~**less** *adj*

²bone *v* **1** to remove the bones from **2** to stiffen (a garment) with bones **3** to try to find out about, esp hurriedly; revise – usu + *up* – ~**d** *adj*

³bone *adv* absolutely, utterly – chiefly in *bone dry*, *bone idle*

bonfire /'bonfaiə⁽r⁾/ *n* a large fire built in the open air

bonnet /'bonɪt/ *n* **1** a cloth or straw hat tied under the chin, now worn chiefly by children **2** *Br* the hinged metal covering over the engine of a motor vehicle

bonus /'bəʊnəs/ *n* sthg given in addition to what is usual or strictly due **2** money or an equivalent given in addition to an employee's usual pay

¹book /bʊk/ *n* **1a** a set of written, printed, or blank sheets bound together into a volume **b** a long written or printed literary composition **c** a major division of a treatise or literary work **d** a record of business transactions – usu *pl* **2** the bets registered by a bookmaker

²book *v* **1a** to reserve or make arrangements for in advance **b** *chiefly Br* to register in a hotel **2a** to take the name of with a view to prosecution **b** to enter the name of (a player) in a book for a violation of the rules usu involving foul play – used with reference to a rugby or soccer player – ~**able** *adj* – ~**ing** *n*

³book *adj* **1** derived from books; theoretical **2** shown by books of account

¹boom /buːm/ *n* **1** a spar at the foot of the mainsail in fore-and-aft rig that is attached at its fore end to the mast **2** a long movable arm used to manipulate a microphone **3** a barrier across a river or enclosing an area of water to keep logs together; *also* the enclosed logs **4** a cable or line of spars extended across a river or the mouth of a harbour as a barrier to navigation

²boom *v* **1** to make a deep hollow sound or cry **2** to experience a rapid increase in activity or importance

³boom /buːm/ *n* **1** a booming sound or cry **2a** a rapid growth or increase in a specified area **b** a rapid widespread expansion of economic activity

boomerang /'bu:məræŋ/ *n* **1** a bent piece of wood shaped so that it returns to its thrower and used by Australian aborigines as a hunting weapon **2** an act or utterance that backfires on its originator

¹**boost** /bu:st/ *v* **1** to push or shove up from below **2** to increase, raise **3** to encourage, promote **4** to raise the voltage of or across (an electric circuit)

²**boost** *n* **1** a push upwards **2** an increase in amount **3** an act that promotes or encourages

¹**boot** *n* **1** a high stout shoe; *also* a shoe for certain sports (e g football) **2** a blow or kick delivered (as if) by a booted foot **3** *Br* the major luggage compartment of a motor car **4** summary discharge or dismissal – slang; chiefly in *give/get the boot*

²**boot** *v* to kick

¹**booze** /bu:z/ *v* to drink intoxicating liquor to excess – slang

²**booze** *n* intoxicating drink; *esp* spirits USE slang

¹**border** /'bɔːdə'/ *n* **1** an outer part or edge **2** a boundary, frontier **3** a narrow bed of planted ground (e g beside a path) **4** an ornamental design at the edge of sthg (e g printed matter, fabric, or a rug)

²**border** *v* **1** to put a border on **2** to adjoin at the edge or boundary

¹**bore** /bɔː'/ *v* **1** to make a hole with a rotary tool **2** to drill a mine or well – ~r *n*

²**bore** *n* **1** a hole made (as if) by boring **2** a barrel (e g of a gun) **3a** the interior diameter of a tube **b** the diameter of an engine cylinder

³**bore** *past of* **bear**

⁴**bore** *n* a tidal flood that moves swiftly as a steep-fronted wave in a channel, estuary, etc

⁵**bore** *n* a tedious person or thing

⁶**bore** *v* to weary by being dull or monotonous – ~dom *n*

born /bɔːn/ *adj* **1a** brought into existence (as if) by birth **b** by birth; native **2** having a specified character or situation from birth

borne /bɔːn/ *past part of* **bear**

borough /'bʌrə/ *n* a British urban constituency; *also* a similar political unit in the USA

borrow /'bɒrəʊ/ *v* **1** to take or receive with the intention of returning **2a** to appropriate for one's own use **b** to copy or imitate – ~er *n* – ~ing *n*

¹**boss** /bɒs/ *n* **1** a protuberant part or body **2** a raised ornamentation **3** a carved ornament concealing the intersection of the ribs of a vault or panelled ceiling

²**boss** *n* **1** one who exercises control or authority; *specif* one who directs or supervises workers **2** a politician who controls a party organization (e g in the USA)

³**boss** *v* to order – often + *about* or *around* USE infml

botany /'bɒtəni/ *n* **1** a branch of biology dealing with plant life **2** the properties and life phenomena exhibited by a plant, plant type, or plant group – **-nist** *n*, **-anic**, **-anical** *adj*, **-anize** *v*

¹**both** /bəʊθ/ *adj* being as one; affecting or involving the one as well as the other

²**both** *pron pl in constr* the one as well as the other

³**both** *conj* – used to indicate and stress the inclusion of each of 2 or more things specified by coordinated words or word groups

¹**bother** /'bɒðə'/ *v* **1** to cause to be troubled or perplexed **2a** to annoy or inconvenience **b** – used as a mild interjection of annoyance **3** to take pains; take the trouble

²**bother** *n* **1** (a cause of) mild discomfort, annoyance, or worry **2** unnecessary fussing **3** a minor disturbance – ~some *adj*

¹**bottle** /'bɒtl/ *n* **1a** a rigid or semirigid container, esp for liquids, usu of glass or plastic, with a comparatively narrow neck or mouth **b** the contents of a bottle **2a** intoxicating drink – slang **b** bottled milk used to feed infants **3** *Br* nerve; guts – slang

²**bottle** *v* **1** to put into a bottle **2** *Br* to preserve (e g fruit) by storage in glass jars

¹**bottom** /'bɒtəm/ *n* **1a** the underside of sthg **b** a surface on which sthg rests **c** the buttocks, rump **2** the ground below a body of water **3** the part of a ship's hull lying below the water **4a** the lowest, deepest, or farthest part or place **b** the lowest or last place in order of precedence **c** the transmission gear of a motor vehicle giving lowest speed of travel **d** the lower part of a two-piece garment – often pl with sing. meaning

²**bottom** *v* to reach the bottom – usu + *out*

bough /baʊ/ *n* a (main) branch of a tree

bought /bɔːt/ *past of* **buy**

¹**bounce** /baʊns/ *v* **1** to cause to rebound **2** to return (a cheque) as not good because of lack of funds in the payer's account – infml

²**bounce** *n* **1a** a sudden leap or bound **b** a rebound **2** verve, liveliness – **bouncy** *adj* – **-ily** *adv* – **-ness**

¹**bound** /baʊnd/ *adj* going or intending to go

²**bound** *n* **1** a limiting line; a boundary **2** sthg that limits or restrains USE usu pl with sing. meaning

³**bound** *v* **1** to set limits to **2** to form the boundary of USE usu pass

⁴**bound** *adj* **1a** confined **b** certain, sure *to* **2** placed under legal or moral obligation

⁵**bound** *n* a leap, jump **2** a bounce

⁶**bound** *v* **1** to move by leaping **2** to rebound, bounce

boundary /'baʊndəri/ *n* **1** sthg, esp a dividing line, that indicates or fixes a limit or extent **2a** the marked limits of a cricket field **b** (the score of 4 or 6 made by) a stroke in cricket that sends the ball over the boundary

bouquet /bəʊ'keɪ, bu:-/ *n* **1** a bunch of flowers fastened together **2** a distinctive

bra

and characteristic fragrance (e g of wine)

¹**bourgeois** /'buəʒwɑː/ n, pl **bourgeois** 1 a middle-class person 2 one whose behaviour and views are influenced by bourgeois values or interests

²**bourgeois** adj 1 middle-class 2 marked by a narrow-minded concern for material interests and respectability 3 capitalist

bout /baut/ n 1 a spell of activity 2 an athletic match (e g of boxing) 3 an outbreak or attack of illness, fever, etc

¹**bow** /bau/ v 1 to submit, yield 2 to bend the head, body, or knee in respect, submission, or greeting – ~ed adj

²**bow** /bau/ n a bending of the head or body in respect, submission, or greeting

³**bow** /bəu/ n 1 a bend, arch 2 a strip of wood, fibreglass, etc held bent by a strong cord and used to shoot an arrow 3 an often ornamental slipknot (e g for tying a shoelace) 4 (a stroke made with) a resilient wooden rod with horsehairs stretched from end to end, used in playing an instrument of the viol or violin family

⁴**bow** /bəu/ v 1 to (cause to) bend into a curve 2 to play (a stringed instrument) with a bow

⁵**bow** /bau/ n 1 the forward part of a ship – often pl with sing. meaning 2 the rower in the front end of a boat

bowels /'bauəlz/ n 1 the gut, intestines 2 the innermost parts

¹**bowl** /bəul/ n 1 any of various round hollow vessels used esp for holding liquids or food or for mixing food 2 the contents of a bowl 3a the hollow of a spoon or tobacco pipe **b** the receptacle of a toilet 4a a bowl-shaped geographical region or formation **b** NAm a bowl-shaped structure; esp a sports stadium – ~ful n

²**bowl** n 1 a ball used in bowls that is weighted or shaped to give it a bias 2 pl but sing in constr a game played typically outdoors on a green, in which bowls are rolled at a target jack in an attempt to bring them nearer to it than the opponent's bowls

³**bowl** v 1 to play or roll a ball in bowls or bowling 2a to play as a bowler in cricket **b** to deliver (a ball) to a batsman in cricket **c** to dismiss (a batsman in cricket) by breaking the wicket – used with reference to a bowled ball or a bowler 3 to travel in a vehicle smoothly and rapidly – often + along

bowling /'bəulɪŋ/ n any of several games in which balls are rolled at 1 or more objects

¹**box** /bɒks/ n any of several evergreen shrubs or small trees used esp for hedges

²**box** n 1a a rigid container having 4 sides, a bottom, and usu a cover **b** the contents of a box 2a a small compartment (e g for a group of spectators in a theatre) **b**(1) the penalty area (2) the penalty box 3a a shield to protect the genitals, worn esp by batsmen and wicketkeepers in cricket **b** a structure that contains a telephone for use by members of a specified organization 4 a small simple sheltering or enclosing structure 5 Br a gift given to tradesmen at Christmas 6 Br television; specif a television set – + the; infml

³**box** v 1 to enclose (as if) in a box – + in or up 2 to hem in (e g an opponent in soccer) – usu + in

⁴**box** 1 to slap (e g the ears) with the hand 2 to engage in boxing

boxing /'bɒksɪŋ/ n the art of attack and defence with the fists practised as a sport

Boxing Day n December 26, observed as a public holiday in Britain (apart from Scotland), on which service workers (e g postmen) were traditionally given Christmas boxes

¹**boy** /bɔɪ/ n 1a a male child from birth to puberty **b** a son **c** an immature male; a youth **d** a boyfriend 2 a fellow, person 3 a male servant – sometimes taken to be offensive – ~hood n – ~ish adj – ~ishly adv – ~ishness n

²**boy** interj, chiefly NAm – used to express excitement or surprise

boycott /'bɔɪkɒt/ v to refuse to have dealings with (e g a person, shop, or organization), usu to express disapproval or to force acceptance of certain conditions – **boycott** n

bra /brɑː/ n, pl **bras** a woman's closely fitting undergarment with cups for supporting the breasts

bracelet /'breɪslɪt/ n 1 an ornamental band or chain worn round the wrist 2 pl handcuffs – infml

¹**bracket** /'brækɪt/ n 1 an overhanging projecting fixture or member that is designed to support a vertical load or strengthen an angle 2a a parenthesis **b** either of a pair of marks ( ) used in writing and printing to enclose matter **c** an angle bracket 3 (the distance between) a pair of shots fired usu in front of and beyond a target to aid in range-finding 4 any of a graded series of income groups

²**bracket** v 1 to place (as if) within brackets 2 to put in the same category; associate – usu + together 3a to get a range by firing in front of and behind (a target) **b** to establish a margin on either side of (e g an estimation)

¹**brag** /bræg/ n a card game resembling poker

²**brag** v to talk or assert boastfully

¹**braid** /breɪd/ v 1 chiefly NAm to plait 2 to ornament, esp with ribbon or braid

²**braid** n 1 a narrow piece of fabric, esp plaited cord or ribbon, used for trimming 2 chiefly NAm a length of plaited hair

¹**brain** /breɪn/ n 1a the portion of the vertebrate central nervous system enclosed within the skull, that constitutes the organ of thought and neural coordination **b** a nervous centre in invertebrates comparable in position and function to the vertebrate brain 2a intellectual endowment; intelligence –

often pl with sing. meaning **b(1)** a very intelligent or intellectual person **(2)** the chief planner of an organization or enterprise – usu pl with sing. meaning but sing. in constr

²**brain** v **1** to kill by smashing the skull **2** to hit hard on the head – infml

brain wave n **1** a rhythmic fluctuation of voltage between parts of the brain **2** a sudden bright idea

¹**brake** /breɪk/ n **1** a device for arresting usu rotary motion, esp by friction **2** sthg that slows down or stops movement or activity

²**brake** v to slow or stop by a brake

³**brake** n an estate car

bramble /'bræmbəl/ n a rough prickly shrub, esp a blackberry

¹**branch** /braːntʃ/ n **1** a secondary shoot or stem (e g a bough) arising from a main axis (e g of a tree) **2a** a tributary **b** a side road or way **3** a distinct part of a complex whole: e g **a** a division of a family descending from a particular ancestor **b** a distinct area of knowledge **c** a division or separate part of an organization

²**branch** v **1** to put forth branches **2** to spring out (e g from a main stem)

¹**brand** /brænd/ n **1** a charred piece of wood **2a** a mark made by burning with a hot iron, or with a stamp or stencil, to identify manufacture or quality or to designate ownership (e g of cattle) **b** a mark formerly put on criminals with a hot iron **3a** a class of goods identified by name as the product of a single firm or manufacturer **b** a characteristic or distinctive kind **4** a sword – poetic

²**brand** v **1** to mark with a brand **2** to stigmatize or impress indelibly

brandy /'brændi/ n a spirit distilled from wine or fermented fruit juice

brass /braːs/ n **1** an alloy of copper and zinc **2** sing or pl in constr the brass instruments of an orchestra or band **3** brazen self-assurance **4** brass, brass hats sing or pl in constr senior military personnel **5** chiefly N Eng money USE (3, 4, & 5) infml

¹**brave** /breɪv/ adj **1** courageous, fearless **2** excellent, splendid – ~ly adv – ~ry n

²**brave** v to face or endure with courage

³**brave** n a N American Indian warrior

¹**bread** /bred/ n **1** a food consisting essentially of flour or meal which is baked and usu leavened, esp with yeast **2** food, sustenance **3a** livelihood **b** money – slang

²**bread** v to cover with breadcrumbs

breadth /bredθ, bretθ/ n **1** distance from side to side **2a** sthg of full width **b** a wide expanse **3** liberality of views or taste

¹**break** /breɪk/ v **broke; broken 1a** to separate into parts with suddenness or violence **b** to come apart or split into pieces; burst, shatter **2** to violate, transgress **3a** to force a way through or into **b** to escape with sudden forceful effort – often + out or away **c** to make a sudden dash **4** to make or effect by cutting or forcing through **5** to disrupt the order or compactness of **6a** to defeat utterly; destroy **b** to give way in disorderly retreat **c** to crush the spirit of **d(1)** to train (an animal, esp a horse) for the service of human beings **(2)** to inure, accustom **e(1)** to exhaust in health, strength, or capacity **(2)** to fail in health, strength, or control **7a** to ruin financially **b** to reduce in rank **8a** to reduce the force or intensity of **b** to cause failure and discontinuance of (a strike) by measures outside bargaining processes **9** to exceed, surpass **10** to ruin the prospects of **11a** to stop or interrupt **b** to destroy the uniformity of **12a** to end a relationship, agreement, etc with **b** to cause to discontinue a habit **13a** to come to pass; occur **b** to make known; tell **14a** to solve or crack (a code or cipher system) **b** to demonstrate the falsity of (an alibi) **15** to split into smaller units, parts, or processes; divide – often + up or down **16** to become inoperative because of damage, wear, or strain **17** to open the operating mechanism of (a gun) **18** to separate after a clinch in boxing **19** of a wave to curl over and disintegrate in surf or foam **20** of weather to change suddenly, esp after a fine spell **21** esp of a ball bowled in cricket to change direction of forward travel on bouncing **22** of a voice to alter sharply in tone, pitch, or intensity; esp to shift abruptly from one register to another **23** to interrupt one's activity for a brief period **24** to make the opening shot of a game of snooker, billiards, or pool **25** of cream to separate during churning into liquid and fat

²**break** n **1** an act or action of breaking **2a** a condition produced (as if) by breaking; a gap **b** a rupture in previously good relations **3** the action or act of breaking in, out, or forth **4** a dash, rush **5a** a change or interruption in a continuous process or trend **b** a respite from work or duty; specif a daily pause for play and refreshment at school **c** a planned interruption in a radio or television programme **6a** the opening shot in a game of snooker, billiards, or pool **b** a slow ball bowled in cricket that deviates in a specified direction on bouncing **c** the act or an instance of breaking an opponent's service in tennis **d** a sequence of successful shots or strokes (e g in snooker) **7** a notable variation in pitch, intensity, or tone in the voice **8a** the point where one musical register changes to another **b** a short ornamental passage inserted between phrases in jazz **9a** a stroke of esp good luck **b** an opportunity, chance

breakdown /'breɪkdaʊn/ n **1** a failure to function **2** a physical, mental, or nervous collapse **3** failure to progress or have effect **4** a division into categories; a classification **5** an account in which the transactions are recorded under various categories

break down v **1a** to divide into (simpler) parts or categories **b** to undergo decomposition **2** to take apart, esp for storage or shipment **3** to become inoperative through breakage or wear **4** to lose one's composure completely

breakfast /'brekfəst/ n (food prepared for) the first meal of the day, esp when taken in the morning

breast /brest/ n **1** either of 2 milk-producing organs situated on the front of the chest in the human female and some other mammals **2** the fore part of the body between the neck and the abdomen **3** sthg (e g a swelling or curve) resembling a breast **4** the seat of emotion and thought; the bosom – fml

breast v **1** to contend with resolutely; confront **2** to meet, lean, or thrust against with the breast or front **3** chiefly Br to climb, ascend

breath /breθ/ n **1** a slight indication; a suggestion **2a** breathing **b** opportunity or time to breathe; respite **3** spirit, animation

breathe /briːð/ v **1a** to draw air into and expel it from the lungs **b** to send out by exhaling **2** to live **3a** to pause and rest before continuing **b** to allow (e g a horse) to rest after exertion **4** of wine to be exposed to the beneficial effects of air after being kept in an airtight container (e g a bottle) **5** to utter, express

breed /briːd/ v bred **1** to rear; bring up **2** to produce, engender **3** to propagate (plants or animals) sexually and usu under controlled conditions – ~er n

breed n **1** a group of animals or plants, often specially selected, visibly similar in most characteristics **2** race, lineage **3** class, kind

breeze /briːz/ n **1** a light gentle wind **2** a slight disturbance or quarrel – infml **3** chiefly NAm sthg easily done; a cinch – infml

breeze v **1** to come in or into, or move along, swiftly and airily **2** to make progress quickly and easily – infml

brew /bruː/ v **1** to prepare (e g beer or ale) by steeping, boiling, and fermentation or by infusion and fermentation **2a** to contrive, plot – often + up **b** to be in the process of formation – often + up **3** to prepare (e g tea) by infusion in hot water

brew n **1** a brewed beverage **2a** an amount brewed at once **b** the quality of what is brewed

bribe /braɪb/ v to induce or influence (as if) by a bribe – ~ry n

bribe n sthg, esp money, given or promised to influence the judgment or conduct of a person

brick /brɪk/ n **1** a usu rectangular unit for building or paving purposes, typically about 8in × 3¾in × 2¼in made of moist clay hardened by heat **2** a rectangular compressed mass (e g of ice cream) **3** a reliable stout-hearted person; a stalwart – infml

brick v to close, face, or pave with bricks – usu + up

bride /braɪd/ n a woman at the time of her wedding – **-dal** adj

bridegroom /'braɪdgruːm, -grʊm/ n a man at the time of his wedding

bridge /brɪdʒ/ n **1a** a structure spanning a depression or obstacle and supporting a roadway, railway, canal, or path **b** a time, place, or means of connection or transition **2a** the upper bony part of the nose **b** an arch serving to raise the strings of a musical instrument **c** a raised platform on a ship from which it is directed **d** the support for a billiards or snooker cue formed esp by the hand **3a** sthg (e g a partial denture permanently attached to adjacent natural teeth) that fills a gap

bridge v to make a bridge over or across; also to cross (e g a river) by a bridge

bridge n any of various card games for usu 4 players in 2 partnerships in which players bid for the right to name a trump suit, and in which the hand of the declarer's partner is exposed and played by the declarer

bridle /'braɪdl/ n a framework of leather straps buckled together round the head of a draught or riding animal, including the bit and reins, used to direct and control it

bridle v **1** to restrain or control (as if) with a bridle **2** to show hostility or resentment (e g because of an affront), esp by drawing back the head and chin

brief /briːf/ adj **1** short in duration or extent **2** in few words; concise – ~ly adv

brief n **1a** a statement of a client's case drawn up for the instruction of counsel **b** a case, or piece of employment, given to a barrister **c** a set of instructions outlining what is required, and usu setting limits to one's powers (e g in negotiating) **2** pl short close-fitting pants

brief v **1** to provide with final instructions or necessary information **2** Br to retain (a barrister) as legal counsel – ~ing n

briefcase /'briːfkeɪs/ n a flat rectangular case for carrying papers or books

brigade /brɪ'geɪd/ n **1** a large section of an army usu composed of a headquarters, several fighting units (e g infantry battalions or armoured regiments), and supporting units **2** an organized or uniformed group of people (e g firemen)

bright /braɪt/ adj **1a** radiating or reflecting light; shining **b** radiant with happiness **2** of a colour of high saturation or brilliance **3a** intelligent, clever **b** lively, charming **c** promising, talented – ~ly adv – ~ness n

brilliant /'brɪlɪənt/ adj **1** very bright; glittering **2** of high quality; good – infml – **-liance, -liancy** n

brim /brɪm/ n **1** the edge or rim of a hollow vessel, a natural depression, or a cavity **2** the projecting rim of a hat

brim v to be full

bring /brɪŋ/ v brought **1a** to convey (sthg) to a place or person; come with or cause to come **b** to cause to achieve a particular condition **2a** to cause to

bri

occur, lead to **b** to offer, present **3** to prefer (a charge or legal case) **4** to sell for (a price)

brink /brɪŋk/ *n* **1** an edge; *esp* the edge at the top of a steep place **2** *the* verge, onset

brisk /brɪsk/ *adj* **1** keenly alert; lively **2** fresh, invigorating **3** energetic, quick – ~**ly** *adv* – ~**ness** *n*

¹**bristle** /'brɪsl/ *n* a short stiff coarse hair or filament

²**bristle** *v* **bristling 1** to rise and stand stiffly erect **2** to take on an aggressive attitude or appearance (e g in response to a slight) **3** to be filled or thickly covered (*with* sthg suggestive of bristles)

British /'brɪtɪʃ/ *n* **1** *pl in constr* the people of Britain **2** *chiefly NAm* English as typically spoken and written in Britain – **British** *adj*

brittle /'brɪtl/ *adj* **1** easily broken or cracked; frail **2** easily hurt or offended; sensitive **3** sharp, tense

¹**broad** /brɔːd/ *adj* **1** having ample extent from side to side **2** extending far and wide; spacious **3** open, full – esp in *broad daylight* **4** marked by lack of restraint or delicacy; coarse **5** liberal, tolerant **6** relating to the main points; general **7** dialectal, esp in pronunciation – ~**ly** *adv* – ~**ness** *n*

²**broad** *n* **1** the broad part **2** *often cap, Br* a large area of fresh water formed by the broadening of a river – usu pl; used chiefly with reference to such formations found in E Anglia **3** *chiefly NAm* a woman – slang

¹**broadcast** /'brɔːdkɑːst/ *adj* cast or scattered in all directions

²**broadcast** *n* **1** the act of transmitting by radio or television **2** a single radio or television programme

³**broadcast** *v* **1** to scatter or sow (seed) broadcast **2** to make widely known **3** to transmit as a broadcast, esp for widespread reception **4** to speak or perform on a broadcast programme – ~**er** *n* – ~**ing** *n*

¹**broke** /brəʊk/ *past of* **break**

²**broke** *adj* penniless – infml

broken /'brəʊkən/ *adj* **1** violently separated into parts; shattered **2a** having undergone or been subjected to fracture **b** *of a land surface* irregular, interrupted, or full of obstacles **c** not fulfilled; violated **d** discontinuous, interrupted **3a** made weak or infirm **b** subdued completely; crushed **c** not working; defective **4** affected by separation or divorce – ~**ly** *adv* – ~**ness** *n*

¹**bronze** /brɒnz/ *v* to make brown or tanned

²**bronze** *n* **1** any of various copper-base alloys; *esp* one containing tin **2** a sculpture or artefact made of bronze **3** a yellowish-brown colour **4** **bronze, bronze medal** an award for coming third in a competition

brooch /brəʊtʃ/ *n* an ornament worn on clothing and fastened by means of a pin

¹**brood** /bruːd/ *n* **1** young birds, insects,

etc hatched or cared for at one time **2** the children in one family – humor

²**brood** *v* **1** *of a bird* to sit on eggs in order to hatch them **2a** to dwell gloomily *on*; worry *over* or *about* **b** to be in a state of depression – ~**er** *n*

³**brood** *adj* kept for breeding

¹**brook** /brʊk/ *v* to tolerate; stand for

²**brook** *n* a usu small freshwater stream

brother /'brʌðə/ *n, pl* **brothers,** (*3, 4, & 5*) **brothers** *also* **brethren 1** a male having the same parents as another person; *also* a half brother or stepbrother **2** a kinsman **3** a fellow member **4** one, esp a male, who is related to another by a common tie or interest **5** a member of a men's religious order who is not in holy orders

brought /brɔːt/ *past of* **bring**

brow /braʊ/ *n* **1a** an eyebrow **b** the forehead **2** the top or edge of a hill, cliff, etc

¹**brown** /braʊn/ *adj* **1** of the colour brown; *esp* of dark or tanned complexion **2** (made with ingredients that are) partially or wholly unrefined or unpolished – ~**ish** *adj*

²**brown** *n* any of a range of dark colours between red and yellow in hue

³**brown** *v* to make or become brown (e g by sautéing)

¹**browse** /braʊz/ *n* a period of time spent browsing

²**browse** *v* **1** *of animals* to nibble at leaves, grass, or other vegetation **2** to read or search idly *through* a book or a mass of things (e g in a shop), in the hope of finding sthg interesting

¹**bruise** /bruːz/ *v* **1** to inflict a bruise on **2** to crush (e g leaves or berries) by pounding **3** to wound, injure; *esp* to inflict psychological hurt on

²**bruise** *n* **1** an injury involving rupture of small blood vessels and discoloration without a break in the skin; *also* a similar plant injury **2** an injury to the feelings

¹**brush** /brʌʃ/ *n* scrub vegetation

²**brush** *n* **1** an implement composed of bristles set into a firm piece of material and used for grooming hair, painting, sweeping, etc **2a** a bushy tail, esp of a fox **3** an act of brushing **4** a quick light touch or momentary contact in passing

³**brush** *v* **1a** to apply a brush to **b** to apply with a brush **2** to remove with sweeping strokes (e g of a brush) – usu + *away* or *off* **3** to pass lightly over or across **4** to move lightly, heedlessly, or rudely – usu + *by* or *past*

⁴**brush** *n* a brief encounter or skirmish

brutal /'bruːtl/ *adj* **1** grossly ruthless or unfeeling **2** cruel, cold-blooded **3** harsh, severe **4** unpleasantly accurate and incisive – -**tality** *n* – -**tally** *adv*

¹**brute** /bruːt/ *adj* **1** characteristic of an animal in quality, action, or instinct: e g **a** cruel, savage **b** not working by reason; mindless **2** purely physical

²**brute** *n* **1** a beast **2** a brutal person – **brutish** *adj* – **brutishly** *adv*

¹**bubble** /'bʌbl/ *v* **1** to form or produce bubbles **2** to make a sound like the

bubbles rising in liquid **3** to be highly excited or overflowing (with a feeling)

²**bubble** *n* **1a** a usu small body of gas within a liquid or solid **b** a thin spherical usu transparent film of liquid inflated with air or vapour **2** sthg that lacks firmness or reality; *specif* an unreliable or speculative scheme **3** a sound like that of bubbling

bucket /'bʌkɪt/ *n* **1** a large open container used esp for carrying liquids **2** the scoop of an excavating machine **3** *pl* large quantities – *infml*

buckle /'bʌkəl/ *n* a fastening consisting of a rigid rim, usu with a hinged pin, used to join together 2 loose ends (e g of a belt or strap) or for ornament

buckle *v* **1** to fasten with a buckle **2** to bend, give way, or crumple

¹**bud** /bʌd/ *n* **1** a small protuberance on the stem of a plant that may develop into a flower, leaf, or shoot **2** sthg not yet mature or fully developed: e g **a** an incompletely opened flower **b** an outgrowth of an organism that becomes a new individual

²**bud** *v* **1** *of a plant* to put forth buds **2** to reproduce asexually by forming and developing buds **3** to graft a bud into (a plant of another kind), usu in order to propagate a desired variety

budget /'bʌdʒɪt/ *n* **1** a statement of a financial position for a definite period of time (e g for the following year), that is based on estimates of expenditures and proposals for financing them **2** a plan of how money will be spent or allocated **3** the amount of money available for, required for, or assigned to a particular purpose – ~**ary** *adj*

budget *v* to plan or provide for the use of (e g money, time, or manpower) in detail

¹**buffet** /'bʌfɪt/ *n* **1** a blow, esp with the hand **2** sthg that strikes with telling force

²**buffet** /'bʌfeɪ/ *v* to strike sharply, esp with the hand; cuff **2** to strike repeatedly; batter **3** to use roughly; treat unpleasantly

³**buffet** /'bʊfeɪ/ *n* **1** a meal set out on tables or a sideboard for diners to help themselves **2** *chiefly Br* a self-service restaurant or snack bar

bug /bʌg/ *n* **1** any of several insects commonly considered obnoxious; *esp* a bedbug **2** an unexpected defect or imperfection **3** a disease-producing germ; *also* a disease caused by it – not used technically **4** a concealed listening device **5** a temporary enthusiasm; a craze – *infml*

bug *v* **1** to plant a concealed listening device in **2** to bother, annoy – *infml*

bugle /'bjuːgəl/ *n* a European annual plant of the mint family that has spikes of blue flowers

bugle *n* a valveless brass instrument that is used esp for military calls

build /bɪld/ *v* **built 1** to construct by putting together materials gradually into a composite whole **2** to develop according to a systematic plan, by a definite process, or on a particular base

3a to increase in intensity **b** to develop in extent – ~**er** *n*

²**build** *n* the physical proportions of a person or animal; *esp* a person's figure of a usu specified type

building /'bɪldɪŋ/ *n* **1** a permanent structure (e g a school or house) usu having walls and a roof **2** the art, business, or act of assembling materials into a structure

bulb /bʌlb/ *n* **1a** a short stem base of a plant (e g the lily, onion, or hyacinth), with 1 or more buds enclosed in overlapping membranous or fleshy leaves, that is formed underground as a resting stage in the plant's development **b** a tuber, corm, or other fleshy structure resembling a bulb in appearance **c** a plant having or developing from a bulb **2** a glass globe containing a filament that produces light when electricity is passed through it – ~**ous** *adj*

¹**bulge** /bʌldʒ/ *n* **1** a swelling or convex curve on a surface, usu caused by pressure from within or below **2** a sudden and usu temporary expansion (e g in population) – **bulgy** *adj* – **bulgily** *adv* – **bulginess** *n*

²**bulge** *v* to jut out; swell

¹**bulk** /bʌlk/ *n* **1a** spatial dimension; *also* volume **b** roughage **2** voluminous or ponderous mass – often used with reference to the shape or size of a corpulent person **3** the main or greater part *of*

²**bulk** *v* **1** to cause to swell or to be thicker or fuller; pad – often + *out* **2** to gather into a mass **3** to appear as a factor; loom

³**bulk** *adj* (of materials) in bulk

¹**bull** /bʊl/ *n* **1a** an adult male bovine animal **b** an adult male elephant, whale, or other large animal **2** one who buys securities or commodities in expectation of a price rise or who acts to effect such a rise **3** a bull's eye – ~**ish** *adj*

²**bull** *n* a papal edict on a subject of major importance

³**bull** *n* **1** empty boastful talk; nonsense **2** *Br* unnecessary or irksome fatigues or discipline, esp in the armed forces *USE* slang

bulldog /'bʊldɒg/ *n* **1** a thickset muscular short-haired dog of an English breed that has widely separated forelegs and a short neck **2** a proctor's attendant at Oxford or Cambridge

bulldozer /'bʊldəʊzə/ *n* a tractor-driven machine with a broad blunt horizontal blade that is used for clearing land, building roads, etc

bullet /'bʊlɪt/ *n* a small round or elongated missile designed to be fired from a firearm; *broadly* a cartridge – ~**proof** *adj*

bulletin /'bʊlətɪn/ *n* a brief public notice; *specif* a brief news item

bull's-eye *n* **1** a small thick disc of glass inserted (e g in a ship's deck) to let in light **2** a very hard round usu peppermint sweet **3a** (a shot that hits) the centre of a target **b** sthg that precisely attains a desired end

¹**bully** /'bʊli/ *n* **1** a browbeating person;

esp one habitually cruel to others weaker than him-/herself **2** a hired ruffian

²**bully** *v* to treat abusively; intimidate

³**bully, bully-off** *v or n* (to perform) a procedure for starting play in a hockey match in which 2 opposing players face each other and alternately strike the ground and the opponent's stick 3 times before attempting to gain possession of the ball

¹**bump** /bʌmp/ *v* **1** to knock against sthg with a forceful jolt – often + *into* **2** to meet, esp by chance

²**bump** *n* **1** a sudden forceful blow or jolt **2** a rounded projection from a surface; *esp* a swelling of tissue **3** a thrusting of the hips forwards in an erotic manner **4** *pl the* act of holding a child by his/her arms and legs and swinging him/her into the air and back to the ground

bun /bʌn/ *n* **1** any of various usu sweet and round small rolls or cakes that may contain added ingredients (e g currants or spice) **2** a usu tight knot of hair worn esp on the back of the head

¹**bunch** /bʌntʃ/ *n* **1** a compact group formed by a number of things of the same kind, esp when growing or held together; a cluster **2** *sing or pl in constr* the main group (e g of cyclists) in a race **3** *pl, Br* a style in which the hair is divided into 2 lengths and tied, usu one on each side of the head **4** *sing or pl in constr* a group of people – *infml*

²**bunch** *v* to form (into) a group or cluster – often + *up*

¹**bundle** /bʌndl/ *n* **1a** a collection of things held loosely together **b** a package **c** a collection, conglomerate **2** a great mass **3** a sizable sum of money – *slang*

²**bundle** *v* **1** to make into a bundle or package **2** to hustle or hurry unceremoniously **3** to hastily deposit or stuff *into* a suitcase, box, drawer, etc

bungalow /bʌŋɡələu/ *n* a usu detached or semidetached 1-storied house

¹**bunk** /bʌŋk/ *n* a built-in bed (e g on a ship) that is often one of a tier of berths

²**bunk** *v* to sleep or bed *down*, esp in a makeshift bed

³**bunk** *n* nonsense, humbug

bunker /bʌŋkəʳ/ *n* **1** a bin or compartment for storage; *esp* one on a ship for storing fuel **2a** a fortified **b** a golf course hazard that is an area of sand-covered bare ground with 1 or more embankments

¹**buoy** /bɔɪ/ *n* a distinctively shaped and marked float moored to the bottom **a** as a navigational aid to mark a channel or hazard **b** for mooring a ship

²**buoy** *v* **1** to mark (as if) by a buoy **2a** to keep afloat **b** to support, sustain **3** to raise the spirits of *USE* (2 & 3) usu + *up* – **~ancy** *n* – **~ant** *adj* – **~antly** *adv*

¹**burden** /bɜːdən/ *n* **1a** sthg that is carried; a load **b** a duty, responsibility **2** sthg oppressive or wearisome; an encumbrance

²**burden** *v* to load, oppress

³**burden** *n* **1** a chorus, refrain **2** a central topic; a theme

bureaucracy /bjuˈrɒkrəsi, bjuə-/ *n* government characterized by specialization of functions, adherence to fixed rules, and a hierarchy of authority; *also* the body of appointed government officials

bureaucrat /ˈbjuərəkræt/ *n* a government official who follows a rigid routine – **~ic** *adj* – **~ically** *adv*

burglar /ˈbɜːɡləʳ/ *n* sby who unlawfully enters a building (e g to steal) – **~y** *n* – **burgle** *v*

burial /ˈberiəl/ *n* the act, process, or ceremony of burying esp a dead body

¹**burn** /bɜːnt/ *n, chiefly Scot* a small stream

²**burn** *v* **burnt, burned 1a** to consume fuel and give off heat, light, and gases **b** to undergo combustion **c** to destroy by fire **d** to use as fuel **2a** *of the ears or face* to become very red and feel uncomfortably hot **b** to produce or undergo a painfully stinging or smarting sensation **c** to be filled *with*; experience sthg strongly **3a** to injure or damage by exposure to fire, heat, radiation, caustic chemicals, or electricity **b** to execute by burning **c** to char or scorch by exposing to fire or heat

³**burn** *n* **1** injury or damage resulting (as if) from burning **2** a burned area **3** a burning sensation

burrow /ˈbʌrəu/ *n* a hole or excavation in the ground made by a rabbit, fox, etc for shelter and habitation

²**burrow** *v* **1a** to make a burrow **b** to progress (as if) by digging **2** to make a motion suggestive of burrowing; snuggle, nestle **3** to make a search as if by digging

¹**burst** /bɜːst/ *v* **burst 1** to break open, apart, or into pieces, usu from impact or because of pressure from within **2a** to give way from an excess of emotion **b** to give vent suddenly to a repressed emotion **3a** to emerge or spring suddenly **b** to launch, plunge **4** to be filled to breaking point or to the point of overflowing

²**burst** *n* **1** an explosion, eruption **2** a sharp temporary increase (of speed, energy, etc) **3** a volley of shots

burst out *v* **1** to begin suddenly **2** to exclaim suddenly

bury /ˈberi/ *v* **1** to dispose of by depositing (as if) in the earth; *esp* to (ceremonially) dispose of a dead body thus **2** to conceal, hide **3** to put completely out of mind **4** to submerge, engross – usu + *in*

¹**bus** /bʌs/ *n* a large motor-driven passenger vehicle operating usu according to a timetable along a fixed route

²**bus** *v* to transport by bus; *specif, chiefly NAm* to transport (children) by bus to a school in another district where the pupils are of a different race, in order to create integrated classes

¹**bush** /buʃ/ *n* **1a** a (low densely branched) shrub **b** a close thicket of shrubs **2** a large uncleared or sparsely

settled area (e g in Africa or Australia), usu scrub-covered or forested **3** a bushy tuft or mass

bush v to extend like or resemble a bush

business /ˈbɪznɪs/ n **1a** a role, function **b** an immediate task or objective **2a** a usu commercial or mercantile activity engaged in as a means of livelihood **b** one's regular employment, profession, or trade **c** a commercial or industrial enterprise; *also* such enterprises **d** economic transactions or dealings **3** an affair, matter **4** movement or action performed by an actor **5a** personal concern **b** proper motive; justifying right **6** serious activity – ∼ **man**, – ∼ **woman** n

bust /bʌst/ n **1** a sculpture of the upper part of the human figure including the head, neck, and usu shoulders **2** the upper part of the human torso between neck and waist; *esp* the (size of the) breasts of a woman

bust v busted *also* bust **1a** to break, smash; *also* to make inoperative **1b** to bring to an end; break up – often + up **c** to burst **d** to break down **2a** to arrest **b** to raid **3** to lose a game or turn by exceeding a limit (e g the count of 21 in pontoon)

bust adj **1** broken – chiefly infml **2** bankrupt – chiefly in go bust; infml

busy /ˈbɪzi/ adj **1** engaged in action; occupied **2** full of activity; bustling **3** foolishly or intrusively active; meddlesome **4** full of detail – **busily** adv – **busyness** n

busy v to make (esp oneself) busy; occupy

but /bət; *strong* bʌt/ conj **1a** were it not **b** without the necessary accompaniment that – used after a negative **2a** on the contrary; on the other hand – used to join coordinate sentence elements of the same class or function expressing contrast **b** and nevertheless; and yet

but prep **1a** with the exception of; barring **b** other than **c** not counting **2** Scot without, lacking

but adv **1** only, merely **2** to the contrary **3** – used for emphasis **4** NE Eng & Aust however, though

butcher /ˈbʊtʃəʳ/ n **1** sby who slaughters animals or deals in meat **2** sby who kills ruthlessly or brutally

butcher v **1** to slaughter and prepare for market **2** to kill in a barbarous manner **3** to spoil, ruin – ∼ **y** n

butt n a blow or thrust, usu with the head or horns – **butt** v

butt n **1a** a target **b** pl a range, specif for archery or rifle practice **c** a low mound, wall, etc from behind which sportsmen shoot at game birds **2** an object of abuse or ridicule; a victim

butt v to abut – usu + against or onto

butt n **1** the end of a plant or tree nearest the roots **2** the thicker or handle end of a tool or weapon **3** the unsmoked remnant of a cigar or cigarette

butt n a large cask, esp for wine, beer, or water

butter /ˈbʌtəʳ/ n **1** a pale yellow solid emulsion made by churning milk or cream and used as food **2** any of various food spreads made with or having the consistency of butter

butterfly /ˈbʌtəflaɪ/ n **1** any of numerous slender-bodied day-flying insects with large broad often brightly coloured wings **2** a swimming stroke executed on the front by moving both arms together forwards out of the water and then sweeping them back through the water **3** pl a feeling of sickness caused esp by nervous tension – infml

buttock /ˈbʌtək/ n the back of a hip that forms one of the 2 fleshy parts on which a person sits

button /ˈbʌtn/ n **1** a small knob or disc secured to an article (e g of clothing) and used as a fastener by passing it through a buttonhole or loop **2** an immature whole mushroom **3** a guard on the tip of a fencing foil

button v to close or fasten (as if) with buttons – often + up

buy /baɪ/ v bought **1** to purchase **2** to obtain, often by some sacrifice **3** to bribe, hire **4** to believe, accept – slang

buy n an act of buying; a purchase

buzz /bʌz/ v **1** to make a low continuous vibratory sound like that of a bee **2** to be filled with a confused murmur **3** to fly over or close to in order to threaten or warn **4** to summon or signal with a buzzer

buzz n **1** a persistent vibratory sound **2a** a confused murmur or flurry of activity **b** rumour, gossip **3** a telephone call – infml **4** a pleasant stimulation; a kick – infml

by /baɪ/ prep **1a** in proximity to; near **b** on the person or in the possession of **2a** through the medium of): via **b** up to and then beyond; past **3a** in the circumstances of; during (e g slept by day) **b** not later than (e g home by dark) **4a(1)** through the instrumentality or use of (e g by bus) **(2)** through the action or creation of (e g a song by Wolf) **b(1)** sired by **(2)** with the participation of (the other parent) (e g a son by an earlier marriage) **5** with the witness or sanction of **6a** in conformity with (e g done by the rules) **b** in terms of (e g paid by the dozen) **c** from the evidence of (e g judge by appearances) **7** with respect to **8** to the amount or extent of **9** in successive units or increments of **10** – used in division as the inverse of into, in multiplication, and in measurements **11** chiefly Scot in comparison with; beside

by adv **1a** close at hand; near **b** at or to another's home (e g by sometime) **2** past **3** aside, away; esp in or into reserve

C

cab /kæb/ n 1 a taxi 2 the part of a locomotive, lorry, crane, etc that houses the driver and operating controls

cabbage /'kæbɪdʒ/ n 1 a cultivated plant that has a short stem and a dense globular head of usu green leaves used as a vegetable 2a one who has lost control of his/her esp mental and physical faculties as the result of illness or accident b an inactive and apathetic person – *USE* (2) infml

cabin /'kæbɪn/ n 1a a room or compartment on a ship or boat for passengers or crew b a compartment in an aircraft for cargo, crew, or passengers 2 a small usu single-storied dwelling of simple construction

cabinet /'kæbɪnɪt, 'kæbnɪt/ n 1a a case for storing or displaying articles b an upright case housing a radio or television set 2 *sing or pl in constr, often cap* a body of advisers of a head of state, who formulate government policy – **cabinet** *adj*

¹cable /'keɪbl/ n 1 a strong thick (wire) rope 2 an assembly of electrical conductors insulated from each other and surrounded by a sheath 3 a telegram 4 a nautical unit of length equal to about a *Br* 185m (202yd) b *NAm* 219m (240yd)

²cable *v* to communicate by means of a telegram

café /'kæfeɪ/ n a small restaurant serving snacks, tea, coffee etc

¹cage /keɪdʒ/ n 1 a box or enclosure of open construction for animals 2 a barred cell or fenced area for prisoners 3 a framework serving as a support

²cage *v* to put or keep (as if) in a cage

¹cake /keɪk/ n 1 (a shaped mass of) any of various sweet baked foods made from a basic mixture of flour and sugar, usu with fat, eggs, and a raising agent 2 a block of compressed or congealed matter

²cake *v* to encrust

calamity /kə'læmɪti/ n 1 a state of deep distress caused by misfortune or loss 2 an extremely grave event; a disaster

calculate /'kælkjʊleɪt, -kjə-/ v 1 to determine by mathematical processes 2 to forecast consequences 3 to count, rely – + *on* or *upon*

calculation /ˌkælkjʊ'leɪʃən, -kjə-/ n 1 (the result of) the process or an act of calculating 2 studied care in planning, esp to promote self-interest

calculator /'kælkjʊleɪtə, -kjə-/ n an electronic or mechanical machine for performing mathematical operations

calendar /'kælɪndə/ n 1 a system for fixing the beginning, length, and divisions of the civil year and arranging days and longer divisions of time (e g weeks and months) in a definite order 2 a usu printed display of the days of 1 year 3 a chronological list of events or activities

¹calf /kɑːf/ n, pl **calves** *also* **calfs**, (2) **calfs** 1a the young of the domestic cow or a closely related mammal (e g a bison) b the young of some large animals (e g the elephant and whale) 2 calfskin – **calve** *v*

²calf n, pl **calves** the fleshy back part of the leg below the knee

¹call /kɔːl/ v 1a to speak loudly or distinctly so as to be heard at a distance b to utter or announce in a loud distinct voice – often + *out* c *of an animal* to utter a characteristic note or cry 2a to command or request to come or be present b to summon to a particular activity, employment, or office 3 to rouse from sleep + with a brief visit – often + *in* or *by* 5 to (try to) get into communication by telephone – often + *up* 6a to make a demand in bridge for (a card or suit) b to require (a player) to show the hand in poker by making an equal bet 7 to speak of or address by a specified name; give a name to 8a to regard or characterize as a certain kind; consider b to consider for purposes of an estimate or for convenience 9 to predict, guess

²call n 1a calling with the voice b the cry of an animal (e g a bird); *also* an imitation of an animal's cry made to attract the animal 2a a request or command to come or assemble b a summons or signal on a drum, bugle, or pipe 3a a divine vocation or stronger inner prompting b the attraction or appeal of a particular activity or place 4a a demand, request b need, justification 5 a short usu formal visit 6 calling in a card game 7 telephoning 8 a direction or a succession of directions for a square dance rhythmically called to the dancers – ~**er** n

¹calm /kɑːm/ n 1a the absence of winds or rough water; stillness b a state in which the wind has a speed of less than 1km/h (about ⅝mph) 2 a state of repose free from agitation

²calm *adj* 1 marked by calm; still 2 free from agitation or excitement

³calm *v* to make or become calm

calves /kɑːvz/ pl of **calf**

came /keɪm/ past of **come**

camel /'kæməl/ n 1 either of 2 large ruminants used as draught and saddle animals in (African and Asian) desert regions: a the 1-humped Arabian camel b the 2-humped Bactrian camel 2 a float used to lift submerged ships 3 a light yellowish brown colour

camera /'kæmərə/ n a lightproof box having an aperture, and esp a lens, for recording the image of an object on a light-sensitive material: e g a one containing photographic film for producing a permanent record b one containing a device which converts the image into an electrical signal (e g for television transmission)

camouflage /'kæməflɑːʒ/ n 1 the disguising of esp military equipment or installations with nets, paint, etc **2** concealment by means of disguise

¹camp /kæmp/ *n* **1a** a temporary shelter (e g a tent) or group of shelters **b** a new settlement (e g in a lumbering or mining region) **2** *sing or pl in constr* a group of people engaged in promoting or defending a theory or position **3** a place where troops are housed or trained

²camp *v* **1** to pitch or occupy a camp **2** to live temporarily in a camp or outdoors – ~er *n*

³camp *adj* **1** exaggeratedly effeminate or deliberately and outrageously artificial, affected, or inappropriate, esp to the point of tastelessness *USE infml*

⁴camp *v* to behave in a camp style, manner, etc – usu + *up; infml*

campaign /kæm'peɪn/ *n* **1** a connected series of military operations forming a distinct phase of a war **2** a connected series of operations designed to bring about a particular result – campaign *v,* – ~er *n*

¹can /kən; *strong* kʌn/ *verbal auxiliary, pres sing & pl* can; *past* could **1a** know how to **b** be physically or mentally able to **c** may perhaps – chiefly in questions **d** be logically inferred or supposed to – chiefly in negatives **e** be permitted by conscience or feeling to **f** be inherently able or designed to **g** be logically able to **h** be enabled by law, agreement, or custom to **2** have permission to – used interchangeably with *may* **3** will – used in questions with the force of a request

²can /kæn/ *n* **1** a usu cylindrical receptacle: **a** a vessel for holding liquids **b** a tin; *esp* a tin containing a beverage (e g beer) **2** *NAm the* toilet – *infml*

³can /kæn/ *v* **1** to pack or preserve in a tin **2** *chiefly NAm* to put a stop or end to – *slang*

canal /kə'næl/ *n* **1** a tubular anatomical channel **2** an artificial waterway for navigation, drainage, or irrigation

canary /kə'neəri/ *n* a small usu green to yellow finch of the Canary islands, widely kept as a cage bird

cancel /'kænsəl/ *v* **1** to mark or strike out for deletion **2a** to make void; countermand, annul **b** to bring to nothingness; destroy **c** to match in force or effect; counterbalance – usu + *out* **3** to call off, usu without intending to reschedule to a later time **4** to deface (a stamp), usu with a set of parallel lines, so as to invalidate reuse

cancer /'kænsə/ *n* **1** *cap* (sby born under) the 4th zodiacal constellation, pictured as a crab **2** (a condition marked by) a malignant tumour of potentially unlimited growth **3** a source of evil or anguish – ~ous *adj* – ~ously *adv*

candidate /'kændɪdɪt/ *n* **1** one who is nominated or qualified for, or aspires to an office, membership, or award **2** one who is taking an examination **3** sthg suitable for a specified action or process – -ature *n*

candle /'kændl/ *n* a usu long slender cylindrical mass of tallow or wax enclosing a wick that is burnt to give light

¹cane /keɪn/ *n* **1a** a hollow or pithy usu flexible jointed stem (e g of bamboo) **b** an elongated flowering or fruiting stem (e g of a raspberry) **c** any of various tall woody grasses or reeds; *esp* sugarcane **2a** a walking stick made of cane **b** (the use of) a cane or rod for flogging **c** a length of split cane for use in basketry

²cane *v* to beat with a cane; *broadly* to punish

cannibal /'kænɪbəl/ *n* **1** a human being who eats human flesh **2** an animal that eats its own kind – ~ism *n* – ~istic *adj*

¹cannon /'kænən/ *n, pl* cannons, cannon **1** a usu large gun mounted on a carriage **2** an automatic shell-firing gun mounted esp in an aircraft

²cannon *n, Br* a shot in billiards in which the cue ball strikes each of 2 object balls

³cannon *v* **1** to collide – usu + *into* **2** to collide with and be deflected *off* sthg

cannot /'kænɒt, -nət/ can not

canoe /kə'nuː/ *n* **1** a long light narrow boat with sharp ends and curved sides usu propelled by paddling **2** *chiefly Br* a kayak

canvas /'kænvəs/ *also* canvass *n* **1** a firm closely woven cloth usu of linen, hemp, or cotton used for clothing, sails, tents etc **2** a set of sails; sail **3** a cloth surface suitable for painting on in oils; *also* the painting on such a surface **4** a coarse cloth so woven as to form regular meshes as a basis for embroidery or tapestry **5** the floor of a boxing or wrestling ring

canvass /'kænvəs/ *v* to seek orders or votes; solicit

¹cap /kæp/ *n* **1a** a soft usu flat head covering with a peak and no brim **b** (one who has gained) selection for an esp national team; *also* a cap awarded as a mark of this **2a** a usu unyielding overlying rock or soil layer **b** (a patch of distinctively coloured feathers on) the top of a bird's head **3** sthg that serves as a cover or protection, esp for the end or top of an object **4** the uppermost part; the top **5** a small container holding an explosive charge (e g for a toy pistol or for priming the charge in a firearm) **6** *Br* a dutch cap

²cap *v* to follow with sthg more noticeable or significant; outdo

capable /'keɪpəbl/ *adj* **1** susceptible **2** having the attributes or traits required to perform a specified deed or action **3** able *USE (except 3) + of* – -bly *adv*

capacity /kə'pæsɪti/ *n* **1a** the ability to accommodate or deal with sthg **b** an ability to contain **c** the maximum amount that can be contained or produced **2** legal competence or power **3a** ability, calibre **b** potential **4** a position or role assigned or assumed

¹capital /'kæpɪtl/ *adj* **1a** punishable by death **b** involving execution **2** *of a letter* of or conforming to the series (e g

A, B, C rather than a, b, c) used to begin sentences or proper names **3a** of the greatest importance or influence **b** being the seat of government **4** excellent – not now in vogue

²**capital** *n* **1a** (the value of) a stock of accumulated goods, esp at a particular time and in contrast to income received during a particular period **b** accumulated possessions calculated to bring in income **c** *sing or pl in constr* people holding capital **d** a sum of money saved **2** an esp initial capital letter **3** a city serving as a seat of government

³**capital** *n* the top part or piece of an architectural column

capitalism /'kæpɪtlɪzəm/ *n* an economic system characterized by private ownership and control of the means of production, distribution, and exchange and by the profit motive

capitalist /'kæpɪtlɪst/ , capitalistic *adj* **1** owning capital **2** practising, advocating, or marked by capitalism – **capitalist** *n*

capsule /'kæpsjuːl/ *n* **1** a closed plant receptacle containing spores or seeds **2** a usu gelatin shell enclosing a drug for swallowing **3** a detachable pressurized compartment, esp in a spacecraft or aircraft, containing crew and controls; *also* a spacecraft **4** a covering that encloses the top of a bottle, esp of wine, and protects the cork

captain /'kæptɪn/ *n* **1a** a middle-ranking military or naval officer **b** an officer in charge of a ship **c** a pilot of a civil aircraft **2** a distinguished military leader **3** a leader of a team, esp a sports team **4** a dominant figure **5** *Br* the head boy or girl at a school

captive /'kæptɪv/ *adj* **1a** taken and held as prisoner, esp by an enemy in war **b** kept within bounds **2** in a situation that makes departure or inattention difficult – **-vity** *n*

capture /'kæptʃə/ *v* **1** to take captive; win, gain **2** to preserve in a relatively permanent form **3** to remove (e g a chess piece) from the playing board according to the rules of a game – **capture** *n*

car /kɑː/ *n* **1a** a railway carriage; *esp* one used for a specific purpose **b** a motor car **2** the passenger compartment of an airship or balloon **3** *NAm* the cage of a lift

caravan /'kærəvæn/ *n* **1a** *sing or pl in constr* a company of travellers on a journey through desert or hostile regions; *also* a train of pack animals **b** a group of vehicles travelling together **2** *Br* a covered vehicle designed to be towed by a motor car or horse and to serve as a dwelling when parked

carbon /'kɑːbən/ *n* **1** a nonmetallic element occurring as diamond, graphite, charcoal, coke, etc and as a constituent of coal, petroleum, carbonates (e g limestone), and organic compounds **2a** a sheet of carbon paper **b** a copy (e g of a letter) made with carbon paper – **~ize** *v*

card *n* **1** a playing card **2** *pl but sing or pl in constr* a game played with cards **3** a valuable asset or right for use in negotiations **4** a flat stiff usu small and rectangular piece of paper or thin cardboard: e g **a** a postcard **b** a visiting card **c** a programme; *esp* one for a sporting event **d** a greeting card **5** *pl, Br* the National Insurance and other papers of an employee, held by his/her employer

¹**cardboard** /'kɑːdbɔːd/ *n* material of similar composition to paper but thicker and stiffer

²**cardboard** *adj* **1** made (as if) of cardboard **2** unreal, insubstantial

cardigan /'kɑːdɪgən/ *n* a knitted garment for the upper body that opens down the front and is usu fastened with buttons

¹**care** /keə/ *n* **1** a cause for anxiety **2** close attention; effort **3** change, supervision; *specif, Br* guardianship and supervision of children by a local authority

²**care** *v* **1** to feel interest or concern – often + *about* **2** to give care – often + *for* **3** to have a liking or taste *for*

¹**career** /kə'rɪə/ *n* a field of employment in which one expects to remain; *esp* such a field which requires special qualifications and training

²**career** *v* to move swiftly in an uncontrolled fashion

careful /'keəfəl/ *adj* **1** exercising or taking care **2a** marked by attentive concern **b** cautious, prudent – often + *to* and an infinitive – **~ly** *adv* – **~ness** *n*

careless /'keəlɪs/ *adj* **1** not taking care **2a** negligent, slovenly **b** unstudied, spontaneous **3a** free from care; untroubled **b** indifferent, unconcerned – **~ly** *adv* – **~ness** *n*

caretaker /'keəteɪkə/ *n* **1** one who takes care of the house or land of an owner, esp during his/her absence **2** one who keeps clean a large and/or public building (e g a school or office), looks after the heating system, and carries out minor repairs **3** sby or sthg temporarily installed in office

cargo /'kɑːgəʊ/ *n* the goods conveyed in a ship, aircraft, or vehicle; freight

carpenter /'kɑːpɪntə/ *n* a woodworker; *esp* one who builds or repairs large-scale structural woodwork – **~try** *n*

¹**carpet** /'kɑːpɪt/ *n* a heavy woven or felted material used as a floor covering; *also* a floor covering made of this fabric

²**carpet** *v* **1** to cover (as if) with a carpet **2** to reprimand – *infml*

carriage /'kærɪdʒ/ *n* **1** the manner of bearing the body; posture **2** (the price or cost of) carrying **3** a wheeled vehicle; *esp* a horse-drawn passenger-carrying vehicle designed for private use **4** a movable part of a machine that supports some other part **5** a railway passenger vehicle; a coach

carrot /'kærət/ *n* **1** (a biennial plant with) a usu orange spindle-shaped root eaten as a vegetable **2** a promised and often illusory reward or advantage

¹**carry** /'kæri/ v **1** to support and move (a load); transport **2** to convey, conduct **3** to lead or influence by appeal to the emotions **4** to transfer from one place to another; *esp* to transfer (a digit corresponding to a multiple of 10) to the next higher power of 10 in addition **5a** to bear on or within oneself **b** to have as a mark, attribute, or property **6** to have as a consequence, esp in law; involve **7** to hold (e g one's person) in a specified manner **8** to keep in stock for sale **9** to maintain through financial support or personal effort **10** to extend or prolong in space, time, or degree **11** to gain victory for **12a** to broadcast or publish **b** to reach or penetrate to a distance **c** to convey itself to a reader or audience **13** to perform with sufficient ability to make up for the poor performance of (e g a partner or teammate)

²**carry** n the range of a gun or projectile

¹**cart** /kɑːt/ n **1** a heavy 2-wheeled or 4-wheeled vehicle used for transporting bulky or heavy loads (e g goods or animal feed) **2** a lightweight 2-wheeled vehicle drawn by a horse or pony **3** a small wheeled vehicle

²**cart** v to take or drag away without ceremony or by force – *infml*; usu + *off*

carton /'kɑːtn/ n a box or container made of plastic, cardboard, etc

cartoon /kɑː'tuːn/ n **1** a preparatory design, drawing, or painting (e g for a fresco) **2** a satirical drawing commenting on political and usu political matters **b** a series of drawings (e g in a magazine) telling a story **3** a film using animated drawings – ~**ist** n

carve /kɑːv/ v **1** to cut so as to shape **2** to make or acquire (a career, reputation, etc) through one's own efforts – often + *out* **3** to cut (food, esp meat) into pieces or slices

¹**case** /keɪs/ n **1** a situation (requiring investigation or action) **2** an (inflectional) form of a noun, pronoun, or adjective indicating its grammatical relation to other words **3a** a suit or action that reaches a court of law **b(1)** the evidence supporting a conclusion **(2)** an argument; *esp* one that is convincing **4a** an instance of disease or injury; *also* a patient suffering from a specific illness **b** an example **5** a peculiar person; a character – *infml*

²**case** n **1** a box or receptacle for holding sthg: e g **a** a glass-panelled box for the display of specimens (e g in a museum) **b** a suitcase **2** an outer covering (e g of a book)

³**case** v to inspect or study (e g a house), esp with intent to rob – *slang*

¹**cash** /kæʃ/ n **1** ready money **2** money or its equivalent paid promptly at the time of purchase

²**cash** v **1** to pay or obtain cash for **2** to lead and win a bridge trick with (the highest remaining card of a suit)

cashier /kæ'ʃɪə/ v to dismiss, usu dis-

honourably, esp from service in the armed forces

²**cashier** n **1** one employed to receive cash from customers, esp in a shop **2** one who collects and records payments (e g in a bank)

¹**cast** /kɑːst/ v **cast 1a** to cause to move (as if) by throwing **b** to place as if by throwing **c** to deposit (a vote) formally **d(1)** to throw off or away **(2)** to shed, moult **(3)** *of an animal* to give birth to (prematurely) **2** to calculate (a horoscope) by means of astrology **3a** to arrange into a suitable form or order **b** to assign a part for (e g a play) or to (e g an actor) **4** to shape (e g metal or plastic) by pouring into a mould when molten **5** to throw out a line and lure with a fishing rod **6** to look round; seek – + *about* or *around*

²**cast** n **1** a throw of a (fishing) line or net **2** *sing or pl in constr* the set of performers in a dramatic production **3** a slight squint in the eye **4a** a reproduction (e g of a statue) formed by casting **b** an impression taken from an object with a molten or plastic substance **c** a plaster covering and support for a broken bone **5** a tinge, suggestion **6** the excrement of an earthworm

¹**castle** /'kɑːsəl/ n **1** a large fortified building or set of buildings **2** a stronghold **3** a rook in chess

²**castle** v to move (a chess king) 2 squares towards a rook and then place the rook on the square on the other side of the king

castrate /kæ'streɪt/ v **1a** to remove the testes of; geld **b** to remove the ovaries of; spay **2** to deprive of vitality or vigour; emasculate – **-tration** n

casual /'kæʒʊəl/ adj **1** subject to, resulting from, or occurring by chance **2a** occurring without regularity; occasional **b** employed for irregular periods **3a** feeling or showing little concern; nonchalant **b** informal, natural; *also* designed for informal wear – ~**ly** adv – ~**ness** n

casualty /'kæʒʊəltɪ/ n **1** a member of a military force killed or wounded in action **2** a person or thing injured, lost, or destroyed

¹**cat** /kæt/ n **1a** a small domesticated flesh-eating mammal kept as a pet or for catching rats and mice **b** any of a family of carnivores that includes the domestic cat, lion, tiger, leopard, jaguar, cougar, lynx, and cheetah **2** a malicious woman **3** a cat-o'-nine-tails **4** a (male) person – *slang*

²**cat** n a catamaran – *infml*

catalogue, NAm chiefly **catalog** n **1** (a pamphlet or book containing) a complete list of items arranged systematically with descriptive details **2** a list, series — **catalogue** v

¹**catapult** /'kætəpʌlt, -pʊlt/ n **1** an ancient military device for hurling missiles **2** *Br* a Y-shaped stick with a piece of elastic material fixed between the 2 prongs, used for shooting small objects (e g stones)

²**catapult** v **1** to throw or launch (a

missile) by means of a catapult **2** to (cause to) move suddenly or abruptly

¹catch /kætʃ/ v **caught 1a** to capture or seize, esp after pursuit **b** to discover unexpectedly; surprise **c** to become entangled, fastened, or stuck **2a** to seize; esp to intercept and keep hold of (a moving object), esp in the hands **b** to dismiss (a batsman in cricket) by catching the ball after it has been hit and before it has touched the ground **3a** to contract; become infected with **b** to hit, strike **c** to receive the force or impact of **4** to attract, arrest **5** to take or get quickly or for a moment **6** to be in time for **7** to grasp with the senses or the mind **8** of a fire to start to burn

²catch n **1** sthg caught; esp the total quantity caught at one time **2** a game in which a ball is thrown and caught **3** sthg that retains or fastens **4** an often humorous or coarse round for 3 or more voices **5** a concealed difficulty; a snag **6** an eligible marriage partner – infml

catch up v **1** to act or move fast enough to draw level with **2** to acquaint oneself or deal with sthg belatedly – + on or with

caterpillar /'kætə,pilə'/ n a wormlike larva, specif of a butterfly or moth

cathedral /kə'θi:drəl/ n a church that is the official seat of a bishop

cattle /'kætl/ n, pl bovine animals kept on a farm, ranch, etc

caught /kɔ:t/ past of **catch**

cauliflower /'kɒli,flauə'/ n (a plant closely related to the cabbage with) a compact head of usu white undeveloped flowers eaten as a vegetable

¹cause /kɔ:z/ n **1a** sby or sthg that brings about an effect **b** a reason for an action or condition; a motive **2a** a ground for legal action **3** a principle or movement worth defending or supporting

²cause v to serve as the cause or occasion of

'cause /kəz/ conj because – nonstandard

¹caution /'kɔ:ʃən/ n **1a** a warning, admonishment; specif an official warning given to sby who has committed a minor offence **b** prudent forethought intended to minimize risk; care **3** sby or sthg that causes astonishment or amusement – infml

²caution v **1a** to advise caution to; warn; specif to warn (sby under arrest) that his/her words will be recorded and may be used in evidence **b** to admonish, reprove; specif to give an official warning to **2** of a soccer referee to book

cautious /'kɔ:ʃəs/ adj careful, prudent – ~ly adv – ~ness n

cavalry /'kævəlri/ n, sing or pl in constr **1** a branch of an army consisting of mounted troops **2** a branch of a modern army consisting of armoured vehicles – ~man n

¹cave /keiv/ n a natural chamber (e g underground or in the side of a hill or cliff) having a usu horizontal opening on the surface

²cave /kei'vi:/ interj, Br – used as a

warning call among schoolchildren, esp at public school

cavern /'kævən/ n a large usu underground chamber or cave

cease v /si:s/ to bring to an end; terminate, discontinue – **cease** n

ceaseless /'si:sləs/ adj continuing endlessly; constant – ~ly adv

ceiling /'si:liŋ/ n **1** the overhead inside surface of a room **2** the height above the ground of the base of the lowest layer of clouds **3** an upper usu prescribed limit

celebrate /'seli,breit/ v **1** to perform (a sacrament or solemn ceremony) publicly and with appropriate rites **2a** to mark (a holy day or feast day) ceremonially **b** to mark (a special occasion) with festivities or suspension of routine activities – **-bration** n

celebrity /si'lebriti/ n **1** the state of being famous **2** a well-known and widely acclaimed person

cell /sel/ n **1** a 1-room dwelling occupied esp by a hermit **2** a small room for a prisoner, monk, etc **3** a small compartment (e g in a honeycomb), receptacle, cavity (e g one containing seeds in a plant ovary), or bounded space **4** the smallest structural unit of living matter consisting of nuclear and cytoplasmic material bounded by a membrane and capable of functioning either alone or with others in all fundamental life processes **5** a vessel (e g a cup or jar) containing electrodes and an electrolyte either for generating electricity by chemical action or for use in electrolysis **6** the primary unit of a political, esp Communist, organization

cellar /'selə'/ n **1** an underground room; esp one used for storage **2** an individual's stock of wine

cellophane /'selə,fein/ n regenerated cellulose in the form of thin transparent sheets, used esp for wrapping goods

¹cement /si'ment/ n **1** a powder consisting of ground alumina, silica, lime, iron oxide, and magnesia burnt in a kiln, that is used as the binding agent in mortar and concrete **2** a substance (e g a glue or adhesive) used for sticking objects together **3** sthg serving to unite firmly **4** concrete – not used technically

²cement v **1** to unite or make firm (as if) by the application of cement **2** to overlay with concrete

cemetery /'semitri/ n a burial ground; esp one not in a churchyard

censor /'sensə'/ n an official who examines publications, films, letters, etc and has the power to suppress objectionable (e g obscene or libellous) matter – ~ship n – ~ious adj – censor v

census /'sensəs/ n **1** a periodic counting of the population and gathering of related statistics (e g age, sex, or social class) carried out by government **2** a usu official count or tally

cent /sent/ n (a coin or note representing) a unit worth ¹/₁₀₀ of the basic money unit of certain countries (e g the American dollar)

centigrade /'senti̱greɪd/ *adj* Celsius

central /'sentrəl/ *adj* **1** containing or constituting a centre **2** of primary importance; principal **3** at, in, or near the centre **4** having overall power or control **5** of, originating in, or comprising the central nervous system – ~**ly** *adv* – ~**ize** *v*

¹**centre** /'sentə'/ *NAm chiefly* **center** *n* **1** the point round which a circle or sphere is described; *broadly* the centre of symmetry **2a** a place, esp a collection of buildings, round which a usu specified activity is concentrated **b** sby or sthg round which interest is concentrated **c** a source from which sthg originates **d** a region of concentrated population **3** the middle part (e g of a stage) **4** *often cap* a group, party, etc holding moderate political views **5** a player occupying a middle position in the forward line of a team (e g in football or hockey) **6** a temporary wooden framework on which an arch is supported during construction

²**centre**, *NAm chiefly* **center** *v* **1** to place, fix, or move in, into, or at a centre or central area **2** to gather to a centre; concentrate **3** to adjust (e g lenses) so that the axes coincide

century /'sentʃəri/ *n* **1** a subdivision of the ancient Roman legion orig consisting of 100 men **2** a group, sequence, or series of 100 like things; *specif* 100 runs made by a cricketer in 1 innings **3** a period of 100 years; *esp* any of the 100-year periods reckoned forwards or backwards from the conventional date of the birth of Christ

cereal /'sɪərɪəl/ *n* **1** (a grass or other plant yielding) grain suitable for food **2** a food made from grain and usu eaten with milk and sugar at breakfast

ceremonial /ˌserɪ'məʊnɪəl/ *n* **1** a usu prescribed system of formalities or rituals **2** (a book containing) the order of service in the Roman Catholic church

ceremony /'serɪməni/ *n* **1** a formal act or series of acts prescribed by ritual, protocol, or convention **2** (observance of) established procedures of civility or politeness – **-nial** *adj* – **-nious** *adj*

certain /'sɜːtn/ *adj* **1a** of a particular but unspecified character, quantity, or degree **b** named but not known **2a** established beyond doubt or question; definite **b** unerring, dependable **3a** inevitable **b** incapable of failing; sure – + *infinitive* **4** assured in mind or action – ~**ly** *adv*

certainty /'sɜːtnti/ *n* **1** sthg certain **2** the quality or state of being certain

¹**certificate** /sə'tɪfɪkət/ *n* a document containing a certified statement; *esp* one declaring the status or qualifications of the holder

²**certificate** /sə'tɪfɪkeɪt/ *v* to testify to with a certificate

¹**chain** /tʃeɪn/ *n* **1a** a series of usu metal links or rings connected to or fitted into one another and used for various purposes (e g support or restraint) **b** a unit of length equal to 66ft (about 20.12m) **2** sthg that confines, restrains, or secures

– usu pl **3a** a series of linked or connected things **b** a group of associated establishments (e g shops or hotels) under the same ownership

²**chain** *v* to fasten, restrict, or confine (as if) with a chain – often + *up* or *down*

¹**chair** /tʃeə'/ *n* **1** a seat for 1 person, usu having 4 legs and a back and sometimes arms **2a** an office or position of authority or dignity; *specif* a professorship **b** a chairman **3** a sedan chair

²**chair** *v* **1** to install in office **2** to preside as chairman of **3** *chiefly Br* to carry shoulder-high in acclaim

chairman /'tʃeəmən/, *fem* **chairlady, chairwoman** *n* **1** one who presides over or heads a meeting, committee, organization, or board of directors **2** a radio or television presenter; *esp* one who coordinates unscripted or diverse material – ~**ship** *n*

¹**chalk** /tʃɔːk/ *n* **1** a soft white, grey, or buff limestone composed chiefly of the shells of small marine organisms **2** a short stick of chalk or chalky material used esp for writing and drawing – ~**y** *adj*

²**chalk** *v* to set down or add up (as if) with chalk – usu + *up*

¹**challenge** /'tʃælɪndʒ/ *v* **1** to order to halt and prove identity **2** to dispute, esp as being unjust, invalid, or outmoded; impugn **3** to defy boldly; dare **b** to call out to duel, combat, or competition **4** to stimulate by testing the skill of (sby or sthg) – ~**r** *n*

²**challenge** *n* **1a** a command given by a sentry, watchman, etc to halt and prove identity **b** a questioning of right or validity **2a** a summons that is threatening or provocative; *specif* a call to a duel **b** an invitation to compete **3** (sthg having) the quality of being demanding or stimulating

champagne /ʃæm'peɪn/ *n* a white sparkling wine made in the old province of Champagne in France

¹**champion** /'tʃæmpɪən/ *n* **1** a militant supporter of, or fighter for, a cause or person **2** one who shows marked superiority; *specif* the winner of a competitive event

²**champion** *v* to protect or fight for as a champion

³**champion** *adj, chiefly N Eng* superb, splendid

¹**chance** /tʃɑːns/ *n* **1** the incalculable (assumed) element in existence; that which determines unaccountable happenings **2** a situation favouring some purpose; an opportunity **3a** the possibility of a specified or favourable outcome in an uncertain situation **b** *pl* the more likely indications **4** a risk – **chance** *adj*

²**chance** *v* **1** to take place or come about by chance; happen **2** to come or light *on* or *upon* by chance **3** to accept the hazard of; risk

¹**change** /tʃeɪndʒ/ *v* **1a** to make or become different **b** to exchange, reverse – often + *over* or *round* **2a** to replace with another **b** to move from one to another **c** to exchange for an equivalent

sum or comparable item **d** to put on fresh clothes or covering **3** to go from one vehicle of a public transport system to another **4** *of the (male) voice* to shift to a lower register; break **5** to undergo transformation, transition, or conversion

²**change** *n* **1a** (a marked) alteration **b** a substitution **2** an alternative set, esp of clothes **3a** money returned when a payment exceeds the amount due **b** coins of low denominations **4** an order in which a set of bells is struck in change ringing

changeable /'tʃeɪndʒəbəl/ *adj* **1** able or apt to vary **2** capable of being altered or exchanged **3** fickle – **-bly** *adv* – **-ness** *n*

¹**channel** /'tʃænl/ *n* **1a** the bed where a stream of water runs **b** the deeper part of a river, harbour, or strait **c** a narrow region of sea between 2 land masses **d** a path along which information passes or can be stored (e g on a recording tape) **e** a course or direction of thought, action, or communication – often *pl* with sing. meaning **f** a television station **2** a usu tubular passage, esp for liquids **3** a long gutter, groove, or furrow

²**channel** *v* to convey into or through a channel; direct

chaos /'keɪ-ɒs/ *n* **1** *often cap* the confused unorganized state of primordial matter before the creation of distinct forms **2** a state of utter confusion – **chaotic** *adj* – **chaotically** *adv*

chapter /'tʃæptə'/ *n* **1a** a major division of a book **b** sthg resembling a chapter in being a significant specified unit **2** (a regular meeting of) the canons of a cathedral or collegiate church, or the members of a religious house **3** a local branch of a society or fraternity

character /'kærˌktə'/ *n* **1a** a distinctive mark, usu in the form of a stylized graphic device **b** a graphic symbol (e g a hieroglyph or alphabet letter) used in writing or printing **2** (any of) qualities that make up and distinguish the individual **3a** a person, esp one marked by notable or conspicuous traits **b** any of the people portrayed in a novel, film, play, etc **4** (good) reputation **5** moral strength; integrity

¹**charge** /tʃɑːdʒ/ *v* **1a** to load or fill to capacity **b(1)** to restore the active materials in (a storage battery) by the passage of a direct current in the opposite direction to that of discharge **(2)** to give an electric charge to **c** to fill with (passionate) emotion, feeling, etc **2** to command or exhort with right or authority **3** to blame or accuse **4** to rush violently at; attack; *also* to rush into (an opponent), usu illegally, in soccer, basketball, etc **5a** to fix or ask as fee or payment **b** to ask payment of (a person) **c** to record (an item) as an expense, debt, obligation, or liability

²**charge** *n* **1** the quantity that an apparatus is intended to receive and fitted to hold; *esp* the quantity of explosive for a gun or cannon **2a** power, force **b** a definite quantity of electricity;

esp the charge that a storage battery is capable of yielding **3a** an obligation, requirement **b** control, supervision **c** sby or sthg committed to the care of another **4** the price demanded or paid for sthg **5** an accusation, indictment, or statement of complaint **6** a violent rush forwards (e g in attack)

charity /'tʃærˌti/ *n* **1** benevolent goodwill towards or love of humanity **2a** kindly generosity and helpfulness, esp towards the needy or suffering; *also* aid given to those in need **b** an institution engaged in relief of the poor, sick, etc **3a** a gift for public benevolent purposes **b** an institution (e g a hospital) funded by such a gift **4** lenient judgment of others

¹**charm** /tʃɑːm/ *n* **1** an incantation **2** sthg worn to ward off evil or to ensure good fortune **3a** a quality that fascinates, allures, or delights **b** *pl* physical graces or attractions, esp of a woman **4** a small ornament worn on a bracelet or chain

²**charm** *v* **1a** to affect (as if) by magic; bewitch **b** to soothe or delight by compelling attraction **2** to control (esp a snake) by the use of rituals (e g the playing of music) – ~**ing** *adj* – ~**ingly** *adv* –

¹**chart** /tʃɑːt/ *n* **1a** an outline map showing the geographical distribution of sthg (e g climatic or magnetic variations) **b** a navigator's map **2a** a sheet giving information in the form of a table; *esp, pl the* list of best-selling popular gramophone records (produced weekly) **b** a graph **c** a schematic, usu large, diagram

²**chart** *v* **1** to make a chart of **2** to lay out a plan for

¹**charter** /'tʃɑːtə'/ *n* **1** a document that creates and defines the rights of a city, educational institution, or company **2** a constitution **3** a special privilege, immunity, or exemption **4** a total or partial lease of a ship, aeroplane, etc for a particular use or group of people

²**charter** *v* **1a** to establish or grant by charter **b** to certify as qualified **2** to hire or lease for usu exclusive and temporary use

¹**chase** /tʃeɪs/ *v* **1a** to follow rapidly or persistently; pursue **b** to hunt, hasten **2** to cause to depart or flee; drive **3** *chiefly Br* to investigate (a matter) or contact (a person, company, etc) in order to obtain information or (hasten) results – usu + *up*

²**chase** *n* **1a** chasing, pursuit **b** *the* hunting of wild animals **2** sthg pursued; a quarry **3** a tract of unenclosed land set aside for the breeding of animals for hunting and fishing **4** a steeplechase

³**chase** *v* to ornament (metal) by indenting with a hammer and tools that have no cutting edge – ~**r** *n*

⁴**chase** *n* a groove cut in a surface for a pipe, wire, etc

¹**chat** /tʃæt/ *v* to talk in an informal or familiar manner

²**chat** *n* (an instance of) light familiar talk; *esp* (a) conversation

chatter /'tʃætə/ v 1 to talk idly, incessantly, or fast; jabber 2a esp of teeth to click repeatedly or uncontrollably (e g from cold) b of a cutting tool (e g a drill) to vibrate rapidly while cutting – ~er n – chatter n

cheap adj 1a (relatively) low in price b charging a low price 2 gained with little effort; esp gained by contemptible means 3a of inferior quality or worth; tawdry, sleazy b contemptible because of lack of any fine or redeeming qualities – ~ly adv – ~ness n

¹cheat /tʃiːt/ n 1 a fraudulent deception; a fraud 2 one who cheats; a pretender, deceiver

²cheat v 1a to practise fraud or deception b to violate rules dishonestly (e g at cards or in an exam) 2 to be sexually unfaithful – usu + on 3 to defeat the purpose or blunt the effects of

¹check /tʃek/ n 1 exposure of a chess king to an attack from which it must be protected or moved to safety – often used interjectionally 2 a sudden stoppage of a forward course or progress; an arrest 3 one who or that which arrests, limits, or restrains; a restraint 4 a criterion 5 an inspection, examination, test, or verification 6a (a square in) a pattern of squares (of alternating colours) b a fabric woven or printed with such a design 7 NAm a cheque 8a chiefly NAm a ticket or token showing ownership or identity b NAm a bill, esp for food and drink in a restaurant

²check v 1 to put (a chess opponent's king) in check 2a to slow or bring to a stop; brake b to block the progress of 3 to restrain or diminish the action or force of 4a to compare with a source, original, or authority; verify b to inspect for satisfactory performance, accuracy, safety, or conformance – sometimes + out or over c chiefly NAm to correspond point for point; tally – often + out 5 to note or mark with a tick – often + off 6 chiefly NAm to leave or accept for safekeeping in a cloakroom or left-luggage office – often + in

cheek /tʃiːk/ n 1 the fleshy side of the face below the eye and above and to the side of the mouth 2 either of 2 paired facing parts (e g the jaws of a vice) 3 insolent boldness; impudence 4 a buttock – infml

cheeky /'tʃiːki/ adj impudent, insolent – cheekily adv – cheekiness n

¹cheer /tʃɪə/ n 1 happiness, gaiety 2 sthg that gladdens 3 a shout of applause or encouragement

²cheer v 1a to instil with hope or courage; comfort b to make glad or happy – usu + up 2 to urge on, encourage, or applaud esp by shouts

cheerful /'tʃɪəfəl/ adj 1 full of good spirits; merry b ungrudging 2 conducive to good cheer; likely to dispel gloom – ~ly adv – ~ness n

¹cheese /tʃiːz/ n 1 (an often cylindrical cake of) a food consisting of coagulated, compressed, and usu ripened milk curds 2 a fruit preserve with the consistency of cream cheese

²cheese n an important person; a boss – slang; chiefly in big cheese

¹chemical /'kemɪkəl/ adj 1 of, used in, or produced by chemistry 2 acting, operated, or produced by chemicals – ~ly adv

²chemical n a substance (e g an element or chemical compound) obtained by a chemical process or used for producing a chemical effect

chemist /'kemɪst/ n 1 one who is trained in chemistry 2 Br (a pharmacist, esp in) a retail shop where medicines and miscellaneous articles (e g cosmetics and films) are sold

chemistry /'kemɪstri/ n 1 a science that deals with the composition, structure, and properties of substances and of the transformations they undergo 2a the composition and chemical properties of a substance b chemical processes and phenomena (e g of an organism)

cheque /tʃek/ n, chiefly Br a written order for a bank to pay money as instructed; also a printed form on which such an order is usually written

cherry /'tʃeri/ n 1 (the wood or small pale yellow to deep red or blackish fruit of) any of numerous trees and shrubs of the rose family, often cultivated for their fruit or ornamental flowers 2 light red

chess /tʃes/ n a game for 2 players each of whom moves his/her 16 chessmen according to fixed rules across a chessboard and tries to checkmate his/her opponent's king

chest /tʃest/ n 1a a box with a lid used esp for the safekeeping of belongings b a usu small cupboard used esp for storing medicines or first-aid supplies 2 the part of the body enclosed by the ribs and breastbone

¹chestnut /'tʃesnʌt/ n 1 (the nut or wood of) a tree or shrub of the beech family 2 reddish brown 3 a horse chestnut 4 a chestnut-coloured animal, specif a horse 5 an often repeated joke or story; broadly anything repeated excessively

²chestnut adj of the colour chestnut

chew /tʃuː/ v to crush, grind, or gnaw (esp food) (as if) with the teeth

chick /tʃɪk/ n 1 a young bird; esp a (newly hatched) chicken 2 a young woman – slang

¹chicken /'tʃɪkɪn/ n 1 the common domestic fowl, esp when young; also its flesh used as food 2 a young person – chiefly in he/she is no chicken – slang

²chicken adj scared – infml

¹chief /tʃiːf/ n the head of a body of people or an organization; a leader

²chief adj 1 accorded highest rank or office 2 of greatest importance or influence

chiefly /'tʃiːfli/ adv 1 most importantly; principally, especially 2 for the most part; mostly, mainly

chieftain /'tʃiːftɪn/ n a chief, esp of a band, tribe, or clan

child /tʃaɪld/ n, pl children 1 an unborn or recently born person 2a a young person, esp between infancy and youth **b** sby under the age of 14 – used in English law **3a** a son or daughter **b** a descendant **4** one strongly influenced by another or by a place or state of affairs **5** a product, result

childhood /'tʃaɪldhʊd/ n **1** the state or period of being a child **2** an early period in the development of sthg

¹**chill** /tʃɪl/ v **1a** to make cold or chilly **b** to make (esp food or drink) cool, esp without freezing **2** to affect as if with cold; dispirit

²**chill** adj chilly

³**chill** n **1** a cold **2** a moderate but disagreeable degree of cold **3** coldness of manner

chilly /'tʃɪli/ adj **1** noticeably (unpleasantly) cold **2** lacking warmth of feeling; distant, unfriendly **3** tending to arouse fear or apprehension – **chilliness** n

chimney /'tʃɪmni/ n **1** a flue or flues for carrying off smoke; esp the part of such a structure extending above a roof **2** a structure through which smoke and gases (e g from a furnace or steam engine) are discharged **3** a tube, usu of glass, placed round a flame (e g of an oil lamp) to serve as a shield

chin /tʃɪn/ n the lower portion of the face lying below the lower lip; the lower jaw

china /'tʃaɪnə/ n **1** porcelain; also vitreous porcelain ware (e g dishes and vases) for domestic use **2** crockery **3** chiefly Br bone china

¹**chip** /tʃɪp/ n **1** a small usu thin and flat piece (e g of wood or stone) cut, struck, or flaked off **2** a counter used as a token for money in gambling games **3** a flaw left after a chip is removed **4** (the small piece of semiconductor, esp silicon, on which is constructed) an integrated circuit **5a** chiefly Br a strip of potato fried in deep fat **b** NAm & Austr a potato crisp

²**chip** v -**pp**- **1a** to cut or hew with an edged tool **b** to cut or break a fragment from **2** to kick or hit a ball, pass, etc in a short high arc

chirp /tʃɜːp/ v or n (to make or speak in a tone resembling) the characteristic short shrill sound of a small bird or insect – **chirp** n

chirpy /'tʃɜːpi/ adj lively, cheerful – infml – **chirpily** adv – **chirpiness** n

¹**chisel** /'tʃɪzəl/ n a metal tool with a cutting edge at the end of a blade used in dressing, shaping, or working wood, stone, metal, etc

²**chisel** v **1** to cut or work (as if) with a chisel **2** to trick, cheat, or obtain (sthg) by cheating – slang – ~**ler** n

chocolate /'tʃɒklɪt/ n **1** a paste, powder, or solid block of food prepared from (sweetened or flavoured) ground roasted cacao seeds **2** a beverage made by mixing chocolate with usu hot water or milk **3** a sweet made or coated with chocolate **4** a dark brown colour

¹**choice** /tʃɔɪs/ n **1** the act of choosing; selection **2** the power of choosing; an option **3** sby or sthg chosen **4** a sufficient number and variety to choose among

²**choice** adj **1** selected with care; well chosen **2** of high quality – ~**ly** adv – ~**ness** n

choir /'kwaɪə/ n **1** sing or pl in constr an organized company of singers **2** the part of a church occupied by the singers or the clergy; specif the part of the chancel between the sanctuary and the nave

¹**choke** /tʃəʊk/ v **1** to check the normal breathing esp by compressing or obstructing the windpipe **2a** to stop or suppress expression of or by; silence – often + back or down **b** to become obstructed or checked **c** to become speechless or incapacitated, esp from strong emotion – usu + up **3a** to restrain the growth or activity of **b** to obstruct by filling up or clogging; jam

²**choke** n sthg that obstructs passage or flow: e g **a** a valve in the carburettor of a petrol engine for controlling the amount of air in a fuel air mixture **b** a narrowing towards the muzzle in the bore of a gun

³**choke** n the fibrous (inedible) central part of a globe artichoke

choose /tʃuːz/ v chose; chosen **1a** to select freely and after consideration **b** to decide on; esp to elect **2a** to decide **b** to wish

¹**chop** /tʃɒp/ v -**pp**- **1a** to cut into or sever, usu by a blow or repeated blows of a sharp instrument **b** to cut into pieces – often + up **2** to make a quick stroke or repeated strokes (as if) with a sharp instrument

²**chop** n **1** a forceful blow (as if) with an axe **2** a small cut of meat often including part of a rib **3** an uneven motion of the sea, esp when wind and tide are opposed **4** abrupt removal; esp the sack – infml

³**chop** n (a licence validated by) a seal or official stamp such as was formerly used in China or India

chopstick /'tʃɒpstɪk/ n either of 2 slender sticks held between thumb and fingers, used chiefly in oriental countries to lift food to the mouth

chore /tʃɔː/ n **1** a routine task or job **2** a difficult or disagreeable task

chorus /'kɔːrəs/ n **1** a character (e g in Elizabethan drama) or group of singers and dancers (e g in Greek drama) who comment on the action **2** sing or pl in constr **a** a body of singers who sing the choral parts of a work (e g in opera) **b** a group of dancers and singers supporting the featured players in a musical or revue **3** a part of a song or hymn recurring at intervals **4** sthg performed, sung, or uttered simultaneously by a number of people or animals

chose /tʃəʊz/ past of choose

chosen /'tʃəʊzən/ adj selected or marked for favour or special privilege

Christ /kraɪst/ n the Messiah; Jesus

christen /'krɪsən/ v **1a** to baptize **b** to name esp at baptism **2** to name or dedicate (e g a ship or bell) by a ceremony suggestive of baptism **3** to use for the first time – infml – ~ **ing** n

¹Christian /'krɪstʃən, -tɪən/ n **1a** an adherent of Christianity **b** a member of a Christian denomination, esp by baptism **2** a good or kind person regardless of religion

²Christian adj **1** of or consistent with Christianity or Christians **2** commendably decent or generous

Christianity /ˌkrɪstɪ'ænətɪ/ n **1** the religion based on the life and teachings of Jesus Christ and the Bible **2** conformity to (a branch of) the Christian religion

Christmas /'krɪsməs/ n **1** a festival of the western Christian churches on December 25 that commemorates the birth of Christ and is usu observed as a public holiday **2** Christmas, **Christmas-tide** the festival season from Christmas Eve till the Epiphany (January 6)

chronic /'krɒnɪk/ adj **1** esp of an illness marked by long duration or frequent recurrence **2a** always present or encountered; esp constantly troubling **b** habitual, persistent **3** Br bad, terrible – infml – ~ **ally** adv

chuckle /'tʃʌkl/ v to laugh inwardly or quietly – **chuckle** n

chunk /tʃʌŋk/ n **1** a lump; esp one of a firm or hard material (e g wood) **2** a (large) quantity – infml

church tʃɜːtʃ/ n **1** a building for public (Christian) worship; esp a place of worship used by an established church **2** often cap institutionalized religion; esp the established Christian religion of a country **3** cap a body or organization of religious believers: e g **a** the whole body of Christians **b** a denomination **c** a congregation **4** an occasion for public worship **5** the clerical profession

cider, cyder /'saɪdə/ n an alcoholic drink made from apples

cigar /sɪ'gɑː/ n a small roll of tobacco leaf for smoking

cigarette /ˌsɪgə'ret/ NAm also **cigaret** n a narrow cylinder of tobacco enclosed in paper for smoking

cinder /'sɪndə/ n **1** a fragment of ash **2** a piece of partly burned material (e g coal) that will burn further but will not flame

cinema /'sɪnɪmə/ n **1a** films considered esp as an art form, entertainment, or industry – usu + the **b** the art or technique of making films **2** a theatre where films are shown

¹circle /'sɜːkl/ n **1a** a closed plane curve every point of which is equidistant from a fixed point within the curve **b** the plane surface bounded by such a curve **2** sthg in the form of (an arc of) a circle **3** a balcony or tier of seats in a theatre **4** cycle, round **5** sing or pl in constr a group of people sharing a common interest, activity, or leader

²circle v **1** to enclose or move (as if) in a circle **2** to move or revolve round

circuit /'sɜːkɪt/ n **1** a closed loop encompassing an area **2a** a course round a periphery **b** a racetrack **3** a regular tour (e g by a judge) round an

assigned area or territory **4a** the complete path of an electric current, usu including the source of energy **b** an array of electrical components connected so as to allow the passage of current **5a** an association or league of similar groups **b** a chain of theatres at which productions are presented successively

¹circular /'sɜːkjʊlə/ adj **1** having the form of a circle **2** moving in or describing a circle or spiral **3** marked by the fallacy of assuming sthg which is to be demonstrated **4** marked by or moving in a cycle **5** intended for circulation

²circular n a paper (e g a leaflet or advertisement) intended for wide distribution

circulate /'sɜːkjʊleɪt/ v **1** to move in a circle, circuit, or orbit; esp to follow a course that returns to the starting point **2a** to flow without obstruction **b** to become well known or widespread **c** to go from group to group at a social gathering **d** to come into the hands of readers; specif to become sold or distributed **3** to cause to circulate

circulation /ˌsɜːkjʊ'leɪʃən/ n **1** a flow **2** orderly movement through a circuit; esp the movement of blood through the vessels of the body induced by the pumping action of the heart **3a** passage or transmission from person to person or place to place; esp the interchange of currency **b** the average number of copies (e g of a newspaper) of a publication sold over a given period

circumstance /-'sɜːkəmstæns, -stəns/ n **1** a condition or event that accompanies, causes, or determines another; also the sum of such conditions or events **2a** a state of affairs; an occurrence – often pl with sing. meaning **b** pl situation with regard to material or financial welfare **3** attendant formalities and ceremony

circus /'sɜːkəs/ n **1a** a large circular or oval stadium used esp for sports contests or spectacles **b** a public spectacle **2a** (the usu covered arena housing) an entertainment in which a variety of performers (e g acrobats and clowns) and performing animals are involved in a series of unrelated acts **b** an activity suggestive of a circus (e g in being a busy scene of noisy or frivolous action) **3** Br a road junction in a town partly surrounded by a circle of buildings – usu in proper names

cistern /'sɪstən/ n an artificial reservoir for storing liquids, esp water

citizen /'sɪtɪzən/ n **1** an inhabitant of a city or town; esp a freeman **2** a (native or naturalized) member of a state – ~ **ship** n

city /'sɪtɪ/ n **1a** a large town **b** an incorporated British town that has a cathedral or has had civic status conferred on it **c** a usu large chartered municipality in the USA **2** a city-state **3a** the financial and commercial area of London **b** cap, sing or pl in constr the influential financial interests of the British economy

civil /'sɪvəl/ *adj* **1** of citizens **2** adequately courteous and polite; not rude **3** relating to private rights as distinct from criminal proceedings **4** of or involving the general public as distinguished from special (e g military or religious) affairs

civilian /sɪ'vɪlɪən/ *n* one who is not in the army, navy, air force, or other uniformed public body

civilization *n* **1** a relatively high level of development of culture and technology **2** the culture characteristic of a time or place

civilize, -ise *v* **1** to cause cultural development, esp along Western or modern lines **2** to educate, refine – ~d *adj*

civil service *n sing or pl in constr* the administrative service of a government or international agency, exclusive of the armed forces

¹claim /kleɪm/ *v* **1a** to ask for, esp as a right **b** to require, demand **c** to take; account for **2** to take as the rightful owner **3** to assert in the face of possible contradiction; maintain

²claim *n* **1** a demand for sthg (believed to be) due **2a** a right or title to sthg **b** an assertion open to challenge **3** sthg claimed; *esp* a tract of land staked out

clang /klæŋ/ *v* **1** to make a loud metallic ringing sound **2** *esp of a crane or goose* to utter a harsh cry **3** to cause to clang – **clang** *n*

¹clap /klæp/ *v* **1** to strike (e g 2 flat hard surfaces) together so as to produce a loud sharp noise **2a** to strike (the hands) together repeatedly, usu in applause **b** to applaud **3** to strike with the flat of the hand in a friendly way **4** to place, put, or set, esp energetically – infml

²clap *n* **1** a loud sharp noise, specif of thunder **2** a friendly slap **3** the sound of clapping hands; *esp* applause

³clap *n* venereal disease; *esp* gonorrhoea – slang

¹clash /klæʃ/ *v* **1** to make a clash **2a** to come into conflict **b** to form a displeasing combination; not match

²clash *n* **1** a noisy usu metallic sound of collision **2a** a hostile encounter **b** a sharp conflict

¹clasp /klɑːsp/ *n* **1** a device for holding objects or parts of sthg together **2** a holding or enveloping (as if) with the hands or arms

²clasp *v* **1** to fasten (as if) with a clasp **2** to enclose and hold with the arms; *specif* to embrace **3** to seize (as if) with the hand; grasp

¹class /klɑːs/ *n* **1a** *sing or pl in constr* a group sharing the same economic or social status in a society consisting of several groups with differing statuses – often pl with sing. meaning **b** the system of differentiating society by classes **c** high quality; elegance **2** *sing or pl in constr* a body of students meeting regularly to study the same subject **3** a group, set, or kind sharing common attributes **4a** a division or rating based on grade or quality **b** *Br* a level of

university honours degree awarded to a student according to merit

²class *v* to classify

¹classic /'klæsɪk/ *adj* **1a** of recognized value or merit; serving as a standard of excellence **b** both traditional and enduring **2** classical **3a** authoritative, definitive **b** being an example that shows clearly the characteristics of some group of things or occurrences

²classic *n* **1a** a literary work of ancient Greece or Rome **b** *pl* Greek and Latin literature, history, and philosophy considered as an academic subject **2a** (the author of) a work of lasting excellence **b** an authoritative source **3** a classic example; archetype **4** an important long-established sporting event; *specif, Br* any of 5 flat races for horses (e g the Epsom Derby)

classify /'klæsɪfaɪ/ *v* **1** to arrange in classes **2** to assign to a category

¹clatter /'klætə/ *v* **1** to make a clatter **2** to move or go with a clatter **3** to cause to clatter

²clatter *n* **1** a rattling sound (e g of hard bodies striking together) **2** a commotion

¹claw /klɔː/ *n* **1** (a part resembling or limb having) a sharp usu slender curved nail on an animal's toe **2** any of the pincerlike organs on the end of some limbs of a lobster, scorpion, or similar arthropod **3** sthg (e g the forked end of a claw hammer) resembling a claw

²claw *v* to rake, seize, dig, pull, or make (as if) with claws

clay /kleɪ/ *n* **1a** (soil composed chiefly of) an earthy material that is soft when moist but hard when fired and is used for making brick, tile, and pottery **b** thick and clinging earth or mud **2a** a substance that resembles clay and is used for modelling **b** the human body as distinguished from the spirit – ~ey *adj*

¹clean /kliːn/ *adj* **1** (relatively) free from dirt or pollution **2** unadulterated, pure **3a** free from illegal, immoral, or disreputable activities or characteristics **b** observing the rules; fair **4** thorough, complete **5** relatively free from error or blemish; clear; *specif* legible **6a** characterized by clarity, precision, or deftness **b** not jagged; smooth – ~ness *n* – ~ly *adv*

²clean *adv* **1a** so as to leave clean **b** in a clean manner **2** all the way; completely

³clean *v* **1** to make clean – often + *up* **2a** to strip, empty **b** to deprive of money or possessions – often + *out*; infml **3** to undergo cleaning

⁴clean *n* an act of cleaning away dirt

clean up *v* to make a large esp sweeping gain (e g in business or gambling)

¹clear /klɪə/ *adj* **1a** bright, luminous **b** free from cloud, mist, haze, or dust **c** untroubled, serene **2** clean, pure: *eg* **a** free from blemishes **b** easily seen through; transparent **3a** easily heard **b** easily visible; plain **c** free from obscurity or ambiguity; easily understood **4a** capable of sharp discernment;

keen **b** free from doubt; sure **5** free from guilt **6a** net **b** unqualified, absolute **c** free from obstruction or entanglement **d** full   – ~**ness** *n* – ~**ly** *adv*

²**clear** *adv* **1** clearly **2** *chiefly NAm* all the way

³**clear** *v* **1a** to make transparent or translucent **b** to free from unwanted material – often + *out* **2a** to free from accusation or blame; vindicate **b** to certify as trustworthy **3a** to rid (the throat) of phlegm; *also* to make a rasping noise in (the throat) **b** to erase accumulated totals or stored data from (e g a calculator or computer memory) **4** to authorize or cause to be authorized **5a** to free from financial obligation **b(1)** to settle, discharge **(2)** to deal with until finished or settled **c** to gain without deduction **d** to put or pass through a clearinghouse **6a** to get rid of; remove – often + *off*, *up*, or *away* **b** to kick or pass (the ball) away from the goal as a defensive measure in soccer **7** to go over without touching **8a** to become clear – often + *up* **b** to go away; vanish – sometimes + *off*, *out*, or *away*

clear up *v* **1** to tidy up **2** to explain

clergyman /ˈklɜːdʒɪmən/ *n* an ordained minister

¹**clerk** /klɑːk/ *n* sby whose occupation is keeping records or accounts or doing general office work

²**clerk** *v* to act or work as a clerk

clever /ˈklevə²/ *adj* skilful or adroit *with* the hands or body; nimble **b** mentally quick and resourceful; intelligent **2** marked by wit or ingenuity; *also* thus marked but lacking depth or soundness – ~**ly** *adv* – ~**ness** *n*

client /ˈklaɪənt/ *n* **1a** sby who engages or receives the advice or services of a professional person or organization **b** a customer

cliff /klɪf/ *n* a very steep high face of rock, earth, ice, etc

climate /ˈklaɪmɪt/ *n* **1** (a region of the earth having a specified) average course or condition of the weather over a period of years as shown by temperature, wind, rain, etc **2** the prevailing state of affairs or feelings of a group or period; a milieu – -**atic** *adj*

¹**climax** /ˈklaɪmæks/ *n* **a** the highest point; a culmination **b** the point of highest dramatic tension or a major turning point in some action (e g of a play) **c** an orgasm

²**climax** *v* to come to a climax

climb /klaɪm/ *v* **1a** to go gradually upwards; rise **b** to slope upwards **2a** to go *up*, *down*, etc on a more or less vertical surface using the hands to grasp or give support **b** *of a plant* to ascend in growth (e g by twining) **c** to get *into* or *out of* clothing, usu with some haste or effort **4** to go upwards on or along, to the top of, or over **5** to draw or pull oneself up, over, or to the top of, by using hands and feet **6** to grow up or over   – ~**er** *n*

cling /klɪŋ/ *v* **clung 1a** to stick as if glued firmly **b** to hold (on) tightly or tenaciously **2a** to have a strong emotional attachment or dependence **b** *esp of a smell* to linger

clinic /ˈklɪnɪk/ *n* **1** a meeting held by an expert or person in authority, to which people bring problems for discussion and resolution **2a** a facility (e g of a hospital) for the diagnosis and treatment of outpatients **b** a usu private hospital

¹**clip** /klɪp/ *v* to clasp or fasten with a clip

²**clip** *n* **1** any of various devices that grip, clasp, or hold **2** (a device to hold cartridges for charging) a magazine from which ammunition is fed into the chamber of a firearm **3** a piece of jewellery held in position by a spring clip

³**clip** *v* **1a** to cut (off) (as if) with shears **b** to excise **2** to abbreviate in speech or writing **3** to hit with a glancing blow; *also* to hit smartly – infml

⁴**clip** *n* **1a** the product of (a single) shearing (e g of sheep) **b** a section of filmed material **2a** an act of clipping **b** the manner in which sthg is clipped **3** a sharp blow **4** a rapid rate of motion *USE (3&4)* infml

clipping /ˈklɪpɪŋ/ *n* a (newspaper) cutting

¹**cloak** /kləʊk/ *n* **1** a sleeveless outer garment that usu fastens at the neck and hangs loosely from the shoulders **2** sthg that conceals; a pretence, disguise

²**cloak** *v* to cover or hide (as if) with a cloak

¹**clock** /klɒk/ *n* **1** a device other than a watch for indicating or measuring time **2** a recording or metering device with a dial and indicator attached to a mechanism **3** *Br* a face – slang

²**clock** *v* **1a** to register on a mechanical recording device **b** *Br* to attain a time, speed, etc, of – often + *up*; infml **2** to hit – infml

³**clock** *n* an ornamental pattern on the outside ankle or side of a stocking or sock

clockwork /ˈklɒk-wɜːk/ *n* machinery that operates in a manner similar to that of a mechanical clock; *specif* machinery powered by a coiled spring

¹**clog** /klɒg/ *n* a shoe, sandal, or overshoe with a thick typically wooden sole

²**clog** *v* **a** to obstruct so as to hinder motion in or through **b** to block or become blocked *up*

¹**close** /kləʊz/ *v* **1a** to move so as to bar passage **b** to deny access to **c** to suspend or stop the operations of; *also* to discontinue or dispose of (a business) permanently – often + *down* **2a** to bring to an end **b** to conclude discussion or negotiation about; *also* to bring to agreement or settlement **3** to bring or bind together the parts or edges of **4a** to contract, swing, or slide so as to leave no opening **b** to cease operation; *specif, Br* to stop broadcasting – usu + *down* **5** to draw near, esp in order to fight – usu + *with* **6** to come to an end

²**close** /kləʊz/ *n* a conclusion or end in time or existence

³**close** /kləʊs/ n **1** a road closed at one end **2** Br the precinct of a cathedral

⁴**close** /kləʊs/ adj **1** having no openings; closed **2** confined, cramped **3** restricted, closed **4** secretive, reticent **5** strict, rigorous **6** hot and stuffy **7** having little space between items or units; compact, dense **8** very short or near to the surface **9** near; esp adjacent **10** intimate, familiar **11a** searching, minute **b** faithful to an original **12** evenly contested or having a (nearly) even score – ~**ly** adv – ~**ness** n

⁵**close** /kləʊs/ adv in or into a close position or manner; near

cloth /klɒθ/ n **1** a pliable material made usu by weaving, felting, or knitting natural or synthetic fibres and filaments **2** a piece of cloth adapted for a particular purpose **3** the distinctive dress (of) a profession or calling distinguished by its dress; specif the clergy

clothes /kləʊðz, kləʊz/ n pl **1** articles of material (e g cloth) worn to cover the body, for warmth, protection, or decoration **2** bedclothes

clothing /ˈkləʊðɪŋ/ n clothes

¹**cloud** /klaʊd/ n **1a** a visible mass of particles of water or ice at a usu great height in the air **b** a light filmy, puffy, or billowy mass seeming to float in the air **2** any of many masses of opaque matter in interstellar space **3** a great crowd or multitude; a swarm, esp of insects **4** sthg that obscures or blemishes

²**cloud** v **1** to grow cloudy – usu + over or up **2a** of facial features to become troubled, apprehensive, etc **b** to become blurred, dubious, or ominous **3a** to envelop or obscure (as if) with a cloud **b** to make opaque or murky by condensation, smoke, etc **4** to make unclear or confused **5** to taint, sully **6** to cast gloom over

cloudy /ˈklaʊdi/ adj **1** (having a sky) overcast with clouds **2** not clear or transparent – **cloudiness** n

clown /klaʊn/ n **1** a jester in an entertainment (e g a play); specif a grotesquely dressed comedy performer in a circus **2** one who habitually plays the buffoon; a joker – **clown** v

¹**club** /klʌb/ n **1a** a heavy stick thicker at one end than the other and used as a hand weapon **b** a stick or bat used to hit a ball in golf and other games **2a** a playing card marked with 1 or more black figures in the shape of a cloverleaf **b** pl but sing or pl in constr the suit comprising cards identified by this figure **3** sing or pl in constr an association of people for a specified object, usu jointly supported and meeting periodically **b** an often exclusive association of people that has premises available as a congenial place of retreat or temporary residence or for dining at **c** a group of people who agree to make regular payments or purchases in order to secure some advantage **d** a nightclub

²**club** v **1** to beat or strike (as if) with a club **2** to combine to share a common expense or object – usu + together

clue /klu:/ n sthg that guides via intricate procedure to the solution of a problem

clumsy /ˈklʌmzi/ adj **1a** awkward and ungraceful in movement or action **b** lacking tact or subtlety **2** awkwardly or poorly made; unwieldy – **clumsily** adv – **clumsiness** n

clung /klʌŋ/ past of cling

¹**cluster** /ˈklʌstə/ n **1a** a compact group formed by a number of similar things or people; a bunch **2** a group of faint stars or galaxies that appear close together and have common properties (e g distance and motion)

²**cluster** v to grow or assemble in or collect into a cluster

¹**clutch** /klʌtʃ/ v **1** to grasp or hold (as if) with the hand or claws, esp tightly or suddenly **2** to seek to grasp and hold – often + at

²**clutch** n **1** (the claws or a hand in) the act of grasping or seizing firmly **2** (a lever or pedal operating) a coupling used to connect and **3** a paper tape on which a certain type of telegraphic receiving disconnect a driving and a driven part of a mechanism

³**clutch** n a nest of eggs or a brood of chicks; broadly a group, bunch

¹**coach** /kəʊtʃ/ n **1a** a large usu closed four-wheeled carriage **b** a railway carriage **c** a usu single-deck bus used esp for long-distance or charter work **2a** a private tutor **b** sby who instructs or trains a performer, sportsman, etc

²**coach** v **1** to train intensively by instruction, demonstration, and practice **2** to act as coach to

coal /kəʊl/ n **1** a piece of glowing, burning, or burnt carbonized material (e g partly burnt wood) **2a** (small piece or broken up quantity of) black or blackish solid combustible mineral consisting chiefly of carbonized vegetable matter and widely used as a natural fuel

coarse /kɔ:s/ adj **1** of ordinary or inferior quality or value; common **2a(1)** composed of relatively large particles **(2)** rough in texture or tone **b** adjusted or designed for heavy, fast, or less delicate work **c** not precise or detailed with respect to adjustment or discrimination **3** crude or unrefined in taste, manners, or language – ~**ly** adv – ~**ness** n

¹**coast** /kəʊst/ n the land near a shore; the seashore – ~**al** adj

²**coast** v **1** to sail along the shore (of) **2a** to slide, glide, etc downhill by the force of gravity **b** to move along (as if) without further application of driving power **c** to proceed easily without special application of effort or concern

¹**coat** /kəʊt/ n **1** an outer garment that has sleeves and usu opens the full length of the centre front **2** the external covering of an animal **3** a protective layer; a coating

²**coat** v to cover or spread with a protective or enclosing layer

coat of arms n a set of distinctive

heraldic shapes or representations, usu depicted on a shield, that is the central part of a heraldic achievement

cobbler /'kɒblə²/ n 1 a mender or maker of leather goods, esp shoes 2 pl, Br nonsense, rubbish – often used interjectionally; infml

cobweb /'kɒbweb/ n 1 (a) spider's web 2 a single thread spun by a spider

¹**cock** /kɒk/ n 1a the (adult) male of various birds, specif the domestic fowl b the male of fish, crabs, lobsters, and other aquatic animals 2 a device (e g a tap or valve) for regulating the flow of a liquid 3 the hammer of a firearm or its position when cocked ready for firing 4 Br – used as a term of infml address to a man 5 the penis – vulg 6 Br nonsense, rubbish – slang

²**cock** v 1a to draw back and set the hammer of (a firearm) for firing b to draw or bend back in preparation for throwing or hitting 2a to set erect b to turn, tip, or tilt, usu to one side 3 to turn up (e g the brim of a hat)

³**cock** n a small pile (e g of hay)

cockerel /'kɒkərəl/ n a young male domestic fowl

cockney /'kɒkni/ n 1 a native of London and now esp the E End of London 2 the dialect of (the E End of) London

cockpit /'kɒk,pɪt/ n 1 a pit or enclosure for cockfights 2a a recess below deck level from which a small vessel (e g a yacht) is steered b a space in the fuselage of an aeroplane for the pilot (and crew) c the driver's compartment in a racing or sports car

cocktail /'kɒkteɪl/ n 1a a drink of mixed spirits or of spirits mixed with flavourings b sthg resembling or suggesting such a drink; esp a mixture of diverse elements 2a an appetizer of tomato juice, shellfish, etc b a dish of finely chopped mixed fruits

cocky /'kɒki/ adj marked by overconfidence or presumptuousness – infml

cocoa /'kəʊkəʊ/ n 1 the cacao tree 2a powdered ground roasted cacao seeds from which some fat has been removed b a beverage made by mixing cocoa with usu hot milk

coconut /'kəʊkənʌt/ also **cocoanut** n the large oval fruit of the coconut palm whose outer fibrous husk yields coir and whose nut contains thick edible meat and a thick sweet milk

¹**cod** /kɒd/ n, pl **cod** (the flesh of) a soft-finned N Atlantic food fish or related Pacific fish

²**cod** n, Br nonsense – slang

¹**code** /kəʊd/ n 1 a systematic body of laws, esp with statutory force 2 a system of principles or maxims 3a a system of signals for communication b a system of symbols used to represent assigned and often secret meanings

²**code** v to put into the form or symbols of a code

coffee /'kɒfi/ n 1 a beverage made from the roasted seeds of a coffee tree; also these seeds either green or roasted

2 a cup of coffee 3 a time when coffee is drunk

coffin /'kɒfᶦn/ n 1 a box or chest for the burial of a corpse 2 the horny body forming the hoof of a horse's foot

coherent /kəʊ'hɪərənt/ adj 1 having the quality of cohering 2a logically consistent b showing a unity of thought or purpose – ~ly adv

¹**coil** /kɔɪl/ v 1 to wind into rings or spirals 2 to move in a circular, spiral, or winding course 3 to form or lie in a coil

²**coil** n 1a (a length of rope, cable, etc gathered into) a series of loops; a spiral b a single loop of a coil 2 a number of turns of wire, esp in spiral form, usu for electromagnetic effect or for providing electrical resistance 3 a series of connected pipes in rows, layers, or windings

¹**coin** /kɔɪn/ n 1 a usu thin round piece of metal issued as money 2 metal money

²**coin** v 1a to make (a coin), esp by stamping; mint b to convert (metal) into coins 2 to create, invent 3 to make or earn (money) rapidly and in large quantity – often in coin it – ~er n

coincide /,kəʊɪn'saɪd/ v 1 to occupy the same place in space or time 2 to correspond in nature, character, function, or position 3 to be in accord or agreement; concur – **dent** adj

coincidence /kəʊ'ɪnsᶦdəns/ n 1 the act or condition of coinciding; a correspondence 2 (an example of) the chance occurrence at the same time or place of 2 or more events that appear to be related or similar – **tal** adj – **tally** adv

¹**cold** /kəʊld/ adj 1 having a low temperature, often below some normal temperature or below that compatible with human comfort 2a marked by lack of warm feeling; unemotional; also unfriendly b marked by deliberation or calculation 3a previously cooked but served cold b not (sufficiently) hot or heated c made cold 4a depressing, cheerless b producing a sensation of cold; chilling c cool 5a dead b unconscious 6a retaining only faint scents, traces, or clues b far from a goal, object, or solution sought 7 presented or regarded in a straightforward way; impersonal 8 unprepared 9 intense yet without the usual outward effects – ~ly adv – ~ness n

²**cold** n 1a a condition of low temperature b cold weather 2 bodily sensation produced by relative lack of heat; chill 3 a bodily disorder popularly associated with chilling; specif an inflamation of the mucous membranes of the nose, throat, etc 4 a state of neglect or deprivation – esp in come/bring in out of the cold

³**cold** adv with utter finality; absolutely

¹**collapse** /kə'læps/ v 1 to break down completely; disintegrate 2 to fall in or give way abruptly and completely (e g through compression) 3 to lose force, value, or effect suddenly 4 to break

down in energy, stamina, or self-control through exhaustion or disease; *esp* to fall helpless or unconscious **5** to fold down into a more compact shape **6** to cause to collapse

²collapse *n* **1a** an (extreme) breakdown in energy, strength, or self-control **b** an airless state of (part of) a lung **2** the act or an instance of collapsing

¹collar /'kɒlə' *n* **1a** a band that serves to finish or decorate the neckline of a garment; *esp* one that is turned over **b** a band fitted about the neck of an animal **c** a part of the harness of draught animals that fits over the shoulders and takes the strain when a load is drawn **d** a protective or supportive device worn round the neck **2** any of various animal structures or markings similar to a collar in appearance or form **3** a cut of bacon from the neck of a pig

²collar *v* **1** to seize by the collar or neck; *broadly* to apprehend **2** to buttonhole *USE* infml

colleague /'kɒliːg/ *n* a fellow worker, esp in a profession

¹collect /'kɒlɪkt/ *n* a short prayer; *specif, often cap* one preceding the Epistle read at Communion

²collect /kə'lekt/ *v* **1a** to bring together into 1 body or place; *specif* to assemble a collection of **b** to gather or exact from a number of sources **2** to accumulate, gather **3** to claim as due and receive possession or payment of **5** to provide transport or escort for **6** *chiefly Br* to gain, obtain **7** to come together in a band, group, or mass; gather **8a** to assemble a collection **b** to receive payment

collection /kə'lekʃən/ *n* sthg collected; *esp* an accumulation of objects gathered for study, comparison, or exhibition

college /'kɒlɪdʒ/ *n* **1** a building used for an educational or religious purpose **2a** a self-governing endowed constituent body of a university offering instruction and often living quarters but not granting degrees **b** an institution offering vocational or technical instruction **3** an organized body of people engaged in a common pursuit **4** *chiefly Br* a public school or private secondary school; *also* a state school for older pupils *USE* (except 1) sing. or pl in constr

collide /kə'laɪd/ *v* **1** to come together forcibly **2** to come into conflict

collision /kə'lɪʒən/ *n* an act or instance of colliding; a clash

colonel /'kɜːnəl/ *n* an officer of middle rank in the army or American air force

colony /'kɒləni/ *n* **1** a body of settlers living in a new territory but subject to control by the parent state; *also* their territory **2** (the area occupied by) a group of individuals with common interests living close together **3** a group of people segregated from the general public **– nize** *vb*

colossal /kə'lɒsəl/ *adj* of or like a colossus; *esp* of very great size or degree **– ly** *adv*

¹colour /'kʌlə' *n* **1** a hue, esp as opposed to black, white, or grey **2** an identifying badge, pennant, or flag (e g of a ship or regiment) **3** character, nature **4** the use or combination of colours (e g by painters) **5** vitality, interest **6** a pigment **7** tonal quality in music **8** skin pigmentation other than white, characteristic of race **9** *Br* the award made to a regular member of a team

²colour *v* **1a** to give colour to **b** to change the colour of **2** to change as if by dyeing or painting: e g **a** to misrepresent, distort **b** to influence, affect **3** to take on or impart colour; *specif* to blush

colourful /'kʌləfəl/ *adj* **1** having striking colours **2** full of variety or interest

column /'kɒləm/ *n* **1a** a vertical arrangement of items or a vertical section of printing on a page **b** a special and usu regular feature in a newspaper or periodical **2** a pillar that usu consists of a round shaft, a capital, and a base **3** sthg resembling a column in form, position, or function **4** a long narrow formation of soldiers, vehicles, etc in rows

¹comb /kəʊm/ *n* **1a** a toothed instrument used esp for adjusting, cleaning, or confining hair **b** a structure resembling such a comb; *esp* any of several toothed devices used in handling or ordering textile fibres **2** a fleshy crest on the head of a domestic fowl or a related bird **3** a honeycomb

²comb *v* **1** to draw a comb through for the purpose of arranging or cleaning **2** to pass across with a scraping or raking action **3** to search or examine systematically **4** to use with a combing action **5** , *of a wave* to roll over or break into foam

¹combat /'kɒmbæt, kəm'bæt/ *v* **1** to fight with; battle **2** to struggle against; *esp* to strive to reduce or eliminate

²combat /'kɒmbæt/ *n* **1** a fight or contest between individuals or groups **2** a conflict, controversy **3** active fighting in a war

combination /,kɒmbɪ'neɪʃən/ *n* **1a** a result or product of combining **b** a group of people working as a team **2** *pl* any of various 1-piece undergarments for the upper and lower parts of the body and legs **3** a (process of) combining, esp to form a chemical compound

¹combine /kəm'baɪn/ *v* **1a** to bring into such close relationship as to obscure individual characters; merge **b** to (cause to) unite into a chemical compound **2** to cause to mix together **3** to possess in combination **4** to become one **5** to act together

²combine /'kɒmbaɪn/ *n* **1** a combination of people or organizations, esp in industry or commerce, to further their interests **2 combine, combine harvester** a harvesting machine that cuts, threshes, and cleans grain while moving over a field

¹come /kʌm/ *v* **1a** to move towards sthg

nearer, esp towards the speaker; approach **b** to move or journey nearer, esp towards or with the speaker, with a specified purpose **c**(1) to reach a specified position in a progression (2) to arrive, appear, occur **d**(1) to approach, reach, or fulfil a specified condition – often + *to* (2) – used with a following infinitive to express arrival at a condition or chance occurrence **2a** to happen, esp by chance **b**(1) to extend, reach (2) to amount **c** to originate, arise, or be the result of **d** to fall within the specified limits, scope, or jurisdiction **e** to issue *from* **f** to be available or turn out, usu as specified **g** to be or belong in a specified place or relation; *also* take place **3** to become; *esp* to reach a culminating state **4** to experience orgasm – *infml* **5a** to move nearer by traversing **b** to reach some state after traversing **6** to take on the aspect of; play the role of – *infml*

²**come** *interj* – used to express encouragement or to urge reconsideration

comedian /kə'miːdiən/, *fem* **comedienne** *n* **1** an actor who plays comic roles **2** one, esp a professional entertainer, who aims to be amusing

comedown /'kʌmdaʊn/ *n* a striking descent in rank or dignity – *infml*

comedy /'kɒmidi/ *n* **1a** a drama of light and amusing character, typically with a happy ending **b** (a work in) the genre of (dramatic) literature dealing with comic or serious subjects in a light or satirical manner **2** a ludicrous or farcical event or series of events **3** the comic aspect of sthg

come to *v* to recover consciousness

¹**comfort** /'kʌmfət/ *n* **1** (sby or sthg that provides) consolation or encouragement in time of trouble or worry **2** contented well-being

²**comfort** *v* **1** to cheer up **2** to ease the grief or trouble of; console – ~**er** *n*

comfortable /'kʌmftəbəl, 'kʌmfət-/ *adj* **1a** providing or enjoying contentment and security **b** enjoying physical comfort **2a** causing no worry or doubt **b** free from stress or tension – **-bly** *adv*

¹**comic** /'kɒmɪk/ *adj* **1** of or marked by comedy **2** causing laughter or amusement; funny

²**comic** *n* **1** a comedian **2** a magazine consisting mainly of strip-cartoon stories

comma /'kɒmə/ *n* **1** a punctuation mark , used esp as a mark of separation within the sentence **2** a butterfly with a silvery comma-shaped mark on the underside of the hind wing

¹**command** /kə'mɑːnd/ *v* **1** to direct authoritatively; order **2a** to have at one's immediate disposal **b** to be able to ask for and receive **c** to overlook or dominate (as if) from a strategic position **d** to have military command of as senior officer **3** to be commander; be supreme

²**command** *n* **1** an order given **2a** the ability or power to control; the mastery **b** the authority or right to command **c**

facility in use **3** *sing or pl in constr* the unit, personnel, etc under a commander

³**command** *adj* done on command or request

commando /kə'mɑːndəʊ/ *n* (a member of) a usu small military unit for surprise raids

commence /kə'mens/ *v* to start, begin – *fml* – ~**ment** *n*

¹**comment** /'kɒment/ *n* **1** a note explaining or criticizing the meaning of a piece of writing **2a** an observation or remark expressing an opinion or attitude **b** a judgment expressed indirectly

²**comment** *v* to explain or interpret sthg by comment; *broadly* to make a comment

commentary /'kɒməntəri/ *n* **1** a systematic series of explanations or interpretations (e g of a piece of writing) **2** a series of spoken remarks and comments used as a broadcast description of some event

commentate /'kɒmənteɪt/ *v* to give a broadcast commentary – **-tator** *n*

commerce /'kɒmɜːs/ *n* the exchange or buying and selling of commodities, esp on a large scale

¹**commercial** /kə'mɜːʃəl/ *adj* **1a**(1) engaged in work designed for the market (2) (characteristic) of commerce (3) having or being a good financial prospect **b** producing work to a standard determined only by market criteria **2a** viewed with regard to profit **b** designed for a large market **3** supported by advertisers – ~**ize** *v*

²**commercial** *n* an advertisement broadcast on radio or television

commit /kə'mɪt/ *v* **1a** to entrust to; place in a prison or mental institution **c** to transfer, consign **2** to carry out (a crime, sin, etc) **3a** to obligate, bind **b** to assign to some particular course or use

committee /kə'mɪti/ *n sing or pl in constr* a body of people delegated **a** to report on, investigate, etc some matter **b** to organize or administrate a society, event, etc

¹**common** /'kɒmən/ *adj* **1** of the community at large; public **2** belonging to or shared by 2 or more individuals or by all members of a group **3a** occurring or appearing frequently; familiar **b** of the familiar kind **4a** widespread, general **b** characterized by a lack of privilege or special status **5** lacking refinement – ~**ness** *n* – ~**ly** *adv*

²**common** *n* **1** *pl but sing or pl in constr, often cap* **a** the political group or estate made up of commoners **b** the House of Commons **2** a piece of land open to use by all: e g **a** undivided land used esp for pasture **b** a more or less treeless expanse of undeveloped land available for recreation **3a** a religious service suitable for any of various festivals **b** the ordinary of the Mass **4** *Br* common sense – *slang*

common market *n* an economic unit formed to remove trade barriers among its members; *specif, often cap C&M the* European economic community

common sense *n* sound and prudent (but often unsophisticated) judgment

commonwealth /'kɒmənwelθ/ *n* 1 **a** a political unit: e g **a** one founded on law and united by agreement of the people for the common good **b** one in which supreme authority is vested in the people 2 *cap* the English state from 1649 to 1660 3 a state of the USA 4 *cap* a federal union of states – used officially of Australia 5 *often cap* a loose association of autonomous states under a common allegiance; *specif* an association consisting of Britain and states that were formerly British colonies

communicate /kə'mju:nɪˌkeɪt/ *v* 1 to convey knowledge of or information about; make known 2 to receive Communion 3 to transmit information, thought, or feeling so that it is satisfactorily received or understood 4 to give access to each other; connect

communication /kəˌmju:nɪˈkeɪʃən/ *n* 1 a verbal or written message 2 (the use of a common system of symbols, signs, behaviour, etc for the) exchange of information 3 *pl* a system (e g of telephones) for communicating 4 *pl but sing or pl in constr* techniques for the effective transmission of information, ideas, etc

communism /'kɒmjʊnɪzəm/ *n* 1 **a** a theory advocating elimination of private property **b** a system in which goods are held in common and are available to all as needed 2 *cap* **a** a doctrine based on revolutionary Marxian socialism and Marxism-Leninism that is the official ideology of the USSR **b** a totalitarian system of government in which a single party controls state-owned means of production – **-ist** *n* – **-istic** *adj*

community /kə'mju:nɪti/ *n* 1 *sing or pl in constr* **a** a group of people living in a particular area **b** a group of individuals or a body of people or nations with some common characteristic 2 society in general 3**a** joint ownership or participation **b** common character; likeness **c** social ties; fellowship **d** the state or condition of living in a society

commute /kə'mju:t/ *v* 1 to convert (e g a payment) into another form 2 to exchange (a penalty) for another less severe 3 to travel back and forth regularly (e g between home and work) – **-muter** *n*

companion /kɒm'pænɪən/ *n* one who accompanies another; a comrade – **~ship** *n*

company /'kʌmpəni/ *n* 1**a** friendly association with another; fellowship **b** companions, associates **c** *sing or pl in constr* visitors, guests 2 *sing or pl in constr* a group of people or things **a** a unit of soldiers composed usu of a headquarters and 2 or more platoons **b** an organization of musical or dramatic performers **d** the officers and men of a ship 3 *sing or pl in constr* an association

of people for carrying on a commercial or industrial enterprise

comparative /kəm'pærətɪv/ *adj* 1 considered as if in comparison to sthg else as a standard; relative 2 characterized by the systematic comparison of phenomena – **~ly** *adv*

¹**compare** /kəm'peə/ *v* 1 to represent as similar; liken 2 to examine the character or qualities of, esp in order to discover resemblances or differences 3 to bear being compared 4 to be equal or alike – + *with*

²**compare** *n* comparison

comparison /kəm'pærɪsən/ *n* 1**a** the representing of one thing or person as similar to or like another **b** an examination of 2 or more items to establish similarities and dissimilarities 2 identity or similarity of features

compartment /kəm'pɑ:tmənt/ *n* 1 any of the parts into which an enclosed space is divided 2 a separate division or section – **~alize** *v*

¹**compass** /'kʌmpəs/ *v* **a** to encompass **b** to travel entirely round *USE fml*

²**compass** *n* 1**a** a boundary, circumference **b** range, scope 2**a** an instrument that indicates directions, typically by means of a freely-turning needle pointing to magnetic north **b** an instrument for drawing circles or transferring measurements that consists of 2 legs joined at 1 end by a pivot – usu pl with sing. meaning

compel /kəm'pel/ *v* 1 to drive or force irresistibly *to* do sthg 2 to cause to occur by overwhelming pressure – **compelling** *adj* – **compellingly** *adv*

compensate /'kɒmpənseɪt/ *v* 1 to have an equal and opposite effect to; counterbalance 2 to make amends to, esp by appropriate payment 3 to supply an equivalent *for* – **-sation** *n* – **-satory** *adj*

compete /kəm'pi:t/ *v* to strive consciously or unconsciously for an objective; *also* to be in a state of rivalry

competition /ˌkɒmpɪˈtɪʃən/ *n* 1 the act or process of competing; rivalry 2 a usu organized test of comparative skill, performance, etc; *also, sing or pl in constr* the others competing with one – **-itive** *adj* – **-itively** *adv* – **-itiveness** *n*

competitor /kəm'petɪtə/ *n* sby who or sthg that competes; a rival

complain /kəm'pleɪn/ *v* 1 to express feelings of discontent 2 to make a formal accusation or charge – **~ing** *adj* – **~ingly** *adv*

complaint /kəm'pleɪnt/ *n* 1 an expression of discontent 2**a** sthg that is the cause or subject of protest or outcry **b** a bodily ailment or disease

¹**complete** /kəm'pli:t/ *adj* 1 having all necessary parts, elements, or steps 2 whole or concluded 3 thoroughly competent; highly proficient 4**a** fully carried out; thorough **b** total, absolute – **~ness** *n*

²**complete** *v* 1 to bring to an end; *esp* to bring to a perfected state 2**a** to make whole or perfect **b** to mark the end of

c to execute, fulfil – ~**ly** *adv*
– **-tion** *n*

complexion /kəm'plekʃən/ *n* **1** the appearance of the skin, esp of the face **2** overall aspect or character

complicated /'kɒmplɪˌkeɪtɪd/ *adj* **1** consisting of parts intricately combined **2** difficult to analyse, understand, or explain – ~**ly** *adv* – ~**ness** *n*

compose /kəm'pəʊz/ *v* **1a** to form by putting together **b** to form the substance of; make up – chiefly passive **2a** to create by mental or artistic labour; produce **b** to formulate and write (a piece of music) **3** to free from agitation; calm, settle

composition /ˌkɒmpə'zɪʃən/ *n* **1** the act or process of composing; *specif* arrangement into proper proportion or relation and esp into artistic form **2** the factors or parts which go to make sthg; *also* the way in which the factors or parts make up the whole **3** a product of mixing or combining various elements or ingredients **4** an intellectual creation: e g **a** a piece of writing; esp a school essay **b** a written piece of music, esp of considerable size and complexity

¹**compound** /kəm'paʊnd/ *v* **1** to put together (parts) so as to form a whole; combine **2** to form by combining parts **3** to add to; augment **4** to become joined in a compound

²**compound** /'kɒmpaʊnd/ *adj* composed of or resulting from union of (many similar) separate elements, ingredients, or parts **2** involving or used in a combination

³**compound** /'kɒmpaʊnd/ *n* **1** a word consisting of components that are words, combining forms, or affixes (e g *houseboat, anthropology*) **2** sthg formed by a union of elements or parts; *specif* a distinct substance formed by combination of chemical elements in fixed proportion by weight

⁴**compound** *n* a fenced or walled-in area containing a group of buildings, esp residences

comprehend /ˌkɒmprɪ'hend/ *v* **1** to grasp the nature, significance, or meaning of; understand **2** to include – fml
– **hensible** *adj* – **hensibility** *n*

¹**comprehensive** /ˌkɒmprɪ'hensɪv/ *adj* **1** covering completely or broadly; inclusive **2** having or exhibiting wide mental grasp **3** *chiefly Br* of or being the principle of educating in 1 unified school nearly all children above the age of 11 from a given area regardless of ability – ~**ly**

²**comprehensive** *n, Br* a comprehensive school

¹**compromise** /'kɒmprəmaɪz/ *n* **1a** the settling of differences through arbitration or through consent reached by mutual concessions **b** a settlement reached by compromise **c** sthg blending qualities of 2 different things **2** a concession to sthg disreputable or prejudicial

²**compromise** *v* **1** to adjust or settle by mutual concessions **2** to expose to

discredit or scandal **3** to come to agreement by mutual concession

compulsory /kəm'pʌlsəri/ *adj* **1** mandatory, enforced **2** involving compulsion or obligation; coercive – **-rily**

computer /kəm'pju:tə'/ *n* a programmable electronic device that can store, retrieve, and process data

comrade /'kɒmrɪd, -reɪd/ *n* **1a** an intimate friend or associate; a companion **b** a fellow soldier **2** a communist
– ~**ship** *n*

conceal /kən'si:l/ *v* **1** to prevent disclosure or recognition of **2** to place out of sight – ~**ment** *n*

concede /kən'si:d/ *v* **1** to grant as a right or privilege **2a** to accept as true, valid, or accurate **b** to acknowledge grudgingly or hesitantly **3** to allow involuntarily – chiefly journ **4** to make concession; yield

conceit /kən'si:t/ *n* **1** excessively high opinion of oneself **2a** a fanciful idea **b** an elaborate, unusual, and cleverly expressed figure of speech – ~**ed** *adj*

conceive /kən'si:v/ *v* **1** to become pregnant (with) **2a** to cause to originate in one's mind **b** to form a conception of; evolve mentally; visualize **3** to be of the opinion – fml

¹**concentrate** /'kɒnsəntreɪt/ *v* **1a** to bring or direct towards a common centre or objective; focus **b** to gather into 1 body, mass, or force **2a** to make less dilute **b** to express or exhibit in condensed form **3** to draw towards or meet in a common centre **4** to gather, collect **5** to concentrate one's powers, efforts, or attention

²**concentrate** *n* sthg concentrated; *esp* a feed for animals rich in digestible nutrients

concentration /ˌkɒnsən'treɪʃən/ *n* **1** direction of attention to a single object **2** a concentrated mass or thing **3** the relative content of a (chemical) component; strength

¹**concern** /kən'sɜːn/ *v* **1** to relate to; be about **2** to have an influence on; involve; *also* to be the business or affair of **3** to be a care, trouble, or distress to **4** to engage, occupy

²**concern** *n* **1** sthg that relates or belongs to one **2** matter for consideration **3** marked interest or regard, usu arising through a personal tie or relationship **4** a business or manufacturing organization or establishment – ~**ed** *adj*
– ~**edly** *adv*

concerning /kən'sɜːnɪŋ/ *prep* relating to; with reference to

concert /'kɒnsət/ *n* **1** an instance of working together; an agreement – esp in *in concert (with)* **2** a public performance of music or dancing; *esp* a performance, usu by a group of musicians, that is made up of several individual compositions

conclude /kən'klu:d/ *v* **1** to bring to an end, esp in a particular way or with a particular action **2a** to arrive at as a logically necessary inference **b** to decide **c** to come to an agreement on; effect **3** to end – **-clusion** *n*

¹concrete /'kɒŋkri:t/ *adj* **a** characterized by or belonging to immediate
experience of actual things or events **b**
specific, particular **c** real, tangible
– ~**ly** *adv*

²concrete *n* a hard strong building
material made by mixing a cementing
material (e g portland cement) and a
mineral aggregate (e g sand and gravel)
with sufficient water to cause the
cement to set and bind the entire
mass

³concrete *v* **1** to form into a solid mass;
solidify **2** to cover with, form of, or set
in concrete

condemn /kən'dem/ *v* **1** to declare to
be utterly reprehensible, wrong, or evil,
usu after considering evidence **2a** to
prescribe punishment for; *specif* to sentence to death **b** to sentence, doom **3** to
declare unfit for use or consumption
– ~**ation** *n*

¹condition /kən'dɪʃən/ *n* **1** sthg essential to the appearance or occurrence of
sthg else; a prerequisite **2** a favourable
or unfavourable state of sthg **3a** a state
of being **b** a usu defective state of health
or appearance **c** a state of physical
fitness or readiness for use **d** *pl* attendant circumstances

²condition *v* **1** to put into a proper or
desired state for work or use **2** to give
a certain condition to **3a** to adapt to a
surrounding culture **b** to modify so that
an act or response previously associated
with one stimulus becomes associated
with another

¹conduct /kən'dʌkt/ *n* **1** the act, manner, or process of carrying on; management **2** a mode or standard of personal
behaviour, esp as based on moral principles

²conduct /kɒndʌkt, -dəkt/ *v* **1** to bring
(as if) by leading; guide **2** to carry on or
out, usu from a position of command or
control **3** to convey in a channel, pipe,
etc **4** to behave in a specified manner **5**
to direct the performance or execution
of (e g a musical work or group of
musicians) **6** to act as leader or director, esp of an orchestra **7** to have the
property of transmitting (heat, sound,
electricity, etc) – ~**ive** *adj*

conductor /kən'dʌktə/ *n* **1** a collector
of fares on a public conveyance, esp a
bus **2** one who directs the performance
of musicians **3** a substance or body
capable of transmitting electricity, heat,
sound, etc

cone /kəʊn/ *n* **1** a mass of overlapping
woody scales that, esp in trees of the
pine family, are arranged on an axis and
bear seeds between them; *broadly* any of
several similar flower or fruit clusters
2a a solid generated by rotating a
right-angled triangle about a side other
than its hypotenuse **b** a solid figure
tapering evenly to a point from a circular base **3a** any of the relatively short
light receptors in the retina of vertebrates that are sensitive to bright light
and function in colour vision **b** a crisp
cone-shaped wafer for holding a portion
of ice cream

conference /'kɒnfərəns/ *n* **1a** a usu
formal interchange of views; a consultation **b** a meeting of 2 or more people for
the discussion of matters of common
concern **2** a representative assembly or
administrative organization of a
denomination, organization, association, etc

confess /kən'fes/ *v* **1** to make known
(e g sthg wrong or damaging to oneself);
admit **2** to declare faith in or adherence
to **3a** to acknowledge (one's sins or the
state of one's conscience) to God or a
priest **b** to hear a confession

confession /kən'feʃən/ *n* **1** a disclosure of one's sins **2** a statement of what
is confessed: e g **a** a written acknowledgment of guilt by a party accused of
an offence **b** a formal statement of religious beliefs **3** an organized religious
body having a common creed

confidence /'kɒnfɪdəns/ *n* **1** faith,
trust **2** a feeling or consciousness of
one's powers being sufficient, or of reliance on one's circumstances **3** the quality or state of being certain **4a** a relationship of trust or intimacy **b** reliance
on another's discretion **5** sthg said in
confidence; a secret

confident /'kɒnfɪdənt/ *adj* **1** characterized by assurance; *esp* self-reliant **2**
full of conviction; certain – ~**ly** *adv*

confidential /,kɒnfɪ'denʃəl/ *adj* **1** private, secret **2** marked by intimacy or
willingness to confide – ~**ity** *n* – ~**ly**
adv

¹confine /kən'faɪn/ *v* **1** to keep within
limits; restrict **2a** to shut up; imprison
b to keep indoors or in bed, esp just
before childbirth – usu passive

²confine /'kɒnfaɪn/ *n* **1** bounds, borders
2 outlying parts; limits *USE* usu pl
with sing. meaning

confirm /kən'fɜːm/ *v* **1** to make firm or
firmer; strengthen **2** to give approval
to; ratify **3** to administer the rite of
confirmation to **4** to make certain of;
remove doubt about by authoritative act
or indisputable fact – **ation** *n*

confiscate /'kɒnfɪskeɪt/ *v* to seize (as
if) by authority – **-cation** *n* – **-catory**
adj

¹conflict /'kɒnflɪkt/ *n* **1** a sharp disagreement or clash (e g between divergent ideas, interests, or people) **2** (distress caused by) mental struggle
resulting from incompatible impulses **3**
a hostile encounter (e g a fight, battle, or
war)

²conflict /kən'flɪkt/ *v* to be in opposition
(to another or each other); disagree

confuse /kən'fjuːz/ *v* **1a** to make
embarrassed; abash **b** to disturb or
muddle in mind or purpose **2a** to make
indistinct; blur **b** to mix indiscriminately; jumble **c** to fail to differentiate
from another often similar or related
thing – ~**d** *adj* – ~**dly** *adv* – **-fusing**
adj – **-fusingly** *adv*

confusion /kən'fjuːʒən/ *n* **1** an
instance of confusing or being confused
2 (a) disorder, muddle

congratulate /kən'grætʃʊleɪt/ *v* to
express pleasure to (a person) on

con

account of success or good fortune – **-lation** n – **-latory** adj

conjure /'kʌndʒə'/ v **1a** to summon by invocation or by uttering a spell, charm, etc **b(1)** to affect or effect (as if) by magical powers **(2)** to imagine, contrive – often + **up 2** to make use of magical powers **3** to use a conjurer's tricks – **-er, -or** n

connect /kə'nekt/ v **1** to join or fasten together, usu by some intervening thing **2** to place or establish in relationship **3** to be or become joined **4** to make a successful hit or shot – **~ed** adj – **~ion** n

conquer /'kɒŋkə'/ v **1** to acquire or overcome by force of arms; subjugate **2** to gain mastery over **3** to be victorious – **~or** n

conquest /'kɒŋkwest/ n **1** conquering **2a** sthg conquered; esp territory appropriated in war – often pl **b** a person who has been won over, esp by love or sexual attraction

conscience /'kɒnʃəns/ n **1** the consciousness of the moral quality of one's own conduct or intentions, together with a feeling of obligation to refrain from doing wrong **2** conformity to the dictates of conscience; conscientiousness

¹conscious /'kɒnʃəs/ adj **1** perceiving with a degree of controlled thought or observation **2** personally felt **3** capable of or marked by thought, will, intention, or perception **4** having mental faculties undulled by sleep, faintness, or stupor; awake **5** done or acting with critical awareness **6** marked by awareness of or concern for sthg specified – **~ness** n

²conscious n consciousness – used in Freudian psychology

¹consent /kən'sent/ v to give assent or approval; agree to

²consent n compliance in or approval of what is done or proposed by another; acquiescence

consequence /'kɒnsɨkwəns/ n **1** sthg produced by a cause or necessarily following from a set of conditions **2** a conclusion arrived at by reasoning **3a** importance in terms of power to produce an effect; moment **b** social importance

consequently /'kɒnsɨkwəntli/ adv as a result; in view of the foregoing

conservation /,kɒnsə'veɪʃən/ n careful preservation and protection, esp of a natural resource, the quality of the environment, or plant or animal species, to prevent exploitation, destruction, etc

conservatism /kən'sɜːvətɪzəm/ n **1** (a political philosophy based on) the disposition to preserve what is established **2** cap the principles and policies of a Conservative party **3** the tendency to prefer an existing situation to change

consider /kən'sɪdə'/ v **1** to think about with care or caution **2** to gaze on steadily or reflectively **3** to think of as specified; regard as being **4** to have as an opinion **5** to reflect, deliberate

considerable /kən'sɪdərəbəl/ adj **1** worth consideration; significant **2** large in extent or degree – **-bly** adv

consideration /kən,sɪdə'reɪʃən/ n **1** continuous and careful thought **2a** sthg considered as a basis for thought or action; a reason **b** a taking into account **3** thoughtful and sympathetic or solicitous regard

consist /kən'sɪst/ v **1** to lie, reside in **2** to be made up or composed of

consistent /kən'sɪstənt/ adj marked by harmonious regularity or steady continuity; free from irregularity, variation, or contradiction – **~ly** adv

conspiracy /kən'spɪrəsi/ n **1** (the offence of) conspiring together **2a** an agreement among conspirators **b** sing or pl in constr a group of conspirators

¹constant /'kɒnstənt/ adj **1** marked by steadfast resolution or faithfulness; exhibiting constancy of mind or attachment **2** invariable, uniform **3** continually occurring or recurring; regular – **~ly** adv

²constant n sthg invariable or unchanging: e g **a** a number that has a fixed value in a given situation or universally or that is characteristic of some substance or instrument **b** a number that is assumed not to change value in a given mathematical discussion **c** a term in logic with a fixed designation

constitute /'kɒnstɨtjuːt/ v **1** to appoint to an often specified office, function, or dignity **2** to establish; set up: e g **a** to establish formally **b** to give legal form to **3** to form, make, be

constitution /,kɒnstɨ'tjuːʃən/ n **1** the act of establishing, making, or setting up **2a** the physical and mental structure of an individual **b** the factors or parts which go to make sthg; composition; also the way in which these parts or factors make up the whole **3** the way in which a state or society is organized **4** (a document embodying) the fundamental principles and laws of a nation, state, or social group

¹construct /kən'strʌkt/ v **1** to make or form by combining parts; build **2** to set in logical order – **~ion** n – **~or** n – **~ional** adj

²construct /'kɒnstrʌkt/ n sthg constructed, esp mentally

constructive /kən'strʌktɪv/ adj **1** (judicially) implied rather than explicit **2** of or involved in construction **3** suggesting improvement or development – **~ly** adv – **~ness** n

consult /kən'sʌlt/ v **1** to ask the advice or opinion of **2** to refer to **3** to deliberate together; confer **4** to serve as a consultant – **~ation** n – **~ative** adj

¹contact /'kɒntækt/ n **1a** (an instance of) touching **b** (a part made to form) the junction of 2 electrical conductors through which a current passes **2a** association, relationship **b** connection, communication **c** the act of establishing communication with sby or observing or receiving a significant signal from a person or object **3** one serving as a carrier or source

²**contact** v 1 to bring into contact 2a to enter or be in contact with; join b to get in communication with

³**contact** adj maintaining, involving, or activated or caused by contact

contain /kən'teɪn/ v 1 to keep within limits; hold back or hold down: e g a to restrain, control b to check, halt c to prevent (an enemy, opponent, etc) from advancing or attacking 2a to have within; hold b to comprise, include

container /kən'teɪnə'/ n 1 a receptacle 2 a metal packing case, standardized for mechanical handling, usu forming a single lorry or rail-wagon load – ~ **ize** v

¹**contemporary** /kən'temprəri, -pəri/ adj 1 happening, existing, living, or coming into being during the same period of time 2 marked by characteristics of the present period; modern

²**contemporary** n sby or sthg contemporary with another; specif one of about the same age as another

¹**content** /kən'tent/ adj happy, satisfied – ~ **ment** n – ~ **ed** adj

²**content** /kən'tent/ v 1 to appease the desires of; satisfy 2 to limit (oneself) in requirements, desires, or actions – usu + **with**

³**content** /'kɒntent/ n freedom from care or discomfort; satisfaction

⁴**content** /'kɒntent/ n 1 that which is contained – usu pl with sing. meaning a pl the topics or matter treated in a written work 2a the substance, gist b the events, physical detail, and information in a work of art 3 the matter dealt with in a field of study 4 the amount of specified material contained; proportion

¹**contest** /'kɒntest/ v 1 to make the subject of dispute, contention, or legal proceedings 2 to strive, vie – ~ **ant** n

²**contest** /kən'test/ n 1 a struggle for superiority or victory 2 a competitive event; a competition; esp one adjudicated by a panel of specially chosen judges

¹**continent** /'kɒntɪnənt/ adj 1 exercising continence 2 not suffering from incontinence of the urine or faeces

²**continent** n 1 any of the (7) great divisions of land on the globe 2 cap the continent of Europe as distinguished from the British Isles

continual /kən'tɪnjʊəl/ adj 1 continuing indefinitely without interruption 2 recurring in steady rapid succession – ~ **ly** adv

continue /kən'tɪnjuː/ v 1 to maintain (a condition, course, or action) without interruption; carry on 2 to remain in existence; endure 3 to remain in a place or condition; stay 4 to resume (an activity) after interruption 5 to cause to continue 6 to stay further – -**uation** n

continuous /kə'tɪnjʊəs/ adj marked by uninterrupted extension in space, time, or sequence – ~ **ly** adv

contraceptive /,kɒntrə'septɪv/ n a method or device used in preventing conception – -**tion** n

¹**contract** /'kɒntrækt/ n 1a (a document containing) a legally binding agreement between 2 or more people or parties b a betrothal 2 an undertaking to win a specified number of tricks in bridge

²**contract** /kən'trækt/ v 1 to undertake by contract 2a to catch (an illness) b to incur as an obligation 3 to knit, wrinkle 4 to reduce to a smaller size (as if by squeezing or forcing together 5 to shorten (e g a word) 6 to make a contract 7 to draw together so as to become smaller or shorter

contradict /,kɒntrə'dɪkt/ v 1 to state the contrary of (a statement or speaker) 2 to deny the truthfulness of (a statement or speaker) – ~ **ion** n – ~ **ory** adj

¹**contrary** /'kɒntrəri/ n 1 a fact or condition incompatible with another 2 either of a pair of opposites 3 either of 2 terms (e g true and false) that cannot both simultaneously be said to be true of the same subject

²**contrary** /'kɒntrəri, sense 4 kən'treəri/ adj 1 completely different or opposed 2 opposite in position, direction, or nature 3 of wind or weather unfavourable 4 obstinately self-willed; inclined to oppose the wishes of others – -**ily** adv – -**iness** n

¹**contrast** /'kɒntrɑːst/ n 1a juxtaposition of dissimilar elements (e g colour, tone, or emotion) in a work of art b degree of difference between the lightest and darkest parts of a painting, photograph, television picture, etc 2 comparison of similar objects to set off their dissimilar qualities 3 a person or thing against which another may be contrasted

²**contrast** /kən'trɑːst/ v 1 to exhibit contrast 2 to put in contrast 3 to compare in respect to differences

contribute /kən'trɪbjuːt/ v 1 to give in common with others 2 to supply (e g an article) for a publication 3 to help bring about an end or result – -**bution** n

¹**control** /kən'trəʊl/ v 1 to check, test, or verify 2a to exercise restraining or directing influence over b to have power over; rule – ~ **ler** n – ~ **able** adj

²**control** n 1 power to control, direct, or command 2a (an organism, culture, etc used in) an experiment in which the procedure or agent under test in a parallel experiment is omitted and which is used as a standard of comparison in judging experimental effects b a mechanism used to regulate or guide the operation of a machine, apparatus, or system – often pl c an organization that directs a space flight

controversy /'kɒntrəvɜːsi, kən'trɒvəsi/ n (a) debate or dispute, esp in public or in the media – -**sial** adj – -**sially** adv

convenience /kən'viːnɪəns/ n 1 fitness or suitability 2 an appliance, device, or service conducive to comfort 3 a suitable time; an opportunity 4 personal comfort or advantage 5 Br a public toilet

convenient /kən'vi:nɪənt/ adj 1 suited to personal comfort or to easy use 2 suited to a particular situation 3 near at hand; easily accessible – ~ly adv

conventional /kən'venʃənəl/ adj 1a conforming to or sanctioned by convention b lacking originality or individuality 2 (of warfare) not using atom or hydrogen bombs – ~ly adv – ize v

conversation /,kɒnvə'seɪʃən/ n 1 (an instance of) informal verbal exchange of feelings, opinions, or ideas 2 an exchange similar to conversation; esp real-time interaction with a computer, esp through a keyboard – ~al adj – ~ally adv – ~alist n

convert /kən'vɜ:t/ v 1a to win over from one persuasion or party to another b to win over to a particular religion or sect 2a to alter the physical or chemical nature or properties of, esp in manufacturing b to change from one form or function to another; esp to make (structural) alterations to (a building or part of a building) c to exchange for an equivalent 3 to gain exxtra points for a try in rugby by kicking the ball between the uprights of the goal above the cross-bar – **version** n

convert /'kɒnvɜ:t/ n a person who has experienced an esp religious conversion

convey /kən'veɪ/ v 1 to take or carry from one place to another 2 to impart or communicate (e g feelings or ideas) 3 to transmit, transfer; specif to transfer (property or the rights to property) to another – ~er, ~or n

convict /kən'vɪkt/ v 1 to find or prove to be guilty 2 to convince of error or sinfulness

convict /'kɒnvɪkt/ n a person serving a (long-term) prison sentence

convince /kən'vɪns/ v to cause to believe; persuade – ~d adj

cook /kʊk/ n sby who prepares food for eating

cook v 1 to prepare food for eating, esp by subjection to heat 2 to undergo the process of being cooked 3 to subject to the action of heat or fire

cooker /'kʊkəʳ/ n 1 an apparatus, appliance, etc for cooking; esp one typically consisting of an oven, hot plates or rings, and a grill fixed in position 2 a variety, esp of fruit, not usu eaten raw

cool /ku:l/ adj 1 moderately cold; lacking in warmth 2a dispassionately calm and self-controlled b lacking friendliness or enthusiasm c of or being an understated, restrained, and melodic style of jazz 3 bringing or suggesting relief from heat 4 showing sophistication by a restrained or detached manner 5 – used as an intensive; infml 6 very good; excellent – slang – ~ish adj – ~ly adv – ~ness n

cool v 1 to become cool; lose heat or warmth 2 to lose enthusiasm or passion 3 to make cool; impart a feeling of coolness to – often + off or down 4 to moderate the excitement, force, or activity of

cool n 1 a cool atmosphere or place 2 poise, composure – infml

cool adv in a casual and nonchalant manner – infml

coop /ku:p/ n 1 a cage or small enclosure or building, esp for housing poultry 2 a confined space

coop v 1 to confine in a restricted space – usu + up 2 to place or keep in a coop – often + up

co-op /'kəʊ-ɒp/ n a cooperative

cooperate /kəʊ'ɒpəreɪt/ v to act or work with others for a common purpose – **ation** n – **ative** adj

cooperative /kəʊ'ɒpərətɪv/ n an enterprise (e g a shop) or organization (e g a society) owned by and operated for the benefit of those using its services

cop /kɒp/ v to get hold of; catch; specif, Br to arrest – slang

cop n, Br a capture, arrest – esp in a fair cop; slang

cop n a policeman – infml

copper /'kɒpəʳ/ n 1 a common reddish metallic element that is ductile and malleable and one of the best conductors of heat and electricity 2 a coin or token made of copper or bronze and usu of low value 3 any of various small butterflies with usu copper-coloured wings 4 chiefly Br a large metal vessel used, esp formerly, for boiling clothes – **copper**, ~y adj

copper n a policeman – infml

copy /'kɒpi/ n 1 an imitation, transcript, or reproduction of an original work 2 any of a series of esp mechanical reproductions of an original impression 3 (newsworthy) material ready to be printed

copy v 1 to make a copy (of) 2 to model oneself on 3 to undergo copying

cord /kɔ:d/ n 1 (a length of) long thin flexible material consisting of several strands (e g of thread or yarn) woven or twisted together 2 a moral, spiritual, or emotional bond 3 an electric flex 4 a unit of cut wood usu equal to 128ft³ (about 3.63m³); also a stack containing this amount of wood 5a a rib like a cord on a textile b(1) a fabric made with such ribs (2) pl trousers made of corduroy

cord v to provide, bind, or connect with a cord

core /kɔ:ʳ/ n 1 a central or interior part, usu distinct from an enveloping part: e g a the usu inedible central part of an apple, pineapple, etc b the portion of a foundry mould that shapes the interior of a hollow casting c a cylindrical portion removed from a mass for inspection; specif such a portion of rock got by boring d a piece of ferromagnetic material (e g iron) serving to concentrate and intensify the magnetic field resulting from a current in a surrounding coil e the central part of a planet, esp the earth f a subject which is central in a course of studies 2 the essential, basic, or central part (e g of an individual, class, or entity)

core v to remove a core from

cork /kɔ:k/ n 1a the elastic tough outer

tissue of the cork oak used esp for stoppers and insulation **b** a layer of similar tissue in other plants **2** a usu cork stopper, esp for a bottle **3** an angling float

²**cork** v to fit or close with a cork

¹**corn** /kɔːn/ n **1** a small hard seed **2** (the seeds of) the important cereal crop of a particular region (e g wheat and barley in Britain) **3** sweet corn, maize **4** sthg corny – infml

²**corn** v to preserve or season with salt or brine

³**corn** n a local hardening and thickening of skin (e g on the top of a toe)

¹**corner** /ˈkɔːnə/ n **1a** the point where converging lines, edges, or sides meet; an angle **b** the place of intersection of 2 streets or roads **c** a piece designed to form, mark, or protect a corner (e g of a book) **2** the angular space between meeting lines, edges, or borders: e g **a** the area of a playing field or court near the intersection of the sideline and the goal line or baseline **b** any of the 4 angles of a boxing ring; *esp* that in which a boxer rests between rounds **3** *sing or pl in constr* a contestant's group of supporters, adherents, etc **4** a corner kick; *also* a corner hit **5a** a private, secret, or remote place **b** a difficult or embarrassing situation; a position from which escape or retreat is difficult **6** control or ownership of enough of the available supply of a commodity or security to permit manipulation of esp the price **7** a point at which significant change occurs – often in *turn a corner*

²**corner** v **1a** to drive into a corner **b** to catch and hold the attention of, esp so as to force into conversation **2** to get a corner on **3** to turn a corner

¹**corporal** /ˈkɔːpərəl/ adj of or affecting the body

²**corporal** n a low-ranking non-commissioned officer in the army or British air force

corporation /ˌkɔːpəˈreɪʃən/ n **1** *sing or pl in constr* the municipal authorities of a town or city **2** a body made up of more than 1 person which is formed and authorized by law to act as a single person with its own legal identity, rights, and duties **3** an association of employers and employees or of members of a profession in a corporate state **4** a potbelly – humor

corpse /kɔːps/ n a dead (human) body

¹**correct** /kəˈrekt/ v **1** to alter or adjust so as to counteract some imperfection or failing **2a** to punish (e g a child) with a view to reforming or improving **b** to point out the faults of – ~ion n – ~ive adj, n

²**correct** adj **1** conforming to an approved or conventional standard **2** true, right – ~ly adv – ~ness n

correspond /ˌkɒrɪˈspɒnd/ v **1a** to be in conformity or agreement; suit, match – usu + *to* or *with* **b** to be equivalent or parallel **2** to communicate *with* a person by exchange of letters – ~ence n – ~ent adj

corridor /ˈkɒrɪdɔː/ n, **1** a passage (e g in a hotel or railway carriage) onto which compartments or rooms open **2** a usu narrow passageway or route: e g **a** a narrow strip of land through foreign-held territory **3** a strip of land that by geographical characteristics is distinct from its surroundings

¹**corrupt** /kəˈrʌpt/ v **1a** to change from good to bad in morals, manners, or actions; *also* to influence by bribery **b** to degrade with unsound principles or moral values **2** to alter from the original or correct form or version **3** to become corrupt – ~ible adj – ~ibility n

²**corrupt** adj **1a** morally degenerate and perverted **b** characterized by bribery **2** having been vitiated by mistakes or changes – ~ly adv – ~ness n

¹**cosmetic** /kɒzˈmetɪk/ n a cosmetic preparation for external use

²**cosmetic** adj of or intended to improve beauty (e g of the hair or complexion); *broadly* intended to improve the outward appearance – ~ian n

cosmos /ˈkɒzmɒs/ n **1** an orderly universe **2** a complex and orderly system that is complete in itself **3** any of a genus of tropical American composite plants grown for their yellow or red flower heads

¹**cost** /kɒst/ n **1a** the price paid or charged for sthg **b** the expenditure (e g of effort or sacrifice) made to achieve an object **2** the loss or penalty incurred in gaining sthg **3** *pl* expenses incurred in litigation

²**cost** v **1** to require a specified expenditure **2** to require the specified effort, suffering, or loss **3** to cause to pay, suffer, or lose **4** to estimate or set the cost of

costly /ˈkɒstli/ adj **1** valuable, expensive **2** made at great expense or with considerable sacrifice – -liness n

¹**costume** /ˈkɒstjuːm/ n **1** a distinctive fashion in coiffure, jewellery, and apparel of a period, country, class, or group **2** a set of garments suitable for a specified occasion, activity, or season **3** a set of garments belonging to a specific time, place, or character, worn in order to assume a particular role (e g in a play or at a fancy-dress party)

²**costume** v **1** to provide with a costume **2** to design costumes for

³**costume** adj characterized by the use of costumes

¹**cot** /kɒt/ n a small house; a cottage – poetic

²**cot** n **1** a lightweight bedstead **2** a small bed with high enclosing sides, esp for a child

cottage /ˈkɒtɪdʒ/ n a small house, esp in the country

¹**cotton** /ˈkɒtn/ n **1** (a plant producing or grown for) a soft usu white fibrous substance composed of the hairs surrounding the seeds of various tropical plants of the mallow family **2a** fabric

made of cotton **b** yarn spun from cotton

cotton v to come to understand; catch on – usu + *on* or *onto*; infml

¹**couch** /kautʃ/ v **1** to phrase in a specified manner **2** *of an animal* to lie down to sleep; *also* to lie in ambush

²**couch** n **1** a piece of furniture for sitting or lying on **a** with a back and usu armrests **b** with a low back and raised head-end **2** a long upholstered seat with a headrest for patients to lie on during medical examination or psychoanalysis **3** the den of an animal (e g an otter)

cough /kɒf/ v **1** to expel air from the lungs suddenly with an explosive noise **2** to make a noise like that of coughing – **cough** n

could /kəd; *strong* kʊd/ *verbal auxiliary* **1** *past of* **can** – used in the past, in the past conditional, as an alternative to *can* suggesting less force or certainty, as a polite form in the present, as an alternative to *might* expressing purpose in the past, and as an alternative to *ought* or *should* **2** feel impelled to

council /'kaunsəl/ n *sing or pl in constr* an elected or appointed body with administrative, legislative, or advisory powers; *esp* a locally-elected body having power over a parish, district, county, etc

council *adj* Br provided, maintained, or operated by local government

counsel /'kaunsəl/ n **1** advice; consultation **2** thoughts or intentions – chiefly in *keep one's own counsel* **3a** a barrister engaged in the trial of a case in court **b** a lawyer appointed to advise a client

counsel v to advise

counsellor /'kaunsələ/ n **1** an adviser **2** NAm a lawyer; *specif* a counsel

¹**count** /kaunt/ v **1a** to reckon by units so as to find the total number of units involved – often + *up* **b** to name the numbers in order **c** to include in a tallying and reckoning **2** to include or exclude (as if) by counting **3** to rely *on* or *upon* sby or sthg **4** to have value or significance – ~**able** *adj*

²**count** n **1** a total obtained by counting **2a** an allegation in an indictment **b** a specific point under consideration; an issue **3** the total number of individual things in a given unit or sample **4** the calling out of the seconds from 1 to 10 when a boxer has been knocked down during which he must rise or be defeated

³**count** n a European nobleman corresponding in rank to a British earl

¹**counter** /'kauntə/ n **1** a small disc of metal, plastic, etc used in counting or in games **2** sthg of value in bargaining; an asset **3** a level surface (e g a table) over which transactions are conducted or food is served or on which goods are displayed

²**counter** v **1** to nullify the effects of; offset **2** to meet attacks or arguments with defensive or retaliatory steps

³**counter** *adv* in an opposite, contrary, or wrong direction

⁴**counter** n **1** the contrary, opposite **2** an

overhanging stern of a vessel **3a** the (blow resulting from the) making of an attack while parrying (e g in boxing or fencing) **b** an agency or force that offsets; a check

⁵**counter** *adj* marked by or tending towards an opposite direction or effect showing opposition, hostility, or antipathy

countess /'kauntɪs/ n **1** the wife or widow of an earl or count **2** a woman having in her own right the rank of an earl or count

countless /'kauntlɪs/ *adj* too numerous to be counted; innumerable

country /'kʌntri/ n **1** an indefinite usu extended expanse of land; a region **2a** the land of a person's birth, residence, or citizenship **b** a political state or nation or its territory **3** *sing or pl in constr* **a** the populace **b** *the* electorate **4** rural as opposed to urban areas

¹**county** /'kaunti/ n any of the territorial divisions of Britain and Ireland constituting the chief units for administrative, judicial, and political purposes; *also* a local government unit in various countries (e g the USA)

²**county** *adj* characteristic of or belonging to the English landed gentry

¹**couple** /'kʌpəl/ v **1** to unite or link **2** to fasten together; connect **3** to copulate

²**couple** n **1** *sing or pl in constr* **2** people paired together; *esp* a married or engaged couple **2a** **2** things considered together; a pair **b** an indefinite small number; a few – infml **3** **2** equal and opposite forces that act along parallel lines and cause rotation

³**couple** *adj* two

coupon /'kuːpɒn/ n **1** a detachable ticket or certificate that entitles the holder to sthg **2** a voucher given with a purchase that can be exchanged for goods **3** a part of a printed advertisement to be cut off for use as an order form or enquiry form **4** a printed entry form for a competition, esp the football pools

courage /'kʌrɪdʒ/ n mental or moral strength to confront danger, fear, etc; bravery – -**ageous** *adj*

¹**course** /kɔːs/ n **1** the moving in a path from point to point **2** the path over which sthg moves: e g **a** a racecourse **b** the direction of travel, usu measured as a clockwise angle from north **c** a golf course **3a** usual procedure or normal action **b** progression through a series of acts or events or a development or period **4a** a series of educational activities relating to a subject, esp when constituting a curriculum **b** a particular medical treatment administered over a designated period **5** a part of a meal served at one time **6** a continuous horizontal layer of brick or masonry throughout a wall

²**course** v **1** to hunt or pursue (e g hares) with dogs that follow by sight **2** *of a liquid* to run or pass rapidly (as if) along an indicated path

¹**court** /kɔːt/ n **1a** the residence or

establishment of a dignitary, esp a sovereign **b** *sing or pl in constr* the sovereign and his officers and advisers who are the governing power **c** a reception held by a sovereign **2a** a manor house or large building (e g a block of flats) surrounded by usu enclosed grounds – archaic except in proper names **b** a space enclosed wholly or partly by a building **c** (a division of) a rectangular space walled or marked off for playing lawn tennis, squash, basketball, etc **d** a yard surrounded by houses, with only 1 opening onto a street **3a** (a session of) an official assembly for the transaction of judicial business **b** *sing or pl in constr* judicial officers in session

²**court** *v* **1** to act so as to invite or provoke **2a** to seek the affections of; woo **b** *of a man and woman* to be involved in a relationship that may lead to marriage **c** *of an animal* to perform actions to attract (a mate) **3** to seek to win the favour of

courteous /'kɜːtɪəs/ *adj* showing respect and consideration for others – ~**ly** *adv* – ~**ness** *n*

¹**courtesy** /'kɜːtl̩si/ *n* courteous behaviour; a courteous act

²**courtesy** *adj* granted, provided, or performed by way of courtesy

cousin /'kʌzən/ *n* **1** a child of one's uncle or aunt **2** a relative descended from one's grandparent or more remote ancestor in a different line

¹**cover** /'kʌvə/ *v* **1a** to guard from attack **b** to have within the range of one's guns **c** to insure **d** to make sufficient provision for (a demand or charge) by means of a reserve or deposit **2a** to hide from sight or knowledge; conceal – usu + *up* **b** to lie or spread over; envelop **3** to lay or spread sthg over **4** to extend thickly or conspicuously over the surface of **5** to include, consider, or take in **6a** to have as one's territory or field of activity **b** to report news about **7** to pass over; traverse **8** to conceal sthg illicit, blameworthy, or embarrassing from notice – usu + *up* **9** to act as a substitute or replacement during an absence – chiefly in *cover for someone*

²**cover** *n* **1a** natural shelter for an animal **b(1)** a position affording shelter from attack **(2)** (the protection offered by) a force supporting a military operation **2** sthg that is placed over or about another thing e g **a** a lid, top **b** (the front or back part of) a binding or jacket of a book **c** a cloth (e g a blanket) used on a bed **d** sthg (e g vegetation or snow) that covers the ground **e** the extent to which clouds obscure the sky **3a** sthg that conceals or obscures **b** a masking device; a pretext **4** an envelope or wrapper for postal use **5a** cover-point, extra cover, or a cricket fielding position between them **b** *pl* the fielding positions in cricket that lie between point and mid-off

¹**cow** /kaʊ/ *n* **1** the mature female of cattle or of any animal the male of which is called *bull* **2** a domestic bovine

animal regardless of sex or age **3** a woman; *esp* one who is unpleasant

²**cow** *v* to intimidate with threats or a show of strength

coward /'kaʊəd/ *n* one who lacks courage or resolve – ~**ly** *adj* – ~**ice** *n* – ~**liness** *n*

cowboy /'kaʊbɔɪ/ *n* **1** a cattle ranch hand in N America **2** one who employs irregular or unscrupulous methods, esp in business

¹**crab** /kræb/ *n* **1** any of numerous chiefly marine crustaceans usu with the front pair of limbs modified as grasping pincers and a short broad flattened carapace; *also* the flesh of this cooked and eaten as food **2** *pl* infestation with crab lice

²**crab** *v* to cause to move sideways or in an indirect or diagonal manner

³**crab** *v* **1** to make sullen; sour **2** to carp grouse

⁴**crab** *n* an ill-tempered person – *infml*

¹**crack** /kræk/ *v* **1** to make a sudden sharp explosive noise **2** to break or split (apart) esp so that fissures appear **3** to lose control or effectiveness under pressure – often + *up* **4a** *esp of hydrocarbons* to break up into simpler chemical compounds when heated, usu with a catalyst **b** to produce (e g petrol) by cracking **5** to tell (a joke) **6a** to puzzle out and expose, solve, or reveal the mystery of **b** to break into **7** to open (e g a can or bottle) for drinking – *infml*

²**crack** *n* **1** a sudden sharp loud noise **2** a narrow break or opening; a chink fissure **3** a sharp resounding blow **4** a witty remark; a quip – *infml* **5** an attempt, try *at* – *infml*

³**crack** *adj* of superior quality or ability

cracker /'krækə/ *n* **1** a brightly coloured paper and cardboard tube that makes an explosive crack when pulled sharply apart and usu contains a toy paper hat, or other party item **2** *pl* a tool for cracking nuts **3** a thin often savoury biscuit **4** *Br* an outstandingly attractive girl or woman – *infml*

¹**crackle** /'krækəl/ *v* to crush or crack with a snapping sound

²**crackle** *n* **1** the noise of repeated small cracks or reports **2** a network of fine cracks on an otherwise smooth surface

¹**cradle** /'kreɪdl/ *n* **1a** a baby's bed or cot, usu on rockers **b** a framework of wood or metal used as a support, scaffold, etc **2a** the earliest period of life infancy **b** a place of origin

²**cradle** *v* **1** to place or keep (as if) in a cradle **2** to shelter or hold protectively

¹**craft** /krɑːft/ *n* **1** skill in planning making, or executing; dexterity – often in combination **2** an activity or trade requiring manual dexterity or artistic skill; *broadly* a trade, profession **3** skill in deceiving to gain an end **4a** a (small boat **b** an aircraft **c** a spacecraft

²**craft** *v* to make (as if) using skill and dexterity

crafty /'krɑːfti/ *adj* showing subtlety and guile – **craftily** *adv* – **craftiness** *n*

¹**cramp** /kræmp/ *n* 1 a painful involuntary spasmodic contraction of a muscle 2 *pl* severe abdominal pain

²**cramp** *n* 1 a usu metal device bent at the ends and used to hold timbers or blocks of stone together 2 a clamp

³**cramp** *v* 1a to confine, restrain b to restrain from free expression – esp in *cramp someone's style* 2 to fasten or hold with a clamp

¹**crane** /kreɪn/ *n* 1 any of a family of tall wading birds 2 a machine for moving heavy weights by means of a projecting swinging arm or a hoisting apparatus supported on an overhead track

²**crane** *v* to stretch one's neck, esp in order to see better

¹**crash** /kræʃ/ *v* 1a to break violently and noisily; smash b to damage (an aircraft) in landing c to damage (a vehicle) by collision 2a to make a crashing noise b to force one's way with loud crashing noises 3 to enter without invitation or payment – *infml* 4 to spend the night in a (makeshift) place; go to sleep – sometimes + *out*; *slang* 5 *esp of a computer system or program* to become (suddenly) completely inoperative – **crash** *adv*

²**crash** *n* 1 a loud noise (e g of things smashing) 2 a breaking to pieces (as if) by collision; *also* an instance of crashing 3 a sudden decline or failure (e g of a business)

³**crash** *adj* designed to achieve an intended result in the shortest possible time

¹**crawl** /krɔːl/ *v* 1 to move slowly in a prone position (as if) without the use of limbs 2 to move or progress slowly or laboriously 3 to be alive or swarming (as if) with creeping things 4 to behave in a servile manner – *infml*

²**crawl** *n* 1a crawling b slow or laborious motion 2 the fastest swimming stroke, executed lying on the front and consisting of alternating overarm strokes combined with kicks with the legs

crayon /'kreɪən, -ɒn/ *v or n* (to draw or colour with) a stick of coloured chalk or wax used for writing or drawing

crazy /'kreɪzi/ *adj* 1 mad, insane 2 impractical, eccentric 3 extremely enthusiastic *about*; very fond – **-zily** *adv* – **-ziness** *n*

creak /kriːk/ *v or n* (to make) a prolonged grating or squeaking noise

¹**cream** /kriːm/ *n* 1 the yellowish part of milk that forms a surface layer when milk is allowed to stand 2a a food (e g a sauce or cake filling) prepared with or resembling cream in consistency, richness, etc b a biscuit, chocolate, etc filled with (a soft preparation resembling) whipped cream c sthg with the consistency of thick cream; *esp* a usu emulsified medicinal or cosmetic preparation 3 the choicest part 4 a pale yellowish white colour – ~ *adj* – ~ **iness** *n*

²**cream** *v* 1 to take away (the choicest part) – usu + *off* 2 to break into a

creamy froth 3 to form a surface layer of or like cream 4 *NAm* to defeat completely

¹**crease** /kriːs/ *n* 1 a line or mark made (as if) by folding a pliable substance 2a an area surrounding the goal in lacrosse, hockey, etc into which an attacking player may not precede the ball or puck b the bowling crease, popping crease, or return crease of a cricket pitch

²**crease** *v* 1 to make a crease in or on; wrinkle 2 *chiefly Br* to cause much amusement to – often + *up*

create /kriˈeɪt/ *v* 1 to bring into existence 2a to invest with a new form, office, or rank b to produce, cause 3 to design, invent 4 to make a loud fuss about sthg – *infml*

creation /kriˈeɪʃən/ *n* 1 *often cap* the act of bringing the world into ordered existence 2 sthg created: e g a creatures singly or collectively b an original work of art c a product of some minor art or craft (e g dressmaking or cookery) showing unusual flair or imagination – often derog – **-tive** *adj*

creature /'kriːtʃə/ *n* 1 a lower animal 2a an animate being; *esp* a non-human one b a human being; a person 3 one who is the servile dependant or tool of another

¹**credit** /'kredɪt/ *n* 1a the balance in a person's favour in an account b a sum loaned by a bank to be repaid with interest c time given for payment for goods or services provided but not immediately paid for 2 credence 3 influence derived from enjoying the confidence of others; standing 4 a source of honour or repute 5 acknowledgment, approval 6 an acknowledgment of a contributor by name that appears at the beginning or end of a film or television programme 7a recognition that a student has fulfilled a course requirement b the passing of an examination at a level well above the minimum though not with distinction

²**credit** *v* 1 to believe 2 to place to the credit of 3 to ascribe some usu favourable characteristic to – + *with*

¹**creep** /kriːp/ *v* **crept** 1 to move along with the body prone and close to the ground 2a to go very slowly b to go timidly or cautiously so as to escape notice 3a to crawl b of a plant to spread or grow over a surface by clinging with tendrils, roots, etc or rooting at intervals

²**creep** *n* 1 a movement of or like creeping 2 *Br* an obnoxious or ingratiatingly servile person – *infml*

cremate /krɪˈmeɪt/ *v* to reduce (a dead body) to ashes by burning – **cremation** *n*

crest /krest/ *n* 1a a showy tuft or projection on the head of an animal, esp a bird b the plume, emblem, etc worn on a knight's helmet c coat of arms – not used technically in heraldry 2 the ridge or top, esp of a wave, roof, or mountain 3 *the* climax, culmination – ~ **ed** *adj*

¹**crew** /kru:/ *chiefly Br past of* **crow**

²**crew** *n sing or pl in constr* **1** a company of men working on 1 job or under 1 foreman **2a** the personnel of a ship or boat (excluding the captain and officers) **b** the people who man an aircraft in flight **3** a number of people temporarily associated – *infml*

¹**cricket** /'krɪkɪt/ *n* a leaping insect noted for the chirping sounds produced by the male

²**cricket** *n* a game played with a bat and ball on a large field with 2 wickets near its centre by 2 sides of 11 players each – ~**er** *n*

crime /kraɪm/ *n* **1 (a)** violation of law **2** a grave offence, esp against morality **3** criminal activity **4** sthg deplorable, foolish, or disgraceful – *infml*

¹**criminal** /'krɪmɪnəl/ *adj* **1** involving or being a crime **2** relating to crime or its punishment **3** guilty of crime **4** disgraceful, deplorable – *infml* – ~**lly** *adv*

²**criminal** *n* one who has committed or been convicted of a crime

crimson /'krɪmzən/ *adj or n* (a) deep purplish red

¹**cripple** /'krɪpl/ *n* a lame or partly disabled person or animal

²**cripple** *v* **1** to make a cripple; lame **2** to deprive of strength, efficiency, wholeness, or capability for service

crisis /'kraɪsɪs/ *n, pl* **crises 1** the turning point for better or worse in an acute disease (e g pneumonia) **2** an unstable or crucial time or situation; *esp* a turning point

¹**crisp** /krɪsp/ *adj* **1a** easily crumbled; brittle **b** desirably firm and fresh **c** newly made or prepared **2** sharp, clean-cut, and clear **3** decisive, sharp **4** *of weather* briskly cold; fresh; *esp* frosty – ~**ly** *adv* – ~**ness** *n*

²**crisp** *n, chiefly Br* a thin slice of (flavoured or salted) fried potato, usu eaten cold

critic /'krɪtɪk/ *n* **1** one who evaluates works of art, literature, or music, esp as a profession **2** one who tends to judge harshly or to be over-critical of minor faults

critical /'krɪtɪkəl/ *adj* **1a** inclined to criticize severely and unfavourably **b** involving careful judgment or judicious evaluation **2a** of a measurement, point, etc at which some phenomenon undergoes a marked change **b** crucial, decisive **c** being in or approaching a state of crisis **3** *of a nuclear reactor* sustaining an energy-producing chain reaction – ~**ly** *adv*

criticism /'krɪtɪsɪzəm/ *n* **1** criticizing, usu unfavourably **2** the art or act of analysing and evaluating esp the fine arts, literature, or literary documents

criticize, -ise /'krɪtɪsaɪz/ *v* **1** to judge the merits or faults of **2** to stress the faults of

¹**croak** /krəʊk/ *v* **1** to utter (gloomily) in a hoarse raucous voice **2** to die – *slang*

²**croak** *n* a deep hoarse cry characteristic of a frog or toad

crockery /'krɒkəri/ *n* earthenware or china tableware, esp for everyday domestic use

crocodile /'krɒkədaɪl/ *n* **1** any of several tropical or subtropical large voracious thick-skinned long-bodied aquatic reptiles **2** (leather prepared from) the skin of a crocodile **3** a line of people (e g schoolchildren) walking in pairs

crooked /'krʊkɪd/ *adj* **1** having a crook or curve; bent **2** not morally straightforward; dishonest – ~**ly** *adv* – ~**ness** *n*

¹**crop** /krɒp/ *n* **1** (the stock or handle of) a riding whip **2** a pouched enlargement of the gullet of many birds in which food is stored and prepared for digestion **3** a short haircut **4** (the total production of) a plant or animal product that can be grown and harvested extensively

²**crop** *v* **1a** to harvest **b** to cut short; trim **2** to grow as or to cause (land) to bear a crop

¹**cross** /krɒs/ *n* **1a** an upright stake with a transverse beam used, esp by the ancient Romans, for execution **b** *often cap* the cross on which Jesus was crucified; *also* the Crucifixion **2** an affliction, trial **3** a design of an upright bar intersected by a horizontal one used esp as a Christian emblem **4** a monument surmounted by a cross **5** a mark formed by 2 intersecting lines crossing at their midpoints that is used as a signature, to mark a position, to indicate that sthg is incorrect, or to indicate a kiss in a letter **6** sby who or sthg that combines characteristics of 2 different types or individuals **7** a hook delivered over the opponent's lead in boxing **8** crossing the ball in soccer

²**cross** *v* **1** to make the sign of the cross on or over **2a** to intersect **b** to move, pass, or extend across sthg – usu + *over* **3** to run counter to; oppose **4** to go across **5** to draw 2 parallel lines across (a cheque) so that it can only be paid directly into a bank account **6** to kick or pass (the ball) across the field in soccer, specif from the wing into the goal area **7** *of letters, travellers, etc* to meet and pass **8** to interbreed, hybridize

³**cross** *adj* **1** lying or moving across **2** mutually opposed **3** involving mutual interchange; reciprocal **4a** irritable, grumpy **b** angry, annoyed **5** crossbred, hybrid – ~**ly** *adv* – ~**ness** *n*

cross-section *n* **1** (a drawing of) a surface made by cutting across sthg, esp at right angles to its length **2** a representative sample

crouch /kraʊtʃ/ *v* to lower the body by bending the legs – **crouch** *n*

¹**crow** /krəʊ/ *n* **1** the carrion or hooded crow or a related large usu entirely glossy black bird **2** a crowbar

²**crow** *v* **crowed**, *(1)* **crowed** *also* **crew 1** to make the loud shrill cry characteristic of a cock **2** *esp of an infant* to utter sounds of happiness or pleasure **3** to

exult gloatingly, esp over another's misfortune

crow n 1 the characteristic cry of the cock 2 a triumphant cry

crowd /kraʊd/ v 1a to collect in numbers; throng b to force or thrust into a small space 2 to hoist more (sail) than usual for greater speed – usu + on 3 to press close to; jostle

crowd n sing or pl in constr 1 a large number of people gathered together without order; a throng 2 people in general – + the 3 a large number of things close together and in disorder

crowded /ˈkraʊdɪd/ 1 filled with numerous people, things, or events 2 pressed or forced into a small space – ~ness n

crown /kraʊn/ n 1 a reward of victory or mark of honour; esp the title representing the championship in a sport 2 a (gold and jewel-encrusted) headdress worn as a symbol of sovereignty 3a the topmost part of the skull or head b the summit of a slope, mountain, etc c the upper part of the foliage of a tree or shrub d the part of a hat or cap that covers the crown of the head e (an artificial substitute for) the part of a tooth visible outside the gum 4 often cap the sovereign as head of state; also sovereignty 5 the high point or culmination 6 a British coin worth 25 pence (formerly 5 shillings)

crown v 1 to invest with a crown 2 to surmount, top 3 to bring to a successful conclusion 4 to put an artificial crown on (a tooth)

crucial /ˈkruːʃəl/ adj 1 essential to the resolving of a crisis; decisive 2 of the greatest importance or significance – ~ly adv

cruel /ˈkruːəl/ adj 1 liking to inflict pain or suffering; pitiless 2 causing suffering; painful – ~ly adv – ~ness n

cruelty /ˈkruːəlti/ n 1 being cruel 2 (an instance of) cruel behaviour

cruise /kruːz/ v 1 to travel by sea for pleasure 2 to go about or patrol the streets without any definite destination 3a of an aircraft to fly at the most efficient operating speed b of a vehicle to travel at an economical speed that can be maintained for a long distance 4 to make progress easily 5 to search (e g in public places) for an esp homosexual partner – slang

crumb /krʌm/ n 1 a small fragment, esp of bread 2 a small amount 3 (loose crumbly soil or other material resembling) the soft part of bread inside the crust 4 a worthless person – slang

crumble /ˈkrʌmbl/ v to break or fall into small pieces; disintegrate – often + away – -ly adj

crumble n a dessert of stewed fruit topped with a crumbly mixture of fat, flour, and sugar

crumple /ˈkrʌmpl/ v 1 to press, bend, or crush out of shape 2 to collapse – often + up

crush /krʌʃ/ v 1 to alter or destroy by pressure or compression 2 to subdue, overwhelm 3 to crowd, push

²**crush** n 1 a crowding together, esp of many people 2 (the object of) an intense usu brief infatuation – infml

crust /krʌst/ n 1 the hardened exterior of bread 2 the pastry cover of a pie 3a the outer rocky layer of the earth b a deposit built up on the inside of a wine bottle during long aging

¹**cry** /kraɪ/ v 1 to call loudly; shout (e g in fear or pain) 2 to weep, sob 3 of a bird or animal to utter a characteristic sound or call 4 to require or suggest strongly a remedy – usu + out for; infml

²**cry** n 1 an inarticulate utterance of distress, rage, pain, etc 2 a loud shout 3 a watchword, slogan 4 a general public demand or complaint 5 a spell of weeping 6 the characteristic sound or call of an animal or bird 7 pursuit – in in full cry

¹**cuckoo** /ˈkʊkuː/ n, pl **cuckoos** 1 (any of a large family of birds including) a greyish brown European bird that lays its eggs in the nests of other birds which hatch them and rear the offspring 2 the characteristic call of the cuckoo

²**cuckoo** adj deficient in sense or intelligence; silly – infml

culprit /ˈkʌlprɪt/ n one guilty of a crime or a fault

cultivate /ˈkʌltɪveɪt/ v 1 to prepare or use (land, soil, etc) for the growing of crops; also to break up the soil about (growing plants) 2a to foster the growth of (a plant or crop) b to improve by labour, care, or study; refine 3 to further, encourage – -vation n

¹**culture** /ˈkʌltʃə/ n 1 enlightenment and excellence of taste acquired by intellectual and aesthetic training 2a the socially transmitted pattern of human behaviour that includes thought, speech, action, institutions, and man-made objects b the customary beliefs, social forms, etc of a racial, religious, or social group 3 (a product of) the cultivation of living cells, tissue, viruses, etc in prepared nutrient media – -al adj – -ally adv

²**culture** v 1 to cultivate 2 to grow (bacteria, viruses, etc) in a culture

¹**cunning** /ˈkʌnɪŋ/ adj 1 dexterous, ingenious 2 devious, crafty – ~ly adv

²**cunning** n craft, slyness

cup /kʌp/ n 1 a small open drinking vessel that is usu bowl-shaped and has a handle on 1 side 2 the consecrated wine of the Communion 3 (a competition or championship with) an ornamental usu metal cup offered as a prize 4 sthg resembling a cup 5 either of 2 parts of a garment, esp a bra, that are shaped to fit over the breasts 6 any of various usu alcoholic and cold drinks made from mixed ingredients

cupboard /ˈkʌbəd/ n a shelved recess or freestanding piece of furniture with doors, for storage of utensils, food, clothes, etc

¹**cure** /kjʊə/ n 1 spiritual or pastoral charge 2 (a drug, treatment, etc that gives) relief or esp recovery from a dis-

ease **3** sthg that corrects a harmful or troublesome situation; a remedy **4** a process or method of curing

²**cure** *v* **1a** to restore to health, soundness, or normality **b** to bring about recovery from **2a** to rectify **b** to free (sby) from sthg objectionable or harmful **3** to prepare by chemical or physical processing; *esp* to preserve (meat, fish, etc) by salting, drying, smoking, etc – **-rable** *adj*

curiosity /ˌkjʊəriˈɒsɪti/ *n* **1** inquisitiveness; nosiness **2** a strange, interesting, or rare object, custom, etc

curious /ˈkjʊərɪəs/ *adj* **1** eager to investigate and learn **2** inquisitive, nosy **3** strange, novel, or odd – ~**ly** *adv*

¹**curl** /kɜːl/ *v* **1a** to grow in coils or spirals **b** to form curls or twists **2** to move or progress in curves or spirals

²**curl** *n* **1** a curled lock of hair **2** sthg with a spiral or winding form; a coil **3** a (plant disease marked by the) rolling or curling of leaves

curly /ˈkɜːli/ *adj* tending to curl; having curls – **curliness** *n*

currant /ˈkʌrənt/ *n* **1** a small seedless type of dried grape used in cookery **2** a redcurrant, blackcurrant, or similar acid edible fruit

currency /ˈkʌrənsi/ *n* **1** (the state of being in) general use, acceptance, or prevalence **2** sthg (e g coins and bank notes) that is in circulation as a medium of exchange

¹**current** /ˈkʌrənt/ *adj* **1** occurring in or belonging to the present time **2** used as a medium of exchange **3** generally accepted, used, or practised at the moment – ~**ly** *adv*

²**current** *n* **1a** the part of a body of gas or liquid that moves continuously in a certain direction **b** the swiftest part of a stream **c** a (tidal) movement of lake, sea, or ocean water **2** a flow of electric charge; *also* the rate of such flow

¹**curse** /kɜːs/ *n* **1** an utterance (of a deity) or a request (to a deity) that invokes harm or injury **2** an evil or misfortune that comes (as if) in response to cursing or as retribution **3** a cause of misfortune **4** menstruation – + *the*; *infml*

²**curse** *v* **1** to call upon divine or supernatural power to cause harm or injury to **2** to use profanely insolent language against **3** to bring great evil upon; afflict

curtain /ˈkɜːtɪn/ *n* **1** a hanging fabric screen (at a window) that can usu be drawn back **2** a device or agency that conceals or acts as a barrier **3** an exterior wall that carries no load **4a** the movable screen separating the stage from the auditorium of a theatre **b** the ascent or opening (e g at the beginning of a play) of a stage curtain; *also* its descent or closing **c** *pl* the end; *esp* death – ~**s**

curtsy, curtsey /ˈkɜːtsi/ *n* an act of respect, made by a woman, performed by bending at the knees and bowing the head – **curtsy** *v*

¹**curve** /kɜːv/ *v* to have or make a turn, change, or deviation from a straight line without sharp breaks or angularity

²**curve** *n* **1** a curving line or surface **2** sthg curved (e g a curving line of the human body) **3** a representation on a graph of a varying quantity (e g speed, force, or weight)

¹**cushion** /ˈkʊʃən/ *n* **1** a soft pillow or padded bag; *esp* one used for sitting, reclining, or kneeling on **2** a bodily part resembling a pad **3** a pad of springy rubber along the inside of the rim of a billiard table off which balls bounce **4** sthg serving to mitigate the effects of disturbances or disorders

²**cushion** *v* **1** to mitigate the effects of **2** to protect against force or shock

¹**custom** /ˈkʌstəm/ *n* **1a** an established socially accepted practice **b** the usual practice of an individual **c** the usages that regulate social life **2a** *pl* duties or tolls imposed on imports or exports **b** *pl* but *sing* or *pl* in *constr* the agency, establishment, or procedure for collecting such customs **3** business patronage

²**custom** *adj, Nam* made or performed according to personal order

customer /ˈkʌstəmər/ *n* **1** one who purchases a commodity or service **2** an individual, usu having some specified distinctive trait

¹**cut** /kʌt/ *v* **-tt-**; **cut** **1a** to penetrate (as if) with an edged instrument **b** to hurt the feelings of **2a** to trim, pare **b** to shorten by omissions **c** to reduce in amount **3a** to mow or reap **b(1)** to divide into parts with an edged instrument **(2)** to fell, hew **c** to make a stroke with a whip, sword, etc **4a** to divide into segments **b** to intersect, cross **c** to break, interrupt **d** to divide (a pack of cards) into 2 portions **5a** to refuse to recognize (an acquaintance) **b** to stop (a motor) by opening a switch **c** to terminate the filming of (a scene in a film) **6a** to make or give shape to (as if) with an edged tool **b** to record sounds on (a gramophone record) **c** to make an abrupt transition from one sound or image to another in film, radio, or television **7a** to perform, make **b** to give the appearance or impression of **8a** to stop, cease – *infml* **b** to absent oneself from (e g a class) – *infml*

²**cut** *n* **1a** a (slice cut from a) piece from a meat carcass or a fish **b** a share **2a** a canal, channel, or inlet made by excavation or worn by natural action **b(1)** an opening made with an edged instrument **(2)** a gash, wound **c** a passage cut as a roadway **3a** a gesture or expression that hurts the feelings **b** a stroke or blow with the edge of sthg sharp **c** a lash (as if) with a whip **d** the act of reducing or removing a part **e** (the result of) a cutting of playing cards **4** an attacking stroke in cricket played with the bat held horizontally and sending the ball on the off side **5** an abrupt transition from one sound or image to another in film, radio, or television **6a** the shape and style in which a thing is cut,

formed, or made **b** a pattern, type **c** a haircut

cutlery /'kʌtləri/ *n* edged or cutting tools; *esp* implements (e g knives, forks, and spoons) for cutting and eating food

cut-price *adj* selling or sold at a discount

¹**cycle** /'saɪkəl/ *n* **1a** (the time needed to complete) a series of related events happening in a regularly repeated order **b** one complete performance of a periodic process (e g a vibration or electrical oscillation) **2** a group of poems, plays, novels, or songs on a central theme **3** a bicycle, motorcycle, tricycle, etc

²**cycle** *v* to ride a bicycle – **-ist** *n*

cynic /'sɪnɪk/ *n* **1** *cap* an adherent of an ancient Greek school of philosophers who held that virtue is the highest good and that its essence lies in mastery over one's desires and wants **2** one who sarcastically doubts the existence of human sincerity or of any motive other than self-interest; *broadly* a pessimist – ~**al** *adj* – ~**ism** *n* – ~**ally** *adv*

D

dad /dæd/ *n* a father – *infml*

daffodil /'dæfədɪl/ *n* any of various plants with flowers that have a large typically yellow corona elongated into a trumpet shape

dagger /'dægə/ *n* a short sharp pointed weapon for stabbing

daily /'deɪli/ *adj* **1a** occurring, made, or acted on every day **b** *of a newspaper* issued every weekday **c** of or providing for every day **2** covering the period of or based on a day

daily *adv* every day; every weekday

daily *n* **1** a newspaper published daily from Monday to Saturday **2** *Br* a charwoman who works on a daily basis

dainty /'deɪnti/ *n* a delicacy

dainty *adj* **1** attractively prepared and served **2** delicately beautiful **3a** fastidious **b** showing avoidance of anything rough – **-tily** *adv* – **-tiness** *n*

dairy /'deəri/ *n* **1** a room, building, etc where milk is processed and butter or cheese is made **2** farming concerned with the production of milk, butter, and cheese **3** an establishment for the sale or distribution of milk and milk products – ~**ing** *n*

daisy /'deɪzi/ *n* a usu white composite plant with a yellow disc and well-developed ray flowers in its flower head

dam /dæm/ *n* a female parent – used esp with reference to domestic animals

dam *n* a barrier preventing the flow of a fluid; *esp* a barrier across a watercourse

dam *v* to stop up; block

damage /'dæmɪdʒ/ *n* **1** loss or harm

resulting from injury to person, property, or reputation **2** *pl* compensation in money imposed by law for loss or injury **3** expense, cost – *infml*

²**damage** *v* to cause damage to

¹**damn** /dæm/ *v* **1** to condemn to a punishment or fate; *esp* to condemn to hell **2** to condemn as a failure by public criticism **3** to bring ruin on **4** to curse – often used as an interjection to express annoyance

²**damn** *n* **1** the utterance of the word *damn* as a curse **2** the slightest bit – chiefly in negative phrases

³**damn** *adj or adv* – used as an intensive

¹**damp** /dæmp/ *n* moisture, humidity

²**damp, dampen** *v* **1a** to diminish the activity or intensity of – often + *down* **b** to reduce progressively the vibration or oscillation of (e g sound waves) **2** to make damp

³**damp** *adj* slightly or moderately wet – ~**ly** *adv*

¹**dance** /dɑːns/ *v* **1** to engage in or perform a dance **2** to move quickly up and down or about – **dancer** *n*

²**dance** *n* **1** (an act or instance or the art of) a series of rhythmic and patterned bodily movements usu performed to music **2** a social gathering for dancing **3** a piece of music for dancing

dandruff /'dændrəf, -drʌf/ *n* a scurf that comes off the scalp in small white or greyish scales

danger /'deɪndʒə/ *n* **1** exposure to the possibility of injury, pain, or loss **2** a case or cause of danger – ~**ous** *adj* – ~**ously** *adv*

dangle /'dæŋgəl/ *v* to hang or swing loosely

¹**dare** /deə/ *v* **dared**, *archaic* **durst** **1** to have sufficient courage or impudence (to) **2a** to challenge to perform an action, esp as a proof of courage **b** to confront boldly; defy

²**dare** *n* a challenge to a bold act

¹**daring** /'deərɪŋ/ *adj* adventurously bold in action or thought

²**daring** *n* venturesome boldness

¹**dark** /dɑːk/ *adj* **1** (partially) devoid of light **2a** (partially) black *of a colour* of (very) low lightness **3a** arising from or showing evil traits or desires; evil **b** dismal, sad **c** lacking knowledge or culture **4** not fair; swarthy – ~**ly** *adv* – ~**ness** *n*

²**dark** *n* a place or time of little or no light; night, nightfall

darken /'dɑːkən/ *v* to make or become dark or darker

¹**darling** /'dɑːlɪŋ/ *n* **1a** a dearly loved person **b** a dear **2** a favourite

²**darling** *adj* **1** dearly loved; favourite **2** charming – used esp by women

¹**dart** /dɑːt/ *n* **1a** a small projectile with a pointed shaft at one end and flights of feather, plastic, etc at the other **b** *pl but sing in constr* a game in which darts are thrown at a dartboard **2** sthg with a slender pointed shaft or outline; *specif* a stitched tapering fold put in a garment to shape it to the figure **3** a quick movement; a dash

²dart *v* to move suddenly or rapidly

¹dash /dæʃ/ *v* 1 to move with sudden speed 2a to strike or knock violently b to break by striking or knocking 3 to destroy, ruin 4 *Br* to damn – euph

²dash *n* 1 (the sound produced by) a sudden burst or splash 2a a stroke of a pen b a punctuation mark – used esp to indicate a break in the thought or structure of a sentence 3 a small but significant addition 4 liveliness of style and action; panache 5 a sudden onset, rush, or attempt 6 a signal (e g a flash or audible tone) of relatively long duration that is one of the 2 fundamental units of Morse code

data /'deɪtə, 'dɑːtə/ *n pl but sing or pl in constr* factual information (e g measurements or statistics) used as a basis for reasoning, discussion, or calculation

¹date /deɪt/ *n* (the oblong edible fruit of) a tall palm

²date *n* 1 the time reckoned in days or larger units at which an event occurs 2 the period of time to which sthg belongs 3a an appointment for a specified time; *esp* a social engagement between 2 people of opposite sex – infml b *NAm* a person of the opposite sex with whom one has a date – infml

³date *v* 1 to determine or record the date of 2a to have been in existence – usu + *from* b to become old-fashioned 3 to mark with characteristics typical of a particular period 4 *chiefly NAm* to make or have a date with (a person of the opposite sex) – infml – **datable, dateable** *adj*

daughter /'dɔːtə'/ *n* 1a a human female having the relation of child to parent b a female descendant – often pl 2a a human female having a specified origin, loyalties, etc b sthg considered as a daughter

dawdle /'dɔːdl/ *v* 1 to spend time idly 2 to move lackadaisically – **~r** *n*

¹dawn /dɔːn/ *v* 1 to begin to grow light as the sun rises 2 to begin to be perceived or understood

²dawn *n* 1 the first appearance of light in the morning 2 a first appearance; beginning

day /deɪ/ *n* 1 the time of light when the sun is above the horizon between one night and the next 2 the time required by a celestial body, specif the earth, to turn once on its axis 3 the solar day of 24 hours beginning at midnight 4 a specified day or date 5 a specified time or period 6 the time established by usage or law for work, school, or business

daze /deɪz/ *v* to stupefy, esp by a blow; stun – **daze** *n* – **~dly** *adv*

dazzle /'dæzl/ *v* 1 to overpower or temporarily blind (the sight) with light 2 to impress deeply, overpower, or confound with brilliance – **dazzle** *n*

¹dead /ded/ *adj* 1 deprived of life; having died 2a(1) having the appearance of death; deathly (2) lacking power to move, feel, or respond; numb b grown cold; extinguished 3 inani-

mate, inert 4a no longer having power or effect, interest or significance b no longer used; obsolete c lacking in activity d lacking elasticity or springiness 5a absolutely uniform b exact c abrupt d complete, absolute – **~ness** *n*

²dead *n* 1 *pl in constr* dead people or animals 2 the time of greatest quiet or inactivity

³dead *adv* 1 absolutely, utterly 2 suddenly and completely 3 directly, exactly 4 *Br* very, extremely – infml

deadline /'dedlaɪn/ *n* a date or time before which sthg (e g the presentation of copy for publication) must be done

¹deadly /'dedli/ *adj* 1 capable of producing death 2a implacable b unerring c marked by determination or extreme seriousness 3 lacking animation; dull 4 intense, extreme – **-liness** *n*

²deadly *adv* 1 suggesting death 2 extremely

deaf /def/ *adj* 1 (partially) lacking the sense of hearing 2 unwilling to hear or listen to; not to be persuaded – **~ness** *n*

¹deal /diːl/ *n* 1 a usu large or indefinite quantity or degree; a lot 2 the act or right of distributing cards to players in a card game; *also* the hand dealt to a player

²deal *v* **dealt** 1 to distribute the cards in a card game 2 to concern oneself or itself 3a to trade b to sell or distribute sthg as a business 4 to take action with regard to sby or sthg – **~er** *n*

³deal *n* 1 a transaction 2 treatment received 3 an arrangement for mutual advantage

⁴deal *n* (a sawn piece of) fir or pine timber

dealing /'diːlɪŋ/ *n* 1 *pl* friendly or business interactions 2 a method of business; a manner of conduct

¹dear /dɪə'/ *adj* 1 highly valued; much loved – often used in address 2 expensive 3 heartfelt – **~ness** *n* – **~ly** *adv*

²dear *n* 1a a loved one; a sweetheart b – used as a familiar or affectionate form of address 2 a lovable person

³dear *interj* – used typically to express annoyance or dismay

death /deθ/ *n* 1 a permanent cessation of all vital functions; the end of life 2 the cause or occasion of loss of life 3 *cap* death personified, usu represented as a skeleton with a scythe 4 the state of being dead 5 extinction, disappearance

¹debate /dɪ'beɪt/ *n* the usu formal discussion of a motion a in parliament b between 2 opposing sides

²debate *v* 1 to argue about 2 to consider – **-table** *adj* – **~r** *n*

debt /det/ *n* 1 a state of owing 2 sthg owed; an obligation

debut /'deɪbjuː, 'debjuː/ *n* 1 a first public appearance 2 a formal entrance into society

decade /'dekeɪd/ *n* 1 a group of 10 years 2 a division of the rosary containing 10 Hail Marys

decay /dɪ'keɪ/ *v* 1 to decline from a

sound or prosperous condition **2** to decrease gradually in quantity, activity, or force; *specif* to undergo radioactive decay **3** to decline in health, strength, or vigour **4** to undergo decomposition

²**decay** *n* **1** a gradual decline in strength, soundness, prosperity, or quality **2** a wasting or wearing away; ruin **3** (a product of) rot; *specif* decomposition of organic matter chiefly by bacteria in the presence of oxygen **4** decrease in quantity, activity, or force; *esp* spontaneous disintegration of an atom or particle usu with the emission of radiation

deceit /dɪ'si:t/ *n* **1** the act or practice of deceiving; deception **2** the quality of being deceitful

deceitful /dɪ'si:tfəl/ *adj* having a tendency or disposition to deceive: **a** not honest **b** deceptive, misleading – ~ly *adv* – ~ness *n*

deceive /dɪ'si:v/ *v* to cause to accept as true or valid what is false or invalid; delude – **deceiver** *n*

December /dɪ'sembə'/ *n* the 12th month of the Gregorian calendar

decent /'di:sənt/ *adj* **1** conforming to standards of propriety, good taste, or morality; *specif* clothed according to standards of propriety **2** adequate, tolerable **3** *chiefly Br* obliging, considerate – *infml* – **decency** *n* – ~ly *adv*

decide /dɪ'saɪd/ *v* **1** to arrive at a solution that ends uncertainty or dispute about **2** to bring to a definitive end **3** to make a choice or judgment

¹**decimal** /'desɪməl/ *adj* **1** numbered or proceeding by tens: **a** based on the number 10 **b** subdivided into units which are tenths, hundredths, etc of another unit **2** using a decimal system (e g of coinage) – ~ly *adv*

²**decimal, decimal fraction** *n* a fraction that is expressed as a sum of integral multiples of powers of $1/10$ by writing a dot followed by 1 digit for the number of tenths, 1 digit for the number of hundredths, and so on (e g $0.25 = {}^{25}/_{100}$)

decision /dɪ'sɪʒən/ *n* **1** deciding **b** a conclusion arrived at after consideration **2** a report of a conclusion **3** promptness and firmness in deciding

¹**deck** /dek/ *n* **1** a platform in a ship serving usu as a structural element and forming the floor for its compartments **2a** a level or floor of a bus with more than 1 floor **b** the part of a record player or tape recorder on which the record or tape is mounted when being played **3** *NAm* a pack of playing cards **4** the ground – *infml*; chiefly in *hit the deck*

²**deck** *v* to array, decorate – often + *out*

declaration /,deklə'reɪʃən/ *n* **1** sthg declared **2** a document containing such a declaration

declare /dɪ'kleə'/ *v* **1** to make known formally or explicitly **2** to make evident; show **3** to state emphatically; affirm **4** to make a full statement of (one's taxable or dutiable income or property) **5** *of a captain or team* to announce one's decision to end one's side's innings in cricket before all the batsmen are out – **declarable** *adj* – **declaratory** *adj*

¹**decline** /dɪ'klaɪn/ *v* **1** to slope or bend down **2a** *of a celestial body* to sink towards setting **b** to draw towards a close; wane **3a** to refuse to undertake, engage in, or comply with **b** to refuse courteously

²**decline** *n* **1a** a gradual physical or mental decay **b** a change to a lower state or level **2** the period during which sthg is approaching its end **3** a downward slope

decorate /'dekəreɪt/ *v* **1a** to add sthg ornamental to **b** to apply new coverings of paint, wallpaper, etc to the interior or exterior surfaces of **2** to award a mark of honour to – **-ation**

¹**decrease** /dɪ'kri:s/ *v* to (cause to) grow progressively less (e g in size, amount, number, or intensity)

²**decrease** *n* **1** the process of decreasing **2** the amount by which sthg decreases

dedicated /'dedɪkeɪtɪd/ *adj* **1** devoted to a cause, ideal, or purpose; zealous **2** given over to a particular purpose – ~ly *adv*

deed /di:d/ *n* **1** an illustrious act or action; a feat, exploit **2** the act of performing **3** a signed (and sealed) written document containing some legal transfer, bargain, or contract

¹**deep** /di:p/ *adj* **1a** extending far downwards **b** (extending) far from the surface of the body **c** extending well back from a front surface **d** near the outer limits of the playing area **2** having a specified extension in an implied direction **3a** difficult to understand **b** capable of profound thought **c** engrossed, involved **d** intense, extreme **4a** *of a colour* high in saturation and low in lightness **b** having a low musical pitch or pitch range – ~ly *adv* – ~ness *n*

²**deep** *adv* **1a(1)** to a great depth **(2)** deep to a specified degree – usu in combination **b** well within the boundaries **2** far on; late **3** in a deep position

³**deep** *n* **1** a vast or immeasurable extent; an abyss **2** the sea

deep-freeze *v* to freeze or store (e g food) in a freezer

deep freeze *n* a freezer

deer /dɪə'/ *n*, *pl deer also* deers any of several ruminant mammals of which most of the males and some of the females bear antlers

¹**defeat** /dɪ'fi:t/ *v* **1a** to nullify or frustrate **2** to win victory over

²**defeat** *n* **1** an overthrow, esp of an army in battle **2** the loss of a contest

¹**defect** /'di:fekt/ *n* an imperfection that impairs worth or usefulness – ~ive *adj*

²**defect** /dɪ'fekt/ *v* to desert a cause or party, often in order to espouse another – ~or *n* – ~ion *n*

defence /dɪ'fens/ *NAm chiefly* **defense** *n* **1** the act or action of defending **2a** a means or method of defending;

also, pl a defensive structure **b** an argument in support or justification **c** a defendant's denial, answer, or strategy **3** *sing or pl in constr* a defending party or group (e g in a court of law) **b** defensive players, acts, or moves in a game or sport **4** the military resources of a country – ~**less** *adj*

defend /dɪˈfend/ *v* **1a** to protect from attack **b** to maintain by argument in the face of opposition or criticism **2a** to play or be in defence **b** to attempt to prevent an opponent from scoring (e g a goal) **3** to act as legal representative in court for

defensive /dɪˈfensɪv/ *adj* **1** serving to defend **2a** disposed to ward off expected criticism or critical inquiry **b** of or relating to the attempt to keep an opponent from scoring

defiance /dɪˈfaɪəns/ *n* a disposition to resist; contempt of opposition

define /dɪˈfaɪn/ *v* **1** to fix or mark the limits of; demarcate **2a** to be the essential quality or qualities of; identify **b** to set forth the meaning of – ~**ly**

definite /ˈdefɪnɪt, ˈdefənɪt/ *adj* **1** having distinct or certain limits **2a** free of all ambiguity, uncertainty, or obscurity **b** unquestionable, decided **3** designating an identified or immediately identifiable person or thing – ~**ly** *adv*

defy /dɪˈfaɪ/ *v* **1** to challenge to do sthg considered impossible; dare **2** to show no fear of nor respect for **3** to resist attempts at

degree /dɪˈɡriː/ *n* **1** a step or stage in a process, course, or order of classification **2a** the extent or measure of an action, condition, or relation **b** a legal measure of guilt or negligence **c** a positive and esp considerable amount **3** the civil condition or status of a person **4** an academic title conferred: **a** on students in recognition of proficiency **b** honorarily **5** a division or interval of a scale of measurement; *specif* any of various units for measuring temperature **6** a 360th part of the circumference of a circle

¹**delay** /dɪˈleɪ/ *n* **1** delaying or (an instance of) being delayed **2** the time during which sthg is delayed

²**delay** *v* **1a** to postpone **b** to move or act slowly **2a** to pause momentarily **b** to stop, detain, or hinder for a time

delete /dɪˈliːt/ *v* to eliminate, esp by blotting out, cutting out, or erasing – -**tion** *n*

¹**deliberate** /dɪˈlɪbərɪt/ *adj* **1** of or resulting from careful and thorough consideration **2** characterized by awareness of the consequences **3** slow, unhurried – ~**ly** *adv* – ~**ness** *n*

²**deliberate** /dɪˈlɪbəreɪt/ *v* to ponder issues and decisions carefully – -**ative** *adj*

delicate /ˈdelɪkɪt/ *adj* **1** pleasing to the senses in a subtle way; dainty, charming **2a** marked by keen sensitivity or subtle discrimination **b** fastidious, squeamish **3** marked by extreme precision or sensitivity **4** calling for or involving

meticulously careful treatment **5a** very finely made **b(1)** fragile **(2)** weak, sickly **c** marked by or requiring tact – ~**ly** *adv*

delicious /dɪˈlɪʃəs/ *adj* **1** affording great pleasure; delightful **2** highly pleasing to one of the bodily senses, esp of taste or smell – ~**ly** *adv* – ~**ness** *n*

¹**delight** /dɪˈlaɪt/ *n* **1** great pleasure or satisfaction; joy **2** sthg that gives great pleasure

²**delight** *v* to take great pleasure *in* doing sthg

delightful /dɪˈlaɪtfəl/ *adj* highly pleasing – ~**ly** *adv*

deliver /dɪˈlɪvə⁄/ *v* **1** to set free **2** to hand over **3a** to aid in the birth of **b** to give birth to **4** to utter **5** to aim or guide (e g a blow) to an intended target or destination **6** to produce the promised, desired, or expected results – infml

¹**deluge** /ˈdeljuːdʒ/ *n* **1a** a great flood; *specif, cap* the Flood recorded in the Old Testament (Gen 6:8) **b** a drenching fall of rain **2** an overwhelming amount or number

²**deluge** *v* **1** to overflow with water; inundate **2** to overwhelm, swamp

delusion /dɪˈluːʒən/ *n* (a mental state characterized by) a false belief (about the self or others) that persists despite the facts and occurs esp in psychotic states – -**sive** *adj*

¹**demand** /dɪˈmɑːnd/ *n* **1** demanding or asking, esp with authority; a claim **2a** an expressed desire for ownership or use **b** willingness and ability to purchase a commodity or service **c** the quantity of a commodity or service wanted at a specified price and time **3** a desire or need *for*; the state of being sought after

²**demand** **1** to make a demand; ask **2** to call for urgently, abruptly, or insistently

democracy /dɪˈmɒkrəsi/ *n* **1a** government by the people **b** (a political unit with) a government in which the supreme power is exercised by the people directly or indirectly through a system of representation usu involving free elections **2** the absence of class distinctions or privileges

democratic /ˌdeməˈkrætɪk/ *adj* **1** of or favouring democracy or social equality **2** *often cap* of or constituting a political party of the USA associated with policies of social reform and internationalism – ~**ally** *adv* – -**ratization** *n*

demolish /dɪˈmɒlɪʃ/ *v* **1** to destroy, smash, or tear down **2** to eat up – infml

demonstrate /ˈdemənstreɪt/ *v* **1** to show clearly **2** to illustrate and explain, esp with many examples **3** to show or prove the application, value, or efficiency of to a prospective buyer **4** to take part in a (political) demonstration – -**tion** *n* – -**strable** *adj*

den /den/ *n* **1** the lair of a wild, usu predatory, animal **2** a centre of secret, esp unlawful, activity **3** a comfortable usu secluded room

des

denial /dɪˈnaɪəl/ n 1 a refusal to satisfy a request or desire 2a a refusal to admit the truth or reality (e g of a statement or charge) b an assertion that an allegation is false 3 a refusal to acknowledge sby or sthg; a disavowal

dense /dens/ adj 1 marked by high density, compactness, or crowding together of parts 2 sluggish of mind; stupid 3 demanding concentration to follow or comprehend – ~ly adv – ~ness n

dent /dent/ n 1 a depression or hollow made by a blow or by pressure 2 an adverse effect – **dent** v

dental /ˈdentl/ adj of the teeth or dentistry

dentist /ˈdentɪst/ n one who treats diseases, injuries, etc of the teeth, and mouth and who makes and inserts false teeth – ~ry n

deny /dɪˈnaɪ/ v 1 to declare to be untrue or invalid; refuse to accept 2a to give a negative answer to b to refuse to grant 3 to restrain (oneself) from self-indulgence

depart /dɪˈpɑːt/ v 1 to leave; go away (from) 2 to turn aside; deviate from – ~ed adj – ~ure n

department /dɪˈpɑːtmənt/ n 1a a division of an institution or business that provides a specified service or deals with a specified subject b a major administrative subdivision (e g in France) c a section of a large store 2 a distinct sphere (e g of activity or thought) – infml – ~al adj

depend /dɪˈpend/ v 1 to be determined by or based on some condition or action 2a to place reliance or trust b to be dependent, esp for financial support USE (1&2) + on or upon

dependence /dɪˈpendəns/ also **dependance** n 1 being influenced by or subject to another 2 reliance, trust 3 psychological need for a drug after a period of use; habituation

dependent /dɪˈpendənt/ adj 1 determined or conditioned by another; contingent 2 relying on another for support 3 subject to another's jurisdiction USE (1&2) + on or upon

¹**deposit** /dɪˈpɒzɪt/ v 1 to place, esp for safekeeping or as a pledge; esp to put in a bank 2 to lay down; place – ~or n

²**deposit** n 1 depositing or being deposited 2a money deposited in a bank b money given as a pledge or down payment 3 a depository 4 sthg laid down; esp (an accumulation of) matter deposited by a natural process

depress /dɪˈpres/ v 1 to push or press down 2 to lessen the activity or strength of 3 to sadden, dispirit – **depressing** adj – **depressingly** adv – **depressed** adj

depression /dɪˈpreʃən/ n 1a a pressing down; a lowering b (a mental disorder marked by inactivity, difficulty in thinking and concentration, and esp by) sadness or dejection 2 a depressed area or part; a hollow 3 an area of low pressure in a weather system 4 a period of low general economic activity marked esp by rising levels of unemployment

depth /depθ/ n 1a a part that is far from the outside or surface b(1) a profound or intense state (of thought or feeling) (2) the worst, most intensive, or severest part 2a the perpendicular measurement downwards from a surface b the distance from front to back 3 the degree of intensity USE (1) often pl with sing. meaning

deputy /ˈdepjʊti/ n 1 a person (e g a second-in-command) appointed as a substitute with power to act for another 2 a member of the lower house of some legislative assemblies – **-tize** v

¹**derelict** /ˈderɪlɪkt/ adj left to decay

²**derelict** n 1 sthg voluntarily abandoned; specif a ship abandoned on the high seas 2 a down-and-out

derive /dɪˈraɪv/ v 1 to obtain or receive, esp from a specified source 2 to infer, deduce from – **-vation** n

descend /dɪˈsend/ v 1 to pass from a higher to a lower level 2 to pass by inheritance 3 to incline, lead, or extend downwards 4 to come down or make a sudden attack – usu + on or upon 5 to sink in status or dignity; stoop

descendant /dɪˈsendənt/ NAm also **descendent** n sby or sthg descended or deriving from another

descent /dɪˈsent/ n 1 the act or process of descending 2 a downward step (e g in status or value) 3a derivation from an ancestor b a transmission from a usu earlier source; a derivation 4 a downward inclination; a slope

describe /dɪˈskraɪb/ v 1 to give an account of in words 2 to trace the outline of

description /dɪˈskrɪpʃən/ n 1 an account 2 kind, sort – **-tive** adj – **-tively** adv – **-tiveness** n

¹**desert** /ˈdezət/ n (a desolate region like) a dry barren region incapable of supporting much life

²**desert** /dɪˈzɜːt/ n deserved reward or punishment – usu pl with sing. meaning

³**desert** v 1 to quit one's post, (military) service, etc without leave or justification 2 to abandon or forsake, esp in time of need – **deserter** n – **desertion** n

Desert /ˈdezət/ trademark – used for an ankle-high laced suede boot with a rubber sole

deserve /dɪˈzɜːv/ v to be worthy of or suitable for (some recompense or treatment) – ~dly adv – **deserving** adj

¹**design** /dɪˈzaɪn/ v 1 to conceive and plan out in the mind 2a to draw the plans for b to create or execute according to a plan; devise – ~er n

²**design** n 1 a mental plan or scheme 2 pl dishonest, hostile, or acquisitive intent – + on 3 (the act of producing) a drawing, plan, or pattern showing the details of how sthg is to be constructed 4 the arrangement of the elements of a work of art or article 5 a decorative pattern

desirable /dɪˈzaɪərəbəl/ adj 1 causing (sexual) desire; attractive 2 worth seeking or doing as advantageous, beneficial, or wise – -**bility** n – -**bly** adv

¹**desire** /dɪ'zaɪə'/ v 1 to long or hope for 2 to express a wish for; request 3 to wish to have sexual relations with – **desirous** adj

²**desire** n 1 a conscious impulse towards something promising enjoyment or satisfaction 2 a (sexual) longing or craving

desk /desk/ n 1a a table with a sloping or horizontal surface and often drawers and compartments, that is designed esp for writing and reading b a music stand 2 a division of an organization specializing in a usu specified phase of activity

¹**despair** /dɪ'speə'/ v to lose all hope or confidence

²**despair** n 1 utter loss of hope 2 a cause of hopelessness

despatch /dɪ'spætʃ/ v or n (to) dispatch

desperate /'despərɪt/ adj 1 being (almost) beyond hope 2a reckless because of despair b undertaken as a last resort 3 suffering extreme need or anxiety – ~**ly** adv – -**ation** n

despise /dɪ'spaɪz/ v 1 to regard with contempt or distaste 2 to regard as negligible or worthless

dessert /dɪ'zɜːt/ n a usu sweet course or dish served at the end of a meal

destination /,destɪ'neɪʃən/ n a place which is set for the end of a journey or to which sthg is sent

destiny /'destɪni/ n 1 the power or agency held to determine the course of events 2 sthg to which a person or thing is destined; fortune 3 a predetermined course of events

destroy /dɪ'strɔɪ/ v 1 to demolish, ruin 2 to put an end to; kill

destruction /dɪ'strʌkʃən/ n 1 destroying or being destroyed 2 a cause of ruin or downfall

¹**detail** /'diːteɪl/ n 1 a small and subordinate part; specif part of a work of art considered or reproduced in isolation 2 an individual relevant part or fact – usu pl 3 sing or pl in constr a small military detachment selected for a particular task

²**detail** v 1 to report in detail 2 to assign to a particular task or place

detain /dɪ'teɪn/ v 1 to hold or retain (as if) in custody 2 to delay; hold back

detect /dɪ'tekt/ v to discover the existence or presence of – **detector** n – ~**ive** adj

detective /dɪ'tektɪv/ n a policeman or other person engaged in investigating crimes, detecting lawbreakers, or getting information that is not readily accessible

detention /dɪ'tenʃən/ n 1 detaining or being detained, esp in custody 2 the keeping in of a pupil after school hours as a punishment

deter /dɪ'tɜː'/ v to discourage or prevent from acting

deteriorate /dɪ'tɪərɪəreɪt/ v to grow or make or worse – -**ration** n

determination /dɪ,tɜːmɪ'neɪʃən/ n 1 firm intention 2 the ability to make and act on firm decisions; resoluteness

determine /dɪ'tɜːmɪn/ v 1 to settle, decide 2a to fix beforehand b to regulate 3 to ascertain the intent, nature, or scope of

deterrent /dɪ'terənt/ n sthg that deters; esp a (nuclear) weapon that is held in readiness by one nation or alliance in order to deter another from attacking – -**rence** n

detest /dɪ'test/ v to feel intense dislike for; loathe – ~**able** adj – ~**ably** adv – ~**ation** n

develop /dɪ'veləp/ v 1a to show signs of b to subject (exposed photograph material) esp to chemicals, in order to produce a visible image 2 to bring out the possibilities of 3a to promote the growth of b to make more available or usable 4 to acquire gradually 5a to go through a process of natural growth, differentiation, or evolution by successive changes b to evolve; broadly to grow

development /dɪ'veləpmənt/ n 1 the act, process, or result of developing; esp economic growth 2 being developed

device /dɪ'vaɪs/ n 1a sthg elaborate or intricate in design b sthg (e g a figure of speech or a dramatic convention) designed to achieve a particular artistic effect c a piece of equipment or a mechanism designed for a special purpose or function 2 pl desire, will

devil /'devəl/ n 1 often cap the supreme spirit of evil in Jewish and Christian belief 2 a malignant spirit 3 an extremely cruel or wicked person 4 a high-spirited, reckless, or energetic person 5a a person of the specified type b sthg provoking, difficult, or trying

devote /dɪ'vəʊt/ v 1 to set apart for a special purpose; dedicate to 2 to give (oneself) wholly to

devoted /dɪ'vəʊtɪd/ adj loyally attached – ~**ly** adv

devour /dɪ'vaʊə'/ v 1 to eat up greedily or ravenously 2 to swallow up; consume 3 to take in eagerly through the mind or senses

dew /djuː/ n moisture that condenses on the surfaces of cool bodies, esp at night – **dewy** adj – **dewily** adv – **dewiness** n

diabolic /,daɪə'bɒlɪk/ adj 1 (characteristic) of the devil; fiendish 2 dreadful, appalling – ~**ally** adv

diagonal /daɪ'ægənəl/ adj 1 joining 2 nonadjacent angles of a polygon or polyhedron 2 running in an oblique direction from a reference line (e g the vertical)

diagram /'daɪəgræm/ n 1 a line drawing made for mathematical or scientific purposes 2 a drawing or design that shows the arrangement and relations (e g of parts) – ~**matic** adj

¹**dial** /'daɪəl/ n 1 the graduated face of a timepiece 2a a face on which some measurement is registered, usu by means of numbers and a pointer b a disc-shaped control on an electrical or

mechanical device **3** *Br* a person's face – *slang*

²**dial** *v* to make a call on the telephone

dialect /'daɪəlekt/ *n* a regional, social, or subordinate variety of a language, usu differing distinctively from the standard or original language – ~**al** *adj*

dialogue /'daɪəlɒg/ *NAm also* **dialog** *n* **1a** a conversation between 2 people or between a person and sthg else (e g a computer) **b** an exchange of ideas and opinions **2** the conversational element of literary or dramatic composition

¹**diamond** /'daɪəmənd/ *n* **1** a (piece of) very hard crystalline carbon that is highly valued as a precious stone, esp when flawless and transparent, and is used industrially as an abrasive and in rock drills **2** a square or rhombus orientated so that the diagonals are horizontal and vertical **3a** a playing card marked with 1 or more red diamond-shaped figures **b** *pl but sing or pl in constr* the suit comprising cards identified by this figure

²**diamond** *adj* of, marking, or being a 60th or 75th anniversary

diary /'daɪəri/ *n* **1** (a book containing) a daily record of personal experiences or observations **2** *chiefly Br* a book with dates marked in which memoranda can be noted

¹**dice** /daɪs/ *n, pl* **dice 1a** a small cube that is marked on each face with from 1 to 6 spots so that spots on opposite faces total 7 and that is used to determine arbitrary values in various games **b** a gambling game played with dice **2** a small square piece (e g of food)

²**dice** *v* **1** to cut (e g food) into small cubes **2** to take a chance

¹**dictate** /dɪk'teɪt/ *v* **1** to speak or read for a person to transcribe or for a machine to record **2** to impose, pronounce, or specify with authority – **-tation** *n*

²**dictate** /'dɪkteɪt/ *n* **1** an authoritative rule, prescription, or command **2** a ruling principle – usu *pl*

dictator /dɪk'teɪtə/ *n* an absolute ruler; *esp* one who has seized power unconstitutionally and uses it oppressively – ~**ial** *adj*

dictionary /'dɪkʃənəri/ *n* **1** a reference book containing the meanings of words or terms often together with information about their pronunciations, etymologies, etc **2** a reference book giving for words of one language equivalents in another

did /dɪd/ *past of* **do**

¹**die** /daɪ/ *v* **dying 1** to stop living; suffer the end of physical life **2** to pass out of existence, cease **3** to long keenly or desperately

²**die** *n* any of various tools or devices for giving a desired shape, form, or finish to a material or for impressing an object or material

diesel engine /'di:zəl ˌendʒɪn/ *n* an internal-combustion engine in which fuel is ignited by air compressed to a sufficiently high temperature

¹**diet** /'daɪət/ *n* **1** the food and drink habitually taken by a group, animal, or individual **2** the kind and amount of food prescribed for a person or animal for a special purpose (e g losing weight) – **dietary** *adj*

²**diet** *n* any of various national or provincial legislatures

difference /'dɪfərəns/ *n* **1a** unlikeness between 2 or more people or things **b** the degree or amount by which things differ **2** a disagreement, dispute; dissension **4** a significant change in or effect on a situation

different /'dɪfərənt/ *adj* **1** partly or totally unlike; dissimilar – + *from*, chiefly *Br to*, or chiefly *NAm than* **2a** distinct **b** various **c** another **3** unusual, special – ~**ly** *adv*

difficult /'dɪfɪkəlt/ *adj* **1** hard to do, make, carry out, or understand **2a** hard to deal with, manage, or please **b** puzzling

difficulty /'dɪfɪkəlti/ *n* **1** being difficult **2** an obstacle or impediment **3** a cause of (financial) trouble or embarrassment – usu *pl* with sing. meaning

¹**dig** /dɪg/ *v* **1** to break up, turn, or loosen earth with an implement **2** to bring to the surface (as if) by digging; unearth **3** to hollow out by removing earth; excavate **4** to drive down into; thrust **5** to poke, prod **6** to understand, appreciate – *slang* – ~**ger** *n*

²**dig** *n* **1a** a thrust, poke **b** a cutting or snide remark **2** an archaeological excavation (site) **3** *pl, chiefly Br* lodgings

¹**digest** /'daɪdʒest, dɪ-/ *n* **1** a systematic compilation of laws **2** a shortened version (e g of a book)

²**digest** *v* **1** to convert (food) into a form the body can use **2** to assimilate mentally **3** to compress into a short summary – ~**ible** *adj* – ~**ibility** *n*

digestion /daɪ'dʒestʃən, dɪ-/ *n* the process or power of digesting sthg, esp food

digit /'dɪdʒɪt/ *n* **1a** any of the Arabic numerals from 1 to 9, usu also including 0 **b** any of the elements that combine to form numbers in a system other than the decimal system **2** a finger or toe – ~**al** *adj*

dignify /'dɪgnɪfaɪ/ *v* to confer dignity or distinction on – **-fied** *adj*

dignity /'dɪgnɪti/ *n* **1** being worthy, honoured, or esteemed **2** high rank, office, or position **3** stillness of manner; gravity

¹**dilute** /daɪ'lu:t/ *v* **1** to make thinner or more liquid by adding another liquid **2** to diminish the strength or brilliance of by adding more liquid, light, etc – **-tion** *n*

²**dilute** *adj* weak, diluted

¹**dim** /dɪm/ *adj* **1** giving out a weak or insufficient light **2a** seen or seeing indistinctly **b** characterized by an unfavourable or pessimistic attitude – esp in *take a dim view of* **3** lacking intelligence; stupid – *infml* – ~**ly** *adv* – ~**ness** *n*

²**dim** *v* to make or become dim

din /dɪn/ *n* a loud continued discordant noise

dine /daɪn/ v to eat dinner – **diner** n

dinner /ˈdɪnə'/ n 1 (the food eaten for) the principal meal of the day taken either in the evening or at midday 2 a formal evening meal or banquet

dinosaur /ˈdaɪnəsɔː'/ n 1 any of a group of extinct, typically very large flesh- or plant-eating reptiles, most of which lived on the land 2 something that is unwieldy and outdated

¹**dip** /dɪp/ v 1a(1) to plunge or immerse in a liquid (e g in order to moisten or dye) (2) to plunge into a liquid and quickly emerge b(1) to immerse sthg in a processing liquid or finishing material (2) to immerse a sheep in an antiseptic or parasite-killing solution 2a to lower and then raise again b to drop down or decrease suddenly 3 to reach inside or below sthg, esp so as to take out part of the contents – usu + in or into 4 to lower (the beam of a vehicle's headlights) so as to reduce glare 5 to incline downwards from the plane of the horizon

²**dip** n 1 a brief bathe for sport or exercise 2 a sharp downward course; a drop 3 a hollow, depression 4a a sauce or soft mixture into which food is dipped before being eaten b a liquid preparation into which an object or animal may be dipped (e g for cleaning or disinfecting)

diplomacy /dɪˈpləʊməsi/ n 1 the art and practice of conducting international relations 2 skill and tact in handling affairs – **-mat** n – **-matic** adj – **-matically** adv

¹**direct** /dɪˈrekt, daɪ-/ v 1 to address or aim a remark 2 to cause to turn, move, point, or follow a straight course 3 to show or point out the way for 4a to supervise b to order or instruct with authority c to produce a play d NAm to conduct an orchestra

²**direct** adj 1 going from one point to another in time or space without deviation or interruption; straight 2 stemming immediately from a source, cause, or reason 3 frank, straightforward 4a operating without an intervening agency b effected by the action of the people or the electorate and not by representatives 5 consisting of or reproducing the exact words of a speaker or writer – **~ness** n

³**direct** adv 1 from point to point without deviation; by the shortest way 2 without an intervening agency or stage

direction /dɪˈrekʃən, daɪ-/ n 1 guidance or supervision of action 2a the act, art, or technique of directing an orchestra, film, or theatrical production b a word, phrase, or sign indicating the appropriate tempo, mood, or intensity of a passage or movement in music 3 pl explicit instructions on how to do sthg or get to a place 4a the line or course along which sby or sthg moves or is aimed b the point towards which sby or sthg faces 5a a tendency, trend b a guiding or motivating purpose

¹**directly** /dɪˈrektli, daɪ-/ adv 1 in a

direct manner 2a without delay; immediately b soon, shortly

²**directly** conj immediately after; as soon as – infml

director /dɪˈrektə', daɪ-/ n 1 the head of an organized group or administrative unit 2 a member of a governing board entrusted with the overall direction of a company 3 sby who has responsibility for supervising the artistic and technical aspects of a film or play – **~ship** n

dirt /dɜːt/ n 1 a filthy or soiling substance (e g mud or grime) b sby or sthg worthless or contemptible 2 soil 3a obscene or pornographic speech or writing b scandalous or malicious gossip

dirty /ˈdɜːti/ adj 1 not clean or pure b causing sby or sthg to become soiled or covered with dirt 2a base, sordid b unsportsmanlike, unfair c low, despicable 3a indecent, obscene b sexually illicit 4 of weather rough, stormy 5 of colour not clear and bright; dull – **dirtily** adv

disability /ˌdɪsəˈbɪlɪti/ n 1a inability to do sthg (e g pursue an occupation) because of physical or mental impairment b a handicap 2 a legal disqualification

disable /dɪsˈeɪbəl/ v 1 to deprive of legal right, qualification, or capacity 2 to cripple – **~ment** n

disadvantage /ˌdɪsədˈvɑːntɪdʒ/ n 1 an unfavourable, inferior, or prejudicial situation 2 a handicap

disagree /ˌdɪsəˈɡriː/ v 1 to be unlike or at variance 2 to differ in opinion – usu + with 3 to have a bad effect – usu + with – **~ment** n

disappear /ˌdɪsəˈpɪə'/ v 1 to pass from view suddenly or gradually 2 to cease to be or to be known 3 to leave or depart, esp secretly – infml – **~ance** n

disappoint /ˌdɪsəˈpɔɪnt/ v to fail to meet the expectation or hope of; also to sadden by so doing – **~ed** adj – **~edly** adv – **~ing** adj – **~ingly** adv – **~ment** n

disapprove /ˌdɪsəˈpruːv/ v to have or express an unfavourable opinion of – **-proval** n – **-provingly** adv

disaster /dɪˈzɑːstə'/ n 1 a sudden event bringing great damage, loss, or destruction 2 a failure – **-trous** adj – **-trously** adv

disc /dɪsk/, NAm chiefly disk n 1 a thin flat circular object 2 any of various round flat anatomical structures; esp any of the cartilaginous discs between the spinal vertebrae 3 a gramophone record 4 a magnetic disc used for the storage of computer data

¹**discipline** /ˈdɪsɪplɪn/ n 1 a field of study 2 training of the mind and character designed to produce obedience and self-control 3 punishment, chastisement 4 order obtained by enforcing obedience (e g in a school or army) – **-plinary** adj

²**discipline** v 1 to punish or penalize for the sake of discipline 2 to train by instruction and exercise, esp in obedi-

ence and self-control **3** to bring (a group) under control

disclose /dɪsˈkləʊz/ v **1** to expose to view **2** to reveal to public knowledge

discotheque /ˈdɪskətek/ n a nightclub for dancing to usu recorded music

discourage /dɪsˈkʌrɪdʒ/ v **1** to deprive of confidence; dishearten **2a** to hinder, deter *from* **b** to attempt to prevent, esp by showing disapproval – **agingly** adv – **~ ment** n

discover /dɪsˈkʌvə/ v **1** to obtain sight or knowledge of for the first time **2** to make known or visible – fml – **~able** adj – **~er** n – **~y** n

discuss /dɪsˈkʌs/ v **1** to consider or examine (a topic) in speech or writing – **~ion** n

disease /dɪˈziːz/ n **1** a condition of (a part of) a living animal or plant body that impairs the performance of a vital function; (a) sickness, malady **2** a harmful or corrupt development, situation, condition, etc – **~d** adj

¹**disgrace** /dɪsˈɡreɪs/ v **1** to bring reproach or shame to **2** to cause to lose favour or standing

²**disgrace** n **1a** loss of favour, honour, or respect; shame **b** the state of being out of favour **2** sby or sthg shameful

¹**disguise** /dɪsˈɡaɪz/ v **1** to change the appearance or nature of in order to conceal identity **2** to hide the true state or character of

²**disguise** n **1** (the use of) sthg (e g clothing) to conceal one's identity **2** an outward appearance that misrepresents the true nature of sthg

disgust /dɪsˈɡʌst, dɪz-/ n strong aversion aroused by sby or sthg physically or morally distasteful – **disgust** v

¹**dish** /dɪʃ/ n **1a** a shallow open often circular or oval vessel used esp for holding or serving food; *broadly* any vessel from which food is eaten or served **b** pl *the* utensils and tableware used in preparing, serving, and eating a meal **2** a type of food prepared in a particular way **3a** a directional aerial, esp for receiving radio or television transmissions or microwaves, having a concave usu parabolic reflector **b** a hollow or depression **4** an attractive person – infml

²**dish** v **1** to make concave like a dish **2** chiefly Br to ruin or spoil (e g a person or his/her hopes) – infml

dishonest /dɪsˈɒnɪst/ adj not honest, truthful, or sincere – **~ly** adv – **~y** n

¹**dislike** /dɪsˈlaɪk/ v to regard with dislike

²**dislike** /ˌdɪsˈlaɪk/ n (an object of) a feeling of aversion or disapproval

dismay /dɪsˈmeɪ/ v or n (to fill with) sudden consternation or apprehension

dismiss /dɪsˈmɪs/ v **1** to remove or send away, esp from employment or service **2** to put out of one's mind; reject as unworthy of serious consideration **3** to refuse a further hearing to (e g a court case) **4** to bowl out (a batsman or side) in cricket – **~al** n

disobedient /ˌdɪsəˈbiːdɪənt, ˌdɪsəʊ-/ adj refusing or failing to obey – **~ly** adv – **-ience** n

disobey /ˌdɪsəˈbeɪ, ˌdɪsəʊ-/ v to fail to obey

disorder /dɪsˈɔːdə/ n **1** lack of order; confusion **2** breach of the peace or public order **3** an abnormal physical or mental condition; an ailment + **disorder** v

¹**dispatch** /dɪˈspætʃ/ v **1** to send off or away promptly, esp on some task **2** to get through or carry out quickly **3** to kill, esp with quick efficiency – euph

²**dispatch** n **1** an important diplomatic or military message **2** a news item sent into a newspaper by a correspondent **3** promptness and efficiency

dispense /dɪˈspens/ v **1a** to deal out, distribute **b** to administer (e g law or justice) **2** to prepare and give out (drugs, medicine, etc on prescription) **3** to do without – usu + *with* – **dispenser** n

¹**display** /dɪˈspleɪ/ v **1** to expose to view; show **2** to exhibit, esp ostentatiously

²**display** n **1** a presentation or exhibition of sthg in open view **b** an esp ostentatious show or demonstration **c** an eye-catching arrangement of sthg (e g goods for sale) **2a** a pattern of behaviour exhibited esp by male birds in the breeding season

disposable /dɪˈspəʊzəbl/ adj **1** available for use; *specif* remaining after deduction of taxes **2** designed to be used once and then thrown away

dispose /dɪˈspəʊz/ v **1** to incline *to* **2** to put in place; arrange **3** to cause to have a specified attitude *towards* **4** to settle a matter finally; *also* get rid *of*

disposition /ˌdɪspəˈzɪʃən/ n **1a** final arrangement; settlement **b** orderly arrangement **2a** natural temperament **b** a tendency, inclination

disprove /dɪsˈpruːv/ v to prove to be false; refute

¹**dispute** /dɪˈspjuːt/ v **1a** to discuss angrily **b** to call into question **2a** to struggle against; resist **b** to struggle over; contest – **disputation** n – **disputable** adj – **disputably** adv

²**dispute** /dɪˈspjuːt, ˈdɪspjuːt/ n **1** controversy, debate **2** a quarrel, disagreement

disqualify /dɪsˈkwɒlɪfaɪ/ v **1** to make or declare unfit or unsuitable to do sthg **2** to declare ineligible (e g for a prize) because of violation of the rules

dissolve /dɪˈzɒlv/ v **1a** to terminate officially **b** to cause to break up; dismiss **2a** to pass into solution **b** to melt, liquefy **3** to fade away; disperse **4** to fade out (one film or television scene) while fading into another

¹**distance** /ˈdɪstəns/ n **1a** (the amount of) separation in space or time between 2 points or things **b** a distant point or place **2a** remoteness in space **b** reserve, coldness **c** difference, disparity

²**distance** v to place or keep physically or mentally at a distance

distant /ˈdɪstənt/ adj **1a** separated in space or time by a specified distance **b** far-off or remote in space or time **2** not closely related **3** different in kind **4** reserved, aloof **5** coming from or going to a remote place – ~**ly** adv

distil /dɪˈstɪl/ v **1** to subject to or transform by heating and condensing the resulting vapour **2a** to obtain or separate *out* or *off* (as if) by distilling **b** to obtain spirits by distilling the products of fermentation **c** to extract the essence of (e g an idea or subject) – ~**lation** n

distinct /dɪˈstɪŋkt/ adj **1** different, separate *from* **2** readily perceptible to the senses or mind; clear – ~**ly** adv – ~**ness** n

distinction /dɪˈstɪŋkʃən/ n **1** a difference made or marked; a contrast **2** a distinguishing quality or mark **3a** outstanding merit, quality, or worth **b** special honour or recognition

distinguish /dɪˈstɪŋgwɪʃ/ v **1a** to mark or recognize as separate or different – often + *from* **b** to recognize the difference *between* **c** to make (oneself) outstanding or noteworthy **d** to mark as different; characterize **2** to discern; make out – ~**able** adj

distinguished /dɪˈstɪŋgwɪʃt/ adj **1** marked by eminence, distinction, or excellence **2** dignified in manner, bearing, or appearance

distress /dɪˈstres/ n **1** mental or physical anguish **2** a state of danger or desperate need

distribute /dɪˈstrɪbjuːt/ v **1** to divide among several or many **2a** to disperse or scatter over an area **b** to give out, deliver – -**bution** n – -**butional** adj

district /ˈdɪstrɪkt/ n **1** a territorial division made esp for administrative purposes **2** an area or region with a specified character or feature

disturb /dɪˈstɜːb/ v **1a** to break in upon; interrupt **b** to alter the position or arrangement of **2a** to destroy the peace of mind or composure of **b** to throw into disorder **c** to put to inconvenience – ~**ance** n

¹ditch /dɪtʃ/ n a long narrow excavation dug in the earth for defence, drainage, irrigation, etc

²ditch v **1** to make a forced landing of (an aircraft) on water **2** to get rid of; abandon

¹dive /daɪv/ v **1a** to plunge into water headfirst **b** to submerge **2a** to descend or fall steeply **b** to plunge one's hand quickly *into* **3** to lunge or dash headlong

²dive n **1a(1)** a headlong plunge into water; *esp* one executed in a prescribed manner **(2)** submerging (e g by a submarine) **b** a sharp decline **2a** a disreputable bar, club, etc – informal

diver /ˈdaɪvə/ n **1** a person who works or explores underwater for long periods, either carrying a supply of air or having it sent from the surface **2** any of various diving birds

divert /daɪˈvɜːt, dɪ-/ v **1a** to turn aside from one course or use to another **b** to distract **2** to entertain, amuse – **diversion** n – **diversionary** adj

¹divide /dɪˈvaɪd/ v **1** to separate into 2

or more parts, categories, divisions, etc **2** to give out in shares; distribute **3a** to cause to be separate; serve as a boundary between **b** to separate into opposing sides or parties **4** to determine how many times a number contains another number by means of a mathematical operation – **divisible** adj

²divide n **1** a watershed **2** a point or line of division

¹divine /dɪˈvaɪn/ adj **1a** of, being, or proceeding directly from God or a god **b** devoted to the worship of God or a god; sacred **2** delightful, superb – infml – ~**ly** adv

²divine n a clergyman; *esp* one skilled in theology

³divine v **1** to discover, perceive, or foresee intuitively or by supernatural means **2** to discover or locate (e g water or minerals) by means of a divining rod – **diviner** n

division /dɪˈvɪʒən/ n **1** dividing or being divided **2** any of the parts or sections into which a whole is divided **3** *sing or pl in constr* a military unit having the necessary tactical and administrative services to act independently **4** an administrative or operating unit of an organization **5** a group of organisms forming part of a larger group **6** a competitive class or category (e g of a soccer league) **7** sthg that divides, separates, or marks off **8** disagreement, disunity **9** the physical separation into different lobbies of the members of a parliamentary body voting for and against a question **10** the mathematical operation of dividing one number by another

divorce /dɪˈvɔːs/ v **1a** to end marriage with (one's spouse) by divorce **b** to dissolve the marriage between **2** to end the relationship or union of; separate – usu + *from* – **divorce** n

¹dizzy /ˈdɪzi/ adj **1** experiencing a whirling sensation in the head with a tendency to lose balance **2** causing or feeling giddiness or mental confusion **3** foolish, silly – infml

²dizzy v to make dizzy; bewilder

do /duː/ v **does** /dʌz/ *strong* duz/; **did** /dɪd/; **done** /dʌn/ **1a** to carry out the task of; effect, perform (e g do some washing) **b** to act, behave (e g do as I say) **2** to put into a specified condition (e g do him to death) **3** to have as a function (e g what's that book *doing* on the floor?) **4** to cause, impart (e g sthg will *do* you good) **5** to bring to an esp unwanted conclusion; finish – used esp in the past participle (e g that's *done* it) **6a** to fare; get along (e g do well at school) **b** to carry on business or affairs; manage (e g we can *do* without you) **7** to be in progress; happen (e g there's nothing *doing*) to expend, exert (e g did their damnedest to hog the game) **8** to provide or have available (e g they *do* teas here) **9** to bring into existence; produce (e g *did* a portrait of his mother) **10** to put on; perform (e g *do* a Shakespearean comedy) **11** to come to or make an end; finish – used in the past participle; (e g have you *done* with the newspaper?) **12** to suffice, serve (e g half of that will *do*) **13** to be fitting; conform to custom or propriety (e g won't *do* to be late) **14a** to put in order, arrange, clean (e g *do* the garden) **b** to cook (e g likes her steak well *done*) **15** to perform the appropriate professional service or services for (e g the barber will *do* you now) **16a** to work at, esp as a course of study or occupation (e g *do* classics) **b** to solve; WORK OUT (e g *do* a sum) **17** to travel at a (maximum) speed of (e g *do* 70 on the motorway) **18** to serve out, esp as a prison sentence (e g *did* 3 years) **19** to suffice, suit (e g that will *do* nicely) **20** – used as a substitute verb to avoid repetition (e g if you must make a noise; *do* it elsewhere) **21** – used to form present and past tenses expressing emphasis (e g *do* be quiet) **22a** *chiefly Br* to arrest, convict – *slang* (e g get *done* for theft) **b** to treat unfairly; *esp* to cheat, deprive (e g *did* him out of his inheritance) – *infml* **c** to rob – *slang* (e g *do* a shop)

²do *n*, **1** sthg one ought to do – usu *pl* **2** *chiefly Br* a festive party or occasion – *infml*

³do /dəʊ/ **doh** *n* the 1st note of the diatonic scale in solmization

¹dock /dɒk/ *n* any of a genus of coarse weeds whose leaves are used to alleviate nettle stings

²dock *v* **1** to cut (e g a tail) short **2** to make a deduction from (e g wages) **3** to take away (a specified amount) from

³dock *n* **1** a usu artificially enclosed body of water in a port or harbour, where a ship can moor (e g for repair work to be carried out) **2** *pl* *the* total number of such enclosures in a harbour, together with wharves, sheds, etc

⁴dock *v* **1** to come or go into dock **2** *of spacecraft* to join together while in space

⁵dock *n* the prisoner's enclosure in a criminal court

¹doctor /'dɒktə'/ *n* **1** a holder of the highest level of academic degree conferred by a university **2** one qualified to practise medicine; a physician or surgeon **3** sby skilled in repairing or treating a usu specified type of machine, vehicle, etc

²doctor *v* **1a** to give medical treatment to **b** to repair, mend **2a** to adapt or modify for a desired end **b** to alter in a dishonest way **3** to castrate or spay – *euph*

¹document /'dɒkjʊmənt/ *n* an original or official paper that gives information about or proof of sthg – ~ary *adj*

²document /'dɒkjʊment/ *v* **1** to provide documentary evidence of **2** to support with factual evidence, references, etc **3** to provide (a ship) with papers required by law recording ownership, cargo, etc

¹dodge /dɒdʒ/ *v* **1** to shift position suddenly (e g to avoid a blow or a pursuer) **2** to evade (a duty) usu by trickery

²dodge *n* **1** a sudden movement to avoid

sthg **2** a clever device to evade or trick

does /dəz; *strong* dʌz/ *pres 3rd sing of* **do**

¹dog /dɒg/ *n* **1a** a 4-legged flesh-eating domesticated mammal occurring in a great variety of breeds and prob descended from the common wolf **b** any of a family of carnivores to which the dog belongs **c** a male dog **2** any of various usu simple mechanical devices for holding, fastening, etc that consist of a spike, rod, or bar **3** *chiefly NAm* sthg inferior of its kind **4** an esp worthless man or fellow **5** *pl* ruin

²dog *v* to pursue closely like a dog; hound

³dog *adj* male

doing /'duːɪŋ/ *n* **1** the act or result of performing; action (e g this must be your *doing*) **2** effort, exertion (e g that will take a great deal of *doing*) **3** *pl* things that are done or that occur; activities

dole /dəʊl/ *n* **1** a distribution of food, money, or clothing to the needy **2** *the* government unemployment benefit

dole out *v* to give, distribute, or deliver, esp in small portions

doll /dɒl/ *n* **1** a small-scale figure of a human being used esp as a child's toy **2a** a (pretty but often silly) young woman – *infml* **b** an attractive person – *slang*

dollar /'dɒlə'/ *n* (a coin or note representing) the basic money unit of the USA, Canada, Australia, etc

¹dome /dəʊm/ *n* a (nearly) hemispherical roof or vault – ~**d** *adj*

²dome *v* to cover with or form into a dome

¹domestic /də'mestɪk/ *adj* **1** of or devoted to the home or the family **2** of one's own or some particular country; not foreign **3a** living near or about the habitations of human beings **b** tame; *also* bred by human beings for some specific purpose (e g food, hunting, etc) – ~**ally** *adv*

²domestic *n* a household servant

dominate /'dɒmɪneɪt/ *v* **1** to exert controlling influence or power over **2** to overlook from a superior height **3** to occupy a commanding or preeminent position in **4** to have or exert mastery or control – **-nation** *n*

donate /dəʊ'neɪt/ *v* to make a gift (of), esp to a public or charitable cause – **-ion** *n*

¹done /dʌn/ **1** *past part of* **do 2** *chiefly dial & NAm past of* **do**

²done *adj* **1** socially conventional or accepted (e g it's not *done* to eat peas off your knife) **2** arrived at or brought to an end; completed **3** physically exhausted; spent **4** no longer involved; through (e g I'm *done* with the Army) **5** doomed to failure, defeat, or death **6** cooked sufficiently **7** arrested, imprisoned – *slang*

³done *interj* – used in acceptance of a bet or transaction

donkey /'dɒŋki/ *n* **1** the domestic ass **2** a stupid or obstinate person

¹doom /duːm/ n 1 God's judgment of the world 2a an (unhappy) destiny b unavoidable death or destruction; also environmental catastrophe – often in combination

²doom v to destine, esp to failure or destruction

door /dɔː/ n 1 a usu swinging or sliding barrier by which an entry is closed and opened; also a similar part of a piece of furniture 2 a doorway 3 a means of access

doorway /'dɔːweɪ/ n an entrance into a building or room that is closed by means of a door

¹dose /dəʊs/ n 1 the measured quantity of medicine to be taken at one time 2 a part of an experience to which one is exposed 3 an infection with a venereal disease – slang

²dose v to give a dose, esp of medicine, to

¹dot /dɒt/ n 1 a small spot; a speck 2a(1) a small point made with a pointed instrument (2) a small round mark used in spelling or punctuation b(1) a point after a note or rest in music indicating lengthening of the time value by one half (2) a point over or under a note indicating that it is to be played staccato 3 a precise point, esp in time 4 a signal (eg a flash or audible tone) of relatively short duration that is one of the 2 fundamental units of Morse code

²dot v 1 to mark with a dot 2 to intersperse with dots or objects scattered at random

¹double /'dʌbəl/ adj 1 twofold, dual 2 consisting of 2, usu combined, similar members or parts 3 being twice as great or as many 4 marked by duplicity; deceitful 5 folded in 2 6 of twofold or extra size, strength, or value

²double n 1 a double amount; esp a double measure of spirits 2a a living person who closely resembles another living person b a ghostly counterpart of a living person c(1) an understudy (2) one who resembles an actor and takes his/her place in scenes calling for special skills 3 a sharp turn or twist 4a a bet in which the winnings and stake from a first race are bet on a second race b two wins in or on horse races, esp in a single day's racing 5 an act of doubling in a card game 6 the outermost narrow ring on a dartboard counting double the stated score; also a throw in darts that lands there

³double adv 1 to twice the extent or amount 2 two together

⁴double v 1a to increase by adding an equal amount b to make a call in bridge that increases the value of tricks won or lost on (an opponent's bid) 2a to make into 2 thicknesses; fold b to clench c to cause to stoop or bend over – usu + up or over 3 to become twice as much or as many 4 to turn back on one's course – usu + back 5 to become bent or folded, usu in the middle – usu + up or over 6 to serve an additional purpose – usu + as

¹doubt /daʊt/ v 1 to be in doubt about 2a to lack confidence in; distrust b to consider unlikely – ~er n

²doubt n 1 (a state of) uncertainty of belief or opinion 2 a lack of confidence; distrust 3 an inclination not to believe or accept; a reservation

doubtful /'daʊtfəl/ adj 1 causing doubt; open to question 2a lacking a definite opinion; hesitant b uncertain in outcome; not settled 3 of questionable worth, honesty, or validity – ~ly adv

doubtless /'daʊtlɪs/ adv 1 without doubt 2 probably

dough /dəʊ/ n 1 a mixture that consists essentially of flour or meal and milk, water, or another liquid and is stiff enough to knead or roll 2 money – slang

dove /dʌv/ n 1 any of various (smaller and slenderer) types of pigeon 2 an advocate of negotiation and compromise; esp an opponent of war – usu contrasted with hawk

¹down /daʊn/ n (a region of) undulating treeless usu chalk uplands, esp in S England – usu pl with sing. meaning

²down adv 1a at or towards a relatively low level (eg down into the cellar) b downwards from the surface of the earth or water c below the horizon d downstream e in or into a lying or sitting position (eg lie down) f to or on the ground, surface, or bottom (eg telephone wires are down) g so as to conceal a particular surface (eg turned it face down) h downstairs 2 on the spot 2; esp as an initial payment (eg paid £10 down) 3a(1) in or into a relatively low condition or status (eg family has come down in the world) – sometimes used interjectionally to express opposition (eg down with the oppressors!) (2) to prison – often + go or send b(1) in or into a state of relatively low intensity or activity (eg calm down) (2) into a slower pace or lower gear (eg changed down into second) c lower in amount, price, figure, or rank (eg prices are down) d behind an opponent (eg we're 3 points down) 4a so as to be known, recognized, or recorded, esp on paper (eg scribbled it down; you're down to speak next) b so as to be firmly held in position (eg stick down the flap of the c to the moment of catching or discovering (eg track the criminal down) 5 in a direction conventionally the opposite of up: eg a to leeward b in or towards the south c chiefly Br away from the capital of a country or from a university city 6 downwards 7a to a concentrated state (eg got his report down to 3 pages) b so as to be flattened, reduced, eroded, or diluted (eg heels worn down) c completely from top to bottom (eg hose the car down)

³down adj 1 directed or going downwards (eg the down escalator) 2a depressed, dejected b ill (eg down with flu) 3 having been finished or dealt with (eg eight down and two to go) 4 with the rudder to windward – used with reference to a ship's helm 5 chiefly Br bound in a direction regarded as down; *esp* travelling away from a large town, esp London

⁴down *prep* **1a** down along, round, through, towards, in, into, or on **b** at the bottom of (e g the bathroom is *down* those stairs) **2** *Br* down to; to (e g going *down* the shops) – nonstandard

⁵down *n* a grudge, prejudice – often in *have a down on*

⁶down *v* **1** to cause to go or come down **2** to drink down; swallow quickly – infml **3** to defeat – infml

⁷down *n* a covering of soft fluffy feathers

¹downhill /ˌdaʊn'hɪl/ *n* a skiing race downhill against time

²downhill /ˌdaʊn'hɪl/ *adv* **1** towards the bottom of a hill **2** towards a lower or inferior state or level – in *go downhill*

³downhill /ˌdaʊn'hɪl/ *adj* sloping downhill

¹downstairs /ˌdaʊn'steəz/ *adv* down the stairs; on or to a lower floor

²downstairs /ˌdaʊn'steəz/ *adj* situated on the main, lower, or ground floor of a building

³downstairs *n, pl* **downstairs** the lower floor of a building

doze /dəʊz/ *v* **1** to sleep lightly **2** to fall into a light sleep – usu + *off* – **doze** *n*

dozen /'dʌzən/ *n, pl* **dozens, dozen 1** a group of 12 **2** an indefinitely large number – usu pl with sing. meaning – **dozen** *adj*

¹drag /dræg/ *n* **1** a device for dragging under water to search for objects **2** sthg that retards motion, action, or progress; a burden **3a** a drawing along or over a surface with effort or pressure **b** motion effected with slowness or difficulty **c** a drawing into the mouth of pipe, cigarette, or cigar smoke – infml **4a** woman's clothing worn by a man – slang; often in *in drag* **b** clothing – slang **5** a dull or boring person or experience – slang

²drag *v* **1a** to draw slowly or heavily; haul **b** to cause to move with painful or undue slowness or difficulty **2a** to search (a body of water) with a drag **b** to catch with a dragnet or trawl **3** to bring by force or compulsion – infml **4** to hang or lag behind **b** to trail along on the ground **6** to move or proceed laboriously or tediously – infml **7** to draw tobacco smoke into the mouth – usu + *on*; infml

³drag *adj* of drag racing

dragon /'drægən/ *n* **1** a mythical winged and clawed monster, often breathing fire **2** a fierce, combative, or very strict person

¹drain /dreɪn/ *v* **1a** to draw off (liquid) gradually or completely **b** to exhaust physically or emotionally **2a** to make gradually dry **b** to carry away the surface water of **c** to deplete or empty (as if) by drawing off gradually **d** to empty by drinking the contents of **3** to flow off gradually **4** to become gradually dry

²drain *n* **1** a means (e g a pipe) by which usu liquid matter is drained away **2** a

gradual outflow or withdrawal **3** sthg that causes depletion; a burden

drama /'drɑːmə/ *n* **1** a composition in verse or prose intended to portray life or character or to tell a story through action and dialogue; *specif* a play **2** dramatic art, literature, or affairs **3** a situation or set of events having the qualities of a drama – ~ **tize** *v*

dramatic /drə'mætɪk/ *adj* **1** of drama **2a** suitable to or characteristic of drama; vivid **b** striking in appearance or effect – ~ **ally** *adv*

drank /dræŋk/ *past of* **drink**

drastic /'dræstɪk/ *adj* radical in effect or action; severe – ~ **ally** *adv*

¹draught /drɑːft/ *n* **1** a team of animals together with what they draw **2** the act or an instance of drinking; *also* the portion drunk in such an act **3** the act of drawing (e g from a cask); *also* a quantity of liquid so drawn **4** the depth of water a ship requires to float in, esp when loaded **5** a current of air in a closed-in space

²draught *adj* **1** used for drawing loads **2** served from the barrel or cask

draughts /drɑːfts/ *n pl but sing or pl in constr, Br* a game for 2 players each of whom moves his/her usu 12 draughtsmen according to fixed rules across a chessboard usu using only the black squares

¹draw /drɔː/ *v* **drawn 1** to pull, haul **2** to cause to go in a certain direction **3a** to attract **b** to bring in, gather, or derive from a specified source **c** to bring on oneself; provoke **d** to bring out by way of response; elicit **4** to inhale **5a** to bring or pull out, esp with effort **b** to disembowel **c** to cause (blood) to flow **6a** to accumulate, gain **b** to take (money) from a place of deposit – often + *out* **c** to use in making a cash demand **d** to receive regularly, esp from a particular source **7a** to take (cards) from a dealer or pack **b** to receive or take at random **8** to strike (a ball) so as to impart a curved motion or backspin **9** to produce a likeness of (e g by making lines on a surface); portray, delineate **10** to formulate or arrive at by reasoning **11** to pull together and close (e g curtains) **12** to stretch or shape (esp metal) by pulling through thin; *also* to produce (e g a wire) thus **13** to come or go steadily or gradually **14** to advance as far as a specified position **15a** to pull back a bowstring **b** to bring out a weapon **16** to produce or allow a draught **17** to sketch **18** to finish a competition or contest without either side winning **19** to obtain resources (e g of information) **20** *chiefly NAm* to suck in sthg, esp tobacco smoke – usu + *on*

²draw *n* **1a** a sucking pull on sthg held between the lips **b** the removing of a handgun from its holster in order to shoot **2** a drawing of lots; a raffle **3** a contest left undecided; a tie **4** sthg that draws public attention or patronage **5** the usu random assignment of starting positions in a competition, esp a competitive sport

drawer /drɔ:ʳ/ n 1 one who draws a bill of exchange or order for payment or makes a promissory note 2 an open-topped box in a piece of furniture which to open and close slides back and forth in its frame 3 pl an undergarment for the lower body – now usu humor

¹**dread** /dred/ v 1 to fear greatly 2 to be extremely apprehensive about

²**dread** n (the object of) great fear, uneasiness, or apprehension

³**dread** adj causing or inspiring dread

dreadful /'dredfəl/ adj 1 inspiring dread; causing great and oppressive fear 2a extremely unpleasant or shocking b very disagreeable (e g through dullness or poor quality) 3 extreme – ~ness n – ~ly adv

¹**dream** /dri:m/ n 1 a series of thoughts, images, or emotions occurring during sleep 2 sthg notable for its beauty, excellence, or enjoyable quality 3 a strongly desired goal; an ambition; also a realization of an ambition – often used attributively

²**dream** v dreamed, dreamt 1 to have a dream (of) 2 to indulge in daydreams or fantasies 3 to consider as a possibility; imagine 4 to pass (time) in reverie or inaction – usu + away

¹**drench** /drentʃ/ n a poisonous or medicinal drink, esp put down the throat of an animal

²**drench** v 1 to administer a drench to (an animal) 2 to make thoroughly wet (e g with falling water or by immersion); saturate

¹**dress** /dres/ v 1a to put clothes on b to provide with clothing 2 to add decorative details or accessories; embellish 3 to prepare for use or service; esp to prepare (e g a chicken) for cooking or eating 4a to apply dressings or medicaments to (e g a wound) b(1) to arrange (the hair) (2) to groom and curry (an animal) c to kill and prepare for market d to cultivate, esp by applying manure or fertilizer e to finish the surface of (e g timber, stone, or textiles) f to arrange goods on a display in (e g a shop window) 5a to put on clothing b to put on or wear formal, elaborate, or fancy clothes 6 of a man to have one's genitals lying on a specified side of the trouser crutch

²**dress** n 1 utilitarian or ornamental covering for the human body; esp clothing suitable for a particular purpose or occasion 2 a 1-piece outer garment including both top and skirt usu for a woman or girl 3 covering, adornment, or appearance appropriate or peculiar to a specified time

³**dress** adj of, being, or suitable for an occasion requiring or permitting formal dress

dressing /'dresɪŋ/ n 1 a seasoning, sauce, or stuffing 2 material applied to cover a wound, sore, etc 3 manure or compost to improve the growth of plants

dressing gown n a loose robe worn esp over nightclothes or when not fully dressed

drew /dru:/ past of draw

¹**dribble** /'drɪbəl/ v 1 to fall or flow in drops or in a thin intermittent stream; trickle 2 to let saliva trickle from the mouth; drool 3 to come or issue in piecemeal or disconnected fashion 4 to propel (a ball or puck) by successive slight taps or bounces with hand, foot, or stick 5 to proceed by dribbling

²**dribble** n 1 a small trickling stream or flow 2 a tiny or insignificant bit or quantity 3 an act or instance of dribbling

¹**drift** /drɪft/ n 1a a mass of sand, snow, etc deposited (as if) by wind or water b rock debris deposited by natural wind, water, etc; specif a deposit of clay, sand, gravel, and boulders transported by (running water from) a glacier 2 a general underlying tendency or meaning, esp of what is spoken or written 3 the motion or action of drifting: e g a a ship's deviation from its course caused by currents b a slow-moving ocean current c an easy, moderate, more or less steady flow along a spatial course d a gradual shift in attitude, opinion, or emotion e an aimless course, with no attempt at direction or control 4 a nearly horizontal mine passage on or parallel to a vein or rock stratum

²**drift** v 1a to become driven or carried along by a current of water or air b to move or float smoothly and effortlessly 2a to move in a random or casual way b to become carried along aimlessly 3 to pile up under the force of wind or water 4 to pile up in a drift

¹**drill** /drɪl/ v 1a to bore or drive a hole in (as if) by the piercing action of a drill b to make (e g a hole) by piercing action 2a to instruct and exercise by repeating b to train or exercise in military drill

²**drill** n 1 (a device or machine for rotating) a tool with an edged or pointed end for making a hole in a solid substance by revolving or by a succession of blows 2 training in marching and the manual of arms 3 a physical or mental exercise aimed at improving facility and skill by regular practice 4 a marine snail that bores through oyster shells and eats the flesh 5 chiefly Br the approved or correct procedure for accomplishing sthg efficiently – infml

³**drill** n 1a a shallow furrow into which seed is sown b a row of seed sown in such a furrow 2 a planting implement that makes holes or furrows, drops in the seed and sometimes fertilizer, and covers them with earth

⁴**drill** v to sow (seeds) by dropping along a shallow furrow

⁵**drill** n a durable cotton fabric in twill weave

¹**drink** /drɪŋk/ v drank; drunk, drank 1a to swallow (a liquid); also to swallow the liquid contents of (e g a cup) b to take in or suck up; absorb c to take in or receive avidly – usu + in 2 to join in (a toast) 3 to take liquid into the mouth

for swallowing **4** to drink alcoholic beverages, esp habitually or to excess

¹drink *n* **1a** liquid suitable for swallowing **b** alcoholic drink **2** a draught or portion of liquid for drinking **3** excessive consumption of alcoholic beverages **4** *the ocean*; *broadly* any large body of water – + *the*; *infml*

¹drip /drɪp/ *v* **1a** to let fall drops of moisture or liquid **b** to overflow (as if) with moisture **2** to fall or let fall (as if) in drops

²drip *n* **1a** the action or sound of falling in drops **b** liquid that falls, overflows, or is forced out in drops **2** a projection for throwing off rainwater **3** a device for the administration of a liquid at a slow rate, esp into a vein **4** a dull or inconsequential person – *infml*

¹drive /draɪv/ *v* **driven 1a** to set in motion by physical force **b** to force into position by blows **c** to repulse or cause to go by force, authority, or influence **d** to set or keep in motion or operation **2a** to control and direct the course of (a vehicle or draught animal) **b** to convey or transport in a vehicle **3** to carry on or through energetically **4a** to exert inescapable or persuasive pressure on; force **b** to compel to undergo or suffer a change (e g in situation, awareness, or emotional state) **c** to urge relentlessly to continuous exertion **5** to cause (e g game or cattle) to move in a desired direction **6a** to propel (an object of play) swiftly **b** to play a drive in cricket at (a ball) or at the bowling of (a bowler) **7** to rush or dash rapidly or with force against an obstruction **8** to imply as an ultimate meaning or conclusion – + *at*

²drive *n* **1** a trip in a carriage or motor vehicle **2** a private road giving access from a public way to a building on private land **3** a (military) offensive, aggressive, or expansionist move **4** a strong systematic group effort; a campaign **5a** a motivating instinctual need or acquired desire **b** great zeal in pursuing one's ends **6a** the means for giving motion to a machine (part) **b** the means by or position from which the movement of a motor vehicle is controlled or directed **7** the act or an instance of driving an object of play; *esp* an attacking cricket stroke played conventionally with a straight bat and designed to send the ball in front of the batsman's wicket

¹droop /druːp/ *v* **1** to (let) hang or incline downwards **2** to become depressed or weakened; languish

²droop *n* the condition or appearance of drooping

¹drop /drɒp/ *n* **1a(1)** the quantity of fluid that falls in 1 spherical mass **(2)** *pl* a dose of medicine measured by drops **b** a minute quantity **2a** an ornament that hangs from a piece of jewellery (e g an earring) **b** a small globular often medicated sweet or lozenge **3a** the act or an instance of dropping; a fall **b** a decline in quantity or quality **4** the distance from a higher to a lower level or

through which sthg drops **5** sthg that drops, hangs, or falls: e g **a** an unframed piece of cloth stage scenery **b** a hinged platform on a gallows **6** a small quantity of drink, esp alcohol; *broadly* an alcoholic drink – *infml* **7** (a secret place used for the deposit and collection of) letters or stolen or illegal goods – *slang*

¹drop *v* **1** to fall in drops **2a(1)** to fall, esp unexpectedly or suddenly **(2)** to descend from one level to another **b** to fall in a state of collapse or death **3a** to cease to be of concern; lapse **b** to become less **4** to let fall; cause to fall **5a** to lower from one level or position to another **b** to cause to lessen or decrease; reduce **6** to set down from a ship or vehicle; unload; *also* to airdrop **7a** to give up (e g an idea) **b** to leave incomplete; cease **c** to break off an association or connection with; *also* to leave out of a team or group **8a** to utter or mention in a casual way **b** to send through the post **9** to lose – *infml*

drought /draʊt/ *n* **1** a prolonged period of dryness **2** a prolonged shortage of sthg

¹drove /drəʊv/ *n* **1** a group of animals driven or moving in a body **2** a crowd of people moving or acting together

²drove *past of* **drive**

drown /draʊn/ *v* **1a** to suffocate by submergence, esp in water **b** to wet thoroughly; drench **2** to engage (oneself) deeply and strenuously **3** to blot out (a sound) by making a loud noise **4** to destroy (e g a sensation or an idea) as if by drowning

¹drug /drʌg/ *n* **1** a substance used as (or in the preparation of) a medication **2** a substance that causes addiction or habituation

²drug *v* **1** to administer a drug to **2** to lull or stupefy (as if) with a drug

¹drum /drʌm/ *n* **1** a percussion instrument usu consisting of a hollow cylinder with a drumhead stretched over each end, that is beaten with a stick or a pair of sticks in playing **2** the tympanic membrane of the ear **3** the sound made by striking a drum; *also* any similar sound **4** a cylindrical container; *specif* a large usu metal container for liquids

²drum *v* **1** to beat a drum **2** to make a succession of strokes, taps, or vibrations that produce drumlike sounds **3** to throb or sound rhythmically **4** to summon or enlist (as if) by beating a drum **5** to instil (an idea or lesson) by constant repetition – usu + *into* or *out of* **6** to strike or tap repeatedly **7** to produce (rhythmic sounds) by such action

¹drunk /drʌŋk/ *past part of* **drink**

²drunk *adj* **1** under the influence of alcohol **2** dominated by an intense feeling

¹dry /draɪ/ *adj* **1a** (relatively) free from a liquid, esp water **b** not in or under water **c** lacking precipitation or humidity **2a** characterized by exhaustion of a supply of water or liquid **b** devoid of natural moisture; *also* thirsty **c** no longer sticky or damp **d** *of a mammal* not giving milk **e** lacking freshness; stale **3** not shedding or accompanied by tears **4** prohibiting the manufacture or distribution of alcoholic beverages **5** lacking sweetness; *sec* **6** functioning without lubrication **7** built or constructed without a process which requires water **8a** not showing or communicating warmth, enthusiasm, or feeling; impassive **b** uninteresting **c** lacking embellishment, bias, or emotional concern; plain **9** not yielding what is expected or desired; unproductive **10** marked by a matter-of-fact, ironic, or terse manner of expression – ~**ly**, **drily** *adv* – ~**ness** *n*

²**dry** *v* to make or become dry – often + **out**

¹**duck** /dʌk/ *n* **1a** any of various swimming birds in which the neck and legs are short, the bill is often broad and flat, and the sexes are almost always different from each other in plumage **b** the flesh of any of these birds used as food **2** a female duck **3** *chiefly Br* dear – often pl with sing. meaning but sing. in constr; *infml*

²**duck** *v* **1** to plunge (something) under the surface of water **2** to move or lower the head or body suddenly, esp as a bow or to avoid being hit **3** to avoid, evade (a duty, question, or responsibility) – **duck** *n*

³**duck** *n* a durable closely woven usu cotton fabric

⁴**duck** *n* a score of nought, esp in cricket

¹**due** /dju:/ *adj* **1** owed or owing as a debt **2a** owed or owing as a natural or moral right (e g got his *due* reward) **b** appropriate (e g after *due* consideration) **3a** (capable of) satisfying a need, obligation, or duty **b** regular, lawful (e g *due* proof of loss) **4** ascribable – + **to** **5** payable **6** required or expected in the prearranged or normal course of events (e g *due* to arrive soon)

²**due** *n* sthg due or owed: e g **a** sthg esp nonmaterial that rightfully belongs to one **b** pl fees, charges

³**due** *adv* directly, exactly – used before points of the compass

¹**duel** /'dju:əl/ *n* **1** a formal combat with weapons fought between 2 people in the presence of witnesses in order to settle a quarrel **2** a conflict between usu evenly matched antagonistic people, ideas, or forces

²**duel** *v* to fight a duel

¹**dug** /dʌg/ *past of* **dig**

²**dug** *n* an udder; *also* a teat – usu used with reference to animals

¹**dull** /dʌl/ *adj* **1** mentally slow; stupid **2a** slow in perception or sensibility; insensible **b** lacking zest or vivacity; listless **3** lacking sharpness of cutting edge or point; blunt **4** not resonant or ringing **5** cloudy, overcast **6** boring, uninteresting – ~**y** *adv* – ~**ness** *n*

²**dull** *v* to make or become dull

dumb /dʌm/ *adj* **1** (temporarily) devoid of the power of speech **2** not expressed in uttered words **3** not willing to speak **4** stupid – ~**ly** *adv* – ~**ness** *n*

¹**dummy** /'dʌmi/ *n* **1** the exposed hand in bridge played by the declarer in addition to his/her own hand; *also* the player whose hand is a dummy **2** an imitation or copy of sthg used to reproduce some of the attributes of the original; e g **a** *chiefly Br* a rubber teat given to babies to suck in order to soothe them **b** a large puppet in usu human form, used by a ventriloquist **c** a model of the human body, esp the torso, used for fitting or displaying clothes **3** a person or corporation that seems to act independently but is in reality acting for or at the direction of another **5** an instance of dummying an opponent in sports **6** a dull or stupid person – *infml*

²**dummy** *adj* resembling or being a dummy: e g **a** sham, artificial **b** existing in name only; fictitious

³**dummy** *v* to deceive an opponent (e g in rugby or soccer) by pretending to pass or release the ball while still retaining possession of it

¹**dump** /dʌmp/ *v* **1a** to unload or let fall in a heap or mass **b** to get rid of unceremoniously or irresponsibly; abandon **2** to sell in quantity at a very low price; *specif* to sell abroad at less than the market price at home

²**dump** *n* **1a** an accumulation of discarded materials (e g refuse) **b** a place where such materials are dumped **2** a quantity of esp military reserve materials accumulated in 1 place **3** a disorderly, slovenly, or dilapidated place – *infml*

dunce /dʌns/ *n* a dull or stupid person

dungeon /'dʌndʒən/ *n* a dark usu underground prison or vault, esp in a castle

¹**duplicate** /'dju:plɪkɨt/ *adj* **1a** consisting of or existing in 2 corresponding or identical parts or examples **b** being the same as another **2** being a card game, *specif* bridge, in which different players play identical hands in order to compare scores

²**duplicate** /'dju:plɪkeɪt/ *n* **1** either of 2 things that exactly resemble each other; *specif* an equally valid copy of a legal document **2** a copy

³**duplicate** *v* to make an exact copy of – ~**cation** *n*

during /'djʊərɪŋ/ *prep* **1** throughout the whole duration of **2** at some point in the course of

dusk /dʌsk/ *n* (the darker part of) twilight

¹**dust** /dʌst/ *n* **1** fine dry particles of any solid matter, esp earth; *specif* the fine particles of waste that settle esp on household surfaces **2** the particles into which sthg, esp the human body, disintegrates or decays **3** sthg worthless **4** the surface of the ground **5a** a cloud of dust **b** confusion, disturbance – esp in **kick up/raise a dust** – ~**less** *adj*

²**dust** *v* **1** to make free of dust (e g by wiping or beating) **2** to prepare to use again – usu + **down** or **off** **3a** to sprinkle

with fine particles **b** to sprinkle in the form of dust **4** *of a bird* to work dust into the feathers **5** to remove dust (e g from household articles), esp by wiping or brushing

dustbin /'dʌst,bɪn/ *n, Br* a container for holding household refuse until collection

dusty /'dʌsti/ *adj* **1** covered with or full of dust **2** consisting of dust; powdery **3** resembling dust, esp in consistency or colour **4** lacking vitality; dry

duty /'dju:ti/ *n* **1** conduct due to parents and superiors; respect **2a** tasks, conduct, service, or functions that arise from one's position, job, or moral obligations **b** assigned (military) service or business **3a** a moral or legal obligation **b** the force of moral obligation **4** a tax, esp on imports

¹**dwarf** /dwɔːf/ *n, pl* **dwarfs, dwarves 1** a person of unusually small stature **2** an animal or plant much below normal size **3** a small manlike creature in esp Norse and Germanic mythology who was skilled as a craftsman

²**dwarf** *v* **1** to stunt the growth of **2** to cause to appear smaller

dwell /dwel/ *v* **dwelt, dwelled 1** to remain for a time **2** to keep the attention directed, esp in speech or writing; linger – + *on* or *upon* **3** to live as a resident; reside – *fml*

dwindle /'dwɪndl/ *v* **dwindling** to become steadily less in quantity; shrink, diminish

¹**dye** /daɪ/ *n* a soluble or insoluble colouring matter

²**dye** *v* to impart a new and often permanent colour to, esp by dipping in a dye – **dyer** *n*

dynamic /daɪ'næmɪk, dɪ-/ *adj* **1a** of physical force or energy in motion **b** of dynamics **2a** marked by continuous activity or change **b** energetic, forceful – ~**ally** *adv*

dynamite /'daɪnəmaɪt/ *n* **1** a blasting explosive that is made of nitroglycerine absorbed in a porous material **2** sby or sthg that has explosive force or effect – *infml*

E

¹**each** /iːtʃ/ *adj* being one of 2 or more distinct individuals considered separately and often forming a group

²**each** *pron* each one

³**each** *adv* to or for each; apiece

each other *pron* each of 2 or more in reciprocal action or relation – not used as subject of a clause (e g wore *each other's* shirts)

eager /'iːgə/ *adj* marked by keen, enthusiastic, or impatient desire or interest – ~**ly** *adv* – ~**ness** *n*

eagle /'iːgl/ *n* **1** any of various large birds of prey noted for their strength, size, gracefulness, keenness of vision,

and powers of flight **2** any of various emblematic or symbolic representations of an eagle: e g **a** the standard of the ancient Romans **b** the seal or standard of a nation (e g the USA) having an eagle as emblem **3** a golf score for 1 hole of 2 strokes less than par

¹**ear** /ɪə/ *n* **1** (the external part of) the characteristic vertebrate organ of hearing and equilibrium **2** the sense or act of hearing **3** sthg resembling an ear in shape or position; *esp* a projecting part (e g a lug or handle) **4a** sympathetic attention **b** *pl* notice, awareness

²**ear** *n* the fruiting spike of a cereal, including both the seeds and protective structures

¹**early** /'ɜːli/ *adv* **1** at or near the beginning of a period of time, a development, or a series **2** before the usual or proper time

²**early** *adj* **1a** of or occurring near the beginning of a period of time, a development, or a series **(2)** primitive **2a** occurring before the usual time **b** occurring in the near future **c** maturing or producing sooner than related forms – **-liness** *n*

earn /ɜːn/ *v* **1** to receive (e g money) as return for effort, esp for work done or services rendered **2** to bring in as income **3a** to gain or deserve because of one's behaviour or qualities **b** to make worthy of or obtain for – ~**er** *n*

¹**earnest** /'ɜːnɪst/ *n* a serious and intent mental state – esp in *in earnest*

²**earnest** *adj* determined and serious – ~**ly** *adv* – ~**ness** *n*

³**earnest** *n* **1** sthg of value, esp money, given by a buyer to a seller to seal a bargain **2** a token of what is to come; a pledge

earnings /'ɜːnɪŋz/ *n pl* money earned; *esp* gross revenue

¹**earth** /ɜːθ/ *n* **1** soil **2** the sphere of mortal or worldly existence as distinguished from spheres of spiritual life **3a** areas of land as distinguished from sea and air **b** the solid ground **4** *often cap* the planet on which we live that is third in order from the sun **5** the people of the planet earth **6** the lair of a fox, badger, etc **7** *chiefly Br* an electrical connection to earth

²**earth** *v* **1** to drive (e g a fox) to hiding in its earth **2** to draw soil about (plants) – usu + *up* **3** *chiefly Br* to connect electrically with earth

earthquake /'ɜːθkweɪk/ *n* a (repeated) usu violent earth tremor caused by volcanic action or processes within the earth's crust

¹**ease** /iːz/ *n* **1** being comfortable: e g **a** freedom from pain, discomfort, or anxiety **b** freedom from labour or difficulty **c** freedom from embarrassment or constraint; naturalness **2** facility, effortlessness **3** easing or being eased

²**ease** *v* **1** to free from sthg that pains, disquiets, or burdens – + *of* **2** to alleviate **3** to lessen the pressure or tension of, esp by slackening, lifting, or shifting **4** to make less difficult **5** to manoeuvre gently or carefully in a specified way **6**

to decrease in activity, intensity, or severity – often + *off* or *up* **7** to manoeuvre oneself gently or carefully

easily /'iːzɪli/ *adv* **1** without difficulty **2** without doubt; by far

¹**east** /iːst/ *adj or adv* towards, at, belonging to, or coming from the east

²**east** *n* **1** (the compass point corresponding to) the direction 90° to the right of north that is the general direction of sunrise **2a** *often cap* regions or countries lying to the east of a specified or implied point of orientation **b** *cap* regions lying to the east of Europe **3** the altar end of a church **4** *sby* (e g a bridge player) occupying a position designated east

Easter /'iːstə/ *n* a feast that commemorates Christ's resurrection and is observed on the first Sunday after the first full moon following March 21

eastern /'iːstən/ *adj* **1** *often cap* (characteristic) of a region conventionally designated east **2** *cap* **3 Eastern, Eastern Orthodox** of the Russian or Greek Orthodox churches

¹**easy** /'iːzɪ/ *adj* **1** causing or involving little difficulty or discomfort **2a** not severe; lenient **b** readily prevailed on; compliant: e g (1) not difficult to deceive or take advantage of (2) readily persuaded to have sexual relations – infml **3a** plentiful in supply at low or declining interest rates **b** less in demand and usu lower in price **4a** marked by peace and comfort **b** not hurried or strenuous **c** free from pain, annoyance, or anxiety **5** marked by social ease **6** not burdensome or difficult **7** marked by ready facility and freedom from constraint **8** *chiefly Br* not having marked preferences on a particular issue – infml – **easiness** *n*

²**easy** *adv* **1** easily **2** without undue speed or excitement; slowly, cautiously

eat /iːt/ *v* ate; eaten **1** to take in through the mouth and swallow as food **2** to consume gradually; corrode **3** to vex, bother – infml **4** to take food or a meal

¹**echo** /'ekəʊ/ *n, pl* echoes **1** the repetition of a sound caused by the reflection of sound waves **2** *sby* or *sthg* that repeats or imitates another **3** a repercussion, result **4** a soft repetition of a musical phrase

²**echo** *v* **1** to resound with echoes **2** to produce an echo **3** to repeat, imitate

¹**eclipse** /'klɪps/ *n* **1a** the total or partial obscuring of one celestial body by another **b** passage into the shadow of a celestial body **2** a falling into obscurity or decay; a decline

²**eclipse** *v* to cause an eclipse of: e g **a** to obscure, darken **b** to surpass

economic /ˌekə'nɒmɪk, ˌiː-/ *adj* **1** of economics **2** of or based on the production, distribution, and consumption of goods and services **3** of an economy **4** having practical or industrial significance or uses; affecting material resources **5** profitable

economics /ˌekə'nɒmɪks, ˌiː-/ *n pl but*

sing or pl in constr **1** a social science concerned chiefly with the production, distribution, and consumption of goods and services **2** economic aspect or significance – **-mist** *n*

economy /ɪ'kɒnəmɪ/ *n* **1** thrifty and efficient use of material resources; frugality in expenditure; *also* an instance or means of economizing **2** efficient and sparing use of nonmaterial resources (e g effort, language, or motion) **3** the structure of economic life in a country, area, or period; *specif* an economic system

¹**edge** /edʒ/ *n* **1a** the cutting side of a blade **b** the (degree of) sharpness of a blade **c** penetrating power; keenness **2a** the line where an object or area begins or ends; a border **b** the narrow part adjacent to a border; the brink, verge **c** a point that marks a beginning or transition; a threshold – esp in *on the edge of* **d** a favourable margin; an advantage **3** a line where 2 planes or 2 plane faces of a solid body meet or cross

²**edge** *v* **1** to give or supply an edge to **2** to move or force gradually in a specified way **3** to incline (a ski) sideways so that 1 edge cuts into the snow **4** to hit (a ball) or the bowling of (a bowler) in cricket with the edge of the bat

edible /'edɪbəl/ *adj* fit to be eaten as food – **edibility** *n* – **~s** *n*

educate /'edjʊkeɪt/ *v* **1** to provide schooling for **2** to develop mentally or morally, esp by instruction **3** to train or improve (faculties, judgment, skills, etc) – **~or** *n*

education /ˌedjʊ'keɪʃən/ *n* **1** educating or being educated **2** the field of study that deals with methods of teaching and learning – **~al** *adj*

¹**effect** /ɪ'fekt/ *n* **1a** the result of a cause or agent **b** the result of purpose or intention **2** the basic meaning; intent – esp in *to that effect* **3** power to bring about a result; efficacy **4** *pl* personal movable property; goods **5a** a distinctive impression on the human senses **b** the creation of an often false desired impression **c** sthg designed to produce a distinctive or desired impression – often *pl* **6** the quality or state of being operative; operation **7** an experimental scientific phenomenon named usu after its discoverer

²**effect** /ə'fekt/ *v* **1** to bring about, often by surmounting obstacles; accomplish **2** to put into effect; carry out

effective /ɪ'fektɪv/ *adj* **1a** producing a decided, decisive, or desired effect **b** impressive, striking **2** ready for service or action **3** actual, real **4** being in effect; operative – **~ly** *adv* – **~ness** *n*

efficient /ɪ'fɪʃənt/ *adj* **1** of a person able and practical; briskly competent **2** productive of desired effects, esp with minimum waste – **~ly** *adv* – **-ency** *n*

effort /'efət/ *n* **1** conscious exertion of physical or mental power **2** a serious attempt; a try **3** sthg produced by exertion or trying **4** the force applied (e g to a simple machine) as distinguished from the force exerted against the load

¹egg /eg/ *v* to incite to action – usu + *on*

²egg *n* **1a** the hard-shelled reproductive body produced by a bird; *esp* that produced by domestic poultry and used as a food **b** an animal reproductive body consisting of an ovum together with its nutritive and protective envelopes that is capable of developing into a new individual **c** an ovum **2** sthg resembling an egg in shape

eight /eɪt/ *n* the number 8 **2** sthg having 8 parts or members or a denomination of 8; *esp* (the crew of) an 8-person racing boat – **eighth** *adj, n, pron, adv*

eighteen /eɪˈtiːn/ *n* the number 18 – ~ **th** *adj, n, pron, adv*

eighty /ˈeɪti/ *n* **1** the number 80 **2** *pl* the numbers 80 to 89; *specif* a range of temperatures, ages, or dates within a century characterized by those numbers – **eightieth** *adj, n, pron, adv*

¹either /ˈaɪðə/ *adj* **1** being the one and the other of 2 (e g flowers blooming on *either* side of the path) **2** being the one or the other of 2 (e g take *either* road)

²either *pron* the one or the other (e g could be happy with *either* of them)

³either *conj* – used before 2 or more sentence elements of the same class or function joined usu by *or* to indicate that what immediately follows is the first of 2 or more alternatives (e g *either* sink or swim)

⁴either *adv* for that matter, likewise – used for emphasis after a negative or implied negation (e g not wise or handsome *either*)

¹elaborate /ɪˈlæbərət/ *adj* **1** planned or carried out with great care and attention to detail **2** marked by complexity, wealth of detail, or ornateness; intricate – ~ **ly** *adv* – ~ **ness** *n*

²elaborate /ɪˈlæbəreɪt/ *v* to work out or go into detail; develop – often + *on* – **-tion** *n*

¹elastic /ɪˈlæstɪk/ *adj* **1** buoyant, resilient **2** capable of being easily stretched or expanded and resuming its former shape **3** capable of ready change; flexible, adaptable – ~ **ity** *n*

²elastic /ɪˈlæstɪk/ *n* **1** an elastic fabric usu made of yarns containing rubber **2** easily stretched rubber, usu prepared in cords, strings, or bands

¹elbow /ˈelbəʊ/ *n* **1** the joint between the human forearm and upper arm **2** the part of a garment that covers the elbow

²elbow *v* to push or shove aside (as if) with the elbow; jostle

¹elder /ˈeldə/ *n* any of several shrubs or small trees of the honeysuckle family

²elder *adj* of earlier birth or greater age, esp than another related person or thing

³elder *n* **1** one who is older; a senior **2** one having authority by virtue of age and experience **3** an official of the early

church or of a Presbyterian congregation

elderly /ˈeldəli/ *adj* rather old

eldest /ˈeldɪst/ *adj* of the greatest age or seniority; oldest

¹elect /ɪˈlekt/ *adj* **1** chosen for salvation through divine mercy **2** chosen for office or position but not yet installed

²elect *v* **1** to be selected by vote for an office, position, or membership **2** to choose, decide – *fml* – ~ **ion** *n*

elector /ɪˈlektə/ *n* **1** sby qualified to vote in an election **2** sby entitled to participate in an election: e g **a** *often cap* any of the German princes entitled to elect the Holy Roman Emperor **b** a member of the electoral college in the USA

electric /ɪˈlektrɪk/ *adj* **1a** of, being, supplying, producing, or produced by electricity **b** operated by or using electricity **2** producing an intensely stimulating effect; thrilling **3** *of a musical instrument* electronically producing or amplifying sound

electrical /ɪˈlektrɪkəl/ *adj* **1** of or connected with electricity **2** producing, produced, or operated by electricity – ~ **ly** *adv*

electricity /ɪˌlekˈtrɪsɪti/ *n* **1** (the study of) the phenomena due to (the flow or accumulation of) positively and negatively charged particles (e g protons and electrons) **2** electric current; *also* electric charge

electron /ɪˈlektrɒn/ *n* a negatively charged elementary particle that occurs in atoms outside the nucleus and the mass movement of which constitutes an electric current in a metal

elegant /ˈelɪgənt/ *adj* **1** gracefully refined or dignified (e g in manners, taste, or style) **2** tastefully rich or luxurious, esp in design or ornamentation **3** *of ideas* neat and simple – ~ **ly** *adv* – **-ance** *n*

element /ˈelɪmənt/ *n* **1a** any of the 4 substances air, water, fire, and earth formerly believed to constitute the physical universe **b** *pl* forces of nature; *esp* violent or severe weather **c** the state or sphere natural or suited to sby or sthg **2** a constituent part: e g **a** *pl* the simplest principles of a subject of study; the rudiments **b** a constituent of a mathematical set **c** any of the factors determining an outcome **d** a distinct part of a composite device; *esp* a resistor in an electric heater, kettle, etc **3** any of more than 100 fundamental substances that consist of atoms of only one kind

elementary /ˌelɪˈmentəri/ *adj* of or dealing with the basic elements or principles of sthg; simple

elephant /ˈelɪfənt/ *n* a very large nearly hairless mammal having the snout prolonged into a muscular trunk and 2 upper incisors developed into long tusks which provide ivory

eleven /ɪˈlevən/ *n* **1** the number 11 **2** *sing or pl in constr* sthg having 11 parts or members or a denomination of 11; *esp* a cricket, soccer, or hockey team – ~ **th** *adj, n, pron, adv*

eliminate /ɪˈlɪmɪ̱neɪt/ v **1a** to cast out or get rid of completely; eradicate **b** to set aside as unimportant; ignore **2** to expel (e g waste) from the living body **3a** to kill (a person), esp so as to remove as an obstacle **b** to remove (a competitor, team, etc) from a competition, usu by defeat – **-nation** n

elm /elm/ n (the wood of) any of a genus of large graceful trees

else /els/ adv **1** apart from the person, place, manner, or time mentioned or understood (e g how else could he have acted) **2** also, besides **3** if not, otherwise – used absolutely to express a threat (e g do what I tell you or else)

elsewhere /els'weə', 'elsweə'/ adv in or to another place

embarrass /ɪm'bærəs/ v **1** to involve in financial difficulties, esp debt **2** to cause to experience a state of self-conscious distress; disconcert – ~ingly adv – ~ment n

¹embrace /ɪm'breɪs/ v **1** to take and hold closely in the arms as a sign of affection; hug **2** to encircle, enclose **3a** to take up, esp readily or eagerly; adopt **b** to avail oneself of; welcome **4** to include as a part or element of a more inclusive whole **5** to join in an embrace; hug one another

²embrace n an act of embracing or gripping

embroider /ɪm'brɔɪdə'/ v **1** to ornament (e g cloth or a garment) with decorative stitches made by hand or machine **2** to elaborate on (a narrative); embellish with exaggerated or fictitious details – ~y n

emerald /'emərəld/ adj or n (of the bright green colour of) a beryl used as a gemstone

emerge /ɪ'mɜːdʒ/ v **1** to rise (as if) from an enveloping fluid; come out into view **2** to become manifest or known **3** to rise from an obscure or inferior condition – **-gence** n

emergency /ɪ'mɜːdʒənsi/ n an unforeseen occurrence or combination of circumstances that calls for immediate action

emigrate /'emɪgreɪt/ v to leave one's home or country for life or residence elsewhere – **-tion** n

emotion /ɪ'məʊʃən/ n **1** excitement **2** a mental and physical reaction (e g anger, fear, or joy) marked by strong feeling and often physiological changes that prepare the body for immediate vigorous action – ~less adj

emotional /ɪ'məʊʃənəl/ adj **1** of the emotions **2** inclined to show (excessive) emotion **3** emotive – ~ly adv

emperor /'empərə'/ n the supreme ruler of an empire

emphasis /'emfəsɪ̱s/ n, pl emphases special consideration of or stress on sthg – **-atic** adj – **-atically** adv – **-asize** v

empire /'empaɪə'/ n **1a** (the territory of) a large group of countries or peoples under 1 authority **b** sthg resembling a political empire; esp an extensive territory or enterprise under single domination or control **2** imperial sovereignty

Empire adj (characteristic) of a style (e g of furniture or interior decoration) popular during the first French Empire (1804-14); specif of a style of women's dress having a high waistline

¹employ /ɪm'plɔɪ/ v **1a** to use in a specified way or for a specific purpose **b** to spend (time) **c** to use **2a** to engage the services of **b** to provide with a job that pays wages or a salary – ~er n

²employ n the state of being employed, esp for wages or a salary – fml

employee /ɪm'plɔɪ-iː, ˌemplɔɪ'iː/ n one employed by another, esp for wages or a salary and in a position below executive level

employment /ɪm'plɔɪmənt/ n (an) activity in which one engages or is employed

¹empty /'empti/ adj **1a** containing nothing; esp lacking typical or expected contents **b** not occupied, inhabited, or frequented **2a** lacking reality or substance; hollow **b** lacking effect, value, or sincerity **c** lacking sense; foolish **3** hungry – infml – **emptily** adv – **emptiness** n

²empty v **1a** to make empty; remove the contents of **b** to deprive, divest **c** to discharge (itself) of contents **2** to remove from what holds, encloses, or contains **3** to transfer by emptying **4** to become empty

³empty n a bottle, container, vehicle, etc that has been emptied

enable /ɪ'neɪbəl/ v **1** to provide with the means or opportunity **2** to make possible, practical, or easy

enclose /ɪn'kləʊz/ also **inclose** v **1a(1)** to close in completely; surround **(2)** to fence off (common land) for individual use **b** to hold in; confine **2** to include in a package or envelope, esp along with sthg else – **-sure** n

¹encounter /ɪn'kaʊntə'/ v **1a** to meet as an adversary or enemy **b** to engage in conflict with **2** to meet or come across, esp unexpectedly

²encounter n **1** a meeting or clash between hostile factions or people **2** a chance meeting

encourage /ɪn'kʌrɪdʒ/ v **1** to inspire with courage, spirit, or hope **2** to spur on **3** to give help or patronage to (a process or action); promote – **-agingly** adv – ~ment n

encyclopedia, **encyclopaedia** /ɪnˌsaɪkləˈpiːdiə/ n a reference book containing information on all branches of knowledge or comprehensive information on 1 branch, usu in articles arranged alphabetically by subject

¹end /end/ n **1a** the part of an area that lies at the boundary; also the farthest point from where or from where sthg **b(1)** the point that marks the extent of sthg in space or time; the limit **(2)** the point where sthg ceases to exist **c** either of the extreme or last parts lengthways of an object that is appreciably longer than it is broad **2a** (the events, sections, etc immediately preceding) the cessation of action, activity, or existence **b** the final condition; esp death **3** sthg left over; remnant

4 an aim or purpose **5** sthg or sby extreme of a kind; *the* ultimate **6a** either half of a games pitch, court, etc **b** a period of action or turn to play in bowls, curling, etc **7** a particular part of an undertaking or organization *USE* (5 & 7) *infml*

²**end** *v* **1** to bring or come to an end **2** to destroy **3** to reach a specified ultimate situation, condition, or rank – often + *up*

³**end** *adj* final, ultimate

¹**endeavour** /ɪn'devə'/ *v* to attempt by exertion or effort; try – usu + infin; *fml*

²**endeavour** *n* serious determined effort ; *also* an instance of this – *fml*

ending /'endɪŋ/ *n* **1** the last part of a book, film, etc **2** one or more letters or syllables added to a word base, esp as an inflection

endless /'endlɪs/ *adj* **1** (seeming) without end **2** extremely numerous **3** of a belt, chain, etc that is joined to itself at its ends – ~**ly** *adv*

endurance /ɪn'djuərəns/ *n* the ability to withstand hardship, adversity, or stress

endure /ɪn'djuə'/ *v* **1** to continue in the same state; last **2** to undergo (e g a hardship), esp without giving in **3** to tolerate, permit – **durable** *adj* – **ring** *adj* – **ringly** *adv*

enemy /'enəmɪ/ *n* **1** one who is antagonistic to another; *esp* one seeking to injure, overthrow, or confound an opponent **2** sthg harmful or deadly **3** a hostile military unit or force

energetic /enə'dʒetɪk/ *adj* **1** marked by energy, activity, or vigour **2** operating with power or effect; forceful – ~**ally** *adv*

energy /'enədʒɪ/ *n* **1** the capacity of acting or being active **2** natural power vigorously exerted **3** the capacity for doing work

engage *v* **1a** to attract and hold (sby's thoughts, attention, etc) **b** to interlock or become interlocked with; cause to mesh **2a** to arrange to employ (sby) **b** to arrange to obtain the services of **c** to order (a room, seat, etc) to be kept for one; reserve **3a** to hold the attention of; engross **b** to induce to participate, esp in conversation **4a** to enter into contest with **b** to bring together or interlock (e g weapons) **5** to pledge oneself; promise **6** to occupy one's time; participate **7** to enter into conflict

engagé /ˌɒŋgæ'ʒeɪ/ *adj* actively involved or committed (politically)

engaged /ɪn'geɪdʒd/ *adj* **1** involved in activity; occupied **2** pledged to be married **3** *chiefly Br* **a** in use **b** reserved, booked

engagement /ɪn'geɪdʒmənt/ *n* **1** an agreement to marry; a betrothal **2** a pledge **3a** a promise to be present at a certain time and place **b** employment, esp for a stated time **4** a hostile encounter between military forces

engine /'endʒɪn/ *n* **1** a mechanical tool **2** a machine for converting any of various forms of energy into mechanical

force and motion **3** a railway locomotive

¹**engineer** /ˌendʒɪ'nɪə'/ *n* **1a** a designer or builder of engines **b** a person who is trained in or follows as a profession a branch of engineering **c** a person who starts or carries through an enterprise, esp by skilful or artful contrivance **2** a person who runs or supervises an engine or apparatus

²**engineer** *v* **1** to lay out, construct, or manage as an engineer **2** to contrive, plan, or guide, usu with subtle skill and craft

engineering /ˌendʒɪ'nɪərɪŋ/ *n* **1** the art of managing engines **2** the application of science and mathematics by which the properties of matter and the sources of energy in nature are made useful to human beings

¹**English** /'ɪŋglɪʃ/ *adj* (characteristic) of England

²**English** *n* **1a** the Germanic language of the people of Britain, the USA, and most Commonwealth countries **b** English language, literature, or composition as an academic subject **2** *pl in constr* the people of England

enjoy /ɪn'dʒɔɪ/ *v* **1** to take pleasure or satisfaction in **2a** to have the use or benefit of **b** to experience – ~**ment** *n*

enlarge /ɪn'lɑːdʒ/ *v* **1** to make larger **2** to reproduce in a larger form; *specif* to make a photographic enlargement of **3** to grow larger **4** to speak or write at length; elaborate – often + *on* or *upon*

enormous /ɪ'nɔːməs/ *adj* marked by extraordinarily great size, number, or degree – ~**ness** *n*

¹**enough** /ɪ'nʌf/ *adj* fully adequate in quantity, number, or degree

²**enough** *adv* **1** to a fully adequate degree; sufficiently **2** to a tolerable degree

³**enough** *pron, pl* **enough** a sufficient quantity or number

enquire /ɪn'kwaɪə'/ *v* to inquire

enquiry /ɪŋ'kwaɪərɪ/ *n* an inquiry

ensure /ɪn'ʃuə'/ *v* to make sure, certain, or safe; guarantee

enter /'entə'/ *v* **1** to go or come in or into **2** to register as candidate in a competition **3** to make a beginning **4** to inscribe, register **5** to cause to be received, admitted, or considered – often + *for* **6** to put in; insert **7** to become a member of or an active participant in **8** to put on record **9a** to make oneself a party to – + *into* **b** to participate or share in – + *into*

enterprise /'entəpraɪz/ *n* **1** a (difficult or complicated) project or undertaking **2** a unit of economic organization or activity; *esp* a business organization **3** readiness to engage in enterprises

entertain /ˌentə'teɪn/ *v* **1** to show hospitality to **2** to be ready and willing to think about (an idea, doubt, suggestion, etc) **3** to hold the attention of, usu pleasantly or enjoyably; divert **4** to invite guests to esp one's home

entertainment /ˌentə'teɪnmənt/ *n* **1**

sthg entertaining, diverting, or engaging **2** a public performance – **-ner** *n*

enthusiasm /ɪn'θjuːziæzəm/ *n* **1** keen and eager interest and admiration – usu + *for* or *about* **2** an object of enthusiasm – **-ast** *n* – **-astic** *adj*

entire /ɪn'taɪə/ *adj* **1** having no element or part left out **2** complete in degree; total **3a** consisting of 1 piece; homogeneous **b** intact – **~ly** *adv*

¹entrance /'entrəns/ *n* **1** the act of entering **2** the means or place of entry **3** power or permission to enter; admission **4** an arrival of a performer onto the stage or before the cameras

²entrance /ɪn'trɑːns/ *v* to fill with delight, wonder, or rapture – **~d** *adj*

entry /'entri/ *n* **1** the act of entering; entrance **2** the right or privilege of entering **3** a door, gate, hall, vestibule, or other place of entrance **4a** a record made in a diary, account book, index, etc **b** a dictionary headword, often with its definition **5** a person, thing, or group entered in a contest; an entrant **6** the total of those entered or admitted

envelope /'envələʊp, 'ɒn-/ *n* **1** sthg that envelops; a wrapper, covering **2** a flat container, usu of folded and gummed paper (e g for a letter) **3** a membrane or other natural covering that encloses

envious /'enviəs/ *adj* feeling or showing envy – **~ly** *adv*

environment /ɪn'vaɪərənmənt/ *n* **1** the circumstances, objects, or conditions by which one is surrounded **2** the complex of climatic, of soil, and biological factors that acts upon an organism or an ecological community – **~al** *adj* – **~ally** *adv*

¹envy /'envi/ *n* painful, resentful, or admiring awareness of an advantage enjoyed by another, accompanied by a desire to possess the same advantage; *also* an object of such a feeling

²envy *v* to feel envy towards or on account of

epidemic /ˌepɪ'demɪk/ *n* or *adj* (an outbreak of a disease) affecting many individuals within a population, community, or region at the same time

equable /'ekwəbəl/ *adj* uniform, even; *esp* free from extremes or sudden changes – **-bly** *adv*

¹equal /'iːkwəl/ *adj* **1a** of the same quantity, amount, or number as another **b** identical in value; equivalent **2a** like in quality, nature, or status **b** like for each member of a group, class, or society **3** evenly balanced or matched **4** capable of meeting the requirements of sthg (e g a situation or task) – + *to* – **~ity** *n* – **~ize** *v*

²equal *v* **1** to be equal to; *esp* to be identical in value to **2** to make or produce sthg equal to

equator /ɪ'kweɪtə/ *n* **1** the great circle of the celestial sphere whose plane is perpendicular to the rotational axis of the earth **2** a great circle; *specif* the one that is equidistant from the 2 poles of the earth and divides the earth's surface

into the northern and southern hemispheres – **~ial** *adj* – **~ially** *adv*

equip /ɪ'kwɪp/ *v* **1** to make ready for service, action, or use; provide with appropriate supplies **2** to dress, array

equipment /ɪ'kwɪpmənt/ *n* **1** the set of articles, apparatus, or physical resources serving to equip a person, thing, enterprise, expedition, etc **2** mental or emotional resources

erase /ɪ'reɪz/ *v* **1** to obliterate or rub out (e g written, painted, or engraved letters) **2** to remove from existence or memory as if by erasing – **~r** *n*

errand /'erənd/ *n* (the object or purpose of) a short trip taken to attend to some business, often for another

erratic /ɪ'rætɪk/ *adj* **1** having no fixed course **2** characterized by lack of consistency, regularity, or uniformity, esp in behaviour – **~ally** *adv*

error /'erə/ *n* **1** a mistake or inaccuracy in speech, opinion, or action **2** the state of being wrong in behaviour or beliefs **3** an act that fails to achieve what was intended

¹escape /ɪ'skeɪp/ *v* **1a** to get away, esp from confinement or restraint **b** to leak out gradually; seep **2** to avoid a threatening evil **3** to get or stay out of the way of; avoid **4** to fail to be noticed or recallable by **5** to be produced or made by (esp a person), usu involuntarily

²escape *n* **1** an act or instance of escaping **2** a means of escape **3** a cultivated plant run wild

³escape *adj* **1** providing a means of escape **2** providing a means of evading a regulation, claim, or commitment

¹escort /'eskɔːt/ *n* **1** a person, group of people, ship, aircraft, etc accompanying sby or sthg to give protection or show courtesy **2** one who accompanies another socially

²escort /ɪ'skɔːt/ *v* to accompany as an escort

especial /ɪ'speʃəl/ *adj* (distinctively or particularly) special

espionage /'espɪɒnɑːʒ/ *n* spying or the use of spies to obtain information

esquire, Esq /ɪ'skwaɪə/ *n* – used as a title equivalent to Mr and placed after the surname

¹essay /e'seɪ/ *v* to attempt – *fml*

²essay /'eseɪ/ *n* **1** a usu short piece of prose writing on a specific topic **2** an (initial tentative) effort or attempt – *fml* – **~ist** *n*

¹essential /ɪ'senʃəl/ *adj* **1** of or being (an) essence; inherent **2** of the utmost importance; basic, necessary – **~ly** *adv*

²essential *n* sthg basic, indispensable, or fundamental

establish /ɪ'stæblɪʃ/ *v* **1** to make firm or stable **2** to enact permanently **3** to bring into existence; found **4a** to set on a firm basis; place (e g oneself) in a permanent or firm usu favourable position **b** to gain full recognition or acceptance of **5** to make (a church or religion) a national institution supported by civil authority **6** to put beyond doubt; prove **7** to cause (a plant) to grow and multiply in a place where previously absent

estate /ɪˈsteɪt/ n **1** a social or political class (e g the nobility, clergy, or commons) **2a(1)** the whole of sby's real or personal property **(2)** the assets and liabilities left by sby at death **b** a large landed property, esp in the country, usu with a large house on it **3** Br a part of an urban area devoted to a particular type of development; specif one devoted to housing

estate agent n, Br **1** an agent who is involved in the buying and selling of land and property (e g houses) **2** one who manages an estate; a steward – **estate agency** n

¹**estimate** /ˈestɪmeɪt/ v **1a** to judge approximately the value, worth, or significance of **b** to determine roughly the size, extent, or nature of **c** to produce a statement of the approximate cost of **2** to judge, conclude – **-tor** n

²**estimate** /ˈestɪmlt/ n **1** the act of appraising or valuing; a calculation **2** an opinion or judgment of the nature, character, or quality of sby or sthg **3** a statement of the expected cost of a job

estimation /ˌestɪˈmeɪʃən/ n **1** an opinion of the worth or character of sby or sthg **2** esteem

et cetera /et ˌet ˈsetərə/ adv and other things, esp of the same kind; broadly and so forth

eternal /ɪˈtɜːnəl/ adj **1** having infinite duration; everlasting **2** incessant, interminable **3** timeless

Eucharist /ˈjuːkərɪst/ n (the bread and wine consecrated in) the Christian sacrament in which bread and wine, being or representing the body and blood of Christ, are ritually consumed in accordance with Christ's injunctions at the Last Supper – ~**ic** adj

¹**even** /ˈiːvən/ n, archaic the evening – poetic

²**even** adj **1a** having a horizontal surface; flat, level **b** without break or irregularity; smooth **c** in the same plane or line – + with **2a** without variation; uniform **b** level **3a** equal also fair **b** being in equilibrium **4** exactly divisible by 2 **5** exact, precise **6** fifty-fifty – ~**ly** adv – ~**ness** n

³**even** adv **1** at the very time – + as **2a** – used as an intensive to emphasize the contrast with a less strong possibility (e g can't even walk, let alone run) **b** – used as an intensive to emphasize the comparative degree

⁴**even** v to make or become even – often + up or out

evening /ˈiːvnɪŋ/ n **1** the latter part of the day and the early part of the night; the time between sunset and bedtime **2** a late period (e g of time or life); the end **3** (the period of) an evening's entertainment

event /ɪˈvent/ n **1a** a (noteworthy or important) happening or occurrence **b** a social occasion or activity **2** a contingency, case – esp in in the event of and in the event that **3** any of the contests in a sporting programme or tournament

eventual /ɪˈventʃʊəl/ adj taking place at an unspecified later time; ultimately resulting

ever /ˈevəʳ/ adv **1** always – now chiefly in certain phrases and in combination (e g an ever-growing need) **2** at any time – chiefly in negatives and questions (e g he won't ever do it) **3** – used as an intensive (e g looks ever so angry)

every /ˈevri/ adj **1** being each member without exception, of a group larger than 2 (e g every word counts) **2** being each or all possible (e g was given every chance) **3** being once in each (e g go every third day)

everybody /ˈevrɪbɒdi/ pron every person

everything /ˈevriθɪŋ/ pron **1a** all that exists **b** all that is necessary or that relates to the subject **2** sthg of the greatest importance; all that counts

everywhere /ˈevriweəʳ/ adv or n (in, at, or to) every place or the whole place

¹**evidence** /ˈevɪdəns/ n **1** an outward sign; an indication **2** sthg, esp a fact, that gives proof or reasons for believing or agreeing with sthg; specif information used (by a tribunal) to arrive at the truth

²**evidence** v to offer evidence of; show

evident /ˈevɪdənt/ adj clear to the vision or understanding – ~**ly** adv

¹**evil** /ˈiːvəl/ adj **1** not good morally; sinful, wicked **b** arising from bad character or conduct **2a** causing discomfort or repulsion; offensive **b** disagreeable **3a** pernicious, harmful **b** marked by misfortune – **evilly** adv

²**evil** n **1** sthg evil; sthg that brings sorrow, distress, or calamity **2a** the fact of suffering, misfortune, or wrongdoing **b** wickedness, sin

¹**exact** /ɪgˈzækt/ v to demand and obtain by force, threats, etc; require – ~**ion** n

²**exact** adj **1** exhibiting or marked by complete accordance with fact **2** marked by thorough consideration or minute measurement of small factual details – ~**ness**, ~**itude** n

exactly /ɪgˈzæktli/ adv **1** altogether, entirely **2** quite so – used to express agreement

exaggerate /ɪgˈzædʒəreɪt/ v **1** to say or believe more than the truth about **2** to make greater or more pronounced than normal; overemphasize – ~**d** adj – ~**dly** adv – **-ation** n

examination /ɪgˌzæmɪˈneɪʃən/ n **1** (an) examining **2** (the taking by a candidate for a university degree, Advanced level, Ordinary level, etc of) a set of questions designed to test knowledge **3** a formal interrogation (in a law court)

examine /ɪgˈzæmɪn/ v **1** to inspect closely; investigate **2a** to interrogate closely **b** to test (e g a candidate for a university degree) by an examination in order to determine knowledge – **-iner** n

example /ig'zɑːmpəl/ n 1 sthg representative of all of the group or type to which it belongs 2 sby or sthg that may be copied by other people 3 (the recipient of) a punishment inflicted as a warning to others

exceed /ik'siːd/ v 1 to extend beyond 2 to be greater than or superior to 3 to act or go beyond the limits of

exceedingly /ik'siːdɪŋli/ **exceeding** adv very, extremely

excel /ik'sel/ v to be superior (to); surpass (others) in accomplishment or achievement – often + at or in

excellent /'eksələnt/ adj outstandingly good – **-ence** n – **-ly** adv

¹except /ik'sept/ v to take or leave out from a number or a whole; exclude – ~**ed** adj – ~**ing** prep

²except also **excepting** prep with the exclusion or exception of

³except also **excepting** conj 1 only, but (e g would go except it's too far) 2 unless (e g except you repent) – fml

exception /ik'sepʃən/ n 1 excepting or excluding 2 sby or sthg excepted; esp a case to which a rule does not apply 3 question, objection

exceptional /ik'sepʃənəl/ adj 1 forming an exception; unusual 2 not average; esp superior – ~**ly** adv

¹excess /ik'ses, 'ekses/ n 1a the exceeding of usual, proper, or specified limits b the amount or degree by which one thing or quantity exceeds another 2 (an instance of) undue or immoderate indulgence; intemperance – ~**ive** adj – ~**ively** adv

²excess /'ekses/ adj more than the usual, proper, or specified amount; extra

¹exchange /iks'tʃeindʒ/ n 1a the act of exchanging one thing for another; a trade b a usu brief interchange of words or blows 2 sthg offered, given, or received in an exchange 3a (the system of settling, usu by bills of exchange rather than money) debts payable currently, esp in a foreign country b(1) change or conversion of one currency into another (2) **exchange, exchange rate** the value of one currency in terms of another 4 a place where things or services are exchanged: e g a an organized market for trading in securities or commodities b a centre or device controlling the connection of telephone calls between many different lines

²exchange v 1a to part with, give, or transfer in return for sthg received as an equivalent b of 2 parties to give and receive (things of the same type) 2 to replace by other goods 3 to engage in an exchange – ~**able** adj

excite /ik'sait/ v 1 to provoke or stir up (action) 2 to rouse to strong, esp pleasurable, feeling 3 to arouse (e g an emotional response) – ~**ment** n

exclude /ik'skluːd/ v 1a to shut out b to bar from participation, consideration, or inclusion 2 to expel, esp from a place or position previously occupied – **-usion** n

excursion /ik'skɜːʃən/ n 1 a (brief) pleasure trip, usu at reduced rates 2 a deviation from a direct, definite, or proper course; esp a digression

¹excuse /ik'skjuːz/ v 1a to make apology for b to try to remove blame from 2 to forgive entirely or overlook as unimportant 3 to allow to leave; dismiss 4 to be an acceptable reason for; justify – usu neg 5 Br to free from (a duty) – usu pass

²excuse /ik'skjuːs/ n 1 sthg offered as grounds for being excused 2 pl an expression of regret for failure to do sthg or esp for one's absence

execute /'eksɪkjuːt/ v 1 to carry out fully; put completely into effect 2 to put to death (legally) as a punishment 3 to make or produce (e g a work of art), esp by carrying out a design 4 to (do what is required to) make valid 5 to play, perform

execution /ˌeksɪ'kjuːʃən/ n 1 a putting to death as a punishment 2 a judicial writ directing the enforcement of a judgment 3 the act, mode, or result of performance

¹executive /ig'zekjutiv/ adj 1 concerned with making and carrying out laws, decisions, etc; specif, Br of or concerned with the detailed application of policy or law rather than its formulation 2 of, for, or being an executive

²executive n 1 the executive branch of a government 2 an individual or group that controls or directs an organization 3 one who holds a position of administrative or managerial responsibility

¹exercise /'eksəsaiz/ n 1 the use of a specified power or right 2 bodily exertion for the sake of developing and maintaining physical fitness 3 sthg performed or practised in order to develop, improve, or display a specific power or skill

²exercise v 1 to make effective in action; use, exert 2a to use repeatedly in order to strengthen or develop b to train (e g troops) by drills and manoeuvres 3 to engage the attention and effort of

exert /ig'zɜːt/ v 1 to bring (e g strength or authority) to bear 2 to take upon (oneself) the effort of doing sthg – ~**ion** n

¹exhaust /ig'zɔːst/ v 1 to empty by drawing off the contents; specif to create a vacuum in 2a to consume entirely; use up b to tire out 3 to develop or deal with to the fullest possible extent

²exhaust n 1 (the escape of) used gas or vapour from an engine 2 the conduit or pipe through which used gases escape

¹exhibit /ig'zibɪt/ v 1 to reveal, manifest 2 to show publicly, esp for purposes of competition or demonstration – ~**or** n

²exhibit n 1 sthg exhibited 2 sthg produced as evidence in a lawcourt

exhibition /ˌeksɪ'biʃən/ n 1 a public showing (e g of works of art or objects of manufacture) 2 Br a grant drawn from the funds of a school or university to help to maintain a student

exile /'eksail, 'egzail/ n 1 enforced or

voluntary absence from one's country or home **2** one who is exiled voluntarily or by authority – **exile** v

exist /ɪg'zɪst/ v **1** to have being esp in specified conditions **2** to continue to be **3a** to have life **b** to live at an inferior level or under adverse circumstances

existence /ɪg'zɪstəns/ n **1a** the totality of existent things **b** the state or fact of existing; life **2** manner of living or being

¹**exit** /'egzɪt, 'eksɪt/ – used as a stage direction to specify who goes off stage

²**exit** n **1** a departure of a performer from a scene **2** the act of going out or away **3** a way out of an enclosed place or space

exorbitant /ɪg'zɔːbɪtənt/ adj, of prices, demands, etc much greater than is reasonable; excessive – **-tance** n – ~**ly** adv

expand /ɪk'spænd/ v **1** to increase the size, extent, number, volume, or scope of **2** to express in detail or in full **3** to grow genial; become more sociable – ~**able** adj – **expansion** n

expect /ɪk'spekt/ v **1** to anticipate or look forward to **2** to be pregnant **a** to consider an event probable or certain **b** to consider reasonable, due, or necessary **3** to suppose, think

expedition /,ekspɪ'dɪʃən/ n **1** a journey or excursion undertaken for a specific purpose (e g for war or exploration) **2** efficient promptness; speed

expel /ɪk'spel/ v **1** to drive or force out **2** to drive away; esp to deport **3** to cut off from membership

expend /ɪk'spend/ v **1** to pay out **2** to consume (e g time, care, or attention)

expense /ɪk'spens/ n **1a** a financial burden or outlay **b** pl the charges incurred by an employee in performing his/her duties **c** an item of business outlay chargeable against revenue in a specific period **2** a cause or occasion of usu high expenditure

expensive /ɪk'spensɪv/ adj **1** involving great expense **2** commanding a high price; dear – ~**ly** adv

experience /ɪk'spɪərɪəns/ n **1** the usu conscious perception or apprehension of reality or of an external, bodily, or mental event **2** (the knowledge, skill, or practice derived from) direct participation or observation **3** sthg personally encountered or undergone – **experience** v

experiment /ɪk'sperɪmənt/ n **1** a tentative procedure or policy that is on trial **2** an operation carried out under controlled conditions in order to test or establish a hypothesis or to illustrate a known law – ~**al** adj

expert /'ekspɜːt/ n or adj (sby or sthg) having or showing special skill or knowledge derived from training or experience – ~**ly** adv – ~**ness** n

expire /ɪk'spaɪə/ v **1** to come to an end **2** to emit the breath **3** to die

explain /ɪk'spleɪn/ v **1** to make sthg plain or understandable **2** to give the reason for or cause of – ~**er** n

explanation /,eksplə'neɪʃən/ n the act or process of explaining; sthg, esp a statement, that explains

explode /ɪk'spləud/ v **1** to give expression to sudden, violent, and usu noisy emotion **2** to burst or expand violently as a result of pressure, or a rapid chemical reaction **3** to bring (e g a belief or theory) into discredit by demonstrating falsity

explore /ɪk'splɔː/ **1** to make or conduct a search **2** to travel into or through for purposes of geographical discovery – ~**r** n – **-ration** n

explosion /ɪk'spləuʒən/ n **1** (a noise caused by something) exploding **2** a rapid large-scale expansion, increase, or upheaval **3** a sudden violent outburst of emotion

¹**explosive** /ɪk'spləusɪv/ adj **1** threatening to burst forth with sudden violence or noise **2** tending to arouse strong reactions – ~**ly** adv – ~**ness** n

²**explosive** n an explosive substance

export /ɪk'spɔːt/ v to carry or send a commodity to another country for purposes of trade – ~**able** adj – ~**ation** n – ~**er** n – **export** n

expose /ɪk'spəuz/ v **1** to submit or subject to an action or influence; specif to subject (a photographic film, plate, or paper) to the action of radiant energy **2a** to exhibit for public veneration **b** to engage in indecent exposure of (oneself) **3** to bring (sthg shameful) to light

exposé /ek'spəuzeɪ/ expose n **1** a formal recital or exposition of facts; a statement **2** an exposure of sthg discreditable

¹**express** /ɪk'spres/ adj **1** firmly and explicitly stated **2a** travelling at high speed **b** to be delivered without delay by special messenger

²**express** n **1** an express vehicle **2** express mail

³**express** v **1** to state **2** to make known the opinions, feelings, etc of (oneself) **3** to represent by a sign or symbol

expression /ɪk'spreʃən/ n **1a** expressing, esp in words **b** a significant word or phrase **2a** a means or manner of expressing sthg; esp sensitivity and feeling in communicating or performing **b** facial aspect or vocal intonation indicative of feeling – ~**less** adj

extend /ɪk'stend/ v **1** to stretch out in distance, space, or time **2** to exert (e g a horse or oneself) to full capacity **3** to give or offer, usu in response to need; proffer **4a** to reach in scope or application **b** to prolong in time **c** to advance, further **5** to increase the scope, meaning, or application of

extension /ɪk'stenʃən/ n **1a** extending or being extended **b** sthg extended **2** extent, scope **3** a straightening of (a joint between the bones of) a limb **4** an increase in length of time **5a** a part added (e g to a building) **b** an extra telephone connected to the principal line

extensive /ɪk'stensɪv/ adj having wide or considerable extent – ~**ly** adv – ~**ness** n

extent /ɪk'stent/ n **1** the range or distance over which sthg extends 2 the point or limit to which sthg extends

¹**exterior** /ɪk'stɪərɪə/ adj 1 on the outside or an outside surface; external 2 suitable for use on outside surfaces

²**exterior** n 1 an exterior part or surface; outside 2 an outward manner or appearance

¹**extra** /'ekstrə/ adj 1 more than is due, usual, or necessary; additional 2 subject to an additional charge

²**extra** n sthg or sby extra or additional: e g a an added charge b a specified edition of a newspaper c a run in cricket (e g a bye, leg bye, no-ball, or wide) that is not credited to a batsman's score d an additional worker; specif one hired to act in a group scene in a film or stage production

³**extra** adv beyond or above the usual size, extent, or amount

extraordinary /ɪk'strɔːdənərɪ/ adj 1 exceptional; remarkable 2 on or for a special function or service – **-rily** adv

¹**extreme** /ɪk'striːm/ adj 1a existing in a very high degree b not moderate c exceeding the usual or expected 2 situated at the farthest possible point from a centre or the nearest to an end 3 most advanced or thoroughgoing – ~**ly** adv

²**extreme** n 1 sthg situated at or marking one or other extreme point of a range 2 a very pronounced or extreme degree 3 an extreme measure or expedient

¹**eye** /aɪ/ n 1a any of various usu paired organs of sight b the faculty of seeing c a gaze, glance 2a the hole through the head of a needle b a loop; esp one of metal or thread into which a hook is inserted c an undeveloped bud (e g on a potato) d a calm area in the centre of a tropical cyclone e the (differently coloured or marked) centre of a flower 3 the direction from which the wind is blowing – ~**less** adj

²**eye** v to watch closely

eyebrow /'aɪbraʊ/ n (hair growing on) the ridge over the eye

eyelash /'aɪlæʃ/ n (a single hair of) the fringe of hair edging the eyelid

eyelid /'aɪ,lɪd/ n a movable lid of skin and muscle that can be closed over the eyeball

F

fable /'feɪbəl/ n 1 a legendary story of supernatural happenings 2 a fictitious account 3 a story conveying a moral; esp one in which animals speak and act like human beings

fabric /'fæbrɪk/ n 1a the basic structure of a building b an underlying structure; a framework 2 cloth

fabulous /'fæbjʊləs/ adj 1 extraordinary, incredible 2 told in or based on fable 3 marvellous, great – infml

¹**face** /feɪs/ n 1 the front part of the (human) head including the chin, mouth, nose, eyes, etc and usu the forehead 2 a facial expression; specif a grimace 3a an outward appearance b effrontery, impudence c dignity, reputation 4a a front, upper, or outer surface b an exposed surface of rock c the right side (e g of cloth or leather) 5 the exposed working surface of a mine or excavation

²**face** v 1 to meet or deal with firmly and without evasion 2 to cover the front or surface of 3 to have the face towards ; also to turn the face in a specified direction

facility /fə'sɪlɪtɪ/ n 1 the ability to perform sthg easily; aptitude 2 sthg (e g equipment) that promotes the ease of an action or operation – usu pl

fact /fækt/ n 1 a thing done; esp a criminal act 2 the quality of having actual existence in the real world; also sthg having such existence 3 an event, esp as distinguished from its legal effect 4 a piece of information presented as having objective reality

factor /'fæktə/ n 1 one who acts for another; an agent 2 a condition, force, or fact that actively contributes to a result 3 any of the numbers or symbols that when multiplied together form a product – ~**ize** v

factory /'fæktərɪ/ n a building or set of buildings with facilities for manufacturing

fade /feɪd/ v 1 to lose freshness or vigour; wither 2 of a brake to lose braking power gradually, esp owing to prolonged use 3 to lose freshness or brilliance of colour 4 to disappear gradually; vanish – often + away

¹**fail** /feɪl/ v 1a to lose strength; weaken b to fade or die away c to stop functioning 2a to fall short b to be unsuccessful (e g in passing a test) c to become bankrupt or insolvent 3a to disappoint the expectations or trust of b to prove inadequate or incapable of carrying out an expected service or function for 4 to leave undone; neglect

²**fail** n 1 failure – chiefly in without fail 2 an examination failure

failure /'feɪljə/ n 1 a failing to perform a duty or expected action 2 lack of success 3a a falling short; a deficiency b deterioration, decay 4 sby or sthg unsuccessful

¹**faint** /feɪnt/ adj 1 cowardly, timid – chiefly in faint heart 2 weak, dizzy, and likely to faint 3 feeble 4 lacking distinctness; esp dim – ~**ly** adv – ~**ness** n

²**faint** v to lose consciousness because of a temporary decrease in the blood supply to the brain (e g through exhaustion or shock) – **faint** n

¹**fair** /feə/ adj 1 attractive, beautiful 2 superficially pleasing 3 clean, clear 4 not stormy or foul; fine 5a free from self-interest or prejudice; honest b conforming with the established rules; allowed 6 light in colour; blond 7 mod-

erately good or large; adequate – ~ **ness** *n*

²**fair** *n* **1** a periodic gathering of buyers and sellers at a particular place and time for trade or a competitive exhibition, usu accompanied by entertainment and amusements **2** *Br* a fun fair

fairly /ˈfeəli/ *adv* **1** completely, quite **2** properly, impartially, or honestly **3** to a full degree or extent **4** for the most part

fairy /ˈfeəri/ *n* a small mythical being having magic powers and usu human form

fairy-tale *adj* marked by a unusual grace or beauty **b** apparently magical success or good fortune

fairy tale *n* **1** a story which features supernatural or imaginary forces and beings **2** a made-up story, usu designed to mislead – **fairy-tale** *adj*

faith /feiθ/ *n* **1a** allegiance to duty or a person; loyalty – chiefly in *good/ bad faith* **b** fidelity to one's promises – chiefly in *keep/ break faith* **2a** belief and trust in and loyalty to God or the doctrines of a religion **b** complete confidence **3** sthg believed with strong conviction; *esp* a system of religious beliefs

¹**faithful** /ˈfeiθfəl/ *adj* **1** showing faith; loyal; *specif* loyal to one's spouse in having no sexual relations outside marriage **2** firm in adherence to promises or in observance of duty **3** true to the facts; accurate – ~ **ness** *n*

²**faithful** *n pl* **1** *the* full church members **2** *the* body of adherents of a religion (e g Islam) **3** loyal followers or members

faithless /ˈfeiθlis/ *adj* **1a** lacking esp religious faith **b** disloyal **2** untrustworthy – ~ **ly** *adv* – ~ **ness** *n*

¹**fake** /feik/ *n* any of the loops of a coiled rope or cable

¹**fake** *v* **1** to alter or treat so as to impart a false character or appearance; falsify **2a** to counterfeit, simulate **b** to feign

²**fake** *n* **1** a worthless imitation passed off as genuine **2** an impostor, charlatan

²**fake** *adj* counterfeit, phoney

fall /fɔːl/ *v* **fell; fallen 1a** to descend freely (as if) by the force of gravity **b** to hang freely **2a** to become less or lower in degree, level, pitch, or volume **b** to be uttered; issue **c** to look down **3a** to come down from an erect to a usu prostrate position suddenly and esp involuntarily **b** to enter an undesirable state; esp unavoidably or unwittingly **c** to drop because wounded or dead; *esp* to die in battle – euph **d** to lose office **4a** to yield to temptation; sin **b** *of a woman* to lose one's virginity, esp outside marriage **5a** to move or extend in a downward direction – often + *off* or *away* **b** to decline in quality or quantity; abate, subside – often + *off* or *away* **c** to assume a look of disappointment or dismay **d** to decline in financial value **6a** to occur at a specified time or place **b** to come (as if) by chance – + *in* or *into* **c** to come or pass by lot, assignment, or

inheritance; devolve – usu + *on*, *to*, or *upon* **7** to come within the limits, scope, or jurisdiction of sthg **8** to begin heartily or actively – usu + *to* **9** to fall in love with – + *for* **10** to be deceived by – + *for*

²**fall** *n* **1** the act of falling by the force of gravity **2a** a falling out, off, or away; a dropping **b** sthg or a quantity that falls or has fallen **3a** a loss of greatness or power; a collapse **b** the surrender or capture of a besieged place **c** *often cap* mankind's loss of innocence through the disobedience of Adam and Eve **4a** a downward slope **b** a cataract – usu pl with sing. meaning but sing. or pl in constr **5** a decrease in size, quantity, degree, or value **6** *chiefly NAm* autumn

false /fɔːls/ *adj* **1** not genuine **2a** intentionally untrue; lying **b** adjusted or made so as to deceive **3** not based on reality; untrue **4** disloyal, treacherous **5** resembling or related to a more widely known kind **6** imprudent, unwise – ~ **ly** *adv* – ~ **ness** *n* – **falsity** *n*

falsehood /ˈfɔːlshʊd/ *n* **1** an untrue statement; a lie **2** absence of truth or accuracy; falsity

fame /feim/ *n* **1** public estimation; reputation **2** popular acclaim; renown – ~ **d** *adj*

¹**familiar** /fəˈmɪliə/ *n* an intimate associate; a companion

²**familiar** *adj* **1** closely acquainted; intimate **2a** casual, informal **b** too intimate and unrestrained; presumptuous **3** frequently seen or experienced; common – ~ **ize** *v*

¹**family** /ˈfæməli/ *n sing or pl in constr* **1** a group of people of common ancestry or common convictions **2** a group of people living under 1 roof; *esp* a set of 2 or more adults living together and rearing their children **3** a group of related languages descended from a single ancestral language **4** a category in the biological classification of living things ranking above a genus and below an order

²**family** *adj* of or suitable for a family or all of its members

famine /ˈfæmɪn/ *n* an extreme scarcity of food; *broadly* any great shortage

famous /ˈfeiməs/ *adj* well-known

¹**fan** /fæn/ *n* **1** a folding circular or semicircular device that consists of material (e g paper or silk) mounted on thin slats that is waved to and fro by hand to produce a cooling current of air **2** a device, usu a series of vanes radiating from a hub rotated by a motor, for producing a current of air

²**fan** *v* **1** to eliminate (e g chaff) by winnowing **2** to move or impel (air) with a fan **3** to stir up to activity as if by fanning a fire; stimulate **4** to spread *out* like a fan

³**fan** *n* an enthusiastic supporter or admirer (e g of a sport, pursuit, or celebrity)

¹**fancy** /ˈfænsi/ *n* **1** an inclination **2** a notion, whim **3a** imagination, esp of a capricious or misleading sort **b** the

power of mental conception and representation, used in artistic expression (e g by a poet) **4** *sing or pl in constr* the group of fanciers of a particular animal or devotees of a particular sport

²**fancy** *v* **1** to believe without knowledge or evidence **2a** to have a fancy for; like, desire **b** to consider likely to do well **3** to form a conception of; imagine

³**fancy** *adj* **1** based on fancy or the imagination; whimsical **2a** not plain or ordinary ; *esp* fine, quality **b** ornamental – **fancily** *adv*

fantastic /fæn'tæstɪk/ *adj* **1a** unreal, imaginary **b** so extreme as to challenge belief; *specif* exceedingly large or great **2** marked by extravagant fantasy or eccentricity **3** – used as a generalized term of approval – ~**ally** *adv*

¹**far** /faːʳ/ *adv* **farther, further; farthest, furthest** **1** to or at a considerable distance in space (e g wandered *far* into the woods) **2** in total contrast (e g *far* from criticizing you, I'm delighted) – + *from* **3** to or at an extent or degree (e g as *far* as I know **4a** to or at a considerable distance or degree (e g a bright student will go *far*) **b** much (e g *far* too hot) **5** to or at a considerable distance in time (e g worked *far* into the night)

²**far** *adj* **farther, further; farthest, furthest** **1** remote in space, time, or degree (e g in the *far* distance) **2** long **3** being the more distant of 2 (e g the *far* side of the lake) **4** *of a political position* extreme

farce /faːs/ *n* **1** forcemeat **2** a comedy with an improbable plot that is concerned more with situation than characterization **3** a ridiculous or meaningless situation or event – **farcical** *adj* – **farcically** *adv*

¹**fare** /feəʳ/ *v* to get along; succeed, do

²**fare** *n* **1a** the price charged to transport sby **b** a paying passenger **2** food provided for a meal

¹**farewell** /feəˈwel/ *interj* goodbye

²**farewell** *n* an act of departure or leave-taking

¹**farm** /faːm/ *n* an area of land devoted to growing crops or raising (domestic) animals

²**farm** *v* **1** to collect and take the proceeds of (e g taxation or a business) on payment of a fixed sum **2** to produce crops or livestock

farmer /ˈfaːməʳ/ *n* **1** sby who pays a fixed sum for some privilege or source of income **2** sby who cultivates land or crops or raises livestock

¹**farther** /ˈfaːðəʳ/ *adv* **1** at or to a greater distance or more advanced point (e g *farther* down the corridor) **2** to a greater degree or extent

²**farther** *adj* **1a** more distant; remoter **b** far (e g the *farther* side) **2** additional

¹**farthest** /ˈfaːðɪst/ *adj* most distant in space or time

²**farthest** *adv* **1** to or at the greatest distance in space, time, or degree **2** by the greatest degree or extent; most

fascinate /ˈfæsɪneɪt/ *v* **1** to transfix by an irresistible mental power **2** to attract strongly, esp by arousing interest; captivate – –**ting** *adj* – –**tingly** *adv*

fascism /ˈfæʃɪzəm/ *n* **1** a political philosophy, movement, or regime that is usu hostile to socialism, exalts nation and race, and stands for a centralized government headed by a dictatorial leader **2** brutal dictatorial control – **facist** *n*, *adj*

¹**fashion** /ˈfæʃən/ *n* **1** a manner, way **2a** a prevailing and often short-lived custom or style **b** the prevailing style or custom, esp in dress

²**fashion** *v* **1** to give shape or form to, esp by using ingenuity; mould, construct **2** to mould into a particular character by influence or training; transform, adapt

¹**fast** /faːst/ *adj* **1a** firmly fixed or attached **b** tightly closed or shut **2a(1)** moving or able to move rapidly; swift **(2)** taking a comparatively short time **(3)** accomplished quickly **(4)** quick to learn **b** conducive to rapidity of play or action or quickness of motion **c** *of a clock* indicating in advance of what is correct **3** *of a colour* permanently dyed; not liable to fade **4** dissipated, wild; *also* promiscuous

²**fast** *adv* **1** in a firm or fixed manner **2** sound, deeply **3a** in a rapid manner; quickly **b** in quick succession **4** in a reckless or dissipated manner **5** ahead of a correct time or posted schedule

³**fast** *v* to abstain from some or all foods or meals

⁴**fast** *n* an act or time of fasting

fasten /ˈfaːsən/ *v* **1** to attach or secure, esp by pinning, tying, or nailing **2** to fix or direct steadily **3** to attach, impose *on* – ~**er** *n*

fastening /ˈfaːsənɪŋ/ *n* a fastener

fastidious /fæˈstɪdɪəs/ *adj* **1** excessively difficult to satisfy or please **2** showing or demanding great delicacy or care – ~**ly** *adv* – ~**ness** *n*

¹**fat** /fæt/ *adj* **1a** plump **b** obese **2a** well filled out; thick, big **b** prosperous, wealthy **3** richly rewarding or profitable; substantial **4** productive, fertile **5** practically nonexistent – infml – ~**ness** *n*

²**fat** *n* **1** (animal tissue consisting chiefly of cells distended with) greasy or oily matter **2** the best or richest part

fatal /ˈfeɪtl/ *adj* **1** fateful, decisive **2a** of fate **b** like fate according to a fixed sequence; inevitable **3a** causing death **b** bringing ruin

fatally /ˈfeɪtli/ *adv* **1** mortally **2** as is or was fatal

¹**fate** /feɪt/ *n* **1** the power beyond human control that determines events; destiny **2a** a destiny **b** a disaster; *esp* death **3** an outcome, end; *esp* one that is adverse and inevitable

²**fate** *v* to destine; *also* to doom – usu pass

¹**father** /ˈfaːðəʳ/ *n* **1a** a male parent of a child; *also* a sire **b** *cap* God; the first person of the Trinity **2** a man receiving filial respect from another **3** *often cap* an early Christian writer accepted by the church as authoritative **4** a source,

origin **5** a priest of the regular clergy – used esp as a title in the Roman Catholic church

²father *v* **1a** to beget **b** to give rise to; initiate **2** to fix the paternity of *on*

¹fault /fɔːlt/ *n* **1a** a failing; a defect **b** a service that does not land in the prescribed area in tennis, squash, etc **2a** a misdemeanour **b** a mistake **3** responsibility for wrongdoing or failure **4** a fracture in the earth's crust accompanied by displacement (e g of the strata) along the fracture line – ~y *adj*

²fault *v* **1** to commit a fault; err **2** to produce a geological fault (in)

favour /'feɪvə'/ *NAm chiefly* **favor** *n* **1a** friendly or approving regard shown towards another; approbation **b** popularity **2** (an act of) kindness beyond what is expected or due **3** a token of allegiance or love (e g a ribbon or badge), usu worn conspicuously **4** consent to sexual activities, esp given by a woman – usu pl with sing. meaning; euph

²favour, *NAm chiefly* **favor** *v* **1a** to regard or treat with favour **b** to do a favour or kindness for; oblige – usu + *by* or *with* **2** to show partiality towards; prefer **3** to sustain; facilitate

favourable /'feɪvərəbəl/ *adj* **1a** disposed to favour; partial **b** giving a result in one's favour **2a** helpful, advantageous **b** successful – -**rably** *adv*

¹favourite /'feɪvərɪt/ *n* **1** sby or sthg favoured or preferred above others; *specif* one unduly favoured **2** the competitor judged most likely to win, esp by a bookmaker

²favourite *adj* constituting a favourite

¹fear /fɪə'/ *n* **1** (an instance of) an unpleasant often strong emotion caused by anticipation or awareness of (a specified) danger **2** anxiety, solicitude **3** profound reverence and awe, esp towards God **4** reason for alarm; danger – ~less *adj*

²fear *v* **1** to have a reverential awe of **2** to be afraid of; consider or expect with alarm

fearful /'fɪəfəl/ *adj* **1** causing or likely to cause fear **2a** showing or arising from fear **b** timid, timorous **3** extremely bad, large, or intense – *infml* – ~**ly** *adv* – ~**ness** *n*

¹feast /fiːst/ *n* **1a** an elaborate often public meal; a banquet **b** sthg that gives abundant pleasure **2** a periodic religious observance commemorating an event or honouring a deity, person, or thing

²feast *v* **1** to take part in a feast; give a feast for **2** to delight, gratify

feat /fiːt/ *n* **1** a notable and esp courageous act or deed **2** an act or product of skill, endurance, or ingenuity

¹feather /'feðə'/ *n* **1a** any of the light outgrowths forming the external covering of a bird's body **b** the vane of an arrow **2** plumage **3** the act of feathering an oar

²feather *v* **1** to cover, clothe, adorn, etc with feathers **2a** to turn (an oar blade)

almost horizontal when lifting from the water **b** to change the angle at which (a propeller blade) meets the air so as to have the minimum wind resistance

¹feature /'fiːtʃə'/ *n* **1** a part of the face; *also, pl* the face **2** a prominent or distinctive part or characteristic **3a** a full-length film **b** a distinctive article or story, in a newspaper, magazine, or on radio

²feature *v* **1** to give special prominence to (e g in a performance or newspaper) **2** to play an important part; be a feature – usu + *in*

February /'februəri/ *n* the 2nd month of the Gregorian calendar

fed up *adj* discontented, bored – *infml*

fee /fiː/ *n* **1** a sum of money paid esp for entrance or for a professional service **2** money paid for education – usu pl with sing. meaning

feeble /'fiːbəl/ *adj* **1** lacking in strength or endurance; weak **2** deficient in authority, force, or effect – **feebly** *adv* – ~**ness** *n*

¹feed /fiːd/ *v* **fed 1a** to give food to **b** to give as food **2** to provide sthg essential to the growth, sustenance, maintenance, or operation of **3** to produce or provide food for **4** to supply for use, consumption, or processing, esp in a continuous manner

²feed *n* **1** an act of eating **2** (a mixture or preparation of) food for livestock **3** a mechanism by which the action of feeding is effected **4** one who supplies cues for another esp comic performer's lines or actions

¹feel /fiːl/ *v* **felt 1a** to handle or touch in order to examine or explore **b** to perceive by a physical sensation coming from discrete end organs (e g of the skin or muscles) **2** to experience actively or passively; be affected by **3** to ascertain or explore by cautious trial – often + *out* **4a** to be aware of by instinct or by drawing conclusions from the evidence available **b** to believe, think **5** to have sympathy or pity *for*

²feel *n* **1** the sense of feeling; touch **2a** the quality of a thing as imparted through touch **b** typical or peculiar quality or atmosphere **3** intuitive skill, knowledge, or ability – usu + *for*

feeling /'fiːlɪŋ/ *n* **1** (a sensation experienced through) one of the 5 basic physical senses **2a** an emotional state or reaction **b** *pl* susceptibility to impression; sensibility **3** a conscious recognition; a sense **4a** an opinion or belief, esp when unreasoned **b** a presentiment **5** capacity to respond emotionally, esp with the higher emotions – **feeling** *adj*

¹fell /fel/ *v* **1** to cut, beat, or knock down **2** to kill

²fell *past of* **fall**

³fell *n* a steep rugged stretch of high moorland, esp in northern England – often pl with sing. meaning

⁴fell *adj* **1** fierce, cruel **2** very destructive; deadly *USE poetic*

¹fellow /'feləʊ/ *n* **1** a comrade, associate – usu pl **2a** an equal in rank, power, or character; a peer **b** either of a pair; a mate **3** a member of an incorporated literary or scientific society **4** a man; *also* a boy **5** an incorporated member of a collegiate foundation **6** a person appointed to a salaried position allowing for advanced research

²**fellow** *adj* being a companion or associate; belonging to the same group – used before a noun

fellowship /'feləʊʃɪp/ *n* **1** the condition of friendly relations between people; companionship **2a** community of interest, activity, feeling, or experience **b** the state of being a fellow or associate **3** *sing or pl in constr* a group of people with similar interests; an association **4** the position of a fellow (e g of a university)

¹**felt** /felt/ *n* a nonwoven cloth made by compressing wool or fur often mixed with natural or synthetic fibres

²**felt** *v* **1** to make into or cover with felt **2** to cause to stick and mat together

³**felt** *past of* feel

¹**female** /'fiːmeɪl/ *n* **1** an individual that bears young or produces eggs; *esp* a woman or girl as distinguished from a man or boy **2** a plant or flower with an ovary but no stamens – **female** *adj*

²**female** *adj* designed with a hole or hollow into which a corresponding male part fits

¹**feminine** /'femɪnɪn/ *adj* **1** of or being a female person **2** characteristic of, appropriate to, or peculiar to women; womanly **3** of or belonging to the gender that normally includes most words or grammatical forms referring to females – **-nity** *n*

²**feminine** *n* **1** the feminine principle in human nature – esp in *eternal feminine* **2** (a word of) the feminine gender

¹**fence** /fens/ *n* **1a** a barrier (e g of wire or boards) intended to prevent escape or intrusion or to mark a boundary **2** a receiver of stolen goods

²**fence** *v* **1a** to enclose with a fence – usu + *in* **b** to separate *off* or keep *out* (as if) with a fence **2a** to practise fencing **b** to use tactics of attack and defence (e g thrusting and parrying) resembling those of fencing **3** to receive or sell stolen goods

¹**ferry** /'feri/ *v* **1** to carry by boat over a body of water **2** to convey (e g by car) from one place to another

²**ferry** *n* (a boat used at) a place where people or things are carried across a body of water (e g a river)

fertile /'fɜːtaɪl/ *adj* **1a** (capable of) producing or bearing fruit (in great quantities); productive **b** characterized by great resourcefulness and activity; inventive **2a** capable of sustaining abundant plant growth **b** affording abundant possibilities for development **c** capable of breeding or reproducing – **-lity** *n* – **-lize** *v*

¹**festival** /'festɪvəl/ *adj* of, appropriate to, or set apart as a festival

²**festival** *n* **1a** a time marked by special (e g customary) celebration **b** a religious feast **2** a usu periodic programme

or season of cultural events or entertainment **3** gaiety, conviviality

fetch /fetʃ/ *v* **1** to go or come after and bring or take back **2a** to cause to come; bring **b** to produce as profit or return; realize **3** to reach by sailing, esp against the wind or tide and without having to tack **4** to strike or deal (a blow, slap, etc) – *infml*

fever /'fiːvə/ *n* **1** a rise of body temperature above the normal, *also* a disease marked by this **2a** a state of intense emotion or activity **b** a contagious usu transient enthusiasm; a craze

feverish /'fiːvərɪʃ/ *also* **feverous** *adj* **1a** having the symptoms of a fever **b** indicating, relating to, or caused by (a) fever **2** marked by intense emotion, activity, or instability

¹**few** /fjuː/ *adj* **1** amounting to only a small number (e g one of his *few* pleasures) **2** at least some though not many – + *a* (e g caught a *few* more fish)

²**few** *n pl in constr* **1** not many (e g *few* of his stories were true) **2** at least some though not many – + *a* (e g a *few* of them) **3** a select or exclusive group of people; an élite

fiancé /fi'ɒnseɪ/ *fem* **fiancée** *n* sby engaged to be married

fibre /'faɪbə/ *NAm chiefly* **fiber** *n* **1** a slender natural or man-made thread or filament (e g of wool, cotton, or asbestos) **2** material made of fibres **3** essential structure or character strength, fortitude

fiction /'fɪkʃən/ *n* **1** an invented story **2** literature (e g novels or short stories) describing imaginary people and events – **~al** *adj* – **~alize** *v* – **~alization** *n*

¹**fidget** /'fɪdʒɪt/ *n* **1** uneasiness or restlessness shown by nervous movements – usu pl with sing. meaning **2** sby who fidgets *USE infml*

²**fidget** *v* to move or act restlessly or nervously – **~y** *adj*

¹**field** /fiːld/ *n* **1a** an (enclosed) area of land free of woods and buildings (used for cultivation or pasture) **b** an area of land containing a natural resource **c** (the place where) a battle is fought; *also* a battle **2a** an area or division of an activity **b** the sphere of practical operation outside a place of work (e g a laboratory) **c** an area in which troops are operating (e g in an exercise or theatre of war) **3** the participants in a sports activity, esp with the exception of the favourite or winner **4** a region or space in which a given effect (e g magnetism) exists **5** *also* **field of view** the area visible through the lens of an optical instrument

²**field** *v* **1a** to stop and pick up a hit ball **b** to deal with by giving an impromptu answer **2** to put into the field of play or battle

fierce /fɪəs/ *adj* **1** violently hostile or aggressive; combative, pugnacious **2a** lacking restraint or control; violent, heated **b** extremely intense or severe **3** furiously active or determined **4** wild or

menacing in appearance – ~ly *adv*
– ~ness *n*

fiery /'faɪəri/ *adj* **1a** consisting of fire **b** burning, blazing **2** very hot **3** of the colour of fire; *esp* red **4a** full of or exuding strong emotion or spirit; passionate **b** easily provoked; irascible

fifteen /fɪf'tiːn/ *n* the number 15; *esp*, *sing* or *pl in constr* a Rugby Union football team

fifth /fɪfθ, fɪθ/ *n* (the combination of 2 notes at) a musical interval of 5 diatonic degrees

fifty /'fɪfti/ *n* **1** the number 50 **2** *pl* the numbers 50 to 59; *specif* a range of temperatures, ages, or dates within a century characterized by those numbers

¹fight /faɪt/ *v* **fought** **1a** to contend in battle or physical combat **b** to attempt to prevent the success, effectiveness, or development of **2** to stand as a candidate for (e g a constituency) in an election **3** to struggle to endure or surmount **4** to resolve or control by fighting – + *out* or *down*

²fight *n* **1a** a battle, combat **b** a boxing match **c** an argument **2** a usu protracted struggle for an objective **3** strength or disposition for fighting; pugnacity

¹figure /'fɪgə/ *n* **1a** an (Arabic) number symbol **b** *pl* arithmetical calculations **c** value, esp as expressed in numbers **2** bodily shape or form, esp of a person **3** a diagram or pictorial illustration **4** an intentional deviation from the usual form or syntactic relation of words **5** an often repetitive pattern in a manufactured article (e g cloth) or natural substance (e g wood) **6a** a series of movements in a dance **b** an outline representation of a form traced by a series of evolutions (e g by a skater on an ice surface) **7** a personage, personality **8** a short musical phrase

²figure *v* **1** to decorate with a pattern **2** to take an esp important or conspicuous part – often + *in* **3** to seem reasonable or expected – *infml*; esp in *that figures* **4a** *chiefly NAm* to conclude, decide **b** *chiefly NAm* to regard, consider

¹file /faɪl/ *n* a tool, usu a bar of hardened steel, with many cutting ridges for shaping or smoothing objects or surfaces

²file *vt* to rub, smooth, or cut away (as if) with a file

³file *v* **1** to arrange in order (e g alphabetically) for preservation and reference **2** to submit or record officially

⁴file *n* **1** a folder, cabinet, etc in which papers are kept in order **2** a collection of papers or publications on a subject, usu arranged or classified

⁵file *n* **1** a row of people, animals, or things arranged one behind the other **2** any of the rows of squares that extend across a chessboard from white's side to black's side

⁶file *v* to march or proceed in file

¹fill /fɪl/ *v* **1a** to put into as much as can be held or conveniently contained **b** to supply with a full complement **c** to repair the cavities of (a tooth) **d** to stop up; obstruct, plug **2a** to feed, satiate **b** to satisfy, fulfil **3a** to occupy the whole of **b** to spread through **4** to possess and perform the duties of; hold

²fill *n* **1** as much as one can eat or drink **2** as much as one can bear

¹film /fɪlm/ *n* **1a** a thin skin or membranous covering **b** an abnormal growth on or in the eye **2a** a thin layer or covering **b** a roll or strip of cellulose acetate or cellulose nitrate coated with a light-sensitive emulsion for taking photographs **3a** a series of pictures recorded on film for the cinema and projected rapidly onto a screen so as to create the illusion of movement (e g of an incident or story) on film **c** cinema – often *pl* with sing. meaning

²film *v* to make a film of or from

¹filter /'fɪltə/ *n* **1** a porous article or mass (e g of paper, sand, etc) through which a gas or liquid is passed to separate out matter in suspension **2** an apparatus containing a filter medium

²filter *v* **1** to remove by means of a filter **2** to move gradually **3** to become known over a period of time **4** *Br, of traffic* to turn left or right in the direction of the green arrow while the main lights are still red

filth /fɪlθ/ *n* **1** foul or putrid matter, esp dirt or refuse **2** sthg loathsome or vile; *esp* obscene or pornographic material – ~y *adj* – ~ily *adv* – ~iness *n*

fin /fɪn/ *n* **1** an external membranous part of an aquatic animal (e g a fish or whale) used in propelling or guiding the body **2a** an appendage of a boat (e g a submarine) **b** a vertical control surface attached to an aircraft for directional stability

¹final /'faɪnl/ *adj* **1** not to be altered or undone; conclusive **2** being the last; occurring at the end **3** of or relating to the ultimate purpose or result of a process – ~ize *v* – ~ly *adv*

²final *n* **1** a deciding match, game, trial, etc in a sport or competition; *also*, *pl* a round made up of these **2** the last examination in a course – usu *pl*

finality /faɪ'nælɪti, fɪ-/ *n* **1** the condition of being at an ultimate point, esp of development or authority **2** a fundamental fact, action, or belief

¹finance /'faɪnæns, fɪ'næns/ *n* **1** *pl* resources of money **2** the system that includes the circulation of money and involves banking, credit, and investment **3** the science of the management of funds **4** the obtaining of funds – **-cial** *adj* – **-cially** *adv*

²finance *v* to raise or provide money for

¹find /faɪnd/ *v* **found** **1a** to come upon, esp accidentally; encounter **b** to meet with (a specified reception) **2a** to come upon or discover by searching, effort, or experiment; obtain **b** to obtain by effort or management **3a** to experience, feel **b** to perceive (oneself) to be in a specified place or condition **c** to gain or regain the use or power of **d** to bring (oneself) to a realization of one's powers or of one's true vocation **4** to provide, supply **5** to determine and announce

²find *n* **1** an act or instance of finding sthg, esp sthg valuable **2** sby or sthg found; *esp* a valuable object or talented person discovered

¹fine /faɪn/ *n* **1** a sum payable as punishment for an offence **2** a forfeiture or penalty paid to an injured party in a civil action

²fine *v* to punish by a fine – **finable**, **fineable** *adj*

³fine *adj* **1** free from impurity **2a** very thin in gauge or texture **b** consisting of relatively small particles **c** very small **d** keen, sharp **3a** subtle or sensitive in perception or discrimination **b** performed with extreme care and accuracy **4a** superior in quality, conception, or appearance; excellent **b** bright and sunny **5** marked by or affecting often excessive elegance or refinement **6** very well **7** awful – used as an intensive – ~ **ly** *adv* – ~**ness** *n*

⁴fine *v* **1** to purify, clarify – often + *down* **2** to make finer in quality or size – often + *down*

¹finger /ˈfɪŋgə/ *n* **1** any of the 5 parts at the end of the hand or forelimb; *esp* one other than the thumb **2a** sthg that resembles a finger, esp in being long, narrow, and often tapering in shape **b** a part of a glove into which a finger is inserted

²finger *v* **1** to play (a musical instrument) with the fingers **2** to touch or feel with the fingers; handle

fingerprint /ˈfɪŋgəprɪnt/ *n* **1** the impression of a fingertip on any surface; *esp* an ink impression of the lines upon the fingertip taken for purposes of identification **2** unique distinguishing characteristics (e g of a recording machine or infrared spectrum)

¹finish /ˈfɪnɪʃ/ *v* **1a** to end, terminate; *also* to end a relationship with sby, sthg, or use entirely – often + *off* or *up* **2a** to bring to completion or issue; complete, perfect – often + *off* **b** to complete the schooling of (a girl), esp in the social graces **3a** to bring to an end the significance or effectiveness of **b** to bring about the death of **4** to arrive, end, or come to rest in a specified position or manner – often + *up*

²finish *n* **1a** the final stage; the end **b** the cause of one's ruin; downfall **2** the texture or appearance of a surface, esp after a coating has been applied **3** the result or product of a finishing process **4** the quality or state of being perfected, esp in the social graces

fir /fɜː/ *n* (the wood of) any of various related evergreen trees of the pine family that have flattish leaves and erect cones

¹fire /faɪə/ *n* **1a** the phenomenon of combustion manifested in light, flame, and heat **b**(1) burning passion or emotion (2) inspiration **2** fuel in a state of combustion (e g in a fireplace or furnace) **3a** a destructive burning (e g of a building or forest) **b** a severe trial or ordeal **4** brilliance, luminosity **5** the

discharge of firearms **6** *Br* a small usu gas or electric domestic heater

²fire *v* **1a** to ignite **b**(1) to inspire (2) to inflame **2** to dismiss from a position **3** to discharge a firearm

firebrand /ˈfaɪəbrænd/ *n* **1** a piece of burning material, esp wood **2** one who creates unrest or strife; an agitator, troublemaker

fire brigade *n* an organization for preventing or extinguishing fires; *esp* one maintained in Britain by local government

fireman /ˈfaɪəmən/ *n, pl* **firemen 1** sby employed to extinguish fires **2** sby who tends or feeds fires or furnaces

fireplace /ˈfaɪəpleɪs/ *n* a usu framed opening made in a chimney to hold a fire; a hearth

firework /ˈfaɪəwɜːk/ *n* **1** a device for producing a striking display (e g of light or noise) by the combustion of explosive or inflammable mixtures **2** *pl* **a** a display of temper or intense conflict **b** pyrotechnics

¹firm /fɜːm/ *adj* **1a** securely or solidly fixed in place **b** not weak or uncertain; vigorous **c** having a solid or compact structure that resists stress or pressure **2** not subject to change, unsteadiness, or disturbance; steadfast **3** indicating firmness or resolution – ~**ly** *adv* – ~**ness** *n*

²firm *v* **1** to make solid, compact, or firm **2** to put into final form; settle **3** to support, strengthen *USE* often + *up*

³firm *n* a business partnership not usu recognized as a legal person distinct from the members composing it; *broadly* any business unit or enterprise

¹first /fɜːst/ *adj* **1** preceding all others in time, order, or importance: e g **a** earliest **b** being the lowest forward gear or speed of a motor vehicle **c** relating to or having the (most prominent and) usu highest part among a group of instruments or voices **2** least, slightest (e g hasn't the *first* idea what to do)

²first *adv* **1** before anything else; at the beginning **2** for the first time **3** in preference to sthg else

³first *n* sthg or sby that is first: e g **a** the first occurrence or item of a kind **b** the first and lowest forward gear or speed of a motor vehicle **c** the winning place in a contest **d** first, first class *often cap* the highest level of an honours degree

first aid *n* emergency care or treatment given to an ill or injured person before proper medical aid can be obtained

first class *n* the first or highest group in a classification: e g **a** the highest of usu 3 classes of travel accommodation **b** the highest level of an honours degree

¹fish /fɪʃ/ *n, pl* **fish, fishes 1a** an aquatic animal – usu in combination **b** (the edible flesh of) any of numerous cold-blooded aquatic vertebrates that typically have gills and an elongated scaly body **2** a person; *esp* a fellow – usu derog

²fish *v* **1** to try to catch fish **2** to seek

sthg by roundabout means **3a** to search for sthg underwater **b** to search (as if) by groping or feeling

³**fish** n a piece of wood or iron fastened alongside another member to strengthen it

fisherman /ˈfiʃəmən/ n **1** fem fisher-woman one who engages in fishing as an occupation or for pleasure **2** a ship used in commercial fishing

fishmonger /ˈfiʃmʌŋgə/ n, chiefly Br a retail fish dealer

fist /fist/ n the hand clenched with the fingers doubled into the palm and the thumb across the fingers

¹**fit** n **1a** a sudden violent attack of a disease (e g epilepsy), esp when marked by convulsions or unconsciousness **b** a sudden but transient attack of a specified physical disturbance **2** a sudden outburst or flurry, esp of a specified activity or emotion

²**fit** adj **1a** adapted or suited to an end or purpose **b** acceptable from a particular viewpoint (e g of competence, morality, or qualifications) **2a** in a suitable state; ready **b** in such a distressing state as to be ready to do or suffer sthg specified **3** healthy – ~ness n

³**fit** v fitted also fit **1** to be suitable for or to; harmonize with **2a** to be of the correct size or shape for **b** to insert or adjust until correctly in place **c** to try on (clothes) in order to make adjustments in size **d** to make a place or room for **3** to be in agreement or accord with **4** to cause to conform to or suit sthg **5** to supply, equip –often + out

⁴**fit** n **1** the manner in which clothing fits the wearer **2** the degree of closeness with which surfaces are brought together in an assembly of parts

five /faiv/ n **1** the number 5 **2** pl but sing in constr any of several games in which players hit a ball with their hands against the front wall of a 3- or 4-walled court

¹**fix** /fiks/ v **1a** to make firm, stable, or stationary **b(1)** to kill, harden, and pre-serve for microscopic study **(2)** to make the image of (a photographic film) per-manent by removing unused sensitive chemicals **c** to fasten, attach **2** to hold or direct steadily **3a** to set or place definitely; establish **b** to assign **4** to set in order; adjust **5** to repair, mend **6** chiefly NAm to get ready or prepare (esp food or drink) **7a** to get even with – infml **b** to influence by illicit means – infml

²**fix** n **1** a position of difficulty or embar-rassment; a trying predicament **2** (a determination of) the position (e g of a ship) found by bearings, radio, etc **3** a shot of a narcotic – slang

fixture /ˈfikstʃə/ n **1** fixing or being fixed **2** sthg fixed (e g to a building) as a permanent appendage or as a struc-tural part **3** (an esp sporting event held on) a settled date or time

¹**flag** /flæg/ n a (wild) iris or similar plant of damp ground with long leaves

²**flag** n a (slab of) hard evenly stratified stone that splits into flat pieces suitable for paving – **flag** v

³**flag** n **1** a usu rectangular piece of fabric of distinctive design that is used as a symbol (e g of a nation) or as a signal-ling device **2** the nationality or registra-tion of a ship, aircraft, etc

⁴**flag** v **1** to put a flag on (e g for identifi-cation) **2a** to signal to (as if) with a flag **b** to signal to stop – usu + down

⁵**flag** v to become feeble, less interesting, or less active; decline

flair /fleə/ n **1** intuitive discernment, esp in a specified field **2** natural apti-tude; talent **3** sophistication or smart-ness USE (1 & 2) usu + for

¹**flake** /fleik/ n a platform, tray, etc for drying fish or produce

²**flake** n **1** a small loose mass or particle **2** a thin flattened piece or layer; a chip **3** a pipe tobacco of small irregularly cut pieces

³**flake** v to form or separate into flakes; chip

¹**flame** /fleim/ n **1** (a tongue of) the glowing gaseous part of a fire **2a** a state of blazing usu destructive combustion – often pl with sing. meaning **b** a condi-tion or appearance suggesting a flame, esp in having red, orange, or yellow colour **c** a bright reddish orange colour **3** a sweetheart – usu in old flame

²**flame** v **1** to burn with a flame; blaze **2** to break out violently or passionately **3** to shine brightly like flame; glow

¹**flap** /flæp/ n **1** sthg broad or flat, flex-ible or hinged, and usu thin, that hangs loose or projects freely: e g **a** an extended part forming a closure (e g of an envelope or carton) **b** a movable control surface on an aircraft wing for increasing lift or lift and drag **2** the motion of sthg broad and flexible (e g a sail); also an instance of the up-and-down motion of a wing (e g of a bird) **3** a state of excitement or panicky confusion; an uproar – infml

²**flap** v **1** to sway loosely, usu with a noise of striking and esp when moved by the wind **2** to beat (sthg suggesting) wings **3** to be in a flap or panic – infml

¹**flare** /fleə/ v **1a** to shine or blaze with a sudden flame – usu + up **b** to become suddenly and often violently excited, angry, or active – usu + up **2** to open or spread outwards; esp to widen gradu-ally towards the lower edge

²**flare** n **1a** (a device or substance used to produce) a fire or blaze of light used to signal, illuminate, or attract attention **b** a temporary outburst of energy from a small area of the sun's surface **2** a sudden outburst (e g of sound, excite-ment, or anger) **3** a spreading out-wards; also a place or part that spreads

¹**flash** /flæʃ/ v **1a** to cause the sudden appearance or reflection of (esp light) **b(1)** to cause (e g a mirror) to reflect light **(2)** to cause (a light) to flash **c** to convey by means of flashes of light **2a** to make known or cause to appear with great speed **b** to display ostentatiously

c to expose to view suddenly and briefly

²flash *n* **1** a sudden burst of light **2** a sudden burst of perception, emotion, etc **3** a short time **4** an esp vulgar or ostentatious display **5a** a brief look; a glimpse **b** a brief news report, esp on radio or television **c** flashlight photography **6** a thin ridge on a cast or forged article, resulting from the hot metal, plastic, etc penetrating between the 2 parts of the mould **7** an indecent exposure of the genitals – *slang*

³flash *adj* **1** of sudden origin or onset and usu short duration; *also* carried out very quickly **2** flashy, showy – *infml*

flask /flɑːsk/ *n* **1** a broad flat bottle, usu of metal or leather-covered glass, used to carry alcohol or other drinks on the person **2** any of several conical, spherical, etc narrow-necked usu glass containers used in a laboratory **3** a vacuum flask

¹flat /flæt/ *adj* **1** having a continuous horizontal surface **2a** lying at full length or spread out on a surface; prostrate **b** resting with a surface against sthg **3** having a broad smooth surface and little thickness; *also* shallow **4a** clearly unmistakable; downright **b(1)** fixed, absolute **(2)** exact **5a** lacking animation; dull, monotonous; *also* inactive **b** having lost effervescence or sparkle **6a** *of a tyre* lacking air; deflated **b** *of a battery* completely or partially discharged **7a** *of a musical note* lowered a semitone in pitch **b** lower than the proper musical pitch **8** having a low trajectory **9a** uniform in colour **b** *of a painting* lacking illusion of depth **c** *esp of paint* having a matt finish – ~ness *n*

²flat *n* **1** a flat part or surface **2** (a character indicating) a musical note 1 semitone lower than a specified or particular note **3** a flat piece of theatrical scenery **4** a flat tyre **5** *often cap* horse racing over courses without jumps; *also* the season for this

³flat *adv* **1** positively, uncompromisingly **2a** on or against a flat surface **b** so as to be spread out; at full length **3** below the proper musical pitch **4** wholly, completely – *infml*

⁴flat *n* a self-contained set of rooms used as a dwelling

flatter /ˈflætəʳ/ *v* **1** to praise excessively, esp from motives of self-interest or in order to gratify another's vanity **2** to raise the hope of or gratify, often groundlessly or with intent to deceive **3** to portray or represent (too) favourably – ~er *n* – ~y *n*

¹flavour /ˈfleɪvəʳ/ *NAm chiefly* **flavor** *n* **1** the blend of taste and smell sensations evoked by a substance in the mouth; *also* a distinctive flavour **2** characteristic or predominant quality – ~less *adj*

²flavour, *NAm chiefly* **flavor** *v* to give or add flavour to

flaw /flɔː/ *n* **1** a blemish, imperfection **2** a usu hidden defect (e g a crack) that may cause failure under stress **3** a

weakness in sthg immaterial (e g an argument or piece of reasoning) – **flaw** *v*

flee /fliː/ *v* **fled 1** to run away from danger, evil, etc **2** to pass away swiftly; vanish

¹fleet /fliːt/ *n* **1** a number of warships under a single command **2** *often cap* a country's navy – usu + *the* **3** a group of ships, aircraft, lorries, etc owned or operated under one management

²fleet *adj* swift in motion; nimble – ~ly *adv* – ~ness *n*

¹flesh /fleʃ/ *n* **1a** the soft, esp muscular, parts of the body of a (vertebrate) animal as distinguished from visceral structures, bone, hide, etc **b** excess weight; fat **2** the edible parts of an animal **3a** the physical being of humans **b** the physical or sensual aspect of human nature **4a** human beings; humankind – esp in *all flesh* **b** kindred, stock **5** a fleshy (edible) part of a plant or fruit – ~y *adj*

²flesh *v* to clothe or cover (as if) with flesh; *broadly* to give substance to – usu + *out*

flew /fluː/ *past of* **fly**

¹flex /fleks/ *v* **1** to bend **2** to move (a muscle or muscles) so as to flex a limb or joint

²flex *n* a length of flexible insulated electrical cable used in connecting a portable electrical appliance to a socket

flexible /ˈfleksɪbəl/ *adj* **1** capable of being bent; pliant **2** yielding to influence; tractable **3** capable of changing in response to new conditions; versatile – ~ibly *adv* – ~ibility *n*

¹flicker /ˈflɪkəʳ/ *v* **1** to move irregularly or unsteadily; quiver **2a** to burn fitfully or with a fluctuating light **b** *of a light* to fluctuate in intensity

²flicker *n* **1** a flickering (movement or light) **2** a momentary quickening or stirring

¹flight /flaɪt/ *n* **1** a passage through the air using wings **2a** a passage or journey through air or space; *specif* any such flight scheduled by an airline **b** swift movement **3** a group of similar creatures or objects flying through the air **4** a brilliant, imaginative, or unrestrained exercise or display **5** (a series of locks, hurdles, etc resembling) a continuous series of stairs from one landing or floor to another **6** any of the vanes or feathers at the tail of a dart, arrow, etc that provide stability **7** a small unit of (military) aircraft or personnel in the Royal Air Force

²flight *n* an act or instance of fleeing

¹flimsy /ˈflɪmzi/ *adj* **1a** lacking in strength or substance **b** of inferior materials or workmanship; easily destroyed or broken **2** having little worth or plausibility – ~sily *adv* – ~siness *n*

²flimsy *n* (a document printed on) a lightweight paper used esp for multiple copies

fling /flɪŋ/ *v* **flung 1** to throw or cast (aside), esp with force or recklessness **2** to place or send suddenly and unceremoniously 3 to cast or direct (oneself or one's efforts) vigorously or unrestrainedly

²**fling** n 1 a period devoted to self-indulgence 2 a casual attempt – chiefly infml

¹**float** /fləʊt/ n 1a a cork or other device used to keep the baited end of a fishing line afloat b (e g a hollow ball) that floats at the end of a lever in a cistern, tank, or boiler and regulates the liquid level c a watertight structure enabling an aircraft to float on water 2 a tool for smoothing a surface of plaster, concrete, etc 3 (a vehicle with) a platform supporting an exhibit in a parade 4 a sum of money available for day-to-day use (e g for expenses or for giving change)

²**float** v 1 to rest on the surface of or be suspended in a fluid 2a to drift (as if) on or through a liquid b to wander aimlessly 3 to lack firmness of purpose; vacillate 4 of a currency to find a level in the international exchange market in response to the law of supply and demand and without artificial support or control 5 to present (e g an idea) for acceptance or rejection – **~er** n

¹**flock** /flɒk/ n sing or pl in constr 1 a group of birds or mammals assembled or herded together 2 a church congregation, considered in relation to its pastor 3 a large group

²**flock** v to gather or move in a crowd

³**flock** n 1 a tuft of wool or cotton fibre 2 woollen or cotton refuse used for stuffing furniture, mattresses, etc 3 very short or pulverized fibre used esp to form a velvety pattern on cloth or paper or a protective covering on metal

flog /flɒg/ v 1 to beat severely with a rod, whip, etc 2 to force into action; drive 3 to repeat (sthg) so frequently as to make uninteresting – esp in flog something to death; infml 4 Br to sell – slang

¹**flood** /flʌd/ n 1 an overflowing of a body of water, esp onto normally dry land 2 an overwhelming quantity or volume 3 a floodlight

²**flood** v 1 to cover with a flood; inundate 2 to fill abundantly or excessively 3 to drive out of a house, village, etc by flooding

¹**floor** /flɔːr/ n 1 the level base of a room 2a the lower inside surface of a hollow structure (e g a cave or bodily part) b a ground surface 3 a structure between 2 storeys of a building; also a storey 4a the part of an assembly in which members sit and speak b the members of an assembly c the right to address an assembly 5 a lower limit

²**floor** v 1 to knock to the floor or ground 2 to reduce to silence or defeat; nonplus

¹**flounder** /ˈflaʊndər/ n, pl **flounder**, esp for different types **flounders** any of various flatfishes including some marine food fishes

²**flounder** v 1 to struggle to move or obtain footing 2 to proceed or act clumsily or feebly

flour /ˈflaʊər/ n 1 finely ground meal, esp of wheat 2 a fine soft powder – **~y** adj

¹**flourish** /ˈflʌrɪʃ/ v 1 to grow luxuriantly; thrive 2a to prosper b to be in good health 3 to wave or wield with dramatic gestures; brandish – **~ingly** adv

²**flourish** n 1 a showy or flowery embellishment (e g in literature or handwriting) or passage (e g in music) 2a an act of brandishing b an ostentatious or dramatic action

¹**flow** /fləʊ/ v 1a to issue or move (as if) in a stream b to circulate 2 of the tide to rise 3 to abound 4a to proceed smoothly and readily b to have a smooth graceful continuity 5 to hang loose or freely

²**flow** n 1a a flowing 2a a smooth uninterrupted movement or supply; the motion characteristic of fluids b a stream or gush of fluid c the direction of (apparent) movement 3 the quantity that flows in a certain time

¹**flower** /ˈflaʊər/ n 1a a blossom b a plant cultivated for its blossoms 2a the finest or most perfect part or example b the finest most vigorous period; prime c a state of blooming or flourishing – esp in in flower – **~less** adj

²**flower** v 1 to produce flowers; blossom 2 to reach a peak condition; flourish

flown /fləʊn/ past part of fly

flu /fluː/ n influenza

fluent /ˈfluːənt/ adj 1 able to speak or write with facility; also spoken or written in this way 2 effortlessly smooth and rapid; polished – **-ency** n – **~ly** adv

¹**fluid** /ˈfluːɪd/ adj 1a able to flow b likely or tending to change or move; not fixed 2 characterized by or employing a smooth easy style 3 easily converted into cash – **~ity** n

²**fluid** n sthg capable of flowing to conform to the outline of its container; specif a liquid or gas

flung /flʌŋ/ past of fling

¹**flutter** /ˈflʌtər/ v 1 to flap the wings rapidly 2a to move with quick wavering or flapping motions b to beat or vibrate in irregular spasms 3 to move about or behave in an agitated aimless manner

²**flutter** n 1 a state of (nervous) confusion, excitement, or commotion 2 chiefly Br a small gamble or bet

¹**fly** /flaɪ/ v flew; flown 1a to move in or through the air by means of wings b to float, wave, or soar in the air 2 to take flight; flee 3a to move, act, or pass swiftly b to move or pass suddenly and violently into a specified state 4 to operate or travel in an aircraft or spacecraft 5 to depart in haste; dash – chiefly infml

²**fly** n 1 pl the space over a stage where scenery and equipment can be hung 2 (a garment) opening concealed by a fold of cloth extending over the fastener; esp, pl such an opening in the front of a pair of trousers

fly

³**fly** *adj, chiefly Br* keen, artful – *infml*

⁴**fly** *n* **1** a winged insect – often in combination (e g *mayfly*) **2** a natural or artificial fly attached to a fishhook for use as bait

¹**foam** /fəʊm/ *n* **1a** (a substance in the form of) a light frothy mass of fine bubbles formed in or on the surface of a liquid (e g by agitation or fermentation) **b** a frothy mass formed in salivating or sweating **c** a chemical froth discharged from fire extinguishers **2** a material in a lightweight cellular form resulting from introduction of gas bubbles during manufacture **3** *the sea* – poetic – **foamy** *adj*

²**foam** *v* **1a** to produce or form foam **b** to froth at the mouth, esp in anger; *broadly* to be angry **2** to gush out in foam **3** to become covered (as if) with foam **4** to cause air bubbles to form in

¹**focus** /'fəʊkəs/ *n, pl* **focuses, foci 1a** a point at which rays (e g of light, heat, or sound) converge or from which they (appear to) diverge after reflection or refraction **b** the point at which an object must be placed for an image formed by a lens or mirror to be sharp **2a** the distance between a lens and the point at which it forms a focus **b** adjustment (e g of the eye) necessary for distinct vision **c** a state in which sthg must be placed in order to be clearly perceived **2** a centre of activity or attention **4** the place of origin of an earthquake – **focal** *adj*

²**focus** *v* **1** to bring or come to a focus; converge **2** to cause to be concentrated **3** to adjust the focus of **4** to bring one's eyes or a camera to a focus

foetus /'fiːtəs/ *fetus n* an unborn or unhatched vertebrate; *specif* a developing human from usu 3 months after conception to birth – **foetal** *adj*

¹**fog** /fɒg/ *n* **1** a murky condition of the atmosphere caused esp by fine particles, specif of water, suspended in the lower atmosphere **2a** a state of confusion or bewilderment **b** sthg that confuses or obscures

²**fog** *v* **1** to envelop or suffuse (as if) with fog **2** to make confused or confusing **3** to produce fog on (e g a photographic film) during development

foggy /'fɒgi/ *adj* **1a** thick with fog **b** covered or made opaque by moisture or grime **2** blurred, obscured – **-ily** *adv* – **-iness** *n*

¹**fold** /fəʊld/ *n* **1** an enclosure for sheep; *also* a flock of sheep **2** *sing or pl in constr* a group of people adhering to a common faith, belief, or enthusiasm

²**fold** *v* to pen (e g sheep) in a fold

³**fold** *v* **1** to lay one part of over another part **2** to reduce the length or bulk of by doubling over – often + *up* **3a** to clasp together; entwine **b** to bring (limbs) to rest close to the body **4a** to clasp closely; embrace **b** to wrap, envelop **5** to gently incorporate (a food ingredient) into a mixture without thorough stirring or beating – usu + *in* **6** to become or be capable of being folded **7** to fail completely; *esp* to stop production or operation because of lack of business or capital – often + *up*; chiefly *infml*

⁴**fold** *n* **1** (a crease made by) a doubling or folding over **2** a part doubled or laid over another part; a pleat **3** (a hollow inside) sthg that is folded or that enfolds **4** *chiefly Br* an undulation in the landscape

folk /fəʊk/ *n* **1** *pl in constr* the great proportion of a people that tends to preserve its customs, superstitions, etc **2** *pl in constr* a specified kind or class of people – often pl with sing. meaning **3** simple music, usu song, of traditional origin or style **4** *pl in constr* people generally – *infml*; often pl with sing. meaning **5** *pl* the members of one's own family; relatives – *infml*

²**folk** *adj* **1** originating or traditional with the common people **2** of (the study of) the common people

follow /'fɒləʊ/ *v* **1** to go, proceed, or come after **2** to pursue, esp in an effort to overtake **3a** to accept as a guide or leader **b** to obey or act in accordance with **4** to copy, imitate **5a** to walk or proceed along **b** to engage in as a calling or way of life; pursue (e g a course of action) **6** to come or take place after in time or order **7** to come into existence or take place as a result or consequence of **8a** to attend closely to; keep abreast of **b** to understand the logic of (e g an argument) **9** to go or come after sby or sthg in place, time, or sequence **10** to result or occur as a consequence or inference

follower /'fɒləʊə'/ *n* **1a** one who follows the opinions or teachings of another **b** one who imitates another **2** a fan

folly /'fɒli/ *n* **1** lack of good sense or prudence **2** a foolish act or idea **3** (criminally or tragically) foolish actions or conduct **4** a usu fanciful structure (e g a summerhouse) built esp for scenic effect or to satisfy a whim

fond /fɒnd/ *adj* **1** foolish, silly **2** having an affection or liking for sthg specified – + *of* **3a** foolishly tender; indulgent **b** affectionate, loving **4** doted on; cherished – ~**ly** *adv* – ~**ness** *n*

food /fuːd/ *n* **1a** (minerals, vitamins, etc together with) material consisting essentially of protein, carbohydrate, and fat taken into the body of a living organism and used to provide energy and sustain processes (e g growth and repair) essential for life **b** inorganic substances absorbed (e g in gaseous form or in solution) by plants **2** nutriment in solid form **3** sthg that sustains or supplies

¹**fool** /fuːl/ *n* **1** a person lacking in prudence, common sense, or understanding **2a** a jester **b** a person who is victimized or made to appear foolish; a dupe **3** a cold dessert of fruit puree mixed with whipped cream or custard

²**fool** *v* **1a** to act or spend time idly or aimlessly **b** to meddle, play, or trifle *with* **2** to play or improvise a comic

role; *specif* to joke **3** to make a fool of; deceive

³fool *adj* foolish, silly – *infml*

foolish /'fuːlɪʃ/ *adj* **1** marked by or proceeding from folly **2** absurd, ridiculous – ~**ly** *adv* – ~**ness** *n*

¹foot /fʊt/ *n, pl* **feet 1** the end part of the vertebrate leg on which an animal stands **2** an organ of locomotion or attachment of an invertebrate animal, esp a mollusc **3** a unit of length equal to ⅓yd (0.305m) **4** the basic unit of verse metre consisting of any of various fixed combinations of stressed and unstressed or long and short syllables **5** manner or motion of walking or running; step **6a** the lower end of the leg of a chair, table, etc **b** the piece on a sewing machine that presses the cloth against the feed **7** the lower edge or lowest part; the bottom **8a** the end that is opposite the head or top or nearest to the human feet **b** the part (e g of a stocking) that covers the human foot

²foot *v* **1** to walk, run, or dance on, over, or through **2** to pay or stand credit for

football /'fʊtbɔːl/ *n* (the inflated round or oval ball used in) any of several games, esp soccer, that are played between 2 teams on a usu rectangular field having goalposts at each end and whose object is to get the ball over a goal line or between goalposts by running, passing, or kicking

footing /'fʊtɪŋ/ *n* **1** a stable position or placing of or for the feet **2** a (condition of a) surface with respect to its suitability for walking or running on **3a** an established position **b** a position or rank in relation to others

footpath /'fʊtpɑːθ/ *n* a narrow path for pedestrians; *also* a pavement

footstep /'fʊtstep/ *n* **1** the sound of a step or tread **2** distance covered by a step

¹for /fə'; *strong* fɔː'/ *prep* **1a** – used to indicate purpose (e g a grant *for* studying medicine) goal or direction (e g left *for* home) or that which is to be had or gained (e g run *for* your life) **b** to belong to (e g the flowers are *for* you) **2** as being or constituting (e g ate it *for* breakfast) **3** because of (e g cried *for* joy) **4a** in place of (e g change *for* a pound) **b** on behalf of; representing (e g acting *for* my client) **c** in support of; in favour of (e g he played *for* England) **5** considered as; considering (e g tall *for* her age) **6** with respect to; concerning (e g famous *for* its scenery) **7** – used to indicate cost, payment, equivalence, or correlation (e g £7 *for* a hat) **8** – used to indicate duration of time or extent of space (e g *for* 10 miles; gone *for* months) **9** on the occasion of or at the time of (e g came home *for* Christmas)

²for *conj* **1** and the reason is that **2** because

³for *adj* being in favour of a motion or measure

forbid /fə'bɪd/ *v* **forbidding; forbade, forbad; forbidden 1a** to refuse (e g by authority) to allow; command against **b**

to refuse access to or use of **2** to make impracticable; hinder, prevent – **-bidden** *adj*

¹force /fɔːs/ *n* **1a** strength or energy exerted or brought to bear; active power **b** moral or mental strength **c** capacity to persuade or convince **d** (legal) validity; operative effect **2a** *pl* the armed services of a nation or commander **b** a body of people or things fulfilling an often specified function **c** an individual or group having the power of effective action **3** violence, compulsion, or constraint exerted on or against a person or thing **4a** (the intensity of) an agency that if applied to a free body results chiefly in an acceleration of the body and sometimes in elastic deformation and other effects **b** an agency or influence analogous to a physical force **5** *cap* a measure of wind strength as expressed by a number on the Beaufort scale

²force *v* **1** to compel by physical, moral, or intellectual means **2** to make or cause through natural or logical necessity **3a** to press, drive, or effect against resistance or inertia **b** to impose or thrust urgently, importunately, or inexorably **4** to break open or through **5a** to raise or accelerate to the utmost **b** to produce only with unnatural or unwilling effort **6** to hasten the growth, onset of maturity, or rate of progress of

¹forecast /'fɔːkɑːst/ *v* **1** to estimate or predict (some future event or condition), esp as a result of rational study and analysis of available pertinent data **2** to serve as a forecast of; presage **3** to calculate or predict the future

²forecast /'fɔːkɑːst/ *n* a prophecy, estimate, or prediction of a future happening or condition; *esp* a weather forecast

forefront /'fɔːfrʌnt/ *n* the foremost part or place; the vanguard

foreground /'fɔːgraʊnd/ *n* **1** the part of a picture or view nearest to and in front of the spectator **2** a position of prominence; the forefront

forehead /'fɔrɪd, 'fɔːhed/ *n* the part of the face above the eyes

foreign /'fɒrɪn/ *adj* **1** (situated) outside a place or country; *esp* (situated) outside one's own country **2** born in, belonging to, or characteristic of some place or country other than the one under consideration **3** alien in character; not connected or pertinent *to* **4** of, concerned with, or dealing with other nations **5** occurring in an abnormal situation in the living body and commonly introduced from outside

foreigner /'fɒrɪnə'/ *n* **1** a person belonging to or owing allegiance to a foreign country; an alien **2** *chiefly dial* a stranger; *esp* a person not native to a community

foreman /'fɔːmən/ *fem* **forewoman** *n* **1** the chairman and spokesman of a jury **2** a person, often a chief worker, who supervises a group of workers, a particular operation, or a section of a plant

¹foremost /'fɔːməʊst/ adj **1** first in a series or progression **2** of first rank or position; preeminent

²foremost adv most importantly

foresee /fɔː'siː/ v foreseeing; foresaw; foreseen to be aware of (e g a development) beforehand – ~able adj

¹forest /'forɪst/ n **1** a tract of wooded land in Britain formerly owned by the sovereign and used for hunting game **2** a dense growth of trees and underbrush covering a large tract of land **3** sthg resembling a profusion of trees

²forest v to cover with trees or forest

foretell /fɔː'tel/ v foretold to tell beforehand; predict

forever /fə'revə/ adv **1** for all future time; indefinitely **2** persistently, incessantly

¹forfeit /'fɔːfɪt/ n **1** sthg lost, taken away, or imposed as a penalty **2** the loss or forfeiting of sthg, esp of civil rights **3a** an article deposited or a task performed in the game of forfeits **b** pl but sing or pl in constr a game in which articles are deposited (e g for making a mistake) and then redeemed by performing a silly task – **forfeit** adj

²forfeit v **1** to lose the right to by some error, offence, or crime **2** to subject to confiscation as a forfeit – ~ure n

¹forge /fɔːdʒ/ n (a workshop with) an open furnace where metal, esp iron, is heated and wrought – ~ing n

²forge v **1** to shape (metal or a metal object) by heating and hammering or with a press **2** to form or bring into being, esp by an expenditure of effort **3** to counterfeit (esp a signature, document, or bank note) **4** to commit forgery – ~r n

³forge v **1** to move forwards slowly and steadily but with effort **2** to move with a sudden increase of speed and power

forget /fə'get/ v forgetting; forgot; forgotten **1** to fail to remember **2** to fail to give attention to; disregard **3** to disregard intentionally

forgive /fə'gɪv/ v forgave; forgiven **1** to cease to resent **2** to pardon – -vable adj – -ving adj

forgiveness /fə'gɪvnɪs/ n forgiving or being forgiven; pardon

¹fork /fɔːk/ n **1** a tool or implement with 2 or more prongs set on the end of a handle: e g **a** an agricultural or gardening tool for digging, carrying, etc **b** a small implement for eating or serving food **2a** a forked part, or piece of equipment **b** a forked support for a cycle wheel – often pl with sing. meaning **3** (a part containing) a division into branches **4** any of the branches into which sthg forks

²fork v **1** to divide into 2 or more branches **2** to make a turn into one of the branches of a fork **3** to pay, contribute – + out, over, or up

forked /fɔːkt/ adj having one end divided into 2 or more branches or points

¹form /fɔːm/ n **1** the shape and structure of sthg as distinguished from its material **2** the essential nature of a thing as distinguished from the matter in which it is embodied **3a** established or correct method of proceeding or behaving **b** a prescribed and set order of words **4** a printed or typed document; esp one with blank spaces for insertion of required or requested information **5** conduct regulated by external controls (e g custom or etiquette); ceremony **6a** the bed or nest of a hare **b** a long seat; a bench **7** sthg (e g shuttering) that holds, supports, and determines shape **8a** the way in which sthg is arranged, exists, or shows itself **b** a kind, variety **9** the structural element, plan, or design of a work of art **10** sing or pl in constr a class organized for the work of a particular year, esp in a British school **11a** the past performances of a competitor considered as a guide to its future performance **b** known ability to perform **c** condition suitable for performing, esp in sports – often + in, out of, or off **12** Br a criminal record – slang – ~less adj

²form v **1** to give form, shape, or existence to **2a** to give a particular shape to; shape or mould into a certain state or after a particular model **b** to model or train by instruction and discipline **3** to develop, acquire **4** to serve to make up or constitute; be a usu essential or basic element of

formal /'fɔːməl/ adj **1a** determining or being the essential constitution or structure **b** of, concerned with, or being the (outward) form of sthg as distinguished from its content **2a** following or based on conventional forms and rules **b** characterized by punctilious respect for correct procedure **3** having the appearance without the substance; ostensible – ~ly adv

¹former /'fɔːmə/ adj **1** of or occurring in the past **2** preceding in time or order **3** first of 2 things (understood to have been) mentioned

²former n, pl former the first mentioned; first

formerly /'fɔːməli/ adv at an earlier time; previously

formula /'fɔːmjʊlə/ n, pl formulas, formulae **1a** a set form of words for use in a ceremony or ritual **b** (a conventionalized statement intended to express) a truth, principle, or procedure, esp as a basis for negotiation or action **2** (a list of ingredients used in) a recipe **3a** a fact, rule, or principle expressed in symbols **b** a symbolic expression of the chemical composition of a substance **4** a prescribed or set form or method (e g of writing); an established rule or custom **5** a classification of racing cars specifying esp size, weight, and engine capacity

fort /fɔːt/ n a strong or fortified place

forth /fɔːθ/ adv **1** onwards in time, place, or order; forwards (e g from this day forth) **2** out into notice or view (e g put forth leaves) **3** away from a centre; abroad (e g went forth to preach)

fortnight /'fɔːtnaɪt/ n, chiefly Br two weeks

fortunate /ˈfɔːtʃənət/ *adj* 1 unexpectedly bringing some good; auspicious 2 lucky

fortune /ˈfɔːtʃən/ *n* 1 *often cap* a supposed (personified) power that unpredictably determines events and issues 2a (prosperity attained partly through) luck b *pl* the favourable or unfavourable events that accompany the progress of an individual or thing 3 destiny, fate 4 material possessions or wealth

forty /ˈfɔːti/ *n* 1 the number 40 2 *pl* the numbers 40 to 49; *specif* a range of temperatures, ages, or dates in a century characterized by those numbers

¹**forward** /ˈfɔːwəd/ *adj* 1a located at or directed towards the front b situated in advance 2a eager, ready b lacking modesty or reserve; pert 3 advanced in development; precocious 4 moving, tending, or leading towards a position in (or at the) front 5 of or getting ready for the future (e g *forward* planning) – ~ly *adv* – ~ness *n*

²**forward** *adv* 1 to or towards what is ahead or in front 2 to or towards an earlier time (e g bring *forward* the date of the meeting) 3 into prominence

³**forward** *n* a mainly attacking player in hockey, soccer, etc stationed at or near the front of his/her side or team

⁴**forward** *v* 1 to help onwards; promote 2a to send (forwards) b to send onwards from an intermediate point in transit – ~ing *n*

fought /fɔːt/ *past of* **fight**

¹**foul** /faul/ *adj* 1 dirty, stained 2 notably offensive, unpleasant, or distressing 3 obscene, abusive 4a treacherous, dishonourable b constituting a foul in a game or sport 5 polluted 6 entangled – ~ly *adv* – ~ness *n*

²**foul** *n* 1 an entanglement or collision in angling, sailing, etc 2 an infringement of the rules in a game or sport

³**foul** *v* 1 to commit a foul in a sport or game 2 to pollute 3 to become entangled with 4 to obstruct, block 5 to dishonour, discredit

¹**found** /faund/ *past of* **find**

²**found** *adj* having all usual, standard, or reasonably expected equipment

³**found** *v* 1 to set or ground on sthg solid – often + *on* or *upon* 2 to establish (e g a city or institution)

foundation /faunˈdeɪʃən/ *n* 1 the act of founding 2 the basis on which sthg stands or is supported 3 an organization or institution established by endowment with provision for future maintenance 4 an underlying natural or prepared base or support; *esp* the whole masonry substructure on which a building rests 5 a cream, lotion, etc applied as a base for other facial make-up

founder /ˈfaundə/ *v* 1 to go lame 2 to collapse; give way 3 to sink 4 to come to grief; fail

¹**fountain** /ˈfauntɪn/ *n* 1 a spring of water issuing from the earth 2 a source 3 (the structure providing) an artificially produced jet of water

²**fountain** *v* to (cause to) flow or spout like a fountain

four /fɔː/ *n* 1 the number 4 2 sthg having 4 parts or members or a denomination of 4; *esp* (the crew of) a 4-person racing rowing boat 3 a shot in cricket that crosses the boundary after having hit the ground and scores 4 runs

fourth /fɔːθ/ *n* 1 (the combination of 2 notes at) a musical interval of 4 diatonic degrees 3 the 4th and usu highest forward gear or speed of a motor vehicle

fowl /faul/ *n* 1 a bird 2 a domestic fowl; *esp* an adult hen 3 the flesh of birds used as food

¹**fox** /fɒks/ *n* 1 (the fur of) a red fox or related flesh-eating mammal of the dog family with a pointed muzzle, large erect ears, and a long bushy tail 2 a clever crafty person

²**fox** *v* 1 to outwit 2 to baffle

fraction /ˈfrækʃən/ *n* 1a a number (e g ¾, ⅝, 0.234) that is expressed as the quotient of 2 numbers b a (small) portion or section 2 an act of breaking up 3 a tiny bit; a little 4 any of several separate portions separable by distillation

¹**fracture** /ˈfræktʃə/ *n* a break or breaking, esp of hard tissue (e g bone)

²**fracture** *v* 1 to cause or undergo fracture 2 to damage or destroy as if by breaking apart; break up

fragile /ˈfrædʒaɪl/ *adj* 1 easily shattered 2 lacking in strength; delicate – -gility *n*

¹**fragment** /ˈfrægmənt/ *n* an incomplete, broken off, or detached part

²**fragment** /frægˈment/ *v* to break up or apart into fragments

frail /freɪl/ *adj* 1 morally or physically weak 2 easily broken or destroyed 3 slight, insubstantial

¹**frame** /freɪm/ *v* 1 to plan, shape 2 to fit or adjust for a purpose 3a to contrive evidence against (an innocent person) b to prearrange the outcome of (e g a contest)

²**frame** *n* 1 the physical structure of a human body 2 a structure that gives shape or strength (e g to a building) 3a an open case or structure made for admitting, enclosing, or supporting sthg b the rigid part of a bicycle c the outer structure of a pair of glasses that holds the lenses 4a an enclosing border b the matter or area enclosed in such a border: e g (1) a single picture of the series on a length of film (2) a single complete television picture made up of lines c a limiting, typical, or esp appropriate set of circumstances; a framework 5 one round of play in snooker, bowling, etc

framework /ˈfreɪmwɜːk/ *n* 1 a skeletal, openwork, or structural frame 2 a basic structure (e g of ideas)

¹**frank** /fræŋk/ *adj* marked by free, forthright, and sincere expression *also* undisguised – ~ness *n* – ~ly *adv*

²**frank** *n* a mark or stamp on a piece of mail indicating postage paid – **frank** *v*

Frank *n* a member of a W Germanic

people that established themselves in the Netherlands and Gaul and on the Rhine in the 3rd and 4th c

fraud /frɔːd/ *n* **1a** deception, esp for unlawful gain **b** a trick **2a** a person who is not what he/she pretends to be **b** sthg that is not what it seems or is represented to be

¹**freak** /friːk/ *n* **1** a person or animal with a physical oddity who appears in a circus, funfair, etc **2** a person seen as being highly unconventional, esp in dress or ideas **3** an ardent enthusiast **4a** a sexual pervert **b** someone addicted to a specified drug – *slang* – **freak** *adj*

²**freak** *v* to freak out – *slang*

¹**free** /friː/ *adj* **1a** enjoying civil and political liberty **b** not subject to the control or domination of another **2a** not determined by external influences **b** voluntary, spontaneous **3a** exempt, relieved, or released, esp from an unpleasant or unwanted condition or obligation – often in combination **b** not bound, confined, or detained by force **4a** having no trade restrictions **b** not subject to government regulation **5** having or taken up with no obligations or commitments **6** having an unrestricted scope **7a** not obstructed or impeded **b** not being used or occupied **8** not fastened **9a** lavish, unrestrained **b** outspoken **c** too familiar or forward **10** not costing or charging anything **11** not (permanently) united with, attached to, or combined with sthg else; separate **12a** not literal or exact **b** not restricted by or conforming to conventional forms – **~ly** *adv*

²**free** *adv* **1** in a free manner **2** without charge

³**free** *v* **1** to cause to be free **2** to relieve or rid of sthg that restrains, confines, restricts, or embarrasses **3** to disentangle, clear

freedom /'friːdəm/ *n* **1a** the absence of necessity or constraint in choice or action **b** liberation from slavery or restraint **c** being exempt or released *from* sthg (onerous) **2a** ease, facility **b** being frank, open, or outspoken **c** improper familiarity **3** boldness of conception or execution **4** unrestricted use *of*

¹**freeze** /friːz/ *v* **froze; frozen 1** to convert from a liquid to a solid by cold **2a** to make extremely cold **b** to anaesthetize (as if) by cold **3a** to become clogged with ice **b** to become fixed or motionless; *esp* to abruptly cease acting or speaking **4** to immobilize the expenditure, withdrawal, or exchange of (foreign-owned bank balances) by government regulation **5** to preserve (e g food) by freezing

²**freeze** *n* **1** freezing cold weather **2** an act or period of freezing sthg, esp wages or prices at a certain level

freezer /'friːzəʳ/ *n* an apparatus that freezes or keeps cool; *esp* an insulated cabinet or room for storing frozen food or for freezing food rapidly

¹**frequent** /'friːkwənt/ *adj* **1** often

repeated or occurring **2** habitual, persistent – **~ly** *adv*

²**frequent** /fri'kwent/ *v* to be in or visit often or habitually

¹**fresh** /freʃ/ *adj* **1a** not salt **b** free from taint; clean **c** *of weather* cool and windy **2a** *of food* not preserved or frozen **b** not stale, sour, or decayed **3a** (different or alternative and) new **b** newly or just come or arrived **4** too forward with a person of the opposite sex – *infml* – **~ness** *n*

²**fresh** *adv* **1** just recently; newly **2** *chiefly NAm* as of a very short time ago

friction /'frɪkʃən/ *n* **1a** the rubbing of one body against another **b** resistance to relative motion between 2 bodies in contact **2** disagreement between 2 people or parties of opposing views

Friday /'fraɪdi/ *n* the day of the week following Thursday

friend /frend/ *n* **1a** a person whose company, interests, and attitudes one finds sympathetic and to whom one is not closely related **b** an acquaintance **2a** sby or sthg not hostile **b** sby or sthg that favours or encourages sthg (e g a charity) **3** *cap* a Quaker

¹**friendly** /'frendli/ *adj* **1a** having the relationship of friends **b** not hostile **c** inclined to be favourable – usu + *to* **2** cheerful, comforting – **-iness** *n*

²**friendly** *n, chiefly Br* a match played for practice or pleasure and not as part of a competition

friendship /'frendʃɪp/ *n* being friends or being friendly

fright /fraɪt/ *n* **1** fear excited by sudden danger or shock **2** sthg unsightly, strange, ugly, or shocking – *infml* – **fright** *v*

frighten /'fraɪtn/ *v* **1** to make afraid; scare **2** to force by frightening – **~ingly** *adv*

frightful /'fraɪtfəl/ *adj* **1** causing intense fear, shock, or horror **2** unpleasant, difficult – *infml* – **~ness** *n* – **~ly** *adv*

¹**fringe** /frɪndʒ/ *n* **1** an ornamental border (e g on a curtain or garment) consisting of straight or twisted threads or tassels **2** the hair that falls over the forehead **3a** sthg marginal, additional, or secondary **b** *sing or pl in constr* a group with marginal or extremist views **c** *often cap* theatre featuring small-scale avant-garde productions

²**fringe** *v* **1** to provide or decorate with a fringe **2** to serve as a fringe for

frog /frɒg/ *n* **1** any of various tailless smooth-skinned web-footed largely aquatic leaping amphibians **2** the triangular horny pad in the middle of the sole of a horse's foot **3** a usu ornamental fastening for the front of a garment consisting of a button and a loop **4** *often cap* a French person – *chiefly derog; infml* **5** the hollow in either or both faces of a brick to take mortar

from /frəm; *strong* frɒm/ *prep* **1** – used to indicate a starting point: e g **a** a place where a physical movement, or an action or condition suggestive of movement, begin (e g came here *from* the

fum

city) **b** a starting point in measuring or reckoning or in a statement of extent or limits (e g lives 5 miles *from* the coast) **c** a point in time after which a period is reckoned (e g a week *from* today) **d** a viewpoint **2** – used to indicate separation: e g **a** physical separation (e g absent *from* school) **b** removal, refraining, exclusion, release, or differentiation (e g relief *from* pain; don't know one *from* the other) **3** – used to indicate the source, cause, agent, or basis (e g a call *from* my lawyer; made *from* flour)

¹**front** /frʌnt/ n **1** (feigned) demeanour or bearing, esp in the face of a challenge, danger, etc **2** *often cap* a zone of conflict between armies **3a** a sphere of activity **b** a movement linking divergent elements to achieve certain common objectives; *esp* a political coalition **4a** the (main) face of a building **b** the forward part or surface: e g **(1)** the part of the human body opposite to the back **(2)** the part of a garment covering the chest **c** *the* beach promenade at a seaside resort **5** the boundary between 2 dissimilar air masses **6a** a position ahead of a person or of the foremost part of a thing **b** a position of importance, leadership, or advantage **7** a person, group, or thing used to mask the identity or true character of the actual controlling agent; *also* a poorly nominal head

²**front** v **1** to face – often + *on* or *onto* **2** to serve as a front – often + *for*

³**front** adj of or situated at the front

frontier /ˈfrʌntɪə/ n **1** a border between 2 countries **2** the boundary between the known and the unknown – often pl with sing. meaning **3** *NAm* a region that forms the margin of settled or developed territory

¹**frost** /frɒst/ n **1a** (the temperature that causes) freezing **b** a covering of minute ice crystals on a cold surface **2** coldness of attitude or manner

²**frost** v **1** to freeze – often + *over* **2a** to produce a fine-grained slightly roughened surface on (metal, glass, etc) **b** to cover (e g a cake or grapes) with sugar; *also, chiefly NAm* to ice (a cake)

frosty /ˈfrɒsti/ adj **1** marked by or producing frost **2** (appearing as if) covered with frost **3** marked by coolness or extreme reserve in manner – **-ily** adv – **-iness** n

¹**frown** /fraʊn/ v **1** to contract the brow **2** to give evidence of displeasure or disapproval – often + *on* or *upon* – **~ingly** adv

²**frown** n **1** a wrinkling of the brow in displeasure, concentration, or puzzlement **2** an expression of displeasure

froze /frəʊz/ *past of* **freeze**

frozen /ˈfrəʊzən/ adj **1a** treated, affected, solidified, or crusted over by freezing **b** subject to long and severe cold **2a** drained or incapable of emotion **b** incapable of being changed, moved, or undone **c** not available for present use

fruit /fruːt/ n **1a** a product of plant growth (e g grain or vegetables) **b** a

succulent edible plant part used chiefly in a dessert or sweet dish **c** the ripened fertilized ovary of a flowering plant together with its contents **2** offspring, progeny **3a** a (favourable) product or result – often pl with sing. meaning – **fruit** v

fruitful /ˈfruːtfəl/ adj **1** (conducive to) yielding or producing (abundant) fruit **2** abundantly productive – **~ly** adv – **~ness** n

frustrate /frʌˈstreɪt/ v **1a** to balk or defeat in an endeavour; foil **b** to induce feelings of discouragement and vexation in **2** to make ineffectual; nullify – **-ation** n

¹**fry** /fraɪ/ v to cook in hot fat

²**fry**, pl **fry** **1a** recently hatched or very small (adult) fishes **b** the young of other animals, esp when occurring in large numbers **2** a member of a group or class; *esp* a person

¹**fuel** /ˈfjuːəl/ n **1a** a material used to produce heat or power by combustion **b** nutritive material **2** a source of sustenance, strength, or encouragement

²**fuel** v **1** to provide with fuel **2** to support, stimulate

¹**fugitive** /ˈfjuːdʒɪtɪv/ adj **1** running away or trying to escape **2a** elusive **b** likely to change, fade, or disappear

²**fugitive** n a person who flees or tries to escape, esp from danger, justice, or oppression

fulfil /fʊlˈfɪl/ *NAm chiefly* **fulfill** v **1a** to cause to happen as appointed or predicted – usu pass **b** to put into effect **c** to measure up to; satisfy **2** to develop the full potential of – **~ment** n

¹**full** /fʊl/ adj **1** possessing or containing a great amount or as much or as many as is possible or normal **2a** complete, esp in detail, number, or duration **b** lacking restraint, check, or qualification **3** at the highest or greatest degree; maximum **4** rounded in outline; *also* well filled out or plump **5a** having an abundance of material (e g in the form of gathers or folds) **b** rich in experience **6** satisfied, esp with food or drink, often to the point of discomfort – usu + *up* **7** filled with excited anticipation or pleasure **8** possessing a rich or pronounced quality – **~ness, fulness** n

²**full** adv exactly, squarely

³**full** n **1** the highest or fullest state, extent, or degree **2** the requisite or complete amount – chiefly in *in full*

⁴**full** v to cleanse and finish (woollen cloth) by moistening, heating, and pressing – **~er** n

full-scale adj **1** identical to an original in proportion and size **2** involving full use of available resources

full stop n a punctuation mark . used to mark the end (e g of a sentence or abbreviation)

fully /ˈfʊli/ adv **1** completely **2** at least

fumble /ˈfʌmbəl/ v **1a** to grope for or handle sthg clumsily or awkwardly **b** to make awkward attempts to do or find sthg **2** to feel one's way or move awkwardly – **~r** n

¹fume /fjuːm/ n 1 an (irritating or offensive) smoke, vapour, or gas – often pl with sing. meaning 2 a state of unreasonable excited irritation or anger

²fume v 1 to emit fumes 2 to be in a state of excited irritation or anger

¹fun /fʌn/ n 1 (a cause of) amusement or enjoyment 2 derisive jest; ridicule 3 violent or excited activity or argument

²fun adj providing entertainment, amusement, or enjoyment – infml

¹function /'fʌŋkʃən/ n 1 an occupational duty 2 the action characteristic of a person or thing or for which a thing exists 3 an impressive, elaborate, or formal ceremony or social gathering 4 a quality, trait, or fact dependent on and varying with another

²function v 1 to have a function; serve 2 to operate

¹fund /fʌnd/ n 1 an available quantity of material or intangible resources 2 (an organization administering) a resource, esp a sum of money, whose principal or interest is set apart for a specific objective 3 pl an available supply of money

²fund v 1 to make provision of resources for discharging the interest or principal of 2 to provide funds for

¹fundamental /ˌfʌndə'mentl/ adj 1 serving as a basis to support existence or to determine essential structure or function – often + to 2 of essential structure, function, or facts 3 of, being, or produced by the lowest component of a complex vibration 4 of central importance; principal

²fundamental n 1 a minimum constituent without which a thing or system would not be what it is 2 the prime tone of a harmonic series 3 the harmonic component of a complex wave that has the lowest frequency

funeral /'fjuːnərəl/ n (a procession connected with) a formal and ceremonial disposing of dead body, esp by burial or cremation

fun fair n, chiefly Br a usu outdoor show offering amusements (e g sideshows, rides, or games of skill)

fungus /'fʌŋgəs/ n, pl fungi also funguses any of a major group of often parasitic organisms lacking chlorophyll and including moulds, rusts, mildews, smuts, mushrooms, and toadstools – -goid adj – -gal adj

¹funnel /'fʌnl/ n 1 a utensil usu having the shape of a hollow cone with a tube extending from the smaller end, designed to direct liquids or powders into a small opening 2 a shaft, stack, or flue for ventilation or the escape of smoke or steam

²funnel v 1 to pass (as if) through a funnel 2 to move to a focal point or into a central channel

funny /'fʌni/ adj 1 causing mirth and laughter; seeking or intended to amuse 2 peculiar, strange, or odd 3 involving trickery, deception, or dishonesty 4 unwilling to be helpful; difficult 5a slightly unwell b slightly mad 6 pleasantly amusing; nice – esp in funny old USE (3, 4, 5, & 6) infml

¹fur /fɜːʳ/ v to (cause to) become coated or clogged (as if) with fur – often + up

²fur n 1 the hairy coat of a mammal, esp when fine, soft, and thrift; also such a coat with the skin 2 an article of clothing made of or with fur 3 a coating resembling fur: e g a a coating of dead cells on the tongue of sby who is unwell b the thick pile of a fabric c a coating formed in vessels (e g kettles or pipes) by deposition of scale from hard water

furious /'fjʊəriəs/ adj 1 exhibiting or goaded by uncontrollable anger 2 giving a stormy or turbulent appearance 3 marked by (violent) noise, excitement, or activity – ~ness n – ~ly adv

furnace /'fɜːnɪs/ n an enclosed apparatus in which heat is produced (e g for heating a building or reducing ore)

furnish /'fɜːnɪʃ/ v to provide or supply (with what is needed); esp to equip with furniture – ~ings n pl

furniture /'fɜːnɪtʃəʳ/ n necessary, useful, or desirable equipment: e g a the movable articles (e g tables, chairs, and beds) that make an area suitable for living in or use b accessories c the whole movable equipment of a ship (e g rigging, sails, anchors, and boats)

¹further /'fɜːðəʳ/ adv 1 farther 2 moreover 3 to a greater degree or extent (e g further annoyed by a second interruption)

²further adj 1 farther 2 extending beyond what exists or has happened; additional (e g further volumes) 3 coming after the one referred to

³further v to help forward

furthermore /ˌfɜːðə'mɔːʳ/ adv in addition to what precedes; moreover – used esp when introducing fresh matter for consideration

fury /'fjʊəri/ n 1 intense, disordered, and often destructive rage 2 cap any of the 3 avenging deities who in Greek mythology punished crimes 3 wild disordered force or activity

¹fuse /fjuːz/ n the detonating device for setting off the charge in a projectile, bomb, etc

²fuse v 1 to become fluid with heat 2 to become blended (as if) by melting together 3 to fail because of the melting of a fuse

³fuse n (a device that includes) a wire or strip of fusible metal that melts and interrupts the circuit when the current exceeds a particular value

¹fuss /fʌs/ n 1a needless or useless bustle or excitement b a show of (affectionate) attention – often in make a fuss of 2a a state of agitation, esp over a trivial matter b an objection, protest

²fuss v 1a to create or be in a state of restless activity; specif to shower affectionate attentions b to pay close or undue attention to small details 2 to become upset; worry

¹future /'fjuːtʃəʳ/ adj 1 that is to be;

gap

specif existing after death **2** of or constituting the future tense

²**future** *n* **1a** time that is to come **b** that which is going to occur **2** sthg (e g a bulk commodity) bought for future acceptance or sold for future delivery – usu pl **3** (a verb form in) a tense indicating the future

G

gadget /'gædʒɪt/ *n* a usu small and often novel device, esp on a piece of machinery – **~ry** *n*

¹**gag** /gæg/ *v* **1** to apply a gag to or put a gag in the mouth of (to prevent speech) **2** to (cause to) retch **3** to prevent from having free speech or expression – chiefly journ

²**gag** *n* **1** sthg thrust into the mouth to keep it open or prevent speech or outcry **2** a joke or trick

gaiety /'geɪəti/ *n* **1** merrymaking; *also* festive activity **2** gay quality, spirits, manner, or appearance

¹**gain** /geɪn/ *n* **1** resources or advantage acquired or increased; a profit **2** the obtaining of profit or possessions **3** an increase in amount, magnitude, or degree

²**gain** *v* **1a(1)** to get possession of or win, usu by industry, merit, or craft **(2)** to increase a lead over or catch up a rival by (esp time or distance) **b** to acquire **2** to increase, specif in weight **3** *of a timepiece* to run fast

galactic /gə'læktɪk/ *adj* of a galaxy, esp the Milky Way

galaxy /'gæləksi/ *n* **1** *often cap* the Milky Way **2** any of many independent systems composed chiefly of stars, dust, and gases and separated from each other in the universe by vast distances

gale /geɪl/ *n* **1** a strong wind **2** a noisy outburst

gallantry /'gæləntri/ *n* **1** (an act of) courteous attention, esp to a lady **2** spirited and conspicuous bravery

gallery /'gæləri/ *n* **1** a covered passage for walking; a colonnade **2** an outdoor balcony **3a** a long and narrow passage, room, or corridor **b** a horizontal subterranean passage in a cave or (military) mining system **4a** a room or building devoted to the exhibition of works of art **b** an institution or business exhibiting or dealing in works of art **5** *sing or pl in constr* **a** (the occupants of) a balcony projecting from 1 or more interior walls of a hall, auditorium, or church, to accommodate additional people, or reserved for musicians, singers, etc **b** the undiscriminating general public **c** the spectators at a tennis, golf, etc match

gallon /'gælən/ *n* a unit of liquid capacity equal to 8pt

¹**gallop** /'gæləp/ *n* **1** a fast bounding gait of a quadruped; *specif* the fastest natural 4-beat gait of the horse **2** a ride or run at a gallop **3** a rapid or hasty progression

²**gallop** *v* to progress or ride at a gallop

gambit /'gæmbɪt/ *n* **1** a chess opening, esp in which a player risks (several) minor pieces to gain an advantage **2a** a remark intended to start a conversation or make a telling point **b** a calculated move; a stratagem

gamble /'gæmbəl/ *v* **1a** to play a game (of chance) for money or property **b** to bet or risk sthg on an uncertain outcome **2** to speculate namely in business – **-bler** *n*

¹**game** /geɪm/ *n* **1a** activity engaged in for diversion or amusement; play **b** often derisive or mocking jesting **2a** a course or plan consisting of (secret) manoeuvres directed towards some end **b** a specified type of activity seen as competitive or governed by rules (and pursued for financial gain) **3a(1)** a physical or mental competition conducted according to rules with the participants in direct opposition to each other; a match **(2)** a division of a larger contest **3** *pl* organized sports, esp athletics **4a** animals under pursuit or taken in hunting; *specif* (the edible flesh of) certain wild mammals, birds, and fish (e g deer and pheasant), hunted for sport or food **b** an object of ridicule or attack – often in *fair game* **5** prostitution – *slang*; often in *on the game*

²**game** *adj* **1** having a resolute unyielding spirit **2** ready to take risks or try sthg new – **~ly** *adv*

³**game** *adj* injured, crippled, or lame

game keeper /'geɪm,kiːpə'/ *n* one who has charge of the breeding and protection of game animals or birds on a private preserve

gammon /'gæmən/ *n* (the meat of) the lower end including the hind leg of a side of bacon removed from the carcass after curing with salt

¹**gander** /'gændə'/ *n* an adult male goose

²**gander** *n* a look, glance

gang /gæŋ/ *n* **1** a combination of similar implements or devices arranged to act together **2** *sing or pl in constr* a group of people **a** associating for criminal, disreputable, etc ends; *esp* a group of adolescents who (disreputably) spend leisure time together **b** that have informal and usu close social relations **c** that have informal and usu close social relations

gangster /'gæŋstə'/ *n* a member of a criminal gang

gaol /dʒeɪl/ *v or n, chiefly Br* (to) jail – **~er** *n*

gap /gæp/ *n* **1** a break in a barrier (e g a wall or hedge) **2a** a mountain pass **b** a ravine **3** an empty space between 2 objects or 2 parts of an object **4** a break in continuity **5** a disparity or difference

gape /geɪp/ *v* **1a** to open the mouth wide **b** to open or part widely **2** to gaze

stupidly or in openmouthed surprise or
wonder

garage /'gærɑ:ʒ, 'gærɪdʒ/ n 1 a building for the shelter of motor vehicles 2
an establishment for providing essential
services (e g the supply of petrol or
repair work) to motor vehicles

¹**garden** /'gɑ:dn/ n 1 a plot of ground
where herbs, fruits, vegetables, or typically flowers are cultivated 2a a public
recreation area or park b an open-air
eating or drinking place

²**garden** v to work in, cultivate, or lay
out a garden – ~er n – ~ing n

³**garden** adj of a cultivated as distinguished from a wild kind grown in the
open

garment /'gɑ:mənt/ n an article of
clothing

gas /gæs/ n 1 a fluid (e g air) that has
neither independent shape nor volume
and tends to expand indefinitely 2a a
gas or gaseous mixture used to produce
general anaesthesia, as a fuel, etc b a
substance (e g tear gas or mustard gas)
that can be used to produce a poisonous,
choking, or irritant atmosphere 3 NAm
petrol 4 empty talk – chiefly infml
– ~eous adj

²**gas** v 1 to poison or otherwise affect
adversely with gas 2 to talk idly –
chiefly infml

gasp /gɑ:sp/ v 1 to catch the breath
suddenly and audibly (e g with shock) 2
to utter with gasps – usu + out
– ~ n

¹**gate** /geɪt/ n 1 (the usu hinged frame or
door that closes) an opening in a wall,
fence, etc 2a a space between 2 markers
through which a skier, canoeist, etc
must pass in a slalom race b a mechanically operated barrier used as a starting device for a race c either of a pair
of barriers that (1) let water in and out
of a lock (2) close a road at a level
crossing 3 an (electronic) device (e g in
a computer) that produces a signal
when specified input conditions are met
4 the total admission receipts or the
number of spectators at a sporting
event

²**gate** v, Br to punish by confinement to
the premises of a school or college

¹**gather** /'gæðə'/ v 1 to bring together;
collect (up) 2 to pick, harvest 3a to
summon up b to accumulate 4a to
bring together the parts of b to draw
about or close to sth c to pull (fabric)
together, esp along a line of stitching, to
create small tucks 5 to reach a conclusion (intuitively from hints or through
inferences)

²**gather** n a tuck in cloth made by gathering

¹**gauge** /geɪdʒ/ n 1 measurement
according to some standard or system 2
an instrument for or a means of measuring or testing sth (e g a dimension or
quantity) 3 relative position of a ship
with reference to another ship and the
wind 4 the distance between the rails of
a railway, wheels on an axle, etc 5a the
thickness of a thin sheet of metal, plastic,etc b the diameter of wire, a screw,

etc c (a measure of) the fineness of a
knitted fabric

²**gauge** v 1 to measure (exactly) the size,
dimensions, capacity, or contents of 2
to estimate, judge

gave /geɪv/ past of give

gay /geɪ/ adj 1 happily excited 2
bright, attractive 3 given to social
pleasures 4 homosexual

gaze /geɪz/ v or n (to fix the eyes in) a
steady and intent look – -er n

¹**gear** /gɪə'/ n 1a clothing, garments b
movable property; goods 2 a set of
equipment usu for a particular purpose
3a(1) a mechanism that performs a
specific function in a complete machine
(2) a toothed wheel (that is one of a set
of interlocking wheels) b any of 2 or
more adjustments of a transmission (e g
of a bicycle or motor vehicle) that determine direction of travel or ratio of
engine speed to vehicle speed

²**gear** v 1a to provide with or connect by
gearing b to put into gear 2 to adjust
to so as to match, blend with, or satisfy
sth

geese /gi:s/ pl of goose

gelignite /'dʒelɪgnaɪt/ n a dynamite in
which the adsorbent base is a mixture of
potassium or sodium nitrate with
wood pulp

gem /dʒem/ n 1 a precious stone, esp
when cut and polished for use in jewellery 2 sby or sth highly prized or
much beloved

gene /dʒi:n/ n a unit of inheritance that
is carried on a chromosome and controls the transmission of hereditary
characteristics

¹**general** /'dʒenərəl/ adj 1 involving or
applicable to the whole 2 of, involving,
or applicable to (what is common to)
every member of a class, kind, or group
3a applicable to or characteristic of the
majority of individuals involved; prevalent b concerned or dealing with universal rather than particular aspects 4
approximate rather than strictly accurate 5 holding superior rank or taking
precedence over others similarly titled

²**general** n a high-ranking officer in the
armed forces; esp one in command of an
army

general election n an election in
which candidates are elected in all con-
stituencies of a nation or state

generally /'dʒenərəli/ adv 1 without
regard to specific instances 2 usually; as
a rule 3 collectively; as a whole

generate /'dʒenəreɪt/ v 1 to bring into
existence or originate produce 2 to
define (a linguistic, mathematical, etc
structure (e g a curve or surface)) by the
application of 1 or more rules or operations to given quantities

generation /ˌdʒenə'reɪʃən/ n 1 sing or
pl in constr a a group of living organisms constituting a single step in the line
of descent from an ancestor b a group
of individuals born and living at the
same time c a type or class of objects
usu developed from an earlier type 2
the average time between the birth of
parents and that of their offspring 3 the

process of coming or bringing into being

generator /'dʒenəreɪtə'/ *n* **1** an apparatus for producing a vapour of gas **2** a machine for generating electricity; *esp* a dynamo

generous /'dʒen(ə)rəs/ *adj* **1** magnanimous, kindly **2** liberal in giving (e g of money or help) **3** marked by abundance, ample proportions, or richness – **-rosity** *n*, ~**ly** *adv*

genetics /dʒɪ'netɪks/ *n pl but sing in constr* **1** the biology of (the mechanisms and structures involved in) the heredity and variation of organisms **2** the genetic make-up of an organism, type, group, or condition – **-icist** *n*

genitals /'dʒenɪt̯lz/ *n pl* the (external) reproductive and sexual organs – **genital** *adj*, ~**ia** *n*

genius /'dʒiːnɪəs/ *n* **1** an attendant spirit of a person or place **2a** a peculiar, distinctive, or identifying character or spirit **b** the associations and traditions of a place **3** a spirit or genie **4a** a single strongly marked capacity or aptitude **b** (a person endowed with) extraordinary intellectual power (as manifested in creative activity)

¹**gentle** /'dʒentl/ *adj* **1a** honourable, distinguished; *specif* of or belonging to a gentleman **b** kind, amiable **2** free from harshness, sternness, or violence; mild, soft; *also* tractable **3** soft, moderate – ~**ness** *n*, **-ly** *adj*

²**gentle** *n* a maggot, esp when used as bait for fish

gentleman /'dʒentlmən/ *n* **1a** a man belonging to the landed gentry or nobility; *also* a man of independent wealth **b** a man who is chivalrous, well-mannered, and honourable **2** a valet – usu in *gentleman's gentleman* **3** a man of social class or condition – ~**ly** *adj*

genuine /'dʒenjuɪn/ *adj* **1** actually produced by or proceeding from the alleged source or author or having the reputed qualities of character **2** free from pretence; sincere ~**ly** *adv*, ~**ness** *n*

geography /dʒɪ'ɒgrəfi, 'dʒɒgrəfi/ *n* **1a** science that deals with the earth and its life; *esp* the description of land, sea, air, and the distribution of plant and animal life including human beings and their industries **2** the geographical features of an area – **-pher** *n*, **-phical** *adj*

geology /dʒɪ'ɒlədʒi/ *n* **1** a science that deals with the history of the earth's crust, esp as recorded in rocks **2** the geological features of an area – **-gical** *adj*

geometry /dʒɪ'ɒmɪtri/ *n* **1** a branch of mathematics that deals with the measurement, properties, and relationships of points, lines, angles, surfaces, and solids **2** (surface) shape **3** an arrangement of objects or parts that suggests geometrical figures

germ /dʒɜːm/ *n* **1a** a small mass of cells capable of developing into (a part of) an organism **b** the embryo of a cereal grain that is usu separated from the starchy parts during milling **2** sthg that serves as an origin **3** a (disease-causing) microorganism

¹**gesture** /'dʒestʃə'/ *n* **1** a movement, usu of the body or limbs, that expresses or emphasizes an idea, sentiment, or attitude **2** sthg said or done for its effect on the attitudes of others or to convey a feeling (e g friendliness)

²**gesture** *v* to make or express (by) a gesture

get /get/ *v* **1** to gain possession of **2a** to receive as a return; earn **b** to become affected by; catch **c** to be subjected to **3a** to cause to come, go, or move **b** to prevail on; induce **4** to make ready; prepare **5a** to have – used in the present perfect tense form with present meaning **b** to have as an obligation or necessity –used in the present perfect tense form with present meaning; + *to* and an understood or expressed infinitive (e g in he's *got* to go) **6a** to puzzle **b** to irritate **7** to affect emotionally **8** to reach or enter into the specified condition or activity (e g in *get* drunk) **9** to contrive by effort, luck, or permission – + *to* and an infinitive

ghastly /'gɑːstli/ *adj* **1a** (terrifyingly) horrible **b** intensely unpleasant, disagreeable, or objectionable **2** pale, wan – **-liness** *n*

ghetto /'getəʊ/ *n* **1** part of a city in which Jews formerly lived **2** an often slum area of a city in which a minority group live, esp because of social, legal, or economic pressures

¹**ghost** /gəʊst/ *n* **1** a disembodied soul; *esp* the soul of a dead person haunting the living **2a** a faint shadowy trace **b** the least bit **3** a false image in a photographic negative or on a television screen – ~**ly** *adj* – ~**liness** *n*

²**ghost, ghostwrite** *v* to write something to appear under another person's name

¹**giant** /'dʒaɪənt/ *n* **1** *fem* **giantess** a legendary human being of great stature and strength **2** sby or sthg extraordinarily large **3** a person of extraordinary powers

²**giant** *adj* extremely large

gift /gɪft/ *n* **1** a natural capacity or talent **2** sthg freely given by one person to another **3** the act, right, or power of giving

gigantic /dʒaɪ'gæntɪk/ *adj* unusually great or enormous – ~**ally** *adv*

¹**gill** /gɪl/ *n* a measure equal to ¼ pint or 0.142 litres

²**gill** /dʒɪl/ *n* **1** an organ, esp of a fish, for oxygenating blood using the oxygen dissolved in water **2** the flesh under or about the chin or jaws – usu pl with sing. meaning **3** any of the radiating plates forming the undersurface of the cap of some fungi (e g mushrooms)

³**gill** /gɪl/ **ghyll** *n*, *Br* **1** a ravine **2** a narrow mountain stream

gimmick /'gɪmɪk/ *n* a scheme, device, or object devised to gain attention or publicity – ~**y** *adj*

ginger /'dʒɪndʒə'/ *n* **1a** (any of several cultivated tropical plants with) a thickened pungent aromatic underground stem used (dried and ground) as a spice, or candied as a sweet **b** the spice usu prepared by drying and grinding ginger **2** a strong brown colour

gipsy /'dʒɪpsɪ/ *NAm* **gypsy** *n* **1** *often cap* **a** a member of a dark Caucasian people coming orig from India to Europe in the 14th or 15th c and leading a migratory way of life **2** a person who moves from place to place; a wanderer

giraffe /dʒɪ'rɑːf/ *n* a large African ruminant mammal with a very long neck and a beige coat marked with brown or black patches

girder /'gɜːdə'/ *n* a horizontal main supporting beam

girl /gɜːl/ *n* **1a** a female child **b** a young unmarried woman **2a** a sweetheart, girlfriend **b** a daughter **3** a woman – *chiefly infml*

¹**give** /gɪv/ *v* **gave; given** **1** to make a present of **2** to grant, bestow, or allot (by formal action) **3a** to administer **b** to commit to another as a trust or responsibility **c** to convey or express to another **4a** to proffer, present (for another to use or act on) **b** to surrender (oneself) to a partner in sexual intercourse **5** to present to view or observation **6a** to present for, or provide by way of, entertainment **b** to present, perform, or deliver in public **7** to attribute, ascribe **8** to yield as a product or effect **9** to yield possession of by way of exchange; pay **10** to make, execute, or deliver (e g by some bodily action) **11** to cause to undergo; impose **12** to award by formal verdict **13** to offer for consideration, acceptance, or use **14a** to cause to have or receive **b** to cause to catch or contract **15** to apply freely or fully; devote **16** to allow, concede **17** to care to the extent of **18** to yield or collapse in response to pressure **19** to impart information; talk – *infml* **20** to happen – *slang* – **giver** *n*

²**give** *n* the capacity or tendency to yield to pressure; resilience, elasticity

glacier /'glæsɪə'/ *n* a large body of ice moving slowly down a slope or spreading outwards on a land surface

glad /glæd/ *adj* **1** expressing or experiencing pleasure, joy, or delight **2** very willing **3** causing happiness and joy

glamour /'glæmə'/ *n* a romantic, exciting, and often illusory attractiveness; *esp* alluring or fascinating personal attraction – **-orize** *v* – **-orous** *adj*

¹**glance** /glɑːns/ *v* **1** to strike a surface obliquely so as to go off at an angle – often + *off* **2** to touch on a subject or refer to it briefly or indirectly **3a** *of the eyes* to move swiftly from one thing to another **b** to take a quick look at sthg

²**glance** *n* **1** a quick intermittent flash or gleam **2** a deflected impact or blow **3a** a swift movement of the eyes **b** a quick or cursory look

¹**glare** /gleə'/ *v* **1** to shine with a harsh

uncomfortably brilliant light **2** to express hostility by staring fiercely

²**glare** *n* **1** a harsh uncomfortably bright light; *specif* painfully bright sunlight **2** an angry or fierce stare

glaring /'gleərɪŋ/ *adj* painfully and obtrusively evident – ~**ly** *adv*

glass /glɑːs/ *n* **1a** a hard brittle usu transparent substance formed by fusing silica sand and other ingredients **b** a substance resembling glass, esp in hardness and transparency **2a** thing made of glass: e g **(1)** a glass drinking vessel (e g a tumbler or wineglass) **(2)** a mirror **(3)** a barometer **b(1)** an optical instrument (e g a magnifying glass) for viewing objects not readily seen **(2)** *pl* a pair of lenses together with a frame to hold them in place for correcting defects of vision or protecting the eyes

¹**gleam** /gliːm/ *n* **1a** a transient appearance of subdued or partly obscured light **b** a glint **2** a brief or faint appearance or occurrence

²**gleam** *v* **1** to shine with subdued steady light or moderate brightness **2** to appear briefly or faintly

glee /gliː/ *n* **1** a feeling of merry high-spirited joy or delight **2** an unaccompanied song for 3 or more usu male solo voices – ~**ful** *adj*

glide /glaɪd/ **1** to move noiselessly in a smooth, continuous, and effortless manner **2** to pass gradually and imperceptibly **3** *of an aircraft* to fly without the use of engines

glider /'glaɪdə'/ *n* an aircraft similar to an aeroplane but without an engine

¹**glimmer** /'glɪmə'/ *v* **1** to shine faintly or unsteadily **2** to appear indistinctly with a faintly luminous quality

²**glimmer** *n* **1** a feeble or unsteady light **2a** a dim perception or faint idea **b** a small sign or amount

¹**glimpse** /glɪmps/ *v* to get a brief look at

²**glimpse** *n* a brief fleeting view or look

¹**glitter** /'glɪtə'/ *v* **1** to shine by reflection with a brilliant or metallic lustre **2** to be brilliantly attractive in a superficial or deceptive way

²**glitter** *n* **1** sparkling brilliance, showiness, or attractiveness **2** small glittering particles used for ornamentation – ~**ing** *adj*

globe /gləʊb/ *n* sthg spherical or rounded: e g **a** a spherical representation of the earth, a heavenly body, or the heavens **b** the earth

gloom /gluːm/ *n* **1** partial or total darkness **2a** lowness of spirits **b** an atmosphere of despondency – ~**y** *adj*

glorious /'glɔːrɪəs/ *adj* **1a** possessing or deserving glory **b** conferring glory **2** marked by great beauty or splendour **3** delightful, wonderful – ~**ly** *adv*

¹**glory** /'glɔːrɪ/ *n* **1** (sthg that secures) praise or renown **2** a (most) commendable asset **3a** (sthg marked by) resplendence or magnificence **b** the splendour, blessedness, and happiness of heaven; eternity **4** a state of great gratification or exaltation

²**glory** v to rejoice proudly

¹**glossy** /'glosi/ adj 1 having a surface lustre or brightness 2 attractive in an artificially opulent, sophisticated, or smoothly captivating manner

²**glossy** n, chiefly Br a magazine expensively produced on glossy paper and often having a fashionable or sophisticated content

glove /glʌv/ n a covering for the hand having separate sections for each of the fingers and the thumb and often extending part way up the arm

¹**glow** /gləu/ v 1 to shine (as if) with an intense heat 2a to experience a sensation (as if) of heat; show a ruddy colour (as if) from being too warm b to show satisfaction or elation

²**glow** n 1 brightness or warmth of colour 2a warmth of feeling or emotion b a sensation of warmth 3 light (as if) from sthg burning without flames or smoke

¹**glue** /glu:/ n any of various strong adhesives; also a solution of glue used for sticking things together – ~y adj

²**glue** v 1 to cause to stick tightly with glue 2 to fix (e g the eyes) on an object steadily or with deep concentration

¹**glut** /glʌt/ v 1 to fill, esp with food, to beyond capacity 2 to flood (the market) with goods so that supply exceeds demand

²**glut** n an excessive supply (e g of a harvested crop) which exceeds market demand

glutton /'glʌtn/ n 1 one given habitually to greedy and voracious eating and drinking 2 one who has a great capacity for accepting or enduring sthg – ~ous adj – ously adv – ~y n

gnat /næt/ n any of various small usu biting 2-winged flies

gnaw /nɔ:/ v 1 to bite or chew on with the teeth; esp to wear away by persistent biting or nibbling 2 to affect as if by continuous eating away; plague 3 to erode, corrode

¹**go** /gəu/ v went; gone 1 to proceed on a course 2a to move out of or away from a place; leave – sometimes used with a further verb to express purpose b to make an expedition for a specified activity 3a to pass by means of a specified process or according to a specified procedure b(1) to proceed in a thoughtless or reckless manner – used to intensify a complementary verb (2) to proceed to do sthg surprising – used with and to intensify a complementary verb c(1) to extend (2) to speak, proceed, or develop in a specified direction or up to a specified limit 4 to travel on foot or by moving the feet 5 to be, esp habitually 6a to become lost, consumed, or spent b to die c to elapse d to be got rid of (e g by sale or removal) e to fail f to succumb; give way 7a to happen, progress – often + on b to be in general or on an average c to turn out (well) 8 to put or subject oneself 9a to begin an action, motion, or process b to maintain or perform an action or motion c to function in a proper or specified way

d to make a characteristic noise e to perform a demonstrated action 10a to be known or identified as specified b to be performed or delivered in a specified manner 11a to act or occur in accordance or harmony b to contribute to a total or result 12 to be about, intending, or destined – + to and an infinitive (e g is it going to rain) 13a to come or arrive at a specified state or condition b to join a specified institution professionally or attend it habitually c to come to be; turn d(1) to become voluntarily (2) to change to a specified system or tendency e to continue to be; remain 14 to be compatible with, harmonize 15a to be capable of passing, extending, or being contained or inserted b to belong 16a to carry authority b to be acceptable, satisfactory, or adequate c to be the case; be valid 17 to empty the bladder or bowels – euph

²**go** n, pl goes 1 energy, vigour 2a a turn in an activity (e g a game) b an attempt, try 3 a spell of activity 4 a success

³**go** adj functioning properly

⁴**go** n an Oriental game of capture and territorial domination played by 2 players with counters on a board covered in a grid

¹**go-ahead** adj energetic and progressive

²**go-ahead** n a sign, signal, or authority to proceed

goal /gəul/ n 1 an end towards which effort is directed 2a an area or object through or into which players in various games attempt to put a ball or puck against the defence of the opposing side b (the points gained by) the act of putting a ball or puck through or into a goal

goalkeeper /'gəul,ki:pə⁊/ n a player who defends the goal in soccer, hockey, lacrosse, etc

goat /gəut/ n 1 any of various long-legged (horned) ruminant mammals smaller than cattle and related to the sheep 2 a lecherous man 3 a foolish person

go at v 1 to attack 2 to undertake energetically

god /gɒd/ n 1 cap the being perfect in power, wisdom, and goodness whom human beings worship as creator and ruler of the universe 2 a being or object believed to have more than natural attributes and powers (e g the control of a particular aspect of reality) and to require human beings' worship 3 pl the highest gallery in a theatre, usu with the cheapest seats

godchild /'gɒdtʃaild/ n sby for whom sby else becomes sponsor at baptism

godparent /'gɒd,peərənt/ n a sponsor at baptism

¹**going** /'gəuɪŋ/ n 1 an act or instance of going – often in combination the condition of the ground (e g for horse racing) 2 advance, progress

²**going** adj 1 current, prevailing 2 profitable, thriving

gold /gəuld/ n 1 a heavy ductile yellow metallic element that occurs chiefly free and is used esp in coins and jewellery 2 a gold medal 3 a deep metallic yellow colour 4 (a shot hitting) the golden or yellow centre spot of an archery target

golden /'gəʊldən/ *adj* 1 consisting of, relating to, or containing gold 2 of the colour of gold 3 prosperous, flourishing 4 favourable, advantageous 5 of or marking a 50th anniversary

goldfish /'gəʊld,fɪʃ/ *n* a small (golden yellow) fish related to the carps and widely kept in aquariums and ponds

golf /gɒlf/ *n* a game in which a player using special clubs attempts to hit a ball into each of the 9 or 18 successive holes on a course with as few strokes as possible – ~er *n*

¹gone /gɒn/ *adj* 1a involved, absorbed b pregnant by a specified length of time c infatuated – often + *on*; *infml* 2 dead – *euph*

²gone *adv*, *Br* past, turned (a certain age)

gong /gɒŋ/ *n* 1 a disc-shaped percussion instrument that produces a resounding tone when struck with a usu padded hammer 2 a flat saucer-shaped bell 3 a medal or decoration – *slang*

¹good /gʊd/ *adj* better; best 1a(1) of a favourable character or tendency (2) bountiful, fertile (3) handsome, attractive b(1) suitable, fit (2) free from injury or disease; whole c(1) agreeable, pleasant; *specif* amusing (2) beneficial to the health or character (3) not rotten; fresh d ample, full e(1) well-founded, true (2) deserving of respect; honourable (3) legally valid 2a(1) morally commendable; virtuous (2) correct; *specif* well-behaved (3) kind, benevolent b reputable; *specif* wellborn c competent, skilful d loyal

²good *n* 1 prosperity, benefit 2a sthg that has economic utility or satisfies an economic want – usu pl b *pl* personal property having intrinsic value but usu excluding money, securities, and negotiable instruments c *pl* wares, merchandise 3 *pl but sing or pl in constr* the desired or necessary article – *infml*

³good *adv* well – *infml*

goodness /'gʊdnɪs/ *n* the nutritious or beneficial part of sthg

¹goose /guːs/ *n, pl* geese; gooses 1 (the female of) any of numerous large long-necked web-footed waterfowl 2 a simpleton, dolt

²goose *v* to poke between the buttocks

gooseberry /'gʊzbəri, 'guːz-, 'gʊs-/ *n* 1 (the shrub that bears) an edible acid usu prickly green or yellow fruit 2 an unwanted companion to 2 lovers – chiefly in *to play gooseberry*

gorgeous /'gɔːdʒəs/ *adj* 1 splendidly beautiful or magnificent 2 very fine; pleasant – ~ly *adv* – ~ness *n*

gorilla /gə'rɪlə/ *n* an anthropoid ape of western equatorial Africa related to but much larger than the chimpanzee

¹gospel /'gɒspəl/ *n* 1 *often cap* the message of the life, death, and resurrection of Jesus Christ; *esp* any of the first 4 books of the New Testament 2 the

message or teachings of a usu religious teacher or movement

²gospel *adj* 1 of the Christian gospel; evangelical 2 of or being usu evangelistic religious songs of American origin

gossip /'gɒsɪp/ *n* 1 sby who habitually reveals usu sensational facts concerning other people's actions or lives 2a (rumour or report of) the facts related by a gossip b a chatty talk – *gossip v*

got /gɒt/ 1 *past of* get 2 *pres pl & 1&2 sing of* get – nonstandard

govern /'gʌvən/ *v* 1 to exercise continuous sovereign authority over 2a to control, determine, or strongly influence b to hold in check; restrain

government /'gʌvəmənt, 'gʌvənmənt/ *n* 1 the office, authority, or function of governing 2 policy making as distinguished from administration 3 the machinery through which political authority is exercised 4 *sing or pl in constr* the body of people that constitutes a governing authority – ~al *adj*

governor /'gʌvənə/ *n* 1a a ruler, chief executive, or nominal head of a political unit b the managing director and usu the principal officer of an institution or organization c a member of a group (e g the governing body of a school) that controls an institution 2 sby (e g a father, guardian, or employer) looked on as governing – *slang* – ~ship *n*

gown /gaʊn/ *n* 1 a loose flowing robe worn esp by a professional or academic person when acting in an official capacity 2 a woman's dress, esp one that is elegant or for formal wear

grab /græb/ *v* -bb- 1 to take or seize hastily; snatch 2 to obtain unscrupulously 3 to forcefully engage the attention of – *infml* – **grab** *n*

¹grace /greɪs/ *n* 1a divine assistance given to human beings b a state of being pleasing to God 2 a short prayer at a meal asking a blessing or giving thanks 3 disposition to or an act or instance of kindness or clemency 4a a charming trait or accomplishment b an elegant appearance or effect; charm c ease and suppleness of movement or bearing 5 – used as a title for a duke, duchess, or archbishop 6 consideration, decency

²grace *v* 1 to confer dignity or honour on 2 to adorn, embellish

graceful /'greɪsfəl/ *adj* displaying grace in form, action, or movement – -fully *adv*

gracious /'greɪʃəs/ *adj* 1a marked by kindness and courtesy b having those qualities (e g comfort, elegance, and freedom from hard work) made possible by wealth 2 merciful, compassionate – used conventionally of royalty and high nobility – ~ly *adv* – ~ness *n*

¹grade /greɪd/ *n* 1 a position in a scale of ranks or qualities 2 a class of things of the same stage or degree 3 *NAm* a school form; a class 4 *NAm* a mark indicating a degree of accomplishment at school

²grade *v* 1 to arrange in grades; sort 2

to arrange in a scale or series **3** *NAm* to assign a mark to

gradual /'grædʒʊəl/ *adj* proceeding or happening by steps or degrees – **-ually** *adv* – ~ **ness** *n*

¹**grain** /greɪn/ *n* **1** a seed or fruit of a cereal grass; *also* (the seeds or fruits collectively of) the cereal grasses or similar food plants **2a** a discrete (small hard) particle or crystal (e g of sand, salt, or a metal) **b** the least amount possible **3** a granular surface, nature, or appearance **4** a small unit of weight, used for medicines (¹/₇₀₀₀ of a pound or 0.0648 gram) **5a** the arrangement of the fibres in wood **b** the direction, alignment, or texture of the constituent particles, fibres, or threads **6** natural disposition or character; temper

²**grain** *v* to paint in imitation of the grain of wood or stone

gram, gramme /græm/ *n* a metric unit of weight equal to about ½, 03

¹**grammar** /'græmə'/ *n* **1** the study of the classes of words, their inflections, and their functions and relations in the sentence; *broadly* this study when taken to include that of phonology and sometimes of usage **2** the characteristic system of inflections and syntax of a language **3** a grammar textbook **4** the principles or rules of an art, science, or technique

²**grammar** *adj* of the type of education provided at a grammar school

gramophone /'græməfəʊn/ *n* a device for reproducing sounds from the vibrations of a stylus resting in a spiral groove on a rotating disc; a record player

¹**grand** /grænd/ *adj* **1** having more importance than others; foremost **2** complete, comprehensive **3** main, principal **4** large and striking in size, extent, or conception **5a** lavish, sumptuous **b** marked by regal form and dignity; imposing **c** lofty, sublime **6** intended to impress **7** very good; wonderful – *infml* – ~ **ly** *adv* – ~ **ness** *n*

²**grand** *n* **1** a grand piano **2a** *Br* a thousand pounds **b** *NAm* a thousand dollars *USE* (2) *slang*

grandchild /'græntʃaɪld/ *n* a child of one's son or daughter

granddaughter /'græn,dɔːtə'/ *n* a daughter of one's son or daughter

grandfather /'græn,fɑːðə'/ *n* the father of one's father or mother; *broadly* a male ancestor

grandmother /'græn,mʌðə'/ *n* the mother of one's father or mother; *broadly* a female ancestor

grandparent /'græn,peərənt/ *n* the parent of one's father or mother

grand piano *n* a piano with horizontal frame and strings

grandson /'grænsʌn/ *n* a son of one's son or daughter

grandstand /'grændstænd/ *n* a usu roofed stand for spectators at a racecourse, stadium, etc in an advantageous position for viewing the contest

granite /'grænɪt/ *n* a very hard granular igneous rock formed of quartz, feldspar, and mica and used esp for building **2** unyielding firmness or endurance

¹**grant** /grɑːnt/ *v* **1a** to consent to carry out or fulfil (e g a wish or request) **b** to permit as a right, privilege, or favour **2** to bestow or transfer formally **3a** to be willing to concede **b** to assume to be true

²**grant** *n* **1** sthg granted; *esp* a gift for a particular purpose **2** a transfer of property; *also* the property so transferred

grape /greɪp/ *n* (any of a genus of widely cultivated woody vines that bear, in clusters,) a smooth-skinned juicy greenish white to deep red or purple berry eaten as a fruit or fermented to produce wine

graph /grɑːf/ *n* a diagram (e g a series of points, a line, a curve, or an area) expressing a relation between quantities or variables

¹**grasp** /grɑːsp/ *v* **1** to take, seize, or clasp eagerly (as if) with the fingers or arms **2** to succeed in understanding; comprehend

²**grasp** *n* **1** a firm hold **2** control, power **3** the power of seizing and holding or attaining **4** comprehension

¹**grass** /grɑːs/ *n* **1** herbage suitable or used for grazing animals **2** any of a large family of plants with slender leaves and flowers in small spikes or clusters, that includes bamboo, wheat, rye, corn, etc **3** land on which grass is grown; *esp* a lawn **4** cannabis; *specif* marijuana – *slang* **5** *Br* a police informer – *slang*

²**grass** *v* **1** to cover or seed with grass – often + *down* **2** *Br* to inform the police; *esp* to betray sby to the police – *slang*

grasshopper /'grɑːs,hopə'/ *n* any of numerous plant-eating insects with hind legs adapted for leaping

grassy /'grɑːsi/ *adj* **1** consisting of or covered with grass **2** (having a smell) like grass

¹**grate** /greɪt/ *n* **1** a frame or bed of metal bars to hold the fuel in a fireplace, stove, or furnace **2** a fireplace

²**grate** *v* **1** to reduce to small particles by rubbing on sthg rough **2a** to gnash or grind noisily **b** to cause to make a rasping sound **3** to cause irritation; jar

grateful /'greɪtfəl/ *adj* **1** feeling or expressing thanks **2** pleasing, comforting – ~ **ly** *adv* – ~ **ness** *n*

gratitude /'grætɪtjuːd/ *n* the state or feeling of being grateful; thankfulness

¹**grave** /greɪv/ *n* an excavation for burial of a body; *broadly* a tomb

²**grave** *adj* **1a** requiring serious consideration; important **b** likely to produce great harm or danger **2** serious, dignified **3** drab in colour; sombre – ~ **ly** *adv*

³**grave** /grɑːv/ *adj or n* (being or marked with) an accent ` used to show that a vowel is pronounced with a fall of pitch (e g in ancient Greek) or has a certain quality (e g è in French)

gravel /'grævəl/ *n* **1** (a stratum or surface of) loose rounded fragments of rock mixed with sand **2** a sandy deposit of small stones in the kidneys and urinary bladder

gravity /ˈgrævˌti/ *n* **1a** dignity or sobriety of bearing **b** significance; *esp* seriousness **2** (the quality of having) weight **3** (the attraction of a celestial body for bodies at or near its surface resulting from) gravitation

gravy /ˈgreɪvi/ *n* the (thickened and seasoned) fat and juices from cooked meat used as a sauce

¹**graze** /greɪz/ *v* **1** to feed on the grass of (e g a pasture) **2** to put to graze

²**graze** *v* **1** to touch (sth) lightly in passing **2** to abrade, scratch

³**graze** *n* (an abrasion, esp of the skin, made by) a scraping along a surface

¹**grease** /griːs/ *n* **1** melted down animal fat **2** oily matter **3** a thick lubricant

²**grease** /griːs, griːz/ *v* **1** to smear, lubricate, or soil with grease **2** to hasten or ease the process or progress of

greasy /ˈgriːsi, -zi/ *adj* **1a** smeared or soiled with grease **b** oily in appearance, texture, or manner **c** slippery **2** containing an unusual amount of grease – **ily** *adv* – **iness** *n*

¹**great** /greɪt/ *adj* **1a** notably large in size or number **b** of a relatively large kind – in plant and animal names **c** elaborate, ample **2a** extreme in amount, degree, or effectiveness **b** of importance; significant **3** eminent, distinguished **4** main, principal **5** removed in a family relationship by at least 3 stages directly or 2 stages indirectly – chiefly in combination **6** markedly superior in character or quality; *esp* noble **7a** remarkably skilled **b** enthusiastic, keen **8** – used as a generalized term of approval; *infml* – **ly** *adv* – **ness** *n*

²**great** *n* one who is great – usu pl

greed /griːd/ *n* **1** excessive acquisitiveness; avarice **2** excessive desire for or consumption of food – **y** *adj* – **ily** *adv* – **ness** *n*

¹**green** /griːn/ *adj* **1** of the colour green **2a** covered by green growth or foliage **b** consisting of green (edible) plants **3a** youthful, vigorous **b** not ripened or matured; immature **c** fresh, new **4** appearing pale, sickly, or nauseated **5** affected by intense envy or jealousy **6** not aged; unseasoned **7** deficient in training, knowledge, or experience – **ness** *n* – **ish** *adj*

²**green** *n* **1** a colour whose hue resembles that of growing fresh grass or the emerald and lies between blue and yellow in the spectrum **2** sth of a green colour **3** *pl* green leafy vegetables (e g spinach and cabbage) the leaves and stems of which are often cooked **4a** a common or park in the centre of a town or village **b** a smooth area of grass for a special purpose (e g bowling or putting)

greengrocer /ˈgriːnˌgrəʊsə/ *n*, *chiefly Br* a retailer of fresh vegetables and fruit

greenhouse /ˈgriːnhaʊs/ *n* a glassed enclosure for the cultivation or protection of tender plants

¹**greet** /griːt/ *v* **1** to welcome with gestures or words **2** to meet or react to in a specified manner

²**greet** *v Scot* to weep, lament

greeting /ˈgriːtɪŋ/ *n* **1** a salutation at meeting **2** an expression of good wishes; regards – usu pl with sing. meaning

grenade /grɪˈneɪd/ *n* **1** a small missile that contains explosive, gas, incendiary chemicals, etc and is thrown by hand or launcher **2** a glass container of chemicals that bursts when thrown, releasing a fire extinguishing agent, tear gas, etc

grew /gruː/ *past of* **grow**

¹**grey** /greɪ/, *NAm chiefly* **gray 1** of the colour grey **2** dull in colour **3a** lacking cheer or brightness; dismal **b** intermediate or unclear in position, condition, or character – **ness** *n* – **ish** *adj*

²**grey**, *NAm chiefly* **gray** *n* **1** any of a series of neutral colours ranging between black and white **2** sth grey; *esp* grey clothes, paint, or horses

grief /griːf/ *n* (a cause of) deep and poignant distress (e g due to bereavement)

grievance /ˈgriːvəns/ *n* **1** a cause of distress (e g unsatisfactory working conditions) felt to afford reason for complaint or resistance **2** the formal expression of a grievance; a complaint

¹**grieve** /griːv/ *v* to (cause to) suffer grief

²**grieve** *n*, *Scot* a farm or estate manager

grievous /ˈgriːvəs/ *adj* **1** causing or characterized by severe pain, suffering, or sorrow **2** serious, grave – **ly** *adv* – **ness** *n*

¹**grill** /grɪl/ *v* **1** to cook on or under a grill by radiant heat **2** to subject to intense and usu long periods of questioning – *infml*

²**grill** *n* **1** a cooking utensil of parallel bars on which food is exposed to heat (e g from burning charcoal) **2** an article or dish of grilled food **3 grill, grillroom** a usu informal restaurant or dining room, esp in a hotel **4** *Br* an apparatus on a cooker under which food is cooked or browned by radiant heat

grim /grɪm/ *adj* **1** fierce or forbidding in disposition, action, or appearance **2** unflinching, unyielding **3** ghastly or sinister in character **4** unpleasant, nasty – *infml* – **ly** *adv* – **ness** *n*

grin /grɪn/ *v* to smile so as to show the teeth

¹**grind** /graɪnd/ *v* **ground 1** to reduce to powder or small fragments by crushing between hard surfaces **2** to wear down, polish, or sharpen by friction; whet **3a** to rub, press, or twist harshly together **b** to press together with a rotating motion **4** to operate or produce by turning a crank **5** to become pulverized, polished, or sharpened by friction **6** to move with difficulty or friction, esp so as to make a grating noise **7** to work monotonously; *esp* to study hard **8** to rotate the hips in an erotic manner

²**grind** *n* **1** dreary monotonous labour or

routine **2** the result of grinding; *esp* material obtained by grinding to a particular degree of fineness **3a** the act of rotating the hips in an erotic manner **b** *Br* an act of sexual intercourse – *vulg*

¹**grip** /grip/ *v* **1** to seize or hold firmly **2** to attract and hold the interest of

¹**grip** *n* **1a** a strong or tenacious grasp **b** manner or style of gripping **2a** control, mastery, power **b** (power of) understanding or doing **3** a part or device that grips **4** a part by which sthg is grasped; *esp* a handle **5** one who handles scenery, properties, lighting, or camera equipment in a theatre or film or television studio **6** a travelling bag

¹**grit** /grit/ *n* **1** a hard sharp granule (e g of sand or stone); *also* material composed of such granules **2** the structure or texture of a stone that adapts it to grinding **3** firmness of mind or spirit; unyielding courage – *infml* – **gritty** *adj*

²**grit** *v* **1** to cover or spread with grit **2** to cause (esp one's teeth) to grind or grate

groan /grəun/ *v* **1** to utter a deep moan **2** to creak under strain

grocer /ˈgrəusə/ *n* a dealer in (packaged or tinned) staple foodstuffs, household supplies, and usu fruit, vegetables, and dairy products

grocery /ˈgrəusəri/ *n* **1** *pl* commodities sold by a grocer **2** a grocer's shop

¹**groom** /gruːm, grum/ *n* **1** one who is in charge of the feeding, care, and stabling of horses **2** a bridegroom

²**groom** /gruːm/ *v* **1** to clean and care for (e g a horse) **2** to make neat or attractive **3** to get into readiness for a specific objective; prepare

¹**groove** /gruːv/ *n* **1a** a long narrow channel or depression **b** the continuous spiral track on a gramophone record whose irregularities correspond to the recorded sounds **2** a fixed routine; a rut **3** top form – *infml* **4** an enjoyable or exciting experience – *infml*; no longer in vogue

²**groove** *v* **1** to make or form a groove (in) **2** to excite pleasurably – *infml*; no longer in vogue **3** to enjoy oneself intensely; *also* to get on well – *infml*; no longer in vogue

grope /grəup/ *v* **1** to feel about or search blindly or uncertainly *for* **2** to touch or fondle the body of (a person) for sexual pleasure – **grope** *n* – **-ingly** *adv*

¹**gross** /grəus/ *adj* **1** glaringly noticeable, usu because excessively bad or objectionable; flagrant **2a** big, bulky; *esp* excessively fat **b** of *vegetation* dense, luxuriant **3** consisting of an overall total before deductions (e g for taxes) are made **4** made up of material or perceptible elements; corporal **5** coarse in nature or behaviour; *specif* crudely vulgar – ~**ly** *adv* – ~**ness** *n*

²**gross** *n* an overall total exclusive of deductions

³**gross** *v* to earn or bring in (an overall total) exclusive of deductions

⁴**gross** *n*, *pl* **gross** a group of 12 dozen things

¹**grotesque** /grəuˈtesk/ *n* a style of decorative art in which incongruous or fantastic human and animal forms are interwoven with natural motifs (e g foliage)

²**grotesque** *adj* (having the characteristics) of the grotesque: e g **a** fanciful, bizarre **b** absurdly incongruous **c** departing markedly from the natural, expected, or typical

¹**ground** /graund/ *n* **1a** the bottom of a body of water **b** *pl* (1) sediment (2) ground coffee beans after brewing **2** a basis for belief, action, or argument – often *pl* with sing. meaning **3a** a surrounding area; a background **b** (material that serves as) a substratum or foundation **4a** the surface of the earth **b** an area used for a particular purpose **c** *pl* the area round and belonging to a house or other building **d** an area to be won or defended (as if) in battle **5a** soil

²**ground** *v* **1** to bring to or place on the ground **2a** to provide a reason or justification for **b** to instruct in fundamentals (e g of a subject) **3** to restrict (e g a pilot or aircraft) to the ground **4** to run aground

³**ground** *past of* **grind**

groundless /ˈgraundlis/ *adj* having no foundation – ~**ly** *adv* – ~**ness** *n*

¹**group** /gruːp/ *n* **1** two or more figures or objects forming a complete unit in a composition **2** *sing or pl in constr* **a** a number of individuals or objects assembled together or having some unifying relationship **b** an operational and administrative unit belonging to a command of an air force

²**group** *v* **1** to combine in a group **2** to assign to a group; classify **3** to form or belong to a group

grovel /ˈgrovəl/ *v* **1** to lie or creep with the body prostrate in token of submission or abasement **2** to abase or humble oneself – ~**ler** *n*

grow /grəu/ *v* **grew; grown 1a** to spring up and develop to maturity (in a specified place or situation) **b** to assume some relation (as if) through a process of natural growth **2a** to increase in size by addition of material (e g by assimilation into a living organism or by crystallization) **b** to increase, expand **3** to develop from a parent source **4** to become gradually **5** to cause to grow; produce **6** to develop

¹**growl** /graul/ *v* **a** to rumble **b** to utter a growl

²**growl** *n* a deep guttural inarticulate sound

grown-up *n or adj* (an) adult

growth /grəuθ/ *n* **1a** (a stage in the process of) growing **b** progressive development **c** an increase, expansion **2a** sthg that grows or has grown **b** a tumour or other abnormal growth of tissue **3** the result of growth; a product

¹**grudge** /grʌdʒ/ *v* to be unwilling or reluctant to give or admit; begrudge

gru

²**grudge** n a feeling of deep-seated resentment or ill will

gruff /grʌf/ adj 1 brusque or stern in manner, speech, or aspect 2 deep and harsh – ~ly adv – ~ness n

grumble /'grʌmbl/ v 1 to mutter in discontent 2 to rumble

¹**grunt** /grʌnt/ v to utter (with) a grunt

²**grunt** n the deep short guttural sound of a pig; also a similar sound

¹**guarantee** /,gærən'tiː/ n 1 one who guarantees 2 a (written) undertaking to answer for the payment of a debt or the performance of a duty of another in case of the other's default 3 an assurance of the quality of or of the length of use to be expected from a product offered for sale, accompanied by a promise to replace it or pay the customer back 4 sth given as security; a pledge

²**guarantee** v 1 to undertake to answer for the debt or default of 2a to undertake to do or secure (sth) b to engage for the existence, permanence, or nature of 3 to give security to

¹**guard** /gɑːd/ n 1 a defensive position in boxing, fencing, etc 2 the act or duty of protecting or defending 3a a person or group whose duty is to protect a place, people, etc b pl troops part of whose duties are to guard a sovereign 4 a protective or safety device; esp a device on a machine for protecting against injury 5 Br the person in charge of a railway train

²**guard** v 1 to protect from danger, esp by watchful attention; make secure 2 to watch over so as to prevent escape, entry, theft, etc; also to keep in check

guardian /'gɑːdiən/ n 1 one who or that which guards or protects 2 sby who has the care of the person or property of another; specif sby entrusted by law with the care of sby who is of unsound mind, not of age, etc – ~ship n

guerilla, guerrilla /gə'rɪlə/ n a member of an irregular, usu politically motivated fighting unit often engaged in harassing stronger regular units

¹**guess** /ges/ v 1 to form an opinion of with little or no consideration of the facts 2 to arrive at a correct conclusion about by conjecture, chance, or intuition 3 chiefly NAm to believe, suppose – infml 4 to make a guess

²**guess** n a surmise, estimate

guest /gest/ n 1a a person entertained in one's home b a person taken out, entertained, and paid for by another c a person who pays for the services of an establishment (e g a hotel) 2 one who is present by invitation

guidance /'gaɪdəns/ n help, advice

¹**guide** /gaɪd/ n 1a one who leads or directs another b one who shows and explains places of interest to travellers, tourists, etc c sth, esp a guidebook, that provides sby with information about a place, activity, etc d sth or sby that directs a person in his/her conduct or course of life 2 a bar, rod, etc for steadying or directing the motion of

sth 3 often cap, chiefly Br a member of a worldwide movement of girls and young women founded with the aim of forming character and teaching good citizenship through outdoor activities and domestic skills

²**guide** v 1 to act as a guide (to); direct in a way or course 2 to direct or supervise, usu to a particular end; also to supervise the training of

guilt /gɪlt/ n 1 the fact of having committed a breach of conduct, esp one that violates law 2a responsibility for a criminal or other offence b feelings of being at fault or to blame, esp for imagined offences or from a sense of inadequacy – ~less adj – ~lessly adv – ~lessness n

guilty /'gɪlti/ adj 1 justly answerable for an offence 2a suggesting or involving guilt b feeling guilt – -ily adv – -iness n

guitar /gɪ'tɑːr/ n a flat-bodied stringed instrument with a long fretted neck, plucked with a plectrum or the fingers

gulf /gʌlf/ n 1 a partially landlocked part of the sea, usu larger than a bay 2 a deep chasm; an abyss 3 an unbridgeable gap

gulp /gʌlp/ v 1 to swallow hurriedly, greedily, or in 1 swallow – often + down 2 to make a sudden swallowing movement as if surprised or nervous

¹**gum** /gʌm/ n (the tissue that surrounds the teeth and covers) the parts of the jaws from which the teeth grow

²**gum** n 1 any of various substances (e g a mucilage or gum resin) that exude from plants 2 a substance or deposit resembling a plant gum (e g in adhesive quality)

³**gum** v 1 to smear or stick (as if) with gum 2 to exude or form gum

¹**gun** /gʌn/ n 1a a rifle, pistol, etc b a device that throws a projectile 2 a discharge of a gun 3 sby who carries a gun in a shooting party

²**gun** v 1 to shoot – often + down 2 to search for or attack

gunpowder /'gʌn,paʊdə'/ n an explosive mixture of potassium nitrate, charcoal, and sulphur used in gunnery and blasting

¹**gush** /gʌʃ/ v 1 to issue copiously or violently 2 to emit (in) a sudden copious flow 3 to make an effusive often affected display of sentiment or enthusiasm – ~ing adj – ~ingly adv

²**gush** n 1 (sth emitted in) a sudden outpouring 2 an effusive and usu affected display of sentiment or enthusiasm

¹**gust** /gʌst/ n 1 a sudden brief rush of (rain carried by the) wind 2 a sudden outburst; a surge

²**gust** v to blow in gusts

¹**gutter** /'gʌtə'/ n 1 a trough just below the eaves or at the side of a street to catch and carry off rainwater, surface water, etc 2 the lowest or most vulgar level or condition of human life

²**gutter** v of a flame to burn fitfully or feebly; be on the point of going out

³**gutter** *adj* (characteristic) of the gutter; *esp* marked by extreme vulgarity or cheapness

gymnasium /dʒɪm'neɪzɪəm/ *n, pl* **gymnasiums, gymnasia** a large room or separate building used for indoor sports and gymnastic activities

gymnast /'dʒɪmnæst, -nəst/ *n* sby trained in gymnastics – ~**ic** *adj* – ~**ically** *adv*

gymnastics /dʒɪm'næstɪks/ *n pl but sing or pl in constr* 1 physical exercises developing or displaying bodily strength and coordination, often performed in competition 2 an exercise in intellectual or physical dexterity

H

habit /'hæbɪt/ *n* 1 a costume characteristic of a calling, rank, or function 2 bodily or mental make-up 3a a settled tendency or usual manner of behaviour b an acquired pattern or mode of behaviour 4 addiction

habitual /hə'bɪtʃʊəl/ *adj* 1 having the nature of a habit 2 by force of habit 3 in accordance with habit; customary – ~**ly** *adv*

had /d, əd, həd; *strong* hæd/ *past of* **have**

haemorrhage /'hemərɪdʒ/ *n* a (copious) loss of blood from the blood vessels

haggle /'hægəl/ *v* to bargain, wrangle

¹**hail** /heɪl/ *n* 1 (precipitation in the form of) small particles of clear ice or compacted snow 2 a group of things directed at sby or sthg and intended to cause hurt, damage, or distress

²**hail** *v* 1 to precipitate hail 2 to pour down or strike like hail

³**hail** *interj* 1 – used to express acclamation 2 *archaic* – used as a salutation

⁴**hail** *v* 1a to salute, greet b to greet with enthusiastic approval; acclaim *as* 2 to greet or summon by calling 3 to come *from*, be a native of

⁵**hail** *n* 1 a call to attract attention 2 hearing distance

hair /heə/ *n* a (a structure resembling) a slender threadlike outgrowth on the surface of an animal; *esp* (any of) the many usu coloured hairs that form the characteristic coat of a mammal b the coating of hairs, esp on the human head or other body part

haircut /'heəkʌt/ *n* (the result of) cutting and shaping of the hair

hairdresser /'heə,dresə/ *n* sby whose occupation is cutting, dressing, and styling the hair – -**sing** *n*

¹**hairpin** /'heə,pɪn/ *n* 1 a 2-pronged U-shaped pin of thin wire for holding the hair in place 2 a sharp bend in a road

²**hairpin** *adj* having the shape of a hairpin

hair-raising *adj* causing terror or astonishment

hairy /'heəri/ *adj* 1 covered with (material like) hair 2 made of or resembling hair 3 frighteningly dangerous – infml – -**iness** *n*

¹**half** /hɑːf/ *n, pl* **halves** /hɑːvz/ 1a either of 2 equal parts into which sthg is divisible; *also* a part of a thing approximately equal to a half b half an hour – used in designation of time 2 either of a pair: e g a a partner b a school term – used esp at some British public schools 3 sthg of (approximately) half the value or quantity: e g a half a pint b a child's ticket

²**half** *adj* 1a being one of 2 equal parts b(1) amounting to approximately half (2) falling short of the full or complete thing (e g a *half* smile) 2 extending over or covering only half (e g *half* sleeves) 3 *Br* half past

³**half** *adv* 1 in an equal part or degree (e g she was *half* laughing, *half* crying) 2 nearly but not completely (e g *half* cooked)

half brother *n* a brother related through 1 parent only

halfhearted /,hɑːf'hɑːtɪd/ *adj* lacking enthusiasm or effort

halfpenny /'heɪpni/ *n* 1 (a British bronze coin representing) one half of a penny 2 a small amount

half sister *n* a sister related through 1 parent only

halftime /,hɑːf'taɪm/ *n* (an intermission marking) the completion of half of a game or contest

halfway /,hɑːf'weɪ/ *adj or adv* 1 midway between 2 points 2 (done or formed) partially

hall /hɔːl/ *n* 1 the house of a medieval king or noble 2 the manor house of a landed proprietor 3 the entrance room or passage of a building 4 a large room for public assembly or entertainment

hallucination /hə,luːsɪ'neɪʃən/ *n* 1 the perception of sthg apparently real to the perceiver but which has no objective reality, *also* the image, object, etc perceived 2 a completely unfounded or mistaken impression or belief – -**atory** *adj*

¹**halt** /hɒlt/ *v* 1 to hesitate between alternative courses; waver 2 to display weakness or imperfection (e g in speech or reasoning); falter

²**halt** *n* 1 a (temporary) stop or interruption 2 *Br* a railway stopping place, without normal station facilities, for local trains

³**halt** to come to a halt 1 to bring to a stop 2 to cause to stop; end

halve /hɑːv/ *v* 1 to divide into 2 equal parts b to reduce to a half 2 to play (e g a hole or match in golf) in the same number of strokes as one's opponent

¹**ham** /hæm/ *n* 1 a buttock with its associated thigh – usu *pl* 2 (the meat of) the rear end of a bacon pig, esp the thigh, when removed from the carcass before curing with salt 3a an inexpert but showy performer; *also* an actor performing in an exaggerated theatrical

style **b** an operator of an amateur radio station

²**ham** v to execute with exaggerated speech or gestures; overact

hamburger /'hæmbɜːgə'/ n a round flat cake of minced beef; also a sandwich of a fried hamburger in a bread roll

¹**hammer** /'hæmə'/ n **1a** a hand tool that consists of a solid head set crosswise on a handle and is used to strike a blow (e g to drive in a nail) **b** a power tool that substitutes a metal block or a drill for the hammerhead **2a** a lever with a striking head for ringing a bell or striking a gong **b** the part of the mechanism of a modern gun whose action ignites the cartridge **c** one of the three bones of the middle ear **d** a gavel **e**(1) a padded mallet in a piano action for striking a string (2) a hand mallet for playing various percussion instruments **3** (an athletic field event using) a metal sphere weighing 16lb (about 7.3kg) attached by a wire to a handle and thrown for distance

²**hammer** v **1** to strike blows, esp repeatedly, (as if) with a hammer; pound **2** to make repeated efforts at; esp to reiterate an opinion or attitude **3** to beat, drive, or shape (as if) with repeated blows of a hammer **4** to force as if by hitting repeatedly **5** to beat decisively – infml

hammock /'hæmək/ n a hanging bed, usu made of netting or canvas and suspended by cords at each end

¹**hamper** /'hæmpə'/ v **1** to restrict the movement or operation of by bonds or obstacles; hinder **2** to interfere with; encumber

²**hamper** n a large basket with a cover for packing, storing, or transporting crockery, food, etc

¹**hand** /hænd/ n **1a** (the segment of the forelimb of vertebrate animals corresponding to) the end of the forelimb of human beings, monkeys, etc when modified as a grasping organ **b** a stylized figure of a hand used as a pointer or marker **c** a forehock of pork **d** an indicator or pointer on a dial **2** either of 2 sides or aspects of an issue or argument **3** a pledge, esp of betrothal or marriage **4** handwriting **5** a unit of measure equal to 4in (about 102mm) used esp for the height of a horse **6a** assistance or aid, esp when involving physical effort **b** a round of applause **7a** (the cards or pieces held by) a player in a card or board game **b** a single round in a game **c** the force or solidity of one's position (e g in negotiations) **d** a turn to serve in a game (e g squash) in which only the server may score points and which lasts as long as the server can win points **8a** a worker, employee ; esp one employed at manual labour or general tasks **b** a member of a ship's crew **c** one skilled in a particular action or pursuit **9a** handiwork **b** style of execution; workmanship

²**hand** v **1** to lead or assist with the hand **2** to give or pass (as if) with the hand

handbag /'hændbæg/ n a bag designed for carrying small personal articles and money, carried usu with women

handful /'hændfʊl/ n, pl **handfuls** also **handsful 1** as much or as many as the hand will grasp **2** a small quantity or number **3** sby or sthg (e g a child or animal) that is difficult to control – infml

¹**handicap** /'hændikæp/ n **1** (a race or contest with) an artificial advantage or disadvantage given to contestants so that all have a more equal chance of winning **2** a (physical) disability or disadvantage that makes achievement unusually difficult

²**handicap** v **1** to assign handicaps to; impose handicaps on **2** to put at a disadvantage

handkerchief /'hæŋkətʃif/ n a small piece of cloth used for various usu personal purposes (e g blowing the nose or wiping the eyes) or as a clothing accessory

¹**handle** /'hændl/ n **1** a part that is designed to be grasped by the hand **2** the feel of a textile **3** a title; also an esp aristocratic or double-barrelled name – infml

²**handle** v **1a** to try or examine (e g by touching or moving) with the hand **b** to manage with the hands **2a** to deal with (e g a subject or idea) in speech or writing, or as a work of art **b** to manage, direct **3** to deal with, act on, or dispose of **4** to engage in the buying, selling, or distributing of (a commodity) **5** to respond to controlling movements in a specified way – ~**able** adj

handshake /'hændʃeik/ n a clasping and shaking of each other's usu right hand by 2 people (e g in greeting or farewell)

handsome /'hænsəm/ adj **1** considerable, sizable **2** marked by graciousness or generosity; liberal **3a** of a man having a pleasing appearance; good-looking **b** of a woman attractive in a dignified statuesque way – ~**ly** adv

handwriting /'hænd,raitiŋ/ n writing done by hand; esp the style of writing peculiar to a particular person

handy /'hændi/ adj **1** convenient for use; useful **2** clever in using the hands, esp in a variety of practical ways **3** conveniently near – infml – **-ily** adv – **-iness** n

¹**hang** /hæŋ/ v **hung, hanged 1a** to fasten to some elevated point by the top so that the lower part is free; suspend **b** to suspend by the neck until dead **c** to fasten on a point of suspension so as to allow free motion within given limits **d** to suspend (meat, esp game) before cooking to make the flesh tender and develop the flavour **2** to decorate, furnish, or cover by hanging sthg up (e g flags or bunting) **3** to hold or bear in a suspended or inclined position **4** to fasten (sthg, esp wallpaper) to a wall (e g with paste) **5** to display (pictures) in a gallery **6** to remain fastened at the top so that the lower part is free; dangle **7**

to remain poised or stationary in the air
8 to stay on; persist 9 to fall or droop
from a usu tense or taut position 10 to
depend 11 to lean, incline, or jut over or
downwards 12 to fall in flowing lines

²**hang** n 1 the manner in which a thing
hangs a downward slope; *also* a droop
3 the special method of doing, using, or
dealing with sth; the knack – chiefly in
get the hang of

hangar /'hæŋə²/ n a shed; *esp* a large
shed for housing aircraft

hanger /'hæŋə²/ n a device (e g a loop
or strap) by which or to which sth is
hung or hangs; *esp* a hook and crosspiece to fit inside the shoulders of a
dress, coat, etc to keep the shape of the
garment when hung up

hangover /'hæŋəʊvə²/ n 1 sth (e g a
custom) that remains from the past 2
the disagreeable physical effects following heavy consumption of alcohol or use
of other drugs

happen /'hæpən/ v 1 to occur by
chance; come *on* or *upon* by chance 2
to come into being as an event; occur 3
to have the luck or fortune *to*; chance

happening /'hæpənɪŋ/ n 1 sth that
happens; an occurrence 2a the creation
or presentation of a nonobjective work
of art (e g an action painting) b a usu
unscripted or improvised public performance in which the audience partici-
pates

happy /'hæpi/ adj 1 favoured by luck
or fortune; fortunate 2 well adapted or
fitting; felicitous 3a enjoying or
expressing pleasure and contentment b
glad, pleased 4 characterized by a
dazed irresponsible state – usu in combination 5 impulsively quick or overin-
clined to use sth – usu in combination
6 having or marked by an atmosphere of
good fellowship; friendly 7 satisfied as
to the fact; confident, sure 8 tipsy –
euph – **-pily** adv – **-piness** n

harass /'hærəs/ v 1 to worry and
impede by repeated raids 2 to annoy or
worry persistently

¹**harbour** /'hɑːbə²/ NAm chiefly **har-
bor** n 1 a place of security and comfort;
a refuge 2 a part of a body of water
providing protection and anchorage for
ships

²**harbour** v 1 to give shelter or refuge to
2 to be the home or habitat of; contain
3 to have or keep (e g thoughts or feelings) in the mind – ~**er** n

¹**hard** /hɑːd/ adj 1 not easily penetrated
or yielding to pressure; firm 2a *of
alcoholic drink* having a high percentage of alcohol b *of water* containing
salts of calcium, magnesium, etc that
inhibit lathering with soap 3 having or
producing relatively great photographic
contrast 4 *of currency* stable in value;
also soundly backed and readily con-
vertible into foreign currencies without
large discounts 5 firmly and closely
twisted 6 physically fit or resistant to
stress 7a not speculative or conjectural;
factual b close, searching 8a(1) difficult to endure (2) oppressive, inequit-
able b lacking consideration or com-

passion c(1) harsh, severe (2) resentful
d not warm or mild e(1) forceful, violent (2) demanding energy or stamina
(3) using or performing with great
energy or effort 9 sharply defined; stark
10a difficult to do, understand, or
explain b having difficulty in doing sth
11a *of a drug* addictive and gravely
detrimental to health b *of pornography*
hard-core – ~**ness** n

²**hard** adv 1a with great or maximum
effort or energy; strenuously b in a
violent manner; fiercely c to the full
extent – used in nautical directions d in
a searching or concentrated manner 2a
in such a manner as to cause hardship,
difficulty, or pain; severely b with bitterness or grief 3 in a firm manner;
tightly 4 to the point of hardness 5
close in time or space

³**hard** n, chiefly Br a firm usu artificial
foreshore or landing place

hardly /'hɑːdli/ adv 1 in a severe manner; harshly 2 with difficulty; painfully
3 only just; barely 4 scarcely

hardship /'hɑːdʃɪp/ n (an instance of)
suffering, privation

hardware /'hɑːdweə²/ n 1 items sold
by an ironmonger 2 the physical components (e g electronic and electrical
devices) of a vehicle (e g a spacecraft) or
an apparatus (e g a computer) 3 tape
recorders, closed-circuit television, etc
used as instructional equipment

hardy /'hɑːdi/ adj 1 bold, audacious
2a inured to fatigue or hardships; robust
b capable of withstanding adverse conditions; *esp* capable of living outdoors
over winter without artificial protection
– **-diness** n

¹**hare** /heə²/ n 1 any of various swift
timid long-eared mammals like large
rabbits with long hind legs 2 a figure of
a hare moved mechanically along a dog
track for the dogs to chase

²**hare** v to run fast – infml

¹**harm** /hɑːm/ n 1 physical or mental
damage; injury 2 mischief, wrong
– ~**ful** adj – ~**fully** adv – ~**fulness** n

²**harm** v to cause harm to

harmless /'hɑːmlɪs/ adj 1 free from
harm, liability, or loss 2 lacking
capacity or intent to injure – ~**ly** adv
– ~**ness** n

harmony /'hɑːməni/ n 1a the (pleas-
ant-sounding) combination of simultaneous musical notes in a chord b (the
science of) the structure of music with
respect to the composition and progression of chords 2a pleasing or con-
gruent arrangement of parts b agreement, accord – **-nious** adj – **-niously**
adv – **-niousness** n – **nize** v

¹**harness** /'hɑːnɪs/ n 1 the gear of a
draught animal other than a yoke 2
sth that resembles a harness (e g in
holding or fastening sth)

²**harness** v 1a to put a harness on (e g
a horse) b to attach (e g a wagon) by
means of a harness 2 to tie together;
yoke 3 to utilize; *esp* to convert (a
natural force) into energy

harp /hɑːp/ n a musical instrument that
has strings stretched across an open

triangular frame, plucked with the fingers

harsh /hɑːʃ/ *adj* **1** having a coarse uneven surface; rough **2** disagreeable or painful to the senses **3** unduly exacting; severe – **~ly** *adv* – **~ness** *n*

¹**harvest** /ˈhɑːvɪst/ *n* **1** (the season for) the gathering in of agricultural crops **2** (the yield of) a mature crop of grain, fruit, etc **3** the product or reward of exertion

²**harvest** *v* to gather in (a crop); reap

has /s, z, əz, həz; *strong* hæz/ *pres 3rd sing of* **have**

¹**haste** /heɪst/ *n* **1** rapidity of motion; swiftness **2** rash or headlong action; precipitateness

²**haste** *v* to move or act swiftly – *fml*

hasten /ˈheɪsən/ *v* **1** to cause to hurry **2** to accelerate **3** to move or act quickly; hurry

hasty /ˈheɪsti/ *adj* **1** done or made in a hurry **2** precipitate, rash – **-ily** *adv* – **-iness** *n*

¹**have** /əv, həv; *strong* hæv/ *v* **has; had 1a** to hold in one's possession or at one's disposal **b** to contain as a constituent or be characterized by **2** to own as an obligation or necessity – + *to* and an expressed or understood infinitive (e g you don't *have* to if you don't want to) **3** to stand in relationship to (e g *have* 2 sisters) **4a** to get, obtain **b** to receive (e g *had* news) **c** to accept; *specif* to accept in marriage **d** to have sexual intercourse with (a woman or sexual partner) **5a** to experience, esp by undergoing or suffering (e g *have* a cold) **b** to undertake and make or perform (e g *have* a look at that) **c** to entertain in the mind (e g *have* an opinion) **d** to engage in; CARRY ON **6a** to cause to by persuasive or forceful means (e g so he would *have* us believe) **b** to cause to be (brought into a specified condition) (e g *have* it finished) **c** to invite as a guest **7** to allow, permit **8a** to hold in a position of disadvantage or certain defeat (e g we *have* him now) **b** to perplex, floor (e g you *have* me there) **9a** to be pregnant with or be the prospective parents of **b** to give birth to **10** to partake of; consume **11** to take advantage of; fool (e g been *had* by his partner) – *infml* **12** – used with the past participle to form perfect tenses (e g we *have* had); used with *got* to express obligation or necessity (e g *have* got to go) **13** would (e g I *had* as soon not) *USE* British speakers in particular often express the idea of momentary as opposed to habitual possession or experience with *have got*

²**have** *n* a wealthy person – usu pl; esp in *the haves and have-nots*

haven /ˈheɪvən/ *n* **1** a harbour, port **2** a place of safety or refuge

havoc /ˈhævək/ *n* **1** widespread destruction; devastation **2** great confusion and disorder

¹**hawk** /hɔːk/ *n* **1** any of numerous medium-sized birds of prey that have (short) rounded wings and long tails and that hunt during the day **2** one who takes a militant attitude; a supporter of

a warlike policy – **~ish** *adj* – **~ishness** *n*

²**hawk** *v* to hunt game with a trained hawk – **~er** *n*

³**hawk** *v* to offer for sale in the street

⁴**hawk** *v* to utter a harsh guttural sound (as if) in clearing the throat

hay /heɪ/ *n* herbage, esp grass, mowed and cured for fodder

haystack /ˈheɪstæk/ *n* a relatively large sometimes thatched outdoor pile of hay

¹**hazard** /ˈhæzəd/ *n* **1** a game of chance played with 2 dice **2a** a risk, peril **b** a source of danger **3** a golf-course obstacle (e g a bunker)

²**hazard** *v* **1** to expose to danger **2** to venture, risk

hazardous /ˈhæzədəs/ *adj* **1** depending on hazard or chance **2** involving or exposing one to risk (e g of loss or harm) – **~ly** *adv* – **~ness** *n*

haze /heɪz/ *n* **1** vapour, dust, smoke, etc causing a slight decrease in the air's transparency **2** vagueness or confusion of mental perception

hazy /ˈheɪzi/ *adj* **1** obscured, cloudy **2** vague, indefinite – **-ily** *adv* – **-iness** *n*

¹**he** /i, hi; *strong* hiː/ *pron* **1** that male person or creature who is neither speaker nor hearer – + *cap* in reference to God **2** – used in a generic sense or when the sex of the person is unspecified

²**he** /hiː/ *n* **1** a male person or creature **2** the player in a children's game who must catch others; it

¹**head** /hed/ *n* **1** the upper or foremost division of the body containing the brain, the chief sense organs, and the mouth **2a** the seat of the intellect; the mind **b** natural aptitude or talent **c** mental or emotional control; composure **3** the obverse of a coin – usu pl with sing. meaning **4a** a person, individual **b** a single individual (domestic animal) out of a number – usu pl **5a** the end that is upper, higher, or opposite the foot **b** the source of a stream, river, etc **6** a director, leader **a** a school principal **b** one in charge of a department in an institution **7** the part of a plant bearing a compact mass of leaves, fruits, flowers, etc **8** the leading part of a military column, procession, etc **9a** the uppermost extremity or projecting part of an object; the top **b** the striking part of a weapon, tool, implement, etc **10** a mass of water in motion **11** (the pressure resulting from) the difference in height between 2 points in a body of liquid **12a** (parts adjacent to) the bow of a ship **b** a (ship's) toilet – usu pl with sing. meaning in British English **13** a measure of length equivalent to a head **14** the place of leadership, honour, or command **15a** a word often in larger letters placed above a passage in order to introduce or categorize **b** a separate part or topic **16** the foam or froth that rises on a fermenting or effervescing liquid **17a** the part of a boil, pimple, etc at which it is likely to break **b** a culminating point; a crisis – esp in *come to*

hea

a **head 18a** a part of a machine or machine tool containing a device (e g a cutter or drill); *also* the part of an apparatus that performs the chief or a particular function **b** any of at least 2 electromagnetic components which bear on the magnetic tape in a tape recorder, such that one can erase recorded material if desired and another may either record or play back **19** one who uses LSD, cannabis, etc habitually or excessively – often in combination; *slang*

²**head** *adj* **1** principal, chief **2** situated at the head

³**head** *v* **1** to cut back or off the upper growth of (a plant) **2a** to provide with or form a head **b** to form the head or top of **3** to be at the head of; lead **4a** to put sthg at the head of (e g a list); *also* to provide with a heading **b** to stand as the first or leading member of **5** to drive (e g a soccer ball) with the head **6** to point or proceed in a specified direction

headache /'hedeɪk/ *n* **1** pain in the head **2** a difficult situation or problem – **-achy** *adj*

headfirst /hed'fɜːst/ *adv* with the head foremost; headlong

heading /'hedɪŋ/ *n* **1** the compass direction in which a ship or aircraft points **2** an inscription, headline, or title standing at the top or beginning (e g of a letter or chapter)

headlight /'hedlaɪt/ *n* (the beam cast by) the main light mounted on the front of a motor vehicle

headline /'hedlaɪn/ *n* a title printed in large type above a newspaper story or article; *also, pl, Br* a summary given at the beginning or end of a news broadcast

headmaster /,hed'mɑːstə/, *fem* **headmistress** *n* one who heads the staff of a school

headquarters /'hed,kwɔːtəz, ,hed'kwɔːtəz/ *n, pl* **headquarters 1** a place from which a commander exercises command **2** the administrative centre of an enterprise *USE* often pl with sing. meaning

headway /'hedweɪ/ *n* **1a** (rate of) motion in a forward direction **b** advance, progress **2** headroom

heal /hiːl/ *v* **1a** to make sound or whole **b** to restore to health **2** to restore to a sound or normal state; mend – ~**er** *n*

health /helθ/ *n* **1a** soundness of body, mind, or spirit **b** the general condition of the body **2** condition ; *esp* a sound or flourishing condition; well-being

healthy /'helθi/ *adj* **1** enjoying or showing health and vigour of body, mind, or spirit **2** conducive to good health **3** prosperous, flourishing – **healthily** *adv* – **healthiness** *n*

¹**heap** /hiːp/ *n* **1** a collection of things lying one on top of another; a pile **2a** a great number or large quantity; a lot – *infml; often pl* with sing. meaning

²**heap** *v* **1a** to throw or lay in a heap; pile *up* **b** to form or round into a heap **2** to

supply abundantly *with*; *also* to bestow lavishly or in large quantities *upon*

hear /hɪə/ *v* **heard 1** to perceive or have the capacity of perceiving (sound) with the ear **2** to learn or gain information (by hearing) **3** to listen to with attention; heed **4** to give a legal hearing to **5** to receive a communication *from*

hearing /'hɪərɪŋ/ *n* **1a** the one of the 5 basic physical senses by which waves received by the ear are interpreted by the brain as sounds varying in pitch, intensity, and timbre **b** earshot **2a** an opportunity to be heard **b** a trial in court

heart /hɑːt/ *n* **1a** a hollow muscular organ that by its rhythmic contraction acts as a force pump maintaining the circulation of the blood **b** the breast, bosom **c** sthg resembling a heart in shape; *specif* a conventionalized representation of a heart **2a** a playing card marked with 1 or more red heart-shaped figures **b** *pl but sing or pl in constr* the suit comprising cards identified by this figure **3a** humane disposition; compassion **b** love, affections **c** courage, spirit **4** one's innermost character or feelings **5a** the central or innermost part (of a lettuce, cabbage, etc) **b** the essential or most vital part

heartbroken /'hɑːt,brəʊkən/ *adj* overcome by sorrow

hearth /hɑːθ/ *n* **1** a brick, stone, or cement area in front of the floor of a fireplace **2** home, fireside

hearty /'hɑːti/ *adj* **1a** enthusiastically or exuberantly friendly; jovial **b** unrestrained, vigorous **2a** robustly healthy **b** substantial, abundant

¹**heat** /hiːt/ *v* to make or become warm or hot – often + *up*

²**heat** *n* **1a** the condition of being hot; warmth; *also* a marked degree of this **b** excessively high bodily temperature **c** any of a series of degrees of heating **2a** intensity of feeling or reaction **b** the height or stress of an action or condition **c** readiness for sexual intercourse in a female mammal – usu in *on heat* or (*chiefly NAm*) *in heat* **3** pungency of flavour **4a** a single round of a contest that has 2 or more rounds for each contestant **b** any of several preliminary contests whose winners go into the final **5** pressure, coercion – *slang*

heated /'hiːtɪd/ *adj* marked by anger – ~**ly** *adv*

heater /'hiːtə/ *n* a device that gives off heat or holds sthg to be heated

heather /'heðə/ *n* a (common usu purplish-pink flowered northern) heath

¹**heave** /hiːv/ *v* **heaved, hove 1** to lift upwards or forwards, esp with effort **2** to throw, cast **3** to utter with obvious effort **4** to cause to swell or rise **5** to haul, draw **6** to rise and fall rhythmically **7** to vomit **8** to pull

²**heave** *n* **1a** an effort to heave or raise **b** a throw, cast **2** an upward motion; *esp* a rhythmical rising

heaven /'hevən/ *n* **1** (any of the spheres of) the expanse of space that surrounds the earth like a dome; the firmament – usu pl with sing. meaning **2** often cap the dwelling place of God, his angels, and the spirits of those who have received salvation; Paradise **3** a place or condition of utmost happiness

heavenly /'hevənli/ adj **1** of heaven or the heavens; celestial **2a** suggesting the blessed state of heaven; divine **b** delightful – infml

¹heavy /'hevi/ adj **1** having great weight in proportion to size **2** hard to bear; specif grievous **3** of weighty import; serious **4** emotionally intense; profound **5** oppressed; burdened **6** lacking sparkle or vivacity; slow, dull **7** dulled with weariness; drowsy **8a** of an unusually large amount **b** of great force **c** overcast **d** of ground or soil full of clay and inclined to hold water; impeding motion **e** loud and deep **f** laborious, difficult **g** of large capacity or output **h** consuming in large quantities – usu + on **9a** digested with difficulty, usu because of excessive richness **b** esp of bread not sufficiently raised or leavened **10** producing heavy usu large goods (e g coal, steel, or machinery) often used in the production of other goods **11a** of the larger variety **b** heavily armoured, armed, or equipped **12** of rock music loud and strongly rhythmic – slang **13** chiefly NAm frighteningly serious; specif threatening – slang; often used as an interjection – **-ily** adv – **-iness** n

²heavy adv in a heavy manner; heavily

³heavy n **1** pl units (e g of bombers, artillery, or cavalry) of the heavy sort **2a** (an actor playing) a villain **b** sby of importance or significance – infml **3** one hired to compel or deter by means of threats or physical violence – slang

¹hedge /hedʒ/ n **1a** a boundary formed by a dense row of shrubs or low trees **b** a barrier, limit **2** a means of protection or defence (e g against financial loss) **3** a calculatedly noncommittal or evasive statement

²hedge v **1** to enclose or protect (as if) with a hedge **2** to hem in or obstruct (as if) with a barrier; hinder **3** to protect oneself against losing (e g a bet), esp by making counterbalancing transactions **4** to plant, form, or trim a hedge **5** to avoid committing oneself to a definite course of action, esp by making evasive statements

hedgehog /'hedʒhog/ n any of a genus of small Old World spine-covered insect-eating mammals that are active at night

¹heel /hiːl/ n **1** (the back part of the hind limb of a vertebrate corresponding to) the back of the human foot below the ankle and behind the arch or an anatomical structure resembling this **2** either of the crusty ends of a loaf of bread **3** the part of a garment or an article of footwear that covers or supports the human heel **4a** the lower end of a mast **b** the base of a tuber or cutting of a plant used for propagation **5** a backward kick with the heel in rugby,

esp from a set scrum **6** a contemptible person – slang

²heel v **1** to supply with a heel; esp to renew the heel of **2** to exert pressure on, propel, or strike (as if) with the heel; specif to kick (a rugby ball) with the heel, esp out of a scrum

³heel v to tilt to one side

⁴heel n (the extent of) a tilt to one side

height /haɪt/ n **1** the highest or most extreme point; the zenith **2a** the distance from the bottom to the top of sthg standing upright **b** the elevation above a level **3** the condition of being tall or high **4a** a piece of land (e g a hill or plateau) rising to a considerable degree above the surrounding country – usu pl with sing. meaning **b** a high point or position

heir /eə/ n **1** sby who inherits or is entitled to succeed to an estate or rank **2** sby who receives or is entitled to receive some position, role, or quality passed on from a parent or predecessor

held /held/ past of **hold**

helicopter /'helɪkɒptə/ n an aircraft which derives both lift and propulsive power from a set of horizontally rotating rotors or vanes and is capable of vertical takeoff and landing

hell /hel/ n **1a** a nether world (e g Hades or Sheol) inhabited by the spirits of the dead **b** the nether realm of the devil in which the souls of those excluded from Paradise undergo perpetual torment **2a** a place or state of torment, misery, or wickedness – often as an interjection, an intensive, or as a generalized term of abuse **b** a place or state of chaos or destruction **c** a severe scolding

hello /hə'ləʊ, he-/ n an expression or gesture of greeting – used interjectionally in greeting, in answering the telephone, to express surprise, or to attract attention

helmet /'helmɪt/ n **1** a covering or enclosing headpiece of ancient or medieval armour **2** any of various protective head coverings, esp made of a hard material to resist impact **3** sthg, esp a hood-shaped petal or sepal, resembling a helmet

¹help /help/ v **1** to give assistance or support to **2** to remedy, relieve **3a** to be of use to; benefit **b** to further the advancement of; promote **4a** to keep from occurring; prevent **b** to restrain (oneself) from taking action **5** to serve with food or drink, esp at a meal **6** to appropriate sthg for (oneself), esp dishonestly **7** to be of use or benefit

²help n **1** aid, assistance **2** remedy, relief **3a** sby, esp a woman, hired to do work, esp housework **b** the services of a paid worker; also, chiefly NAm the workers providing such services

helpful /'helpfəl/ adj of service or assistance; useful – ~ly adv – ~ness n

helping /'helpɪŋ/ n a serving of food

helpless /'helplɪs/ adj **1** lacking protection or support; defenceless **2** lack-

ing strength or effectiveness; powerless
– ~ly adv – ~ness n

¹**hem** /hem/ n 1 the border of a cloth
article when turned back and stitched
down; esp the bottom edge of a garment
finished in this manner 2 a similar
border on an article of plastic, leather,
etc

²**hem** v 1a to finish (e g a skirt) with a
hem b to border, edge 2 to enclose,
confine – usu + in or about 3 to make
a hem in sewing

¹**hen** /hen/ n 1a a female bird, specif a
domestic fowl (over a year old) b a
female lobster, crab, fish, or other
aquatic animal 2 an esp fussy woman –
infml 3 chiefly Scot dear – used to girls
and women

²**hen** adj relating to or intended for
women only

hence /hens/ adv 1 from this time;
later than now 2 because of a preceding
fact or premise 3 from here; away – fml;
sometimes + from; sometimes used as an
interjection

¹**her** /ə, hə; strong hɜː/ adj of her or
herself, esp as possessor, agent, or object
of an action – used in titles of females
(e g her Majesty)

²**her** pron, objective case of **she** (e g older
than her; that's her)

herb /hɜːb/ n 1 a seed plant that does
not develop permanent woody tissue
and dies down at the end of a growing
season 2 a plant (part) valued for its
medicinal, savoury, or aromatic qualities

¹**herd** /hɜːd/ n 1 a number of animals of
1 kind kept together or living as a group
2a sing or pl in constr a group of people
usu having a common bond – often
derog b the masses – derog

²**herd** v 1 to keep or move (animals)
together 2 to gather, lead, or drive as if
in a herd

¹**here** /hɪə/ adv 1 in or at this place –
often interjectional, esp in answering a
roll call 2 to this point or particular (e g here we agree) 3 to this place or
position (e g come here) 4 – used when
introducing, offering, or drawing attention (e g here she comes) 5 – used
interjectionally to attract attention

²**here** adj 1 – used for emphasis, esp after
a demonstrative (e g this book here) 2
– used for emphasis between a demonstrative and the following noun; substandard (e g this here book)

³**here** n this place or point

heresy /ˈherɪsi/ n 1 (adherence to) a
religious belief or doctrine contrary to
or incompatible with an explicit church
dogma 2 an opinion or doctrine contrary to generally accepted belief

heretic /ˈherɪtɪk/ n 1 a dissenter from
established church dogma; esp a bap-
tized member of the Roman Catholic
church who disavows a revealed truth 2
one who dissents from an accepted
belief or doctrine – ~al adj – ~ally
adv

heritage /ˈherɪtɪdʒ/ n 1 sthg transmitted by or acquired from a predecessor;
a legacy 2 a birthright

hermit /ˈhɜːmɪt/ n 1 one who retires
from society and lives in solitude, esp
for religious reasons 2 a recluse

hero /ˈhɪərəʊ/ fem **heroine** n, pl **heroes**
1a a mythological or legendary figure
often of divine descent endowed with
great strength or ability b an illustrious
warrior c a person, esp a man, admired
for noble achievements and qualities
(e g courage) 2 the principal (male)
character in a literary or dramatic
work

heroic /hɪˈrəʊɪk/ also **heroical** adj 1 of
or befitting heroes 2a showing or
marked by courage b grand, noble
– ~ally adv

heroism /ˈherəʊɪzəm/ n heroic conduct
or qualities; esp extreme courage

herring /ˈherɪŋ/ n, pl herring, esp for
different types **herrings** a N Atlantic
food fish that is preserved in the adult
state by smoking or salting

hers /hɜːz/ pron, pl **hers** that which or
the one who belongs to her – used
without a following noun as a pronoun
equivalent in meaning to the adjective
her (e g the car is hers)

herself /əˈself, hə-; strong hɜː-/ pron 1
that identical female person or creature
used reflexively, for emphasis , or in
absolute constructions (e g herself an
orphan, she understood the situation) 2
her normal self (e g isn't quite herself)

hesitate /ˈhezɪteɪt/ v 1 to hold back,
esp in doubt or indecision 2 to be reluctant or unwilling to 3 to stammer
– -tating adj – -tion n

¹**hide** /haɪd/ v hid; hidden, hid 1 to put
out of sight; conceal 2 to keep secret 3
to screen from view 4 to conceal oneself
5 to remain out of sight – often + out

²**hide** n, chiefly Br a camouflaged hut or
other shelter used for observation, esp
of wildlife or game

³**hide** n the raw or dressed skin of an
animal – used esp with reference to
large heavy skins

¹**high** /haɪ/ adj 1a extending upwards
for a considerable or above average distance b situated at a considerable
height above a base (e g the ground) c
of physical activity extending to or
from, or taking place at a considerable
height above, a base (e g the ground or
water) d having a specified elevation;
tall – often in combination 2 at the
period of culmination or fullest development 3 elevated in pitch 4 relatively far
from the equator 5 of meat, esp game
slightly decomposed or tainted 6a
exalted in character; noble b good,
favourable 7 of greater degree, amount,
cost, value, or content than average 8a
foremost in rank, dignity, or standing b
critical, climactic c marked by sublime
or heroic events or subject matter 9
forcible, strong 10a showing elation or
excitement b intoxicated by alcohol or
a drug 11 advanced in complexity,
development, or elaboration 13 of a
gear designed for fast speed

²**high** adv at or to a high place, altitude,
or degree

³**high** n 1 a region of high atmospheric

pressure **2** a high point or level; a height

highland /'haɪlənd/ n high or mountainous land – usu pl with sing. meaning

Highland /'haɪlənd/ adj relating to or being a member of a shaggy long-haired breed of hardy beef cattle

¹**highlight** /'haɪlaɪt/ n **1** the lightest spot or area (e g in a painting or photograph) **2** an event or detail of special significance or interest **3** a contrasting brighter part in the hair or on the face that reflects or gives the appearance of reflecting light

²**highlight** v **1** to focus attention on; emphasize **2** to emphasize (e g a figure) with light tones in painting, photography, etc

highly /'haɪli/ adv **1** to a high degree; extremely **2** with approval; favourably

Highness /'haɪnɪs/ n – used as a title for a person of exalted rank (e g a king or prince)

hijack /'haɪdʒæk/ high-jack v **1a** to stop and steal from (a vehicle in transit) **b** to seize control of, and often divert, (a means of transport) by force **2** to steal, rob, or kidnap as if by hijacking – **hijack** n – ~ **er** n – ~ **ing** n

¹**hike** /haɪk/ v to go on a hike – **hiker** n – **hiking** n

²**hike** n **1** a long walk in the country, esp for pleasure or exercise **2** chiefly NAm an increase or rise

¹**hill** /hɪl/ n **1** a usu rounded natural rise of land lower than a mountain **2** an artificial heap or mound (e g of earth) **3** an esp steep slope

²**hill** v to draw earth round the roots or base of (plants)

hilt /hɪlt/ n a handle, esp of a sword or dagger

him /ɪm; strong hɪm/ pron, objective case of **he** (e g threw it at him, it's him)

himself /ɪm'self; strong hɪm-/ pron **1a** that identical male person or creature used reflexively, for emphasis, or in absolute constructions (e g himself a rich man, he knew the pitfalls) **b** – used reflexively when the sex of the antecedent is unspecified (e g everyone must fend for himself) **2** his normal self (e g isn't quite himself)

¹**hind** /haɪnd/ n, pl **hinds** also **hind** a female (red) deer

²**hind** adj situated at the back or behind; rear

¹**hinder** /'hɪndə/ vt **1** to retard or obstruct the progress of; hamper **2** to restrain, prevent – often + from

²**hinder** adj situated behind or at the rear; posterior

hindrance /'hɪndrəns/ n **1** the action of hindering **2** an impediment, obstacle

hindsight /'haɪndsaɪt/ n the grasp or picture of a situation that one has after it has occurred

¹**hinge** /hɪndʒ/ n **1a** a jointed or flexible device on which which a swinging part (e g a door or lid) turns **b** a flexible joint in which bones are held together by ligaments **c** a small piece of thin gummed paper used in fastening a postage stamp in an album **2** a point or principle on which sthg turns or depends

²**hinge** v **1** to attach by or provide with hinges **2** to hang or turn (as if) on a hinge **3** to depend or turn on a single consideration or point

¹**hint** /hɪnt/ n **1** a brief practical suggestion or piece of advice **2** an indirect or veiled statement; an insinuation **3** a slight indication or trace; a suggestion – usu + of

²**hint** v **1** to indicate indirectly or by allusion **2** to give a hint

¹**hip** /hɪp/ n the ripened fruit of a rose

²**hip** n **1** the projecting region at each side of the lower or rear part of the mammalian trunk formed by the pelvis and upper part of the thigh; also the joint or socket where the thighbone articulates with the pelvis **2** an external angle between 2 adjacent sloping sides of a roof

³**hip** adj keenly aware of or interested in the newest developments; broadly trendy – infml

hippopotamus /ˌhɪpə'pɒtəməs/ n, pl **hippopotamuses**, **hippopotami** any of several large plant-eating 4-toed chiefly aquatic mammals, with an extremely large head and mouth, very thick hairless skin, and short legs

¹**hire** /haɪə/ n **1** payment for the temporary use of sthg **2** hiring or being hired

²**hire** v **1a** to engage the services of for a set sum **b** to engage the temporary use of for an agreed sum **2** to grant the services of or temporary use of for a fixed sum

hire purchase n, chiefly Br a system of paying for goods by instalments

¹**his** /ɪz; strong hɪz/ adj of him or himself, esp as possessor, agent, or object of an action – used in titles of males (e g his Majesty)

²**his** /hɪz/ pron, pl **his** that which or the one who belongs to him – used without a following noun as a pronoun equivalent in meaning to the adjective his (e g the house is his)

hiss /hɪs/ v **1** to make a sharp voiceless sound like a prolonged s, esp in disapproval **2** to show disapproval of by hissing – ~ n

history /'hɪstəri/ n **1** (a chronological record of) significant past events **2a** a treatise presenting systematically related natural phenomena **b** an account of sby's medical, sociological, etc background **3** a branch of knowledge that records the past **4a** past events ⟨that's all ~ now⟩ **b** an unusual or interesting past **c** previous treatment, handling, or experience – **-rical** adj – **-rically** adv

¹**hit** /hɪt/ v **1a** to reach (as if) with a blow; strike (a blow) **b** to make sudden forceful contact with **2a** to bring or come into contact (with) **b** to deliver, inflict **3** to have a usu detrimental effect or impact on **4** to discover or meet, esp

by chance **5a** to reach, attain **b** to cause a propelled object to strike (e g a target), esp for a score in a contest **c** *of a batsman* to score (runs) in cricket; *also* to score runs off a ball bowled by (a bowler) **6** to indulge in, esp excessively **7** to arrive at or in **8** to rob – infml **9** *chiefly NAm* to kill – slang **10a** to attack **b** to happen or arrive, esp with sudden or destructive force **11** to come, esp by chance; arrive at or find sthg – + *on* or *upon*

²**hit** *n* **1** a blow; *esp* one that strikes its target **2a** a stroke of luck **b** sthg (e g a popular tune) that enjoys great success **3** a telling remark **4** a robbery **5** *chiefly NAm* an act of murder *USE (4 & 5)* slang

¹**hive** /haɪv/ *n* **1** (a structure for housing) a colony of bees **2** a place full of busy occupants

²**hive 1** to collect into a hive **2** *of bees* to enter and take possession of a hive

¹**hoard** /hɔːd/ *n* **1** an often secret supply (e g of money or food) stored up for preservation or future use **2** a cache of valuable archaeological remains

²**hoard** *v* to lay up a hoard (of) – ~**er** *n*

hoarding /ˈhɔːdɪŋ/ *n* **1** a temporary fence put round a building site **2** *Br* a large board designed to carry outdoor advertising

hoarse /hɔːs/ *adj* **1** rough or harsh in sound; grating **2** having a hoarse voice – ~**ly** *adv* – ~**ness** *n*

¹**hoax** /həʊks/ *v* to play a trick on; deceive

²**hoax** *n* an act of deception; a trick – ~**er** *n*

¹**hobby** /ˈhɒbɪ/ *n* a leisure activity or pastime engaged in for interest or recreation

²**hobby** *n* a small Old World falcon that catches small birds while in flight

¹**hoe** /həʊ/ *n* any of various implements, esp one with a long handle and flat blade, used for tilling, weeding, etc

²**hoe** *v* **1** to weed or cultivate (land or a crop) with a hoe **2** to remove (weeds) by hoeing

¹**hog** /hɒg/ *n* **1** a young unshorn sheep **2** a warthog or other wild pig **3** *Br* a castrated male pig raised for slaughter **4** a selfish, gluttonous, or filthy person – slang

²**hog** *v* to appropriate a selfish or excessive share of; monopolize – infml

¹**hoist** /hɔɪst/ *v* to raise into position (as if) by means of tackle; *broadly* to raise

²**hoist** *n* an apparatus for hoisting

¹**hold** /həʊld/ *v* **held 1a** to have in one's keeping; possess **b** to retain by force **c** to keep by way of threat or coercion **2a** to keep under control; check **b** to stop the action of temporarily; delay **c** to keep from advancing or from attacking successfully **d** to restrict, limit **e** to bind legally or morally **3a** to have, keep, or support in the hands or arms; grasp **b** to keep in a specified situation, position, or state **c** to support, sustain **d** to retain **e** to keep in custody **f** to set

aside; reserve **4** to bear, carry **5a** to keep up without interruption; continue **b** to keep the uninterrupted interest or attention of **6a** to contain or be capable of containing **b** to have in store **7a** to consider to be true; believe **b** to have in regard **8a** to engage in with sby else or with others **b** to cause to be conducted; convene **9a** to occupy as a result of appointment or election **b** to have earned or been awarded **10a** to maintain position **b** to continue unchanged; last **11** to withstand strain without breaking or giving way **12** to bear or carry oneself **13** to be or remain valid; apply **14** to maintain a course; continue

²**hold** *n* **1a** a manner of grasping an opponent in wrestling **b** influence, control **c** possession **2** sthg that may be grasped as a support

³**hold** *n* **1** a space below a ship's deck in which cargo is stored **2** the cargo compartment of a plane

¹**hole** /həʊl/ *n* **1** an opening into or through a thing **2a** a hollow place; *esp* a pit or cavity **b** a deep place in a body of water **3** an animal's burrow **4** a serious flaw (e g in an argument) **5a** the unit of play from the tee to the hole in golf **b** a cavity in a putting green into which the ball is to be played in golf **6** a dirty or dingy place **7** an awkward position; a fix *USE (6 & 7)* infml

²**hole** *v* **1** to make a hole in **2** to drive into a hole **3** to make a hole in sthg

¹**holiday** /ˈhɒlɪdɪ/ *n* **1** a day, often in commemoration of some event, on which no paid employment is carried out **2** a period of relaxation or recreation spent away from home or work – often pl with sing. meaning

²**holiday** *v* to take or spend a holiday

¹**hollow** /ˈhɒləʊ/ *adj* **1a** having a recessed surface; sunken **b** curved inwards; concave **2** having a cavity within **3** echoing like a sound made in or by beating on an empty container; muffled **4a** deceptively lacking in real value or significance **b** lacking in truth or substance; deceitful – ~**ly** *adv* – ~**ness** *n*

²**hollow** *v* to make or become hollow

³**hollow** *n* **1** a depressed or hollow part of a surface; *esp* a small valley or basin **2** an unfilled space; a cavity

⁴**hollow** *adv* **1** in a hollow manner **2** completely, totally – infml

holly /ˈhɒlɪ/ *n* (the foliage of) any of a genus of trees and shrubs with thick glossy spiny-edged leaves and usu bright red berries

holy /ˈhəʊlɪ/ *adj* **1** set apart to the service of God or a god; sacred **2a** characterized by perfection and transcendence; commanding absolute adoration and reverence **b** spiritually pure; godly **3** terrible, awful – used as an intensive

home /həʊm/ *n* **1a** a family's place of residence; a domicile **b** a house **2** the social unit formed by a family living together **3a** a congenial environment **b** a habitat **4a** a place of origin; *also* one's native country **b** the place where sthg originates or is based **5** an establishment providing residence and often care for children, convalescents, etc – **~ less** *adj* – **~ lessness** *n*

²**home** *adv* **1** to or at home **2** to a final, closed, or standard position (e g drive a nail *home*) **3** to an ultimate objective (e g a finishing line) **4** to a vital sensitive core (e g the truth struck *home*)

³**home** *adj* **1** of or being a home, place of origin, or base of operations **2** prepared, carried out, or designed for use in the home **3** operating or occurring in a home area

⁴**home** *v* **1** to go or return home **2** *of an animal* to return accurately to one's home or birthplace from a distance **3** to be directed *in on* a target

homemade /ˌhəʊmˈmeɪd/ *adj* made in the home, on the premises, or by one's own efforts

homesick /ˈhəʊmˌsɪk/ *adj* longing for home and family while absent from them – **~ ness** *n*

homework /ˈhəʊmwɜːk/ *n* **1** work done in one's own home for pay **2** an assignment given to a pupil to be completed esp away from school **3** preparatory reading or research (e g for a discussion)

homosexual /ˌheʊmə'sekʃʊəl/ *adj or n* (of, for, or being) sby having a sexual preference for members of his/her own sex

honest /ˈɒnɪst/ *adj* **1** free from fraud or deception; legitimate, truthful **2** respectable or worthy **3a** marked by integrity **b** frank, sincere – **~ y** *n*

honestly /ˈɒnɪstli/ *adv* to speak in an honest way

honey /ˈhʌni/ *n* **1** (a pale golden colour like that typical of) a sweet viscous sticky liquid formed from the nectar of flowers in the honey sac of various bees **2** sthg sweet or agreeable; sweetness **3** a superlative example – chiefly infml

¹**honeycomb** /ˈhʌnikəʊm/ *n* (sthg resembling in shape or structure) a mass of 6-sided wax cells built by honeybees in their nest to contain their brood and stores of honey

²**honeycomb** *v* **1** to cause to be chequered or full of cavities like a honeycomb **2** to penetrate into every part; riddle

honeymoon /ˈhʌnimuːn/ *n* **1** the period immediately following marriage, esp when taken as a holiday by the married couple **2** a period of unusual harmony following the establishment of a new relationship

¹**honour** /ˈɒnə/ *n* **1a** good name or public esteem **b** outward respect; recognition **2** a privilege **3** *cap* a person of superior social standing – now used esp as a title for a holder of high office (e g a judge in court) **4** one who brings respect or fame **5** a mark or symbol of distinction: e g **a** an exalted title or rank **b** a ceremonial rite or observance – usu pl **6** *pl* a course of study for a university degree more exacting and specialized than that leading to a pass degree **7** (a

woman's) chastity or purity **8a** a high standard of ethical conduct; integrity **b** one's word given as a pledge

²**honour** *v* **1a** to regard or treat with honour or respect **b** to confer honour on **2a** to live up to or fulfil the terms of **b** to accept and pay when due

honourable /ˈɒnərəbl/ *adj* **1** worthy of honour **2** performed or accompanied with marks of honour or respect **3** entitled to honour – used as a title for the children of certain British noblemen and for various government officials **4a** bringing credit to the possessor or doer **b** consistent with blameless reputation **5** characterized by (moral) integrity – **-bly** *adv*

¹**hood** /hʊd/ *n* **1a** a loose often protective covering for the top and back of the head and neck that is usu attached to the neckline of a garment **b** a usu leather covering for a hawk's head and eyes **2a** an ornamental scarf worn over an academic gown that indicates by its colour the wearer's university and degree **b** a hoodlike marking, crest, or expansion on the head of an animal (e g a cobra or seal) **3a** a folding waterproof top cover for an open car, pram, etc **b** a cover or canopy for carrying off fumes, smoke, etc

²**hood** *n* a hoodlum or gangster – infml

¹**hoof** /huːf/ *n, pl* **hooves, hoofs** (a foot with) a curved horny casing that protects the ends of the digits of a horse, cow, or similar mammal and that corresponds to a nail or claw

²**hoof** *v* **1** to kick **2** to go on foot – usu + *it USE* infml

¹**hook** /hʊk/ *n* **1** (sthg shaped like) a curved or bent device for catching, holding, or pulling **2a** (a flight of) a ball in golf that deviates from a straight course in a direction opposite to the dominant hand of the player propelling it **b** an attacking stroke in cricket played with a horizontal bat aimed at a ball of higher than waist height and intended to send the ball on the leg side **3** a short blow delivered in boxing with a circular motion while the elbow remains bent and rigid

²**hook** *v* **1** to form (into a) hook (shape) **2** to seize, make fast, or connect (as if) by a hook **3** to hit or throw (a ball) so that a hook results **4** to become hooked

hooligan /ˈhuːlɪgən/ *n* a young ruffian or hoodlum – **~ ism** *n*

¹**hoop** /huːp/ *n* **1** a large (rigid) circular strip used esp for holding together the staves of containers, as a child's toy, or to expand a woman's skirt **2** a circular figure or object **3** an arch through which balls must be hit in croquet

²**hoop** *v* to bind or fasten (as if) with a hoop

¹**hoot** /huːt/ *v* **1** to utter a loud shout, usu in contempt **2a** to make (a sound similar to) the long-drawn-out throat noise of an owl **b** to sound the horn, whistle, etc of a motor car or other vehicle **3** to laugh loudly – infml

²**hoot** *n* **1** a sound of hooting **2** a damn

3 a source of laughter or amusement USE (2, 3) infml

¹**hop** /hɒp/ v 1 to move by a quick springy leap or in a series of leaps; hop to jump on 1 foot 2 to make a quick trip, esp by air 3 to board or leave a vehicle 4 to jump over

²**hop** n 1a a short leap, esp on 1 leg b a bounce, a rebound 2 a short or long flight between 2 landings 3 a dance – infml

³**hop** n 1 a climbing plant of the hemp family with inconspicuous green flowers of which the female ones are in cone-shaped catkins 2 pl the ripe dried catkins of a hop used esp to impart a bitter flavour to beer

¹**hope** /həʊp/ 1 to wish or long for with expectation of fulfilment 2 to expect with desire; trust

²**hope** n 1 trust, reliance 2a desire accompanied by expectation of or belief in fulfilment b sby or sthg on which hopes are centred c sthg hoped for

¹**hopeful** /ˈhəʊpfəl/ adj 1 full of hope 2 inspiring hope – ~**ness** n

²**hopeful** n a person who aspires to or is likely to succeed

hopefully /ˈhəʊpfəli/ adv 1 in a hopeful manner 2 it is hoped – disapproved of by some speakers

hopeless /ˈhəʊpl̩s/ adj 1 having no expectation of success 2a giving no grounds for hope b incapable of solution, management, or accomplishment 3 incompetent, useless – chiefly infml – ~**ly** adv – ~**ness** n

horde /hɔːd/ n 1 a (Mongolian) nomadic people or tribe 2 a crowd, swarm

horizon /həˈraɪzən/ n 1a the apparent junction of earth and sky b(1) the plane that is tangent to the earth's surface at an observer's position (2) (the great circle formed by the intersection with the celestial sphere of) the plane parallel to such a plane but passing through the earth's centre 2 range of perception, experience, or knowledge

horizontal /ˌhɒrɪˈzɒntl̩/ adj 1a near the horizon b in the plane of or (operating in a plane) parallel to the horizon or a base line; level 2 of or concerning relationships between people of the same rank in different hierarchies – ~**ly** adv

horn /hɔːn/ n 1a(1) any of the usu paired bony projecting parts on the head of cattle, giraffes, deer, and similar hoofed mammals and some extinct mammals and reptiles (2) a permanent solid pointed part attached to the nasal bone of a rhinoceros b a natural projection from an animal (e g a snail or owl) resembling or suggestive of a horn c the tough fibrous material consisting chiefly of keratin that covers or forms the horns and hooves of cattle and related animals, or other hard parts (e g claws or nails) d a hollow horn used as a container 2 sthg resembling or suggestive of a horn; esp either of the curved ends of a crescent 3a an animal's horn used as a wind instrument

b(1) a hunting horn (2) a French horn c a wind instrument used in a jazz band; esp a trumpet d a device (e g on a motor car) for making loud warning noises – ~**like**, ~**ed** adj

horrible /ˈhɒrəbəl/ adj 1 marked by or arousing horror 2 extremely unpleasant or disagreeable – chiefly infml – **-bly** adv

horrid /ˈhɒrɪd/ adj 1 horrible, shocking 2 repulsive, nasty – ~**ly** adv – ~**ness** n

horrify /ˈhɒrɪfaɪ/ v 1 to cause to feel horror 2 to fill with distaste; shock – ~**ingly**, **-fically** adv – **-fic** adj

horror /ˈhɒrə/ n 1a intense fear, dread, or dismay b intense aversion or repugnance 2 (sby or sthg that has) the quality of inspiring horror

horse /hɔːs/ n 1a(1) a large solid-hoofed plant-eating quadruped mammal domesticated by humans since prehistoric times and used as a beast of burden, a draught animal, or for riding (2) a racehorse b a male horse; a stallion or gelding 2a a usu 4-legged frame for supporting sthg (e g planks) b a padded obstacle for vaulting over 3 sing or pl in constr the cavalry 4 heroin – slang

horseman /ˈhɔːsmən/, fem **horsewoman** n 1 a rider on horseback 2 a (skilled) breeder, tender, or manager of horses – ~**ship** n

horsepower /ˈhɔːspaʊə/ n an imperial unit of power equal to about 746W

horseshoe /ˈhɔːʃuː, ˈhɔːs-/ n (sthg with a shape resembling) a shoe for horses, usu consisting of a narrow U-shaped plate of iron fitting the rim of the hoof

horticulture /ˈhɔːtɪˌkʌltʃə/ n the science and art of growing fruits, vegetables, and flowers – **-tural** adj – **-turalist** n

¹**hose** /həʊz/ n 1 a leg covering that sometimes covers the foot 2 a flexible tube for conveying fluids (e g from a tap or in a car engine)

²**hose** v to spray, water, or wash with a hose

hospitable /ˈhɒspɪtəbəl, hɒˈspɪ-/ adj 1a offering a generous and cordial welcome (to guests or strangers) b offering a pleasant or sustaining environment 2 readily receptive – **-bly** adv

hospital /ˈhɒspɪtl/ n 1 an institution where the sick or injured are given medical care – often used in British English without an article 2 a repair shop for specified small objects – ~**ize** v

hospitality /ˌhɒspɪˈtæl̩ti/ n hospitable treatment or reception

¹**host** /həʊst/ n 1 a very large number; a multitude 2 an army – chiefly poetic or archaic

²**host** n 1a an innkeeper b one who receives or entertains guests socially or officially c sby or sthg that provides facilities for an event or function 2a a living animal or plant on or in which a parasite or smaller organism lives b an

individual into which a tissue or part is transplanted from another

³**host** *v* to act as host at or of

⁴**host** *n, often cap* the bread consecrated in the Eucharist

hostage /'hɒstɪdʒ/ *n* a person held by one party as a pledge that promises will be kept or terms met by another party

hostel /'hɒstl/ *n* 1 *chiefly Br* a supervised residential home: e g **a** an establishment providing accommodation for nurses, students, etc **b** an institution for junior offenders, ex-offenders, etc, encouraging social adaptation 2 a Youth Hostel 3 an inn – chiefly poetic or archaic

hostess /'həʊstɪs/ *n* 1 a woman who entertains socially or acts as host 2a a female employee on a ship, aeroplane, etc who manages the provisioning of food and attends to the needs of passengers **b** a woman who acts as a companion to male patrons, esp in a nightclub; *also* a prostitute

hostile /'hɒstaɪl/ *adj* 1 of or constituting an enemy 2 antagonistic, unfriendly 3 not hospitable

hostility /hɒ'stɪlɪti/ *n* 1 *pl* overt acts of warfare 2 antagonism, opposition, or resistance

¹**hot** /hɒt/ *adj* 1a having a relatively high temperature **b** capable of giving a sensation of heat or of burning, searing, or scalding **c** having a temperature higher than normal body temperature 2a vehement, fiery **b** sexually excited; *also* sexually arousing **c** eager, enthusiastic **d** of or being an exciting style of jazz with strong rhythms 3 severe, stringent – usu + *on* 4 having or causing the sensation of an uncomfortable degree of body heat 5a very recent; fresh **b** close to sthg sought 6a suggestive of heat or of burning objects **b** pungent, peppery 7a of intense and immediate interest; sensational **b** performing well or strongly fancied to win (e g in a sport) **c** currently popular; selling very well **d** very good – used as a generalized term of approval 9a recently and illegally obtained **b** wanted by the police *USE* (2b, 2c, & 7d) *infml*, (9) *slang*

²**hot** *adv* hotly

hotel /həʊ'tel/ *n* a usu large establishment that provides meals and (temporary) accommodation for the public, esp for people travelling away from home

hotly /'hɒtli/ *adv* in a hot or fiery manner

¹**hound** /haʊnd/ *n* 1 a dog; *esp* one of any of various hunting breeds typically with large drooping ears and a deep bark that track their prey by scent 2 a mean or despicable person 3 one who is devoted to the pursuit of sthg specified

²**hound** *v* 1 to pursue (as if) with hounds 2 to harass persistently

hour /aʊə'/ *n* 1 (any of the 7 times of day set aside for) a daily liturgical devotion 2 the 24th part of a day; a period of 60 minutes 3a *the* time of day reckoned in hours and minutes by the clock; *esp* the beginning of each full hour measured by the clock **b** *pl* the time reckoned in one 24-hour period from midnight to midnight 4a a fixed or customary period of time set aside for a usu specified purpose – often *pl* **b** a particular, usu momentous, period or point of time **c** *the* present 5 the work done or distance travelled at normal rate in an hour

¹**house** /haʊs/ *n* 1 a building designed for people to live in 2a an animal's shelter or refuge (e g a nest or den) **b** a building in which sthg is housed or stored **c** a building used for a particular purpose, esp eating, drinking, or entertainment 3 any of the 12 equal sectors into which the celestial sphere is divided in astrology 4a *sing or pl in constr* the occupants of a house **b** a family including ancestors, descendants, and kindred 5a (a residence of) a religious community **b** any of several groups into which a British school may be divided for social purposes or games 6 (the chamber of) a legislative or deliberative assembly; *esp* a division of a body consisting of 2 chambers 7 a business organization or establishment 8 (the audience in) a theatre or concert hall

²**house** /haʊz/ *v* 1 to provide with accommodation or storage space 2 to serve as shelter for; contain

¹**household** /'haʊshəʊld/ *n sing or pl in constr* all the people who live together in a dwelling

²**household** *adj* 1 domestic 2 familiar, common

householder /'haʊs,həʊldə'/ *n* a person who occupies a dwelling as owner or tenant

housekeeper /'haʊs,ki:pə'/ *n* sby, esp a woman, employed to take charge of the running of a house

housekeeping /'haʊs,ki:pɪŋ/ *n* 1 (money used for) the day-to-day running of a house and household affairs 2 the general management of an organization which ensures its smooth running (e g the provision of equipment, keeping of records, etc)

housewife /'haʊs-waɪf; *sense* 2 'hʌzɪf/ *n* 1 a usu married woman who runs a house 2 a small container for needlework articles (e g thread) – ~ly *adj*

housework /'haʊsw3:k/ *n* the work (e g cleaning) involved in maintaining a house

housing /'haʊzɪŋ/ *n* 1 (the provision of) houses or dwelling-places collectively 2 a protective cover for machinery, sensitive instruments, etc

hover /'hɒvə'/ *v* 1 to hang in the air or on the wing 2a to linger or wait restlessly around a place **b** to be in a state of uncertainty, indecision, or suspense

hovercraft /'hɒvəkrɑ:ft/ *n, pl* **hovercraft** a vehicle supported on a cushion of air provided by fans and designed to travel over both land and sea

¹**how** /haʊ/ *adv* 1a in what manner or way (e g *how* do you spell it?) **b** with what meaning; to what effect (e g *how*

can you explain it?) **c** for what reason; why (e g *how* could you do it?) **2** by what measure or quantity (e g *how* much does it cost) – often used in an exclamation as an intensive (e g *how* nice of you!) **3** in what state or condition (e g *how* are you?)

²**how** *conj* **1a** the way, manner, or state in which (e g remember *how* they fought?) **b** that (e g do you remember *how* he arrived right at the end?) **2** however, as (e g do it *how* you like)

³**how** *n* the manner in which sthg is done

¹**however** /hau'evə/ *conj* in whatever manner or way (e g can go *however* he likes)

²**however** *adv* **1** to whatever degree or extent; no matter how (e g *however* hard I try) **2** in spite of that; nevertheless (e g would like to; *however*, I'd better not) **3** how in the world (e g *however* did you manage it?) – *infml*

howl /haul/ *v* **1a** *esp of dogs, wolves, etc* to make a loud sustained doleful cry **b** *of wind* to make a sustained wailing sound **2** to cry loudly and without restraint (e g with pain or laughter) **3** to utter with a loud sustained cry

hub /hʌb/ *n* **1** the central part of a wheel, propeller, or fan through which the axle passes **2** the centre of activity or importance

¹**huddle** /'hʌdl/ *v* **1** to crowd together **2** to draw or curl (oneself) up

²**huddle** *n* **1** a closely-packed group; a bunch **2** a secretive or conspiratorial meeting

¹**hug** /hʌg/ *v* **1** to hold or press tightly, esp in the arms **2a** to feel very pleased with (oneself) **b** to cling to; cherish **3** to stay close to

²**hug** *n* a tight clasp or embrace

huge /hju:dʒ/ *adj* great in size, scale, degree, or scope; enormous – **~ness** *n*

hum /hʌm/ *v* **1a** to utter a prolonged /m/ sound **b** to make the characteristic droning noise of an insect in motion or a similar sound **2** to be lively or active – *infml* **3** to have an offensive smell – *slang* **4** to sing with the lips closed and without articulation – **hum** *n*

¹**human** /'hju:mən/ *adj* **1** (characteristic) of humans **2** consisting of men and women **3a** having the esp good attributes (e g kindness and compassion) thought to be characteristic of humans **b** having, showing, or concerned with qualities or feelings characteristic of mankind – **~ize** *v*

²**human, human being** *n* a man, woman, or child; a person

humane /hju:'mein/ *adj* **1a** marked by compassion or consideration for other human beings or animals **b** causing the minimum pain possible **2** characterized by broad humanistic culture; liberal

humanity /hju:'mænɪti/ *n* **1** the quality of being humane **2** the quality or state of being human **3** *pl* the cultural branches of learning **4** mankind

¹**humble** /'hʌmbl/ *adj* **1** having a low opinion of oneself; unassertive **2**

marked by deference or submission **3a** ranking low in a hierarchy or scale **b** modest, unpretentious – **~bly** *adv*

¹**humble** *v* **1** to make humble in spirit or manner; humiliate **2** to destroy the power, independence, or prestige of

humid /'hju:mɪd/ *adj* containing or characterized by perceptible moisture

humiliate /hju:'mɪlieit/ *v* to cause to feel humble; lower the dignity or self-respect of – **-ation** *n*

humility /hju:'mɪlɪti/ *n* the quality or state of being humble

humorous /'hju:mərəs/ *adj* full of, characterized by, or expressing humour – **~ly** *adv*

¹**humour** /'hju:mə/ *n* **1** any of the 4 fluids of the body (blood, phlegm, and yellow and black bile) formerly held to determine, by their relative proportions, a person's health and temperament **2** characteristic or habitual disposition **3** a state of mind; a mood **4** a sudden inclination; a caprice **5a** (sthg having) the quality of causing amusement **b** the faculty of expressing or appreciating what is comic or amusing

²**humour** *v* to comply with the mood or wishes of; indulge

¹**hump** /hʌmp/ *n* **1** a rounded protuberance: **a a** a humped or crooked back **b** a fleshy protuberance on the back of a camel, bison, etc **2** a difficult, trying, or critical phase **3** *Br* a fit of depression or sulking – *infml*; + *the*

²**hump** *v* **1** to form or curve into a hump **2** *chiefly Br* to carry with difficulty **3** to have sexual intercourse (with) – *slang*

hundred /'hʌndrɪd/ *n, pl* **hundreds, hundred 1** the number 100 **2** the number occupying the position 3 to the left of the decimal point in Arabic notation; *also, pl* this position **3** 100 units or digits; *specif* £100 **4** *pl* the numbers 100 to 999 **5** a score of 100 or more runs made by a batsman in cricket **6** *pl* the 100 years of a specified century **7** a historical subdivision of a county **8** an indefinitely large number – *infml*; often pl with sing. meaning – **~th** *adj, n, pron, adv*

hundredweight /'hʌndrɪdweit/ *n, pl* **hundredweight, hundredweights** a British unit of weight equal to 112lb (about 50.80kg)

hung /hʌŋ/ *past of* **hang**

¹**hunger** /'hʌŋgə/ *n* **1** (a weakened condition or unpleasant sensation arising from) a craving or urgent need for food **2** a strong desire; a craving

²**hunger** *v* to have an eager desire – usu + *for* or *after* *n*

hungry /'hʌŋgri/ *adj* **1a** feeling hunger **b** characterized by or indicating hunger or appetite **2** eager, avid – **-grily** *adv*

¹**hunt** /hʌnt/ *v* **1a** to pursue for food or enjoyment **b** to use (e g hounds) in the search for game **2a** to pursue with intent to capture **b** to search out; seek **3** to persecute or chase, esp by harrying **4** to take part in a hunt, esp regularly **5** to attempt to find sthg

²**hunt** *n* **1** the act, the practice, or an instance of hunting **2** *sing or pl in*

constr a group of usu mounted hunters and their hounds

hunter /'hʌntəʳ/, *fem* (*1a&2*) **huntress** *n* **1a** sby who hunts game, esp with hounds **b** a usu fast strong horse used in hunting **2** a person who hunts or seeks sthg, esp overeagerly **3** a watch with a hinged metal cover to protect it

¹**hurdle** /'hɜ:d/ *n* **1a** a portable framework, usu of interlaced branches and stakes, used esp for enclosing land or livestock **b** a frame formerly used for dragging traitors to execution **2a** a light barrier jumped by men, horses, dogs, etc in certain races **b** *pl* any of various races over hurdles **3** a barrier, obstacle

²**hurdle** *v* **1** to jump over, esp while running **2** to overcome, surmount **3** to run in hurdle races – **~r** *n*

hurl /hɜ:l/ *v* **1** to drive or thrust violently **2** to throw forcefully **3** to utter or shout violently

hurricane /'hʌrɪkən/ *n* (a usu tropical cyclone with) a wind of a velocity greater than 117km/h (73 to 136mph)

hurried /'hʌrid/ *adj* done in a hurry – **~ly** *adv*

¹**hurry** /'hʌri/ *v* **1a** to transport or cause to go with haste; rush **b** to cause to move or act with (greater) haste **2** to hasten the progress or completion of **3** to move or act with haste – often + *up*

²**hurry** *n* **1** flurried and often bustling haste **2** a need for haste; urgency

hurt /hɜ:t/ *v* **1a** to afflict with physical pain; wound **b** to cause mental distress to; offend **2** to be detrimental to **3** to feel pain; suffer **4** to cause damage, distress, or pain

²**hurt** *n* **1** (a cause of) mental distress **2** wrong, harm

¹**husband** /'hʌzbənd/ *n* a married man, esp in relation to his wife

²**husband** *v* to make the most economical use of; conserve

¹**hush** /hʌʃ/ *v* to make or become quiet or calm

²**hush** *n* a silence or calm, esp following noise

¹**husky** /'hʌski/ *adj* of, resembling, or containing husks

²**husky** *adj* hoarse, breathy – **-kily** *adv* – **-kiness** *n*

³**husky** *adj* burly, hefty – *infml*

⁴**husky** *n* (any of) a breed of sledge dogs native to Greenland

hut /hʌt/ *n* a small often temporary dwelling of simple construction

hydrogen /'haidrədʒən/ *n* the simplest and lightest of the elements that is normally a highly inflammable gas

hygiene /'haidʒi:n/ *n* (conditions or practices, esp cleanliness, conducive to) the establishment and maintenance of health

hymn /him/ *n* **1** a song of praise to God; *esp* a metrical composition that can be included in a religious service **2** a song of praise or joy

hypnosis /hip'nəʊsɪs/ *n* any of various conditions that (superficially) resemble

sleep; *specif* one induced by a person to whose suggestions the subject is then markedly susceptible – **-notic** *adj* – **-notically** *adv*

hypnotism /'hipnətizəm/ *n* **1** the induction of hypnosis **2** hypnosis – **-tist** *n*, **-ize** *v*

hypocrisy /hɪ'pɒkrəsi/ *n* the feigning of virtues, beliefs, or standards, esp in matters of religion or morality

hypocrite /'hipəkrɪt/ *n* one given to hypocrisy – **-critical** *adj*

hysteria /hɪ'stɪərɪə/ *n* **1** a mental disorder marked by emotional excitability and disturbances (e g paralysis) of the normal bodily processes **2** unmanageable emotional excess – **-ric** *n*, **-rical** *adj*

hysterics /hɪ'steriks/ *n pl but sing or pl in constr* a fit of uncontrollable laughter or crying; hysteria

I

i /ai/ *n, pl* **i's**, *is often cap* **1** (a graphic representation of or device for reproducing) the 9th letter of the English alphabet **2** one

I /ai/ *pron* the one who is speaking or writing

¹**ice** /ais/ *n* **1a** frozen water **b** a sheet or stretch of ice **2** a substance reduced to the solid state by cold **3** (a serving of) a frozen dessert: e g **a** an ice cream **b** a water ice **4** *NAm* diamonds – *slang*

²**ice** *v* **1a** to coat with or convert into ice **b** to supply or chill with ice **2** to cover (as if) with icing **3** to become ice-cold **4** to become covered or clogged with ice

iceberg /'aisbɜːg/ *n* **1** a large floating mass of ice detached from a glacier **2** an emotionally cold person

ice cream *n* a sweet flavoured frozen food containing cream (substitute) and often eggs

icicle /'aisɪkəl/ *n* a hanging tapering mass of ice formed by the freezing of dripping water

icy /'aisi/ *adj* **1a** covered with, full of, or consisting of ice **b** intensely cold **2** characterized by personal coldness – **icily** *adv* – **iciness** *n*

idea /ai'dɪə/ *n* **1a** a transcendent entity of which existing things are imperfect representations **b** a plan of action **2a** an indefinite or vague impression **b** sthg (e g a thought, concept, or image) actually or potentially present in the mind **3** a formulated thought or opinion **4** whatever is known or supposed about sthg **5** an individual's conception of the perfect or typical example of sthg specified **6** the central meaning or aim of a particular action or situation

¹**ideal** /ai'dɪəl/ *adj* **1a** existing only in the mind; *broadly* lacking practicality **b** relating to or constituting mental images, ideas, or conceptions **2** of or

embodying an ideal; perfect – ~**ly** *adv*

²**ideal** *n* **1** a standard of perfection, beauty, or excellence **2** one looked up to as embodying an ideal or as a model for imitation **3** an ultimate object or aim – ~**ize** *v*

identical /aɪˈdentɪkəl/ *adj* **1** being the same **2** being very similar or exactly alike **3** *of twins, triplets, etc* derived from a single egg

identification /aɪˌdentɪfɪˈkeɪʃən/ *n* **1a** identifying or being identified **b** evidence of identity **2a** the putting of oneself mentally in the position of another

identify /aɪˈdentɪfaɪ/ *v* **1a** to cause to be or become identical **b** to associate or link closely **2** to establish the identity of

identity /aɪˈdentɪti/ *n* **1** the condition of being exactly alike **2** the distinguishing character or personality of an individual **3** the condition of being the same as sthg or sby known or supposed to exist **4** *Austr & NZ* a person, character

idiot /ˈɪdɪət/ *n* **1** a person suffering from accute mental deficiency, esp from birth **2** a silly or foolish person – ~**ic** *adj* – ~**ically** *adv*

¹**idle** /ˈaɪdl/ *adj* **1** having no particular purpose or value **2** groundless **3** not occupied or employed: e g **a** not in use or operation **b** not turned to appropriate use **4** lazy – ~**ness** *n* – **idly** *adv*

²**idle** *v* **1a** to spend time in idleness **b** to move idly **2** *esp of an engine* to run without being connected to the part (e g the wheels of a car) that is driven, so that no useful work is done

idol /ˈaɪdl/ *n* **1** an image or symbol used as an object of worship; *broadly* a false god **2** an object of passionate or excessive devotion – ~**ize** *v*

¹**if** /ɪf/ *conj* **1a** in the event that (e g *if* she should call, let me know) **b** supposing (e g *if* you'd listened, you'd know) **c** on condition that **2** whether (e g asked *if* the mail had come) **3** – used to introduce an exclamation expressing a wish (e g *if* only it would rain) **4** even if; although (e g an interesting *if* irrelevant point) **5** that – used after expressions of emotion (e g I don't car *if* she's cross) **6** – used with a negative when an expletive introduces startling news (e g blow me *if* he didn't hit her)

²**if** *n* **1** a condition, stipulation **2** a supposition

igloo /ˈɪgluː/ *n* an Eskimo dwelling, usu made of snow blocks and in the shape of a dome

ignite /ɪgˈnaɪt/ *v* **1a** to set fire to; *also* to kindle **b** to cause (a fuel mixture) to burn **c** to catch fire **2** to spark off; excite, esp suddenly

ignition /ɪgˈnɪʃən/ *n* **1** the act or action of igniting **2** the process or means (e g an electric spark) of igniting a fuel mixture

ignorance /ˈɪgnərəns/ *n* the state of being ignorant

ignorant /ˈɪgnərənt/ *adj* **1** lacking knowledge, education, or comprehension (of sthg specified) **2** caused by or showing lack of knowledge **3** lacking social training; impolite – chiefly infml

ignore /ɪgˈnɔː/ *v* to refuse to take notice of; disregard

¹**ill** /ɪl/ *adj* **worse; worst 1** bad: e g **a** morally evil **b** malevolent, hostile **c** attributing evil or an objectionable quality **2a** causing discomfort or inconvenience; disagreeable **b(1)** not normal or sound **(2)** not in good health; *also* nauseated **3** unlucky, disadvantageous **4** socially improper **5a** unfriendly, hostile **b** harsh

²**ill** *adv* **worse; worst 1a** with displeasure or hostility **b** in a harsh manner **c** so as to reflect unfavourably **2** in a reprehensible, harsh, or deficient manner **3** hardly, scarcely (e g can *ill* afford it) **4a** in an unfortunate manner; badly, unluckily **b** in a faulty, imperfect, or unpleasant manner *USE* often in combination

³**ill** *n* **1** the opposite of good; evil **2a** (a) misfortune, trouble **b(1)** an ailment **(2)** sthg that disturbs or afflicts **3** sthg that reflects unfavourably

ill-bred *adj* having or showing bad upbringing; impolite

illegal /ɪˈliːgəl/ *adj* not authorized by law – ~**ity** *n*

illegible /ɪˈledʒəbəl/ *adj* not legible – -**bility** *n* – -**bly** *adv*

illiterate /ɪˈlɪtərɪt/ *adj* **1** unable to read or write **2** showing lack of education – -**racy** *n*

illness /ˈɪlnɪs/ *n* an unhealthy condition of body or mind

ill-treat *v* to treat cruelly or improperly – ~**ment** *n*

illuminate /ɪˈluːmɪneɪt, ɪˈljuː-/ *v* **1a(1)** to cast light on; fill with light **(2)** to brighten **b** to enlighten spiritually or intellectually **2** to elucidate **3** to decorate (a manuscript) with elaborate initial letters or marginal designs in gold, silver, and brilliant colours – -**ation** *n*

illusion /ɪˈluːʒən/ *n* **1** a false impression or notion **2a(1)** a misleading image presented to the vision **(2)** sthg that deceives or misleads intellectually **b** perception of an object in such a way that it presents a misleading image

illustrate /ˈɪləstreɪt/ *v* **1a** to clarify (by giving or serving as an example or instance) **b** to provide (e g a book) with visual material **2** to show clearly; demonstrate – -**ive** *adj* – -**ively** *adv*

illustration /ˌɪləˈstreɪʃən/ *n* **1** illustrating or being illustrated **2** sthg that serves to illustrate: e g **a** an example that explains or clarifies sthg **b** a picture or diagram that helps to make sthg clear or attractive

image /ˈɪmɪdʒ/ *n* **1** a reproduction (e g a portrait or statue) of the form of a person or thing **2a** the optical counterpart of an object produced by a lens, mirror, etc or an electronic device **b** a likeness of an object produced on a photographic material **3a** exact likeness **b** a person who strikingly resembles another specified person **4** a typical example or embodiment (e g of a quality) **5a** a mental picture of sthg (not actually present) **b** an idea, concept **6** a figure of speech, esp a metaphor or simile

imaginary /ɪˈmædʒənəri/ *adj* existing only in imagination; lacking factual reality

imagination /ɪˌmædʒɪˈneɪʃən/ *n* **1** the act or power of forming a mental image of sthg not present to the senses or never before wholly perceived in reality **2** creative ability **3** a fanciful or empty notion

imaginative /ɪˈmædʒənətɪv/ *adj* **1** of or characterized by imagination **2** given to imagining; having a lively imagination **3** of images; *esp* showing a command of imagery

imagine /ɪˈmædʒɪn/ *v* **1** to form a mental image of (sthg not present) **2** to suppose, think **3** to believe without sufficient basis **4** to use the imagination

imitate /ˈɪmɪteɪt/ *v* **1** to follow as a pattern, model, or example **2** to reproduce **3** to resemble **4** to mimic – **-ation**, **-ativeness** *n* – **-ative** *adj*

immaculate /ɪˈmækjʊlɪt/ *adj* **1** without blemish; pure **2** free from flaw or error **3** spotlessly clean

immature /ˌɪməˈtʃʊə/ *adj* **1** lacking complete growth, differentiation, or development **2a** not having arrived at a definitive form or state **b** exhibiting less than an expected degree of maturity – **-turity** *n*

immediate /ɪˈmiːdɪət/ *adj* **1a** acting or being without any intervening agency or factor **b** involving or derived from a single premise **2** next in line or relationship **3** occurring at once or very shortly **4** in close or direct physical proximity **5** directly touching or concerning a person or thing

¹**immediately** /ɪˈmiːdɪətli/ *adv* **1** in direct relation or proximity; directly **2** without delay

²**immediately** *conj* as soon as

immense /ɪˈmens/ *adj* very great, esp in size, degree, or extent – **-ensity** *n*

immerse /ɪˈmɜːs/ *v* **1** to plunge into sthg, esp a fluid, that surrounds or covers **2** to baptize by complete submergence **3** to engross, absorb – **-sion** *n*

immigrate /ˈɪmɪɡreɪt/ to come into a country of which one is not a native for permanent residence – **-gration** *n* – **-grant** *n*

immoral /ɪˈmɒrəl/ *adj* not conforming to conventional moral standards, esp in sexual matters – **~ity** *n*

¹**immortal** /ɪˈmɔːtəl/ *adj* **1** exempt from death **2** enduring forever; imperishable

²**immortal** *n* **1a** one exempt from death **b** *pl, often cap* the gods of classical antiquity **2** a person of lasting fame – **~ize** *v*

immune /ɪˈmjuːn/ *adj* **1** free, exempt **2** having a high degree of resistance to a disease **3a** having or producing antibodies to a corresponding antigen **b**

concerned with or involving immunity – **immunity** *n* – **immunize** *v*

¹**impact** /ɪmˈpækt/ *v* **1** to fix or press firmly (as if) by packing or wedging **2** to impinge or make contact, esp forcefully

²**impact** /ˈɪmpækt/ *n* **1a** an impinging or striking, esp of one body against another **b** (the impetus produced by or as if by) a violent contact or collision **2** a strong or powerful effect or impression

impartial /ɪmˈpɑːʃəl/ *adj* not biased – **~ity** *n*

impatient /ɪmˈpeɪʃənt/ *adj* **1a** restless or quickly roused to anger or exasperation **b** intolerant **2** showing or caused by a lack of patience **3** eagerly desirous; anxious – **-ience** *n*

impede /ɪmˈpiːd/ *v* to interfere with or retard the progress of – **-iment** *n*

¹**imperfect** /ɪmˈpɜːfikt/ *adj* **1** not perfect: e g **a** defective **b** not having the stamens and carpels in the same flower **2** of or being a verb tense expressing a continuing state or an incomplete action, esp in the past – **~ion** *n* – **~ly**

²**imperfect** *n* (a verb form expressing) the imperfect tense

impertinent /ɪmˈpɜːtɪnənt/ *adj* **1** not restrained within due or proper bounds; *also* rude, insolent **2** irrelevant – chiefly *fml* – **-nence** *n*

impetus /ˈɪmpɪtəs/ *n* **1a** a driving force **b** an incentive, stimulus **2** the energy possessed by a moving body

¹**implement** /ˈɪmplɪmənt/ *n* **1** an article serving to equip **2** (sby or sthg that serves as) a utensil or tool

²**implement** /ˈɪmplɪment/ *v* to carry out; *esp* to give practical effect to

implore /ɪmˈplɔː/ *v* **1** to call on in supplication; beseech **2** to call or beg for earnestly; entreat

imply /ɪmˈplaɪ/ *v* **1** to involve or indicate as a necessary or potential though not expressly stated consequence **2** to express indirectly; hint at

impolite /ˌɪmpəˈlaɪt/ *adj* not polite; rude – **~ness** *n*

¹**import** /ɪmˈpɔːt/ *v* **1** to bring from a foreign or external source; *esp* to bring (e g merchandise) into a place or country from another country **2** to convey as meaning or portent; signify – chiefly *fml* – **~er** *n*

²**import** /ˈɪmpɔːt/ *n* **1** sthg imported **2** importing, esp of merchandise **3** purport, meaning **4** (relative) importance USE (3 & 4) *fml*

important /ɪmˈpɔːtənt/ *adj* of considerable significance or consequence – **-ance** *n*

impose /ɪmˈpəʊz/ *v* **1a** to establish or apply as compulsory **b** to establish or make prevail by force **2** to force into the company or on the attention of another **3** to take unwarranted advantage; *also* to be an excessive requirement or burden – **-sition** *n*

impossible /ɪmˈpɒsɪbl/ *adj* **1a** incapable of being or occurring; not possible **b** seemingly incapable of being done, attained, or fulfilled; insuperably difficult **c** difficult to believe **2** extremely undesirable or difficult to put up with **– bility** *n*

impostor /ɪmˈpɒstə/ , **imposter** *n* one who assumes a false identity or title for fraudulent purposes

¹**impress** /ɪmˈpres/ *v* **1a** to apply with pressure so as to imprint **b** to mark (as if) by pressure or stamping **2a** to fix strongly or deeply (e g in the mind or memory) **b** to produce a deep and usu favourable impression (on) **3** to transmit (force or motion) by pressure

²**impress** /ˈɪmpres/ *n* **1** the act of impressing **2** a mark made by pressure **3** an impression, effect

³**impress** /ɪmˈpres/ *v* to procure or enlist by forcible persuasion

impression /ɪmˈpreʃən/ *n* **1** the act or process of impressing **2** the effect produced by impressing: e g **a** a stamp, form, or figure produced by physical contact **b** a (marked) influence or effect on the mind or senses; *esp* a favourable impression **3a** an effect of alteration or improvement **b** a telling image impressed on the mind or senses **4a** (a print or copy made from) the contact of a printing surface and the material being printed **b** all the copies of a publication (e g a book) printed in 1 continuous operation **5** a usu indistinct or imprecise notion or recollection **6** an imitation or representation of salient features in an artistic or theatrical medium; *esp* an imitation in caricature of a noted personality as a form of theatrical entertainment

impressive /ɪmˈpresɪv/ *adj* making a marked impression; stirring deep feelings, esp of awe or admiration **– ~ ly** *adv* **– ~ ness** *n*

imprison /ɪmˈprɪzən/ *v* to put (as if) in prison **– ~ ment** *n*

improper /ɪmˈprɒpə/ *adj* **1** not in accordance with fact, truth, or correct procedure **2** not suitable or appropriate **3** not in accordance with propriety or modesty; indecent **– -priety** *n*

improve /ɪmˈpruːv/ *v* **1** to enhance in value or quality; make better **2** to use to good purpose **3** to advance or make progress in what is desirable **4** to make useful additions or amendments **– ~ ment** *n*

improvise /ˈɪmprəvaɪz/ *v* **1** to compose, recite, or perform impromptu or without a set script, musical score, etc **2** to make, devise, or provide (sthg) without preparation (from what is conveniently to hand) **– -visation** *n*

impulse /ˈɪmpʌls/ *n* **1a** (motion produced by) the act of driving onwards with sudden force **b** a wave of excitation transmitted through a nerve that results in physiological (e g muscular) activity or inhibition **2a** a force so communicated as to produce motion suddenly **b** inspiration, stimulus **3a** a sudden spontaneous inclination or incitement to some usu unpremeditated action **b** a propensity or natural tendency, usu other than rational

impulsive /ɪmˈpʌlsɪv/ *adj* **1** having the power of driving or impelling **2** actuated by or prone to act on impulse **– ~ ness** *n*

¹**in** /ɪn/ *prep* **1a(1)** – used to indicate location within or inside sthg three-dimensional (e g swimming in the lake) **(2)** – used to indicate location within or not beyond limits (e g in sight) **(3)** at – used with the names of cities, countries, and seas (e g in London) **(4)** during (e g in the summer) **(5)** by or before the end of (e g will come in an hour) **b** into (e g come in the kitchen and get warm) **2a** – used to indicate means, instrumentality, or medium of expression (e g written in French) **b** – used to describe costume (e g a girl in red) **3a** – used to indicate qualification, manner, circumstance, or condition (e g in fun; in a hurry) **b** so as to be **c** – used to indicate occupation or membership (e g a job in insurance) **4a** as regards (e g equal in distance) **b** by way of (e g said in reply) **5a** – used to indicate division, arrangement, or quantity (e g standing in a circle) **b** – used to indicate the larger member of a ratio (e g one in six is eligible) **6** *of an animal* pregnant with (e g in calf) **7** – used to introduce indirect objects (e g rejoice in) or to form adverbial phrases

²**in** *adv* **1a** to or towards the inside or centre (e g come in out of the rain) **b** so as to incorporate (e g mix in the flour) **c** to or towards home, the shore, or one's destination (e g 3 ships came sailing in) **d** at a particular place, esp at one's home or business (e g be in for lunch) **e** into concealment (e g the sun went in) **2a** so as to be added or included (e g fit a piece in) **b** in or into political power (e g voted them in) **c(1)** on good terms (e g in with the boss) **(2)** in a position of assured success **(3)** into a state of efficiency or proficiency (e g work a horse in) **d** in or into vogue or fashion **e** in or into a centre, esp a central point of control (e g letters pouring in)

³**in** *adj* **1a** located inside **b** being in operation or power (e g the fire's still in) **c** shared by a select group (e g an in joke) **2** directed or serving to direct inwards (e g the in tray) **3** extremely fashionable

inability /ˌɪnəˈbɪlɪti/ *n* lack of sufficient power, resources, or capacity

inaction /ɪnˈækʃən/ *n* lack of action or activity **– -tive** *adj* **– -tivity** *n*

inadequate /ɪnˈædɪkwɪt/ *adj* not adequate: e g **a** insufficient **b** characteristically unable to cope **– -acy** *n*

incapable /ɪnˈkeɪpəbəl/ *adj* lacking capacity, ability, or qualification for the purpose or end in view: e g **a** not in a state of or of a kind to admit of **b** not able or fit for the doing or performance of **– -bility** *n* **– -bly** *adv*

incentive /ɪnˈsentɪv/ *n* sthg that motivates or spurs one on (e g to action or effort)

¹**inch** /ɪntʃ/ *n* **1** a unit of length equal to ¹⁄₃₆ yd (about 25.4mm) **2** a small

amount, distance, or degree **3** *pl* stature, height **4** a fall of rain, snow, etc enough to cover a surface to the depth of 1 in

²**inch** *v* to move by small degrees

³**inch** *n, chiefly Scot* an island – usu in place-names

¹**incident** /'ɪnsɪdənt/ *n* **1** an occurrence of an action or situation that is a separate unit of experience **2** an occurrence that is a cause of conflict or disagreement **3** an event occurring as part of a series or as dependent on or subordinate to sthg else

²**incident** *adj* **1** that is a usual accompaniment or consequence **2** dependent on another thing in law

¹**incidental** /ˌɪnsɪˈdentl/ *adj* **1** occurring merely by chance **2** likely to ensue as a chance or minor consequence

²**incidental** /ˌɪnsɪˈdentl/ *n* **1** sthg incidental **2** *pl* minor items (e g of expenses)

incite /ɪnˈsaɪt/ *v* to move to action; stir up – ~**ment** *n*

¹**incline** /ɪnˈklaɪn/ *v* **1** to (cause to) lean, tend, or become drawn towards an opinion or course of conduct **2** to (cause to) deviate or move from a line, direction, or course, esp from the vertical or horizontal – **-nation** *n*

²**incline** /ˈɪnklaɪn/ *n* an inclined surface; a slope

include /ɪnˈkluːd/ *v* **1** to contain, enclose **2** to take in or comprise as a part of a larger group, set, or principle – **-ding** *prep* – ~**d** *adj* – **-usion** *n*

inclusive /ɪnˈkluːsɪv/ *adj* **1a** broad in orientation or scope **b** covering or intended to cover all or the specified items, costs, or services **2** including the stated limits or extremes

income /'ɪŋkʌm, 'ɪn-/ *n* (the amount of) a usu periodic gain or recurrent benefit usu measured in money that derives from one's work, property, or investment

incompetent /ɪnˈkɒmpɪtənt/ *adj* **1** lacking the qualities needed for effective action **2** not legally qualified **3** inadequate to or unsuitable for a particular purpose – **-ence**, **-ency** *n*

incomplete /ˌɪnkəmˈpliːt/ *adj* **1** unfinished **2** lacking a part – ~**ness** *n*

incongruous /ɪnˈkɒŋgruəs/ *adj* out of place; discordant or disagreeing – ~**ness** *n* – **-uity** *n*

inconsistent /ˌɪnkənˈsɪstənt/ *adj* **1** not compatible; containing incompatible elements **2** not consistent or logical in thought or actions – ~**ency** *n*

inconvenient /ˌɪnkənˈviːnɪənt/ *adj* not convenient, esp in causing difficulty, discomfort, or annoyance – ~**ly** *adv* – **-ence** *n*

incorporate /ɪnˈkɔːpəreɪt/ *v* **1a** to unite thoroughly with or work indistinguishably into sthg **b** to admit to membership in a corporate body **2a** to combine thoroughly to form a consistent whole **b** to form into a legal corporation **3** to unite in or as 1 body – **-ration** *n*

incorrect /ˌɪnkəˈrekt/ *adj* **1** inaccurate; factually wrong **2** not in accordance with an established norm; improper – ~**ly** *adv* – ~**ness** *n*

¹**increase** /ɪnˈkriːs/ *v* **1** to make or become (progressively) greater (e g in size, amount, quality, number, or intensity) **2** to multiply by the production of young

²**increase** /'ɪnkriːs/ *n* **1** (an) addition or enlargement in size, extent, quantity, etc **2** sthg (e g offspring, produce, or profit) added to an original stock by addition or growth – **-singly** *adv*

incredible /ɪnˈkredəbl/ *adj* **1** too extraordinary and improbable to be believed; *also* hard to believe **2** – used as a generalized term of approval – **-bility** *n* – **-bly** *adv*

indebted /ɪnˈdetɪd/ *adj* **1** owing money **2** owing gratitude or recognition to another – ~**ness** *n*

indecisive /ˌɪndɪˈsaɪsɪv/ *adj* **1** giving an uncertain result **2** marked by or prone to indecision – ~**ly** *adv* – ~**ness** *n*

indeed /ɪnˈdiːd/ *adv* **1** without any question; truly – often used in agreement **2** – used for emphasis after *very* and an adjective or adverb **3** in point of fact; actually **4** – expressing irony, disbelief, or surprise

indefinite /ɪnˈdefənɪt/ *adj* **1** designating an unidentified or not immediately identifiable person or thing **2** not precise; vague **3** having no exact limits – ~**ness** *n* – ~**ly** *adv*

¹**independent** /ˌɪndɪˈpendənt/ *adj* **1** not dependent: e g **a**(1) self-governing **(2)** not affiliated with a larger controlling unit **b**(1) not relying on sthg else **(2)** not committed to a political party **c**(1) not requiring or relying on, or allowing oneself to be controlled by, others (e g for guidance or care) **(2)** having or providing enough money to live on, esp without working **2** of a clause able to stand alone as a complete statement – **-ence** *n* – ~**ly** *adv*

²**independent** /ˌɪndɪˈpendənt/ *n, often cap* sby not bound by a political party

¹**index** /'ɪndeks/ *n, pl* **indexes**, **indices** **1** a guide or list to aid reference; e g *esp* an alphabetical list of items (e g topics or names) treated in a printed work that gives with each item the page number where it appears **2** sthg that points towards or demonstrates a particular state of affairs **3** a list of restricted or prohibited material; *specif, cap* the list of books banned by the Roman Catholic church **4** a character ☞ used to direct attention (e g to a note or paragraph)

²**index** *v* **1** to provide with or list in an index **2** to serve as an index of **3** to cause to be index-linked **4** to prepare an index

indicate /'ɪndɪkeɪt/ *v* **1a**(1) to point to; point out **(2)** to show or demonstrate as or by means of a sign or pointer **b** to be a sign or symptom of **c** to demonstrate or suggest the necessity or advisability of – chiefly pass **2** to state or express briefly; suggest – **-ation** *n*

indicator /'ɪndɪkeɪtə/ *n* **1a** a hand or needle on an instrument (e g a dial) **b**

an instrument for giving visual readings attached to a machine or apparatus **c** a device (e g a flashing light) on a vehicle that indicates an intention to change direction **2a** a substance (e g litmus) that shows, esp by change of colour, the condition (e g acidity or alkalinity) of a solution **b** a chemical tracer (e g an isotope) **3** a statistic (e g the level of industrial production) that gives an indication of the state of a national economy

indifferent /ɪnˈdɪfərənt/ *adj* **1** that does not matter one way or the other **2** not interested in or concerned about sthg **3a** neither good nor bad; mediocre **b** not very good; inferior – ~ly *adv* – -ence *n*

indigestible /ˌɪndɪˈdʒestəbəl/ *adj* not (easily) digested – -bility *n*, -bly *adv*

indigestion /ˌɪndɪˈdʒestʃən/ *n* (pain in the digestive system usu resulting from) difficulty in digesting sthg

indignant /ɪnˈdɪɡnənt/ *adj* angry because of sthg judged unjust, mean, etc – -ation *n* – ~ly *adv*

indirect /ˌɪndɪˈrekt/ *adj* **1a** deviating from a direct line or course **b** not going straight to the point **2** not straightforward or open **3** not directly aimed at **4** stating what a real or supposed original speaker said but with changes of tense, person, etc – ~ly *adv* – ~ness *n*

indispensable /ˌɪndɪˈspensəbəl/ *adj* that cannot be done without – -bility *n* – -bly *adv*

¹**individual** /ˌɪndɪˈvɪdʒuəl/ *adj* **1a** of or being an individual **b** intended for 1 person **2** existing as a distinct entity; separate **3** having marked individuality – ~ly *adv*

²**individual** *n* **1** a particular person, being, or thing (as distinguished from a class, species, or collection) **2** a person

indoctrinate /ɪnˈdɒktrɪˌneɪt/ *v* to imbue with a usu partisan or sectarian opinion, point of view, or ideology – -nation *n*

indoor /ˈɪndɔːʳ/ *adj* **1** of the interior of a building **2** done, living, or belonging indoors

indoors /ˌɪnˈdɔːz/ *adv* in or into a building

indulge /ɪnˈdʌldʒ/ *v* **1a** to give free rein to (e g a taste) **b** to allow (oneself) to do sthg pleasurable or gratifying **2** to treat with great or excessive leniency, generosity, or consideration – ~nt *adj* – ~ntly *adv*

industrial /ɪnˈdʌstriəl/ *adj* **1** of, involved in, or derived from industry **2** characterized by highly developed industries **3** used in industry

industrious /ɪnˈdʌstriəs/ *adj* **1** persistently diligent **2** constantly, regularly, or habitually occupied – ~ly *adv* – ~ness *n*

industry /ˈɪndəstri/ *n* **1** diligence in an employment or pursuit **2a** systematic work, esp for the creation of value **b(1)** a usu specified group of productive or profit-making enterprises **(2)** an organized field of activity regarded in its

commercial aspects **c** manufacturing activity as a whole – -rialize *v*

inefficient /ˌɪnɪˈfɪʃənt/ *adj* not producing the effect intended or desired, esp in a capable or economical way – ~ly *adv* – -ciency *n*

inept /ɪˈnept/ *adj* **1** not suitable or apt to the time, place, or occasion **2** lacking sense or reason **3** generally incompetent – ~ly *adv* – ~itude, ~ness *n*

inertia /ɪˈnɜːʃə/ *n* **1** a property of matter by which it remains at rest or in uniform motion in the same straight line unless acted on by some external force **2** indisposition to motion, exertion, or change

inevitable /ɪˈnevɪtəbəl/ *adj* incapable of being avoided or evaded; bound to happen or to confront one – -bility *n* – -bly *adv*

inexpensive /ˌɪnɪkˈspensɪv/ *adj* reasonable in price; cheap – ~ly *adv*

infallible /ɪnˈfæləbəl/ *adj* **1** incapable of error; *esp, of the Pope* incapable of error in defining dogma **2** not liable to fail – -bility *n*

¹**infant** /ˈɪnfənt/ *n* **1** a child in the first period of life **2** a minor

²**infant** *adj* **1** in an early stage of development **2** concerned with or intended for young children, esp those aged from 5 to 7 or 8

infantry /ˈɪnfəntri/ *n sing or pl in constr* (a branch of an army containing) soldiers trained, armed, and equipped to fight on foot – ~man *n*

infect /ɪnˈfekt/ *v* **1** to contaminate (e g air or food) with a disease-causing agent **2a** to pass on a disease or a disease-causing agent to **b** to invade (an individual or organ), usu by penetration – used with reference to a disease-causing organism **3** to transmit or pass on sthg (e g an emotion) to

infection /ɪnˈfekʃən/ *n* **1** infecting **2** (an agent that causes) a contagious or infectious disease **3** the communication of emotions or qualities through example or contact

infectious /ɪnˈfekʃəs/ *adj* **1a** infectious, infective capable of causing infection **b** communicable by infection **2** readily spread or communicated to others – ~ly *adj* – ~ness *n*

infer /ɪnˈfɜːʳ/ *v* **1** to derive as a conclusion from facts or premises **2** to suggest, imply – disapproved of by some speakers – ~ence *n* – ~ential *adj* – ~entially *adv*

inferior /ɪnˈfɪəriəʳ/ *adj* **1** situated lower down **2** of low or lower degree or rank **3** of little or less importance, value, or merit **4** *of a planet* nearer the sun than the earth is

infernal /ɪnˈfɜːnəl/ *adj* **1** of hell **2** hellish, diabolical **3** damned – *infml*

infest /ɪnˈfest/ *v* **1** to spread or swarm in or over in a troublesome manner **2** to live in or on as a parasite – ~ation *n*

¹**infinite** /ˈɪnfɪnɪt/ *adj* **1** subject to no limitation or external determination **2** extending indefinitely **3** immeasurably or inconceivably great or extensive **4a**

extending beyond, lying beyond, or being greater than any arbitrarily chosen finite value, however large **b** extending to infinity

²**infinite** *n* **1** divineness, sublimity – + *the* **3** an infinite quantity or magnitude

infinity /ɪnˈfɪnɪti/ *n* **1a** the quality of being infinite **b** unlimited extent of time, space, or quantity **2** an indefinitely great number or amount

inflammable /ɪnˈflæməbəl/ *adj* **1** capable of being easily ignited and of burning rapidly **2** easily inflamed, excited, or angered

inflate /ɪnˈfleɪt/ *v* **1** to swell or distend (with air or gas) **2** to increase (a price level) or cause (a volume of credit or the economy) to expand **3** to become inflated – **-atable** *adj*

inflation /ɪnˈfleɪʃən/ *n* inflating or being inflated; *esp* a substantial and continuing rise in the general level of prices, caused by or causing an increase in the volume of money and credit or an expansion of the economy

inflict /ɪnˈflɪkt/ *v* to force or impose (sthg damaging or painful) on sby

¹**influence** /ˈɪnfluəns/ *n* **1** the power to achieve sthg desired by using wealth or position **2** the act, power, or capacity of causing or producing an effect in indirect or intangible ways **3** sby or sthg that exerts influence; *esp* sby or sthg that tends to produce a moral or immoral effect on another – **-ential** *adj* **-entially** *adv*

²**influence** *v* to affect, alter, or modify by indirect or intangible means

influenza /ˌɪnfluˈenzə/ *n* **1** a highly infectious virus disease characterized by sudden onset, fever, severe aches and pains, and inflammation of the respiratory mucous membranes **2** any of numerous feverish usu virus diseases of domestic animals marked by respiratory symptoms

inform /ɪnˈfɔːm/ *v* **1** to impart an essential quality or character to **2** to communicate knowledge to **3** to give information or knowledge **4** to act as an informer *against* or *on* – ~**ant** *n* – ~**ative** *adj* – ~**atively** *adv*

informal /ɪnˈfɔːməl/ *adj* marked by an absence of formality or ceremony; everyday – ~**ity** *n* – ~**ly** *adv*

information /ˌɪnfəˈmeɪʃən/ *n* **1** the communication or reception of facts or ideas **2a** knowledge obtained from investigation, study, or instruction **b** news **c** (significant) facts or data **3** a formal accusation presented to a magistrate

ingenious /ɪnˈdʒiːnɪəs/ *adj* marked by originality, resourcefulness, and cleverness – ~**ly** *adv* – **ingenuity** *n*

ingenuous /ɪnˈdʒenjuəs/ *adj* showing innocent or childlike simplicity; frank, candid – ~**ly** *adv* – ~**ness** *n*

ingredient /ɪnˈɡriːdɪənt/ *n* sthg that forms a component part of a compound, combination, or mixture

inhabit /ɪnˈhæbɪt/ *v* to occupy or be present in – ~**able** *adj* – ~**ant** *n*

inherit /ɪnˈherɪt/ *v* **1** to receive, either by right or from an ancestor at his/her death **2** to receive by genetic transmission – ~**ance** *n*

¹**initial** /ɪˈnɪʃəl/ *adj* **1** of the beginning **2** first

²**initial** *n* **1** the first letter of a name **2** *pl* the first letter of each word in a full name

³**initial** *v* to put initials (indicating ownership or authorization) on

¹**initiate** /ɪˈnɪʃieɪt/ *v* **1** to cause or enable the beginning of; start **2** to instil with rudiments or principles (of sthg complex or obscure) **3** to induct into membership (as if) by formal rites

²**initiate** /ɪˈnɪʃiɪt/ *n* **1** sby who is undergoing or has undergone initiation **2** sby who is instructed or proficient in a complex or specialized field

¹**initiative** /ɪˈnɪʃiətɪv/ *adj* introductory, preliminary

²**initiative** *n* **1** a first step, esp in the attainment of an end or goal **2** energy or resourcefulness displayed in initiation of action **3** a procedure enabling voters to propose a law by petition

inject /ɪnˈdʒekt/ *v* **1a** to throw, drive, or force into sthg **b** to force a fluid into **2** to introduce as an element or factor

injection /ɪnˈdʒekʃən/ *n* **1** injecting **2** sthg (e g a medication) that is injected

injure /ˈɪndʒə/ *v* **1** to do injustice to **2a** to inflict bodily hurt on **b** to impair the soundness of **c** to inflict damage or loss on – **-rious** *adj* – **-riously** *adv*

injury /ˈɪndʒəri/ *n* **1** a wrong **2** hurt, damage, or loss sustained

¹**ink** /ɪŋk/ *n* **1** a coloured liquid used for writing and printing **2** the black secretion of a squid, octopus, etc that hides it from a predator or prey

²**ink** *v* to apply ink to

¹**inland** /ˈɪnlənd/ *adv or n* (into or towards) the interior part of a country

²**inland** /ɪnˈlænd/ *adj* **1** of the interior of a country **2** *chiefly Br* not foreign; domestic

inn /ɪn/ *n* **1a** an establishment (e g a small hotel) providing lodging and food, esp for travellers **b** a public house **2** a residence formerly provided for students in London

inner /ˈɪnə/ *adj* **1a** situated within; internal **b** situated near to a centre, esp of influence **2** of the mind or soul

innings /ˈɪnɪŋz/ *n* **1a** any of the alternating divisions of a cricket match during which one side bats and the other bowls **b** the (runs scored in or quality of the) turn of 1 player to bat **2a** a period in which sby has opportunity for action or achievements **b** *chiefly Br* the duration of sby's life

innocent /ˈɪnəsənt/ *adj* **1a** free from guilt or sin; pure **b** harmless in effect or intention **c** free from legal guilt **2** lacking or deprived of sthg **3a** artless, ingenuous **b** ignorant, unaware

innocuous /ɪˈnɒkjuəs/ *adj* **1** having no harmful effects **2** inoffensive, insipid – ~**ly** *adv* – ~**ness** *n*

innovate /'ɪnəveɪt/ *v* to make changes; introduce sthg new – **-vator** *n*

innuendo /ˌɪnjʊ'endəʊ/ *n* an oblique allusion; *esp* a veiled slight on sby's character or reputation

inquest /'ɪŋkwest/ *n* **1** a judicial inquiry, esp by a coroner, into the cause of a death **2** an inquiry or investigation, esp into sthg that has failed

inquire, enquire /ɪn'kwaɪə/ *v* to seek information; ask about

inquiry, enquiry *n* **1** a request for information **2** a thorough or systematic investigation

inquisitive /ɪn'kwɪzɪtɪv/ *adj* **1** eager for knowledge or understanding **2** fond of making inquiries; *esp* unduly curious about the affairs of others – **~ly** *adv* – **~ness** *n*

insane /ɪn'seɪn/ *adj* **1** mentally disordered; exhibiting insanity **2** typical of or intended for insane people **3** utterly absurd – **~ly** *adv* – **-anity** *n*

inscrutable /ɪn'skruːtəbəl/ *adj* hard to interpret or understand; enigmatic – **-bility** *n* – **-bly** *adv*

insect /'ɪnsekt/ *n* **1** any of a class of arthropods with a well-defined head, thorax, and abdomen, only 3 pairs of legs, and typically 1 or 2 pairs of wings **2** any of various small invertebrate animals (e g woodlice and spiders) – not used technically

¹insert /ɪn'sɜːt/ *v* **1** to put or thrust in **2** to put or introduce into the body of sthg **3** to set in and make fast; *esp* to insert by sewing between 2 cut edges – **~ion** *n*

²insert /'ɪnzɜːt, -sɜːt/ *n* sthg (esp written or printed) inserted

¹inside /ɪn'saɪd/ *n* **1** an inner side or surface **2a** an interior or internal part **b** inward nature, thoughts, or feeling **c** viscera, entrails – usu pl with sing. meaning **3** a position of confidence or of access to confidential information **4** the middle portion of a playing area

²inside /ɪn'saɪd/ *adj* **1** of, on, near, or towards the inside **2** of or being the inner side of a curve or being near the side of the road nearest the kerb or hard shoulder

³inside *prep* **1a** in or into the interior of **b** on the inner side of **2** within (e g *inside* an hour)

⁴inside *adv* **1** to or on the inner side **2** in or into the interior **3** indoors **4** *chiefly Br* in or into prison – slang

insist /ɪn'sɪst/ *v* **1** to take a resolute stand **2** to place great emphasis or importance *on* sthg **3** to maintain persistently – **~ence** *n*, **~ency** *n*

insolent /'ɪnsələnt/ *adj* showing disrespectful rudeness; impudent – **~ly** *adv* – **-solence** *n*

insomnia /ɪn'sɒmnɪə/ *n* prolonged (abnormal) inability to obtain adequate sleep – **~c** *n*, *adj*

inspect /ɪn'spekt/ *v* **1** to examine closely and critically; scrutinize **2** to view or examine officially – **~ion** *n*

inspector /ɪn'spektə/ *n* a police officer ranking immediately above a sergeant;

also, an official who inspects – **~ate,** **~ship** *n*

inspiration /ˌɪnspɪ'reɪʃən/ *n* **1a** a divine influence or action on a person which qualifies him/her to receive and communicate sacred revelation **b** the action or power of stimulating the intellect or emotions **2** an inspired idea **3** an inspiring agent or influence – **~al** *adj*

inspire /ɪn'spaɪə/ *v* **1** to influence or guide by divine inspiration **2** to exert an animating or exalting influence on **3** to act as a stimulus for **4** to affect – usu + *with*

install /ɪn'stɔːl/ *v* **1** to induct into an office, rank, or order, esp with ceremonies or formalities **2** to establish in a specified place, condition, or status **3** to place in usu permanent position for use or service

instalment /ɪn'stɔːlmənt/ *n* **1** any of the parts into which a debt is divided when payment is made at intervals **2** any of several parts (e g of a publication) presented at intervals

¹instance /'ɪnstəns/ *n* **1** an example cited as an illustration or proof **2** the institution of a legal action **3** a situation viewed as 1 stage in a process or series of events

²instance *v* to put forward as a case or example; cite

¹instant /'ɪnstənt/ *n* **1** an infinitesimal space of time; *esp* a point in time separating 2 states **2** the present or current month

²instant *adj* **1a** present, current **b** of or occurring in the present month – used in commercial communications **2** immediate **3a**(1) premixed or precooked for easy final preparation **(2)** appearing (as if) in ready-to-use form **b** immediately soluble in water **4** demanding, urgent – *fml* – **~ly** *adv* – **~aneous** *adj* – **~aneously** *adv* – **~aneousness** *n*

instead /ɪn'sted/ *adv* as a substitute or alternative (e g sent his son *instead*)

instinct /'ɪnstɪŋkt/ *n* **1** a natural or inherent aptitude, impulse, or capacity **2** (a largely inheritable tendency of an organism to make a complex and specific) response to environmental stimuli without involving reason + **~ive** *adj*

¹institute /'ɪnstɪtjuːt/ *v* to originate and establish; inaugurate

²institute *n* **1** (the premises used by) an organization for the promotion of a cause **2** an educational institution

institution /ˌɪnstɪ'tjuːʃən/ *n* **1** an established practice in a culture; *also* a familiar object **2** an established organization or (public) body (e g a university or hospital) – **~al** *adj*

instruct /ɪn'strʌkt/ *v* **1** to teach **2a** to direct authoritatively **b** to command **3** to engage (a lawyer, specif a barrister) for a case – **~or** *n*

instruction /ɪn'strʌkʃən/ *n* **1a** an order, a command – often pl with sing. meaning **b** *pl* an outline or manual of technical procedure **2** teaching – **~al** *adj*

¹instrument /'ɪnstrəmənt/ n **1a** a means whereby sthg is achieved, performed, or furthered **b** a dupe; a tool of another **2** an implement, tool, or device designed esp for delicate work or measurement **3** a device used to produce music **4** a formal legal document **5** an electrical or mechanical device used in navigating an aircraft

²instrument v to orchestrate

insufficient /,ɪnsə'fɪʃənt/ adj deficient in power, capacity, or competence – ~ly adv – -ciency n

¹insult /ɪn'sʌlt/ v to treat with insolence, indignity, or contempt; also to cause offence or damage to

²insult /'ɪnsʌlt/ n an act of insulting; sthg that insults

insurance /ɪn'ʃʊərəns/ n **1** insuring or being insured **2a** the business of insuring people or property **b** (the protection offered by) a contract whereby one party undertakes to indemnify or guarantee another against loss by a particular contingency or risk **c(1)** the premium demanded under such a contract **(2)** the sum for which sthg is insured

insure /ɪn'ʃʊə/ v **1** to give, take, or procure insurance on or for **2** to contract to give or take insurance; specif to underwrite

intact /ɪn'tækt/ adj untouched, esp by anything that harms or diminishes; whole, uninjured – ~ness n

intake /'ɪnteɪk/ n **1** an opening through which liquid or gas enters an enclosure or system **2a** a taking in **b(1)** sing or pl in constr an amount or number taken in **(2)** sthg taken in

intellect /'ɪntɪlekt/ n the capacity for intelligent thought, esp when highly developed

¹intellectual /,ɪntɪ'lektʃʊəl/ adj **1a** of the intellect **b** developed or chiefly guided by the intellect rather than by emotion or experience **2** given to or requiring the use of the intellect – ~ly adv

²intellectual n an intellectual person

intelligence /ɪn'telɪdʒəns/ n **1** the ability to learn, apply knowledge, or think abstractly, esp in allowing one to deal with new or trying situations; also the skilled use of intelligence or reason **2** the act of understanding **3a** news; information **b** (a group of people who gather) information concerning an enemy – -gent adj – -gently adv

intend /ɪn'tend/ v **1** to mean, signify **2a** to have in mind as a purpose or goal **b** to design for a specified use or future

intense /ɪn'tens/ adj **1a** existing or occurring in an extreme degree **b** having or showing a usual characteristic in extreme degree **2** intensive **3a** feeling emotion deeply, esp by nature or temperament **b** deeply felt – ~ly adv – -sity n

¹intent /ɪn'tent/ n **1a** the act or fact of intending **b** the state of mind with which an act is done **2** criminal intention **3** meaning, significance

²intent adj **1** directed with strained or eager attention; concentrated **2** having the mind, attention, or will concentrated on sthg or some end or purpose – ~ly adv – ~ness n

intention /ɪn'tenʃən/ n **1** a determination to act in a certain way; a resolve **2** pl purpose with respect to proposal of marriage **3a** what one intends to do or bring about; an aim **b** the object for which religious devotion is offered **4** a concept

intentional /ɪn'tenʃənəl/ adj done by intention or design + ~ly adv

intercede /,ɪntə'siːd/ v to beg or plead on behalf of another with a view to reconciling differences + -cession n

¹interest /'ɪntrɪst/ n **1a(1)** right, title, or legal share in sthg **(2)** participation in advantage and responsibility **b** a business in which one has an interest **2** benefit; advantage; specif self-interest **3a** a charge for borrowed money, generally a percentage of the amount borrowed **b** sthg added above what is due **4** a financially interested group **5a** readiness to be concerned with, moved by, or have one's attention attracted by sthg; curiosity **b** (the quality in) a thing that arouses interest

²interest v **1** to induce or persuade to participate or engage, esp in an enterprise **2** to concern or engage (sby, esp oneself) in an activity or cause **3** to engage the attention or arouse the interest of – ~ing adj – ~ingly adv

interfere /,ɪntə'fɪə/ v **1** to get in the way of, hinder, or impede another – + with **2** to enter into or take a part in matters that do not concern one **3** to hinder illegally an attempt of a player to catch or hit a ball or puck – usu + with

interference /,ɪntə'fɪərəns/ n **1** the phenomenon resulting from the meeting of 2 wave trains (e g of light or sound) with an increase in intensity at some points and a decrease at others **2** the illegal hindering of an opponent in hockey, ice hockey, etc **3** (sthg that produces) the confusion of received radio signals by unwanted signals or noise

¹interior /ɪn'tɪərɪə/ adj **1** lying, occurring, or functioning within the limits or interior **2** away from the border or shore **3** of the mind or soul

²interior n **1** the internal or inner part of a thing; also the inland **2** internal affairs **3** a representation of the interior of a building or room

internal /ɪn'tɜːnl/ adj **1** existing or situated within the limits or surface of sthg **2** of or existing within the mind **3** depending only on the properties of the thing under consideration without reference to things outside it **4** (present or arising) within (a part of) the body or an organism **5** within a state ~ize v – ~ly adv

¹international /,ɪntə'næʃənəl/ adj **1** affecting or involving 2 or more nations **2** known, recognized, or renowned in more than 1 country ~ize v

²international n **1** (sby who plays or has played in) a sports, games, etc match between 2 national teams **2** also **internationale** often cap any of several socialist or communist organizations of international scope

interpret /ɪnˈtɜːprɪt/ v **1** to expound the meaning of **2** to conceive of in the light of one's beliefs, judgments, or circumstances; construe **3** to represent by means of art; bring to realization by performance **4** to act as an interpreter – ~**er** n – ~**ative**, ~**ive** adj

interpretation /ɪnˌtɜːprɪˈteɪʃən/ n an instance of artistic interpreting in performance or adaptation

interrogate /ɪnˈterəgeɪt/ v to question formally – –**gation** n – –**gator** n

interrupt /ˌɪntəˈrʌpt/ v **1** to break the flow or action of (a speaker or speech) **2** to break the uniformity or continuity of (sthg) **3** to interrupt an action; esp to interrupt another's utterance with one's own – ~**ion** n

interval /ˈɪntəvəl/ n **1** an intervening space: e g **a** a time between events or states; a pause **b** a distance or gap between objects, units, or states **c** the difference in pitch between 2 notes **2** Br a break in the presentation of an entertainment (e g a play)

intervene /ˌɪntəˈviːn/ v **1** to enter or appear as sthg irrelevant or extraneous **2** to occur or come between 2 things, esp points of time or events **3** to come in or between so as to hinder or modify **4a** to enter a lawsuit as a third party **b** to interfere in another nation's internal affairs – –**vention** n

interview /ˈɪntəvjuː/ n **1** a formal consultation usu to evaluate qualifications (e g of a prospective student or employee) **2** (a report of) a meeting at which information is obtained (e g by a journalist) from sby

intestine /ɪnˈtestɪn/ n the tubular part of the alimentary canal that extends from the stomach to the anus –**inal** adj

¹intimate /ˈɪntɪmɪt/ v to make known: e g **a** to announce **b** to hint; imply – –**mation** n

²intimate /ˈɪntɪmeɪt/ adj **1a** intrinsic, essential **b** belonging to or characterizing one's deepest nature **2** marked by very close association, contact, or familiarity **3** suggesting informal warmth or privacy **4** of a very personal or private nature **5** involved in a sexual relationship; specif engaging in an act of sexual intercourse – euph – ~**ly** adv – –**macy** n

³intimate /ˈɪntɪmɪt/ n a close friend or confidant

intimidate /ɪnˈtɪmɪdeɪt/ v to frighten; esp to compel or deter (as if) by threats – –**dation** n

into /ˈɪntə; before consonants ˈɪntu; strong ˈɪntuː/ prep **1a** so as to be inside (e g come into the house) **b** so as to be (e g grow into a woman) **c** so as to be in (a state) (e g shocked into silence) **d** so as to be expressed in, dressed in, engaged in, or a member of (e g translate into French; enter into an alliance) **e** – used in division as the inverse of by or divided by (e g divide 35 into 70) **2** – used to indicate a partly elapsed period of time or a partly traversed extent of space (e g far into the night; deep into the jungle) **3** in the direction of; esp towards the centre of (e g look into the sun) **4** to a position of contact with; against (e g ran into the wall) **5** involved with; esp keen on (e g are you into meditation?) – infml

intricate /ˈɪntrɪkɪt/ adj **1** having many complexly interrelating parts or elements **2** difficult to resolve or analyse – ~**ly** adv – –**cacy** n

¹intrigue /ˈɪntriːg/ v **1** to arouse the interest or curiosity of **2** to captivate; fascinate **3** to carry on an intrigue; esp to plot, scheme

²intrigue /ˈɪntriːg, ɪnˈtriːg/ n **1** a secret scheme or plot **2** a clandestine love affair

introduce /ˌɪntrəˈdjuːs/ v **1** to lead or bring in, esp for the first time **2a** to bring into play **b** to bring into practice or use; institute **3** to lead to or make known by a formal act, announcement, or recommendation **c** to cause to be acquainted; make (oneself or sby) known to another **b** to make preliminary explanatory or laudatory remarks about (e g a speaker) **4** to place, insert **5** to bring to a knowledge or discovery of sthg – –**ductory** adj

introduction /ˌɪntrəˈdʌkʃən/ n **1a** a preliminary treatise or course of study **b** a short introductory musical passage **2** sthg introduced; specif a plant or animal new to an area

intuition /ˌɪntjuˈɪʃən/ n **1a** (knowledge gained by) immediate apprehension or cognition **b** the power of attaining direct knowledge without evident rational thought and the drawing of conclusions from evidence available **2** quick and ready insight – –**tive** adj – –**tively** adv

invade /ɪnˈveɪd/ v **1** to enter (e g a country) for hostile purposes **2** to encroach on **3** to spread over or into as if invading – ~**r** n

¹invalid /ɪnˈvælɪd/ adj **1** without legal force **2** logically inconsistent – ~**ly** adv – ~**ity** n

²invalid /ˈɪnvəliːd, -lɪd/ adj **1** suffering from disease or disability **2** of or suited to an invalid – ~**ism** n

³invalid /ˈɪnvəlɪd/ n one who is sickly or disabled

⁴invalid /ˈɪnvəlɪd, ˌɪnvəˈliːd/ v to remove from active duty by reason of sickness or disability

invaluable /ɪnˈvæljuəbəl/ adj valuable beyond estimation; priceless

invariable /ɪnˈveəriəbəl/ adj not (capable of) changing; constant – –**bly** adv – –**bility** n

invasion /ɪnˈveɪʒən/ n **1** an invading, esp by an army **2** the incoming or spread of sthg usu harmful

invent /ɪnˈvent/ v **1** to think up **2** to produce (e g sthg useful) for the first time – ~**or** n

invention /ɪnˈvenʃən/ *n* **1** productive imagination; inventiveness **2a** a (misleading) product of the imagination **b** a contrivance or process devised after study and experiment

invert /ɪnˈvɜːt/ *v* **1a** to turn inside out or upside down **b** to turn (e g a foot) inwards **2a** to reverse in position, order, or relationship **b** to subject to musical inversion

¹**invest** /ɪnˈvest/ *v* **1** to confer (the symbols of) authority, office, or rank on **2** to clothe, endow, or cover (as if) *with* sthg

²**invest** *v* **1** to commit (money) to a particular use (e g buying shares or new capital outlay) in order to earn a financial return **2** to devote (e g time or effort) to sthg for future advantages **3** to make an investment

investigate /ɪnˈvestɪɡeɪt/ *v* **1** to make a systematic examination or study (of) **2** to conduct an official inquiry (into) – **-gator** *n* – **-gation** *n*

investment /ɪnˈvestmənt/ *n* (a sum of) money invested for income or profit; *also* the asset (e g property) purchased

invisible /ɪnˈvɪzəbəl/ *adj* **1** incapable (by nature or circumstances) of being seen **2a** not appearing in published financial statements **b** not reflected in statistics **3** too small or unobtrusive to be seen or noticed; inconspicuous – **-bility** *n* – **-bly** *adv*

invitation /ˌɪnvɪˈteɪʃən/ *n* **1** an often formal request to be present or participate **2** an incentive, inducement

invite /ɪnˈvaɪt/ *v* **1a** to offer an incentive or inducement to **b** to (unintentionally) increase the likelihood of **2** to request (the presence of) formally or politely

involve /ɪnˈvɒlv/ *v* **1a** to cause to be associated or take part **b** to occupy (oneself) absorbingly; *esp* to commit (oneself) emotionally **2** to relate closely **3a** to have within or as part of itself **b** to require as a necessary accompaniment – **~ment** *n*

inward /ˈɪnwəd/ *adj* **1** situated within or directed towards the inside **2** of or relating to the mind or spirit (e g struggled to achieve *inward* peace) – **~ly** *adv*

inwards /ˈɪnwədz/ *adv* **1** towards the inside, centre, or interior **2** towards the inner being

IOU *n* (a written acknowledgment of) a debt

iris /ˈaɪərɪs/ *n*, *pl* (*I*) **irises, irides** **1** the opaque contractile diaphragm perforated by the pupil that forms the coloured portion of the eye **2** any of a large genus of plants with long straight leaves and large showy flowers

¹**iron** /ˈaɪən/ *n* **1** a heavy malleable ductile magnetic silver-white metallic element that readily rusts in moist air, occurs in most igneous rocks, and is vital to biological processes **2a** sthg used to bind or restrain – usu pl **b** a heated metal implement used for branding or cauterizing **c** a metal implement with a smooth flat typically triangular base that is heated (e g by electricity) and used to smooth or press clothing **d** a stirrup **e** any of a numbered series of usu 9 golf clubs with metal heads of varying angles for hitting the ball to various heights and lengths

²**iron** *adj* **1** (made) of iron **2** resembling iron (e g in appearance, strength, solidity, or durability)

³**iron** *v* to smooth (as if) with a heated iron

ironic /aɪˈrɒnɪk/ **ironical** *adj* **1** of, containing, or constituting irony **2** given to irony – **~ally** *adv*

irony /ˈaɪərəni/ *n* **1** the use of words to express a meaning other than and esp the opposite of the literal meaning **2** (an event or situation showing) incongruity between actual circumstances and the normal, appropriate, or expected result **3** an attitude of detached awareness of incongruity

irregular /ɪˈreɡjʊlə/ *adj* **1a** contrary to rule, custom, or moral principles **b** not inflected in the normal manner **c** inadequate because of failure to conform **2** lacking symmetry or evenness **3** lacking continuity or regularity, esp of occurrence or activity – **~ly** *adv*

irregularity /ɪˌreɡjʊˈlærɪti/ *n* sthg irregular (e g contrary to accepted professional or ethical standards)

irrelevant /ɪˈreləvənt/ *adj* not relevant; inapplicable – **~ly** *adv* – **-vance, -vancy** *n* *adv*

irresistible /ˌɪrɪˈzɪstəbəl/ *adj* impossible to resist successfully; highly attractive or enticing – **-bly** *adv*

irrespective /ˌɪrɪˈspektɪv/ *adv*/ *prep* without regard or reference to; in spite of

irresponsible /ˌɪrɪˈspɒnsəbəl/ **1** showing no regard for the consequences of one's actions **2** unable to bear responsibility – **-bility** *n* – **-bly** *adv*

irrigate /ˈɪrɪɡeɪt/ *v* **1** to supply (e g land) with water by artificial means **2** to flush (e g an eye or wound) with a stream of liquid – **-gable** *adj* – **-gation** *n*

irritable /ˈɪrɪtəbəl/ *adj* capable of being irritated: e g **a** easily exasperated or excited **b** (excessively) responsive to stimuli – **-bility** *n* – **-bly** *adv*

irritate /ˈɪrɪteɪt/ *v* **1** to excite impatience, anger, or displeasure (in) **2** to induce a response to a stimulus in or of – **-tant** *n* **-tion** *n*

is /s, z, əz; *strong* ɪz/ *v pres 3 sing of* be, *dial pres 1&2 sing of* be, *substandard pres pl of* be

island /ˈaɪlənd/ *n* **1** an area of land surrounded by water and smaller than a continent **2** sthg like an island (e g in being isolated or surrounded) **3** a traffic island **4** an isolated superstructure on the deck of a ship, esp an aircraft carrier

isle /aɪl/ *n* a (small) island – used in some names

isolate /ˈaɪsəleɪt/ *v* **1** to set apart from others; *also* to quarantine **2** to separate from another substance so as to obtain in a pure form **3** to insulate – **-lation** *n*

¹issue /'ɪʃuː, 'ɪsjuː/ *n* **1** the action of going, coming, or flowing out **2** a means or place of going out **3** offspring **4** an outcome that usu resolves or decides a problem **5** a matter that is in dispute between 2 or more parties; a controversial topic **6** sthg coming out from a usu specified source **7a** the act of publishing, giving out, or making available **b** the thing or the whole quantity of things given out, published, or distributed at 1 time

²issue *v* **1a** to go, come, or flow out **b** to emerge **2** to appear or become available through being given out, published, or distributed **3a** to give out, distribute, or provide officially **b** to send out for sale or circulation

¹it /ɪt/ *pron* **1a** that thing, creature, or group – used as subject or object; (e g noticed that *it* was old; had a baby but lost *it*) **b** the person in question **2** – used as subject of an impersonal verb (e g *it's* raining) **3a** – used to highlight part of a sentence (e g *it* was yesterday that he arrived) **b** – used with many verbs and prepositions as a meaningless object (e g run for *it*) **4** – used to refer to an explicit or implicit state of affairs (e g how's *it* going?) **5** that which is available, important, or appropriate (e g one boiled egg and that's *it*; a bit brighter, that's *it*)

²it *n* **1** the player in a usu children's game who performs a unique role (e g trying to catch others in a game of tag) **2** sex appeal; *also* sexual intercourse – *infml*

¹itch /ɪtʃ/ *v* **1** to have or produce an itch **2** to have a restless desire – *infml*

²itch *n* **1a** an irritating sensation in the upper surface of the skin that makes one want to scratch **b** a skin disorder characterized by such a sensation **2** a restless desire – *infml*

item /'aɪtəm/ *n* **1** a separate unit in an account or series **2** a separate piece of news or information ~**ize** *v*

its /ɪts/ *adj* relating to it or itself, esp as possessor, agent, or object of an action

itself /ɪt'self/ *pron* **1** that identical thing, creature, or group **2** its normal self

ivory /'aɪvəri/ *n* **1** the hard creamy-white form of dentine of which the tusks of elephants and other tusked mammals are made **2** a creamy slightly yellowish white colour **3** *pl* things (e g dice or piano keys) made of (sthg resembling) ivory – *infml*

ivy /'aɪvi/ *n* a very common and widely cultivated Eurasian woody climbing plant with evergreen leaves, small yellowish flowers, and black berries

J

¹jab /dʒæb/ *v* **1a** to pierce (as if) with a sharp object **b** to poke quickly or abruptly **2** to strike (sby) with a short straight blow **3** to make quick or abrupt thrusts (as if) with a sharp or pointed object

²jab *n* a hypodermic injection – *infml*

¹jack /dʒæk/ *n* **1** any of various portable mechanisms for exerting pressure or lifting a heavy object a short distance **2a** a small white target ball in lawn bowling **b(1)** *pl but sing in constr* a game in which players toss and pick up small bone or metal objects in a variety of shapes in between throws of a ball **(2)** a small 6-pointed metal object used in the game of jacks **3** a playing card carrying the figure of a soldier or servant and ranking usu below the queen **4** a single-pronged electric plug

²jack *v* **1** to move or lift (as if) by a jack **2** to raise the level or quality of **3** give up – usu + *in*; *infml* USE (*1&2*) usu + *up*

¹jacket /'dʒækɪt/ *n* **1** an outer garment for the upper body opening down the full length of the centre front **2** the skin of a (baked) potato **3a** a thermally insulating cover (e g for a hot water tank) **b(1)** a dust jacket **(2)** the cover of a paperback book

²jacket *v* to put a jacket on; enclose in or with a jacket

jackpot /'dʒækpɒt/ *n* **1** (a combination that wins) a top prize on a fruit machine **2** a large prize (e g in a lottery), often made up of several accumulated prizes that have not been previously won

jagged /'dʒægɪd/ *adj* having a sharply uneven edge or surface – ~**ly** *adv*

¹jail /dʒeɪl/ *Br also* **gaol** *n* a prison

²jail, *Br also* **gaol** *v* to confine (as if) in a jail

¹jam /dʒæm/ *v* **1a** to press, squeeze, or crush into a close or tight position **b** to (cause to) become wedged or blocked so as to be unworkable **c** to block passage of or along **d** to fill (to excess) **2** to crush; *also* to bruise by crushing **3** to send out interfering signals or cause reflections so as to make unintelligible **4** to become blocked or wedged **5** to take part in a jam session – *slang*

²jam *n* **1** a crowded mass that impedes or blocks **2** the pressure or congestion of a crowd **3** a difficult state of affairs – *infml*

³jam *n* a preserve made by boiling fruit and sugar to a thick consistency

January /'dʒænjʊəri/ *n* the 1st month of the Gregorian calendar

¹jar /dʒɑːr/ *v* **1a** to make a harsh or discordant noise **b** to have a harshly disagreeable effect – + *on* or *upon* **2** to vibrate **3** to cause to jar, esp by shaking or causing a shock to

²**jar** n **1** a jarring noise **2a** a sudden or unexpected shake **b** an unsettling shock (e g to nerves or feelings)

³**jar** n **1a** usu cylindrical short-necked and wide-mouthed container, made esp of glass **b** the contents of or quantity contained in a jar **2** a glass of an alcoholic drink, esp beer – infml

¹**jaw** /dʒɔ:/ n **1** either of 2 cartilaginous or bony structures that in most vertebrates form a framework above and below the mouth in which the teeth are set **2** pl **a** the entrance of a narrow pass or channel **b** the 2 parts of a machine, tool, etc between which sth may be clamped or crushed **c** a position or situation of imminent danger

²**jaw** v to talk or gossip for a long time or long-windedly – infml

jay /dʒeɪ/ n an Old World bird of the crow family with a dull pink body, black, white, and blue wings, and a black-and-white crest

jazz /dʒæz/ n **1** music developed esp from ragtime and blues and characterized by syncopated rhythms and individual or group improvisation around a basic theme or melody **2** similar but unspecified things – infml

jealous /'dʒeləs/ adj **1a** intolerant of rivalry or unfaithfulness **b** apprehensive of and hostile towards a (supposed) rival **2** resentful, envious of **3** vigilant in guarding a possession, right, etc **4** distrustfully watchful – ~ly adv – ~y n

jeans /dʒi:nz/ n pl in constr, pl jeans casual usu close-fitting trousers, made esp of blue denim

jeep /dʒi:p/ n a small rugged general-purpose motor vehicle with 4-wheel drive, used esp by the armed forces

jeer /dʒɪə/ v to laugh mockingly or scoff (at) – jeer n

¹**jelly** /'dʒeli/ n **1a** a soft fruit-flavoured transparent dessert set with gelatin **b** a savoury food product of similar consistency, made esp from meat stock and gelatin **2** a clear fruit preserve made by boiling sugar and the juice of fruit **3** a substance resembling jelly in consistency

²**jelly 1** to bring to the consistency of jelly; cause to set **2** to set in a jelly

¹**jerk** /dʒɜ:k/ v **1** to give a quick suddenly arrested push, pull, twist, or jolt to **2** to propel with short abrupt motions **3** to utter in an abrupt or snappy manner **4** to make a sudden spasmodic motion **5** to move in short abrupt motions

²**jerk** n **1** a single quick motion (e g a pull, twist, or jolt) **2** an involuntary spasmodic muscular movement due to reflex action **3** chiefly NAm a stupid, foolish, or naive person – infml

jerky /'dʒɜ:ki/ adj **1** marked by irregular or spasmodic movements **2** marked by abrupt or awkward changes – -ily adv – -iness n

jersey /'dʒɜ:zi/ n **1** a plain weft-knitted fabric made of wool, nylon, etc and used esp for clothing **2** a jumper **3** often cap any of a breed of small short-horned cattle noted for their rich milk

¹**jest** /dʒest/ n **1** an amusing or mocking act or utterance; a joke **2** a frivolous mood or manner

²**jest** v **1** to speak or act without seriousness **2** to make a witty remark

¹**jet** /dʒet/ n **1a** a hard black form of coal that is often polished and used for jewellery **2** an intense black

²**jet** v **1** to emit in a jet or jets **2** to direct a jet of liquid or gas at

³**jet** n **1a** a forceful stream of fluid discharged from a narrow opening or a nozzle **b** a nozzle or other narrow opening for emitting a jet of fluid **2** (an aircraft powered by) a jet engine

⁴**jet** v to travel by jet aircraft

jet engine n an engine that produces motion in one direction as a result of the discharge of a jet of fluid in the opposite direction; specif an aircraft engine that discharges the hot air and gases produced by the combustion of a fuel to produce propulsion or lift

jetty /'dʒeti/ n **1** a structure (e g a pier or breakwater) extending into a sea, lake, or river to influence the current or tide or to protect a harbour **2** a small landing pier

jew /dʒu:/ v to get the better of financially, esp by hard bargaining – often + out of; derog

Jew /dʒu:/ fem **Jewess** n **1** a member of a Semitic people existing as a nation in Palestine from the 6th c BC to the 1st c AD, some of whom now live in Israel and others in various countries throughout the world **2** a person whose religion is Judaism **3** sby given to hard financial bargaining – derog – ~ish adj

jewel /'dʒu:əl/ n **1** an ornament of precious metal often set with stones and worn as an accessory **2** sby or sth highly esteemed **3** a precious stone **4** a bearing for a pivot (e g in a watch or compass) made of crystal, precious stone, or glass

jeweller /'dʒu:ələ/ n sby who deals in, makes, or repairs jewellery and often watches, silverware, etc – ~y n

¹**jig** /dʒɪg/ n **1** (a piece of music for) any of several lively springy dances in triple time **2a** any of several fishing lures that jerk up and down in the water **b** a device used to hold a piece of work in position (e g during machining or assembly) and to guide the tools working on it **c** a device in which crushed ore or coal is separated from waste by agitating in water

²**jig** v **1** to dance (in the rapid lively manner of) a jig **2a** (cause to) make a rapid jerky movement **b** to separate (a mineral from waste) with a jig **3** to catch (a fish) with a jig **4** to work with or machine by using a jig

jigsaw /'dʒɪgsɔ:/ n **1** a power-driven fretsaw **2** jigsaw, jigsaw puzzle a puzzle consisting of small irregularly cut pieces, esp of wood or card, that are fitted together to form a picture for amusement; *broadly* sthg composed of many disparate parts or elements

¹jingle /'dʒɪŋgəl/ *v* to (cause to) make a light clinking or tinkling sound

²jingle *n* **1** a light, esp metallic clinking or tinkling sound **2** a short catchy song or rhyme characterized by repetition of phrases and used esp in advertising

¹job /dʒɒb/ *n* **1a** a piece of work; *esp* a small piece of work undertaken at a stated rate **b** sthg produced by work **2a**(1) a task (2) sthg requiring unusual exertion **b** a specific duty, role, or function **c** a regular paid position or occupation **d** *chiefly Br* a state of affairs – + *bad* or *good* **3** an object of a usu specified type **4a** a plan or scheme designed or carried out for private advantage **b** a crime; *specif* a robbery *USE* (3&4) *infml*

²job *v* **1** to do odd or occasional pieces of work, usu at a stated rate **2** to carry on public business for private gain **3a** to carry on the business of a middleman or wholesaler **b** to work as a stockjobber **4** to buy and sell (e g shares) for profit **5** to hire or let for a definite job or period of service **6** to get, deal with, or effect by jobbery **7** to subcontract – usu + *out*

Job /dʒəʊb/ *n* (a narrative and poetic book of the Old Testament which tells of) a Jewish patriarch who endured afflictions with fortitude and faith – usu *the patience of Job*

¹jockey /'dʒɒki/ *n* sby who rides a horse, esp as a professional in races

²jockey *v* **1** to manoeuvre or manipulate by adroit or devious means **2** to act as a jockey

¹jog /dʒɒg/ *v* **1** to give a slight shake or push to; nudge **2** to rouse (the memory) **3** to move up and down or about with a short heavy motion **4** to run or ride at a slow trot – ~ **ger** *n*

²jog *n* **1** a slight shake **2a** a jogging movement or pace **b** a slow trot

¹join /dʒɔɪn/ *v* **1a** to put or bring together so as to form a unit **b** to connect (e g points) by a line **c** to adjoin; meet **2** to put, bring, or come into close association or relationship **3a** to come into the company of **b** to become a member of (a group) **4** to come together so as to be connected **5** to take part in a collective activity – usu + *in*

²join *n* a joint

¹joint /dʒɔɪnt/ *n* **1a**(1) a point of contact between 2 or more bones of an animal skeleton together with the parts that surround and support it **b** a part or space included between 2 articulations, knots, or nodes **c** a large piece of meat (for roasting) cut from a carcass **2a** a place where 2 things or parts are joined **b** an area at which 2 ends, surfaces, or edges are attached **c** the hinge of the binding of a book along the back edge of each cover **3** a shabby or disreputable place of entertainment – *infml* **4** a marijuana cigarette – *slang*

²joint *adj* **1** united, combined **2** common to 2 or more: e g **a** involving the united

activity of 2 or more **b** held by, shared by, or affecting 2 or more **3** sharing with another – ~ **ly** *adv*

³joint *v* **1** to fit together **2** to provide with a joint **3** to prepare (e g a board) for joining by planing the edge **4** to separate the joints of (e g meat)

¹joke /dʒəʊk/ *n* **1a** sthg said or done to provoke laughter; *esp* a brief oral narrative with a humorous twist **b** the humorous or ridiculous element in sthg **c** an instance of joking or making fun **d** a laughingstock

²joke *v* to make jokes – **jokingly** *adv*

joker /'dʒəʊkə/ *n* **1** sby given to joking **2** a playing card added to a pack usu as a wild card **3** sthg (e g an expedient or stratagem) held in reserve to gain an end or escape from a predicament **4** a fellow; *esp* an insignificant, obnoxious, or incompetent person – *infml*

¹jolly /'dʒɒli/ *adj* **1a** full of high spirits **b** given to conviviality **c** expressing, suggesting, or inspiring gaiety **2** extremely pleasant or agreeable – *infml* **3** *Br* slightly drunk – *euph* – **jollity, jolliness** *n*

²jolly *adv* very – *infml*

³jolly *v* **1** to (try to) put in good humour, esp to gain an end – usu + *along* **2** to make cheerful or bright – + *up*; *infml*

¹jolt /dʒəʊlt/ *v* **1** to (cause to) move with a sudden jerky motion **2** to give a (sudden) knock or blow to **3** to abruptly disturb the composure of

²jolt *n* an unsettling blow, movement, or shock

¹jot /dʒɒt/ *n* the least bit

²jot *v* to write briefly or hurriedly

journal /'dʒɜːnəl/ *n* **1a** an account of day-to-day events **b** a private record of experiences, ideas, or reflections kept regularly **c** a record of the transactions of a public body, learned society, etc **2a** a daily newspaper **b** a periodical dealing esp with matters of current interest or specialist subjects

journalism /'dʒɜːnəl-ɪzəm/ *n* **1** (the profession of) the collecting and editing of material of current interest for presentation through news media **2a** writing designed for publication in a newspaper or popular magazine **b** writing characterized by a direct presentation of facts or description of events without an attempt at interpretation – **-ist** *n* – **-istic** *adj*

journey /'dʒɜːni/ *n* **1** travel from one place to another, esp by land and over a considerable distance **2** the distance involved in a journey, or the time taken to cover it

joy /dʒɔɪ/ *n* **1** (the expression of) an emotion or state of great happiness, pleasure, or delight **2** a source or cause of delight **3** *Br* success, satisfaction – *infml*

joyful /'dʒɔɪfəl/ *adj* filled with, causing, or expressing joy – ~ **ness** *n*

jubilee /'dʒuːbɪˌliː, ˌdʒuːbɪˈliː/ *n* **1** (a celebration of) a special anniversary (e g of a sovereign's accession) **2** a season or occasion of celebration

¹judge /dʒʌdʒ/ *v* **1** to form an opinion

about through careful weighing of evidence 2 to sit in judgment on 3 to determine or pronounce after deliberation 4 to decide the result of (a competition or contest) 5 to form an estimate or evaluation of 6 to hold as an opinion 7 to act as a judge

²judge n sby who judges: e g **a** a public official authorized to decide questions brought before a court **b** sby appointed to decide in a competition or (sporting) contest (e g diving) **c** sby who gives an (authoritative) opinion

judgment, judgement /'dʒʌdʒmənt/ n **1** a formal decision by a court **2** (the process of forming) an opinion or evaluation based on discerning and comparing **3** the capacity for judging **4 Judgement, Judgement Day** the final judging of mankind by God

¹jug /dʒʌg/ n **1a** chiefly Br a vessel for holding and pouring liquids that typically has a handle and a lip or spout **b** the contents of or quantity contained in a jug; a jugful **2** prison – infml

²jug v to stew (e g a hare) in an earthenware vessel

juggle /'dʒʌgəl/ v **1** to perform the tricks of a juggler **2** to manipulate, esp in order to achieve a desired end **3** to hold or balance precariously

juice /dʒuːs/ n **1** the extractable fluid contents of cells or tissues **2a** pl the natural fluids of an animal body **b** the liquid or moisture contained in sthg **3** the inherent quality of sthg; esp the basic force or strength of sthg **4** a medium (e g electricity or petrol) that supplies power – infml

juicy /'dʒuːsi/ adj **1** succulent **2** financially rewarding or profitable – infml **3** rich in interest; esp interesting because of titillating content – infml – **-iness** n

jukebox /'dʒuːkbɒks/ n a coin-operated record player that automatically plays records chosen from a restricted list

July /dʒuˈlaɪ/ n the 7th month of the Gregorian calendar

¹jumble /'dʒʌmbəl/ v to mix up in a confused or disordered mass

²jumble n **1** a mass of things mingled together without order or plan **2** Br articles for a jumble sale

jumble sale n, Br a sale of donated secondhand articles, usu conducted to raise money for some charitable purpose

¹jump /dʒʌmp/ v **1a** to spring into the air, esp using the muscular power of feet and legs **b** to move suddenly or involuntarily from shock, surprise, etc **c** to move quickly or energetically (as if) with a jump; also to act with alacrity **2** to pass rapidly, suddenly, or abruptly (as if) over some intervening thing: e g **a** to skip **b** to rise suddenly in rank or status **c** to make a mental leap **d** to come to or arrive at a position or judgment without due deliberation **e** to undergo a sudden sharp increase **3** to make a sudden verbal or physical attack – usu + on or upon **4a** to (cause to) leap

over **b** to pass over, esp to a point beyond; skip, bypass **c** to act, move, or begin before (e g a signal) **5a** to escape or run away from **b** to leave hastily or in violation of an undertaking **c** to depart from (a normal course) **6** to make a sudden or surprise attack on

²jump n **1a(1)** an act of jumping; a leap **(2)** a sports contest (e g the long jump) including a jump **(3)** a space, height, or distance cleared by a jump **(4)** an obstacle to be jumped over (e g in a horse race) **b** a sudden involuntary movement; a start **2a** a sharp sudden increase (e g in amount, price, or value) **b** a sudden change or transition; esp one that leaves a break in continuity **c** any of a series of moves from one place or position to another; a move

¹jumper /'dʒʌmpə/ n a jumping animal; esp a horse trained to jump obstacles

²jumper n Br a knitted or crocheted garment worn on the upper body

junction /'dʒʌŋkʃən/ n **1** joining or being joined **2a** a place of meeting **b** an intersection of roads, esp where 1 terminates **3** sthg that joins

June /dʒuːn/ n the 6th month of the Gregorian calendar

jungle /'dʒʌŋgəl/ n **1** an area overgrown with thickets or masses of (tropical) trees and other vegetation **2a** a confused, disordered, or complex mass **b** a place of ruthless struggle for survival

¹junior /'dʒuːnɪə/ n **1** a person who is younger than another **2a** a person holding a lower or subordinate position in a hierarchy of ranks **b** a member of a younger form in a school **3** NAm a male child; a son – infml

²junior adj **1** younger – used, esp in the USA, to distinguish a son with the same name as his father **2** lower in standing or rank **3** for children aged from 7 to 11

¹junk /dʒʌŋk/ n **1a** secondhand or discarded articles or material; broadly rubbish **1 b** sthg of little value or inferior quality **2** narcotics; esp heroin – slang

²junk n a sailing ship used in the Far East with a high poop and overhanging stem, little or no keel, and sails that are often stiffened with horizontal battens

jury /'dʒʊəri/ n **1** a body of usu 12 people who hear evidence in court and are sworn to give an honest verdict, esp of guilty or not guilty, based on this evidence **2** a committee for judging a contest or exhibition

¹just /dʒʌst/ adj **1a** conforming (rigidly) to fact or reason **b** conforming to a standard of correctness; proper **2a(1)** acting or being in conformity with what is morally upright or equitable **(2)** being what is merited; deserved **b** legally correct – ~ **ly** adv – ~ **ness** n

²just /dʒəst; strong dʒʌst/ adv **1a** exactly, precisely – not following not (e g just right) **b** at this moment and not sooner (e g he's only just arrived) – sometimes used with the past tense **c** only at this moment and not later (e g

I'm *just* coming) **2a** by a very small margin; immediately, barely (e g only *just* possible) **b** only, simply (e g *just* a short note) **3** quite (e g not *just* yet) **4** perhaps, possibly (e g it might *just* snow) **5** very, completely (e g *just* wonderful) **6** indeed – sometimes expressing irony (e g didn't he *just*!) *USE* (5, 6) infml

justice /'dʒʌstɪs/ *n* **1a** the maintenance or administration of what is just **b** the administration of law **2a** the quality of being just, impartial, or fair **b** (conformity to) the principle or ideal of just dealing or right action **3** conformity to truth, fact, or reason **4** *Br* – used as a title for a judge

jut /dʒʌt/ *v* to stick *out*; project

¹**juvenile** /'dʒuːvənaɪl/ *adj* **1** physiologically immature or undeveloped **2** (characteristic) of or suitable for children or young people

²**juvenile** *n* **1** a young person **2** a young individual resembling an adult of its kind except in size and reproductive activity **3** an actor who plays youthful parts

K

kaleidoscope /kə'laɪdəskəʊp/ *n* **1** a tubular instrument containing loose chips of coloured glass between mirrors so placed that an endless variety of symmetrical patterns is produced as the instrument is rotated and the chips of glass change position **2** sthg that is continually changing; *esp* a variegated changing pattern, scene, or succession of events – **-scopic** *adj* – **-scopically** *adv*

kangaroo /ˌkæŋgə'ruː/ *n* any of various plant-eating marsupial mammals of Australia, New Guinea, and adjacent islands that hop on their long powerful hind legs

¹**keel** /kiːl/ *n* a flat-bottomed ship; *esp* a barge used on the river Tyne to carry coal

²**keel** *n* **1a** a timber or plate which extends along the centre of the bottom of a vessel and usu projects somewhat from the bottom **b** the main load-bearing member (e g in an airship) **2** a projection (e g the breastbone of a bird) suggesting a keel

³**keel 1** to (cause to) turn over **2** to fall *over* (as if) in a faint

¹**keen** /kiːn/ *adj* **1a** having or being a fine edge or point; sharp **b** affecting one as if by cutting or piercing **2a** enthusiastic, eager **b** *of emotion or feeling* intense **3a** intellectually alert; *also* shrewdly astute **b** sharply contested; competitive; *specif, Br, of prices* low in order to be competitive **c** extremely sensitive in perception – **~ly** *adv* – **keenness** *n*

²**keen** *v or n* (to utter) a loud wailing

lamentation for the dead, typically at Irish funerals

¹**keep** /kiːp/ *v* kept **1a** to take notice of by appropriate conduct; fulfil (the obligations of) **b** to act fittingly in relation to (a feast or ceremony) **c** to conform to in habits or conduct **d** to stay in accord with (a beat) **2a** to watch over and defend; guard **b**(1) to take care of, esp as an owner; tend **(2)** to support **(3)** to maintain in a specified condition – often in combination **c** to continue to maintain **d**(1) to cause to remain in a specified place, situation, or condition **(2)** to store habitually for use **(3)** to preserve (food) in an unspoilt condition **e** to have or maintain in one's service, employment, or possession or at one's disposal – often + *on* **f** to record by entries in a book **g** to have customarily in stock for sale **3a** to delay, detain **b** to hold back; restrain **c** to save, reserve **d** to refrain from revealing or releasing **4** to retain possession or control of **5a** to continue to follow **b** to stay or remain on or in, often against opposition **6** to manage, run **7a** to maintain a course **b** to continue, usu without interruption **c** to persist in a practice **8a** to stay or remain in a specified desired place, situation, or condition **b** to remain in good condition **c** to be or remain with regard to health **d** to call for no immediate action **9** to act as wicketkeeper or goalkeeper – infml

²**keep** *n* **1** a castle, fortress, or fortified tower **2** the means (e g food) by which one is kept – infml

keeper /'kiːpə'/ *n* **1a** a protector, guardian, or custodian **b** a gamekeeper **c** a curator **2** any of various devices (e g a latch or guard ring) for keeping sthg in position **3a** a goalkeeper **b** a wicket-keeper

keep on *v* to talk continuously; *esp* to nag

keep up *v* **1** to persist or persevere in; continue **2** to preserve from decline **3** to maintain an equal pace or level of activity, progress, or knowledge (e g with another) **4** to continue without interruption

¹**kennel** /'kenl/ *n* **a** a shelter for a dog **b** an establishment for the breeding or boarding of dogs – often pl with sing. meaning but sing. or pl in constr

²**kennel** *v* to put or keep (as if) in a kennel

kept /kept/ *past of* **keep**

kerb /kɜːb/ *n, Br* the edging, esp of stone, to a pavement, path, etc

kernel /'kɜːnl/ *n* **1** the inner softer often edible part of a seed, fruit stone, or nut **2** a whole seed of a cereal **3** a central or essential part; core

kettle /'ketl/ *n* a metal vessel used esp for boiling liquids; *esp* one with a lid, handle, and spout that is placed on top of a stove or cooker or contains an electric heating-element and is used to boil water

¹**key** /kiː/ *n* **1a** a usu metal instrument by which the bolt of a lock is turned **b** sthg having the form or function of such

a key **2a** a means of gaining or preventing entrance, possession, or control **b** an instrumental or deciding factor **3a** sthg that gives an explanation or identification or provides a solution **b** a list of words or phrases explaining symbols or abbreviations **c** an arrangement of the important characteristics of a group of plants or animals used for identification **4a** any of the levers of a keyboard musical instrument that is pressed by a finger or foot to actuate the mechanism and produce the notes **b** a lever that controls a vent in the side of a woodwind instrument or a valve in a brass instrument **c** a small button or knob on a keyboard (e g of a typewriter) designed to be pushed down by the fingers **5** a dry usu single-seeded fruit (e g of an ash or elm tree) **6** a particular system of 7 musical notes forming a scale

²**key** *v* **1** to roughen (a surface) to improve adhesion of plaster, paint, etc **2** to bring into harmony or conformity; make appropriate **3** to make nervous, tense, or excited – usu + *up* **4** to keyboard

³**key** *adj* of basic importance; fundamental

⁴**key** *n* a low island or reef, esp in the Caribbean area

khaki /ˈkɑːki/ *n* **1** a dull yellowish brown colour **2** a khaki-coloured cloth made usu of cotton or wool and used esp for military uniforms

¹**kick** /kɪk/ *v* **1a** to strike (out) with the foot or feet **b** to make a kick in football **2** to show opposition; rebel **3** *of a fire-arm* to recoil when fired **4** to free oneself of (a drug or drug habit) – *infml*

²**kick** *n* **1a** a blow or sudden forceful thrust with the foot; *specif* one causing the propulsion of an object **b** the power to kick **c** a repeated motion of the legs used in swimming **d** a sudden burst of speed, esp in a footrace **2** the recoil of a gun **3a** a stimulating effect or quality **b** a stimulating or pleasurable experience or feeling – often *pl* **c** an absorbing or obsessive new interest

¹**kid** /kɪd/ *n* **1** the young of a goat or related animal **2** the flesh, fur, or skin of a kid **3** a child; *also* a young person (e g a teenager) – *infml*

²**kid** *v* **1a** to mislead as a joke **b** to convince (oneself) of sthg untrue or improbable **2** to make fun of **3** to engage in good-humoured fooling

kidnap /ˈkɪdnæp/ *v* to seize and detain (a person) by force and often for ransom – ~ *n*

kidney /ˈkɪdni/ *n* **1a** either of a pair of organs situated in the body cavity near the spinal column that excrete waste products of metabolism in the form of urine **b** an excretory organ of an invertebrate **2** the kidney of an animal eaten as food **3** sort, kind, or type, esp with regard to temperament

¹**kill** /kɪl/ *v* **1** to deprive of or destroy life **2a** to put an end to **b** to defeat, veto **3a** to destroy the vital, active, or essential quality of **b** to spoil, subdue, or neutralize the effect of **4** to cause (time) to pass

(e g while waiting) **5** to cause (e g an engine) to stop **6** to cause extreme pain to **7** to overwhelm with admiration or amusement **8** to discard or abandon further investigation of (a story) – *journ*

²**kill** *n* **1** a killing or being killed **2** sthg killed: e g **a** animals killed in a shoot, hunt, season, or particular period of time **b** an enemy aircraft, submarine, etc destroyed by military action

kilogram /ˈkɪləgræm/ *n* **1** the SI unit of mass and weight equal to the mass of a platinum-iridium cylinder kept near Paris, and approximately equal to the weight of a litre of water **2** a unit of force equal to the weight of a kilogram mass under the earth's gravitational attraction

kilometre /ˈkɪlə,miːtə/, kɪˈlɒmɪtə/ *n* 1000 metres

kilt /kɪlt/ *n* a skirt traditionally worn by Scotsmen that is formed usu from a length of tartan, is pleated at the back and sides, and is wrapped round the body and fastened at the front

¹**kind** /kaɪnd/ *n* **1** fundamental nature or quality **2a** a group united by common traits or interests **b** a specific or recognized variety – often in combination

²**kind** *adj* **1** disposed to be helpful and benevolent **2** forbearing, considerate, or compassionate **3** cordial, friendly **4** not harmful; mild, gentle – ~ **ness** *n*

kindle /ˈkɪndl/ *v* **1** to set (a fire, wood, etc) burning **2** to stir up (e g emotion) **3** to catch fire

¹**kindly** /ˈkaɪndli/ *adj* **1** agreeable, beneficial **2** sympathetic, generous – **-liness** *n*

²**kindly** *adv* **1** in an appreciative or sincere manner **2** – used (1) to add politeness or emphasis to a request (2) to convey irritation or anger in a command

king /kɪŋ/ *n* **1** a male monarch of a major territorial unit; *esp* one who inherits his position and rules for life **2** the holder of a preeminent position **3** the principal piece of each colour in a set of chessmen that has the power to move 1 square in any direction and must be protected against check **4** a playing card marked with a stylized figure of a king and ranking usu below the ace **5** a draughtsman that has reached the opposite side of the board and is empowered to move both forwards and backwards – ~ **ly** *adj* – ~ **ship** *n*

kingdom /ˈkɪŋdəm/ *n* **1** a territorial unit with a monarchical form of government **2** *often cap* the eternal kingship of God **3** an area or sphere in which sby or sthg holds a preeminent position

kiosk /ˈkiːɒsk/ *n* **1** an open summerhouse or pavilion common in Turkey or Iran **2** a small stall or stand used esp for the sale of newspapers, cigarettes, and sweets **3** *Br* a public telephone box

¹**kipper** /ˈkɪpə/ *n* a kippered fish, esp a herring

²**kipper** *v* to cure (split dressed fish) by salting and drying, usu by smoking

¹kiss /kɪs/ v 1 to touch with the lips, esp as a mark of affection or greeting 2 to touch one another with the lips, esp as a mark of love or sexual desire 3 to touch gently or lightly – ~able adj

²kiss n an act or instance of kissing

¹kit /kɪt/ n 1 a set of tools or implements 2 a set of parts ready to be assembled 3 a set of clothes and equipment for use in a specified situation; esp the equipment carried by a member of the armed forces

²kit v chiefly Br to equip, outfit; esp to clothe – usu + out or up

kitchen /ˈkɪtʃɪn/ n a place (e g a room in a house or hotel) where food is prepared

kite /kaɪt/ n 1 any of various hawks with long narrow wings, a deeply forked tail, and feet adapted for taking insects and small reptiles as prey 2 a light frame covered with thin material (e g paper or cloth), designed to be flown in the air at the end of a long string

kitten /ˈkɪtn/ n the young of a cat or other small mammal

kitten v to give birth to kittens

kitty /ˈkɪti/ n a jointly held fund of money (e g for household expenses)

knack /næk/ n a special ability, capacity, or skill that enables sthg, esp of a difficult or unusual nature, to be done with ease

knead /niːd/ v to work and press into a mass (as if) with the hands

knee /niː/ n a (the part of the leg that includes) a joint in the middle part of the human leg that is the articulation between the femur, tibia, and kneecap b a corresponding joint in an animal, bird, or insect

knee v to strike with the knee

kneel /niːl/ v knelt, kneeled to fall or rest on the knee or knees

knew /njuː/ past of know

knickers /ˈnɪkəz/ n pl Br women's pants

¹knife /naɪf/ n, pl knives 1a a cutting implement consisting of a more or less sharp blade fastened to a handle b such an instrument used as a weapon 2 a sharp cutting blade or tool in a machine

²knife v 1 to cut, slash, or wound with a knife 2 to cut, mark, or spread with a knife

¹knight /naɪt/ n 1a(1) a mounted man-at-arms serving a feudal superior (2) a man honoured by a sovereign for merit, ranking below a baronet b a man devoted to the service of a lady (e g as her champion) 2 either of 2 pieces of each colour in a set of chessmen that move from 1 corner to the diagonally opposite corner of a rectangle of 3 by 2 squares over squares that may be occupied – ~hood n – ~ly adj

²knight v to make a knight of

¹knit /nɪt/ v 1a to link firmly or closely b to unite intimately 2a to (cause to) grow together b to contract into wrinkles 3 to form (e g a fabric, garment, or design) by working 1 or more yarns into a series of interlocking loops using 2 or more needles or a knitting machine 4 to make knitted fabrics or articles

²knit, knit stitch n a basic knitting stitch that produces a raised pattern on the front of the work

knitting /ˈnɪtɪŋ/ n work that has been or is being knitted

knob /nɒb/ n 1a a rounded protuberance b a small rounded ornament, handle, or control (for pushing, pulling, or turning) 2 a small piece or lump (e g of coal or butter) – ~bly adj

¹knock /nɒk/ v 1 to strike sthg with a sharp (audible) blow; esp to strike a door seeking admittance 2 to (cause to) collide with sthg 3 to be in a place, often without any clearly defined aim or purpose – usu + about or around 4a to make a sharp pounding noise b of an internal-combustion engine to make a series of sharp popping noises because of faulty combustion of the fuel-air mixture 5 to find fault (with) 6a(1) to strike sharply (2) to drive, force, make, or take (as if) by striking 7 to set forcibly in motion with a blow

²knock n 1a (the sound of) a knocking or a sharp blow or rap b a piece of bad luck or misfortune 2 a harsh and often petty criticism

knock off 1 to stop doing sthg, esp one's work 2 to do hurriedly or routinely 3 to deduct 4 to kill; esp to murder 5 to steal 6 Br to have sexual intercourse with USE (4&5) infml, (6) slang

knockout /ˈnɒk-aʊt/ n 1 a blow that knocks out an opponent (or knocks him down for longer than a particular time, usu 10s, and results in the termination of a boxing match) 2 a competition or tournament with successive rounds in which losing competitors are eliminated until a winner emerges in the final 3 sby or sthg that is sensationally striking or attractive – infml

knock out v 1a to defeat (a boxing opponent) by a knockout b to make unconscious 2 to tire out; exhaust 3 to eliminate (an opponent) from a knock-out competition 4 to overwhelm with amazement or pleasure – infml

¹knot /nɒt/ n 1a an interlacing of (parts of) 1 or more strings, threads, etc that forms a lump or knob b a piece of ribbon, braid etc tied as an ornament c a (sense of) tight constriction 2 sthg hard to solve 3 a bond of union; esp the marriage bond 4a a protuberant lump or swelling in tissue b (a rounded cross-section in timber of) the base of a woody branch enclosed in the stem from which it arises 5 a cluster of people or things 6 a speed of 1 nautical mile per hour

²knot v 1 to tie in or with a knot 2 to unite closely or intricately 3 to form a knot or knots

know /nəʊ/ v knew, known 1a(1) to perceive directly; have direct cognition of (2) to have understanding of (3) to recognize or identify b(1) to be acquainted or familiar with (2) to have experience of **2a** to be aware of the truth or factual nature of; be convinced or certain of **b** to have a practical understanding of **3** to (come to) have knowledge (of sthg)

knowledge /'nɒlɪdʒ/ n **1a** the fact or condition of knowing sthg or sby through experience or association **b** acquaintance with, or understanding or awareness of, sthg **2** the range of a person's information, perception, or understanding **3** the sum of what is known; the body of truth, information, and principles acquired by mankind (on some subject)

knuckle /'nʌkəl/ n **1** the rounded prominence formed by the ends of the 2 bones at a joint; *specif* any of the joints between the hand and the fingers or the finger joints closest to these **2** a cut of meat consisting of the lowest leg joint of a pig, sheep, etc with the adjoining flesh

L

¹label /'leɪbəl/ n **1** a slip (e g of paper or cloth), inscribed and fastened to sthg to give information (e g identification or directions) **2** a descriptive or identifying word or phrase: e g **a** an epithet **b** a word or phrase used with a dictionary definition to provide additional information (e g level of usage) **3** an adhesive stamp **4** a trade name; *specif* a name used by a company producing commercial recordings

²label v **a** to fasten a label to **b** to describe or categorize (as if) with a label

laboratory /lə'bɒrətri/ n a place equipped for scientific experiment, testing, or analysis; *broadly* a place providing opportunity for research in a field of study

laborious /lə'bɔːrɪəs/ adj involving or characterized by effort – ~ly adv – ~ness n

¹labour /'leɪbə'/ n **1a** expenditure of effort, esp when difficult or compulsory; toil **b** human activity that provides the goods or services in an economy **c** (the period of) the physical activities involved in the birth of young **2** an act or process requiring labour; a task **3** workers **4** *sing or pl in constr, cap* the Labour party

²labour v **1** to exert one's powers of body or mind, esp with great effort; work, strive **2** to move with great effort **4** to suffer from some disadvantage or distress **5** to treat in laborious detail

Labour adj of or being a political party, specif one in the UK, advocating a planned socialist economy and associated with working-class interests – ~ite n

labourer /'leɪbərə'/ n one who does unskilled manual work, esp outdoors

labyrinth /'læbərɪnθ/ n **1** a place that is a network of intricate passageways, tunnels, blind alleys, etc **2** sthg perplexingly complex or tortuous in structure, arrangement, or character **3** (the tortuous anatomical structure in) the ear or its bony or membranous part – ~ine n

¹lace /leɪs/ n **1** a cord or string used for drawing together 2 edges (e g of a garment or shoe) **2** an ornamental braid for trimming coats or uniforms **3** an openwork usu figured fabric made of thread, yarn, etc, used for trimmings, household furnishings, garments, etc

²lace v **1** to draw together the edges of (as if) by means of a lace passed through eyelets **2** to draw or pass (e g a lace) through sthg **3** to confine or compress by tightening laces, esp of a corset **4a** to add a dash of an alcoholic drink to **b** to give savour or variety to

¹lack /læk/ v **1** to be deficient or missing **2** to be short or have need of sthg – usu + for

²lack n **1** the fact or state of being wanting or deficient **2** sthg lacking

lad /læd/ n **1** a male person between early boyhood and maturity **2** a fellow, chap **3** Br a stable lad

ladder /'lædə'/ n **1** a structure for climbing up or down that has 2 long sidepieces of metal, wood, rope, etc joined at intervals by crosspieces on which one may step **2a** sthg that resembles or suggests a ladder in form or use **b** chiefly Br a vertical line in hosiery or knitting caused by stiches becoming unravelled **3** a series of ascending steps or stages

¹ladle /'leɪdl/ n a deep-bowled long-handled spoon used esp for taking up and conveying liquids or semiliquid foods (e g soup)

²ladle v to take up and convey (as if) in a ladle

lady /'leɪdi/ n **1a** a woman with authority, esp as a feudal superior **b** a woman receiving the homage or devotion of a knight or lover **2a** a woman of refinement or superior social position **b** a woman – often in courteous reference or usu pl in address **3** a wife **4a** cap any of various titled women in Britain – used as a title **b** cap a female member of an order of knighthood

¹lag /læg/ v to stay or fall behind; fail to keep pace – often + behind

²lag n **1** the act or an instance of lagging **2** an interval between related events; specif a time lag

³lag n a convict or an ex-convict

⁴lag v to cover or provide with lagging

laid /leɪd/ past of lay

lain /leɪn/ past part of lie

lair /leə'/ n **1** the resting or living place of a wild animal **2** a refuge or place for hiding

laissez-faire /ˌleɪseɪ 'feə'/ n a doctrine opposing government regulation of economic affairs – laissez-faire adj

lake /leɪk/ n a large inland body of water; also a pool of oil, pitch, or other liquid

²**lake** *n* **1** a deep purplish red pigment orig prepared from cochineal **2** any of numerous usu bright pigments composed essentially of a soluble dye absorbed in or combined with an inorganic carrier

¹**lamb** /læm/ *n* **1a** a young sheep, esp one that is less than a year old **b** the young of various animals (e g the smaller antelopes) other than sheep **2** a gentle, meek, or innocent person **3** the flesh of a lamb used as food

²**lamb** *v* to give birth to a lamb

¹**lame** /leɪm/ *adj* **1** having a body part, esp a leg, so disabled as to impair freedom of movement; *esp* having a limp caused by a disabled leg **2** weak, unconvincing – ~ly *adv* – ~ness *n*

²**lame** *v* to make lame

lamé /ˈlɑːmeɪ/ *n* a brocaded clothing fabric made from any of various fibres combined with tinsel weft threads often of gold or silver

¹**lament** /ləˈment/ *v* to feel or express grief or deep regret; mourn aloud – often + *for* or *over* – ~ation *n*

²**lament** *n* **1** an expression of grief **2** a dirge, elegy

lamp /læmp/ *n* **1** any of various devices for producing visible light: e g **a** a vessel containing an inflammable substance (e g oil or gas) that is burnt to give out artificial light **b** a usu portable electric device containing a light bulb **2** any of various light-emitting devices (e g a sunlamp) which produce electromagnetic radiation (e g heat radiation)

lampoon /læmˈpuːn/ *v or n* (to make the subject of) a harsh satire – ~ist *n*

¹**lance** /lɑːns/ *n* **1** a weapon having a long shaft with a sharp steel head carried by horsemen for use when charging **2a** a lancet

²**lance** *v* **1** to pierce (as if) with a lance **2** to open (as if) with a lancet

¹**land** /lænd/ *n* **1a** the solid part of the surface of a celestial body, esp the earth **b** ground or soil of a specified situation, nature, or quality **2** (*the* way of life in) *the* rural and esp agricultural regions of a country **3** (the people of) a country, region, etc **4** a realm, domain **5** ground owned as property – often pl with sing. meaning

²**land** *v* **1** to set or put on shore from a ship **2a** to set down (e g passengers or goods) after conveying **b** to bring to or cause to reach a specified place, position, or condition **c** to bring (e g an aeroplane) to a surface from the air **3a** to catch and bring in (e g a fish) **b** to gain, secure – infml **4** to strike, hit – infml **5** to present or burden *with* sthg unwanted – infml **6a** to go ashore from a ship; disembark **b** *of a boat, ship, etc* to come to shore; *also* to arrive on shore in a boat, ship, etc **7a** to end up – usu + *up* **b** to strike or come to rest on a surface (e g after a fall) **c** *of an aircraft, spacecraft, etc* to alight on a surface; *also* to arrive in an aircraft, spacecraft, etc which has alighted on a surface

landing /ˈlændɪŋ/ *n* **1** the act of going

or bringing to a surface from the air or to shore from the water **2** a place for discharging and taking on passengers and cargo **3** a level space at the end of a flight of stairs or between 2 flights of stairs

landlady /ˈlændˌleɪdi/ *n* **1** a female landlord **2** the female proprietor of a guesthouse or lodging house

landlord /ˈlændlɔːd/ *n* **1** sby who owns land, buildings, or accommodation for lease or rent **2** sby who owns or keeps an inn; an innkeeper

landmark /ˈlændmɑːk/ *n* **1a** an object (e g a stone) that marks a boundary **b** a conspicuous object that can be used to identify a locality **2** an event that marks a turning point or new development

¹**landscape** /ˈlændskeɪp/ *n* **1** natural, esp inland scenery **2a** a picture, drawing, etc of landscape **b** the art of depicting landscape

²**landscape** *v* to improve or modify the natural beauties of

landslide /ˈlændslaɪd/ *n* **1** a usu rapid movement of rock, earth, etc down a slope; *also* the moving mass **2** an overwhelming victory, esp in an election

lane /leɪn/ *n* **1** a narrow passageway, road, or street **2a** a fixed ocean route used by ships **b** a strip of road for a single line of vehicles **c** any of several marked parallel courses to which a competitor must keep during a race (e g in running or swimming) **d** a narrow hardwood surface down which the ball is sent towards the pins in tenpin bowling

language /ˈlæŋgwɪdʒ/ *n* **1a** those words, their pronunciation, and the methods of combining them used by a particular people, nation, etc **b(1)** (the faculty of making and using) audible articulate meaningful sound **(2)** a systematic means of communicating using conventionalized signs, gestures, or marks **(3)** the suggestion by objects, actions, or conditions of associated ideas or feelings **2a** a particular style or manner of verbal expression **b** the specialized vocabulary and phraseology belonging to a particular group or profession

lantern /ˈlæntən/ *n* **1** a portable protective case with transparent windows that houses a light (e g a candle) **2a** the chamber in a lighthouse containing the light **b** a structure above an opening in a roof which has glazed or open sides for light or ventilation

¹**lap** /læp/ *n* (the clothing covering) the front part of the lower trunk and thighs of a seated person

²**lap** *v* **1** to fold or wrap over or round **2a** to place or lie so as to (partly) cover (one another) **b** to unite (e g beams or timbers) so as to preserve the same breadth and depth throughout **3a** to overtake and thereby lead or increase the lead over (another contestant) by a full circuit of a racetrack **b** to complete a circuit of (a racetrack)

³**lap** *n* **1** the amount by which one object overlaps another **2a** (the distance

covered during) the act or an instance of moving once round a closed course or track **b** one stage or segment of a larger unit (e g a journey) **c** one complete turn (e g of a rope round a drum)

⁴**lap** *v* **1** to take in (liquid) with the tongue **2** to move in little waves, usu making a gentle splashing sound **3** to take in eagerly or quickly – usu + *up*

⁵**lap** *n* **1** an act or instance of lapping **2** a gentle splashing sound

lapel /lə'pel/ *n* a fold of the top front edge of a coat or jacket that is continuous with the collar

¹**lapse** /læps/ *n* **1** a slight error (e g of memory or in manners) **2a** a drop; *specif* a drop in temperature, humidity, or pressure with increasing height **b** an esp moral fall or decline **3a(1)** the legal termination of a right or privilege through failure to exercise it **(2)** the termination of insurance coverage for nonpayment of premiums **b** a decline into disuse **4** an abandonment of religious faith **5** a continuous passage or elapsed period

²**lapse** *v* **1a** to fall or depart from an attained or accepted standard or level (e g of morals) – usu + *from* **b** to sink or slip gradually **2** to go out of existence or use **3** to pass to another proprietor by omission or negligence **4** *of time* to run its course; pass

larder /'lɑːdə'/ *n* a place where food is stored; a pantry

large /lɑːdʒ/ *adj* **1** having more than usual power, capacity, or scope **2** exceeding most other things of like kind (in quantity or size) **3** dealing in great numbers or quantities; operating on an extensive scale

largely /'lɑːdʒli/ *adv* to a large extent

¹**lark** /lɑːk/ *n* any of numerous brown singing birds mostly of Europe, Asia, and northern Africa; *esp* a skylark

²**lark** *v* to have fun – usu + *about* or *around*

³**lark** *n* **1** a lighthearted adventure; *also* a prank **2** *Br* a type of activity; *esp* a business, job *USE* infml

laser /'leizə'/ *n* a device that generates an intense beam of light or other electromagnetic radiation of a single wavelength by using the natural oscillations of atoms or molecules

¹**lash** /læʃ/ *v* **1** to move violently or suddenly **2** to beat, pour **3** to attack physically or verbally, (as if) with a whip – often + *at, against,* or *out* **4** to strike quickly and forcibly (as if) with a lash **5** to drive (as if) with a whip; rouse

²**lash** *n* **1a(1)** a stroke (as if) with a whip **(2)** (the flexible part of) a whip **b** a sudden swinging movement or blow **2** violent beating **3** an eyelash

³**lash** *v* to bind or fasten with a cord, rope, etc

lass /læs/, **lassie** *n* a young woman; a girl

¹**lasso** /lə'suː, 'læsəʊ/ *n, pl* **lassos, lassoes** a rope or long thong of leather with a running noose that is used esp for catching horses and cattle

²**lasso** *v* to catch (as if) with a lasso

¹**last** /lɑːst/ *v* **1** to continue in time **2a** to remain in good or adequate condition, use, or effectiveness **b** to manage to continue (e g in a course of action) **3** to continue in existence or action as long as or longer than – often + *out* **4** to be enough for the needs of

²**last** *adj* **1** following all the rest: e g **a** final, latest **b** being the only remaining **2** of the final stage of life (e g *last* rites) **3** next before the present; most recent **4a** lowest in rank or standing; *also* worst **b** least suitable or likely (e g the *last* person you'd think of) **5a** conclusive, definitive (e g the *last* word) **b** single – used as an intensive (e g ate every *last* scrap)

³**last** *adv* **1** after all others; at the end **2** on the most recent occasion **3** in conclusion; lastly

⁴**last** *n* sby or sthg last

⁵**last** *n* a form (e g of metal) shaped like the human foot, over which a shoe is shaped or repaired

¹**latch** /lætʃ/ *v* **1** to attach oneself **2** to gain understanding or comprehension *USE* + *on* or *onto*

²**latch** *n* a fastener (e g for a door)

¹**late** /leit/ *adj* **1a** occurring or arriving after the expected time **b** of the end of a specified time span **2a** (recently) deceased – used with reference to names, positions or specified relationships **b** just prior to the present, esp as the most recent of a succession **3** far on in the day or night

²**late** *adv* **1a** after the usual or proper time **b** at or near the end of a period of time or of a process – often + *on* **2** until lately – **~ness** *n*

lately /'leitli/ *adv* recently; of late

¹**Latin** /'lætin/ *adj* **1** of Latium or the Latins **2a** of or composed in Latin **b** Romance **3** of the part of the Christian church using a Latin liturgy; *broadly* Roman Catholic **4** of the peoples or countries using Romance languages **5** *chiefly NAm* of the peoples or countries of Latin America

²**Latin** *n* **1** the language of ancient Latium and of Rome **2** a member of the people of ancient Latium **3** a member of any of the Latin peoples **4** *chiefly NAm* a native or inhabitant of Latin America

latitude /'lætɪˌtjuːd/ *n* **1a** the angular distance of a point on the surface of a celestial body, esp the earth, measured N or S from the equator **b** the angular distance of a celestial body from the ecliptic **2** a region as marked by its latitude – often *pl* with sing. meaning **3** (permitted) freedom of action or choice

¹**latter** /'lætə'/ *adj* **1** of the end; later, final **2** recent, present (e g in *latter* years) **3** second of 2 things, or last of several things mentioned or understood

²**latter** *n, pl* **latter** the second or last mentioned

¹**laugh** /lɑːf/ *v* **1a** to make the explosive vocal sounds characteristically express-

ing amusement, mirth, joy, or derision **b** to experience amusement, mirth, joy, or derision **2** to dismiss as trivial – + *off* or *away*

²**laugh** *n* **1** the act or sound of laughing **2** an expression of mirth or scorn **3** a means of entertainment; a diversion – often pl with sing. meaning **4** a cause for derision or merriment; a joke – *infml*

laughter /'lɑːftəʳ/ *n* **1** a sound (as if) of laughing **2** the action of laughing

¹**launch** /lɔːntʃ/ *v* **1a** to throw forward; hurl **b** to release or send off (e g a self-propelled object) **2a** to set (an esp newly built boat or ship) afloat **b** to start or set in motion (e g on a course or career) **c** to introduce (a new product) onto the market **3** to throw oneself energetically – + *into* or *out into* **4** to make a start – usu + *out* or *forth*

²**launch** *n* an act or instance of launching

³**launch** *n* **1** the largest boat carried by a warship **2** a large open or half-decked motorboat

laundry /'lɔːndri/ *n* **1** clothes or cloth articles that have been or are to be laundered, esp by being sent to a laundry **2** a place where laundering is done; *esp* a commercial laundering establishment

lavatory /'lævətəri/ *n* a toilet

lavender /'lævɪndəʳ/ *n* **1** a Mediterranean plant of the mint family widely cultivated for its narrow aromatic leaves and spikes of lilac-purple flowers which are dried and used in perfume sachets **2** a pale purple colour

¹**lavish** /'lævɪʃ/ *adj* **1** expending or bestowing profusely **2** expended, bestowed, or produced in abundance – ~ly *adv*

²**lavish** *v* to expend or bestow *on* with profusion

law /lɔː/ *n* **1a(1)** a rule of conduct formally recognized as binding or enforced by authority **(3)** the whole body of such rules **(3)** common law **b** the control brought about by such law – esp in *law and order* **c** litigation **2a** a rule one should observe **b** control, authority **3** *often cap* the revelation of the will of God set out in the Old Testament **4** a rule of action, construction, or procedure **5** the law relating to one subject **6** *often cap the* legal profession **7a** a statement of an order or relation of natural phenomena **b** a necessary relation between mathematical or logical expressions **8** *sing or pl in constr, often cap the* police – *infml*

lawful /'lɔːfəl/ *adj* **1** allowed by law **2** rightful – ~ly *adv* – ~ness *n*

¹**lawn** /lɔːn/ *n* a fine sheer linen or cotton fabric of plain weave that is thinner than cambric

²**lawn** *n* an area of ground (e g around a house or in a garden or park) that is covered with grass and is kept mowed

lawyer /'lɔːjəʳ/ *n* sby whose profession is to conduct lawsuits or to advise on legal matters

¹**lay** /leɪ/ *v* **laid** **1** to beat or strike down with force **2a** to put or set down **b** to place for rest or sleep; *esp* to bury **3** *of a bird* to produce (an egg) **4** to calm, allay **5** to bet, wager **6a** to dispose or spread over or on a surface **b** to set in order or position **7** to put or impose a duty, burden, or punishment – esp + *on* or *upon* **8** to prepare, contrive **9a** to bring into position or against or into contact with sthg **b** to prepare or position for action or operation **10** to bring to a specified condition **11a** to assert, allege **b** to submit for examination and judgment **12** to put aside for future use; store, reserve – + *aside, by, in,* or *up* **13** to put out of use or consideration – + *aside* or *by* **14** to copulate with – *slang*

²**lay** *past of* lie

³**lay** *n* a simple narrative poem intended to be sung; a ballad

⁴**lay** *adj* **1** of or performed by the laity **2** of domestic or manual workers in a religious community **3** not belonging to a particular profession

¹**layer** /'leɪəʳ/ *n* **1a** a single thickness of some substance spread or lying over or under another **b** any of a series of gradations or depths **2** a branch or shoot of a plant treated to induce rooting while still attached to the parent plant

²**layer** *v* **1** to propagate (a plant) by means of layers **2** to arrange or form (as if) in layers **3** to form out of or with layers

layman /'leɪmən/ *fem* **laywoman** *n* **1** a person not of the clergy **2** a person without special (e g professional) knowledge of some field

layout /'leɪaʊt/ *n* the plan, design, or arrangement of sthg (e g rooms in a building or matter to be printed) laid out

lay out *v* **1** to prepare (a corpse) for a funeral **2** to knock flat or unconscious

lazy /'leɪzi/ *adj* **1a** disinclined or averse to activity; indolent; *also* not energetic or vigorous **b** encouraging inactivity or indolence **2** moving slowly – -**zily** *adv* – -**ziness** *n*

¹**lead** /liːd/ *v* **led** **1a(1)** to guide on a way, esp by going in advance **(2)** to cause to go with one (under duress) **b** to direct or guide on a course or to a state or condition; influence **c** to serve as a channel or route for **d(1)** to lie or run in a specified place or direction **(2)** to serve as an entrance or passage **2** to go through; live **3a** to direct the operations, activity, or performance of; have charge of **b** to go or be at the head or ahead of **c** to be first or ahead **4a** to begin, open – usu + *off* **b** to play the first card of a trick, round, or game **5** to tend or be directed towards a specified result **6** to direct the first of a series of blows at an opponent in boxing (*with the right or left hand*)

²**lead** /liːd/ *n* **1a(1)** position at the front or ahead **(2)** the act or privilege of leading in cards; *also* the card or suit led

b guidance, direction; (an) example **c** a margin or position of advantage or superiority **2a** an indication, clue **b** (one who plays) a principal role in a dramatic production **c** a line or strap for leading or restraining an animal (e g a dog) **d** a news story of chief importance **3** an insulated electrical conductor

³lead /led/ *n* **1** a heavy soft malleable bluish-white metallic element used esp in pipes, cable sheaths, batteries, solder, type metal, and shields against radioactivity **2** the (lead) weight on a sounding line **3** a thin stick of graphite or crayon in or for a pencil **4** *pl, Br* (a usu flat roof covered with) thin lead sheets

leader /'liːdə'/ *n* **1a** a main or end shoot of a plant **b** a blank section at the beginning or end of a reel of film or recorded tape **2** sby or sthg that ranks first, precedes others, or holds a principal position **3** *chiefly Br* a newspaper editorial **4** *Br* the principal first violinist and usu assistant conductor of an orchestra – ~**ship** *n*

leading /'liːdɪŋ/ *adj* coming or ranking first; foremost, principal

¹leaf /liːf/ *n, pl* **leaves 1a** any of the usu green flat and typically broad-bladed outgrowths from the stem of a plant that function primarily in food manufacture by photosynthesis **b** (the state of having) foliage **2a** a part of a book or folded sheet of paper containing a page on each side **b** a part (e g of a window shutter, folding door, or table) that slides or is hinged **c** metal (e g gold or silver) in sheets, usu thinner than foil

²leaf *v* **1** to shoot out or produce leaves **2** to glance quickly *through* a book, magazine, etc

leafy /'liːfi/ *adj* **1** having or thick with leaves **2** consisting chiefly of leaves

¹league /liːg/ *n* any of various units of distance of about 3mi (5km)

²league *n* **1a** an association of nations, groups, or people for a common purpose or to promote a common interest **b** (a competition for an overall title, in which each person or team plays all the others at least once, held by) an association of people or sports clubs **2** a class, category

¹leak /liːk/ *v* **1** to (let a substance) enter or escape through a crack or hole **2** to become known despite efforts at concealment – often + *out* **3** to give out (information) surreptitiously

²leak *n* **1a** a crack or hole through which sthg (e g a fluid) is admitted or escapes, usu by mistake **b** a means by which sthg (e g secret information) is admitted or escapes, usu with prejudicial effect **2** a leaking or that which is leaked; *esp* a disclosure **3** an act of urinating – *slang*

¹lean /liːn/ *v* **leant, leaned 1a** to incline or bend from a vertical position **b** to rest supported *on/against* sthg **2** to rely for support or inspiration – + *on* or *upon* **3** to incline in opinion, taste, etc **4** to exert pressure; use coercion – + *on*; *infml*

²lean *adj* **1a** lacking or deficient in flesh or bulk **b** *of meat* containing little or no fat **2** *esp of a fuel mixture* low in the combustible component – ~**ness** *n*

³lean *n* the part of meat that consists principally of fat-free muscular tissue

¹leap /liːp/ *v* **leapt, leaped 1** to jump **2a** to pass abruptly from one state or topic to another; *esp* to rise quickly **b** to seize eagerly *at* an opportunity, offer, etc

²leap *n* **1a** (the distance covered by) a jump **b** a place leapt over or from **2** a sudden transition, esp a rise or increase

leap year *n* a year with an extra day added to make it coincide with the solar year

learn /lɜːn/ *v* **learnt, learned 1a** to gain knowledge of or skill in **b** to memorize **2** to come to be able – + infinitive **3** to come to realize or know – ~**er** *n*

learning /'lɜːnɪŋ/ *n* **1** acquired knowledge or skill **2** modification of a behavioural tendency by experience (e g exposure to conditioning)

¹lease /liːs/ *n* **1** a contract putting the land or property of one party at the disposal of another, usu for a stated period and rent **2** a (prospect of) continuance – *chiefly in* lease *of* life

²lease *v* to grant by or hold under lease

¹least /liːst/ *adj* **1** lowest in rank, degree, or importance **2a** smallest in quantity or extent **c** smallest possible; slightest

²least *n* the smallest quantity, number, or amount

³least *adv* to the smallest degree or extent

¹leather /leðə'/ *n* **1** animal skin dressed for use **2** sthg wholly or partly made of leather; *esp* a piece of chamois, used esp for polishing metal or glass

²leather *v* to beat with a strap; thrash

¹leave /liːv/ *v* **left 1a** to bequeath **b** to cause to remain as an aftereffect **2a** to cause or allow to be or remain in a specified or unaltered condition **b** to fail to include, use, or take along – sometimes + *off* or *out* **c** to have remaining or as a remainder **d** to allow to do or continue sthg without interference **3a** to go away from; *also* set out *for* **b** to desert, abandon **c** to withdraw from **4** to put, station, deposit, or deliver, esp before departing

²leave *n* **1** permission to do sthg **2** authorized (extended) absence (e g from employment)

leaves /liːvz/ *pl of* leaf

¹lecture /'lektʃə'/ *n* **1** a discourse given to an audience, esp for instruction **2** a reproof delivered at length; a reprimand

²lecture *v* to deliver a lecture or series of lectures; *specif* to work as a teacher at a university or college – **r** *n*

led /led/ *past of* lead

LED *n* a diode that emits light when an electric current is passed through it and that is used esp to display numbers, symbols, etc on a screen (e g in a pocket calculator)

ledge /ledʒ/ n 1 a (narrow) horizontal surface that projects from a vertical or steep surface (e g a wall or rock face) 2 an underwater ridge or reef

leek /li:k/ n an onion-like vegetable with a white cylindrical edible bulb

¹**left** /left/ adj 1a of, situated on, or being the side of the body in which most of the heart is located b located nearer to the left hand than to the right; esp located on the left hand when facing in the same direction as an observer often cap of the Left in politics

²**left** n 1a (a blow struck with) the left hand b the location or direction of the left side c the part on the left side 2 sing or pl in constr, cap those professing socialist or radical political views

³**left** past of **leave**

left-handed adj 1 using the left hand habitually or more easily than the right 2 of, designed for, or done with the left hand 3 clumsy, awkward 4 ambiguous, double-edged – ~ly adv – ~ness n

¹**leg** /leg/ n 1 a limb of an animal used esp for supporting the body and for walking: e g a (an artificial replacement for) either of the lower limbs of a human b a (hind) leg of a meat animal, esp above the hock c any of the appendages on each segment of an arthropod (e g an insect or spider) used in walking and crawling 2 the part of a garment that covers (part of) the leg 3 the side of a cricket pitch to the left of a right-handed batsmen or to the right of a left-handed one 4a the course and distance sailed on a single tack b a portion of a trip; a stage c the part of a relay race run by 1 competitor d any of a set of events or games that must all be won to decide a competition

²**leg** adj in, on, through, or towards the leg side of a cricket field

legal /ˈliːgəl/ adj 1 of law 2a deriving authority from law b established by or having a formal status derived from law 3 permitted by law – ~ly adv – ~ity n – ~ize v

legend /ˈledʒənd/ n 1a a story coming down from the past; esp one popularly regarded as historical b a person, act, or thing that inspires legends 2a an inscription or title on an object (e g a coin) b a caption c the key to a map, chart, etc – ~ary adj

legible /ˈledʒəbəl/ adj capable of being read or deciphered – -bility n – -bly adv

legislation /ˌledʒɨsˈleɪʃən/ n (the making of) laws + -tive adj

¹**legitimate** /lɨˈdʒɪtɨmɨt/ adj 1 lawfully begotten; specif born in wedlock 2 neither spurious nor false; genuine 3a in accordance with law b ruling by or based on the strict principle of hereditary right 4 conforming to recognized principles or accepted rules and standards

²**legitimate** /lɨˈdʒɪtɨmeɪt/ legitimatize, legitimize v 1a to give legal status to b to justify 2 to give (an illegitimate child) the legal status of one legitimately born

leisure /ˈleʒəʳ/ n 1 freedom provided by the cessation of activities; esp time free from work or duties 2 unhurried ease – ~d adj

¹**leisurely** /ˈleʒəli/ adv without haste; deliberately

²**leisurely** adj characterized by leisure; unhurried

lemon /ˈlemən/ n 1 (a stout thorny tree that bears) an oval yellow acid citrus fruit 2 a pale yellow colour 3 one who or that which is unsatisfactory or worthless; a dud – infml

lemonade /ˌleməˈneɪd/ n a (carbonated) soft drink made or flavoured with lemon

lend /lend/ v lent 1a to give for temporary use on condition that the same or its equivalent be returned b to let out (money) for temporary use on condition of repayment with interest 2 to give the assistance or support of; afford, contribute – ~er n

length /leŋθ/ n 1a(1) the longer or longest dimension of an object (2) the extent from end to end b a measured distance or dimension c the quality or state of being long 2 duration or extent in or with regard to time 3 distance or extent in space 4 the degree to which sthg (e g a course of action or a line of thought) is carried; a limit, extreme – often pl with sing. meaning 5a a long expanse or stretch b a piece, esp of a certain length (being or usable as part of a whole or of a connected series) 6 the vertical extent of sthg (e g an article of clothing), esp with reference to the position it reaches on the body – usu in combination

lengthen /ˈleŋθən/ v to make or become longer

lengthy /ˈleŋθi/ adj of great or unusual length; long; also excessively or tediously protracted – -ily adv – -iness n

lenient /ˈliːnɪənt/ adj of a mild or merciful nature; not severe – -ience n – ~ly adv

lens /lenz/ n 1 a piece of glass or other transparent material with 2 opposite regular surfaces, at least 1 of which is curved, that is used either singly or combined in an optical instrument to form an image by focussing rays of light 2 a device for directing or focussing radiation other than light (e g sound waves or electrons)

Lent n the 40 weekdays from Ash Wednesday to Easter observed by Christians as a period of penitence and fasting

leopard /ˈlepəd/ fem **leopardess** n 1 a big cat of southern Asia and Africa that is usu tawny or buff with black spots arranged in broken rings or rosettes 2 a heraldic figure of a lion with the farther forepaw raised and its head turned towards the observer

¹**less** /les/ adj 1 fewer (e g less than 3) – disapproved of by some speakers 2 lower in rank, degree, or importance (e g no less a person than the President himself(3 smaller in quantity or extent (e g of less importance)

²**less** adv to a lesser degree or extent

³**less** prep diminished by; minus (e g £100 less tax)

⁴**less** n, pl **less** a smaller portion or quantity

lessen /'lesən/ v to reduce in size, extent, etc; diminish, decrease

lesson /'lesən/ n 1 a passage from sacred writings read in a service of worship 2a a reading or exercise to be studied b period of instruction 3 sthg, esp a piece of wisdom, learned by study or experience

lest /lest/ conj so that not; for fear that (e g obeyed her lest she should be angry)

¹**let** /let/ n 1 a serve or rally in tennis, squash, etc that does not count and must be replayed 2 sthg that impedes; an obstruction – fml

²**let** v let; -tt- 1 to offer or grant for rent or lease 2 to give opportunity to, whether by positive action or by failure to prevent; allow to 3 – used in the imperative to introduce a request or proposal, a challenge, or a command;

³**let** n, Br 1 an act or period of letting premises (e g a flat or bed-sitter) 2 premises rented or for rent

letdown /'letdaʊn/ n a disappointment, disillusionment – infml

let down v 1 to make (a garment) longer 2 to fail in loyalty or support; disappoint

lethal /'liːðəl/ adj relating to or (capable of) causing death

let off v 1 to cause to explode 2 to excuse from punishment

letter /'letə'/ n 1 a symbol, usu written or printed, representing a speech sound and constituting a unit of an alphabet 2 a written or printed message addressed to a person or organization and usu sent through the post 3 pl but sing or pl in constr a literature; writing b learning; esp scholarly knowledge of or achievement in literature 4 the precise wording; the strict or literal meaning

lettuce /'letɪs/ n a common garden vegetable whose succulent edible leaves are used esp in salads

¹**level** /'levəl/ n 1 a device (e g a spirit level) for establishing a horizontal line or plane 2a a horizontal state or condition b an (approximately) horizontal line, plane, or surface 3a a position of height in relation to the ground; height b a practically horizontal or flat area, esp of land 4 a position or place in a scale or rank (e g of value or importance) 5 the (often measurable) size or amount of sthg specified

²**level** v 1a to make (a line or surface) horizontal; make level, even, or uniform b to raise or lower to the same height – often + up c to attain or come to a level – usu + out or off 2 to aim, direct – + at or against 3 to bring to a common level, plane, or standard; equalize 4 to lay level with the ground; raze

³**level** adj 1a having no part higher than another b parallel with the plane of the horizon 2a even, unvarying b equal in

advantage, progression, or standing c steady, unwavering

¹**lever** /'liːvə'/ n 1 a bar used for prizing up or dislodging sthg 2a a rigid bar used to exert a pressure or sustain a weight at one end by applying force at the other and turning it on a fulcrum b a projecting part by which a mechanism is operated or adjusted

²**lever** v to prize, raise, or move up (as if) with a lever – + up

liable /'laɪəbəl/ adj 1 legally responsible 2 exposed or subject to 3 habitually likely to – -**bility** n

liar /'laɪə'/ n one who (habitually) tells lies

¹**liberal** /'lɪbərəl/ adj 1a generous, open-handed b abundant, ample 2 broad-minded, tolerant; esp not bound by authoritarianism, orthodoxy, or tradition 3 cap of a political party in the UK advocating economic freedom and moderate reform – ~**ize** v, ~**ly** adv

²**liberal** n 1 one who is not strict in the observance of orthodox ways (e g in politics or religion) 2 cap a supporter of a Liberal party – ~**ism** n

liberate /'lɪbəreɪt/ v 1 to set free; specif to free (a country) from foreign domination 2 to steal – euph or humor – -**rator** n

liberation /ˌlɪbə'reɪʃən/ n the seeking of equal rights and status; also a movement dedicated to seeking these for a specified group

liberty /'lɪbəti/ n 1a freedom from physical restraint or dictatorial control b the power of choice 2 a right or immunity awarded or granted; a privilege 3 a breach of etiquette or propriety

librarian /laɪ'breərɪən/ n sby who manages or assists in a library – ~**ship** n

library /'laɪbrəri/ n 1 a place in which books, recordings, films, etc are kept for reference or for borrowing by the public 2 a collection of such books, recordings, etc

licence /'laɪsəns/ NAm chiefly **license** n 1 (a certificate giving evidence of) permission granted by authority to engage in an otherwise unlawful activity, esp the sale of alcoholic drink 2a freedom that allows or is used with irresponsibility b disregard for rules of propriety or personal conduct

license, licence v to give official permission to or for

¹**lick** /lɪk/ v 1 to lap up (as if) with the tongue; also to dart like a tongue 2 to get the better of; overcome – ~**ing** n

²**lick** n 1 a small amount; a touch 2 a stroke or blow 3 a place to which animals regularly go to lick a salt deposit 4 speed, pace – infml

lid /lɪd/ n a hinged or detachable cover (for a receptacle)

¹**lie** /laɪ/ v **lying; lay; lain** 1a to be or to stay at rest in a horizontal position; rest, recline b to assume a horizontal position – often + down 2a of sthg inanimate to be or remain in a flat or horizontal position on a surface b of snow to remain on the ground without melt-

ing **3** to have as a direction **4a** to occupy a specified place or position **b** *of an action, claim, etc in a court of law* to be sustainable or admissible

²**lie** *n* **1** the way, position, or situation in which sthg lies **2** a haunt of an animal or fish

³**lie** *v* **lying 1** to make an untrue statement with intent to deceive; speak falsely **2** to create a false or misleading impression

⁴**lie** *n* **1** an untrue or false statement, esp when made with intent to deceive **2** sthg that misleads or deceives

lieutenant /lef'tenənt/ *n* **1** an official empowered to act for a higher official; a deputy or representative **2** a low-ranking officer in the navy, British army, etc

¹**life** /laɪf/ *n, pl* **lives 1** the quality that distinguishes a vital and functional being from a dead body **b** a state of matter (e g a cell or an organism) characterized by capacity for metabolism, growth, reaction to stimuli, and reproduction **2** an aspect of the process of living **3** a biography **4** a state or condition of existence; a manner of living **5a** the period from birth to death or to the present time **b** the period from an event or the present time until death **c** a sentence of imprisonment for life **6** the period of usefulness, effectiveness, or functioning of sthg inanimate **7** living beings (e g of a specified kind or environment) **8** any of several chances to participate given to a contestant in some games, 1 of which is forfeited each time he/she loses

²**life** *adj* **1** using a living model **2** of, being, or provided by life insurance

lifeless /'laɪflɪs/ *adj* **1a** dead **b** inanimate **2** having no living beings **3** lacking qualities expressive of life and vigour; dull – **~ly** *adv* – **~ness** *n*

lifelike /'laɪflaɪk/ *adj* accurately representing or imitating (the appearance of objects in) real life

lifelong /'laɪflɒŋ/ *adj* lasting or continuing throughout life

¹**lift** /lɪft/ *v* **1** to raise from a lower to a higher position; elevate **2** to put an end to (a blockade or siege) by withdrawing the surrounding forces **3** to revoke, rescind **4a** to copy without acknowledgement **b** to take out of normal setting **5** *of bad weather* to cease temporarily **6** to steal – *infml*

²**lift** *n* **1** a (device for) lifting or (the amount) being lifted **2** a usu free ride as a passenger in a motor vehicle **3** a slight rise or elevation of ground **4** the distance or extent to which sthg (e g water in a canal lock) rises **5** a usu temporary feeling of cheerfulness, pleasure, or encouragement **6** any of the ropes by which the yard is suspended from the mast on a square-rigged ship **7** *chiefly Br* a device for conveying people or objects from one level to another, esp in a building

¹**light** /laɪt/ *n* **1** an electromagnetic radiation in the wavelength range including infrared, visible, ultraviolet, and X rays;

specif the part of this range that is visible to the human eye **2** daylight **3** an electric light **4a** spiritual illumination **b** understanding, knowledge **c** *the* truth **5a** public knowledge **b** a particular aspect or appearance in which sthg is viewed **6** a medium (e g a window) through which light is admitted **7** *pl* a set of principles, standards, or opinions **8** the representation in art of the effect of light on objects or scenes **9** a flame or spark for lighting sthg (e g a cigarette)

²**light** *adj* **1** having plenty of light; bright **2a** pale in colour or colouring **b** *of colours* medium in saturation and high in lightness

³**light** *v* **lit, lighted 1** to set fire to **2** to conduct (sby) with a light; guide

⁴**light** *adj* **1a** having little weight; not heavy **b** designed to carry a comparatively small load **c** (made of materials) having relatively little weight in proportion to bulk **d** containing less than the legal, standard, or usual weight **2a** of little importance; trivial **b** not abundant **3a** *of sleep or a sleeper* easily disturbed **b** exerting a minimum of force or pressure; gentle, soft **c** faint **4a** easily endurable **b** requiring little effort **5** nimble **6** lacking seriousness; frivolous **7** free from care; cheerful **8** intending or intended chiefly to entertain **9** *of a drink* having a comparatively low alcoholic content or a mild flavour **10** easily digested **11** producing light usu small goods often for direct consumption – **~ness** *n* – **~ly** *adv*

⁵**light** *adv* **1** lightly **2** with the minimum of luggage

⁶**light** *v* **lighted, lit 1** to settle, alight **2** to arrive by chance; happen

¹**lighter** /'laɪtə/ *n* a large usu flat-bottomed barge used esp in unloading or loading ships

²**lighter** *n* a device for lighting (a cigar, cigarette, etc)

lighthearted /laɪt'hɑːtɪd/ *adj* free from care or worry; cheerful

lighthouse /'laɪthaʊs/ *n* a tower, mast, etc equipped with a powerful light to warn or guide shipping at sea

¹**lightning** /'laɪtnɪŋ/ *n* (the brilliant light flash resulting from) an electric discharge between 2 clouds or between a cloud and the earth

²**lightning** *adj* very quick, short, or sudden

¹**like** /laɪk/ *v* **1a** to find agreeable, acceptable, or pleasant; enjoy **b** to feel towards; regard **2** to wish or choose to have, be, or do; want – **~kable** *adj* – **-king** *n*

²**like** *adj* **1a** alike in appearance, character, or quantity (e g suits of *like* design) **b** bearing a close resemblance; *esp* faithful (e g his portrait is very *like*) **2** likely

³**like** *prep* **1a** having the characteristics of; similar to **b** typical of **2a** in the manner of; similarly to **b** to the same degree as (e g fits *like* a glove) **c** close to (e g cost something *like* £5) **3** appearing to be, threaten, or promise

(e g you seem *like* a sensible man) **4** – used to introduce an example (e g a subject *like* physics)

⁴like *n* one who or that which is like another, esp in high value; a counterpart

⁵like *adv* **1** likely, probably (e g he'll come *like* as not) **2** so to speak (e g went up to her casually, *like*) – nonstandard

⁶like *conj* **1** in the same way as (e g if she can sing *like* she can dance) **2** *chiefly NAm* as if (e g acts *like* he knows what he's doing)

likelihood /'laɪklihud/ *n* probability

¹likely /'laɪkli/ *adj* **1** having a high probability of being or occurring **2** reliable, credible **3** seeming appropriate; suitable **4** promising

²likely *adv* probably – often in *most/very/more/quite likely*

lilac /'laɪlək/ *n* **1** a shrub with large clusters of fragrant white or (pale pinkish) purple flowers **2** a pale pinkish purple colour

lily /'lɪli/ *n* **1** any of a genus of plants that grow from bulbs and are widely cultivated for their variously coloured showy flowers **2** a water lily

¹limb /lɪm/ *n* **1** any of the projecting paired appendages of an animal body used esp for movement and grasping but sometimes modified into sensory or sexual organs; *esp* a leg or arm of a human being **2** a large primary branch of a tree **3** an extension, branch; *specif* any of the 4 branches or arms of a cross

²limb *n* **1** the outer edge of the apparent disc of a celestial body **2** the broad flat part of a petal or sepal furthest from its base

¹lime /laɪm/ *n* **1** a caustic solid consisting of calcium (and some magnesium) oxide, obtained by heating calcium carbonate (e g in the form of shells or limestone) to a high temperature, and used in building (e g in plaster) and in agriculture **2** calcium hydroxide (occurring as a dry white powder), made by treating caustic lime with water

²lime *v* to treat or cover with lime

³lime *n* (the light fine-grained wood of) any of a genus of widely planted (ornamental) trees that usu have heart-shaped leaves

⁴lime *n* a (spiny tropical citrus tree cultivated for its) small spherical greenish-yellow fruit

limelight /'laɪmlaɪt/ *n* **1** (the white light produced by) a stage lighting instrument producing illumination by means of an intense flame directed on a cylinder of lime **2** *the* centre of public attention

limestone /'laɪmstəʊn/ *n* a widely-occurring rock consisting mainly of calcium carbonate

¹limit /'lɪmɪt/ *n* **1a** a boundary **b** *pl* the place enclosed within a boundary **2a** sthg that bounds, restrains, or confines **b** a line or point that cannot or should not be passed **3** a prescribed maximum or minimum amount, quantity, or number **4** sby or sthg exasperating or intolerable – + *the*; infml

²limit *v* **1** to restrict to specific bounds or limits **2** to curtail or reduce in quantity or extent; curb – ~**ation** *n*

limited /'lɪmɪtɪd/ *adj* **1** confined within limits; restricted **2** restricted as to the scope of powers **3** lacking the ability to grow or do better

¹limp /lɪmp/ *v* **1** to walk in a manner that avoids putting the full weight of the body on **1** (injured) leg **2** to proceed slowly or with difficulty – **limp** *n*

²limp *adj* **1a** lacking firmness and body; drooping or shapeless **b** not stiff or rigid **2** lacking energy – ~**ly** *adv*, ~**ness** *n*

¹line /laɪn/ *v* **1** to cover the inner surface of; provide with a lining **2** to fill

²line *n* **1a** a cord or rope; *esp* one on a ship **b** a device for catching fish consisting of a usu single-filament cord with hooks, floats, a reel, etc **c** a length of material (e g cord) used in measuring and levelling **d** piping for conveying a fluid (e g steam or compressed air) **e(1)** (a connection for communication by means of) a set of wires connecting one telephone or telegraph (exchange) with another **(2)** the principal circuits of an electric power distribution system **2a** a horizontal row of written or printed characters **b** a single row of words in a poem **c** a short letter; a note **d** a short sequence of words spoken by an actor playing a particular role; *also, pl* all of the sequences making up a particular role **3a** sthg (e g a ridge, seam, or crease) that is distinct, elongated, and narrow **b** a wrinkle (e g on the face) **c** the course or direction of sthg in motion **d** (a single set of rails forming) a railway track **4a** a course of conduct, action, or thought **b** a field of activity or interest **5a** a related series of people or things coming one after the other in time; a family, lineage **b** a linked series of trenches and fortifications, esp facing the enemy – usu pl with sing. meaning **c** the regular and numbered infantry regiments of the army as opposed to auxiliary forces or household troops **d** a rank of objects of 1 kind; a row **e** (the company owning or operating) a group of vehicles, ships, aeroplanes, etc carrying passengers or goods regularly over a route **f** an arrangement of operations in manufacturing allowing ordered occurrence of various stages of production **6** a narrow elongated mark drawn, projected, or imagined (e g on a map): e g **a** a boundary, contour, circle of latitude or longitude, etc **b** the equator **c** a mark (e g in pencil) that forms part of the formal design of a picture; *also* an artist's use of such lines **d** a limit or farthest edge with reference to which the playing of some game or sport is regulated – usu in combination **7** a straight or curved geometric element, generated by a moving point (continually satisfying a particular condition), that has length but no breadth **8** merchandise or services of the same general class for sale or regularly available **9** *pl, Br* a (specified) number of lines of writing, esp to be copied as a school punishment

³**line** *v* **1** to mark or cover with a line or lines **2** to place or form a line along **3** to form *up* into a line or lines

linen /'lɪnɪn/ *n* **1** cloth or yarn made from flax **2** clothing or household articles (e g sheets and tablecloths) made of a usu washable cloth, esp linen

¹**liner** /'laɪnə²/ *n* a passenger ship belonging to a shipping company and usu sailing scheduled routes

²**liner** *n* a replaceable (metal) lining (for reducing the wear of a mechanism)

linger /'lɪŋgə²/ *v* **1a** to delay going; tarry **b** to dwell on a subject – usu + *over, on,* or *upon* **2** to continue unduly or unhappily in a failing or moribund state – often + *on* **3** to be slow to act; procrastinate **4** to be slow in disappearing – ~**er** *n* – ~**ing** *adj* – ~**ingly** *adv*

lining /'laɪnɪŋ/ *n* **1** (a piece of) material used to line sthg (e g a garment) **2** providing sthg with a lining

¹**link** /lɪŋk/ *n* **1** a connecting structure: e g **a** a single ring or division of a chain **b** the fusible part of an electrical fuse **2** sthg analogous to a link of a chain; a connecting element

²**link** *v* to join, connect to become connected by a link – often + *up* – ~**age** *n*

linoleum /lɪ'nəʊlɪəm/ *n* a floor covering with a canvas back and a coloured or patterned surface of hardened linseed oil and a filler (e g cork dust)

lion /'laɪən/, *fem* **lioness** *n* **1a** a flesh-eating big cat of open or rocky areas of Africa and formerly southern Asia that has a tawny body with a tufted tail and in the male a shaggy blackish or dark brown mane **b** *cap* Leo **2** a person of interest or importance

lip /lɪp/ *n* **1** either of the 2 fleshy folds that surround the mouth **2** a fleshy fold surrounding some other body opening (e g the vagina) **3** the edge of a hollow vessel or cavity; *esp* one shaped to make pouring easy **4** impudent or insolent talk, esp in reply – *slang*

liquid /'lɪkwɪd/ *adj* **1** flowing freely like water **2** neither solid nor gaseous **3a** shining and clear **b** *of a sound* flowing, pure, and free of harshness **c** smooth and unconstrained in movement **4** consisting of or capable of ready conversion into cash – ~ *n*

liquorice /'lɪkərɪs, -rɪʃ/ *n* a sweet, black highly-flavoured plant-extract used in brewing, medicine and confectionery

¹**list** /lɪst/ *n, pl but sing or pl in constr* **1** (the fence surrounding) a court or yard for jousting **2** a scene of competition

²**list** *n* a roll or catalogue of words or numbers (e g representing people or objects belonging to a class), usu arranged in order so as to be easily found

³**list** *v* **1** to make a list of **2** to include on a list; *specif, Br* to include (a building)

in an official list as being of architectural or historical importance and hence protected from demolition

⁴**list** *v* to (cause to) lean to one side

listen /'lɪsən/ *v* **1** to pay attention to sound **2** to hear or consider with thoughtful attention; heed **3** to be alert to catch an expected sound

lit /lɪt/ *past of* **light**

¹**literal** /'lɪtərəl/ *adj* **1a** according with the exact letter of a written text **b** having the factual or ordinary construction or primary meaning of a term or expression **c** characterized by a lack of imagination **2** of or expressed in letters **3** reproduced word for word; exact, verbatim – ~**ly** *adv*

²**literal** *n* a misprint involving a single letter

literary /'lɪtərəri/ *adj* **1a** of, being, or concerning literature **b** characteristic of or being in a formal, rather than colloquial, style **2a** well-read **b** producing, well versed in, or connected with literature

literate /'lɪtərɪt/ *adj* **1a** educated, cultured **b** able to read and write **2** versed in literature or creative writing

literature /'lɪtərətʃə²/ *n* **1** writings in prose or verse; *esp* writings having artistic value or expression and expressing ideas of permanent or universal interest **2** the body of writings on a particular subject **3** printed matter (e g leaflets or circulars)

litre /'liːtə²/ *NAm chiefly* **liter** *n* a metric unit of capacity equal to 1.000 028dm³ (about 0.220gal)

¹**litter** /'lɪtə²/ *n* **1a** a covered and curtained couch carried by people or animals **b** a stretcher or other device for carrying a sick or injured person **2a** material used as bedding for animals **b** the uppermost slightly decayed layer of organic matter on the forest floor **3** a group of offspring of an animal, born at 1 birth **4a** rubbish or waste products, esp in a public place **b** an untidy accumulation of objects (e g papers)

²**litter** *v* **1** to give birth to a litter **2** to strew with litter **3** to scatter about in disorder

¹**little** /'lɪtl/ *adj* **littler, less, lesser; littlest, least** **1a** amounting to only a small quantity **b** *of a plant or animal* small in comparison with related forms – used in vernacular names **c** small in condition, distinction, or scope **2** not much: e g **a** existing only in a small amount or to a slight degree **b** short in duration; brief **c** existing to an appreciable though not extensive degree or amount – + *a* **3** small in importance or interest; trivial

²**little** *adv* **less; least** **1** to no great degree or extent; not much (+ *a* *little-known*) **2** not at all (e g cared *little* for his neighbours)

³**little** *n* **1a** only a small portion or quantity; not much **b** at least some, though not much – + *a* (e g have a *little* of this cake) **2** a short time or distance

¹**live** /lɪv/ *v* **1** to be alive; have the life of an animal or plant **2** to continue alive

3 to maintain oneself; subsist **4** to conduct or pass one's life **5** to occupy a home; dwell **6** to have a life rich in experience **7** to cohabit – + *together* or *with* **8** *chiefly Br*, *of a thing* to be found in a specified place – *infml*

²**live** /laɪv/ *adj* **1** having life **2** containing living organisms **3** exerting force or containing energy: e g **a** glowing **b** connected to electric power **c** *of ammunition, bombs, etc* unexploded, unfired **4** of continuing or current interest

³**live** *adv* during, from, or at a live production

lively /'laɪvli/ *adj* **1** briskly alert and energetic; vigorous, animated **2** quick to rebound; resilient **3** full of life, movement, or incident – **-liness** *n*

¹**liver** /'lɪvə/ *n* **1a** a large organ of vertebrates that secretes bile and causes changes in the blood (e g by acting upon blood sugar) **b** any of various large digestive glands of invertebrates **2** the liver of an animal (e g a calf or pig) eaten as food **3** a greyish reddish brown colour

²**liver** *n* one who lives, esp in a specified way

livid /'lɪvɪd/ *adj* **1** discoloured by bruising **2** ashen, pallid **3** reddish **4** very angry; enraged – **~ly** *adv*

¹**living** /'lɪvɪŋ/ *adj* **1a** having life; alive **b** existing in use **2** true to life; exact – esp in the *living image of* **3** – used as an intensive **4** *of feelings, ideas, etc* full of power and force

²**living** *n* **1** the condition of being alive **2** a manner of life **3** means of subsistence; a livelihood

living room *n* a room in a residence used for everyday activities

lizard /'lɪzəd/ *n* any of a suborder of reptiles distinguished from the snakes by 2 pairs of well differentiated functional limbs (which may be lacking in burrowing forms), external ears, and eyes with movable lids

¹**load** /ləʊd/ *n* **1a** an amount, esp large or heavy, that is (to be) carried, supported, or borne **b** the quantity that can be carried at 1 time by a specified means – often in combination **2** the forces to which a structure is subjected **3** a burden of responsibility, anxiety, etc **4** external resistance overcome by a machine or other source of power **5** power output (e g of a power plant) **6** the amount of work to be performed by a person, machine, etc **7** a large quantity or amount; a lot – usu pl with sing. meaning; *infml*

²**load** *v* **1a** to put a load in or on **b** to place in or on a means of conveyance **2** to encumber or oppress with sthg heavy, laborious, or disheartening; burden **3a** to weight or shape (dice) to fall unfairly **b** to charge with hidden implications; *also* to bias **4** to put a load or charge in a device or piece of equipment; esp to insert the charge in a firearm

¹**loaf** /ləʊf/ *n*, *pl* **loaves 1** a mass of bread often having a regular shape and standard weight **2** a shaped or moulded often symmetrical mass of food (e g sugar or chopped cooked meat) **3** *Br* head, brains – slang; esp in *use one's loaf*

²**loaf** *v* to spend time in idleness – **~er** *n*

¹**loan** /ləʊn/ *n* **1a** money lent at interest **b** sthg lent, usu for the borrower's temporary use **2** the grant of temporary use

²**loan** *v* to lend

loath, loth /ləʊθ/ unwilling, reluctant

loathe /ləʊð/ *v* to dislike greatly, often with disgust or intolerance – **-thing** *n*

loathsome /'ləʊðsəm/ *adj* giving rise to loathing; disgusting – **~ly** *adv* – **~ness** *n*

¹**lobby** /'lɒbi/ *n* **1** a porch or small entrance hall **2** an anteroom of a legislative chamber to which members go to vote during a division **3** *sing* or *pl in constr* a group of people engaged in lobbying

²**lobby** *v* to try to influence (e g a member of a legislative body) towards an action

lobster /'lɒbstə/ *n* any of a family of large edible 10-legged marine crustaceans that have stalked eyes, a pair of large claws, and a long abdomen

¹**local** /'ləʊkəl/ *adj* **1** (characteristic) of or belonging to a particular place; not general or widespread **2a** primarily serving the needs of a particular limited district **b** *of a public conveyance* making all the stops on a route – **~ize** *v* – **~ly** *adv*

²**local** *n*, *Br* the neighbourhood pub

locate /ləʊ'keɪt/ *v* **1** to determine or indicate the place, site, or limits of **2** to set or establish in a particular spot – **-d** *adj*

location /ləʊ'keɪʃən/ *n* **1** a particular place or position **2** a place outside a studio where a (part of a) picture is filmed

¹**lock** /lɒk/ *n* a curl, tuft, etc of hair

²**lock** *n* **1** a fastening that can be opened and often closed only by means of a particular key or combination **2** an enclosed section of waterway (e g a canal) which has gates at each end and in which the water level can be raised or lowered to move boats from one level to another **3** a hold in wrestling secured on a usu specified body part **4** *chiefly Br* the maximum extent to which the front wheels of a vehicle can be turned

³**lock** *v* **1a** to fasten the lock of **b** to make fast (as if) with a lock **2a** to shut in or out or make secure or inaccessible (as if) by means of locks **b** to hold fast or inactive; fix in a particular situation or method of operation **3a** to make fast by the interlacing or interlocking of parts **b** to grapple in combat; *also* to bind closely – often pass – **~able** *adj*

locomotive /ˌləʊkə'məʊtɪv/ *n* an engine that moves under its own power; esp one that moves railway carriages and wagons

locust /'ləʊkəst/ *n* **1** a migratory grasshopper that often travels in vast swarms stripping the areas passed of all vegetation 2 any of various hard-wooded leguminous trees

lodge /lodʒ/ *v* **1a** to provide temporary, esp rented, accommodation for **b** to establish or settle in a place **2** to serve as a receptacle for; contain, house **3** to fix in place **4** to deposit for safeguard or preservation **5** to place or vest (e g power), esp in a source, means, or agent **6** to lay (e g a complaint) before authority

lodge *n* **1** the meeting place of a branch of an esp fraternal organization **2** a house set apart for residence in a particular season (e g the hunting season) **3a** a house orig for the use of a gamekeeper, caretaker, porter, etc **b** a porter's room (e g at the entrance to a college, block of flats, etc) **c** the house where the head of a university college lives, esp in Cambridge **4** a den or lair of an animal or a group of animals (e g beavers or otters)

lodger /'lodʒə'/ *n* one who occupies a rented room in another's house

lodging /'lodʒɪŋ/ *n* **1** a place to live; a dwelling **2a** a temporary place to stay **b** a rented room or rooms for residing in, usu in a private house rather than a hotel – usu pl with sing. meaning

loft /loft/ *n* **1** an attic **2a** a gallery in a church or hall **b** an upper floor in a barn or warehouse used for storage – sometimes in combination

loft *v* to propel through the air or into space – ~ed *adj*

lofty /'lofti/ *adj* **1** having a haughty overbearing manner; supercilious **2a** elevated in character and spirit; noble **b** elevated in position; superior **3** impressively high – **-ily** *adv* – **-iness** *n*

log /log/ *n* **1a** usu bulky piece or length of unshaped timber (ready for sawing or for use as firewood) **2** an apparatus for measuring the rate of a ship's motion through the water **3a** the full nautical record of a ship's voyage **b** the full record of a flight by an aircraft

log *v* **1** to cut trees for timber **2** to enter details of or about in a log **3a** to move or attain (e g an indicated distance, speed, or time) as noted in a log **b** to have (an indicated record) to one's credit; achieve

log *n* a logarithm

logarithm /'logərɪðəm/ *n* the exponent that indicates the power to which a number is raised to produce a given number – **~ic** *adj* – **~ically** *adv*

logic /'lodʒɪk/ *n* **1a** a science that deals with the formal principles and structure of thought and reasoning **b** a particular mode of reasoning viewed as valid or faulty **2** the interrelation or sequence of facts or events when seen as inevitable or predictable – **~al** *adj* – **~ally** *adv*

loiter /'loɪtə'/ *v* **1** to remain in an area for no obvious reason **2** to dawdle – **~er** *n*

lone /ləʊn/ *adj* **1** only, sole **2** situated alone or separately; isolated **3** having no company; solitary – *fml*

lonely /'ləʊnli/ *adj* **1** cut off from others; solitary **2** not frequented by people; desolate **3** sad from being alone or without friends – **-liness** *n*

¹long /loŋ/ *adj* **1a** extending for a considerable distance **b** having greater length than usual **2** having a specified length **3** extending over a considerable or specified time **4** containing a large or specified number of items or units **5** reaching or extending a considerable distance **6** *of betting odds* greatly differing in the amounts wagered on each side

²long *adv* **1** for or during a long or specified time **2** at a point of time far before or after a specified moment or event **3** after or beyond a specified time

³long *v* to feel a strong desire or craving, esp *for* sthg not likely to be attained – **~ing** *n*, *adj* – **~ingly** *adv*

longitude /'londʒɪtjuːd/ *n* the (time difference corresponding to) angular distance of a point on the surface of a celestial body, esp the earth, measured E or W from a prime meridian (e g that of Greenwich)

long-winded *adj* tediously long in speaking or writing

¹look /lʊk/ *v* **1a** to use the power of sight; esp to make a visual search *for* **b** to direct one's attention **c** to direct the eyes **2** to have the appearance of being; appear, seem **3** to have a specified outlook

²look *n* **1a** the act of looking **b** a glance **2a** a facial expression **b** (attractive) physical appearance – usu pl with sing. meaning **3** the state or form in which sthg appears

look after *v* to take care of

lookout /'lʊk-aʊt/ *n* **1** one engaged in keeping watch **2** a place or structure affording a wide view for observation **3** a careful looking or watching **4** a matter of care or concern **5** *chiefly Br* a future possibility; a prospect

look out *v* **1** to take care – often imper **2** to keep watching

¹loom /luːm/ *n* a frame or machine for weaving together yarns or threads into cloth

²loom *v* **1** to come into sight indistinctly, in enlarged or distorted and menacing form, often as a result of atmospheric conditions **2** to appear in an impressively great or exaggerated form

¹loop /luːp/ *n* **1 a** (partially) closed figure that has a curved outline surrounding a central opening **2** a zigzag-shaped intrauterine contraceptive device **3** a ring or curved piece used to form a fastening or handle **4** a piece of film or magnetic tape whose ends are spliced together so as to reproduce the same material continuously

²loop *v* **1a** to make a loop in, on, or about **b** to fasten with a loop **2** to form a loop with

loophole /'luːphəʊl/ *n* **1** a small opening through which missiles, firearms, etc may be discharged or light and air admitted **2** a means of escape; esp an ambiguity or omission in a text through which its intent may be evaded

¹loose /luːs/ *adj* **1a** not rigidly fastened or securely attached **b** having worked partly free from attachments **c** not tight-fitting **2a** free from a state of confinement, restraint, or obligation **b** not brought together in a bundle, container, or binding **3** not dense, close, or compact in structure or arrangement **4a** lacking in (power of) restraint **b** dissolute, promiscuous **5** not tightly drawn or stretched; slack **6a** lacking in precision, exactness, or care **b** permitting freedom of interpretation – ~ly *adv* – ~n v – ~ness n

²loose *v* **1a** to let loose; release **b** to free from restraint **2** to make loose; untie **3** to cast loose; detach **4** to let fly; discharge (e g a bullet)

³loose *adv* in a loose manner; loosely

¹loot /luːt/ *n* **1** goods, usu of considerable value, taken in war; spoils **2** sthg taken illegally (e g by force or deception)

²loot *v* to seize and carry away (sthg) by force or illegally, esp in war or public disturbance – ~er n

¹lord /lɔːd/ *n* **1** one having power and authority over others **2** *cap* **a** God **b** Jesus – often + *Our* **3** a man of rank or high position: e g **a** a feudal tenant holding land directly from the king **b** a British nobleman **4** *pl* the House of Lords

²lord *v* to act like a lord; *esp* to put on airs – usu + *it*

lorry /'lori/ *n*, *Br* a large motor vehicle for carrying loads by road

lose /luːz/ *v* **lost 1** to miss from one's possession or from a customary or supposed place; *also* to fail to find **2** to suffer deprivation of; part with, esp in an unforeseen or accidental manner **3** to suffer loss through the death of or final separation from (sby) **4a** to fail to use; let slip by **b** to be defeated in (a contest for) **c** to fail to catch with the senses or the mind **5** to fail to keep or maintain **6** to fail to keep in sight or in mind **7** to free oneself from; get rid of **8** to run slow by the amount of – used with reference to a timepiece

loss /lɒs/ *n* **1a** the act or an instance of losing possession **b** the harm or privation resulting from loss or separation **2** a person, thing, or amount lost; esp *pl* killed, wounded, or captured soldiers **3a** failure to gain, win, obtain, or use sthg **b** an amount by which cost exceeds revenue **4** decrease in amount, size, or degree **5** destruction, ruin

lost /lɒst/ *adj* **1a** unable to find the way **b** bewildered, helpless **2** ruined or destroyed physically or morally **3a** no longer possessed **b** no longer known **4** rapt, absorbed

lot /lɒt/ *n* **1** an object used as a counter in deciding a question by chance **2** (the use of lots as a means of making) a choice **3a** sthg that falls to sby by lot; a share **b** one's way of life or worldly fate; fortune **4** a film studio and its adjoining property **5** an article or a

number of articles offered as 1 item (e g in an auction sale) **6a** *sing or pl in constr* a number of associated people; a set (e g you *lot*) **b** a kind, sort – chiefly in a *bad lot* **7** a considerable amount or number – often pl with sing. meaning **8** *chiefly Br* the whole amount or number (e g ate up the whole *lot*) *USE (6a&8)* infml – chiefly infml

lottery /'lotəri/ *n* **1** (a way of raising money by the sale or) the distribution of numbered tickets some of which are later randomly selected to entitle the holder to a prize **2** an event or affair whose outcome is (apparently) decided by chance

loud /laʊd/ *adj* **1** marked by or producing a high volume of sound **2** clamorous, noisy **3** obtrusive or offensive in appearance; flashy – ~ly *adv*

loudspeaker /,laʊd'spiːkə, 'laʊd-,spiːkə'/ *n* an electromechanical device that converts electrical energy into acoustic energy and that is used to reproduce audible sounds

¹lounge /laʊndʒ/ *v* to act or move idly or lazily; loll – ~r n

²lounge *n* **1** a room in a private house for sitting in **2** a room in a public building providing comfortable seating; *also* a waiting room (e g at an airport)

lour /laʊə/ *also* **lower** *v* **1** to look sullen; frown **2** to become dark, gloomy and threatening – **lour** n

¹love /lʌv/ *n* **1a** strong affection for another **b** attraction based on sexual desire **2** warm interest in, enjoyment of, or attraction to sthg **3a** the object of interest and enjoyment **b** a person who is loved; a dear (one) **4** unselfish loyal and benevolent concern for the good of another **5** a god or personification of love **6** an amorous episode; a love affair **7** a score of zero in tennis, squash, etc **8** sexual intercourse – euph

²love *v* **1** to hold dear; cherish **2a** to feel a lover's passion, devotion, or tenderness for **b** to have sexual intercourse with **3** to like or desire actively; take pleasure in **4** to thrive in – **-vable** *adj*

¹lovely /'lʌvli/ *adj* **1** delicately or delightfully beautiful **2** very pleasing; fine – **-liness** n

²lovely *n* a beautiful woman – infml

lover /'lʌvə'/ *n* **1a** a person in love **b** a man with whom a woman has sexual relations, esp outside marriage **c** *pl* **2** people in love with each other; *esp* **2** people who habitually have sexual relations **2** a devotee

¹low /ləʊ/ *v or n* (to make) the deep sustained throat sound characteristic of esp a cow

²low *adj* **1** not measuring much from the base to the top; not high **2a** situated or passing below the normal level or below the base of measurement **b** marking a nadir or bottom **3** *of sound* not shrill or loud; soft **4** near the horizon **5** humble in character or status **6a** weak **b** depressed **7** of less than usual degree, size, amount, or value **8a** lacking dignity or formality **b** morally reprehensible **c** coarse, vulgar **9** unfavourable, disparaging 10 *of a gear* designed for slow speed – ~**ness** *n*

³**low** *n* sthg low: e g **a** a depth, nadir **b** a region of low atmospheric pressure

⁴**low** *adv* at or to a low place, altitude, or degree

¹**lower** /'ləʊə/ *adj* 1 relatively low in position, rank, or order 2 less advanced in the scale of evolutionary development 3 constituting the popular, more representative, and often (e g in Britain) more powerful branch of a legislative body consisting of 2 houses 4a beneath the earth's surface **b** *often cap* being an earlier division of the named geological period or series

²**lower** /'ləʊə/ *v* 1a to cause to descend **b** to reduce the height of 2a to reduce in value, amount, degree, strength, or pitch **b** to degrade; *also* to humble

¹**lowly** /'ləʊli/ *adv* 1 in a humble or meek manner 2 in a low position, manner, or degree

²**lowly** *adj* 1 humble and modest in manner or spirit 2 low in the scale of biological or cultural evolution 3 ranking low in a social or economic hierarchy – **-liness** *n*

loyal /'lɔɪəl/ *adj* unswerving in allegiance (e g to a person, country, or cause) – ~**ly** *adv*, *adv*, *n* ~**ty** *n*

loyalist /'lɔɪəlɪst/ *n* sby loyal to a government or sovereign, esp in time of revolt

LP *n* a gramophone record designed to be played at 33⅓ revolutions per minute and typically having a diameter of 12in (30.5cm) and a playing time of 20–25min

lubricate /'lu:brɪkeɪt/ *v* 1 to make smooth or slippery 2 to act as a lubricant – **-cation** *n* – **-cator** *n*

luck /lʌk/ *n* 1 whatever good or bad events happen to a person by chance 2 the tendency for a person to be consistently fortunate or unfortunate 3 success as a result of good fortune

lucky /'lʌki/ *adj* having, resulting from, or bringing good luck – **-ily** *adv* – **-iness** *n*

luggage /'lʌgɪdʒ/ *n* (cases, bags, etc containing) the belongings that accompany a traveller

lukewarm /,luː'kwɔːm/ *adj* 1 moderately warm; tepid 2 lacking conviction; indifferent

lullaby /'lʌləbaɪ/ *n* a song to quieten children or lull them to sleep

¹**lumber** /'lʌmbə/ *v* to move heavily or clumsily

²**lumber** /'lʌmbə/ *n* 1 surplus or disused articles (e g furniture) that are stored away 2 *NAm* timber or logs, esp when dressed for use

³**lumber** *v* to clutter, encumber

luminous /'luːmɪnəs/ *adj* 1 emitting or full of light; bright 2 easily understood; *also* explaining clearly – ~**ly** *adv* – **-nosity** *n*

¹**lump** /lʌmp/ *n* 1 a usu compact piece or mass of indefinite size and shape 2 an abnormal swelling 3 a heavy thickset person 4 *Br* *the* whole group of casual nonunion building workers

²**lump** *v* to group without discrimination

³**lump** *adj* not divided into parts; entire

⁴**lump** *v* to put up with – chiefly in *like it or lump it*

lunatic /'luːnətɪk/ *adj* 1a insane **b** of or designed for the care of insane people 2 wildly foolish

lunch /lʌntʃ/ **luncheon** *n* a midday meal – **lunch** *v*

lung /lʌŋ/ *n* 1 either of the usu paired organs in the chest that constitute the basic respiratory organ of air-breathing vertebrates 2 any of various respiratory organs of invertebrates

lurk /lɜːk/ *v* 1 to lie hidden, esp with evil intent 2 to move furtively or inconspicuously

¹**lush** /lʌʃ/ *adj* 1 producing or covered by luxuriant growth 2 opulent, sumptuous

²**lush** *n, chiefly NAm* a heavy drinker; an alcoholic

¹**lust** /lʌst/ *n* 1 strong sexual desire, esp as opposed to love 2 an intense longing; a craving

²**lust** *v* to have an intense (sexual) desire or craving

luxury /'lʌkʃəri/ *n* 1 great ease or comfort based on habitual or liberal use of expensive items without regard to cost 2a sthg desirable but costly or difficult to obtain **b** sthg relatively expensive adding to pleasure or comfort but not indispensable

lynch /lɪntʃ/ *v* to put to death illegally by mob action

M

macaroni /,mækə'rəʊni/ *n* 1 pasta made from hard wheat and shaped in hollow tubes that are wider in diameter than spaghetti 2 an English dandy of the late 18th and early 19th c who affected continental ways

¹**machine** /mə'ʃiːn/ *n* 1a a combination of parts that transmit forces, motion, and energy one to another in a predetermined manner **b** an instrument (e g a lever or pulley) designed to transmit or modify the application of power, force, or motion **c** a combination of mechanically, electrically, or electronically operated parts for performing a task 2 a person or organization that acts like a machine

²**machine** *v* 1 to shape, finish, or operate on by a machine 2 to act on, produce, or perform a particular operation or activity on, using a machine; *esp* to sew using a sewing machine

machinery /mə'ʃiːnəri/ *n* 1a machines in general or as a functioning unit **b** the working parts of a machine 2 the means by which sthg is kept in action or a desired result is obtained 3 the system or organization by which an activity or process is controlled

mackintosh /'mækɪntɒʃ/ *also* **macintosh** *n, chiefly Br* a raincoat

mad /mæd/ *adj* 1 mentally disordered; insane 2 utterly foolish; senseless 3 carried away by intense anger 4 carried away by enthusiasm or desire 5 intensely excited or distraught; frantic 6 marked by intense and often chaotic hectic activity

madam /'mædəm/ *n* 1 a lady – used without a name as a form of respectful or polite address to a woman 2 a female brothel keeper 3 a conceited pert young lady or girl

madden /'mædn/ *v* 1 to drive mad; craze 2 to exasperate, enrage

made /meɪd/ *adj* 1 assembled or prepared, esp by putting together various ingredients 2 assured of success – infml

madly /'mædli/ *adv* to a degree suggestive of madness: e g a with great energy; frantically b without restraint; passionately

madness /'mædnɪs/ *n* 1 insanity 2 extreme folly

magazine /ˌmægə'ziːn/ *n* 1 a storeroom for arms, ammunition, or explosives 2a a usu illustrated periodical, bound in paper covers, containing miscellaneous pieces by different authors b a television or radio programme containing a number of usu topical items, often without a common theme 3 a supply chamber: e g a a holder from which cartridges can be fed into a gun chamber automatically b a lightproof chamber for films or plates in a camera or for film in a film projector

¹magic /'mædʒɪk/ *n* 1 (rites, incantations, etc used in) the art of invoking supernatural powers to control natural forces by means of charms, spells, etc 2a an extraordinary power or influence producing results which defy explanation b sthg that seems to cast a spell 3 the art of producing illusions by sleight of hand – ~al *adj*

²magic *adj* 1 of, being, or used in magic 2 having seemingly supernatural qualities 3 – used as a general term of approval; infml

³magic *v* -ck- to affect, influence, or take away (as if) by magic

magician /mə'dʒɪʃən/ *n* 1 one skilled in magic 2 a conjurer

magistrate /'mædʒɪstreɪt, -strɪt/ *n* a civil legislative or executive official: e g a a principal official exercising governmental powers b a paid or unpaid local judicial officer who presides in a magistrates' court – **-acy** *n, n,* – **-terial** *adj*

magnet /'mægnɪt/ *n* 1 a body (of iron, steel, etc) that has an (artificially imparted) magnetic field external to itself and attracts iron 2 sthg that attracts – **~ic** *adj* – **~ically** *adv* – **~ism** *n* – **~ize** *v*

magnificent /mæg'nɪfɪsənt/ *adj* 1 marked by stately grandeur and splendour 2a sumptuous in structure and adornment b strikingly beautiful or impressive 3 sublime 4 exceptionally fine or excellent – **-cence** *n* – **~ly** *adv*

magnify /'mægnɪfaɪ/ *v* 1 to have the power of causing objects to appear larger than they are 2 to enlarge in fact or in appearance – **-fier** *n*

magnifying glass *n* a single optical lens for magnifying

magpie /'mægpaɪ/ *n* 1 any of numerous birds of the crow family with a very long tail and black-and-white plumage 2 one who chatters noisily 3 one who collects objects in a random fashion

maid /meɪd/ *n* 1 an unmarried girl or woman; *also* a female virgin 2 a female servant

¹maiden /'meɪdn/ *n* 1 an unmarried girl or woman 2 **maiden, maiden over** an over in cricket in which no runs are credited to the batsman

²maiden *adj* 1a(1) not married (2) virgin b *of a female animal* never having borne young or been mated c that has not been altered from its original state 2 being the first or earliest of its kind

maiden name *n* the surname of a woman prior to marriage

¹mail /meɪl/ *n* 1 the postal matter that makes up 1 particular consignment 2 a conveyance that transports mail 3 a postal system

²mail *v* to post

³mail *n* 1 armour made of interlocking metal rings, chains, or sometimes plates 2 a hard enclosing covering of an animal

⁴mail *v* to clothe (as if) with mail

mail order *n* an order for goods that is received and fulfilled by post

¹main /meɪn/ *n* 1 physical strength – in with might and main 2 the chief or essential part – chiefly in in the main 3 the chief pipe, duct, or cable of a public service (e g gas, electricity, or water) – often *pl* with *sing.* meaning 4 the high sea

²main *adj* 1 chief, principal 2 fully exerted 3 connected with or located near the mainmast or mainsail

mainland /'meɪnlənd/ *n* the largest land area of a continent, country, etc, considered in relation to smaller offshore islands

mainstream /'meɪnstriːm/ *n* a prevailing current or direction of activity or influence

maintain /meɪn'teɪn, mən-/ *v* 1 to keep in an existing state (e g of operation, repair, efficiency, or validity) 2 to sustain against opposition or danger 3 to continue or persevere in 4 to support, sustain, or provide for 5 to affirm (as if) in argument – **~able** *adj*

maintenance /'meɪntənəns/ *n* 1 maintaining or being maintained 2 (payment for) the upkeep of property or equipment 3 payments for the support of one spouse by another, esp of a woman by a man, pending or following legal separation or divorce

maize /meɪz/ *n* (the ears or edible seeds of) a tall widely cultivated cereal grass bearing seeds on elongated ears

majesty /'mædʒɪsti/ *n* 1 sovereign

power **2a** impressive bearing or aspect **b** greatness or splendour of quality or character – **-tic** *adj* – **-tically** *adv*

¹**major** /'meɪdʒə/ *adj* **1a** greater in importance, size, rank, or degree **b** of considerable importance **2** notable or conspicuous in effect or scope **3** involving serious risk to life; serious **4** *esp of a scale* having semitones between the third and fourth and the seventh and eighth notes

²**major** *n* **1** a major musical interval, scale, key, or mode **2** a middle-ranking officer in the army

majority /mə'dʒɒrˌti/ *n* **1** the (status of one who has attained the) age at which full legal rights and responsibilities are acquired **2** a number greater than half of a total **3** the greatest in number of 2 or more groups constituting a whole; *specif* (the excess of votes over its rival obtained by) a group having sufficient votes to obtain control **4** the military office, rank, or commission of a major

¹**make** /meɪk/ *v* **made** *v* **1a** to create or produce (for someone) by work or action **b** to cause; bring about **2** to formulate in the mind **3** to put together from ingredients or components – often + *up* **4** to compute or estimate to be **5a** to assemble and set alight the materials for (a fire) **b** to renew or straighten the bedclothes on (a bed) **6a** to cause to be or become **b** to cause (sthg) to appear or seem to; represent as **c(1)** to change, transform **(2)** to produce as an end product **7a** to enact, establish **b** to draft or produce a version of **8** to perform; carry out **9** to put forward for acceptance **10** to cause to act in a specified way; compel **11a** to amount to; count as **b** to combine to form **12** to be capable of becoming or of serving as **13** to reach, attain – often + *it* **14** to gain (e g money) by working, trading, dealing, etc **15a** to act so as to acquire **b** to score (points, runs, etc) in a game or sport

²**make** *n* **1** the manner or style in which sthg is constructed **b** a place or origin of manufacture; a brand **2** the physical, mental, or moral constitution of a person

make out *v* **1** to complete (e g a printed form or document) by writing information in appropriate spaces **2** to find or grasp the meaning of **3** to claim or pretend to be true **4** to identify (e g by sight or hearing) with difficulty or effort

makeshift /'meɪk,ʃɪft/ *adj or n* (being) a crude and temporary expedient

make-up *n* **1** the way in which the parts of sthg are put together **2a** cosmetics (e g lipstick and mascara) applied, esp to the face, to give colour or emphasis **b** materials (e g wigs and cosmetics) used for special costuming (e g for a play)

make up *v* **1** to invent (e g a story), esp in order to deceive **2** to arrange typeset matter into (columns or pages) for printing **3** to wrap or fasten up **4** to become reconciled; *also* to attempt to

ingratiate **5** to compensate *for* **6** to put on costumes or make-up (e g for a play)

malady /'mælədi/ *n* a disease or disorder

¹**male** /meɪl/ *adj* **1a(1)** of or being the sex that produces sperm or spermatozoa by which the eggs of a female are made fertile **(2)** *of a plant or flower* having stamens but no ovaries **b(1)** (characteristic) of the male sex **(2)** made up of male individuals **2** designed for fitting into a corresponding hollow part

²**male** *n* a male person, animal, or plant

malice /'mælɪs/ *n* conscious desire to harm; *esp* a premeditated desire to commit a crime – **-cious** *adj*

¹**malign** /mə'laɪn/ *adj* **1** harmful in nature, influence, or effect **2** bearing or showing (vicious) ill will or hostility – **-ity** *n*

²**malign** *v* to utter injuriously (false) reports about; speak ill of

¹**malt** /mɔːlt, mɒlt/ *n* **1** grain softened in water, allowed to germinate, then roasted and used esp in brewing and distilling **2** unblended malt whisky produced in a particular area

mammal /'mæml/ *n* any of a class of higher vertebrates comprising humans and all other animals that have mammary glands and nourish their young with milk

¹**mammoth** /'mæməθ/ *n* any of numerous extinct large hairy elephants

²**mammoth** *adj* of very great size

¹**man** /mæn/ *n, pl* **men** **1a(1)** a human being; *esp* an adult male as distinguished from a woman or child **(2)** a husband – esp in *man and wife* **b** the human race **c** any ancestor of modern man **d** one possessing the qualities associated with manhood (e g courage and strength) **e** a fellow, chap – used interjectionally **2a** *pl* the members of (the ranks of) a military force **b** *pl* the working force as distinguished from the employer and usu the management **3** any of the pieces moved by each player in chess, draughts, etc – ∼**like** *adj* – ∼**ly** *adj* – ∼**liness** *n*

²**man** *v* **1** to supply with the man or men necessary **2** to take up station by (e g in 'man the pumps!')

manage /'mænɪdʒ/ *v* **1a** to make and keep submissive **b** to use (e g money) economically **2** to succeed in handling (e g a difficult situation or person) **3** to succeed in accomplishing **4** to conduct the running of (esp a business); *also* to have charge of (e g a sports team or athlete)

management /'mænɪdʒmənt/ *n* **1** the act or art of managing **2** *sing or pl in constr* the collective body of those who manage or direct an enterprise

manager /'mænɪdʒə/ *fem* **manageress** *n* **1** one who conducts business affairs **2** sby who directs a sports team, player, entertainer, etc

mane /meɪn/ *n* **1** long thick hair growing about the neck of a horse, male lion, etc 2 long thick hair on a person's head

¹mangle /'mæŋgəl/ v 1 to hack or crush (as if) by repeated blows 2 to spoil by poor work, errors, etc

²mangle v or n (to pass through) a machine with rollers for squeezing water from and pressing laundry

manhood /'mænhʊd/ n 1 manly qualities 2 the condition of being an adult male as distinguished from a child or female

mania /'meiniə/ n 1 abnormal excitement and euphoria marked by mental and physical hyperactivity and disorganization of behaviour 2 excessive or unreasonable enthusiasm – often in combination

maniac /'meiniæk/ n one who is or acts as if (violently) insane; a lunatic – ~al adj – ~ally adv

manifesto /,mæni'festəʊ/ n a public declaration of intentions, esp a political party before an election

manipulate /mə'nipjʊleit/ v 1 to handle or operate, esp skilfully 2a to manage or use skilfully b to control or influence by artful, unfair, or insidious means, esp to one's own advantage 3 to examine and treat (a fracture, sprain, etc) by moving bones into the proper position manually – -lative adj – -lation n

mankind /,mæn'kaind/ n sing but sing or pl in constr the human race

manner /'mænə/ n 1 a kind, sort; also sorts 2a the mode or method in which sthg is done or happens b a method of artistic execution; a style 3 pl social behaviour evaluated as to politeness; esp conduct indicating good background 4 characteristic or distinctive bearing, air, or deportment

mannered /'mænəd/ adj 1 having manners of a specified kind – usu in combination 2 having an artificial or stilted character

¹manoeuvre /mə'nu:və/ n 1a a military or naval movement b a (large-scale) training exercise for the armed forces 2 an intended and controlled deviation from a straight and level flight path in the operation of an aircraft 3 a skilful or dexterous movement 4 an adroit and clever management of affairs, often using deception

²manoeuvre v 1 to perform a military or naval manoeuvre (to secure an advantage) 2 to perform a manoeuvre 3 to cause (e g troops) to execute manoeuvres 4 to manipulate with adroitness – -vrer n

manslaughter /'mæn,slɔːtə/ n the unlawful killing of sby without malicious intent

mantelpiece /'mæntlpiːs/, mantel n an ornamental structure round a fireplace

¹manual /'mænjʊəl/ adj 1 of or involving the hands 2 requiring or using physical skill and energy 3 worked or done by hand and not by machine or automatically – ~ly adv

²manual n 1 a book of instructions; a handbook 2 a keyboard for the hands; specif any of the several keyboards of an organ that control separate divisions of the instrument

¹manufacture /,mænjʊ'fæktʃə/ n 1 the esp large-scale making of wares by hand or by machinery 2 the act or process of producing sthg

²manufacture v 1 to make (materials) into a product suitable for use 2 to make (wares) from raw materials by hand or by machinery, esp on a large scale 3 to invent, fabricate

manure /mə'njʊə/ n material that fertilizes land; esp the faeces of domestic animals

manuscript /'mænjʊskript/ n or adj (a composition or document) written by hand or typed as distinguished from a printed copy

¹many /'meni/ adj more /mɔː/; most /mohst/ 1 consisting of or amounting to a large but unspecified number 2 being one of a large number (e g many a man)

²many pron pl in constr a large number of people or things

³many n pl in constr 1 a large but indefinite number 2 the great majority

⁴many adv to a considerable degree or amount; far – with plurals

¹map /mæp/ n 1 a representation, usu on a flat surface, of (part of) the earth's surface, the celestial sphere, etc 2 sthg that represents with a clarity suggestive of a map

²map v 1 to make a map of b to survey in order to make a map 2 to plan in detail – often + out

marathon /'mærəθən/ n 1 a long-distance race; specif a foot race of 26mi 385yd (about 42.2km) that is contested on an open course in major athletics championships 2a an endurance contest b an event or activity characterized by great length or concentrated effort

¹marble /'mɑːbəl/ n 1a (more or less) crystallized limestone that can be highly polished and is used esp in building and sculpture b a sculpture or carving made of marble 2 a little ball made of a hard substance, esp glass, and used in children's games 3 pl elements of common sense; esp sanity – infml

²marble v marbling to give a veined or mottled appearance to (e g the edges of a book)

¹march /mɑːtʃ/ n, often cap a border region; esp a tract of land between 2 countries whose ownership is disputed – usu pl

²march v 1 to move along steadily, usu in step with others 2a to move in a direct purposeful manner b to make steady progress 3 to cause to march 4 to cover by marching – ~er n

³march n 1a the action of marching b the distance covered within a specified period of time by marching c a regular measured stride or rhythmic step used in marching d steady forward movement 2 a musical composition with a

strongly accentuated beat and is designed or suitable to accompany marching

March *n* the 3rd month of the Gregorian calendar

mare /mea⁰/ *n* a female equine animal, esp when fully mature or of breeding age; *esp* a female horse

margarine /ˌmɑːdʒəˈriːn, ˌmɑːgə-/ *n* a substitute for butter made usu from vegetable oils churned with ripened skimmed milk to a smooth emulsion

¹**margin** /ˈmɑːdʒɪn/ *n* **1** the part of a page outside the main body of printed or written text **2** the outside limit and adjoining surface of sthg **3a** a spare amount or measure or degree allowed (e g in case of error) **b(1)** a bare minimum below which or an extreme limit beyond which sthg becomes impossible or is no longer desirable **(2)** the limit below which economic activity cannot be continued under normal conditions **4** the difference between net sales and the cost of merchandise sold **5** measure or degree of difference

²**margin** *v* to provide with a border

¹**marine** /məˈriːn/ *adj* **1** of or (living) in the sea **2** of or used in the navigation or commerce of the sea

²**marine** *n* **1** seagoing ships (of a specified nationality or class) **2a** any of a class of soldiers serving on shipboard or in close association with a naval force **b** a soldier who serves on a ship or in the navy

mariner /ˈmærɪnə⁰/ *n* a seaman, sailor

marital /ˈmærɪtl/ *adj* of marriage – ~ly *adv*

¹**mark** /mɑːk/ *n* **1a** sthg (e g a line, notch, or fixed object) designed to record position **b** a target **c** the starting line or position in a track event **d** a goal or desired object **2a(1)** a sign or token **(2)** an impression on the surface of sthg; *esp* a scratch, stain, etc that spoils the appearance of a surface **(3)** a distinguishing characteristic **b** a symbol used for identification or indication of ownership **c** a written or printed symbol **d** *cap* – used with a numeral to designate a particular model of a weapon or machine **e** a point or level (reached) **3** an assessment of (educational) merits **4** an object of attack; *specif* a victim of a swindle – *infml*

²**mark** *v* **1a(1)** to fix or trace *out* the limits of **(2)** to plot the course of **b** to set apart (as if) by a line or boundary – usu + *off* **2a(1)** to designate, identify or indicate (as if) by a mark **(2)** to make or leave a mark on **(3)** to add appropriate symbols, characters, or other marks to or on – usu + *up* **b(1)** to register, record **(2)** to evaluate by marks **c(1)** to characterize, distinguish **(2)** to be the occasion of (sthg notable); to indicate as a particular time **3** to take notice of **4** *Br* to stay close to (an opposing player) in hockey, soccer, etc so as to hinder the getting or play of the ball **5** to become or make sthg stained, scratched, etc **6** to evaluate sthg by marks – ~er *n*

³**mark** *n often cap* (a note or coin representing) the basic money unit of either East or West Germany

Mark *n* the 2nd Gospel in the New Testament

¹**market** /ˈmɑːkɪt/ *n* **1a** a meeting together of people for the purpose of trade, by private purchase and sale **b** an open space, building, etc where a market (e g for trading in provisions or livestock) is held **2a** (a geographical area or section of the community in which there is) demand for commodities **b** commercial activity; extent of trading **c** an opportunity for selling **d** the area of economic activity in which the forces of supply and demand affect prices

²**market** *v* **1** to deal in a market **2** to sell – ~able *adj* – ~ability – ~er, eer *n*

marketplace /ˈmɑːkɪtpleɪs/ *n* **1** an open place in a town where markets are held **2** somewhere where there is a demand of commodities

market research *n* research (e g the collection and analysis of information about consumer preferences) dealing with the patterns or state of demand (for a particular product) in a market

marksman /ˈmɑːksmən/, *fem* **markswoman** *n* a person skilled in hitting a mark or target – ~ship *n*

¹**marmalade** /ˈmɑːməleɪd/ *n* a clear sweetened preserve made from oranges, lemons, etc and usu containing pieces of fruit peel

²**marmalade** *adj, esp of cats* brownish orange

¹**maroon** /məˈruːn/ *v* **1** to abandon on a desolate island or coast **2** to isolate in a helpless state

²**maroon** *n* **1** a dark brownish red colour **2** an explosive rocket used esp as a distress signal

Maroon *n* (a descendant of) a fugitive Negro slave of the W Indies and Guiana in the 17th and 18th c

marriage /ˈmærɪdʒ/ *n* **1a** the state of being or mutual relation of husband and wife **b** the institution whereby a man and a woman are joined in a special kind of social and legal dependence **2** an act or the rite of marrying; *esp* the wedding ceremony **3** an intimate or close union

married /ˈmærɪd/ *adj* **1a** joined in marriage **b** of married people **2** united, joined

marrow /ˈmærəʊ/ *n* **1a** a soft tissue that fills the cavities and porous part of most bones and contains many blood vessels **b** the substance of the spinal cord **2** the inmost, best, or essential part; the core **3** *chiefly Br* a vegetable marrow

marry /ˈmærɪ/ *v* **1a** to give in marriage **b** to take as spouse **c** to perform the ceremony of marriage for **d** to obtain by marriage **2** to bring together closely, harmoniously, and usu permanently **3a** to take a spouse **b** to become husband and wife

marsh /mɑːʃ/ *n* (an area of) soft wet

land usu covered with sedges, rushes, etc

martial /'mɑːʃəl/ adj of or suited to war or a warrior; also warlike

¹martyr /'mɑːtəʳ/ n 1 one who is put to death for adherence to a cause, esp a religion 2 a victim, esp of constant (self-inflicted) suffering

²martyr v 1 to put to death as a martyr 2 to inflict agonizing pain on

¹marvel /'mɑːvəl/ n one who or that which is marvellous

²marvel v to become filled with surprise, wonder, or amazed curiosity

marvellous /'mɑːvələs/ adj 1 causing wonder 2 of the highest kind or quality – ~ly adv

mascot /'mæskət/ n a person, animal, or object adopted as a (good luck) symbol

masculine /'mæskjʊlɪn/ adj 1a male b having qualities appropriate to a man 2 of, belonging to, or being the gender that normally includes most words or grammatical forms referring to males 3 having or occurring in a stressed final syllable

¹mask /mɑːsk/ n 1a a (partial) cover for the face used for disguise or protection b(1) a figure of a head worn on the stage in ancient times to identify the character (2) a grotesque false face worn at carnivals or in rituals c a copy of a face made by sculpting or by means of a mould 2a sthg that disguises or conceals; esp a pretence, facade b a translucent or opaque screen to cover part of the sensitive surface in taking or printing a photograph 3 a device covering the mouth and nose used a to promote breathing (e g by connection to an oxygen supply) b to remove noxious gas from air c to prevent breathing out of infective material (e g during surgery) 4 the head or face of a fox, dog, etc – ~ed adj

²mask v 1 to provide, cover, or conceal (as if) with a mask: e g a to make indistinct or imperceptible b to cover up 2 to cover for protection 3 to modify the shape of (e g a photograph) by means of a mask

¹masquerade /,mæskə'reɪd/ n a social gathering of people wearing masks and often fantastic costumes

²masquerade v 1 to disguise oneself; also to wear a disguise 2 to assume the appearance of sthg that one is not – usu + as – -rader n

¹mass /mæs, mɑːs/ n 1 cap the liturgy or a celebration of the Eucharist, esp in Roman Catholic and Anglo-Catholic churches 2 a musical setting of the Mass

²mass /mæs/ n 1a a quantity of matter or the form of matter that holds together in 1 body b(1) an (unbroken) expanse (2) the principal part or main body c the property of a body that is a measure of its inertia, causes it to have weight in a gravitational field, and is commonly taken as a measure of the amount of material it contains 2 a large quantity, amount, or number – often pl

with sing. meaning 3 pl the body of ordinary people as contrasted with the élite

³mass /mæs/ v to assemble in or collect into a mass

⁴mass /mæs/ adj 1a of, designed for, or consisting of the mass of the people b participated in by or affecting a large number of individuals c large scale 2 viewed as a whole; total

¹massacre /'mæsəkəʳ/ v 1 to kill (as if) in a massacre 2 to defeat severely – infml

²massacre n 1 the ruthless and indiscriminate killing of large numbers 2 complete defeat or destruction

massage /'mæsɑːʒ/ n (an act of) kneading, rubbing, etc of the body in order to relieve aches, tone muscles, give relaxation, etc – massage v

massive /'mæsɪv/ adj 1a large, solid, or heavy b impressively large or ponderous 2 large or impressive in scope or degree – ~ly adv – ~ness n

mass media n pl broadcasting, newspapers, and other means of communication designed to reach large numbers of people

mass-produce v to produce (goods) in large quantities by standardized mechanical processes – -duction n

¹mast /mɑːst/ n 1 a tall pole or structure rising from the keel or deck of a ship, esp for carrying sails 2 a vertical pole or lattice supporting a radio or television aerial

²mast n beechnuts, acorns, etc accumulated on the forest floor and often serving as food for animals (e g pigs)

¹master /'mɑːstəʳ/ n 1a(1) a male teacher (2) a person holding an academic degree higher than a bachelor's but lower than a doctor's b a workman qualified to teach apprentices c an artist, performer, player, etc of consummate skill 2a one having control or authority over another b one who or that which conquers or masters c a person qualified to command a merchant ship d an owner, esp of a slave or animal e an employer 3 cap a youth or boy too young to be called mister – used as a title 4 a presiding officer in an institution or society (e g a Masonic lodge) or at a function 5 an original from which copies (e g of film or gramophone records) can be made – ~y n

²master v 1 to become master of; overcome 2a to become skilled or proficient in the use of b to gain a thorough understanding of

³master adj 1 having chief authority; controlling 2 principal, main

masterpiece /'mɑːstəpiːs/ n a work done with extraordinary skill; esp the supreme creation of a type, period, or person

¹mat /mæt/ n 1a a piece of coarse usu woven, felted, or plaited fabric (e g of rushes or rope) used esp as a floor covering b a doormat c an often decorative piece of material used to protect a surface from heat, moisture, etc caused by an object placed on it 2 sthg made up of many intertwined or tangled strands

²**mat** v to become tangled or intertwined

³**mat** v, adj, or n (to) matt

¹**match** /mætʃ/ n **1a** one who or that which is equal to or able to contend with another **b** a person or thing exactly like another **2** two people, animals, or things that go well together **3** a contest between 2 or more teams or individuals **4a** a marriage union **b** a prospective partner in marriage

²**match** v **1** to be a counterpart or equal **2** to harmonize

³**match** n a short slender piece of wood, cardboard, etc tipped with a mixture that ignites when subjected to friction

¹**mate** /meɪt/ v or n (to) checkmate

²**mate** n **1a** an associate, companion – usu in combination **b** an assistant to a more skilled workman **2** a deck officer on a merchant ship ranking below the captain **3a** either of a pair: e g (1) either member of a breeding pair of animals (2) either of 2 matched objects **b** a marriage partner

³**mate** **1** to join or fit together **2** to copulate

maté /ˈmɑːteɪ/ **mate** n **1** a tealike aromatic beverage used chiefly in S America **2** (the leaves and shoots, used in making maté, of) a S American holly

¹**material** /məˈtɪərɪəl/ adj **1a(1)** of, derived from, or consisting of matter; esp physical (2) bodily **b** of matter rather than form **2** important, significant **3** of or concerned with physical rather than spiritual things – ~ly adv

²**material** n **1a** the elements, constituents, or substances of which sthg is composed or can be made **b(1)** data that may be worked into a more finished form (2) a person considered with a view to his/her potential for successful training **c** cloth **2** pl apparatus necessary for doing or making sthg

mathematics /ˌmæðəˈmætɪks/ n pl but sing or pl in constr the science of numbers and their operations, interrelations, and combinations and of space configurations and their structure, measurement, etc – ~ical adj – ~ically adv – ~ician n

matron /ˈmeɪtrən/ n **1a** a (dignified mature) married woman **b** a woman in charge of living arrangements in a school, residential home, etc **2** Br a woman in charge of the nursing in a hospital – not now used technically

¹**matter** /ˈmætə/ n **1a** a subject of interest or concern or which merits attention **b** an affair, concern **c** material (for treatment) in thought, discourse, or writing **d** a condition (unfavourably) affecting a person or thing **2a** the substance of which a physical object is composed **b** material substance that occupies space and has mass **c** sthg of a specified kind or for a specified purpose **d** material discharged by suppuration; pus

²**matter** v to be of importance

mattress /ˈmætrɪs/ n a fabric casing filled with resilient material (e g foam rubber or an arrangement of coiled springs) used esp on a bed

¹**mature** /məˈtʃʊə/ adj **1** based on careful consideration **2a** having completed natural growth and development; adult **b** having attained a final or desired state **3** older or more experienced than others of his/her kind – **-rity** n – ~ly adv

²**mature** v **1** to bring to full development or completion **2** to become due for payment – **-ration** n

mauve /məʊv/ n or adj bluish purple

maximum /ˈmæksɪməm/ n, pl **maxima, maximums** **1** the greatest quantity or value attainable or attained **2** the period of highest or most extreme development – **-mize** v

may /meɪ/ verbal auxiliary, pres sing & pl **may**; past **might** **1a** have permission to; have liberty to **b** be in some degree likely to **2** – used to express a wish or desire, esp in prayer, curse, or benediction (e g long may he reign) **3** – used to express purpose or expectation (e g sit here so I may you better) contingency (e g he'll do his duty come what may); or concession (e g he may be slow, but he's thorough); used in questions to emphasize ironic uncertainty (e g and who may you be)

May n **1** the 5th month of the Gregorian calendar **2** not cap (the blossom of) hawthorn

maybe /ˈmeɪbi/ adv perhaps

mayor /meə/ n the chief executive or nominal head of a city or borough – ~al adj

mayoress /ˈmeərɪs/ n **1** the wife or hostess of a mayor **2** a female mayor

maze n **1** (a drawn representation of) a network of paths designed to confuse and puzzle those who attempt to walk through it **2** sthg intricately or confusingly complicated

¹**me** /mi/ pron; strong miː/ pron, objective case of I (e g fatter than me; its me)

²**me** n sthg suitable for me (e g that dress isn't really me)

³**me** n the 3rd note of the diatonic scale in solmization

meadow /ˈmedəʊ/ n (an area of moist low-lying usu level) grassland

¹**meal** /miːl/ n **1** the portion of food taken or provided at 1 time to satisfy appetite **2** (the time of) eating a meal

²**meal** n (a product resembling, esp in texture) the usu coarsely ground seeds of a cereal grass or pulse

¹**mean** /miːn/ adj **1** lacking distinction or eminence; merely ordinary or inferior **2** of poor shabby inferior quality or status **3** not honourable or worthy; base; esp small-minded **4a** not generous **b** characterized by petty malice; spiteful **c** chiefly NAm particularly bad-tempered, unpleasant, or disagreeable – ~ly adv – ~ness n

²**mean** v **meant** **1** to have in mind as a purpose; intend **2** to serve or intend to convey, produce, or indicate; signify **3** to intend for a particular use or purpose

4 to have significance or importance to the extent or degree of

³mean *n* **1a** a middle point between extremes **b** a value that lies within a range of values and is computed according to a prescribed law; *esp* an average **2** *pl but sing or pl in constr* that which enables a desired purpose to be achieved; *also* the method used to attain an end **3** *pl* resources available for disposal; *esp* wealth

⁴mean *adj* **1** occupying a middle position; intermediate in space, order, time, kind, or degree **2** being the mean of a set of values

¹meaning /'miːnɪŋ/ *n* **1** that which is conveyed or which one intends to convey, esp by language **2** significant quality; value **3** implication of a hidden or special significance – ~less *adj*

²meaning *adj* significant, expressive

means test *n* an examination into sby's financial state to determine whether he/she should receive public assistance, a student grant, etc

¹meantime /'miːntaɪm/ *n* the intervening time

²meantime *adv* meanwhile

mean time *n* time that is based on the motion of the mean sun and that has the mean solar second as its unit

¹meanwhile /'miːnwaɪl/ *n* the meantime

²meanwhile *adv* **1** during the intervening time **2** during the same period (e g *meanwhile*, down on the farm)

measles /'miːzəlz/ *n pl but sing or pl in constr* an infectious virus disease marked by a rash of distinct red circular spots

¹measure /'meʒə'/ *n* **1a(1)** an appropriate or due portion **(2)** a (moderate) extent, amount, or degree **(3)** a fixed, suitable, or conceivable limit **b(1)** the dimensions, capacity, or amount of sthg ascertained by measuring **(2)** the character, nature, or capacity of sby or sthg ascertained by assessment – esp in *get the measure of* **c** a measured quantity **2a** an instrument or utensil for measuring **b** a standard or unit of measurement **3a** a (slow and stately) dance **b(1)** poetic rhythm measured by quantity or accent **(2)** musical time **c(1)** the notes and rests that form a bar of music **(2)** a metrical unit; a foot **4** a basis or standard of comparison **5a** a step planned or taken to achieve an end **b** a proposed legislative act

²measure *v* **1** to take or allot in measured amounts – usu + *out* **2** to mark off by making measurements – often + *off* **3** to ascertain the measurements of **4** to estimate or appraise by a criterion – usu + *against* or *by*

measurement /'meʒəmənt/ *n* **1** measuring **2** a figure, extent, or amount obtained by measuring

meat /miːt/ *n* **1** food; esp solid food as distinguished from drink **2** animal tissue used as food **3** the core or essence of sthg

mechanic /mɪ'kænɪk/ *n* a skilled worker who repairs or maintains machinery

mechanical /mɪ'kænɪkəl/ *adj* **1a** of or using machinery **b** made, operated by, or being a machine or machinery **2** done as if by machine; lacking in spontaneity **3** of, dealing with, or in accordance with (the principles of) mechanics – ~ly

mechanics /mɪ'kænɪks/ *n pl but sing or pl in constr* **1** the physics and mathematics of (the effect on moving and stationary bodies of) energy and forces **2** the practical application of mechanics to the design, construction, or operation of machines or tools

mechanism /'mekənɪzəm/ *n* **1** a piece of machinery **2** mechanical operation or action **3** a theory that all natural processes are mechanically determined and can be explained by the laws of physics and chemistry – **-istic** *adj* – **-istically** *adv* – **-ize** *v*

medal /'medl/ *n* a piece of metal with a (stamped) design, emblem, inscription, etc that commemorates a person or event or is awarded for excellence or achievement

media /'miːdɪə/ *pl of* **medium**

¹medical /'medɪkəl/ *adj* **1** of or concerned with physicians or the practice of medicine **2** requiring or devoted to medical treatment – ~ly *adv*

²medical *n* an examination to determine sby's physical fitness

medicine /'medsən/ *n* **1** a substance or preparation used (as if) in treating disease **2** the science and art of the maintenance of health and the prevention and treatment of disease (using nonsurgical methods)

mediocre /,miːdɪ'əʊkə'/ *adj* **1** neither good nor bad; indifferent; *esp* conspicuously lacking distinction or imagination **2** not good enough; fairly bad – **-crity** *n*

meditate /'medɪteɪt/ **1** to engage in deep or serious reflection **2** to empty the mind of thoughts and fix the attention on 1 matter, esp as a religious exercise – **-tion** *n* – **-tive** *adj* – **-tively** *adv*

¹medium /'miːdɪəm/ *n, pl* **mediums, media** **1** (sthg in) a middle position or state **2** a means of effecting or conveying sthg: e g **a(1)** a substance regarded as the means of transmission of a force or effect **(2)** a surrounding or enveloping substance **b** a mode of artistic expression or communication **c** one through whom others seek to communicate with the spirits of the dead **3a** a condition or environment in which sthg may function or flourish **b** a nutrient for the artificial cultivation of bacteria and other (single-celled) organisms **c** a liquid with which dry pigment can be mixed

²medium *adj* intermediate in amount, quality, position, or degree

meek /miːk/ *adj* **1** patient and without resentment **2** lacking spirit and courage; timid – ~ly *adv* – ~ness *n*

¹meet /miːt/ *v* **met 1a** to come into the

presence of by accident or design **b** to be present to greet the arrival of **c** to come into contact or conjunction with **2** to encounter as antagonist or foe **3** to answer, esp in opposition **4** to conform to, esp exactly and precisely; satisfy **5** to pay fully **6** to become acquainted with **7** to experience during the course of sthg

²**meet** *n* the assembling of participants for a hunt or for competitive sports

³**meet** *adj* suitable, proper – *fml*

meeting /'mi:tɪŋ/ *n* **1** a coming together: e g **a** an assembly of people for a common purpose **b** a session of horse or greyhound racing **2** a permanent organizational unit of the Quakers **3** an intersection, junction

¹**melancholy** /'melənkəli/ *n* **1** (a tendency to) bad temper or depression; melancholia **2a** depression of mind or spirits **b** a sad pensive mood – *-ic adj*

²**melancholy** *adj* **1** depressed in spirits; dejected **2** causing, tending to cause, or expressing sadness or depression

melody /'melədi/ *n* **1** an agreeable succession or arrangement of sounds **2a** a rhythmic succession of single notes organized as an aesthetic whole **b** the chief part in a harmonic composition – *-ic adj*

melon /'melən/ *n* (any of various plants of the cucumber family having) a fruit (e g a watermelon) containing sweet edible flesh and usu eaten raw

¹**melt** /melt/ *v* **1** to become altered from a solid to a liquid state, usu by heating **2a** to dissolve, disintegrate **b** to disappear as if by dissolving **3** to be or become mild, tender, or gentle

²**melt** *n* the spleen, esp when used as food

member /'membə'/ *n* **1** a part or organ of the body: e g **a** a limb **b** the penis – *euph* **2a** an individual or other belonging to or forming part of a group or organization **b** *often cap* one who is entitled to sit in a legislative body; *esp* a member of Parliament **3a** a constituent part of a whole **b** a beam or similar (load-bearing) structure, esp in a building

membership /'membəʃɪp/ *n sing or pl in constr* the body of members

memorable /'memərəbəl/ *adj* worth remembering; notable – *-bly adv*

¹**memorial** /mɪˈmɔːrɪəl/ *adj* serving to commemorate a person or event

²**memorial** *n* sthg, a monument, that commemorates a person or event

memory /'memərɪ/ *n* **1** (the power or process of recalling or realizing) the store of things learned and retained from an organism's experience **2** commemorative remembrance **3a** (the object of) recall or recollection **b** the time within which past events can be or are remembered **4** (the capacity of) a device in which information, esp for a computer, can be inserted, stored, and extracted when wanted – *-orize v*

men /men/ *pl of* **man**

¹**menace** /'menᵻs/ *n* **1** a show of intention to inflict harm; a threat **2a** a source

of danger **b** a person who causes annoyance

²**menace** *v* to threaten or show intent to harm – *-acingly adv*

¹**mend** /mend/ *v* **1** to improve or rectify **2** to restore to sound condition or working order; repair – *~er n*

²**mend** *n* a mended place or part

mental /'mentl/ *adj* **1a** of the mind or its activity **b** of intellectual as contrasted with emotional or physical activity **c** (performed or experienced) in the mind **2** of, being, or (intended for the care of people) suffering from a psychiatric disorder **3** crazy; *also* stupid – *infml* – *~ly adv*

mentality /men'tælᵻti/ *n* **1** mental power or capacity; intelligence **2** a mode of thought; mental disposition or outlook

¹**mention** /'menʃən/ *n* **1** a brief reference to sthg; a passing remark **2** a formal citation for outstanding achievement

²**mention** *v* to make mention of; refer to

menu /'menju:/ *n* (a list of) the dishes that may be ordered (e g in a restaurant) or that are to be served (e g at a banquet)

¹**mercenary** /'mɜːsənəri/ *n* a hired soldier in foreign service

²**mercenary** *adj* **1** serving merely for (financial) reward **2** hired for service in the army of a foreign country

merchandise /'mɜːtʃəndaɪs, -daɪz/ *n* **1** the commodities that are bought and sold in commerce **2** wares for sale

¹**merchant** /'mɜːtʃənt/ *n* **1** a wholesaler; *also, chiefly NAm* a shopkeeper **2** a person who is given to a specified activity – *chiefly derog*

²**merchant** *adj* of or used in commerce; *esp* of a merchant navy

mercury /'mɜːkjʊri/ *n* **1** a heavy silverwhite poisonous univalent or bivalent metallic element that is liquid at ordinary temperatures and used in thermometers, barometers, etc **2** *cap* the planet nearest the sun

mercy /'mɜːsi/ *n* **1** compassion or forbearance shown esp to an offender **2a** an act of divine compassion; a blessing **b** a fortunate circumstance **3** compassionate treatment of those in distress – *merciful adj*

¹**mere** /mɪə'/ *n* a (small) lake

²**mere** *adj* being what is specified and nothing else; nothing more than – *~ly adv*

merge /mɜːdʒ/ *v* **1** to (cause to) combine or unite **2** to blend or (cause to) come together gradually without abrupt change

meridian /məˈrɪdɪən/ *n* **1** a great circle passing through the poles of the celestial sphere and the zenith of a given place **2** a high point, esp of success or greatness

¹**merit** /'merᵻt/ *n* **1a** the quality of deserving well or ill **b** a praiseworthy quality; virtue **c** worth, excellence **2** *pl* the intrinsic rights and wrongs of a (legal) case

²**merit** v to be worthy of or entitled to

merry /'meri/ adj 1 full of gaiety or high spirits 2 marked by festivity 3 slightly drunk; tipsy – infml – **-rily** adv – **-riness** n

¹**mess** /mes/ n 1 a prepared dish of soft or liquid food; also a usu unappetizing mixture of ingredients eaten together 2 sing or pl in constr a group of people (e g servicemen or servicewomen) who regularly take their meals together 3a a confused, dirty, or offensive state or condition b a disordered situation resulting from misunderstanding, blundering, or misconduct

²**mess** v 1 to take meals with a mess 2 to make a mess 3a to dabble, potter b to handle or play with sthg, esp carelessly c to interfere, meddle USE (3) often + about or around

message /'mesɪdʒ/ n 1 a communication in writing, in speech, or by signals 2 a central theme or idea intended to inspire, urge, warn, enlighten, advise, etc

messenger /'mesəndʒə'/ n one who bears a message or does an errand: e g a a dispatch bearer in government or military service b an employee who carries messages

Messrs /'mesəz/ pl of **Mr**

¹**met** /met/ past of **meet**

²**met** adj meteorological

metal /'metl/ n any of various opaque, fusible, ductile, and typically lustrous substances (e g iron, copper, or mercury), esp chemical elements, that are good conductors of electricity and heat

metallic /mɪ'tælɪk/ adj 1 of, containing, or being (a) metal 2 yielding metal 3 having an acrid quality

metaphor /'metəfə', -fɔː'/ n (an instance of) a figure of speech in which a word or phrase literally denoting one kind of object or idea is applied to another to suggest a likeness or analogy between them (e g in the ship ploughs the sea) – **~ical** adj

meteor /'miːtɪə'/ n (the streak of light produced by the passage of) any of many small particles of matter in the solar system observable only when heated by friction so that they glow as they fall into the earth's atmosphere

meteoric /,miːti'ɒrɪk/ adj resembling a meteor in speed or in sudden and temporary brilliance – **~ally** adv

meteorology /,miːtɪə'rolədʒi/ n the science of the atmosphere and its phenomena, esp weather and weather forecasting – **-gical** adj – **-gist** n

¹**meter** /'miːtə'/ n, NAm a metre

²**meter** n an instrument for measuring (and recording) the amount of sthg (e g gas, electricity, or parking time) used

³**meter** v 1 to measure by means of a meter 2 to supply in a measured or regulated amount

method /'meθəd/ n 1a a systematic procedure for doing sthg b a regular way of doing sthg 2a an orderly arrangement or system b the habitual practice of orderliness and regularity

methodical /mɪ'θɒdɪkəl/ adj 1 arranged, characterized by, or performed with method or order 2 habitually proceeding according to method; systematic – **~ly** adv

¹**metre** /'miːtə'/ NAm chiefly **meter** n the SI unit of length equal to a certain number of wavelengths of a specific radiation of the krypton isotope ₃₆Kr⁸⁶ (about 1.094yd)

²**metre** /, NAm chiefly **meter** n 1 systematically arranged and measured rhythm in verse 2 a basic recurrent rhythmical pattern of accents and beats per bar in music

metric /'metrɪk/ adj (using or being units) based on the metre, litre, and kilogram as standard of measurement – **~ize** v

mice /maɪs/ pl of **mouse**

microfilm /'maɪkrəʊ,fɪlm/ n a film bearing a photographic record on a reduced scale of graphic matter (e g printing)

microphone /'maɪkrəfəʊn/ n a device that converts sounds into electrical signals, esp for transmission or recording

microprocessor /,maɪkrəʊ'prəʊsesə'/ n a very small computer composed of 1 or more integrated circuits functioning as a unit

microscope /'maɪkrəskəʊp/ n an instrument consisting of (a combination of) lenses for making enlarged images of minute objects using light or other radiations – **-py** n

¹**mid** /mɪd/ adj 1 being the part in the middle or midst – often in combination 2 occupying a middle position

²**mid** prep amid

midday /,mɪd'deɪ/ n the middle part of the day; noon

¹**middle** /'mɪdl/ adj 1 equally distant from the extremes; central 2 at neither extreme

²**middle** n 1 a middle part, point, or position 2 the waist 3 the position of being among or in the midst of sthg 4 sthg intermediate between extremes; a mean

Middle Ages n pl the period of European history from about AD 500 to about 1500

middle class n a class occupying a position between upper and lower; esp a fluid heterogeneous grouping of business and professional people, bureaucrats, and some farmers and skilled workers – often pl with sing. meaning

midget /'mɪdʒɪt/ n 1 a very small person; a dwarf 2 sthg (e g an animal) much smaller than usual

midnight /'mɪdnaɪt/ n the middle of the night; specif 12 o'clock at night

midst /mɪdst/ n 1 the inner or central part or point; the middle 2 a position near to the members of a group 3 the condition of being surrounded or beset (e g by problems) 4 a period of time about the middle of a continuing act or state

midway /,mɪd'weɪ/ adv halfway

¹**might** /maɪt/ past of **may** – used to express permission or liberty in the past

(e g asked whether he *might* come), a past or present possibility contrary to fact (e g I *might* well have been killed) purpose or expectation in the past (e g wrote it down so that I *might* not forget it), less probability or possibility than may (e g *might* get there before it rains), a polite request (e g you *might* post this letter for me), or as a polite or ironic alternative to *may* (e g who *might* you be?) or to *ought* or *should* (e g you *might* at least apologize)

²**might** *n* **1** power, authority, or resources wielded individually or collectively **2a** physical strength **b** all the power or effort one is capable of

¹**mighty** /'maɪti/ *adj* **1** powerful **2** accomplished or characterized by might **3** imposingly great

²**mighty** *adv* to a great degree; extremely

migrate /maɪ'greɪt/ *v* **1** to move from one country or locality to another **2** *of an animal* to pass usu periodically from one region or climate to another for feeding or breeding – **-ory** *adj* – **-tion** *n*

¹**mild** /maɪld/ *adj* **1** gentle in nature or manner **2a** not strong in flavour or effect **b** not being or involving what is extreme **3** not severe; temperate – **~ly** *adv* – **~ness** *n*

²**mild** *n, Br* a dark-coloured beer not flavoured with hops

mile /maɪl/ *n* **1** any of various units of distance: **a** a unit equal to 1760yd (about 1.61km) **b** a nautical mile **2** a large distance or amount – often pl with sing. meaning

milestone /'maɪlstəʊn/ *n* **1** a stone serving as a milepost **2** a crucial stage in sthg's development

militant /'mɪlɪtənt/ *adj* **1** engaged in warfare or combat **2** aggressively active (e g in a cause); combative

¹**military** /'mɪlɪtəri/ *adj* **1** (characteristic) of soldiers, arms, or war **2** carried on or supported by armed force **3** of the army or armed forces

²**military** *n* *pl in constr* soldiers **1** *sing or pl in constr* the army (as opposed to civilians or police)

¹**milk** /mɪlk/ *n* **1** **a** (white or creamy) liquid secreted by the mammary glands of females for the nourishment of their young (and used as a food by humans) **2** a milklike liquid: e g **a** the latex of a plant **b** the juice of a coconut **c** a cosmetic lotion, esp a cleanser

²**milk** *v* **1** to draw milk from the breasts or udder of **2** to draw sthg from as if by milking: e g **a** to induce (a snake) to eject venom **b** to compel or persuade to yield illicit or excessive profit or advantage

milkman /'mɪlkmən/ *n* one who sells or delivers milk

¹**mill** /mɪl/ *n* **1** a building provided with machinery for grinding grain into flour **2a** a machine or apparatus for grinding grain **b** a machine or hand-operated device for crushing or grinding a solid substance (e g coffee beans or peppercorns) **3** a building or collection of

buildings with machinery for manufacturing

²**mill** *v* **1a** to grind into flour, meal, or powder **b** to shape or dress by means of a rotary cutter **2** to give a raised rim or a ridged edge to (a coin) **4** to move in a confused swirling mass – usu + *about* or *around*

milligram /'mɪlɪgræm/ *n* one thousandth of a gram (about 0.015 grain)

millilitre /'mɪlɪˌliːtə/ *n* a thousandth of a litre (.002pt)

millimetre /'mɪlɪˌmiːtə/ *n* one thousandth of a metre (about 0.039in)

million /'mɪljən/ *n* **1** the number 1,000,000 **2** an indefinitely large number – infml; often pl with sing. meaning – **~th** *adj, n, pron, adv*

millionaire /ˌmɪljə'neə/ *n* sby whose wealth is estimated at a million or more money units

¹**mimic** /'mɪmɪk/ *adj* **1** imitation, mock **2** of mime or mimicry

²**mimic** *v* **-ck-** **1** to imitate slavishly; ape **2** to ridicule by imitation **3** to simulate

¹**mince** /mɪns/ *v* **1** to cut or chop into very small pieces **2** to walk with short affected steps

²**mince** *n* minced meat

¹**mind** /maɪnd/ *n* **1** the (capabilities of the) organized conscious and unconscious mental processes of an organism that result in reasoning, thinking, perceiving, etc **2a** recollection, memory **b** attention, concentration **3** the normal condition of the mental faculties **4** a disposition, mood **5** the mental attributes of a usu specified group **6a** the intellect and rational faculties as contrasted with the emotions **b** the human spirit and intellect as opposed to the body and the material world

²**mind** *v* **1** to pay attention to or follow (advice, instructions, or orders) **2a** to be concerned about; care **b** to object to **3a** to be careful **b** to be attentive or wary – often + *out* **4** to give protective care to; look after

¹**mine** *pron, pl* **mine** that which or the one who belongs to me – used without a following noun as a pronoun equivalent in meaning to the adjective *my* (e g children younger than *mine*; that brother of *mine*)

²**mine** *n* **1** an excavation from which mineral substances are taken **2** an encased explosive designed to destroy enemy personnel, vehicles, or ships **3** a rich source of

³**mine** *v* **1** to dig an underground passage to gain access to or cause the collapse of (an enemy position) **2** to place military mines in, on, or under **3** to dig into for ore, coal, etc

mineral /'mɪnərəl/ *n* **1** any of various naturally occurring substances (e g stone, coal, and petroleum) obtained by drilling, mining, etc **2** sthg neither animal nor vegetable

mingle /'mɪŋgəl/ *v* **1** to bring or mix together or with sthg else **2** to mix with or go among a group of people

¹**miniature** /'mɪnɪətʃə, 'mɪnɪtʃə/ *n* **1a** a

copy or representation on a much reduced scale **b** sthg small of its kind **2** a very small painting (e g a portrait on ivory or metal)

²**miniature** *adj* (represented) on a small or reduced scale or smaller

minimum /'mɪnɪməm/ *n, pl* **minima, minimums 1** the least quantity or value assignable, admissible, or possible **2** the lowest degree or amount reached or recorded – **-mize** *v*

¹**minister** /'mɪnɪstə/ *n* **1** an agent **2** a clergyman, *esp* of a Protestant or nonconformist church **3** a high officer of state managing a division of government **4** a diplomatic representative accredited to a foreign state – ~ **ial** *adj* – ~ **ially** *adv*

²**minister** *v* **1** to perform the functions of a minister of religion **2** to give aid or service

ministration /,mɪnɪ'streɪʃən/ *n* the act or process of ministering, esp in religious matters – **-trant** *n*

ministry /'mɪnɪstri/ *n* **1** service, ministration **2** the office, duties, or functions of a minister **3** the body of ministers of religion or government **4** the period of service or office of a minister or ministry **5** a government department presided over by a minister

¹**minor** /'maɪnə/ *adj* **1a** inferior in importance, size, rank, or degree **b** comparatively unimportant **2** not having attained majority **3a** *esp of a scale or mode* having semitones between the second and third, fifth and sixth, and sometimes seventh and eighth steps **b** being or based on a (specified) minor scale **4** not serious or involving risk to life

²**minor** *n* **1** sby who has not attained majority **2** a minor musical interval, scale, key, or mode

minority /maɪ'nɒrɪti/ *n* **1a** the period before attainment of majority **b** the state of being a legal minor **2** the smaller of 2 groups constituting a whole; *specif* a group with less than the number of votes necessary for control **3** *sing or pl in constr* a group of people who share common characteristics or interests differing from those of the majority of a population

¹**mint** /mɪnt/ *n* **1** a place where money is made **2** a vast sum or amount – infml

²**mint** *v* **1** to make (e g coins) by stamping metal **2** to fabricate, invent

³**mint** *adj* unspoilt as if fresh from a mint; pristine

⁴**mint** *n* **1** any of a genus of plants that have leaves with a characteristic strong taste and smell, used esp as a flavouring **2** a sweet, chocolate, etc flavoured with mint

¹**minus** /'maɪnəs/ *prep* **1** diminished by **2** without

²**minus** *n* **1** a negative quantity **2** a deficiency, defect

³**minus** *adj* **1** negative **2** having negative qualities; *esp* involving a disadvantage

minuscule /'mɪnəskjuːl/ *adj* very small

¹**minute** /'mɪnɪt/ *n* **1** the 60th part of an hour of time or of a degree **2** a short space of time; a moment **3a** a memorandum **b** *pl* the official record of the proceedings of a meeting

²**minute** /maɪ'njuːt/ *v* to make notes or a brief summary (of)

³**minute** /maɪ'njuːt/ *adj* **1** extremely small **2** of minor importance; petty **3** marked by painstaking attention to detail – ~ **ness** *n*

miracle /'mɪrəkəl/ *n* **1** an extraordinary event manifesting divine intervention in human affairs **2** an astonishing or unusual event, thing, or accomplishment **3** a person or thing that is a remarkable example or instance of sthg

miraculous /mɪ'rækjʊləs/ *adj* **1** of the nature of a miracle; supernatural **2** evoking wonder like a miracle; marvellous – ~ **ly**

¹**mirror** /'mɪrə/ *n* **1** a smooth surface (e g of metal or silvered glass) that forms images by reflection **2** sthg that gives a true representation

²**mirror** *v* to reflect (as if) in a mirror

misadventure /,mɪsəd'ventʃə/ *n* a misfortune, mishap

misbehave /,mɪsbɪ'heɪv/ *v* to behave badly – **-d** *adj* – **-iour**

miscalculate /,mɪs'kælkjʊleɪt/ *v* to calculate wrongly – **-lation** *n*

miscellaneous /,mɪsə'leɪnɪəs/ *adj* **1** consisting of diverse items or members **2** having various characteristics or capabilities – ~ **ly** *adv* – ~ **ness** *n*

mischief /'mɪstʃɪf/ *n* **1** sthg or esp sby that causes harm or annoyance **2** often playful action that annoys or irritates, usu without causing or intending serious harm

mischievous /'mɪstʃɪvəs/ *adj* **1** harmful, malicious **2** able or tending to cause annoyance, unrest, or minor injury **3a** playfully provocative; arch **b** disruptively playful – ~ **ly** *adv* – ~ **ness** *n*

misdirect /,mɪsdɪ'rekt/ *v* **1** to give a wrong direction to **2** to address (mail) wrongly – ~ **ion** *n*

miser /'maɪzə/ *n* a mean grasping person; *esp* one who hoards wealth – ~ **ly** *adj* – ~ **liness** *n*

miserable /'mɪzərəbəl/ *adj* **1a** wretchedly inadequate or meagre **b** causing extreme discomfort or unhappiness **2** in a pitiable state of distress or unhappiness **3** shameful, contemptible

misery /'mɪzəri/ *n* **1** (a cause of) physical or mental suffering or discomfort **2** great unhappiness and distress **3** *chiefly Br* a grumpy or querulous person; *esp* a killjoy – infml

misfire /,mɪs'faɪə/ *v* **1** *of an engine, rocket etc* to have the explosive or propulsive charge fail to ignite at the proper time **2** *esp of a firearm* to fail to fire **3** to fail to have an intended effect – **misfire** *n*

misfit /'mɪs,fɪt/ *n* **1** sthg that fits badly **2** a person poorly adjusted to his/her environment

misfortune /mɪs'fɔːtʃən/ *n* **1** bad luck

2 a distressing or unfortunate incident or event

misgiving /ˌmɪsˈgɪvɪŋ/ n a feeling of doubt, suspicion, or apprehension, esp concerning a future event

misguide /ˌmɪsˈgaɪd/ v to lead astray – ~d adj – ~dly adv

misjudge /ˌmɪsˈdʒʌdʒ/ v 1 to estimate wrongly 2 to have an unjust opinion of – ~ment n

mislay /mɪsˈleɪ/ v to leave in an unremembered place

mislead /mɪsˈliːd/ v to lead in a wrong direction or into a mistaken action or belief – ~ingly adv

¹**miss** /mɪs/ v 1 to fail to hit, reach, contact, or attain 2 to discover or feel the absence of, esp with regret 3 to escape, avoid 4 to leave out; omit – often + out 5 to fail to perform or attend 6 to fail to take advantage of

²**miss** n 1 a failure to hit 2 a failure to attain a desired result 3 a deliberate avoidance or omission of sthg

³**miss** n 1 – used as a title preceding the name of an unmarried woman or girl 2 a young unmarried woman or girl – chiefly infml

missile /ˈmɪsaɪl/ n an object thrown or projected, usu so as to strike sthg at a distance; also a self-propelled weapon that travels through the air

missing /ˈmɪsɪŋ/ adj absent; also lost

mission /ˈmɪʃən/ n 1a a ministry commissioned by a religious organization to propagate its faith or carry on humanitarian work, usu abroad b a mission establishment c a campaign to increase church membership or strengthen Christian faith 2a a group sent to a foreign country to negotiate, advise, etc b a permanent embassy or legation 3 a specific task with which a person or group is charged 4 a definite military, naval, or aerospace task

¹**missionary** /ˈmɪʃənəri/ adj relating to, engaged in, or devoted to missions 2 characteristic of a missionary

²**missionary** n a person undertaking a mission; esp one in charge of a religious mission in some remote part of the world

mist /mɪst/ n 1 water in the form of diffuse particles in the atmosphere, esp near the earth's surface 2 sthg that dims or obscures 3 a film, esp of tears, before the eyes

¹**mistake** /mɪˈsteɪk/ v mistook; mistaken 1 to choose wrongly 2a to misunderstand the meaning, intention, or significance of b to estimate wrongly 3 to identify wrongly; confuse with another

²**mistake** n 1 a misunderstanding of the meaning or significance of sthg 2 a wrong action or statement arising from faulty judgment, inadequate knowledge, or carelessness

mistaken /mɪˈsteɪkən/ adj 1 of a person wrong in opinion 2 of an action, idea, etc based on wrong thinking; incorrect – ~ly

mistress /ˈmɪstrɪs/ n 1a a woman in a position of power or authority b the

female head of a household 2 a woman who has achieved mastery of a subject or skill 3 a woman with whom a man has a continuing sexual relationship outside marriage 4 chiefly Br a schoolmistress

mistrust /mɪsˈtrʌst/ v 1 to have little trust in; be suspicious of 2 to doubt the reliability or effectiveness of – mistrust n

misunderstand /ˌmɪsʌndəˈstænd/ v 1 to fail to understand 2 to interpret incorrectly

misunderstanding /ˌmɪsʌndəˈstændɪŋ/ n 1 a failure to understand; a misinterpretation 2 a disagreement, dispute

¹**mix** /mɪks/ v 1a(1) to combine or blend into a mass (2) to combine with another – often + in b to bring into close association 2 to prepare by mixing different components or ingredients 3 to control the balance of (various sounds), esp during the recording of a film, broadcast, record, etc 4 to seek or enjoy the society of others

²**mix** n 1 an act or process of mixing 2 a product of mixing; specif a commercially prepared mixture of food ingredients 3 a combination 4 a combination in definite proportions of 2 or more recordings (e g of a singer and an accompaniment)

mixed /mɪkst/ adj 1 combining diverse elements 2 made up of or involving people of different races, national origins, religions, classes, or sexes 3 including or accompanied by conflicting or dissimilar elements

mixture /ˈmɪkstʃə/ n 1a mixing or being mixed b the relative proportions of constituents; specif the proportion of fuel to air produced in a carburettor 2a (a portion of) matter consisting of 2 or more components in varying proportions that retain their own properties b a combination of several different kinds; a blend

¹**moan** /məʊn/ n a low prolonged sound of pain or grief

²**moan** v 1 to produce (a sound like) a moan 2 to complain, grumble – ~er n

¹**mob** /mɒb/ n 1 the masses, populace 2 a disorderly riotous crowd 3 a criminal gang 4 chiefly Austr a flock, drove, or herd of animals 5 sing or pl in constr, chiefly Br a crowd, bunch – infml – mob adj

²**mob** v 1 to attack in a large crowd or group 2 to crowd round, esp out of curiosity or admiration

¹**mobile** /ˈməʊbaɪl/ adj 1 capable of moving or being moved 2 changing quickly in expression or mood 3 (capable of) undergoing movement into a different social class – -ility n

²**mobile** /ˈməʊbail/ n a structure (e g of cardboard or metal) with usu suspended parts that are moved in different planes by air currents or machinery

¹**mock** /mɒk/ v 1 to treat with contempt or ridicule 2 to disappoint the hopes of

3 to mimic in fun or derision – ~**er** n – ~**ingly** adv

²**mock** n a school examination used as a rehearsal for an official one

³**mock** adj (having the character) of an imitation or simulation

⁴**mock** adv in an insincere or pretended manner – usu in combination

mockery /'mɒkəri/ n 1 jeering or contemptuous behaviour or words 2 an object of laughter or derision 3 a deceitful or contemptible imitation; a travesty

¹**model** /'mɒdl/ n 1 structural design 2 a replica of sthg in relief or 3 dimensions; also a representation of sthg to be constructed 3 an example worthy of imitation or emulation 4 sby or sthg that serves as a pattern for an artist; esp one who poses for an artist 5 one who is employed to wear merchandise, esp clothing, in order to display it 6 a type or design of an article or product (e g a garment or car)

²**model** v 1 to plan or form after a pattern 2 to shape in a mouldable material; broadly to produce a representation or simulation of 3 to construct or fashion in imitation of a particular model 4 to display, esp by wearing

³**model** adj 1 (worthy of) being a pattern for others 2 being a miniature representation of sthg

¹**moderate** /'mɒdərɪt/ adj 1a avoiding extremes of behaviour or expression b not violent; temperate 2 being (somewhat less than) average in quality, amount, or degree – -**tion** n – ~**ly** adv

²**moderate** /'mɒdəreɪt/ v 1 to lessen the intensity or extremeness of 2 to preside over

³**moderate** /'mɒdərɪt/ n one who holds moderate views or favours a moderate course

modern /'mɒdn/ adj 1a (characteristic) of a period extending from a certain point in the past to the present time b (characteristic) of the present or the immediate past; contemporary 2 involving recent techniques, styles, or ideas – ~**ize** v

modest /'mɒdɪst/ adj 1 having a moderate estimate of one's abilities or worth; not boastful or self-assertive 2 (characteristic) of a modest nature 3 carefully observant of proprieties of dress and behaviour 4 small or limited in size, amount, or aim – ~**ly** adv – ~**y** n

modify /'mɒdɪfaɪ/ v 1 to make less extreme 2 to undergo change 3a to make minor changes in b to make basic changes in, often for a specific purpose – -**fication** n

moist /mɔɪst/ adj 1 slightly wet; damp 2 highly humid – ~**en** v – ~**ly** adv – ~**ness** n

moisture /'mɔɪstʃə/ n liquid diffused, condensed, or absorbed in relatively small amounts

molecule /'mɒlɪkjuːl/ n the smallest particle of a substance that retains its characteristic properties, consisting of 1 or more atoms

moment /'məʊmənt/ n 1 a very brief interval or point of time 2a present time b a time of excellence or prominence 3 importance in influence or effect 4 a stage in historical or logical development 5 (a measure of) the tendency of a force to produce turning motion

momentary /'məʊməntəri/ adj lasting a very short time – -**rily** adv

momentum /məʊ'mentəm, mə-/ n the product of the mass of a body and its velocity

monarch /'mɒnək/ n 1 sby who reigns over a kingdom or empire 2 sby or sthg occupying a commanding or preeminent position – ~**ic, ~ical** adj

monarchy /'mɒnəki/ n (a government or state with) undivided rule by a monarch

monastery /'mɒnəstri/ n a residence occupied by a religious community, esp of monks

Monday /'mʌndi, -deɪ/ n the day of the week following Sunday

monetary /'mʌnɪtəri/ adj of money or its behaviour in an economy

money /'mʌni/ n 1 sthg generally accepted as a means of payment; esp officially printed, coined, or stamped currency 2 a form or denomination of coin or paper money 3 the first, second, and third places in a race on whose result money is betted – usu in in/out of the money – ~**less** adj

mongrel /'mʌŋgrəl/ n a dog or other individual (of unknown ancestry) resulting from the interbreeding of diverse breeds

monk /mʌŋk/ n a male member of a religious order, living apart from the world under vows of poverty, chastity, etc – ~**ish** adj

¹**monkey** /'mʌŋki/ n 1 any small long-tailed primate mammal 2a a mischievous child; a scamp b a ludicrous figure; a fool USE (2) infml

²**monkey** v 1 to act in an absurd or mischievous manner 2 to mess around with USE infml; often + about or around

mono /'mɒnəʊ/ adj or n monophonic (sound reproduction)

monopolize, -ise /mə'nɒpəlaɪz/ v to assume complete possession or control of

monopoly /mə'nɒpəli/ n 1 (a person or group having) exclusive ownership or control (through legal privilege, command of the supply of a commodity, concerted action, etc) 2 sthg, esp a commodity, controlled by one party

monotonous /mə'nɒtənəs/ adj 1 uttered or sounded in 1 unvarying tone 2 tediously uniform or repetitive – -**ny**, ~**ness** n – ~**ly** adv

monster /'mɒnstə/ n 1a an animal or plant of (grotesquely) abnormal form or structure b an (imaginary) animal of incredible shape or form that is usu dangerous or horrifying 2 one exceptionally large for its kind 3 sthg monstrous; *esp* a person of appalling ugliness, wickedness, or cruelty

monstrous /'mɒnstrəs/ *adj* **1** having the qualities or appearance of a monster; extraordinarily large **2a** extraordinarily ugly or vicious **b** outrageously wrong or ridiculous – ~ly *adv*

month /mʌnθ/ *n* **1a** any of the 12 divisions of the year in the Julian or Gregorian calendars corresponding roughly with the period of the moon's rotation; *also* any similar division of the year in other calendars **b** 28 days or 4 weeks; *also* the interval between the same date in adjacent months **2** *pl* an indefinite usu protracted period of time

monthly /'mʌnθli/ *n* a monthly periodical **2** *pl* a menstrual period – *infml*

monument /'mɒnjʊmənt/ *n* **1a** a lasting evidence or reminder of sby or sthg notable or influential **b** a memorial stone, sculpture, or structure erected to commemorate a person or event **2** a structure or site of historical or archaeological importance

monumental /ˌmɒnjʊ'mentl/ *adj* **1a** of, serving as, or resembling a monument **b** occurring or used on a monument **2** very great in degree; imposing, outstanding

moo /mu:/ *v or n* (to) low

mood /mu:d/ *n* **1a** (the evocation, esp in art or literature, of) a predominant emotion, feeling, or frame of mind **b** the right frame of mind **2** a fit of often silent anger or bad temper

²mood *n* a distinct form or set of inflectional forms of a verb indicating whether the action or state it denotes is considered a fact, wish, possibility, etc

moody /'mu:di/ *adj* **1** sullen or gloomy **2** temperamental – **moodily** *adv* – **moodiness** *n*

moon /mu:n/ *n* **1** the earth's natural satellite that shines by reflecting the sun's light **2** a satellite

²moon *v* **1** to move about listlessly **2** to spend time in idle gazing or daydreaming *USE* often – *around* or *about*; *infml*

moonlight /'mu:nlaɪt/ *v* to hold a second job in addition to a regular one

¹moor /mʊə/ *n, chiefly Br* an expanse of open peaty infertile usu heath-covered upland

²moor *v* to make (e g a boat or buoy) fast with cables, lines, or anchors

Moor *n* a member of the mixed Arab and Berber people that conquered Spain in the 8th c AD

¹moot /mu:t/ *n* **1** an early English assembly to decide points of community and political interest **2** a mock court in which law students argue hypothetical cases

²moot *v* to put forward for discussion

³moot *adj* open to question; debatable – usu in *moot point*

¹mop /mɒp/ *n* **1** an implement consisting of a head made of absorbent material fastened to a long handle and used esp for cleaning floors **2** a shock of untidy hair

²mop *v* **1** to clean (a floor or other surface) with a mop **2** to wipe (as if) with a mop

¹moral /'mɒrəl/ *adj* **1a** of or being principles of right and wrong in conduct; ethical **b** conforming to a standard of right conduct **c** capable of distinguishing right and wrong **2** of, occurring in, or acting on the mind, emotions, or will – ~ly *adv*

²moral *n* **1** (a concluding passage pointing out) the moral significance or practical lesson **2** *pl* a standards of esp sexual conduct **b** ethics

morale /mə'rɑ:l/ *n* the mental and emotional condition (e g of enthusiasm or loyalty) of an individual or group with regard to the function or tasks at hand

morality /mə'ræləti/ *n* **1** a system or sphere of moral conduct **2** (degree of conformity to standards of) right conduct or moral correctness

morbid /'mɔ:bɪd/ *adj* **1** of, affected with, induced by, or characteristic of disease **2** abnormally susceptible to or characterized by gloomy feelings; *esp* having an unnatural preoccupation with death **3** grisly, gruesome – ~ity *n* – ~ly *adv*

¹more /mɔ:r/ *adj* **1** greater in quantity or number **2** additional, further

²more *adv* **1a** as an additional amount **b** moreover, again **2** to a greater degree or extent – often used with an adjective or adverb to form the comparative (e g much *more* even)

³more *n, pl* **more 1** a greater or additional quantity, amount, or part **2** *pl* additional ones

moreover /mɔ:'rəʊvə/ *adv* in addition to what has been said – used to introduce new matter

morning /'mɔ:nɪŋ/ *n* **1a** the dawn **b** the time from midnight or sunrise to noon **2** an early period (e g of time or life); the beginning

¹mortal /'mɔ:tl/ *adj* **1** causing or about to cause death; fatal **2** not living forever; subject to death **3** marked by relentless hostility **4** of or connected with death – *infml*

²mortal *n* **1** a human being **2** a person of a specified kind

mortality /mɔ:'tæləti/ *n* **1** being mortal **2** the death of large numbers of people, animals, etc; *also* the number of deaths in a given time or place **3** the human race

mortally /'mɔ:təli/ *adv* **1** in a deadly or fatal manner **2** to an extreme degree; intensely

¹mortgage /'mɔ:gɪdʒ/ *n* a transfer of the ownership of property (e g for security on a loan) on condition that the transfer becomes void on payment

²mortgage *v* **1** to transfer the ownership of (property) by a mortgage **2** to make subject to a claim or obligation

mosque /mɒsk/ *n* a building used for public worship by Muslims

mosquito /mə'ski:təʊ/ *n* any of numerous 2-winged flies with females that suck the blood of animals and often transmit diseases (e g malaria) to them

moss /mɒs/ n **1** any of a class of primitive plants with small leafy stems bearing sex organs at the tip; *also* many of these plants growing together and covering a surface **2** *chiefly Scot* a (peat) bog – ~y *adj*

¹most /məʊst/ *adj* **1** the majority of **2** greatest in quantity or extent

²most *adv* **1** to the greatest degree or extent – often used with an adjective or adverb to form the superlative (e g the *most* challenging job he ever had) **2** very (e g shall *most* certainly come)

³most *n, pl* **most** the greatest quantity, number, or amount

⁴most *adv, archaic, dial, or NAm* almost

mostly /məʊstli/ *adv* for the greatest part; mainly; *also* in most cases; usually

moth /mɒθ/ n **1** a clothes moth **2** a usu night-flying insect with feathery antennae and a stouter body and duller colouring than the butterflies

¹mother /ˈmʌðə⁄/ n **1a** a female parent **b** an old or elderly woman **2** a source, origin – ~less *adj*

²mother *adj* **1a** of or being a mother **b** bearing the relation of a mother **2** derived (as if) from one's mother **3** acting as or providing a parental stock – used without reference to sex

³mother *vt* **1a** to give birth to **b** to give rise to; initiate, produce **2** to care for or protect like a mother – often derog

mother-in-law *n, pl* **mothers-in-law** the mother of one's spouse

¹motion /ˈməʊʃən/ n **1a** a formal proposal made in a deliberative assembly **b** an application to a court or judge for an order, ruling, or direction **2a** an act, process, or instance of changing position; movement **b** an active or functioning state or condition **3a** an act or instance of moving the body or its parts; a gesture **b** pl actions, movements; *esp* merely simulated or mechanical actions – often in *go through the motions* **4** an evacuation of the bowels – usu pl with sing. meaning – ~less *adj*

²motion *v* to direct by a gesture

¹motive /ˈməʊtɪv/ n **1** a need, desire, etc that causes sby to act **2** a recurrent phrase or figure that is developed through the course of a musical composition – ~less *adj*

²motive *adj* **1** moving or tending to move to action **2** of (the causing of) motion

¹motor /ˈməʊtə⁄/ n **1** sthg or sby that imparts motion **2a** an internal-combustion engine **b** a rotating machine that transforms electrical energy into mechanical energy **3** a motor vehicle; *esp* a motor car

²motor *adj* **1a** causing or imparting motion **b** of or involving muscular movement **2a** equipped with or driven by a motor **b** of or involving motor vehicles

³motor *v* to travel by motor car; *esp* to drive – ~ist *n*

motor bike *n* a motorcycle – infml

motorboat /ˈməʊtəbəʊt⁄ n a usu small boat propelled by a motor

motorcycle /ˈməʊtəˌsaɪkəl⁄ n a 2-wheeled motor vehicle that can carry 1 or sometimes 2 people astride the engine – **-clist** n

motorway /ˈməʊtəweɪ⁄ n, Br a major road designed for high-speed traffic that has separate carriageways for different directions and certain restrictions on the types of vehicle and driver allowed on it

motto /ˈmɒtəʊ⁄ n, pl **mottoes 1** a sentence, phrase, or word inscribed on sthg as appropriate to or indicative of its character or use **2** a short expression of a guiding principle; a maxim **3** (a piece of paper printed with) a usu humorous or sentimental saying

¹mould /məʊld⁄ NAm chiefly **mold** n crumbling soft (humus-rich) soil suited to plant growth

²mould, *NAm chiefly* **mold** n **1** the frame on or round which an object is constructed **2** a cavity or form in which a substance (e g a jelly or a metal casting) is shaped **3** a fixed pattern or form

³mould, *NAm chiefly* **mold** v **1** to give shape to **2** to form in a mould **3** to exert a steady formative influence on **4** to fit closely to the contours of

⁴mould, *NAm chiefly* **mold** n (a fungus producing) an often woolly growth on the surface of damp or decaying organic matter

mouldy /ˈməʊldi⁄ *adj* **1** of, resembling, or covered with a mould-producing fungus **2** old and mouldering; fusty, crumbling **3a** miserable, nasty **b** stingy USE (3) infml – **mouldiness** n

mound /maʊnd⁄ n **1a** an artificial bank of earth or stones **b** a small hill **2** a heap, pile

¹mount /maʊnt⁄ n a high hill; a mountain – usu before a name

²mount v **1** to increase in amount, extent, or degree **2** to rise, ascend **3a** to get up on or into sthg above ground level; *esp* to seat oneself (e g on a horse) for riding **b** to go up; climb **c** *of a male animal* to copulate with (a female animal) **4** to initiate and carry out (e g an assault or strike) **5** to station for defence or observation or as an escort **6a** to attach to a support **b** to arrange or assemble for use or display **7a** to prepare (e g a specimen) for examination or display **b** to organize and present for public viewing or performance; stage

³mount n **1a** the material (e g cardboard) on which a picture is mounted **b** a jewellery setting **c** a hinge, card, etc for mounting a stamp in a stamp collection **2** a horse for riding

mountain /ˈmaʊntɪn⁄ n **1a** a landmass that projects conspicuously above its surroundings and is higher than a hill **2a** a vast amount or quantity – often pl with sing. meaning **b** a supply, esp of a specified usu agricultural commodity, in excess of demand – ~**ous** *adj*

mountainous /'maʊntɪnəs/ *adj* **1** containing many mountains **2** resembling a mountain; huge

mourn /mɔːn/ *v* to feel or express (e g in a conventional manner) grief or sorrow, esp for a death

mourning /'mɔːnɪŋ/ *n* **1** the act or state of one who mourns **2a** an outward sign (e g black clothes or an armband) of grief for a person's death **b** a period of time during which signs of grief are shown

¹**mouse** /maʊs/ *n, pl* **mice 1** any of numerous small rodents with a pointed snout, rather small ears, and slender tail **2** a timid person

²**mouse** *v* **1** to hunt for mice **2** *chiefly NAm* to search for carefully – usu + out

moustache /məˈstɑːʃ/ *NAm chiefly* **mustache** *n* the hair growing or allowed to grow on sby's upper lip

¹**mouth** /maʊθ/ *n* **1a** the opening through which food passes into an animal's body; *also* the cavity in the head of the typical vertebrate animal bounded externally by the lips that encloses the tongue, gums, and teeth **b** an individual, esp a child, requiring food **2** sthg like a mouth, esp in affording entrance or exit: e g **a** the place where a river enters a sea, lake, etc **b** the opening of a cave, volcano, etc **c** the opening of a container **3** a tendency to talk too much

²**mouth** /maʊð/ *v* **1** to utter pompously **2** to repeat without comprehension or sincerity **3** to form (words) soundlessly with the lips

mouthful /'maʊθfʊl/ *n* **1** a quantity that fills the mouth **2** a small quantity **3** a word or phrase that is very long or difficult to pronounce

mouthpiece /'maʊθpiːs/ *n* **1** sthg placed at or forming a mouth **2** a part (e g of a musical instrument or a telephone) that goes in the mouth or is put next to the mouth **3** sby or sthg that expresses or interprets another's views

¹**move** /muːv/ *v* **1a(1)** to go or pass with a continuous motion **(2)** to proceed or progress towards a (specified) place or condition – often + *on* **b** to change the place or position of **c(1)** to transfer a piece in a board game (e g in chess) from one position to another **(2)** *of a piece in board games* to travel or be capable of travelling to another position **d** to change one's residence **2** to pass one's life in a specified environment **3** to (cause to) change position or posture **4a** to take action; act **b** to prompt to action **5a** to make a formal request, application, or appeal **b** to propose formally in a deliberative assembly **6** to affect in such a way as to lead to a show of emotion or of a specified emotion **7** *of the bowels* to evacuate **8a** to (cause to) operate or function, esp mechanically **b** to show marked activity or speed – *infml* – ~**r** *n adj*

²**move** *n* **1a** the act of moving a piece (e g

in chess) **b** the turn of a player to move **2a** a step taken so as to gain an objective **b** a movement **c** a change of residence or official location

movement /'muːvmənt/ *n* **1a** the act or process of moving; *esp* change of place, position, or posture **b** an action, activity – usu pl with sing. meaning **2a** a trend, specif in prices **b** an organized effort to promote an end **3** the moving parts of a mechanism that transmit motion **4** a unit or division having its own key, rhythmic structure, and themes and forming a separate part of an extended musical composition

moving /'muːvɪŋ/ *adj* **1** marked by or capable of movement **b** of a change of residence or official location **2a** producing or transferring motion or action **b** evoking a deep emotional response – ~**ly** *adv*

¹**mow** /maʊ/ *n* the part of a barn where hay or straw is stored

²**mow** /məʊ/ *v* **mowed; mowed, mown 1** to cut down a crop, esp grass **2** to cut down the standing herbage, esp grass, of (e g a field) – ~**er** *n*

Mrs /'mɪsɪz/ *n* **1** – used as a conventional title of courtesy before a married woman's surname where no other title is appropriate **2** a wife – *infml*

Ms /mɪz, məz/ *n* – used instead of Mrs or Miss, esp when marital status is unknown or irrelevant

¹**much** /mʌtʃ/ *adj* **more** /'maw/; **most** /məʊst/ **1** great in quantity or extent (e g how *much* milk it is) **2** excessive, immoderate (e g it's a bit *much*)

²**much** *adv* **more; most 1a(1)** to a great degree or extent; considerably (e g was *much* happier) **(2)** very – with verbal adjectives (e g was *much* amused) **b** frequently, often (e g *much* married) **c** by far (e g *much* the fatter) **2** nearly, approximately (e g looks *much* the same)

³**much** *n* **1** a great quantity, amount, or part **2** sthg considerable or impressive (e g wasn't *much* to look at) **3** a relative quantity or part (e g I'll say this *much* for him)

mud /mʌd/ *n* **1** (a sticky mixture of a solid and a liquid resembling) soft wet earth **2** abusive and malicious remarks or charges

¹**muddle** /'mʌdl/ *v* **1** to stupefy, esp with alcohol **2** to mix confusedly in one's mind – often + *up* **3** to proceed or get along in a confused aimless way – + *along* or *on*

²**muddle** *n* **1** a state of (mental) confusion **2** a confused mess

¹**muddy** /'mʌdi/ *adj* **1** lacking in clarity or brightness **2** obscure in meaning; muddled, confused

²**muddy** *v* to make cloudy, dull, or confused

¹**mug** /mʌg/ *n* **1** a large usu cylindrical drinking cup **2** the face or mouth of sby **3** sby easily deceived; a sucker *USE* (2 & 3) *infml*

²**mug** *v* to assault, esp in the street with intent to rob – **mugger** *n* – **mugging** *n*

¹**multiple** /'mʌltɪpəl/ *adj* **1** consisting

of, including, or involving more than 1
2 many, manifold **3** shared by many

²**multiple** *n* **1** the product of a quantity
by an integer **2 multiple, multiple store**
a chain store

multiplication /ˌmʌltɪplɪˈkeɪʃən/ *n* **1**
multiplying or being multiplied **2** a
mathematical operation that at its simplest is an abbreviated process of adding
an integer to itself a specified number of
times

multiply /ˈmʌltɪplaɪ/ *v* **1a** to become
greater in number; spread **b** to breed or
propagate **2** to perform multiplication

multitude /ˈmʌltɪtjuːd/ *n* **1** a great
number; a host **2** a crowd – chiefly fml
3 *the* populace, masses

mumble /ˈmʌmbəl/ *v* to say (words) in
an inarticulate usu subdued voice

municipal /mjuːˈnɪsɪpəl/ *adj* **1a** of a
municipality **b** having local
self-government **2** restricted to 1 locality – **~ly** *adv*

¹**murder** /ˈmɜːdəʳ/ *n* the crime of unlawfully and intentionally killing sby

²**murder** *v* **1** to kill (sby) unlawfully and
intentionally **2** to slaughter brutally **3**
to mutilate, mangle – **~er** *n*
– **~ess** *n*

murderous /ˈmɜːdərəs/ *adj* **1** having
the purpose or capability of murder or
characterized by or causing murder or
bloodshed – **~ly** *adv* – **~ness** *n*

¹**murmur** /ˈmɜːməʳ/ *n* **1** a
half-suppressed or muttered complaint
2a a low indistinct (continuous) sound
b a subdued or gentle utterance

²**murmur** *v* **1** to make a murmur **2** to
complain, grumble – **~ing** *n*

muscle /ˈmʌsəl/ *n* **1** (an organ that
moves a body part, consisting of) a
tissue made of modified elongated cells
that contract when stimulated to produce motion **2** muscular strength; brawn
– **~d** *adj*

muscular /ˈmʌskjʊləʳ/ *adj* **1a** of, constituting, or performed by muscle or the
muscles **b** having well-developed
muscles **2** having strength of expression
or character; vigorous – **~ly** *adv*

museum /mjuːˈzɪəm/ *n* an institution
devoted to the acquiring, care, study,
and display of objects of interest or
value; *also* a place exhibiting such
objects

¹**mushroom** /ˈmʌʃruːm, -rʊm/ *n* the
enlarged, esp edible, fleshy fruiting
body of a fungus, consisting typically of
a stem bearing a flattened cap

²**mushroom** *v* **1** to spring up suddenly
or multiply rapidly **2** to flatten at the
end on impact **3** to pick wild mushrooms

music /ˈmjuːzɪk/ *n* **1** vocal, instrumental, or mechanical sounds having
rhythm, melody, or harmony **2** an
agreeable sound **3** the score of a musical composition set down on paper

¹**musical** /ˈmjuːzɪkəl/ *adj* **1** having the
pleasing harmonious qualities of music
2 having an interest in or talent for
music **3** set to or accompanied by music
4 of music, musicians, or music lovers
– **-ly** *adv*

²**musical** *n* a film or theatrical production containing songs, dances, and
dialogue

musician /mjuːˈzɪʃən/ *n* a composer,
conductor, or performer of music; *esp*
an instrumentalist

Muslim /ˈmʌzlɪm, ˈmʊz-, ˈmʊs-/ *n* an
adherent of Islam

¹**must** /məst; *strong* mʌst/ *verbal auxiliary, pres & past all persons* **must 1a** be
commanded or requested to (e g you
must stop) **b** certainly should; ought by
all means to (e g I *must* read that book)
2 be compelled by physical, social, or
legal necessity to (e g man *must* eat to
live); be required by need or purpose to
(e g we *must* hurry if we want to catch
the bus) – past often replaced by *had to*
except in reported speech; used in the
negative to express the idea of prohibition (e g we *must* not park here) **3** be
unreasonably or perversely compelled
to (e g why *must* you be so stubborn?)
4 be logically inferred or supposed to
(e g it *must* be time) **5** was presumably
certain to; was or were bound to (e g if
he really was there, I *must* have seen
him)

²**must** *n* an essential or prerequisite

³**must** *n* grape juice before and during
fermentation

mustard /ˈmʌstəd/ *n* a pungent yellow
powder used as a condiment or in medicine, esp as an emetic; *also* any of several related plants with lobed leaves,
yellow flowers, and straight pods that
product seeds from which mustard is
prepared

mutilate /ˈmjuːtɪleɪt/ *v* **1** to cut off or
permanently destroy or damage a limb
or essential part of **2** to damage or
deface – **-tion** *n*

mutiny /ˈmjuːtɪni, -tənɪ/ *n* concerted
revolt (e g of a naval crew) against discipline or a superior officer

mutter /ˈmʌtəʳ/ *v* to utter, esp in a low
or indistinct voice

mutton /ˈmʌtn/ *n* the flesh of a mature
sheep used as food

mutual /ˈmjuːtʃʊəl/ *adj* **1a** directed by
each towards the other **b** having the
same specified feeling for each other **2**
shared by 2 or more in common – **~ity**
n – **~ly** *adv*

my /maɪ/ *adj* **1** of me or myself, esp as
possessor, agent, or object of an action
– sometimes used with vocatives (e g *my*
lord) **2** – used interjectionally to
express surprise, in certain fixed exclamations (e g *my* God!), and with names
of certain parts of the body to express
doubt or disapproval (e g *my* foot!)

myself /maɪˈself/ *pron* **1** that identical
one that is I – used reflexively, for
emphasis, or in absolute constructions
(e g *myself* a tourist, I nevertheless
avoided other tourists) **2** my normal
self (e g I'm not quite *myself* today)

mysterious /mɪˈstɪərɪəs/ *adj* **1** difficult
to comprehend **2** containing, suggesting, or implying mystery – **~ly** *adv*
– **~ness** *n*

mystery /ˈmɪstərɪ/ *n* **1a** a religious
truth disclosed by revelation alone **b** a

secret religious rite **2a** sthg not understood or beyond understanding **b** a fictional work dealing usu with the solution of a mysterious crime **3** an enigmatic or secretive quality *adj*

myth /mɪθ/ *n* **1** a traditional story that embodies popular beliefs or explains a practice, belief, or natural phenomenon **2** a parable, allegory **3a** a person or thing having a fictitious existence **b** a belief subscribed to uncritically by an (interested) group – ~ical *adj*

N

¹**nag** /næg/ *n* a horse; *esp* one that is old or in poor condition

²**nag** *v* **1** to subject to constant scolding or urging **2** to be a persistent source of annoyance or discomfort – ~ger *n*

³**nag** *n* a person, esp a woman, who nags habitually

¹**nail** /neɪl/ *n* **1** a horny sheath protecting the upper end of each finger and toe of human beings and other primates **2** a slender usu pointed and headed spike designed to be driven in, esp with a hammer, to join materials, act as a support, etc

²**nail** *v* **1** to fasten (as if) with a nail **2** to fix steadily **3** to catch, trap **4** to detect and expose (e g a lie or scandal) so as to discredit

naive, naïve /naɪˈiːv/ *adj* **1** ingenuous, unsophisticated **2** lacking worldly wisdom or experience; *esp* credulous – ~ty *n*

naked /ˈneɪkɪd/ *adj* **1** having no clothes on **2a** of a knife or sword not enclosed in a sheath or scabbard **b** exposed to the air or to full view **3** without furnishings or ornamentation **4** unarmed, defenceless **5** not concealed or disguised **6** unaided by any optical device – ~ly *adv* – ~ness *n*

¹**name** /neɪm/ *n* **1** a word or phrase designating an individual person or thing **2** a descriptive usu disparaging epithet **3a** reputation **b** a famous or notorious person or thing

²**name** *v* **1** to give a name to; call **2** to identify by name **3** to nominate, appoint **4** to decide on; choose **5** to mention explicitly; specify

namely /ˈneɪmli/ *adv* that is to say

namesake /ˈneɪmseɪk/ *n* sby or sthg that has the same name as another

narrate /nəˈreɪt/ *v* to recite the details of (a story)

narrative /ˈnærətɪv/ *n* **1** sthg (e g a story) that is narrated **2** the art or practice of narration

¹**narrow** /ˈnærəʊ/ *adj* **1** of little width, esp in comparison with height or length **2** limited in size or scope; restricted **3** inflexible, hidebound **4** only just sufficient or successful – ~ness *n*

²**narrow** *n* a narrow part or (water) passage – usu pl with sing. meaning

³**narrow** *v* to make or become narrow or narrower

narrow-minded *adj* lacking tolerance or breadth of vision; bigoted – ~ness *n*

nasty /ˈnɑːsti/ *adj* **1** repugnant, esp to smell or taste **2** obscene, indecent **3** mean, tawdry **4a** harmful, dangerous **b** disagreeable, dirty **5** giving cause for concern or anxiety **6** spiteful, vicious – -tily *adv* – -tiness *n*

nation /ˈneɪʃən/ *n* **1** a people with a common origin, tradition, and language (capable of) constituting a nation-state **2** a community of people possessing a more or less defined territory and government

nationalism /ˈnæʃənəlɪzəm/ *n* loyalty and devotion to a nation; *esp* the exalting of one nation above all others – -list, *adj* – -listic *adj* – -listically *adv*

nationality /ˌnæʃəˈnælɪti/ *n* **1** national character **2** national status **3** citizenship of a particular nation **4** existence as a separate nation

nationalize, -ise /ˈnæʃənəlaɪz/ *v* to invest control or ownership of in the national government

¹**native** /ˈneɪtɪv/ *adj* **1** inborn, innate **2** belonging to a particular place by birth **3a** belonging to or being the place of one's birth **b** of or being one's first language or sby using his/her first language **4** living (naturally), grown, or produced in a particular place; indigenous **5** found in nature, esp in a pure form

²**native** *n* **1** one born or reared in a particular place **2a** an original or indigenous (non-European) inhabitant **b** a plant, animal, etc indigenous to a particular locality **3** a local resident

¹**natural** /ˈnætʃərəl/ *adj* **1** based on an inherent moral sense **2** in accordance with or determined by nature **3** related by blood rather than by adoption **4** innate, inherent **5** of nature as an object of study **6** having a specified character or attribute by nature **7** happening in accordance with the ordinary course of nature **8** normal or expected **9** of the physical as opposed to the spiritual world **10a** true to nature; lifelike **b** free from affectation or constraint **c** not disguised or altered in appearance or form **11** (containing only notes that are) neither sharp nor flat – ~ness *n*

²**natural** *n* **1** (a note affected by) a sign placed on the musical staff to nullify the effect of a preceding sharp or flat **2** one having natural skills or talents

naturalist /ˈnætʃərəlɪst/ *n* a student of natural history

naturally /ˈnætʃərəli/ *adv* **1** by nature **2** as might be expected **3** in a natural manner

nature /ˈneɪtʃəʳ/ *n* **1** the inherent character or constitution of a person or thing **2** a creative and controlling force in the universe **3** the physical constitution of an organism **4** the external world in its entirety **5** natural scenery

naughty /ˈnɔːti/ *adj* **1** badly behaved;

wicked 2 slightly improper – euph or humor – **-tily** adv – **-tiness** n

nauseate /'nɔːzɪeɪt, -sɪ-/ v to (cause to) become affected with nausea or disgust

nautical /'nɔːtɪkəl/ adj of or associated with seamen, navigation, or ships – **~ly** adv

naval /'neɪvəl/ adj 1 of a navy 2 consisting of or involving warships

navigate /'nævɪgeɪt/ v 1 to steer a course through a medium (e g water) 2 to perform the activities (e g taking sightings and making calculations) involved in navigation 3a to steer or manage (a boat) in sailing b to operate or direct the course of (e g an aircraft) – **-ion** n

navy /'neɪvi/ n 1 a nation's ships of war and support vessels together with the organization needed for maintenance 2 sing or pl in constr the personnel manning a navy 3 navy blue

¹**near** /nɪə/ adv 1 in or into a near position or manner (e g came near to tears) 2 closely approximating; nearly (e g a near-perfect performance)

²**near** prep near to (e g went too near the edge)

³**near** adj 1 intimately connected or associated 2a not far distant in time, space, or degree b close, narrow (e g a near miss) 3a being the closer of 2 (e g the near side) b being the left-hand one of a pair (e g the near wheel of a cart) – **-ness** n

⁴**near** v to approach

nearby /nɪə'baɪ/ adv or adj close at hand

nearly /'nɪəli/ adv 1 in a close manner or relationship (e g nearly related) 2 almost but not quite

¹**neat** /niːt/ adj 1 without addition or dilution 2 elegantly simple 3a precise, well-defined b skilful, adroit 4 (habitually) tidy and orderly 5 chiefly NAm fine, excellent – infml

²**neat** adv without addition or dilution; straight

necessarily /'nesɪsərɪli, ˌnesɪ'serɪli/ adv as a necessary consequence; inevitably

¹**necessary** /'nesəsəri/ n an indispensable item; an essential

²**necessary** adj 1a inevitable, inescapable b logically unavoidable 2 essential, indispensable

necessity /nɪ'sesɪti/ n 1 the quality of being necessary, indispensable, or unavoidable 2 impossibility of a contrary order or condition 3 poverty, want 4a sthg necessary or indispensable b a pressing need or desire

¹**neck** /nek/ n 1a the part of an animal that connects the head with the body; also a cut of meat taken from this part b the part of a garment that covers the neck; also the neckline 2a a narrow part, esp shaped like a neck b the part of a stringed musical instrument extending from the body and supporting the fingerboard and strings

²**neck** v to kiss and caress in sexual play – infml

necklace /'nek-lɪs/ n a string of jewels, beads, etc worn round the neck as an ornament

¹**need** /niːd/ n 1a a lack of sthg necessary, desirable, or useful b a physiological or psychological requirement for the well-being of an organism 2 a condition requiring supply or relief 3 poverty, want

²**need** v 1 to be in need of; require 2 to be constrained (e g I'll need to work hard) va 3 be under necessity or obligation to

¹**needle** /'niːdl/ n 1a a small slender usu steel instrument with an eye for thread at one end and a sharp point at the other, used for sewing b any of various similar larger instruments without an eye, used for carrying thread and making stitches (e g in crocheting or knitting) c the slender hollow pointed end of a hypodermic syringe for injecting or removing material 2 a slender, usu sharp-pointed, indicator on a dial; esp a magnetic needle 3 a needle-shaped leaf, esp of a conifer 4 Br a feeling of enmity or ill will – infml

²**needle** v to provoke by persistent teasing or gibes

needless /'niːdlɪs/ adj not needed; unnecessary – **~ly** adv

¹**negative** /'negətɪv/ adj 1a marked by denial, prohibition, or refusal b expressing negation 2 lacking positive or agreeable features 3 less than zero and opposite in sign to a positive number that when added to the given number yields zero 4 having lower electric potential and constituting the part towards which the current flows from the external circuit 5 having the light and dark parts in approximately inverse order to those of the original photographic subject – **~ly** adv

²**negative** n 1 a negative reply 2 sthg that is the negation or opposite of sthg else 3 an expression (e g the word no) of negation or denial 4 the side that upholds the contradictory proposition in a debate 5 the plate of an electric cell that is at the lower potential 6 a negative photographic image on transparent material used for printing positive pictures

¹**neglect** /nɪ'glekt/ v 1 to pay insufficient attention to; disregard 2 to leave undone or unattended to

²**neglect** n neglecting or being neglected

negligent /'neglɪdʒənt/ adj 1 (habitually or culpably) neglectful 2 pleasantly casual in manner – **~ly** adv – **-gence** n

negligible /'neglɪdʒəbəl/ adj trifling, insignificant – **-bly** adv

negotiate /nɪ'gəʊʃieɪt/ v 1 to confer with another in order to reach an agreement 2a to transfer (e g a bill of exchange) to another by delivery or endorsement b to convert into cash or the equivalent value 3a to travel successfully along or over b to complete or deal with successfully – **-ation** n – **-ator** n

Negress /'niːgrɪs/ n a female Negro – chiefly derog

Negro /'niːgrəʊ/ n a member of the esp African branch of the black race of mankind

¹**neighbour** /'neɪbə/ n 1 one living or situated near another 2 a fellow human being

²**neighbour** v to adjoin or lie near to

neighbourhood /'neɪbəhʊd/ n 1 an adjacent or surrounding region 2 an approximate amount, extent, or degree 3 (the inhabitants of) a district of a town, city etc, forming a distinct community

¹**neither** /'naɪðə/ pron not the one or the other (e g neither of us)

²**neither** conj 1 not either (e g neither here nor there) 2 also not; nor (e g he didn't go and neither did I)

³**neither** adj not either (e g neither hand)

⁴**neither** adv 1 similarly not; also not (e g I can't swim. Neither can I) 2 chiefly dial either

nephew /'nevjuː, 'nef-/ n a son of one's brother or sister or of one's brother-in-law or sister-in-law

¹**nerve** /nɜːv/ n 1 any of the filaments of nervous tissue that conduct nervous impulses to and from the nervous system and are made up of axons and dendrites 2 fortitude, tenacity 3 (disrespectful) assurance or boldness 4a a sore or sensitive subject – esp in hit/touch a nerve b pl acute nervousness or anxiety

²**nerve** v 1 to give strength and courage to 2 to prepare (oneself) psychologically for – often + up

nervous /'nɜːvəs/ adj 1 of, affected by, or composed of (the) nerves or neurons 2a easily excited or agitated b timid, apprehensive – ~ly adv – ~ness n

nervous system n the brain, spinal cord, or other nerves and nervous tissue together forming a system for interpreting stimuli from the sense organs and transmitting impulses to muscles, glands, etc

¹**nest** /nest/ n 1a a bed or receptacle prepared by a bird for its eggs and young b a place or structure in which animals live, esp in their immature stages 2a a place of rest, retreat, or lodging b a den or haunt 3 a series of objects made to fit close together or one inside another

²**nest** v 1 to build or occupy a nest 2 to fit compactly together

¹**net** /net/ n 1 an open meshed fabric twisted, knotted, or woven together at regular intervals and used for a variety of purposes, e g fishing or as a barrier in various games 2 (the fabric that encloses the sides and back of) a soccer, hockey, etc goal 3a a practice cricket pitch surrounded by nets – usu pl b a period of practice in such a net

²**net** v 1 to cover or enclose (as if) with a net 2 to hit (a ball) into the net for the loss of a point in a game

³**net** adj remaining after all deductions (e g for taxes, outlay, or loss) 2 final, ultimate

⁴**net** v 1 to make by way of profit 2 to get possession of

¹**nettle** /'netl/ n any of a genus of widely distributed green-flowered plants covered with (stinging) hairs

²**nettle** v 1 to strike or sting (as if) with nettles 2 to arouse to annoyance or anger

network /'netwɜːk/ n 1 a fabric or structure of cords or wires that cross at regular intervals and are knotted or secured at the crossings 2 a system of crisscrossing lines or channels 3 an interconnected chain, group, or system 4a a group of radio or television stations linked together so that they can broadcast the same programmes if desired b a radio or television company that produces programmes for broadcast over such a network

¹**neuter** /'njuːtə/ adj 1 of or belonging to the gender that is neither masculine nor feminine 2 lacking generative organs or having nonfunctional ones – neuter n

²**neuter** v to castrate

¹**neutral** /'njuːtrəl/ adj 1 (of or being a country, person, etc) not engaged on either side of a war, dispute, etc 2a indifferent, indefinite b without colour c neither acid nor alkaline d not electrically charged or positive or negative; not live – ~ity n – ~ly adv

²**neutral** n 1 a neutral country, person, etc 2 a neutral colour 3 a position (of a gear lever) in which gears are disengaged

neutron /'njuːtrɒn/ n an uncharged elementary particle with a mass about that of the proton, present in the nuclei of all atoms except those of normal hydrogen

never /'nevə/ adv 1 not ever; at no time 2 not in any degree; not under any condition (e g this will never do) 3 surely not (e g you're never 18!) – chiefly infml

nevertheless /,nevəðə'les/ adv in spite of that; yet

¹**new** /njuː/ adj 1 not old; not used previously; recent 2a only recently discovered, recognized, or in use; novel b different from or replacing a former one of the same kind 3 having been in the specified condition or relationship for only a short time; unaccustomed 4 cap modern; esp in use after medieval times

²**new** adv newly, recently – usu in combination

news /njuːz/ n pl but sing in constr 1 (a report or series of reports of) recent (notable) events; new information about sthg 2a news reported in a newspaper, a periodical, or a broadcast b material that is newsworthy 3 a radio or television broadcast of news

newsagent /'njuːz,eɪdʒənt/'nuːz- Brə/ n, chiefly Br a retailer of newspapers and magazines

newspaper /'njuːs,peɪpə/ n (an organization that publishes) a paper printed and distributed usu daily or weekly and containing news, articles of opinion, features, and advertising

¹**next** /nekst/ *adj* **1** immediately adjacent or following (e g in place or order) **2** immediately after the present or a specified time

²**next** *adv* **1** in the time, place, or order nearest or immediately succeeding **2** on the first occasion to come (e g when we *next* meet)

³**next** *prep* nearest or adjacent to (e g wear wool *next* to the skin)

⁴**next** *n* the next occurrence, item, or issue of a kind

next-door *adj* situated or living in the next building, room, etc

next door *adv* in or to the next building, room, etc – **next-door** *adj*

next of kin *n, pl* **next of kin** the person most closely related to another person

nib /nɪb/ *n* **1** a bill or beak **2** the writing point of a pen **3** a small pointed or projecting part or article

¹**nibble** /'nɪbəl/ *v* **1** to take gentle, small, or cautious bites **2** to show cautious or qualified interest *USE* often + *at*

²**nibble** *n* **1** an act of nibbling **2** a very small amount (e g of food) *USE* infml

nice /naɪs/ *adj* **1** showing or requiring fine discrimination or treatment **2a** pleasant, agreeable **b** well done; well-executed **3** inappropriate or unpleasant – usu ironic **4a** socially acceptable; well-bred **b** decent, proper – ~**ly** *adv* – ~**ness** *n*

nickname /'nɪkneɪm/ *n* **1** a name used in place of or in addition to a proper name **2** a familiar form of a proper name, esp of a person

nicotine /'nɪkətiːn/ *n* an alkaloid that is the chief drug in tobacco

niece /niːs/ *n* a daughter of one's brother or sister or of one's brother-in-law or sister-in-law

night /naɪt/ *n* **1** the period of darkness from dusk to dawn caused by the earth's daily rotation **2** an evening characterized by a specified event or activity **3a** darkness **b** a state of affliction, ignorance, or obscurity

nightingale /'naɪtɪŋgeɪl/ *n* any of several Old World thrushes noted for the sweet usu nocturnal song of the male

nightmare /'naɪtmeə/ *n* **1** a frightening dream that usu awakens the sleeper **2** an experience, situation, or object that causes acute anxiety or terror – **-marish** *adj* – **-marishly** *adv* – **-marishness** *n*

nil /nɪl/ *n* nothing, zero

nimble /'nɪmbəl/ *adj* **1** quick, light, and easy in movement **2** quick and clever in thought and understanding – ~**ness** *n* – **-bly** *adv*

nine /naɪn/ *n* **1** the number 9 **2** the first or last 9 holes of an 18-hole golf course **3** *pl in constr, cap* the Common Market countries between 1973 and 1981

nineteen /,naɪn'tiːn/ *n* the number 19 – ~**th** *adj, adv, n, pron*

ninety /'naɪnti/ *n* **1** the number 90 **2** *pl* (a range of temperatures, ages, or dates within a century characterized by) the numbers 90 to 99 – **-tieth** *adj, n, adv, pron*

ninth /naɪnθ/ *n* **1** 9th **2a** (a chord containing) a musical interval of an octave and a second **b** the note separated by this interval from a lower note

¹**nip** /nɪp/ *v* **1** to catch hold of and squeeze sharply; pinch **2** to sever (as if) by pinching sharply – often + *off* **3** to injure or make numb with cold **4** to go quickly or briefly; hurry – infml

²**nip** *n* **1** a sharp stinging cold **2** (an instance of) nipping; a pinch

³**nip** *n* a small measure or drink of spirits

Nip *n* a Japanese – derog

nitrogen /'naɪtrədʒən/ *n* a trivalent gaseous chemical element that constitutes about 78 per cent by volume of the atmosphere and is found in combined form as a constituent of all living things

¹**no** /nəʊ/ *adv* **1** – used to negate an alternative choice **2** in no respect or degree – in comparisons **3** – used in answers expressing negation, dissent, denial, or refusal; contrasted with *yes* **4** – used like a question demanding assent to the preceding statement **5** nay **6** – used as an interjection to express incredulity **7** *chiefly Scot* not

²**no** *adj* **1a** not any (e g *no* money) **b** hardly any; very little (e g I'll be finished in *no* time) **2a** not a; quite other than a (e g he's *no* expert) **b** – used before a noun phrase to give force to an opposite meaning (e g in *no* uncertain terms)

³**no** *n, pl* **noes, nos** a negative reply or vote

No, Noh *n* a classic Japanese (form of) dance-drama

nobility /nəʊ'bɪləti, nə-/ *n* **1** being noble **2** *sing or pl in constr* the people making up a noble class

¹**noble** /'nəʊbəl/ *adj* **1a** gracious and dignified in character or bearing **b** famous, notable **2** of or being high birth or exalted rank **3** imposing, stately **4** having or showing a magnanimous character or high ideals – **nobly** *adv*

²**noble** *n* a person of noble rank or birth

¹**nobody** /'nəʊbədi/ *pron* not anybody

²**nobody** *n* a person of no influence or consequence

¹**nod** /nɒd/ *v* **1** to make a short downward movement of the head (e g in assent or greeting) **2** to become drowsy or sleepy **3** to make a slip or error in a moment of inattention

²**nod** *n* **1** (an instance of) nodding **2** an unconsidered indication of agreement, approval, etc – infml

¹**noise** /nɔɪz/ *n* **1** loud confused shouting or outcry **2a** (a harsh or unwanted) sound **b** unwanted signals or fluctuations in an electrical circuit

²**noise** *v* to spread by gossip or hearsay – usu + *about* or *abroad*

noisy /'nɔɪzi/ *adj* **1** making noise **2** full of or characterized by noise – **noisily** *adv* – **noisiness** *n*

nomad /'nəʊmæd/ n 1 a member of a people that wanders from place to place, usu seasonally 2 one who wanders aimlessly from place to place – ~ic adj – ~ically adv

nominate /'nɒmɪneɪt/ v 1 to designate, specify 2a to appoint or recommend for appointment b to propose for an honour, award, or as a candidate – -tion n

noncommittal /,nɒnkə'mɪtl/ adj giving no clear indication of attitude or feeling – ~ly adv

¹**none** /nʌn/ pron, pl none 1 not any; not part or thing 2 not one person; nobody (e g it's none other than Tom) 3 not any such thing or person

²**none** adv 1 by no means; not at all 2 in no way; to no extent

nonentity /nɒ'nentɪti/ n sby or sthg of little importance or interest

nonsense /'nɒnsəns/ n 1a meaningless words or language b foolish or absurd language, conduct, or thought 2 frivolous or insolent behaviour 3 – used interjectionally to express forceful disagreement

nonstop /,nɒn'stɒp/ adj done or made without a stop – **nonstop** adv

noon /nuːn/ n 1 noon, noonday the middle of the day; midday 2 the highest or culminating point

no one pron nobody

noose /nuːs/ n a loop with a running knot that tightens as the rope is pulled – **noose** v

nor /nɔː/ conj 1 – used to join 2 sentence elements of the same class or function (e g not done by you nor me) 2 also not; neither (e g it didn't seem hard, nor was it)

nor' n north – often in combination

normal /'nɔːməl/ adj 1 conforming to or constituting a norm, rule, or principle; not odd or unusual 2 occurring naturally 3a having average intelligence or development b free from mental disorder – ~ize v – ~ly adv

north /nɔːθ/ adj or adv towards, at, belonging to, or coming from the north

¹**north** n 1 (the compass point corresponding to) the direction of the north terrestrial pole 2 often cap regions or countries lying to the north of a specified or implied point of orientation

¹**northeast** /,nɔː'θiːst/ adj or adv towards, at, belonging to, or coming from the northeast

²**northeast** /,nɔː'θiːst/ n 1 (the general direction corresponding to) the compass point midway between north and east 2 often cap regions or countries lying to the northeast of a specified or implied point of orientation

¹**northerly** /'nɔːðəli/ adj or adv north

²**northerly** n a wind from the north

northern /'nɔːðən/ adj 1 often cap (characteristic) of a region conventionally designated North 2 north

north pole n 1a often cap N&P the northernmost point of the rotational axis of the earth b the northernmost point on the celestial sphere, about

which the stars seem to revolve 2 the northward-pointing pole of a magnet

¹**northwest** /,nɔː'θwest/ adj or adv towards, at, belonging to, or coming from the northwest

²**northwest** n 1 (the general direction corresponding to) the compass point midway between north and west 2 often cap regions or countries lying to the northwest of a specified or implied point of orientation

¹**nose** /nəʊz/ n 1a the part of the face that bears the nostrils and covers the front part of the nasal cavity b a snout, muzzle 2a the sense or (vertebrate) organ of smell b aroma, bouquet 3 the projecting part or front end of sthg 4a the nose as a symbol of undue curiosity or interference b a knack for detecting what is latent or concealed

²**nose** v 1 to use the nose in examining, smelling, etc; to sniff or nuzzle 2a to pry – often + into b to search or look inquisitively – usu + about or around 3 to move ahead slowly or cautiously

nostalgia /nɒ'stældʒə/ n 1 homesickness 2 a wistful or excessively sentimental yearning for sthg past or irrecoverable – -gic adj – -gically adv

nostril /'nɒstrɪl/ n the opening of the nose to the outside

nosy, nosey /'nəʊzi/ adj prying, snooping – infml

not /nɒt/ adv 1 – used to negate a (preceding) word or word group (e g not thirsty; will it rain? I hope not) 2 – used to give force to an opposite meaning (e g not without – reason)

¹**notable** /'nəʊtəbl/ adj 1 worthy of note; remarkable 2 distinguished, prominent – -bly adv – -bility n

²**notable** n 1 a prominent person 2 pl, often cap a group of people summoned, esp in France when it was a monarchy, to act as a deliberative body

¹**notch** /nɒtʃ/ n 1 a V-shaped indentation 2 a degree, step

²**notch** v 1 to make a notch in 2 to score or achieve – usu + up

¹**note** /nəʊt/ v 1a to take due or special notice of b to record in writing 2 to make special mention of; remark

²**note** n 1a(1) a sound having a definite pitch (2) a call, esp of a bird b a written symbol used to indicate duration and pitch of a tone by its shape and position on the staff 2a a characteristic feature of smell, flavour, etc b a mood or quality 3a a memorandum b a brief comment or explanation c a piece of paper money d(1) a short informal letter (2) a formal diplomatic communication 4a distinction, reputation b observation, notice

notebook /'nəʊtbʊk/ n a book for notes or memoranda

noted /'nəʊtɪd/ adj well-known, famous

¹**nothing** /'nʌθɪŋ/ pron 1 not any thing; no thing 2 sthg of no consequence 3 no truth or value (e g there's nothing in this rumour)

²**nothing** adv not at all; in no degree

³**nothing** n 1 sthg that does not exist 2

sby or sthg of no or slight value or size

⁴nothing *adj* of no account; worthless

¹notice /ˈnəʊtɪs/ *n* **1a** warning of a future occurrence **b** notification of intention of terminating an agreement at a particular time **2** attention, heed **3** a written or printed announcement **4** a review (e g of a play)

²notice *v* **1** to comment upon; refer to **2** to take notice of; mark

notification /ˌnəʊtɪfɪˈkeɪʃən/ *n* **1** (an instance of) notifying **2** sthg written that gives notice

notify /ˈnəʊtɪfaɪ/ *v* **1** to give (official) notice to **2** to make known

notion /ˈnəʊʃən/ *n* **1a** a broad general concept **b** a conception, impression **2** a whim or fancy

notorious /nəʊˈtɔːrɪəs, nə-/ *adj* well-known, esp for a specific (unfavourable) quality or trait – ~**ly** *adv*

nought /nɔːt/ *n* **1** naught; nothing **2** the arithmetical symbol 0; zero

noun /naʊn/ *n* a word that is the name of a person, place, thing, substance, or state and that belongs to 1 of the major form classes in grammar

nourish /ˈnʌrɪʃ/ *v* **1** to nurture, rear **2** to encourage the growth of; foster **3** to provide or sustain with nutriment; feed – ~**ment** *n*

¹novel /ˈnɒvəl/ *adj* **1** new and unlike anything previously known **2** original and striking, esp in conception or style

²novel *n* an invented prose narrative that deals esp with human experience and social behaviour – ~**ist** *n*

novelty /ˈnɒvəlti/ *n* **1** sthg new and unusual **2** a small manufactured often cheap article for personal or household adornment

November /nəʊˈvembə, nə-/ *n* the 11th month of the Gregorian calendar

novice /ˈnɒvɪs/ *n* **1** a person admitted to probationary membership of a religious community **2** a beginner

¹now /naʊ/ *adv* **1a** at the present time **b** in the immediate past **c** in the time immediately to follow; forthwith **2** – used with the sense of present time weakened or lost **a** to introduce an important point or indicate a transition (e g *now* if we turn to the next aspect of the problem) **b** to express command, request, or warning (e g *now*, don't squabble) **3** sometimes – linking 2 or more coordinate words or phrases (e g *now* one and *now* another) **4** under the changed or unchanged circumstances (e g he'll never believe me *now*) **5** at the time referred to (e g *now* the trouble began) **6** up to the present or to the time referred to (e g haven't been for years *now*)

²now *conj* in view of the fact that; since

³now *n* **1** the present time **2** the time referred to

nowadays /ˈnaʊədeɪz/ *adv* in these modern times; today

¹nowhere /ˈnəʊweə/ *adv* **1** not anywhere **2** to no purpose or result

²nowhere *n* a nonexistent place

nuclear /ˈnjuːklɪə/ *adj* **1** of or constituting a nucleus **2** of, using, or being the atomic nucleus, atomic energy, the atom bomb, or atomic power

nucleus /ˈnjuːklɪəs/ *n*, *pl* **nuclei** a central point, mass, etc about which gathering, concentration, etc takes place: e g **a** a usu round membrane-surrounded cell part that contains the chromosomes **b** the positively charged central part of an atom that accounts for nearly all of the atomic mass and consists of protons and usu neutrons

¹nude /njuːd/ *adj* without clothing or covering; naked, bare – **nudity** *n*

²nude *n* **1a** a representation of a nude human figure **b** a nude person **2** the state of being nude

nudge /nʌdʒ/ *v* **1** to touch or push gently; *esp* to catch the attention of by a push of the elbow **2** to move (as if by) pushing gently or slowly

nuisance /ˈnjuːsəns/ *n* **1** (legally actionable) harm or injury **2** an annoying or troublesome person or thing

numb /nʌm/ *adj* **1** devoid of sensation, esp as a result of cold or anaesthesia **2** devoid of emotion

¹number /ˈnʌmbə/ *n* **1a(1)** *sing* or *pl* in *constr* an indefinite, usu large, total **(2)** *pl* a numerous group; many; *also* an instance of numerical superiority **b(1)** any of an ordered set of standard names or symbols (e g 2, 5, 27th) used in counting or in assigning a position in an order **(2)** an element (e g 6, -3, ⅝, √7) belonging to an arithmetical system based on or analogous to the numbers used in counting and subject to specific rules of addition, subtraction, and multiplication **2a** a word, symbol, letter, or combination of symbols representing a number **b** one or more numerals or digits used to identify or designate **3** a group of individuals **4a** sthg viewed in terms of the advantage or enjoyment obtained from it **b** an article of esp women's clothing **c** a person or individual, esp an attractive girl **5** insight into a person's motives or character

²number *v* **1** to include as part of a whole or total **2** to assign a number to **3** to comprise in number; total

numeral /ˈnjuːmərəl/ *n* a conventional symbol that represents a natural number or zero *n*

numerous /ˈnjuːmərəs/ *adj* consisting of many units or individuals – ~**ly** *adv* – ~**ness** *n*

nun /nʌn/ *n* a female member of a religious order living in a convent and often engaged in educational or nursing work

¹nurse /nɜːs/ *n* **1** a woman employed to take care of a young child **2** sby skilled or trained in caring for the sick or infirm, esp under the supervision of a physician

²nurse *v* **1** to suckle an offspring **2** to encourage the development of; nurture **3a** to attempt to cure (e g an illness or injury) by appropriate treatment **b** to care for and wait on (e g a sick person) **4** to hold in one's mind; harbour **5** to hold (e g a baby) lovingly or caressingly

nursery /'nɜːsəri/ *n* **1** a child's bedroom or playroom **2** a place where small children are looked after in their parents' absence **3** an area where plants, trees, etc are grown for propagation, sale, or transplanting

nut /nʌt/ *n* **1** (the often edible kernel of) a dry fruit or seed with a hard separable rind or shell **2** a difficult person, problem, or undertaking **3** a typically hexagonal usu metal block with an internal screw thread cut on it that can be screwed onto a bolt to tighten or secure sthg **4** a small piece or lump **5** a person's head **6a** an insane or wildly eccentric person **b** an ardent enthusiast

nutrition /njuː'trɪʃən/ *n* all the processes by which an organism takes in and uses food

nylon /'nailon/ *n* **1** any of numerous strong tough elastic synthetic fibres used esp in textiles and plastics **2** *pl* stockings made of nylon

O

oak /əʊk/ *n, pl* **oaks, oak** (the tough hard durable wood of) any of various trees or shrubs of the beech family, usu having lobed leaves and producing acorns as fruits

oar /ɔːʳ/ *n* a long usu wooden shaft with a broad blade at one end used for propelling or steering a boat

oasis /əʊ'eɪsɪs/ *n, pl* **oases** a fertile or green area in a dry region

oath /əʊθ/ *n* **1** a solemn calling upon God or a revered person or thing to witness to the true or binding nature of one's declaration **2** an irreverent use of a sacred name; *broadly* a swearword

oatmeal /'əʊtmiːl/ *n* **1** meal made from oats, used esp in porridge **2** a greyish beige colour

oats /əʊts/ *n pl* a widely cultivated cereal grass that does not form a tight head like wheat or barley

obedient /ə'biːdɪənt/ *adj* submissive to the will or authority of a superior; willing to obey – ~**ly** *adv* – –**ence** *n*

obey /əʊ'beɪ, ə-/ *v* **1** to submit to the commands or guidance of **2** to comply with; execute

object /'ɒbdʒɪkt/ *n* **1** sthg that is (capable of) being sensed physically or examined mentally **2** sthg or sby that arouses an emotion or provokes a reaction or response **3** an end towards which effort, action, etc is directed; a goal **4** a noun or noun equivalent appearing in a prepositional phrase or representing the goal or the result of the

action of its verb (e g *house* in *we built a house*)

²object /əb'dʒekt/ *v* **1** to oppose sthg with words or arguments **2** to feel dislike or disapproval – ~**ion** *n* – ~**or** *n*

obligation /,ɒblɪ'geɪʃən/ *n* **1** (e g a contract or promise) that binds one to a course of action **2** (the amount of) a financial commitment **3** sthg one is bound to do; a duty

oblige /ə'blaɪdʒ/ *v* **1** to constrain by force or circumstance **2** to do sthg as a favour; be of service to

obliterate /ə'blɪtəreɪt/ *v* **1** to make illegible or imperceptible **2** to destroy all trace or indication of – –**ation** *n*

oblivion /ə'blɪvɪən/ *n* **1** the state of forgetting or being oblivious **2** the state of being forgotten

oblivious /ə'blɪvɪəs/ *adj* lacking conscious knowledge; completely unaware – usu + *of* or *to* – ~**ly** *adv* – ~**ness** *n*

oblong /'ɒblɒŋ/ *adj* rectangular with adjacent sides unequal

obscene /əb'siːn/ *adj* **1** offending standards of sexual propriety or decency **2** (morally) repugnant – ~**ly** *adv* – –**nity** *n*

¹obscure /əb'skjʊəʳ/ *adj* **1** hard to understand; abstruse **2** not well-known or widely acclaimed **3** faint, indistinct – ~**ly** *adv* – –**rity** *n*

²obscure *v* **1** to conceal (as if) by covering **2** to make indistinct or unintelligible

observe /əb'zɜːv/ *v* **1a** to act in due conformity with **b** to celebrate or perform (e g a ceremony or festival) **2** to perceive or take note of, esp for scientific purposes **3** to utter as a comment – –**vable** *adj* – –**vably** *adv* – –**vant** *adj* – –**vation** *n* – ~**r** *n*

obsess /əb'ses/ *v* to preoccupy intensely or abnormally

obsession /əb'seʃən/ *n* a persistent (disturbing) preoccupation with an often unreasonable idea – –**ive** *adj*

obsolete /'ɒbsəliːt/ *adj* **1** no longer in use **2** outdated, outmoded

obstacle /'ɒbstəkəl/ *n* sthg that hinders or obstructs

obstinate /'ɒbstɪnɪt/ *adj* clinging stubbornly to an opinion or course of action; not yielding to arguments or persuasion – ~**ly** *adv* – –**nacy** *n*

obstruct /əb'strʌkt/ *v* **1** to block or close up by an obstacle **2** to hinder, impede – ~**ion** *n*

obtain /əb'teɪn/ *v* **1** to acquire or attain **2** to be generally accepted or practised – *fml* – ~**able**

obvious /'ɒbvɪəs/ *adj* **1** evident to the senses or understanding **2** unsubtle – ~**ly** *adv*

¹occasion /ə'keɪʒən/ *n* **1** a suitable opportunity or circumstance **2** a state of affairs that provides a reason or grounds **3** the immediate or incidental cause **4** a time at which sthg occurs **5** a special event or ceremony

²occasion *v* to bring about; cause – *fml*

occasional /ə'keɪʒənəl/ *adj* **1** of a particular occasion **2** composed for a particular occasion **3** occurring at irregular or infrequent intervals **4** acting in a specified capacity from time to time **5** designed for use as the occasion demands – ~**ly** *adv*

occupation /ˌɒkjʊˈpeɪʃən/ *n* **1** an activity in which one engages, esp to earn a living **2a** the occupancy of land **b** tenure **3** taking possession or the holding and control of a place or area, esp by a foreign military force – ~**al** *adj*

occupy /ˈɒkjʊpaɪ/ *v* **1** to engage the attention or energies of **2** to fill up (a portion of space or time) **3** to take or maintain possession of **4** to reside in or use as an owner or tenant – -**pant** *n* – -**pancy** *n*

occur /əˈkɜː/ *v* -**rr**- **1** to be found; exist **2** to become the case; happen **3** to come to mind

occurrence /əˈkʌrəns/ *n* sthg that takes place; an event

ocean /ˈəʊʃən/ *n* **1** (any of the large expanses that together constitute) the whole body of salt water that covers nearly ¾ of the surface of the globe **2** *pl* a huge amount – *infml* – ~**ic** *adj*

o'clock /əˈklɒk/ *adv* according to the clock – used in specifying the exact hour

October /ɒkˈtəʊbə/ *n* the 10th month of the Gregorian calendar

octopus /ˈɒktəpəs/ *n, pl* **octopuses,** **octopi** any of a genus of molluscs related to the squids and cuttlefishes with 8 muscular arms equipped with 2 rows of suckers

odd /ɒd/ *adj* **1a** left over when others are paired or grouped **b** not matching **2** not divisible by 2 without leaving a remainder **3** somewhat more than the specified number – *usu in combination* **4** not regular or planned; casual, occasional **5** different from the usual or conventional; strange – ~**ly** *adv*

odds /ɒdz/ *n pl but sing or pl in concord* **1** the probability (expressed as a ratio) that one thing will happen rather than another **2** disagreement, variance **3** the ratio between the amount to be paid off for a winning bet and the amount of the bet

odds and ends *n pl* miscellaneous items or remnants

odour /ˈəʊdə/ *NAm chiefly* **odor** *n* **1** (the sensation resulting from) a quality of sthg that stimulates the sense of smell **2** repute, favour – *fml* **3** a characteristic quality; a savour – *chiefly derog* – ~**less** *adj* – **odorous** *adj*

of /əv, ə; *strong* ɒv/ *prep* **1a** – used to indicate origin or derivation (e g a man *of* noble birth) **b** – used to indicate cause, motive, or reason (e g died *of* pneumonia) **c** proceeding from; on the part of (e g very kind *of* him) **d** by (e g the plays *of* Shaw) **2a** composed or made from (e g a crown *of* gold) **b** containing (e g a cup *of* water) **c** – used to indicate the mass noun or class that includes the part denoted by the previous word (e g an inch *of* rain; a blade *of*

grass) **d** from among (e g one *of* his poems) **3a** belonging to; related to (e g the leg *of* the chair) **b** that is or are – used before possessive forms (e g a friend *of* John's) **c** characterized by; with, having (e g a man *of* courage) **d** connected with (e g a teacher *of* French) **e** existing or happening in or on (e g the battle *of* Blenheim; my letter *of* the 19th) **4a** relating to (a topic); concerning (e g stories *of* his travels) **b** in respect to (e g slow *of* speech) **c** directed towards (e g love *of* nature) **d** – used to show separation or removal (e g eased *of* pain) **e** – used as a function word to indicate a whole or quantity from which a part is removed or expended **5** – used to indicate apposition (e g the art *of* painting) **6** in, during (e g go there *of* an evening) – *infml*

¹**off** /ɒf/ *adv* **1a(1)** from a place or position; *specif* away from land (e g the ship stood *off* to sea) **(2)** away in space or ahead in time (e g Christmas is a week *off*) **b** from a course; aside; (e g turned *off* into a lay-by) *specif* away from the wind **c** into sleep or unconsciousness (e g dozed *off*) **2a** so as to be not supported, not in close contact, or not attached (e g the hands came *off*; took his coat *off*) **b** so as to be divided (e g a corner screened *off*) **3a** to or in a state of discontinuance or suspension (e g the radio is *off*) **b** so as to be completely finished or no longer existent (e g kill them *off*) **c** in or into a state of putrefaction (e g the cream's gone *off*) **d** (as if) by heart (e g knew it *off* pat) **4** away from an activity or function (e g the night shift went *off*) **5** offstage (e g noises *off*) **6** to a sexual climax (e g brought him *off*) – *slang*

²**off** *prep* **1a** – used to indicate physical separation or distance from (e g take it *off* the table) **b** to seaward of (e g 2 miles *off* shore) **c** lying or turning aside from; adjacent to (e g a shop just *off* the high street) **d** (slightly) away from – *often in combination* (a week *off* work; *off*-target) **2** – used to indicate the source from which sthg derives or is obtained (e g bought it *off* a friend) **3a** not occupied in (e g *off* duty) **b** tired of; no longer interested in or using (e g he's *off* drugs) **c** below the usual standard or level of (e g *off* his game)

³**off** *adj* **1a** being the most distant of 2 **b** seaward **c** being the right-hand one of a pair (e g the *off* wheel of a cart) **d** situated to one side; adjoining (e g bedroom with dressing room *off*) **2a** started on the way (e g *off* on a spree) **b** not taking place or staying in effect; cancelled (e g the match is *off*) **c** *of a dish on a menu* no longer being served **3a** not up to standard; unsatisfactory in terms of achievement (e g an *off* day) **b** slack (e g *off* season) **4** affected (as if) with putrefaction **5** provided (e g how are you *off* for socks?) **6a** in, on, through, or towards the *off* side of a cricket field **b** *esp of a ball bowled in cricket* moving or tending to move in

the direction of the leg side **7** *of behaviour* not what one has a right to expect; *esp* rather unkind or dishonest – *infml*

⁴off *n* the start or outset; *also* a starting signal

offence /ə'fens/ *NAm chiefly* **offense** *n* **1** sthg that occasions a sense of outrage **2** (an) attack, assault **3** displeasure, resentment **4a** a sin or misdeed **b** an illegal act; a crime

offend /ə'fend/ *v* **1** to break a moral or divine law – often + *against* **2** to cause displeasure, difficulty, or discomfort to – ~ **er** *n*

¹offensive /ə'fensɪv/ *adj* **1** of or designed for aggression or attack **2** arousing physical disgust; repellent **3** causing indignation or outrage – ~ **ly** *adv* – ~ **ness** *n*

²offensive *n* **1** the position or attitude of an attacking party **2** an *esp* military attack on a large scale

¹offer /'ɒfə'/ *v* **1** to present (e g a prayer or sacrifice) in an act of worship – often + *up* **2** to present (e g for acceptance, rejection, or consideration) **3** to declare one's willingness **4** to make available **5** to present (goods) for sale **6** to tender as payment; bid

²offer *n* **1a** a proposal; *specif* a proposal of marriage **b** an undertaking to do or give sthg on a specific condition **2** a price named by a prospective buyer

office /'ɒfɪs/ *n* **1** an *esp* beneficial service or action carried out for another **2** a position with special (public) duties or responsibilities **3** a prescribed form or service of worship **4a** a place, *esp* a large building, where the business of a particular organization is carried out **b** (a group of people sharing) a room in which the administrative, clerical, or professional work of an organization is performed

officer /'ɒfɪsə'/ *n* **1** a policeman **2** one who holds a position with special duties or responsibilities (e g in a government or business) **3a** one who holds a position of authority or command in the armed forces; *specif* a commissioned officer **b** a master or any of the mates of a merchant or passenger ship – **officer** *v*

¹official /ə'fɪʃəl/ *n* one who holds an *esp* public office – ~ **dom** *n*

²official *adj* **1** of an office and its duties **2** holding an office **3** authoritative, authorized **4** suitable for or characteristic of a person in office; formal – ~ **ly** *adv*

often /'ɒfən, 'ɒftən/ *adv* **1** (at) many times **2** in many cases

¹oil /ɔɪl/ *n* **1** any of numerous smooth greasy combustible liquids or low melting-point solids that are insoluble in water but dissolve in organic solvents **2a** *pl* oil paint **b** an oil painting **3** petroleum – **oily** *adj*

²oil *v* to treat or lubricate with oil

ointment /'ɔɪntmənt/ *n* a soothing or healing salve for application to the skin

¹old /əʊld/ *adj* **1a** dating from the *esp* remote past **b** persisting from an earlier time **c** of long standing **2** having existed for a specified period of time **3** advanced in years or age **4** former **5a** made long ago; *esp* worn with time or use **b** no longer in use; discarded **6** long familiar

²old *n* **1** old or earlier time **2** one of a specified age – usu in combination

old-fashioned *adj* **1** (characteristic) of a past era; outdated **2** clinging to customs of a past era

omen /'əʊmən/ *n* an event or phenomenon believed to be a sign of some future occurrence

ominous /'ɒmɪnəs/ *adj* portentous; *esp* foreboding evil or disaster – ~ **ly** *adv*

omit /əʊ'mɪt, ə-/ *v* **1** to leave out or unmentioned **2** to fail to do or perform – **omission** *n*

¹omnibus /'ɒmnɪbəs/ *n* **1** a book containing reprints of a number of works, usu by 1 author **2** a bus

²omnibus *adj* of, containing, or providing for many things at once

¹on /ɒn/ *prep* **1a**(1) in contact with or supported from below by (e g *on* the table) (2) attached or fastened to (e g a dog *on* a lead) (3) carried on the person of (e g have you a match *on* you?) (4) very near to, esp along an edge or border (e g towns *on* the frontier) (5) within the limits of a usu specified area (*on* page 17) **b** at the usual standard or level of (e g *on* form) **c**(1) in the direction of (e g *on* the right) (2) into contact with (e g jumped *on* the horse) (3) with regard to; concerning (e g keen *on* sports) (4) with a specified person or thing as object (e g try it out *on* her) (5) having as a topic; about (e g a book *on* India) (6) staked on the success of (e g put £5 *on* a horse) (7) doing or carrying out a specified action or activity (e g here *on* business) (8) working for, supporting, or belonging to (e g *on* a committee) (9) working at; in charge of (e g the man *on* the gate) **2a** having as a basis or source (e g of knowledge or comparison) (e g have it *on* good authority) **b** at the expense of (e g drinks are *on* the house) **3a** in the state or process of (e g *on* strike) **b** in the specified manner (e g *on* the cheap) **c** using as a medium (e g played it *on* the clarinet); *esp* over **4b** (e g talking *on* the telephone) **d** using by way of transport (e g arrived *on* foot) **e** sustained or powered by (e g car runs *on* petrol) **f** regularly taking (e g *on* valium) **4** through contact with (e g cut himself *on* a piece of glass) **5a** at the time of (e g every hour *on* the hour) **b** on the occasion of or immediately after and usu in consequence of (e g fainted *on* hearing the news) **c** in the course of (e g *on* a journey) **d** after (e g blow *on* blow)

²on *adv* **1** so as to be supported from below, in close contact, or attached (e g put the top *on*) **2a** ahead or forwards in space or time (e g do it later *on*) **b** with the specified part forward (e g cars crashed head *on*) **c** without interruption (e g chattered *on*) **d** in continuance or succession **3a** in or into (a state permitting) operation (e g put a record *on*) **b** in or into an activity or function (e g the night shift came *on*)

³**on** *adj* **1a** *cricket* leg (e g *on* drive) **b** taking place (e g the game is *on*) **c** performing or broadcasting (e g we're *on* in 10 minutes) **d** intended, planned (e g has nothing *on* for tonight) **e** worn as clothing (e g just a cardigan *on*) **2a** committed to a bet **b** in favour of a win (e g the odds are 2 to 1 *on*) **3** *chiefly Br* possible, practicable – usu neg (e g it's just not *on*) **4a** *chiefly Br* nagging (e g always *on* at him) **b** talking dully, excessively, or incomprehensibly (e g what's he *on* about) *USE* (3&4) infml

¹**once** /wʌns/ *adv* **1** one time and no more **2** even 1 time; ever (e g if *once* we lose the key) **3** at some indefinite time in the past; formerly **4** by 1 degree of relationship (e g second cousin *once* removed)

²**once** *n* one single time

³**once** *conj* from the moment when; as soon as

¹**one** /wʌn/ *adj* **1a** being a single unit or thing **b** being the first – used after the noun modified (e g on page *one*) **2** being a particular but unspecified instance (e g saw her *one* morning) **3a**(1) the same; identical (e g both of *one* mind) (2) constituting a unified entity (e g all shouted with *one* voice) **b** being in a state of agreement; united **4** being some unspecified instance – used esp of future time (e g we might try it *one* weekend) **5a** being a particular object or person (e g close first *one* eye, then the other) **b** being the only individual of an indicated or implied kind (e g the *one* and only person she wanted)

²**one** *pron, pl* **ones 1** a single member or specimen of a usu specified class or group **2** an indefinitely indicated person; anybody at all (e g has a duty to *one's* public) **3** – used to refer to a noun or noun phrase previously mentioned or understood (e g 2 grey shirts and 3 red *ones*) *USE* used as a subject or object; no pl for sense 2

³**one** *n* **1** the number 1 **2** the number denoting unity **3** the first in a set or series (e g takes a *one* in shoes) **4a** a single person or thing **b** a unified entity (e g is secretary and treasurer in *one*) **c** a particular example or instance (e g *one* of the coldest nights this year) **d** a certain specified person (e g *one* George Hopkins) **5a** a person with a liking or interest for a specified thing; an enthusiast (e g he's rather a *one* for bikes) **b** a bold, amusing, or remarkable character (e g oh! you are a *one*) **6a** a blow, stroke **7** sthg having a denomination of 1 (e g I'll take the money in *ones*)

oneself /wʌn'self/ *pron* **1** a person's self; one's own self – used reflexively (e g one should wash *oneself*) or for emphasis (e g to do it *oneself*) **2** one's normal state or condition **5** not feeling quite *oneself*)

onion /ˈʌnjən/ *n* (a plant with) a pun-

gent usu white bulb much used in cooking

¹**only** /ˈəʊnli/ *adj* **1** unquestionably the best **2** alone in its class or kind; sole

²**only** *adv* **1a** nothing more than; merely **b** solely, exclusively **2** nothing other than (e g it was *only* too true) **3a** in the final outcome (e g will *only* make you sick) **b** with nevertheless the final result (e g won the battle, *only* to lose the war) **4** no earlier than (e g *only* last week)

³**only** *conj* **1** but, however (e g they look very nice, *only* we can't use them) **2** were it not for the fact that *USE* infml

onto /ˈɒntʊ, -tə/ *prep* **1** to a position on **2** in or into a state of awareness about (e g put the police *onto* him) **3** *chiefly Br* in or into contact with (e g been *onto* him about the drains); *esp on* at; nagging

onward /ˈɒnwəd/ *adj* directed or moving onwards; forward

onwards /ˈɒnwədz/, **onward** *adv* towards or at a point lying ahead in space or time; forwards

opaque /əʊ'peɪk/ *adj* **1** not transmitting radiant energy, esp light; not transparent **2** hard to understand; unintelligible – **-acity** *n* – **~ly** *adv* – **~ness** *n*

¹**open** /ˈəʊpən/ *adj* **1** having no enclosing or confining barrier **2** allowing passage; not shut or locked **3** exposed to general view or knowledge; public **b** vulnerable to attack or question **4a** not covered or protected **b** not fastened or sealed **5** not restricted to a particular category of participants; *specif* contested by both amateurs and professionals **6** presenting no obstacle to passage or view **7** having the parts or surfaces spread out or unfolded **8a** not finally decided or settled **b** available for a qualified applicant; vacant **c** remaining available for use or filling until cancelled **9** willing to consider new ideas; unprejudiced **10** candid, frank **11** having relatively wide spacing between words or lines **12a** of a string on a musical instrument not stopped by the finger **b** of a note produced on a musical instrument without fingering the strings, valves, slides, or keys **13** in operation; *esp* ready for business or use **14** free from checks or restraints **15** *Br, of a cheque* payable in cash to the person, organization, etc named on it; not crossed

²**open** *v* **1a** to change or move from a closed position **b** to permit entry *into* or *onto* **c** to gain access to the contents of **2a** to make available for or active in a particular use or function; *specif* to establish **b** to declare available for use, esp ceremonially **c** to make the necessary arrangements for (e g a bank account), esp by depositing money **3** to disclose, reveal – often + *up* **4** to make 1 or more openings in **5** to unfold; spread out **6** to begin, commence

³**open** *n* **1** outdoors **2** *often cap* an open contest, competition, or tournament

opening /ˈəʊpənɪŋ/ *n* **1** an act of making or becoming open **2** a breach, aperture **3a** an often standard series of moves made at the beginning of a game of chess or draughts **b** a first performance **4a** a favourable opportunity; a chance **b** an opportunity for employment; a vacancy

openly /'əupənli/ *adv* in an open and frank manner – **openness** *n*

¹**opera** /'ɒpərə/ *pl of* **opus**

²**opera** *n* **1** (the performance of or score for) a drama set to music and made up of vocal pieces with orchestral accompaniment and usu other orchestral music (e g an overture) **2** the branch of the arts concerned with such works **3** a company performing operas +– ~ **tic** *adj*

operate /'ɒpəreit/ *v* **1a** one who exert power or influence; act **2** to produce a desired effect **3a** to work; (cause to) function **b** to perform surgery – usu + *on* **c** to carry on a military or naval action or mission **4** to be in action; *specif* to carry out trade or business

operation /ˌɒpə'reifən/ *n* **1a** the act, method, or process of operating **b** sthg (to be) done; an activity **2** the state of being functional or operative **3** a surgical procedure carried out on a living body for the repair of damage or the restoration of health **4** any of various mathematical or logical processes (e g addition) carried out to derive one expression from others according to a rule **5** a usu military action, mission, or manoeuvre and its planning **6** a business or financial transaction

operator /'ɒpəreitə'/ *n* **1a** one who operates a machine or device **b** one who owns or runs a business, organization, etc **c** one who is in charge of a telephone switchboard **2** a shrewd and skilful manipulator – *infml*

opinion /ə'pinjən/ *n* **1** a view or judgment formed about a particular matter **2** a generally held view **3** a formal expression by an expert of his/her professional judgment or advice; *esp* a barrister's written advice to a client

opponent /ə'pəunənt/ *n* one who takes the opposite side in a contest, conflict, etc

opportunity /ˌɒpə'tju:niti/ *n* **1** a favourable set of circumstances **2** a chance for advancement or progress

oppose /ə'pəuz/ *v* **1** to place opposite or against sthg so as to provide counterbalance, contrast, etc **2** to offer resistance to

¹**opposite** /'ɒpəzit/ *n* sthg or sby opposed or contrary

²**opposite** *adj* **1** set over against sthg that is at the other end or side of an intervening line or space **2a** occupying an opposing position; diametrically different; contrary **3** being the other of a matching or contrasting pair

³**opposite** *adv* on or to an opposite side

⁴**opposite** *prep* **1** across from and usu facing **2** in a role complementary to

opposition /ˌɒpə'zifən/ *n* **1** placing opposite or being so placed **2** hostile or contrary action **3** *sing of pl in constr* **a**

the body of people opposing sthg **b** *often cap* a political party opposing the party in power

oppress /ə'pres/ *v* **1** to crush by harsh or authoritarian rule **2** to weigh heavily on the mind or spirit of – ~ **ion**, ~ **iveness** *n*, **-ive** *adj*, **-ively** *adv*, **-~or** *n*

optic /'ɒptik/ **optical** *adj* of vision or the eye

optician /ɒp'tifən/ *n* one who prescribes spectacles for eye defects or supplies lenses for spectacles on prescription

optimism /'ɒptimizəm/ *n* a tendency to emphasize favourable aspects of situations or events or to expect the best possible outcome – **-mist** *n* – **-mistic** *adj* – **-mistically** *adv*

option /'ɒpfən/ *n* **1** an act of choosing **2** (a contract conveying) a right to buy or sell designated securities or commodities at a specified price during a stipulated period **3a** an alternative course of action **b** an item offered in addition to or in place of standard equipment

optional /'ɒpfənəl/ *adj* not compulsory; available as a choice – ~ **ly** *adv*

¹**or** /ə'/ *strong* ɔ:'/ *conj* **1a** – used to join 2 sentence elements of the same class or function and often introduced by *either* to indicate that what immediately follows is another or a final alternative **b** – used before the second and later of several suggestions to indicate approximation or uncertainty (e g 5 *or* 6 days) **2** and *not* – used after a neg (e g never drinks *or* smokes) **3** that is – used to indicate equivalence or elucidate meaning (e g a heifer *or* a young cow) **4** – used to indicate the result of rejecting a preceding choice (e g hurry *or* you'll be late)

²**or** *n* a gold colour; *also* yellow – used in heraldry

¹**oral** /'ɔ:rəl/ *adj* **1** uttered in words; spoken **2a** of, given through, or affecting the mouth **b** of or characterized by (passive dependency, aggressiveness, or other personality traits typical of) the first stage of sexual development in which gratification is derived from eating, sucking, and later by biting

²**oral** *n* an oral examination

¹**orange** /'ɒrindʒ/ *n* **1** a spherical fruit with a reddish yellow leathery aromatic rind and sweet juicy edible pulp; *also* the tree that bears this **2** a colour whose hue resembles that of the orange and lies between red and yellow in the spectrum

²**orange** *adj* of the colour orange

Orange *adj* of Orangemen

oration /ə'reifən, ɔ:-/ *n* a speech delivered in a formal and dignified manner

orator /'ɒrətə'/ *n* a skilled public speaker

¹**orbit** /'ɔ:bit/ *n* **1** the bony socket of the eye **2** a path described by one body in its revolution round another (e g that of the earth round the sun) **3** a sphere of influence – ~ **al** *adj*

²**orbit** *v* to revolve in an orbit round

orchard /'ɔːtʃəd/ n a usu enclosed area in which fruit trees are planted

orchestra /'ɔːkɪstrə/ n 1 the space in front of the stage in a modern theatre that is used by an orchestra 2 a group of musicians including esp string players organized to perform ensemble music – ~l adj

ordeal /ɔːˈdiːl, 'ɔːdiːl/ n a severe or testing experience

¹**order** /'ɔːdə'/ n 1a a religious body or community often required to take vows of renunciation of earthly things b a military decoration 2 pl the office of a person in the Christian ministry 3a a rank or group in a community b a category in the classification of living things ranking above the family and below the class 4a a rank, level, or category b arrangement of objects or events according to sequence in space, time, value, etc 5a (a rank in) a social or political system b regular or harmonious arrangement 6 customary procedure, esp in debate 7 the rule of law or proper authority 8 a proper, orderly, or functioning condition 9a a direction to purchase, sell, or supply goods or to carry out work b goods bought or sold

²**order** v 1 to put in order; arrange 2a to give an order to; command b to place an order for

¹**orderly** /'ɔːdəli/ adj 1a arranged in order; neat, tidy b liking or exhibiting order; methodical 2 well behaved; peaceful – -liness n

²**orderly** n 1 a soldier assigned to carry messages, relay orders, etc for a superior officer 2 a hospital attendant who does routine or heavy work (e g carrying supplies or moving patients)

ordinary /'ɔːdənri/ adj 1 routine, usual 2 not exceptional; commonplace – -rily adv

organ /'ɔːgən/ n 1 a wind instrument consisting of sets of pipes made to sound by compressed air and controlled by keyboards; also an electronic keyboard instrument producing a sound approximating to that of an organ 2 a differentiated structure (e g the heart or a leaf) consisting of cells and tissues and performing some specific function in an organism 3 a periodical

organism /'ɔːgənɪzəm/ n 1 a complex structure of interdependent and subordinate elements 2 a living being

organization, -isation /ˌɔːgənaɪˈzeɪʃən/ n 1 the arrangement of parts so as to form an effective whole 2 a an association, society b an administrative and functional body

organize, -ise /'ɔːgənaɪz/ v 1 to arrange into a functioning whole 2a to set up an administrative structure for b to cause to form an association, esp a trade union 3 to arrange by systematic planning and effort

orgy /'ɔːdʒi/ n 1a a drunken revelry b an instance (e g a party) of wild sexual activity 2 an excessive or frantic indulgence in a specified activity – -giastic adj

¹**orient** /'ɔːrɪənt, 'ɒri-/ n cap the East

²**orient** /'ɔːrɪent, 'ɒri-/ v 1 to set in a definite position, esp in relation to the points of the compass 2 to adjust to an environment or a situation b to acquaint (oneself) with the existing situation or environment

origin /'ɒrɪdʒɪn/ n 1 ancestry, parentage 2 a source or starting-point

¹**original** /əˈrɪdʒɪnəl, -dʒənəl/ n 1 that from which a copy, reproduction, or translation is made 2 an eccentric person – ~ity n

²**original** adj 1 initial, earliest; not secondary or derivative 2 being the first instance or source of a copy, reproduction, or translation 3 inventive, creative

¹**ornament** /'ɔːnəmənt/ n 1 sthg that lends grace or beauty; (a) decoration or embellishment 2 an embellishing note not belonging to the essential harmony or melody – ~al adj – ~ally adv

²**ornament** /'ɔːnəment/ v to add ornament to; embellish – ~ation n

¹**orphan** /'ɔːfən/ n a child 1 or both of whose parents are dead

²**orphan** v to cause to be an orphan

orphanage /'ɔːfənɪdʒ/ n an institution for the care of orphans

orthodox /'ɔːθədɒks/ adj 1a conforming to established, dominant, or official doctrine (e g in religion) b conventional 2 cap (consisting of) the Eastern churches headed by the patriarch of Constantinople which separated from the Western church in the 9th c – ~y n

ostensible /ɒˈstensɪbəl/ adj being such in appearance rather than reality; professed, declared – -bly adv

ostrich /'ɒstrɪtʃ/ n 1 a swift-footed 2-toed flightless bird that has valuable wing and tail plumes and is the largest of existing birds 2 one who refuses to face up to unpleasant realities

¹**other** /ˈʌðə'/ adj 1a being the 1 left of 2 or more (e g held on with one hand and waved with the other) b being the ones distinct from that or those first mentioned (e g taller than the other boys) c second (e g every other day) 2a not the same; different (e g schools other than hers) b far, opposite (e g lives on the other side of town) 3 additional, further (e g John and 2 other boys) 4 recently past (e g the other evening)

²**other** pron, pl others also other 1 the remaining or opposite one (e g went from one side to the other) 2 a different or additional one (e g some film or other)

³**other** adv otherwise – + than

¹**otherwise** /ˈʌðəwaɪz/ adv 1 in a different way 2 in different circumstances 3 in other respects 4 if not; or else 5 not – used to express the opposite (e g mothers, whether married or otherwise) 6 alias

²**otherwise** adj of a different kind (e g how can I be otherwise than grateful?)

ought /ɔːt/ verbal auxiliary – used to

express moral obligation (e g *ought* to pay our debts), advisability (*ought* to be boiled for 10 minutes), enthusiastic recommendation (you *ought* to hear her *sing*), natural expectation (e g *ought* to have arrived by now) or logical consequence (e g the result *ought* to be infinity) used in the negative to express moral condemnation of an action (e g you *ought* not to treat him like that); often used with the perfect infinitive to express unfulfilled obligation (e g *ought* never to have been allowed)

¹**ounce** /aʊns/ *n* ¹/₁₆ of a pound avoirdupois or ¹/₁₂ of a pound troy weight

²**ounce** *n* a snow leopard

our /ɑːʳ; *strong* aʊəʳ/ *adj* of us, ourself, or ourselves, esp as possessors or possessor, agents or agent, or objects or object of an action; of everybody

ours /aʊəz/ *pron, pl* ours that which or the one who belongs to us – used without a following noun as a pronoun equivalent in meaning to the adjective *our*

ourselves /aʊə'selvz/ *pron, pl in constr* 1 those identical people that are we – used reflexively (e g we're doing it for *ourselves*) or for emphasis (e g we *ourselves* will never go) 2 our normal selves (e g not feeling quite *ourselves*)

¹**out** /aʊt/ *adv* 1a away from the inside or centre (e g went *out* into the garden) b from among other things (e g separate *out* the bad apples) c away from the shore, the city, or one's homeland (e g live *out* in the country) d away from a particular place, esp of one's home or business (e g move *out* into lodgings) e(1) clearly in or into view (e g when the sun's *out*) (2) *of a flower* in or into full bloom 2a(1) out of the proper place (e g left a word *out*) (2) amiss in reckoning b in all directions from a central point of control (e g lent *out* money) c from political power (e g voted them *out*) d into shares or portions e out of vogue or fashion 3a to or in a state of extinction or exhaustion (e g before the year is *out*) b to the fullest extent or degree; completely (e g hear me *out*) c in or into a state of determined effort (e g *out* to fight pollution) 4a aloud b in existence; ever – with a superlative; *infml* (e g the funniest thing *out*) 5 so as to be put out of a game 6 – used on a 2-way radio circuit to indicate that a message is complete and no reply is expected

²**out** *v* to become publicly known

³**out** *adj* 1 located outside; external 2 located at a distance; outlying 3 not being in operation or power 4 directed or serving to direct outwards (e g the *out* tray) 5 not allowed to continue batting 6 out of the question

⁴**out** *n* a way of escaping from an embarrassing or difficult situation

outbreak /'aʊtbreɪk/ *n* 1a a sudden or violent breaking out b a sudden increase in numbers of a harmful organism or in sufferers from a disease within a particular area 2 an insurrection, revolt

outburst /'aʊtbɜːst/ *n* 1 a violent expression of feeling 2 a surge of activity or growth

outcaste /'aʊtkɑːst/ *n* a Hindu who has been ejected from his/her caste

outcome /'aʊtkʌm/ *n* a result, consequence

outcry /'aʊtkraɪ/ *n* 1 a loud cry; a clamour 2 a public expression of anger or disapproval

outdated /ˌaʊt'deɪtᵻd/ *adj* outmoded

outdo /aʊt'duː/ *v* to surpass in action or performance

outdoor /'aʊt'dɔːʳ/ *adj* 1 of or performed outdoors 2 not enclosed; without a roof

outdoors /ˌaʊt'dɔːz/ *adv* outside a building; in or into the open air

²**outdoors** *n pl but sing in constr* 1 the open air 2 the world remote from human habitation

outer /'aʊtəʳ/ *adj* 1 existing independently of the mind; objective 2a situated farther out b away from a centre c situated or belonging on the outside

outfit /'aʊt,fɪt/ *n* 1a a complete set of equipment needed for a particular purpose b a set of garments worn together, often for a specified occasion or activity 2 *sing or pl in constr* a group that works as a team – *infml* – **outfit** *v*

outgrow /aʊt'grəʊ/ *v* 1 to grow or increase faster than 2 to grow too large or too old for

outlandish /aʊt'lændɪʃ/ *adj* strikingly unusual; bizarre – ~ly *adv* – ~ness *n*

¹**outlaw** /'aʊtlɔː/ *n* a fugitive from the law

²**outlaw** *v* 1 to deprive of the protection of law 2 to make illegal

outlet /'aʊtlet, -lᵻt/ *n* 1a an exit or vent b a means of release or satisfaction for an emotion or drive 2 an agency (e g a shop or dealer) through which a product is marketed

¹**outline** /'aʊtlaɪn/ *n* 1 a line bounding the outer limits of sthg; shape 2 (a) drawing with no shading 3 a condensed treatment or summary 4 a preliminary account of a project

²**outline** *v* 1 to draw the outline of 2 to indicate the principal features of

outlook /'aʊtlʊk/ *n* 1 an attitude; point of view 2 a prospect for the future

output /'aʊtpʊt/ *n* 1 mineral, agricultural, or industrial production 2 mental or artistic production 3 the amount produced by sby in a given time 4 sthg (e g energy, material, or data) produced by a machine or system

outrageous /aʊt'reɪdʒəs/ *adj* 1 not conventional or moderate; extravagant 2 going beyond all standards of propriety, decency, or taste; shocking, offensive – ~ly *adv*

¹**outright** /aʊt'raɪt/ *adv* 1 completely 2 instantaneously

²**outright** /'aʊtraɪt/ *adj* being completely or exactly what is stated

¹**outside** /aʊt'saɪd, 'aʊtsaɪd/ *n* 1a an external part; the region beyond a boundary b the area farthest from a point of reference: e g (1) the section of a playing area towards the sidelines;

also a corner (2) the side of a pavement nearer the traffic **2** an outer side or surface **3** an outer manifestation; an appearance **4** the extreme limit of an estimation or guess; a maximum

²**outside** /'autsaɪd/ *adj* **1a** of or being on, near, or towards the outside **b** of or being the outer side of a curve or near the middle of the road **2** maximum **3a** originating elsewhere (e g an *outside* broadcast) **b** not belonging to one's regular occupation or duties **4** barely possible; remote

³**outside** /aut'saɪd/ *adv* **1** on or to the outside **2** outdoors **3** *chiefly Br* not in prison – *slang*

⁴**outside** /'autsaɪd/ *prep* **1** on or to the outside of **2** beyond the limits of **3** except, besides (e g few interests *outside* her children)

outsider /aut'saɪdə'/ *n* **1** sby who does not belong to a particular group **2** a competitor who has only an outside chance of winning

outspoken /aut'spəukən/ *adj* direct and open in speech or expression; frank – ~ ly *adv* – ~ ness *n*

outstanding /aut'stændɪŋ/ *adj* **1a** unpaid **b** continuing, unresolved **2a** standing out from a group; conspicuous **b** marked by eminence and distinction – ~ ly *adv*

outward /'autwəd/ *adj* **1a** situated at or directed towards the outside **b** being or going away from home **2** of the body or external appearances

outwardly /'autwədli/ *adv* in outward appearance; superficially

outwards /'autwədz/ *adv* towards the outside

¹**oval** /'əuvəl/ *adj* having the shape of an egg; *also* elliptical

²**oval** *n* an oval figure or object

oven /'ʌvn/ *n* a chamber used for baking, heating, or drying

¹**over** /'əuvə'/ *adv* **1a** across a barrier **b** across an intervening space **c** downwards from an upright position (e g fell *over*) **d** across the brim or brink (e g the soup boiled *over*) **e** so as to bring the underside up **f** so as to be reversed or folded **g** from one person or side to another **h** across (e g got his point *over*) **2a(1)** beyond some quantity or limit (2) excessively, inordinately – often in combination (3) in excess; remaining **b** till a later time (e g stay *over* till Monday) **3** so as to cover the whole surface (e g windows boarded *over*) **4a** at an end **b** – used on a two-way radio circuit to indicate that a message is complete and a reply is expected **5** – used to show repetition (e g told you *over* and *over*)

²**over** *prep* **1a** higher than; above **b** vertically above but not touching **c** – used to indicate movement down upon (e g hit him *over* the head) or down across the edge of (e g fell *over* the cliff) **d** across (e g climbed *over* the gate) **e** so as to cover **f** divided by (e g 6 *over* 2 is 3) **2a** with authority, power, or jurisdiction in relation to **b** – used to indicate superiority, advantage, or preference (e g a big lead *over* the others) **3** more than **4a** all

through or throughout (e g showed me all *over* the house) **b** by means of (a medium or channel of communication) (e g *over* the radio) **5a** in the course of; during **b** until the end of (stay *over* Sunday) **c** past, beyond **6** – used to indicate an object of occupation or activity or reference (e g sitting *over* their wine, laughed *over* the incident)

³**over** *adj* **1** upper, higher (e g *over*lord) **2** outer, covering (e g *over*coat) **3** excessive (e g *over*confident) *USE* often in combination

⁴**over** *n* any of the divisions of an innings in cricket during which 1 bowler bowls 6 or 8 balls from the same end of the pitch

¹**overall** /,əuvər'ɔ:l/ *adv* **1** as a whole **2** from end to end, esp of a ship

²**overall** *n* **1** *pl* a protective garment resembling a boiler suit or dungarees **2** *chiefly Br* a usu loose-fitting protective coat worn over other clothing

³**overall** *adj* including everything

overboard /'əuvəbɔ:d/ *adv* **1** over the side of a ship or boat into the water **2** to extremes of enthusiasm

overcoat /'əuvəkəut/ *n* **1** a warm usu thick coat for wearing outdoors over other clothing **2** a protective coat (e g of paint)

overcome /,əuvə'kʌm/ *v* **1** to get the better of; surmount **2** to overpower, overwhelm

overdo /,əuvə'du:/ *v* **1a** to do or use in excess **b** to exaggerate **2** to cook too much

overdose /'əuvədəus/ *v or n* (to give or take) too great a dose of drugs, medicine, etc

overdraft /'əuvədra:ft/ *n* an act of overdrawing at a bank; the state of being overdrawn; *also* the sum overdrawn

¹**overflow** /,əuvə'fləu/ *v* to flow over or beyond a brim, edge, or limit

²**overflow** /'əuvəfləu/ *n* **1** a flowing over; an inundation **2** sthg that flows over; *also, sing or pl in constr* the excess members of a group **3** an outlet or receptacle for surplus liquid

overhaul /,əuvə'hɔ:l/ *v* **1** to examine thoroughly and carry out necessary repairs **2** to overtake

¹**overhead** /,əuvə'hed/ *adv* above one's head

²**overhead** /'əuvəhed/ *adj* **1** operating, lying, or coming from above **2** of overhead expenses

³**overhead** /'əuvəhed/ *n* **1** a business expense (e g rent, insurance, or heating) not chargeable to a particular part of the work or product **2** a stroke in squash, tennis, etc made above head height

overhear /,əuvə'hɪə'/ *v* to hear (sby or sthg) without the speaker's knowledge or intention

overlap /,əuvə'læp/ *v* to extend over and cover a part of; partly coincide

overlook /,əuvə'luk/ *v* **1** to have or provide a view of from above **2a** to fail to notice; miss **b** to ignore **c** to excuse

overnight /,əυvə'naɪt/ *adj or adv* **1** during or throughout the evening or night **2** suddenly

overreach /,əυvə'riːtʃ/ *v* to defeat (oneself) by trying to do or gain too much

¹**override** /,əυvə'raɪd/ *v* **1a** to prevail over; dominate **b** to set aside or annul; *also* to neutralize the action of (e g an automatic control) **2** to overlap

²**override** /'əυvəraɪd/ *n* a device or system used to override a control

¹**overseas** /,əυvə'siːz/, **oversea** *adv* beyond or across the seas

²**overseas** /'əυvəsiːz/ **oversea** *adj* **1** of transport across the seas **2** of, from, or in (foreign) places across the seas

overshadow /,əυvə'ʃædəυ/ *v* **1** to cast a shadow over **2** to exceed in importance; outweigh

oversight /'əυvəsaɪt/ *n* **1** supervision **2** an inadvertent omission or error

oversleep /,əυvə'sliːp/ *v* to sleep beyond the intended time

overtake /,əυvə'teɪk/ *v* **1** to catch up with (and pass beyond), esp a motor vehicle **2** to come upon suddenly

overthrow /,əυvə'θrəυ/ *v* **1** to overturn, upset **2** to cause the downfall of; defeat

overtime /'əυvətaɪm/ *n* time in excess of a set limit; *esp* working time in excess of a standard working day or week **2** the wage paid for overtime

overturn /,əυvə'tɜːn/ *v* **1** to cause to turn over; upset **2** to overthrow

overweight /,əυvə'weɪt/ *adj* exceeding the expected, normal, or proper (bodily) weight

overwhelm /,əυvə'welm/ *v* **1** to cover over completely; submerge **2** to overcome by superior force or numbers **3** to overpower with emotion – ~**ing** *adj* – ~**ingly** *adv*

owe /əυ/ *v* **1a** to be under obligation to pay or render **b** to be indebted to **2** to have or enjoy as a result of the action or existence of sthg or sby else – **owing** *adj*

owing to *prep* because of

owl /aυl/ *n* any of an order of chiefly nocturnal birds of prey with large head and eyes and a short hooked bill – ~**ish** *adj* – ~**ishly** *adv*

¹**own** /əυn/ *adj* belonging to, for, or relating to oneself or itself – usu after a possessive pronoun (e g cooked his *own* dinner)

²**own** *v* **1** to have or hold as property; possess **2** to acknowledge, admit – often + *to* – ~**er** *n* – ~**ership** *n*

³**own** *pron*, *pl* **own** one belonging to oneself or itself – usu after a possessive pronoun

ox /ɒks/ *n*, *pl* **oxen** **1** a (domestic species of) bovine mammal **2** an adult castrated male domestic ox

oxygen /'ɒksɪdʒən/ *n* a bivalent gaseous chemical element that forms about 21 per cent by volume of the atmosphere and is essential for the life of all plants and animals

P

¹**pace** /peɪs/ *n* **1** rate of movement or activity **2** a manner of walking **3** the distance covered by a single step in walking, usu taken to be about 0.75m (about 30in) **4a** a gait; *esp* a fast 2-beat gait of a horse in which the legs move in lateral pairs **b** *pl* an exhibition of skills or abilities

²**pace** *v* **1** to walk with a slow or measured tread **2** to measure by pacing – often + *out* or *off* **3** to set or regulate the pace of; *specif* to go ahead of (e g a runner) as a pacemaker

³**pace** *prep* with due respect to

pacific /pə'sɪfɪk/ *adj* **1** having a mild peaceable nature **2** *cap* of (the region round) the Pacific ocean – ~**ally** *adv*

pacifism /'pæsɪfɪzəm/ *n* opposition to war as a means of settling disputes; *specif* refusal to bear arms on moral or religious grounds

pacify /'pæsɪfaɪ/ *v* **1** to allay the anger or agitation of **2a** to restore to a peaceful state; subdue **b** to reduce to submission – -**fication, -fier** *n*

¹**pack** /pæk/ *n* **1** a bundle or bag of things carried on the shoulders or back **2a** a large amount or number **b** a full set of playing cards **3** an organized troop (e g of cub scouts) **4** *sing or pl in constr* the forwards in a rugby team, esp when acting together **5** *sing or pl in constr* **a** a group of domesticated animals trained to hunt or run together **b** a group of (predatory) animals of the same kind **6** wet absorbent material for application to the body as treatment (e g for a bruise)

²**pack** *v* **1a** to stow (as if) in a container, esp for transport or storage – often + *up* **b** to cover, fill, or surround with protective material **2a** to crowd together so as to fill; cram **b** to force into a smaller volume; compress **3** to bring to an end; finish – + *up* or *in* **4** to gather into a pack **5** to cover or surround with a pack

³**pack** *v* to influence the composition of (e g a jury) so as to bring about a desired result

package /'pækɪdʒ/ *n* **1a** a small or medium-sized pack; a parcel **b** sthg wrapped or sealed **2** a wrapper or container in which sthg is packed **3** **package, package holiday** a holiday, booked through a single agent, including transport, accommodation and (some) meals at an all-in price – **package** *v*

packed /pækt/ *adj* **1a** that is crowded or stuffed – often in combination **b** compressed **2** filled to capacity

packet /'pækɪt/ *n* **1** a small pack or parcel **2** a passenger boat carrying mail and cargo on a regular schedule **3** *Br* a large sum of money – infml

pack up v 1 to finish work 2 to cease to function

¹**pad** /pæd/ n 1 a thin flat mat or cushion: e g a a padding used to shape an article of clothing b a padded guard worn to shield body parts, esp the legs of a batsman, against impact c a piece of absorbent material used as a surgical dressing or protective covering 2 (the cushioned thickening of the underside of) the foot of an animal 3 a number of sheets of paper (e g for writing or drawing) fastened together at 1 edge 4 a flat surface for a vertical takeoff or landing 5 living quarters – infml

²**pad** v 1 to provide with a pad or padding 2 to expand or fill out (speech or writing) with superfluous matter – often + out

³**pad** v to walk with a muffled step

¹**paddle** /pædl/ n 1a a usu wooden implement similar to but smaller than an oar, used to propel and steer a small craft (e g a canoe) b an implement with a short handle and broad flat blade used for stirring, mixing, hitting, etc 2 any of the broad boards at the circumference of a paddle wheel or waterwheel

²**paddle** v to go on or through water (as if) by means of paddling a craft

³**paddle** v to walk, play, or wade in shallow water

padlock /pædlok/ n a portable lock with a shackle that can be passed through a staple or link and then secured

¹**page** /peidʒ/ n 1a a youth attending on a person of rank; esp one in the personal service of a knight b a boy serving as an honorary attendant at a formal function (e g a wedding) 2 sby employed to deliver messages or run errands

²**page** v to summon esp by repeatedly calling out the name of (e g over a public-address system)

³**page** n (a single side of) a leaf of a book, magazine, etc

pageant /pædʒənt/ n 1 an ostentatious display 2 a show, exhibition; esp a colourful spectacle with a series of tableaux, dramatic presentations, or a procession, expressing a common theme

paid /peid/ past of **pay**

pail /peil/ n (the contents of or quantity contained in) an esp wooden or metal bucket

¹**pain** /pein/ n 1a a basic bodily sensation induced by a noxious stimulus or physical disorder and characterized by physical discomfort (e g pricking, throbbing, or aching) b acute mental or emotional distress 2 pl trouble or care taken 3 sby or sthg that annoys or is a nuisance – infml

²**pain** v to make suffer or cause distress to; hurt

painful /peinfəl/ adj 1a feeling or giving pain b irksome, annoying 2 requiring effort or exertion – ~ly adv – ~ness n

¹**paint** /peint/ v 1 to apply colour, etc to 2a to represent in colours on a surface by applying pigments b to decorate by

painting 3 to depict as having specified or implied characteristics

²**paint** n a mixture of a pigment and a suitable liquid which forms a closely adherent coating when spread on a surface

¹**painter** /peintə'/ n 1 an artist who paints 2 sby who applies paint (e g to a building), esp as an occupation

²**painter** n a line used for securing or towing a boat

painting /peintiŋ/ n 1 a product of painting; esp a painted work of art 2 the art or occupation of painting

¹**pair** /peə'/ n sing or pl in constr 1a(1) two corresponding things usu used together (2) two corresponding bodily parts b a single thing made up of 2 connected corresponding pieces 2a two similar or associated things: e g (1) a couple in love, engaged, or married (2) two playing cards of the same value in a hand (3) two horses harnessed side by side (4) two mated animals b a partnership between 2 people, esp in a contest against another partnership

²**pair** v to arrange in pairs

¹**palace** /pælɪs/ n 1 the official residence of a ruler (e g a sovereign or bishop) 2a a large public building b a large and often ornate place of public entertainment

²**palace** adj 1 of a palace 2 of or involving the intimates of a chief executive

¹**pale** /peil/ adj 1 deficient in (intensity of) colour 2 not bright or brilliant; dim 3 feeble, faint – ~ly adv – ~ness n

²**pale** n 1 a slat in a fence 2 a territory under a particular jurisdiction

¹**palm** /pɑːm/ n 1 any of a family of tropical or subtropical trees, shrubs, etc usu having a simple stem and a crown of large leaves 2 (a leaf of the palm as) a symbol of victory, distinction, or rejoicing

²**palm** n the concave part of the human hand between the bases of the fingers and the wrist

³**palm** v 1a to conceal in or with the hand b to pick up stealthily 2 to impose by fraud

pamper /pæmpə'/ v to treat with extreme or excessive care and attention

pamphlet /pæmflɪt/ n a usu small unbound printed publication with a paper cover, often dealing with topical matters

¹**pan** /pæn/ n 1a any of various usu broad shallow open receptacles: e g (1) a dustpan (2) a round metal container or vessel usu with a long handle, used to heat or cook food 2 a hollow or depression in land 3 chiefly Br the bowl of a toilet 4 chiefly NAm a baking tin

²**pan** v 1 to wash earth, gravel, etc in search of metal (e g gold) 2 to separate (e g gold) by panning 3 to criticize severely – infml

³**pan** n (a substance for chewing consisting of betel nut and various spices etc wrapped in) a betel leaf

⁴**pan** v to rotate a film or television cam-

era so as to keep a moving object in view

⁵pan *n* the act or process of panning a camera; the movement of the camera in a panning shot

panda /'pændə/ *n* **1** a long-tailed Himalayan flesh-eating mammal resembling the American racoon and having long chestnut fur spotted with black **2** a large black-and-white plant-eating mammal of western China resembling a bear but related to the racoons

pander /'pændə'/ *v* to provide gratification for other's desires – *usu* + *to*

pane /peɪn/ *n* **1** a framed sheet of glass in a window or door **2** any of the sections into which a sheet of postage stamps is cut for distribution

¹panel /'pænl/ *n* **1a** a list of people summoned for jury service **b** a group of people selected to perform some service (e g investigation or arbitration), or to discuss or compete on radio or television programme **2** a separate or distinct part of a surface: e g **a** a thin usu rectangular board set in a frame (e g in a door) **b** a vertical section of fabric **3** a thin flat piece of wood on which a picture is painted **4a** a flat often insulated support (e g for parts of an electrical device) usu with controls on 1 face **b** a usu vertical mount for controls or dials (e g in a car or aircraft)

²panel *v* to furnish or decorate with panels

¹panic /'pænɪk/ *n* **1** a sudden overpowering fright; *esp* a sudden unreasoning terror that spreads rapidly through a group **2** a sudden widespread fright concerning financial affairs and resulting in a depression in values – ~**ky** *adj*

²panic *v* to (cause to) be affected with panic

panorama /ˌpænə'rɑːmə/ *n* **1a** a large pictorial representation encircling the spectator **b** a picture exhibited by being unrolled before the spectator **2a** an unobstructed or complete view of a landscape or area **b** a comprehensive presentation or survey of a series of events – -**mic** *adj* – -**mically** *adv*

pansy /'pænzi/ *n* **1** (a flower of) a garden plant derived from wild violets **2** an effeminate male or male homosexual – *derog*

¹pant /pænt/ *v* **1a** to breathe quickly, spasmodically, or in a laboured manner **b** to make a puffing sound **2** to long eagerly; yearn – ~**ingly** *adv*

²pant *n* **1** a panting breath **2** a puffing sound

panther /'pænθə'/ *n* **1** a leopard, esp of the black colour phase **2** *NAm* a puma

panties /'pæntiz/ *n pl* pants for women or children; *also* knickers

pantomime /'pæntəmaɪm/ *n* **1a** any of various dramatic or dancing performances in which a story is told by bodily or facial movements **b** a British theatrical and musical entertainment of the Christmas season based on a nursery tale with stock roles and topical jokes **2** mime

pantry /'pæntri/ *n* **1** a room or cupboard used for storing provisions or tableware **2** a room (e g in a hotel or hospital) for preparation of cold foods to order

pants /pænts/ *n pl* **1** *chiefly Br* an undergarment that covers the crotch and hips and that may extend to the waist and partly down each leg **2** *chiefly NAm* trousers

¹paper /'peɪpə'/ *n* **1** a sheet of closely compacted vegetable fibres (e g of wood or cloth) **2a** a piece of paper containing a written or printed statement; a document; *specif* a document carried as proof of identity or status – often *pl* **b** a piece of paper containing writing or print **c** the question set or answers written in an examination in 1 subject **3** a paper container or wrapper **4** a newspaper **5** wallpaper

²paper *v* to cover or line with paper; *esp* to apply wallpaper to

³paper *adj* **1a** made of paper, thin cardboard, or papier-mâché **b** papery **2** of clerical work or written communication **3** existing only in theory; nominal

paperweight /'peɪpəweɪt/ *n* a usu small heavy object used to hold down loose papers (e g on a desk)

par /pɑː'/ *n* **1** the money value assigned to each share of stock in the charter of a company **2** a common level; equality – esp in *on a par with* **3a** an amount taken as an average or norm **b** an accepted standard; *specif* a usual standard of physical condition or health **4** the standard score (of a good player) for each hole of a golf course

parachute /'pærəʃuːt/ *n* a folding device of light fabric used esp for ensuring a safe descent of a person or object from a great height (e g from a aeroplane) – -**chutist** *n*

¹parade /pə'reɪd/ *n* **1** an ostentatious show **2** the (ceremonial) ordered assembly of a body of troops before a superior officer **3** a public procession **4** *chiefly Br* a row of shops, esp with a service road

²parade *v* **1** to march in a procession **2** to promenade **3** to show off

paradise /'pærədaɪs/ *n* **1** *often cap* **a** the garden of Eden **b** Heaven **2** a place of bliss, felicity, or delight

paraffin /ˌpærə'fɪn, 'pærəfɪn/ *n* **1** a usu waxy inflammable mixture of hydrocarbons used chiefly in candles, cosmetics, and in making other chemicals **2** an inflammable liquid hydrocarbon obtained by distillation of petroleum and used esp as a fuel

paragraph /'pærəgrɑːf/ *n* a usu indented division of a written composition that develops a single point or idea

¹parallel /'pærəlel/ *adj* **1a** extending in the same direction, everywhere equidistant, and not meeting **b** everywhere equally distant **2** analogous, comparable

²parallel *n* **1** a parallel line, curve, or

surface **2** sby or sthg equal or similar in all essential particulars; a counterpart, analogue **3** a comparison to show resemblance **4** the arrangement of 2-terminal electrical devices in which one terminal of each device is joined to one conductor and the others are joined to another conductor

³**parallel** *v* **1** to compare **2a** to equal, match **b** to correspond to

¹**paralytic** /ˌpærəˈlɪtɪk/ *adj* **1** of, resembling, or affected with paralysis **2** *chiefly Br* very drunk – *infml*

²**paralytic** *n* one suffering from paralysis

parasite /ˈpærəsaɪt/ *n* **1** an organism living in or on another organism to its own benefit **2** sthg or sby depending on sthg or sby else for existence or support without making a useful or adequate return – **-sitic, -sitical** *adj* – **-sitically** *adv* – **-sitism** *n*

paratroops /ˈpærətruːps/ *n pl* troops trained and equipped to parachute from an aeroplane – **-trooper** *n*

¹**parcel** /ˈpɑːsəl/ *n* a wrapped bundle; a package

²**parcel** *v* **1** to divide into parts; distribute – often + *out* **2** to make up into a parcel; wrap – often + *up*

¹**pardon** /ˈpɑːdn/ *n* **1** a release from legal penalties **2** excuse or forgiveness for a fault, offence, or discourtesy

²**pardon** *v* **1** to absolve from the consequences of a fault or crime **2** to allow (an offence) to pass without punishment

¹**parent** /ˈpeərənt/ *n* **1** sby who begets or brings forth offspring; a father or mother **2a** an animal or plant regarded in relation to its offspring **b** the material or source from which sthg is derived – **-al** *adj*

²**parent** *v* to be or act as the parent of

parish /ˈpærɪʃ/ *n* **1** the subdivision of a diocese served by a single church or clergyman **2** a unit of local government in rural England

¹**park** /pɑːk/ *n* **1** an area of land for recreation in or near a city or town **2** an area maintained in its natural state as a public property **3** an assigned space for military animals, vehicles, or materials

²**park** *v* **1** to leave or place (a vehicle) for a time, esp at the roadside or in a car park or garage **2** to set and leave temporarily

parliament /ˈpɑːləmənt/ *n* **1** a formal conference for the discussion of public affairs **2** *often cap* the supreme legislative body of the UK that consists of the House of Commons and the House of Lords; *also* a similar body in another nation or state – **-ary** *adj*

¹**parody** /ˈpærədi/ *n* **1** a literary or musical work in which the style of an author is imitated for comic or satirical effect **2** a feeble or ridiculous imitation

²**parody** *v* to compose a parody on – **-dist** *n*

¹**parrot** /ˈpærət/ *n* **1** any of numerous chiefly tropical birds that have a distinctive stout hooked bill, are often crested and brightly coloured, and are excellent mimics **2** a person who parrots another's words

²**parrot** *v* to repeat or imitate (e g another's words) without understanding or thought

parsnip /ˈpɑːsnɪp/ *n* (the long edible tapering root of) a European plant of the carrot family with large leaves and yellow flowers

¹**part** /pɑːt/ *n* **1a** any of the often indefinite or unequal subdivisions into which sthg is (regarded as) divided and which together constitute the whole **b** an amount equal to another amount **c** an organ, member, or other constituent element of a plant or animal body **d** a division of a literary work **e** a vocal or instrumental line or melody in music or harmony **f** a constituent member of an apparatus (e g a machine); *also* a spare part **2** sthg falling to one in a division or apportionment; a share **3** any of the opposing sides in a conflict or dispute **4** a function or course of action performed **5a** an actor's lines in a play **b** a role

²**part** *v* **1** to separate from or take leave of sby **2** to become separated, detached, or broken **3** to separate (the hair) by combing on each side of a line

³**part** *adv* partly

⁴**part** *adj* partial

partial /ˈpɑːʃəl/ *adj* **1** inclined to favour one party more than the other; biased **2** markedly fond of sby or sthg – + *to* **3** of a part rather than the whole; not general or total – **~ly** *adv*

participate /pɑːˈtɪsɪpeɪt/ *v* **1** to take part **2** to have a part or share in sthg – **-pant** *n* – **-pation** *n*

participle /ˈpɑːtɪsɪpəl/ *n* a verbal form (e g *singing* or *sung*) that has the function of an adjective and at the same time can be used in compound verb forms

particle /ˈpɑːtɪkəl/ *n* **1** a minute subdivision of matter (e g an electron, atom or molecule) **2** a minute quantity or fragment **3** a minor unit of speech including all uninflected words or all words except nouns and verbs; *esp* a function word

¹**particular** /pəˈtɪkjʊlə/ *adj* **1** of or being a single person or thing; specific **2** detailed, exact **3** worthy of notice; special, unusual **4a** concerned over or attentive to details; meticulous **b** hard to please; exacting – **~ity** *n* – **~ly** *adv*

²**particular** *n* an individual fact, point, circumstance, or detail

¹**partition** /pɑːˈtɪʃən/ *n* **1** division into parts **2** sthg that divides; *esp* a light interior dividing wall

²**partition** *v* **1** to divide into parts or shares **2** to divide or separate *off* by a partition

partly /ˈpɑːtli/ *adv* in some measure or degree; partially

¹**partner** /ˈpɑːtnə/ *n* **1a** either of a couple who dance together **b** sby who plays with 1 or more others in a game against an opposing side **c** a person with whom one is having a sexual relationship; a spouse, lover, etc **2** any of

the principal members of a joint business – ~**ship** n

²**partner** v to act as a partner to

part-time adj involving or working less than customary or standard hours

party /'paːti/ n **1a** a person or group taking 1 side of a question, dispute, or contest **b** sing or pl constr a group of people organized to carry out an activity or fulfil a function together **2** sing or pl constr a group organized for political involvement **3** one who is involved; a participant – usu + to **4** a (festive) social gathering

¹**pass** /paːs/ v **1** to move, proceed **2a** to go away – often + off **b** to die – often + on or away; euph **3a** to go by; move past; also surpass **b** of time to elapse **c** to overtake another vehicle **4a** to go across, over, or through **b** to emit or discharge from a bodily part, esp the bowels or bladder **c** to go uncensured or unchallenged **5** to go from one quality, state, or form to another **6a** to pronounce a judgment **b** to utter – esp in pass a comment, pass a remark **7** to go from the control or possession of one person or group to that of another **8** to take place as a mutual exchange or transaction **9a** to become approved by a body (e g a legislature) **b** to undergo an inspection, test, or examination successfully **10a** to be accepted or regarded as adequate or fitting **b** to resemble or act the part of so well as to be accepted – usu + for **11** to kick, throw, or hit a ball or puck to a teammate **12** to decline to bid, bet, or play in a card game

²**pass** n a narrow passage over low ground in a mountain range

³**pass** n **1** a usu distressing or bad state of affairs – often in come to a pretty pass **2a** a written leave of absence from a military post or station for a brief period **b** a permit or ticket allowing free transport or free admission **3** the passing of an examination **4** an act of passing in cards, soccer, rugby, etc; also a ball or puck passed **b** a ball hit to the side and out of reach of an opponent, esp in tennis **5** a sexually inviting gesture or approach – usu in make a pass at

passage /'pæsidʒ/ n **1** the action or process of passing from one place or condition to another **2a** a way of exit or entrance; a road, path, channel, or course by which sth passes **b** passage, passageway a corridor or lobby giving access to the different rooms or parts of a building or apartment **3a** a specified act of travelling or passing, esp by sea or air **b** the passing of a legislative measure **4** a right, liberty, or permission to pass **5a** a brief noteworthy portion of a written work or speech **b** a phrase or short section of a musical composition

passenger /'pæsɪndʒə', -sən-/ n **1** sby who travels in, but does not operate, a public or private conveyance **2** chiefly Br a member of a group who contributes little or nothing to the functioning or productivity of the group

passerby /,paːsə'baɪ/ n a person who happens by chance to pass by a particular place

passion /'pæʃən/ n **1** often cap **a** the sufferings of Christ between the night of the Last Supper and his death **b** a musical setting of a gospel account of the Passion story **2a** intense, driving, or uncontrollable feeling **b** an outbreak of anger **3** ardent affection; also strong sexual desire **b** (the object of) a strong liking, devotion, or interest – ~**less** adj – ~**lessly** adv

passionate /'pæʃənɪt/ adj **1** easily aroused to anger **2a** capable of, affected by, or expressing intense feeling, esp love, hatred, or anger **b** extremely enthusiastic; keen – ~**ly** adv

passive /'pæsɪv/ adj **1a** acted on, receptive to, or influenced by external forces or impressions **b** of a verb form or voice expressing an action that is done to the grammatical subject of a sentence (e g was hit in 'the ball was hit') **c** of a person lacking in energy, will, or initiative; meekly accepting **2a** not active or operative; inert **b** of or characterized by chemical inactivity **3** offering no resistance; submissive – ~**ly** adv

passport /'paːspɔːt/ n **1** an official document issued by a government as proof of identity and nationality to one of its citizens for use when leaving or reentering the country **2a** a permission or authorization to go somewhere **b** sth that secures admission or acceptance

¹**past** /paːst/ adj **1a** just gone or elapsed **b** having gone by; earlier **2** finished, ended **3** of or constituting the past tense expressing elapsed time **4** preceding, former

²**past** prep **1a** beyond the age of or for **b** subsequent to in time (e g half past 2) **2a** at the farther side of; beyond **b** up to and then beyond (e g drove past the house) **3** beyond the capacity, range, or sphere of

³**past** n **1a** time gone by **b** sth that happened or was done in the past **2** a past life, history, or course of action; esp one that is kept secret

⁴**past** adv so as to pass by the speaker (e g children ran past)

pasta /'pæstə/ n any of several (egg or oil enriched) flour and water doughs that are usu shaped and used fresh or dried (e g as spaghetti)

¹**paste** /peɪst/ n **1a** a fat-enriched dough used esp for pastry **b** a usu sweet doughy confection **c** a smooth preparation of meat, fish, etc used as a spread **2a** a preparation of flour or starch and water used as an adhesive **b** clay or a clay mixture used in making pottery or porcelain **3** a brilliant glass used in making imitation gems

²**paste** v **1** to stick with paste **2** to cover with sth pasted on

pastime /'paːstaɪm/ n sth (e g a hobby, game, etc) that amuses and serves to make time pass agreeably

pastry /'peɪstri/ n **1** a dough containing

fat esp when baked (e g for piecrust) 2 (an article of) usu sweet food made with pastry

pasture /'pɑːstʃəʳ/ n 1 plants (e g grass) grown for feeding (grazing) animals 2 (a plot of) land used for grazing 3 the feeding of livestock; grazing – pasture v

¹pasty /'pæsti/ n a small filled usu savoury pie or pastry case baked without a container

²pasty /'peisti/ adj resembling paste; esp pallid and unhealthy in appearance

¹pat /pæt/ n 1 a light tap, esp with the hand or a flat instrument 2 a small mass of sthg (e g butter) shaped (as if) by patting

²pat v 1 to strike lightly with the open hand or some other flat surface 2 to flatten, smooth, or put into place or shape with light blows 3 to tap or stroke gently with the hand to soothe, caress, or show approval

³pat adv in a pat manner; aptly, promptly

⁴pat adj 1 prompt, immediate 2 suspiciously appropriate; contrived 3 learned, mastered, or memorized exactly

¹patch /pætʃ/ n 1 a piece of material used to mend or cover a hole or reinforce a weak spot 2 a tiny piece of black silk worn on the face, esp by women in the 17th and 18th c, to set off the complexion 3a a small piece; a scrap b a small piece of land usu used for growing vegetables 4 chiefly Br a usu specified period 5 chiefly Br an area for which a particular individual or unit (e g of police) has responsibility

²patch v 1 to mend or cover (a hole) with a patch 2 to mend or put together, esp in a hasty or shabby fashion – usu + up

patchwork /'pætʃwɜːk/ n 1 sthg composed of miscellaneous or incongruous parts 2 work consisting of pieces of cloth of various colours and shapes sewn together

¹patent /'peitnt, 'pæ-/ adj 1a secured by or made under a patent b proprietary 2 made of patent leather 3 readily visible or intelligible; not hidden or obscure

²patent n 1 (a formal document securing to an inventor) the exclusive right to make or sell an invention 2 a patented invention 3 a privilege, licence

³patent v to obtain a patent for (an invention)

path /pɑːθ/ n 1 a track formed by the frequent passage of people or animals 2 a course, route 3 a way of life, conduct, or thought – ~ less adj

pathetic /pə'θetik/ adj 1 pitiful 2 marked by sorrow or melancholy; sad – ·ically adv

patience /'peiʃəns/ n 1 the capacity, habit, or fact of being patient 2 chiefly Br any of various card games that can be played by 1 person and usu involve the arranging of cards into a prescribed pattern

¹patient /'peiʃənt/ adj 1 bearing pains or trials calmly or without complaint 2

not hasty or impetuous 3 steadfast despite opposition, difficulty, or adversity – ~ly adv

²patient n an individual awaiting or under medical care

patriot /'pætriət, -triot, 'pei-/ n one who loves and zealously supports his/her country – ~ism n – ~ic adj – ~ically adv

¹patrol /pə'trəʊl/ n 1a traversing a district or beat or going the rounds of a garrison or camp for observation or the maintenance of security b sing or pl in constr a detachment of men employed for reconnaissance, security, or combat 2 sing or pl in constr a subdivision of a scout troop or guide company that has 6 to 8 members

²patrol v to carry out a patrol (of)

patron /'peitrən/ fem patroness n 1 a wealthy or influential supporter of an artist or writer 2 sby who uses his/her wealth or influence to help an individual, institution, or cause 3 a customer 4 the proprietor of an establishment (e g an inn), esp in France

patronize, -ise /'pætrənaiz/ v 1 to be or act as a patron of 2 to adopt an air of condescension towards

¹patter /'pætəʳ/ n 1 the sales talk of a street hawker 2 empty chattering talk 3 the talk with which an entertainer accompanies his/her routine

²patter v 1 to strike or tap rapidly and repeatedly 2 to run with quick light-sounding steps

¹pattern /'pætn/ n 1 a form or model proposed for imitation; an example 2 a design, model, or set of instructions for making things 3 a specimen, sample 4 a usu repeated decorative design (e g on fabric) 5 a (natural or chance) configuration

²pattern v 1 to make or model according to a pattern 2 to decorate with a design

¹pause /pɔːz/ n 1 a temporary stop 2 temporary inaction, esp as caused by uncertainty; hesitation

²pause v 1 to stop temporarily 2 to linger for a time

pavement /'peivmənt/ n a paved surface for pedestrians at the side of a road

pavilion /pə'viljən/ n 1 a large often sumptuous tent 2 a light sometimes ornamental structure in a garden, park, etc 3 chiefly Br a permanent building on a sports ground, specif a cricket ground, containing changing rooms and often also seats for spectators

¹paw /pɔː/ n 1 the (clawed) foot of a lion, dog, or other (quadruped) animal 2 a human hand – infml; chiefly humor

²paw v 1 to feel or touch clumsily, rudely, or indecently 2 to touch or strike at with a paw 3 to scrape or strike (as if) with a hoof

¹pawn /pɔːn/ n 1 sthg delivered to or deposited with another as a pledge or security (e g for a loan) 2 the state of being pledged – usu + in

²**pawn** v to deposit in pledge or as security

³**pawn** n 1 any of the 8 chessmen of each colour of least value that have the power to move only forwards usu 1 square at a time 2 sby or sthg that can be used to further the purposes of another

pawnbroker /'pɔːn,brəʊkəʳ/ n one who lends money on the security of personal property pledged in his/her keeping

¹**pay** /peɪ/ v **paid** 1 to make due return for services done or property received 2a to give in return for goods or service **b** to discharge indebtedness for 3 to give or forfeit in reparation or retribution 4 to requite according to what is deserved 5 to give, offer, or make willingly or as fitting 6 to be profitable to 7 to be worth the expense or effort to 7 to slacken (e g a rope) and allow to run out – usu + out – ~**er** n

²**pay** n 1 the status of being paid by an employer; employ 2 sthg paid as a salary or wage

³**pay** adj 1 equipped with a coin slot for receiving a fee for use 2 requiring payment

payment /'peɪmənt/ n 1 the act of paying 2 sthg that is paid 3 a recompense (e g a reward or punishment)

pea /piː/ n 1 (a leguminous climbing plant that bears) an edible rounded protein-rich green seed 2 any of various leguminous plants related to or resembling the pea – usu with a qualifying term

peace /piːs/ n 1 a state of tranquillity or quiet 2 freedom from disquieting or oppressive thoughts or emotions 3 harmony in personal relations 4a mutual concord between countries **b** an agreement to end hostilities

peaceful /'piːsfəl/ adj 1 peaceable 2 untroubled by conflict, agitation, or commotion; quiet, tranquil 3 of a state or time of peace – ~**ly** adv – ~**ness** n

¹**peach** /piːtʃ/ n 1 (a low spreading tree that bears) an edible fruit with a large stone, thin downy skin, and sweet white or yellow flesh 2 a light yellowish pink colour 3 a particularly excellent person or thing; specif an unusually attractive girl or young woman – infml

²**peach** v to turn informer on

peacock /'piːkɒk/ n a bird the male of which has very large tail feathers that are usu tipped with eyelike spots and can be erected and spread in a fan shimmering with iridescent colour

¹**peak** /piːk/ n 1 to grow thin or sickly

²**peak** n 1 a projecting part on the front of a cap or hood 2 a sharp or pointed end 3 (the top of) a hill or mountain ending in a point 4 the upper aftermost corner of a 4-cornered fore-and-aft sail 5 the highest level or greatest degree, esp as represented on a graph

³**peak** v to reach a maximum

⁴**peak** adj at or reaching the maximum of capacity, value, or activity

peal /piːl/ n 1a a complete set of changes on a given number of bells **b** a set of bells tuned to the notes of the major scale for change ringing 2a a loud prolonged sound – **peal** v

pear /peəʳ/ n (a tree that bears) a large fleshy edible fruit wider at the end furthest from the stalk

¹**pearl** /pɜːl/ n 1 a dense usu milky white lustrous mass of mother-of-pearl layers, formed as an abnormal growth in the shell of some molluscs, esp oysters, and used as a gem 2 sby or sthg rare or precious

²**pearl** adj 1a of or resembling pearl **b** made of or adorned with pearls 2 having medium-sized grains

peasant /'pezənt/ n 1 a small landowner or farm labourer 2 a usu uneducated person of low social status

pebble /'pebəl/ n a small usu rounded stone, often worn smooth by the action of water

¹**peck** /pek/ n a unit of volume or capacity equal to 2gall (about 9.1l)

²**peck** v 1a to strike or pierce (repeatedly) with the beak or a pointed tool **b** to kiss perfunctorily 2 to eat reluctantly and in small bites

³**peck** v, of a horse to stumble on landing from a jump

peculiar /pɪ'kjuːliəʳ/ adj 1 belonging exclusively to 1 person or group 2 distinctive 3 different from the usual or normal; strange, curious

peculiarity /pɪ,kjuːliˈærⁱ̩ti/ n a distinguishing characteristic

¹**pedal** /'pedl/ n 1 a lever pressed by the foot in playing a musical instrument 2 a foot lever or treadle by which a part is activated in a mechanism

²**pedal** adj of the foot

³**pedal** v 1 to use or work a pedal or pedals 2 to ride a bicycle

pedant /'pednt/ n one who is unimaginative or unnecessarily concerned with detail, esp in academic matters – ~**ic** adj – ~**ically** adv

pedestal /'pedⁱ̩stl/ n 1 a base supporting a column, statue, etc 2 a position of esteem or idealized respect

¹**pedestrian** /pⁱ̩'destriən/ adj 1 commonplace, unimaginative 2a going or performed on foot **b** of or designed for walking

²**pedestrian** n sby going on foot; a walker

¹**peel** /piːl/ v 1 to strip off an outer layer 2a to come off in sheets or scales **b** to lose an outer layer (e g of skin) 3 to take off one's clothes – usu + off; infml

²**peel** n the skin or rind of a fruit

³**peel** also **pele** n a small fortified tower built in the 16th c along the Scottish-English border

⁴**peel** n a usu long-handled (baker's) shovel for getting bread, pies, etc into or out of an oven

¹**peep** /piːp/ v 1 to utter a feeble shrill sound characteristic of a newly hatched bird; cheep 2 to utter a slight sound

²**peep** n 1 a cheep 2 a slight sound, esp spoken – infml

³**peep** v 1 to look cautiously or slyly, esp through an aperture 2 to begin to

emerge (as if) from concealment; show slightly

⁴peep *n* **1** the first faint appearance **2** a brief or furtive look; a glance

¹peer /pɪə/ *n* **1** sby who is of equal standing with another **2** a duke, marquess, earl, viscount, or baron of the British peerage

²peer *adj* belonging to the same age, grade, or status group

³peer *v* to look narrowly or curiously; *esp* to look searchingly at sth difficult to discern

¹peg /peg/ *n* **1** a small usu cylindrical pointed or tapered piece of wood, metal, or plastic used to pin down or fasten things or to fit into or close holes; a pin **2a** a projecting piece used to hold or support **b** sth (e g a fact or opinion) used as a support, pretext, or reason **3a** any of the wooden pins set in the head of a stringed instrument and turned to regulate the pitch of the strings **b** a step or degree, esp in estimation – esp in *take sby down a peg (or two)*

²peg *v* **1** to put a peg into **2** to pin down; restrict **3** to fix or hold (e g prices) at a predetermined level **4** *Br* to fasten (e g washing) to a clothesline with a clothes peg – often + *out*

pellet /'pelɪt/ *n* **1** a usu small rounded or spherical body (e g of food or medicine) **2** a piece of small shot

¹pelt /pelt/ *n* **1** a usu undressed skin with its hair, wool, or fur **2** a skin stripped of hair or wool before tanning

²pelt *v* **1** *of rain* to fall heavily and continuously **2** to move rapidly and vigorously; hurry **3** to hurl, throw **4** to strike with a succession of blows or missiles

pelvis /'pelvɪs/ *n, pl* **pelvises, pelves** (the cavity of) a basin-shaped structure in the skeleton of many vertebrates that is formed by the pelvic girdle and adjoining bones of the spine – **pelvic** *adj*

¹pen /pen/ *n* **1** a small enclosure for animals **2** a small place of confinement or storage

²pen *v* to shut in a pen

³pen *n* **1** an implement for writing or drawing with fluid (e g ink) **2a** a writing instrument as a means of expression **b** a writer – fml

⁴pen *v* to write – fml

⁵pen *n* a female swan

penal /'pi:nl/ *adj* **1** of punishment **2** liable to punishment – **penally** *adv*

penalize, -ise /'pi:nəlaɪz/ *v* **1** to inflict a penalty on **2** to put at a serious disadvantage

penalty /'penlti/ *n* **1** a punishment legally imposed or incurred **2** a forfeiture to which a person agrees to be subject if conditions are not fulfilled **3a** disadvantage, loss, or suffering due to some action **b** a disadvantage imposed for violation of the rules of a sport

pence /pens/ *pl of* **penny**

¹pencil /'pensl/ *n* **1** an implement for writing, drawing, or marking consisting of or containing a slender cylinder or strip of a solid marking substance (e g graphite) **2** a set of light rays, esp when diverging from or converging to a point **3** sth long and thin like a pencil

²pencil *v* to draw, write, or mark with a pencil

penetrate /'penɪtreɪt/ *v* **1a** to pass into or through **b** to enter, esp by overcoming resistance; pierce **2** to see into or through; discern **3** to be absorbed by the mind; be understood – **-tration** *n* – **-trable, -trative** *adj* – **-trability** *n*

penetrating /'penɪtreɪtɪŋ/ *adj* **1** having the power of entering, piercing, or pervading **2** acute, discerning – ~**ly** *adv*

penguin /'peŋgwɪn/ *n* any of various erect short-legged flightless aquatic birds of the southern hemisphere

penicillin /,penɪ'sɪlɪn/ *n* any of several antibiotics or antibacterial drugs orig obtained from moulds

peninsula /pɪ'nɪnsjʊlə/ *n* a piece of land jutting out into or almost surrounded by water; *esp* one connected to the mainland by an isthmus – ~**r** *adj*

penis /'pi:nɪs/ *n, pl* **penes, penises** the male sexual organ by means of which semen is introduced into the female during coitus

penknife /'pen-naɪf/ *n* a small pocket-knife

penniless /'penɪlɪs/ *adj* lacking money; poor

penny /'peni/ *n, pl* **pennies, pence 1a** (a usu bronze coin representing) (1) a former British money unit worth £¹⁄₂₄₀ (2) a British money unit in use since 1971 that is worth £¹⁄₁₀₀ **b** a unit of currency of the Irish Republic, Gibraltar and the Falkland Islands **2** *NAm* a cent

¹pension /'penʃən/ *n* a fixed sum paid regularly to a person (e g following retirement or as compensation for a wage-earner's death) – ~**able** *adj*

²pension /'pɒnsɪɒn/ *n* (bed and board provided by) a hotel or boardinghouse, esp in continental Europe

penultimate /pen'ʌltɪmɪt/ *adj* next to the last

¹people /'pi:pl/ *n* **1** human beings in general **2** a group of persons considered collectively **3** the members of a family or kinship **4** the mass of a community **5** a body of persons that are united by a common culture and that often constitute a politically organized group

²people *v* **1** to supply or fill with people **2** to dwell in; inhabit

¹pepper /'pepə/ *n* **1a** any of a genus of tropical mostly climbing shrubs with aromatic leaves; *esp* one with red berries from which black pepper and white pepper are prepared **b** a condiment made from ground dried pepper berries **2** any of various products similar to pepper; *esp* a pungent condiment obtained from capsicums – used with a qualifying term **3** (the usu red or green fruit of) a capsicum whose fruits are not hot peppers or sweet peppers

²pepper *v* **1a** to sprinkle, season, or cover (as if) with pepper **b** to shower with shot or other missiles **2** to sprinkle

pep talk *n* a usu brief, high-pressure, and emotional talk designed esp to encourage

per /pə⁻; *strong* pɜ⁻/ *prep* **1** by the means or agency of; through **2** with respect to every; for each **3** according to (e g *per* list price)

perceive /pə'siːv/ *v* **1** to understand, realize **2** to become aware of through the senses; *esp* to see, observe – -**ceivable** *adj*

per cent /pə 'sent/ *adv* in or for each 100

per cent *n, pl* **per cent 1** one part in a 100 **2** a percentage

per cent *adj* reckoned on the basis of a whole divided into 100 parts

percentage /pə'sentɪdʒ/ *n* **1** a proportion (expressed as per cent of a whole) **2** a share of winnings or profits **3** an advantage, profit – *infml*

perceptive /pə'septɪv/ *adj* **1** capable of or exhibiting (keen) perception; observant, discerning **2** characterized by sympathetic understanding or insight – ~**ly** *adv* – ~**ness** *n* – -**tivity** *n*

perch /pɜːtʃ/ *n* **1** a roost for a bird **2** *chiefly Br* a unit of length equal to 5½ yds; a rod **3a** a resting place or vantage point; a seat **b** a prominent position *USE* (*3*) *infml*

perch *v* to alight, settle, or rest, esp briefly or precariously

perch *n* a small European freshwater spiny-finned fish

perennial /pə'renɪəl/ *adj* **1** present at all seasons of the year **2** *of a plant* living for several years, usu with new herbaceous growth each year **3** lasting for a long time or forever; constant

perfect /'pɜːfɪkt/ *adj* **1a** entirely without fault or defect; flawless **b** corresponding to an ideal standard or abstract concept **2a** accurate, exact **b** lacking in no essential detail; complete **c** absolute, utter **3** of or constituting a verb tense or form that expresses an action or state completed at the time of speaking or at a time spoken of

perfect /pə'fekt/ *v* **1** to make perfect; improve, refine **2** to bring to final form – ~**ible** *adj* – ~**ibility** *n*

perfectly /'pɜːfɪktli/ *adv* to an adequate extent; quite

perforate /'pɜːfəreɪt/ *v* to make a hole through; *specif* to make a line of holes in or between (e g rows of postage stamps in a sheet) to make separation easier

perform /pə'fɔːm/ *v* **1** to do; carry out **2a** to do in a formal manner or according to prescribed ritual **b** to give a rendering of; present – ~**er** *n*

performance /pə'fɔːməns/ *n* **1a** the execution of an action **b** sthg accomplished; a deed, feat **2** the fulfilment of a claim, promise, etc **3** a presentation to an audience of (a character in a) play, a piece of music, etc **4** the ability to perform or work (efficiently or well) **5a** a lengthy or troublesome process or activity **b** a display of bad behaviour

perfume /'pɜːfjuːm/ *n* **1** a sweet or pleasant smell; a fragrance **2** a pleasant-smelling (liquid) preparation (e g of floral essences)

perfume /pə'fjuːm/ *v* to fill or imbue with a sweet smell

perhaps /pə'hæps/ *adv* possibly but not certainly; maybe

peril /'perɪl/ *n* **1** exposure to the risk of being injured, destroyed, or lost; danger **2** sthg that imperils; a risk

period /'pɪərɪəd/ *n* **1a** the full pause at the end of a sentence; *also, chiefly NAm* a full stop **b** a stop, end **2a** a portion of time **b** the (interval of) time that elapses before a cyclic motion or phenomenon begins to repeat itself; the reciprocal of the frequency **c** (a single cyclic occurrence of) menstruation **3** a chronological division; a stage (of history) **4** any of the divisions of the school day

period *adj* of, representing, or typical of a particular historical period

periodic /,pɪərɪ'ɒdɪk/ *adj* **1** recurring at regular intervals **2** consisting of or containing a series of repeated stages – ~**ally** *adv*

periodical /,pɪərɪ'ɒdɪkəl/ *adj* **1** periodic **2** *of a magazine or journal* published at fixed intervals (e g weekly or quarterly)

periodical *n* a periodical publication

periscope /'perɪskəʊp/ *n* a tubular optical instrument containing lenses, mirrors, or prisms for seeing objects not in the direct line of sight

perish /'perɪʃ/ *v* **1a** to be destroyed or ruined **b** to die, esp in a terrible or sudden way – *poetic or journ* **2** *chiefly Br* to deteriorate, spoil

perjure /'pɜːdʒə⁻/ *v* to make (oneself) guilty of perjury – ~**r** *n*

perjury /'pɜːdʒəri/ *n* the voluntary violation of an oath, esp by a witness

permanent /'pɜːmənənt/ *adj* **1** continuing or enduring without fundamental or marked change; lasting, stable **2** not subject to replacement according to political circumstances – ~**ly** *adv*

permission /pə'mɪʃən/ *n* formal consent; authorization

permit /pə'mɪt/ *v* **1** to consent to, usu expressly or formally **2** to give leave; authorize **3** to make possible

permit /'pɜːmɪt/ *n* a written warrant allowing the holder to do or keep sthg

perpendicular /,pɜːpən'dɪkjʊlə⁻/ *adj* **1** being or standing at right angles to the plane of the horizon or a given line or plane **2** *cap of, being, or built in a late Gothic style of architecture prevalent in England from the 15th to the 16th c characterized by large windows, fan vaults, and an emphasis on vertical lines – ~**ly** *adv*

perpendicular *n* a line, plane, or surface at right angles to the plane of the horizon or to another line or surface

perpetual /pə'petʃʊəl/ *adj* **1a** everlasting; holding sthg (e g an office) for life or for an unlimited time **2** occurring continually; constant **3** *of a plant* blooming continuously throughout the season – **~ly** adv

perplex /pə'pleks/ v 1 to puzzle, confuse 2 to complicate

persecute /'pɜːsɪkjuːt/ v 1 to cause to suffer because of race, religion, political beliefs, etc 2 to pester – **-cution** n – **-cutor** n

persevere /,pɜːsɪ'vɪə/ v to persist in a state, enterprise, or undertaking in spite of adverse influences, opposition, or discouragement – **-verance** n

persist /pə'sɪst/ v 1 to go on resolutely or stubbornly in spite of opposition or warning 2 to be insistent in the repetition or pressing of an utterance (e g a question or opinion) 3 to continue to exist, esp past a usual, expected, or normal time

persistent /pə'sɪstənt/ adj 1 continuing to exist in spite of interference or treatment 2 remaining a beyond the usual period b without change in function or structure – **~ly** adv – **-tence** n

person /'pɜːsən/ n 1 a human being (considered as being different from all others) 2 any of the 3 modes of being in the Trinity as understood by Christians 3 a living human body or its outward appearance

personal /'pɜːsənəl/ adj 1 of or affecting a person; private 2a done in person without the intervention of another b carried on between individuals directly 3 of the person or body 4 of or referring to (the character, conduct, motives, or private affairs of) an individual, often in an offensive manner

personality /,pɜːsə'nælɪti/ n 1 the totality of an individual's behavioural and emotional tendencies; broadly a distinguishing complex of individual or group characteristics 2a (sby having) distinction or excellence of personal and social traits b a person of importance, prominence, renown, or notoriety

personally /'pɜːsənəli/ adv 1 in person 2 as a person; in personality 3 for oneself; as far as oneself is concerned 4 as directed against oneself in a personal way

personnel /,pɜːsə'nel/ n 1 sing or pl in constr a body of people employed (e g in a factory, office, or organization) or engaged on a project 2 a division of an organization concerned with the employees and their welfare at work

'perspective /pə'spektɪv/ adj of, using, or seen in perspective

'perspective n 1a the visual appearance of solid objects with respect to their relative distance and position b a technique for representing this, esp by showing parallel lines as converging 2 the aspect of an object of thought from a particular standpoint

perspiration /,pɜːspə'reɪʃən/ n 1 sweating 2 sweat

perspire /pə'spaɪə/ v to sweat

persuade /pə'sweɪd/ v 1 to move by argument, reasoning, or entreaty to a belief, position, or course of action 2 to

get (sthg) with difficulty out of or from

persuasion /pə'sweɪʒən/ n 1a persuading or being persuaded b persuasiveness 2a an opinion held with complete assurance b (a group adhering to) a particular system of religious beliefs

perverse /pə'vɜːs/ adj 1a obstinate in opposing what is right, reasonable, or accepted; wrongheaded b arising from or indicative of stubbornness or obstinacy 2 unreasonably opposed to the wishes of others; uncooperative, contrary – **~ly** adv – **~ness** n – **-sity** n

'pervert /pə'vɜːt/ v 1 to cause to turn aside or away from what is good, true, or morally right; corrupt 2a to divert to a wrong end or purpose; misuse b to twist the meaning or sense of; misinterpret

'pervert /'pɜːvɜːt/ n a person given to some form of sexual perversion

pessimism /'pesɪmɪzəm/ n a tendency to stress the adverse aspects of a situation or event or to expect the worst possible outcome – **-mist** n – **-mistic** adj – **-mistically** adv

pest /pest/ n 1 a plant or animal capable of causing damage or carrying disease 2 sby or sthg that pesters or annoys; a nuisance

pester /'pestə/ v to harass with petty irritations; annoy

'pet /pet/ n 1 a domesticated animal kept for companionship rather than work or food 2 sby who is treated with unusual kindness or consideration; a favourite 3 chiefly Br darling – used chiefly by women as an affectionate form of address

'pet adj 1a kept or treated as a pet b for pet animals 2 expressing fondness or endearment 3 favourite

'pet v 1 to treat with unusual kindness and consideration; pamper 2 to engage in amorous embracing, caressing, etc

'pet n a fit of peevishness, sulkiness, or anger

petal /'petl/ n any of the modified often brightly coloured leaves making up the flower head of a plant

'petition /pɪ'tɪʃən/ n 1 an earnest request; an entreaty 2 (a document embodying) a formal written request to a superior – **~er** n

'petition v to make an esp formal written request (to or for)

petrol /'petrəl/ n, chiefly Br a volatile inflammable liquid used as a fuel for internal-combustion engines

petroleum /pɪ'trəʊliəm/ n an oily inflammable usu dark liquid widely occurring in the upper strata of the earth that is refined to produce petrol and other products

petty /'peti/ adj 1 having secondary rank or importance; also trivial 2 small-minded – **-tily** adv – **-tiness** n

'phantom /'fæntəm/ n 1 sthg (e g a ghost) apparent to the senses but with no substantial existence 2 sthg existing only in the imagination

²**phantom** adj 1 of or being a phantom 2 fictitious, dummy

pharmacist /fɑːməs¦ɪst/ n sby who prepares and sells drugs – **-cy** n

pharmacy /ˈfɑːməsi/ n 1 the preparation, compounding, and dispensing of drugs 2 a place where medicines are compounded or dispensed

¹**phase** /feɪz/ n **1a** a discernible part or stage in a course, development, or cycle **b** an aspect or part (e g of a problem) under consideration 2 a stage of a regularly recurring motion or cyclic process (e g an alternating electric current) with respect to a starting point or standard position

²**phase** v 1 to conduct or carry out by planned phases 2 to schedule (e g operations) or contract for (e g goods or services) to be performed or supplied as required

phenomenal /fɪˈnɒm¦nəl/ adj extraordinary, remarkable

phenomenon /fɪˈnɒm¦nən/ n, pl **phenomena** 1 an object of sense perception rather than of thought or intuition 2 a fact or event that can be scientifically described and explained 3 a rare, exceptional, unusual, or abnormal person, thing, or event – **-enal** adj

philosopher /fɪˈlɒsəfə/ n 1 a specialist in philosophy 2 a person whose philosophical viewpoint enables him/her to meet trouble with equanimity

philosophical /ˌfɪləˈsɒfɪkəl/ adj 1 of philosophers or philosophy 2 calm in the face of trouble – **~ly** adv

philosophy /fɪˈlɒsəfi/ n 1 the study of the nature of knowledge and existence and the principles of moral and aesthetic value 2 the philosophical principles, teachings, or beliefs of a specified individual, group, or period 3 equanimity in the face of trouble or stress

phobia /ˈfəʊbɪə/ n an exaggerated and illogical fear of sthg – **phobic** n, adj

¹**phone** /fəʊn/ n a telephone

²**phone** v to telephone – often + up

¹**photo** /ˈfəʊtəʊ/ v or n (to) photograph

²**photo** adj photographic

¹**photocopy** /ˈfəʊtəʊˌkɒpi/ n a photographic reproduction of graphic matter

²**photocopy** v to make a photocopy (of) – **-ier** n

¹**photograph** /ˈfəʊtəgrɑːf/ n a picture or likeness obtained by photography

²**photograph** v to take a photograph – **~er** n – **~ic** adj – **~ically** adv

photography /fəˈtɒgrəfi/ n the art or process of producing images on a sensitized surface (e g a film) by the action of radiant energy, esp light

¹**phrase** /freɪz/ n 1 a brief usu idiomatic or pithy expression; esp a catchphrase 2 a group of musical notes forming a natural unit of melody 3 a group of 2 or more grammatically related words that do not form a clause

²**phrase** v 1 to express in words or in appropriate or telling terms 2 to divide into melodic phrases

physical /ˈfɪzɪkəl/ adj 1 having material existence; perceptible, esp through the senses, and subject to the laws of nature 2 of natural science or physics 3 of the body, esp as opposed to the spirit – **~ly** adv

physician /fɪˈzɪʃən/ n a person skilled in the art of healing

physics /ˈfɪzɪks/ n pl but sing or pl in constr 1 a science that deals with (the properties and interactions of) matter and energy in such fields as mechanics, heat, electricity, magnetism, atomic structure, etc 2 the physical properties and phenomena of a particular system

pianist /ˈpɪən¦ɪst, ˈpjɑː-/ n a performer on the piano

¹**piano** /ˈpjɑːnəʊ, piˈænəʊ/ adv or adj in a soft or quiet manner

²**piano** n, pl **pianos** a stringed instrument having steel wire strings that sound when struck by felt-covered hammers operated from a keyboard

¹**pick** /pɪk/ v **1a** to remove bit by bit **b** to remove covering or clinging matter from 2a to gather by plucking **b** to choose, select 3 to provoke **4a** to dig into, esp in order to remove unwanted matter; probe **b** to pluck with a plectrum or with the fingers 5 to unlock with a device (e g a wire) other than the key 6 to make (one's way) carefully on foot

²**pick** n 1 the act or privilege of choosing or selecting; a choice 2 sing or pl in constr the best or choicest

³**pick** n 1 pick, pickaxe a heavy wooden-handled tool with a head that is pointed at one or both ends 2 a plectrum

pickle /ˈpɪkəl/ n 1 a brine or vinegar solution in which meat, fish, vegetables, etc are preserved 2 (an article of) food preserved in a pickle; esp chutney – often pl 3 a difficult situation – infml – **pickle** v

¹**picnic** /ˈpɪknɪk/ n 1 (the food eaten at) an outing that includes an informal meal, usu lunch, eaten in the open 2 a pleasant or amusingly carefree experience; also an easily accomplished task or feat – infml

²**picnic** v **-ck-** to go on a picnic – **picnicker** n

¹**picture** /ˈpɪktʃə/ n 1 a design or representation made by painting, drawing, etc **2a** a description so vivid or graphic as to suggest a mental image or give an accurate idea of sthg **b** a presentation of the relevant or characteristic facts concerning a problem or situation **3a** a film **b** pl, chiefly Br the cinema

²**picture** v 1 to paint or draw a representation, image, or visual conception of; depict 2 to describe graphically in words 3 to form a mental image of; imagine

¹**pie** /paɪ/ n 1 a magpie 2 a variegated animal

²**pie** n a dish consisting of a sweet or savoury filling covered or encased by pastry and baked in a container

¹piece /piːs/ n 1 a part of a whole; *esp* a part detached, cut, etc from a whole 2 an object or individual regarded as a unit of a kind or class 3 a standard quantity (e g of length, weight, or size) in which sthg is made or sold 4a a literary, artistic, dramatic, or musical work b a passage to be recited 5 a man used in playing a board game; *esp* a chessman of rank superior to a pawn

²piece v 1 to repair, renew, or complete by adding pieces; patch – often + *up* 2 to join into a whole – often + *together*

pier /pɪə/ n 1 an intermediate support for the adjacent ends of 2 bridge spans 2 a structure extending into navigable water for use as a landing place, promenade, etc

pierce /pɪəs/ v 1 to enter or thrust into sharply or painfully 2 to make a hole in or through 3 to penetrate with the eye or mind 4 to move or affect the emotions, esp sharply or painfully

piercing /ˈpɪəsɪŋ/ adj penetrating: e g a loud, shrill b perceptive c penetratingly cold; biting d cutting, incisive – ~ly adv

¹pig /pɪg/ n 1 *chiefly Br* any of various (domesticated) stout-bodied short-legged omnivorous mammals with a thick bristly skin and a long mobile snout 2 sby like or suggestive of a pig in habits or behaviour (e g in dirtiness, greed, or selfishness) 3 a policeman – slang; derog

²pig v 1 to live like a pig – + *it* 2a to eat (food) greedily b to overindulge (oneself)

pigeon /ˈpɪdʒ³n/ n any of a family of birds with a stout body and smooth and compact plumage, many of which are domesticated or live in urban areas

pigmy, pygmy /ˈpɪgmi/ n 1 a member of a people of equatorial Africa who are under 5ft in height 2 a dwarf; *also* sby markedly inferior or insignificant in a particular area

pigsty /ˈpɪgstaɪ/ n 1 an enclosure with a covered shed for pigs 2 a dirty, untidy, or neglected place

pigtail /ˈpɪgteɪl/ n 1 a tight plait of hair, esp at the back of the head 2 either of 2 bunches of hair worn loose or plaited at either side of the head by young girls – ~ed adj

¹pile /paɪl/ n a beam of timber, steel, reinforced concrete, etc driven into the ground to carry a vertical load

²pile n 1a a quantity of things heaped together b a large quantity, number, or amount 2 a large building or group of buildings 3 a great amount of money; a fortune 4 an atomic reactor

³pile v 1 to lay or place in a pile; stack – often + *up* 2 to move or press forwards (as if) in a mass; crowd

⁴pile n a soft raised surface on a fabric or carpet consisting of cut threads or loops

⁵pile n a haemorrhoid – usu pl

pilgrim /ˈpɪlgr³m/ n a person making a pilgrimage

pilgrimage /ˈpɪlgr³mɪdʒ/ n a journey to a shrine or sacred place as an act of devotion, in order to acquire spiritual merit, or as a penance

pill /pɪl/ n 1a a small rounded solid mass of medicine to be swallowed whole b an oral contraceptive taken daily by a woman over a monthly cycle – + *the* 2 sthg repugnant or unpleasant that must be accepted or endured

pillar /ˈpɪlə/ n 1a a firm upright support for a superstructure b an usu ornamental column or shaft 2 a chief supporter; a prop

pillar box n a red pillar-shaped public letter box

¹pillow /ˈpɪləʊ/ n a usu rectangular cloth bag (e g of cotton) filled with soft material (e g down) and used to support the head of a reclining person

²pillow v 1 to rest or lay (as if) on a pillow 2 to serve as a pillow for

¹pilot /ˈpaɪlət/ n 1 sby qualified and usu licensed to conduct a ship into and out of a port or in specified waters 2 a guide, leader 3 sby who handles or is qualified to handle the controls of an aircraft or spacecraft

²pilot v 1 to act as a guide to; lead or conduct over a usu difficult course 2a to direct the course of b to act as pilot of

³pilot adj serving as a guide, activator, or trial

pimple /ˈpɪmpəl/ n a small solid inflamed (pus-containing) swelling – **-ply** adj – ~**d** adj

¹pin /pɪn/ n 1 a piece of solid material (e g wood or metal) used esp for fastening separate articles together or as a support 2a a small thin pointed piece of metal with a head used esp for fastening cloth, paper, etc b sthg of small value; a trifle 3 a projecting metal bar on a plug which is inserted into a socket 4 a leg – infml; usu pl

²pin v 1a to fasten, join, or secure with a pin b to hold fast or immobile 2a to attach, hang b to assign the blame or responsibility for

¹pinch /pɪntʃ/ v 1a to squeeze or compress painfully (e g between the finger and thumb) b to prune the tip of (a plant or shoot), usu to induce branching – + *out* or *back* 2 to subject to strict economy or want 3a to steal – slang b to arrest – slang – ~ed adj

²pinch n 1a a critical juncture; an emergency b(1) pressure, stress (2) hardship, privation 2a an act of pinching b as much as may be taken between the finger and thumb

¹pine /paɪn/ v 1 to lose vigour or health (e g through grief) – often + *away* 2 to yearn intensely and persistently, esp for sthg unattainable

²pine n 1 (any of various trees related to) any of a genus of coniferous evergreen trees which have slender elongated needles 2 the straight-grained white or yellow usu durable and resinous wood of a pine

pineapple /ˈpaɪnæpəl/ n (the large oval edible succulent yellow-fleshed fruit of) a tropical plant with rigid spiny leaves and a dense head of small flowers

¹**pink** /piŋk/ v to cut a zigzag or saw-toothed edge on

²**pink** n any of a genus of plants related to the carnation and widely grown for their white, pink, red, or variegated flowers

³**pink** adj 1 of the colour pink 2 holding moderately radical political views

⁴**pink** n 1 any of various shades of pale red 2 (the scarlet colour of) a fox hunter's coat

⁵**pink** v, Br, of an internal-combustion engine to make a series of sharp popping noises because of faulty combustion of the fuel-air mixture

pinnacle /'pinəkəl/ n 1 an architectural ornament resembling a small spire and used esp to crown a buttress 2 a lofty mountain 3 the highest point of development or achievement

pint /paint/ n 1 a unit of liquid capacity equal to ⅛gal 2 a pint of liquid, esp milk or beer

pioneer /,paɪə'nɪə/ n 1 a member of a military unit (e g engineers) engaging in light construction and defensive works 2a a person or group that originates or helps open up a new line of thought or activity or a new method or technical development b any of the first people to settle in a territory

pioneer adj 1 original, earliest 2 (characteristic) of early settlers or their time

³**pioneer** v 1 to open or prepare for others to follow; esp to settle 2 to originate or take part in the development of

pious /'paɪəs/ adj 1 devout 2 sacred or devotional as distinct from the profane or secular 3 dutiful 4 sanctimonious – ~ly adv – ~ness n

¹**pip** /pip/ n a fit of irritation, low spirits, or disgust – chiefly infml; esp in to give one the pip

²**pip** n 1 any of the dots on dice and dominoes that indicate numerical value 2 a star worn, esp on the shoulder, to indicate an army officer's rank

³**pip** v to beat by a narrow margin – infml

⁴**pip** n a small fruit seed of an apple, orange, etc

⁵**pip** n a short high-pitched tone, esp broadcast in a series as a time signal

¹**pipe** /paɪp/ n 1a a tubular wind instrument b a bagpipe – usu pl with sing. meaning 2 a long tube or hollow body for conducting a liquid, gas, etc 3a a tubular or cylindrical object, part, or passage 4 a large cask used esp for wine (e g port) 5 a wood, clay, etc tube with a mouthpiece at one end, and at the other a small bowl in which tobacco is burned for smoking

²**pipe** v 1 to play on a pipe 2a to speak in a high or shrill voice b to make a shrill sound 3a to trim with piping b to force (e g cream or icing) through a piping tube or nozzle in order to achieve a decorative effect

¹**pirate** /'paɪərət/ n sby who commits

piracy 2 an unauthorized radio station; esp one located on a ship in international waters – **-ratical** adj – **-ratically** adv

²**pirate** v 1 to commit piracy on 2 to take or appropriate by piracy 3 to reproduce without authorization

pistol /'pistl/ n a short firearm intended to be aimed and fired with 1 hand

¹**pit** /pit/ n 1a a hole, shaft, or cavity in the ground b a mine 2 an area often sunken or depressed below the adjacent floor area; esp one in a theatre housing an orchestra 3 a hollow or indentation, esp in the surface of a living plant or animal; esp a natural hollow in the surface of the body 4 any of the areas alongside a motor-racing track used for refuelling and repairing the vehicles during a race – usu pl with sing. meaning; + the

²**pit** v 1 to make pits in; esp to scar or mark with pits 2 to set into opposition or rivalry; oppose – often + against

³**pit** n, NAm a fruit stone

¹**pitch** /pitʃ/ n 1 a black or dark viscous substance obtained as a residue in the distillation of tar 2 resin obtained from various conifers

²**pitch** v 1 to erect and fix firmly in place 2 to throw, fling 3a(1) to cause to be at a particular level or of a particular quality (2) to set in a particular musical pitch or key b to cause to be set at a particular angle; slope 4a to fall precipitately or headlong b of a ship to move so that the bow is alternately rising and falling 5 of a ball to bounce

³**pitch** n 1 pitching; esp an up-and-down movement 2a a slope; also the degree of slope b distance from any point on the thread of a screw to the corresponding point on an adjacent thread measured parallel to the axis c the distance advanced by a propeller in 1 revolution d the number of teeth on a gear or of threads on a screw per unit distance 3a the relative level, intensity, or extent of some quality or state b(1) the property of a sound, esp a musical note, that is determined by the frequency of the waves producing it; highness or lowness of sound (2) a standard frequency for tuning instruments 4 an often high-pressure sales talk or advertisement 5 a wicket 6 chiefly Br a a usu specially marked area used for playing soccer, rugby, hockey, etc b an area or place, esp in a street, to which a person lays unofficial claim for carrying out business or activities

piteous /'pitiəs/ adj causing or deserving pity or compassion – ~ly adv – ~ness n

pitfall /'pitfɔːl/ n 1 a trap or snare; specif a camouflaged pit used to capture animals 2 a hidden or not easily recognized danger or difficulty

pitiful /'pitifəl/ adj 1 deserving or arousing pity or sympathy 2 exciting pitying contempt (e g by meanness or inadequacy) – ~ly adv – ~ness n

¹**pity** /'piti/ n 1a (the capacity to feel)

sympathetic sorrow for one suffering, distressed, or unhappy **b** a contemptuous feeling of regret aroused by the inferiority or inadequacy of another **2** sthg to be regretted

²**pity** v to feel pity (for)

¹**pivot** /'pivət/ n **1** a shaft or pin on which sthg turns **2a** a person, thing, or factor having a major or central role, function, or effect **b** a key player or position – ~**al** adj

²**pivot** v to turn (as if) on a pivot

placard /'plækɑːd/ n a notice for display or advertising purposes, usu printed on or fixed to a stiff backing material

¹**place** /pleɪs/ n **1a** physical environment; a space **b** physical surroundings; atmosphere **c** an indefinite region or expanse; an area **3** a particular region or centre of population **4** a particular part of a surface or body; a spot **5** relative position in a scale or series: eg **a** a particular part in a piece of writing; esp the point at which a reader has temporarily stopped **b** an important or valued position **c** degree of prestige **6** a leading place, being second or third, in a competition **7a** a proper or designated niche **b** an appropriate moment or point **8** an available seat or accommodation **9a** employment; a job; esp public office **b** prestige accorded to one of high rank; status **10** a public square

²**place** v **1** to distribute in an orderly manner **2a** to put in, direct to, or assign to a particular place **b** to put in a particular state **3** to appoint to a position **4** to find employment or a home for **5a** to assign to a position in a series or category **b** to identify by connecting with an associated context **c** to put, lay **6** to give (an order) to a supplier

¹**plague** /pleɪg/ n **1a** a disastrous evil or affliction; a calamity **b** a large destructive influx **2** any of several epidemic virulent diseases that cause many deaths **3** a cause of irritation; a nuisance

²**plague** v **1** to cause worry or distress to **2** to disturb or annoy persistently

plaice /pleɪs/ n, pl **plaice** any of various flatfishes; a flounder

¹**plain** /pleɪn/ n **1** an extensive area of level or rolling treeless country **2** a broad unbroken expanse

²**plain** adj **1** lacking ornament; undecorated **2** free of added substances; pure **3a** evident to the mind or senses; obvious **b** clear **4** free from deceitfulness or subtlety; candid **5** lacking special distinction; ordinary **6a** not complicated **b** not rich or elaborately prepared or decorated **7** unremarkable either for physical beauty or for ugliness **8** of flour not containing a raising agent

³**plain, plainly** adv in a plain manner; clearly, simply; also totally, utterly

¹**plait** /plæt/ n a length of plaited material, esp hair

²**plait** v **1** to interweave the strands of **2** to make by plaiting

¹**plan** /plæn/ n **1** a drawing or diagram: eg **a** a top or horizontal view of an

object **b** a large-scale map of a small area **2a** a method for achieving an end **b** a customary method of doing sthg **c** a detailed formulation of a programme of action

²**plan** v **1** to design **2** to arrange in advance **3** to have in mind; intend – ~**ner** n

¹**plane** /pleɪn/ v **1** to make flat or even with a plane **2** to remove by planing – often + away or down

²**plane, plane tree** n any of a genus of trees with large deeply cut lobed leaves and flowers in spherical heads

³**plane** n a tool with a sharp blade protruding from the base of a flat metal or wooden stock for smoothing or shaping a wood surface

⁴**plane** n **1** a surface such that any 2 included points can be joined by a straight line lying wholly within the surface **2** a level of existence, consciousness, or development **3** an aeroplane; also any of the surfaces that support it in flight

⁵**plane** adj **1** having no elevations or depressions; flat **2a** of or dealing with geometric planes **b** lying in a plane

planet /'plænɪt/ n any of the bodies, except a comet, meteor, or satellite, that revolve round a star, esp the sun in our solar system **2** a star held to have astrological significance – ~**ary** adj

¹**plank** /plæŋk/ n **1** a long flat piece of wood **2** a (principal) item of a political policy or programme

²**plank** v to cover or floor with planks

¹**plant** /plɑːnt/ v **1a** to put in the ground, soil, etc for growth **b** to set or sow (land) with seeds or plants **2** to establish, institute **3** to place firmly or forcibly **4** to position secretly; specif to conceal in order to observe or deceive

²**plant** n **1** any of a kingdom of living things (eg a green alga, moss, fern, conifer, or flowering plant) typically lacking locomotive movement or obvious nervous or sensory organs **2a** the buildings, machinery, etc employed in carrying on a trade or an industrial business **b** a factory or workshop for the manufacture of a particular product

plantation /plæn'teɪʃən, plɑːn-/ n **1** (a place with) a usu large group of plants, esp trees, under cultivation **2** a settlement in a new country or region; a colony **3** an agricultural estate, usu worked by resident labour

plaque /plæk/ n **1** a commemorative or decorative inscribed tablet of ceramic, wood, metal, etc **2** a film of mucus on a tooth that harbours bacteria

¹**plaster** /'plɑːstə/ n **1** a medicated or protective dressing **2** a pastelike mixture (e g of lime, water, and sand) that hardens on drying and is used esp for coating walls, ceilings, and partitions **3** **plaster, plaster cast** a rigid dressing of gauze impregnated with plaster of paris for immobilizing a diseased or broken body part

²**plaster** v **1** to overlay or cover with (a)

plaster **2a** to cover over or conceal as if with a coat of plaster **b** to smear (sthg) thickly; coat **3** to fasten (sthg) (to) or place (sthg) (on), esp conspicuously or in quantity **4** to inflict heavy damage, injury, or casualties on, esp by a concentrated or unremitting attack – infml

¹**plastic** /'plæstɪk/ adj **1** capable of being moulded or modelled **2** supple, pliant **3** sculptural **4** made or consisting of a plastic **5** formed by or adapted to an artificial or conventional standard; synthetic – chiefly derog – ~**ally** adv – ~**ity** n

²**plastic** n any of numerous (synthetic) organic polymers that can be moulded, cast, extruded, etc into objects, films, or filaments

Plasticine /'plæstɪˌsiːn/ trademark – used for a modelling substance that remains plastic for a long period

¹**plate** /pleɪt/ n **1a** a smooth flat thin usu rigid piece of material **b** an (external) scale or rigid layer of bone, horn, etc forming part of an animal body **2a** domestic utensils and tableware made of or plated with gold, silver, or base metals **b** a shallow usu circular vessel, made esp of china, from which food is eaten or served **3a** a prepared surface from which printing is done **b** a sheet of material (e g glass) coated with a light-sensitive photographic emulsion **c** an electrode in an accumulator **4** a horizontal structural member (e g a timber) that provides bearing and anchorage, esp for rafters or joists **5** the part of a denture that fits to the mouth **6** a full-page book illustration

²**plate** v to cover permanently with an adherent layer, esp of metal; also to deposit (e g a layer) on a surface – **plating** n

plateau /'plætəʊ/ n, pl **plateaus** or **plateaux 1** a usu extensive relatively flat land area raised sharply above adjacent land on at least **1** side **2** a relatively stable level, period, or condition

platform /'plætfɔːm/ n **1** a declaration of (political) principles and policies **2a** a raised surface at a railway station to facilitate access to trains **b** a raised flooring (e g for speakers) **3** a place or opportunity for public discussion **4** chiefly Br the area next to the entrance or exit of a bus

platinum /'plætɪnəm/ n a heavy precious greyish white noncorroding metallic element used esp as a catalyst and for jewellery

plausible /'plɔːzəbəl/ adj **1** apparently fair, reasonable, or valid but often deceptive **2** of a person persuasive but deceptive – **bly** adv – **bility** n

¹**play** /pleɪ/ n **1** the conduct, course, or (a particular) action in or of a game **2a** (children's spontaneous) recreational activity **b** the absence of serious or harmful intent; jest **3a** operation, activity **b** light, quick, transitory, or fitful movement **c** free or unimpeded motion **4a** the dramatized representation of an action or story on stage **b** a

dramatic composition (for presentation in a theatre)

²**play** v **1a** to engage in sport or recreation **b(1)** to deal or behave frivolously, mockingly, or playfully – often + around or about **(2)** to make use of double meaning or of the similarity of sound of 2 words for stylistic or humorous effect – usu in play on words **c(1)** to deal with, handle, or manage – often + it **(2)** to exploit, manipulate **d** to pretend to engage in **e(1)** to perform or execute for amusement or to deceive or mock **(2)** to wreak **2a** to take advantage **b** to move or operate in a lively, irregular, or intermittent manner **c** to move or function freely within prescribed limits **d** to discharge repeatedly or in a stream **3** to act with special consideration so as to gain favour, approval, or sympathy – usu + up to **4a** to put on a performance of (a play) **b** to act or perform in or as a **5a(1)** to contend against in a game **(2)** to perform the duties associated with (a certain position) **b(1)** to make bets on **(2)** to operate on the basis of **c** to put into action in a game **d** to direct the course of (e g a ball); hit **6a** to perform music on an instrument **b** to perform music on **c** to perform music of a specified composer **d** to reproduce sounds, esp music, on (an apparatus) **7** to have (promiscuous or illicit) sexual relations – euph; usu in play around – ~**er** n

playful /'pleɪfəl/ adj **1** full of fun; frolicsome **2** humorous, lighthearted – ~**fully** adv – ~**ness** n

plaything /'pleɪˌθɪŋ/ n a toy

plea /pliː/ n **1** an accused person's answer to an indictment **2** sthg offered by way of excuse or justification **3** an earnest entreaty; an appeal

plead /pliːd/ v **1** to make or answer an allegation in a legal proceeding **2** to make a specified plea **3a** to urge reasons for or against sthg **b** to entreat or appeal earnestly; implore – ~**ing** n

pleasant /'plezənt/ adj **1** having qualities that tend to give pleasure; agreeable **2** of a person likable, friendly – ~**ly** adv

please /pliːz/ v **1** to afford or give pleasure or satisfaction **2** to like, wish **3** to be willing – usu used in the imperative **(1)** to express a polite request (e g please come in) **(2)** to turn an apparent question into a request (e g can you shut it, please?) **4** to be the will or pleasure of – fml

pleasure /'pleʒə/ n **1** (a state of) gratification **2** enjoyment, recreation **3** a source of delight or joy **4** a wish, desire – fml – ~ v – **-rable** adj

¹**pledge** /pledʒ/ n **1** sthg delivered as security for an obligation (e g a debt) **2** the state of being held as a security **3a** a token, sign, or earnest of sthg else **4** a binding promise to do or forbear

²**pledge** v **1** to deposit as security for fulfilment of a contract or obligation **2** to drink the health of **3** to bind by a pledge **4** to give a promise of

¹**plenty** /'plenti/ n **1a** sing or pl in constr

a full or more than adequate amount or supply **b** a large number or amount **2** copiousness, plentifulness – **-tiful** *adj*

²**plenty** *adv* **1** quite, abundantly **2** *chiefly NAm* to a considerable or extreme degree; very (e g *plenty* hungry) *USE* infml

pliable /'plaɪəbəl/ *adj* **1** easily bent without breaking; flexible **2** yielding readily to others; compliant – **-bility** *n*

pliers /'plaɪəz/ *n pl* a pair of pincers with long jaws for holding small objects or for bending and cutting wire

plod /plɒd/ *v* **1** to tread slowly or heavily along or over **2** to work laboriously and monotonously

¹**plot** /plɒt/ *n* **1** a small piece of land, esp one used or designated for a specific purpose **2** the plan or main story of a literary work **3** a secret plan for accomplishing a usu evil or unlawful end; an intrigue

²**plot** *v* **1** to make a plot, map, or plan of **2** to draw (a curve) by means of plotted points **3** to plan or contrive, esp secretly **4** to invent or devise the plot of (a literary work) – **~ter** *n*

¹**plough** /plaʊ/, *NAm* **plow** *n* **1** an implement used to cut, lift, and turn over soil, esp in preparing ground for sowing **2** ploughed land

²**plough** *v* **1** to make or work with a plough **2** to cut into, open, or make furrows or ridges in (as if) with a plough – often + *up* **3** to force a way, press violently **4** to proceed steadily and laboriously; plod **5** to fail an exam

¹**pluck** /plʌk/ *v* **1** to pull or pick off or out **2** to pick, pull, or grasp at; *also* to play (an instrument) in this manner

²**pluck** *n* **1** an act or instance of plucking or pulling **2** courage and determination

plucky /'plʌki/ *adj* marked by courage; spirited – **-ily** *adv* – **-iness** *n*

¹**plug** /plʌg/ *n* **1** a stopper **2** a flat compressed cake of (chewing) tobacco **3** a small core or segment removed from a larger object **4** a device having usu 3 pins projecting from an insulated case for making electrical connection with a suitable socket; *also* the electrical socket **5** a piece of favourable publicity (e g for a commercial product) usu incorporated in general matter – infml

²**plug** *v* **1** to block, close, etc (as if) by inserting a plug **2** to hit with a bullet **3** to advertise or publicize insistently **4** to work doggedly and persistently *on*

plum /plʌm/ *n* **1** (any of numerous trees that bear) an edible globular to oval smooth-skinned fruit with an oblong seed **2** sthg excellent or superior; *esp* an opportunity or position offering exceptional advantages **3** a dark reddish purple colour

plumber /'plʌmə/ *n* sby who installs, repairs, and maintains water piping and fittings

plumbing /'plʌmɪŋ/ *n* the apparatus (e g pipes and fixtures) concerned in the distribution and use of water in a building

plume /pluːm/ *n* **1** a usu large feather or cluster of feathers esp worn as an ornament **2** sthg resembling a feather (e g in shape, appearance, or lightness): e g **a** a feathery or feather-like animal or plant part; *esp* a full bushy tail **b** a trail of smoke, blowing snow, etc – **~d** *adj*

¹**plump** /plʌmp/ *v* to drop or sink suddenly or heavily

²**plump** *adj* having a full rounded form; slightly fat

¹**plunder** /'plʌndə/ *v* **1** to pillage, sack **2** to take, esp by force (e g in war); steal – **~er** *n*

²**plunder** *n* sthg taken by force, theft, or fraud; loot

¹**plunge** /plʌndʒ/ *v* **1** to thrust or cast oneself (as if) into water **2** to cause to penetrate quickly and forcibly **3a** to be thrown headlong or violently forwards and downwards; *also* to move oneself in such a manner **b** to act with reckless haste; enter suddenly or unexpectedly **4** to descend or dip suddenly

²**plunge** *n* a dive; *also* a swim

plural /'plʊərəl/ *adj* **1** of or being a word form (e g *we*, *houses*, *cattle*) denoting more than 1, or in some languages more than 2 or 3, persons, things, or instances **2** consisting of or containing more than 1 (kind or class) – **~ly** *adv*

¹**plus** /plʌs/ *prep* **1** increased by; with the addition of **2** and also

²**plus** *n* an added quantity **2** a positive factor, quantity, or quality

³**plus** *adj* **1** algebraically or electrically positive **2** additional and welcome **3** greater than that specified

⁴**plus** *conj* and moreover

¹**ply** /plaɪ/ *n* **1a** a strand in a yarn, wool, etc **b** any of several layers (e g of cloth) usu sewn or laminated together **2** (any of the veneer sheets forming) plywood

²**ply** *v* **1** to apply oneself steadily **2** *of a boatman, taxi driver, etc* to wait regularly in a particular place for custom – esp in *ply for hire* **3** to go or travel regularly

pneumatic /njuːˈmætɪk/ *adj* **1** moved or worked by air pressure **2** adapted for holding or inflated with compressed air – **~ally** *adv*

¹**poach** /pəʊtʃ/ *v* to cook (e g fish or an egg) in simmering liquid

²**poach** *v* **1** to take game or fish illegally **2** to trespass on or *upon*

¹**pocket** /'pɒkɪt/ *n* **1** a small bag that is sewn or inserted in a garment so that it is open at the top or side **2** any of several openings at the corners or sides of a billiard table into which balls are propelled **3** a small isolated area or group

²**pocket** *v* **1** to appropriate to one's own use; steal **2** to accept; put up with **3** to drive (a ball) into a pocket of a billiard table

³**pocket** *adj* small, miniature

¹**pod** /pɒd/ *n* **1** a long seed vessel or fruit, esp of the pea, bean, or other leguminous plant **2** an egg case of a locust or similar insect

pod v to remove (e g peas) from the pod

poem /'pəʊɪm/ n 1 an individual work of poetry 2 a creation, experience, or object suggesting a poem

poet /'pəʊɪt/ fem **poetess** n 1 one who writes poetry 2 a creative artist with special sensitivity to his/her medium – ~ical adj – ~ic adj – ~ically adv

poetry /'pəʊɪtri/ n 1a metrical writing; verse b a poet's compositions; poems 2 writing that is arranged to formulate a concentrated imaginative awareness of experience through meaning, sound, and rhythm 3 a quality of beauty, grace, and great feeling

point /pɔɪnt/ n 1a an individual detail; an item b the most important essential in a discussion or matter 2 an end or object to be achieved; a purpose 3a a geometric element that has a position but no extent or magnitude b a precisely indicated position c an exact moment; esp the moment before sthg d a particular step, stage, or degree in development 4a the sharp or narrowly rounded end of sthg; a tip b the tip of the toes – used in ballet; usu pl 5a a projecting usu tapering piece of land b(1) the tip of a projecting body part (2) a tine 6a a very small mark b(1) a punctuation mark; esp full stop (2) a decimal point 7 any of the 32 evenly spaced compass directions; also the 11° 15' interval between 2 successive points 8 a unit of counting in the scoring of a game or contest 9 a fielding position in cricket near to the batsman on the off side 10 pl, Br a device made of usu 2 movable rails and necessary connections and designed to turn a locomotive or train from one track to another

point v 1 to give added force, emphasis, or piquancy to 2 to scratch out the old mortar from the joints of (e g a brick wall) and fill in with new material 3a to indicate the position or direction of sthg, esp by extending a finger b of a gundog to indicate the presence and place of (game) for a hunter 4 to lie extended, aimed, or turned in a particular direction

pointed /'pɔɪntɪd/ adj 1 having a point 2a pertinent b aimed at a particular person or group 3 conspicuous, marked – ~ly adv

pointless /'pɔɪntlɪs/ adj devoid of meaning, relevance, or purpose; senseless – ~ly adv – ~ness n

point of view n a position from which sthg is considered or evaluated

poison /'pɔɪzən/ n a substance that through its chemical action kills, injures, or impairs an organism

poison v 1 to injure, kill, treat, etc with poison 2 to exert a harmful influence on; corrupt – ~er n

poisonous /'pɔɪzənəs/ adj having the properties or effects of poison – ~ly adv

poke /pəʊk/ n, chiefly dial NAm a bag, sack

poke v 1a to prod, jab b to stir the coals or logs of (a fire) so as to promote burning 2a to look about or through sthg without system; rummage b to meddle 3 to become stuck out or forwards; protrude 4 of a man to have sexual intercourse with – vulg

³poke n 1a a quick thrust; a jab 2a a punch – infml 3 an act of sexual intercourse – vulg

¹poker /'pəʊkəʳ/ n a metal rod for poking a fire

²poker n any of several card games in which a player bets that the value of his/her hand is greater than that of the hands held by others

polar /'pəʊləʳ/ adj 1a of, coming from, or characteristic of (the region round) a geographical pole b esp of an orbit passing over a planet's N and S poles 2 of 1 or more poles (e g of a magnet) 3 resembling a pole or axis round which all else revolves; pivotal

¹pole /pəʊl/ n 1a a long slender usu cylindrical object (e g a length of wood) b a shaft which extends from the front axle of a wagon between the draught animals 2 a unit of length equal to 5½yd (about 5m) 3 the most favourable front-row position on the starting line of a (motor) race

²pole v to push or propel (e g a boat) with poles

³pole n 1 either extremity of an axis of (a body, esp the earth, resembling) a sphere 2a either of 2 related opposites b a point of guidance or attraction 3a either of the 2 terminals of an electric cell, battery, or dynamo b any of 2 or more regions in a magnetized body at which the magnetic flux density is concentrated

Pole n a native or inhabitant of Poland

police /pə'liːs/ n 1 the department of government concerned with maintenance of public order and enforcement of laws 2a sing or pl in constr a police force b pl in constr policemen – police n

policeman /pə'liːsmən/ fem **policewoman** n a member of a police force

¹policy /'pɒlɪsi/ n 1 a definite course of action selected from among alternatives to guide and determine present and future decisions 2 an overall plan embracing general goals and procedures, esp of a governmental body

²policy n (a document embodying) a contract of insurance

¹polish /'pɒlɪʃ/ v 1 to make smooth and glossy, usu by friction 2 to refine in manners or condition 3 to bring to a highly developed, finished, or refined state; perfect – often + up – ~er n

²polish n 1a a smooth glossy surface b freedom from rudeness or coarseness 2 a preparation used to produce a gloss and often a colour for the protection and decoration of a surface

¹Polish /'pəʊlɪʃ/ adj (characteristic) of Poland

²Polish n the language of the Poles

polite /pə'laɪt/ adj 1 showing or characterized by correct social usage; refined 2 marked by consideration and deference; courteous – ~ly adv – ~ness n

political /pə'lɪtɪkəl/ adj 1 of government 2a of (party) politics b sensitive to politics – ~ly adv

politician /ˌpɒlɪ'tɪʃən/ n a person experienced or engaged in politics

politics /'pɒlɪtɪks/ n pl but sing or pl in constr 1 the art or science of government 2a political affairs; specif competition between interest groups in a government b political life as a profession 3 sby's political sympathies

¹**poll** /pəʊl/ n 1 (the hairy top or back of) the head 2 the broad or flat end of the head of a striking tool (e g a hammer) 3a the casting of votes b the place where votes are cast – usu pl with sing. meaning c the number of votes recorded 4 a survey conducted by the questioning of people selected at random or by quota

²**poll** v 1 to cut off or cut short the horns of (a cow) 2 to pollard (a tree) 3 to receive and record the votes of; also to cast one's vote 4 to question in a poll

³**poll** n a polled animal

pollute /pə'luːt/ v 1 to make morally impure; defile 2 to make physically impure or unclean; esp to contaminate (an environment), esp with man-made waste – -tion n

polythene /'pɒlɪθiːn/ n any of various lightweight plastics used esp for packaging and bowls, buckets, etc

pompous /'pɒmpəs/ adj 1 self-important, pretentious 2 excessively elevated or ornate – ~ly adv – -posity, ~ness n

pond /pɒnd/ n a body of (fresh) water usu smaller than a lake

ponder /'pɒndə/ v 1 to weigh in the mind; assess 2 to review mentally; think over

pony /'pəʊni/ n a small horse; esp a member of any of several breeds of very small stocky horses under 14.2 hands in height

¹**pool** /puːl/ n 1 a small and relatively deep body of usu fresh water (e g a still place in a stream or river) 2 a small body of standing liquid; a puddle

²**pool** n 1 an aggregate stake to which each player of a game has contributed 2 any of various games played on a billiard table with 6 pockets and often 15 numbered balls 3 a facility, service, or group of people providing a service for a number of people (e g the members of a business organization) 4 pl the football pools

³**pool** v to contribute to a common stock (e g of resources or effort)

poor /pʊə/ adj 1 lacking material possessions 2 less than adequate; meagre 3 exciting pity 4 inferior in quality, value, or workmanship 5 humble, unpretentious

poorly /'pʊəli, 'pɔːli/ adj somewhat ill

¹**pop** /pɒp/ v 1 to push, put, or thrust out suddenly 2 to cause to explode or burst open 3 to protrude from the sockets 4 Br to pawn

²**pop** n 1 a popping sound 2 a flavoured fizzy drink

³**pop** adv like or with a pop; suddenly – infml

⁴**pop** n, chiefly NAm a father – infml

⁵**pop** adj popular: e g a of pop music b of or constituting a mass culture widely disseminated through the mass media

⁶**pop** n pop music

pope /pəʊp/ n 1 often cap the prelate who as bishop of Rome is the head of the Roman Catholic church 2 a priest of an Eastern church

poppy /'pɒpi/ n any of several genera of plants with showy flowers and capsular fruits including the opium poppy and several other plants cultivated for their ornamental value

popular /'pɒpjʊlə/ adj 1 (suited to the needs, means, tastes, or understanding) of the general public 2 having general currency 3 commonly liked or approved – ~ity n – ~ize v – ~ly adv

populate /'pɒpjʊleɪt/ v 1 to have a place in; occupy, inhabit 2 to supply or provide with inhabitants; people

population /ˌpɒpjʊ'leɪʃən/ n 1 sing or pl in constr the whole number of people or inhabitants in a country or region 2 sing or pl in constr a body of people or individuals having a quality or characteristic in common 3 a set (e g of individual people or items) from which samples are taken for statistical measurement

porch /pɔːtʃ/ n 1 a covered usu projecting entrance to a building 2 NAm a veranda

porcupine /'pɔːkjʊpaɪn/ n any of various large rodents with stiff sharp erectile bristles mingled with the hair

¹**pore** /pɔː/ v 1 to study closely or attentively 2 to reflect or meditate steadily USE usu + on, over, or upon

²**pore** n a minute opening; esp one (e g in a membrane, esp the skin, or between soil particles) through which fluids pass or are absorbed

pork /pɔːk/ n the flesh of a pig used as food

pornography /pɔː'nɒgrəfi/ n (books, photographs, films, etc containing) the depiction of erotic behaviour intended to cause sexual excitement – -pher n – -phic adj – -phically adv

porridge /'pɒrɪdʒ/ n 1 a soft food made by boiling oatmeal in milk or water until thick 2 Br time spent in prison – slang

¹**port** /pɔːt/ n 1 a town or city with a harbour where ships may take on or discharge cargo or passengers

²**port** n 1 an opening (e g in machinery) for intake or exhaust of a fluid 2 an opening in a ship's side to admit light or air or to load cargo 3 a hole in an armoured vehicle or fortification through which guns may be fired

³**port** adj or n (of or at) the left side of a ship or aircraft looking forwards

⁴**port** v to turn or put (a helm) to the left – used chiefly as a command

port *n* a fortified sweet wine of rich taste and aroma made in Portugal

portable /'pɔːtəbəl/ *n or adj* (sthg) capable of being carried or moved about – **-bility** *n*

porter /'pɔːtə/ *n* a gatekeeper or doorkeeper, esp of a large building, who usu regulates entry and answers enquiries

porter *n* **1** sby who carries luggage; *specif* sby employed to carry luggage **2** a heavy dark brown beer – ~ **age** *n*

porthole /'pɔːthəʊl/ *n* a usu glazed opening, esp in the side of a ship or aircraft

portion /'pɔːʃən/ *n* **1** a part or share of sthg; *esp* a helping of food **2** an individual's lot or fate

portion *v* to divide into portions; distribute – often + *out*

portrait /'pɔːtrɪt/ *n* **1** a pictorial likeness of a person **2** a verbal portrayal or representation

portray /pɔː'treɪ/ *v* **1** to make a picture of; depict **2a** to describe in words **b** to play the role of – ~ **al** *n*

pose /pəʊz/ *v* **1** to assume a posture or attitude, usu for artistic purposes **2** to affect an attitude or character; posture – usu + *as* **3** to present for attention or consideration

pose *n* **1** a sustained posture; *esp* one assumed for artistic purposes **2** an assumed attitude of mind or mode of behaviour

posh /pɒʃ/ *adj* **1** very fine; splendid **2** socially exclusive or fashionable – often derog *USE* infml

position /pə'zɪʃən/ *n* **1** an opinion; point of view **2** a market commitment in securities or commodities **3** the place occupied by sby or sthg; *also* the proper place **4a** a condition, situation **b** social or official rank or status **5** a post, job – fml

position *v* to put in a proper or specified position

positive /'pɒzɪtɪv/ *adj* **1** fully assured; confident **2** incontestable **3** utter **4** real, active **5a** capable of being constructively applied; helpful **b** concentrating on what is good or beneficial **6** having or expressing actual existence or quality as distinguished from deficiency **7** having the light and dark parts similar in tone to those of the original photographic subject **8** in a direction arbitrarily or customarily taken as that of increase or progression **9** numerically greater than zero **10a** charged with electricity **b** having higher electric potential and constituting the part from which the current flows to the external circuit **11** marked by or indicating acceptance, approval, or affirmation – ~ *n* – ~ **ly** *adv*

possess /pə'zes/ *v* **1** to make the owner or holder – + *of* or *with* **2a** to have and hold as property; own **b** to have as an attribute, knowledge, or skill **3** to influence so strongly as to direct the actions; *also, of a demon, evil spirit, etc* to enter into and control – ~ **or** *n*

possession /pə'zeʃən/ *n* **1a** having or taking into control **b** ownership **2a**

sthg owned, occupied, or controlled **b** *pl* wealth, property **3** domination by sthg (e g an evil spirit or passion)

possibility /,pɒsɪ'bɪlɪti/ *n* **1** the condition or fact of being possible **2** sthg possible **3** potential or prospective value – usu *pl* with sing. meaning

possible /'pɒsɪbəl/ *adj* **1** within the limits of ability, capacity, or realization **2** capable of being done or occurring according to nature, custom, or manners **3** that may or may not occur – **possible** *n*

possibly /'pɒsɪbli/ *adv* **1** it is possible that; maybe **2** – used as an intensifier with *can* or *could*

post /pəʊst/ *n* **1** a piece of timber, metal, etc fixed firmly in an upright position, esp as a stay or support **2** a pole marking the starting or finishing point of a horse race **3** a goalpost

post *v* **1** to fasten to a wall, board, etc in order to make public – often + *up* **2** to publish, announce, or advertise (as if) by use of a placard

post *n* **1** a (single despatch or delivery of) the mail handled by a postal system **2** *chiefly Br* a postal system or means of posting

post *v* **1** to send by post **2** to provide with the latest news; inform

post *n* **1a** the place at which a soldier or body of troops is stationed **b** a station or task to which one is assigned **2** an office or position to which a person is appointed **3** a trading post, settlement **4** *Br* either of 2 bugle calls giving notice of the hour for retiring at night

post *v* to station

postage /'pəʊstɪdʒ/ *n* (markings or stamps representing) the fee for a postal service

postcard /'pəʊstkɑːd/ *n* a card that can be posted without an enclosing envelope

postdate /,pəʊst'deɪt/ *v* **1** to date with a date later than that of execution **2** to assign (an event) to a date subsequent to that of actual occurrence

poster /'pəʊstə/ *n* a (decorative) bill or placard for display often in a public place

postman /'pəʊstmən/ *n* sby who delivers the post

post meridiem /,pəʊst mə'rɪdɪəm/ *adj* being after noon – abbr **pm**

postmortem /,pəʊst'mɔːtəm/ *adj* occurring after death

postmortem *n* **1** an examination of a body after death for determining the cause of death or the character and extent of changes produced by disease **2** an examination of a plan or event that failed, in order to discover the cause of failure

post office *n* **1** a national usu governmental organization that runs a postal system **2** a local branch of a national post office

postpone /pəʊs'pəʊn/ *v* to hold back to a later time; defer – ~ **ment** *n*

posture /'pɒstʃə/ *n* **1** the position or bearing of (relative parts) of the body **2** a frame of mind; an attitude

²**posture** v 1 to assume a posture; esp to strike a pose for effect 2 to assume an artificial or insincere attitude; attitudinize

¹**pot** /pɒt/ n 1 any of various usu rounded vessels (e g of metal or earthenware) used for holding liquids or solids, esp in cooking 2 an enclosed framework for catching fish or lobsters 3 a drinking vessel (e g of pewter) used esp for beer 4 the total of the bets at stake at 1 time 5 Br a shot in billiards or snooker in which an object ball is pocketed 6 NAm the common fund of a group 7 a large amount (of money) – usu pl with sing. meaning; infml 8 a potbelly – infml 9 cannabis; specif marijuana – slang

²**pot** v 1 to preserve in a sealed pot, jar, or can 2 to make or shape (earthenware) as a potter

potato /pə'teɪtəʊ/ n, pl **potatoes** 1 a sweet potato, yam 2 a plant widely cultivated in temperate regions for its edible starchy tubers; also a potato tuber eaten as a vegetable

¹**potential** /pə'tenʃəl/ adj existing in possibility; capable of being made real – ~ly adv

²**potential** n 1 sthg that can develop or become actual; possible capacity or value 2 the difference between the voltages at 2 points (e g in an electrical circuit or in an electrical field)

¹**potter** /'pɒtə'/ n one who makes pottery

²**potter** v 1 to spend time in aimless or unproductive activity – often + around or about 2 to move or travel in a leisurely or random fashion – **potter** n

pottery /'pɒtəri/ n 1 a place where ceramic ware is made and fired 2 articles of fired clay; esp coarse or hand-made ceramic ware

pouch /paʊtʃ/ n 1 a small drawstring bag carried on the person 2 a lockable bag for mail or diplomatic dispatches 3 an anatomical structure resembling a pouch: e g a a pocket of skin in the abdomen of marsupials for carrying their young b a pocket of skin in the cheeks of some rodents used for storing food

poultry /'pəʊltri/ n domesticated birds (e g chickens) kept for eggs or meat

pounce /paʊns/ v 1 to swoop on and seize sthg (as if) with talons 2 to make a sudden assault or approach – ~ n

¹**pound** /paʊnd/ n 1 a unit of mass and weight equal to 16oz avoirdupois (about 0.453kg) 2 the basic money unit of the UK and many other countries

²**pound** v 1 to reduce to powder or pulp by beating or crushing 2 to strike heavily or repeatedly 3 to move or run along with heavy steps

³**pound** n 1 an enclosure for animals; esp a public enclosure for stray or unlicensed animals 2 a place for holding personal property until redeemed by the owner

pour /pɔː'/ v 1 (to cause) to flow in a stream 2 to dispense (a drink) into a container 3 to supply or produce freely or copiously 4 to rain hard – often + down

poverty /'pɒvəti/ n 1a the lack of sufficient money or material possessions b the renunciation of individual property by a person entering a religious order 2 the condition of lacking desirable elements; deficiency, death

¹**powder** /'paʊdə'/ n 1 matter reduced to a state of dry loose particles (e g by crushing or grinding) 2 a preparation in the form of fine particles, esp for medicinal or cosmetic use 3 any of various solid explosives used chiefly in gunnery and blasting

²**powder** v 1 to sprinkle or cover (as if) with powder 2 to reduce or convert to powder

¹**power** /'paʊə'/ n 1a possession of control, authority, or influence over others b a sovereign state c a controlling group – often in the powers that be 2 ability to act or produce or undergo an effect 3a physical might b mental or moral efficacy; vigour c political control or influence 4 the number of times, as indicated by an exponent, that a number has to be multiplied by itself 5a electricity b the rate at which work is done or energy emitted or transferred 6 magnification 7 a large amount of – infml

²**power** v 1 to supply with esp motive power 2 to make (one's way) in a powerful and vigorous manner

³**power** adj driven by a motor

powerful /'paʊəfəl/ adj having great power, prestige, or influence – ~ly adv

¹**practical** /'præktikəl/ adj 1a of or manifested in practice or action b being such in practice or effect; virtual 2 capable of being put to use or account; useful 3 suitable for use 4 disposed to or capable of positive action as opposed to speculation; also prosaic – ~ity n

²**practical** n a practical examination or lesson

practically /'præktikəli/ adv almost, nearly

practice /'præktɪs/ , NAm also **practise** n 1a actual performance or application b a repeated or customary action; a habit c the usual way of doing sthg d dealings, conduct – esp in sharp practice 2 (an instance of) regular or repeated exercise in order to acquire proficiency; also proficiency or experience gained in this way 3 a professional business

practise /'præktɪs/ , NAm chiefly **practice** v 1 to perform or work at repeatedly so as to become proficient 2 to be professionally engaged in

prairie /'preəri/ n an extensive area of level or rolling (practically) treeless grassland, esp in N America

¹**praise** /preɪz/ v 1 to express a favourable judgment of; commend 2 to glorify or extol (e g God or a god)

²**praise** n 1 expression of approval; commendation 2 worship

¹**pram** /præm/ n a small lightweight

nearly flat-bottomed boat with a broad transom and low squared-off bow

pram *n* a usu 4-wheeled carriage for babies that is pushed by a person on foot

prance /prɑ:ns/ *v* to walk or move in a gay, lively, or haughty manner – **prance** *n*

pray /preɪ/ *v* **1** to request earnestly or humbly **2** to address prayers to God or a god

prayer /preə'/ *n* **1a** an address to God or a god in word or thought, with a petition, confession, thanksgiving, etc **b** an earnest request **2** the act or practice of praying **3** a religious service consisting chiefly of prayers – often *pl* with *sing.* meaning

preach /pri:tʃ/ *v* **1** to deliver a sermon **2** to urge acceptance or abandonment of an idea or course of action, esp in an officious manner – **~er** *n*

precarious /prɪ'keəriəs/ *adj* **1** dependent on chance or uncertain circumstances; doubtful **2** characterized by a lack of security or stability; dangerous – **~ly** *adv* – **~ness** *n*

precaution /prɪ'kɔ:ʃən/ *n* **1** care taken in advance; foresight **2** a measure taken beforehand to avoid possible harmful consequences; a safeguard – **~ary** *adj*

precede /prɪ'si:d/ *v* **1** to surpass in rank, dignity, or importance **2** to be, go, or come before, ahead, or in front of

precedent /'presɪdənt/ *n* **1** an earlier occurrence of sthg similar **2** a judicial decision that serves as a rule for subsequent similar cases

precious /'preʃəs/ *adj* **1** of great value or high price **2** highly esteemed or cherished; dear **3** excessively refined; affected – **~ly** *adv* – **~ness** *n*

precious *adv* very, extremely

precious *n* a dear one; darling

precipice /'presɪpɪs/ *n* **1** a very steep, perpendicular, or overhanging surface (e g of a rock or mountain) **2** the brink of disaster

precise /prɪ'saɪs/ *adj* **1** exactly or sharply defined or stated **2** highly exact **3** strictly conforming to a rule, convention, etc; punctilious **4** distinguished from every other; very – **~ly** *adv* – **~ness** *n*

precision /prɪ'sɪʒən/ *n* **1** being precise; exactness **2** the degree of refinement with which an operation is performed or a measurement stated

precision *adj* **1** adapted for extremely accurate measurement or operation **2** marked by precision of execution

predecessor /'pri:dɪsesə'/ *n* **1** the previous occupant of a position or office to which another has succeeded **2** an ancestor

predicament /prɪ'dɪkəmənt/ *n* a (difficult, perplexing, or trying) situation

predict /prɪ'dɪkt/ *v* to foretell (sthg) on the basis of observation, experience, or scientific reason

prediction /prɪ'dɪkʃən/ *n* sthg that is predicted; a forecast – **-tive** *adj* – **-tively** *adv*

preface /'prefɪs/ *n* **1** an introduction

to a book, speech, etc **2** sthg that precedes or heralds; a preliminary

²**preface** *v* to introduce *by* or provide *with* a preface – **-atory** *adj*

prefect /'pri:fekt/ *n* **1** a chief officer or chief magistrate (e g in France or Italy) **2** a monitor in a secondary school, usu an older pupil with some authority over other pupils

prefer /prɪ'fɜ:'/ *v* **1** to choose or esteem above another; like better **2** to bring (a charge) against sby

preference /'prefərəns/ *n* **1** the power or opportunity of choosing **2** sby or sthg preferred; a choice **3** priority in the settlement of an obligation

pregnant /'pregnənt/ *adj* **1** full of ideas or resourcefulness; inventive **2** containing unborn young within the body **3** showing signs of the future; portentous **4** full, teeming – usu + *with* – **~ly** *adv*

¹**prejudice** /'predʒədɪs/ *n* **1** (an instance of) a preconceived judgment or opinion; esp a biased and unfavourable one formed without sufficient reason or knowledge **2** an irrational attitude of hostility directed against an individual, group, or race

²**prejudice** *v* **1** to injure by some judgment or action **2** to cause (sby) to have an unreasonable bias

¹**preliminary** /prɪ'lɪmɪnəri/ *n* sthg that precedes or is introductory or preparatory: e g **a** a preliminary scholastic examination **b** *pl, Br* matter (e g a list of contents) preceding the main text of a book

²**preliminary** *adj* preceding and preparing for what is to follow

prelude /'prelju:d/ *n* **1** an introductory or preliminary performance, action, or event; an introduction **2a** a musical section or movement introducing the theme or chief subject or serving as an introduction (e g to an opera) **b** a short separate concert piece, usu for piano or orchestra – **prelude** *v*

premature /'premətʃə', -tʃuə', ˌpremə'tʃuə'/ *adj* happening, arriving, existing, or performed before the proper or usual time; esp, of a human born after a gestation period of less than 37 weeks – **~ly** *adv*

premeditate /pri:'medɪteɪt/ *v* to think over and plan beforehand – **-tation** *n* – **~d** *adj*

premises /'premɪsɪz/ *n pl* a piece of land with the buildings on it; *also* (part of) a building

¹**premium** /'pri:mɪəm/ *n* **1a** a sum above a fixed price or wage, paid chiefly as an incentive **b** a sum in advance of or in addition to the nominal value of sthg **2** the sum paid for a contract of insurance **3** a high value or a value in excess of that normally expected

²**premium** *adj* of exceptional quality

preoccupy /pri:'ɒkjupaɪ/ *v* to engage or engross the attention of to the exclusion of other things – **-pied** *adj*

preparation /ˌprepə'reɪʃən/ *n* **1** preparing **2** a state of being prepared; readiness **3** a preparatory act or

appearance of; feign 2 to claim or assert falsely; profess

²**pretend** adj make-believe – used esp by children

pretentious /prɪˈtenʃəs/ adj making usu unjustified or excessive claims (e g of value or standing) – ~ness n – ~ly adv

pretext /ˈpriːtekst/ n a false reason given to disguise the real one; an excuse

¹**pretty** /ˈprɪti/ adj 1a attractive or aesthetically pleasing, esp because of delicacy or grace, but less than beautiful b outwardly pleasant but lacking strength, purpose, or intensity 2 miserable, terrible 3 moderately large; considerable – -tily adv – -tiness n

²**pretty** adv 1a in some degree; esp somewhat excessively b very – used to emphasize much or nearly 2 in a pretty manner; prettily – infml

prevent /prɪˈvent/ v 1 to keep from happening or existing 2 to hold or keep back; stop – often + from – ~able adj – ~ion n

previous /ˈpriːvɪəs/ adj 1 going before in time or order 2 acting too soon; premature – ~ly adv

¹**prey** /preɪ/ n 1 an animal taken by a predator as food 2 sby or sthg helpless or unable to resist attack; a victim

²**prey** v 1 to seize and devour prey – often + on or upon 2 to live by extortion, deceit, or exerting undue influence 3 to have continuously oppressive or distressing effect

price /praɪs/ n 1 the money, or amount of goods or services, that is exchanged or demanded in barter or sale 2 the terms for the sake of which sthg is done or undertaken: e g a an amount sufficient to bribe sby b a reward for the catching or killing of sby 3 the cost at which sthg is done or obtained – ~ v – ~d adj

priceless /ˈpraɪsl̩s/ adj 1 having a worth beyond any price; invaluable 2 particularly amusing or absurd – infml

¹**prick** /prɪk/ n 1 a mark or shallow hole made by a pointed instrument 2a a nagging or sharp feeling of sorrow or remorse b a sharp localized pain 3 the penis – infml 4 a disagreeable person – infml

²**prick** v 1 to pierce slightly with a sharp point 2 to trace or outline with punctures 3 to cause to be or stand erect – often + up

¹**prickle** /ˈprɪkəl/ n 1 a sharp pointed spike arising from the skin or bark of a plant 2 a prickling sensation

²**prickle** v to cause or feel a stinging sensation; tingle

prickly /ˈprɪkli/ adj 1 full of or covered with prickles 2 prickling, stinging 3a troublesome, vexatious b easily irritated – -liness n

¹**pride** /praɪd/ n 1a inordinate self-esteem; conceit b a reasonable or justifiable self-respect c delight or satisfaction arising from some act, pos-

session, or relationship 2 sing or pl in constr a group of lions

²**pride** v to be proud of (oneself) – + on or upon

priest /priːst/ n a person authorized to perform the sacred rites of a religion – ~hood n – ~ly adj – ~liness n

¹**primary** /ˈpraɪməri/ adj 1a of first rank, importance, or value; principal b basic, fundamental 2a direct, firsthand b not derivable from other colours, odours, or tastes c of or at a primary school 3 of or being an industry that produces raw materials

²**primary** n 1 sthg that stands first in rank, importance, or value; a fundamental – usu pl 2 any of the usu 9 or 10 strong feathers on the joint of a bird's wing furthest from the body 3 a primary colour 4 a caucus 5 a primary school

¹**prime** /praɪm/ n 1 the most active, thriving, or successful stage or period 2 the chief or best individual or part; the pick 3 prime, prime number a positive integer that has no factor except itself and 1

²**prime** adj 1 having no factor except itself and 1 2 first in rank, authority, or significance; principal 3 of meat of the highest grade or best quality 4 not deriving from sthg else; primary

³**prime** v 1 to fill, load; esp to fill or ply (a person) with liquor 2 to prepare (a firearm or charge) for firing by supplying with priming or a primer 3 to apply a first coat (e g of paint or oil) to (a surface) 4 to put into working order by filling or charging with sthg, esp a liquid 5 to instruct beforehand; prepare

prime minister n the chief executive of a parliamentary government – ~ship n

¹**primitive** /ˈprɪmɪtɪv/ adj 1 original, primary 2a of the earliest age or period; primeval b belonging to or characteristic of an early stage of development or evolution 3a of or produced by a relatively simple people or culture b lacking in sophistication or subtlety; crude; also uncivilized – ~ly adv – ~ness n

²**primitive** n 1a a primitive concept, term, or proposition 2a an artist of an early, esp pre-Renaissance, period b an artist, esp self-taught, whose work is marked by directness and naiveté 3 a member of a primitive people

prince /prɪns/ n 1 a sovereign ruler, esp of a principality 2 a foreign nobleman of varying rank and status

¹**princess** /prɪnˈses/ n 1 a female member of a royal family; esp a daughter of a sovereign 2 the wife or widow of a prince 3 a woman having in her own right the rank of a prince

²**princess** adj closely fitting at the top, flared from the hips to the hemline, and having gores or panels

¹**principal** /ˈprɪnsɪpəl/ adj most important, consequential, or influential; chief – ~ly adv

²**principal** n 1 a person who has controlling authority or is in a leading position: e g a the head of an educational institu-

tion **b** one who employs another to act for him/her **c** a leading performer **2 a** capital sum placed at interest, due as a debt, or used as a fund

principle /ˈprɪnsₔpəl/ *n* **1a** a universal and fundamental law, doctrine, or assumption **b** a rule or code of conduct **c** the laws or facts of nature underlying the working of an artificial device **2 a** primary source; a fundamental element **3** an underlying faculty or endowment

¹print /prɪnt/ *n* **1a** a mark made by pressure **b** sthg impressed with a print or formed in a mould **2** printed state or form **3** printed matter or letters **4a(1)** a copy made by printing (e g from a photographic negative) (2) a reproduction of an original work of art (e g a painting) (3) an original work of art (e g a woodcut or lithograph) intended for graphic reproduction **b** (an article made from) cloth with a pattern applied by printing **c** a photographic copy, esp from a negative

²print *v* **1** to stamp (e g a mark or design) in or on sthg **2a** to make a copy of by impressing paper against an inked printing surface **b** to impress with a design or pattern **c** to publish in print **3** to write each letter of separately, not joined together **4** to make (a positive picture) on sensitized photographic surface from a negative or a positive

printer /ˈprɪntəʳ/ *n* **1** a person engaged in printing **2** a machine for printing from photographic negatives **3** a device (e g a line printer) that produces printout

printing /ˈprɪntɪŋ/ *n* **1** reproduction in printed form **2** the art, practice, or business of a printer

priority /praɪˈɒrₔti/ *n* **1a** being prior **b** superiority in rank **2** sthg meriting prior attention

prior to *prep* before in time; in advance of – fml

prison /ˈprɪzən/ *n* a place of enforced confinement; *specif* a building in which people are confined for safe custody while on trial or for punishment after conviction

prisoner /ˈprɪzənəʳ/ *n* sby kept under involuntary confinement; *esp* sby on trial or in prison

¹private /ˈpraɪvₔt/ *adj* **1a** intended for or restricted to the use of a particular person, group, etc **b** belonging to or concerning an individual person, company, or interest **c** of or receiving medical treatment in Britain outside the National Health Service and paying fees for it **2** not related to one's official position; personal **3a** withdrawn from company or observation **b** not (intended to be) known publicly; secret – **~ly** *adv*

²private *n* a soldier of the lowest rank

privilege /ˈprɪvₔlɪdʒ/ *n* a right, immunity, or advantage granted exclusively to a particular person, class, or group; a prerogative; *esp* such an advantage attached to a position or office

¹prize /praɪz/ *n* **1** sthg offered or striven for in competition or in a contest of

chance **2** sthg exceptionally desirable or precious

²prize *adj* **1a** awarded or worthy of a prize **b** awarded as a prize **2** outstanding of a kind

³prize *v* **1** to estimate the value of; rate **2** to value highly; esteem

⁴prize *n* property or shipping lawfully captured at sea in time of war

⁵prize, *Br also* **prise** *v* **1** to press, force, or move with a lever **2** to open, obtain, or remove with difficulty

¹probable /ˈprɒbəbl/ *adj* **1** supported by evidence strong enough to establish likelihood but not proof **2** likely to be or become true or real

²probable *n* sby or sthg probable; *esp* sby who will probably be selected

¹probe /prəʊb/ *n* **1** a slender surgical instrument for examining a cavity **2** a device used to investigate or send back information, esp from interplanetary space **3a** a tentative exploratory survey **b** a penetrating or critical investigation; an inquiry – *journ*

²probe *v* **1** to investigate thoroughly – *journ* **2** to make an exploratory investigation – **probing** *adj* – **probingly** *adv*

problem /ˈprɒbləm/ *n* **1a** a question raised for inquiry, consideration, or solution **b** a proposition in mathematics or physics stating sthg to be done **2a** a situation or question that is difficult to understand or resolve **b** sby who is difficult to deal with or understand

²problem *adj* difficult to deal with; presenting a problem

procedure /prəˈsiːdʒəʳ/ *n* **1** a particular way of acting or accomplishing sthg **2** an established method of doing things

proceed /prəˈsiːd/ *v* **1** to arise from a source; originate **2** to continue after a pause or interruption **3** to begin and carry on an action, process, or movement **4** to move along a course; advance

proceeding /prəˈsiːdɪŋ/ *n* **1** a procedure **2** *pl* events, goings-on **3** *pl* legal action **4** *pl* an official record of things said or done

proceeds /ˈprəʊsiːdz/ *n pl* **1** the total amount brought in **2** the net amount received

¹process /ˈprəʊses/ *n* **1** sthg going on; a proceeding **2a** a natural phenomenon marked by gradual changes that lead towards a particular result **b** a series of actions or operations designed to achieve an end; *esp* a continuous operation or treatment (e g in manufacture) **3** a whole course of legal proceedings **4** a prominent or projecting part of a living organism or an anatomical structure

²process *v* **1** to subject to a special process or treatment (e g in the course of manufacture) **2** to take appropriate action on

³process *v* to move in a procession

procession /prəˈseʃən/ *n* **1** a group of individuals moving along in an orderly way, esp as part of a ceremony or demonstration **2** a succession, sequence

proclaim /prə'kleɪm/ v 1 to declare publicly and usu officially; announce 2 to give outward expression of; show

proclamation /ˌprɒklə'meɪʃən/ n 1 proclaiming or being proclaimed 2 an official public announcement

procure /prə'kjʊə/ v 1 to get and provide (esp women) to act as prostitutes 2 to obtain, esp by particular care and effort 3 to achieve – **-curable** adj – ~ment n – ~r n

¹**prod** /prɒd/ v 1 to poke or jab (as if) with a pointed instrument, esp repeatedly 2 to incite to action; stir

²**prod** n 1 a prodding action; a jab 2 an incitement to act

prodigy /'prɒdɪdʒi/ n 1 sthg extraordinary, inexplicable, or marvellous 2 a person, esp a child, with extraordinary talents

¹**produce** /prə'djuːs/ v 1 to give birth or rise to 2 to act as a producer of 3 to give being, form, or shape to; make; esp to manufacture 4 to (cause to) accumulate

²**produce** /'prɒdjuːs/ n agricultural products; esp fresh fruits and vegetables as distinguished from grain and other staple crops

product /'prɒdʌkt/ n 1 the result of the multiplying together of 2 or more numbers or expressions 2 sthg produced by a natural or artificial process; esp a marketable commodity

production /prə'dʌkʃən/ n 1a a literary or artistic work b a work presented on the stage or screen or over the air 2 the making of goods available for human wants 3 total output, esp of a commodity or an industry

productive /prə'dʌktɪv/ adj 1 having the quality or power of producing, esp in abundance 2 effective in bringing about; being the cause of 3a yielding or furnishing results or benefits b yielding or devoted to the satisfaction of wants or the creation of utilities – ~ly adv – ~ness n

profession /prə'feʃən/ n 1 an act of openly declaring or claiming a faith, opinion, etc 2 an avowed religious faith 3 a calling requiring specialized knowledge and often long and intensive academic preparation

professional /prə'feʃənəl/ adj 1a (characteristic) of a profession b engaged in 1 of the learned professions c(1) characterized by or conforming to the technical or ethical standards of a profession (2) characterized by conscientious workmanship 2 engaging for gain or livelihood in an activity or field of endeavour often engaged in by amateurs 3 following a line of conduct as though it were a profession 4 of a breaking of rules, esp in sport intentional – euph – ~ly adv

professional n 1 one who engages in a pursuit or activity professionally 2 one with sufficient experience or skill in an occupation or activity to resemble a professional – infml

profile /'prəʊfaɪl/ n 1 a side view, esp of the human face 2 an outline seen or represented in sharp relief; a contour 3 a side or sectional elevation 4 a concise written or spoken biographical sketch – **profile** v

¹**profit** /'prɒfɪt/ n 1 a valuable return; a gain 2 the excess of returns over expenditure – ~able adj – ~ably adv – ~less adj – ~lessly adv

²**profit** v to derive benefit; gain – usu + from or by

profound /prə'faʊnd/ adj 1a having intellectual depth and insight b difficult to fathom or understand 2 coming from, reaching to, or situated at a depth; deep-seated 3a characterized by intensity of feeling or quality b all encompassing; complete – ~ly adv

¹**program** /'prəʊɡræm/ n 1 a sequence of coded instructions that can be inserted into a mechanism (e g a computer) or that is part of an organism 2 chiefly NAm a programme

²**program** v to work out a sequence of operations to be performed by (a computer or similar mechanism); provide with a program

¹**programme** /'prəʊɡræm/ NAm chiefly **program** n 1a a brief usu printed (pamphlet containing a) list of the features to be presented, the people participating, etc (e g in a public performance or entertainment) b a radio or television broadcast characterized by some feature (e g a presenter, a purpose, or a theme) giving it coherence and continuity 2 a systematic plan of action 3 a curriculum 4 a prospectus, syllabus

²**programme**, NAm chiefly **program** v to cause to conform to a pattern (e g of thought or behaviour); condition

¹**progress** /'prəʊɡres/ n 1 a ceremonial journey; esp a monarch's tour of his/her dominions 2 a forward or onward movement (e g to an objective or goal); an advance 3 gradual improvement; esp the progressive development of mankind

²**progress** /prə'ɡres/ v 1 to move forwards; proceed 2 to develop to a higher, better, or more advanced stage

¹**progressive** /prə'ɡresɪv/ adj 1a making use of or interested in new ideas, findings, or opportunities b of or being an educational theory marked by emphasis on the individual, informality, and self-expression 2 moving forwards continuously or in stages; advancing – ~ly adv

²**progressive** n 1 sby or sthg progressive 2 sby believing in moderate political change, esp social improvement

prohibit /prə'hɪbɪt/ v 1 to forbid by authority 2 to prevent from doing sthg

¹**project** /'prɒdʒekt/ n 1 a specific plan or design; a scheme 2a a large undertaking, esp a public works scheme b a task or problem engaged in by usu a group of pupils, esp to supplement and apply classroom studies

²**project** /prə'dʒekt/ v 1 to plan, figure, or estimate for the future 2 to throw forwards or upwards, esp by mech-

anical means **3** to present or transport in imagination **4** to cause to protrude **5** to cause (light or an image) to fall into space or on a surface **6a** to cause (one's voice) to be heard at a distance **b** to communicate vividly, esp to an audience **7** to attribute (sthg in one's own mind) to a person, group, or object

projector /prə'dʒektə/ *n* an apparatus for projecting films or pictures onto a surface

prolific /prə'lɪfɪk/ *adj* **1** producing young or fruit (freely) **2** marked by abundant inventiveness or productivity – ~**ally** *adv*

prolong /prə'lɒŋ/ *v* to lengthen – ~**ation** *n*

prominent /'prɒmɪnənt/ *adj* **1** projecting beyond a surface or line; protuberant **2a** readily noticeable; conspicuous **b** widely and popularly known; leading – ~**ly** *adv*

¹**promise** /'prɒmɪs/ *n* **1** a declaration that one will do or refrain from doing sthg specified **2** grounds for expectation usu of success, improvement, or excellence **3** sthg promised

²**promise** *v* **1** to pledge oneself to do, bring about, or provide (sthg for) **2** to assure **3** to suggest beforehand; indicate

promising /'prɒmɪsɪŋ/ *adj* likely to succeed or to yield good results – ~**ly** *adv*

promote /prə'məʊt/ *v* **1** to advance in station, rank, or honour; raise **2a** to contribute to the growth or prosperity of; further **b** to help bring (e g an enterprise) into being; launch **c** to present (e g merchandise) for public acceptance through advertising and publicity – ~**r** *n*

promotion /prə'məʊʃən/ *n* **1** being raised in position or rank **2a** the act of furthering the growth or development of sthg, esp sales or public awareness **b** sthg (e g a price reduction or free sample) intended to promote esp sales of merchandise – ~**al** *adj*

¹**prompt** /prɒmpt/ *v* **1** to move to action; incite **2** to assist (sby acting or reciting) by saying the next words of sthg forgotten or imperfectly learnt

²**prompt** *adj* of or for prompting actors – ~**ly** *adv* – ~**ness** *n*

³**prompt** *adj* **1a** ready and quick to act as occasion demands **b** punctual **2** performed readily or immediately

⁴**prompt** *n* the act or an instance of prompting; a reminder

prone /prəʊn/ *adj* **1** having a tendency or inclination; disposed *to* **2** having the front or ventral surface downwards; prostrate – ~**ness** *n*

pronoun /'prəʊnaʊn/ *n* a word used as a substitute for a noun or noun equivalent and referring to a previously named or understood person or thing

pronounce /prə'naʊns/ *v* **1** to pass judgment; declare one's opinion definitely or authoritatively – often + *on* or *upon* **2** to produce speech sounds; *also* to say correctly

pronunciation /prə,nʌnsi'eɪʃən/ *n* the act or manner of pronouncing sthg

¹**proof** /pruːf/ *n* **1** the cogency of evidence that compels acceptance of a truth or a fact **2** an act, effort, or operation designed to establish and discover a fact or the truth; a test **3a** an impression (e g from type) taken for examination or correction **b** a proof impression of an engraving, lithograph, etc **4** the alcoholic content of a beverage compared with the standard for proof spirit

²**proof** *adj* **1** designed for or successful in resisting or repelling; impervious – often in combination **2** used in proving or testing or as a standard of comparison **3** of standard strength or quality or alcoholic content

³**proof** *v* **1** to make or take a proof of **2** to give a resistant quality to; make (sthg) proof *against*

¹**prop** /prɒp/ *n* **1** a rigid usu auxiliary vertical support (e g a pole) **2** a source of strength or support

²**prop** *v* **1** to support by placing sthg under or against **2** to support by placing against sthg *USE* often + *up*

³**prop** *n* any article or object used in a play or film other than painted scenery or costumes

propaganda /,prɒpə'gændə/ *n* (the usu organized spreading of) ideas, information, or rumour designed to promote or damage an institution, movement, person, etc

propel /prə'pel/ *v* **1** to drive forwards by means of a force that imparts motion **2** to urge on; motivate – ~**lant** *adj* or *n*

propeller /prə'pelə/ *n* a device consisting of a central hub with radiating blades that is used to propel a ship, aeroplane, etc

¹**proper** /'prɒpə/ *adj* **1** suitable, appropriate **2** belonging to one; own **3** belonging characteristically to a species or individual; peculiar **4** being strictly so-called **5** strictly decorous; genteel **6** *chiefly Br* thorough, complete

²**proper** *adv, chiefly dial* in a thorough manner; completely

properly /'prɒpəli/ *adv* **1** in a fit manner; suitably **2** strictly in accordance with fact; correctly **3** *chiefly Br* to the full extent; completely

property /'prɒpəti/ *n* **1a** a quality, attribute, or power inherent in sthg **b** an attribute common to all members of a class **2a** sthg owned or possessed; *specif* a piece of real estate **b** sthg to which a person has a legal title **3** a prop

prophecy /'prɒfɪsi/ *n* **1** (the capacity to utter) an inspired declaration of divine will and purpose **2** a prediction of an event

prophesy /'prɒfɪsaɪ/ *v* **1** to speak as if divinely inspired **2** to make a prediction

prophet /'prɒfɪt/ *n* **1** a person who utters divinely inspired revelations **2** one who foretells future events; a predictor **3** a spokesman for a doctrine, movement, etc – ~ical *adj* – ~ically *adv*

¹**proportion** /prə'pɔːʃənəl/ *n* 1 the relation of one part to another or to the whole with respect to magnitude, quantity, or degree 2 harmonious relation of parts to each other or to the whole; balance 3a proper or equal share b a quota, percentage 4 *pl* size, dimension

²**proportion** *v* 1 to adjust (a part or thing) in proportion to other parts or things 2 to make the parts of harmonious or symmetrical

proposal /prə'pəʊzəl/ *n* 1 an act of putting forward or stating sthg for consideration 2a a proposed idea or plan of action; a suggestion b an offer of marriage 3 an application for insurance

propose /prə'pəʊz/ *v* 1 to present for consideration or adoption 2 to make an offer of marriage 3a to recommend to fill a place or vacancy; nominate b to offer as a toast – ~r *n*

¹**proposition** /ˌprɒpə'zɪʃən/ *n* 1 sthg offered for consideration or acceptance; *specif* a proposal of sexual intercourse 2 an expression, in language or signs, of sthg that can be either true or false 3 a project, situation, or individual requiring to be dealt with

²**proposition** *v* to make a proposal to; *specif* to propose sexual intercourse to

proprietor /prə'praɪətə/ *n* an owner

¹**prospect** /'prɒspekt/ *n* 1 an extensive view; a scene 2 *pl* a financial and social expectations b chances, esp of success 3 a potential client, candidate, etc

²**prospect** /prə'spekt/ *v* to explore (an area), esp for mineral deposits – ~or *n*

prospective /prə'spektɪv/ *adj* 1 likely to come about; expected 2 likely to be or become

prosper /'prɒspə/ *v* to succeed, thrive; *specif* to achieve economic success

prosperous /'prɒspərəs/ *adj* marked by esp financial success – ~ly *adv* – ~rity *n*

¹**prostitute** /'prɒstɪtjuːt/ *v* to devote to corrupt or unworthy purposes; debase

²**prostitute** *n* a person, esp a woman, who engages in sex for money – ~tion *n*

protect /prə'tekt/ *v* 1 to cover or shield from injury or destruction; guard against 2 to shield or foster (a home industry) by a protective tariff – ~ive *adj*

protection /prə'tekʃən/ *n* 1 protecting or being protected 2 sthg that protects 3 the shielding of the producers of a country from foreign competition by import tariffs 4a immunity from threatened violence, often purchased under duress b money extorted by racketeers posing as a protective association

protector /prə'tektə/ *n* 1a a guardian b a device used to prevent injury; a guard 2 *often cap* the executive head of the Commonwealth from 1653 to 1659

protein /'prəʊtiːn/ *n* any of numerous extremely complex combinations of amino acids that are essential constituents of all living cells and are an essential part of the diet of animals and humans

¹**protest** /'prəʊtest/ *n* 1 a formal declaration of disapproval 2 protesting; *esp* an organized public demonstration of disapproval 3 an objection or display of unwillingness

²**protest** /prə'test/ *v* to make formal or solemn declaration or affirmation of 2 to enter a protest – ~er *n*

protestant /'prɒtɪstənt/ *n cap* a Christian who denies the universal authority of the pope and affirms the principles of the Reformation – **protestant** *adj* – ~ism *n*

protocol /'prəʊtəkɒl/ *n* 1 an original draft or record of a document or transaction 2 a code of correct etiquette and precedence

proton /'prəʊtɒn/ *n* an elementary particle identical with the nucleus of the hydrogen atom, that carries a positive charge numerically equal to the charge of an electron and has a mass of 1.672 × 10⁻²⁷kg

prototype /'prəʊtətaɪp/ *n* 1 sby or sthg that exemplifies the essential or typical features of a type 2 a first full-scale and usu operational form of a new type or design of a construction (e g an aeroplane)

proud /praʊd/ *adj* 1a having or displaying excessive self-esteem b much pleased; exultant 2a stately; magnificent b giving reason for pride; glorious 3 projecting slightly from a surrounding surface

prove /pruːv/ *v* **proved, proven** 1a to test the quality of; try out b to subject to a testing process 2 to establish the truth or validity of by evidence or demonstration 3 to turn out, esp after trial 4 to allow (bread dough) to rise and become light before baking – ~**vable** *adj* – ~**vably** *adv*

proverb /'prɒvɜːb/ *n* a brief popular epigram or maxim; an adage

provide /prə'vaɪd/ *v* 1 to furnish, equip with 2 to supply what is needed for sustenance or support 3 to stipulate

province /'prɒvɪns/ *n* 1a an administrative district of a country b *pl* all of a country except the metropolis – usu + *the* 2 a field of knowledge or activity; sphere

¹**provision** /prə'vɪʒən/ *n* 1a providing b a measure taken beforehand; a preparation 2 *pl* a stock of food or other necessary goods 3 a proviso, stipulation

²**provision** *v* to supply with provisions

provisional /prə'vɪʒənəl/ *adj* serving for the time being; *specif* requiring later confirmation – ~ly *adv*

Provisional *adj* of or being the secret terrorist wing of the IRA

proviso /prə'vaɪzəʊ/ *n* 1 a clause that introduces a condition 2 a conditional stipulation

provocation /ˌprɒvə'keɪʃən/ *n* 1 an act of provoking; incitement 2 sthg that provokes or arouses

provoke /prə'vəʊk/ *v* 1 to incite to

anger; incense **2a** to call forth; evoke **b** to stir up on purpose; induce

¹prowl /praʊl/ v to move about (in) or roam (over) in a stealthy or predatory manner

²prowl n an act or instance of prowling

prudence /'pru:dəns/ n **1** discretion or shrewdness **2** caution or circumspection with regard to danger – **-ent** adj – **-ently** adv

pry /praɪ/ v **1** to inquire in an overinquisitive or impertinent manner *into* **2** to look closely or inquisitively at sby's possessions, actions, etc

psychiatry /saɪ'kaɪətri/ n a branch of medicine that deals with mental, emotional, or behavioural disorders – **-trist** n – **-tric** adj – **-trically** adv

psychological /ˌsaɪkə'lɒdʒɪkəl/ adj **1a** of psychology **b** mental **2** directed towards or intended to affect the will or mind – **~ly** adv

psychology /saɪ'kɒlədʒi/ n the science or study of mind and behaviour – **-logist** n

pub /pʌb/ n an establishment where alcoholic beverages are sold and consumed

¹public /'pʌblɪk/ adj **1** of or being in the service of the community **2** general, popular **3** of national or community concerns as opposed to private affairs **4** accessible to or shared by all members of the community **5a** exposed to general view; open **b** well-known, prominent – **~ly** adv

²public n **1** the people as a whole; the populace **2** a group or section of people having common interests or characteristics

publication /ˌpʌblɪ'keɪʃən/ n **1** the act or process of publishing **2** a published work

publicity /pʌ'blɪsɪti/ n **1a** paid advertising **b** the dissemination of information or promotional material **2** public attention or acclaim – **-cize** v

publish /'pʌblɪʃ/ v **1** to make generally known **2a** to produce or release for publication; *specif* to print **b** to issue the work of (an author) – **~er** n

pudding /'pʊdɪŋ/ n **1a** a sausage **2** any of various sweet or savoury dishes of a soft to spongy or fairly firm consistency that are made from rice, tapioca, flour, etc and are cooked by boiling, steaming, or baking **3** dessert

¹puddle /'pʌdl/ n a small pool of liquid; *esp* one of usu muddy rainwater

²puddle v to work (a wet mixture of earth or concrete) into a dense impervious mass

¹puff /pʌf/ v **1a(1)** to blow in short gusts **(2)** to exhale or blow forcibly **b** to breathe hard and quickly; pant **c** to draw on (a pipe, cigarette, etc) with intermittent exhalations of smoke **2a** to become distended; swell **b** to distend (as if) with air or gas; inflate **c** to make proud or conceited USE **(2)** + *up*

²puff n **1a** an act or instance of puffing **b** a small cloud (e g of smoke) emitted

in a puff **2** a light round hollow pastry made of puff paste **3** a highly favourable notice or review, esp one that publicizes sthg or sby **4** *chiefly Br* a breath of wind – *infml*

¹pull /pʊl/ v **1a** to exert force upon so as to (tend to) cause motion towards the force; tug at **b** to move, esp through the exercise of mechanical energy **2** to strain (a muscle) **3** to hit (e g a ball in cricket or golf) towards the left from a right-handed swing or towards the right from a left-handed swing **4** to draw apart; tear **5** to print (e g a proof) by impression **6** to bring out (a weapon) ready for use **7** to draw from the barrel, esp by pulling a pump handle **8a** to carry out, esp with daring and imagination – usu + *off* **b** to do, perform, or say with a deceptive intent **9** to draw or inhale hard in smoking

²pull n **1a** the act or an instance of pulling **b(1)** a draught of liquid **(2)** an inhalation of smoke (e g from a cigarette) **2** (special influence exerted to obtain) an advantage **3** a force that attracts, compels, or influences

pullover /'pʊlˌəʊvə/ n a garment for the upper body, esp a jumper, put on by being pulled over the head

pull over v, *of a driver or vehicle* to move towards the side of the road, esp in order to stop

¹pulp /pʌlp/ n **1a** the soft juicy or fleshy part of a fruit or vegetable **b** a material prepared by chemical or mechanical means from rags, wood, etc that is used in making paper **2** a soft shapeless mass, esp produced by crushing or beating **3** a magazine or book cheaply produced on rough paper and containing sensational material – **~y** adj

²pulp v **1** to reduce to pulp **2** to remove the pulp from

¹pulse /pʌls/ n the edible seeds of any of various leguminous crops (e g peas, beans, or lentils); *also* the plant yielding these

²pulse n **1** a regular throbbing caused in the arteries by the contractions of the heart; *also* a single movement of such throbbing **2a** (an indication of) underlying sentiment or opinion **b** a feeling of liveliness; vitality **3a** rhythmical vibrating or sounding **b** a single beat or throb

³pulse v to pulsate, throb

¹pump /pʌmp/ n a device that raises, transfers, or compresses fluids or that reduces the density of gases, esp by suction or pressure or both

²pump v **1a** to raise (e g water) with a pump **b** to draw fluid from with a pump – often + *out* **2** to question persistently **3** to move (sthg) rapidly up and down as if working a pump handle **4** to inflate by means of a pump or bellows – usu + *up*

³pump n **1** a low shoe without fastenings that grips the foot chiefly at the toe and heel **2** *Br* a plimsoll

¹punch /pʌntʃ/ v **1** to strike, esp with a hard and quick thrust of the fist **2** to drive or push forcibly (as if) by a punch

3 to emboss, cut, or make (as if) with a punch – ~**er** n

²**punch** n 1 a blow (as if) with the fist 2 effective energy or forcefulness

³**punch** n 1 a tool, usu in the form of a short steel rod, used esp for perforating, embossing, cutting, or driving the heads of nails below a surface 2 a device for cutting holes or notches in paper or cardboard

⁴**punch** n a hot or cold drink usu made from wine or spirits mixed with fruit, spices, water, and occas tea

punctual /'pʌŋktʃʊəl/ adj (habitually) arriving, happening, performing, etc at the exact or agreed time – ~**ity** n – ~**ly** adv

punctuate /'pʌŋktʃʊeɪt/ v 1 to mark or divide with punctuation marks 2 to break into or interrupt at intervals

punctuation /ˌpʌŋktʃʊ'eɪʃən/ n the dividing of writing with marks to clarify meaning; also a system of punctuation

¹**puncture** /'pʌŋktʃə'/ n a hole, narrow wound, etc made by puncturing; esp a small hole made accidentally in a pneumatic tyre

²**puncture** v 1 to pierce with a pointed instrument or object 2 to make useless or deflate as if by a puncture

punish /'pʌnɪʃ/ v 1 to impose a penalty on (an offender) or for (an offence) 2 to treat roughly or damagingly – infml

punishment /'pʌnɪʃmənt/ n 1 a punishing or being punished b a judicial penalty 2 rough or damaging treatment – infml

¹**pupil** /'pjuːpəl/ n 1 a child or young person at school or receiving tuition 2 one who has been taught or influenced by a distinguished person

²**pupil** n the contractile usu round dark opening in the iris of the eye

puppet /'pʌpɪt/ n 1a a small-scale toy figure (e g of a person or animal) usu with a cloth body and hollow head that fits over and is moved by the hand b a marionette 2 one whose acts are controlled by an outside force or influence

puppy /'pʌpɪ/ n 1 a young dog (less than a year old) 2 a conceited or ill-mannered young man

¹**purchase** /'pɜːtʃɪs/ v 1 to obtain by paying money or its equivalent; buy 2 to obtain by labour, danger, or sacrifice – -**chasable** adj – ~**r** n

²**purchase** n 1 sthg obtained by payment of money or its equivalent 2a a mechanical hold or advantage (e g that applied through a pulley or lever); broadly an advantage used in applying power or influence b a means, esp a mechanical device, by which one gains such an advantage

pure /pjʊə'/ adj 1a(1) unmixed with any other matter (2) free from contamination (3) free from moral fault b of a musical sound being in tune and free from harshness 2a sheer, unmitigated b abstract, theoretical 3a free from anything that vitiates or weakens b containing nothing that does not properly belong 4a chaste b ritually clean

purely /'pjʊəli/ adv 1 simply, merely 2 in a chaste or innocent manner 3 wholly, completely

¹**purge** /pɜːdʒ/ v 1a to clear of guilt b to free from moral or physical impurity 2a to cause evacuation from (e g the bowels) b to rid (e g a nation or party) of unwanted or undesirable members, often summarily or by force – -**gation** n

²**purge** n 1 an (esp political) act of purging 2 a purgative

¹**purple** /'pɜːpəl/ adj 1 of the colour purple 2 highly rhetorical; ornate – **purplish** adj

²**purple** n 1 a colour falling about midway between red and blue in hue 2 imperial, regal, or very high rank

¹**purpose** /'pɜːpəs/ n 1 the object for which sthg exists or is done; the intention 2 resolution, determination

²**purpose** v to have as one's intention – fml

purposely /'pɜːpəsli/ adv with a deliberate or express purpose

purr /pɜː'/ v to make the low vibratory murmur of a contented cat

¹**purse** /pɜːs/ n 1 a small flattish bag for money; esp a wallet with a compartment for holding change 2 a sum of money offered as a prize or present; also the total amount of money offered in prizes for a given event 3 NAm a handbag

²**purse** v to pucker, knit

pursue /pə'sjuː/ v 1 to follow in order to overtake, capture, kill, or defeat 2 to find or employ measures to obtain or accomplish 3a to engage in b to follow up 4 to continue to afflict; haunt – ~**r** n

pursuit /pə'sjuːt/ n 1 an act of pursuing 2 an activity that one regularly engages in (e g as a pastime or profession)

¹**push** /pʊʃ/ v 1 to apply a force to (sthg) in order to cause movement away from the person or thing applying the force 2a to develop (e g an idea or argument), esp to an extreme degree b to urge or press the advancement, adoption, or practice of; specif to make aggressive efforts to sell c to press or urge (sby) to sthg; pressurize 3 to press forwards energetically against obstacles or opposition 4 to exert oneself continuously or vigorously to achieve an end 5 to approach in age or number – infml 6 to engage in the illicit sale of (drugs) – slang 7 to press against sthg with steady force (as if) in order to move it away

²**push** n 1 a vigorous effort to attain an end; a drive 2a an act or action of pushing b vigorous enterprise or energy 3a an exertion of influence to promote another's interests b stimulation to activity; an impetus 4 Br dismissal – esp in get/give the push

¹**put** /pʊt/ v 1a to place in or move into a specified position or relationship b to bring into a specified condition 2a to cause to endure or undergo; subject b to impose, establish 3a to formulate for judgment or decision b to express, state

4a to turn into language or literary form **b** to adapt, set **5a** to devote, apply **b** to impel, incite **6a** to repose, rest **b** to invest **7** to give as an estimate; *also* to imagine as being **8** to write, inscribe **9** to bet, wager

²**put** *n* a throw made with an overhand pushing motion; *specif* the act or an instance of putting the shot

³**put** *adj* in the same position, condition, or situation – in **stay put**

put forward *v* **1** to propose (e g a theory) **2** to bring into prominence

put off *v* **1** to disconcert, distract **2a** to postpone **b** to get rid of or persuade to wait, esp by means of excuses or evasions

¹**put-on** *adj* pretended, assumed

²**put-on** *n* an instance of deliberately misleading sby; *also, chiefly NAm* a parody, spoof

put on *v* **1a** to dress oneself in; don **b** to feign, assume **2** to cause to act or operate; apply **3** to come to have an increased amount of **4** to stage, produce (e g a play) **5** to bet (a sum of money)

put out *v* **1** to extinguish **2** to publish, issue **3** to produce for sale **4a** to disconcert, confuse **b** to annoy, irritate **c** to inconvenience **5** to give or offer (a job of work) to be done by another outside the premises **6** to set out from shore

¹**putty** /'pʌti/ *n* a dough-like cement, usu made of whiting and boiled linseed oil, used esp in fixing glass in sashes and stopping crevices in woodwork

²**putty** *v* to use putty on or apply putty to

put-up *adj* contrived secretly beforehand – *infml*

put up *v* **1** to nominate for election – often + *for* **2** to offer for public sale **3** to give food and shelter to; accommodate **4** to build, erect **5** to offer as a prize or stake **6** to increase the amount of; raise

¹**puzzle** /'pʌzəl/ *v* to offer or represent a problem difficult to solve or a situation difficult to resolve; perplex; *also* to exert (e g oneself) *over* or *about* such a problem or situation – **puzzled** *adj* – **puzzler** *n*

²**puzzle** *n* a problem, contrivance, etc designed for testing one's ingenuity – ~**ment** *n*

pygmy /'pɪgmi/ *n* **1** a member of a very small people of equatorial Africa **2** an insignificant or worthless person in a specified sphere

pyjamas /pə'dʒɑːməz/ *NAm chiefly* **pajamas** *n pl* **1** loose lightweight trousers traditionally worn in the East **2** a suit of loose lightweight jacket and trousers for sleeping in

pylon /'paɪlən/ *n* a tower for supporting either end of a wire, esp electricity power cables, over a long span

pyramid /'pɪrəmɪd/ *n* **1** an ancient massive structure having typically a square ground plan and tapering smooth or stepped walls that meet at the top **2** a polyhedron having for its base a polygon and for faces triangles with a common vertex **3** a nonphysical structure or system (e g a social or organizational hierarchy) having a broad supporting base and narrowing gradually to an apex

Q

¹**quack** /kwæk/ *v or n* (to make) the characteristic cry of a duck

²**quack** *n* **1** one who has or pretends to have medical skill **2** a charlatan *USE* *infml* – ~**ery** *n*

quadruped /'kwɒdruped/ *n* an animal having 4 feet

quaint /kweɪnt/ *adj* **1** unusual or different in character or appearance; odd **2** pleasingly or strikingly old-fashioned or unfamiliar – ~**ly** *adv* – ~**ness** *n*

¹**quake** /kweɪk/ *v* **1** to shake or vibrate, usu from shock or instability **2** to tremble or shudder, esp inwardly from fear

²**quake** *n* **1** a quaking **2** an earthquake – *infml*

qualification /ˌkwɒlɪfɪ'keɪʃən/ *n* **1** a restriction in meaning or application **2a** a quality or skill that fits a person (e g for a particular task or appointment) **b** a condition that must be complied with (e g for the attainment of a privilege)

qualified /'kwɒlɪfaɪd/ *adj* **1a** fitted (e g by training or experience) for a usu specified purpose; competent **b** complying with the specific requirements or conditions (e g for appointment to an office); eligible **2** limited or modified in some way

qualify /'kwɒlɪfaɪ/ *v* **1a** to reduce from a general to a particular or restricted form; modify **b** to make less harsh or strict; moderate **2** to reach an accredited level of competence **3** to exhibit a required degree of ability or achievement in a preliminary contest

¹**quality** /'kwɒlɪti/ *n* **1a** peculiar and essential character; nature **b** an inherent feature; a property **2a** degree of excellence; grade **b** superiority in kind **3** a distinguishing attribute; a characteristic

²**quality** *adj* **1** concerned with or displaying excellence **2** *of a newspaper* aiming to appeal to an educated readership

quandary /'kwɒndəri/ *n* a state of perplexity or doubt

quantity /'kwɒntɪti/ *n* **1a** an indefinite amount or number **b** a known, measured or estimated amount **c** the total amount or number **d** a considerable amount or number – often pl with sing. meaning **2** the character of a logical proposition as universal, particular, or singular

¹**quarantine** /'kwɒrəntiːn/ *n* **1** (the period of) a restraint on the activities or communication of people or the transport of goods or animals, designed to

prevent the spread of disease or pests **2** a state of enforced isolation

²quarantine v **1** to detain in or exclude by quarantine **2** to isolate from normal relations or communication

¹quarrel /'kwɒrəl/ n **1** a reason for dispute or complaint **2** a usu verbal conflict between antagonists; a dispute

²quarrel v **1** to find fault with **2** to contend or dispute actively; argue

¹quarry /'kwɒri/ n the prey or game of a predator, esp a hawk, or of a hunter

²quarry n **1** an open excavation from which building materials (e g stone, slate, and sand) are obtained **2** a source from which useful material, esp information, may be extracted – **quarry** v

quart /kwɔːt/ n a unit of liquid capacity equal to 2pt

¹quarter /'kwɔːtə/ n **1** any of 4 equal parts into which sthg is divisible **2** any of various units equal to or derived from a fourth of some larger unit **3** a fourth of a measure of time: e g **a** any of 4 3-month divisions of a year **b** a quarter of an hour – used in designation of time **4** (a coin worth) a quarter of a (US) dollar **5** a hindquarter, rump **6** (the direction of or region round) a (cardinal) compass point **7** pl living accommodation; lodgings; esp accommodation for military personnel or their families **8** merciful consideration of an opponent; specif the clemency of not killing a defeated enemy **9** the part of a ship's side towards the stern

²quarter v **1** to divide into 4 (almost) equal parts **2** to provide with lodgings or shelter; esp to assign (a member of the armed forces) to accommodation **3** to crisscross (an area) in many directions

³quarter adj consisting of or equal to a quarter

quash /kwɒʃ/ v **1a** to nullify (by judicial action) **b** to reject (a legal document) as invalid **2** to suppress or extinguish summarily and completely

quay /kiː/ n an artificial landing place beside navigable water for loading and unloading ships

queen /kwiːn/ n **1** the wife or widow of a king **2** a female monarch **3** the most powerful piece of each colour in a set of chessmen, which has the power to move any number of squares in any direction **4** a playing card marked with a stylized figure of a queen and ranking usu below the king **5** the fertile fully developed female in a colony of bees, ants, or termites

¹queer /kwɪə/ adj **1a** eccentric, unconventional **b** mildly insane **2** questionable, suspicious **3** not quite well; queasy – infml **4** homosexual – derog

²queer v to spoil the effect or success of

quench /kwentʃ/ v **1** to put out (the light or fire of) **2a** to terminate (as if) by destroying; eliminate **b** to relieve or satisfy with liquid

¹query /'kwɪəri/ a question, esp expressing doubt or uncertainty

²query v **1** to put as a question **2** to question the accuracy of (e g a statement)

¹quest /kwest/ n **1** (the object of) a pursuit or search **2** an adventurous journey undertaken by a knight in medieval romance

²quest v to search for – chiefly poetic

¹question /'kwestʃən/ n **1a** an interrogative expression used to elicit information or test knowledge **b** an interrogative sentence or clause **2** an act or instance of asking; an inquiry **3a** a subject or concern that is uncertain or in dispute **b** the specific point at issue **4a** (room for) doubt or objection **b** chance, possibility

²question v **1a** to ask a question of **b** to interrogate **2** to doubt, dispute – ~ing adj – ~ingly adv – ~er n

questionable /'kwestʃənəbəl/ adj **1** open to doubt or challenge; not certain or exact **2** of doubtful morality or propriety; shady – -bly adv

¹queue /kjuː/ n **1** a pigtail **2** a waiting line, esp of people or vehicles

²queue v to line up or wait in a queue

¹quick /kwɪk/ adj **1a** fast in understanding, thinking, or learning; mentally agile **b** reacting with speed and keen sensitivity **2a** fast in development or occurrence **b** done or taking place with rapidity **c** inclined to hastiness (e g in action or response) **d** capable of being easily and speedily prepared – ~ly adv – ~ness n

²quick adv in a quick manner

³quick n **1** painfully sensitive flesh, esp under a fingernail, toenail, etc **2** the inmost sensibilities

¹quiet /'kwaɪət/ n being quiet; tranquillity

²quiet adj **1a** marked by little or no motion or activity; calm **b** free from noise or uproar; still **c** secluded **2a** gentle, reserved **b** unobtrusive, conservative **3** private, discreet – ~ly adv – ~ness n

³quiet adv in a quiet manner

⁴quiet v to calm, soothe

¹quilt /kwɪlt/ n **1** a thick warm top cover for a bed consisting of padding held in place between 2 layers of cloth by lines of stitching **2** a bedspread

²quilt v to stitch or sew together in layers with padding in between

¹quit /kwɪt/ adj released from obligation, charge, or penalty – + of

²quit v **1** to cease doing sthg; specif **1** to give up one's job **2** of a tenant to vacate occupied premises **3** to admit defeat; give up

quite /kwaɪt/ adv or adj **1a** wholly, completely **b** positively, certainly **2** more than usually; rather **3** chiefly Br to only a moderate degree

¹quiver /'kwɪvə/ n a case for carrying or holding arrows

²quiver v to shake or move with a slight trembling motion

¹quiz /kwɪz/ n -zz- a public test of (general) knowledge, esp as a television or radio entertainment

²quiz v to question closely – journ

quota /'kwəʊtə/ n 1 a proportional part or share; esp the share or proportion to be either contributed or received by an individual or body 2 a numerical limit set on some class of people or things

quotation /kwəʊ'teɪʃən/ n 1 sthg quoted; esp a passage or phrase quoted from printed literature 2 quoting 3a current bids and offers for or prices of shares, securities, commodities, etc b an estimate

quotation mark n either of a pair of punctuation marks ' ' or ' ' used to indicate the beginning and end of a direct quotation

¹**quote** /kwəʊt/ v 1 to repeat a passage or phrase previously said or written, esp by writing or speech, esp in substantiation or illustration and usu with an acknowledgment 2 to cite in illustration 3 to make an estimate of or give exact information on (e g the price of a commodity or service)

²**quote** n 1 a quotation 2 quotation mark

R

¹**rabbit** /'ræbɪt/ n 1 (the fur of) a small long-eared mammal that is related to the hares but differs from them in producing naked young and in its burrowing habits 2 Br an unskilful player (e g in golf, cricket, or tennis)

²**rabbit** v, Br to talk aimlessly or inconsequentially – infml; often + on

¹**race** /reɪs/ n 1a a strong or rapid current of water in the sea, a river, etc b a watercourse used to turn the wheel of a mill 2a a contest of speed (e g in running or riding) b pl a meeting in which several races (e g for horses) are run

²**race** v 1 to compete in a race 2 to go or move at top speed or out of control 3 of a motor, engine, etc to revolve too fast under a diminished load – ~ r n

³**race** n 1 a family, tribe, people, or nation belonging to the same stock 2 an actually or potentially interbreeding group within a species 3a a division of mankind having traits that are sufficient to characterize it as a distinct human type b human beings collectively – race, racial adj – racially adv

racialism /'reɪʃəlɪzəm/ racism n 1 racial prejudice or discrimination 2 the belief that racial differences produce an inherent superiority for a particular race – racialist, racist adj, n

¹**rack** /ræk/ n 1 an instrument of torture on which the victim's body is stretched – usu + the 2 a framework, stand, or grating on or in which articles are placed

²**rack** v 1 to torture on the rack 2 to cause to suffer torture, pain, or anguish 3 to raise (rents) oppressively 4 to place in a rack

³**rack** v to draw off (e g wine) from the lees

⁴**rack** n the front rib section of lamb used for chops or as a roast

⁵**rack** n destruction – chiefly in rack and ruin

¹**racket, racquet** /'rækɪt/ n 1 a lightweight implement consisting of netting stretched in an open frame with a handle attached that is used for striking the ball, shuttle, etc in various games 2 pl, but sing in constr a game for 2 or 4 players play on a 4-walled court

²**racket** n 1 a loud and confused noise 2a a fraudulent enterprise made workable by bribery or intimidation b an easy and lucrative occupation or line of business – infml

radar /'reɪdɑː/ n an electronic device that generates high-frequency radio waves and locates objects in the vicinity by analysis of the radio waves reflected back from them

radiant /'reɪdɪənt/ adj 1a radiating rays or reflecting beams of light b vividly bright and shining; glowing 2 of or emitting radiant heat

radiate /'reɪdɪeɪt/ v 1 to send out rays of light, heat, or any other form of radiation 2 to proceed in a direct line from or towards a centre 3 to show or display clearly

radiation /,reɪdɪ'eɪʃən/ n 1 the action or process of radiating; esp the process of emitting radiant energy in the form of waves or particles 2 electromagnetic radiation (e g light) or emission from radioactive sources (e g alpha rays)

radiator /'reɪdɪeɪtə/ n 1 a room heater through which hot water or steam circulates as part of a central-heating system 2 a device with a large surface area used for cooling an internal-combustion engine by means of water circulating through it

¹**radical** /'rædɪkəl/ adj 1a of or growing from the root or the base of a stem b designed to remove the root of a disease or all diseased tissue 2 essential, fundamental 3a departing from the usual or traditional; extreme b of or constituting a political group advocating extreme measures – ~ly adv

²**radical** n sby who is a member of a radical party or who holds radical views

¹**radio** /'reɪdɪəʊ/ n 1 the system of wireless transmission and reception of signals by means of electromagnetic waves 2 a radio receiver 3a a radio transmitter (e g in an aircraft) b a radio broadcasting organization or station c the radio broadcasting industry

²**radio** v to send or communicate sthg by radio

radioactivity /,reɪdɪəʊæk'tɪvɪti/ n the property possessed by some elements (e g uranium) of spontaneously emitting alpha or beta rays and sometimes also gamma rays by the disintegration of the nuclei of atoms – -tive adj

radish /'rædɪʃ/ n (a plant of the mustard family with) a pungent fleshy typically dark red root, eaten raw as a salad vegetable

radium /'reɪdɪəm/ n an intensely radio-active metallic element that occurs naturally and is used chiefly in lumi-nous materials and in the treatment of cancer

radius /'reɪdɪəs/ n, pl **radii** 1 a straight line extending from the centre of a circle or sphere to the circumference or sur-face 2 a bounded or circumscribed area

raffle /'ræfəl/ v or n (to dispose of by means of) a lottery in which the prizes are usually goods

raft /rɑːft/ n 1 a flat usu wooden struc-ture designed to float on water and used as a platform or vessel 2 a foundation slab for a building, usu made of reinforced concrete – **raft** v

rafter /'rɑːftə/ n any of the parallel beams that form the framework of a roof

¹rag /ræg/ n **1a** (a waste piece of) worn cloth **b** pl clothes, esp when in poor or ragged condition **2** a usu sensational or poorly written newspaper

²rag v to torment, tease; also to engage in horseplay

³rag n, chiefly Br **1** an outburst of bois-terous fun; a prank **2** a series of pro-cessions and stunts organized by stu-dents to raise money for charity

⁴rag n (a composition or dance in) rag-time

¹rage /reɪdʒ/ n **1** (a fit or bout of) violent and uncontrolled anger **2** (an object of) fashionable and temporary enthusiasm

²rage v **1** to be in a rage **2** to be unchecked in violence or effect

ragged /'rægɪd/ adj **1** having an irregular edge or outline **2** torn or worn to tatters **3** straggly – **~ly** adv – **~ness** n

¹raid /reɪd/ n **1a** a usu hostile incursion made in order to seize sby or sthg **b** a surprise attack by a small force **2** a sudden invasion by the police (e g in search of criminals or stolen goods)

²raid v to make or take part in a raid

¹rail /reɪl/ n **1** an esp horizontal bar, usu supported by posts, which may serve as a barrier (e g across a balcony) or as a support on or from which sthg (e g a curtain) may be hung **2a** a railing **b** either of the fences on each side of a horse-racing track – usu pl with sing. meaning **3a** either of a pair of lengths of rolled steel forming a guide and running surface (e g a railway) for wheeled vehicles **b** the railway

²rail v to enclose or separate with a rail or rails – often + off

³rail n any of numerous wading birds of small or medium size, usu having very long toes which enable them to run on soft wet ground

⁴rail v to utter angry complaints or abuse – often + against or at

railing /'reɪlɪŋ/ n **1a** a usu vertical rail in a fence or similar barrier **2** (material for making) rails

railway /'reɪlweɪ/ n, chiefly Br **1** a line of track usu having 2 parallel lines or

rails fixed to sleepers on which vehicles run to transport goods and passengers **2** an organization which runs a railway network

¹rain /reɪn/ n **1** (a descent of) water falling in drops condensed from vapour in the atmosphere **2** pl the rainy season **3** a dense flow or fall of sthg – **~less** adj

²rain v **1** of rain to fall in drops from the clouds **2** to cause to fall; pour or send down **3** to bestow abundantly

rainbow /'reɪnbəʊ/ n **1** an arch in the sky consisting of a series of concentric arcs of the colours red, orange, yellow, green, blue, indigo, and violet, formed esp opposite the sun by the refraction, reflection, and interference of light rays in raindrops, spray, etc **2** an array of bright colours

raincoat /'reɪnkəʊt/ n a coat made from waterproof or water-resistant material

rainy /'reɪnɪ/ adj **1** having or character-ized by heavy rainfall **2** wet with rain

¹raise /reɪz/ v **1** to cause or help to rise to an upright or standing position **2** to stir up; incite **3** to lift up **4a** to levy, obtain **b** to assemble, collect **5a** to grow, cultivate **b** to rear (e g a child) **6** to give rise to; provoke **7** to bring up for consideration or debate **8** to increase the strength, intensity, degree, or pitch of

²raise n **1** an act of raising or lifting **2** an increase of a bet or bid

¹rake /reɪk/ n **1** a long-handled imple-ment with a head on which a row of projecting prongs is fixed for gathering hay, grass, etc or for loosening or level-ling the surface of the ground **2** a mech-anical implement, usu with rotating pronged wheels, used for gathering hay

²rake v **1** to gather, loosen, or level (as if) with a rake **2** to search through, esp in a haphazard manner – often + through or among **3** to sweep the length of, esp with gunfire

³rake n (to cause) to incline from the perpendicular

⁴rake n **1** the overhang of a ship's bow or stern **2** the angle of inclination or slope, esp of a stage in a theatre

⁵rake n a dissolute man, esp in fashion-able society – **rakish** adj – **rakishly** adv

¹rally /'rælɪ/ v **1** to bring together for a common cause **2a** to come together again to renew an effort **b** to arouse for or recall to order or action **3** to recover, revive

²rally n **1a** a mustering of scattered forces to renew an effort **b** a recovery of strength or courage after weakness or dejection **c** an increase in price after a decline **2** a mass meeting of people sharing a common interest or support-ing a common, usu political, cause **3** a series of strokes interchanged between players (e g in tennis) before a point is won **4** also **rallye** a motor race, usu over public roads, designed to test both speed and navigational skills

¹**ram** /ræm/ n **1** an uncastrated male sheep **2a** a battering ram **b** a heavy beak on the prow of a warship for piercing enemy vessels

²**ram** v to strike against violently and usu head-on

¹**ramble** /'ræmbəl/ v **1** to walk for pleasure, esp without a planned route **2** to talk or write in a disconnected long-winded fashion **3** to grow or extend irregularly

²**ramble** n a leisurely walk taken for pleasure and often without a planned route – ~**r** n

rampant /'ræmpənt/ adj **1** of a heraldic animal rearing upon the hind legs with forelegs extended – used after a noun **2** characterized by wildness or absence of restraint – ~**ly** adv

ran /ræn/ past of **run**

random adj **1** lacking a definite plan, purpose, or pattern **2** (of, consisting of, or being events, parts, etc) having or relating to a probability of occurring equal to that of all similar parts, events, etc

rang /ræŋ/ past of **ring**

¹**range** /reɪndʒ/ n **1a** a series of mountains **b** a number of objects or products forming a distinct class or series **c** a variety, cross-section **2** a usu solid-fuel fired cooking stove with 1 or more ovens, a flat metal top, and 1 or more areas for heating pans **3a** an open region over which livestock may roam and feed, esp in N America **b** the region throughout which a kind of living organism or ecological community naturally lives or occurs **4a(1)** the distance to which a projectile can be propelled **(2)** the distance between a weapon and the target **b** the maximum distance a vehicle can travel without refuelling **c** a place where shooting (e g with guns or missiles) is practised **5a** the space or extent included, covered, or used **b** the extent of pitch within a melody or within the capacity of a voice or instrument **6a** a sequence, series, or scale between limits **b** (the difference between) the least and greatest values of an attribute or series

²**range** v **1** to set in a row or in the proper order **2** to roam over or through **3** to determine or give the elevation necessary for (a gun) to propel a projectile to a given distance **4** to extend in a usu specified direction **5** to change or differ within limits

¹**rank** /ræŋk/ adj **1** excessively vigorous and often coarse in growth **2** offensively gross or coarse **3a** shockingly conspicuous; flagrant **b** complete – used as an intensive **4** offensive in odour or flavour – ~**ly** adv – ~**ness** n

²**rank** n **1a** a row, line, or series of people or things **b(1)** sing or pl in constr a line of soldiers ranged side by side in close order **(2)** pl rank and file **c** any of the 8 rows of squares that extend across a chessboard perpendicular to the files **2** an esp military formation – often pl with sing. meaning **3a** a degree or position in a hierarchy or order; specif an

official position in the armed forces **b** (high) social position **4** Br a place where taxis wait to pick up passengers

³**rank** v **1** to take or have a position in relation to others **2** to determine the relative position of; rate

ransack /'rænsæk/ v **1** to search in a disordered but thorough manner **2** to rob, plunder

¹**ransom** /'rænsəm/ n a price paid or demanded for the release of a captured or kidnapped person

²**ransom** v to free from captivity or punishment by paying a ransom – ~**er** n

¹**rap** /ræp/ n **1** (the sound made by) a sharp blow or knock **2** blame, punishment – infml

²**rap** v **1** to strike with a sharp blow **2** to utter (e g a command) abruptly and forcibly – usu + out **3** to criticize sharply – journ

³**rap** n the least bit (e g of care or consideration) – infml

⁴**rap** n, chiefly NAm talk, conversation – slang – **rap** v

¹**rape** /reɪp/ n a European plant of the mustard family grown as a forage crop and for its oil-producing seeds

²**rape** v **1** to despoil **2** to commit rape on – rapist n

³**rape** n **1** an act or instance of robbing, despoiling, or violating **2** the crime of forcing a woman to have sexual intercourse against her will **3** an outrageous violation

¹**rapid** /'ræpɪd/ adj moving, acting, or occurring with speed; swift – ~**ity** n – ~**ly** adv

²**rapid** n a part of a river where the water flows swiftly over a steep usu rocky slope in the river bed – usu pl with sing. meaning

¹**rare** /reə/ adj, of meat cooked so that the inside is still red

²**rare** adj **1** lacking in density; thin **2** marked by unusual quality, merit, or appeal **3** seldom occurring or found – ~**ness** n

¹**rash** /ræʃ/ adj acting with, characterized by, or proceeding from undue haste or impetuosity – ~**ly** adv – ~**ness** n

²**rash** n **1** an outbreak of spots on the body **2** a large number of instances of a specified thing during a short period

raspberry /'rɑːzbəri/ n **1** (a widely grown shrub that bears) any of various usu red edible berries **2** a rude sound made by sticking the tongue out and blowing noisily – slang

¹**rat** /ræt/ n **1** any of numerous rodents that are considerably larger than the related mice **2** a contemptible or wretched person; specif one who betrays or deserts his party, friends, or associates

²**rat** v to betray, desert, or inform on one's associates – usu + on

¹**rate** /reɪt/ n **1** valuation **2a** a fixed ratio between 2 things **b** a charge, payment, or price fixed according to a ratio, scale, or standard **c** Br a tax levied by a local authority – usu pl with sing. meaning **3**

a quantity, amount, or degree of sthg measured per unit of sthg else

²**rate** v 1 to consider to be; value as 2 to determine or assign the relative rank or class of 3 to be worthy of; deserve 4 to think highly of; consider to be good – *infml*

rather /ˈrɑːðə/ *adv or adj* 1 more readily or willingly; sooner 2 more properly, reasonably, or truly 3 to some degree; somewhat; *esp* somewhat excessively 4 on the contrary

ratio /ˈreɪʃɪəʊ/ *n* 1 the indicated division of one mathematical expression by another 2 the relationship in quantity, number, or degree between things or between one thing and another

¹**ration** /ˈræʃən/ *n* a share or amount (e g of food) which one permits oneself or which one is permitted

²**ration** v 1 to distribute or divide (e g commodities in short supply) in fixed quantities – often + *out* 2 to use sparingly

rat race *n the* struggle to maintain one's position in a career or survive the pressures of modern urban life

¹**rattle** /ˈrætl/ v 1 to (cause to) make a rapid succession of short sharp sounds 2 to chatter incessantly and aimlessly – often + *on* 3 to say or perform in a brisk lively fashion – often + *off* 4 to upset to the point of loss of poise and composure

²**rattle** *n* 1 a rattling sound 2a a child's toy consisting of loose pellets in a hollow container that rattles when shaken b a device that consists of a springy tongue in contact with a revolving ratchet wheel which is rotated or shaken to produce a loud noise 3 a throat noise caused by air passing through mucus and heard esp at the approach of death

¹**rave** /reɪv/ v 1 to talk irrationally (as if) in delirium; *broadly* to rage, storm 2 to talk with extreme or passionate enthusiasm

²**rave** *n* 1 a raving 2 an extravagantly favourable review

raw /rɔː/ *adj* 1 not cooked 2 not processed or purified 3 having the surface abraded or chafed 4 lacking experience, training, etc; new 5 disagreeably damp or cold – ~**ness** *n*

¹**ray** /reɪ/ *n* any of numerous fishes having the eyes on the upper surface of a flattened body and a long narrow tail

²**ray** *n* 1a any of the lines of light that appear to radiate from a bright object b a narrow beam of radiant energy (e g light or X rays) c a stream of (radioactive) particles travelling in the same line 2 any of a group of lines diverging from a common centre 3a any of the bony rods that support the fin of a fish b any of the radiating parts of the body of a radially symmetrical animal (e g a starfish) 4 a slight manifestation or trace (e g of intelligence or hope)

razor /ˈreɪzə/ *n* a sharp-edged cutting implement for shaving or cutting (facial) hair

¹**reach** /riːtʃ/ v 1 to stretch out 2a to touch or grasp by extending a part of the body (e g a hand) or an object b to pick up and draw towards one; pass c(1) to extend to (2) to get up to or as far as; arrive at d to contact or communicate with

²**reach** *n* 1a the action or an act of reaching b the distance or extent of reaching or of ability to reach c a range; *specif* comprehension 2 a straight uninterrupted portion of a river or canal 3 the tack sailed by a vessel with the wind blowing more or less from the side

react /riˈækt/ v 1 to exert a reciprocal or counteracting force or influence – often + *on* or *upon* 2 to respond to a stimulus 3 to act in opposition to a force or influence – usu + *against* 4 to undergo chemical reaction

reaction /riˈækʃən/ *n* 1a a reacting b tendency towards a former and usu outmoded (political or social) order or policy 2 bodily response to or activity aroused by a stimulus: e g a the response of tissues to a foreign substance (e g an antigen or infective agent) b a mental or emotional response to circumstances 3 the force that sthg subjected to the action of a force exerts equally in the opposite direction 4a a chemical transformation or change; an action between atoms, molecules, etc to form new substances b a process involving change in atomic nuclei resulting from interaction with a particle or another nucleus

¹**read** /riːd/ v **read** 1a(1) to look at or otherwise sense (e g letters, symbols, or words) with mental assimilation of the communication represented (2) to utter aloud (interpretatively) the printed or written words of – often + *out* b to study (a subject), esp for a degree 2a to understand, comprehend b to interpret the meaning or significance of

²**read** /riːd/ *n* 1 sthg to read with reference to the interest, enjoyment, etc it provides 2 *chiefly Br* a period of reading

³**read** /red/ *adj* instructed by or informed through reading

reader /ˈriːdə/ *n* 1a one who reads and corrects proofs b one who evaluates manuscripts 2 a member of a British university staff between the ranks of lecturer and professor 3 a usu instructive (introductory) book or anthology

readily /ˈredɪli/ *adv* 1 without hesitating 2 without much difficulty

reading /ˈriːdɪŋ/ *n* 1a material read or for reading b the extent to which a person has read c an event at which a play, poetry, etc is read to an audience d an act of formally reading a bill that constitutes any of 3 successive stages of approval by a legislature, *specif* Parliament 2a a form or version of a particular (passage in a) text b the value indicated or data produced by an instrument 3 a particular interpretation

¹**ready** /ˈredi/ *adj* 1a prepared mentally or physically for some experience or

action **b** prepared or available for immediate use **2a**(1) willingly disposed (2) likely or about to do the specified thing **b** spontaneously prompt – ~ *adv* – **-iness** *n*

²**ready** *v* to make ready

³**ready** *n* (ready) money

⁴**ready** *adv* in advance

real /rɪəl/ *adj* **1a** not artificial, fraudulent, illusory, fictional, etc; *also* being precisely what the name implies; genuine **b** of practical or everyday concerns or activities **2** measured by purchasing power rather than the paper value of money **3** complete, great – used chiefly for emphasis

realism /ˈrɪəlɪzəm/ *n* **1** concern for fact or reality and rejection of the impractical and visionary **2** the belief that objects of sense perception have real existence independent of the mind **3** fidelity in art, literature, etc to nature and to accurate representation without idealization – **-list** *n*

realistic /rɪəˈlɪstɪk/ *adj* **1** not impractical or over optimistic; sober **2** of realism

reality /rɪˈælɪti/ *n* **1** being real **2a** a real event, entity, or state of affairs **b** the totality of real things and events

realize, -ise /ˈrɪəlaɪz/ *v* **1** to accomplish **2** to bring or get by sale, investment or effort **3** to be fully aware of – **-zation** *n*

really /ˈrɪəli/ *adv* **1a** in reality, actually **b** without question; thoroughly **2** more correctly – used to give force to an injunction (e g you *really* should have asked me first) **3** – expressing surprise or indignation

realm /relm/ *n* **1** a kingdom **2** a sphere, domain – often pl with sing. meaning

reap /riːp/ *v* **1** to cut a crop; *also* to harvest **2** to obtain or win, esp as the reward for effort – ~ **er** *n*

¹**rear** /rɪə/ *v* **1a** to breed and tend (an animal) or grow (e g a crop) for use or sale **b** to bring up **2** to rise to a height **3** *of a horse* to rise up on the hind legs

²**rear** *n* **1** the back part of sthg: e g **a** the part (e g of an army) away from the enemy **b** the part of sthg located opposite its front **c** the buttocks **2** the space or position at the back

³**rear** *adj* at the back

¹**reason** /ˈriːzən/ *n* **1a** (a statement offered as) an explanation or justification **b** a rational ground or motive **2a** proper exercise of the mind; *also* the intelligence **b** sanity

²**reason** *v* **1** to use the faculty of reason so as to arrive at conclusions **2** to talk or argue *with* another so as to influence his/her actions or opinions **3** to formulate, assume, analyse, or conclude by the use of reason – often + *out* – ~ **er** *n*

reasonable /ˈriːzənəbəl/ *adj* **1a** in accord with reason **b** not extreme or excessive **c** moderate, fair **d** inexpensive **2a** having the faculty of reason;

rational **b** sensible – **-bleness** *n* – **-bly** *adv*

reassure /ˌriːəˈʃʊə/ *v* to restore confidence to – **-surance** *n* – **-suringly** *adv*

¹**rebel** /ˈrebəl/ *adj* **1** in rebellion **2** of rebels

²**rebel** /rɪˈbel/ *n* one who rebels against a government, authority, convention, etc

³**rebel** /rɪˈbel/ *v* **1** to oppose or disobey (one in) authority or control, esp a government **2** to act in or show opposition

rebellion /rɪˈbeljən/ *n* **1** opposition to (one in) authority or dominance **2** (an instance of) open armed resistance to an established government

¹**rebound** /rɪˈbaʊnd/ *v* **1** to spring back (as if) on collision or impact with another body **2** to return with an adverse effect to a source or starting point

²**rebound** /ˈriːbaʊnd/ *n* **1** a rebounding, recoil **2** a recovery

rebuke /rɪˈbjuːk/ *v or n* (to) reprimand

¹**recall** /rɪˈkɔːl/ *v* **1a** to call or summon back **b** to bring back to mind **2** to cancel, revoke – ~ **able** *adj*

²**recall** /rɪˈkɔːl/ *n* **1** a call or summons to return **2** remembrance of what has been learned or experienced **3** the act of revoking or the possibility of being revoked

recede /rɪˈsiːd/ *v* **1a** to move back or away; withdraw **b** to slant backwards **2** to grow less, smaller, or more distant; diminish

receipt /rɪˈsiːt/ *n* **1** the act or process of receiving **2** sthg (e g goods or money) received – usu pl with sing. meaning **3** a written acknowledgment of having received goods or money

receive /rɪˈsiːv/ *v* **1** to (willingly) come into possession of or be provided with **2a** to act as a receptacle or container for; *also* to take (an impression, mark, etc) **b** to assimilate through the mind or senses **3** to welcome, greet; *also* to entertain **4a** to take the force or pressure of **b** to suffer the hurt or injury of

receiver /rɪˈsiːvə/ *n* **1** a person appointed to hold in trust and administer property of a bankrupt or insane person or property under litigation **2** one who receives stolen goods **3a** a radio, television, or other part of a communications system that receives the signal **b** the part of a telephone that contains the mouthpiece and earpiece

recent /ˈriːsənt/ *adj* **1** of a time not long past **2** having lately come into existence – ~ **ly** *adv*

reception /rɪˈsepʃən/ *n* **1** receiving or being received: e g **a** an admission **b** a response, reaction **c** the receiving of a radio or television broadcast **2** a formal social gathering during which guests are received **3** *Br* an office or desk where visitors or clients (e g to an office, factory, or hotel) are received on arrival

¹**recess** /rɪˈses, ˈriːses/ *n* **1** a hidden, secret, or secluded place – usu pl **2** an

alcove 3 a suspension of business or activity, usu for a period of rest or relaxation

²**recess** /rɪ'ses/ v 1 to put in a recess 2 to make a recess in 3 to interrupt for a recess

recession /rɪ'seʃən/ n 1 a withdrawal 2 a period of reduced economic activity

recipe /'resɪˌpi/ n 1 a list of ingredients and instructions for making sthg, specif a food dish 2 a procedure for doing or attaining sthg

recital /rɪ'saɪtl/ n 1 a reciting 2 a concert or public performance given by a musician, small group of musicians, or dancer

recite /rɪ'saɪt/ v 1 to repeat from memory or read aloud, esp before an audience 2 to relate in detail; enumerate – -tation n – ~ r n

reckless /'reklɪs/ adj marked by lack of proper caution; careless of consequences – ~ly adv – ~ness n

reckon /'rekən/ v 1a to count – usu + up b to estimate, compute 2 to consider or think of in a specified way 3 to suppose, think 4 to esteem highly – infml 5 to place reliance on 6 to take into account – + with – ~ er n

recognition /ˌrekəɡ'nɪʃən/ n 1 recognizing or being recognized 2 special notice or attention

recognize, -ise /'rekəɡnaɪz/ v 1 to perceive to be something already known 2 to show appreciation of 3 to admit as being of a particular status or having validity

recollect /ˌrekə'lekt/ v 1 to bring back to the level of conscious awareness; remember, recall 2 to bring (oneself) back to a state of composure or concentration – ~ion n

recommend /ˌrekə'mend/ v 1 to endorse as fit, worthy, or competent 2 to advise – ~ation n

reconcile /'rekənsaɪl/ v 1 to restore to friendship or harmony 2 to make consistent or congruous 3 to cause to submit to or accept – -cilable adj – -liation n

reconsider /ˌriːkən'sɪdə/ v to consider (sthg) again with a view to change, revision, or revocation – ~ation n

reconstruct /ˌriːkən'strʌkt/ v 1a to restore to a previous condition b to recreate 2 to build up a mental image or physical representation of (e g a crime or a battle) from the available evidence – ~ion n

¹**record** /rɪ'kɔːd/ v 1a to commit to writing so as to supply written evidence b to register by mechanical or other means 2 to give evidence of; show 3 to convert (e g sound) into a permanent form fit for reproduction

²**record** /'rekɔːd/ n 1a sthg recorded or on which information, evidence, etc has been registered b sthg that recalls, relates, or commemorates past events or feats c an authentic official document 2a(1) a body of known or recorded facts regarding sthg or sby (2) a list of previous criminal convictions b the best

recorded performance in a competitive sport 3 a flat usu plastic disc with a spiral groove whose undulations represent recorded sound for reproduction on a gramophone

recover /rɪ'kʌvə/ v 1a to get back b to regain a normal or stable position or condition (e g of health) 2 to obtain by legal action – ~able adj

recovery /rɪ'kʌvəri/ n a recovering: e g a a return to normal health b a regaining of balance or control (e g after a stumble or mistake) c an economic upturn (e g after a depression)

recreation /ˌrekrɪ'eɪʃən/ n (a means of) pleasurable activity, diversion, etc

¹**recruit** /rɪ'kruːt/ n a newcomer to a field or activity; specif a newly enlisted member of the armed forces

²**recruit** v 1 to enlist recruits 2 to secure the services of; hire – ~ment n

rectangle /'rektæŋɡəl/ n a parallelogram all of whose angles are right angles; esp one that is not a square – -gular adj

recur /rɪ'kɜː/ v to occur again, esp repeatedly or after an interval: e g a to come up again for consideration b to come again to mind – ~rence n

¹**red** /red/ adj 1 of the colour red 2a flushed, esp with anger or embarrassment b tinged with or rather red 3 failing to show a profit 4 often cap communist – infml – ~ness n – ~dish adj

²**red** n 1 a colour whose hue resembles that of blood or of the ruby or is that of the long-wave extreme of the visible spectrum 2 the condition of being financially in debt or of showing a loss – usu in/out of the red 3 a red traffic light meaning 'stop' 4 cap a communist USE (4) chiefly derog

red-handed adv or adj in the act of committing a crime or misdeed

reduce /rɪ'djuːs/ v 1 to diminish in size, amount, extent, or number; also to lose weight by dieting 2 to bring or force to a specified state or condition 3 to force to capitulate 4 to bring to a systematic form or character 5 to lower in grade, rank, status, or condition 6a to diminish in strength, density, or value b to lower the price of – reducible adj

reduction /rɪ'dʌkʃən/ n 1 a reducing or being reduced 2a sthg made by reducing; esp a reproduction (e g of a picture) in a smaller size b the amount by which sthg is reduced

redundant /rɪ'dʌndənt/ adj 1a superfluous b excessively verbose 2 chiefly Br unnecessary, unfit, or no longer required for a job – ~ly adv

reed /riːd/ n 1 (the slender, often prominently jointed, stem of) any of various tall grasses that grow esp in wet areas 2 a growth or mass of reeds; specif reeds for thatching 3a a thin elastic tongue or flattened tube (e g of cane) fastened over an air opening in a musical instrument (e g an organ or clarinet) and set in vibration by an air current **b** a woodwind instrument having a reed

¹reel /ˈriːl/ *n* a revolvable device on which sthg flexible is wound: e g **a** a small wheel at the butt of a fishing rod for winding the line **b** a flanged spool for photographic film, magnetic tape, etc **c** *chiefly Br* a small spool for sewing thread – **reel** *v*

²reel *v* **1** to be giddy; be in a whirl **2** to waver or fall back (e g from a blow) **3** to walk or (appear to) move unsteadily (e g from dizziness or intoxication)

³reel *n* (the music for) a lively esp Scottish-Highland or Irish dance in which 2 or more couples perform a series of circular figures and winding movements

refer /rɪˈfɜː/ *v* **1** to explain in terms of a general cause **2** to send or direct for information, aid, treatment, etc **3** to relate *to* sthg; *also* allude *to* **4** to have recourse; glance briefly for information

¹referee /ˌrefəˈriː/ *n* **1a** one to whom a legal matter is referred for investigation or settlement **b** (character) reference **2** an official who supervises the play and enforces the laws in any of several sports (e g football and boxing)

²referee *v* to act as a referee (in or for)

¹reference /ˈrefərəns/ *n* **1** referring or consulting **2** (a) bearing on or connection with a matter – often in *in/with reference to* **3a** an allusion, mention **b** sthg that refers a reader to another source of information (e g a book or passage); *also* the other source of information **4a** a person to whom inquiries as to character or ability can be made **b** a statement of the qualifications of a person seeking employment or appointment given by sby familiar with him/her **c** a standard for measuring, evaluating, etc

²reference *v* to provide (e g a book) with references to authorities and sources of information

refine /rɪˈfaɪn/ *v* **1** to free from impurities **2** to improve or perfect by pruning or polishing **3** to free from imperfection, esp from what is coarse, vulgar, or uncouth

refined /rɪˈfaɪnd/ *adj* **1** fastidious, cultivated **2** *esp of food* processed to the extent that desirable ingredients may be lost in addition to impurities or imperfections

reflect /rɪˈflekt/ *v* **1** to send or throw (light, sound, etc) back or at an angle **2** to show as an image or likeness; mirror **3** to make manifest or apparent **4** to consider **5** to tend to bring reproach or discredit – usu + *on* or *upon*

reflection /rɪˈflekʃən/ *n* **1** a reflecting of light, sound, etc **2a** an image given back (as if) by a reflecting surface **b** an effect produced by or related to a specified influence or cause **3** an often obscure or indirect criticism **4** consideration of some subject matter, idea, or purpose

¹reflex /ˈriːfleks/ *n* **1** an automatic response to a stimulus that does not reach the level of consciousness **2** *pl* the power of acting or responding with adequate speed **3** an (automatic) way of behaving or responding

²reflex *adj* **1** bent, turned, or directed back **2** occurring as an (automatic) response **3** *of an angle* greater than 180° but less than 360°

reflexive /rɪˈfleksɪv/ *adj* **1** directed or turned back on itself **2** of, denoting, or being an action (e g in *he perjured himself*) directed back upon the agent or the grammatical subject – **-ly** *adv*

¹reform /rɪˈfɔːm/ *v* **1** to amend or alter for the better **2** to put an end to (an evil) by enforcing or introducing a better method or course of action **3** to induce or cause to abandon evil ways – **~er** *n*

²reform *n* **1** amendment of what is defective or corrupt **2** (a measure intended to effect) a removal or correction of an abuse, a wrong, or errors

refrain /rɪˈfreɪn/ *v* to keep oneself from doing, feeling, or indulging in sthg, esp from following a passing impulse – usu + *from*

²refrain *n* (the musical setting of) a regularly recurring phrase or verse, esp at the end of each stanza or division of a poem or song; a chorus

refresh /rɪˈfreʃ/ *v* **1** to restore strength or vigour to; revive (e g by food or rest) **2** to arouse, stimulate (e g the memory)

refreshing /rɪˈfreʃɪŋ/ *adj* agreeably stimulating because of freshness or newness – **~ly** *adv*

refreshment /rɪˈfreʃmənt/ *n* **1** refreshing or being refreshed **2** assorted foods, esp for a light meal – usu *pl* with sing. meaning

refrigerator /rɪˈfrɪdʒəreɪtə/ *n* an insulated cabinet or room for keeping food, drink, etc cool

refuge /ˈrefjuːdʒ/ *n* **1** (a place that provides) shelter or protection from danger or distress **2** a person, thing, or course of action that offers protection or is resorted to in difficulties

refugee /ˌrefjʊˈdʒiː/ *n* one who flees for safety, esp to a foreign country to escape danger or persecution

refusal /rɪˈfjuːzəl/ *n* **1** a refusing, denying, or being refused **2** the right or option of refusing or accepting sthg before others

¹refuse /rɪˈfjuːz/ *v* **1** to express oneself as unwilling to accept **2a** to show or express unwillingness to do or comply with **b** *of a horse* to decline to jump a fence, wall, etc

²refuse /ˈrefjuːs/ *n* worthless or useless stuff; rubbish, garbage

regain /rɪˈɡeɪn/ *v* to gain or reach again; recover

¹regard /rɪˈɡɑːd/ *n* **1** a gaze, look **2** attention, consideration **3a** a feeling of respect and affection **b** *pl* friendly greetings

²regard *v* **1** to pay attention to; take into consideration or account **2** to look steadily at **3** to consider and appraise in a specified way or from a specified point of view

regarding /rɪ'gɑ:dɪŋ/ *prep* with regard to

¹**regardless** /rɪ'gɑ:dl̩s/ *adj* heedless, careless

²**regardless** *adv* despite everything

¹**regiment** /'redʒ₁mənt/ *n sing or pl in constr* 1 a permanent military unit consisting usu of a number of companies, troops, batteries, or sometimes battalions 2 a large number or group – ~ **al** *adj*

²**regiment** /'redʒ₁ment/ *v* to subject to strict and stultifying organization or control – ~ **ation** *n*

region /'ri:dʒən/ *n* 1 an administrative area 2 an indefinite area of the world or universe; *esp* an area with broadly uniform features 3 an indefinite area surrounding a specified body part 4 a sphere of activity of interest – ~ **al** *adj* – ~ **ally** *adv*

¹**register** /'redʒ₁stə'/ *n* 1 a written record containing (official) entries of items, names, transactions, etc 2a a roster of qualified or available individuals b a school attendance record 3 (a part of) the range of a human voice or a musical instrument 4 a device registering a number or a quantity 5 a condition of correct alignment or proper relative position (e g of the plates used in colour printing) – often in *in/out of register*

²**register** *v* 1a to enrol formally b to record automatically; indicate c to make a (mental) record of; note 2 to secure special protection for (a piece of mail) by prepayment of a fee 3 to convey an impression of 4 to achieve, win

¹**regret** /rɪ'gret/ *v* to be very sorry about

²**regret** *n* 1 grief or sorrow tinged esp with disappointment, longing, or remorse 2 *pl* a conventional expression of disappointment, esp on declining an invitation – ~ **ful** *adj* – ~ **fully** *adv* – ~ **fulness** *n*

¹**regular** /'regjʊlə'/ *adj* 1a formed, built, arranged, or ordered according to some rule, principle, or type b(1) with equilateral and equiangular (2) having faces that are identical regular polygons with identical angles between them c perfectly (radially) symmetrical or even 2a steady or uniform in course, practice, or occurrence; habitual, usual, or constant b recurring or functioning at fixed or uniform intervals 3 constituted, conducted, or done in conformity with established or prescribed usages, rules, or discipline 4 of being a permanent standing army – *infml* – ~ **ity** *n* – ~ **ize** *v* – ~ **ly** *adv*

²**regular** *n* 1 a soldier in a regular army 2 one who is usu present or participating; *esp* one who habitually visits a particular place

regulate /'regjʊleɪt/ *v* 1 to govern or direct according to rule 2 to bring order, method, or uniformity to 3 to fix

or adjust the time, amount, degree, or rate of

¹**regulation** /,regjʊ'leɪʃən/ *n* 1 regulating or being regulated 2a an authoritative rule or order

²**regulation** *adj* conforming to regulations; official

rehearsal /rɪ'hɜ:səl/ *n* a practice session, esp of a play, concert, etc preparatory to a public appearance

rehearse /rɪ'hɜ:s/ *v* 1 to present an account of (again) 2 to give a rehearsal of; practice

¹**reign** /reɪn/ *n* the time during which sby or sthg reigns

²**reign** *v* 1 to hold office as head of state; rule 2 to be predominant or prevalent

¹**rein** /reɪn/ *n* 1 a long line fastened usu to both sides of a bit, by which a rider or driver controls an animal 2 controlling or guiding power – usu pl

²**rein** *v* to check or stop (as if) by pulling on reins – often + *in*

reindeer /'reɪndɪə'/ *n* any of several deer that inhabit N Europe, Asia, and America, have antlers in both sexes, and are often domesticated

reinforce /,ri:ɪn'fɔ:s/ *v* 1 to make stronger or more pronounced 2 to strengthen or increase (e g an army) by fresh additions 3 to stimulate (an experimental subject) with a reward following a correct or desired performance

¹**reject** /rɪ'dʒekt/ *v* 1a to refuse to accept, consider, submit to, or use b to refuse to accept or admit 2 to fail to accept (e g a skin graft or transplanted organ) as part of the organism because of immunological differences – ~ **ion** *n*

²**reject** /'ri:dʒekt/ *n* a rejected person or thing; *esp* a substandard article of merchandise

rejoice /rɪ'dʒɔɪs/ *v* to feel or express joy or great delight

relate /rɪ'leɪt/ *v* 1 to give an account of; tell 2 to show or establish logical or causal connection between 3 to respond, esp favourably – often + *to*

related /rɪ'leɪt₁d/ *adj* 1 connected by reason of an established or discoverable relation 2 connected by common ancestry or sometimes by marriage – ~ **ness** *n*

relation /rɪ'leɪʃən/ *n* 1 the act of telling or recounting 2 an aspect or quality (e g resemblance) that connects 2 or more things as belonging or working together or as being of the same kind 3 a relative 4 reference, respect, or connection 5 the interaction between 2 or more people or groups – usu pl with sing. meaning 6 *pl* a dealings, affairs b communication, contact

relationship /rɪ'leɪʃənʃɪp/ *n* 1 the state or character of being related or interrelated 2 (a specific instance or type of) kinship 3 a state of affairs existing between those having relations or dealings

¹**relative** /'relətɪv/ *n* 1 a word referring grammatically to an antecedent 2a a person connected with another by blood

relationship or marriage **b** an animal or plant related to another by common descent

²**relative** *adj* **1** introducing a subordinate clause qualifying an expressed or implied antecedent; *also* introduced by such a connective **2a** not absolute or independent; comparative **b** expressing, having, or existing in connection with or with reference to sthg else (e g a standard) *adv*

relativity /ˌrelə'tɪvᵻti/ *n* **1** being relative **2a** *also* **special theory of relativity** a theory (based on the 2 postulates (1) that the speed of light in a vacuum is constant and independent of the source or observer and (2) that all motion is relative) that leads to the assertion that mass and energy are equivalent and that mass, dimension, and time will change with increased velocity **b** *also* **general theory of relativity** an extension of this theory to include gravitation and related acceleration phenomena

relax /rɪ'læks/ *v* **1** to make less tense, rigid or severe **2** to cast off inhibition, nervous tension, or anxiety **3** to seek rest or recreation

¹**relay** /'riːleɪ/ *n* **1** a number of people who relieve others in some work **2** a race between teams in which each team member successively covers a specified portion of the course **3** the act of passing sthg along by stages; *also* such a stage

²**relay** /'riːleɪ/ *v* **1** to provide with relays **2** to pass along by relays

¹**release** /rɪ'liːs/ *v* **1** to set free from restraint, confinement, or servitude **2** to relieve from sthg that confines, burdens, or oppresses **3** to relinquish (e g a claim or right) in favour of another **4** to give permission for publication, performance, exhibition, or sale of, on but not before a specified date; *also* to publish, issue

²**release** *n* **1** relief or deliverance from sorrow, suffering, or trouble **2** discharge from obligation or responsibility **3** freeing or being freed; liberation (e g from jail) **4a** (the act of permitting) performance or publication **b(1)** a statement prepared for the press **(2)** a (newly issued) gramophone record

relegate /'relɪgeɪt/ *v* **1** to assign to a place of insignificance or oblivion; put out of sight or mind; *specif* to demote to a lower division of a sporting competition (e g a football league) **2** to submit or refer to sby or sthg for appropriate action – **-gation** *n*

relevant /'relɪvənt/ *adj* **1** having significant and demonstrable bearing on the matter at hand **2** having practical application, esp to the real world – **~ly** *adv* – **-vance, -vancy** *n*

reliable /rɪ'laɪəbəl/ *adj* suitable or fit to be relied on; dependable – **-bly** *adv*

relic /'relɪk/ *n* **1** a part of the body of or some object associated with a saint or martyr, that is preserved as an object of reverence **2** sthg left behind after decay, disintegration, or disappearance; *also* an outmoded custom, belief, or practice

relief /rɪ'liːf/ *n* **1a** removal or lightening of sthg oppressive, painful, or distressing **b** aid in the form of money or necessities, esp for the poor **c** military assistance to an endangered or surrounded post or force **d** a means of breaking or avoiding monotony or boredom **2** (release from a post or duty by) one who takes over the post or duty of another **3** (a method of) sculpture in which the design stands out from the surrounding surface **4** sharpness of outline due to contrast **5** the differences in elevation of a land surface

relieve /rɪ'liːv/ *v* **1a** to free from a burden; give aid or help to **b** to set free from an obligation, condition, or restriction – often + *of* **2** to bring about the removal or alleviation of **3** to release from a post, station, or duty **4** to remove or lessen the monotony of **5** to give relief to (oneself) by urinating or defecating

religion /rɪ'lɪdʒən/ *n* **1a** the (organized) service and worship of a god, gods, or the supernatural **b** personal commitment or devotion to religious faith or observance **2** a cause, principle, or system of beliefs held to with ardour and faith; sthg considered to be of supreme importance

religious /rɪ'lɪdʒəs/ *adj* **1** of or manifesting faithful devotion to an acknowledged ultimate reality or deity **2** of, being, or devoted to the beliefs and observances of a religion **3** scrupulously and conscientiously faithful

relinquish /rɪ'lɪŋkwɪʃ/ *v* **1** to renounce or abandon **2** to give over possession or control of

reluctant /rɪ'lʌktənt/ *adj* holding back; unwilling – **~ly** *adv*

rely /rɪ'laɪ/ *v* **1** to have confidence based on experience **2** to be dependent *USE* + *on* or *upon*

remain /rɪ'meɪn/ *v* **1** to be sthg or a part not destroyed, taken, or used up **2** to stay behind (with) **3** to continue to be

remainder /rɪ'meɪndə'/ *n* **1a** a remaining group, part, or trace **b(1)** the number left after a subtraction **(2)** the final undivided part after division, that is less than the divisor **2** a book sold at a reduced price by the publisher after sales have fallen off

remains /rɪ'meɪnz/ *n* **1** a remaining part or trace **2** a dead body

¹**remark** /rɪ'mɑːk/ *v* to notice sthg and make a comment or observation *on* or *upon*

²**remark** *n* **1** mention or notice of that which deserves attention **2** a casual expression of an opinion or judgment

remarkable /rɪ'mɑːkəbəl/ *adj* worthy of being or likely to be noticed, esp being uncommon or extraordinary – **-bly** *adv*

remedy /'remᵻdi/ *n* **1** a medicine, application, or treatment that relieves or cures a disease **2** sthg that corrects or counteracts an evil or deficiency

²**remedy** v to provide or serve as a remedy for

remember /rɪˈmembə/ v 1 to bring to mind or think of again (for attention or consideration) 2 to retain in the memory 3 to convey greetings from

remind /rɪˈmaɪnd/ v to cause to remember – ~**er** n

remnant /ˈremnənt/ n 1a a usu small part or trace remaining b a small surviving group – often pl 2 an unsold or unused end of fabric

remote /rɪˈməʊt/ adj 1 far removed in space, time, or relation 2 out-of-the-way, secluded 3 small in degree 4 distant in manner – ~**ly** adv – ~**ness** n

removal /rɪˈmuːvəl/ n 1 Br the moving of household goods from one residence to another 2 removing or being removed

¹**remove** /rɪˈmuːv/ v 1 to change the location, position, station, or residence of 2 to move by lifting, pushing aside, or taking away or off 3 to get rid of – **removable** adj

²**remove** n 1a a distance or interval separating one person or thing from another b a degree or stage of separation 2 a form intermediate between 2 others in some British schools

render /ˈrendə/ v 1 to melt down; extract by melting 2a to yield; give up b to deliver for consideration, approval, or information 3a to give in return or retribution b to restore; give back 4a to cause to be or become b to reproduce or represent by artistic or verbal means 5 to apply a coat of plaster or cement directly to

rendezvous /ˈrɒndɪvuː, -deɪ-/ n, pl **rendezvous** 1 a place (appointed) for assembling or meeting 2 a meeting at an appointed place and time

renew /rɪˈnjuː/ v 1 to restore to freshness, vigour, or perfection 2 to revive 3 to make changes in; rebuild 4 to make or do again 5 to begin again; resume 6 to replace, replenish 7 to grant or obtain an extension of or on (e g a subscription, lease, or licence) – ~**able** adj – ~**al** n

renown /rɪˈnaʊn/ n a state of being widely acclaimed; fame – ~**ed** adj

¹**rent** /rent/ n 1 a usu fixed periodical payment made by a tenant or occupant of property or user of goods to the owner for the possession and use thereof 2 the portion of the income of an economy (e g of a nation) attributable to land as a factor of production in addition to capital and labour

²**rent** v 1 to take and hold under an agreement to pay rent 2 to grant the possession and use of for rent – ~**able** adj

³**rent** past of rend

⁴**rent** n 1 an opening or split made (as if) by rending 2 an act or instance of rending

¹**repair** /rɪˈpeə/ v to go; take oneself off to – fml

²**repair** v 1 to restore by replacing a part or putting together what is torn or broken 2 to restore to a sound or healthy state – ~**able** adj – ~**er** n

³**repair** n 1 an instance or the act or process of repairing 2 relative condition with respect to soundness or need of repairing

repay /rɪˈpeɪ/ v 1a to pay back b to give or inflict in return or requital 2 to compensate, requite 3 to recompense – ~**able** adj – ~**ment** n

repeal /rɪˈpiːl/ v to revoke (a law) – **repeal** n

¹**repeat** /rɪˈpiːt/ v 1a to say or state again b to say through from memory c to say after another 2 to make, do, perform, present, or broadcast again 3 to express or present (oneself or itself) again in the same words, terms, or form – ~**ed** adj – ~**edly** adv

²**repeat** n 1 the act of repeating 2a a television or radio programme that has previously been broadcast at least once b (a sign placed before or after) a musical passage to be repeated in performance

repel /rɪˈpel/ v 1 to drive back; repulse 2a to be incapable of sticking to, mixing with, taking up, or holding b to (tend to) force away or apart by mutual action at a distance 3 to cause aversion in; disgust

repent /rɪˈpent/ v to feel sorrow, regret, or contrition for

repercussion /ˌriːpəˈkʌʃən/ n 1 an echo, reverberation 2 a widespread, indirect, or unforeseen effect of an act, action, or event

repetition /ˌrepɪˈtɪʃən/ n 1 repeating or being repeated 2 a reproduction, copy – **-tive** adj

repetitious /ˌrepɪˈtɪʃəs/ adj tediously repeating – ~**ness** n

replace /rɪˈpleɪs/ v 1 to restore to a former place or position 2 to take the place of, esp as a substitute or successor 3 to put sthg new in the place of – ~**able** adj

replacement /rɪˈpleɪsmənt/ n 1 replacing or being replaced 2 sthg or sby that replaces another

replica /ˈreplɪkə/ n a copy, duplicate

¹**reply** /rɪˈplaɪ/ v 1 to respond in words or writing 2 to do sthg in response 3 to give as an answer

²**reply** n sthg said, written, or done in answer or response

¹**report** /rɪˈpɔːt/ n 1 (an account spread by) common talk 2a a usu detailed account or statement b a usu formal record of the proceedings of a meeting or inquiry c a statement of a pupil's performance at school usu issued every term to the pupil's parents or guardian 3 a loud explosive noise

²**report** v 1 to give information about; relate 2a to convey news of b to make a written record or summary of c to present the newsworthy aspects or developments of in writing or for broadcasting 3a to make known to the relevant authorities b to make a charge of misconduct against

reporter /rɪˈpɔːtə/ n sby who or sthg that reports: e g a one who makes a shorthand record of a proceeding **b** a journalist who writes news stories **c** one who gathers and broadcasts news

represent /ˌreprɪˈzent/ *v* **1** to convey a mental impression of **2** to serve as a sign or symbol of **3** to portray or exhibit in art; depict **4a** to take the place of in some respect; stand in for **b** to serve, esp in a legislative body, by delegated authority **5** to serve as a specimen, exemplar, or instance of

representation /ˌreprɪzenˈteɪʃən/ *n* **1a** an artistic likeness or image **b** a usu formal protest **2** representing or being represented on or in some formal, esp legislative, body

¹**representative** /ˌreprɪˈzentətɪv/ *adj* **1** serving to represent **2a** standing or acting for another, esp through delegated authority **b** of or based on representation of the people in government by election **3** serving as a typical or characteristic example

²**representative** *n* **1** a typical example of a group, class, or quality **2a(1)** one who represents a constituency **(2)** a member of a House of Representatives or of a US state legislature **b** a deputy, delegate **c** one who represents a business organization

repress /rɪˈpres/ *v* **1a** to curb **b** to put down by force **2a** to hold in or prevent the expression of, by self-control **b** to exclude (e g a feeling) from consciousness – ~**ive** *adj* – ~**ively** *adv*

¹**reprimand** /ˈreprɪˌmɑːnd/ *n* a severe (and formal) reproof

²**reprimand** *v* to criticize sharply or formally censure, usu from a position of authority

¹**reproach** /rɪˈprəʊtʃ/ *n* **1** (a cause or occasion of) discredit or disgrace **2** an expression of rebuke or disapproval – ~**ful** *adj* – ~**fully** *adv*

²**reproach** *v* to express disappointment and displeasure with (a person) for conduct that is blameworthy or in need of amendment

reproduce /ˌriːprəˈdjuːs/ *v* **1** to produce (new living things of the same kind) by a sexual or asexual process **2** to imitate closely **3** to make an image or copy of – -**ducible** *adj*

reproduction /ˌriːprəˈdʌkʃən/ *n* **1** the sexual or asexual process by which plants and animals give rise to offspring **2** sthg (e g a painting) that is reproduced – -**tive** *adj*

reptile /ˈreptaɪl/ *n* **1** any of a class of vertebrates that include the alligators and crocodiles, lizards, snakes, turtles, and extinct related forms (e g the dinosaurs) and have a bony skeleton and a body usu covered with scales or bony plates **2** a grovelling or despicable person – -**tilian** *adj, n*

republic /rɪˈpʌblɪk/ *n* **1** a state in which supreme power resides in the people and is exercised by their elected representatives governing according to law **2** a body of people freely and equally engaged in a common activity

repulsion /rɪˈpʌlʃən/ *n* **1** repulsing or being repulsed **2** a force (e g between

like electric charges or like magnetic poles) tending to produce separation **3** a feeling of strong aversion – -**sive** *adj* – ~**sively** *adv* – ~**siveness** *n*

reputation /ˌrepjʊˈteɪʃən/ *n* **1** overall quality or character as seen or judged by others **2** a place in public esteem or regard; good name

reputed /rɪˈpjuːtɪd/ *adj* being such according to general or popular belief – ~**ly** *adv*

¹**request** /rɪˈkwest/ *n* **1** the act or an instance of asking for sthg **2** sthg asked for

²**request** *v* **1** to make a request to or of **2** to ask as a favour or privilege **3** to ask for

require /rɪˈkwaɪə/ *v* **1a** to call for as suitable or appropriate **b** to call for as necessary or essential; have a compelling need for **2** to impose an obligation or command on; compel – ~**ment** *n*

rescue /ˈreskjuː/ *v* to free from confinement, danger, or evil

¹**research** /rɪˈsɜːtʃ, ˈriːsɜːtʃ/ *n* scientific or scholarly inquiry; *esp* study or experiment aimed at the discovery, interpretation, reinterpretation, or application of (new) facts, theories, or laws

²**research** *v* **1** to search or investigate thoroughly **2** to engage in research on or for – ~**er** *n*

resemble /rɪˈzembl/ *v* to be like or similar to – -**blance** *n*

resent /rɪˈzent/ *v* to harbour or express ill will or bitterness at – ~**ful** *adj* – ~**fully** *adv* – ~**fulness** *n* – ~**ment** *n*

reservation /ˌrezəˈveɪʃən/ *n* **1** an act of reserving sthg; *esp* (a promise, guarantee, or record of) an arrangement to have sthg (e g a hotel room) held for one's use **2** a tract of land set aside; *specif* one designated for the use of American Indians by treaty **3** a specific doubt or objection **4** a strip of land separating carriageways **5** *chiefly NAm* an area in which hunting is not permitted; *esp* one set aside as a secure breeding place

¹**reserve** /rɪˈzɜːv/ *v* to hold in reserve; keep back

²**reserve** *n* **1** sthg retained for future use or need **2** sthg reserved or set aside for a particular use or reason: e g **a(1)** a military force withheld from action for later use – usu pl with sing. meaning **(2)** the military forces of a country not part of the regular services; *also* a reservist **b** *chiefly Br* a tract (e g of public land) set apart for the conservation of natural resources or (rare) flora and fauna **3** restraint, closeness, or caution in one's words and actions **4** money, gold, foreign exchange, etc kept in hand or set apart usu to meet liabilities – often pl with sing. meaning **5** a player or participant who has been selected to substitute for another if the need should arise

reserved /rɪˈzɜːvd/ *adj* **1** restrained in speech and behaviour **2** kept or set apart or aside for future or special use

reservoir /'rezəvwɑː/ n **1a** an artificial lake where water is collected and kept in quantity for use **b** a part of an apparatus in which a liquid is held **2** an available but unused extra source or supply

reside /rɪ'zaɪd/ v **1a** to dwell permanently or continuously; occupy a place as one's legal domicile **b** to make one's home for a time **2** to be present as an element or quality

residence /'rezɪdəns/ n **1** the act or fact of dwelling in a place **2a** a (large or impressive) dwelling **3** the period of abode in a place

¹**resident** /'rezɪdənt/ adj **1** living in a place, esp for some length of time **2** of an animal not migratory

²**resident** n one who resides in a place

resign /rɪ'zaɪn/ **1** to give up one's office or position **2** to reconcile, consign; esp to give (oneself) over without resistance

resignation /,rezɪg'neɪʃən/ n **1a** an act or instance of resigning sthg **b** a formal notification of resigning **2** the quality or state of being resigned

resigned /rɪ'zaɪnd/ adj marked by or expressing submission to sthg regarded as inevitable – ~ly adv

resist /rɪ'zɪst/ v **1a** to withstand the force or effect of **b** to exert force in opposition **2** to refrain from

resistance /rɪ'zɪstəns/ n **1** an act or instance of resisting **2** the ability to resist **3** an opposing or retarding force **4** the opposition offered to the passage of a steady electric current through a substance, usu measured in ohms **5** often cap an underground organization of a conquered country engaging in sabotage – ~tant adj

resolute /'rezəluːt/ adj **1** firmly resolved; determined **2** bold, unwavering – ~ly adv – ~ness n

resolution /,rezə'luːʃən/ n **1a** the act of making a firm decision **b** the act of finding out sthg (e g the answer to a problem); solving **c** the process or capability (e g of a microscope) of making individual parts or closely adjacent images distinguishable **2a** sthg that is resolved **b** firmness of resolve **3** a formal expression of opinion, will, or intent voted by a body or group

¹**resolve** /rɪ'zɒlv/ v **1** to break up or separate into constituent parts **2** to cause or produce the resolution of **3a** to deal with successfully **b** to find an answer to **4** to reach a firm decision about

²**resolve** n **1** sthg that is resolved **2** fixity of purpose

¹**resort** /rɪ'zɔːt/ n **1** sby who or sthg that is looked to for help **2** a frequently visited place (e g a village or town), esp providing accommodation and recreation for holidaymakers

²**resort** v **1** to go, esp frequently or in large numbers **2** to have recourse to

resource /rɪ'zɔːs, -'sɔːs/ n **1a** a natural source of wealth or revenue **b** a source of information or expertise **2** a means of

occupying one's spare time **3** the ability to deal with a difficult situation

resourceful /rɪ'zɔːsfəl, -'sɔːs-/ adj skilful in handling situations; capable of devising expedients – ~ly adv – ~ness n

¹**respect** /rɪ'spekt/ n **1** a relation to or concern with sthg usu specified; reference – in with/in respect to **2a** high or special regard; esteem **b** pl expressions of respect or deference **3** an aspect; detail

²**respect** v **1a** to consider worthy of high regard **b** to refrain from interfering with **2** to have reference to

respectable /rɪ'spektəbəl/ adj **1** decent or conventional in character or conduct **2a** acceptable in size or quantity **b** fairly good; tolerable **3** presentable – -bly adv – ~ness n – -ability n

respectful /rɪ'spektfəl/ adj marked by or showing respect or deference – ~ly adv – ~ness n

respectively /rɪ'spektɪvli/ adv **1** in particular; separately **2** in the order given

respond /rɪ'spɒnd/ v **1** to write or speak in reply; make an answer **2** to show a (favourable) reaction

response /rɪ'spɒns/ n **1** an act of responding **2a** sthg (e g a verse) sung or said by the people or choir after or in reply to the officiant in a liturgical service **b** a change in the behaviour of an organism resulting from stimulation

responsibility /rɪ,spɒnsə'bɪlɪti/ n **1a** moral or legal obligation **b** reliability, trustworthiness **2** sthg or sby that one is responsible for

responsible /rɪ'spɒnsəbəl/ adj **1a** liable to be required to justify **b** being the reason or cause **2a** able to answer for one's own conduct **b** able to discriminate between right and wrong – -ibly adv

¹**rest** /rest/ n **1** repose, sleep **2a** freedom or a break from activity or labour **b** a state of motionlessness or inactivity **3** peace of mind or spirit **4** a silence in music of a specified duration **5** sthg (e g an armrest) used for support

²**rest** v **1a** to relax by lying down; esp to sleep **b** to lie dead **2** to cease from action or motion; desist from labour or exertion **3** to be free from anxiety or disturbance **4** to be set or lie fixed or supported **5** to be based or founded **6** to depend for action or accomplishment **7** to stop introducing evidence in a law case

³**rest** n a collection or quantity that remains over

restaurant /'restər̄, -rɒnt/ n a place where refreshments, esp meals, are sold usu to be eaten on the premises

restless /'restləs/ adj **1** affording no rest **2** continuously agitated **3** characterized by or manifesting unrest, esp of mind; also changeful, discontented – ~ly adv – ~ness n

restore /rɪ'stɔː/ v **1** to give back **2** to bring back into existence or use **3** to

bring back to or put back into a former
or original (unimpaired) state

restrain /rɪ'streɪn/ v 1 to prevent from
doing sthg 2 to limit, repress, or keep
under control

restraint /rɪ'streɪnt/ n 1a restraining
or being restrained b a means of
restraining; a restraining force or influence 2 moderation of one's behaviour;
self-restraint

restrict /rɪ'strɪkt/ v to regulate or limit
as to use or distribution – ~ed adj
– ~ion n

¹**result** /rɪ'zʌlt/ v 1 to proceed or arise
as a consequence, effect, or conclusion
2 to have a usu specified outcome or
end

²**result** n 1 sthg that results as a (hoped
for or required) consequence, outcome,
or conclusion 2 sthg obtained by calculation or investigation

resume /rɪ'zjuːm/ v 1 to take or
assume again 2 to return to or begin
again after interruption
– **resumption** n

résumé /'rezjʊmeɪ, 'reɪ-/ resumé n a
summing up of sthg (e g a speech or
narrative)

retain /rɪ'teɪn/ v 1a to keep in possession or use b to engage by paying a
retainer c to keep in mind or memory
2 to hold secure or intact; contain in
place – **retention** n – **retentive** adj
– **retentively** adv

retaliate /rɪ'tælieɪt/ v 1 to return like for
like; esp to get revenge – **-ation** n
– **-atory, -ative** adj

retire /rɪ'taɪə/ v 1 to withdraw a from
action or danger b for rest or seclusion;
go to bed 2 to recede; fall back 3 to give
up one's position or occupation; conclude one's working or professional
career

retired /rɪ'taɪəd/ adj 1 remote from the
world; secluded 2 having concluded
one's career 3 received or due in retirement – **-rement** n

retract /rɪ'trækt/ v 1 to draw back or
in 2 to withdraw; take back – ~ion n
– ~able adj

¹**retreat** /rɪ'triːt/ n 1 an act or process
of withdrawing, esp from what is difficult, dangerous, or disagreeable; specif
(a signal for) the forced withdrawal of
troops from an enemy or position 2 a
place of privacy or safety; a refuge 3 a
period of usu group withdrawal for
prayer, meditation, and study

²**retreat** v 1 to make a retreat; withdraw
2 to recede

retrieve /rɪ'triːv/ v 1a to get back again;
recover (and bring back) b to rescue,
save 2 to remedy the ill effects of 3 to
recover (e g information) from storage,
esp in a computer memory 4, esp of a
dog to retrieve game; also to bring back
an object thrown by a person – **-vable**
adj – **-val** n

retrospect /'retrəspekt/ n a survey or
consideration of past events

¹**return** /rɪ'tɜːn/ v 1a to go back or come
back again b to go back to in thought,
conversation, or practice 2 to pass back
to an earlier possessor 3 to reply, retort

– fml 4a to elect a candidate b to bring
in (a verdict) 5 to restore to a former or
proper place, position, or state 6 to
bring in (e g a profit) 7 to give or send
back, esp to an owner

²**return** n 1 the act or process of coming
back to or from a place or condition 2a
a (financial) account or formal report b
a report or declaration of the results of
an election – usu pl with sing. meaning
3 the profit from labour, investment, or
business – often pl with sing. meaning 4
the act of returning sthg, esp to a former
place, condition, or owner 5 Br a ticket
bought for a trip to a place and back
again

³**return** adj 1 doubled back on itself 2
played, delivered, or given in return;
taking place for the second time 3 used
or followed on returning 4 permitting
return 5 of or causing a return to a
place or condition

reunite /,riːjuː'naɪt/ v to come or bring
together again

¹**reveal** /rɪ'viːl/ v 1 to make known (sthg
secret or hidden) 2 to open up to
view

²**reveal** n the side of an opening (e g for
a window) between a frame and the
outer surface of a wall; also a jamb

revelation /,revə'leɪʃən/ n 1 cap a pro-
phetic book of the New Testament –
often pl with sing. meaning but sing. in
constr 2 a revealing or sthg revealed;
esp a sudden and illuminating disclosure

¹**revenge** /rɪ'vendʒ/ v 1 to inflict injury
in return for (an insult, slight, etc) 2 to
avenge (e g oneself) usu by retaliating in
kind or degree

²**revenge** n 1 (a desire for) retaliating in
order to get even 2 an opportunity for
getting satisfaction or requital – ~ful
adj – ~fully adv – ~fulness n

revenue /'revɪnjuː/ n 1 the total yield
of income; esp the income of a national
treasury 2 a government department
concerned with the collection of revenue

¹**reverence** /'revərəns/ n 1 honour or
respect felt or shown; esp profound
respect accorded to sthg sacred 2 a
gesture (e g a bow) denoting respect 3
being revered 4 – used as a title for a
clergyman

²**reverence** v to regard or treat with
reverence

¹**reverse** /rɪ'vɜːs/ adj 1a (acting, operating, or arranged in a manner) opposite
or contrary to a previous, normal, or
usual condition b having the front
turned away from an observer or opponent 2 effecting reverse movement

²**reverse** v 1a to turn or change completely about in position or direction b
to turn upside down 2a to overthrow (a
legal decision) b to change (e g a policy)
to the contrary 3 to cause (e g a motor
car) to go backwards or in the opposite
direction – **reversal** n – **reversible** adj
– **reversibility** n

³**reverse** n 1 the opposite of sthg 2
reversing or being reversed 3 a misfortune 4a the side of a coin, medal, or

currency note that does not bear the principal device **b** the back part of sthg; *esp* the back cover of a book **5** a gear that reverses sthg

¹review /rɪ'vju:/ *n* **1** a revision **2** a formal military or naval inspection **3** a general survey (e g of current affairs) **4** an act of inspecting or examining **5** judicial reexamination of a case **6a** a critical evaluation of a book, play, etc **b** (a part of) a magazine or newspaper devoted chiefly to reviews and essays

²review *v* **1a** to go over (again) or examine critically or thoughtfully **b** to give a review of (a book, play, etc) **2** to hold a review of (troops, ships, etc)

revise /rɪ'vaɪz/ *v* **1** to look over again in order to correct or improve **2** to make an amended, improved, or up-to-date version of **3** *Br* to refresh knowledge of (e g a subject), esp before an exam – **reviser** *n* – **revision** *n*

revival /rɪ'vaɪvəl/ *n* **1** renewed attention to or interest in sthg **2** a new presentation or production (e g of a play) **3** an often emotional evangelistic meeting or series of meetings **4** restoration of an earlier fashion, style, or practice

revive /rɪ'vaɪv/ *v* to return to consciousness, life, health, (vigorous) activity, or current use

revolt /rɪ'vəʊlt/ *v* **1** to renounce allegiance or subjection to a government; rebel **2** to experience or recoil from disgust or abhorrence

²revolt *n* **1** a (determined armed) rebellion **2** a movement or expression of vigorous opposition

revolting /rɪ'vəʊltɪŋ/ *adj* extremely offensive; nauseating – **~ly** *adv*

revolution /,revə'lu:ʃən/ *n* **1a** the action of or time taken by a celestial body in going round in an orbit **b** the motion of a figure or object about a centre or axis **2a** a sudden or far-reaching change **b** the overthrow of one government and the substitution of another by the governed

¹revolutionary /,revə'lu:ʃənəri/ *adj* **1a** of or being a revolution **b** promoting or engaging in revolution; *also* extremist **2** completely new and different

²revolutionary *n* sby who advocates or is engaged in a revolution

revolve /rɪ'vɒlv/ *v* **1** to move in a curved path round (and round) a centre or axis; turn round (as if) on an axis **2** to be centred on a specified theme or main point

¹reward /rɪ'wɔ:d/ *v* **1** to give a reward to or for **2** to recompense

²reward *n* sthg that is given in return for good or evil done or received; *esp* sthg offered or given for some service, effort, or achievement

rhinoceros /raɪ'nɒsərəs/ *n* any of various large plant-eating very thick-skinned hoofed African or Asian mammals with 1 or 2 horns on the snout

rhubarb /'ru:bɑ:b/ *n* **1** (the thick succulent stems, edible when cooked, of) any of several plants of the dock family **2** *chiefly Br* – used by actors to suggest the sound of (many) people talking in the background

¹rhyme /raɪm/ *n* **1a** correspondence in the sound of (the last syllable of) words, esp those at the end of lines of verse **b** a word that provides a rhyme for another **2** (a) rhyming verse

²rhyme *v* **1** to compose rhyming verse **2a** *of a word or (line of) verse* to end in syllables that rhyme

rhythm /'rɪðəm/ *n* **1** the pattern of recurrent alternation of strong and weak elements in the flow of sound and silence in speech **2a** (the aspect of music concerning) the regular recurrence of a pattern of stress and length of notes **b** a characteristic rhythmic pattern **c** **rhythm, rhythm section** *sing or pl in constr* the group of instruments in a band (e g the drums, piano, and bass) supplying the rhythm **3** movement or fluctuation marked by a regular recurrence of elements (e g pauses or emphases) **4** a regularly recurrent change in a biological process or state (e g with night and day) **5** **rhythm, rhythm method** birth control by abstinence from sexual intercourse during the period when ovulation is most likely to occur – **~ic**, **~ical** *adj* – **~ically** *adv*

¹rib /rɪb/ *n* **1** any of the paired curved rods of bone or cartilage that stiffen the body walls of most vertebrates and protect the heart, lungs, etc **2a** a transverse member of the frame of a ship that runs from keel to deck **b** any of the stiff strips supporting an umbrella's fabric **c** an arched support or ornamental band in Romanesque and Gothic vaulting **3a** a vein of a leaf or insect's wing **b** any of the ridges in a knitted or woven fabric; *also* ribbing – **~bed** *adj*

²rib *v* to form a pattern of vertical ridges in by alternating knit stitches and purl stitches

³rib *v* to tease – *infml*

ribbon /'rɪbən/ *n* **1a** a (length of a) narrow band of decorative fabric used for ornamentation (e g of hair), fastening, tying parcels, etc **b** a piece of usu multicoloured ribbon worn as a military decoration or in place of a medal **2** *pl* tatters, shreds

rice /raɪs/ *n* (the seed, important as a food, of) a cereal grass widely cultivated in warm climates

rich /rɪtʃ/ *adj* **1** having abundant possessions, esp material and financial wealth **2** well supplied or endowed – often + *in* **3** sumptuous **4a** vivid and deep in colour **b** full and mellow in tone and quality **5** highly productive or remunerative; giving a high yield **6a** (of food that is) highly seasoned, fatty, oily, or sweet **b** *esp of mixtures of fuel with air* containing more petrol than normal **7** highly amusing; *also* laughable – *infml* – **~ly** *adv* – **~ness** *n*

riches /'rɪtʃɪz/ *n pl* (great) wealth

¹ricochet /'rɪkəʃeɪ/ *n* the glancing rebound of a projectile (e g a bullet) off a hard or flat surface

²ricochet v to proceed (as if) with glancing rebounds

rid /rɪd/ v to relieve, disencumber

riddance /ˈrɪdəns/ n deliverance, relief – often in *good riddance*

¹riddle /ˈrɪdl/ n **1a** a short and esp humorous verbal puzzle **2** sthg or sby mystifying or difficult to understand

²riddle v to speak in or propound riddles

³riddle n a coarse sieve (e g for sifting grain or gravel)

⁴riddle v **1** to separate (e g grain from chaff) with a riddle; sift **2** to cover *with* holes **3** to spread through, esp as an affliction

ride /raɪd/ v **rode**, **ridden** **1a** to sit and travel mounted on and usu controlling an animal **b** to travel on or in a vehicle **2a** to lie moored or anchored **b** to appear to float **3** to be contingent; depend *on* **4** to work *up* or *down* the body **5** to survive without great damage or loss; last *out* **6** to obsess, oppress **7** to give with (a punch) to soften the impact

²ride n **1** a trip on horseback or by vehicle **2** a usu straight road or path in a wood, forest, etc used for riding, access, or as a firebreak **3** *chiefly NAm* a trip on which gangsters take a victim to murder him/her – *euph*

rider /ˈraɪdə/ n **1** sby who rides; *specif* sby who rides a horse **2** sthg added by way of qualification or amendment **3** sthg used to overlie another or to move along on another piece

ridge /rɪdʒ/ n **1a** a range of hills or mountains **b** an elongated elevation of land **2** the line along which 2 upward-sloping surfaces meet; *specif* the top of a roof **3** an elongated part that is raised above a surrounding surface (e g the raised part between furrows on ploughed ground)

ridiculous /rɪˈdɪkjʊləs/ adj arousing or deserving ridicule – ~ly adv – ~ness n

¹rifle /ˈraɪfl/ v to search through, esp in order to break and carry away sthg

²rifle v to cut spiral grooves into the bore of (a rifle, cannon, etc)

³rifle n **1** a shoulder weapon with a rifled bore **2** *pl* a body of soldiers armed with rifles

¹right /raɪt/ adj **1** in accordance with what is morally good, just, or proper **2** conforming to facts or truth **3** suitable, appropriate **4** straight **5a** of, situated on, or being the side of the body that is away from the heart **b** located on the right hand when facing in the same direction as an observer **c** being the side of a fabric that should show or be seen when made up **6** having its axis perpendicular to the base **7** acting or judging in accordance with truth or fact; not mistaken **8** in a correct, proper, or healthy state **9** *often cap* of the Right, esp in politics **10** *chiefly Br* real, utter – *infml*

²right n **1** qualities (e g adherence to duty) that together constitute the ideal of moral conduct or merit moral approval **2a** a power, privilege, interest, etc to which one has a just claim **b** a property interest in sthg – often pl with sing. meaning **3** sthg one may legitimately claim as due **4** the cause of truth or justice **5** the quality or state of being factually or morally correct **6a** *sing or pl in constr, cap* those professing conservative political views **b** *often cap* a conservative position

³right adv **1** in a right, proper, or correct manner **2** in the exact location or position **3** in a direct line or course; straight **4** all the way; completely **5a** without delay; straight **b** immediately **6** to the full (e g entertained *right* royally) – often in British titles **7** on or to the right – ~**ness** n

⁴right v **1** to avenge **2a** to adjust or restore to the proper state or condition; correct **b** to bring or restore (e g a boat) to an upright position

right angle n the angle bounded by 2 lines perpendicular to each other; an angle of 90° – **right-angled** adj

rigid /ˈrɪdʒɪd/ adj **1** deficient in or devoid of flexibility **2a** inflexibly set in opinions or habits **b** strictly maintained **3** precise and accurate in procedure – ~**ly** adv – ~**ity** n

rim /rɪm/ n **1** an outer usu curved edge or border **2** the outer ring of a wheel not including the tyre – ~**less** adj

rind /raɪnd/ **1** the bark of a tree **2** a usu hard or tough outer layer of fruit, cheese, bacon, etc

¹ring /rɪŋ/ n **1** a circular band for holding, connecting, hanging, moving, fastening, etc or for identification **2** a circlet usu of precious metal, worn on the finger **3a** a circular line, figure, or object **b** an encircling arrangement **4a** an often circular space, esp for exhibitions or competitions; *esp* such a space at a circus **b** a square enclosure in which boxers or wrestlers contest **5** any of the concentric bands that revolve round some planets (e g Saturn or Uranus) **6** an electric element or gas burner in the shape of a circle, set into the top of a cooker, stove, etc, which provides a source of heat for cooking

²ring v **1** to place or form a ring round; encircle **2** to attach a ring to

³ring v **rang**; **rung** **1** to sound resonantly **2a** to sound a bell as a summons **b** to announce (as if) by ringing – often + *in* or *out* **3a** to be filled with talk or report **b** to sound repeatedly **4** *chiefly Br* to telephone – often + *up*

⁴ring n **1** a set of bells **2** a clear resonant sound made by vibrating metal **3** resonant tone **4** a loud sound continued, repeated, or reverberated **5** a sound or character suggestive of a particular quality or feeling **6** a telephone call – usu in *give somebody a ring*

ringleader /ˈrɪŋˌliːdə/ n a leader of a group that engages in objectionable activities

¹rinse /rɪns/ v **1** to cleanse (e g from soap) with liquid (e g clean water) – often + *out* **2** to remove (dirt or impurities) by washing lightly

²rinse n **1** (a) rinsing **2a** liquid used for rinsing **b** a solution that temporarily tints the hair

riot /'raɪət/ n **1** unrestrained revelry **2** (a) violent public disorder **3** a profuse and random display **4** sby or sthg wildly funny

riotous /'raɪətəs/ adj **1** participating in a riot **2a** wild and disorderly **b** exciting, exuberant – **~ly** adv – **~ness** n

¹rip /rɪp/ v **1a** to tear or split apart, esp in a violent manner **b** to saw or split (wood) along the grain **2** to rush along **3** to remove by force – + out or off

²rip n a rough or violent tear

³rip n a body of rough water formed a by the meeting of opposing currents, winds, etc **b** by passing over ridges

⁴rip n a mischievous usu young person

ripe /raɪp/ adj **1** fully grown and developed; mature **2** mature in knowledge, understanding, or judgment **3** of advanced years **4** fully prepared; ready for **5** brought by aging to full flavour or the best state; mellow – **~ly** adv – **~n** v – **~ness** n

¹ripple /'rɪpəl/ v **1** to cover with small waves **2a** to proceed with an undulating motion (so as to cause ripples) **b** to impart a wavy motion or appearance to **3** to spread irregularly outwards, esp from a central point

²ripple n **1** a small wave or succession of small waves **2** a sound like that of rippling water

¹rise /raɪz/ v rose; risen **1a** to assume an upright position, esp from lying, kneeling, or sitting **b** to get up from sleep or from one's bed **2** to take up arms **3** to respond warmly or readily; applaud – usu + to **4** to respond to nasty words or behaviour, esp by annoyance or anger **5** to appear above the horizon **6a** to move upwards; ascend **b** to increase in height or volume **7** to extend above other objects or people **8** to increase in fervour or intensity **9** to attain a higher office or rank **10** to increase in amount or number **11** to come into being; originate **12** to show oneself equal to a challenge

²rise n **1a** a movement upwards **b** emergence (e g of the sun) above the horizon **c** the upward movement of a fish to seize food or bait **2** origin **3** the vertical height of sthg, esp a step **4a** an increase, esp in amount, number, or intensity **b** an increase in pay **5a** an upward slope or gradient **b** a spot higher than surrounding ground

risk /rɪsk/ n **1** possibility of loss, injury, or damage **2** a dangerous element or factor; hazard **3** the chance of loss or the dangers to that which is insured in an insurance contract – **~y** adj – **~iness** n

²risk v **1** to expose to hazard or danger **2** to incur the risk or danger of

¹rival /'raɪvəl/ n **1a** any of 2 or more competing for a single goal **b** sby who tries to compete with and be superior to another **2** sby who or sthg that equals another in desirable qualities – **~ry** n

²rival adj having comparable pretensions or claims

³rival v **1** to be in competition with; contend with **2** to strive to equal or excel **3** to possess qualities that approach or equal (those of another)

river /'rɪvə'/ n **1** a natural stream of water of considerable volume **2** a copious or overwhelming quality – often pl

road /rəʊd/ n **1** a relatively sheltered stretch of water near the shore where ships may ride at anchor – often pl with sing. meaning **2** an open usu paved way for the passage of vehicles, people, and animals **3** a route or path – **~less** adj

road hog n a driver of a motor vehicle who obstructs or intimidates others

roadworthy /'rəʊd,wɜː'ðɪ/ adj, of a vehicle in a fit condition to be used on the roads; in proper working order – **-thiness** n

roam /rəʊm/ v **1** to go aimlessly from place to place; wander **2** to travel unhindered through a wide area – **~er** n

¹roar /rɔː'/ v **1** to give a roar **2** to laugh loudly and deeply **3** to be boisterous or disorderly – usu + about

²roar n **1** the deep prolonged cry characteristic of a wild animal **2** a loud cry, call, etc (e g of pain, anger, or laughter) **3** a loud continuous confused sound

¹roast /rəʊst/ v **1a** to cook by exposing to dry heat (e g in an oven) **b** to dry and brown slightly by exposure to heat **2** to heat to excess **3** chiefly NAm to criticize severely

²roast n a piece of meat roasted or suitable for roasting

³roast adj roasted

rob /rɒb/ v **1** to steal sthg from (a person or place), esp by violence or threat **2** to deprive of sthg due, expected, or desired – **~ber** n

robbery /'rɒbərɪ/ n theft accompanied by violence or threat

robe /rəʊb/ n **1** a long flowing outer garment; esp one used for ceremonial occasions or as a symbol of office or profession **2** NAm a woman's dressing gown – **robe** v

robin /'rɒbᵻn/ robin redbreast n a small brownish European thrush resembling a warbler and having an orange red throat and breast; also a larger but similarly coloured N American bird

robot /'rəʊbɒt/ n **1a** a (fictional) humanoid machine that walks and talks **b** sby efficient or clever who lacks human warmth or sensitivity **2** an automatic apparatus or device that performs functions ordinarily performed by human beings **3** sthg guided by automatic controls

¹rock /rɒk/ v **1** to become moved rapidly or violently backwards and forwards (e g under impact) **2a** to move rhythmically back and forth **b**(1) to daze or stun (2) to disturb, upset

²rock, rock and roll, rock 'n' roll n music usu played on electronically amplified instruments, with a persistent heavily accented beat and often country, folk, and blues elements

³rock n 1 a large mass of stone forming a cliff, promontory, or peak 2 a large mass of stony material 3 a firm or solid foundation or support 4 a coloured and flavoured sweet produced in the form of a usu cylindrical stick

¹rocket /'rɒkɪt/ n any of numerous plants of the mustard family

²rocket n 1a a firework consisting of a long case filled with a combustible material fastened to a guiding stick and projected through the air by the rearward discharge of gases released in combustion b such a device used as an incendiary weapon or as a propelling unit (e g for a lifesaving line or whaling harpoon) 2 a jet engine that carries with it everything necessary for its operation and is thus independent of the oxygen in the air 3 a rocket-propelled bomb, missile, or projectile 4 chiefly Br a sharp reprimand – infml

³rocket v 1 to rise or increase rapidly or spectacularly 2 to travel with the speed of a rocket

rod /rɒd/ n 1a(1) a straight slender stick (2) (a stick or bundle of twigs used for) punishment (3) a pole with a line for fishing b a slender bar (e g of wood or metal) 2 a unit of length equal to 5½yd (about 5m) 3 any of the relatively long rod-shaped light receptors in the retina that are sensitive to faint light

rode /rəʊd/ past of ride

¹rogue /rəʊg/ n 1 a wilfully dishonest or corrupt person 2 a mischievous person; scamp

²rogue adj, of an animal (roaming alone and) vicious and destructive

role /rəʊl/ rôle n 1a a socially expected behaviour pattern, usu determined by an individual's status in a particular society b a part played by an actor or singer 2 a function

¹roll /rəʊl/ n 1a a written document that may be rolled up; specif one bearing an official or formal record. b a list of names or related items; a catalogue c an official list of people (e g members of a school or of a legislative body) 2a a quantity (e g of fabric or paper) rolled up to form a single package b any of various food preparations rolled up for cooking or serving; esp a small piece of baked yeast dough

²roll v 1a to propel forwards by causing to turn over and over on a surface b to cause to move in a circular manner; turn over and over c to form into a mass by revolving and compressing d to carry forwards with an easy continuous motion 2 to move onwards in a regular cycle or succession 3 to flow with an undulating motion 4a to become carried on a stream b to move on wheels 5a to take the form of a cylinder or ball – often + up b to wrap round on itself; shape into a ball or roll – often + up 6 to press, spread, or level with a roller; make thin, even, or compact 7 to luxuriate in an abundant supply; wallow 8a

to make a deep reverberating sound b to utter with a trill 9a to rock from side to side b to walk with a swinging gait c to move so as to reduce the impact of a blow – + with 10a to begin to move or operate b to move forwards; develop and maintain impetus 11 NAm to rob (sby sleeping or unconscious) – infml

³roll n 1a a sound produced by rapid strokes on a drum b a reverberating sound 2a a swaying movement of the body (e g in walking or dancing) b a side-to-side movement (e g of a ship) c a flight manoeuvre in which a complete revolution about the longitudinal axis of an aircraft is made with the horizontal direction of flight being approximately maintained

¹Roman Catholic n a member of the Roman Catholic church

²Roman Catholic adj of the body of Christians headed by the pope, with a liturgy centred on the Mass and a body of dogma formulated by the church as the infallible interpreter of revealed truth

¹romance /rəʊ'mæns, rə-/ n 1a a medieval usu verse tale dealing with courtly love and adventure b a prose narrative dealing with imaginary characters involved in usu heroic, adventurous, or mysterious events that are remote in time or place; broadly a love story 2 sthg lacking any basis in fact 3 an emotional aura attaching to an enthralling era, adventure, or pursuit 4 a love affair

²romance v 1 to exaggerate or invent detail or incident 2 to entertain romantic thoughts or ideas

³romance n a short instrumental piece of music in ballad style

Romance adj of or constituting the languages developed from Latin

¹romantic /rəʊ'mæntɪk, rə-/ adj 1 consisting of or like a romance 2 having no basis in real life 3 impractical or fantastic in conception or plan 4a marked by the imaginative appeal of the heroic, remote, or mysterious b often cap of romanticism c of or being (a composer of) 19th-c music characterized by an emphasis on subjective emotional qualities and freedom of form 5a having an inclination for romance b marked by or constituting strong feeling, esp love – ~ally adv – ~ize v

²romantic n 1 a romantic person 2 cap a romantic writer, artist, or composer

romanticism /rəʊ'mæntɪˌsɪzəm/ n, often cap a chiefly late 18th- and early 19th-c literary, artistic, and philosophical movement that reacted against neoclassicism by emphasizing individual aspirations, nature, the emotions, and the remote and exotic – -cist n

¹roof /ruːf/ n 1a the upper usu rigid cover of a building b a dwelling, home 2 the highest point or level 3 the vaulted or covering part of the mouth, skull, etc

²roof v 1 to cover (as if) with a roof 2 to serve as a roof over

room /ruːm, rʊm/ n 1 an extent of

space occupied by, or sufficient or available for, sthg **2a** a partitioned part of the inside of a building **b** such a part used as a separate lodging – often pl **3** suitable or fit occasion; opportunity + *for*

oot /ruːt/ n **1a** the (underground) part of a flowering plant that usu anchors and supports it and absorbs and stores food **b** a (fleshy and edible) root, bulb, tuber, or other underground plant part **2** the part of a tooth, hair, the tongue, etc by which it is attached to the body **3a** sthg that is an underlying cause or basis **b** pl a feeling of belonging established through close familiarity or family ties with a particular place **4** a number which produces a given number when taken an indicated number of times as a factor **5** the basis from which a word is derived

oot v **1** to grow roots or take root **2** to have an origin or base

oot v **1** esp of a pig to dig with the snout **2** to poke or dig about *in*; search (unsystematically) for sthg

oot v to lend vociferous or enthusiastic support to sby or sthg – + *for*

ope /rəʊp/ n **1** a strong thick cord composed of strands of fibres or wire twisted or braided together **2** a row or string consisting of things united (as if) by braiding, twining, or threading **3** pl special methods or procedures

ope v **1** to bind, fasten, or tie with a rope **2** to enlist (sby reluctant) *in* a group or activity

ose /rəʊz/ past of *rise*

ose n **1** (the showy often double flower of) any of a genus of widely cultivated usu prickly shrubs **2a** a compass card **b** a perforated outlet for water (e g from a shower or watering can) **c** an electrical fitting that anchors the flex of a suspended light bulb to a ceiling **3** a pale to dark pinkish colour – **rose** adj

osé /ˈrəʊzeɪ/ n a light pink table wine made from red grapes by removing the skins after fermentation has begun

ot /rɒt/ v **1a** to undergo decomposition, esp from the action of bacteria or fungi – often + *down* **b** to become unsound or weak (e g from chemical or water action) **2** to go to ruin

ot n **1** (sthg) rotting or being rotten; decay **2** any of several plant or animal diseases, esp of sheep, with breakdown and death of tissues **3** nonsense, rubbish – often used interjectionally

otate /rəʊˈteɪt/ v **1** to turn about an axis or a centre; revolve **2a** to take turns at performing an act or operation **b** to perform an ordered series of actions or functions

otation /rəʊˈteɪʃən/ n **1a** a rotating or being rotated (as if) on an axis or centre **b** one complete turn **2a** recurrence in a regular series **b** the growing of different crops in succession in 1 field, usu in a regular sequence

otten /ˈrɒtn/ adj **1** having rotted; putrid **2** morally or politically corrupt **3** extremely unpleasant or inferior **4** marked by illness, discomfort, or

unsoundness *USE* (*3, 4*) infml – ~ **ly** adv – ~ **ness** n

¹rough /rʌf/ adj **1a** not smooth **b** covered with or made up of coarse hair **c** covered with boulders, bushes, etc **2a** turbulent, stormy **b(1)** harsh, violent **(2)** requiring strenuous effort **(3)** unfortunate and hard to bear – often + *on* **3a** harsh to the ear **b** crude in style or expression **c** ill-mannered, uncouth **4a** crude, unfinished **b** executed hastily or approximately **5** *Br* poorly or exhausted, esp through lack of sleep or heavy drinking – infml

²rough n **1** uneven ground bordering a golf fairway **2** the rugged or disagreeable side or aspect **3a** sthg, esp written or illustrated, in a crude or preliminary state **b** broad outline **c** a quick preliminary drawing or layout

³rough adv, chiefly *Br* in want of material comforts; without proper lodging – esp in *live/sleep rough*

roughly /ˈrʌfli/ adv **1a** with insolence or violence **b** in primitive fashion; crudely **2** without claim to completeness or exactness

¹round /raʊnd/ adj **1a** having every part of the surface or circumference equidistant from the centre **b** cylindrical **2** well filled out; plump **3a** complete, full **b** approximately correct; esp exact only to a specific decimal **c** substantial in amount **4** direct in expression **5a** moving in or forming a ring or circle **b** following a roughly circular route **6** presented with lifelike fullness **7** having full resonance or tone – ~ **ness** n

²round adv **1a** in a circular or curved path **b** with revolving or rotating motion **c** in circumference **d** in, along, or through a circuitous or indirect route **e** in an encircling position **2a** in close from all sides so as to surround (e g the children crowded *round*) **b** near, about **c** here and there in various places **3a** in rotation or recurrence **b** from beginning to end; through (e g all year *round*) **c(1)** in or to the other or a specified direction (e g turn *round*) **(2)** to (e g came *round* after fainting) **(3)** in the specified order or relationship (e g got the story the wrong way *round*) **4** about, approximately **5** to a particular person or place (e g invite them *round* for drinks)

³round prep **1a** so as to revolve or progress about (a centre) **b** so as to encircle or enclose **c** so as to avoid or get past; beyond the obstacle of **d** near to; about **2a** in all directions outwards from (e g looked *round* her) **b** here and there in or throughout (e g travel *round* Europe) **3** so as to have a centre or basis in (e g a movement organized *round* the idea of service) **4** continuously during; throughout

⁴round n **1a** sthg round (e g a circle, curve, or ring) **b** a circle of people or things **2** a musical canon sung in unison in which each part is continuously repeated **3a** a circling or circuitous path or course **b** a route or assigned territory habitually traversed (e g by a milkman or policeman) **c** a series of visits made by (1) a general practitioner to patients in their homes (2) a hospital doctor to the patients under his/her care **4** a set of usu alcoholic drinks served at 1 time to each person in a group **5** a unit of ammunition consisting of the parts necessary to fire 1 shot **6** a division of a tournament in which each contestant plays 1 other **7** a prolonged burst (e g of applause) **8** a single slice of bread or toast; *also* a sandwich made with 2 whole slices of bread

⁵**round** *v* **1** to make round or rounded **2** to go round (e g a bend, corner) **3** to bring to completion or perfection – often + *off* or *out* **4** to express as a round number – often + *off, up,* or *down* **5** to turn *on* suddenly and attack

rouse /raʊz/ *v* **1** to stir up; provoke **2** to arouse from sleep or apathy

¹**rout** /raʊt/ *n* a disorderly crowd of people; a mob

²**rout** *n* **1** a state of wild confusion; *specif* a confused retreat; headlong flight **2** a disastrous defeat

³**rout** *v* **1** to disorganize completely; wreak havoc among **2** to put to headlong flight **3** to defeat decisively or disastrously

¹**route** /ruːt/ *n* **1a** a regularly travelled way **b** a means of access **2** a line of travel **3** an itinerary

²**route** *v* to send by a selected route; direct

¹**routine** /ruːˈtiːn/ *n* **1a** a regular course of procedure **b** habitual or mechanical performance of an established procedure **2** a fixed piece of entertainment often repeated

²**routine** *adj* **1** commonplace or repetitious in character **2** of or in accordance with established procedure – ~**ly** *adv*

¹**row** /raʊ/ *v* **1** to propel a boat by means of oars **2** to occupy a specified position in a rowing crew – ~**er** *n* – ~**ing** *adj*

²**row** /raʊ/ *n* an act of rowing a boat

³**row** *n* **1** a number of objects arranged in a (straight) line; *also* the line along which such objects are arranged **2** a way, street

⁴**row** /raʊ/ *n* **1** a noisy quarrel or stormy dispute **2** excessive or unpleasant noise

⁵**row** /raʊ/ *v* to engage in quarrelling

¹**royal** /ˈrɔɪəl/ *adj* **1a** of monarchical ancestry **b** of the crown **c** in the crown's service **2** of superior size, magnitude, or quality **3** of or being a part of the rigging of a sailing ship next above the topgallant – ~**ly** *adv*

²**royal** *n* **1** a royal sail or mast **2** a size of paper usu 25 x 20in (635 × 508mm)

royalty /ˈrɔɪəlti/ *n* **1** royal sovereignty **2** people of royal blood **3** a share of the product or profit reserved by one who grants esp an oil or mining lease **4** a payment made to an author, composer, or inventor for each copy or example of his/her work sold

¹**rub** /rʌb/ *v* **1** to subject to pressure and friction, esp with a back-and-forth

motion **2a** to cause (a body) to move with pressure and friction along a surface **b** to treat in any of various ways by rubbing

²**rub** *n* **1a** an obstacle, difficulty – usu + *the* **b** sthg grating to the feelings (e g a gibe or harsh criticism) **2** the application of friction and pressure

¹**rubber** /ˈrʌbə⁽ʳ⁾/ *n* **1a** an instrument or object used in rubbing, polishing, or cleaning **b** *Br* a small piece of rubber or plastic used for rubbing out esp pencil marks on paper, card, etc **2** (any of various synthetic substances like) an elastic substance obtained by coagulating the milky juice of the rubber tree or other plant that is used, esp when toughened by chemical treatment, in car tyres, waterproof materials, etc

²**rubber** /ˈrʌbə⁽ʳ⁾/ *n* a contest consisting of an odd number of games won by the side that takes a majority

¹**rubbish** /ˈrʌbɪʃ/ *n* **1** worthless or rejected articles; trash **2** sthg worthless; nonsense – often used interjectionally – ~**y** *adj*

²**rubbish** *v* **1** to condemn as rubbish **2** to litter with rubbish

rudder /ˈrʌdə⁽ʳ⁾/ *n* **1** a flat piece or structure of wood or metal hinged vertically to a ship's stern for changing course with **2** a movable auxiliary aerofoil, usu attached to the fin, that serves to control direction of flight of an aircraft in the horizontal plane – ~**less** *adj*

¹**rude** /ruːd/ *adj* **1a** in a rough or unfinished state **b** primitive, undeveloped **2a** discourteous **b** vulgar, indecent **c** ignorant, unlearned **3** showing or suggesting lack of training or skill **4** robust, vigorous – esp in *rude health* **5** sudden and unpleasant; abrupt – ~**ly** *adv* – ~**ness** *n*

¹**ruffle** /ˈrʌfəl/ *v* **1a** to disturb the smoothness of **b** to trouble, vex **2** to erect (e g feathers) (as if) in a ruff **3** to make into a ruffle

²**ruffle** *n* **1** a disturbance of surface evenness (e g a ripple or crumple) **2a** a strip of fabric gathered or pleated on 1 edge **b** a ruff

rug /rʌg/ *n* **1** a heavy mat, usu smaller than a carpet and with a thick pile which is used as a floor covering **2a** a woollen blanket, often with fringes on 2 opposite edges, used as a wrap esp when travelling **b** a blanket for an animal (e g a horse)

rugby /ˈrʌgbi/ *n, often cap* a football game that is played with an oval football, that features kicking, lateral hand-to-hand passing, and tackling and in which forward passing is prohibited

rugged /ˈrʌgɪd/ *adj* **1** having a rough, uneven surface or outline **2** seamed with wrinkles and furrows **3** austere, stern; *also* uncompromising **4** strongly built or constituted; sturdy – ~**ly** *adv* – ~**ness** *n*

¹**ruin** /ˈruːɪn/ *n* **1** physical, moral, economic, or social collapse **2a** the state of being wrecked or decayed **b** the

remains of sthg destroyed – usu pl with sing. meaning **3** (a cause of) destruction or downfall **4** a ruined person or structure

uin v **1** to reduce to ruins **2a** to damage irreparably; spoil **b** to reduce to financial ruin

ule n **1a** a prescriptive specification of conduct or action **b** an established procedure, custom, or habit **2a** a usu valid generalization **b** a standard of judgment **c** a regulating principle, esp of a system **3** the exercise or a period of dominion **4** a strip or set of jointed strips of material marked off in units and used for measuring or marking off lengths

ule v **1a** to exercise power or firm authority over **b** to be preeminent in; dominate **2** to lay down authoritatively, esp judicially **3** to mark with lines drawn (as if) along the straight edge of a ruler

uler /'ru:lə'/ n **1** sby, specif a sovereign, who rules **2** a smooth-edged strip of material that is usu marked off in units (e g centimetres) and is used for guiding a pen or pencil in drawing lines, for measuring, or for marking off lengths

uling /'ru:lɪŋ/ n an official or authoritative decision

uling adj **1** exerting power or authority **2** chief, predominant

umble /'rʌmbəl/ v **1** to make a low heavy rolling sound **2** to reveal or discover the true character of – infml

umble n **1** a rumbling sound **2** NAm a street fight, esp between gangs – infml

umour /'ru:mə'/ n **1** a statement or report circulated without confirmation of its truth **2** talk or opinion widely disseminated but with no identifiable source

umour v to tell or spread by rumour

un /rʌn/ v ran; run **1a** to go faster than a walk; specif to go steadily by springing steps so that both feet leave the ground for an instant in each step **b** to flee, escape **2a** to contend in a race; also to finish a race in the specified place **b** to put forward as a candidate for office **3a** to move (as if) on wheels **b** to pass or slide freely or cursorily **4a** to slip through or past **b** to smuggle **5** to sing or play quickly **6a** to go back and forth; ply **b** of fish to ascend a river to spawn **7a** to function, operate **b** to carry on, manage, or control **8** to own and drive **9** to continue in force **10** to pass, esp by negligence or indulgence, into a specified state **11a(1)** to flow **(2)** to be full of; flow with **b** to discharge liquid **c** to melt **d** to spread, dissolve **12** to have a tendency; be prone **13a** to lie or extend in a specified position, direction, or relation to sthg **b** to extend in a continuous range **14** to occur persistently **15** to make oneself liable to **16** to carry in a printed medium; print **17** to spread quickly from point to point **18** to ladder

un n **1a** an act or the activity of running; continued rapid movement **b** the gait of a runner **c** (a school of fish) migrating or ascending a river to spawn **2a** the direction in which sthg (e g a vein of ore or the grain of wood) lies **b** general tendency or direction **3** a continuous series or unbroken course, esp of identical or similar things: e g **a** a rapid passage up or down a musical scale **b** an unbroken course of performances or showings **c** a persistent and heavy commercial or financial demand **4** the quantity of work turned out in a continuous operation **5** the average or prevailing kind or class **6a** the distance covered in a period of continuous journeying **b** a short excursion in a car **c** freedom of movement in or access to a place **7** an enclosure for domestic animals where they may feed or exercise **8a** an inclined course (e g for skiing) **b** a support or channel (e g a track, pipe, or trough) along which sthg runs **9** a unit of scoring in cricket made typically by each batsman running the full length of the wicket **10** a ladder (e g in a stocking)

rundown /'rʌndaʊn/ n an item-by-item report; a résumé

run-down adj **1** in a state of disrepair **2** in poor health

run down v **1** to knock down, esp with a motor vehicle **2a** to chase to exhaustion or until captured **b** to find by searching **3** to disparage **4** to allow the gradual decline or closure of **5** to cease to operate because of the exhaustion of motive power **6** to decline in physical condition

¹rung /rʌŋ/ past part of ring

²rung n **1a** a rounded part placed as a crosspiece between the legs of a chair **b** any of the crosspieces of a ladder **2** a level or stage in sthg that can be ascended

runner /'rʌnə'/ n **1** an entrant for a race who actually competes in it **2** sby who smuggles or distributes illicit or contraband goods – usu in combination **3** a straight piece on which sthg slides: e g **a** a longitudinal piece on which a sledge or ice skate slides **b** a groove or bar along which sthg (e g a drawer or sliding door) slides **4a** a long narrow carpet (e g for a hall or staircase) **b** a narrow decorative cloth for a table or dresser top

runner-up n a competitor other than the outright winner whose attainment still merits a prize

¹running /'rʌnɪŋ/ n **1** the state of competing, esp with a good chance of winning – in in/out of the running **2** management, operation

²running adj **1** runny **2a** having stages that follow in rapid succession **b** made during the course of a process or activity **3** being part of a continuous length **4** cursive, flowing

³running adv in succession

runway /'rʌnweɪ/ n an artificially surfaced strip of ground on an airfield for the landing and takeoff of aeroplanes

rural /'rʊərəl/ adj of the country, coun-

try people or life, or agriculture – ~ly
adv

¹rush /rʌʃ/ n any of various often tufted
marsh plants with cylindrical (hollow)
leaves, used for the seats of chairs and
for plaiting mats – **rushy** adj

²rush v 1 to push or impel forwards with
speed or violence 2 to perform or finish
in a short time or without adequate
preparation 3 to run against in attack,
often with an element of surprise

³rush n 1a a rapid and violent forward
motion b a sudden onset of emotion 2
a surge of activity; also busy or hurried
activity 3 a great movement of people,
esp in search of wealth 4 the unedited
print of a film scene processed directly
after shooting – usu pl

⁴rush adj requiring or marked by special
speed or urgency

¹rust /rʌst/ n 1 a brittle reddish coating
on iron, esp iron chemically attacked by
moist air 2 corrosive or injurious influence or effect 3 (a fungus causing) any
of numerous destructive diseases of
plants in which reddish brown blisters
form 4 a reddish brown to orange colour

²rust v 1 to form rust; become oxidized
2 to degenerate, esp through lack of use
or advancing age 3 to become reddish
brown as if with rust

¹rustle /'rʌsəl/ v 1a to make or cause a
rustle b to move with a rustling sound
2 chiefly NAm to steal cattle or
horses

²rustle n a quick succession or confusion
of faint sounds

rusty /'rʌsti/ adj 1 affected (as if) by
rust; esp stiff (as if) with rust 2 inept
and slow through lack of practice or
advanced age 3a of the colour rust b
dulled in colour by age and use; shabby
– **rustiness** n

S

¹sabotage /'sæbətɑːʒ/ n 1 destructive
or obstructive action carried on by a
civilian or enemy agent, intended to
hinder military activity 2 deliberate
subversion (e g of a plan or project)

²sabotage v to practise sabotage on
– **-teur** n

¹sack /sæk/ n 1a a usu rectangular large
bag (e g of paper or canvas) 2a garment
without shaping; esp a loosely fitting
dress 3 dismissal from employment –
usu + get or give + the; infml

²sack v to dismiss from a job – infml

³sack n any of various dry white wines
formerly imported to England from S
Europe

⁴sack n the plundering of a place captured in war

⁵sack v 1 to plunder (e g a town) after
capture 2 to strip (a place) of valuables

sacred /'seikrɪd/ adj 1 dedicated or set

apart for the service or worship of a god
or gods 2a worthy of religious veneration b commanding reverence and
respect 3 of religion; not secular or
profane – ~ly adv – ~ness n

¹sacrifice /'sækrɪfaɪs/ n 1 an act of
offering to a deity; esp the killing of a
victim on an altar 2a destruction or
surrender of one thing for the sake of
another of greater worth or importance
b sthg given up or lost – **-ficial** adj

²sacrifice v 1 to offer as a sacrifice 2 to
give up or lose for the sake of an ideal
or end

sacrilege /'sækrɪlɪdʒ/ n 1 a violation
of what is sacred 2 gross irreverence
toward sby or sthg sacred – **-legious** adj
– **-legiously** adv

sad /sæd/ adj 1a affected with or
expressing unhappiness b deplorable,
regrettable 2 of a dull sombre colour 3
of baked goods heavy – ~ly adv
– ~ness n

sadden /'sædn/ v to make or become
sad

¹saddle /'sædl/ n 1a a usu padded and
leather-covered seat secured to the back
of a horse, donkey, etc for the rider to
sit on b a seat in certain types of
vehicles (e g a bicycle or agricultural
tractor) 2a ridge connecting 2 peaks 3
a large cut of meat from a sheep, hare,
rabbit, deer, etc consisting of both sides
of the unsplit back including both
loins

²saddle v to encumber

sadism /'seidizəm/ n a sexual perversion in which pleasure is obtained by
inflicting physical or mental pain on
others; broadly delight in inflicting pain
– **sadist** n – **sadistic** adj – **sadistically**
adv

¹safari /sə'fɑːri/ n (the caravan and
equipment of) a hunting or scientific
expedition, esp in E Africa

²safari adj made of lightweight material,
esp cotton, and typically having 2 breast
pockets and a belt

safe /seif/ adj 1 freed from harm or risk
2 secure from threat of danger, harm, or
loss 3 affording safety from danger 4a
not threatening or entailing danger b
unlikely to cause controversy 5a not
liable to take risks b trustworthy, reliable – ~ly adv – ~ness n

²safe n 1 a room or receptacle for the
safe storage of valuables 2 a receptacle,
esp a cupboard, for the temporary storage of fresh and cooked foods that typically has at least 1 side of wire mesh to
allow ventilation while preventing flies
from entering

safety /'seifti/ n the condition of being
safe from causing or suffering hurt,
injury, or loss

¹sag /sæg/ v 1 to droop, sink, or settle
(as if) from weight, pressure, or loss of
tautness 2 to lose firmness or vigour 3
to fail to stimulate or retain interest

²sag n 1a sagging part 2 an instance or
amount of sagging

said /sed/ adj aforementioned

¹sail /seil/ n 1 an expanse of fabric
which is spread to catch or deflect the

wind as a means of propelling a ship, sand yacht, etc **2** a voyage by ship

sail v **1** to travel in a boat or ship **2a** to travel on water, esp by the action of wind on sails **b** to move without visible effort or in a stately manner **3** to begin a journey by water

sailor /ˈseɪlə/ n **1a** a seaman, mariner **b** a member of a ship's crew other than an officer **2** a traveller by water; esp one considered with reference to any tendency to seasickness

saint /seɪnt/ n **1** a person officially recognized through canonization as being outstandingly holy and so worthy of veneration **2** any of the spirits of the departed in heaven **b** an angel **3** a person of exceptional piety or virtue – ~**ly** adj – ~**liness** n

sake /seɪk/ n **1** the purpose of – in for the sake of **2** interest, benefit or advantage – in for someone's/something's sake

sake, saki /ˈsɑːki/ n a Japanese alcoholic drink of fermented rice

salad /ˈsæləd/ n **1a** (mixed) raw vegetables (e g lettuce, watercress, or tomato) often served with a dressing **b** a dish of raw or (cold) cooked foods often cut into small pieces and combined with a dressing **2** a vegetable or herb eaten raw (in salad); esp lettuce

salary /ˈsæləri/ n a fixed usu monthly payment for regular services, esp of a nonmanual kind

sale /seɪl/ n **1** the act or an instance of selling **2** quantity sold – often pl with sing. meaning **3** an event at which goods are offered for sale **4** public disposal to the highest bidder **5** a selling of goods at bargain prices **6a** pl operations and activities involved in promoting and selling goods or services **b** gross receipts obtained from selling

sales /seɪlz/ adj of, engaged in, or used in selling

saliva /səˈlaɪvə/ n a liquid secreted into the mouth by glands that lubricates ingested food and often begins the breakdown of starches – **-vary** adj

salmon /ˈsæmən/ n **1** (any of various fishes related to) a large soft-finned game and food fish of the N Atlantic that is highly valued for its pink flesh **2** an orangy-pink colour

saloon /səˈluːn/ n **1a** a stately apartment or hall (e g a ballroom, exhibition room, or shipboard social area) **2** Br an enclosed motor car having no partition between the driver and passengers **3** NAm a room or establishment in which alcoholic beverages are sold and consumed

salt /sɔːlt/ n **1a** sodium chloride, occurring naturally esp as a mineral deposit and dissolved in sea water, and used esp for seasoning or preserving **b** any of numerous compounds resulting from replacement of (part of) the hydrogen ion of an acid by a (radical acting like a) metal **c** pl (**1**) a mixture of the salts of alkali metals or magnesium (e g Epsom salts) used as a purgative (**2**) smelling salts **2a** an ingredient that

imparts savour, piquancy, or zest **b** sharpness of wit **3** an experienced sailor

²**salt** v **1** to treat, provide, season, or preserve with common salt or brine **2** to give flavour or piquancy to (e g a story)

³**salt** adj **1a** saline, salty **b** being or inducing a taste similar to that of common salt that is one of the 4 basic taste sensations **2** cured or seasoned with salt; salted **3** containing, overflowed by, or growing in salt water **4** sharp, pungent – ~**ness** n

salty /ˈsɔːlti/ adj **1** of, seasoned with, or containing salt **2** having a taste of (too much) salt **3a** piquant, witty **b** earthy, coarse – **saltiness** n

¹**salute** /səˈluːt/ v **1** to address with expressions of greeting, goodwill, or respect **2a** to honour by a conventional military or naval ceremony **b** to show respect and recognition to (a military superior) by assuming a prescribed position

²**salute** n **1** a greeting, salutation **2a** a sign or expression conveying goodwill or respect **b** an act of saluting a military superior; also the position (e g of the hand or weapon) or the entire attitude of a person saluting a superior

¹**salvage** /ˈsælvɪdʒ/ n **1a** compensation paid to those who save property from loss or damage; esp compensation paid for saving a ship from wreckage or capture **b** the act of saving or rescuing a ship or its cargo **c** the act of saving or rescuing property in danger (e g from fire) **2a** property saved from a calamity (e g a wreck or fire) **b** sthg of use or value extracted from waste material

²**salvage** v to rescue or save (e g from wreckage or ruin)

salvation /sælˈveɪʃən/ n **1** deliverance from the power and effects of sin **2** deliverance from danger, difficulty, or destruction

¹**same** /seɪm/ adj **1** being 1 single thing, person, or group; identical – often as an intensive (e g born in this very same house) **2** being the specified one or ones – + as or that **3** corresponding so closely as to be indistinguishable

²**same** pron, pl **same 1** the same thing, person, or group (e g do the same for you) **2** sthg previously mentioned (e g ordered a drink and refused to pay for same)

³**same** adv in the same manner – + the

¹**sample** /ˈsɑːmpəl/ n **1** an item serving to show the character or quality of a larger whole or group **2** a part of a statistical population whose properties are studied to gain information about the whole

²**sample** v to take a sample of or from; esp to test the quality of by a sample

³**sample** adj intended as an example

¹**sanction** /ˈsæŋkʃən/ n **1** a penalty annexed to an offence **2a** a consideration that determines moral action or judgment **b** a mechanism of social control (e g shame) for enforcing a society's standards **c** official permission or

authoritative ratification **3** an economic or military coercive measure adopted to force a nation to conform to international law

²**sanction** v **1** to make valid; ratify **2** to give authoritative consent to

sanctuary /'sæŋktʃʊəri/ n **1** a consecrated place: e g **a** the ancient temple at Jerusalem or its holy of holies **b** the part of a Christian church in which the altar is placed **2a** a place of refuge and protection **b** a refuge for (endangered) wildlife where predators are controlled and hunting is illegal

¹**sand** /sænd/ n **1** loose granular particles smaller than gravel and coarser than silt that result from the disintegration of (silica-rich) rocks **2** an area of sand; a beach – usu pl with sing. meaning **3** moments of time measured (as if) with an hourglass – usu pl with sing. meaning **4** a yellowish grey colour

²**sand** v **1** to sprinkle (as if) with sand **2** to cover or choke with sand – usu + up **3** to smooth or dress by grinding or rubbing with an abrasive (e g sandpaper) – often + down

sandal /'sændl/ n a shoe consisting of a sole held on to the foot by straps or thongs

¹**sandwich** /'sænwɪdʒ/ n **1a** two slices of usu buttered bread containing a layer of filling **b** a sponge cake containing a filling **2** sthg like a sandwich in having a layered or banded arrangement

²**sandwich** v **1** to insert between 2 things of a different quality or character **2** to create room or time for – often + in or between

³**sandwich** adj **1** of or used for sandwiches **2** Br of a sandwich course

sandy /'sændi/ adj **1** consisting of, containing, or sprinkled with sand **2** resembling sand in colour or texture – **sandiness** n

sane /sein/ adj mentally sound; able to anticipate and appraise the effect of one's actions – ~**ly** adv – -**ity** n

sang /sæŋ/ past of **sing**

sank /sæŋk/ past of **sink**

¹**sap** /sæp/ n **1a** a watery solution that circulates through a plant's vascular system **b** (a fluid essential to life or) bodily health and vigour **2** a foolish gullible person – infml

²**sap** n the extension of a trench from within the trench itself to a point near an enemy's fortifications

³**sap** v **1** to destroy (as if) by undermining **2** to weaken or exhaust gradually **3** to operate against or pierce by a sap

sarcasm /'sɑːkæzəm/ n (the use of) caustic and often ironic language to express contempt or bitterness, esp towards an individual – -**castic** adj – -**castically** adv

¹**sash** /sæʃ/ n a band of cloth worn round the waist or over 1 shoulder as a dress accessory or as the emblem of an honorary or military order

²**sash** n, pl **sash** also **sashes** the framework in which panes of glass are set in a window or door; also such a frame-

work forming a sliding part of a window

sat /sæt/ past of **sit**

satellite /'sætəlaɪt/ n **1** an obsequious follower **2a** a celestial body orbiting another of larger size **b** a man-made object or vehicle intended to orbit a celestial body **3** a country subject to another more powerful country **4** an urban community that is physically separate from an adjacent city but dependent on it

¹**satin** /'sætɪn/ n a fabric (e g of silk) with lustrous face and dull back

²**satin** adj **1** made of satin **2** like satin, esp in lustrous appearance or smoothness

satire /'sætaɪə/ n **1** a literary work holding up human vices and follies to ridicule or scorn **2** biting wit, irony, or sarcasm intended to expose foolishness or vice – -**rical** adj – -**rize** v

satisfaction /,sætɪs'fækʃən/ n **1a** fulfilment of a need or want **b** being satisfied **c** a source of pleasure or fulfilment **2a** compensation for a loss, insult, or injury **b** vindication of one's honour, esp through a duel **3** full assurance or certainty

satisfactory /,sætɪs'fæktəri/ adj satisfying needs or requirements; adequate – -**rily** adv

satisfy /'sætɪsfaɪ/ v **1a** to discharge; carry out **2a** to make content **b** to meet the requirements of **3** to convince **4** to conform to (e g criteria) – ~**ing** adj

saturate /'sætʃəreɪt/ v **1** to treat or provide with sthg to the point where no more can be absorbed, dissolved, or retained **2** to cause to combine chemically until there is no further tendency to combine

Saturday /'sætədi, -deɪ/ n the day of the week following Friday

¹**sauce** /sɔːs/ n **1** a liquid or soft preparation used as a relish, dressing, or accompaniment to food **2** sthg adding zest or piquancy **3** cheek – infml

²**sauce** v to be impudent to – infml

saucepan /'sɔːspən/ n a deep usu cylindrical cooking pan typically having a long handle and a lid

saucer /'sɔːsə/ n **1** a small usu circular shallow dish with a central depression in which a cup is set **2** a flying saucer

sausage /'sɒsɪdʒ/ n (sthg shaped like) a fresh, precooked, or dried cylindrical mass of seasoned minced pork or other meat often mixed with a filler (e g bread) and enclosed in a casing usu of prepared animal intestine

¹**savage** /'sævɪdʒ/ adj **1** not domesticated or under human control; untamed **2** rugged, rough **3** boorish, rude **4** lacking a developed culture – now usu taken to be offensive – ~**ly** adv – ~**ness**, ~**ry** n

²**savage** n **1** a member of a primitive society **2** a brutal, rude, or unmannerly person

³**savage** v to attack or treat brutally; esp to maul

¹**save** /seɪv/ v **1** to rescue from danger or

harm **2a** to put aside as a store or for a particular use – usu + *up* **b** to economize in the use of; conserve **3a** to make unnecessary **b** to prevent an opponent from scoring, winning, or scoring with – ~**r** *n*

save *prep* except – chiefly *fml*

save *conj* were it not; only – chiefly *fml*

saving /'seɪʋɪŋ/ *n* **1** preservation from danger or destruction **2** sthg saved **3a** *pl* money put by over a period of time **b** the excess of income over expenditures – often *pl*

saving *prep* **1** except, save **2** without disrespect to

saviour /'seɪvjə/ *NAm chiefly* **savior** *n* **1** one who brings salvation; *specif, cap* Jesus **2** one who saves sby or sthg from danger or destruction

saw /sɔː/ *past of* **see**

saw *n* a hand or power tool with a toothed part (e g a blade or disc) used to cut wood, metal, bone, etc

saw *v* **sawed, sawn 1** to cut or shape with a saw **2** to make motions as though using a saw

saw *n* a maxim, proverb

say /seɪ/ *v* **says; said 1a** to state in spoken words **1b** to form an opinion as to **2** to utter, pronounce **3a** to indicate, show **b** to give expression to; communicate **4a** to suppose, assume **b** to allege – usu *pass*

say *n* **1** an expression of opinion – esp in *have one's say* **2** a right or power to influence action or decisions; *esp* the authority to make final decisions

say *adv* **1** at a rough estimate **2** for example

saying /'seɪ-ɪŋ/ *n* a maxim, proverb

scab /skæb/ *n* **1** scabies of domestic animals **2** a crust of hardened blood and serum over a wound **3** a blackleg **4** any of various plant diseases characterized by crusted spots; *also* any of these spots

scab *v* to act as a scab

scaffold /'skæfəld, -fəʊld/ *n* a platform on which a criminal is executed

scaffolding /'skæfəldɪŋ/ *n* **1** a supporting framework **2** a temporary platform for workmen working above the ground

scald /skɔːld/ *v* **1** to burn (as if) with hot liquid or steam **2a** to subject to boiling water or steam **b** to heat to just short of boiling

scald *n* an injury to the body caused by scalding

scale /skeɪl/ *n* **1a** either pan of a balance **b** a beam that is supported freely in the centre and has 2 pans of equal weight suspended from its ends **2** an instrument or machine for weighing *USE* (*1b, 2*) usu *pl* with sing. meaning

scale *n* **1** (a small thin plate resembling) a small flattened rigid plate forming part of the external body covering of a fish, reptile, etc **2** a small thin dry flake shed from the skin **3** a thin coating, layer, or incrustation; *esp* a hard incrustation usu of calcium sulphate or car-

bonate that is deposited on the inside of a kettle, boiler, etc by the evaporation or constant passage of hard water **4** a usu thin, membranous, chaffy, or woody modified leaf

³scale *v* **1** to cover with scale **2** to shed or separate or come off in scales; flake

⁴scale *n* **1** a graduated series of musical notes ascending or descending in order of pitch according to a specified scheme of their intervals **2** sthg graduated, esp when used as a measure or rule: e g **a** a linear region divided by lines into a series of spaces and used to register or record sthg (e g the height of mercury in a barometer) **b** a graduated line on a map or chart indicating the length used to represent a larger unit of measure **c** an instrument having a scale for measuring or marking off distances or dimensions **3** a graduated system **4** a proportion between 2 sets of dimensions (e g between those of a drawing and its original) **5** a graded series of tests

⁵scale *v* **1** to climb up or reach (as if) by means of a ladder **2a** to change the scale of **b** to pattern, make, regulate, set, or estimate according to some rate or standard *USE* (*2*) often + *up* or *down*

¹scalp /skælp/ *n* **1** the skin of the human head, usu covered with hair in both sexes **2a** a part of the human scalp with attached hair cut or torn from an enemy as a trophy, esp formerly by N American Indian warriors **b** a trophy of victory

²scalp *v* **1** to remove the scalp of **2** *NAm* **a** to buy and sell to make small quick profits **b** to obtain speculatively and resell at greatly increased prices *USE* (*2*) *infml*

¹scamper /'skæmpə/ *v* to run about nimbly and playfully

²scamper *n* a playful scurry

¹scan /skæn/ *v* **1** to check or read hastily or casually **2a** to traverse (a region) with a controlled beam (e g radar) **b** to make a detailed examination of (e g the human body) using any of a variety of sensing devices (e g ones using ultrasonics, thermal radiation, X-rays, or radiation from radioactive materials) **3** of *verse* to conform to a metrical pattern

²scan *n* **1** a scanning **2** a radar or television trace

scandal /'skændl/ *n* **1** a circumstance or action that causes general offence or indignation or that disgraces those associated with it **2** malicious or defamatory gossip **3** indignation, chagrin, or bewilderment brought about by a flagrant violation of propriety or religious opinion – **-ize** *v*

scandalous /'skændələs/ *adj* **1** libellous, defamatory **2** offensive to propriety – ~**ly** *adv*

scanty /'skænti/ *adj* scant; *esp* deficient in coverage – **-tily** *adv* – **-tiness** *n*

scapegoat /'skeɪpgəʊt/ *n* sby or sthg made to bear the blame for others' faults

¹scar /skɑː'/ n a steep rocky place on a mountainside

²scar n 1 a mark left (e g on the skin) by the healing of injured tissue 2 a mark left on a stem after the fall of a leaf 3 a mark of damage or wear 4 a lasting moral or emotional injury

³scar v to do lasting injury to

scarce /skeəs/ adj 1 not plentiful or abundant 2 few in number; rare

scarcely /'skeəsli/ adv 1a by a narrow margin; only just b almost not 2 not without unpleasantness or discourtesy

¹scare /skeə'/ v 1 to frighten suddenly 2 to drive off by frightening – **~d** adj

²scare n 1 a sudden or unwarranted fright 2 a widespread state of alarm or panic

¹scarf /skɑːf/ n, pl **scarves** a strip or square of cloth worn round the shoulders or neck or over the head for decoration or warmth

²scarf n, pl **scarfs** 1 either of the chamfered or cut away ends that fit together to form a scarf joint 2 **scarf, scarf joint** a joint made by chamfering, halving, or notching 2 pieces to correspond and lapping and bolting them

³scarf, scarph v 1 to unite by a scarf joint 2 to form a scarf on

scarlet /'skɑːlɪt/ adj or n (of) a vivid red colour tinged with orange

scatter /'skætə'/ v 1 to cause (a group or collection) to separate widely 2a to distribute at irregular intervals b to distribute recklessly or at random 3 to sow (seed) by casting in all directions 4 to reflect or disperse (e g a beam of radiation or particles) irregularly and diffusely – **scatter** n

scene /siːn/ n 1 any of the smaller subdivisions of a dramatic work: e g a a division of an act presenting continuous action in 1 place b an episode, sequence, or unit of dialogue in a play, film, or television programme 2 a vista suggesting a stage setting 3 the place of an occurrence or action 4 an exhibition of unrestrained feeling 5 a sphere of activity or interest – slang

scenery /'siːnəri/ n 1 the painted scenes or hangings and accessories used on a theatre stage 2 landscape, esp when considered attractive

¹scent /sent/ v 1 to get or have an inkling of 2 to fill with a usu pleasant smell

²scent n 1 odour: e g a a smell left by an animal on a surface it passes over b a characteristic or particular, esp agreeable, smell c a perfume 2a power of smelling; sense of smell b power of detection; a nose 3 a course of pursuit or discovery 4 a hint, suggestion – **~less** adj

sceptical /'skeptɪkəl/ adj relating to, characteristic of, or marked by scepticism – **~ly** adv

¹schedule /'ʃedjuːl/ n 1 a statement of supplementary details appended to a document 2 a list, catalogue, or inventory 3 (the times fixed in) a timetable 4

a programme, proposal 5 a body of items to be dealt with

²schedule v 1a to place on a schedule b to make a schedule of 2 to appoint or designate for a fixed time 3 Br to place on a list of buildings or historical remains protected by state legislation

¹scheme /skiːm/ n 1 a concise statement or table 2 a plan or programme of action; a project 3 a crafty or secret strategy 4 a systematic arrangement of parts or elements

²scheme v to make plans; also to plot, intrigue – **schemer** n

scholar /'skɒlə'/ n 1 one who attends a school or studies under a teacher 2 one who has done advanced study 3 the holder of a scholarship

school /skuːl/ n 1a an institution for the teaching of children b a part of a university c an establishment offering specialized instruction d NAm a college, university 2a a session of a school b a school building 3a people with a common doctrine or teacher (e g in philosophy or theology) b a group of artists under a common stylistic influence 4 a body of people with similar opinions

²school v 1 to educate in an institution of learning 2a to teach or drill in a specific knowledge or skill b to discipline or habituate to sthg

³school n a large number of fish or aquatic animals of 1 kind swimming together

⁴school v to swim or feed in a school

science /'saɪəns/ n 1a a department of systematized knowledge b sthg (e g a skill) that may be learned systematically c any of the natural sciences 2a coordinated knowledge of the operation of general laws, esp as obtained and tested through scientific method b such knowledge of the physical world and its phenomena; natural science 3 a system or method (purporting to be) based on scientific principles – **scientist** n

scientific /ˌsaɪən'tɪfɪk/ adj of or exhibiting the methods of science – **~ally** adv

scissors /'sɪzəz/ n pl a cutting instrument with 2 blades pivoted so that their cutting edges slide past each other

¹scoff /skɒf/ n an expression of scorn, derision, or contempt – **~er** n

²scoff v to show contempt by derisive acts or language – often + at

³scoff vt, chiefly Br to eat, esp greedily, rapidly, or in an ill-mannered way – infml

¹scold /skəʊld/ n a woman who habitually nags or quarrels

²scold v 1 to find fault noisily and at length 2 to reprove sharply – **~ing** n

¹scoop /skuːp/ n 1a a large ladle for taking up or skimming liquids b a deep shovel for lifting and moving granular material (e g corn or sand) c a handled utensil of shovel shape or with a hemispherical bowl for spooning out soft food (e g ice cream) 2a an act or the action of scooping b the amount held by a scoop 3 a cavity 4 material for publication or broadcast, esp when obtained ahead or to the exclusion of competitors

scoop v 1 to take out or up (as if) with a scoop 2 to empty by scooping 3 to make hollow; dig out 4 to obtain a news story in advance or to the exclusion of (a competitor)

scope /skəʊp/ n 1 space or opportunity for unhampered action, thought, or development 2a extent of treatment, activity, or influence b extent of understanding or perception

scope n a periscope, telescope, or other optical instrument – infml

scorch /skɔːtʃ/ v 1 to burn so as to produce a change in colour and texture 2a to parch (as if) with intense heat b to criticize or deride bitterly 3 to devastate completely, esp before abandoning – used in scorched earth, of property of possible use to an enemy 4 to travel at (excessive) speed

scorch n a mark resulting from scorching

score /skɔː/ n 1a twenty b a group of 20 things – used in combination with a cardinal number c pl an indefinite large number 2 a line (eg a scratch or incision) made (as if) with a sharp instrument 3 an account of debts 4 a grudge 5a a reason, ground b a subject, topic 6a the copy of a musical composition in written or printed notation b the music for a film or theatrical production 7a a number that expresses accomplishment (eg in a game or test) b an act (eg a goal, run, or try) in any of various games or contests that increases such a number 8 the inescapable facts of a situation

score v 1a to enter (a debt) in an account – usu + to or against b to cancel or strike out (eg a record of a debt) with a line or notch – often + out 2 to mark with grooves, scratches, or notches 3a(1) to gain (e g points) in a game or contest (2) to have as a value in a game or contest b to gain, win c to gain or have an advantage or a success d to obtain illicit drugs – slang e to achieve a sexual success – slang 4 to write or arrange (music) for specific voice or instrumental parts

scorn /skɔːn/ n 1 vigorous contempt; disdain 2 an object of extreme disdain or derision – ~ful adj – ~fully adv

scorn v to reject with outspoken contempt

scorpion /ˈskɔːpɪən/ n any of an order of arachnids having an elongated body and a narrow tail bearing a venomous sting at the tip

scourge /skɜːdʒ/ n 1 a means of vengeance or criticism 2 a cause of affliction

scourge v 1 to punish severely 2 to subject to affliction; devastate

scout /skaʊt/ v 1 to observe or explore in order to obtain information 2 to find by making a search – often + out or up

scout n 1 sby or sthg sent to obtain (military) information 2 often cap a

member of a worldwide movement of boys and young men that was founded with the aim of developing leadership and comradeship and that lays stress on outdoor activities

scowl /skaʊl/ v 1 to frown or wrinkle the brows in expression of displeasure 2 to exhibit a gloomy or threatening aspect

scowl n an angry frown

scramble /ˈskræmbəl/ v 1a to move or climb using hands and feet, esp hastily b to move with urgency or panic 2 to struggle eagerly or chaotically for possession of sthg 3a to toss or mix together b to prepare (eggs) in a pan by stirring during cooking 4 esp of an aircraft or its crew to take off quickly in response to an alert 5 to collect by scrambling – + up or together 6 to encode (the elements of a telecommunications transmission) in order to make unintelligible on unmodified receivers

scramble n 1 a scrambling movement or struggle 2 a disordered mess; a jumble 3 a rapid emergency takeoff of aircraft 4 a motorcycle race over very rough ground

scrap /skræp/ n 1 pl fragments of leftover food 2a a small detached fragment b the smallest piece 3a the residue from a manufacturing process b manufactured articles or parts, esp of metal, rejected or discarded and useful only for reprocessing

scrap v 1 to convert into scrap 2 to abandon or get rid of, as without further use

scrap v or n (to engage in) a minor fight or dispute – infml

scrape /skreɪp/ v 1a to remove (clinging matter) from a surface by usu repeated strokes of an edged instrument b to make (a surface) smooth or clean with strokes of an edged or rough instrument 2 to grate harshly over or against 3 to collect or procure (as if) by scraping – often + up or together 4 to get by with difficulty or succeed by a narrow margin – often + in, through, or by

scrape n 1a an act, process, or result of scraping b the sound of scraping 2 a disagreeable predicament, esp as a result of foolish behaviour – infml

scratch /skrætʃ/ v 1 to use the claws or nails in digging, tearing, or wounding 2 to scrape or rub oneself (e g to relieve itching) 3 to acquire money by hard work and saving 4 to make a thin grating sound 5 to withdraw (an entry) from competition

scratch n 1 a mark, injury, or slight wound (produced by scratching) 2 the sound of scratching 3 the most rudimentary beginning – in from scratch 4 standard or satisfactory condition or performance

scratch adj 1 arranged or put together haphazardly or hastily 2 without handicap or allowance

scrawl /skrɔːl/ v to write or draw awkwardly, hastily, or carelessly – scrawl n

¹scream /skri:m/ *v* **1a** to voice a sudden piercing cry, esp in alarm or pain **b** to move with or make a shrill noise like a scream **2** to produce a vivid or startling effect

²scream *n* **1** a shrill penetrating cry or noise **2** sby or sthg that provokes screams of laughter – infml

¹screech /skri:tʃ/ *v* **1** to utter a shrill piercing cry; cry out, esp in terror or pain **2** to make a sound like a screech

²screech *n* a shrill sound or cry

¹screen /skri:n/ *n* **1** a usu movable piece of furniture that gives protection from heat or draughts or is used as an ornament **2a** sthg that shelters, protects, or conceals **b** a shield for secret usu illicit practices **3** a frame holding a netting used esp in a window or door to exclude mosquitoes and other pests **4a** a surface on which images are projected or reflected **b** the surface on which the image appears in a television or radar receiver **5a** *the* films industry; films

²screen *v* **1** to guard from injury, danger, or punishment **2** to examine systematically so as to separate into different groups **3** to show or broadcast a film or television programme

¹screw /skru:/ *n* **1a** a usu pointed tapering metal rod having a raised thread along all or part of its length and a usu slotted head which may be driven into a body by rotating (e g with a screwdriver) **b** a screw-bolt that can be turned by a screwdriver **2** sthg like a screw in form or function; a spiral **3** a propeller **4** *chiefly Br* a small twisted paper packet (e g of tobacco) **5** sby who drives a hard bargain – slang **6** a prison guard – slang **7** an act of sexual intercourse – vulg

²screw *v* **1a** to attach, close, operate, adjust, etc by means of a screw **b** to unite or separate by means of a screw or a twisting motion **2a** to contort (the face) or narrow (the eyes) (e g with effort or an emotion) – often + *up* **b** to crush into irregular folds – usu + *up* **3** to increase the intensity, quantity, or effectiveness of – usu + *up* **4a** to make oppressive demands on **b** to extract by pressure or threat – usu + *from* or *out of* **5** to copulate with – vulg

screwdriver /ˈskruːˌdraɪvə/ *n* a tool for turning screws

scribble /ˈskrɪbəl/ *v* to write or draw without regard for legibility or coherence – **scribble** *n*

¹script /skrɪpt/ *n* **1a** sthg written; text **b** an original document **c** the written text of a stage play, film, or broadcast (used in production or performance) **2a** (printed lettering resembling) handwriting **b** the characters used in the alphabet of a particular language

²script *v* to prepare a script for or from

¹scrub /skrʌb/ *n* (an area covered with) vegetation consisting chiefly of stunted trees or shrubs

²scrub *v* **1** to clean by rubbing, esp with

a stiff brush **2** to abolish; do away with *also* to cancel – infml

scrupulous /ˈskruːpjʊləs/ *adj* **1** inclined to have moral scruples **2** painstakingly exact – ~**ly** *adv* – ~**ness** *n*

scrutiny /ˈskruːtɪni/ *n* **1** a searching study, inquiry, or inspection **2** a searching or critical look **3** close watch – **-nize** *v*

sculptor /ˈskʌlptə/, *fem* **sculptress** *n* an artist who sculptures

¹sculpture /ˈskʌlptʃə/ *n* **1** the art of creating three-dimensional works of art out of mouldable or hard materials by carving, modelling, casting, etc **2** (a piece of) work produced by sculpture – **-ral** *adj*

²sculpture *v* **1a** to represent in sculpture **b** to form (e g wood or stone) into a sculpture **2** to shape (as if) by carving or moulding

scum /skʌm/ *n* **1** pollutants or impurities risen to or collected on the surface of a liquid **2** *pl in constr* the lowest class; the dregs

sea /si:/ *n* **1** an ocean; *broadly* the waters of the earth as distinguished from the land and air **2** sthg vast or overwhelming likened to the sea **3** the seafaring life **4** any of several dark areas on the surface of the moon or Mars

seafood /ˈsiːfuːd/ *n* edible marine fish, shellfish, crustaceans, etc

¹seal /si:l/ *n* **1** any of numerous marine flesh-eating mammals chiefly of cold regions with limbs modified into webbed flippers for swimming **2** sealskin

²seal *n* **1a** an emblem or word impressed or stamped on a document as a mark of authenticity **b** an article used to impress such a word or emblem (e g on wax); *also* a disc, esp of wax, bearing such an impression **2a** a closure (e g a wax seal on a document or a strip of paper over the cork of a bottle) that must be broken in order to give access, and so guarantees that the item so closed has not been tampered with **b** a tight and effective closure (e g against gas or liquid)

⁴seal *v* **1** to confirm or make secure (as if) by a seal **2** to attach an authenticating seal to; *also* to authenticate, ratify **3** to close or make secure against access, leakage, or passage by a fastening or coating; *esp* to make airtight **4** to determine irrevocably

¹seam /si:m/ *n* **1** a line of stitching joining 2 separate pieces of fabric, esp along their edges **2** a line, groove, or ridge formed at the meeting of 2 edges **3** a layer or stratum of coal, rock, etc – ~**less** *adj*

²seam *v* **1** to join (as if) by sewing **2** to mark with a seam, furrow, or scar

seaman /ˈsiːmən/ *n* **1** a sailor, mariner **2** a member of the navy holdng any of the lowest group of ranks below Petty Officer

¹search /sɜːtʃ/ *v* **1a** to look through or over carefully or thoroughly in order to find or discover sthg **b** to examine (a person) for concealed articles (e g weapons or drugs) **c** to scrutinize, esp in order to discover intention or nature **2** to uncover or ascertain by investigation – usu + *out* – ~**er** *n*

search *n* **1** an act or process of searching; *esp* an organized act of searching **2** an exercise of the right of search

searching /'sɜːtʃɪŋ/ *adj* piercing, penetrating – ~**ly** *adv*

seashore /'siːʃɔː/ *n* land (between high and low water marks) next to the sea

seaside /'siːsaɪd/ *n* (a holiday resort or beach on) land bordering the sea

season /'siːzən/ *n* **1** any of the 4 quarters into which the year is commonly divided **2** a period characterized by a particular kind of weather **3** the time of year when a place is most frequented

season *v* **1** to give (food) more flavour by adding seasoning or savoury ingredients **2a** to treat or expose (e g timber) over a period so as to prepare for use **b** to make fit or expert by experience

seat /siːt/ *n* **1a** a piece of furniture (e g a chair, stool, or bench) for sitting on or on **b** the part of sthg on which one rests when sitting; *also* the buttocks **2a** a special chair (e g a throne) of sby in authority; *also* the status symbolized by it **b** a large country mansion **3a** a place where sthg is established or practised **b** a place from which authority is exercised **4** a bodily part in which a particular function, disease, etc is centred **5** posture in or a way of sitting on horseback

seat *v* **1a** to cause to sit or assist in finding a seat **b** to put (e g oneself) in a sitting position **2** to fit to or with a seat **3** , *of a garment* to become baggy in the area covering the buttocks

seaweed /'siːwiːd/ *n* (an abundant growth of) a plant, specif an alga, growing in the sea, typically having thick slimy fronds

secluded /sɪ'kluːdɪd/ *adj* **1** screened or hidden from view **2** living in isolation – –**usion** *n*

'second /'sekənd/ *adj* **1a** next to the first in place or time **b**(1) next to the first in value, quality, or degree (2) inferior, subordinate **c** standing next below the top in authority or importance **2** alternate, other **3** resembling or suggesting a prototype **4** being the forward gear or speed 1 higher than first in a motor vehicle

'second *n* **1a** 2nd **b** sthg that is next after the first in rank, position, authority, or precedence **2** sby who aids, supports, or stands in for another; *esp* the assistant of a duellist or boxer **3** a slightly flawed or inferior article (e g of merchandise) **4a** a place next below the first in a contest **b** *also* **second class** *often cap* the second level of British honours degree **5** the second forward gear or speed of a motor vehicle **6** *pl a* second helping of food – *infml*

'second *n* **1** a 60th part of a minute of time or of a minute of angular measure **2** a moment

'second /sɪ'kɒnd/ *v* **1** to give support or encouragement to **2** to endorse (a motion or nomination) – ~**er** *n* – ~**ment** *n*

'second /sɪ'kɒnd/ *v* to release (e g a teacher, businessman, or military officer) from a regularly assigned position for temporary duty with another organization

secondary /'sekəndəri/ *adj* **1** of second rank or importance **2** immediately derived from sthg primary or basic; derivative **3a** not first in order of occurrence or development **b** of the second order or stage in a series or sequence

'secondhand /ˌsekənd'hænd/ *adj* **1** not original; derivative **2** acquired after being owned by another

'secondhand /ˌsekənd'hænd/ *adv* indirectly; at second hand

secrecy /'siːkrɪsi/ *n* **1** the habit or practice of keeping secrets or maintaining privacy or concealment **2** the condition of being hidden or concealed

'secret /'siːkrɪt/ *adj* **1a** kept or hidden from knowledge or view **b** conducted in secret **2** revealed only to the initiated; esoteric **3** containing information whose unauthorized disclosure could endanger national security – ~**ly** *adv*

'secret *n* **1** sthg kept hidden or unexplained **2** a fact concealed from others or shared confidentially with a few

secretary /'sekrətəri/ *n* **1** sby employed to handle correspondence and manage routine work for a superior **2** an officer of an organization or society responsible for its records and correspondence **3** an officer of state who superintends a government administrative department – –**rial** *adj*

secretive /'siːkrɪtɪv, sɪ'kriːtɪv/ *adj* inclined to secrecy; not open or outgoing in speech or behaviour – ~**ly** *adv* – ~**ness** *n*

'section /'sekʃən/ *n* **1** the action or an instance of (separating by) cutting; *esp* the action of dividing sthg (e g tissues) surgically **2a** a distinct part or portion of sthg written; *esp* a subdivision of a chapter **3** the profile of sthg as it would appear if cut through by an intersecting plane **4** a distinct part of an area, community, or group **5** *sing or pl in constr* a subdivision of a platoon, troop, or battery that is the smallest tactical military unit **6** any of several component parts that may be separated and reassembled **7** a division of an orchestra composed of 1 class of instruments

'section *v* **1** to cut or separate into sections **2** to represent in sections (e g by a drawing)

'secure /sɪ'kjʊə/ *adj* **1a** free from danger **b** free from risk of loss **c** firm, dependable; *esp* firmly fastened **2** assured, certain – ~**ly** *adv*

'secure *v* **1** to make safe from risk or danger **b** to guarantee against loss **c** to give pledge of payment to (a creditor) or of (an obligation) **2** to make fast; shut tightly **3** to obtain or bring about, esp as the result of effort

security /sɪ'kjʊərɪti/ *n* **1a** freedom from danger, fear, or anxiety **b** stability, dependability **2** sthg pledged to guarantee the fulfilment of an obligation 3 an evidence of debt or of ownership (e g a stock certificate) 4a protection b measures taken to protect against esp espionage or sabotage

seduce /si'dju:s/ v 1 to incite to disobedience or disloyalty 2 to lead astray, esp by false promises 3 to effect the physical seduction of – **seducer** n

seductive /si'dʌktɪv/ adj tending to seduce; alluring – ~**ly** adv – ~**ness** n

¹**see** /si:/ v **saw; seen 1a** to perceive by the eye **b** to look at; inspect **2a** to have experience of; undergo **b** to (try to) find out or determine **3** to form a mental picture of; imagine, envisage **4** to perceive the meaning or importance of; understand **5a** to observe, watch **b** to be a witness of **6** to ensure; make certain **7** of a period of time to be marked by **8a** to call on; visit **b** to keep company with **c** to grant an interview to **9** to meet (a bet) in poker or equal the bet of (a player)

²**see** n a bishopric

¹**seed** /si:d/ n **1a** the grains or ripened ovules of plants used for sowing **b** the fertilized ripened ovule of a (flowering) plant that contains an embryo and is capable of germination to produce a new plant **c** semen or milt **2** a source of development or growth **3** a competitor who has been seeded in a tournament – ~**less** adj

²**seed** v **1** to sow seed **2** of a plant to produce or shed seeds **3** to extract the seeds from (e g raisins) **4** to schedule (tournament players or teams) so that superior ones will not meet in early rounds

seek /si:k/ v **sought 1a** to go in search of – often + out **b** to try to discover **2** to ask for **3** to try to acquire or gain **4** to make an effort; aim – + infinitive – ~**er** n

seem /si:m/ v **1** to give the impression of being **2** to appear to the observation or understanding **3** to give evidence of existing

seeming /'si:mɪŋ/ adj apparent rather than real

seemingly /'si:mɪŋli/ adv **1** so far as can be seen or judged **2** to outward appearance only

seemly /'si:mli/ adj in accord with good taste or propriety – **seemliness** n

¹**seesaw** /'si:sɔ:/ n **1** an alternating up-and-down or backwards-and-forwards movement; also anything (e g a process or movement) that alternates **2** (a game in which 2 or more children ride on opposite ends of) a plank balanced in the middle so that one end goes up as the other goes down

²**seesaw** v **1a** to move backwards and forwards or up and down **b** to play at seesaw **2a** to alternate **b** to vacillate

see-through adj transparent

see through v to undergo or endure to the end

¹**segment** /'segmənt/ n **1a** a separated piece of sthg **b** any of the constituent parts into which a body, entity, or quantity is divided or marked off **2** a portion cut off from a geometrical figure by 1 or more points, lines, or planes

²**segment** /seg'ment/ v to separate into segments

seize /si:z/ v **1a** to confiscate, esp by legal authority **b** to lay hold of sthg suddenly, forcibly, or eagerly – usu + on or upon **2a** to take possession of by force **b** to take prisoner **3** to take hold of abruptly or eagerly **4** to attack or afflict physically or mentally **5** of brakes, pistons, etc to become jammed through excessive pressure, temperature, or friction – often + up

¹**seldom** /'seldəm/ adv in few instances; rarely, infrequently

²**seldom** adj rare, infrequent

¹**select** /si'lekt/ adj **1** picked out in preference to others **2a** of special value or quality **b** exclusively or fastidiously chosen, esp on the basis of social characteristics **3** judicious in choice

²**select** v to take according to preference from among a number; pick out – ~**or** n

selection /si'lekʃən/ n **1** sby or sthg selected; also a collection of selected items **2** a range of things from which to choose

selective /si'lektɪv/ adj of or characterized by selection; selecting or tending to select – ~**ly** adv – ~**ness** n – **-tivity** n

¹**self** /self/ pron myself, himself, herself

²**self** adj identical throughout, esp in colour

³**self** n, pl **selves 1** the entire being of an individual **2** a (part or aspect of a) person's individual character **3** the body, emotions, thoughts, sensations, etc that constitute the individuality and identity of a person **4** personal interest, advantage, or welfare

self-confidence n confidence in oneself and one's powers and abilities – **-dent** adj

self-control n restraint of one's own impulses or emotions – **-trolled** adj

self-defence n **1** the act of defending or justifying oneself **2** the legal right to defend oneself with reasonable force

self-employed adj earning income directly from one's own business, trade, or profession rather than as salary or wages from an employer

self-government n control of one's own (political) affairs – **self-governing** adj

selfish /'selfɪʃ/ adj concerned with or directed towards one's own advantage, pleasure, or well-being without regard for others – ~**ly** adv – ~**ness** n

selfless /'selflɪs/ adj having no concern for self; unselfish – ~**ly** adv – ~**ness** n

self-respect n a proper respect for one's human dignity

self-service n the serving of oneself (e g in a cafeteria or supermarket) with things to be paid for at a cashier's desk, usu upon leaving

¹**sell** /sel/ v **sold 1** to deliver or give up

in violation of duty, trust, or loyalty; betray – often + *out* **2a** to give up (property) in exchange, esp for money **b** to give up or dispose of foolishly or dishonourably (in return for sthg else) **3** to cause or promote the sale of **4a** to make acceptable, believable, or desirable by persuasion **b** to persuade to accept or enjoy sthg – usu + *on*; infml

¹**sell** *n* **1** the act or an instance of selling **2** a deliberate deception; a hoax – infml

seller /'selə/ *n* a product offered for sale and selling well, to a specified extent, or in a specified manner

sellotape /'seləteɪp, 'seləʊ-/ *v* to fix (as if) with Sellotape

Sellotape /'seləteɪp/ *trademark* – used for a usu transparent adhesive tape

semicircle /'semɪ,sɜːkəl/ *n* (an object or arrangement in the form of) a half circle – **-cular** *adj*

semidetached /ˌsemɪdɪ'tætʃt/ *adj* forming 1 of a pair of residences joined into 1 building by a common wall – **semidetached** *adj*

¹**semifinal** /ˌsemi'faɪnl/ *adj* **1** next to the last in a knockout competition **2** of or participating in a semifinal

²**semifinal** /ˌsemi'faɪnl/ *n* a semifinal match or round – often pl with sing. meaning

semitone /'semɪtəʊn/ *n* the musical interval (e g E–F or F–F♯) equal to the interval between 2 adjacent keys on a keyboard instrument

send /send/ *v* **sent 1** *of God, fate, etc* to cause to be; grant; bring about **2** to dispatch by a means of communication **3a** to cause, direct, order, or request to go **b** to dismiss **4** to cause to assume a specified state **5a** to pour out; discharge **b** to emit (e g radio signals) **c** to grow out (parts) in the course of development **6** to consign to a destination (e g death or a place of imprisonment)

¹**senior** /'siːnɪə/ *n* **1** sby who is older than another **2** sby of higher standing or rank

²**senior** *adj* **1** elder – used, chiefly in the USA, to distinguish a father with the same name as his son **2** higher in standing or rank

sensation /sen'seɪʃən/ *n* **1a** a mental process (e g seeing or hearing) resulting from stimulation of a sense organ **b** a state of awareness of a usu specified type resulting from internal bodily conditions or external factors; a feeling or sense **2a** a surge of intense interest or excitement **b** a cause of such excitement; *esp* sby or sthg in some respect remarkable or outstanding

sensational /sen'seɪʃənəl/ *adj* **1** arousing an immediate, intense, and usu superficial interest or emotional reaction **2** exceptionally or unexpectedly excellent or impressive – infml – **~ly** *adv*

¹**sense** /sens/ *n* **1** a meaning conveyed or intended; *esp* any of a range of meanings a word or phrase may bear, esp as isolated in a dictionary entry **2** any of

the senses of feeling, hearing, sight, smell, taste, etc **3** soundness of mind or judgment – usu pl with sing. meaning **4a** an ability to use the senses for a specified purpose **b** a definite but often vague awareness or impression **c** an awareness that motivates action or judgment **d** a capacity for discernment and appreciation **5** an ability to put the mind to effective use; practical intelligence

²**sense** *v* **1a** to perceive by the senses **b** to be or become conscious of **2** to grasp, comprehend

senseless /'sensl̩s/ *adj* deprived of, deficient in, or contrary to sense: e g **a** unconscious **b** foolish, stupid **c** meaningless, purposeless – **~ly** *adv* – **~ness** *n*

sensible /'sensəbl/ *adj* **1** having, containing, or indicative of good sense or sound reason **2a** perceptible to the senses or to understanding **b** large enough to be observed or noticed; considerable – **-bly** *adv*

sensitive /'sensɪtɪv/ *adj* **1** capable of being stimulated or excited by external agents (e g light, gravity, or contact) **2** highly responsive or susceptible: e g **a(1)** easily provoked or hurt emotionally **(2)** finely aware of the attitudes and feelings of others or of the subtleties of a work of art **b** capable of registering minute differences; delicate **3** concerned with highly classified information – **~ly** *adv* – **-tivity** *n*

sent /sent/ *past of* **send**

¹**sentence** /'sentəns/ *n* **1a** a judgment formally pronounced by a court and specifying a punishment **b** the punishment so imposed **2** a grammatically self-contained speech unit that expresses an assertion, a question, a command, a wish, or an exclamation and is usu shown in writing with a capital letter at the beginning and with appropriate punctuation at the end

²**sentence** *v* **1** to impose a judicial sentence on **2** to consign to a usu unpleasant fate

sentiment /'sentɪmənt/ *n* **1a** (an attitude, thought, or judgment prompted or coloured by) feeling or emotion **b** a specific view or attitude; an opinion – usu pl with sing. meaning **2** indulgently romantic or nostalgic feeling

sentimental /ˌsentɪ'mentl/ *adj* **1** resulting from feeling rather than reason **2** having an excess of superficial sentiment – **~ly** *adv* – **~ism**, **~ity**, **~ist** *n* – **-ize** *v*

¹**separate** /'sepəreɪt/ *v* **1a** to set or keep apart; detach, divide **b** to make a distinction between; distinguish **c** to disperse in space or time; scatter **2a** to isolate from a mixture or compound – often + *out* **b** to divide into constituent parts or types **3** to cease to live together as man and wife, esp by formal arrangement **4** to go in different directions

²**separate** /'sepər̩t/ *adj* **1** set or kept apart; detached, separated **2** not shared with another; individual **3a** existing independently; autonomous **b** different

in kind; distinct – **~ness** *n* – **~ly** *adv*

separation /ˌsepəˈreɪʃən/ *n* **1a** a point, line, or means of division **b** an intervening space; a gap, break **2** cessation of cohabitation between husband and wife by mutual agreement or judicial decree

sepsis /ˈsepsɪs/ *n, pl* **sepses** the spread of bacteria from a focus of infection

September /sepˈtembə/ *n* the 9th month of the Gregorian calendar

septic /ˈseptɪk/ *adj* relating to, involving, or characteristic of sepsis

sequel /ˈsiːkwəl/ *n* **1** a consequence, result **2a** subsequent development or course of events **b** a play, film, or literary work continuing the course of a narrative begun in a preceding one

sequence /ˈsiːkwəns/ *n* **1** a continuous or connected series **2** an episode, esp in a film **3** order of succession **4** a continuous progression – **sequence** *v*

sergeant /ˈsɑːdʒənt/ *n* **1** a police officer ranking in Britain between constable and inspector **2** a non-commissioned officer of upper rank in the army, airforce, or marines

¹**serial** /ˈsɪəriəl/ *adj* **1** of or constituting a series, rank, or row **2** appearing in successive instalments **3** of or being music based on a series of notes in an arbitrary but fixed order without regard for traditional tonality – **~ly** *adv*

²**serial** *n* **1** a work appearing (e g in a magazine or on television) in parts at usu regular intervals **2** a publication issued as 1 of a consecutively numbered continuing series

series /ˈsɪəriːz/ *n* **1** a number of things or events of the same kind following one another in spatial or temporal succession **2** a usu infinite mathematical sequence whose terms are to be added together **3** a succession of issues of volumes published with continuous numbering or usu related subjects or authors and format **4** a division of rock formations that comprises the rocks deposited during an epoch **5** an arrangement of devices in an electrical circuit in which the whole current passes through each device

serious /ˈsɪəriəs/ *adj* **1** grave or thoughtful in appearance or manner; sober **2a** requiring careful attention and concentration **b** of or relating to a weighty or important matter **3** not jesting or deceiving; in earnest **4** having important or dangerous consequences; critical – **~ly** *adv* – **~ness** *n*

sermon /ˈsɜːmən/ *n* **1** a religious discourse delivered in public, usu by a clergyman as a part of a religious service **2** a speech on conduct or duty; *esp* one that is unduly long or tedious

servant /ˈsɜːvənt/ *n* sby who or sthg that serves others; *specif* sby employed to perform personal or domestic duties for another

¹**serve** /sɜːv/ *v* **1a** to act as a servant **b** to do military or naval service **c** to undergo a term of imprisonment **2a** to be of use; fulfil a specified purpose – often + *as* **b** to be favourable, opportune, or convenient **c** to hold a post or office; discharge a duty **3** to prove adequate or satisfactory; suffice **4** to distribute drinks or helpings of food **5** to attend to customers in a shop **6** to put the ball or shuttle in play in any of various games (e g tennis or volleyball)

²**serve** *n* the act of putting the ball or shuttle in play in any of various games (e g volleyball, badminton, or tennis)

¹**service** /ˈsɜːvɪs/ *n* **1a** work or duty performed by sby **b** employment as a servant **2a** the function performed by sby who or sthg that serves **b** help, use, benefit **c** disposal for use or assistance **3a** a form followed in a religious ceremony **b** a meeting for worship **4a** a helpful act; a favour **b** a piece of useful work that does not produce a tangible commodity – usu pl with sing. meaning **c** a serve **5** a set of articles for a particular use; *specif* a set of matching tableware **6** any of a nation's military forces (e g the army or navy) **7a(1)** a facility supplying some public demand **(2)** *pl* utilities (e g gas, water sewage, or electricity) available or connected to a building **b** the usu routine repair and maintenance of a machine or motor vehicle **c** a facility providing broadcast programmes **8** the bringing of a legal writ, process, or summons to notice as prescribed

²**service** *adj* **1** of the armed services **2** used in serving or delivering **3** providing services

³**service** *v* to perform services for: e g **a** to repair or provide maintenance for **b** to meet interest and sinking fund payments on (e g government debt) **c** to perform any of the business functions auxiliary to production or distribution of **d** *of a male animal* to copulate with

⁴**service, service tree** *n* an Old World tree resembling the related mountain ashes but with larger flowers and larger edible fruits

session /ˈseʃən/ *n* **1a** a meeting or series of meetings of a body (e g a court or council) for the transaction of business; a sitting **2** a period devoted to a particular activity, esp by a group of people

¹**set** /set/ *v* **-tt-; set 1** to cause to sit; place in or on a seat **2a** to place with care or deliberate purpose and with relative stability **b** to transplant **3** to cause to assume a specified condition **4a** to appoint or assign to an office or duty **b** to post, station **5a** to place in a specified relation or position **b** to place in a specified setting **6a** to fasten **b** to apply **7** to fix or decide on as a time, limit, or regulation; prescribe **8a** to establish as the most extreme, esp the highest, level **b** to provide as a pattern or model **c** to allot as or compose for a task **9a** to adjust (a device, esp a measuring device) to a desired position **b** to restore to normal position or connection after dislocation or fracturing **c** to spread to the wind **10** to divide (an age-group of pupils) into sets **11a** to make ready for

use **b** to provide music or instrumentation for (a text) **c** to arrange (type) for printing **12a** to put a fine edge on by grinding or honing **b** to bend slightly the alternate teeth of (a saw) in opposite directions **13** to fix in a desired position **14** to fix (the hair) in a desired style by waving, curling, or arranging, usu while wet **15** to fix a gem in a metal setting **16a** to fix at a specified amount **b** to value, rate **17** to place in relation for comparison; *also* to offset **18a** to put into activity or motion **b** to incite to attack or antagonism **c** to make an attack – + *on* or *upon* **19** to fix firmly; give rigid form to **20** to cause to become firm or solid **21** to cause fruit to develop **22** to pass below the horizon; go down **23** – used as an interjection to command runners to put themselves into the starting position before a race

²**set** *adj* **1** intent, determined **2** fixed by authority or binding decision; prescribed, specified **3** *of a meal* consisting of a specified combination of dishes available at a fixed price **4** reluctant to change; fixed by habit **5** immovable, rigid **6** ready, prepared

³**set** *n* **1** setting or being set **2** a mental inclination, tendency, or habit **3** a number of things, usu of the same kind, that belong or are used together or that form a unit **4** the arrangement of the hair by curling or waving **5** a young plant, rooted cutting, etc ready for transplanting **6** an artificial setting for a scene of a theatrical or film production **7** a division of a tennis match won by the side that wins at least 6 games beating the opponent by 2 games or that wins a tie breaker **8** *sing or pl in constr* a group of people associated by common interests **9** a collection of mathematical elements (e g numbers or points) **10** an apparatus of electronic components assembled so as to function as a unit **11** *sing or pl in constr* a group of pupils of roughly equal ability in a particular subject who are taught together **12** a sett

setback /'setbæk/ *n* **1** an arresting of or hindrance in progress **2** a defeat, reverse

set back *v* **1** to prevent or hinder the progress of; impede, delay **2** to cost – *infml*

set-off *n* **1a** a decoration, adornment **b** a counterbalance, compensation **2** the discharge of a debt by setting against it a sum owed by the creditor to the debtor

set off *v* **1a** to put in relief; show up by contrast **b** to make distinct or outstanding; enhance **2** to treat as a compensating item **3a** to set in motion; cause to begin **b** to cause to explode; detonate **4** to start out on a course or journey

settee /se'tiː/ *n* a long often upholstered seat with a back and usu arms for seating more than 1 person; *broadly* a sofa

setting /'setɪŋ/ *n* **1** the manner, position, or direction in which sthg (e g a dial) is set **2** the (style of) frame in

which a gem is mounted **3a** the background, surroundings **b** the time and place of the action of a literary, dramatic, or cinematic work **the** music composed for a text (e g a poem)

¹**settle** /'setl/ *n* a wooden bench with arms, a high solid back, and an enclosed base which can be used as a chest

²**settle** *v* **1** to place firmly or comfortably **2a** to establish in residence **b** to supply with inhabitants; colonize **3a** to cause to sink and become compacted **b** to clarify by causing the sediment to sink **4** to come to rest **5** to free from pain, discomfort, disorder, or disturbance **6** to fix or resolve conclusively **7** to bestow legally for life – usu + *on* **8a** to become calm or orderly – often + *down* **b** to adopt an ordered or stable life-style – usu + *down* **9a** to adjust differences or accounts; pay – often + *with* or *up* **b** to end a legal dispute by the agreement of both parties, without court action

settlement /'setlmənt/ *n* **1** settling **2** an estate, income, etc legally bestowed on sby **3a** a newly settled place or region **b** a small, esp isolated, village **4** an agreement resolving differences

set-up *n* **1** an arrangement; *also* an organization **2** a task or contest with a prearranged or artificially easy course – chiefly *infml*

set up *v* **1** to put forward (e g a theory) for acceptance; propound **2** to assemble and prepare for use or operation **3** to give voice to, esp loudly; raise **4** to claim (oneself) to be a specified thing **5** to found, institute **6** to provide with what is necessary or useful – usu + *with* or *for*

seven /'sevən/ *n* **1** the number 7 **2** the seventh in a set or series **3** sthg having 7 parts or members or a denomination of 7 – ~ **th** *adj, n, pron, adv*

seventeen /,sevən'tiːn/ *n* the number 17 – ~ **th** *adj, n, pron, adv*

seventy /'sevənti/ *n* **1** the number 70 **2** *pl* the numbers 70 to 79; *specif* a range of temperatures, ages, or dates within a century characterized by those numbers – -**tieth** *adj, n, pron, adv*

¹**several** /'sevərəl/ *adj* **1** more than 2 but fewer than many **2** separate or distinct from one another; respective – chiefly *fml*

²**several** *pron, pl in constr* an indefinite number more than 2 and fewer than many

severe /sɪ'vɪər/ *adj* **1** having a stern expression or character; austere **2** rigorous in judgment, requirements, or punishment; stringent **3** strongly critical or condemnatory; censorious **4** sober or restrained in decoration or manner; plain **5** marked by harsh or extreme conditions **6** serious, grave – ~ **ly** *adv* – -**rity** *n*

sew /səʊ/ *v* **sewed; sewn** **1** to unite, fasten, or attach by stitches made with a needle and thread **2** to close or enclose by sewing **3** to make or mend by sewing – ~ **er** *n*

sewage /'sju:ɪdʒ, 'su:-/ n waste matter carried off by sewers

sewer /'sju:ə', 'su:ə'/ n an artificial usu underground conduit used to carry off waste matter, esp excrement, from houses, schools, towns, etc and surface water from roads and paved areas

sex /seks/ n 1 either of 2 divisions of organisms distinguished as male or female 2 the structural, functional, and behavioural characteristics that are involved in reproduction and that distinguish males and females 3 sexual intercourse – **sex, sexual** adj – **∼ually** adv

sexism /'seksızəm/ n 1 a belief that sex determines intrinsic capacities and role in society and that sexual differences produce an inherent superiority of one sex, usu the male 2 discrimination on the basis of sex; esp prejudice against women on the part of men – **-ist** adj, n

sexless /'sekslɪs/ adj 1 lacking sexuality or sexual intercourse 2 lacking sex appeal

sexy /'seksi/ adj sexually suggestive or stimulating; erotic – **sexily** adv – **sexiness** n

shabby /'ʃæbi/ v 1a threadbare or faded from wear b dilapidated, run-down 2 dressed in worn or grubby clothes; seedy 3 shameful, despicable – **-bily** adv – **-biness** n

¹**shade** /ʃeɪd/ n 1a partial darkness caused by the interception of rays of light b relative obscurity or insignificance 2a a transitory or illusory appearance b a ghost 3 sthg that intercepts or diffuses light or heat; e g a a lampshade b chiefly NAm pl sunglasses – infml 4 a particular level of depth or brightness of a colour 5 a minute difference or amount

²**shade** v 1 to shelter or screen by intercepting radiated light or heat 2 to darken or obscure (as if) with a shadow 3 to mark with shading or gradations of colour 4 to pass by slight changes or imperceptible degrees – usu + into or off into

shadow /'ʃædəʊ/ n 1 partial darkness caused by an opaque body interposed so as to cut off rays from a light source 2 a faint representation or suggestion; an imitation 3 a dark figure cast on a surface by a body intercepting light rays 4 a phantom 5 pl darkness 6 a shaded or darker portion of a picture 7a an inseparable companion or follower b one (e g a spy or detective) who shadows 8 a small degree or portion; a trace 9 a source of gloom or disquiet

shadow v 1 to cast a shadow over 2 to follow (a person) secretly; keep under surveillance 3 to shade

shadow adj 1 identical with another in form but without the other's power or status; specif of or constituting the probable cabinet when the opposition party is returned to power 2 shown by throwing the shadows of performers or puppets on a screen

shadowy /'ʃædəʊi/ adj 1a of the nature of or resembling a shadow, insubstantial b scarcely perceptible; indistinct 2 lying in or obscured by shadow

shaft /ʃɑːft/ n 1a (the long handle of) a spear, lance, or similar weapon b either of 2 poles between which a horse is hitched to a vehicle 2 a sharply delineated beam of light shining from an opening 3a the trunk of a tree b the cylindrical pillar between the capital and the base of a column c the handle of a tool or implement (e g a hammer or golf club) d a usu cylindrical bar used to support rotating pieces or to transmit power or motion by rotation e a man-made vertical or inclined opening leading underground to a mine, well, etc f a vertical opening or passage through the floors of a building 4 a scornful, satirical, or pithily critical remark; a barb

¹**shake** /ʃeɪk/ v shook; shaken 1a to move to and fro with rapid usu irregular motion b to brandish, wave, or flourish, esp in a threatening manner 2 to vibrate, esp from the impact of a blow or shock 3a to tremble as a result of physical or emotional disturbance b to cause to quake, quiver, or tremble 4 to cause to waver; weaken 5 to clasp (hands) in greeting or farewell or to convey goodwill or agreement 6 to agitate the feelings of; upset

²**shake** n 1 an act of shaking 2 pl a condition of trembling (e g from chill or fever); specif delirium tremens 3 a wavering, vibrating, or alternating motion caused by a blow or shock 4 a trill 5 chiefly NAm a milk shake 6 a moment – (6) infml

shaky /'ʃeɪki/ adj 1a lacking stability; precarious b lacking in firmness (e g of beliefs or principals) 2 unsound in health; poorly 3 likely to give way or break down; rickety – **shakily** adv – **shakiness** n

shall /ʃəl; strong ʃæl/ verbal auxiliary pres sing & pl shall; past should 1 – used to urge or command or denote what is legally mandatory 2a –used to express what is inevitable or seems likely to happen in the future b – used in the question form to express simple futurity or with the force of an offer or suggestion 3 – used to express determination

¹**shallow** /'ʃæləʊ/ adj 1 having little depth 2 superficial in knowledge, thought, or feeling 3 not marked or accentuated – **∼ly** adv – **∼ness** n

²**shallow** n a shallow place in a body of water – usu pl with sing. meaning but sing. or pl in constr

¹**sham** /ʃæm/ n 1 cheap falseness; hypocrisy 2 an imitation or counterfeit purporting to be genuine 3 a person who shams

²**sham** v to act so as to counterfeit; also to give a deliberately false impression

shambles /'ʃæmblz/ n 1 a slaughter-house 2a a place of carnage b a scene or a state of chaos or confusion; a mess

shame /ʃeɪm/ n 1 a painful emotion caused by consciousness of guilt, shortcomings, impropriety, or disgrace 2 humiliating disgrace or disrepute; ignominy 3 sthg bringing regret or disgrace

¹**shame** v 1 to bring shame to; disgrace 2 to put to shame by outdoing 3 to fill with a sense of shame 4 to compel by causing to feel guilty

shameful /ˈʃeɪmfəl/ adj 1 bringing disrepute or ignominy; disgraceful 2 arousing the feeling of shame – ~ly adv – ~ness n

¹**shampoo** /ʃæmˈpuː/ v 1 to clean (esp the hair or a carpet) with shampoo 2 to wash the hair of

²**shampoo** n 1 a washing of the hair esp by a hairdresser 2 a soap, detergent, etc used for shampooing

¹**shape** /ʃeɪp/ v 1 to form, create; esp to give a particular form or shape to 2 to adapt in shape so as to fit neatly and closely 3 to guide or mould into a particular state or condition 4 to determine or direct the course of (e g a person's life)

²**shape** n 1a the visible or tactile form of a particular (kind of) item b spatial form 2 the contour of the body, esp of the trunk; the figure 3 an assumed appearance; a guise 4 definite form (e g in thought or words) 5 a general structure or plan 6 sthg made in a particular form 7 the condition of a person or thing, esp at a particular time – shape adj – ~lessly adv – ~lessness n

¹**share** /ʃeəʳ/ n 1a a portion belonging to, due to, or contributed by an individual b a full or fair portion 2a the part allotted or belonging to any of a number owning property or interest together b any of the equal portions into which property or invested capital is divided c pl, chiefly Br the proprietorship element in a company, usu represented by transferable certificates

²**share** v 1 to divide and distribute in shares; apportion – usu + out 2 to partake of, use, experience, or enjoy with others 3 to have a share or part – often + in

³**share** n a ploughshare

shark /ʃɑːk/ n 1 any of numerous mostly large typically grey marine fishes that are mostly active, voracious, and predators and have gill slits at the sides and a mouth on the under part of the body 2 a greedy unscrupulous person who exploits others by usury, extortion, or trickery

¹**sharp** /ʃɑːp/ adj 1 (adapted to) cutting or piercing: e g a having a thin keen edge or fine point b bitingly cold; icy 2a keen in intellect, perception, attention, etc b paying shrewd usu selfish attention to personal gain 3a brisk, vigorous b capable of acting or reacting strongly; esp caustic 4a marked by irritability or anger; fiery b causing intense usu sudden anguish 5 affecting the senses or sense organs intensely; e g a(1) pungent, tart, or acid, esp in flavour (2) acrid b shrill, piercing 6a

characterized by hard lines and angles b involving an abrupt change in direction c clear in outline or detail; distinct 7 of a musical note raised a semitone in pitch 8 stylish, dressy – infml – ~ly adv – ~ness n

²**sharp** adv 1 in an abrupt manner 2 exactly, precisely 3 above the proper musical pitch

³**sharp** n 1 a musical note 1 semitone higher than another indicated or previously specified note 2 a relatively long needle with a sharp point and a small rounded eye for use in general sewing 3 chiefly NAm a swindler, sharper

sharpen /ˈʃɑːpən/ v to make or become sharp or sharper – ~er n

shatter /ˈʃætəʳ/ v 1 to break suddenly apart; disintegrate 2 to have a forceful or violent effect on the feelings of 3 to cause to be utterly exhausted

¹**shave** /ʃeɪv/ v shaved, shaven 1a to remove in thin layers or shreds – often + off b to cut or trim closely 2 to cut off (hair or beard) close to the skin 3 to come very close to or brush against in passing

²**shave** n 1 a tool or machine for shaving 2 an act or process of shaving

shawl /ʃɔːl/ n a usu decorative square, oblong, or triangular piece of fabric that is worn to cover the head or shoulders

¹**she** /ʃi; strong ʃiː/ pron 1 that female person or creature who is neither speaker nor hearer 2 – used to refer to sthg (e g a ship) regarded as feminine

²**she** n a female person or creature – often in combination

sheaf /ʃiːf/ n, pl **sheaves** 1 a quantity of plant material, esp the stalks and ears of a cereal grass, bound together 2 a collection of items laid or tied together

¹**shear** /ʃɪəʳ/ v **sheared, shorn** 1 to cut or clip (hair, wool, a fleece, etc) from sby or sthg; also to cut from 2 to cut with sthg sharp 3 to deprive of sthg as if by cutting off – usu passive + of 4 to become divided or separated under the action of a shear force

²**shear** n 1a a cutting implement similar to a pair of scissors but typically larger b any of various cutting tools or machines operating by the action of opposed cutting edges of metal 2 an action or force that causes or tends to cause 2 parts of a body to slide on each other in a direction parallel to their plane of contact – (1a, b) usu pl with sing. meaning

sheath /ʃiːθ/ n 1 a case or cover for a blade (e g of a knife or sword) 2 a cover or case of (a part of) a plant or animal body 3 a condom

¹**shed** /ʃed/ v **shed** 1 to be incapable of holding or absorbing; repel 2a to cause (blood) to flow by wounding or killing b to pour forth; let flow 3 to cast off hairs, threads etc; moult

²**shed** n a usu single-storied building for shelter, storage, etc, esp with 1 or more sides open

she'd /ʃid; *strong* ʃiːd/ she had; she would

sheep /ʃiːp/ *n, pl* **sheep** 1 any of numerous ruminant mammals related to the goats but stockier and lacking a beard in the male; *specif* one domesticated, esp for its flesh and wool 2 an inane or docile person; *esp* one easily influenced or led

¹**sheer** /ʃɪə/ *adj* 1 transparently fine; diaphanous 2a unqualified, utter b not mixed or mingled with anything else; pure, unadulterated 3 marked by great and unbroken steepness; precipitous

²**sheer** *adv* 1 altogether, completely 2 straight up or down without a break

³**sheer** *v* to (cause to) deviate from a course

⁴**sheer** *n* a turn, deviation, or change in a course (e g of a ship)

¹**sheet** /ʃiːt/ *n* 1 a broad piece of cloth; *specif* a rectangle of cloth (e g of linen or cotton) used as an article of bed linen 2a a usu rectangular piece of paper b a printed section for a book, esp before it has been folded, cut, or bound – usu pl 3 a broad usu flat expanse 4 a suspended or moving expanse 5 a piece of sthg that is thin in comparison to its length and breadth

²**sheet** *v* 1 to form into, provide with, or cover with a sheet or sheets 2 to come down in sheets

³**sheet** *adj* rolled into or spread out in a sheet

⁴**sheet** *n* 1 a rope that regulates the angle at which a sail is set in relation to the wind 2 *pl* the spaces at either end of an open boat

shelf /ʃelf/ *n, pl* **shelves** 1 a thin flat usu long and narrow piece of material (e g wood) fastened horizontally (e g on a wall or in a cupboard, bookcase, etc) at a distance from the floor to hold objects 2a (partially submerged) sandbank or ledge of rocks b a flat projecting layer of rock

¹**shell** /ʃel/ *n* 1 a hard rigid often largely calcium-containing covering of a (sea) animal b the hard or tough outer covering of an egg, esp a bird's egg 2 the covering or outside part of a fruit or seed, esp when hard or fibrous 4a a framework or exterior structure; *esp* the outer frame of a building that is unfinished or has been destroyed (e g by fire) b a hollow form devoid of substance c an edible case for holding a filling 5 a cold and reserved attitude that conceals the presence or absence of feeling 6a a projectile for a cannon containing an explosive bursting charge b a metal or paper case which holds the charge in cartridges, fireworks, etc

²**shell** *v* 1 to take out of a natural enclosing cover, esp a pod 2 to fire shells at, on, or into

she'll /ʃil; *strong* ʃiːl/ she will; she shall

¹**shelter** /ʃeltə/ *n* 1 sthg. or a structure, affording cover or protection 2 the state of being covered and protected; refuge

²**shelter** *v* 1 to take shelter 2 to keep concealed or protected

¹**shepherd** /ʃepəd/ *n* 1 *fem* **shepherdess** one who tends sheep 2 a pastor

²**shepherd** *v* to tend as a shepherd 2 to guide, marshal, or conduct (people) like sheep

sherry /ʃeri/ *n* a blended fortified wine from S Spain that varies in colour from very light to dark brown

¹**shield** /ʃiːld/ *n* 1 a piece of armour (e g of wood, metal, or leather) carried on the arm or in the hand and used esp for warding off blows 2 sby or sthg that protects or defends; a defence 3 a piece of material or a pad attached inside a garment (e g a dress) at the armpit to protect the garment from perspiration 4 sthg designed to protect people from injury from moving parts of machinery, live electrical conductors, etc 5 the Precambrian central rock mass of a continent

²**shield** *v* 1 to protect (as if) with a shield; provide with a protective cover or shelter 2 to cut off from observation; hide

¹**shift** /ʃift/ *v* 1 to exchange for or replace by another; change 2 to change the place, position, or direction of; move 3 to get rid of; dispose of 4 to assume responsibility for

²**shift** *n* 1 a loose unfitted slip or dress 2a a change in direction b a change in emphasis, judgment, or attitude 3 *sing or pl in constr* a group who work (e g in a factory) in alternation with other groups 4 a change in place or position

shilling /ʃilɪŋ/ *n* 1 (a coin representing) a former money unit of the UK worth 12 old pence or £½₀ 2 a money unit equal to £½₀ of any of various other countries (formerly) in the Commonwealth

¹**shin** /ʃin/ *n* the front part of the leg of a vertebrate animal below the knee; *also* a cut of meat from this part, esp from the front leg

²**shin** *v* to climb by gripping with the hands or arms and the legs and hauling oneself up or lowering oneself down

¹**shine** /ʃain/ *v* **shone** 1 to emit light 2 to be bright with reflected light 3 to be outstanding or distinguished 4 to make bright by polishing 5 to direct the light of

²**shine** *n* 1 brightness caused by the emission or reflection of light 2 brilliance, splendour 3 fine weather; sunshine 4 an act of polishing shoes 5 a fancy, crush –esp in *take a shine to*; *infml*

shiny /ʃaini/ *adj* 1 bright or glossy in appearance; lustrous, polished 2 *of material, clothes etc* rubbed or worn to a smooth surface that reflects light

¹**ship** /ʃip/ *n* 1 a large seagoing vessel 2 a boat (propelled by power or sail) 3 *sing or pl in constr* a ship's crew 4 an airship, aircraft, or spacecraft

²**ship** *v* 1 to place or receive on board a ship for transportation 2 to put in place for use 3 to take into a ship or boat 4

to engage for service on a ship **5** to cause to be transported or sent

shipment /'ʃipmənt/ n **1** the act or process of shipping **2** the quantity of goods shipped

shipwreck /'ʃip-rek/ n **1** a wrecked ship or its remains **2** the destruction or loss of a ship **3** an irrevocable collapse or destruction

shipwreck v **1** to cause to undergo shipwreck **2** to ruin

shirk /ʃɜːk/ v to evade or dodge a duty, responsibility, etc

shirt /ʃɜːt/ n an (esp man's) garment for the upper body; esp one that opens the full length of the centre front and has sleeves and a collar

shiver /'ʃivə/ n any of the small pieces that result from the shattering of sthg brittle

¹**shiver** v to break into many small fragments; shatter

²**shiver** v to tremble, esp with cold or fever

³**shiver** n an instance of shivering; a tremor

¹**shock** /ʃɒk/ n a pile of sheaves of grain or stalks of maize set upright in a field

²**shock** n **1** a violent shaking or jarring **2a** a disturbance in the equilibrium or permanence of sthg (e g a system) **b** a sudden or violent disturbance of thoughts or emotions **3** a state of serious depression of most bodily functions associated with reduced blood volume and pressure and caused usu by severe injuries, bleeding, or burns **4** sudden stimulation of the nerves and convulsive contraction of the muscles caused by the passage of electricity through the body

³**shock** v **1a** to cause to feel sudden surprise, terror, horror, or offence **b** to cause to undergo a physical or nervous shock **2** to cause (e g an animal) to experience an electric shock

⁴**shock** n a thick bushy mass, usu of hair

shocking /'ʃɒkiŋ/ adj **1** giving cause for indignation or offence **2** very bad – infml

¹**shoddy** /'ʃɒdi/ n a fabric often of inferior quality manufactured wholly or partly from reclaimed wool

²**shoddy** adj **1** made wholly or partly of shoddy **2a** cheaply imitative; vulgarly pretentious **b** hastily or poorly done; inferior **c** shabby

¹**shoe** /ʃuː/ n **1a** an outer covering for the human foot that does not extend above the ankle and has a thick or stiff sole and often an attached heel **b** a metal plate or rim for the hoof of an animal **2** sthg resembling a shoe in shape or function **3** pl a situation, position; also a predicament **4** the part of a vehicle braking system that presses on the brake drum

²**shoe** v shoeing; shod **1** to fit (e g a horse) with a shoe **2** to protect or reinforce with a usu metal shoe

shoelace /'ʃuːleis/ n a lace or string for fastening a shoe

shone /ʃɒn/ past of shine

shook /ʃʊk/ past & chiefly dial past part of shake

¹**shoot** /ʃuːt/ v shot **1a** to eject or impel by a sudden release of tension (e g of a bowstring or by a flick of a finger) **b** to drive forth **(1)** by an explosion (e g of a powder charge in a firearm or of ignited fuel in a rocket) **(2)** by a sudden release of gas or air **c** to drive the ball or puck in football, hockey, etc towards a goal **d** to send forth with suddenness or intensity **2** to wound or kill with a bullet, arrow, shell, etc shot from a gun, bow, etc **3a** to push or slide (a bolt) in order to fasten or unfasten a door **b** to pass (a shuttle) through the warp threads in weaving **c** to push or thrust forwards; stick out –usu + out **d** to put forth in growing – usu + out **4** to score by shooting **5** to hunt over with a firearm or bow **6** to cause to move suddenly or swiftly forwards **7** to pass swiftly by, over, or along **8** to take a picture or series of pictures or television images of; film; also to make (a film, videotape, etc)

²**shoot** n **1** a stem or branch with its leaves, buds, etc, esp when not yet mature **2a** a shooting trip or party **b** (land over which is held) the right to shoot game **3** (a rush of water down) a descent in a stream

¹**shop** /ʃɒp/ n **1** a building or room for the retail sale of merchandise or for the sale of services **2** a place or part of a factory where a particular manufacturing or repair process takes place **3** the jargon or subject matter peculiar to an occupation or sphere of interest – chiefly in talk shop

²**shop** v **1** to visit a shop with intent to purchase goods **2** to make a search; hunt **3** to inform on; betray

shop assistant n, Br one employed to sell goods in a retail shop

shopfloor /ˌ-'flɔː/ n the area in which machinery or workbenches are located in a factory or mill, esp considered as a place or work; also, sing or pl in constr the workers in an establishment as distinct from the management

shoplift /'-ˌlift/ v to steal from a shop – ~ing n

¹**shore** /ʃɔː/ n **1** the land bordering the sea or another (large) body of water **2** land as distinguished from the sea

²**shore** v **1** to support with shores; prop **2** to give support to; brace, sustain – usu + up

³**shore** n a prop for preventing sinking or sagging

¹**short** /ʃɔːt/ adj **1** having little or insufficient length or height **2a** not extended in time; brief **b** of the memory not retentive **c** quick, expeditious **3a** seeming to pass quickly **a** of a speech sound having a relatively short duration **b** of a syllable in prosody unstressed **4** limited in distance **5a** not coming up to a measure or requirement **b** insufficiently supplied **6a** abrupt, curt **b** quickly provoked **7** of pastry, biscuits, etc crisp and easily broken owing to the presence of

fat **8** made briefer; abbreviated **9** being or relating to a sale of securities or commodities that the seller does not possess at the time of the sale

²**short** *adv* **1** curtly **2** for or during a brief time **3** in an abrupt manner; suddenly **4** at a point or degree before a specified or intended goal or limit

³**short** **1** *pl* knee-length or less than knee-length trousers **2** *pl* short-term bonds **3** a short circuit **4** a brief often documentary or educational film **5** *Br* a drink of spirits

⁴**short** *v* to short-circuit

shortage /'ʃɔːtɪdʒ/ *n* a lack, deficit

shortcoming /'ʃɔːt,kʌmɪŋ/ *n* a deficiency, defect

shortcut /,ʃɔːt'kʌt/ *n* a route or procedure quicker and more direct than one customarily followed

shorten /'ʃɔːtn/ *v* **1** to make short or shorter **2** to add fat to (e g pastry dough) **3** to reduce the area or amount of (sail that is set)

shorthand /'ʃɔːthænd/ *n* **1** a method of rapid writing that substitutes symbols and abbreviations for letters, words, or phrases **2** a system or instance of rapid or abbreviated communication

short-lived *adj* not living or lasting long

shortly /'ʃɔːtli/ *adv* **1a** in a few words; briefly **b** in an abrupt manner **2a** in a short time **b** at a short interval

shortsighted /,ʃɔːt'saɪtɪd/ *adj* **1** able to see near objects more clearly than distant objects **2** lacking foresight

¹**shot** /ʃɒt/ *n* **1a** an action of shooting **b** a directed propelling of a missile; *specif* a directed discharge of a firearm **c** a stroke or throw in a game (e g tennis, cricket, or basketball); *also* an attempt to kick the ball into the goal in soccer **d** a hypodermic injection **2a(1)** small lead or steel pellets (for a shotgun) **(2)** a single (nonexplosive) projectile for a gun or cannon **b** a metal sphere that is thrown for distance as an athletic field event **3** one who shoots; *esp* a marksman **4a** an attempt, try **b** a guess, conjecture **5a** a single photographic exposure **b** an image or series of images in a film or a television programme shot by a camera from 1 angle without interruption **6** a small amount applied at one time; a dose

²**shot** *adj* **1a** *of a fabric* having contrasting and changeable colour effects; iridescent **b** infused or permeated *with* a quality or element **2** utterly exhausted or ruined

should /ʃəd; *strong* ʃʊd/ *past of* **shall** **1** – used (e g in the main clause of a conditional sentence) to introduce a contingent fact, possibility, or presumption **2** ought to **3** used in reported speech to represent *shall* or *will* **4** will probably **5** –used to soften a direct statement

¹**shoulder** /'ʃəʊldə/ *n* **1** the part of the human body formed of bones, joints, and muscles that connects the arm to the trunk; *also* a corresponding part of another animal **2** *pl* **a** the 2 shoulders and the upper part of the back **b** capacity for bearing a burden (e g of blame or responsibility) **3** a cut of meat including the upper joint of the foreleg and adjacent parts **4** an area adjacent to a higher, more prominent, or more important part; e g **a(1)** the slope of a mountain near the top **(2)** a lateral protrusion of a mountain **b** that part of a road to the side of the surface on which vehicles travel **5** a rounded or sloping part (e g of a stringed instrument or a bottle) where the neck joins the body

²**shoulder** *v* **1** to push or thrust (as if) with the shoulder **2a** to place or carry on the shoulder **b** to assume the burden or responsibility of

shout /ʃaʊt/ *v* **1** to utter a sudden loud cry or in a loud voice **2** to buy a round of drinks

shove /ʃʌv/ *v* **1** to push along with steady force **2** to push in a rough, careless, or hasty manner; thrust **3** to force a way forwards – **shove** *n*

¹**shovel** /'ʃʌvl/ *n* **1a** an implement consisting of a broad scoop or a dished blade with a handle, used to lift and throw loose material **b** (a similar part on) a digging or earth-moving machine **2** a shovelful

²**shovel** *v* **1** to dig, clear, or shift with a shovel **2** to convey clumsily or in a mass as if with a shovel

¹**show** /ʃəʊ/ *v* **shown, showed 1a** to cause or permit to be seen; exhibit **b** to be or come in view **c** to appear in a specified way **2** to present as a public spectacle **3** to reveal by one's condition **4** to demonstrate by one's achievements **5a** to point out to sby **b** to conduct, usher **6** to make evident; indicate **7a** to establish or make clear by argument or reasoning **b** to inform, instruct

²**show** *n* **1** a display – often + *on* **2a** a false semblance; a pretence **b** a more or less true appearance of sthg **c** an impressive display of sthg **d** ostentation **3a** a large display or exhibition arranged to arouse interest or stimulate sales **b** a competitive exhibition of animals, plants, etc to demonstrate quality in breeding, growing, etc **4a** a theatrical presentation **b** a radio or television programme **5** an enterprise, affair

¹**shower** /'ʃaʊə/ *n* **1** a fall of rain, snow, etc of short duration **2** sthg like a rain shower **3** an apparatus that provides a stream of water for spraying on the body; *also* an act of washing oneself using such an apparatus **4** *sing or pl in constr*, *Br* a motley or inferior collection of people – infml

²**shower** *v* **1a** to wet copiously (e g with water) in a spray, fine stream, or drops **b** to descend (as if) in a shower **c** to cause to fall in a shower **2** to bestow or present in abundance **3** to take a shower

showing /'ʃəʊɪŋ/ *n* **1** an act of putting sthg on view; a display, exhibition **2** performance in competition

show off *v* **1** to exhibit proudly **2** to

seek attention or admiration by conspicuous behaviour – **show-off** n

shrank /ʃræŋk/ past of **shrink**

¹**shred** /ʃred/ n a narrow strip cut or torn off; also a fragment, scrap

²**shred** v to cut or tear into shreds – ~**der** n

shrewd /ʃru:d/ adj 1 marked by keen discernment and hardheaded practicality 2 wily, artful – ~**ly** adv – ~**ness** n

¹**shriek** /ʃri:k/ v 1 to utter or make a shrill piercing cry; screech 2 to utter with a shriek or sharply and shrilly – often + out

²**shriek** n (a sound similar to) a shrill usu wild cry

¹**shrill** /ʃrɪl/ v to utter or emit a high-pitched piercing sound

²**shrill** adj having, making, or being a sharp high-pitched sound

¹**shrimp** /ʃrɪmp/ n 1 any of numerous mostly small marine 10-legged crustacean animals with a long slender body, compressed abdomen, and long legs 2 a very small or puny person – infml; humor

²**shrimp** v to fish for or catch shrimps – usu in **go shrimping**

shrink /ʃrɪŋk/ v **shrank**, also **shrunk; shrunk, shrunken** 1 to draw back or cower away (e g from sthg painful or horrible) 2 to contract to a smaller volume or extent (e g as a result of heat or moisture) 3 to show reluctance (e g before a difficult or unpleasant duty); recoil

²**shrink** n 1 shrinkage 2 a psychoanalyst or psychiatrist – humor

shrub /ʃrʌb/ n a low-growing usu several-stemmed woody plant – ~**by** adj

shrug /ʃrʌg/ v to lift and contract (the shoulders), esp to express aloofness, aversion, or doubt – **shrug** n

shudder /ʃʌdə⁻/ v 1 to tremble with a sudden brief convulsive movement 2 to quiver, vibrate – **shudder** n

¹**shuffle** /ʃʌfəl/ v 1 to rearrange (e g playing cards or dominoes) to produce a random order 2 to move or walk by sliding or dragging the feet – ~**r** n

²**shuffle** /ʃʌfəl/ n **1a** shuffling (e g of cards) **b** a right or turn to shuffle **2** (a dance characterized by) a dragging sliding movement

shun /ʃʌn/ v to avoid deliberately, esp habitually

shut /ʃʌt/ v **shut** 1 to place in position to close an opening 2 to confine (as if) by enclosure 3 to fasten with a lock or bolt 4 to close by bringing enclosing or covering parts together 5 to cause to cease or suspend operation – usu + down

¹**shutter** /ʃʌtə⁻/ n 1 a usu hinged outside cover for a window, often fitted as one of a pair 2 a device that opens and closes the lens aperture of a camera

²**shutter** v to provide or close with shutters

¹**shy** /ʃaɪ/ adj 1 easily alarmed; timid, distrustful – often in combination 2 wary of 3 sensitively reserved or retiring; bashful; also expressive of such a state or nature – ~**ly** adv – ~**ness** n

²**shy** v 1 to start suddenly aside in fright or alarm; recoil 2 to move or dodge to evade a person or thing – usu + away or from

³**shy** v to throw with a jerking movement; fling

⁴**shy** n 1 a toss, throw 2 a verbal sally or a stall (e g at a fairground) in which people throw balls at targets (e g coconuts) in order to knock them down 4 an attempt

¹**sick** /sɪk/ adj **1a** ill, ailing **b** queasy, nauseated; likely to vomit – often in combination **2a** disgusted or weary, esp because of surfeit **b** distressed and longing for sthg that one has lost or been parted from **3** mentally or emotionally disturbed; also macabre – ~**en** v

²**sick** n, Br vomit

sicken /sɪkən/ v 1 to become ill; show signs of illness 2 to drive to the point of despair or loathing

sickly /sɪkli/ adj 1 somewhat unwell; also habitually ailing 2 feeble, weak 3 mawkish, saccharine

sickness /sɪknɪs/ n 1 ill health 2 a specific disease 3 nausea, queasiness

¹**side** /saɪd/ n **1a** the right or left part of the wall or trunk of the body **b** the right or left half of the animal body or of a meat carcass 2 a location, region, or direction considered in relation to a centre or line of division 3 a surface forming a border or face of an object 4 a slope of a hill, ridge, etc 5 a bounding line or surface of a geometrical figure **6a** sing or pl in constr a person or group in competition or dispute with another **b** the attitude or activity of such a person or group; a part **7** a line of descent traced through a parent **8** an aspect or part of sthg viewed in contrast with some other aspect or part

²**side** adj 1 at, from, towards, etc the side **2a** incidental, subordinate **b** made on the side, esp in secret **c** additional to the main part or portion

³**side** v to take sides; join or form sides

sidelight /saɪdlaɪt/ n 1 incidental or additional information **2a** the red port light or the green starboard light carried by ships travelling at night **b** a light at the side of a (motor) vehicle

sideshow /saɪdʃəʊ/ n 1 a fairground booth or counter offering a game of luck or skill 2 an incidental diversion

sidestep /saɪdstep/ v 1 to step sideways or to one side 2 to evade an issue or decision

sideways /saɪdweɪz/, NAm also sideway adv or adj 1 to or from the side; also askance 2 with 1 side forward (e g turn it sideways) 3 to a position of equivalent rank (e g he was promoted sideways)

siege /si:dʒ/ n a military blockade of a city or fortified place to compel it to surrender

¹**sieve** /sɪv/ n a device with a meshed or perforated bottom that will allow the passage of liquids or fine solids while retaining coarser material or solids

²**sieve** v to sift

sift /sift/ v **1a** to put through a sieve **b** to separate (out) (as if) by passing through a sieve **2** to scatter (as if) with a sieve

¹**sigh** /sai/ v **1** to take a long deep audible breath (e g in weariness or grief) **2** esp of the wind to make a sound like sighing **3** to grieve, yearn – usu + for

²**sigh** n an act of sighing, esp when expressing an emotion or feeling (e g weariness or relief)

¹**sight** /sait/ n **1** sthg seen; esp a spectacle **2a** a thing (e g an impressive or historic building) regarded as worth seeing – often pl **b** sthg ridiculous or displeasing in appearance **3** the process, power, or function of seeing **4** a view, glimpse **5** the range of vision **6a** a device for guiding the eye (e g in aiming a firearm or bomb) **b** a device with a small aperture through which objects are to be seen and by which their direction is ascertained **7** a great deal; a lot – infml

²**sight** v **1** to get or catch sight of **2** to aim (e g a weapon) by means of sights – ~**ing** n

sightseeing /'saitsi:iŋ/ n the act or pastime of touring interesting or attractive sights – often in go sightseeing – **-seer** n

¹**sign** /sain/ n **1a** a motion or gesture by which a thought, command, or wish is made known **b** a signal **2** a mark with a conventional meaning, used to replace or supplement words **3** a character (e g ÷) indicating a mathematical operation; also either of 2 characters + and – that form part of the symbol of a number and characterize it as positive or negative **4** a board or notice bearing information or advertising matter or giving warning, command, or identification **5a** sthg serving to indicate the presence or existence of sby or sthg **b** a presage, portent

²**sign** v **1** to indicate, represent, or express by a sign **2** to put one's signature to **3** to engage by securing the signature on a contract of employment – often + on or up

¹**signal** /'signəl/ n **1** sthg that occasions action **2** a conventional sign (e g a siren or flashing light) made to give warning or command **3** an object used to transmit or convey information beyond the range of human voice **4** the sound or image conveyed in telegraphy, telephony, radio, radar, or television

²**signal** v **1** to warn, order, or request by a signal **2** to communicate by signals **3** to be a sign of; mark

³**signal** adj **1** used in signalling **2** distinguished from the ordinary; conspicuous – chiefly fml

signature /'signətʃər/ n **1** the name of a person written with his/her own hand **2** a letter or figure placed usu at the bottom of the first page on each sheet of printed pages (e g of a book) as a direction to the binder in gathering the sheets

significance /sig'nifikəns/ n **1** sthg conveyed as a meaning, often latently or indirectly **2** the quality of being important; consequence

significant /sig'nifikənt/ adj **1** having meaning; esp expressive **2** suggesting or containing a veiled or special meaning **3a** having or likely to have influence or effect; important **b** probably caused by sthg other than chance – ~**ly** adv

signify /'signifai/ v **1** to mean, denote **2** to show, esp by a conventional token (e g a word, signal, or gesture)

¹**signpost** /'sainpəust/ n a post (e g at a road junction) with signs on it to direct travellers

²**signpost** v **1** to provide with signposts or guides **2** to indicate, mark, esp conspicuously

¹**silence** /'sailəns/ n **1** forbearance from speech or noise; muteness – often interjectional **2** absence of sound or noise; stillness **3** failure to mention a particular thing **4a** oblivion, obscurity **b** secrecy

²**silence** v **1** to put or reduce to silence; still **2** to restrain from expression; suppress **3** to cause (a gun, mortar, etc) to cease firing by return fire, bombing, etc

silent /'sailənt/ adj **1a** mute, speechless; also not talkative **2** free from sound or noise; also without spoken dialogue **3a** endured without utterance **b** conveyed by refraining from reaction or comment; tacit – ~**ly** adv

silk /silk/ n **1** a fibre produced by various insect larvae, usu for cocoons; esp a lustrous tough elastic fibre produced by silkworms and used for textiles **2** thread, yarn, or fabric made from silk filaments

silly /'sili/ adj **1a** showing a lack of common sense or sound judgment **b** trifling, frivolous **2** stunned, dazed

¹**silver** /'silvə'/ n **1** a white ductile and malleable metallic element that takes a very high degree of polish and has the highest thermal and electrical conductivity of any substance **2** coins made of silver or cupro-nickel **3** articles, esp tableware, made of or plated with silver; also cutlery made of other metals **4** a whitish grey colour **5** a silver medal for second place in a competition

²**silver** adj **1** made of silver **2** resembling silver, esp in having a white lustrous sheen **3** consisting of or yielding silver **4** of or marking a 25th anniversary

similar /'similə', 'similə'/ adj **1** marked by correspondence or resemblance, esp of a general kind **2** alike in 1 or more essential aspects – ~**ity** n – ~**ly** adv

simile /'simili/ n a figure of speech explicitly comparing 2 unlike things (e g in cheeks like roses)

simmer /'simə'/ v **1** to bubble gently below or just at the boiling point **2** to be agitated by suppressed emotion – **simmer** n

simple /'simpəl/ adj **1a** free from guile or vanity; unassuming **b** free from elaboration or showiness; unpretentious **2** lacking intelligence; esp mentally retarded **b** naive **3a** sheer, unqualified

b composed essentially of 1 substance **4** not subdivided **5** readily understood or performed; straightforward

simplicity /sɪm'plɪsₑti/ *n* **1** the state or quality of being simple **2** naivety **3** freedom from affectation or guile **4a** directness of expression; clarity **b** restraint in ornamentation

simplify /'sɪmplₑfaɪ/ *v* to make or become simple or simpler – **-fication** *n*

simply /'sɪmpli/ *adv* **1a** without ambiguity; clearly **b** without ornamentation or show **c** without affectation or subterfuge; candidly **2a** solely, merely **b** without any question

simultaneous /ˌsɪmᵊl'teɪnɪəs/ *adj* existing, occurring, or functioning at the same time – **~ly** *adv* – **-neity**, **~ness** *n*

¹**sin** /sɪn/ *n* **1** an offence against moral or religious law or divine commandments **2** an action considered highly reprehensible

²**sin** *v* to commit a sin or an offence – often + *against* – **~ner** *n*

¹**since** /sɪns/ *adv* **1** continuously from then until now (e g has stayed here ever *since*) **2** before now; ago (e g should have done it long *since*) **3** between then and now; subsequently (e g has *since* become rich) *USE* + tenses formed with *to have*

²**since** *prep* in the period between (a specified past time) and now (e g haven't met *since* 1973); from (a specified past time) until now (e g it's a long time *since* breakfast) – + present tenses and tenses formed with *to have*

³**since** *conj* **1** between now and the past time when (e g has held 2 jobs *since* he left school); continuously from the past time when (e g ever *since* he was a child) **2** in view of the fact that; because (e g more interesting, *since* rarer)

sincere /sɪn'sɪə'/ *adj* free from deceit or hypocrisy; honest, genuine – **~ly** *adv* – **-rity** *n*

sing /sɪŋ/ *v* **sang, sung 1a** to produce musical sounds by means of the voice **b** to utter words in musical notes and with musical inflections and modulations **2** to make a loud clear sound or utterance **3a** to relate or celebrate in verse **b** to express vividly or enthusiastically **4** to give information or evidence – slang – **~able** *adj* – **~er** *n*

¹**single** /'sɪŋgᵊl/ *adj* **1** not married **2** not accompanied by others; sole **3** consisting of or having only 1 part or feature **4** consisting of a separate unique whole; individual **5** of *combat* involving only 2 people

²**single** *n* **1** a single person, thing or amount **2** a single run scored in cricket **3** a gramophone record, esp of popular music, with a single short track on each side **4** *Br* a ticket bought for a trip to a place but not back again

³**single** *v* to select or distinguish from a number or group – usu + *out*

single file *n* a line (e g of people) moving one behind the other

single-handed *adj* **1** performed or

achieved by 1 person or with 1 on a side **2** working or managing alone or unassisted by others

single-minded *adj* having a single overriding purpose – **~ly** *adv* – **~ness** *n*

¹**singular** /'sɪŋgjʊlə'/ *adj* **1a** of a separate person or thing; individual **b** of or being a word form denoting 1 person, thing, or instance **2** distinguished by superiority; exceptional **3** not general **4** very unusual or strange; peculiar

²**singular** *n* the singular number, the inflectional form denoting it, or a word in that form

sinister /'sɪnₑstə'/ *adj* **1** (darkly or insidiously) evil or productive of evil or ill fortune; ominous **3** of or situated on the left side or to the left of sthg, esp in heraldry

¹**sink** /sɪŋk/ *v* **sank, sunk 1a** to go down below a surface (e g of water or a soft substance) **b** to cause sthg to penetrate **2a** to fall or drop to a lower place or level **b** to disappear from view **c** to take on a hollow appearance **3** to be or become deeply absorbed *in* **4** to dig or bore (a well or shaft) in the earth **5** to invest – **~able** *adj*

²**sink** *n* **1** a basin, esp in a kitchen, connected to a drain and usu a water supply for washing up **2** a place of vice or corruption **3** a depression in which water (e g from a river) collects and becomes absorbed or evaporated

¹**sip** /sɪp/ *v* to drink (sthg) delicately or a little at a time

²**sip** *n* (a small quantity imbibed by) sipping

sir /sə'; *strong* sɜ:'/ *n* **1** a man entitled to be addressed as *sir* – used as a title before the Christian name of a knight or baronet **2a** – used as a usu respectful form of address to a male **b** *cap* – used as a conventional form of address at the beginning of a letter

siren /'saɪərən/ *n* **1** *often cap* any of a group of mythological partly human female creatures that lured mariners to destruction by their singing **2** a dangerously alluring or seductive woman; a temptress **3** a usu electrically operated device for producing a penetrating warning sound

¹**sister** /'sɪstə'/ *n* **1a** a female having the same parents as another person **b** a half sister **2** *often cap* **a** (the title given to) a Roman Catholic nun **b** a female fellow member of a Christian church **3** a woman related to another person by a common tie or interest (e g adherence to feminist principles) **4** *chiefly Br* a female nurse; *esp* one who is next in rank below a nursing officer and is in charge of a ward or a small department – **~hood** *n*

²**sister** *adj* related (as if) by sisterhood; essentially similar

sister-in-law *n, pl* **sisters-in-law 1** the sister of one's spouse **2** the wife of one's brother

sit /sɪt/ *v* **sat 1a** to rest on the buttocks or haunches **b** to perch, roost **2** to occupy a place as a member of an official body **3** to be in session for official business **4** to cover eggs for hatching **5a** to take up a position for being photographed or painted **b** to act as a model **6** to lie or hang relative to a wearer **7** to take an examination

¹**site** /saɪt/ *n* **1** an area of ground that was, is, or will be occupied by a structure or set of structures (e g a building, town, or monument) **2** the place, scene, or point of sth

²**site** *v* to place on a site or in position; locate

situated /'sɪtʃʊeɪtɪd/ *adj* **1** located **2** supplied to the specified extent with money or possessions **3** being in the specified situation

situation /ˌsɪtʃʊ'eɪʃən/ *n* **1a** the way in which sth is placed in relation to its surroundings **b** a locality **2** position with respect to conditions and circumstances **3** the circumstances at a particular moment; *esp* a critical or problematic state of affairs **4** a position of employment; a post – *chiefly fml*

six /sɪks/ *n* **1** the number 6 **2** the sixth in a set or series **3** sth having 6 parts or members or a denomination of 6: e g **a** a shot in cricket that crosses the boundary before it bounces and so scores 6 runs **b** *pl in constr, cap* the Common Market countries before 1973 – ~**th** *adj, n, pron, adv*

sixteen /ˌsɪk'stiːn/ *n* **1** the number 16 **2** *pl but sing in constr* a book format in which a folded sheet forms 16 leaves – ~**th** *adj, n, pron, adv*

sixty /'sɪksti/ *n* **1** the number 60 **2** *pl* the numbers 60-69; *specif* a range of temperatures, ages, or dates in a century characterized by those numbers – **-tieth** *adj, n, pron, adv*

¹**size** /saɪz/ *n* **1a** physical magnitude, extent, or bulk **b** relative amount or number **c** bigness **2** any of a series of graduated measures, esp of manufactured articles (e g of clothing), conventionally identified by numbers or letters

²**size** *v* to arrange or grade according to size or bulk

³**size** *n* any of various thick and sticky materials used for filling the pores in surfaces (e g of paper, textiles, leather, or plaster) or for applying colour or metal leaf (e g to book edges or covers)

⁴**size** *v* to cover, stiffen, or glaze (as if) with size

¹**skate** /skeɪt/ *n* any of numerous rays that have greatly developed pectoral fins and many of which are important food fishes

²**skate** *n* **1** a roller skate **2** an ice skate

³**skate** *v* **1** to glide along on skates propelled by the alternate action of the legs **2** to glide or slide as if on skates **3** to proceed in a superficial manner – ~**r** *n*

skeleton /'skelɪtn/ *n* **1** a supportive or protective usu rigid structure or framework of an organism; *esp* the bony or more or less cartilaginous framework supporting the soft tissues and protecting the internal organs of a fish or mammal **2** sth reduced to its bare essentials **3** an emaciated person or animal **4** a secret cause of shame, esp in a family – often in *skeleton in the cupboard*

¹**sketch** /sketʃ/ *n* **1** a preliminary study or draft; *esp* a rough often preliminary drawing representing the chief features of an object or scene **2** a brief description or outline **3** a short theatrical piece having a single scene; *esp* a comic variety act

²**sketch** *v* to make a sketch, rough draft, or outline of – ~**er** *n*

ski /skiː/ *n, pl* **skis** **1a** a long narrow strip usu of wood, metal, or plastic that curves upwards in front and is typically one of a pair used esp for gliding over snow **b** a water ski **2** a runner on a vehicle – **ski** *v* – ~**er** *n*

¹**skid** /skɪd/ *n* **1** a device placed under a wheel to prevent its turning or used as a drag **2** the act of skidding; a slide

²**skid** *v of a vehicle, wheel, driver, etc* to slip or slide, esp out of control

skilful /'skɪlfəl/ *NAm chiefly* **skillful** *adj* possessing or displaying skill; expert – ~**ly** *adv*

skill /skɪl/ *n* **1** the ability to utilize one's knowledge effectively and readily **2** a developed aptitude or ability in a particular field – ~**ed** *adj*

skim /skɪm/ *v* **1a** to remove (e g film or scum) from the surface of a liquid **b** to remove cream from (milk) **c** to remove (the choicest part or members) from sth; cream **2** to glance through (e g a book) for the chief ideas or the plot **3** to glide lightly or smoothly along or just above a surface

¹**skin** /skɪn/ *n* **1a** the external covering of an animal (e g a fur-bearing mammal or a bird) separated from the body, usu with its hair or feathers; pelt **b(1)** the pelt of an animal prepared for use as a trimming or in a garment **(2)** a container (e g for wine or water) made of animal skin **2a** the external limiting layer of an animal body, esp when forming a tough but flexible cover **b** any of various outer or surface layers (e g a rind, husk, or film) **3** the life or welfare of a person – esp in *save one's skin* **4** a sheathing or casing forming the outside surface of a ship, aircraft, etc – ~**less** *adj*

²**skin** *v* **1a** to strip, scrape, or peel away an outer covering (e g the skin or rind) of **b** to cut, graze, or damage the surface of **2** to strip of money or property; fleece – *infml*

¹**skip** /skɪp/ *v* **-pp-** **1a** to swing a rope round the body from head to toe, making a small jump each time it passes beneath the feet **b** to rebound from one point or thing after another; ricochet **2** to leave hurriedly or secretly; abscond **3** to leave out (a step in a progression or series); omit **4** to fail to attend

²**skip** *n* **1** a light bounding step or gait **2** an act of omission (e g in reading)

³**skip** *n* **1** a bucket or cage for carrying

men and materials (e g in mining or quarrying) **2** a large open container for waste or rubble

¹skipper /'skɪpə'/ n any of numerous small butterflies that differ from the typical butterflies in the arrangement of the veins in the wings and the form of the antennae

²skipper n **1** the master of a fishing, small trading, or pleasure boat **2** the captain or first pilot of an aircraft **3** Br the captain of a sports team – USE (2&3) infml

¹skirmish /'skɜːmɪʃ/ n **1** a minor or irregular fight in war, usu between small outlying detachments **2** a brief preliminary conflict; broadly any minor or petty dispute

²skirmish v to engage in a skirmish – ~er n

¹skirt /skɜːt/ n **1a(1)** a free-hanging part of a garment (e g a coat) extending from the waist down **(2)** a garment or undergarment worn by women and girls that hangs from and fits closely round the waist **b** either of 2 usu leather flaps on a saddle covering the bars on which the stirrups are hung **2** the borders or outer edge of an area or group – often pl with sing. meaning

²skirt v **1** to extend along or form the border or edge of; border **2** to go or pass round; specif to avoid through fear of difficulty, danger, or dispute

skulk /skʌlk/ v **1** to move in a stealthy or furtive manner **2** to hide or conceal oneself, esp out of cowardice or fear or for a sinister purpose – ~er n

skull /skʌl/ n the skeleton of the head of a vertebrate animal forming a bony or cartilaginous case that encloses and protects the brain and chief sense organs and forms the jaws

¹sky /skaɪ/ n **1** the upper atmosphere when seen as an apparent great vault over the earth; the firmament, heavens **2** weather as manifested by the condition of the sky

²sky v chiefly Br to throw, toss, or hit (e g a ball) high in the air

skyline /'skaɪlaɪn/ n **1** the apparent juncture of earth and sky; the horizon **2** an outline (e g of buildings or a mountain range) against the background of the sky

skyscraper /'skaɪ,skreɪpə'/ n a many-storeyed building

slab /slæb/ n a thick flat usu large plate or slice (e g of stone, wood, or bread)

¹slack /slæk/ adj **1** insufficiently prompt, diligent, or careful; negligent **2a** characterized by slowness, indolence, or languor **b** of tide flowing slowly; sluggish **3a** not taut; relaxed **b** lacking in usual or normal firmness and steadiness – ~ly adv – ~ness n

²slack v **1** to be or become slack **2** to shirk or evade work or duty

³slack n **1** cessation in movement or flow **2** a part of sthg (e g a sail or a rope) that hangs loose without strain **3** pl trousers, esp for casual wear **4** a lull or decrease in activity; a dull season or period

⁴slack n the finest particles of coal produced at a mine

slain /sleɪn/ past part of slay

¹slam /slæm/ n a banging noise; esp one made by a door

²slam v **1** to shut forcibly and noisily; bang **2** to put or throw down noisily and violently **3** to criticize harshly – infml

¹slander /'slɑːndə'/ n the utterance of false charges which do damage to another's reputation

²slander v to utter slander against – ~er n – ~ously adv

slang /slæŋ/ n **1** language peculiar to a particular group **2** informal usu spoken vocabulary – ~y adj – ~iness n

¹slant /slɑːnt/ v **1** to turn or incline from a horizontal or vertical line or a level **2** to take a diagonal course, direction, or path **3** to interpret or present in accord with a particular interest; bias – ~ingly adv

²slant n **1** a slanting direction, line, or plane; a slope **2a** a particular or personal point of view, attitude, or opinion **b** an unfair bias or distortion (e g in a piece of writing)

¹slap /slæp/ n a quick sharp blow, esp with the open hand

²slap v **1** to strike sharply (as if) with the open hand **2** to put, place, or throw with careless haste or force

³slap adv directly, smack

¹slash /slæʃ/ v **1** to cut with violent usu random sweeping strokes **2** esp of rain to fall hard and slantingly **3** to cut slits in (e g a garment) so as to reveal an underlying fabric or colour **4** to criticize cuttingly **5** to reduce drastically; cut

²slash n **1** the act of slashing; also a long cut or stroke made (as if) by slashing **2** an ornamental slit in a garment **3** chiefly Br an act of urinating – infml

¹slate /sleɪt/ n **1** a piece of slate rock used as roofing material **2** a fine-grained metamorphic rock consisting of compressed clay, shale, etc and easily split into (thin) layers **3** a tablet of material, esp slate, used for writing on **4** a dark bluish or greenish grey colour

²slate v, chiefly Br to criticize or censure severely – infml

¹slaughter /'slɔːtə'/ n **1** the act of killing; specif the butchering of livestock for market **2** killing of many people (e g in battle); carnage

²slaughter v **1** to kill (animals) for food **2** to kill violently or in large numbers

¹slave /sleɪv/ n **1** sby held in servitude as the property of another **2** sby who is dominated by a specified thing or person **3** a drudge

²slave v to work like a slave; toil

slavery /'sleɪvəri/ n **1** drudgery, toil **2a** being a slave **b** owning slaves

slay /sleɪ/ v slew; slain **1** to kill violently or with great bloodshed; slaughter **2** to affect overpoweringly (e g with awe or delight) – infml – ~er n

¹sledge /sledʒ/ n a sledgehammer

²**sledge** *n* a vehicle with runners that is pulled by reindeer, horses, dogs, etc and is used esp over snow or ice; *also* a toboggan

sledgehammer /'sledʒ,hæmə'/ *n* a large heavy hammer that is wielded with both hands

sledge-hammer *adj* clumsy, heavy-handed

¹**sleep** /sli:p/ *n* 1 the natural periodic suspension of consciousness that is essential for the physical and mental well-being of higher animals 2 a sleep-like state: e g **a** a state marked by a diminution of feeling followed by tingling **b** the state of an animal during hibernation **c** death – euph 3 a period spent sleeping

²**sleep** *v* **slept** 1 to rest in a state of sleep 2 to have sexual relations – + *with* or *together*

sleepless /'sli:plɪs/ *adj* 1 not able to sleep 2 unceasingly active – ~ly *adv* – ~ness *n*

sleepy /'sli:pi/ *adj* 1 ready to fall asleep 2 lacking alertness; sluggish, lethargic 3 sleep-inducing – **sleepily** *adv* – **sleepiness** *n*

¹**sleet** /sli:t/ *n* precipitation in the form of partly frozen rain, or snow and rain falling together – ~y *adj*

²**sleet** *v* to send down sleet

sleeve /sli:v/ *n* 1 a part of a garment covering the arm 2 a paper or often highly distinctive cardboard covering that protects a gramophone record when not in use – ~**less** *adj*

slender /'slendə'/ *adj* **1a** gracefully slim **b** small or narrow in circumference or width in proportion to length or height **2a** flimsy, tenuous **b** limited or inadequate in amount; meagre – ~ly *adv* – ~ness *n*

¹**slew** /slu:/ *past of* **slay**

²**slew** *v* 1 to turn, twist, or swing about 2 to skid

¹**slice** /slaɪs/ *n* **1a** a thin broad flat piece cut from a thing larger whole **b** a wedge-shaped piece (e g of pie or cake) 2 an implement with a broad blade used for lifting, turning, or serving food 3 a portion, share

²**slice** *v* 1 to cut through (as if) with a knife 2 to cut into slices

¹**slide** /slaɪd/ *v* **slid** **1a** to move in continuous contact with a smooth surface **b** to glide over snow or ice **c** to pass quietly and unobtrusively; steal 3 to pass by smooth or imperceptible gradations

²**slide** *n* 1 an act or instance of sliding 2 a sliding part or mechanism: e g **a** a U-shaped section of tube in the trombone that is pushed out and in to produce notes of different pitch **b** a moving piece of a mechanism that is guided by a part along which it slides **3a**(1) a track or slope suitable for sliding or tobogganing (2) a chute with a slippery surface down which children slide in play **b** a channel or track down or along which sthg is slid **4a** a flat piece of glass on which an object is mounted for examination using a light microscope **b**

a photographic transparency on a small plate or film suitably mounted for projection 5 *Br* a hair-slide

¹**slight** /slaɪt/ *adj* **1a** having a slim or frail build **b** lacking strength or bulk; flimsy **c** trivial; minor 2 scanty, meagre – ~ly *adv* – ~ness *n*

²**slight** *v* 1 to treat as slight or unimportant 2 to treat with disdain or pointed indifference; snub – ~**ingly** *adv*

³**slight** *n* 1 an act of slighting 2 a humiliating affront

¹**slim** /slɪm/ *adj* 1 of small or narrow circumference or width, esp in proportion to length or height 2 slender in build 3 scanty, slight – ~ly *adv* – ~ness *n*

²**slim** *v* to become thinner (e g by dieting) – ~**mer** *n* – ~**ming** *n*

slime /slaɪm/ *n* 1 soft moist soil or clay; *esp* viscous mud 2 mucus or a mucus-like substance secreted by slugs, catfish, etc

slimy /'slaɪmi/ *adj* 1 of or resembling slime; viscous; *also* covered with or yielding slime 2 characterized by obsequious flattery; offensively ingratiating – **sliminess** *n*

¹**sling** /slɪŋ/ *v* **slung** 1 to cast with a careless and usu sweeping or swirling motion; fling 2 *Br* to cast forcibly and usu abruptly – *infml* – ~**er** *n*

²**sling** *n* an act of slinging or hurling a stone or other missile

³**sling** *n* 1 a device that gives extra force to a stone or other missile thrown by hand and usu consists of a short strap that is looped round the missile, whirled round, and then released at 1 end **2a** a usu looped line used to hoist, lower, or carry sthg (e g a rifle); *esp* a bandage suspended from the neck to support an arm or hand **b** a device (e g a rope net) for enclosing material to be hoisted by a tackle or crane

¹**slip** /slɪp/ *v* **1a** to move with a smooth sliding motion **b** to move quietly and cautiously; steal 2 *of time* to elapse, pass **3a** to slide out of place or away from a support or one's grasp **b** to slide on or down a slippery surface 4 to get speedily *into* or *out of* clothing 5 to fall off from a standard or accustomed level by degrees 6 to escape from (one's memory or notice) **7a** to cause to slip open; release, undo **b** to let go of **8a** to insert, place, or pass quietly or secretly **b** to give or pay on the sly 9 to dislocate

²**slip** *n* 1 a sloping ramp extending out into the water to serve as a place for landing, repairing, or building ships 2 *the* act or an instance of eluding or evading **3a** a mistake in judgment, policy, or procedure; a blunder **b** an inadvertent and trivial fault or error 4 (a movement producing) a small geological fault 5 a fall from some level or standard 6 a women's sleeveless undergarment with shoulder straps that resembles a light dress 7 any of several fielding positions in cricket that are close to the batsman and just to the (off) side of the wicketkeeper

³**slip** n **1** a long narrow strip of material (e g paper or wood) **2** a young and slim person

⁴**slip** n a semifluid mixture of clay and water used by potters (e g for coating or decorating ware)

slipper /'slɪpəʳ/ n a light shoe that is easily slipped on the foot; esp a flat-heeled shoe that is worn while resting at home

slippery /'slɪpəri/ adj **1a** causing or tending to cause sthg to slide or fall **b** tending to slip from the grasp **2** not to be trusted; shifty – **-iness** n

¹**slit** /slɪt/ v **slit 1** to make a slit in **2** to cut or tear into long narrow strips

²**slit** n a long narrow cut or opening

slogan /'sləʊgən/ n **1** a phrase used to express and esp make public a particular view, position, or aim **2** a brief catchy phrase used in advertising or promotion

¹**slope** /sləʊp/ v to lie at a slant; incline

²**slope** n **1** a piece of inclined ground **2** upward or downward inclination or (degree of) slant

sloppy /'slɒpi/ adj **1a** wet so as to splash; slushy **b** wet or smeared (as if) with sthg slopped over **2** slovenly, careless **3** disagreeably effusive – **-pily** adv – **-piness** n

¹**slot** /slɒt/ n **1a** a narrow opening, groove, or passage; a slit **2** a place or position in an organization or sequence; a niche

²**slot** v **1** to cut a slot in **2** to place in or assign to a slot – often + in or into

¹**slow** /sləʊ/ adj **1a** lacking in intelligence; dull **b** naturally inert or sluggish **2a** lacking in readiness, promptness, or willingness **b** not quickly aroused or excited **3a** flowing or proceeding with little or less than usual speed **b** exhibiting or marked by retarded speed **c** low, feeble **4** requiring a long time; gradual **5a** having qualities that hinder or prevent rapid movement **b** (designed) for slow movement **6** registering a time earlier than the correct one **7** lacking in liveliness or variety; boring – **~ly** adv – **~ness** n

²**slow** adv in a slow manner; slowly

³**slow** v to make or become slow or slower – often + down or up

¹**slug** /slʌg/ n any of numerous slimy elongated chiefly ground-living gastropod molluscs that are found in most damp parts of the world and have no shell

²**slug** n **1** a lump, disc, or cylinder of material (e g plastic or metal): e g **a** a bullet – slang **b** NAm a disc for insertion in a slot machine; esp one used illegally instead of a coin **2** chiefly NAm a quantity of spirits that can be swallowed at a single gulp – slang

³**slug** n a heavy blow, esp with the fist – infml

⁴**slug** v to hit hard (as if) with the fist – infml

¹**slum** /slʌm/ n **1** a poor overcrowded run-down area, esp in a city – often pl

with sing. meaning **2** a squalid disagreeable place to live – **~my** adj

²**slum** v **1** to live in squalor or on very slender means – often + it **2** to amuse oneself by visiting a place on a much lower social level; also to affect the characteristics of a lower social class

¹**slump** /slʌmp/ v **1a** to fall or sink abruptly **b** to drop down suddenly and heavily; collapse **2** to assume a drooping posture or carriage; slouch

²**slump** n a marked or sustained decline, esp in economic activity or prices

slung /slʌŋ/ past of **sling**

sly /slaɪ/ adj **slier** also **slyer; sliest** also **slyest 1a** clever in concealing one's ends or intentions; furtive **b** lacking in integrity and candour; crafty **2** humorously mischievous; roguish – **~ly** adv – **~ness** n

¹**smack** /smæk/ n (a slight hint of) a characteristic taste, flavour, or aura

²**smack** v **1** to slap smartly, esp in punishment **2** to open (the lips) with a sudden sharp sound, esp in anticipation of food or drink

³**smack** n **1** a sharp blow, esp from sthg flat; a slap **2** a noisy parting of the lips **3** a loud kiss **4** chiefly NAm heroin – slang

⁴**smack** adv squarely and with force; directly – infml

⁵**smack** n a small inshore fishing vessel

¹**small** /smɔːl/ adj **1a** having relatively little size or dimensions **b** immature, young **2a** little in quantity, value, amount, etc **b** made up of few individuals or units **3** lower-case **4** lacking in strength **5a** operating on a limited scale **b** minor in power, influence, etc **c** limited in degree **6** of little consequence; trivial **7a** mean, petty **b** reduced to a humiliating position – **~ness** n

²**small** adv **1** in or into small pieces **2** in a small manner or size

³**small** n **1** a part smaller and esp narrower than the remainder; specif the narrowest part of the back **2** pl, Br small articles of underwear – infml

¹**smart** /smɑːt/ v **1** (to be the cause or seat of) a sharp pain **2** to feel or endure mental distress

²**smart** adj **1** making one smart; causing a sharp stinging **2** forceful, vigorous **3** brisk, spirited **4a** mentally alert; bright **b** clever, shrewd **5** witty, persuasive **6a** neat or stylish in dress or appearance **b** characteristic of or frequented by fashionable society – **~ly** adv – **~ness** n

³**smart** adv in a smart manner; smartly

⁴**smart** n **1** a smarting pain; esp a stinging local pain **2** poignant grief or remorse

¹**smash** /smæʃ/ v **1** to break in pieces by violence; shatter **2a** to drive, throw, or hit violently, esp causing breaking or shattering **b** to hit (e g a ball) with a forceful stroke, specif a smash **3** to destroy utterly; wreck – often + up **4** to crash into; collide

²**smash** n **1a(1)** a smashing blow, attack, or collision **(2)** the result of smashing; esp a wreck due to collision **b** a forceful

overhand stroke (e g in tennis or badminton) **2** utter collapse; ruin; *esp* bankruptcy

³smash *adv* with a resounding crash

smashing /'smæʃɪŋ/ *adj* extremely good; excellent – *infml*

¹smear /smɪə/ *n* **1** a mark or blemish made (as if) by smearing a substance **2** material taken or prepared for microscopic examination by smearing on a slide **3** a usu unsubstantiated accusation

²smear *v* **1** to spread with sthg sticky, greasy, or viscous **2a** to stain or dirty (as if) by smearing **b** to sully, besmirch; *specif* to blacken the reputation of

¹smell /smel/ *v* **smelled, smelt 1a** to have a usu specified smell **b** to have a characteristic aura; be suggestive *of* **c** to have an offensive smell; stink **2** to perceive the odour of (as if) by use of the sense of smell **3** to detect or become aware of by instinct

²smell *n* **1** the one of the 5 basic physical senses by which the qualities of gaseous or volatile substances in contact with certain sensitive areas in the nose are interpreted by the brain as characteristic odours **2** an odour **3** a pervading quality; an aura

¹smile /smaɪl/ *v* **1** to have or assume a smile **2a** to look with amusement or scorn **b** to bestow approval **c** to appear pleasant or agreeable – **smilingly** *adv*

²smile *n* **1** a change of facial expression in which the corners of the mouth curve slightly upwards and which expresses esp amusement, pleasure, approval, or sometimes scorn **2** a pleasant or encouraging appearance

¹smoke /sməʊk/ *n* **1** the gaseous products of burning carbon-containing materials made visible by the presence of small particles of carbon **2** fumes or vapour resembling smoke **3** an act or spell of smoking esp tobacco – ~**less** *adj*

²smoke *v* **1** to emit smoke **2** to (habitually) inhale and exhale the fumes of burning tobacco **3a** to fumigate **b** to drive *out* or away by smoke **4** to colour or darken (as if) with smoke **5** to cure (e g meat or fish) by exposure to smoke, traditionally from green wood or peat

smoker /'sməʊkə/ *n* **1** sby who regularly or habitually smokes tobacco **2** a carriage or compartment in which smoking is allowed

smoky /'sməʊki/ *also* **smokey** *adj* **1** emitting smoke, esp in large quantities **2** suggestive of smoke, esp in flavour, smell, or colour **3a** filled with smoke **b** made black or grimy by smoke – **smokiness** *n*

¹smooth /smuːð/ *adj* **1a** having a continuous even surface **b** free from hair or hairlike projections **c** *of liquid* of an even consistency; free from lumps **d** giving no resistance to sliding; frictionless **2** free from difficulties or obstructions **3** even and uninterrupted in movement or flow **4a** urbane, courteous **b** excessively and often artfully

suave; ingratiating **5** not sharp or acid – ~**ly** *adv* – ~**ness** *n*

²smooth *v* **1** to make smooth **2** to free from what is harsh or disagreeable **3** to dispel or alleviate (e g enmity or perplexity) – often + *away* or *over* **4** to free from obstruction or difficulty **5** to press flat – often + *out* **6** to cause to lie evenly and in order – often + *down*

¹smother /'smʌðə/ *n* a confused mass of things; a welter

²smother *v* **1** to overcome or kill with smoke or fumes **2** to overcome or discomfort (as if) through lack of air **3a** to suppress expression or knowledge of; conceal **b** to prevent the growth or development of; suppress **4a** to cover thickly; blanket **b** to overwhelm

smoulder /'sməʊldə/ *NAm chiefly* **smolder** *v* **1** to burn feebly with little flame and often much smoke **2** to exist in a state of suppressed ferment

smuggle /'smʌgəl/ *v* **1** to import or export secretly contrary to the law, esp without paying duties **2** to convey or introduce surreptitiously – **-gler** *n* – **-gling** *n*

snack /snæk/ *n* a light meal; food eaten between regular meals

snag /snæg/ *n* **1** a sharp or jagged projecting part **2** a concealed or unexpected difficulty or obstacle **3** an irregular tear or flaw made (as if) by catching on a snag

snail /sneɪl/ *n* **1** a gastropod mollusc; *esp* one that has an external enclosing spiral shell **2** a slow-moving or sluggish person or thing

¹snake /sneɪk/ *n* **1** any of numerous limbless scaly reptiles with a long tapering body and with salivary glands often modified to produce venom which is injected through grooved or tubular fangs **2** a sly treacherous person **3** *often cap* a system in which the values of the currencies of countries in the European Economic Community are allowed to vary against each other within narrow limits

²snake *v* to wind in the manner of a snake – **snaky** *adj*

¹snap /snæp/ *v* **1** to grasp or snatch at sthg eagerly **2** to utter sharp biting words; give an irritable retort **3a** to break suddenly, esp with a sharp cracking sound **b** to close or fit in place with an abrupt movement or sharp sound **4** to take possession or advantage of suddenly or eagerly – usu + *up* **5** to photograph

²snap *n* **1** an abrupt closing (e g of the mouth in biting or of scissors in cutting) **2** an act or instance of seizing abruptly; a sudden snatch or bite **3** a sharp curt retort **4a** a sound made by snapping **b** a sudden sharp breaking of sthg thin or brittle **5** a sudden spell of harsh weather **6** a thin brittle biscuit **7** a snapshot **8** a card game in which each player tries to be the first to shout 'snap' when 2 cards of identical value are laid successively

³snap *interj, Br* – used to draw attention to an identity or similarity

⁴snap *adv* with (the sound of) a snap

⁵snap *adj* performed suddenly, unexpectedly, or without deliberation

snapshot /'snæpʃɒt/ *n* a casual photograph made typically by an amateur with a small hand-held camera and without regard to technique

¹snare /sneə'/ *n* **1a** a trap often consisting of a noose for catching animals **b** sthg by which one is trapped or deceived **2** any of the catgut strings or metal spirals of a snare drum which produce a rattling sound

²snare *v* **1** to procure by artful or skilful actions **2** to entangle or hold as if in a snare

¹snarl /snɑːl/ *n* **1** a tangle, esp of hair or thread; a knot **2** a confused or complicated situation

²snarl *v* **1** to cause to become knotted and intertwined; tangle **2** to make excessively confused or complicated *USE* often + *up*

³snarl *v* **1** to growl with bared teeth **2** to speak in a vicious or bad-tempered manner – **snarl** *n*

¹snatch /snætʃ/ *v* to attempt to seize sthg suddenly – often + *at* – **~er** *n*

²snatch *n* **1** a snatching at or of sthg **2a** a brief period of time or activity **b** sthg fragmentary or hurried **3** a robbery – *infml*

¹sneak /sniːk/ *v* **1** to go or leave stealthily or furtively; slink **2** to behave in a furtive or servile manner **3** *Br* to tell tales – *infml*

²sneak *n* **1** a person who acts in a stealthy or furtive manner **2** the act or an instance of sneaking **3** *Br* a person, esp a schoolchild, who tells tales against others – *infml*

sneaking /'sniːkɪŋ/ *adj* **1** furtive, underhand **2** mean, contemptible **3** instinctively felt but unverified

¹sneer /snɪə'/ *v* **1** to smile or laugh with a curl of the lips to express scorn or contempt **2** to speak or write in a scornfully jeering manner – **~er** *n* – **~ingly** *adv*

²sneer *n* a sneering expression or remark

sneeze /sniːz/ *v or n* (to make) a sudden violent involuntary audible expiration of breath

sniff /snɪf/ *v* **1** to draw air audibly up the nose, esp for smelling **2** to show or express disdain or scorn *at* **3** to detect or become aware of (as if) by smelling – **~er** *n*

¹sniff *n* **1** an act or sound of sniffing **2** a quantity that is sniffed

snob /snɒb/ *n* **1** one who blatantly attempts to cultivate or imitate those he/she admires as social superiors **2** one who has an air of smug superiority in matters of knowledge or taste – **~bish** *adj* – **~bishly** *adv* – **~bishness** *n*

snore /snɔː'/ *v or n* (to breathe with) a rough hoarse noise due to vibration of the soft palate during sleep

snort /snɔːt/ *v* **1** to force air violently through the nose with a rough harsh sound **2** to express scorn, anger, or

surprise by a snort **3** to take in (a drug) by inhalation – *infml*

²snort *n* **1** an act or sound of snorting **2** a snifter – *infml*

¹snow /snəʊ/ *n* **1a** (a descent of) water falling in the form of white flakes consisting of small ice crystals formed directly from vapour in the atmosphere **b** fallen snow **2** cocaine – *slang*

²snow *v* **1** to fall in or as snow **2** to cover, shut in, or block (as if) with snow – usu + *in* or *up*

¹snowball /'snəʊbɔːl/ *n* a round mass of snow pressed or rolled together for throwing

²snowball *v* **1** to throw snowballs at **2** to increase or expand at a rapidly accelerating rate

¹snug /snʌg/ *adj* **1** fitting closely and comfortably **2a** enjoying or affording warm secure comfortable shelter **b** marked by relaxation and cordiality **3** affording a degree of comfort and ease – **~ly** *adv*

²snug *v* to snuggle

³snug *n, Br* a small private room or compartment in a pub

¹so /səʊ/ *adv* **1a(1)** in this way; thus – often used as a substitute for a preceding word or word group (e g do you really think so?) **(2)** most certainly; indeed (e g I hope to win and so I shall) **b(1)** in the same way; also – used after *as* to introduce a parallel (e g as the French drink wine, so the British love their beer) **(2)** as an accompaniment – after *as* **c** in such a way – used esp before *as* or *that*, to introduce a result or to introduce the idea of purpose **2a** to such an extreme degree – used before *as* to introduce a comparison, esp in the negative (e g not so fast as mine), or, esp before *as* or *that*, to introduce a result (e g so tired that I went to bed) **b** very **c** to a definite but unspecified extent or degree (e g can only do so much in a day) **3** therefore, consequently **4** then, subsequently **5** *chiefly dial & NAm* – used esp by children, to counter a negative charge

²so *conj* **1** with the result that **2** in order that **3a** for that reason; therefore **b(1)** – used as an introductory particle (e g so here we are) often to belittle a point under discussion (e g so what?)

³so *adj* **1** conforming with actual facts; true **2** disposed in a definite order (e g his books were always exactly so)

⁴so *pron* such as has been specified or suggested; the same

so, soh *n* the musical note sol

¹soak /səʊk/ *v* **1** to lie immersed in liquid (e g water), esp so as to become saturated or softened **2** to become fully felt or appreciated – usu + *in* or *into* **3** to intoxicate (oneself) with alcohol – *infml* **4** to charge an excessive amount of money – *infml* – **~ed** *adj* – **~ing** *adj*

²soak *n* **1a** soaking or being soaked **b** that (e g liquid) in which sthg is soaked **2** a drunkard – *infml*

so-and-so *n, pl* **so-and-sos, so-and-so's** **1** an unnamed or unspecified person or

thing 2 a disliked or unpleasant person
– euph

¹**soap** /səup/ *n* a cleansing and emulsifying agent that lathers when rubbed in water – **soapy** *adj*

²**soap** *v* 1 to rub soap over or into 2 to flatter – often + *up*; *infml*

¹**soar** /sɔː/ *v* 1a to fly high in the air b to sail or hover in the air, often at a great height 2 to rise rapidly or to a very high level 3 to be of imposing height or stature; tower

²**soar** *n* (the range, distance, or height attained in) soaring

¹**sob** /sɒb/ *v* 1 to weep with convulsive catching of the breath 2 to make a sound like that of a sob or sobbing

²**sob** *n* an act or sound of sobbing; *also* a similar sound

¹**sober** /'səubə/ *adj* 1 not drunk or addicted to drink 2 gravely or earnestly thoughtful 3 calmly self-controlled; sedate 4a well balanced; realistic b sane, rational 5 subdued in tone or colour – ~**ly** *adv*

²**sober** *v* to make or become sober – usu + *up*

so-called *adj* 1 commonly named; popularly so termed 2 falsely or improperly so named

soccer /'sɒkə/ *n* a football game that is played with a round ball between teams of 11 players each, that features the kicking and heading of the ball, and in which use of the hands and arms is prohibited except to the goalkeepers

sociable /'səuʃəbəl/ *adj* 1 inclined to seek or enjoy companionship; companionable 2 conducive to friendliness or cordial social relations – -**bility** *n* – -**bly** *adv*

¹**social** /'səuʃəl/ *adj* 1 of or promoting companionship or friendly relations 2a tending to form cooperative relationships; gregarious b living and breeding in more or less organized communities 3 of human society – ~**ly** *adv*

²**social** *n* a social gathering, usu connected with a church or club

socialism /'səuʃəlizəm/ *n* 1 an economic and political theory advocating, or a system based on, collective or state ownership and administration of the means of production and distribution of goods 2 a transitional stage of society in Marxist theory distinguished by unequal distribution of goods according to work done

¹**socialist** /'səuʃəlist/ *n* 1 one who advocates or practises socialism 2 *cap* a member of a socialist party or group

²**socialist** *adj* 1 of socialism 2 *cap* of or constituting a party advocating socialism

¹**society** /sə'saiəti/ *n* 1 companionship or association with others; company 2a *often cap* the human race considered in terms of its structure of social institutions b(1) a community having common traditions, institutions, and collective interests (2) an organized group working together or periodically meeting because of common interests,

beliefs, or profession 3 a fashionable leisure class

²**society** *adj* (characteristic) of fashionable society

sociology /,səusi'ɒlədʒi, ,səuʃi-/ *n* the science of social institutions and relationships; *specif* the study of the often changing behaviour of organized human groups – -**gical** *adj* – -**gically** *adv* – -**gist** *n*

¹**sock** /sɒk/ *n* a knitted or woven covering for the foot usu extending above the ankle and sometimes to the knee

²**sock** *v* to hit or apply forcefully – *infml*

³**sock** *n* a vigorous or forceful blow; a punch – *infml*

socket /'sɒkit/ *n* an opening or hollow that forms a holder for sthg; *also* an electrical plug

sofa /'səufə/ *n* a long upholstered seat with a back and 2 arms or raised ends that typically seats 2 to 4 people

¹**soft** /sɒft/ *adj* 1a yielding to physical pressure b of a consistency that may be shaped, moulded, spread, or easily cut c lacking in hardness 2a pleasing or agreeable to the senses; bringing ease or quiet b having a bland or mellow taste c not bright or glaring; subdued d(1) quiet in pitch or volume; not harsh (2) *of c and g* pronounced /s/ and /j/ respectively (e g in *acid* and *age*) – not used technically e(1) *of the eyes* having a liquid or gentle appearance (2) having a gently curved outline f smooth or delicate in texture falling or blowing with slight force or impact 3a marked by a kindness, lenience, or moderation: e g b mild, low-key; *specif* not of the most extreme or harmful kind 4a lacking resilience or strength, esp as a result of having led a life of ease b mentally deficient; feebleminded 5 amorously attracted, esp covertly – + *on*

²**soft** *n* a soft object, material, or part

³**soft** *adv* in a soft or gentle manner; softly

soften /'sɒfən/ *v* 1 to make soft or softer 2a to weaken the military resistance or the morale of b to impair the strength or resistance of USE (2) often + *up*

softhearted /,sɒft'hɑːtid/ *adj* kind, compassionate – ~**ness** *n*

software /'sɒftweə/ *n* 1 the entire set of programs and procedures associated with a system, esp a computer system 2 sthg contrasted with hardware; *esp* materials for use with audiovisual equipment

soggy /'sɒgi/ *adj* 1a waterlogged, soaked b sodden 2 heavily dull – -**gily** *adv* – -**giness** *n*

¹**soil** /sɔil/ *v* 1 to stain or make unclean, esp superficially; dirty 2 to defile morally; corrupt 3 to blacken or tarnish (e g a person's reputation)

²**soil** *n* 1 firm land; earth 2 the upper layer of earth that may be dug or ploughed and in which plants grow 3 country, land 4 refuse or sewage 5 a medium in which sthg takes hold and develops

solar /'səulə/ *adj* 1 of or derived from

the sun, esp as affecting the earth **2** (of or reckoned by time) measured by the earth's course in relation to the sun **3** produced or operated by the action of the sun's light or heat; *also* using the sun's rays

solar system *n* the sun together with the group of celestial bodies that are held by its attraction and revolve round it

sold /sohld/ *past of* **sell**

¹**soldier** /'sohldzə'/ *n* **1** sby engaged in military service, esp in the army **2** any of a caste of ants or wingless termites having a large head and jaws

²**soldier** *v* **1** to serve as a soldier **2** to press doggedly forward – usu + *on*

¹**sole** /sohl/ *n* **1a** the undersurface of a foot **b** the part of a garment or article of footwear on which the sole rests **2** the usu flat bottom or lower part of sthg or the base on which sthg rests

²**sole** *v* to provide with a (new) sole

³**sole** *n* any of several flatfish including some valued as superior food fishes

⁴**sole** *adj* **1** being the only one; only **2** belonging or relating exclusively to 1 individual or group – ~**ly** *adv*

solemn /'soləm/ *adj* **1** performed so as to be legally binding **2** celebrated with full liturgical ceremony **3a** conveying a deep sense of reverence or exaltation; sublime **b** marked by seriousness and sobriety **c** sombre, gloomy – ~**ly** *adv* – ~**ness** *n*

solicitor /sə'lisitə'/ *n* a qualified lawyer who advises clients, represents them in the lower courts, and prepares cases for barristers to try in higher courts

¹**solid** /'solid/ *adj* **1a** without an internal cavity **b** having no opening or division **2** of uniformly close and coherent texture; compact **3** of good substantial quality or kind: e g **a** well constructed from durable materials **b** sound, cogent **4a** having, involving, or dealing with 3 dimensions or with solids **b** neither gaseous nor liquid **5** without interruption; full **6** of a single substance or character: e g **a** (almost) entirely of 1 metal **b** of uniform colour or tone **7** reliable, reputable, or acceptable – ~**ity** *n* – ~**ly** *adv* – ~**ness** *n*

²**solid** *adv* in a solid manner; *also* unanimously

³**solid** *n* **1** a substance that does not flow perceptibly under moderate stress **2** sthg solid; *esp* a solid colour

¹**solitary** /'solitəri/ *adj* **1a** (fond of) being or living alone or without companions **b** lonely **2** taken, spent, or performed without companions **3** being the only one; sole **4** unfrequented, remote

²**solitary** *n* one who habitually seeks solitude

solitude /'solitjuːd/ *n* **1** being alone or remote from society; seclusion **2** a lonely place; a fastness

¹**solo** /'sohloh/ *n* **1** a (musical composition for) performance by a single voice or instrument with or without accompaniment **2** a flight by 1 person alone in

an aircraft; *esp* a person's first solo flight

²**solo** *adv* without a companion; alone

soluble /'soljubl/ *adj* **1** capable of being dissolved (as if) in a liquid **2** capable of being solved or explained – -**bility** *n*

solution /sə'luːʃən/ *n* **1a** an act or the process by which a solid, liquid, or gaseous substance is uniformly mixed with a liquid or sometimes a gas or solid **b** a typically liquid uniform mixture formed by this process **c** a liquid containing a dissolved substance **2a** an action or process of solving a problem **b** an answer to a problem

solve /solv/ *v* to find a solution for sthg – **solvable** *adj* – **solver** *n*

¹**some** /sʌm/ *adj* **1a** being an unknown, undetermined, or unspecified unit or thing (e g *some* film or other) **b** being an unspecified member of a group or part of a class (e g *some* gems are hard) **c** being an appreciable number, part, or amount of (e g have *some* consideration for others) **d** being of an unspecified amount or number (e g give me *some* water) – used as an indefinite pl of **a** (e g have *some* apples) **2a** an important, striking, or excellent (e g that was *some* party) – chiefly infml **b** no kind of (e g *some* friend you are) – chiefly infml

²**some** /sam; *strong* sʌm/ *pron* **1** *sing or pl in constr* some part, quantity, or number but not all **2** *chiefly NAm* an indefinite additional amount (e g ran a mile and then *some*)

³**some** /sʌm/ *adv* **1** about (e g *some* 80 houses) **2** somewhat – used in Br English in *some more* and more widely in NAm

¹**somebody** /'sʌmbɒdi/ *pron* some indefinite or unspecified person

²**somebody** *n* a person of position or importance

somehow /'sʌmhau/ *adv* **1a** by some means not known or designated **b** no matter how **2** for some mysterious reason

somersault /'sʌməsɔːlt/ *n* a leaping or rolling movement in which a person turns forwards or backwards in a complete revolution bringing the feet over the head and finally landing on the feet

¹**something** /'sʌmθəŋ/ *pron* **1a** some indeterminate or unspecified thing – used to replace forgotten matter or to express vagueness (e g he's *something* or other in the Foreign Office) **b** some part; a certain amount (e g seen *something* of her work) **2a** a person or thing of consequence (e g their daughter is quite *something*) **b** some truth or value (e g there's *something* in what you say)

²**something** *adv* **1** in some degree; somewhat – also used to suggest approximation (e g *something* like 1,000 people) **2** to an extreme degree (e g swears *something* awful) – infml

¹**sometime** /'sʌmtaim/ *adv* **1** at some unspecified future time **2** at some point of time in a specified period

²sometime *adj* having been formerly; late (e g the *sometime* chairman)

sometimes /'sʌmtaɪmz/ *adv* at intervals; occasionally; now and again

somewhat /'sʌmwɒt/ *adv* to some degree; slightly

¹somewhere /'sʌmweə'/ *adv* **1** in, at, or to some unknown or unspecified place **2** to a place or state symbolizing positive accomplishment or progress (e g at last we're getting *somewhere*) **3** in the vicinity of; approximately

²somewhere *n* an undetermined or unnamed place

son /sʌn/ *n* **1a** a male offspring, esp of human beings **b** a male adopted child **c** a male descendant – often pl **2** *cap* the second person of the Trinity; Christ

song /sɒŋ/ *n* **1** the act, art, or product of singing **2** poetry **3** (the melody of) a short musical composition usu with words **4** a very small sum

¹soon /suːn/ *adv* **1** before long; without undue time lapse **2** in a prompt manner; speedily **3** in agreement with one's preference; willingly – in comparisons (e g I'd *sooner* walk than drive)

²soon *adj* advanced in time; early

soot /sʊt/ *n* a fine black powder that consists chiefly of carbon and is formed by combustion, or separated from fuel during combustion

soothe /suːð/ *v* **1** to calm (as if) by showing attention or concern; placate **2** to relieve, alleviate **3** to bring comfort or reassurance to – **soothingly** *adv*

sophisticated /sə'fɪstɪkeɪtɪd/ *adj* **1a** highly complicated or developed; complex **b** worldly-wise, knowing **2** intellectually subtle or refined – **-cation** *n*

¹sore /sɔː'/ *adj* **1a** causing pain or distress **b** painfully sensitive **c** hurt or inflamed so as to be or seem painful **2a** causing irritation or offence **b** causing great difficulty or anxiety; desperate **3** *chiefly NAm* angry, vexed – **~ness** *n*

²sore *n* **1** a localized sore spot on the body **2** a source of pain or vexation; an affliction

¹sorrow /'sɒrəʊ/ *n* **1** deep distress and regret (e g over the loss of sthg precious) **2** a cause or display of grief or sadness – **~ful** *adj* – **~fully** *adv* – **~fulness** *n*

²sorrow *v* to feel or express sorrow

sorry /'sɒri/ *adj* **1** feeling regret, penitence, or pity **2** inspiring sorrow, pity, or scorn

¹sort /sɔːt/ *n* **1** a group constituted on the basis of any common characteristic; a class, kind **b** an instance of a kind **2** nature, disposition **3** a person, individual – *infml*

²sort *v* **1** to put in a rank or particular place according to kind, class, or quality – often + *through* **2** *chiefly Scot* to put in working order; mend – **~er** *n*

sort of *adv* **1** to a moderate degree; rather **2** kind of *USE infml*

sought /sɔːt/ *past of* seek

¹soul /səʊl/ *n* **1** the immaterial essence or animating principle of an individual life **2** all that constitutes a person's self **3a** an active or essential part **b** a moving spirit; a leader **4** a person **5** exemplification, personification **6a** a strong positive feeling esp of intense sensitivity and emotional fervour conveyed esp by American Negro performers **b** music that originated in American Negro gospel singing, is closely related to rhythm and blues, and is characterized by intensity of feeling and earthiness

²soul *adj* (characteristic) of American Negroes or their culture

¹sound /saʊnd/ *adj* **1a** healthy **b** free from defect or decay **2** solid, firm; *also* stable **3a** free from error, fallacy, or misapprehension **b** exhibiting or grounded in thorough knowledge and experience **c** conforming to accepted views; orthodox **4a** deep and undisturbed **b** thorough, severe – **~ly** *adv* – **~ness** *n*

²sound *adv* fully, thoroughly

³sound *n* **1a** the sensation perceived by the sense of hearing **b** energy that is transmitted by longitudinal pressure waves in a material medium (e g air) and is the objective cause of hearing **2** a speech sound **3** a characteristic musical style **4** radio broadcasting as opposed to television – **~less** *adj* – **~lessly** *adv*

⁴sound *v* **1a** to make a sound **b** to resound **c** to give a summons by sound **2** to have a specified import when heard; seem

⁵sound *n* **1** a long broad sea inlet **2a** a long passage of water connecting **2** larger bodies or separating a mainland and an island

⁶sound *v* **1** to determine the depth of water, esp with a sounding line **2** *of a fish or whale* to dive down suddenly

soup /suːp/ *n* **1** a liquid food typically having a meat, fish, or vegetable stock as a base and often thickened and containing pieces of solid food **2** an awkward or embarrassing predicament – *infml*

¹sour /saʊə'/ *adj* **1** being or inducing one of the 4 basic taste sensations that is produced chiefly by acids **2a** having the acid taste or smell (as if) of fermentation **b** smelling or tasting of decay; rotten **c** wrong, awry **3a** unpleasant, distasteful **b** morose, bitter – **~ly** *adv* – **~ness** *n*

²sour *n* the primary taste sensation produced by sthg sour

source /sɔːs/ *n* **1** the point of origin of a stream of water **2a(1)** a generative force; a cause **(2)** a means of supply **b(1)** a place of origin; a beginning **(2)** sby or sthg that initiates **(3)** a person, publication, etc that supplies information, esp at firsthand

¹south /saʊθ/ *adj or adv* towards, at, belonging to, or coming from the south

²south *n* **1** (the compass point corresponding to) the direction of the south terrestrial pole **2** *often cap* regions or countries lying to the south of a specified or implied point of orientation

¹southeast /saʊθ'iːst/ *adj or adv* towards, at, belonging to, or coming from the southeast

²southeast /ˌsaʊθˈiːst/ *n* **1** (the general direction corresponding to) the compass point midway between south and east **2** *often cap* regions or countries lying to the southeast of a specified or implied point of orientation

¹southerly /ˈsʌðəli/ *adj or adv* south

²southerly *n* a wind from the S

southern /ˈsʌðən/ *adj* **1** *often cap* (characteristic) of a region conventionally designated South **2** south

¹southwest /ˌsaʊθˈwest/ *adj or adv* towards, at, belonging to, or coming from the southwest

²southwest /ˌsaʊθˈwest/ *n* **1** (the general direction corresponding to) the compass point midway between south and west **2** *often cap* regions or countries lying to the southwest of a specified or implied point of orientation

souvenir /ˌsuːvəˈnɪə/ *n* sthg that serves as a reminder (e g of a place or past event); a memento

¹sovereign /ˈsɒvrɪn/ *n* **1** a ruler **2** a former British gold coin worth 1 pound

²sovereign /ˈsɒvrɪn/ *adj* **1a** possessing supreme (political) power **b** unlimited in extent; absolute **c** enjoying political autonomy **2a** of outstanding excellence or importance **b** of an unqualified nature; utmost **3** (characteristic) of or befitting a sovereign – **~ty** *n*

soviet /ˈsəʊɪət, ˈsɒ-/ *n* **1** an elected council in a Communist country **2** *pl, cap* the people, esp the leaders, of the USSR

¹sow /saʊ/ *n* an adult female pig; *also* the adult female of various other animals (e g the grizzly bear)

²sow /səʊ/ *v* **sowed; sown, sowed 1a** to scatter (e g seed) on the earth for growth **b** to strew (as if) with seed **2** to implant, initiate – **~er** *n*

¹space /speɪs/ *n* **1** (the duration of) a period of time **2a** a limited extent in 1, 2, or 3 dimensions; distance, area, or volume **b** an amount of room set apart or available **3a** a boundless 3-dimensional extent in which objects and events occur and have relative position and direction **b** physical space independent of what occupies it **4** the region beyond the earth's atmosphere **5** (a piece of type giving) a blank area separating words or lines (e g on a page)

²space *v* to place at intervals or arrange with space between

spacecraft /ˈspeɪs-krɑːft/ *n* a device designed to travel beyond the earth's atmosphere

spaceship /ˈspeɪsˌʃɪp/ *n* a manned spacecraft

spacious /ˈspeɪʃəs/ *adj* **1** containing ample space; roomy **2a** broad or vast in area **b** large in scale or space; expansive – **~ly** *adv* – **~ness** *n*

¹spade /speɪd/ *n* a digging implement that can be pushed into the ground with the foot

²spade *n* **1a** a playing card marked with 1 or more black figures shaped like a spearhead **b** *pl but sing or pl in constr*

the suit comprising cards identified by these figures **2** a Negro – *derog*

spaghetti /spəˈgeti/ *n* pasta in the form of thin often solid strings of varying widths smaller in diameter than macaroni

¹span /spæn/ *archaic past of* **spin**

²span *n* **1** the distance from the end of the thumb to the end of the little finger of a spread hand **2** an extent, distance, or spread between 2 limits: e g **a** a limited stretch (e g of time); *esp* an individual's lifetime **b** the full reach or extent **c** the distance or extent between supports (e g of a bridge); *also* a part of a bridge between supports **d** a wingspan

³span *v* **1** to extend across **2** to form an arch over

spaniel /ˈspænjəl/ *n* **1** any of several breeds of small or medium-sized mostly short-legged dogs usu having long wavy hair, feathered legs and tail, and large drooping ears **2** a fawning servile person

¹spank /spæŋk/ *v* to strike, esp on the buttocks, (as if) with the open hand – **spank** *n* – **~ing** *n*

²spank *v* to move quickly or spiritedly

spanner /ˈspænə/ *n chiefly Br* a tool with 1 or 2 ends shaped for holding or turning nuts or bolts with nut-shaped heads

¹spare /speə/ *v* **1** to refrain from destroying, punishing, or harming **2** to relieve of the necessity of doing, undergoing, or learning sthg **3** to refrain from; avoid **4** to use or dispense frugally – *chiefly neg* **5** to give up as surplus to requirements

²spare *adj* **1** not in use; *esp* reserved for use in emergency **2a** in excess of what is required; surplus **b** not taken up with work or duties; free **3** healthily lean; wiry **4** not abundant; meagre – *infml* **5** *Br* extremely angry or distraught – *infml*

³spare *n* a spare or duplicate item or part; *specif* a spare part for a motor vehicle

spark /spɑːk/ *n* **1a** a small particle of a burning substance thrown out by a body in combustion or remaining when combustion is nearly completed **b** a hot glowing particle struck from a larger mass **2** a luminous disruptive electrical discharge of very short duration between 2 conductors of opposite high potential separated by a gas (e g air) **3** a sparkle, flash **4** sthg that sets off or stimulates an event, development, etc

²spark *v* **1** to produce or give off sparks **2** to cause to be suddenly active; precipitate – *usu* + *off*

³spark *n* a lively and usu witty person – esp in *bright spark*

¹sparkle /ˈspɑːkəl/ *v* **1** to give off or reflect glittering points of light **2** to effervesce **3** to show brilliance or animation

²sparkle *n* **1** a little spark **2** sparkling **3a** vivacity, gaiety **b** effervescence

sparrow /ˈspærəʊ/ *n* any of several

small dull-coloured songbirds related to the finches

sparse /spɑːs/ *adj* of few and scattered elements; *esp* not thickly grown or settled – ~**ly** *adv* – ~**ness**, **sparsity** *n*

spasm /'spæzəm/ *n* **1** an involuntary and abnormal muscular contraction **2 a** sudden violent and brief effort or emotion

¹**spastic** /'spæstɪk/ *adj* **1** of or characterized by spasm **2** suffering from a form of paralysis marked by involuntary jerks and twitches

²**spastic** *n* **1** one who is suffering from spastic paralysis **2** an ineffectual person – used esp by children

spate /speɪt/ *n* **1** flood **2a** a large number or amount, esp occurring in a short space of time **b** a sudden or strong outburst; a rush

speak /spiːk/ *v* spoke; spoken **1** to utter words with the ordinary voice; talk **b**(1) to give voice to thoughts or feelings (2) to be on speaking terms **c** to address a group **2** to act as spokesman *for* **3** to make a claim *for*; reserve **4** to make a characteristic or natural sound **5** to be indicative or suggestive

speaker /'spiːkə/ *n* **1a** one who speaks, esp at public functions **b** one who speaks a specified language **2** the presiding officer of a deliberative or legislative assembly **3** a loudspeaker

speak out **1** to speak loudly enough to be heard **2** to speak boldly; express an opinion frankly

speak up *v* **1** to speak more loudly – often imper **2** to express an opinion boldly

¹**spear** /spɪə/ *n* a thrusting or throwing weapon with long shaft and sharp head or blade used esp by hunters or foot soldiers

²**spear** *v* to pierce, strike, or take hold of (as if) with a spear

³**spear** *n* a usu young blade, shoot, or sprout (e g of asparagus or grass)

¹**special** /'speʃəl/ *adj* **1** distinguished from others of the same category, esp because in some way superior **2** held in particular esteem **3** specific **4** other than or in addition to the usual **5** designed, undertaken, or used for a particular purpose or need – ~**ly** *adv*

²**special** *n* **1** sthg that is not part of a series **2** sby or sthg maintained or produced for a particular use or occasion

specialist /'speʃəlɪst/ *n* **1** one who devotes him-/herself to a special occupation or branch of knowledge **2** a medical practitioner limiting his/her practice to a specific group of complaints

speciality /ˌspeʃɪ'ælɪti/ *n* **1** (the state of having) a distinctive mark or quality **2** a product or object of particular quality **3a** a special aptitude or skill **b** a particular occupation or branch of knowledge

species /'spiːʃiːz/ *n* **1a** a class of individuals having common attributes and designated by a common name **b** a category in the biological classification of living things that ranks immediately below a genus, comprises related organisms or populations potentially capable of interbreeding, and is designated by a name (e g *Homo sapiens*) that consists of the name of a genus followed by a Latin or latinized uncapitalized noun or adjective **2** a kind, sort – chiefly derog

¹**specific** /spɪ'sɪfɪk/ *adj* **1** being or relating to those properties of sthg that allow it to be assigned to a particular category **2** confined to a particular individual, group, or circumstance **3** free from ambiguity; explicit **4** of or constituting a (biological) species – ~**ally** *adv*

²**specific** *n* **1** a characteristic quality or trait **2** *pl, chiefly NAm* particulars

specify /'spesɪfaɪ/ *v* **1** to name or state explicitly or in detail **2** to include as an item in a specification

specimen /'spesɪmən/ *n* **1** an item, part, or individual typical of a group or category; an example **2** a person, individual – chiefly derog

¹**speck** /spek/ *n* **1** a small spot or blemish, esp from stain or decay **2** a small particle

²**speck** *v* to mark with specks

spectacle /'spektəkəl/ *n* **1a** sthg exhibited as unusual, noteworthy, or entertaining **b** an object of scorn or ridicule, esp due to odd appearance or behaviour **2** *pl* glasses

¹**spectacular** /spek'tækjʊlə/ *adj* of or being a spectacle; sensational – ~**ly** *adv*

²**spectacular** *n* sthg (e g a stage show) that is spectacular

spectator /spek'teɪtə/ *n* **1** one who attends an event or activity in order to watch **2** one who looks on without participating; an onlooker

spectrum /'spektrəm/ *n, pl* **spectra 1a** a series of images formed when a beam of radiant energy is subjected to dispersion and brought to focus so that the component waves are arranged in the order of their wavelengths (e g when a beam of sunlight that is refracted and dispersed by a prism forms a display of colours) **b** the range of frequencies of electromagnetic or sound waves **2** a sequence, range

speculate /'spekjʊleɪt/ *v* **1** to meditate *on* or ponder *about* sthg; reflect **2** to buy or sell in expectation of profiting from market fluctuations – -**lation** *n* – -**lator** *n*

speech /spiːtʃ/ *n* **1a** the communication or expression of thoughts in spoken words **b** conversation **2a** a public discourse; an address **3** a language, dialect

¹**speed** /spiːd/ *n* **1a** moving swiftly; swiftness **b** rate of motion **2** rate of performance or execution **3a** the sensitivity of a photographic film, plate, or paper expressed numerically **b** the duration of a photographic exposure **4** an amphetamine drug – slang

²**speed** *v* sped, speeded **1** to move or go quickly **2** to travel at excessive or illegal speed **3** to promote the success or development of

¹**spell** /spel/ *n* **1a** a spoken word or form of words held to have magic power **b** a state of enchantment **2** a compelling influence or attraction

²**spell** *v* spelt **1** to name, *also*, to write the letters of (e g a word) **d** **2** to amount to; mean **er** *n*

³**spell** *v* **1** stand in for **retie** **2** to give a brief rest to

⁴**spell** *n* **1** a period spent in a job or **2** a short or indefinite phase

...ing /'spelɪŋ/ *n* **1** the forming of or by to form words from letters **2** the ...ence of letters that make up a particular word

...nd /spend/ *v* spent **1** to use up or ...y out; expend **2** to wear out, exhaust ... to cause or permit to elapse; pass

...phagnum /'sfægnəm, 'sfæg-/ *n* any of a large genus of atypical mosses that grow only in wet acid areas (e g bogs) where their remains become compacted with other plant debris to form peat

sphere /sfɪə/ *n* **1a** a globular body; a ball **b** (a space or solid enclosed by) a surface, all points of which are equidistant from the centre **2** natural or proper place; *esp* social position or class **3** a field of action, existence, or influence

¹**spice** /spaɪs/ *n* **1** any of various aromatic vegetable products (e g pepper, ginger, or nutmeg) used to season or flavour foods **2** sthg that adds zest or relish **3** a pungent or aromatic smell

²**spice** *v* **1** to season with spice **2** to add zest or relish to

spicy /'spaɪsi/ *adj* **1** lively, spirited **2** piquant, zestful **3** somewhat scandalous; risqué – **spicily** *adv* – **-iness** *n*

spider /'spaɪdə/ *n* any of an order of arachnids having a body with 2 main divisions, 4 pairs of walking legs, and 2 or more pairs of abdominal glands for spinning threads of silk used for cocoons, nests, or webs

¹**spike** /spaɪk/ *n* **1** a very large nail **2a** any of a row of pointed iron pieces (e g on the top of a wall or fence) **b(1)** any of several metal projections set in the sole and heel of a shoe to improve traction **(2)** *pl* a pair of (athletics) shoes having spikes attached

²**spike** *v* **1** to fasten or provide with spikes **2** to disable (a muzzle-loading cannon) by driving a spike into the vent **3** to pierce with or impale on a spike; *specif* to reject (newspaper copy), orig by impaling on a spike **4** to add spirits to (a nonalcoholic drink)

³**spike** *n* **1** an ear of grain **2** an elongated plant inflorescence with the flowers stalkless on a single main axis

¹**spill** /spɪl/ *v* spill **1** to cause or allow to fall or flow out so as to be lost or wasted, esp accidentally **2** to spread profusely or beyond limits

²**spill** *n* **1** a fall from a horse or vehicle **2** a quantity spilt

³**spill** *n* a thin twist of paper or sliver of wood used esp for lighting a fire

¹**spin** /spɪn/ *v* spun **1** to draw out and twist fibre into yarn or thread **2** *esp of*

a spider or insect to form a thread by forcing out a sticky rapidly hardening fluid **3a** to revolve rapidly; whirl **b** to have the sensation of spinning; reel **4** to move swiftly, esp on wheels or in a vehicle **5** to compose and tell (a usu involved or fictitious story)

²**spin** *n* **1a** the act or an instance of spinning sthg **b** the whirling motion imparted (e g to a cricket ball) by spinning **c** a short excursion, esp in or on a motor vehicle **2** a state of mental confusion; a panic – *infml*

spinach /'spɪnɪdʒ, -ɪtʃ/ *n* a plant cultivated for its edible leaves

spindly /'spɪndli/ *adj* having an unnaturally tall or slender appearance, esp suggestive of physical weakness

spine /spaɪn/ *n* **1a** the spinal column **b** the back of a book, usu lettered with the title and author's name **2** a stiff pointed plant part **3** a sharp rigid part of an animal or fish

spinster /'spɪnstə/ *n* an unmarried woman; *esp* a woman who is past the usual age for marrying or who seems unlikely to marry – **~hood** *n*

¹**spiral** /'spaɪərəl/ *adj* **1a** winding round a centre or pole and gradually approaching or receding from it **b** helical **2** of the advancement to higher levels through a series of cyclical movements

²**spiral** *n* **1a** the path of a point in a plane moving round a central point while continuously receding from or approaching it **b** a 3-dimensional curve (e g a helix) with 1 or more turns about an axis **2** a single turn or coil in a spiral object **3** a continuously expanding and accelerating increase or decrease – **spiral** *v*

spire /spaɪə/ *n* a tall tapering roof or other construction on top of a tower

¹**spirit** /'spɪrɪt/ *n* **1** a supernatural being or essence: e g **a** *cap* the Holy Spirit **b** the soul **c** a ghost **d** a malevolent being that enters and possesses a human being **2** temper or state of mind – often pl with sing. meaning **3** the immaterial intelligent or conscious part of a person **4** the attitude or intention characterizing or influencing sthg **5** liveliness, energy; *also* courage **6** a person of a specified kind or character **7** distilled liquor of high alcoholic content – usu pl with sing. meaning **8a** prevailing characteristic **b** the true meaning of sthg (e g a rule or instruction) in contrast to its verbal expression

²**spirit** *v* to carry off, esp secretly or mysteriously – usu + *away* or *off*

spirited /'spɪrɪtɪd/ *adj* **1** full of energy, animation, or courage **2** having a specified frame of mind – often in combination

¹**spiritual** /'spɪrɪtʃʊəl/ *adj* **1** (consisting) of spirit; incorporeal **2** ecclesiastical rather than lay or temporal **3** concerned with religious values **4** of supernatural beings or phenomena – **~ly** *adv*

²**spiritual** *n* a usu emotional religious song of a kind developed esp among Negroes in the southern USA

spi

¹spit /spɪt/ n **1** a slender pointed rod for holding meat over a source of heat (e g an open fire) **2a** a small point of land, esp of sand or gravel, running into a river mouth, bay, etc

²spit v to fix (as if) on a spit; impale

³spit v **spat, spit 1** to eject saliva from the mouth (as an expression of aversion or contempt); *also* to get rid of something in the mouth by ejecting it with some force **2** to express (hostile or malicious feelings) (as if) by spitting **3** to rain or snow slightly or in flurries **4** to sputter

⁴spit n **1a** spittle, saliva **b** the act or an instance of spitting **2** a frothy secretion exuded by some insects

¹spite /spaɪt/ n petty ill will or malice – ~**ful** adj – ~**fully** adv – ~**fulness** n

²spite v to treat vindictively or annoy out of spite

¹splash /splæʃ/ v **1a** to strike and move about a liquid **b** to move through or into a liquid and cause it to spatter **2a** to dash a liquid or semiliquid substance on or against **b** to soil or stain with splashed liquid; spatter **3a** to spread or scatter in the manner of splashed liquid **b** to flow, fall, or strike with a splashing sound **4** chiefly Br to spend money liberally; splurge – usu + out

²splash n **1a** a spot or daub (as if) from splashed liquid **b** a usu vivid patch of colour or of sthg coloured **2a** (the sound of) splashing **b** a short plunge **3** (a vivid impression created esp by) an ostentatious display **4** a small amount, esp of a mixer added to an alcoholic drink; a dash

splendid /'splendɪd/ adj **1** magnificent, sumptuous **2** illustrious, distinguished **3** of the best or most enjoyable kind; excellent – ~**ly** adv

splendour /'splendə'/ n **1a** great brightness or lustre; brilliance **b** grandeur, pomp **2** sthg splendid

splint /splɪnt/ n material or a device used to protect and immobilize a body part (e g a broken arm)

¹splinter /'splɪntə'/ n **1** a sharp thin piece, esp of wood or glass, split or broken off lengthways **2** a small group or faction broken away from a parent body

²splinter v **1** to split or rend into long thin pieces; shatter **2** to split into fragments, parts, or factions

¹split /splɪt/ v **split 1a** to divide, esp lengthways or into layers **b** to break apart; burst **2** to subject (an atom or atomic nucleus) to artificial disintegration, by fission **3** to divide into parts or portions: e g **a** to divide between people; share **b** to divide into opposing factions, parties, etc **4** to sever relations or connections – often + up **5** to share sthg (e g loot or profits) with others – often + with **6** to let out a secret; act as an informer – often + on **7** to leave, esp hurriedly; depart – infml

²split n **1** a narrow break made (as if) by splitting **2** a piece broken off by splitting **3** a division into divergent groups or elements; a breach **4a** splitting **b** pl

but sing in constr the act of lowering oneself to the floor or leaping into the air with legs extended at right angles to the trunk **5** a wine bottle holding a quarter of a usual amount; *also* a small bottle **6** a mineral water, tonic water, etc **6** a mineral water, tonic sliced fruit, esp a rich composed of syrup, and often nuts, ice cream, cream

split adj **1** divided, fractured pared for use by splitting **2** pre-

split second n a fractional second; a flash – **split-second** adj

¹spoil /spɔɪl/ n plunder taken enemy in war or a victim in loot – often pl with sing. mean

²spoil v **spoilt, spoiled 1a** to seriously; ruin **b** to impair the ment of; mar **2a** to impair the cha of by overindulgence or excessive p **b** to treat indulgently; pamper **3** to good or useful qualities, usu as a result of decay **4** to have an eager desire for – esp in *spoiling for a fight* – ~**er** n

¹spoke /spəʊk/ past & archaic past part of **speak**

²spoke n **1** any of the small radiating bars inserted in the hub of a wheel to support the rim **2** a rung of a ladder

spoken /'spəʊkən/ adj **1a** delivered by word of mouth; oral **b** used in speaking or conversation; uttered **2** characterized by speaking in a specified manner – in combination

spokesman /'spəʊksmən/ n one who speaks on behalf of another or others

¹sponge /spʌndʒ/ n **1a(1)** an elastic porous mass of interlacing horny fibres that forms the internal skeleton of various marine animals and is able when wetted to absorb water **(2)** a porous rubber or cellulose product used similarly to a sponge **b** any of a group of aquatic lower invertebrate animals that are essentially double-walled cell colonies and permanently attached as adults **2** a sponger **3** a cake or sweet steamed pudding made from a light-textured mixture

²sponge v **1** to cleanse, wipe, or moisten (as if) with a sponge **2** to obtain esp financial assistance by exploiting natural generosity or organized welfare facilities – usu + on – ~**r** n

¹sponsor /'sponsə'/ n **1** sby who presents a candidate for baptism or confirmation and undertakes responsibility for his/her religious education or spiritual welfare **2** sby who assumes responsibility for some other person or thing **3** sby who or sthg that pays for a project or activity – ~**ship** n

²sponsor v to be or stand as sponsor for

spontaneous /spɒn'teɪnɪəs/ adj **1** proceeding from natural feeling or innate tendency without external constraint **2** springing from a sudden impulse **3** controlled and directed internally **4** developing without apparent external influence, force, cause, or treatment – ~**ly** adv – ~**ness, -neity** n

¹spoon /spuːn/ n **1** an eating, cooking,

or serving implement consisting of a small shallow round or oval bowl with a handle

²**spoon** v 1 to take up and usu transfer (as if) in a spoon 2 to propel (a ball) weakly upwards 3 to indulge in caressing and amorous talk – not now in vogue

spoonful /'spuːnfʊl/ n, pl **spoonfuls** also **spoonsful** as much as a spoon will hold

¹**sport** /spɔːt/ v 1 to exhibit for all to see; show off 2 to play about happily; frolic 3 to speak or act in jest; trifle

²**sport** n 1a a source of diversion or recreation; a pastime b physical activity engaged in for recreation 2a pleasantry, jest b mockery, derision 3 sby who is fair, generous, and esp a good loser 4 an individual exhibiting a sudden deviation from type beyond the normal limits of individual variation

sporting /'spɔːtɪŋ/ adj 1 concerned with, used for, or suitable for sport 2 marked by or calling for sportsmanship 3 involving such risk as a sports competitor might take or encounter 4 fond of or taking part in sports – ~ly adv

¹**spot** /spɒt/ n 1a a blemish on character or reputation; a stain 2a a small usu round area different (e g in colour or texture) from the surrounding surface b(1) an area marred or marked (e g by dirt) (2) a pimple c a conventionalized design used on playing cards to distinguish suits and indicate values 3 a small amount; a bit 4 a particular place or area 5 a place on an entertainment programme 6 a spotlight 7 a usu difficult or embarrassing position; a fix

²**spot** v 1 to mark or mar (as if) with spots 2a to single out; identify b to detect, notice c to watch for and record the sighting of 3 chiefly Br to fall lightly in scattered drops

³**spot** adj 1a available for immediate delivery after sale b involving immediate cash payment 2 given on the spot or restricted to a few random places or instances; also selected at random or as a sample

spotless /'spɒtlɪs/ adj 1 free from dirt or stains; immaculate 2 pure, unblemished – ~ly adv – ~ness n

spotlight /'spɒtlaɪt/ n 1a a projected spot of light used for brilliant illumination of a person or object on a stage b a light designed to direct a narrow intense beam on a small area 2 full public attention – **spotlight** v

spotted /'spɒtɪd/ adj 1 marked with spots 2 sullied, tarnished

¹**spout** /spaʊt/ v 1 to eject (e g liquid) in a copious stream 2 to speak or utter in a strident, pompous, or hackneyed manner; declaim – infml – ~er n

²**spout** n 1 a projecting tube or lip through which liquid issues from a teapot, roof, kettle, etc 2 a discharge or jet of liquid (as if) from a pipe

sprain /spreɪn/ n a sudden or violent twist or wrench of a joint with stretching or tearing of ligaments – **sprain** v

sprang /spræŋ/ past of **spring**

¹**sprawl** /sprɔːl/ v 1 to lie or sit with arms and legs spread out carelessly or awkwardly 2 to spread or develop irregularly

²**sprawl** n 1 a sprawling position 2 an irregular spreading mass or group

¹**spray** /spreɪ/ n 1 a usu flowering branch or shoot 2 a decorative arrangement of flowers and foliage (e g on a dress)

²**spray** n 1 fine droplets of water blown or falling through the air 2 a jet of vapour or finely divided liquid b a device (e g an atomizer or sprayer) by which a spray is dispersed or applied

³**spray** v 1 to discharge, disperse, or apply as a spray 2 to direct a spray on – ~er n

¹**spread** /spred/ v **spread** 1a to open or extend over a larger area – often + out b to stretch out; extend 2a to distribute over an area b to distribute over a period or among a group c to apply as a layer or covering 3a to make widely known b to extend the range or incidence of 4 to force apart – ~able adj

²**spread** n 1 (extent of) spreading 2 sthg spread out: e g a a surface area; an expanse b (the matter occupying) 2 facing pages, usu with printed matter running across the fold 3a a food product suitable for spreading b a sumptuous meal; a feast c a cloth cover; esp a bedspread

spring /sprɪŋ/ v **sprang; sprung** 1a(1) to dart, shoot (2) to be resilient or elastic; also to move by elastic force b to become warped 2 to issue suddenly and copiously; pour out 3a to issue by birth or descent b to come into being; arise 4a to make a leap or leaps b to rise or jump up suddenly 5 to produce or disclose suddenly or unexpectedly 6 to release from prison – infml

²**spring** n 1a a source of supply; esp an issue of water from the ground b an ultimate source, esp of thought or action 2 a time or season of growth or development; specif the season between winter and summer comprising, in the northern hemisphere, the months of March, April, and May 3 a mechanical part that recovers its original shape when released after deformation 4a the act or an instance of leaping up or forward; a bound b(1) capacity for springing; resilience (2) bounce, energy – ~less adj

¹**sprinkle** /'sprɪŋkəl/ v 1 to scatter in fine drops or particles 2a to distribute (sthg) at intervals (as if) by scattering b to occur at (random) intervals on; dot c to wet lightly

²**sprinkle** n 1 an instance of sprinkling; specif a light fall of rain 2 a sprinkling

¹**sprint** /sprɪnt/ v to run or ride a bicycle at top speed, esp for a short distance – ~er n

²**sprint** n 1 (an instance of) sprinting 2a a short fast running, swimming, or bicycle race b a burst of speed

sprung /sprʌŋ/ *adj,* **1** *past of* **spring** **2** equipped with springs

spun /spʌn/ *past of* **spin**

¹spur /spɜːʳ/ *n* **1a** a pointed device secured to a rider's heel and used to urge on a horse **b** *pl* recognition and reward for achievement **2** a goad to action; a stimulus **3a** a stiff sharp spine (e g on the wings or legs of a bird or insect); *esp* one on a cock's leg **b** a hollow projection from a plant's petals or sepals (e g in larkspur or columbine) **4** a lateral projection (e g a ridge) of a mountain (range)

²spur *v* to incite to usu faster action or greater effort; stimulate – usu + *on*

¹spurt /spɜːt/ *v or n* (to make) a sudden brief burst of increased effort, activity, or speed

²spurt *v* to (cause to) gush out in a jet

³spurt *n* a sudden forceful gush; a jet

¹spy /spaɪ/ *v* **1** to catch sight of; see **2** to watch secretly; act as a spy – often + *on*

²spy *n* **1** one who keeps secret watch on sby or sthg **2** one who attempts to gain information secretly from a country, company, etc and communicate it to another

squabble /ˈskwɒbəl/ *v or n* (to engage in) a noisy or heated quarrel, esp over trifles

squad /skwɒd/ *n* **1** a small group of military personnel assembled for a purpose **2** a small group working as a team

squadron /ˈskwɒdrən/ *n* a unit of military organization: **a** a unit of cavalry or of an armoured regiment, usu consisting of 3 or more troops **b** a variable naval unit consisting of a number of warships on a particular operation **c** a unit of an air force consisting usu of between 10 and 18 aircraft

squalid /ˈskwɒlɪd/ *adj* **1** filthy and degraded from neglect or poverty **2** sordid – ~ly *adv*

¹squall /skwɔːl/ *v* to cry out raucously; scream – **squall, ~er** *n*

²squall *n* **1** a sudden violent wind, often with rain or snow **2** a short-lived commotion – **squally** *adj*

squalor /ˈskwɒləʳ/ *n* the quality or state of being squalid

squander /ˈskwɒndəʳ/ *v* to spend extravagantly, foolishly, or wastefully; dissipate – ~er *n*

¹square /skweəʳ/ *n* **1** an instrument (e g a set square or T square) with at least 1 right angle and 2 straight edges, used to draw or test right angles or parallel lines **2** a rectangle with all 4 sides equal **3a** a square scarf **b** an area of ground for a particular purpose (e g military drill) **4** any of the rectangular, square, etc spaces marked out on a board used for playing games **5** the product of a number multiplied by itself **6** an open space in a town, city, etc formed at the meeting of 2 or more streets, and often laid out with grass and trees **7** one who is excessively conventional or conservative in tastes or outlook – *infml*; no longer in vogue

²square *adj* **1a** having 4 equal sides and 4 right angles **b** forming a right angle **2a** approximating to a cube **b** of a shape or build suggesting strength and solidity; broad in relation to length or height **c** square in cross section **3** *of a unit of length* denoting the area equal to that of a square whose edges are of the specified length **4a** exactly adjusted, arranged, or aligned; neat and orderly **b** fair, honest, or straightforward **c** leaving no balance; settled **d** even, tied **5** excessively conservative; dully conventional – *infml*; no longer in vogue – ~ly *adv* – ~ness *n*

³square *v* **1a** to make square or rectangular **b** to test for deviation from a right angle, straight line, or plane surface **2** to multiply (a number) by the same number; to raise to the second power **3a** to balance, settle up; *esp* to pay the bill **b** to even the score of (a contest) **4** to mark off into squares or rectangles **5a** to bring into agreement *with*; match **b** to bribe – *infml*

⁴square *adv* **1** in a straightforward or honest manner **2a** so as to face or be face to face **b** at right angles

¹squash /skwɒʃ/ *v* **1a** to press or beat into a pulp or a flat mass; crush **b** to apply pressure to by pushing or squeezing **2** to reduce to silence or inactivity

²squash *n* **1** the act or soft dull sound of squashing **2** a crushed mass; *esp* a mass of people crowded into a restricted space **3** *also* **squash rackets** a game played in a 4-walled court with long-handled rackets and a rubber ball that can be played off any number of walls **4** *Br* a beverage made from sweetened and often concentrated citrus fruit juice, usu drunk diluted

³squash *n, pl* **squashes, squash** any of various (plants of the cucumber family bearing) fruits widely cultivated as vegetables

¹squat /skwɒt/ *v* **1** to crouch close to the ground as if to escape detection **2** to assume or maintain a position in which the body is supported on the feet and the knees are bent, so that the haunches rest on or near the heels **3** to occupy property as a squatter

²squat *n* **1a** squatting **b** the posture of sby or sthg that squats **2** an empty building occupied by or available to squatters – *infml*

³squat *adj* **1** with the heels drawn up under the haunches **2** disproportionately short or low and broad

¹squeak /skwiːk/ *v* to utter or make a squeak – ~er *n*

²squeak *n* **1** a short shrill cry or squeak **2** an escape – usu in *a narrow squeak*; *infml*

¹squeal /skwiːl/ *v* **1** to utter or make a squeal **2a** to turn informer – *infml* **b** to complain, protest – *infml* – ~er *n*

²squeal *n* a shrill sharp cry or noise

¹squeeze /skwiːz/ *v* **1a** to apply physical pressure to; compress the (opposite) sides of **b** to extract or discharge under pressure **c** to force one's way **2a** to obtain by force or extortion **b** to cause (economic) hardship to **3** to fit into a limited time span or schedule – usu + *in* or *into* **4** to pass, win, or get by narrowly

²**squeeze** *n* **1a** a squeezing or compressing **b** a handshake; *also* an embrace **2** a condition of being crowded together; a crush **3a** a financial pressure caused by narrowing margins or by shortages **b** pressure brought to bear on sby – chiefly in *put the squeeze on*; *infml*

¹**squint** /skwɪnt/ *adj* having a squint; squinting

²**squint** *v* **1** to have or look with a squint **2** to look or peer with eyes partly closed

³**squint** *n* **1** an inability to direct both eyes to the same object because of imbalance of the muscles of the eyeball **2** a glance, look – esp in *have/take a squint at*; *infml*

squirrel /ˈskwɪrəl/ *n* (the usu grey or red fur of) any of various New or Old World small to medium-sized tree-dwelling rodents that have a long bushy tail and strong hind legs

¹**squirt** /skwɜːt/ *v* **1** to issue in a sudden forceful stream from a narrow opening **2** to direct a jet or stream of liquid at

²**squirt** *n* **1** a small rapid stream of liquid; a jet **2** a small or insignificant (impudent) person – *infml*

¹**stab** /stæb/ *n* **1** a wound produced by a pointed weapon **2a** a thrust (as if) with a pointed weapon **b(1)** a sharp spasm of pain **(2)** a pang of intense emotion **3** an attempt, try – *infml*

²**stab** *v* **1** to pierce or wound (as if) with a pointed weapon **2** to thrust, jab – **~ber** *n*

¹**stable** /ˈsteɪbəl/ *n* **1** a building in which domestic animals, esp horses, are sheltered and fed – often pl with sing. meaning **2** *sing or pl in constr* **a** the racehorses or racing cars owned by one person or organization **b** a group of athletes (e g boxers) or performers under one management

²**stable** *v* to put or keep in a stable

³**stable** *adj* **1a** securely established; fixed **b** not subject to change or fluctuation; unvarying **2** not subject to feelings of mental or emotional insecurity **3a** placed or constructed so as to resist forces tending to cause (change of) motion **b** able to resist alteration in chemical, physical, or biological properties – **-bility** *n* – **-bly** *adv*

¹**stack** /stæk/ *n* **1** a large usu circular or square pile of hay, straw, etc **2** an (orderly) pile or heap **3** a chimney stack **4** a high pillar of rock rising out of the sea, that was detached from the mainland by the erosive action of waves **5** a large quantity or number – often pl with sing. meaning; *infml*

²**stack** *v* **1** to arrange in a stack; pile **2** to arrange (cards) secretly for cheating **3** to assign (an aircraft) to a particular altitude and position within a group of aircraft circling before landing

stadium /ˈsteɪdɪəm/ *n, pl* **stadiums** *also* **stadia** a sports ground surrounded by a large usu unroofed building with tiers of seats for spectators

¹**staff** /stɑːf/ *n, pl* **staffs, staves,** (4) **staffs 1a** a long stick carried in the hand for use in walking or as a weapon **b** sthg which gives strength or sustains **2** a rod carried as a symbol of office or authority **3** a set of usu 5 parallel horizontal lines on which music is written **4** *sing or pl in constr* **a** the body of people in charge of the internal operations of an institution, business, etc **b** a group of officers appointed to assist a military commander **c** the teachers at a school or university

²**staff** *v* **1** to supply with a staff or with workers **2** to serve as a staff member of

¹**stage** /steɪdʒ/ *n* **1a** a raised platform **b(1)** the area of a theatre where the acting takes place, including the wings and storage space **(2)** the acting profession; *also the* theatre as an occupation or activity **2** a centre of attention or scene of action **3a** a place of rest formerly provided for those travelling by stagecoach **b** the distance between 2 stopping places on a road **c** a stagecoach **4** a period or step in a progress, activity, or development **5** any of the divisions (e g 1 day's riding or driving between predetermined points) of a race or rally that is spread over several days

²**stage** *v* **1** to produce (e g a play) on a stage **2** to produce and organize, esp for public view

stagger /ˈstægəʳ/ *v* **1** to reel from side to side (while moving); totter **2** to dumbfound, astonish **3** to arrange in any of various alternating or overlapping positions or times **stagger** *n*

stagnant /ˈstægnənt/ *adj* **1a** not flowing in a current or stream; motionless **b** stale **2** dull, inactive – **~ly** *adv*

¹**stain** /steɪn/ *v* **1** to discolour, soil **2** to taint with guilt, vice, corruption, etc; bring dishonour to

²**stain** *n* **1** a soiled or discoloured spot **2** a moral taint or blemish **3a** a preparation (e g of dye or pigment) used in staining; *esp* one capable of penetrating the pores of wood **b** a dye or mixture of dyes used in microscopy to make minute and transparent structures visible, to differentiate tissue elements, or to produce specific chemical reactions

stair /steəʳ/ *n* **1** a series of (flights of) steps for passing from one level to another – usu pl with sing. meaning **2** any step of a stairway

staircase /ˈsteəkeɪs/ *n* **1** the structure or part of a building containing a stairway **2** a flight of stairs with the supporting framework, casing, and balusters

¹**stake** /steɪk/ *n* **1** a pointed piece of material (e g wood) for driving into the ground as a marker or support **2a** a post to which sby was bound for execution by burning **b** execution by burning at a stake – + *the* **3a** sthg, esp money, staked for gain or loss **b** the prize in a contest, esp a horse race – often pl with sing. meaning **c** an interest or share in

an undertaking (e g a commercial venture)

²**stake** v 1 to mark the limits of (as if by stakes – often + *off* or *out* 2 to tether to a stake 3 to bet, hazard 4 to fasten up or support (e g plants) with stakes

stale /steɪl/ adj 1a tasteless or unpalatable from age b *of air* musty, foul 2 tedious from familiarity 3 impaired in vigour or effectiveness, esp from overexertion – **stale** v

stalemate /'steɪlmeɪt/ v or n (to bring into) a a drawing position in chess in which only the king can move and although not in check can move only into check b a deadlock

¹**stalk** /stɔːk/ v 1 to pursue or approach quarry or prey stealthily 2 to walk stiffly or haughtily – ~**er** n

²**stalk** n 1 the stalking of quarry or prey 2 a stiff or haughty walk

³**stalk** n 1 the main stem of a herbaceous plant, often with its attached parts 2 a slender upright supporting or connecting (animal) structure

¹**stall** /stɔːl/ n 1 any of usu several compartments for domestic animals in a stable or barn 2a a wholly or partly enclosed seat in the chancel of a church b a church pew 3a a booth, stand, or counter at which articles are displayed or offered for sale b a sideshow 4 Br a seat on the main floor of an auditorium (e g in a theatre)

²**stall** v 1 to put or keep in a stall 2a to bring to a standstill; block b to cause (e g a car engine) to stop, usu inadvertently

³**stall** n the condition of an aerofoil or aircraft when the airflow is so obstructed (e g from moving forwards too slowly) that lift is lost

⁴**stall** v to play for time; delay

stamina /'stæmɪnə/ n (capacity for) endurance

stammer /'stæmə/ v to speak or utter with involuntary stops and repetitions

¹**stamp** /stæmp/ v 1 to bring down the foot forcibly on 2a to impress, imprint b(1) to attach a (postage) stamp to (2) to mark with an (official) impression, device, etc 3 to provide with a distinctive character

²**stamp** n 1 a device or instrument for stamping 2 the impression or mark made by stamping or imprinting 3a a distinctive feature, indication, or mark b a lasting imprint 4 a printed or stamped piece of paper that for some restricted purpose is used as a token of credit or occasionally of debit: e g a a postage stamp b a stamp used as evidence that tax has been paid

¹**stampede** /stæm'piːd/ n 1 a wild headlong rush or flight of frightened animals 2 a sudden mass movement of people

²**stampede** v to (cause to) run away or rush in panic or on impulse

stance /stɑːns/ n 1a a way of standing or being placed b intellectual or emotional attitude 2 the position of body or feet from which a sportsman (e g a batsman or golfer) plays

¹**stand** /stænd/ v stood 1a to support oneself on the feet in an erect position b to rise to or maintain an erect or upright position 2 to take up or maintain a specified position or posture 3 to be in a specified state or situation 4 to be in a position to gain or lose because of an action taken or a commitment made 5 to occupy a place or location 6 to remain stationary or inactive 7 to agree, accord – chiefly in *it stands to reason* 8a to exist in a definite (written or printed) form b to remain valid or effective 9 *chiefly Br* to be a candidate in an election 10a to endure or undergo b to tolerate, bear; put up with 11 to remain firm in the face of 12 to pay the cost of; pay for – *infml* – ~**er** n

²**stand** n 1 an act, position, or place of standing 2a a usu defensive effort of some length or success b a stop made by a touring theatrical company, rock group, etc to give a performance 3 a strongly or aggressively held position, esp on a debatable issue 4a a structure of tiered seats for spectators – often *pl* with *sing*. meaning b a raised platform serving as a point of vantage or display (e g for a speaker or exhibit) 5 a small usu temporary and open-air stall where goods are sold or displayed 6 a place where a passenger vehicle awaits hire 7 a frame on or in which sthg may be placed for support 8 a group of plants or trees growing in a continuous area 9 *NAm the* witness-box

¹**standard** /'stændəd/ n 1 a (long narrow tapering) flag 2a sthg established by authority, custom, or general consent as a model or example; a criterion b a (prescribed) degree of quality or worth 3 *pl* moral integrity; principles 4 sthg set up and established by authority as a rule for the measure of quantity, weight, value, or quality 5 the basis of value in a money system 6 a shrub or herbaceous plant grown with an erect main stem so that it forms or resembles a tree

²**standard** adj 1a being or conforming to a standard, esp as established by law or custom b sound and usable but not of top quality 2a regularly and widely used, available, or supplied b well established and familiar 3 having recognized and permanent value – ~**ize** v

standard of living n a level of welfare or subsistence maintained by an individual, group, or community and shown esp by the level of consumption of necessities, comforts, and luxuries

standpoint /'stændpɔɪnt/ n a position from which objects or principles are viewed and according to which they are compared and judged

¹**star** /stɑː/ n 1 any natural luminous body visible in the sky, esp at night 2a a planet or a configuration of the planets that is held in astrology to influence a person's destiny – often *pl* b a waxing or waning fortune or fame 3a an often star-shaped ornament or medal worn as a badge of honour, authority, or rank or

as the insignia of an order **b** any of a group of stylized stars used to place sthg in a scale of value or quality – often in combination **4a** a (highly publicized) performer in the cinema or theatre who plays leading roles **b** an outstandingly talented performer ~**ry**, ~**less** adj

²**star** v to play the most prominent or important role

³**star** adj of, being, or appropriate to a star

¹**stare** /steə'/ v to look fixedly, often with wide-open eyes

²**stare** n a staring look

¹**start** /stɑːt/ v **1** to react with a sudden brief involuntary movement **2** to come into being, activity, or operation **3a** to begin a course or journey **b** to range from a specified initial point **4** to begin an activity or undertaking; esp to begin work **5a** to cause to move, act, operate, or do sthg specified **b** to cause to enter or begin a game, contest, or business activity; broadly to put in a starting position **6** to perform or undergo the first stages or actions of; begin

²**start** n **1** a sudden involuntary bodily movement or reaction (e g from surprise or alarm) **2** a beginning of movement, activity, or development **3a** a lead conceded at the start of a race or competition **b** an advantage, lead; a head start **4** a place of beginning

startle /stɑːtl/ v to (cause to) be suddenly frightened or surprised and usu to (cause to) make a sudden brief movement – **lingly** adv

starve /stɑːv/ v **1** to suffer or feel extreme hunger **2** to suffer or perish from deprivation

¹**state** /steit/ n **1a** a mode or condition of being (with regard to circumstances, health, temperament, etc) **b** a condition of abnormal tension or excitement **2** a condition or stage in the physical being of sthg **3a** luxurious style of living **b** formal dignity; pomp – usu + in **4** a politically organized (sovereign) body, usu occupying a definite territory; also its political organization **5** the operations of the government **6** often cap a constituent unit of a nation having a federal government

²**state** v **1** to set, esp by regulation or authority; specify **2** to express the particulars of, esp in words; broadly to express in words

statement /steitmənt/ n **1** stating orally or on paper **2** sthg stated: e g **a** a report of facts or opinions **b** a single declaration or remark; an assertion **3** a proposition (e g in logic) **4** the presentation of a theme in a musical composition **5** a summary of a financial account **6** an outward expression of thought, feeling, etc made without words

statesman /steitsmən/ n one versed in or esp engaged in the business of a government **2** one who exercises political leadership wisely and without narrow partisanship – ~**ship** n

¹**static** /stætik/ adj **1** exerting force by reason of weight alone without motion

2 of or concerned with bodies at rest or forces in equilibrium **3** characterized by a lack of movement, animation, progression, or change **4** of, producing, or being stationary charges of electricity

²**static** n (the electrical disturbances causing) unwanted signals in a radio or television system; atmospherics

¹**station** /steiʃən/ n **1** the place or position in which sthg or sby stands or is assigned to stand or remain **2** a stopping place; esp (the buildings at) a regular or major stopping place for trains, buses, etc **3a** a post or sphere of (naval or military) duty or occupation **b** a stock farm or ranch in Australia or New Zealand **4** standing, rank **5** a place for specialized observation and study of scientific phenomena **6** a place established to provide a public service; esp a police station **7** an establishment equipped for radio or television transmission or reception

²**station** v to assign to or set in a station or position; post

stationary /steiʃənəri/ adj **1** having a fixed position; immobile **2** unchanging in condition

stationery /steiʃənəri/ n materials (e g paper) for writing or typing; specif paper and envelopes for letter writing

statistics /stə'tistiks/ n pl but sing or pl in constr **1** a branch of mathematics dealing with the collection, analysis, interpretation, and presentation of masses of numerical data **2** a collection of quantitative data – **tical** adj – **tically** adv – **tician** n

statue /stætjuː/ n a likeness (e g of a person or animal) sculptured, cast, or modelled in a solid material (e g bronze or stone)

stature /stætʃə'/ n **1** natural height (e g of a person) in an upright position **2** quality or status gained by growth, development, or achievement

status /steitəs/ n **1** the condition of sby or sthg (in the eyes of the law) **2** (high) position or rank in relation to others or in a hierarchy

¹**stay** /stei/ n a strong rope, now usu of wire, used to support a ship's mast or similar tall structure (e g a flagstaff)

²**stay** v to support (e g a chimney) (as if) with stays

³**stay** v **1** to continue in a place or condition; remain **2** to take up temporary residence; lodge **3** of a racehorse to run well over long distances **4** to stop or delay the proceeding, advance, or course of; halt

⁴**stay** n **1a** stopping or being stopped **b** a suspension of judicial procedure **2** a residence or sojourn in a place

⁵**stay** n **1** sby who or sthg that serves as a prop; a support **2** a corset stiffened with bones – usu pl with sing. meaning

¹**steady** /stedi/ adj **1a** firm in position; not shaking, rocking, etc **b** direct or sure; unfaltering **2** showing or continuing with little variation or fluctuation **3a** not easily moved or upset; calm **b** dependable, constant **c** not given to

dissipation; sober – **steadily** adv
– **steadiness** n

²**steady** v to make, keep, or become
steady

³**steady** adv in a steady manner;
steadily

⁴**steady** n a regular boy/girl friend

steak /steɪk/ n **1a** a slice of meat cut
from a fleshy part (e g the rump) of a
(beef) carcass and suitable for grilling or
frying **b** a poorer-quality less tender
beef cut, usu from the neck and shoulder, suitable for braising or stewing **2a** a
cross-sectional slice from between the
centre and tail of a large fish

steal /stiːl/ v **stole; stolen 1** to take (the
property of another) **2** to come or go
secretly or unobtrusively

stealth /stelθ/ n **1** the act or action of
proceeding furtively or unobtrusively **2**
the state of being furtive or unobtrusive
– ~**y** adj – ~**ily** adv

¹**steam** /stiːm/ n **1** a vapour given off by
a heated substance; esp the vapour into
which water is converted when heated
to its boiling point **2a** energy or power
generated (as if) by steam under pressure **b** driving force; power – infml

²**steam** /stiːm/ v **1** to give off steam or
vapour **2** to apply steam to; esp to
expose to the action of steam (e g for
softening or cooking) **3** to proceed
quickly **4** to be angry; boil **5** to become
covered up or over with steam or condensation

¹**steamroller** /ˈstiːmˌrəʊləʳ/ n **1** a
machine equipped with wide heavy rollers for compacting the surfaces of roads,
pavements, etc **2** a crushing force, esp
when ruthlessly applied to overcome
opposition

²**steamroller** also **steamroll** v to force to
a specified state or condition by the use
of overwhelming pressure

¹**steel** /stiːl/ n **1** commercial iron distinguished from cast iron by its malleabil-
ity and lower carbon content **2a** a
fluted round steel rod with a handle for
sharpening knives **b** a piece of steel for
striking sparks from flint **3** a quality
(e g of mind or spirit) that suggests
steel, esp in strength or hardness

²**steel** v **1** to make unfeeling; harden **2**
to fill with resolution or determination

¹**steep** /stiːp/ adj **1** making a large angle
with the plane of the horizon; almost
vertical **2** being or characterized by a
rapid and severe decline or increase **3**
difficult to accept, comply with, or
carry out; excessive – infml – ~**ly** adv
– ~**ness** n

²**steep** v **1** to cover with or plunge into
a liquid (e g in rinsing, bleaching or
soaking) **2** to imbue with or subject
thoroughly to – usu + in

steeple /ˈstiːpəl/ n (a tower with) a tall
spire on a church

¹**steer** /stɪəʳ/ n a male bovine animal
castrated before sexual maturity

²**steer** v **1** to direct the course of; esp to
guide a ship by means of a rudder **2** to
set and hold to (a course)

¹**stem** /stem/ n **1a** the main trunk of a
plant **b** a branch or other plant part
that supports a leaf, fruit, etc **2** the bow
or prow of a vessel **3** a line of ancestry;
esp a fundamental line from which
others have arisen **4** that part of a word
which has unchanged spelling when the
word is inflected **5a** the tubular part of
a tobacco pipe from the bowl outwards,
through which smoke is drawn **b** the
often slender and cylindrical upright
support between the base and bowl of a
wineglass

²**stem** v **1** to make headway against (e g
an adverse tide, current, or wind) **2** to
check or go counter to (sth adverse)

³**stem** v **1** to originate – usu + from

⁴**stem** v to stop or check (as if by dam-
ming)

¹**step** /step/ n **1** a rest for the foot in
ascending or descending: e g **a** a single
tread and riser on a stairway; a stair **b**
a ladder rung **2a(1)** an advance or
movement made by raising the foot and
bringing it down at another point (2) a
combination of foot (and body) movements constituting a unit or a repeated
pattern **b** the sound of a footstep **3** a
short distance **4** pl a course, way **5a** a
degree, grade, or rank in a scale **b** a
stage in a process **c** an action, proceeding, or measure often occurring as 1 in
a series – often pl with sing. meaning **6**
pl a stepladder

²**step** v **1** to move by raising the foot and
bringing it down at another point or by
moving each foot in succession **2a** to go
on foot; walk **b** to be on one's way;
leave – often + along **3** to press down
on sth with the foot **4** to measure by
steps – usu + off or out

stepchild /ˈsteptʃaɪld/ n a child of
one's wife or husband by a former marriage

stepladder /ˈstepˌlædəʳ/ n a portable
set of steps with a hinged frame

stepparent /ˈstepˌpeərənt/ n the husband or wife of one's parent by a subsequent marriage

stepping-stone n **1** a stone on which
to step (e g in crossing a stream) **2** a
means of progress or advancement

stereo /ˈsteriə, ˈstɑr-/ n a device (e g a
record player) for reproducing sound in
which the sound is split into and reproduced by 2 different channels to give a
special effect – ~ adj

sterile /ˈsteraɪl/ adj **1** failing or not able
to produce or bear fruit, crops, or offspring **2a** deficient in ideas or originality **b** free from living organisms, esp
microorganisms **3** bringing no rewards
or results; not productive – **-ization** n
– **-ize** v

¹**stern** /stɜːn/ adj **1a** hard or severe in
nature or manner; austere **b** expressive
of severe displeasure; harsh **2** forbidding or gloomy in appearance **3** inexorable, relentless – ~**ly** adv – ~**ness** n

²**stern** n **1** the rear end of a ship or boat
2 a back or rear part; the last or latter
part

¹**stew** /stjuː/ n **1a** a savoury dish, usu of
meat and vegetables stewed and served
in the same liquid **b** a mixture com-

posed of many usu unrelated parts 2 a
state of excitement, worry, or confusion
– infml

²**stew** v to cook (e g meat or fruit) slowly
by boiling gently or simmering in
liquid

¹**steward** /'stjuːəd/ n 1 one employed
to look after a large household or estate
2a one who manages the provisioning of
food and attends to the needs of passengers (e g on an airliner, ship, or train) b
one who supervises the provision and
distribution of food and drink in a club,
college, etc 3 an official who actively
directs affairs (e g at a race meeting)

²**steward** v to act as a steward (for)

stewardess /ˌstjuːəˈdes/ n a woman
who performs the duties of a steward

¹**stick** /stɪk/ n 1a (a dry and dead) cut or
broken branch or twig 2a a walking
stick b an implement used for striking
an object in a game (e g hockey) 3 sthg
prepared (e g by cutting, moulding, or
rolling) in a relatively long and slender
often cylindrical form 4 a person of a
specified type 5 a stick-shaped plant
stalk (e g of rhubarb or celery) 6 several
bombs, parachutists, etc released from
an aircraft in quick succession 7 pl the
wooded or rural and usu backward
districts

²**stick** v stuck 1 to fasten in position (as
if) by piercing 2 to push, thrust 3 to
attach (as if) by causing to adhere to a
surface 4 to become blocked, wedged,
or jammed 5 to project, protrude –
often + out or up 6a to halt the movement or action of b to baffle, stump 7
to put or set in a specified place or
position 8 to saddle with sthg disadvantageous or disagreeable 9 chiefly Br to
bear, stand

³**stick** n adhesive quality or substance

sticky /'stɪki/ adj 1a adhesive b viscous, gluey 2 humid, muggy; also
clammy 3a disagreeable, unpleasant b
awkward, stiff c difficult, problematic
– **stickily** adv – **stickiness** n

¹**stiff** /stɪf/ adj 1a not easily bent; rigid
b lacking in suppleness and often painful 2a firm, unyielding b(1) marked by
reserve or decorum; formal (2) lacking
in ease or grace; stilted 3 hard fought 4
exerting great force; forceful 5 of a
dense or glutinous consistency; thick 6a
harsh, severe b arduous 7 expensive,
steep – **~en** v – **~ly** adv – **~ness** n

²**stiff** adv in a stiff manner; stiffly

³**stiff** n a corpse – slang

stifle /'staɪfəl/ v 1a to overcome or kill
by depriving of oxygen; suffocate,
smother b to muffle 2a to cut off (e g
the voice or breath) b to prevent the
development or expression of; check,
suppress

¹**still** /stɪl/ adj 1a devoid of or abstaining
from motion b having no effervescence;
not carbonated 2 uttering no sound;
quiet 3a calm, tranquil b free from
noise or turbulence – **~ness** n

²**still** v 1a to allay, calm b to put an end
to; settle 2 to arrest the motion or noise
of; quiet

³**still** adv 1 as before; even at this or that

time 2 in spite of that; nevertheless 3a
even (e g a still more difficult problem)
b yet

⁴**still** n 1 a still photograph; specif a
photograph of actors or of a scene from
a film 2 quiet, silence – chiefly poetic

⁵**still** n an apparatus used in distillation,
esp of spirits, consisting of either the
chamber in which the vaporization is
carried out or the entire equipment

stillborn /'stɪlbɔːn, ˌstɪlˈbɔːn/ adj 1
dead at birth 2 failing from the start;
abortive

stimulate /'stɪmjʊleɪt/ v to excite to
(greater) activity – **-lation** n

¹**sting** /stɪŋ/ v stung 1a to give an irritating or poisonous wound to, esp with a
sting b to affect with sharp quick pain
2 to cause to suffer acute mental pain;
also to incite or goad thus 3 to over-
charge, cheat – infml

²**sting** n 1a a stinging; specif the thrust
of a sting into the flesh b a wound or
pain caused (as if) by stinging 2 also
stinger a sharp organ of a bee, scorpion,
stingray, etc that is usu connected with
a poison gland or otherwise adapted to
wound by piercing and injecting a
poisonous secretion

stipulate /'stɪpjʊleɪt/ v 1 to specify as
a condition or requirement of an agreement or offer 2 to give a guarantee of
in making an agreement – **-ation** n

¹**stir** /stɜː/ v 1a to make or cause a slight
movement or change of position b to
disturb the quiet of; agitate 2a to disturb the relative position of the particles
or parts of (a fluid or semifluid), esp by
a continued circular movement in order
to make the composition homogeneous
b to mix (as if) by stirring 3 to bestir,
exert 4a to rouse to activity; produce
strong feelings in b to provoke – often
+ up

²**stir** n 1a a state of disturbance, agitation, or brisk activity b widespread
notice or discussion 2 a slight movement 3 a stirring movement

¹**stitch** /stɪtʃ/ n 1 a local sharp and
sudden pain, esp in the side 2a a single
in-and-out movement of a threaded
needle in sewing, embroidering, or closing (surgical) wounds b a portion of
thread left in the material after 1 stitch
3 a single loop of thread or yarn round
a stitching implement (e g a knitting
needle) 4 the least scrap of clothing –
usu neg; infml

²**stitch** v 1a to fasten, join, or close (as if)
with stitches; sew 2 to work on or
decorate (as if) with stitches

¹**stock** /stɒk/ n 1a pl a wooden frame
with holes for the feet (and hands) in
which offenders are held for public punishment b the part to which the barrel
and firing mechanism of a gun are
attached 2a the main stem of a plant or
tree b(1) a plant (part) consisting of
roots and lower trunk onto which a
graft is made (2) a plant from which
cuttings are taken 3a the original (e g a
man, race, or language) from which
others derive; a source b the descendants of an individual; family, lineage 4a

sing or pl in constr livestock **b** a store or supply accumulated (e g of raw materials or finished goods) **5a** a debt or fund due (e g from a government) for money loaned at interest; *also, Br* capital or a debt or fund which continues to bear interest but is not usually redeemable as far as the original sum is concerned **b** (preference) shares – often pl **6** any of a genus of plants with usu sweet-smelling flowers **7** a wide band or scarf worn round the neck, esp by some clergymen **8** the liquid in which meat, fish, or vegetables have been simmered that is used as a basis for soup, gravy, etc **9a** an estimate or appraisal of sthg **b** the estimation in which sby or sthg is held

²**stock** *v* **1** to provide with (a) stock; supply **2** to procure or keep a stock of **3** to take in a stock – often + *up*

³**stock** *adj* **1a** kept in stock regularly **b** regularly and widely available or supplied **2** used for (breeding and rearing) livestock **3** commonly used or brought forward; standard – chiefly derog

stock exchange *n* (a building occupied by) an association of people organized to provide an auction market among themselves for the purchase and sale of securities

stocking /'stɒkɪŋ/ *n* a usu knitted close-fitting often nylon covering for the foot and leg

stockpile /'stɒkpaɪl/ *n* an accumulated store; *esp* a reserve supply of sthg essential accumulated for use during a shortage – **stockpile** *v*

stodgy /'stɒdʒi/ *adj* **1** *of food* heavy and filling **2** dull, boring – *infml* – **stodginess** *n*

¹**stole** /stəʊl/ *past of* **steal**

²**stole** *n* **1** a long usu silk band worn traditionally over both shoulders and hanging down in front by priests **2** a long wide strip of material worn by women usu across the shoulders, esp with evening dress

stolen /'stəʊlən/ *past part of* **steal**

¹**stomach** /'stʌmək/ *n* **1a** (a cavity in an invertebrate animal analogous to) a sac-like organ formed by a widening of the alimentary canal of a vertebrate, that is between the oesophagus at the top and the duodenum at the bottom and in which the first stages of digestion occur **b** the part of the body that contains the stomach; belly, abdomen **2a** desire for food; appetite **b** inclination, desire – usu neg

²**stomach** *v* **1** to find palatable or digestible **2** to bear without protest or resentment *USE* usu neg

¹**stone** /stəʊn/ *n* **1** a concretion of earthy or mineral matter: **a(1)** a piece of this, esp one smaller than a boulder **(2)** rock **b(1)** a building or paving block **(2)** a gem **(3)** a sharpening stone **2** the hard central portion of a fruit (e g a peach or date) **3** an imperial unit of weight equal to 14lb (about 6.35kg)

²**stone** *v* **1** to hurl stones at; *esp* to kill by pelting with stones **2** to face, pave, or fortify with stones **3** to remove the stones or seeds of (a fruit)

³**stone** *adj* (made) of stone

stony /'stəʊni/ *adj* **1** containing many stones or having the nature of stone **2a** insensitive to pity or human feeling **b** showing no movement or reaction; dumb, expressionless – **stonily** *adv*

stood /stʊd/ *past of* **stand**

stool /stuːl/ *n* **1a** a seat usu without back or arms supported by 3 or 4 legs or a central pedestal **b** a low bench or portable support for the feet or for kneeling on **2** a discharge of faecal matter

¹**stoop** /stuːp/ *v* **1a** to bend the body forwards and downwards, sometimes simultaneously bending the knees **b** to stand or walk with a temporary or habitual forward inclination of the head, body, or shoulders **2a** to condescend **b** to lower oneself morally **3** *of a bird* to fly or dive down swiftly, usu to attack prey

²**stoop** *n* **1a** an act of bending the body forwards **b** a temporary or habitual forward bend of the back and shoulders **2** the descent of a bird, esp on its prey

³**stoop** *n, chiefly NAm* a porch, platform, entrance stairway, or small veranda at a house door

¹**stop** /stɒp/ *v* **1a** to close by filling or obstructing **b** to hinder or prevent the passage of **2a** to restrain, prevent **b** to withhold **3a** to cause to cease; check, suppress **b** to discontinue; come to an end **4** to instruct one's bank not to honour or pay **5a** to arrest the progress or motion of; cause to halt **b** to cease to move on; halt **c** to pause, hesitate **6a** to break one's journey – often + *off* **b** *chiefly Br* to remain **c** *chiefly NAm* to make a brief call; drop in – usu + *by* **7** to get in the way of, esp so as to be wounded or killed – *infml* – **~pable** *adj*

²**stop** *n* **1** a cessation, end **2** a graduated set of organ pipes of similar design and tone quality **3a** sthg that impedes, obstructs, or brings to a halt; an impediment, obstacle **b** (any of a series of markings, esp f-numbers, for setting the size of) the circular opening of an optical system (e g a camera lens) **4** a device for arresting or limiting motion **5** stopping or being stopped **6a** a halt in a journey **b** a stopping place **7** *chiefly Br* any of several punctuation marks; *specif* full stop

stoppage /'stɒpɪdʒ/ *n* **1** a deduction from pay **2** a concerted cessation of work by a group of employees that is usu more spontaneous and less serious than a strike

stopper /'stɒpə/ *n* sby or sthg that closes, shuts, or fills up; *specif* sthg (e g a bung or cork) used to plug an opening

storage /'stɔːrɪdʒ/ *n* **1** (a) space for storing **2a** storing or being stored (e g in a warehouse) **b** the price charged for keeping goods in storage

¹**store** /stɔː/ *v* **1** to collect as a reserve supply – often + *up* or *away* **2** to place

or leave in a location (e g a warehouse, library, or computer memory) for preservation or later use or disposal **3** to provide storage room for; hold

²**store** *n* **1a** sthg stored or kept for future use **b** *pl* articles accumulated for some specific object and drawn on as needed **c** a source from which things may be drawn as needed; a reserve fund **2** storage – usu + *in* **3** a large quantity, supply, or number **4** a warehouse **5** a large shop

storey /'stɔːri/ *n* (a set of rooms occupying) a horizontal division of a building

¹**storm** /stɔːm/ *n* **1** a violent disturbance of the weather marked by high winds, thunder and lightning, rain or snow, etc **2** a disturbed or agitated state; a sudden or violent commotion **3** a tumultuous outburst **4** a violent assault on a defended position

²**storm** *v* **1a** of wind to blow with violence **b** to rain, hail, snow, or sleet **2** to be in or to exhibit a violent passion; rage **3** to rush about or move impetuously, violently, or angrily **4** to attack or take (e g a fortified place) by storm

stormy /'stɔːmi/ *adj* marked by turmoil or fury – **stormily** *adv*

story /'stɔːri/ *n* **1a** an account of incidents or events **b** a statement of the facts of a situation in question **c** an anecdote; *esp* an amusing one **2a** a short fictional narrative **b** the plot of a literary work **3** a widely circulated rumour **4** a lie **5** a news article or broadcast

¹**stout** /staʊt/ *adj* **1** firm, resolute **2** physically or materially strong: **a** sturdy, vigorous **b** staunch, enduring **3** corpulent, fat – ~**ly** *adv* – ~**ness** *n*

²**stout** *n* a dark sweet heavy-bodied beer

¹**stove** /staʊv/ *n* **1** an enclosed appliance that burns fuel or uses electricity to provide heat chiefly for domestic purposes **2** a cooker

²**stove** *past of* **stave**

¹**straight** /streɪt/ *adj* **1a** free from curves, bends, angles, or irregularities **b** generated by a point moving continuously in the same direction **2** direct, uninterrupted: e g **a** holding to a direct or proper course or method **b** candid, frank **c** coming directly from a trustworthy source **3a** honest, fair **b** properly ordered or arranged (e g with regard to finance) **c** correct **4** unmixed **5a** not deviating from the general norm or prescribed pattern **b** accepted as usual, normal, or proper **6a** conventional in opinions, habits, appearance etc **b** heterosexual *USE* (6) *infml* – ~**ness** *n*

²**straight** *adv* **1** in a straight manner **2** without delay or hesitation; immediately

³**straight** *n* **1** sthg straight: e g **a** a straight line or arrangement **b** a straight part of sthg; *esp* a home straight **2** a poker hand containing 5 cards in sequence but not of the same suit **3a** a

conventional person **b** a heterosexual *USE* (3) *infml*

straightaway /ˌstreɪtə'weɪ/ *adv* without hesitation or delay; immediately

straighten /'streɪtn/ *v* to make or become straight – usu + *up* or *out*

straightforward /ˌstreɪt'fɔːwəd/ *adj* **1** free from evasiveness or ambiguity; direct, candid **2** presenting no hidden difficulties **3** clear-cut, precise – ~**ly** *adv*

¹**strain** /streɪn/ *n* **1a** a lineage, ancestry **b** a kind, sort **2** a passage of verbal or musical expression – usu *pl* with sing. meaning

²**strain** *v* **1** to stretch to maximum extension and tautness **2a** to exert (e g oneself) to the utmost **b** to injure by overuse, misuse, or excessive pressure **3** to cause to pass through a strainer; filter **4** to stretch beyond a proper limit

³**strain** *n* straining or being strained: e g **a** (a force, influence, or factor causing) physical or mental tension **b** excessive or difficult exertion or labour **c** a wrench, twist, or similar bodily injury resulting esp from excessive stretching of muscles or ligaments

¹**strand** /strænd/ *n* a shore, beach

²**strand** *v* to leave in a strange or unfavourable place, esp without funds or means to depart

³**strand** *n* **1** any of the threads, strings, or wires twisted or laid parallel to make a cord, rope, etc **2** an elongated or twisted and plaited body resembling a rope **3** any of the elements interwoven in a complex whole

strange /streɪndʒ/ *adj* **1** not native to or naturally belonging in a place; of external origin, kind, or character **2a** not known, heard, or seen before **b** exciting wonder or surprise **3** lacking experience or acquaintance; unaccustomed *to* – ~**ly** *adv* – ~**ness** *n*

stranger /'streɪndʒə/ *n* **1a** a foreigner, alien **b** sby who is unknown or with whom one is unacquainted **2** one ignorant of or unacquainted with sby or sthg

strangle /'stræŋgəl/ *v* **1** to choke (to death) by compressing the throat; throttle **2** to suppress or hinder the rise, expression, or growth of

¹**strap** /stræp/ *n* **1** a strip of metal or a flexible material, esp leather, for holding objects together or in position **2** (*the* use of, or punishment with) a strip of leather for flogging

²**strap** *v* **1a** to secure with or attach by means of a strap **b** to support (e g a sprained joint) with adhesive plaster **2** to beat with a strap

stratagem /'strætədʒəm/ *n* **1** an artifice or trick for deceiving and outwitting the enemy **2** a cleverly contrived trick or scheme

strategy /'strætɪdʒi/ *n* **1** the science and art of military command exercised to meet the enemy in combat under advantageous conditions **2a** a clever plan or method **b** the art of employing plans towards achieving a goal – –**gic** *adj* – –**gically** *adv* – –**gist** *n*

¹straw /strɔː/ *n* **1** dry stalky plant residue, specif stalks of grain after threshing, used for bedding, thatching, fodder, making hats, etc **2** a dry coarse stem, esp of a cereal grass **3** sthg of small value or importance **4** a tube of paper, plastic, etc for sucking up a drink

²straw *adj* of or resembling the (colour of) straw

strawberry /'strɔːbəri/ *n* (the juicy edible usu red fruit of) any of several white-flowered creeping plants

¹stray /streɪ/ *v* **1** to wander from a proper place, course, or line of conduct or argument **2** to roam about without fixed direction or purpose

²stray *n* a domestic animal wandering at large or lost

³stray *adj* **1** having strayed; wandering, lost **2** occurring at random or sporadically

¹streak /striːk/ *n* **1** a line or band of a different colour from the background **2** an inherent quality; *esp* one which is only occasionally manifested

²streak *v* **1** to make streaks on or in **2** to move swiftly **3** to run through a public place while naked

¹stream /striːm/ *n* **1** a body of running water, esp one smaller than a river **2a** a steady succession of words, events, etc **b** a continuous moving procession **3** an unbroken flow (e g of gas or particles of matter) **4** a prevailing attitude or direction of opinion – esp in *go against/with the stream* **5** *Br* a group of pupils of the same general academic ability

²stream *v* **1** to flow (as if) in a stream **2** to run with a fluid **3** to trail out at full length **4** to pour in large numbers in the same direction **5** *Br* to practise the division of pupils into streams

¹streamline /'striːmlaɪn/ *n* a contour given to a car, aeroplane, etc so as to minimize resistance to motion through a fluid (e g air)

²streamline *v* to make simpler, more efficient, or better integrated

street /striːt/ *n* **1** a thoroughfare, esp in a town or village, with buildings on either side **2** the part of a street reserved for vehicles

strength /streŋθ/ *n* **1** the quality of being strong; capacity for exertion or endurance **2** solidity, toughness **3a** legal, logical, or moral force **b** a strong quality or inherent asset **4a** degree of potency of effect or of concentration **b** intensity of light, colour, sound, or smell **5** force as measured in members **6** a basis – chiefly in *on the strength of*

strengthen /'streŋðən, 'strenðən/ *v* to make or become stronger

strenuous /'strenjʊəs/ *adj* **1** vigorously active **2** requiring effort or stamina – ~ly *adv* – ~ness *n*

¹stress /stres/ *n* **1a** the force per unit area producing or tending to produce deformation of a body; *also* the state of a body under such stress **b** (a physical or emotional factor that causes) bodily or mental tension **c** strain, pressure **2** emphasis, weight **3** intensity of utterance given to a speech sound, syllable, or word so as to produce relative loudness

²stress *v* **1** to subject to physical or mental stress **2** to lay stress on; emphasize

¹stretch /stretʃ/ *v* **1** to extend in a reclining position – often + *out* **2** to extend to full length **3** to extend (oneself or one's limbs), esp so as to relieve muscular stiffness **4** to pull taut **5** to strain **6** to cause to reach (e g from one point to another or across a space) **7** to fell (as if) with a blow – often + *out*; infml – ~able *adj*

²stretch *n* **1** the extent to which sthg may be stretched **2** stretching or being stretched **3** a continuous expanse of time or space **4** elasticity **5** a term of imprisonment – infml

stretcher /'stretʃə'/ *n* **1** a brick or stone laid with its length parallel to the face of the wall **2** a device, consisting of a sheet of canvas or other material stretched between 2 poles, for carrying a sick, injured, or dead person **3** a rod or bar extending between 2 legs of a chair or table

strict /strɪkt/ *adj* **1a** stringent in requirement or control **b** severe in discipline **2a** inflexibly maintained or kept to; complete **b** rigorously conforming to rules or standards **3** exact, precise – ~ly *adv* – ~ness *n*

¹stride /straɪd/ *v* strode to walk (as if) with long steps

²stride *n* **1** a long step **2** an advance – often pl with sing. meaning **3** (the distance covered in) an act of movement completed when the feet regain the initial relative positions **4** a striding gait

strife /straɪf/ *n* bitter conflict or dissension

¹strike /straɪk/ *v* struck; struck *also* stricken **1a** to aim a blow at; hit **b** to make an attack **2a** to haul down **b** to take down the tents of a camp **3a** to collide forcefully **b** to afflict suddenly **4** to delete, cancel **5** to penetrate painfully **6** *of the time* to be indicated by the sounding of a clock, bell, etc **7a** *of light* to fall on **b** *of a sound* to become audible to **8** to cause suddenly to become **9** to cause (a match) to ignite **10a** to make a mental impact on **b** to occur suddenly to **11** to make and ratify (a bargain) **12** *of a fish* to snatch at (bait) **13** to arrive at (a balance) by computation **14** to assume (a pose) **15** to place (a plant cutting) in a medium for rooting **16** to engage in a strike against

²strike *n* **1** a work stoppage by a body of workers, made as a protest or to force an employer to comply with demands **2** a success in finding or hitting sthg; *esp* a discovery of a valuable mineral deposit **3** the opportunity to receive the bowling by virtue of being the batsman at the wicket towards which the bowling is being directed **4** an (air) attack on a target

striking /'straɪkɪŋ/ *adj* attracting attention, esp because of unusual or impressive qualities – ~ly adv

¹**string** /striŋ/ n 1 a narrow cord used to bind, fasten, or tie 2a the gut or wire cord of a musical instrument b a stringed instrument of an orchestra – usu pl 3a a group of objects threaded on a string b (a set of things arranged in) a sequence c a group of usu scattered business concerns d the animals, esp horses, belonging to or used by sby 4 pl conditions or obligations attached to sthg

²**string** v strung 1 to equip with strings 2a to thread (as if) on a string b to tie, hang, or fasten with string 3 to remove the strings of

³**string** adj made with wide meshes and usu of string

¹**strip** /strip/ v 1 to remove clothing, covering, or surface or extraneous matter from; esp to undress (2) to perform a striptease b to deprive of possessions, privileges, or rank 2 to remove furniture, equipment, or accessories from 3 to damage the thread or teeth of (a screw, cog, etc)

²**strip** n 1a a long narrow piece of material b a long narrow area of land or water 2 Br clothes worn by a rugby or soccer team

stripe /straip/ n 1 a line or narrow band differing in colour or texture from the adjoining parts 2 a bar, chevron, etc of braid or embroidery worn usu on the sleeve of a uniform to indicate rank or length of service

strive /straiv/ v stroved; striven 1 to struggle in opposition; contend 2 to endeavour; try hard – ~r n

strode /stroud/ past of stride

¹**stroke** /strouk/ v to pass the hand over gently in 1 direction

²**stroke** n 1 the act of striking; esp a blow with a weapon or implement 2 a single unbroken movement; esp one that is repeated 3 a striking of the ball in a game (e g cricket or tennis); specif an (attempted) striking of the ball that constitutes the scoring unit in golf 4 an unexpected occurrence 5 (an attack of) sudden usu complete loss of consciousness, sensation, and voluntary motion caused by rupture, thrombosis, etc of a brain artery 6a (the technique or mode used for) a propelling beat or movement against a resisting medium b an oarsman who sits at the stern of a racing rowing boat and sets the pace for the rest of the crew 7 (the distance of) the movement in either direction of a reciprocating mechanical part (e g a piston rod) 8 the sound of a striking clock 9 a mark or dash made by a single movement of an implement

stroll /stroul/ v to walk in a leisurely or idle manner – stroll n – ~er n

strong /stroŋ/ adj 1 having or marked by great physical power 2 having moral or intellectual power 3 of a specified number 4a striking or superior of its kind b effective or efficient, esp in a specified area 5 forceful, cogent 6a rich in some active agent (e g a flavour or

extract) b of a colour intense 7 moving with vigour or force 8 ardent, zealous 9 well established; firm 10 having a pungent or offensive smell or flavour 11 of or being a verb that forms inflections by internal vowel change (e g drink, drank, drunk) – ~ly adv

strove /strouv/ past of strive

¹**structure** /'strʌktʃə/ n 1a sthg (e g a building) that is constructed b sthg organized in a definite pattern 2a the arrangement of particles or parts in a substance or body b arrangement or interrelation of elements – -ral adj – -rally adv

²**structure** v to form into a structure

¹**struggle** /'strʌgl/ v 1 to make violent or strenuous efforts against opposition 2 to proceed with difficulty or great effort

²**struggle** n 1 a violent effort; a determined attempt in adverse circumstances 2 a hard-fought contest

¹**stub** /stʌb/ n 1 a short blunt part of a pencil, cigarette, etc left after a larger part has been broken off or used up 2a a small part of a leaf or page (e g of a chequebook) left on the spine as a record of the contents of the part torn away b the part of a ticket returned to the user after inspection

²**stub** v 1 to extinguish (e g a cigarette) by crushing – usu + out 2 to strike (one's foot or toe) against an object

stubborn /'stʌbən/ adj (unreasonably) unyielding or determined 2 refractory, intractable – ~ly adv – ~ness n

stuck /stʌk/ past of stick

student /'stju:dənt/ n 1 a scholar, learner; esp one who attends a college or university 2 an attentive and systematic observer

studio /'stju:diəu/ n 1a the workroom of a painter, sculptor, or photographer b a place for the study of an art (e g dancing, singing, or acting) 2 a place where films are made; also, sing or pl in constr a film production company including its premises and employees 3 a room equipped for the production of radio or television programmes

¹**study** /'stʌdi/ n 1a the application of the mind to acquiring (specific) knowledge b a careful examination or analysis of a subject 2 a room devoted to study 3 a branch of learning 4 a literary or artistic work intended as a preliminary or experimental interpretation

²**study** v 1 to engage in the study of 2 to consider attentively or in detail

¹**stuff** /stʌf/ n 1a materials, supplies, or equipment used in various activities b personal property; possessions 2 a finished textile suitable for clothing; esp wool or worsted material 3 an unspecified material substance 4 the essence of a usu abstract thing 5a subject matter

²**stuff** v 1a to fill (as if) by packing things in; cram b to gorge (oneself) with food c to fill (e g meat or vegetables) with a stuffing d to fill with stuffing or pad-

ding **e** to fill out the skin of (an animal) for mounting **2** to choke or block *up* (the nasal passages) **3** to force into a limited space; thrust

stuffing /'stʌfɪŋ/ *n* material used to stuff sthg; *esp* a seasoned mixture used to stuff meat, eggs, etc

stuffy /'stʌfɪ/ *adj* **1a** badly ventilated; close **b** stuffed up **2** stodgy, dull **3** prim, straitlaced – **stuffily** *adv* – **stuffiness** *n*

stumble /'stʌmbəl/ *v* **1** to trip in walking or running **2a** to walk unsteadily or clumsily **b** to speak or act in a hesitant or faltering manner **3** to come unexpectedly or by chance – + *upon*, *on*, or *across* – **stumble** *n*

¹stump /stʌmp/ *n* **1** the part of an arm, leg, etc remaining attached to the trunk after the rest is removed **2** the part of a plant, esp a tree, remaining in the ground attached to the root after the stem is cut **3** any of the 3 upright wooden rods that together with the bails form the wicket in cricket

²stump *v* **1** to walk heavily or noisily **2** *of a wicketkeeper* to dismiss (a batsman who is outside his popping crease but not attempting to run) by breaking the wicket with the ball before it has touched another fieldsman **3** to baffle, bewilder – *infml*

stun /stʌn/ *v* **1** to make dazed or dizzy (as if) by a blow **2** to overcome, esp with astonishment or disbelief

stung /stʌŋ/ *past of* **sting**

¹stunt /stʌnt/ *v* to hinder or arrest the growth or development of

²stunt *n* an unusual or difficult feat performed to gain publicity

stupid /'stjuːpɪd/ *adj* **1** slow-witted, obtuse **2** dulled in feeling or perception; torpid **3** annoying, exasperating – *infml* – **~ity** *n* – **~ly** *adv*

sturdy /'stɜːdɪ/ *adj* **1** strongly built or constituted; stout, hardy **2a** having physical strength or vigour; robust **b** firm, resolute – **sturdily** *adv* – **sturdiness** *n*

¹sty /staɪ/ *n*, *pl* **sties** a pigsty

²sty, stye *n*, *pl* **styes** an inflamed swelling of a sebaceous gland at the margin of an eyelid

¹style /staɪl/ *n* **1** a prolongation of a plant ovary bearing a stigma at the top **2a** a manner of expressing thought in language, esp when characteristic of an individual, period, etc **b** the custom or plan followed in spelling, capitalization, punctuation, and typographic arrangement and display **3** mode of address; a title **4a** a distinctive or characteristic manner of doing sthg **b** excellence or distinction in social behaviour, manners, or appearance – **~less** *adj*

²style *v* **1** to designate by an identifying term; name **2** to fashion according to a particular mode

subconscious /ˌsʌb'kɒnʃəs/ *adj* existing in the mind but not immediately available to consciousness – **~ly** *adv*

subdue /səb'djuː/ *v* **1** to conquer and bring into subjection **2** to bring under

control; curb **3** to reduce the intensity or degree of (e g colour)

subdued /səb'djuːd/ *adj* **1** brought under control (as if) by military conquest **2** reduced or lacking in force, intensity, or strength

¹subject /'sʌbdʒɪkt/ *n* **1a** sby subject to a ruler and governed by his/her law **b** sby who enjoys the protection of and owes allegiance to a sovereign power or state **2a** that of which a quality, attribute, or relation may be stated **b** the entity (e g the mind or ego) that sustains or assumes the form of thought or consciousness **3a** a department of knowledge or learning **b** an individual whose reactions are studied **c**(1) sthg concerning which sthg is said or done (2) sby or sthg represented in a work of art **d**(1) the term of a logical proposition denoting that of which sthg is stated, denied, or predicated (2) the word or phrase in a sentence or clause denoting that of which sthg is predicated or asserted **e** the principal melodic phrase on which a musical composition or movement is based

²subject *adj* **1** owing obedience or allegiance to another **2a** liable or exposed to **b** having a tendency or inclination; prone to **3** dependent or conditional on sthg *USE* usu + *to*

³subject /səb'dʒekt/ *v* **1** to bring under control or rule **2** to make liable; expose **3** to cause to undergo sthg *USE* usu + *to* – **~ion** *n*

¹submarine /'sʌbməriːn, ˌsʌbmə'riːn/ *adj* being, acting, or growing under water, esp in the sea

²submarine *n* a vessel designed for undersea operations; *esp* a submarine warship that is typically armed with torpedoes or missiles and uses electric, diesel, or nuclear propulsion

submerge /səb'mɜːdʒ/ *v* **1** to go or put under water **2** to cover (as if) with water; inundate – **~nce** *n*

submission /səb'mɪʃən/ *n* **1** an act of submitting sthg for consideration, inspection, etc **2** the state of being submissive, humble, or compliant **3** an act of submitting to the authority or control of another

submit /səb'mɪt/ *v* **1a** to yield to the authority or will of another **b** to subject to a process or practice **2a** to send or commit to another for consideration, inspection, etc **b** to put forward as an opinion; suggest

¹subordinate /sə'bɔːdɪnət/ *adj* **1** occupying a lower class or rank; inferior **2** subject to or controlled by authority **3** *of a clause* functioning as a noun, adjective, or adverb in a complex sentence (e g the clause *'when he heard'* in *'he laughed when he heard'*) – **~ly** *adv*

²subordinate /sə'bɔːdɪneɪt/ *v* **1** to place in a lower order or class **2** to make subject or subservient; subdue

subscribe /səb'skraɪb/ *v* **1a** to give consent or approval to sthg written by signing **b** to give money (e g to charity) **c** to pay regularly in order to receive a periodical or service **2** to feel favourably disposed *USE* usu + *to*

subscription /səb'skrɪpʃən/ *n* **1** a sum subscribed **2a** a purchase by prepayment for a certain number of issues (e g of a periodical) **b** *Br* membership fees paid regularly

subsequent /'sʌbsɪkwənt/ *adj* following in time or order; succeeding – ~**ly** *adv*

subside /səb'saɪd/ *v* **1** to sink or fall to the bottom; settle **2a** to descend; *esp* to sink so as to form a depression **b** of *ground* to cave in; collapse **3** to become quiet; abate – – ~**nce** *n*

¹subsidiary /səb'sɪdɪəri/ *adj* **1** serving to assist or supplement; auxiliary **2** of secondary importance

²subsidiary *n* sby or sthg subsidiary; *esp* a company wholly controlled by another

subsidy /'sʌbsɪdi/ *n* a grant or gift of money (e g by a government to a person or organization, to assist an enterprise deemed advantageous to the public) – –**dize** *v*

substance /'sʌbstəns/ *n* **1a** a fundamental or essential part or import **b** correspondence with reality **2** ultimate underlying reality **3a** (a) physical material from which sthg is made **b** matter of particular or definite chemical constitution **4** material possessions; property

substantial /səb'stænʃəl/ *adj* **1a** having material existence; real **b** important, essential **2** ample to satisfy and nourish **3a** well-to-do, prosperous **b** considerable in quantity; significantly large **4** firmly constructed; solid

¹substitute /'sʌbstɪtjuːt/ *n* sby or sthg that takes the place of another

²substitute *v* **1** to exchange for another **2** to take the place of; *also* to introduce a substitute for – –**tution** *n*

subtle /'sʌtl/ *adj* **1** delicate, elusive **2** cleverly contrived; ingenious **3** artful, cunning – –**tly** *adv*

subtract /səb'trækt/ *v* to take away (a quantity or amount) from another – – ~**ion** *n*

suburb /'sʌbɜːb/ *n* an outlying part of a city or large town

suburbia /sə'bɜːbɪə/ *n* (the inhabitants of) the suburbs of a city

succeed /sək'siːd/ *v* **1a** to inherit sthg, esp sovereignty, rank, or title **b** to follow after another in order **2** to have a favourable or desired result; turn out well

success /sək'ses/ *n* **1** a favourable outcome to an undertaking **2** the attainment of wealth or fame **3** sby or sthg that succeeds – – ~**ful** *adj* – – ~**fully** *adv*

succession /sək'seʃən/ *n* **1** the order or right of succeeding to a property, title, or throne **2a** the act of following in order; a sequence **b** the act or process of becoming entitled to a deceased person's property or title

successor /sək'sesə⁰/ *n* sby or sthg that follows another; *esp* a person who succeeds to throne, title, or office

¹such /sətʃ, sʌtʃ; *strong* sʌtʃ/ *adj or adv* **1a** of the kind, quality, or extent – used before *as* to introduce an example or comparison **b** of the same sort **2** of so extreme a degree or extraordinary a nature – used before *as* to suggest that a name is unmerited (e g we forced down the soup, *such* as it was)

²such /sʌtʃ/ *pron, pl* **such 1** *pl* such people; those **2** that thing, fact, or action (e g *such* was the result) **3** *pl* similar people or things (e g tin and glass and *such*)

¹suck /sʌk/ *v* **1** to draw sthg into the mouth by suction; *esp* to draw milk from a breast or udder with the mouth **2** to act in an obsequious manner – *infml*; usu + *up*

²suck *n* **1** the act of sucking **2** a sucking movement

sudden /'sʌdn/ *adj* **1a** happening or coming unexpectedly **b** abrupt, steep **2** marked by or showing haste – ~**ly** *adv* – ~**ness** *n*

sue /suː, sjuː/ *v* **1** to bring a legal action against **2** to make a request or application – usu + *for* or *to*

suffer /'sʌfə⁰/ *v* **1** to submit to or be forced to endure pain, distress, etc **2** to allow, permit **3** to sustain loss or damage **4** to be handicapped or at a disadvantage

suffering /'sʌfərɪŋ/ *n* the state of one who suffers

sufficient /sə'fɪʃənt/ *adj* enough to meet the needs of a situation – ~**ly** *adv*

suffocate /'sʌfəkeɪt/ *v* **1** to stop the breathing of (e g by asphyxiation) **2** to make uncomfortable by want of cool fresh air – –**cation** *n*

¹sugar /'ʃʊgə⁰/ *n* any of a class of water-soluble carbohydrates that are of varying sweetness and include glucose, ribose, and sucrose; *specif* a sweet crystallizable material that consists of sucrose, is colourless or white when pure tending to brown when less refined, is obtained commercially esp from sugarcane or sugar beet, and is used as a sweetener and preservative of other foods – ~**less** *adj*

²sugar *v* to make palatable or attractive

suggest /sə'dʒest/ *v* **1** to put forward as a possibility or for consideration **2a** to call to mind by thought or association; evoke **b** to indicate the presence of

suggestion /sə'dʒestʃən/ *n* **1** sthg suggested; a proposal **2a** indirect means (e g the natural association of ideas) to evoke ideas or feeling **b** the impressing of an idea, attitude, desired action, etc on the mind of another **3** a slight indication; a trace

suicidal /ˌsuːɪ'saɪdl, ˌsjuː-/ *adj* **1** dangerous, esp to life **2** harmful to one's own interests – ~**ly** *adv*

suicide /'suːɪsaɪd, 'sjuː-/ *n* **1a** (an) act of taking one's own life intentionally **b** ruin of one's own interests **2** one who commits or attempts suicide

¹suit /suːt, sjuːt/ *n* **1** a legal action **2** a

petition or appeal; *specif* courtship **3** a group of things forming a unit or constituting a collection – used chiefly with reference to suites **4a** an outer costume of 2 or more matching pieces that are designed to be worn together **b** a costume to be worn for a specified purpose **5** all the playing cards in a pack bearing the same symbol (i e hearts, clubs, diamonds, or spades)

²suit *v* **1** to be appropriate or satisfactory **2a** to be good for the health or well-being of **b** to be becoming to; look right with **3** to satisfy, please

suitable /'su:təbəl, 'sju:-/ *adj* appropriate, fitting – **-bility** *n* – ~**ness** *n* – **-bly** *adv*

suitcase /'su:tkeɪs, 'sju:t-/ *n* a rectangular usu rigid case with a hinged lid and a handle, used for carrying articles (e g clothes)

suite /swi:t/ *n* **1** *sing or pl in constr* a retinue; *esp* the personal staff accompanying an official or dignitary on business **2a** a group of rooms occupied as a unit **b** a musical composition consisting of several loosely connected instrumental pieces **c** a set of matching furniture (e g a settee and 2 armchairs) for a room

¹sulk /sʌlk/ *v* to be moodily silent

²sulk *n* a fit of sulking – usu pl with sing. meaning

sulphur /'sʌlfə'/ *n* **1** a nonmetallic element chemically resembling oxygen that occurs esp as yellow crystals **2** a pale greenish yellow colour

sum /sʌm/ *n* **1** a (specified) amount of money **2** the whole amount; the total **3a** the result of adding numbers **b** numbers to be added; *broadly* a problem in arithmetic – **sum** *v*

¹summary /'sʌməri/ *adj* **1** concise but comprehensive **2a** done quickly without delay or formality **b** of or using a summary proceeding; *specif* tried or triable in a magistrates' court – **-rily** *adv*

²summary *n* a brief account covering the main points of sthg – **-ize** *v*

¹summer /'sʌmə'/ *n* **1** the season between spring and autumn comprising in the northern hemisphere the months of June, July, and August **2** a period of maturity **3** a year – chiefly poetic

²summer *adj* sown in the spring and harvested in the same year as sown

summit /'sʌmɪt/ *n* **1** a top; *esp* the highest point or peak **2** the topmost level attainable; the pinnacle **3** a conference of highest-level officials

summon /'sʌmən/ *v* **1** to command by a summons to appear in court **2** to call upon to come; send for

summons /'sʌmənz/ *n, pl* **summonses** a written notification warning sby to appear in court

¹sun /sʌn/ *n* **1a** the star nearest to the earth, round which the earth and other planets revolve **b** a star or other celestial body that emits its own light **2** the heat or light radiated from the sun

²sun *v* to expose oneself to the rays of the sun

sunbathe /'sʌnbeɪð/ *v* to expose the

body to the rays of the sun or a sunlamp – ~**r** *n*

sunburn /'sʌnbɜːn/ *v* to burn or tan by exposure to sunlight – **sunburn** *n*

¹Sunday /'sʌndeɪ, -di/ *n* **1** the day of the week falling between Saturday and Monday, observed by Christians as a day of worship **2** a newspaper published on Sundays

²Sunday *adj* **1** of or associated with Sunday **2** amateur – *derog*

sung /sʌŋ/ *past of* sing

sunglasses /'sʌn,glɑːsɪz/ *n pl* glasses to protect the eyes from the sun

sunk /sʌŋk/ *past of* sink

sunlight /'sʌnlaɪt/ *n* sunshine

sunny /'sʌni/ *adj* **1** bright with sunshine **2** cheerful, optimistic **3** exposed to or warmed by the sun – **-nily** *adv* – **-niness** *n*

sunrise /'sʌnraɪz/ *n* (the time of) the rising of the topmost part of the sun above the horizon as a result of the rotation of the earth

sunset /'sʌnset/ *n* (the time of) the descent of the topmost part of the sun below the horizon as a result of the rotation of the earth

sunshine /'sʌnʃaɪn/ *n* the sun's light or direct rays

¹super /'su:pə', 'sju:-/ *n* **1** a superfine grade or extra large size **2** a police or other superintendent – *infml*

²super *adj* – used as a general term of approval; *infml*

superb /su:'pɜːb, sju:-/ *adj* **1** marked by grandeur or magnificence **2** of excellent quality – ~**ly** *adv*

superficial /,su:pə'fɪʃəl, ,sju:-/ *adj* **1** not penetrating below the surface **2a** not thorough or profound; shallow **b** apparent rather than real – ~**ity** *n* – ~**ly** *adv*

superfluous /su:'pɜːfluəs, sju:-/ *adj* exceeding what is sufficient or necessary – ~**ly** *adv* – ~**ness, -fluity** *n*

¹superior /su:'pɪərɪə', sju:-/ *adj* **1** situated higher up; upper **2** of higher rank or status **3a** greater in quality, amount, or worth **b** excellent of its kind **4** of an *animal or plant part* situated above or at the top of another (corresponding) part **5** thinking oneself better than others; supercilious – ~**ity** *n*

²superior *n* **1** a person who is above another in rank or office **2** sby or sthg that surpasses another in quality or merit

superman /'su:pəmæn, 'sju:-/ *n* a person of extraordinary power or achievements – *infml*

supermarket /'su:pə,mɑːkɪt, 'sju:-/ *n* a usu large self-service retail shop selling foods and household merchandise

supernatural /,su:pə'nætʃərəl, ,sju:-/ *adj* **1** of an order of existence or an agency (e g a god or spirit) not bound by normal laws of cause and effect **2a** departing from what is usual or normal, esp in nature **b** attributed to an invisible agent (e g a ghost or spirit) – ~**ly** *adv*

supersonic /,su:pə'sɒnɪk, ,sju:-/ *adj* **1** (using, produced by, or relating to waves or vibrations) having a frequency above the upper threshold of human hearing of about 20,000Hz 2 of, being, or using speeds from 1 to 5 times the speed of sound in air

superstition /ˌsuːpəˈstɪʃən, ˌsjuː-/ n 1 a belief or practice resulting from ignorance, fear of the unknown, trust in magic or chance, or a false conception of causation 2 an irrational abject attitude of mind towards the supernatural, nature, or God resulting from superstition – **-tious** adj – **-tiously** adv

supervise /ˈsuːpəvaɪz, ˈsjuː-/ v to superintend, oversee – **-vision** n – **-visor** n – **-visory** adj

supper /ˈsʌpə/ n (the food for) a usu light evening meal or snack – ~**less** n

supplement /ˈsʌplɪmənt/ n 1 sthg that completes, adds, or makes good a deficiency, or makes an addition 2 a part issued to update or extend a book or periodical – **supplement** v

¹**supply** /səˈplaɪ/ v 1 to provide for; satisfy 2 to provide, furnish – **-ier** n

²**supply** n 1a the quantity or amount needed or available b provisions, stores – usu pl with sing. meaning 2 the quantities of goods and services offered for sale at a particular time or at one price 3 supply, supply teacher Br a teacher who fills a temporary vacancy

¹**support** /səˈpɔːt/ v 1 to bear, tolerate 2a(1) to promote the interests of; encourage (2) to argue or vote for b to assist, help 3 to provide livelihood or subsistence for 4 to hold up or serve as a foundation or prop for – ~**ive** adj

²**support** n 1 supporting or being supported 2 maintenance, sustenance 3 a device that supports sthg 4 sing or pl in constr a body of supporters

supporter /səˈpɔːtə/ n 1 an adherent or advocate 2 either of 2 figures (e g of men or animals) placed one on each side of a heraldic shield as if holding or guarding it

suppose /səˈpəʊz/ v 1a to lay down tentatively as a hypothesis, assumption, or proposal b(1) to hold as an opinion; believe (2) to conjecture, think 2 to devise for a purpose; intend 3 to presuppose 4 to allow, permit – used negatively 5 to expect because of moral, legal, or other obligations USE (2, 4, & 5) chiefly in be supposed to

suppress /səˈpres/ v 1 to put down by authority or force 2 to stop the publication or revelation of 3 to hold back, check 4 to inhibit the growth or development of – ~**ion** n

supreme /suːˈpriːm, sjuː-, sə-/ adj 1 highest in rank or authority 2 highest in degree or quality – ~**ly** adv

¹**sure** /ʃʊə/ adj 1 firm, secure 2 reliable, trustworthy 3 assured, confident 4 bound, certain – ~**ness** n

²**sure** adv, chiefly NAm surely, certainly – infml

surely /ˈʃʊəli/ adv 1 without doubt; certainly 2 it is to be believed, hoped, or expected that

¹**surface** /ˈsɜːfɪs/ n 1 the external or

upper boundary or layer of an object or body 2 (a portion of) the boundary of a three-dimensional object 3 the external or superficial aspect of sthg

²**surface** 1 to come to the surface; emerge 2 to wake up; also get up – infml

³**surface** adj 1 situated or employed on the surface, esp of the earth or sea 2 lacking depth; superficial

¹**surge** /sɜːdʒ/ v to rise and move (as if) in waves or billows

²**surge** n the motion of swelling, rolling, or sweeping forwards like a wave

surgeon /ˈsɜːdʒən/ n a medical specialist who practises surgery

surgery /ˈsɜːdʒəri/ n 1 medicine that deals with diseases and conditions requiring or amenable to operative or manual procedures 2 a surgical operation 3 Br (the hours of opening of) a doctor's, dentist's, etc room where patients are advised or treated 4 Br a session at which an elected representative (e g an MP) is available for usu informal consultation

surly /ˈsɜːli/ adj irritably sullen and churlish

surname /ˈsɜːneɪm/ n the name shared in common by members of a family

surpass /səˈpɑːs/ v 1 to go beyond in quality, degree, or performance; exceed 2 to transcend the reach, capacity, or powers of – ~**ing** adj – ~**ingly** adv

surplus /ˈsɜːpləs/ n 1 the amount in excess of what is used or needed 2 an excess of receipts over disbursements

¹**surprise** /səˈpraɪz/ n 1 an act of taking unawares 2 sthg unexpected or surprising 3 the feeling caused by an unexpected event; astonishment

²**surprise** v 1 to take unawares 2 to fill with wonder or amazement

surprising /səˈpraɪzɪŋ/ adj causing surprise; unexpected – ~**ly** adv

¹**surrender** /səˈrendə/ 1a to give oneself up into the power of another; yield b to relinquish; give up 2 to abandon (oneself) to sthg unrestrainedly

²**surrender** n 1 the act or an instance of surrendering oneself or sthg 2 the voluntary cancellation of an insurance policy by the party insured in return for a payment

¹**surround** /səˈraʊnd/ v 1a to enclose on all sides b to be part of the environment of; be present round 2 to form a ring round; encircle – ~**ing** adj

²**surround** n a border or edging

surroundings /səˈraʊndɪŋz/ n pl the circumstances, conditions, or objects by which one is surrounded

¹**survey** /səˈveɪ/ v 1a to look over and examine closely b to examine the condition of and often give a value for (a building) 2 to determine and portray the form, extent, and position of (e g a tract of land) 3 to view as a whole or from a height

²**survey** /ˈsɜːveɪ/ n a surveying or being surveyed; also sthg surveyed

survival /səˈvaɪvəl/ n 1a the condition of living or continuing b the continuation of life or existence 2 sby or sthg that survives, esp after others of its kind have disappeared

survive /sə'vaɪv/ v to remain alive or in existence; live on – **-vivor** n

¹**suspect** /sə'spekt/ adj (deserving to be) regarded with suspicion

²**suspect** /'sʌspekt/ n sby who is suspected

³**suspect** /sə'spekt/ v 1 to be suspicious of; distrust 2 to believe to be guilty without conclusive proof 3 to imagine to be true, likely, or probable

suspend /sə'spend/ v 1 to debar temporarily from a privilege, office, membership, or employment 2 to make temporarily inoperative 3 to defer till later on certain conditions 4 to hang, so as to be free on all sides

suspense /sə'spens/ n a state of uncertain expectation as to a decision or outcome

suspension /sə'spenʃən/ n 1a temporary removal from office or privileges b temporary withholding or postponement c temporary abolishing of a law or rule 2a hanging or being hung b a solid that is dispersed, but not dissolved, in a solid, liquid, or gas 3 the system of devices supporting the upper part of a vehicle on the axles

suspicion /sə'spɪʃən/ n 1a suspecting or being suspected b a feeling of doubt or mistrust 2 a slight touch or trace

suspicious /sə'spɪʃəs/ adj 1 tending to arouse suspicion; dubious 2 inclined to suspect; distrustful – **~ly** adv

sustain /sə'steɪn/ v 1 to give support or relief to 2 to cause to continue; prolong 3 to buoy up the spirits of 4 to suffer, undergo

¹**swagger** /'swægə'/ v to behave or esp walk in an arrogant or pompous manner – **~er** n **~ingly** adv

²**swagger** n 1 an act or instance of swaggering 2 arrogant or conceitedly self-assured behaviour

¹**swallow** /'swɒləʊ/ n any of numerous small long-winged migratory birds noted for their graceful flight, that have a short bill, a forked tail, and feed on insects caught while flying

²**swallow** v 1 to take through the mouth into the stomach 2 to envelop, engulf 3 to accept without question or protest; also to believe naively 4 to refrain from expressing or showing – **~er** n

³**swallow** n an amount that can be swallowed at one time

swam /swæm/ past of **swim**

¹**swamp** /swɒmp/ n (an area of) wet spongy land sometimes covered with water – **~y** adj

²**swamp** v 1 to inundate, submerge 2 to overwhelm by an excess of work, difficulties, etc

swap /swɒp/ n 1 an art of exchanging one thing for another 2 sthg so exchanged – **~** v

¹**swarm** /swɔːm/ n 1 a colony of honeybees, esp when emigrating from a hive with a queen bee to start a new colony elsewhere 2 sing or pl in constr a group of animate or inanimate things, esp when massing together

²**swarm** v 1 to collect together and depart from a hive 2 to move or assemble in a crowd 3 to contain a swarm; teem

³**swarm** v to climb, esp with the hands and feet – usu + up

¹**sway** /sweɪ/ v 1 to swing slowly and rhythmically back and forth 2 to fluctuate or alternate between one attitude or position and another 3 to change the opinions of, esp by eloquence or argument

²**sway** n 1 swaying or being swayed 2a controlling influence or power b rule, dominion

swear /sweə'/ v swore; sworn 1 to utter or take (an oath) solemnly 2 to promise emphatically or earnestly 3 to use profane or obscene language – **~er** n

¹**sweat** /swet/ v 1 to excrete sweat in visible quantities 2a to emit or exude moisture b to gather surface moisture as a result of condensation 3 to undergo anxiety or tension 4 to exact work from under sweatshop conditions

²**sweat** n 1 the fluid excreted from the sweat glands of the skin; perspiration 2 moisture gathering in drops on a surface 3 hard work; drudgery 4 a state of anxiety or impatience USE (3&4) infml – **~y** adj

sweater /'swetə'/ n a pullover

¹**sweep** /swiːp/ v swept 1a to remove or clean (as if) by brushing b to destroy completely – usu + away c to drive or carry along with irresistible force 2 to move through or along with overwhelming speed or violence 3 to go with stately or sweeping movements 4 to cover the entire range of 5 to move or extend in a wide curve

²**sweep** n 1a a long oar b a windmill sail 2 a clearing out or away (as if) with a broom 3a a curving course or line b a broad extent 4 a sweepstake

sweeping /'swiːpɪŋ/ adj 1 extending in a wide curve or over a wide area 2a extensive, wide-ranging b marked by wholesale and indiscriminate inclusion – **~ly** adv

¹**sweet** /swiːt/ adj 1a being or inducing the one of the 4 basic taste sensations that is typically induced by sugar b of a beverage containing a sweetening ingredient; not dry 2a delightful, charming b marked by gentle good humour or kindliness c fragrant d pleasing to the ear or eye 3 much loved 4a not sour, rancid, decaying, or stale b not salt or salted; fresh – **~ly** adv – **~ness** n – **~ish** adj

²**sweet** n 1 a darling or sweetheart 2 Br a dessert b a toffee, truffle, or other small piece of confectionery prepared with (flavoured or filled) chocolate or sugar; esp one made chiefly of (boiled and crystallized) sugar

sweeten /'swiːtn/ v 1 to make (more) sweet 2 to soften the mood or attitude of 3 to make less painful or trying – **~er** n

sweetheart /'swiːthɑːt/ n a darling, lover

¹**swell** /swel/ v swollen, swelled 1a to

expand gradually beyond a normal or original limit **b** to be distended or puffed up **c** to curve outwards or upwards; bulge **2** to become charged with emotion

²**swell** *n* **1** a rounded protuberance or bulge **2** a (massive) surge of water, often continuing beyond or after its cause (e g a gale) **3** a gradual increase and decrease of the loudness of a musical sound **4** a person of fashion or high social position – *infml*

³**swell** *adj, chiefly NAm* excellent

swelling /'swelɪŋ/ *n* an abnormal bodily protuberance or enlargement

swerve /swɜːv/ *v* to (cause to) turn aside abruptly from a straight line or course

¹**swift** /swɪft/ *adj* **1** (capable of) moving at great speed **2** occurring suddenly or within a very short time **3** quick to respond; ready – ~**ly** *adv* – ~**ness** *n*

²**swift** *n* any of numerous dark-coloured birds that resemble swallows and are noted for their fast darting flight in pursuit of insects

¹**swim** /swɪm/ *v* **swam; swum 1** to propel oneself in water by bodily movements (e g of the limbs, fins, or tail) **2** to surmount difficulties; not go under **3** to have a floating or dizzy effect or sensation – ~**mer** *n*

²**swim** *n* **1** an act or period of swimming **2** the main current of events

swimming /'swɪmɪŋ/ *adj* capable of, adapted to, or used in or for swimming

swimmingly /'swɪmɪŋli/ *adv* very well; splendidly – *infml*

¹**swindle** /'swɪndl/ *v* to obtain property or take property from by fraud – ~**r** *n*

²**swindle** *n* a fraud, deceit

swine /swaɪn/ *n, pl* **swine 1** a pig – used esp technically or in literature **2a** a contemptible person **3** sthg unpleasant *USE* (2 & 3) *infml* – **-nish** *adj*

¹**swing** /swɪŋ/ *v* **swung 1** to move freely to and fro, esp when hanging from an overhead support **2** to turn (as if) on a hinge or pivot **3a** to influence decisively **b** to manage; bring about **4** to play or sing with a lively compelling rhythm; *specif* to play swing music **5** to shift or fluctuate between 2 moods, opinions, etc **6a** to move along rhythmically **b** to start up in a smooth rapid manner **7** to engage freely in sex, *specif* wife-swapping – *slang*

²**swing** *n* **1a** a sweeping or rhythmic movement of the body or a bodily part **b** the regular movement of a freely suspended object to and fro along an arc **c** a steady vigorous rhythm or action **2** the progression of an activity; course **3** the arc or range through which sthg swings **4** a suspended seat on which one may swing to and fro **5** jazz played usu by a large dance band and characterized by a steady lively rhythm, simple harmony, and a basic melody often submerged in improvisation

¹**switch** /swɪtʃ/ *n* **1** a slender flexible twig or rod **2** a shift or change from one

to another **3** a tuft of long hairs at the end of the tail of an animal (e g a cow) **4** a device for making, breaking, or changing the connections in an electrical circuit

²**switch** *v* **1** to shift, change **2a** to shift to another electrical circuit by means of a switch **b** to operate an electrical switch so as to turn *off* or *on* **3** to lash from side to side – ~**able** *adj*

swollen /'swəʊlən/ *past part of* **swell**

¹**swoop** /swuːp/ *v* **1** to make a sudden attack or downward sweep **2** to carry off abruptly; snatch – ~**er** *n*

²**swoop** *n* an act of swooping

sword /sɔːd/ *n* **1** a cutting or thrusting weapon having a long usu sharp-pointed and sharp-edged blade **2** death caused (as if) by a sword – usu + *the* – ~**sman** *n* ~**smanship** *n*

swore /swɔː/ *past of* **swear**

sworn /swɔːn/ *past part of* **swear**

swum /swʌm/ *past part of* **swim**

swung /swʌŋ/ *past of* **swing**

syllable /'sɪləbəl/ *n* (a letter or symbol representing) an uninterruptible unit of spoken language that usu consists of 1 vowel sound either alone or with a consonant sound preceding or following – **-abic** *adj*

symbol /'sɪmbəl/ *n* **1** sthg that stands for or suggests sthg else by reason of association, convention, etc **2** a sign used in writing or printing to represent operations, quantities, elements, relations, or qualities in a particular field (e g chemistry or music) – ~**ic**, ~**ical** *adj* – ~**ically** *adv* – ~**ize** *v*

sympathetic /ˌsɪmpə'θetɪk/ *adj* **1** appropriate to one's mood or temperament; congenial **2** given to or arising from compassion and sensitivity to others' feelings **3** favourably inclined – ~**ally** *adv*

sympathy /'sɪmpəθi/ *n* **1a** relationship between people or things in which each is simultaneously affected in a similar way **b** unity or harmony in action or effect **2a** inclination to think or feel alike **b** tendency to favour or support – often *pl* with *sing.* meaning **3** (the expression of) pity or compassion – **-thize** *v*

symphony /'sɪmfəni/ *n* **1** a usu long and complex sonata for symphony orchestra **2** sthg of great harmonious complexity or variety – **-onic** *adj*

symptom /'sɪmptəm/ *n* **1** sthg giving (subjective) evidence or indication of disease or physical disturbance **2** sthg that indicates the existence of sthg else – ~**atic** *adj* – ~**atically** *adv*

synchronize, -ise /'sɪŋkrənaɪz/ *v* **1** to happen at the same time; *esp* to make sound and image coincide (e g with a film) **2** to make synchronous in operation; *esp* to set clocks or watches to the same time

syndrome /'sɪndrəʊm/ *n* a group of signs and symptoms that occur together and characterize a particular (medical) abnormality

synthesize, -ise /'sɪnθɪ̩saɪz/ *v* to make,

esp by combining parts or in imitation of a natural product

synthetic /sɪn'θetɪk/ *adj* 1 asserting of a subject a predicate that is not part of the meaning of that subject 2 produced artificially; man-made

syrup /'sɪrəp/ *n* 1a a thick sticky solution of (flavoured, medicated, etc) sugar and water b the raw sugar juice obtained from crushed sugarcane after evaporation and before crystallization in sugar manufacture 2 cloying sweetness or sentimentality – ~y *adj*

system /'sɪstᵻm/ *n* 1a a group of body organs that together perform 1 or more usu specified functions b a group of interrelated and interdependent objects or units c a form of social, economic, or political organization 2 an organized set of doctrines or principles usu intended to explain the arrangement or working of a systematic whole 3 a manner of classifying, symbolizing, or formalizing 4 orderly methods

systematic /ˌsɪstᵻ'mætɪk/ *adj* 1 relating to, consisting of, or presented as a system 2 methodical in procedure or plan; thorough 3 of or concerned with classification; *specif* taxonomic – ~ally *adv* – -tize *v*

T

table /'teɪbəl/ *n* 1 a piece of furniture consisting of a smooth flat slab (e g of wood) fixed on legs 2 a systematic arrangement of data usu in rows and columns 3 sthg having a flat level surface

tablespoon /'teɪbəlspuːn/ *n* a large spoon used for serving – ~ful *n*

tablet /'tæblᵻt/ *n* 1 a flat slab or plaque suitable for or bearing an inscription 2a a compressed block of a solid material b a small solid shaped mass or capsule of medicinal material

¹**taboo** /tə'buː, tæ'buː/ *also* tabu *adj* 1a too sacred or evil to be touched, named, or used b set apart as unclean or accursed 2 forbidden, esp on grounds of morality, tradition, or social usage

²**taboo** *also* tabu *n* 1 a prohibition against touching, saying, or doing sthg for fear of harm from a supernatural force 2 a prohibition imposed by social custom

³**taboo** *also* tabu *v* 1 to set apart as taboo 2 to avoid or ban as taboo

¹**tack** /tæk/ *n* 1 a small short sharp-pointed nail, usu with a broad flat head 2 the lower forward corner of a fore-and-aft sail 3a the direction of a sailing vessel with respect to the direction of the wind b a change of course from one tack to another c a course of action 4 a long loose straight stitch usu used to hold 2 or more layers of fabric together temporarily 5 saddlery

²**tack** *v* 1a to fasten or attach with tacks

b to sew with long loose stitches in order to join or hold in place temporarily before fine or machine sewing 2 to add as a supplement 3a to change the course of (a close-hauled sailing vessel) from one tack to the other by turning the bow to windward b to follow a zigzag course c to change one's policy or attitude abruptly

¹**tackle** /'tækəl/ *n* 1 a set of equipment used in a particular activity 2 an assembly of ropes and pulleys arranged to gain mechanical advantage for hoisting and pulling 3 an act of tackling

²**tackle** *v* 1a to take hold of or grapple with, esp in an attempt to stop or restrain b(1) to (attempt to) take the ball from (an opposing player) in hockey or soccer (2) to seize and pull down or stop (an opposing player with the ball) in rugby or American football 2 to set about dealing with

tact /tækt/ *n* a keen sense of how to handle people or affairs so as to avoid friction or giving offence – ~ful *adj* – ~fully *adv* – ~less *adj* – ~lessly *adv* – ~lessness *n*

tactic /'tæktɪk/ *n* 1 a method of employing forces in combat 2 a device for achieving an end

tactics /'tæktɪks/ *n pl but sing or pl in constr* 1 the science and art of disposing and manoeuvring forces in combat 2 the art or skill of employing available means to accomplish an end – -tical *adj* – -tically *adv*

tadpole /'tædpəʊl/ *n* a frog or toad larva with a rounded body, a long tail, and external gills

¹**tag** /tæg/ *n* 1 a loose hanging piece of torn cloth 2 a rigid binding on an end of a shoelace 3 a piece of hanging or attached material; *specif* a flap on a garment that carries information (e g washing instructions) 4 a trite quotation used for rhetorical effect 5 a marker of plastic, metal, etc used for identification or classification

²**tag** *v* 1a to provide with an identifying marker b to label, brand 2 to attach, append

³**tag** *n* a game in which one player chases others and tries to make one of them it by touching him/her

¹**tail** /teɪl/ *n* 1 (an extension or prolongation of) the rear end of the body of an animal 2 sthg resembling an animal's tail in shape or position 3 *pl* a tailcoat; *broadly* formal evening dress for men including a tailcoat and a white bow tie 4 the last, rear, or lower part of sthg 5 the reverse of a coin – usu *pl* with sing. meaning 6 the stabilizing assembly (e g fin, rudder, and tailplane) at the rear of an aircraft 7 sby who follows or keeps watch on sby – *infml* – ~less *adj*

²**tail** *v* 1 to remove the stalk of (e g a gooseberry) 2 to diminish gradually in strength, volume, quantity, etc – usu + off or away 3a to follow for purposes of surveillance – *infml* b to follow closely

¹**tailor** /'teɪlə'/ *n* sby whose occupation is

making or altering esp men's garments

²**tailor** v 1 to make or fashion as the work of a tailor; *specif* to cut and stitch (a garment) so that it will hang and fit well 2 to make or adapt to suit a special need or purpose

¹**take** /teɪk/ v took; taken 1 to seize or capture physically 2 to grasp, grip 3a to catch or attack through a sudden effect b to surprise; come upon suddenly c to attract, delight 4a to receive into one's body, esp through the mouth b to eat or drink habitually 5 to bring or receive into a relationship or connection 6a to acquire, borrow, or use without authority or right b to pay to have (e g by contract or subscription) 7a to assume b to perform or conduct (e g a lesson) as a duty, task, or job c to commit oneself to d to involve oneself in e to consider or adopt as a point of view f to claim as rightfully one's own 8 to obtain by competition 9 to pick out; choose 10 to adopt or avail oneself of for use: e g a to have recourse to as an instrument for doing sthg b to use as a means of transport or progression 11a to derive, draw b(1) to obtain or ascertain by testing, measuring, etc (2) to record in writing (3) to get or record by photography 12a to receive or accept either willingly or reluctantly b to have the natural or intended effect or reaction c to begin to grow; strike root 13a to accommodate b to be affected injuriously by (e g a disease) 14a to apprehend, understand b to look upon; consider c to feel, experience 15a to lead, carry, or remove with one to another place b to require or cause to go 16a to obtain by removing b to subtract 17 to undertake and make, do, or perform 18a to deal with b to consider or view in a specified relation c to apply oneself to the study of or undergo examination in – ~r n

²**take** n 1 the uninterrupted recording, filming, or televising of sthg (e g a gramophone record or film sequence); *also* the recording or scene produced 2 proceeds, takings

take in v 1a to furl b to make (a garment) smaller (e g by altering the positions of the seams or making tucks) 2 to offer accommodation or shelter to 3 to include 4 to perceive, understand 5 to deceive, trick – infml

takeoff /ˈteɪk-ɒf/ n 1 an imitation; *esp* a caricature 2 an act of leaving or a rise from a surface (e g in making a jump, dive, or flight or in the launching of a rocket) 3 a starting point

take off v 1a to deduct b to remove (e g clothing) 2 to take or spend (a period of time) as a holiday, rest, etc 3 to mimic 4 to start off or away 5 to begin a leap or spring 6 to leave the surface; begin flight

takeover /ˈteɪkˌəʊvə/ n an act of gaining control of a business company by buying a majority of the shares

take over v to assume control or possession (of) or responsibility (for)

tale /teɪl/ n 1 a series of events or facts told or presented; an account 2a a usu fictitious narrative; a story b a lie, a falsehood

talent /ˈtælənt/ n 1a any of several ancient units of weight b a unit of money equal to the value of a talent of gold or silver 2a a special often creative or artistic aptitude b general ability or intelligence 3 sexually attractive members of the opposite sex – slang – ~ed adj

¹**talk** /tɔːk/ v 1 to express or exchange ideas verbally or by other means 2 to use speech; speak 3 to use a particular, esp foreign language for conversing or communicating 4a to gossip b to reveal secret or confidential information

²**talk** n 1 a verbal exchange of thoughts or opinions; a conversation 2 meaningless speech; verbiage 3 a formal discussion or exchange of views – often pl with sing. meaning 4 an often informal address or lecture

talkative /ˈtɔːkətɪv/ adj given to talking – ~ness n

tall /tɔːl/ adj 1a of above average height b of a specified height 2 of a plant of a higher growing variety or species 3 highly exaggerated; incredible – ~ish adj – ~ness n

tame /teɪm/ adj 1 changed from a state of native wildness, esp so as to be trainable and useful to human beings 2 made docile and submissive 3 lacking spirit, zest, or interest – ~ly adv – ~ness n

tame v 1 to make tame; domesticate 2 to deprive of spirit; subdue – tamable or tameable adj – tamer n

tamper /ˈtæmpə/ v to interfere or meddle with without permission

¹**tan** /tæn/ v 1 to convert (hide) into leather, esp by treatment with an infusion of tannin-rich bark 2 to make (skin) tan-coloured, esp by exposure to the sun 3 to thrash, beat – infml

²**tan** n 1 a brown colour given to the skin by exposure to sun or wind 2 (a) light yellowish brown colour – tan adj

tangible /ˈtændʒəbəl/ adj 1a capable of being perceived, esp by the sense of touch b substantially real; material 2 capable of being appraised at an actual or approximate value – -bility n – -bly adv

¹**tangle** /ˈtæŋgəl/ v 1 to involve or so as to be trapped or hampered 2 to bring together or intertwine in disordered confusion 3 to engage in conflict or argument – usu + with; infml

²**tangle** n 1 a confused twisted mass 2 a complicated or confused state

tank /tæŋk/ n 1 a large receptacle for holding, transporting, or storing liquids or gas 2 an enclosed heavily armed and armoured combat vehicle that moves on caterpillar tracks

tanker /ˈtæŋkə/ n a ship, aircraft, or road or rail vehicle designed to carry fluid, esp liquid, in bulk (e g an aircraft used for transporting fuel and usu capable of refuelling other aircraft in flight)

tantalize, -ise /'tæntlaɪz/ v to tease or frustate by offering sthg just out of reach

¹tap /tæp/ n **1a** a plug designed to fit an opening, esp in a barrel **b** a device consisting of a spout and valve attached to a pipe, bowl, etc to control the flow of a fluid **2** a tool for forming an internal screw thread **3** the act or an instance of tapping a telephone, telegraph, etc; *also* an electronic listening device used to do this

²tap v **1** to let out or cause to flow by piercing or by drawing a plug from the containing vessel **2a** to pierce so as to let out or draw off a fluid (e g from a body cavity) **b** to draw from or upon **c** to connect an electronic listening device to (e g a telegraph or telephone wire), esp in order to acquire secret information **3** to form an internal screw thread in (e g a nut) by means of a special tool **4** to get money from as a loan or gift – *infml*

³tap v **1** to strike lightly, esp with a slight sound **2** to produce by striking in this manner – often + *out*

⁴tap n (the sound of) a light blow

¹tape /teɪp/ n **1** a narrow band of woven fabric **2** the string stretched above the finishing line of a race **3** a narrow flexible strip or band; *esp* magnetic tape **4** a tape recording

²tape v **1** to fasten, tie, or bind with tape **2** to record on tape, esp magnetic tape

¹taper /'teɪpə/ n **1a** a slender candle **b** a long waxed wick used esp for lighting candles, fires, etc **2** gradual diminution of thickness, diameter, or width

²taper v to decrease gradually in thickness, diameter, or width towards one end; *broadly* to diminish gradually

tape recorder n a device for recording on magnetic tape

tapestry /'tæpɪstri/ n **1** a heavy hand-woven textile used for hangings, curtains, and upholstery, characterized by complicated pictorial designs **2** a machine-made imitation of tapestry used chiefly for upholstery – **-tried** *adj*

¹tar /tɑː/ n **1a** a dark bituminous usu strong-smelling viscous liquid obtained by heating and distilling wood, coal, peat, etc **b** a residue present in smoke from burning tobacco that contains resins, acids, phenols, etc **2** a sailor – *infml*

²tar v to smear with tar

target /'tɑːgɪt/ n **1** a small round shield **2a** an object to fire at in practice or competition; *esp* one consisting of a series of concentric circles with a bull's-eye at the centre **b** sthg (e g an aircraft or installation) fired at or attacked **3a** an object of ridicule, criticism, etc **b** a goal, objective

tarnish /'tɑːnɪʃ/ v **1** to dull the lustre of (as if) by dirt, air, etc **2a** to mar, spoil **b** to bring discredit on – **tarnish** n

tarpaulin /tɑː'pɔːlɪn/ n (a piece of) heavy waterproof usu tarred canvas material used for protecting objects or ground exposed to the elements

¹tart /tɑːt/ adj **1** agreeably sharp or acid to the taste **2** caustic, cutting – ~**ly** adv – ~**ness** n

²tart n **1** a pastry shell or shallow pie containing a usu sweet filling (e g jam or fruit) **2** a sexually promiscuous girl or woman; *also* a prostitute – *infml*

tartan /'tɑːtn/ n (a usu twilled woollen fabric with) a plaid textile design of Scottish origin consisting of checks of varying width and colour usu patterned to designate a distinctive clan

task /tɑːsk/ n **1** an assigned piece of work; a duty **2** sthg hard or unpleasant that has to be done; a chore

¹taste /teɪst/ v **1** to test the flavour of sthg by taking a little into the mouth **2** to have perception, experience, or enjoyment – usu + *of* **3** to eat or drink, esp in small quantities **4** to have a specified flavour – often + *of*

²taste n **1a** the act of tasting **b** a small amount tasted **c** a first acquaintance or experience of sthg **2** (the quality of a dissolved substance as perceived by) the basic physical sense by which the qualities of dissolved substances in contact with taste buds on the tongue are interpreted by the brain as a sensation of sweet, bitter, sour, or salt **3** individual preference; inclination **4** (a manner or quality indicative of) critical judgment or discernment esp in aesthetic or social matters

tasteful /'teɪstfəl/ adj showing or conforming to good taste – ~**ly** adv – ~**ness** n

tasteless /'teɪstləs/ adj **1** having no taste; insipid **2** showing poor taste – ~**ly** adv – ~**ness** n

tasty /'teɪsti/ adj having an appetizing flavour – **tastily**

tattered /'tætəd/ adj (dressed in clothes which are) old and torn

¹tattoo /tə'tuː, tæ'tuː/ n **1a** an evening drum or bugle call sounded as notice to soldiers to return to quarters **b** an outdoor military display given by troops as a usu evening entertainment **2** a rapid rhythmic beating or rapping

²tattoo n (an indelible mark made by) tattooing

³tattoo v to mark (the body) by inserting pigments under the skin – ~**ist** n

taught /tɔːt/ past & past part of **teach**

taut /tɔːt/ adj **1** tightly drawn; tensely stretched **2** showing anxiety; tense – ~**ly** adv – ~**ness** n

¹tax /tæks/ v **1** to levy a tax on **2** to charge, accuse *with* **3** to make strenuous demands on – ~**ability** n – ~**able** adj

²tax n a charge, usu of money, imposed by a government on individuals, organizations, or property, esp to raise revenue

taxation /tæk'seɪʃən/ n **1** the action of taxing; *esp* the imposition of taxes **2** revenue obtained from taxes **3** the amount assessed as a tax

¹taxi /'tæksi/ n, pl **taxis** a motor car that

may be hired to carry passengers short distances, esp in towns

²**taxi** v of an aircraft to go at low speed along the surface of the ground or water

tea /tiː/ n **1a** a shrub grown esp in China, Japan, and the E Indies **b** the leaves of the tea plant prepared for the market, classed according to method of manufacture (e g green tea or oolong), and graded according to leaf size (e g pekoe) **2** an aromatic beverage prepared from tea leaves by infusion with boiling water **3a** refreshments including tea with sandwiches, cakes, etc served in the late afternoon **b** a late-afternoon or early-evening meal that is usu less substantial than the midday meal

teach /tiːtʃ/ v taught **1** to provide instruction in **2** to guide the studies of **3** to impart the knowledge of **4** to instruct by precept, example, or experience

teacher /'tiːtʃəʳ/ n sby whose occupation is teaching

¹**team** /tiːm/ n **1** two or more draught animals harnessed together **2** sing or pl in constr a group formed for work or activity: e g **a** a group on 1 side (e g in a sporting contest or debate) **b** a crew, gang

²**team** v **1** to come together (as if) in a team – often + up **2** to form a harmonizing combination

teapot /'tiːpɒt/ n a usu round pot with a lid, spout, and handle in which tea is brewed and from which it is served

¹**tear** /tɪəʳ/ n **1** a drop of clear salty fluid secreted by the lachrymal gland that lubricates the eye and eyelids and is often shed as a result of grief or other emotion **2** a transparent drop of (hardened) fluid (e g resin)

²**tear** /teəʳ/ v tore; torn **1a** to pull apart by force **b** to wound by tearing; lacerate **2** to move or act with violence, haste, or force

³**tear** /teəʳ/ n **1** damage from being torn – chiefly in wear and tear **2** a hole or flaw made by tearing

¹**tease** /tiːz/ v **1** to disentangle and straighten by combing or carding **2a** to (attempt to) disturb or annoy by persistently irritating or provoking **b** to persuade to acquiesce, esp by persistent small efforts; coax; also to obtain by repeated coaxing

²**tease** n sby or sthg that teases

teaspoon /'tiːspuːn/ n a small spoon used esp for eating soft foods and stirring beverages – ~ful n

tea towel n a cloth for drying the dishes

technical /'teknɪkəl/ adj **1a** having special and usu practical knowledge, esp of a mechanical or scientific subject **b** marked by or characteristic of specialization **2** of a particular subject; esp of a practical subject organized on scientific principles – ~ly adv

technicality /ˌteknɪ'kælɪti/ n sthg technical; esp a detail meaningful only to a specialist

technique /tek'niːk/ n **1** the manner in which an artist, performer, or athlete displays or manages the formal aspect of his/her skill **2a** a body of technical methods (e g in a craft or in scientific research) **b** a method of accomplishing a desired aim

technology /tek'nɒlədʒi/ n **1** (the theory and practice of) applied science **2** the totality of the means and knowledge used to provide objects necessary for human sustenance and comfort – **-gical** adj – **-gically** adv – **-gist** n

tedious /'tiːdɪəs/ adj tiresome because of length or dullness – ~**ly** adv – ~**ness** n

teenage /'tiːneɪdʒ/, **teenaged** adj of or being people in their teens

teens /tiːnz/ n pl the numbers 13 to 19 inclusive; specif the years 13 to 19 in a lifetime

tee shirt /'tiː ʃɜːt/ n a short-sleeved vest worn in place of a shirt

teeth /tiːθ/ pl of tooth

teetotal /ˌtiː'təʊtl/ adj practising complete abstinence from alcoholic drinks – ~**ler** n

telegram /'telɪɡræm/ n a message sent by telegraph and delivered as a written or typed note

¹**telegraph** /'telɪɡrɑːf/ n an apparatus or system for communicating at a distance, esp by making and breaking an electric circuit

²**telegraph** v **1** to send or communicate (as if) by telegraph **2** to make known by signs, esp unknowingly and in advance

telegraphese /ˌtelɪɡrɑː'fiːz/ n the terse and abbreviated language characteristic of telegrams

telegraphic /ˌtelɪ'ɡræfɪk/ adj concise, terse – ~**ally** adv

¹**telephone** /'telɪfəʊn/ n **1** a device for reproducing sounds at a distance; specif one for converting sounds into electrical impulses for transmission, usu by wire, to a particular receiver **2** the system of communications that uses telephones

telephone v to make a telephone call

telephoto /ˌtelɪ'fəʊtəʊ/ adj being a lens (system) designed to give enlarged images of distant objects

teleprinter /'telɪˌprɪntəʳ/ n a typewriter keyboard that transmits telegraphic signals, a typewriting device activated by telegraphic signals, or a machine that combines both these functions

¹**telescope** /'telɪskəʊp/ n **1** a usu tubular optical instrument for viewing distant objects by means of the refraction of light rays through a lens or the reflection of light rays by a concave mirror **2** a radio telescope

²**telescope** v **1** to slide one part within another like the cylindrical sections of a hand telescope **2** to become compressed under impact **3** to become condensed or shortened

televise /'telɪvaɪz/ v to broadcast (an event or film) by television

television /'telɪˌvɪʒən, ˌtelɪ'vɪʒən/ n **1** an electronic system of transmitting changing images together with sound by converting the images and sounds into electrical signals **2** a television receiving set **3a** the television broadcasting industry **b** a television broadcasting organization or station

telex /'teleks/ *n* a communications service involving teleprinters connected by wire through automatic exchanges; *also* a message by telex

tell /tel/ *v* **told 1a** to relate in detail; narrate **b** to give utterance to; express in words **2** to make known; divulge **3a** to report to; inform; *also* to inform *on* **b** to assure emphatically **4** to order **5a** to ascertain by observing **b** to distinguish, discriminate **6** to take effect **7** to serve as evidence or indication

¹**temper** /'tempə'/ *v* **1** to moderate (sthg harsh) *with* the addition of sthg less severe **2** to bring (esp steel) to the right degree of hardness by reheating (and quenching) after cooling **3** to strengthen the character of through hardship

²**temper** *n* **1** the state of a substance with respect to certain desired qualities (e g the degree of hardness or resilience given to steel by tempering) **2a** a characteristic cast of mind or state of feeling **b** composure, equanimity **c** (proneness to displays of) an uncontrolled and often disproportionate rage

temperament /'tempərəmənt/ *n* **1a** a person's peculiar or distinguishing mental or physical character **b** excessive sensitiveness or irritability **2** the modification of the musical intervals of the pure scale to produce a set of 12 fixed notes to the octave which enables a keyboard instrument to play in more than 1 key

temperamental /ˌtempərə'mentl/ *adj* **1** of or arising from individual character or constitution **2a** easily upset or irritated; liable to sudden changes of mood **b** unpredictable in behaviour or performance – ~**ly** *adv*

temperate /'tempərit/ *adj* **1** moderate: e g **a** not extreme or excessive **b** abstemious in the consumption of alcohol **2a** having a moderate climate **b** found in or associated with a temperate climate

temperature /'tempərətʃə'/ *n* **1a** degree of hotness or coldness as measured on an arbitrary scale (e g in degrees Celsius) **b** the degree of heat natural to the body of a living being **2** an abnormally high body heat

tempest /'tempist/ *n* **1** a violent storm **2** a tumult, uproar

tempestuous /tem'pestʃʊəs/ *adj* turbulent, stormy – ~**ly** *adv*

¹**temple** /'templ/ *n* **1** a building dedicated to worship among any of various ancient civilizations (e g the Egyptians, the Greeks, and the Romans) and present-day non-Christian religions (e g Hinduism and Buddhism) **2** a place devoted or dedicated to a specified purpose

²**temple** *n* the flattened space on either side of the forehead of some mammals (e g human beings)

tempo /'tempəʊ/ *n, pl* **tempi 1** the speed of a musical piece or passage indicated by any of a series of directions and often by an exact metronome marking **2** rate of motion or activity

¹**temporary** /'tempərəri/ *adj* lasting for a limited time

²**temporary** *n* a temp

tempt /tempt/ *v* **1** to entice, esp to evil, by promise of pleasure or gain **2** to risk provoking the disfavour of **3a** to induce to do sthg **b** to cause to be strongly inclined **c** to appeal to; entice – ~**er** *n* – ~**ingly** *adv*

temptation /temp'teiʃən/ *n* **1** tempting or being tempted, esp to evil **2** sthg tempting

ten /ten/ *n* **1** the number 10 **2** the tenth in a set or series **3** sthg having 10 parts or members or a denomination of 10 **4** the number occupying the position 2 to the left of the decimal point in the Arabic notation; *also, pl* this position – **tenth** *adj, n, pron, adv*

tenant /'tenənt/ *n* **1** an occupant of lands or property of another; *specif* sby who rents or leases a house or flat from a landlord **2** an occupant, dweller – **tenant** *v*

¹**tend** /tend/ *v* to have charge of; take care of

²**tend** *v* **1** to move, direct, or develop one's course in a specified direction **2** to show an inclination or tendency – + *to*, *towards*, or *to* and an infinitive

tendency /'tendənsi/ *n* **1** a general trend or movement **2** an inclination or predisposition to some particular end, or towards a particular kind of thought or action

¹**tender** /'tendə'/ *adj* **1** having a soft or yielding texture; easily broken, cut, or damaged **2a** physically weak **b** immature, young **3** fond, loving **4a** showing care **b** highly susceptible to impressions or emotions **5** gentle, mild **6a** sensitive to touch **b** sensitive to injury or insult – ~**ly** *adv* – ~**ness** *n*

²**tender** *n* **1a** a ship employed to attend other ships (e g to supply provisions) **b** a boat or small steamer for communication between shore and a larger ship **2** a vehicle attached to a locomotive for carrying a supply of fuel and water

³**tender** *v* **1** to make a bid **2** to present for acceptance

⁴**tender** *n* **1a** a formal esp written offer or bid for a contract **b** a public expression of willingness to buy not less than a specified number of shares at a fixed price from shareholders **2** sthg that may be offered in payment; *specif* money

tendon /'tendən/ *n* a tough cord or band of dense white fibrous connective tissue that connects a muscle with a bone or other part and transmits the force exerted by the muscle

tenement /'tenimənt/ *n* (a flat in) a large building; *esp* one meeting minimum standards and typically found in the poorer parts of a large city

tennis /'tenɪs/ n a singles or doubles game that is played with rackets and a light elastic ball on a flat court divided by a low net

tenor /'tenə/ n 1 the course of thought of sthg spoken or written 2a (sby with) the highest natural adult male singing voice b a member of a family of instruments having a range next lower than that of the alto 3 a continuance in a course or activity

¹**tense** /tens/ n (a member of) a set of inflectional forms of a verb that express distinctions of time

²**tense** adj 1 stretched tight; made taut 2a feeling or showing nervous tension b marked by strain or suspense – ~ly adv – – ~ness n

³**tense** v to make or become tense – often + up

¹**tension** /'tenʃən/ n 1a stretching or being stretched to stiffness b stress 2 either of 2 balancing forces causing or tending to cause extension 3a inner striving, unrest, or imbalance, often with physiological indication of emotion b latent hostility c a balance maintained in an artistic work between opposing forces or elements

²**tension** v to tighten to a desired or appropriate degree

tent /tent/ n 1 a collapsible shelter (e g of canvas) stretched and supported by poles 2 a canopy or enclosure placed over the head and shoulders to retain vapours or oxygen during medical treatment

tentative /'tentətɪv/ adj 1 not fully worked out or developed 2 hesitant, uncertain – ~ly adv – ~ness n

tepid /'tepɪd/ adj 1 moderately warm 2 not enthusiastic – ~ity n – ~ly adv – ~ness n

¹**term** /tɜːm/ n 1a an end, termination; also a time assigned for sthg (e g payment) b the time at which a pregnancy of normal length ends 2a a limited or definite extent of time; esp the time for which sthg lasts b any one of the periods of the year during which the courts are in session c any of the usu 3 periods of instruction into which an academic year is divided 3 an expression that forms part of a fraction or proportion or of a series or sequence 4 a word or expression with a precise meaning; esp one peculiar to a restricted field 5 pl provisions relating to an agreement; also agreement on such provisions 6 pl mutual relationship

²**term** v to apply a term to; call

¹**terminal** /'tɜːmɪnl/ adj 1a of or being an end, extremity, boundary, or terminus b growing at the end of a branch or stem 2a of or occurring in a term or each term b occurring at or causing the end of life 3 occurring at or being the end of a period or series – ~ly adv

²**terminal** n 1 a device attached to the end of a wire or cable or to an electrical apparatus for convenience in making connections 2 the end of a carrier line (e g shipping line or airline) with its associated buildings and facilities 3 a

device (e g a teleprinter) through which a user can communicate with a computer

terminate /'tɜːmɪneɪt/ v 1 to bring to an end; form the conclusion of 2 to come to an end in time; form an ending or outcome – often + in or with – -ation n

terminus /'tɜːmɪnəs/ n, pl termini, terminuses 1 a finishing point; an end 2 a post or stone marking a boundary 3 (the station, town, or city at) the end of a transport line or travel route

terrace /'terɪs/ n 1 a relatively level paved or planted area adjoining a building 2 a raised embankment with a level top 3a a row of houses or flats on raised ground or a sloping site b a row of similar houses joined into 1 building by common walls

terrestrial /tɪˈrestrɪəl/ adj 1a of the earth or its inhabitants b mundane, prosaic 2a of land as distinct from air or water b of organisms living on or in land or soil – ~ly adv

terrible /'terəbl/ adj 1a exciting intense fear; terrifying b formidable in nature c requiring great fortitude; also severe 2 extreme, great 3 of very poor quality; awful; also highly unpleasant USE (2&3) infml

terribly /'terəblɪ/ adv very – infml

terrier /'terɪə/ n (a member of) any of various breeds of usu small dogs, orig used by hunters to drive out small furred game from underground

terrific /təˈrɪfɪk/ adj 1 exciting fear or awe 2 extraordinarily great or intense 3 unusually fine USE (2&3) infml

terrify /'terɪfaɪ/ v 1 to fill with terror or apprehension 2 to drive or impel by menacing; scare, deter

territory /'terɪtərɪ/ n 1a a geographical area under the jurisdiction of a government b an administrative subdivision of a country 2a a geographical area; esp one having a specified characteristic b a field of knowledge or interest 3a an assigned area; esp one in which an agent or distributor operates b an area, often including a nesting site or den, occupied and defended by an animal or group of animals

terror /'terə/ n 1 a state of intense fear 2 sby or sthg that inspires fear 3 revolutionary violence (e g the planting of bombs) 4 an appalling person or thing; esp a brat – infml

terrorism /'terərɪzəm/ n the systematic use of terror, esp as a means of coercion – -ist adj, n – -ize v

¹**test** /test/ n 1a a critical examination, observation, or evaluation b a basis for evaluation 2a a procedure used to identify a substance b a series of questions or exercises for measuring the knowledge, intelligence, etc of an individual or group c a test match

²**test** v to put to the test; try to apply a test as a means of analysis or diagnosis – often + for – ~er n

³**test** n an external hard or firm covering (e g a shell) of an invertebrate (e g a mollusc)

testify /'testɪfaɪ/ v **1a** to make a statement based on personal knowledge or belief **b** to serve as evidence or proof **2a** to make a solemn declaration under oath **b** to make known (a personal conviction)

¹**testimonial** /ˌtestɪ'məʊnɪəl/ adj **1** of or constituting testimony **2** expressive of appreciation, gratitude, or esteem

²**testimonial** n **1** a letter of recommendation **2** an expression of appreciation or esteem (e g in the form of a gift)

testimony /'testɪməni/ n **1a** firsthand authentication of a fact **b** an outward sign; evidence **c** a sworn statement by a witness **2** a public declaration of religious experience

test-tube adj, of a baby conceived by artificial insemination, esp outside the mother's body

test tube n a thin glass tube closed at 1 end and used in chemistry, biology, etc

¹**tether** /'teðə/ n **1** a rope, chain, etc by which an animal is fastened so that it can move only within a set radius **2** the limit of one's strength or resources – chiefly in the end of one's tether

²**tether** v to fasten or restrain (as if) by a tether

text /tekst/ n **1** (a work containing) the original written or printed words and form of a literary composition **2** the main body of printed or written matter, esp on a page or in a book **3a** a passage of Scripture chosen esp for the subject of a sermon or in authoritative support of a doctrine **b** a passage from an authoritative source providing a theme (e g for a speech)

¹**textbook** /'tekstbʊk/ n a book used in the study of a subject; specif one containing a presentation of the principles of a subject and used by students

²**textbook** adj conforming to the principles or descriptions in textbooks: e g **a** ideal **b** typical

textile /'tekstaɪl/ n **1a** (a woven or knitted) cloth **2** a fibre, filament, or yarn used in making cloth

¹**texture** /'tekstʃə/ n **1** identifying quality; character **2a** the size or organization of the constituent particles of a body or substance **b** the visual or tactile surface characteristics of sthg, esp fabric **3** the distinctive or identifying part or quality

²**texture** v to give a particular texture to

¹**than** /ðən; strong ðæn/ conj **1a** – used with comparatives to indicate the second member or the member taken as the point of departure in a comparison (e g older than I am) **b** – used to indicate difference of kind, manner, or degree (e g would starve rather than beg) **2** rather than – usu only after prefer, preferable **3** other than; (e g no alternative than to sack) **4** chiefly NAm from – usu only after different, differently

²**than** prep in comparison with

thank /θæŋk/ v **1** to express gratitude to – used in thank you, usu without a

subject, to express gratitude politely; used in such phrases as thank God, thank heaven, usu without a subject, to express the speaker's or writer's pleasure or satisfaction in sthg **2** to hold responsible

thankful /'θæŋkfəl/ adj **1** conscious of benefit received; grateful **2** feeling or expressing thanks **3** well pleased; glad – ~ly adv – ~ness n

thankless /'θæŋklɪs/ adj **1** not expressing or feeling gratitude **2** not likely to obtain thanks; unappreciated; also unprofitable, futile – ~ly adv – ~ness n

thanks /θæŋks/ n pl **1** kindly or grateful thoughts; gratitude **2** an expression of gratitude – often in an utterance containing no verb and serving as a courteous and somewhat informal expression of gratitude

thank-you n a polite expression of one's gratitude

¹**that** /ðæt/ pron, pl those **1a** the thing or idea just mentioned (e g after that we went to bed) **b** a relatively distant person or thing introduced for observation or discussion (e g who's that?) **c** the thing or state of affairs then (e g look at that) – sometimes used disparagingly of a person **d** the kind or thing specified as follows (e g the purest water is that produced by distillation) **e** what is understood from the context (e g take that!) **2** one of such a group; such (e g that's life) **3** – used to indicate emphatic repetition of an idea previously presented (e g is he capable? He is that) **4** pl the people; such (e g those who think the time has come)

²**that** /ðæt/ adj, pl those **1** being the person, thing, or idea specified, mentioned, or understood (e g that cake we bought) **2** the farther away or less immediately under observation (e g this chair or that one)

³**that** /ðət; strong ðæt/ conj **1** – used to introduce a noun clause as subject, object, or complement (e g said that he was afraid; the fact that you're here) **2** – used to introduce a subordinate clause expressing (1) purpose, (2) reason, or (3) result (e g worked harder that he might win; glad that you are free of it)

⁴**that** /ðət; strong ðæt/ pron **1** – used to introduce some relative clauses (e g it was George that told me; the house that Jack built) or as object of a verb or of a following preposition **2a** at, in, on, by, with, for, or to which (e g the reason that he came; the way that he spoke) **b** according to what; to the extent of what – used after a negative (e g has never been there that I know of)

⁵**that** /ðæt/ adv **1** to the extent indicated or understood (e g a nail about that long) **2** very, extremely – usu with the negative (e g not really that expensive) **3** dial Br to such an extreme degree (e g I'm that hungry I could eat a horse)

¹**thatch** /θætʃ/ v to cover (as if) with thatch

²**thatch** n **1** plant material (e g straw)

used as a roof covering **2** the hair of one's head; *broadly* anything resembling the thatch of a house

¹thaw /θɔ:/ *v* **1a** to go from a frozen to a liquid state **b** to become free of the effect (e g stiffness, numbness, or hardness) of cold as a result of exposure to warmth – often + *out* **2** to be warm enough to melt ice and snow – used in reference to the weather **3** to become less hostile **4** to become less aloof, cold, or reserved

²thaw *n* **1** the action, fact, or process of thawing **2** a period of weather warm enough to thaw ice

¹the /ðə, ði; *strong* ði:/ *definite article* **1a** – used before nouns when the referent has been previously specified by context or circumstance (e g put the cat out; ordered bread and cheese, but didn't eat *the* cheese) **b** – indicating that a following noun is unique or universally recognized (e g the Pope; *the* south) **c** – used before certain proper names (e g the Rhine; *the* MacDonald) **d** – designating 1 of a class as the best or most worth singling out (e g you can't be *the* Elvis Presley) **e** – used before the pl form of a number that is a multiple of 10 to denote a particular decade of a century or of a person's life (e g life in *the* twenties) **2** – used before a singular noun to indicate generic use (e g a history of *the* novel) **3a** that which is (e g nothing but *the* best) **b** those who are (e g *the* elite) **c** he or she who is (e g *the* accused stands before you) **4** – used after *how, what, where, who,* and *why* to introduce various expletives (e g *who the* devil are you?)

²the *adv* **1** than before; than otherwise – with comparatives (e g so much *the* worse) **2a** to what extent (e g *the* sooner the better) **b** to that extent (e g the sooner *the* better) **3** beyond all others – with superlatives (e g likes this *the* best)

³the *prep* per (e g 50p the dozen)

theatre /ˈθɪətə'/ *NAm chiefly* **theater** *n* **1** a building for dramatic performances **2** a room with rising tiers of seats (e g for lectures) **3** a place of enactment of significant events or action **4** *the* theatrical world **5** *Br* an operating theatre

theft /θeft/ *n* the act of stealing; *specif* dishonest appropriation of property with the intention of keeping it

their /ðə'; *strong* ðeə'/ *adj* **1** of them or themselves, esp as possessors, agents, or objects of an action **2** his or her; his, her, its *USE* used attributively

theirs /ðeəz/ *pron, pl* **theirs 1** that which or the one who belongs to them – used without a following noun as a pronoun equivalent in meaning to the adjective *their* **2** his or hers; his, hers

¹them /ðəm; *strong* ðem/ *pron, objective case of* **they**

²them /ðem/ *adj* those – nonstandard

theme /θi:m/ *n* **1** a subject of artistic representation or a topic of discourse **2** a melodic subject of a musical composition or movement

themselves /ðəmˈselvz/ *pron pl in constr* **1a** those identical people, creatures, or things that are they – used reflexively or for emphasis **b** himself or herself; himself, herself (e g hoped nobody would hurt *themselves*) **2** their normal selves (e g soon be *themselves* again)

¹then /ðen/ *adv* **1** at that time **2a** soon after that; next in order (of time) **b** besides; in addition **3a** in that case **b** as may be inferred (e g your mind is made up *then?*) **c** accordingly, so – indicating casual connection in speech or writing (e g our hero, *then* was greatly relieved) **d** as a necessary consequence **e** – used after *but* to offset a preceding statement (e g he lost the race, but *then* he never expected to win)

²then *n* that time

³then *adj* existing or acting at that time (e g the *then* secretary of state)

thence /ðens/ *adv* **1** from there **2** from that preceding fact or premise – chiefly *fml*

theology /θiˈɒlədʒi/ *n* **1** the study of God, esp by analysis of the origins and teachings of an organized religion **2** a theological theory, system, or body of opinion **– -ogical** *adj* **– -ogically** *adv* **– -ogian** *n*

theoretical /θɪəˈretɪkəl/ *adj* **1a** relating to or having the character of theory; abstract **b** confined to theory or speculation; speculative **2** existing only in theory; hypothetical **– ~ly** *adv*

theory /ˈθɪəri/ *n* **1a** a belief, policy, or procedure forming the basis for action **b** an ideal or supposed set of facts, principles, or circumstances – often in *in theory* **2** the general or abstract principles of a subject **3** a scientifically acceptable body of principles offered to explain a phenomenon **4a** a hypothesis assumed for the sake of argument or investigation **b** an unproved assumption; a conjecture **– -rize** *v*

therapy /ˈθerəpi/ *n* therapeutic treatment of bodily, mental, or social disorders

¹there /ðeə'/ *adv* **1** in or at that place – often used to draw attention or to replace a name **2** thither **3a** now (e g *there* goes the hooter) **b** at or in that point or particular (e g *there* is where I disagree with you) **4** – used interjectionally to express satisfaction, approval, encouragement, or defiance

²there /ðeə', ðə'/ *pron* – used to introduce a sentence or clause expressing the idea of existence (e g *there* shall come a time)

³there *n* that place or point

⁴there *adj* – used for emphasis, esp after a demonstrative (e g those men *there* can tell you)

thereabouts /ˌðeərəˈbaʊts/, *NAm also* **thereabout** *adv* **1** in that vicinity **2** near that time, number, degree, or quantity

thereby /ðeə'baɪ, 'ðeəbaɪ/ *adv* **1** by that means; resulting from which **2** in which connection (e g *thereby* hangs a tale)

therefore /ˈðeəfɔ:'/ *adv* **1** for that

reason; to that end **2** by virtue of that; consequently (e g I was tired and *therefore* irritable) **3** as this proves (e g I think *therefore* I exist)

thermometer /θə'mɒmɪtə⁻/ *n* an instrument for measuring temperature; *esp* a glass bulb attached to a fine graduated tube of glass and containing a liquid (e g mercury) that rises and falls with changes of temperature

Thermos /'θɜːməs/ *trademark* – used for an insulated flask used for keeping liquids, etc hot or cold

thermostat /'θɜːməstæt/ *n* an automatic device for regulating temperature

these /ðiːz/ *pl of* this

they /ðeɪ/ *pron pl in constr* **1a** those people, creatures, or things; *also, chiefly Br* that group **b** he (e g if anyone has found it, *they* will hand it in) **2a** people (e g *they* say that there's no truth in it) **b** the authorities

¹**thick** /θɪk/ *adj* **1a** having or being of relatively great depth or extent between opposite surfaces **b** of comparatively large diameter in relation to length **2a** closely-packed; dense **b** great in number **c** viscous in consistency **d** foggy or misty **3a** imperfectly articulated **b** plainly apparent; marked **4a** sluggish, dull **b** obtuse, stupid **5** on close terms; intimate **6** unreasonable, unfair *USE* (4, 5, & 6) *infml* – ~ly *adv*

²**thick** *n* **1** the most crowded or active part **2** the part of greatest thickness

thickness /'θɪknɪs/ *n* **1** the smallest of the 3 dimensions of a solid object **2** the thick part of sthg **3** a layer, ply

thief /θiːf/ *n, pl* **thieves** sby who steals, esp secretly and without violence

thieve /θiːv/ *v* to steal, rob – **-ving** *n, adj* – **-vish** *adj* – **-vishly** *adv* – **-vishness** *n*

thigh /θaɪ/ *n* the segment of the vertebrate hind limb nearest the body that extends from the hip to the knee and is supported by a single large bone

thimble /'θɪmbəl/ *n* **1** a pitted metal or plastic cap or cover worn to protect the finger and to push the needle in sewing **2** a movable ring, tube, or lining in a hole

¹**thin** /θɪn/ *adj* **1a** having little depth between opposite surfaces **b** measuring little in cross section **2** not dense or closely-packed **3** without much flesh; lean **4a** more rarefied than normal **b** few in number **5** lacking substance or strength **6** flimsy, unconvincing **7** somewhat feeble and lacking in resonance **8** lacking in intensity or brilliance **9** disappointingly poor or hard – ~ly *adv* – ~ness *n*

²**thin** *v* **1** to reduce in thickness or depth; attenuate **2** to reduce in strength or density **3** to reduce in number or bulk

thing /θɪŋ/ *n* **1a** a matter, affair, concern **b** an event, circumstance **2a(1)** a deed, act, achievement **(2)** an activity, action **b** a product of work or activity **c** the aim of effort or activity **d** sthg necessary or desirable **3a** a separate and

distinct object of thought (e g a quality, fact, idea, etc) **b** an inanimate object as distinguished from a living being **c** *pl* imaginary objects or entities **4a** *pl* possessions, effects **b** an article of clothing **c** *pl* equipment or utensils, esp for a particular purpose **5** an object or entity not (capable of being) precisely designated **6** *the* proper or fashionable way of behaving, talking, or dressing **7a** a preoccupation (e g a mild obsession or phobia) of a specified type **b** an intimate relationship; *esp* a love affair

¹**think** /θɪŋk/ *v* **thought** **1a** to exercise the powers of judgment, conception, or inference **b** to have in mind or call to mind a thought or idea – *usu* + *of* **2** to have as an opinion; consider **3a** to reflect on – often + *over* **b** to determine by reflecting – often + *out* **c** to have the mind engaged in reflection – usu + *of* or *about* **4** to call to mind; remember **5** to devise by thinking – usu + *up* **6** to have as an expectation **7** to subject to the processes of logical thought – usu + *out* or *through* – ~er *n*

²**think** *n* an act of thinking – *infml*

¹**thinking** /'θɪŋkɪŋ/ *n* **1** the action of using one's mind to produce thoughts **2** opinion that is characteristic (e g of a period, group, or individual)

²**thinking** *adj* marked by use of the intellect

¹**third** /θɜːd/ *adj* **1a** next after the second in place or time **b** ranking next to second in authority or precedence **2a** being any of 3 equal parts into which sthg is divisible **b** being the last in each group of 3 in a series

²**third** *n* **1a** 3rd **b** sthg or sby that is next after second in rank, position, authority, or precedence **c** third, third class *often cap* the third and usu lowest level of British honours degree **2** any of 3 equal parts of sthg **3** (the combination of 2 notes at) a musical interval of 3 diatonic degrees

¹**thirst** /θɜːst/ *n* **1** (the sensation of dryness in the mouth and throat associated with) a desire or need to drink **2** an ardent desire; a craving

²**thirst** *v* **1** to feel thirsty **2** to crave eagerly

thirsty /'θɜːsti/ *adj* **1a** feeling thirst **b** deficient in moisture; parched **2** having a strong desire; avid – **thirstily** *adv*

thirteen /ˌθɜː'tiːn/ *n* the number 13 – ~th *adj, n*

thirty /'θɜːti/ *n* **1** the number 30 **2** *pl* the numbers 30 to 39; *specif* a range of temperatures, ages, or dates in a century characterized by these numbers – **-tieth** *adj, n*

¹**this** /ðɪs/ *pron, pl* **these** **1a** the thing or idea that has just been mentioned **b** what is to be shown or stated (e g do it like *this*) **c** this time or place **2a** a nearby person or thing introduced for observation or discussion **b** the thing or state of affairs here (e g what's all *this*?; please carry *this*)

²**this** *adj, pl* **these** **1a** being the person, thing, or idea that is present or near in time or thought (e g early *this* morning;

who's *this* Mrs Fogg anyway?) **b** the nearer at hand or more immediately under observation (e g *this* chair or that one) **c** constituting the immediate past or future period (e g have lived here *these* 10 years) **d** constituting what is to be shown or stated (e g have you heard *this* one?) **2** a certain (e g there was *this* Irishman ...)

³**this** *adv* **1** to this extent (e g known her since she was *this* high) **2** to this extreme degree – usu + the negative (e g didn't expect to wait *this* long)

thistle /ˈθɪsəl/ *n* any of various prickly composite plants with (showy) heads of mostly tubular flowers

thorn /θɔːn/ *n* **1** a woody plant (of the rose family) bearing sharp prickles of thorns **2** a short hard sharp-pointed plant part, specif a leafless branch **3** sby or sthg that causes irritation

thorny /ˈθɔːni/ *adj* **1** full of or covered in thorns **2** full of difficulties or controversial points – **thorniness** *n prep or adv*,

thorough /ˈθʌrə/ *adj* **1** marked by full detail **2** painstaking **3** being fully and without qualification as specified – ~**ly** *adv*

thoroughfare /ˈθʌrəfeə/ *n* **1** a public way (e g a road, street, or path); *esp* a main road **2** passage, transit

those /ðəʊz/ *pl of* **that**

¹**though** /ðəʊt/ *also* **tho** *adv* however, nevertheless

²**though** /ðəʊ/ *also* **tho** *conj* **1** in spite of the fact that; while **2** in spite of the possibility that; even if **3** and yet; but

¹**thought** /θɔːt/ *past of* **think**

²**thought** *n* **1a** thinking **b** serious consideration **2** reasoning or conceptual power **3a** an idea, opinion, concept, or intention **b** the intellectual product or the organized views of a period, place, group, or individual

thoughtful /ˈθɔːtfəl/ *adj* **1a** having thoughts; absorbed in thought **b** showing careful reasoned thinking **2** showing careful concern for others – ~**ly** *adv* – ~**ness** *n*

thoughtless /ˈθɔːtlɪs/ *adj* **1** lacking forethought; rash **2** lacking concern for others – ~**ly** *adv* – ~**ness** *n*

thousand /ˈθaʊzənd/ *n*, *pl* **thousands**, **thousand 1** the number 1,000 **2** the number occupying the position 4 to the left of the decimal point in the Arabic notation; *also*, *pl* this position **3** an indefinitely large number – often pl with sing. meaning – ~**th** *adj*, *n*, *pron*, *adv*

¹**thrash** /θræʃ/ *v* **1** to thresh **2a** to beat soundly (as if) with a stick or whip **b** to defeat heavily or decisively **3** to move or stir about violently; toss about – usu + *around* or *about*

²**thrash** *n* **1** an act of thrashing, esp in swimming **2** a wild party – *infml*

thrash out *v* to discuss (e g a problem) exhaustively with a view to finding a solution; *also* to arrive at (e g a decision) in this way

¹**thread** /θred/ *n* **1** a filament, group of filaments twisted together, or continu- ous strand (formed by spinning and twisting together short textile fibres) **2a** sthg (e g a thin stream of liquid) like a thread in length and narrowness **b** a projecting spiral ridge (e g on a bolt or pipe) by which parts can be screwed together **3** sthg continuous or drawn out: e g **a** a train of thought **b** a pervasive recurring element **4** a precarious or weak support

²**thread** *v* **1a** to pass a thread through the eye of (a needle) **b** to arrange a thread, yarn, or lead-in piece in working position for use in (a machine) **2a(1)** to pass sthg through the entire length of (2) to pass (e g a tape or film) into or through sthg **b** to make one's way cautiously through or between **3** to string together (as if) on a thread

threadbare /ˈθredbeə/ *adj* **1** having the nap worn off so that the threads show; worn, shabby **2** hackneyed

threat /θret/ *n* **1** an indication of sthg, usu unpleasant, to come **2** an expression of intention to inflict punishment, injury, or damage **3** sthg that is a source of imminent danger or harm

threaten /ˈθretn/ *v* **1** to utter threats against **2a** to give ominous signs of **b** to be a source of harm or danger to **3** to announce as intended or possible – ~**ingly** *adv*

three /θriː/ *n* **1** the number 3 **2** the third in a set or series **3** sthg having 3 parts or members or a denomination of 3

three-dimensional *adj* **1** having 3 dimensions **2** giving the illusion of depth – used of an image or pictorial representation, esp when this illusion is enhanced by stereoscopic means

threshold /ˈθreʃhəʊld, -ʃəʊld/ *n* **1a** the doorway or entrance to a building **b** the point of entering or beginning **2** a level, point, or value above which sthg is true or will take place

threw /θruː/ *past of* **throw**

thrice /θraɪs/ *adv* **1** three times **2** in a threefold manner or degree

thrift /θrɪft/ *n* **1** careful management, esp of money; frugality **2** any of a genus of tufted herbaceous plants; *esp* a sea-pink – ~**y** *adj* – **ily** *adv*

thrill /θrɪl/ *v* **1** to (cause to) experience a sudden tremor of excitement or emotion **2** to tingle, throb

thrive /θraɪv/ *v* **throve, thrived; thriven 1** to grow vigorously **2** to gain in wealth or possessions

throat /θrəʊt/ *n* **1a** the part of the neck in front of the spinal column **b** the passage through the neck to the stomach and lungs **2** sthg throatlike, esp in being a constricted passageway

¹**throb** /θrɒb/ *v* **1** to pulsate with unusual force or rapidity **2** to (come in waves that seem to) beat or vibrate rhythmically

²**throb** *n* a beat, pulse

throne /θrəʊn/ *n* **1** the chair of state of a sovereign or bishop **2** sovereignty

¹**throng** /θrɒŋ/ *n sing or pl in constr* **1** a multitude of assembled people, esp

when crowded together **2** a large number

²**throng** *v* **1** to crowd upon (esp a person) **2** to crowd into

¹**throttle** /ˈθrɒtl/ *v* **1a** to compress the throat of; *also* to kill in this way **b** to suppress **2** to regulate, esp reduce the speed of (e g an engine), by means of a throttle – usu + *back* or *down*

²**throttle** *n* **1** the windpipe **2** (the lever or pedal controlling) a valve for regulating the supply of a fluid (e g fuel) to an engine

¹**through** /θru:/ *also* **thro**, *NAm also* **thru** *prep* **1a(1)** into at one side or point and out at the other **(2)** past (e g saw *through* the deception) **b** – used to indicate passage into and out of a treatment, handling, or process (e g flashed *through* my mind) **2** – used to indicate means, agency, or intermediacy: e g **a** by means of; by the agency of **b** because of (e g failed *through* ignorance) **c** by common descent from or relationship with (e g related *through* their grandfather) **3a** over the whole surface or extent of (e g homes scattered *through* the valley) **b** – used to indicate movement within a large expanse (e g flew *through* the air) **c** among or between the parts or single members of (e g search *through* my papers) **4** during the entire period of (e g all *through* her life) **5a** – used to indicate completion, exhaustion, or accomplishment (e g got *through* the book) **b** – used to indicate acceptance or approval, esp by an official body (e g got the bill *through* Parliament) **6** *chiefly NAm* up till and including (e g Saturday *through* Sunday)

²**through**, *NAm also* **thru** *adv* **1** from one end or side to the other **2a** all the way from beginning to end **b** to a favourable or successful conclusion (e g see it *through*) **3** to the core; completely (e g met *through*) **4** into the open; out (e g break *through*) **5** *chiefly Br* in or into connection by telephone (e g put me *through* to him)

³**through**, *NAm also* **thru** *adj* **1a** extending from one surface to the other (e g a *through* beam) **b** direct (e g a *through* road) **2a** allowing a continuous journey from point of origin to destination without change or further payment (e g a *through* train) **b** starting at and destined for points outside a local zone (e g *through* traffic) **3** arrived at completion, cessation, or dismissal; finished (e g I'm *through* with man)

¹**throughout** /θru:ˈaʊt/ *adv* **1** in or to every part; everywhere (e g of 1 colour *throughout*) **2** during the whole time or action; from beginning to end

²**throughout** *prep* **1** in or to every part of **2** during the entire period of

¹**throw** /θrəʊ/ *v* **threw**; **thrown** **1** to propel through the air in some manner, esp by a forward motion of the hand and arm **2** to cause to fall **3a** to fling (oneself) abruptly **b** to hurl violently **4** to put *on* or *off* hastily or carelessly **5** to shape by hand on a potter's wheel **6**

to deliver (a punch) **7** to send forth; cast, direct **8** to commit (oneself) for help, support, or protection **9** to bring forth; produce **10** to move (a lever or switch) so as to connect or disconnect parts of a mechanism **11** to project (the voice) **12** to give by way of entertainment **13** to disconcert – *infml* – ~**er** *n*

²**throw** *n* **1a** an act of throwing **b** a method or instance of throwing an opponent in wrestling or judo **2** (the distance of) the extent of movement of a cam, crank, or other pivoted or reciprocating piece

¹**thrust** /θrʌst/ *v* **thrust** **1** to force an entrance or passage – often + *into* or *through* **2** to stab, pierce **3** to put (an unwilling person) into a course of action or position **4** to press, force, or impose the acceptance of *on* or *upon* sby

²**thrust** *n* **1a** a push or lunge with a pointed weapon **b(1)** a verbal attack **(2)** a concerted military attack **2a** a strong continued pressure **b** the force exerted by a propeller, jet engine, etc to give forward motion **3a** a forward or upward push **b** a movement (e g by a group of people) in a specified direction

¹**thud** /θʌd/ *v* to move or strike with a thud

²**thud** *n* **1** a blow **2** a dull thump

thug /θʌg/ *n* **1** *often cap* a member of a former religious sect in India given to robbery and murder **2** a violent criminal – ~**gery** *n*

¹**thumb** /θʌm/ *n* the short thick digit of the hand that is next to the forefinger; *also* the part of a glove, etc that covers this

²**thumb** *v* **1** to leaf through pages **2** to request or obtain a lift in a passing vehicle; hitchhike

¹**thump** /θʌmp/ *v* **1** to strike or knock with a thump **2** to thrash **3** to produce (music) mechanically or in a mechanical manner

²**thump** *n* (a sound of) a blow or knock (as if) with sthg blunt or heavy

³**thump** *adv* with a thump

¹**thunder** /ˈθʌndə/ *n* **1** the low loud sound that follows a flash of lightning and is caused by sudden expansion of the air in the path of the electrical discharge **2** a loud reverberating noise

²**thunder** *v* **1a** to give forth thunder – usu impersonally **b** to make a sound like thunder **2** to roar, shout – ~**er** *n*

thunderbolt /ˈθʌndəbəʊlt/ *n* **1** a single discharge of lightning with the accompanying thunder **2** sthg like lightning in suddenness, effectiveness, or destructive power

thundering /ˈθʌndərɪŋ/ *adv*, *Br* very; thumping – *infml*

thunderstruck /ˈθʌndəstrʌk/ *adj* dumbfounded; astonished

Thursday /ˈθɜːzdi, -deɪ/ *n* the day of the week following Wednesday

thus /ðʌs/ *adv* **1** in the manner indicated; in this way **2** to this degree or extent; so **3** because of this preceding fact or premise; consequently **4** as an example

¹**tick** /tɪk/ *n* **1** any of numerous related bloodsucking arachnids that feed on warm-blooded animals and often transmit infectious diseases **2** any of various usu wingless parasitic insects (e g the sheep ked)

²**tick** *n* **1** a light rhythmic audible tap or beat; *also* a series of such sounds **2** a small spot or mark, typically ✓ ; *esp* one used to mark sthg as correct, to draw attention to sthg, to check an item on a list, or to represent a point on a scale **3** *Br* a moment, second – *infml*

³**tick** /tɪk/ *v* **1** to make the sound of a tick **2** to function or behave characteristically **3** to mark or count (as if) by ticks – usu + *off*

⁴**tick** *n* credit, trust – *infml*

ticket /'tɪkɪt/ *n* **1a** a mariner's or pilot's certificate **b** a tag, label **2** an official notification issued to sby who has violated a traffic regulation **3** a usu printed card or piece of paper entitling its holder to the use of certain services (e g a library), showing that a fare or admission has been paid, etc **4** *Br* a certificate of discharge from the armed forces **5** *chiefly NAm* a list of candidates for nomination or election **6** the correct, proper, or desirable thing – *infml*

tickle /'tɪkəl/ *v* **1** to provoke to laughter **2** to touch (e g a body part) lightly and repeatedly so as to excite the surface nerves and cause uneasiness, laughter, or spasmodic movements – **tickle** *n*

tide /taɪd/ *n* **1a** (a current of water resulting from) the periodic rise and fall of the surface of a body of water, specif the sea, that occurs twice a day and is caused by the gravitational attraction of the sun and moon **b** the level or position of water on a shore with respect to the tide; *also* the water at its highest level **2** a flowing stream; a current

¹**tidy** /'taɪdɪ/ *adj* **1a** neat and orderly in appearance or habits; well ordered and cared for **b** methodical, precise **2** large, substantial – *infml* – **-dily** *adv* – **-diness** *n*

²**tidy** *v* to put (things) in order; make (things) neat or tidy

³**tidy** *n* a receptacle for odds and ends (e g kitchen scraps)

¹**tie** /taɪ/ *n* **1a** a line, ribbon, or cord used for fastening or drawing sthg together **b** a structural element (e g a rod or angle iron) holding 2 pieces together **2a** a moral or legal obligation to sby or sthg that restricts freedom of action **b** a bond of kinship or affection **3** a curved line that joins 2 musical notes of the same pitch to denote a single sustained note with the time value of the 2 **4a** a match or game between 2 teams, players, etc **b** (a contest that ends in) a draw or dead heat **5** a narrow length of material designed to be worn round the neck and tied in a knot in the front

²**tie** *v* **1a** to fasten, attach, or close by

knotting **b** to form a knot or bow in **2a** to unite in marriage **b** to unite (musical notes) by a tie **3** to restrain from independence or from freedom of action or choice; constrain (as if) by authority or obligation – often + *down* **4a** to even the score in a game or contest

tiger /'taɪgə'/ *n* **1** a very large Asiatic cat having a tawny coat transversely striped with black **2** a fierce and often bloodthirsty person

¹**tight** /taɪt/ *adj* **1** so close or solid in structure as to prevent passage (e g of a liquid or gas) – often in combination **2a** fixed very firmly in place **b** firmly stretched, drawn, or set **c** fitting (too) closely **3** set close together **4** difficult to get through or out of **5** evenly contested **6** packed, compressed or condensed to (near) the limit **7** stingy, miserly **8** intoxicated, drunk *USE* (7&8) *infml* – ~ **en** *v* – ~ **ly** *adv* – ~ **ness** *n*

²**tight** *adv* **1** fast, tightly **2** in a sound manner

tighten /'taɪtn/ *v* to make or become tight or tighter or more firm or severe – often + *up*

tights /taɪts/ *n pl* a skintight garment covering each leg (and foot) and reaching to the waist

¹**tile** /taɪl/ *n* **1** a thin slab of fired clay, stone, or concrete shaped according to use : e g **·a** a flat or curved slab for use on roofs **b** a flat and often ornamented slab for floors, walls, or surrounds **2a** a thin piece of resilient material (e g cork or linoleum) used esp for covering floors or walls

²**tile** *v* to cover with tiles – **tiler** *n*

¹**till** /tɪl/ *prep* until

²**till** *conj* until

³**till** /tɪl, tl/ *v* to work (e g land) by ploughing, sowing, and raising crops

⁴**till** *n* **1a** a receptacle (e g a drawer or tray) in which money is kept in a shop or bank **b** a cash register **2** the money contained in a till

¹**tilt** /tɪlt/ *v* **1** to cause to slope **2** to point or thrust (as if) in a joust

²**tilt** *n* **1** a military exercise in which a mounted person charges at an opponent or mark **2** speed – in *at full tilt* **3** a written or verbal attack – + *at* **4** a sloping surface

¹**timber** /'tɪmbə'/ *n* **1** growing trees or their wood **2** wood suitable for carpentry or woodwork **3** material, stuff; *esp* personal character or quality

²**timber** *v* to frame, cover, or support with timbers

¹**time** /taɪm/ *n* **1a** the measurable period during which an action, process, or condition exists or continues **b** a continuum in which events succeed one another **2a** the point or period when sthg occurs **b** the period required for an action **3a** a period set aside or suitable for an activity or event **b** an appointed, fixed, or customary moment for sthg to happen, begin, or end; *esp*, *Br* closing time in a public house as fixed by law **4a** a historical period – often *pl* with *sing*. meaning **b** conditions or circum-

stances prevalent during a period – usu pl with sing. meaning **5** a term of imprisonment – infml **6** a season **7a** a tempo **b** the grouping of the beats of music; a rhythm, metre **8** a moment, hour, day, or year as measured or indicated by a clock or calendar **9a** any of a series of recurring instances or repeated actions **b** pl (1) multiplied instances (2) equal fractional parts of which a specified number equal a comparatively greater quantity (e g 7 times smaller) **10** the end of the playing time of a (section of a) game – often used as an interjection

²**time** v **1** to arrange or set the time of **2** to regulate the moment, speed, or duration of, esp to achieve the desired effect **3** to determine or record the time, duration, or speed of

³**time** adj (able to be) set to function at a specific moment

timely /'taımli/ adv or adj at an appropriate time – **-liness** n

times /taımz/ prep multiplied by

¹**timetable** /'taım,teıbəl/ n **1** a table of departure and arrival times of public transport **2** a schedule showing a planned order or sequence of events, esp of classes (e g in a school)

²**timetable** v to arrange or provide for in a timetable

timid /'tımɪd/ adj lacking in courage, boldness, or self-confidence – ~**ity** n – ~**ly** adv – ~**ness** n

¹**tin** /tın/ n **1** a soft lustrous metallic element that is malleable and ductile at ordinary temperatures and is used as a protective coating, in tinfoil, and in soft solders and alloys **2** a box, can, pan, vessel, or sheet made of tinplate: e g **a** a hermetically sealed tinplate container for preserving foods **b** any of various usu tinplate or aluminium containers of different shapes and sizes in which food is cooked, esp in an oven

²**tin** v, chiefly Br to can

¹**tinge** /tındʒ/ v **1** to colour with a slight shade **2** to impart a slight smell, taste, or other quality to

²**tinge** n **1** a slight staining or suffusing colour **2** a slight modifying quality; a trace

tingle /'tıŋgəl/ v or n (to feel or cause) a stinging, prickling, or thrilling sensation

¹**tinkle** /'tıŋkəl/ v to make (a sound suggestive of) a tinkle

²**tinkle** n **1** a series of short light ringing or clinking sounds **2** a jingling effect in verse or prose **3** Br a telephone call – infml

¹**tinsel** /'tınsəl/ n **1** a thread, strip, or sheet of metal, plastic, or paper used to produce a glittering and sparkling effect (e g in fabrics or decorations) **2** sthg superficial, showy, or glamorous

²**tinsel** adj cheaply gaudy; tawdry

¹**tint** /tınt/ n **1** a usu slight or pale coloration; a hue **2** any of various lighter or darker shades of a colour; esp one produced by adding white

²**tint** v to apply a tint to – ~**er** n

tiny /'taıni/ adj very small or diminutive

¹**tip** /tıp/ n **1** the usu pointed end of sthg **2** a small piece or part serving as an end, cap, or point – **tip** v

²**tip** v **1** to overturn, upset – usu + over **2** to cant, tilt **3** to deposit or transfer by tilting

³**tip** n a place for tipping sthg (e g rubbish or coal); a dump – ~**per** n

⁴**tip** v to strike lightly

⁵**tip** v or n **-pp-** (to give or present with) a sum of money in appreciation of a service performed

⁶**tip** n **1** a piece of useful or expert information **2** a piece of inside information which, acted upon, may bring financial gain (e g by betting or investment) – **tip** v

¹**tiptoe** /'tıptəʊ/ n the tip of a toe; also the ends of the toes

²**tiptoe** adv (as if) on tiptoe

³**tiptoe** adj **1** standing or walking (as if) on tiptoe **2** cautious, stealthy

⁴**tiptoe** v **1** to stand, walk, or raise oneself on tiptoe **2** to walk silently or stealthily as if on tiptoe

¹**tire** /taıə/ v **1** to fatigue **2** to wear out the patience of

²**tire** n, chiefly NAm a tyre

tired /taıəd/ adj **1** weary, fatigued **2** exasperated; fed up **3a** trite, hackneyed **b** lacking freshness – ~**ly** adv – ~**ness** n

tiresome /'taıəsəm/ adj wearisome, tedious – ~**ly** adv

tissue /'tıʃuː, -sjuː/ n **1a** a fine gauzy often sheer fabric **b** a mesh, web **2** a paper handkerchief **3** a cluster of cells, usu of a particular kind, together with their intercellular substance that form any of the structural materials of a plant or animal

titbit /'tıt,bıt/, chiefly NAm **tidbit** n a choice or pleasing piece (e g of food or news)

¹**title** /'taıtl/ n **1** (a document giving proof of) legal ownership **2** an alleged or recognized right **3a** a descriptive or general heading (e g of a chapter in a book) **b** a title page and the printed matter on it **c** written material introduced into a film or television programme to represent credits, dialogue, or fragments of narrative – usu pl with sing. meaning **4** the distinguishing name of a work of art (e g a book, picture or musical composition) **5** a descriptive name **6** designation as champion **7** a hereditary or acquired appellation given to a person or family as a mark of rank, office, or attainment

²**title** v **1** to provide a title for **2** to designate or call by a title

¹**to** /tə, tu/; strong tuː/ prep **1** – used to indicate a terminal point or destination: e g **a** a place where a physical movement or an action or condition suggestive of movement ends (e g drive to the city) **b** a direction (e g turned his back to the door) **c** a terminal point in measuring or reckoning or in a statement of extent or limits (e g 10 miles to

the nearest town; not *to* my knowledge) **d** a point in time before which a period is reckoned (e g how long *to* dinner?) **e** a point of contact or proximity (e g pinned it *to* my coat) **f** a purpose, intention, tendency, result, or end (e g a temple *to* Mars; held them *to* ransom; broken *to* pieces) **g** the one to or for which sthg exists or is done or directed (e g kind *to* animals) **2** – used to indicate addition, attachment, connection, belonging, or possession (e g add 17 *to* 20; the key *to* the door) **3** – used to indicate relationship or conformity: e g **a** relative position (e g next door *to* me) **b** proportion or composition (e g 400 *to* the box; won by 17 points *to* 11) **c** correspondence to a standard (e g second *to* none) **4a** – used to indicate that the following verb is an infinitive (e g wants *to* go); often used by itself at the end of a clause in place of an infinitive suggested by the preceding context (e g knows more than he seems *to*) **b** for the purpose of (e g did it *to* annoy)

²**to** *adv* **1a** – used to indicate direction towards; chiefly in *to and fro* **b** close to the wind (e g the ship hove *to*) **2** *of a door or window* into contact, esp with the frame **3** – used to indicate application or attention **4** back into consciousness or awareness **5** at hand (e g saw her close *to*)

toad /təʊd/ *n* **1** any of numerous tailless leaping amphibians that differ from the related frogs by living more on land and in having a shorter squatter body with a rough, dry, and warty skin **2** a loathsome and contemptible person or thing

¹**toast** /təʊst/ *v* **1** to make (e g bread) crisp, hot, and brown by heat **2** to warm thoroughly (e g at a fire)

²**toast** *n* **1** sliced bread browned on both sides by heat **2** sthg in honour of which people drink **3** an act of drinking in honour of sby or sthg

³**toast** *v* to drink to as a toast

tobacco /tə'bækəʊ/ *n* **1** a tall erect annual S American herb cultivated for its leaves **2** the leaves of cultivated tobacco prepared for use in smoking or chewing or as snuff; *also* cigars, cigarettes, or other manufactured products of tobacco

tobacconist /tə'bækənɪst/ *n* a seller of tobacco, esp in a shop

today /tə'deɪ/ *adv or n* **1** (on) this day **2** (at) the present time or age

toddle /'tɒdl/ *v* **1** to walk haltingly in the manner of a young child **2a** to take a stroll; saunter **b** *Br* to depart *USE* (2) *infml*

toddler /'tɒdlə/ *n* a young child

toe /təʊ/ *n* **1a** any of the digits at the end of a vertebrate's foot **b** the fore end of a foot or hoof **2** the front of sthg worn on the foot – **toe** *v*

toffee,toffy /'tɒfɪ/ *n* a sweet with a texture from chewy to brittle, made by boiling sugar, water, and often butter

together /tə'geðə/ *adv* **1a** in or into 1 place, mass, collection, or group **b** in joint agreement or cooperation; as a group **2a** in or into contact (e g connection, collision, or union) (e g mix the ingredients *together*) **b** in or into association, relationship, or harmony (e g colours that go well *together*) **3a** at one time; simultaneously **b** in succession; without intermission (e g was depressed for days *together*) **4** *of a single unit* in or into an integrated whole (e g pull yourself *together*) **5a** to or with each other **b** considered as a unit; collectively (e g these arguments taken *together* make a convincing case)

¹**toil** /tɔɪl/ *n* long strenuous fatiguing labour

²**toil** *v* **1** to work hard and long **2** to proceed with laborious effort

³**toil** *n* sthg by or with which one is held fast or inextricably involved – usu pl with sing. meaning

toilet /'tɔɪlɪt/ *n* **1** the act or process of dressing and grooming oneself **2a** a fixture or arrangement for receiving and disposing of faeces and urine **b** a room or compartment containing a toilet and sometimes a washbasin **3** formal or fashionable (style of) dress – *fml*

¹**token** /'təʊkən/ *n* **1** an outward sign or expression (e g of an emotion) **2** a characteristic mark or feature **3a** a souvenir, keepsake **b** sthg given or shown as a guarantee (e g of authority, right, or identity) **4** a coinlike object used in place of money (e g to pay a milkman) **5** a certified statement redeemable for a usu specified form of merchandise to the amount stated thereon

²**token** *adj* **1** done or given as a token, esp in partial fulfilment of an obligation or engagement **2** done or given merely for show

tolerable /'tɒlərəbəl/ *adj* **1** capable of being borne or endured **2** moderately good or agreeable

tolerance /'tɒlərəns/ *n* **1a** indulgence for beliefs or practices differing from one's own **b** the act of allowing sthg; toleration **2** an allowable variation from a standard dimension

tolerant /'tɒlərənt/ *adj* inclined to tolerate; *esp* marked by forbearance or endurance – **~ly** *adv*

tolerate /'tɒləreɪt/ *v* to allow to be (done) without prohibition, hindrance, or contradiction

¹**toll** /təʊl/ *n* **1** a fee paid for some right or privilege (e g of passing over a highway or bridge) or for services rendered **2** a grievous or ruinous price; *esp* cost in life or health

²**toll** *v* **1** to sound (a bell) by pulling the rope **2** to signal, announce, or summon (as if) by means of a tolled bell

tomato /tə'mɑːtəʊ/ *n, pl* **tomatoes** **1** any of a genus of S American plants of the nightshade family; *esp* one widely cultivated for its edible fruits **2** the usu large and rounded red, yellow, or green pulpy fruit of a tomato

tomb /tuːm/ *n* **1** an excavation in which a corpse is buried **2** a chamber or vault for the dead, built either above or below ground and usu serving as a memorial

tomorrow /tə'mɒrəʊ/ *adv or n* **1** (on) the day after today **2** (in) the future

ton /tʌn/ *n* **1** any of various units of weight; *esp* one equal to 2,240 lbs **2a** a great quantity – often *pl* with sing. meaning **b** a great weight **3** a group, score, or speed of 100 *USE* (2&3) *infml*

¹tone /təʊn/ *n* **1** a vocal or musical sound; *esp* one of a specified quality **2** a sound of a definite frequency with relatively weak overtones **3** an accent or inflection of the voice expressive of a mood or emotion **4** (a change in) the pitch of a word often used to express differences of meaning **5** style or manner of verbal expression **6** the colour that appreciably modifies a hue or white or black **7** the general effect of light, shade, and colour in a picture **8** the state of (an organ or part of) a living body in which the functions are healthy and performed with due vigour **9** prevailing character, quality, or trend (e g of morals)

²tone *v* to blend or harmonize in colour

tongs /tɒŋz/ *n pl* any of various grasping devices consisting commonly of 2 pieces joined at 1 end by a pivot or hinged like scissors

¹tongue /tʌŋ/ *n* **1a** a fleshy muscular movable organ of the floor of the mouth in most vertebrates that bears sensory end organs and small glands and functions esp in tasting and swallowing food and in human beings as a speech organ **b** a part of various invertebrate animals that is analogous to the tongue of vertebrates **2** the tongue of an ox, sheep, etc used as food **3** the power of communication through speech **4a** a (spoken) language **b** the cry (as if) of a hound pursuing or in sight of game – esp in *give tongue* **5** sthg like an animal's tongue (e g elongated and fastened at 1 end only):e g **a** a piece of metal suspended inside a bell so as to strike against the sides as the bell is swung **b** the flap under the lacing or buckles on the front of a shoe or boot **6** the rib on one edge of a board that fits into a corresponding groove in an edge of another board to make a flush joint

²tongue *v* **1** to touch or lick (as if) with the tongue **2** to articulate notes on a wind instrument by successively interrupting the stream of wind with the action of the tongue

¹tonic /'tɒnɪk/ *adj* **1** increasing or restoring physical or mental tone **2** of or based on the first note of a scale

²tonic *n* **1a** sthg that invigorates, refreshes, or stimulates **b tonic, tonic water** a carbonated drink flavoured with a small amount of quinine, lemon, and lime **2** the first note of a diatonic scale

tonight /tə'naɪt/ *adv or n* (on) this night or the night following today

tonsil /'tɒnsəl/ *n* either of a pair of prominent oval masses of spongy tissue that lie 1 on each side of the throat at the back of the mouth – ~litis *n*

too /tuː/ *adv* **1** also; in addition **2a** to a regrettable degree; excessively **b** to a higher degree than meets a standard **3** indeed, so – used to counter a negative charge (e g he did *too*!)

took /tʊk/ *past of* **take**

¹tool /tuːl/ *n* **1a** an implement that is used, esp by hand, to carry out work of a mechanical nature (e g cutting, levering, or digging) – not usu used with reference to kitchen utensils or cutlery **b** (the cutting or shaping part in) a machine tool **2** sthg (e g an instrument or apparatus) used in performing an operation, or necessary for the practice of a vocation or profession **3** sby who is used or manipulated by another **4** a penis – *vulg*

²tool *v* **1** to work, shape, or finish with a tool; *esp* to letter or ornament (e g leather) by means of hand tools **2** to equip (e g a plant or industry) with tools, machines, and instruments for production – often + *up*

tooth /tuːθ/ *n, pl* **teeth 1a** any of the hard bony structures that are borne esp on the jaws of vertebrates and serve esp for the seizing and chewing of food and as weapons **b** any of various usu hard and sharp projecting parts about the mouth of an invertebrate **2** a taste, liking **3** any of the regular projections on the rim of a cogwheel **4** *pl* effective means of enforcement

toothy /'tuːθɪ/ *adj* having or showing prominent teeth

¹top /tɒp/ *n* **1a(1)** the highest point, level, or part of sthg **(2)** (the top of the) head – esp in *top to toe* **(3)** the head of a plant, esp one with edible roots **(4)** a garment worn on the upper body **b(1)** the highest or uppermost region or part **(2)** the upper end, edge, or surface **2** a fitted or attached part serving as an upper piece, lid, or covering **3** the highest degree or pitch conceivable or attained **4** (sby or sthg in) the highest position (e g in rank or achievement) **5** *Br* the transmission gear of a motor vehicle giving the highest ratio of propeller-shaft to engine-shaft speed and hence the highest speed of travel

²top *v* **1a** to cut the top off **b** to shorten or remove the top of (a plant); *also* to remove the calyx of (e g a strawberry) **2a** to cover with a top or on the top; provide, form, or serve as a top for **b** to complete the basic structure of (e g a high-rise building) by putting on a cap or uppermost section – usu + *out* or *off* **3** to be or become higher than; overtop **4** to go over the top of; clear, surmount

³top *adj* **1** of or at the top **2** foremost, leading **3** of the highest quality, amount, or degree

⁴top *n* a child's toy that has a tapering point on which it is made to spin

top-heavy *adj* **1** having the top part too heavy for or disproportionate to the lower part **2** capitalized beyond what is prudent

topic /'tɒpɪk/ *n* **1a** a heading in an outlined argument or exposition **b** the subject of a (section of a) discourse **2** a subject for discussion or consideration

topical /'tɒpɪkəl/ *adj* **1a** of a place **2a** of or arranged by topics **b** referring to the topics of the day; of current interest – ~**ly** *adv* – ~**ity** *n*

topple /'tɒpəl/ *v* **1** to fall (as if) from being top-heavy **2** to overthrow

torch /tɔːtʃ/ *n* **1** a burning stick of resinous wood or twist of tow used to give light **2** *Br* a small portable electric lamp powered by batteries

¹torment /'tɔːment/ *n* **1** extreme pain or anguish of body or mind **2** a source of vexation or pain

²torment /tɔː'ment/ *v* to cause severe usu persistent distress of body or mind to – ~**or** *n*

tornado /tɔː'neɪdəʊ/ *n* a violent or destructive whirlwind, usu progressing in a narrow path over the land and accompanied by a funnel-shaped cloud

¹torpedo /tɔː'piːdəʊ/ *n, pl* **torpedoes 1** an electric ray **2** a self-propelling cigar-shaped submarine explosive projectile used for attacking ships

²torpedo *v* **1** to hit or destroy by torpedo **2** to destroy or nullify (e g a plan) – *infml*

torrent /'tɒrənt/ *n* **1** a violent stream of water, lava, etc **2** a raging tumultuous flow – ~**ial** *adj*

tortoise /'tɔːtəs/ *n* **1** any of an order of land and freshwater (and marine) reptiles with a toothless horny beak and a bony shell which encloses the trunk and into which the head, limbs, and tail may be withdrawn **2** sby or sthg slow or laggard

¹torture /'tɔːtʃə/ *n* **1** the infliction of intense physical or mental suffering as a means of punishment, coercion, or sadistic gratification **2** (sthg causing) anguish of body or mind

²torture *v* **1** to subject to torture **2** to cause intense suffering to **3** to twist or wrench out of shape; *also* to pervert (e g the meaning of a word) – ~**r** *n*

Tory /'tɔːri/ *n* **1** a member of a major British political group of the 18th and early 19th c favouring at first the Stuarts and later royal authority and the established church and seeking to preserve the traditional political structure and defeat parliamentary reform **2** a Conservative – ~**ism** *n*

¹toss /tɒs/ *v* **1** to fling or heave repeatedly about; *also* to bandy **2a** to throw with a quick, light, or careless motion **b** to throw up in the air **c** to flip (a coin) to decide an issue **3** to lift with a sudden jerking motion

²toss *n* **1** a fall, esp from a horse – chiefly in *take a toss* **2a** an abrupt tilting or upward fling **b** an act or instance of deciding by chance, esp by tossing a coin **c** a throw

¹total /'təʊtl/ *adj* **1** comprising or constituting a whole; entire **2** complete **3**

concentrating all available personnel and resources on a single objective – ~**ly** *adv*

²total *n* **1** a product of addition **2** an entire quantity

³total *v* to amount to

¹totter /'tɒtə/ *v* **1a** to tremble or rock as if about to fall **b** to become unstable; threaten to collapse **2** to move unsteadily; stagger

²totter *n* an unsteady gait

tot up *v* to add together; *also* to increase by additions

¹touch /tʌtʃ/ *v* **1** to bring a bodily part into contact with, esp so as to perceive through the sense of feeling; feel **2** to strike or push lightly, esp with the hand or foot or an implement **3** to take into the hands or mouth **4** to put hands on in any way or degree; *esp* to commit violence against **5** to concern oneself with **6** to cause to be briefly in contact with sthg **7** to affect the interest of; concern **8** to move to esp sympathetic feeling **9** to speak or tell of, esp in passing **10** to rival **11** to induce to give or lend – ~**able** *adj* – ~**er** *n*

²touch *n* **1** a light stroke, tap, or push **2** the act or fact of touching **3** the sense of feeling, esp as exercised deliberately with the hands, feet, or lips **4** mental or moral sensitivity, responsiveness, or tact **5** sthg slight of its kind: e g **a** a light attack **b** a small amount; a trace **6a** a manner or method of touching or striking esp the keys of a keyboard instrument **b** the relative resistance to pressure of the keys of a keyboard (e g of a piano or typewriter) **7** an effective and appropriate detail; *esp* one used in an artistic composition **8** a distinctive or characteristic manner, trait, or quality **9** the state or fact of being in contact or communication **10** the area outside the touchlines in soccer or outside and including the touchlines in rugby **11** sby who can be easily induced to part with money – chiefly in *a soft/easy touch*

¹tough /tʌf/ *adj* **1a** strong and flexible; not brittle or liable to cut, break, or tear **b** not easily chewed **2** capable of enduring great hardship or exertion **3** very hard to influence **4** extremely difficult or testing **5** aggressive or threatening in behaviour **6** without softness or sentimentality **7** unfortunate, unpleasant – *infml* – ~**ly** *adv* – ~**ness** *n*

²tough *n* a tough person; *esp* sby aggressively violent

³tough *adv* in a tough manner

¹tour /tʊə/ *n* **1** a period during which an individual or unit is engaged on a specific duty, esp in 1 place **2a** a journey (e g for business or pleasure) in which one returns to the starting point **b** a visit (e g to a historic site or factory) for pleasure or instruction **c** a series of professional engagements involving travel

²tour *v* **1** to make a tour of **2** to present (e g a theatrical production or concert) on a tour

tourism /'tʊərɪzəm/ *n* **1** the practice of

travelling for recreation 2 the organizing of tours for commercial purposes 3 the provision of services (e g accommodation) for tourists

tourist /'tʊərɪst/ *n* 1 sby who makes a tour for recreation or culture 2 a member of a sports team that is visiting another country to play usu international matches

tournament /'tʊənəmənt, 'tɔː-/ *n* 1 a contest between 2 parties of mounted knights armed with usu blunted lances or swords 2 a series of games or contests for a championship

¹**tow** /təʊ/ *v* to draw or pull along behind, esp by a rope or chain

²**tow** *n* 1 a rope or chain for towing 2 towing or being towed 3 sthg towed (e g a boat or car)

³**tow** *n* short or broken fibre (e g of flax or hemp) prepared for spinning

towards /tə'wɔːdz/ *prep* 1 moving or situated in the direction of 2a along a course leading to b in relation to (e g an attitude *towards* life) 3 turned in the direction of 4 not long before (e g *towards* evening) 5 for the partial financing of (e g gave her £5 *towards* a new dress)

¹**towel** /'taʊəl/ *n* an absorbent cloth or paper for wiping or drying sthg (e g crockery or the body) after washing

²**towel** *v* to rub or dry (e g the body) with a towel

¹**tower** /'taʊə/ *n* 1 a building or structure typically higher than its diameter and high relative to its surroundings that may stand apart or be attached to a larger structure and that may be fully walled in or of skeleton framework 2 **tower block, tower** a tall multi-storey building, often containing offices

²**tower** *v* to reach or rise to a great height

town /taʊn/ *n* 1a a compactly settled area as distinguished from surrounding rural territory; *esp* one larger than a village but smaller than a city b a city 2 the city or urban life as contrasted with the country or rural life

town hall *n* the chief administrative building of a town

toxic /'tɒksɪk/ *adj* 1 of or caused by a poison or toxin 2 poisonous – ~ity *n*

¹**toy** /tɔɪ/ *n* 1 a trinket, bauble 2a sthg for a child to play with b sthg designed for amusement or diversion rather than practical use 3 an animal of a breed or variety of exceptionally small size

²**toy** *v* to act or deal *with* sthg without purpose or conviction

³**toy** *adj* 1 designed or made for use as a toy 2 toylike, esp in being small

¹**trace** /treɪs/ *n* 1 a mark or line left by sthg that has passed 2 a vestige of some past thing 3 sthg traced or drawn (e g the graphic record made by a seismograph) 4 a minute and often barely detectable amount or indication, esp of a chemical

²**trace** *v* 1a to delineate, sketch b to copy (e g a drawing) by following the lines or letters as seen through a semi-

transparent superimposed sheet 2a to follow back or study in detail or step by step b to discover signs, evidence, or remains of – ~able *adj*

³**trace** *n* either of 2 straps, chains, or lines of a harness for attaching a vehicle to a horse

¹**track** /træk/ *n* 1a detectable evidence (e g a line of footprints or a wheel rut) that sthg has passed b a path beaten (as if) by feet c a specially laid-out course, esp for racing d(1) the parallel rails of a railway (2) a rail or length of railing along which sthg, esp a curtain, moves or is pulled e a more or less independent sequence of recording (e g a single song) visible as a distinct band on a gramophone record 2 a footprint 3 the course along which sthg moves 4 the condition of being aware of a fact or development 5a the width of a wheeled vehicle from wheel to wheel, usu from the outside of the rims b either of 2 endless usu metal belts on which a tracklaying vehicle travels

²**track** *v* 1 to follow the tracks or traces of 2 to observe or plot the course of (e g a spacecraft) instrumentally 3 to move a film or television camera towards, beside, or away from a subject while shooting a scene – ~er *n*

track suit *n* a warm loose-fitting suit worn by athletes when training

tractor /'træktə/ *n* 1 a 4-wheeled or tracklaying vehicle used esp for pulling or using farm machinery 2 a truck with a short chassis and no body except a driver's cab, used to haul a large trailer or trailers

¹**trade** /treɪd/ *n* 1a the business or work in which one engages regularly b an occupation requiring manual or mechanical skill; a craft c the people engaged in an occupation, business, or industry 2a the business of buying and selling or bartering commodities b business, market 3 *sing or pl in constr* the people or group of firms engaged in a particular business or industry

²**trade** *v* to give in exchange for another commodity; *also* to make an exchange of – ~r *n*

³**trade** *adj* 1 of or used in trade 2 intended for or limited to people in a business or industry

trademark /'treɪdmɑːk/ *n* 1 a name or distinctive symbol or device attached to goods produced by a particular firm or individual and legally reserved to the exclusive use of the owner of the mark as maker or seller 2 a distinguishing feature firmly associated with sby or sthg

tradesman /'treɪdzmən/ *n* 1 a shopkeeper 2 one who delivers goods to private houses

trade union *also* **trades union** *n* an organization of workers formed for the purpose of advancing its members' interests – ~ism *n* – ~ist *n*

tradition /trə'dɪʃən/ *n* 1 the handing down of information, beliefs, and customs by word of mouth or by example from one generation to another 2a an inherited practice or opinion **b** conventions associated with a group or period **3** cultural continuity in attitudes and institutions – ~ **al** *adj* – ~ **ally** *adv*

traffic /'træfik/ *n* **1a** the business of bartering or buying and selling **b** illegal or disreputable trade **2a** the movement (e g of vehicles or pedestrians) through an area or along a route **b** the vehicles, pedestrians, ships, or aircraft moving along a route **3** dealings between individuals or groups – *fml*

tragedy /'trædʒɨdi/ *n* **1** (a) serious drama in which destructive circumstances result in adversity for and usu the deaths of the main characters **2** a disastrous event; a calamity **3** tragic quality or element

tragic /'trædʒik/ *adj* **1** (expressive) of tragedy **2** of, appropriate to, dealing with, or treated in tragedy **3** deplorable, lamentable – ~ **ally** *adv*

¹**trail** /treɪl/ *v* **1** to hang down so as to sweep the ground **2a** to walk or proceed draggingly or wearily – usu + *along* **b** to lag behind; do poorly in relation to others **3** to dwindle **4** to follow a trail; to trail game

²**trail** *n* **1a** sthg that follows as if being drawn behind **b** the streak of light produced by a meteor **2a** a trace or mark left by sby or sthg that has passed or is being followed **b(1)** a track made by passage, esp through a wilderness **(2)** a marked path through a forest or mountainous region

¹**train** /treɪn/ *n* **1** a part of a gown that trails behind the wearer **2a** a retinue, suite **b** a moving file of people, vehicles, or animals **3** the vehicles, men, and sometimes animals that accompany an army with baggage, supplies, ammunition, or siege artillery **4** a connected series of ideas, actions, or events **5** a connected line of railway carriages or wagons with or without a locomotive

²**train** *v* **1** to direct the growth of (a plant), usu by bending, pruning, etc **2a** to form by instruction, discipline, or drill **b** to teach so as to make fit or proficient **3** to prepare (e g by exercise) for a test of skill **4** to aim at an object or objective – ~ **able** *adj* – ~ **er** *n*

training /'treɪnɪŋ/ *n* **1** the bringing of a person or animal to a desired degree of proficiency in some activity or skill **2** the condition of being trained, esp for a contest

traitor /'treɪtə/ *n* **1** sby who betrays another's trust **2** sby who commits treason

¹**tramp** /træmp/ *v* **1** to walk or tread, esp heavily **2a** to travel about on foot **b** to journey as a tramp

²**tramp** *n* **1** a wandering vagrant who survives by taking the occasional job or by begging or stealing money and food **2a** usu long and tiring walk **3** the heavy rhythmic tread of feet **4** a merchant vessel that does not work a regular route but carries general cargo to any port as required

trample /'træmpəl/ *v* **1** to tread heavily so as to bruise, crush, or injure **2** to

treat destructively with ruthlessness or contempt – usu + *on*, *over*, or *upon*

trance /trɑːns/ *n* **1** a state of semiconsciousness or unconsciousness with reduced or absent sensitivity to external stimulation **2** a state of profound abstraction or absorption

transact /træn'zækt/ *v* to perform; carry out; *esp* to conduct – ~ **ion** *n*

transatlantic /,trænzət'læntɪk/ *adj* **1** crossing or extending across the Atlantic ocean **2** situated beyond the Atlantic ocean **3** (characteristic) of people or places situated beyond the Atlantic ocean; *specif, chiefly Br* American

¹**transfer** /træns'fɜː/ *v* **1a** to convey or cause to pass from one person, place, or situation to another **b** to move or send to another location; *specif* to move (a professional soccer player) to another football club **2** to make over the possession or control of – ~ **ability** *n* – ~ **able** *adj* – ~ **ence** *n*

²**transfer** /'trænsfɜː/ *n* **1** conveyance of right, title, or interest in property **2** transferring

transform /træns'fɔːm/ *v* **1** to change radically (e g in structure, appearance, or character) **2** to subject to mathematical transformation **3** to change (a current) in potential (e g from high voltage to low) or in type (e g from alternating to direct)

transformation /,trænsfə'meɪʃən/ *n* the operation of changing one configuration or expression into another in accordance with a mathematical rule

transfuse /træns'fjuːz/ *v* **1** to diffuse into or through; *broadly* to spread across **2** to transfer (e g blood) into a vein – -**fusion** *n*

transistor /træn'zɪstə, -'sɪstə/ *n* any of several semiconductor devices that have usu 3 electrodes and make use of a small current to control a larger one; *also* a radio using using such devices

transition /træn'zɪʃən, -'sɪ-/ *n* **1a** passage from one state or stage to another **b** a movement, development, or evolution from one form, stage, or style to another **2** a musical passage leading from one section of a piece to another – ~ **al** *adj* – ~ **ally** *adv*

translate /trænz'leɪt, træns-/ *v* **1a** to bear, remove, or change from one place, state, form, or appearance to another **b** to transfer (a bishop) from one see to another **2a** to turn into another language **b** to express in different or more comprehensible terms – -**latable** *adj* – -**lator** *n*

translation /trænz'leɪʃən, træns-/ *n* **1** (a version produced by) a rendering from one language into another **2** a change to a different substance or form

transmission /trænz'mɪʃən/ *n* **1** transmitting; *esp* transmitting by radio waves or over a wire **2** the assembly by which the power is transmitted from a motor vehicle engine to the axle

transmit /trænz'mɪt/ *v* **1a** to send or transfer from one person or place to another **b** to convey (as if) by inheritance or heredity **2a** to cause (e g light or force) to pass or be conveyed through a medium **b** to send out (a signal) either by radio waves or over a wire

transmitter /trænz'mitə'/ n 1 the portion of a telegraphic or telephonic instrument that sends the signals **2** a radio or television transmitting station or set

transparent /træn'spærənt, -'speər-/ adj **1a(1)** transmitting light without appreciable scattering so that bodies lying beyond are entirely visible **(2)** penetrable by a specified form of radiation (e g X rays or ultraviolet) **b** fine or sheer enough to be seen through **2a** free from pretence or deceit **b** easily detected or seen through **c** readily understood – ~**ly** adv

¹**transplant** /trænz'plɑ:nt/ v **1** to lift and reset (a plant) in another soil or place **2** to remove from one place and settle or introduce elsewhere **3** to transfer (an organ or tissue) from one part or individual to another – ~**ation** n

²**transplant** /'trænzplɑ:nt/ n **1** transplanting **2** sthg transplanted

¹**transport** /træn'spɔ:t/ v **1** to transfer or convey from one place to another **2** to carry away with strong and often pleasurable emotion **3** to send to a penal colony overseas – ~**able** adj

²**transport** /træn'spɔ:t/ n **1** the conveying of goods or people from one place to another **2** strong and often pleasurable emotion – often pl with sing. meaning **3** a ship or aircraft for carrying soldiers or military equipment **4** a mechanism for moving a tape, esp a magnetic tape, or disk past a sensing or recording head

¹**trap** /træp/ n **1** a device for taking animals; esp one that holds by springing shut suddenly **2a** sthg designed to catch sby unawares **b** a situation from which it is impossible to escape; also a plan to trick a person into such a situation **3a** a trapdoor **b** a device from which a greyhound is released at the start of a race **4** a light usu 1-horse carriage with springs **5** the mouth – slang

²**trap** v **1** to catch or take (as if) in a trap **2** to provide or set (a place) with traps **3** to stop, retain

¹**travel** /'trævəl/ v **1a** to go (as if) on a tour **b** to go as if by travelling **c** to go from place to place as a sales representative **2a** to move or be transmitted from one place to another **b** esp of machinery to move along a specified direction or path **c** to move at high speed – infml

²**travel** n **1** a journey, esp to a distant or unfamiliar place – often pl **2** movement, progression

traveller /'trævələ'/ NAm chiefly **traveler** n **1** a sales representative **2** any of various devices for handling sthg that is being moved laterally **3** dial Br a gipsy

¹**travesty** /'trævɪsti/ n **1** a crude or grotesque literary or artistic parody **2a** a debased, distorted, or grossly inferior imitation

²**travesty** v to make a travesty of

tray /treɪ/ n an open receptacle with a

flat bottom and a low rim for holding, carrying, or exhibiting articles

treacherous /'tretʃərəs/ adj **1** characterized by treachery; perfidious **2a** of uncertain reliability **b** marked by hidden dangers or hazards – ~**ly** adv

treachery /'tretʃəri/ n (an act of) violation of allegiance; (a) betrayal of trust

treacle /'tri:kəl/ n, chiefly Br **1** any of the edible grades of molasses that are obtained in the early stages of sugar refining **2** golden syrup

¹**tread** /tred/ v trod; trodden, trod **1a** to step or walk on or over **b** to walk along **2** to beat or press with the feet **3** of a male bird to copulate with **4** to execute by stepping or dancing

²**tread** n **1** an imprint made (as if) by treading **2** the sound or manner of treading **3a** the part of a wheel or tyre that makes contact with a road or rail **b** the pattern of ridges or grooves made or cut in the face of a tyre **4** (the width of) the upper horizontal part of a step

treason /'tri:zən/ n **1** the betrayal of a trust **2** the offence of violating the duty of allegiance owed to one's crown or government – ~**able** adj – ~**ably** adv

¹**treasure** /'treʒə'/ n **1** wealth, esp in a form which can be accumulated or hoarded **2** sthg of great worth or value; also sby highly valued or prized

²**treasure** v to hold or preserve as precious

treasurer /'treʒərə'/ n the financial officer of an organization (e g a society)

treasury /'treʒəri/ n **1a** a place in which stores of wealth are kept **b** the place where esp public funds that have been collected are deposited and disbursed **2** often cap a government department in charge of finances, esp the collection, management, and expenditure of public revenues

¹**treat** /tri:t/ v **1** to deal with **2a** to behave oneself towards **b** to regard and deal with in a specified manner – usu + as **3** to provide with free food, drink, entertainment, etc – usu + to **4** to care for or deal with medically or surgically **5** to act on with some agent, esp so as to improve or alter – ~**able** adj – ~**er** n

²**treat** n **1** an entertainment given free of charge to those invited **2** a source of pleasure or amusement; esp an unexpected one

treatment /'tri:tmənt/ n **1a** treating sby or sthg **b** the actions customarily applied in a particular situation **2** a substance or technique used in treating

treaty /'tri:ti/ n (a document setting down) an agreement or contract made by negotiation (e g between states)

¹**treble** /'trebəl/ n **1a** the highest voice part in harmonic music; also sby, esp a boy, who performs this part **b** a member of a family of instruments having the highest range **c** the upper half of the whole vocal or instrumental tonal range **2** sthg treble in construction, uses,

amount, number, or value: e g **a** a type of bet in which the winnings and stake from a previous race are bet on the next of 3 races **b** (a throw landing on) the middle narrow ring on a dart board counting treble the stated score

²**treble** *adj* **1a** having 3 parts or uses **b** triple **2a** relating to or having the range or part of a treble **b** high-pitched, shrill

tree /triː/ *n* **1** a tall woody perennial plant having a single usu long and erect main stem, generally with few or no branches on its lower part **2** a device for inserting in a boot or shoe to preserve its shape when not being worn **3** a diagram or graph that branches, usu from a single stem

¹**tremble** /ˈtrembəl/ *v* **1** to shake involuntarily (e g with fear or cold) **2** to be affected with fear or apprehension – **-blingly** *adv*

²**tremble** *n* **1** a fit or spell of involuntary shaking or quivering **2** a tremor or series of tremors

tremendous /trɪˈmendəs/ *adj* **1** such as to arouse awe or fear **2** of extraordinary size, degree, or excellence – ~ **ly** *adv*

¹**trench** /trentʃ/ *n* a deep narrow excavation (e g for the laying of underground pipes); *esp* one used for military defence

²**trench** *v* to dig a trench (in)

¹**trend** /trend/ *v* **1** to show a general tendency to move or extend in a specified direction **2** to deviate, shift

²**trend** *n* **1** a line of general direction **2a** a prevailing tendency or inclination **b** a general movement, esp in taste or fashion

¹**trendy** /ˈtrendi/ *adj, chiefly Br* characterized by uncritical adherence to the latest fashions or progressive ideas – *infml* – **trendiness** *n*

²**trendy** *n, chiefly Br* sby trendy – *chiefly derog*

¹**trespass** /ˈtrespəs, -pæs/ *n* **1** a violation of moral or social ethics; *esp* a sin **2** any unlawful act that causes harm to the person, property, or rights of another; *esp* wrongful entry on another's land

²**trespass** *v* **1a** to err, sin **b** to make an unwarranted or uninvited intrusion on **2** to commit a trespass; *esp* to enter sby's property unlawfully

¹**trial** /ˈtraɪəl/ *n* **1** trying or testing **2** the formal examination and determination by a competent tribunal of the matter at issue in a civil or criminal cause **3** a test of faith, patience, or stamina by suffering or temptation; *broadly* a source of vexation or annoyance **4** an experiment to test quality, value, or usefulness **5** an attempt, effort

²**trial** *adj* **1** of a trial **2** made or done as, or used or tried out in, a test or experiment

triangle /ˈtraɪæŋɡəl/ *n* **1** a polygon of 3 sides and 3 angles **2** a percussion instrument consisting of a steel rod bent into the form of a triangle open at 1

angle and sounded by striking with a small metal rod

triangular /traɪˈæŋɡjʊlə/ *adj* **1** (having the form) of a triangle **2** between or involving 3 elements, things, or people

tribe /traɪb/ *n sing or pl in constr* **1** a social group comprising numerous families, clans, or generations together with slaves, dependants, or adopted strangers **2** a group of people having a common character or interest **3** a category in the classification of living things ranking above a genus and below a family – **tribal** *adj*

tribunal /traɪˈbjuːnəl/ *n* a court of justice; *specif* a board appointed to decide disputes of a specified kind

¹**tributary** /ˈtrɪbjʊtəri/ *adj* **1** paying tribute to another; subject **2** paid or owed as tribute **3** providing with material or supplies

²**tributary** *n* **1** a tributary ruler or state **2** a stream feeding a larger stream or a lake

tribute /ˈtrɪbjuːt/ *n* **1** a payment by one ruler or nation to another in acknowledgment of submission or as the price of protection **2a** sthg (e g a gift or formal declaration) given or spoken as a testimonial of respect, gratitude, or affection **b** evidence of the worth or effectiveness of sthg specified – chiefly in *a tribute to*

¹**trick** /trɪk/ *n* **1a** a crafty practice or stratagem meant to deceive or defraud **b** a mischievous act **c** a deceptive, dexterous, or ingenious feat designed to puzzle or amuse **2a** a habitual peculiarity of behaviour or manner **b** a deceptive appearance, esp when caused by art or sleight of hand **3a** a quick or effective way of getting a result **b** a technical device or contrivance (e g of an art or craft) **4** the cards played in 1 round of a card game, often used as a scoring unit – ~ **ery** *n*

²**trick** *adj* **1** of or involving tricks or trickery **2** skilled in or used for tricks

³**trick** *v* **1** to deceive by cunning or artifice – often + *into, out of* **2** to dress or embellish showily – usu + *out* or *up*

¹**trickle** /ˈtrɪkəl/ *v* **1** to flow in drops or a thin slow stream **2** to move or go gradually or one by one

²**trickle** *n* a thin slow stream or movement

tricky /ˈtrɪki/ *adj* **1** inclined to or marked by trickery **2** containing concealed difficulties or hazards **3** requiring skill, adroitness, or caution (e g in doing or handling) – **trickiness** *n*

tricycle /ˈtraɪsɪkəl/ *n* a 3-wheeled pedal-driven vehicle

tried /traɪd/ *adj* **1** found to be good or trustworthy through experience or testing **2** subjected to trials or severe provocation – often in combination

¹**trifle** /ˈtraɪfəl/ *n* **1** sthg of little value or importance; *esp* an insignificant amount (e g of money) **2** *chiefly Br* a dessert typically consisting of sponge cake soaked in wine (e g sherry), spread with

jam or jelly, and topped with custard and whipped cream

²**trifle** *v* **1** to act heedlessly or frivolously – often + *with* **2** to handle sthg idly **3** to spend or waste in trifling or on trifles

¹**trigger** /'trɪgə/ *n* a device (e g a lever) connected with a catch as a means of release; *esp* the tongue of metal in a firearm which when pressed allows the gun to fire

²**trigger** *v* **1a** to release, activate, or fire by means of a trigger **b** to cause the explosion of **2** to initiate or set off as if by pulling a trigger – often + *off*

¹**trim** /trɪm/ *v* **1** to decorate (e g clothes) with ribbons, lace, or ornaments; adorn **2** to make trim and neat, esp by cutting or clipping **3a** to cause (e g a ship, aircraft, or submarine) to assume a desired position by arrangement of ballast, cargo, passengers, etc **b** to adjust (e g a sail) to a desired position **4** to maintain a neutral attitude towards opposing parties or favour each equally

²**trim** *adj* appearing neat or in good order; compact or clean-cut in outline or structure – ~ly *adv* – ~ness *n*

³**trim** *n* **1** the readiness or fitness of a person or thing for action or use; *esp* physical fitness **2a** material used for decoration or trimming **b** the decorative accessories of a motor vehicle **3a** the position of a ship or boat, esp with reference to the horizontal **b** the inclination of an aircraft or spacecraft in flight with reference to a fixed point (e g the horizon), esp with the controls in some neutral position

trinket /'trɪŋkɪt/ *n* a small (trifling) article; *esp* an ornament or piece of (cheap) jewellery

trio /'triːəʊ/ *n* **1a** (a musical composition for) 3 instruments, voices, or performers **b** the secondary division of a minuet, scherzo, etc **2** *sing or pl in constr* a group or set of 3

¹**trip** /trɪp/ *v* **1a** to dance, skip, or walk with light quick steps **b** to proceed smoothly, lightly, and easily; flow **2a** to catch the foot against sthg so as to stumble **b** to detect in a fault or blunder; catch out – usu + *up* **3** to stumble in articulation when speaking **4** to make a journey **5** to release or operate (a device or mechanism), esp by releasing a catch or producing an electrical signal **6** to get high on a psychedelic drug (e g LSD) – slang

²**trip** *n* **1a** a voyage, journey, or excursion **b** a single round or tour (e g on a business errand) **2** an error, mistake **3** a quick light step **4** a faltering step caused by stumbling **5** a device (e g a catch) for tripping a mechanism **6** an intense, often visionary experience undergone by sby who has taken a psychedelic drug (e g LSD) **7** a self-indulgent or absorbing course of action, way of behaving, or frame of mind *USE* (6&7) *infml*

tripe /traɪp/ *n* **1** the stomach tissue of an ox, cow, etc for use as food **2** sthg

inferior, worthless, or offensive – *infml*

¹**triple** /'trɪpəl/ *v* to make or become 3 times as great or as many

²**triple** *n* **1** a triple sum, quantity, or number **2** a combination, group, or series of 3

³**triple** *adj* **1** having 3 units or members **2** being 3 times as great or as many **3** marked by 3 beats per bar of music **4** having units of 3 components

tripod /'traɪpɒd/ *n* **1** a stool, table, or vessel (e g a cauldron) with 3 legs **2** a 3-legged stand (e g for a camera)

trite /traɪt/ *adj* hackneyed from much use – ~ly *adv* – ~ness *n*

¹**triumph** /'traɪəmf, -ʌmf/ *n* **1** the joy or exultation of victory or success **2** (a) notable success, triumph, or achievement – ~al *adj*

²**triumph** /'traɪəmf/ *v* **1** to celebrate victory or success boastfully or exultantly **2** to obtain victory – often + *over*

triumphant /traɪ'ʌmfənt/ *adj* **1** victorious, conquering **2** rejoicing in or celebrating victory – ~ly *adv*

trivial /'trɪvɪəl/ *adj* **1** commonplace, ordinary **2** of little worth or importance; insignificant – ~ly *adv* – ~ity *n* – ~ize *v*

trod /trɒd/ *past of* **tread**

trodden /'trɒdn/ *past part of* **tread**

trolley /'trɒli/ *n* **1** a device (e g a grooved wheel or skid) attached to a pole that collects current from an overhead electric wire for powering an electric vehicle **2** *chiefly Br* **a** a shelved stand mounted on castors used for conveying sthg (e g food or books) **b** a basket on wheels that is pushed or pulled by hand and used for carrying goods (e g purchases in a supermarket)

¹**troop** /truːp/ *n* **1** *sing or pl in constr* **a** a military subunit (e g of cavalry) corresponding to an infantry platoon **b** a collection of people or things **c** a unit of scouts under a leader **2** *pl* the armed forces

²**troop** *v* to move in a group, esp in a way that suggests regimentation

trophy /'trəʊfi/ *n* sthg gained or awarded in victory or conquest, esp when preserved as a memorial

tropic /'trɒpɪk/ *n* **1** either of the 2 small circles of the celestial sphere on each side of and parallel to the equator at a distance of 23½ degrees, which the sun reaches at its greatest declination N or S **2** *pl, often cap* the region between the 2 terrestrial tropics

tropical /'trɒpɪkəl/ *adj* **1** *also* **tropic** of, occurring in, or characteristic of the tropics **2** *of a sign of the zodiac* beginning at either of the tropics – ~ly *adv*

¹**trot** /trɒt/ *n* **1** a moderately fast gait of a horse or other quadruped in which the legs move in diagonal pairs **2** *pl but sing or pl in constr* diarrhoea – usu + *the*; humor

²**trot** *v* **1** to ride, drive, or proceed at a trot **2** to proceed briskly

Trot *n* a Trotskyite; *broadly* any adherent of the extreme left – chiefly derog

¹**trouble** /'trʌbəl/ *v* **troubling 1a** to agitate mentally or spiritually; worry **b** to produce physical disorder or discomfort in **c** to put to exertion or inconvenience **2** to make (e g the surface of water) turbulent

²**trouble** *n* **1a** being troubled **b** an instance of distress, annoyance, or disturbance **2** a cause of disturbance, annoyance, or distress: e g **a** public unrest or demonstrations of dissatisfaction – often pl with sing. meaning **b** effort made; exertion **3** a problem, snag

troublesome /'trʌbəlsəm/ *adj* giving trouble or anxiety; annoying or burdensome

trough /trɒf/ *n* **1** a long shallow receptacle for the drinking water or feed of farm animals **2** a long narrow or shallow trench between waves, ridges, etc **3a** (the region round the) lowest point of a regularly recurring cycle of a varying quantity (e g a sine wave) **b** an elongated area of low atmospheric pressure

trousers /'trauzəz/ *pl, pl* **trousers** a 2-legged outer garment extending from the waist to the ankle or sometimes only to the knee – **trouser** *adj*

trout /traut/ *n* **1** any of various food and sport fishes of the salmon family restricted to cool clear fresh waters; *esp* any of various Old World or New World fishes some of which ascend rivers from the sea to breed **2** an ugly unpleasant old woman – slang

trowel /'trauəl/ *n* any of various smooth-bladed hand tools used to apply, spread, shape, or smooth loose or soft material; *also* a scoop-shaped or flat-bladed garden tool for taking up and setting small plants

truant /'tru:ənt/ *n* one who shirks duty; *esp* one who stays away from school without permission – **-ancy** *n*

truce /tru:s/ *n* a (temporary) suspension of fighting by agreement of opposing forces

¹**truck** /trʌk/ *n* **1** close association; dealings – chiefly in *have no truck with* **2** payment of wages in goods instead of cash

²**truck** *n* **1a** a usu 4- or 6-wheeled vehicle for moving heavy loads; a lorry **b** a usu 2- or 4-wheeled cart for carrying heavy articles (e g luggage at railway stations) **2** *Br* an open railway goods wagon – **truck** *v*

¹**trudge** /trʌdʒ/ *v* to walk steadily and laboriously (along or over)

²**trudge** *n* a long tiring walk

¹**true** /tru:/ *adj* **1** steadfast, loyal **2a** in accordance with fact or reality **b** being that which is the case rather than what is claimed or assumed **c** consistent, conforming **3** genuine, real **4a** accurately fitted, adjusted, balanced, or formed **b** exact, accurate

²**true** *n* the state of being accurate (e g in alignment or adjustment) – chiefly in *in/out of true*

³**true** *adv* **1** truly **2a** without deviation; straight **b** without variation from type

truly /'tru:li/ *adv* **1** in accordance with fact or reality; truthfully **2** accurately, exactly **3a** indeed **b** genuinely, sincerely **4** properly, duly

¹**trump** /trʌmp/ *n* a trumpet (call) – chiefly poetic

²**trump** *n* **1a** a card of a suit any of whose cards will win over a card that is not of this suit **b** *pl* the suit whose cards are trumps for a particular hand **2** a worthy and dependable person – infml

³**trump** *v* to play a trump on (a card or trick) when another suit was led

¹**trumpet** /'trʌmpɪt/ *n* **1** a wind instrument consisting of a usu metal tube, a cup-shaped mouthpiece, and a flared bell; *specif* a valved brass instrument having a cylindrical tube and a usual range from F sharp below middle C upwards for 2½ octaves **2** sthg that resembles (the flared bell or loud penetrating sound of) a trumpet; *esp* the loud cry of an elephant

²**trumpet** *v* to sound or proclaim loudly (as if) on a trumpet – ~ **er** *n*

trunk /trʌŋk/ *n* **1a** the main stem of a tree as distinguished from branches and roots **b** the human or animal body apart from the head and limbs **2** a large rigid box used usu for transporting clothing and personal articles **3** the long muscular proboscis of the elephant **4** *pl* men's usu close-fitting shorts worn chiefly for swimming or sports

¹**trust** /trʌst/ *n* **1** confident belief in or reliance on (the ability, character, honesty, etc of) sby or sthg **2a** a property interest held by one person for the benefit of another **b** a combination of companies formed by a legal agreement **3a** responsible charge or office **b** care, custody

²**trust** *v* **1** to place confidence in; rely on **2** to expect or hope, esp confidently

trustworthy /'trʌst,wɜːði/ *adj* dependable, reliable – **-thiness** *n*

truth /tru:θ/ *n* **1** sincerity, honesty **2a(1)** the state or quality of being true or factual **(2)** reality, actuality **b** a judgment, proposition, idea, or body of statements that is (accepted as) true **3** conformity to an original or to a standard

¹**try** /trai/ *v* **1a** to investigate judicially **b** to conduct the trial of **2a** to test by experiment or trial – often + *out* **b** to subject to sthg that tests the patience or endurance **3** to make an attempt at

²**try** *n* **1** an experimental trial; an attempt **2** a score in rugby that is made by touching down the ball behind the opponent's goal line

T-shirt *n* a vest-like garment worn casually as a shirt

tub /tʌb/ *n* **1a** any of various wide low often round vessels typically made of wood, metal, or plastic, and used industrially or domestically (e g for washing clothes or holding soil for shrubs) **b** a small round (plastic) container in which

tub

cream, ice cream, etc may be bought **2** a bath **3** an old or slow boat – *infml*

tube /tju:b/ *n* **1** a hollow elongated cylinder; *esp* one to convey fluids **2** any of various usu cylindrical structures or devices: e g **a** a small cylindrical container of soft metal or plastic sealed at one end, and fitted with a cap at the other, from which a paste is dispensed by squeezing **b** the basically cylindrical section between the mouthpiece and bell of a wind instrument **3** *Br* (a train running in) an underground railway running through deep bored tunnels – **-bular** *adj*

tuberculosis /tjuːˌbɜːkjʊˈləʊsɪs/ *n* a serious infectious disease of human beings and other vertebrates caused by the tubercle bacillus and characterized by fever and the formation of abnormal lumps in the body – **-lar** *adj*

¹**tuck** /tʌk/ *v* **1** to draw into a fold or folded position **2** to place in a snug often concealed or isolated spot **3a** to push in the loose end or ends of so as to make secure or tidy **b** to cover snugly by tucking in bedclothes **4a** to eat – usu + *away* **b** to eat heartily – usu + *in* or *into*

²**tuck** *n* **1** a (narrow) fold stitched into cloth to shorten, decorate, or reduce fullness **2** (an act of) eating **b** *Br* food, esp chocolate, pastries, etc, as eaten by schoolchildren – *infml*

Tuesday /'tju:zdɪ, -deɪ/ *n* the day of the week following Monday

¹**tuft** /tʌft/ *n* **1** a small cluster of long flexible hairs, feathers, grasses, etc attached or close together at the base **2** a clump, cluster

²**tuft** *v* **1** to adorn with a tuft or tufts **2** to make (e g a mattress) firm by stitching at intervals and sewing on tufts

¹**tug** /tʌg/ *v* to pull hard (at)

²**tug** *n* **1a** a hard pull or jerk **b** a strong pulling force **2** a struggle between 2 people or opposite forces **3a** tug, **tug-boat** a strongly built powerful boat used for towing or pushing large ships (e g in and out of dock) **b** an aircraft that tows a glider

tug-of-war *n* **1** a struggle for supremacy **2** a contest in which teams pulling at opposite ends of a rope attempt to pull each other across a line marked between them

tulip /'tjuːlɪp/ *n* (the flower of) any of a genus of Eurasian bulbous plants widely grown for their showy flowers

¹**tumble** /'tʌmbəl/ *v* **1** to turn end over end in falling or flight **2a** to fall suddenly and helplessly **b** to suffer a sudden overthrow or defeat **c** to decline suddenly and sharply **3** to roll over and over, to and fro, or around **4** to realize suddenly – often + *to*; *infml*

²**tumble** *n* a confused heap **2** an act of tumbling; *specif* a fall

tumbler /'tʌmblə*r*/ *n* **1a** an acrobat **b** any of various domestic pigeons that tumble or somersault backwards in flight or on the ground **2** a relatively large drinking glass without a foot, stem, or handle

tumour /'tjuːmə*r*/ *n* an abnormal mass of tissue that arises without obvious cause from cells of existing tissue and possesses no physiological function

tumult /'tjuːmʌlt/ *n* **1a** commotion, uproar (e g of a crowd) **b** a turbulent uprising; a riot **2** violent mental or emotional agitation

¹**tune** /tjuːn/ *n* **1a** a pleasing succession of musical notes; a melody **b** *the* dominant tune in a musical composition **2** correct musical pitch (with another instrument, voice, etc) **3a** accord, harmony **b** general attitude; approach

²**tune** *v* **1** to bring a musical instrument or instruments into tune, esp with a standard pitch – usu + *up* **2** to adjust for optimum performance – often + *up* **3** to adjust a receiver for the reception of a particular broadcast or station – + *in* or *to*

tunic /'tjuːnɪk/ *n* **1** a simple (hip- or knee-length) slip-on garment usu belted or gathered at the waist **2** a close-fitting jacket with a high collar worn esp as part of a uniform

¹**tunnel** /'tʌnl/ *n* **1** a hollow conduit or recess (e g for a propeller shaft) **2a** a man-made horizontal passageway through or under an obstruction **b** a subterranean passage (e g in a mine)

²**tunnel** *v* **1** to make a passage through or under **2** to make (e g one's way) by excavating a tunnel – ~ **ler** *n*

turban /'tɜːbən/ *n* **1** (a headdress, esp for a lady, resembling) a headdress worn esp by Muslims and Sikhs and made of a long cloth wound round a cap or directly round the head – ~ **ed** *adj*

turbine /'tɜːbaɪn/ *n* a rotary engine whose central driving shaft is fitted with vanes whirled round by the pressure of water, steam, exhaust gases, etc

¹**turf** /tɜːf/ *n*, *pl* **turfs, turves 1** the upper layer of soil bound by grass and plant roots into a thick mat **2** (a piece of dried) peat **3** *the sport* or business of horse racing or the course on which horse races are run

²**turf** *v* to cover with turf

turkey /'tɜːkɪ/ *n* (the flesh of) a large orig American bird that is farmed for its meat in most parts of the world

turmoil /'tɜːmɔɪl/ *n* an extremely confused or agitated state

¹**turn** /tɜːn/ *v* **1a(1)** to (make) rotate or revolve **(2)** to alter the functioning of (as if) by turning a knob **b** to perform by rotating or revolving **c(1)** to become giddy or dizzy **(2)** *of the stomach* to feel nauseated **d** to centre or hinge on sthg **2a(1)** to dig or plough so as to bring the lower soil to the surface **(2)** to renew (e g a garment) by reversing the material and resewing **b** to cause to change or reverse direction **c** to direct one's course **3a** to change position so as to face another way **b** to change one's attitude to one of hostility **c** to make a sudden violent physical or verbal assault – usu + *on* or *upon* **4a** to direct, present, or point (e g the face) in a specified direction **b** to aim, train **c** to direct, induce, or influence in a specified

direction, esp towards or away from sby or sthg **d** to apply, devote; *also* resort, have recourse to **e** to direct into or out of a receptacle (as if) by inverting **5a** to become changed, altered, or transformed: e g (1) to change colour (2) to become acid or sour **b** to become by change **6a** to give a rounded form to **b** to fashion elegantly or neatly **7** to fold, bend **8** to gain in the course of business – esp in *turn an honest penny*

²**turn** *n* **1a** a turning about a centre or axis; (a) rotation **b** any of various rotating or pivoting movements (in dancing) **2a** a change or reversal of direction, stance, position, or course **b** a deflection, deviation **3** a short trip out and back or round about **4** an act or deed of a specified kind **5a** a place, time, or opportunity granted in succession or rotation **b** a period of duty, action, or activity **6a** an alteration, change **b** a point of change in time **7** a style of expression **8** a single coil (e g of rope wound round an object) **9** a bent, inclination **10a** a spell or attack of illness, faintness, etc **b** a nervous start or shock

turndown /'tɜ:ndaʊn/ *adj* worn turned down

turn down *v* **1** to reduce the intensity, volume, etc of (as if) by turning a control **2** to decline to accept; reject

turning /'tɜ:nɪŋ/ *n* **1a** a place of turning, turning off, or turning back, esp on a road **2a** a forming or being formed by use of a lathe **b** *pl* waste produced in turning sthg on a lathe **3** the width of cloth that is folded under for a seam or hem

turnip /'tɜːnᵻp/ *n* (a plant of the mustard family with) a thick white-fleshed root eaten as a vegetable or fed to stock

turnout /'tɜːnaʊt/ *n* **1** people in attendance (e g at a meeting) **2** manner of dress; getup

turn out *v* **1** to empty the contents of, esp for cleaning **2** to produce often rapidly or regularly (as if) by machine **3** to equip or dress in a specified way **4** to put out (esp a light) by turning a switch **5** to leave one's home for a meeting, public event, etc **6** to get out of bed – *infml*

turntable /'tɜːn,teɪbəl/ *n* **1** a circular platform for turning wheeled vehicles, esp railway engines **2** the platform on which a gramophone record is rotated while being played

turret /'tʌrᵻt/ *n* **1** a little tower, often at the corner of a larger building **2** a rotatable holder (e g for a tool or die) in a lathe, milling machine, etc **3** a usu revolving armoured structure on warships, forts, tanks, aircraft, etc in which guns are mounted

turtle /'tɜːtl/ *n* any of several marine reptiles of the same order as and similar to tortoises but adapted for swimming

tusk /tʌsk/ *n* a long greatly enlarged tooth of an elephant, boar, walrus, etc, that projects when the mouth is closed

and serves for digging food or as a weapon

¹**tutor** /'tjuːtə²/ *n* **1** a private teacher **2** a British university teacher who **a** gives instruction to students, esp individually **b** is in charge of the social and moral welfare of a group of students **3** *Br* an instruction book

²**tutor** *v* to teach or guide usu individually; coach

tweed /twiːd/ *n* **1** a rough woollen fabric made usu in twill weaves and used esp for suits and coats **2** *pl* tweed clothing; *specif* a tweed suit

tweezers /'twiːzəz/ *n pl* a small metal instrument that is usu held between thumb and forefinger, is used for plucking, holding, or manipulating, and consists of 2 prongs joined at 1 end

twelfth /twelfθ, twelθ/ *n* **1** 12th **2** *often cap, Br* the twelfth of August on which the grouse-shooting season begins

twelve /twelv/ *n* **1** the number 12 **2** the twelfth in a set or series **3** sthg having 12 parts or members or a denomination of 12

twenty /'twentɪ/ *n* **1** the number 20 **2** *pl* the numbers 20 to 29; *specif* a range of temperature, ages, or dates in a century characterized by those numbers **3** sthg (e g a bank note) having a denomination of 20 – **-tieth** *n, adj, adv*

twice /twaɪs/ *adv* **1** on 2 occasions **2** two times; in doubled quantity or degree

¹**twig** /twɪg/ *n* a small woody shoot or branch, usu without its leaves – **twiggy** *adj*

²**twig** *v* to catch on; understand – *infml*

twilight /'twaɪlaɪt/ *n* **1a** the light from the sky between full night and sunrise or esp between sunset and full night **b** the period between sunset and full night **2a** a shadowy indeterminate state **b** a period or state of decline

¹**twin** /twɪn/ *adj* **1** born with one other or as a pair at 1 birth **2** having or made up of 2 similar, related, or identical units or parts

²**twin** *n* **1** either of 2 offspring produced at 1 birth **2** either of 2 people or things closely related to or resembling each other

³**twin** *v* **1** to become paired or closely associated **2** to give birth to twins

¹**twine** /twaɪn/ *n* a strong string of 2 or more strands twisted together

²**twine** *v* **1** to twist together **2** to twist or coil round sthg

¹**twinkle** /'twɪŋkəl/ *v* **1** to shine with a flickering or sparkling light **2** to appear bright with gaiety or amusement

²**twinkle** *n* **1** an instant, twinkling **2** an (intermittent) sparkle or gleam

¹**twist** /twɪst/ *v* **1** to join together by winding; *also* to mingle by interlacing **2** to wind or coil round sthg **3a** to wring or wrench so as to dislocate or distort **b** to distort the meaning of; pervert **c** to pull off, turn, or break by a turning force **d** to warp **4** to follow a winding course; snake

²twist n 1 sthg formed by twisting: e g a thread, yarn, or cord formed by twisting 2 or more strands together **b** a screw of paper used as a container **2a** a twisting or being twisted **b** a dance popular esp in the 1960s and performed with gyrations, esp of the hips **c** a spiral turn or curve **3a** a turning off a straight course; a bend **b** a distortion of meaning or sense **4** an unexpected turn or development – **twisty** adj

¹twitch /twɪtʃ/ v 1 to pull, pluck 2 to move jerkily or involuntarily – ~**er** n

²twitch n 1 a short sudden pull or jerk 2 a physical or mental pang 3 (the recurrence of) a short spasmodic contraction or jerk; a tic

¹twitter /'twɪtə'/ v 1 to utter twitters 2 to talk in a nervous chattering fashion 3 to tremble with agitation; flutter – ~**er** n

²twitter n 1 a nervous agitation – esp in all of a twitter 2 a small tremulous intermittent sound characteristic of birds – ~**y** adj

¹two /tu:/ pron, pl in constr 1 two unspecified countable individuals 2 a small approximate number of indicated things

²two n, pl **twos** 1 the number 2 2 the second in a set or series 3 sthg having 2 parts or members or a denomination of 2

tycoon /taɪ'ku:n/ n a businessman of exceptional wealth and power

¹type /taɪp/ n **1a** a model, exemplar, or characteristic specimen (possessing the distinguishing or essential qualities of a class) **b** a lower taxonomic category selected as reference for a higher category **2a** (any of) a collection of usu rectangular blocks or characters bearing a relief from which an inked print can be made **b** printed letters **3a** a person of a specified nature **b** a particular kind, class, or group with distinct characteristics **c** sthg distinguishable as a variety; a sort

²type v to write with a typewriter; also to keyboard

typewriter /'taɪp,raɪtə'/ n a machine with a keyboard for writing in characters resembling type

typhoon /taɪ'fu:n/ n a tropical cyclone occurring in the Philippines or the China sea

typical /'tɪpɪkəl/ adj 1 being or having the nature of a type; symbolic, representative 2a having or showing the essential characteristics of a type **b** showing or according with the usual or expected (unfavourable) traits – ~**ly** adv

typist /'taɪpɪst/ n one who uses a typewriter, esp as an occupation

tyranny /'tɪrəni/ n 1 a government in which absolute power is vested in a single ruler 2 oppressive power (exerted by a tyrant) 3 sthg severe, oppressive, or inexorable in effect – **-nical** adj – **-nically** adv – **-nize** v

tyrant /'taɪərənt/ n 1 a ruler who exercises absolute power, esp oppressively or brutally 2 one who exercises authority harshly or unjustly

tyre /taɪə'/, n a continuous solid or inflated hollow rubber cushion set round a wheel to absorb shock

U

ugly /'ʌgli/ adj 1 frightful, horrible 2 offensive or displeasing to any of the senses, esp to the sight 3 morally offensive or objectionable **4a** ominous, threatening **b** surly, quarrelsome – **-liness** n

¹ultimate /'ʌltɪmɪt/ adj **1a** last in a progression or series **b** eventual **2a** fundamental, basic **b** incapable of further analysis, division, or separation 3 maximum, greatest

²ultimate n sthg ultimate; the highest point

ultimately /'ʌltɪmɪtli/ adv finally; at last

ultimatum /,ʌltɪ'meɪtəm/ n, pl **ultimatums, ultimata** a final proposition or demand; esp one whose rejection will end negotiations and cause a resort to direct action

umbrella /ʌm'brelə/ n 1 a collapsible shade for protection against weather, consisting of fabric stretched over hinged ribs radiating from a central pole 2 the bell-shaped or saucer-shaped largely gelatinous structure that forms the chief part of the body of most jellyfishes

¹umpire /'ʌmpaɪə'/ n 1 one having authority to settle a controversy or question between parties 2 a referee in any of several sports (e g cricket, table tennis, badminton, and hockey)

²umpire v to act as or supervise (e g a match) as umpire

unaccustomed /,ʌnə'kʌstəmd/ adj 1 not customary; not usual or common 2 not used to

unanimous /ju:'nænɪməs/ adj 1 being of one mind; agreeing 2 characterized by the agreement and consent of all – ~**ly** adv – **-mity** n

unarmed /,ʌn'ɑ:md/ adj not armed or armoured

unawares /,ʌnə'weəz/ adv 1 without noticing or intending 2 suddenly, unexpectedly

uncanny /ʌn'kæni/ adj 1 eerie, mysterious 2 beyond what is normal or expected – **-nily** adv

uncertain /ʌn's3:tn/ adj 1 not reliable or trustworthy **2a** not definitely known; undecided, unpredictable **b** not confident or sure; doubtful 3 variable, changeable – ~**ly** adv – ~**ness** n – ~**ty** n

uncle /'ʌŋkəl/ n **1a** the brother of one's father or mother **b** the husband of one's aunt 2 a man who is a very close friend of a young child or its parents

unconcerned /,ʌnkən's3:nd/ adj 1 not involved or interested 2 not anxious or worried – ~**ly** adv

unconditional /ˌʌnkən'dɪʃənəl/ adj absolute, unqualified – ~**ly** adv

¹**unconscious** /ʌn'kɒnʃəs/ adj **1** not knowing or perceiving **2a** not possessing mind or having lost consciousness **b** not marked by or resulting from conscious thought, sensation, or feeling **3** not intentional or deliberate – ~**ly** adv – ~**ness** n

²**unconscious** n the part of the mind that does not ordinarily enter a person's awareness but nevertheless influences behaviour and may be manifested in dreams or slips of the tongue

uncouth /ʌn'kuːθ/ adj awkward and uncultivated in speech or manner; boorish – ~**ly** adv – ~**ness** n

uncover /ʌn'kʌvə'/ v to disclose, reveal

¹**under** /'ʌndə'/ adv **1** in or to a position below or beneath sthg **2a** in or to a lower rank or number (e g £10 or under) **b** to a subnormal degree; deficiently – often in combination (e g under-financed) **3** in or into a condition of subjection, subordination, or unconsciousness **4** so as to be covered, buried, or sheltered

²**under** prep **1a** below or beneath so as to be overhung, surmounted, covered, protected, or hidden **b** using as a pseudonym or alias **2a**(1) subject to the authority, control, guidance, or instruction of (2) during the rule or control of **b** receiving or undergoing the action or effect of (e g under treatment) **3** within the group or designation of (e g under this heading) **4** less than or inferior to; esp falling short of (a standard or required degree)

³**under** adj **1a** lying or placed below, beneath, or on the lower side **b** facing or pointing downwards **2** lower in rank or authority; subordinate **3** lower than usual, proper, or desired in amount or degree USE often in combination

undercarriage /'ʌndəˌkærɪdʒ/ n the part of an aircraft's structure that supports its weight, when in contact with the land or water

undercover /ˌʌndə'kʌvə'/ adj acting or done in secret; specif engaged in spying

undergo /ˌʌndə'gəʊ/ v to be subjected to; experience

¹**underground** /'ʌndəgraʊnd/ adv **1** beneath the surface of the earth **2** in or into hiding or secret operation

²**underground** /'ʌndəgraʊnd/ adj **1** growing, operating, or situated below the surface of the ground **2a** conducted in hiding or in secret **b** existing or operated outside the establishment, esp by the avant-garde

³**underground** /'ʌndəgraʊnd/ n **1** sing or pl in constr **a** a secret movement or group esp in an occupied country, for concerted resistive action **b** a usu avant-garde group or movement that functions outside the establishment **2** Br a usu electric underground urban railway; also a train running in an underground

underline /ˌʌndə'laɪn/ v to emphasize, stress

undermine /ˌʌndə'maɪn/ v to weaken or destroy gradually or insidiously

¹**underneath** /ˌʌndə'niːθ/ prep directly below; close under

²**underneath** adv **1** under or below an object or a surface; beneath **2** on the lower side

underpants /'ʌndəpænts/ n pl men's pants

understand /ˌʌndə'stænd/ v **1a** to grasp the meaning of; comprehend **b** to have a thorough knowledge of or expertise in **2** to assume, suppose **3** to interpret in one of a number of possible ways **4** to show a sympathetic or tolerant attitude – ~**able** adj – ~**ably** adv

¹**understanding** /ˌʌndə'stændɪŋ/ n **1a** a mental grasp; comprehension **2** the power of comprehending; intelligence; esp the power to make experience intelligible by applying concepts **3a** a friendly or harmonious relationship **b** an informal mutual agreement

²**understanding** adj tolerant, sympathetic

understate /ˌʌndə'steɪt/ v **1** to state as being less than is the case **2** to present with restraint, esp for greater effect – ~**ment**

undertake /ˌʌndə'teɪk/ v **1** to take upon oneself as a task **2** to put oneself under obligation to do; contract **3** to guarantee, promise

undertaker /'ʌndəˌteɪkə'/ n sby whose business is preparing the dead for burial and arranging and managing funerals

underwater /ˌʌndə'wɔːtə'/ adj **1** situated, used, or designed to operate below the surface of the water **2** being below the waterline of a ship

underwear /'ʌndəweə'/ n clothing worn next to the skin and under other clothing

underworld /'ʌndəwɜːld/ n **1** the place of departed souls; Hades **2** the world of organized crime

undesirable /ˌʌndɪ'zaɪərəbəl/ n or adj (sby or sthg) unwanted or objectionable

undo /ʌn'duː/ v **1** to open or loosen by releasing a fastening **2** to reverse or cancel out the effects of **3** to destroy the standing, reputation, hopes, etc of

undoing /ʌn'duːɪŋ/ n (a cause of) ruin or downfall

undoubted /ʌn'daʊtɪd/ adj not disputed; genuine – ~**ly** adv

¹**undress** /ʌn'dres/ v to take off (one's) clothes

²**undress** n a state of having little or no clothing on

undue /ʌn'djuː/ adj **1** not yet due **2** excessive, immoderate

uneasy /ʌn'iːzi/ adj **1** uncomfortable, awkward **2** apprehensive, worried **3** precarious, unstable – ~**ily** adv – ~**iness** n

unemployed /ˌʌnɪm'plɔɪd/ adj **1** not engaged in a job **2** not invested

unemployment /ˌʌnɪm'plɔɪmənt/ n the state of being unemployed; lack of available employment

unfold /ʌn'fəʊld/ v **1** to open from a folded state **2** to open out gradually to the mind or eye

¹**unfortunate** /ʌn'fɔːtʃʊn‚t/ adj **1a** unsuccessful, unlucky **b** accompanied by or resulting in misfortune **2** unsuitable, inappropriate

²**unfortunate** n an unfortunate person

unfortunately /ʌn'fɔːtʃʊn‚tli/ adv **1** in an unfortunate manner **2** as is unfortunate

unheard-of adj previously unknown; unprecedented

¹**uniform** /'juːn‚fɔːm/ adj **1** not varying in character, appearance, quantity, etc **2** conforming to a rule, pattern, or practice; consonant – ~ **ity** n – ~ **ly** adv

²**uniform** n dress of a distinctive design or fashion worn by members of a particular group and serving as a means of identification – ~ **ed** adj

unilateral /ˌjuːn‚'lætərəl/ adj **1a** done or undertaken by 1 person or party **b** of or affecting 1 side **2** produced or arranged on or directed towards 1 side – ~ **ly** adv

¹**union** /'juːnɪən/ n **1a(1)** the formation of a single political unit from 2 or more separate and independent units **(2)** a uniting in marriage; also sexual intercourse **b** combination, junction **2a** an association of independent individuals (e g nations) for some common purpose **b** a trade union

²**union** adj of, dealing with, or constituting a union

unique /juː'niːk/ adj **1** sole, only **2** without a like or equal; unequalled **3** very rare or unusual – disapproved of by some speakers – ~ **ly** adv – ~ **ness** n

unit /'juːn‚t/ n **1a(1)** the first and lowest natural number; one **(2)** a single quantity regarded as a whole in calculation **b** the number occupying the position immediately to the left of the decimal point in the Arabic notation; also, pl this position **2** a determinate quantity (e g of length, time, heat, value, or housing) adopted as a standard of measurement **3** a part of a military establishment that has a prescribed organization (e g of personnel and supplies)

unite /juː'naɪt/ **1** to join together to form a single unit **2** to link by a legal or moral bond **3** to act in concert

united /juː'naɪt‚d/ adj **1** combined, joined **2** relating to or produced by joint action **3** in agreement; harmonious – ~ **ly** adv

unity /'juːn‚ti/ n **1a** the state of being 1 or united **b** a definite amount taken as 1 or for which 1 is made to stand in calculation **2a** concord, harmony **b** continuity and agreement in aims and interests

¹**universal** /ˌjuːn‚'vɜːsəl/ adj **1** including or covering all or a whole without limit or exception **2** present or occurring everywhere or under all conditions

²**universal** n a general concept or term

universe /'juːn‚vɜːs/ n **1a** all things that exist; the cosmos **b** a galaxy **2** the whole world; everyone

university /ˌjuːn‚'vɜːs‚ti/ n (the premises of) an institution of higher learning that provides facilities for full-time teaching and research and is authorized to grant academic degrees

¹**unknown** /ˌʌn'nəʊn/ adj not known; also having an unknown value

²**unknown** n a person who is little known (e g to the public)

unless /ʌn'les, ən-/ conj **1** except on the condition that **2** without the necessary accompaniment that; except when

¹**unlike** /ʌn'laɪk/ prep **1** different from **2** not characteristic of **3** in a different manner from

²**unlike** /ʌn'laɪk/ adj **1** marked by dissimilarity; different **2** unequal

unlikely /ʌn'laɪkli/ adj **1** having a low probability of being or occurring **2** not believable; improbable **3** likely to fail; unpromising **4** not foreseen (e g the unlikely result) – **liness, -lihood** n

unload /ʌn'ləʊd/ v **1a** to take (cargo) off or out **b** to give vent to; pour forth **2** to relieve of sthg burdensome **3** to draw the charge from – ~ **er** n

unlock /ʌn'lɒk/ v **1** to unfasten the lock of **2** to open, release

unmistakable /ˌʌnm‚'steɪkəbəl/ adj clear, obvious – **bly** adv

unpleasant /ʌn'plezənt/ adj not pleasant or agreeable; displeasing – ~ **ly** adv – ~ **ness** n

unreasonable /ʌn'riːzənəbəl/ adj **1** not governed by or acting according to reason **2** excessive, immoderate – **bly** adv – ~ **ness** n

untie /ʌn'taɪ/ v **1** to free from sthg that fastens or restrains **2a** to separate out the knotted parts of **b** to disentangle, resolve

¹**until** /ʌn'tɪl, ən-/ prep **1** up to as late as **2** up to as far as

²**until** conj up to the time that; until such time as

unusual /ʌn'juːʒʊəl, -ʒəl/ adj **1** uncommon, rare **2** different, unique – ~ **ly** adv

unwell /ʌn'wel/ adj in poor health

¹**up** /ʌp/ adv **1a** at or towards a relatively high level **b** from beneath the ground or water to the surface **c** above the horizon **d** upstream **e** in or to a raised or upright position; specif out of bed **f** off or out of the ground or a surface (e g pull up a daisy) **g** to the top; esp so as to be full **2a** into a state of, or with, greater intensity or activity (e g speak up) **b** into a faster pace or higher gear **3a** in or into a relatively high condition or status – sometimes used interjectionally as an expression of approval (e g up BBC2!) **b** above a normal or former level: e g **(1)** upwards **(2)** higher in price **c** ahead of an opponent (e g we're 3 points up) **4a(1)** in or into existence, prominence, or prevalence (e g new houses haven't been up long) **(2)** in or into operation or full power (e g get up steam) **b** under consideration or attention; esp before a court **5** so as to be together (e g add up

the figures) **6a** entirely, completely (e g eat *up* your spinach) **b** so as to be firmly closed, joined, or fastened **c** so as to be fully inflated **7** in or into storage **8** in a direction conventionally the opposite of down: **a**(1) to windward (2) with rudder to leeward – used with reference to a ship's helm **b** in or towards the north **c** so as to arrive or approach (e g walked *up* to her) **d** to or at the rear of a theatrical stage **e** *chiefly Br* to or in the capital of a country or a university city (e g *up* in London) **9** in or into parts (e g chop *up*) **10** to a stop – usu + *draw, bring, fetch,* or *pull*

²**up** *adj* **1** moving, inclining, bound, or directed upwards or up **2** ready, prepared (e g dinner's *up*) **3** going on, taking place; *esp* being the matter (e g what's *up*?) **4** at an end; *esp* hopeless (e g it's all *up* with him now) **5** well informed **6** *of a road* being repaired; having a broken surface **7** ahead of an opponent **8** *of a ball in court games* having bounced only once on the ground or floor after being hit by one's opponent and therefore playable **9** *Br, of a train* travelling towards a large town; *specif* travelling towards London

³**up** *v* **1** – used with *and* and another verb to indicate that the action of the following verb is either surprisingly or abruptly initiated (e g he *upped* and married) **2** to increase

⁴**up** *prep* **1a** up along, round, through, towards, in, into, or on **b** at the top of (e g the office is *up* those stairs) **2** *Br* (up) to (e g going *up* the West End) – nonstandard

⁵**up** *n* **1** (sthg in) a high position or an upward incline **2** a period or state of prosperity or success

upheaval /ʌp'hiːvəl/ *n* (an instance of) extreme agitation or radical change

¹**uphill** /ʌp'hil/ *adv* upwards on a hill or incline

²**uphill** /ʌp'hil/ *adj* **1** situated on elevated ground **2** going up; ascending **3** difficult, laborious

uphold /ʌp'həʊld/ *v* **1** to give support to; maintain **2** to support against an opponent or challenge – ~ **er** *n*

upon /ə'pɒn/ *prep* on – chiefly *fml*

¹**upper** /'ʌpə/ *adj* **1a** higher in physical position, rank, or order **b** farther inland **2** being the branch of a legislature consisting of 2 houses that is usu more restricted in membership, is in many cases less powerful, and possesses greater traditional prestige than the lower house

²**upper** *n* the parts of a shoe or boot above the sole

³**upper** *n* a stimulant drug; *esp* amphetamine – *infml*

¹**upright** /'ʌp-raɪt/ *adj* **1a** perpendicular, vertical **b** erect in carriage or posture **2** marked by strong moral rectitude – ~ **ly** *adv* – ~ **ness** *n*

²**upright** *adv* in an upright or vertical position

³**upright** *n* **1** sthg that stands upright **2**

upright, upright piano a piano with vertical frame and strings

uprising /'ʌp,raɪzɪŋ/ *n* a usu localized rebellion

uproar /'ʌp-rɔː/ *n* a state of commotion or violent disturbance

¹**upset** /ʌp'set/ *v* **1** to overturn, knock over **2a** to trouble mentally or emotionally **b** to throw into disorder **3** to make somewhat ill

²**upset** /'ʌp'set/ *n* **1** a minor physical disorder **2** an emotional disturbance **3** an unexpected defeat (e g in politics)

upside down /ʌpsaɪd 'daʊn/ *adv* **1** with the upper and the lower parts reversed **2** in or into great disorder or confusion

¹**upstairs** /ʌp'steəz/ *adv* **1** up the stairs; to or on a higher floor **2** to or at a higher position

²**upstairs** *adj* situated above the stairs, esp on an upper floor

³**upstairs** *n pl but sing or pl in constr* the part of a building above the ground floor

up to *prep* **1** – used to indicate an upward limit or boundary **2** as far as; until **3a** equal to **b** good enough for **4** engaged in (a suspect activity) (e g what's he *up* to?) **5** being the responsibility of (e g it's *up* to me)

up-to-date *adj* **1** including the latest information **2** abreast of the times; modern

upward /'ʌpwəd/ *adj* moving or extending upwards; ascending

upwards /'ʌpwədz/-ər-/ *adv* **1a** from a lower to a higher place, condition, or level; in the opposite direction from down **b** so as to expose a particular surface (e g turned the cards *upwards*) **2a** to an indefinitely greater amount, price, figure, age, or rank (e g from £5 *upwards*)

urban /'ɜːbən/ *adj* (characteristic) of or constituting a city or town

¹**urge** /ɜːdʒ/ *v* **1** to advocate or demand earnestly or pressingly **2** to try to persuade **3** to force or impel in a specified direction or to greater speed

²**urge** *n* a force or impulse that urges

urgent /'ɜːdʒənt/ *adj* **1** calling for immediate attention; pressing **2** conveying a sense of urgency – ~ **ly** *adv* – **-gency** *n*

urine /'juərɪn/ *n* waste material that is secreted by the kidney in vertebrates and forms a clear amber and usu slightly acid fluid

us /əs, s; *strong* ʌs/ *pron* **1** *objective case of* **we 2** *chiefly Br* me – nonstandard

¹**use** /juːs/ *n* **1a** using or being used **b** a way of using sthg **2** habitual or customary usage **3a** the right or benefit of using sthg **b** the ability or power to use sthg (e g a limb) **4a** a purpose or end **b** practical worth or application

²**use** /juːz/ *v* **1** to put into action or service **2** to carry out sthg by means of **3** to expend or consume **4** to treat in a specified manner **5** – used in the past with *to* to indicate a former fact or state – **user** *n* – **usable** *adj*

used /ju:zd; *sense* 3 ju:st/ *adj* **1** employed in accomplishing sthg **2** that has endured use; *specif* secondhand **3** accustomed

useful /'ju:sfəl/ *adj* **1** having utility, esp practical worth or applicability; *also* helpful **2** of highly satisfactory quality – ~ **ly** *adv* – ~ **ness** *n*

useless /'ju:sl̵ɪs/ *adj* having or being of no use **2** inept – infml – ~ **ly** *adv* – ~ **ness** *n*

usual /'ju:ʒəl, 'ju:ʒəl/ *adj* **1** in accordance with usage, custom, or habit; normal **2** commonly or ordinarily used – ~ **ly** *adv*

utensil /ju:'tensəl/ *n* **1** an implement, vessel, or device used in the household, esp the kitchen **2** a useful tool or implement

¹utmost /'ʌtməʊst/ *adj* **1** situated at the farthest or most distant point; extreme **2** of the greatest or highest degree

²utmost *n* **1** the highest point or degree **2** the best of one's abilities, powers, etc

¹utter /'ʌtə'/ *adj* absolute, total – ~ **ly** *adv*

²utter *v* **1** to emit as a sound **2** to give (verbal) expression to – ~ **ance** *n*

V

vacancy /'veɪkənsi/ *n* **1** physical or mental inactivity; idleness **2** a vacant office, post, or room **3** an empty space

vacant /'veɪkənt/ *adj* **1** without an occupant **2** free from activity or work **3a** stupid, foolish **b** expressionless – ~ **ly** *adv*

vacate /və'keɪt, veɪ-/ *v* to give up the possession or occupancy of

¹vacation /və'keɪʃən/ *n* **1** a scheduled period during which activity (e g of a university) is suspended **2** *chiefly NAm* a holiday

²vacation *v, chiefly NAm* to take or spend a holiday

vaccinate /'væksl̵neɪt/ *v* to administer a vaccine to, usu by injection – -**ation** *n*

vaccine /'væksi:n/ *n* material (e g a preparation of killed or modified virus or bacteria) used in vaccinating to produce an immunity

¹vacuum /'vækjʊəm/ *n* **1a** a space absolutely devoid of matter **b** an air pressure below atmospheric pressure **2a** a vacant space; a void **b** a state of isolation from outside influences **3** a vacuum cleaner

²vacuum *v* to clean using a vacuum cleaner

vacuum cleaner *n* an (electrical) appliance for removing dust and dirt (e g from carpets or upholstery) by suction

vague /veɪg/ *adj* **1a** not clearly defined, expressed, or understood; indistinct **b** not clearly felt or sensed **2** not thinking or expressing one's thoughts clearly – ~ **ly** *adv* – ~ **ness** *adv*

vain /veɪn/ *adj* **1** unsuccessful, ineffectual **2** having or showing excessive pride in one's appearance, ability, etc; conceited – ~ **ly** *adv*

valiant /'væliənt/ *adj* characterized by or showing valour; courageous – ~ **ly** *adv*

valid /'væll̵d/ *adj* **1** having legal efficacy; *esp* executed according to the proper formalities **2** well-grounded or justifiable; relevant and meaningful – ~ **ity** *n* – ~ **ly** *adv*

valley /'væli/ *n* **1** an elongated depression of the earth's surface, usu between hills or mountains **2** a hollow, depression

¹valuable /'væljʊəbəl/ *adj* **1** having (high) money value **2** of great use or worth

²valuable *n* a usu personal possession of relatively great money value – usu *pl*

¹value /'vælju:/ *n* **1** a fair return or equivalent for sthg exchanged **2** the worth in money or commodities of sthg **3** relative worth, utility, or importance **4** a numerical quantity assigned or computed **5** sthg (e g a principle or quality) intrinsically valuable or desirable – ~ **less** *adj*

²value *v* **1a** to estimate the worth of in terms of money **b** to rate in terms of usefulness, importance, etc **2** to consider or rate highly; esteem – ~ **ation** *n*

valve /vælv/ *n* **1** a structure, esp in the heart or a vein, that closes temporarily to obstruct passage of material or permits movement of fluid in 1 direction only **2a** any of numerous mechanical devices by which the flow of liquid, gas, or loose material in bulk may be controlled, usu to allow movement in 1 direction only **b** a device in a brass musical instrument for quickly varying the tube length in order to change the fundamental tone by a definite interval **3** any of the separate joined pieces that make up the shell of an (invertebrate) animal; *specif* either of the 2 halves of the shell of a bivalve mollusc **4** *chiefly Br* a vacuum- or gas-filled device for the regulation of electric current by the control of free electrons or ions

¹van *n* the vanguard

²van *n* **1** an enclosed motor vehicle used for transport of goods, animals, furniture, etc **2** *chiefly Br* an enclosed railway goods wagon

vandal /'vændl/ *n* **1** *cap* a member of a Germanic people who overran Gaul, Spain, and N Africa in the 4th and 5th c AD and in 455 sacked Rome **2** one who wilfully or ignorantly destroys or defaces (public) property

vandalism /'vændəl-ɪzəm/ *n* wilful destruction or defacement of property – -**ize** *v*

vanguard /'vængɑ:d/ *n* **1** *sing or pl in constr* the troops moving at the head of an army **2** the forefront of an action or movement

vanish /'vænɪʃ/ 1 to pass quickly from sight; disappear 2 to cease to exist

vanity /'vænₔti/ n 1 worthlessness 2 excessive pride in oneself; conceit

vapour /'veɪpə/, n 1 smoke, fog, etc suspended floating in the air and impairing its transparency 2 a substance in the gaseous state; esp such a substance that is liquid under normal conditions – -ize v

¹**variable** /'veəriəbəl/ adj 1 subject to variation or changes 2 having the characteristics of a variable – -bly adv – ~ness n

²**variable** n 1 sthg (e g a variable star) that is variable 2 (a symbol representing) a quantity that may assume any of a set of values

variation /,veəri'eɪʃən/ n 1a varying or being varied b an instance of varying c the extent to which or the range in which a thing varies 2 the repetition of a musical theme with modifications in rhythm, tune, harmony, or key 3 divergence in characteristics of an organism or genotype from those typical or usual of its group 4 a solo dance in ballet

varied /'veəriɪd/ adj 1 having numerous forms or types; diverse 2 variegated

variety /vɔ'raɪɔti/ n 1 the state of having different forms or types; diversity 2 an assortment of different things, esp of a particular class 3a sthg differing from others of the same general kind; a sort b any of various groups of plants or animals ranking below a species 4 theatrical entertainment consisting of separate performances (e g of songs, skits, acrobatics, etc)

various /'veəriɔs/ adj 1a of differing kinds; diverse b dissimilar in nature or form; unlike 2 having a number of different aspects or characteristics 3 more than one; several

¹**varnish** /'vɑːnɪʃ/ n 1 a liquid preparation that forms a hard shiny transparent coating on drying 2 outside show

²**varnish** v 1 to apply varnish to 2 to gloss over

vary /'veəri/ v 1 to exhibit or undergo change 2 to deviate

vase /vɑːz/ n an ornamental vessel usu of greater depth than width, used esp for holding flowers

vast /vɑːst/ adj very great in amount, degree, intensity, or esp in extent or range

¹**vault** /vɔːlt/ n 1 an arched structure of masonry, usu forming a ceiling or roof 2a an underground passage, room, or storage compartment b a room or compartment for the safekeeping of valuables 3 a burial chamber, esp beneath a church or in a cemetery

²**vault** v to form or cover (as if) with a vault

³**vault** v to bound vigorously (over); esp to execute a leap (over) using the hands or a pole – ~er n

⁴**vault** n an act of vaulting

veal /viːl/ n the flesh of a young calf used as food

¹**vegetable** /'vedʒtəbəl/ adj 1a of, constituting, or growing like plants b consisting of plants 2 made or obtained from plants or plant products

²**vegetable** n 1a a plant 2 a plant (e g the cabbage, bean, or potato) grown for an edible part which is usu eaten with the principal course of a meal; also this part of the plant 3 a person whose physical and esp mental capacities are severely impaired by illness or injury

vegetation /,vedʒₔ'teɪʃən/ n plant life or total plant cover (e g of an area)

vehicle /'viːₔkəl/ n 1 any of various usu liquid media acting esp as solvents, carriers, or binders for active ingredients (e g drugs) or pigments 2 a means of transmission; a carrier 3 a medium through which sthg is expressed or communicated 4 a motor vehicle

¹**veil** /veɪl/ n 1a a length of cloth worn by women as a covering for the head and shoulders and often, esp in eastern countries, the face b a piece of sheer fabric attached for protection or ornament to a hat or headdress 2 the cloistered life of a nun 3 a concealing curtain or cover of cloth 4 a disguise, pretext – ~ed adj

²**veil** v to cover, provide, or conceal (as if) with a veil

vein /veɪn/ n 1 a deposit of ore, coal, etc, esp in a rock fissure 2 any of the tubular converging vessels that carry blood from the capillaries towards the heart 3a any of the vascular bundles forming the framework of a leaf b any of the ribs that serve to stiffen the wings of an insect 4 a streak or marking suggesting a vein (e g in marble) 5 a distinctive element or quality; a strain

²**vein** v to pattern (as if) with veins

velvet /'velvₔt/ n 1 a fabric (e g of silk, rayon, or cotton) characterized by a short soft dense pile 2 sthg suggesting velvet in softness, smoothness, etc – ~y adj

vend /vend/ v to sell, esp by means of a vending machine – ~or n

¹**veneer** /vₔ'nɪə/ n 1 a thin layer of wood of superior appearance or hardness used esp to give a decorative finish (e g to joinery) 2 a protective or ornamental facing (e g of brick or stone) 3 a superficial or deceptively attractive appearance

²**veneer** v 1 to overlay (e g a common wood) with veneer; broadly to face with a material giving a superior surface 2 to conceal under a superficial and deceptive attractiveness

venereal disease /vₔ'nɪəriəl/ n a contagious disease (e g gonorrhoea or syphilis) that is typically acquired during sexual intercourse

vengeance /'vendʒₔns/ n punishment inflicted in retaliation for injury or offence

venom /'venₔm/ n 1 poisonous matter normally secreted by snakes, scorpions, bees, etc and transmitted chiefly by biting or stinging 2 ill will, malevolence

venomous /'venₔmₔs/ adj 1a poisonous b spiteful, malevolent 2 able to inflict a poisoned wound – ~ly adv

ventilate /'ventᵻleɪt/ v 1 to examine freely and openly; expose publicly 2 to cause fresh air to circulate through – -lation n

ventriloquism /ven'trɪləkwɪzəm/ n the production of the voice in such a manner that the sound appears to come from a source other than the vocal organs of the speaker and esp from a dummy manipulated by the producer of the sound – -ist n

¹**venture** /'ventʃə'/ 1 to proceed despite danger; dare to go or do 2 to offer at the risk of opposition or censure

²**venture** n 1 an undertaking involving chance, risk, or danger, esp in business 2 sthg (e g money or property) at risk in a speculative venture – ~ r n

veranda n a usu roofed open structure attached to the outside of a building

verb /vɜːb/ n any of a class of words that characteristically are the grammatical centre of a predicate and express an act, occurrence, or mode of being

¹**verbal** /'vɜːbəl/ adj 1 of, involving, or expressed in words 2 of or formed from a verb 3 spoken rather than written; oral 4 verbatim, word-for-word

²**verbal** n Br a spoken statement; esp one made to the police admitting or implying guilt and used in evidence

verdict /'vɜːdɪkt/ n 1 the decision of a jury on the matter submitted to them 2 an opinion, judgment

¹**verge** /vɜːdʒ/ n 1 an outer margin of an object or structural part 2 the brink, threshold 3 Br a surfaced or planted strip of land at the side of a road

²**verge** v to move or extend towards a specified condition

verify /'verᵻfaɪ/ v 1 to ascertain the truth, accuracy, or reality of 2 to bear out, fulfil – -fiable adj – -fication n

vermin /'vɜːmᵻn/ n 1 pl lice, rats, or other common harmful or objectionable animals 2 an offensive person – ~ous adj

versatile /'vɜːsətaɪl/ adj 1 embracing a variety of subjects, fields, or skills; also turning with ease from one thing to another 2 having many uses or applications – -tility n

verse /vɜːs/ n 1 a line of metrical writing 2 poetry; esp undistinguished poetry 3 a stanza 4 any of the short divisions into which a chapter of the Bible is traditionally divided

version /'vɜːʃən/ n 1 an account or description from a particular point of view, esp as contrasted with another account 2 an adaptation of a work of art into another medium 3 a form or variant of a type or original

versus /'vɜːsəs/ prep 1 against 2 in contrast to or as the alternative of

vertical /'vɜːtɪkəl/ adj 1 situated at the highest point; directly overhead or in the zenith 2 perpendicular to the plane of the horizon 3 of or concerning the relationships between people of different rank in a hierarchy – ~ly adv

¹**very** /'veri/ adj 1 properly so called; actual, genuine 2 absolute (e g the very

thing for the purpose) 3 being no more than; mere (e g the very thought terrified me) USE used attributively

²**very** adv 1 to a high degree; exceedingly 2 – used as an intensive to emphasize same, own, as or the superlative degree

vessel /'vesəl/ n 1 a hollow utensil (e g a jug, cup, or bowl) for holding esp liquid 2 a large hollow structure designed to float on and move through water carrying a crew, passengers, or cargo 3a a tube or canal (e g an artery) in which a body fluid is contained and conveyed or circulated b a conducting tube in a plant

¹**vest** /vest/ v 1 to endow with a particular authority, right, or property 2 to robe in ecclesiastical vestments

²**vest** n 1 chiefly Br a usu sleeveless undergarment for the upper body 2 chiefly NAm a waistcoat

vestige /'vestɪdʒ/ n 1a a trace or visible sign left by sthg vanished or lost b a minute remaining amount 2 a small or imperfectly formed body part or organ that remains from one more fully developed in an earlier stage of the individual, in a past generation, or in closely related forms – -gial adj

¹**vet** /vet/ n sby qualified and authorized to treat diseases and injuries of animals

²**vet** v chiefly Br to subject to careful and thorough appraisal

veteran /'vetərən/ n 1 sby who has had long experience of an occupation, skill, or (military) service 2 veteran, veteran car Br an old motor car; specif one built before 1916 3 NAm a former serviceman

vex /veks/ v vexed also vext 1a to bring distress, discomfort, or agitation to b to irritate or annoy by petty provocations; harass 2 to puzzle, baffle – ~ation n – ~atious adj – ~atiously

via /'vaɪə/ prep 1 passing through or calling at (a place) on the way 2 through the medium of; also by means of

viable /'vaɪəbəl/ adj 1 (born alive and developed enough to be) capable of living 2 capable of working; practicable – -bility n – -bly adv

vibrate /vaɪ'breɪt/ v 1 to move to and fro; oscillate 2 to have an effect as of vibration; throb 3 to be in a state of vibration; quiver 4 to emit (e g sound) (as if) with a vibratory motion

vibration /vaɪ'breɪʃən/ n 1a a periodic motion of the particles of an elastic body or medium in alternately opposite directions from a position of equilibrium b an oscillation or quivering 2 a distinctive usu emotional atmosphere capable of being sensed – usu pl with sing. meaning – -tory adj

vicar /'vɪkə'/ n a Church of England incumbent receiving a stipend but formerly not the tithes of a parish

¹**vice** /vaɪs/ n 1a moral depravity or corruption; wickedness b a habitual and usu minor fault or shortcoming 2 sexual immorality; esp prostitution

²**vice, NAm chiefly vise** n any of various

tools, usu attached to a workbench, that have 2 jaws that close for holding work by operation of a screw, lever, or cam

vice versa /ˌvaɪs 'vɜːsə, ˌvaɪsɪ-/ *adv* with the order changed and relations reversed; conversely

vicinity /vɪ'sɪnɪti/ *n* **1** a surrounding area or district **2** being near; proximity – *fml*

vicious /'vɪʃəs/ *adj* **1** having the nature or quality of vice; depraved **2** unpleasantly fierce, malignant, or severe **3** malicious, spiteful – ~ly *adv* – ~ness *n*

victim /'vɪktɪm/ *n* sby or sthg that is adversely affected by a force or agent: e g **a** one who or that which is injured, destroyed, or subjected to oppression or mistreatment **b** a dupe, prey – ~ize *v*

victor /'vɪktə/ *n* a person, country, etc that defeats an enemy or opponent; a winner

victorious /vɪk'tɔːrɪəs/ *adj* **1a** having won a victory **b** (characteristic) of victory **2** successful, triumphant – ~ly *adv*

victory /'vɪktəri/ *n* **1** the overcoming of an enemy or antagonist **2** achievement of mastery or success in a struggle or endeavour

¹video /'vɪdɪəʊ/ *adj* of a form of magnetic recording for reproduction on a television screen

²video *n* video, videorecorder, videocassette recorder a machine for videotaping

videotape /'vɪdɪəʊteɪp/ *v* to make a recording of (e g sthg that is televised) on magnetic tape

¹view /vjuː/ *n* **1** the act of seeing or examining; inspection; *also* a survey **2** a way of regarding sthg; an opinion **3** a scene, prospect; *also* an aspect **4** extent or range of vision; sight **5** an intention, object **6** a pictorial representation

²view *v* **1a** to see, watch; *also* to watch television **b** to look on in a specified way; regard **2** to look at attentively; inspect

viewpoint /'vjuːpɔɪnt/ *n* a standpoint; point of view

vigilant /'vɪdʒɪlənt/ *adj* alert and watchful, esp to avoid danger – ~ly *adv* – -ance *n*

vigorous /'vɪgərəs/ *adj* **1** possessing or showing vigour; full of active strength **2** done with vigour; carried out forcefully and energetically – ~ly *adv*

vigour /'vɪgə/ *n* **1** active physical or mental strength or force **2** active healthy well-balanced growth, esp of plants **3** intensity of action or effect; force

vile /vaɪl/ *adj* **1a** morally despicable or abhorrent **b** physically repulsive; foul **2** tending to degrade **3** disgustingly or utterly bad; contemptible – ~ly *adv* – ~ness *n*

village /'vɪlɪdʒ/ *n* a group of dwellings in the country, larger than a hamlet and smaller than a town

villain /'vɪlən/ *n* **1** a scoundrel, rascal; *also* a criminal **2** a character in a story or play whose evil actions affect the plot – ~ous *adj*

vine /vaɪn/ *n* **1** the climbing plant that bears grapes **2** (a plant with) a stem that requires support and that climbs by tendrils or twining

vinegar /'vɪnɪgə/ *n* a sour liquid obtained esp by acetic fermentation of wine, cider, etc and used as a condiment or preservative – ~y *adj*

¹vintage /'vɪntɪdʒ/ *n* **1a** wine, specif one of a particular type, region, and year and usu of superior quality that is dated and allowed to mature **b** a collection of contemporary and similar people or things; a crop **2** the act or time of harvesting grapes or making wine

²vintage *adj* **1** of a vintage; *esp* being a product of 1 particular year rather than a blend of wines from different years **2** of the best and most characteristic; classic **3** *Br, of a motor vehicle* built between 1917 and 1930

violate /'vaɪəleɪt/ *v* **1** to fail to comply with; infringe **2** to do harm to; *specif* to rape – -lation *n*

violence /'vaɪələns/ *n* **1** (an instance of) exertion of physical force so as to injure or abuse **2** (an instance of) unjust or unwarranted distortion; outrage **3a** intense or turbulent action or force **b** (an instance of) vehement feeling or expression; fervour

violent /'vaɪələnt/ *adj* **1** marked by extreme force or sudden intense activity **2** notably furious or vehement; *also* excited or mentally disordered to the point of loss of self-control – ~ly *adv*

violet /'vaɪələt/ *n* **1** any of a genus of plants with often sweet-scented flowers, usu all 1 colour, esp as distinguished from the usu larger-flowered violas and pansies **2** a bluish purple colour

violin /ˌvaɪə'lɪn/ *n* a bowed stringed instrument having a fingerboard with no frets, 4 strings, and a usual range from G below middle C upwards for more than 4½ octaves – ~ist *n*

VIP *n, pl* **VIPs** a person of great influence or prestige

¹virgin /'vɜːdʒɪn/ *n* a person, esp a girl, who has not had sexual intercourse – ~ity *n*

²virgin *adj* **1** free of impurity or stain; unsullied **2** being a virgin **3** characteristic of or befitting a virgin; modest **4** untouched, unexploited; *specif* not altered by human activity

virtual /'vɜːtʃʊəl/ *adj* that is such in essence or effect though not formally recognized or admitted

virtually /'vɜːtʃʊəli/ *adv* almost entirely; for all practical purposes

virtue /'vɜːtʃuː/ *n* **1a** conformity to a standard of right; morality **b** a particular moral excellence **2** a beneficial or commendable quality **3** a capacity to act; potency **4** chastity, esp in a woman

virus /'vaɪərəs/ *n* (a disease caused by) any of a large group of submicroscopic often disease-causing agents that typically consist of a protein coat surrounding an RNA or DNA core and that multiply only in living cells

visibility /ˌvizəˈbilɪti/ n 1 being visible 2 the clearness of the atmosphere as revealed by the greatest distance at which prominent objects can be identified visually with the naked eye

visible /ˈvizəbəl/ adj 1 capable of being seen 2 exposed to view 3 capable of being perceived; noticeable 4 of or being trade in goods rather than services

vision /ˈviʒən/ n 1 sthg (revelatory) seen in a dream, trance, or ecstasy 2 discernment, foresight 3a the act or power of seeing; sight b the sense by which the qualities of an object (e g colour, luminosity, shape, and size) constituting its appearance are perceived and which acts through the eye 4 a lovely or charming sight

¹visit /ˈvizɪt/ v 1a to afflict b to inflict punishment for 2a to pay a call on for reasons of kindness, friendship, ceremony, or business b to go or come to look at or stay at (e g for business or sightseeing)

²visit n 1a an act of visiting; a call b an extended but temporary stay 2 an official or professional call; a visitation

visitor /ˈvizɪtə/ n sby who or sthg that makes (formal) visits

visual /ˈviʒuəl/ adj 1 visible 2 producing mental images; vivid 3 done or executed by sight only

vital /ˈvaitl/ adj 1 concerned with or necessary to the maintenance of life 2 full of life and vigour; animated 3 of the utmost importance; essential to continued worth or well-being

vitality /vaiˈtælɪti/ n 1a the quality which distinguishes the living from the dead or inanimate b capacity to live and develop; also physical or mental liveliness 2 power of enduring

vitamin /ˈvitəmɪn, ˈvai-/ n any of various organic compounds that are essential in minute quantities to the nutrition of most animals and regulate metabolic processes

vivid /ˈvivɪd/ adj 1 of a colour very intense 2 producing a strong or clear impression on the senses; specif producing distinct mental images – ~ly adv – ~ness n

vocabulary /vəˈkæbjuləri, vəʊ-/ n 1 a list of words, and sometimes phrases, usu arranged alphabetically and defined or translated 2 the words employed by a language, group, or individual or in a field of work or knowledge 3 a supply of expressive techniques or devices (e g of an art form)

¹vocal /ˈvəʊkəl/ adj 1 uttered by the voice; oral 2 of, composed or arranged for, or sung by the human voice 3a having or exercising the power of producing voice, speech, or sound b given to strident or insistent expression; outspoken – ~ly adv

²vocal n 1 a vocal sound 2 a usu accompanied musical composition or passage for the voice

vocation /vəʊˈkeiʃən/ n 1 a summons or strong inclination to a particular state or course of action; esp a divine call to the religious life 2 the work in which a person is regularly employed; a career

¹voice /vɔis/ n 1a sound produced by humans, birds, etc by forcing air from the lungs through the larynx in mammals or syrinx in birds b(1) (the use, esp in singing or acting, of) musical sound produced by the vocal cords and resonated by the cavities of the head, throat, lungs, etc (2) any of the melodic parts in a vocal or instrumental composition c the faculty of utterance; speech 2a the expressed wish or opinion b right of expression; say 3 distinction of form or a particular system of inflections of a verb to indicate whether it is the subject of the verb that acts

²voice v 1 to express (a feeling or opinion) in words; utter 2 to adjust (e g an organ pipe) in manufacture, for producing the proper musical sounds

volcano /vɒlˈkeinəʊ/ n, pl volcanoes, volcanos 1 (a hill or mountain surrounding) an outlet in a planet's crust from which molten or hot rock and steam issue 2 a dynamic or violently creative person; also a situation liable to become violent

¹volley /ˈvɒli/ n 1a simultaneous discharge of a number of missile weapons b a return or succession of returns made by hitting a ball, shuttle, etc before it touches the ground 2 a burst or emission of many things at once or in rapid succession

²volley v 1 to discharge (as if) in a volley 2 to propel (an object that has not yet hit the ground), esp with an implement or the hand or foot

volt /vəʊlt/ n the derived SI unit of electrical potential difference and electromotive force equal to the difference of potential between 2 points in a conducting wire carrying a constant current of 1 ampere when the power dissipated between these 2 points is equal to 1 watt

voltage /ˈvəʊltɪdʒ/ n an electric potential difference; electromotive force

volume /ˈvɒljuːm/ n 1a a series of printed sheets bound typically in book form; a book b a series of issues of a periodical 2 space occupied as measured in cubic units (e g litres); cubic capacity 3a an amount; also a bulk, mass b (the representation of) mass in art or architecture c a considerable quantity; a great deal – often pl with sing. meaning; esp in speak volumes for 4 the degree of loudness or the intensity of a sound

voluminous /vəˈluːmɪnəs, vəˈljuː-/ adj 1 having or containing a large volume; specif, of a garment very full 2 writing much or at great length – ~ly adv – ~ness n

¹voluntary /ˈvɒləntəri/ adj 1 proceeding from free choice or consent 2 intentional 3 provided or supported by voluntary action – -tarily adv

²**voluntary** n an organ piece played before or after a religious service

¹**volunteer** /ˌvɒlən'tɪə/ n one who undertakes a service of his/her own free will; *esp* sby who enters into military service voluntarily

²**volunteer** adj being, consisting of, or engaged in by volunteers

³**volunteer** v 1 to communicate voluntarily; say 2 to offer oneself as a volunteer

¹**vomit** /'vɒmɪt/ n a vomiting; *also* the vomited matter

²**vomit** /'vɒmɪt/ v 1 to disgorge (the contents of the stomach) through the mouth 2 to eject (sthg) violently or abundantly; spew

¹**vote** /vəʊt/ n 1 a ballot 2 the collective verdict of a body of people expressed by voting 3 *the* franchise 4 a sum of money voted for a special use

²**vote** v 1 to cast one's vote; *esp* to exercise a political franchise 2a to judge by general agreement; declare b to offer as a suggestion; propose

voucher /'vaʊtʃə/ n, *Br* a ticket that can be exchanged for specific goods or services

¹**vow** /vaʊ/ n a solemn and often religiously binding promise or assertion; *specif* one by which a person binds him-/herself to an act, service, or condition

²**vow** v 1 to promise solemnly; swear 2 to resolve to bring about

vowel /'vaʊəl/ n (a letter, in English usu a, e, i, o, u, and sometimes y, representing) any of a class of speech sounds (e g /i:, a:, ʌ, etc/) characterized by lack of closure in the breath channel or lack of audible friction

¹**voyage** /'vɔɪ-ɪdʒ/ n a considerable course or period of travelling by other than land routes; *broadly* a journey

²**voyage** v to make a voyage (across) – ~**r** n

vulgar /'vʌlgə/ adj 1 generally used, applied, or accepted 2a of or being the common people; plebeian b generally current; public 3a lacking in cultivation, breeding, or taste; coarse b ostentatious or excessive in expenditure or display; pretentious 4 lewdly or profanely indecent; obscene – ~**ize** v – ~**ly** adv

vulnerable /'vʌlnərəbəl/ adj 1 capable of being physically or mentally wounded 2 open to attack or damage; assailable – -**bility** n – -**bly** adv

vulture /'vʌltʃə/ n any of various large usu bald-headed birds of prey that are related to the hawks, eagles, and falcons and feed on carrion

W

¹**wad** /wɒd/ n 1a a soft mass, esp of a loose fibrous material, variously used (e g to stop an aperture or pad a gar-

ment) b a soft plug used to retain a powder charge, esp in a muzzle-loading cannon or gun 2 a roll of paper money

²**wad** v 1 to form into a wad or wadding 2 to stuff, pad, or line with some soft substance

¹**waddle** /'wɒdl/ v 1 to walk with short steps swinging the forepart of the body from side to side 2 to move clumsily in a manner suggesting a waddle

²**waddle** n an awkward clumsy swaying gait

¹**wade** /weɪd/ v 1 to walk through water 2 to proceed with difficulty or effort 3 to attack with determination or vigour – + *in* or *into*

²**wade** n an act of wading

wafer /'weɪfə/ n 1a a thin crisp biscuit; *also* a biscuit consisting of layers of wafer sometimes sandwiched with a filling b a round piece of thin unleavened bread used in the celebration of the Eucharist 2 an adhesive disc of dried paste used, esp formerly, as a seal

¹**wag** /wæg/ v 1 to move to and fro, esp with quick jerky motions 2 to move in chatter or gossip

²**wag** n an act of wagging; a shake

³**wag** n a wit, joker

¹**wage** /weɪdʒ/ v to engage in or carry on (a war, conflict, etc)

²**wage** n 1a a payment for services, esp of a manual kind, usu according to contract and on an hourly, daily, weekly, or piecework basis – usu pl with sing. meaning b pl the share of the national product attributable to labour as a factor in production 2 a recompense, reward

¹**wager** /'weɪdʒə/ n 1 sthg (e g a sum of money) risked on an uncertain event 2 sthg on which bets are laid

²**wager** v to lay as or make a bet

waggon, wagon /'wægən/ n 1 a usu 4-wheeled vehicle for carrying bulky or heavy loads; esp one drawn by horses 2 a railway goods vehicle

¹**wail** /weɪl/ v 1 to express sorrow by uttering mournful cries; lament 2 to express dissatisfaction plaintively; complain

²**wail** n 1 a usu loud prolonged high-pitched cry expressing grief or pain 2 a sound suggestive of wailing

waist /weɪst/ n 1a the (narrow) part of the body between the chest and hips b the greatly constricted part of the abdomen of a wasp, fly, etc 2 the part of sthg corresponding to or resembling the human waist; *esp* the middle part of a sailing ship between foremast and mainmast 3 the part of a garment covering the body at the waist or waistline

waistcoat /'weɪskəʊt, 'weskət/ n, *chiefly Br* a sleeveless garment that fastens down the centre front and usu has a V-neck; *esp* such a garment worn under a jacket as part of a man's suit

¹**wait** /weɪt/ v to remain stationary in readiness or expectation b to pause for another to catch up 2a to look forward expectantly b to hold back expectantly

3 to serve at meals – usu in *wait at table* 4 to be ready and available

wait *n* 1 any of a group who serenade for gratuities, esp at the Christmas season 2 an act or period of waiting

waiter /'weɪtəʳ/ *n fem* **waitress** one who waits at table (e g in a restaurant), esp as a regular job

¹**wake** /weɪk/ *v* **waked, woke; waked, woken, woke** 1 to rouse (as if) from sleep; awake – often + *up* 2 to arouse, evoke 3 to arouse conscious interest in; alert – usu + *to*

²**wake** *n* 1 a watch held over the body of a dead person prior to burial and sometimes accompanied by festivity; *broadly* any festive leavetaking 2 *Br* an annual holiday in northern England – usu pl but sing. or pl in constr

³**wake** *n* the track left by a ship

¹**walk** /wɔːk/ 1a to move along on foot; advance by steps, in such a way that at least 1 foot is always in contact with the ground b to go on foot for exercise or pleasure 2 to take (an animal) for a walk 3 to follow on foot for the purposes of examining, measuring, etc – ~**er** *n*

²**walk** *n* an act or instance of going on foot, esp for exercise or pleasure 2 a route for walking 3 a railed or colonnaded platform 4 distance to be walked 5a the gait of a 2-legged animal in which the feet are lifted alternately with 1 foot always (partially) on the ground b the slow 4-beat gait of a quadruped, specif a horse, in which there are always at least 2 feet on the ground c a low rate of speed 6 a route regularly traversed by a person (e g a postman or policeman) in the performance of a particular activity 7 an occupation, calling – chiefly in *walk of life*

walkover /'wɔːk,əʊvəʳ/ *n* an easily won contest; *also* an advance from one round of a competition to the next without contest, due to the withdrawal or absence of other entrants

¹**wall** /wɔːl/ *n* 1 a usu upright and solid structure, esp of masonry or concrete, having considerable height and length in relation to width and serving esp to divide, enclose, retain, or support: e g a a structure bounding a garden, park, or estate b any of the upright enclosing structures of a room or house 2 a material layer enclosing space 3a an almost vertical rock surface b sthg that acts as a barrier or defence

²**wall** *v* 1a to protect or surround (as if) with a wall b to separate or shut out (as if) by a wall 2a to immure b to close (an opening) (as if) with a wall *USE* (2) usu + *up*

wallet /'wɒlɪt/ *n* 1 a holder for paper money, usu with compartments for other items (e g credit cards and stamps) 2 a flat case or folder

wallflower /'wɔːlflaʊəʳ/ *n* 1 any of several Old World perennial plants of the mustard family; *esp* a hardy erect plant with showy fragrant flowers 2 a woman who fails to get partners at a dance – *infml*

¹**wallpaper** /'wɔːlpeɪpəʳ/ *n* decorative paper for the walls of a room

²**wallpaper** *v* to apply wallpaper to (the walls of a room)

walnut /'wɔːlnʌt/ *n* (an edible nut or the wood of) any of a genus of trees with richly grained wood used for cabinet-making and veneers

¹**waltz** /wɔːls/ *n* (music for or in the tempo of) a ballroom dance in ³₄ time with strong accent on the first beat

²**waltz** *v* 1 to dance a waltz 2 to move *along* in a lively or confident manner 3 to grab and lead (e g a person) unceremoniously; march

wand /wɒnd/ *n* a slender rod a carried as a sign of office b used by conjurers and magicians

wander /'wɒndəʳ/ *v* 1 to go or travel idly or aimlessly 2 to follow or extend along a winding course; meander 3a to deviate (as if) from a course; stray b to lose concentration; stray in thought c to think or speak incoherently or illogically

¹**wandering** /'wɒndərɪŋ/ *n* 1 a going about from place to place 2 movement away from the proper or usual course or place *USE* often pl with sing. meaning

²**wandering** *adj* 1 winding, meandering 2 not keeping a rational or sensible course 3 nomadic

wanderlust /'wɒndəlʌst/ *n* eager longing for or impulse towards travelling

¹**wane** /weɪn/ *v* 1 to decrease in size or extent; dwindle 2 to fall gradually from power, prosperity, or influence; decline

²**wane** *n* 1 the act or process of waning 2 a time of waning; *specif* the period from full phase of the moon to the new moon

¹**want** /wɒnt/ *v* 1 to fail to possess, esp in customary or required amount; lack 2a to have a desire for b to have an inclination to; like 3a to have need of; require b to suffer from the lack of; need 4 to wish or demand the presence of 5 ought – + *to* and infinitive

²**want** *n* 1a the quality or state of lacking sthg required or usual b extreme poverty 2 sthg wanted; a need

¹**war** /wɔːʳ/ *n* 1 a state or period of usu open and declared armed hostile conflict between states or nations 2 a struggle between opposing forces or for a particular end

²**war** *v* 1 to engage in warfare 2 to be in active or vigorous conflict

ward /wɔːd/ *n* 1 a division of a prison or hospital 2 a division of a city or town for electoral or administrative purposes 3 a person under guard, protection, or surveillance; *esp* one under the care or control of a legal guardian

warden /'wɔːdn/ *n* 1 one having care or charge of sthg; a guardian 2 the governor of a town, district, or fortress 3 an official charged with special supervisory duties or with the enforcement of specified laws or regulations 4 any of various British college officials

wardrobe /'wɔːdrəʊb/ *n* 1 a room or

(movable) cupboard, esp fitted with shelves and a rail or pegs, where clothes are kept **2a** a collection of clothes (e g belonging to 1 person) **b** a collection of stage costumes and accessories

warehouse /'weəhaus/ *v or n* (to deposit, store, or stock in) a structure or room for the storage of merchandise or commodities

warfare /'wɔːfeər/ *n* **1** hostilities, war **2** struggle, conflict

warlike /'wɔːlaɪk/ *adj* **1** fond of war **2** of or useful in war **3** hostile

¹**warm** /wɔːm/ *adj* **1a** having or giving out heat to a moderate or adequate degree; *also* experiencing heat to this degree **b** feeling or causing sensations of heat brought about by strenuous exertion **2a** marked by enthusiasm; cordial **b** marked by excitement, disagreement, or anger **3** affectionate and outgoing in temperament **4** dangerous, hostile **5** *of a colour* producing an impression of being warm; *specif* in the range yellow to red **6** near to a goal, object, or solution sought – chiefly in children's games – – ~ish *adj* – ~ly *adv* – – ~ness *n*

²**warm** *v* **1** to make warm **2** to become filled with interest, enthusiasm, or affection – + *to or towards* **3** to reheat (cooked food) for eating – often + *up*

warmth /wɔːmθ/ *n* the quality or state of being warm **a** in temperature **b** in feeling

warn /wɔːn/ *v* **1a** to give notice to beforehand, esp of danger or evil **b** to give admonishing advice to; counsel **2** to order to go or stay away – often + *off or away*

warning /'wɔːnɪŋ/ *n* sthg that warns; *also* a notice

¹**warp** /wɔːp/ *n* **1** a series of yarns extended lengthways in a loom and crossed by the weft **2** a rope for warping a ship or boat **3a** a twist or curve that has developed in sthg formerly flat or straight **b** a mental twist or aberration

²**warp** *v* **1a** to turn or twist (e g planks) out of shape, esp out of a plane **b** to cause to think or act wrongly; pervert **2** to manoeuvre (e g a ship) by hauling on a line attached to a fixed object

¹**warrant** /'wɒrənt/ *n* **1a** a sanction, authorization; *also* evidence for or token of authorization **b** a guarantee, security **c** a ground, justification; *also* proof **2a** a document authorizing an officer to make an arrest, a search, etc **b** an official certificate of appointment issued to a noncommissioned officer

²**warrant** *v* **1** to declare or maintain with certainty **2** to guarantee to be as represented **3** to give sanction to **4a** to prove or declare the authenticity or truth of **b** to give assurance of the nature of or for the undertaking of; guarantee **5** to serve as or give adequate ground or reason for

warrior /'wɒrɪə/ *n* a man engaged or experienced in warfare

wart /wɔːt/ *n* **1** a horny projection on the skin, usu of the hands or feet, caused

by a virus; *also* a protuberance, esp on a plant, resembling this **2** an ugly or objectionable man or boy – chiefly Br schoolboy slang – ~ y *adj*

wary /'weəri/ *adj* marked by caution and watchful prudence in detecting and escaping danger – **warily** *adv* – **wariness** *n*

was /wəz; *strong* wɒz/ *past 1 & 3 sing of* be

¹**wash** /wɒʃ/ *v* **1a** to cleanse (as if) by the action of liquid (e g water) **b** to remove (e g dirt) by applying liquid **c** to wash articles; do the washing **2** *of an animal* to cleanse (fur or a furry part) by licking or by rubbing with a paw moistened with saliva **3** to suffuse with light **4** to flow along, over, or against **5** to move, carry, or deposit (as if) by the force of water in motion **6** to cover or daub lightly with a thin coating (e g of paint or varnish) **7** to gain acceptance; inspire belief – *infml*

²**wash** *n* **1a** (an instance of) washing or being washed **b** articles for washing **2** the surging action of waves **3a** a thin coat of paint (e g watercolour) **4** a lotion

washbasin /'wɒʃ,beɪsən/ *n* a basin or sink usu connected to a water supply for washing the hands and face

washing /'wɒʃɪŋ/ *n* articles, esp clothes, that have been or are to be washed

washing-up *n, chiefly Br* the act or process of washing dishes and kitchen utensils; *also* the dishes and utensils to be washed

wasp /wɒsp/ *n* any of numerous largely flesh-eating slender narrow-waisted insects many of which have an extremely painful sting; *esp* one with black and yellow stripes

WASP, Wasp /wɒsp/ *n* an American of N European, esp British, stock and of Protestant background; *esp* one in North America considered to be a member of the dominant and most privileged class

wastage /'weɪstɪdʒ/ *n* **1a** loss, decrease, or destruction of sthg (e g by use, decay, or leakage); *esp* wasteful or avoidable loss of sthg valuable **b** waste, refuse **2** reduction or loss in numbers (e g of employees or students), usu caused by individuals leaving or retiring voluntarily – esp in *natural wastage*

¹**waste** /weɪst/ *n* **1a** uncultivated land **b** a broad and empty expanse (e g of water) **2** wasting or being wasted **3** gradual loss or decrease by use, wear, or decay **4** material rejected during a textile manufacturing process and used usu for wiping away dirt and oil **5** human or animal refuse

²**waste** *v* **1** to lose weight, strength, or vitality – often + *away* **2** to spend or use carelessly or inefficiently; squander

³**waste** *adj* **1a** uninhabited, desolate **b** not cultivated or used; not productive **2** discarded as refuse **3** serving to conduct or hold refuse material; *specif* carrying off superfluous fluid

wasteful /'weɪstfəl/ *adj* given to or

marked by waste; prodigal -- ~**ly** adv
-- ~**ness** n

waste product n 1 debris resulting from a process (e g of manufacture) that is of no further use to the system producing it 2 material (e g faeces) discharged from, or stored in an inert form in, a living body as a by-product of metabolic processes

¹**watch** /wɒtʃ/ v 1 to remain awake during the night, esp in order to keep vigil 2a to be attentive or vigilant; wait for **b** to keep guard 3a to observe closely, esp in order to check on action or change **b** to look at (an event or moving scene) 4a to take care of; tend **b** to be careful of **c** to take care that 5 to be on the alert for -- ~**er** n

²**watch** n 1a the act of keeping awake or alert to guard, protect, or attend **b** a state of alert and continuous attention; lookout 2 a watchman; also, sing or pl in constr a body of watchmen, specif those formerly assigned to patrol the streets of a town at night 3a a period of keeping guard **b(1)** a period of time during which a part of a ship's company is on duty while another part rests **(2)** sing or pl in constr the part of a ship's company on duty during a particular watch 4 a small portable timepiece powered esp by a spring or battery and usu worn on a wrist

watchdog /'wɒtʃdɒg/ n 1 a dog kept to guard property 2 a person or group (e g a committee) that guards against inefficiency, undesirable practices, etc

watchful /'wɒtʃfəl/ adj carefully observant or attentive -- ~**ly** adv -- ~**ness** n

watchman /'wɒtʃmən/ n sby who keeps watch; a guard

¹**water** /'wɔːtə/ n 1a the colourless odourless liquid that descends from the clouds as rain, forms streams, lakes, and seas, is a major constituent of all living matter, and is an oxide of hydrogen which freezes at 0°C and boils at 100°C 2a(1) pl the water occupying or flowing in a particular bed **(2)** chiefly Br a stretch of sea surrounding and controlled by a country **(2)** the sea of a specified part of the earth -- often pl with sing. meaning **c** a water supply 3 the level of water at a specified state of the tide 4 liquid containing or resembling water; esp a pharmaceutical or cosmetic preparation 5 a wavy lustrous pattern (e g of a textile)

²**water** v 1a to moisten, sprinkle, or soak with water **b** to form or secrete water or watery matter (e g tears or saliva) 2a to supply with water for drink **b** to supply water to 3 to be a source of water for 4 to impart a lustrous appearance and wavy pattern to (cloth) by calendering 5 to dilute (as if) by the addition of water -- often + **down**

water closet n (a room or structure containing) a toilet with a bowl that can be flushed with water

waterfall /'wɔːtəfɔːl/ n a vertical or steep descent of the water of a river or stream

watering can n a vessel having a handle and a long spout often fitted with a rose, used for watering plants

waterlogged /'wɔːtəlɒgd/ adj filled or soaked with water; specif, of a vessel so filled with water as to be (almost) unable to float

¹**waterproof** /'wɔːtəpruːf/ adj impervious to water; esp covered or treated with a material to prevent passage of water

²**waterproof** n (a garment made of) waterproof fabric

³**waterproof** v to make waterproof

watertight /'wɔːtətaɪt/ adj 1 of such tight construction or fit as to be impermeable to water 2 esp of an argument impossible to disprove; without loopholes

watt /wɒt/ n the SI unit of power equal to the power that in 1s gives rise to an energy of 1J

¹**wave** /weɪv/ v 1 to flutter or sway to and fro 2 to direct by waving; signal 3 to move (the hand or an object) to and fro in greeting, farewell, or homage 4 to brandish; flourish

²**wave** n 1 a moving ridge or swell on the surface of a liquid (e g the sea) 2a a shape or outline having successive curves **b** a waviness of the hair **c** an undulating line or streak 3 sthg that swells and dies away: e g **a** a surge of sensation or emotion **b** a movement involving large numbers of people in a common activity 4 a sweep of the hand or arm or of some object held in the hand, used as a signal or greeting 5 a rolling or undulatory movement or any of a series of such movements passing along a surface or through the air 6 a movement like that of an ocean wave: e g **a** a surging movement; an influx **b** sing or pl in constr a line of attacking or advancing troops, aircraft, etc 7 (a complete cycle of) a periodic variation of pressure, electrical or magnetic intensity, electric potential, etc by which energy is transferred progressively from point to point without a corresponding transfer of a medium

wavelength /'weɪvlɛŋð/ n the distance in the line of advance of a wave from any 1 point to the next point of corresponding phase (e g from 1 peak to the next)

waver /'weɪvə/ v 1 to vacillate between choices; fluctuate 2a to sway unsteadily to and fro **b** to hesitate as if about to give way; falter 3 to make a tremulous sound; quaver -- ~**er** n -- ~**ingly** adv

wavy /'weɪvi/ adj 1 having waves 2 having a wavelike form or outline -- **waviness** n

¹**wax** /wæks/ n 1 beeswax 2a any of numerous plant or animal substances that are harder, more brittle, and less greasy than fats **b** a pliable or liquid composition used esp for sealing, taking impressions, or polishing

²**wax** v 1 to increase in size and strength

to increase in phase or intensity **2** *archaic* to assume a specified quality or state; become

³**wax** *n* a fit of temper – *infml*

¹**way** /weɪ/ *n* **1a** a thoroughfare for travel or transport from place to place **b** an opening for passage **c** space or room, esp for forward movement **2** the course to be travelled from one place to another; a route **3a** a course leading in a direction or towards an objective **b** what one desires, or wants to do **4a** the manner in which sthg is done or happens **b** a method of doing or accomplishing; a means **c** a characteristic, regular, or habitual manner or mode of being, behaving, or happening **5** the distance to be travelled in order to reach a place or point **6a** a direction – often in combination **b** (the direction of) the area in which one lives **7** a state of affairs; a condition **8** motion or speed of a ship or boat through the water

²**way** *adv* **1** away **2** *chiefly NAm* all the way

waylay /weɪˈleɪ/ *v* **1** to attack from ambush **2** to accost

wayside /ˈweɪsaɪd/ *n* the side of or land adjacent to a road

we /wi; *strong* wiː/ *pron pl in constr* **1** I and one or more other people **2** I – used, esp formerly, by sovereigns; used by writers to maintain an impersonal character

weak /wiːk/ *adj* **1a** deficient in physical vigour; feeble **b** not able to sustain or exert much weight, pressure, or strain **c** not able to resist external force or withstand attack **2a** lacking determination or decisiveness; ineffectual **b** unable to withstand temptation or persuasion **3** not factually grounded or logically presented **4a** unable to function properly **b** lacking skill or proficiency **5a** deficient in a specified quality or ingredient **b** lacking normal intensity or potency **c** mentally or intellectually deficient **d** deficient in strength or flavour; dilute **6** not having or exerting authority or political power **7** of or constituting a verb (conjugation) that in English forms inflections by adding the suffix *-ed* or *-d* or *-t* – ~**ly** *adv* – ~**en** *v*

weakness /ˈwiːknɪs/ *n* **1** a fault, defect **2** (an object of) a special desire or fondness

wealth /welθ/ *n* **1** the state of being rich **2** abundance of money and valuable material possessions **3** abundant supply; a profusion – ~**y** *adj*

weapon /ˈwepən/ *n* an instrument of offensive or defensive combat – ~**less** *adj* – ~**ry** *n*

¹**wear** /weə/ *v* **wore**; **worn 1a** to have or carry on the body as clothing or adornment **b** to dress in (a particular manner, colour, or garment), esp habitually **2** to have or show on the face **3** to impair, damage, or diminish by use or friction **4** to produce gradually by friction or attrition **5** to exhaust or lessen the strength of; weary **6** *chiefly Br* to find

(a claim, proposal etc) acceptable – *infml* – ~**able** *adj* – ~**er** *n*

²**wear** *n* **1** clothing, usu of a specified kind **2** capacity to withstand use; durability **3** minor damage or deterioration through use

¹**weary** /ˈwɪəri/ *adj* **1** exhausted, tired **2** having one's patience, tolerance, or pleasure exhausted – + *of* **3** wearisome – **wearily** *adv* – **weariness** *n*

²**weary** *v* to make or become weary

weasel /ˈwiːzəl/ *n* any of various small slender flesh-eating mammals with reddish brown fur which, in northern forms, turns white in winter

¹**weather** /ˈweðə/ *n* the prevailing (bad) atmospheric conditions, esp with regard to heat or cold, wetness or dryness, calm or storm, and clearness or cloudiness

²**weather** *v* **1** to expose or subject to atmospheric conditions **2** to bear up against and come safely through

¹**weave** /wiːv/ *v* **wove**; **woven**; **weaved 1a** to form (cloth) by interlacing strands (e g of yarn), esp on a loom **b** to interlace (e g threads) into a fabric, design, etc **c** to make (e g a basket) by intertwining **2a** to produce by elaborately combining elements into a coherent whole **b** to introduce; work in – usu + *in* or *into* – **weave** *n*

²**weave** *v* **weaved** to direct (e g the body or one's way) in a winding or zigzag course, esp to avoid obstacles

¹**web** /web/ *n* **1** a woven fabric; esp a length of fabric still on the loom **2** a spider's web; *also* a similar network spun by various insects **3** a tissue or membrane; *esp* that uniting fingers or toes either at their bases (e g in human beings) or for most of their length (e g in many water birds) **4** an intricate structure suggestive of sthg woven; a network **5** a continuous sheet of paper for use in a printing press

²**web** *v* to entangle, ensnare

wedding /ˈwedɪŋ/ *n* **1** a marriage ceremony, usu with its accompanying festivities **2** a joining in close association **3** a wedding anniversary or its celebration – usu in combination

¹**wedge** /wedʒ/ *n* **1** a piece of wood, metal, etc tapered to a thin edge and used esp for splitting wood or raising heavy objects **2a** (a shoe with) a wedge-shaped sole raised at the heel and tapering towards the toe **b** an iron golf club with a broad face angled for maximum loft **3** sthg causing a breach or separation

²**wedge** *v* **1** to fasten or tighten by driving in a wedge **2** to force or press into a narrow space; cram – usu + *in* or *into*

Wednesday /ˈwenzdi,-deɪ/ *n* the day of the week following Tuesday

¹**weed** /wiːd/ *n* **1** an unwanted wild plant which often overgrows or chokes out more desirable plants **2** an obnoxious growth or thing **3** *Br* a weedy person – *infml*

²**weed** *v* **1** to clear of weeds **2** to remove the undesirable parts of

week /wi:k/ *n* **1a** any of several 7-day cycles used in various calendars **b** a week beginning with a specified day or containing a specified event **2** a period of 7 consecutive days

weekday /'wi:kdeɪ/ *n* any day of the week except (Saturday and) Sunday

¹**weekend** /wi:k'end/ *n* the end of the week; *specif* the period from Friday night to Sunday night

²**weekend** *v* to spend the weekend (e g at a place)

¹**weekly** /'wi:kli/ *adv* every week; once a week; by the week

²**weekly** *adj* **1** occurring, appearing, or done weekly **2** calculated by the week

³**weekly** *n* a weekly newspaper or periodical

¹**weep** /wi:p/ *v* **wept** **1a** to express deep sorrow for, usu by shedding tears; bewail **b** to mourn *for* sby or sthg **2** to pour (tears) from the eyes **3** to exude (a fluid) slowly; ooze

²**weep** *n* a fit of weeping

weeping /'wi:pɪŋ/ *adj, of a tree* (being a variety) having slender drooping branches

weigh /weɪ/ *v* **1** to ascertain the weight of (as if) on a scale to have weight or a specified weight **2** to consider carefully; evaluate – often + *up* **3** to measure (a definite quantity) (as if) on a scale – often + *out* **4** to be a burden or cause of anxiety to – often + *on* or *upon*

weigh down *v* **1** to make heavy **2** to oppress, burden

weigh in *v* to have oneself or one's possessions (e g luggage) weighed; *esp* to be weighed after a horse race or before a boxing or wrestling match

¹**weight** /weɪt/ *n* **1a** the amount that a quantity or body weighs, as measured on a particular scale **b** any of the classes into which contestants in certain sports (e g boxing and wrestling) are divided according to body weight **2a** a quantity weighing a certain amount **b** a heavy object thrown or lifted as an athletic exercise or contest **3a** a system of units of weight **b** any of the units of weight used in such a system **c** a piece of material (e g metal) of known weight for use in weighing articles **4a** sthg heavy; a load **b** a heavy object to hold or press sthg down or to counterbalance **5a** a burden, pressure **b** corpulence **6** relative heaviness **7a** relative importance, authority, or influence **b** *the* main force or strength

²**weight** *v* **1** to load or make heavy (as if) with a weight **2** to oppress with a burden **3** to arrange in such a way as to create a bias

weird /wɪəd/ *adj* of a strange or extraordinary character; odd – *infml* – ~**ly** *adv* – ~**ness** *n*

¹**welcome** /'welkəm/ *interj* – used to express a greeting to a guest or newcomer on his/her arrival

²**welcome** *v* **1** to greet hospitably and with courtesy **2** to greet or receive in the specified, esp unpleasant, way **3** to receive or accept with pleasure

³**welcome** *adj* **1** received gladly into one's presence or companionship **2** giving pleasure; received with gladness, esp because fulfilling a need

⁴**welcome** *n* **1** a greeting or reception on arrival or first appearance **2** the hospitable treatment that a guest may expect

¹**weld** /weld/ *v* **1a** to fuse (metallic parts) together by heating and allowing the metals to flow together or by hammering or compressing with or without previous heating **b** to unite (plastics) in a similar manner by heating or by using a chemical solvent **2** to unite closely or inseparably – ~**er** *n*

²**weld** *n* a welded joint

welfare /'welfeə/ *n* **1** well-being **2** organized efforts to improve the living conditions of the poor, elderly, etc

welfare state *n* (a country operating) a social system based on the assumption by the state of responsibility for the individual and social welfare of its citizens

¹**well** /wel/ *n* **1** (a pool fed by) a spring of water **2** a pit or hole sunk into the earth to reach a supply of water **3** a shaft or hole sunk in the earth to reach a natural deposit (e g oil or gas) **4** an open space extending vertically through floors of a structure **5** a source from which sthg springs **6** *Br* the open space in front of the judge in a law court

²**well** *v* **1** to rise to the surface and usu flow forth **2** to rise to the surface like a flood of liquid

³**well** *adv* **better; best** **1** in a good or proper manner; rightly **2** in a way appropriate to the circumstances; satisfactory, skilfully **3** in a kind or friendly manner; favourably **4** in a prosperous manner (e g he lives *well*) **5a** to an extent approaching completeness; thoroughly (e g after being well dried with a towel) **b** on a close personal level; intimately **6a** easily, fully (e g *well* worth the price) **b** much, considerably (e g *well* over a million) **c** in all likelihood; indeed (e g *well* may be true)

⁴**well** *interj* **1** – used to express surprise, indignation, or resignation **2** – used to indicate a pause in talking or to introduce a remark

⁵**well** *adj* **1** satisfactory, pleasing **2** advisable, desirable **3** prosperous, well-off **4** healthy **5** being a cause for thankfulness; fortunate (e g it is *well* that this has happened)

well-being *n* the state of being happy, healthy, or prosperous

well-known *adj* fully or widely known; *specif* famous

well-off *adj* **1** well-to-do, rich **2** in a favourable or fortunate situation **3** well provided

went /went/ *past of* go

were /wə/; *strong* wɜː/ *past 2 sing, past pl, substandard past 1 & 3 sing, or past subjunctive of* be

¹**west** /west/ *adj or adv* towards, at, belonging to, or coming from the west

²**west** *n* **1** (the compass point corresponding to) the direction 90° to the left

of north that is the general direction of sunset **2** *often cap* regions or countries lying to the west of a specified or implied point of orientation; *esp* the non-Communist countries of Europe and America **3** European civilization in contrast with that of the Orient

¹westerly /'westəli/ *adj or adv* west

²westerly *n* a wind from the west

¹western /'westən/ *adj* **1** *often cap* (characteristic) of a region conventionally designated West: e g **a** of or stemming from European traditions in contrast with those of the Orient **b** of the non-Communist countries of Europe and America **2** west

²western *n*, *often cap* a novel, film, etc dealing with cowboys, frontier life, etc in the W USA, esp during the latter half of the 19th c

¹wet /wet/ *adj* **1** consisting of, containing, or covered with liquid (e g water) **2** rainy **3** still moist enough to smudge or smear **4** involving the use or presence of liquid **5** *chiefly Br* feebly ineffectual or dull – *infml* – ~**ly** *adv* – ~**ness** *n*

²wet *n* **1** moisture, wetness **2** rainy weather; rain **3** *chiefly Br* a wet person; a drip – *infml*

³wet *v* **1** to make wet **2** to urinate in or on

¹whack /wæk/ *vt* **1** to strike with a smart or resounding blow **2** to get the better of; defeat *USE infml*

²whack *n* **1** (the sound of) a smart resounding blow **2** a portion, share **3** an attempt, go *USE infml*

whale /weil/ *n* any of an order of often enormous aquatic mammals that superficially resemble large fish, have tails modified as paddles, and are frequently hunted for oil, flesh, or whalebone

¹what /wɒt/ *pron* **1a(1)** – used as an interrogative expressing inquiry about the identity, nature, purpose, or value of sthg or sby (e g *what* is this?) **(2)** – used to ask for repetition of sthg not properly heard or understood **b** – used as an exclamation expressing surprise or excitement and frequently introducing a question **c** *chiefly Br* – used in demanding assent (e g a clever play, *what*?); not now in vogue **2** that which; the one that (e g no income but *what* he gets from his writing) **3a** WHATEVER 1a **b** how much – used in exclamations (e g *what* it must cost!)

²what *adv* in what respect?; how much?

³what *adj* **1a** which **b** how remarkable or striking – used esp in exclamatory utterances and dependent clauses (e g *what* a suggestion!) **2** the that; as much or as many (e g told him *what* little I knew)

¹whatever /wɒ'tevə'/ *pron* **1a** anything or everything that **b** no matter what **2** what in the world? – *infml*

²whatever *adj* **1a** any that; all that (e g buy peace on *whatever* possible terms) **b** no matter what **2** of any kind at all – used after a noun with *any* or with a negative

wheat /wiːt/ *n* (any of various grasses cultivated in most temperate areas for) a cereal grain that yields a fine white flour and is used for making bread and pasta, and in animal feeds

¹wheel /wiːl/ *n* **1** a circular frame of hard material that may be (partly) solid or spoked and that is capable of turning on an axle **2** a contrivance or apparatus having as its principal part a wheel; *esp* a chiefly medieval instrument of torture to which the victim was tied while his/her limbs were broken by a metal bar **3** sthg resembling a wheel in shape or motion; *esp* a catherine wheel **4a** a curving or circular movement **b** a rotation or turn, usu about an axis or centre; *specif* a turning movement of troops or ships in line in which the units preserve alignment and relative positions **5** *pl* the workings or controlling forces of sthg **6** *pl* a motor vehicle, esp a motor car *USE* (6) *infml*

²wheel *v* **1** to turn (as if) on an axis; revolve **2** to change direction as if revolving on a pivot **3** to move or extend in a circle or curve **4** to alter or reverse one's opinion – often + *about* or *round* **5** to convey or move (as if) on wheels; *esp* to push (a wheeled vehicle or its occupant)

wheelbarrow /'wiːl,bærəʊ/ *n* a load-carrying device that consists of a shallow box supported at 1 end by usu 1 wheel and at the other by a stand when at rest or by handles when being pushed

wheelchair /'wiːltʃeə'/ *n* an invalid's chair mounted on wheels

¹when /wen/ *adv* **1** at what time? **2a** at or during which time **b** and then; whereupon 1

²when *conj* **1a** at or during the time that **b** as soon as **c** whenever **2** in the event that; if **3a** considering that (e g why smoke *when* you know it's bad for you?) **b** in spite of the fact that; although (e g he gave up politics *when* he might have done well)

³when *pron* what or which time (e g since *when* have you known that?)

⁴when *n* a date, time

whence /wens/ *adv or conj* **1a** from where?; from which place, source, or cause? **b** from which place, source, or cause **2** to the place from which *USE* chiefly *fml*

¹whenever /we'nevə'/ *conj* **1** at every or whatever time **2** in any circumstance

²whenever *adv* when in the world? – *infml*

¹where /weə'/ *adv* **1a** at, in, or to what place? (e g *where* is the house?) **b** at, in, or to what situation, direction, circumstances, or respect? (e g *where* does this plan lead?) **2** at, in, or to which (place) (e g the town *where* he lives)

²where *conj* **1a** at, in, or to the place at which (e g stay *where* you are) **b** wherever **c** in a case, situation, or respect in which (e g outstanding *where* endurance is called for) **2** whereas, while

³**where** n 1 what place or point? 2 a place, point – infml

¹**whereabouts** /ˌweərəˈbaʊts/ also **whereabout** adv or conj in what vicinity

²**whereabouts** /ˈweərəbaʊts/ n pl but sing or pl in constr the place or general locality where a person or thing is

whereas /weəˈræz/ conj 1 in view of the fact that; since – used, esp formally, to introduce a preamble 2 while on the contrary; although

whereby /weəˈbaɪ/ conj 1 in accordance with which (e g a law whereby children receive cheap milk) 2 by which means – chiefly fml

whereupon /ˌweərəˈpɒn/ adv or conj closely following and in consequence of which – chiefly fml

¹**wherever** /weəˈrevə/ adv where in the world? – chiefly infml

²**wherever** conj at, in, or to every or whatever place

whether /ˈweðə/ conj – used usu with correlative or or with or whether to indicate a an indirect question involving alternatives (e g decide whether he should protest) b indifference between alternatives (e g seated him next to her, whether by accident or design)

¹**which** /wɪtʃ/ adj 1 being what one or ones out of a known or limited group? (e g which tie should I wear?) 2 whichever 3 – used to introduce a relative clause by modifying the noun which refers either to a preceding word or phrase or to a whole previous clause (e g he may come, in which case I'll ask him)

²**which** pron, pl **which** 1 what one out of a known or specified group? (e g which of those houses do you live in?) 2 whichever 3 – used to introduce relative clause (e g the office in which I work)

¹**whichever** /wɪˈtʃevə/ pron, pl **whichever** 1 whatever one out of a group 2 no matter which 3 which in the world? – chiefly infml

²**whichever** adj being whatever one or ones out of a group; no matter which

¹**whiff** /wɪf/ n 1a a quick puff, slight gust, or inhalation, esp of air, a smell, smoke, or gas 2 a slight trace

²**whiff** v to smell unpleasant – ~y adj

¹**while** /waɪl/ n 1 a period of time, esp when short and marked by the occurrence of an action or condition; a time (e g stay here for a while) 2 the time and effort used; trouble (e g it's worth your while)

²**while** conj 1a during the time that b providing that; as long as 2a when on the other hand; whereas b in spite of the fact that; although (e g while respected, he is not liked)

³**while** prep, archaic or dial until

¹**whine** /waɪn/ v to utter or make a whine

²**whine** n 1 (a sound like) a prolonged high-pitched cry, usu expressive of distress or pain 2 a querulous or peevish complaint

¹**whip** /wɪp/ v 1 to take, pull, jerk, or move very quickly 2a to strike with a whip or similar slender flexible implement, esp as a punishment; also to spank b to drive or urge on (as if) by using a whip 3 to bind or wrap (e g a rope or rod) with cord for protection and strength 4 to oversew (an edge, hem, or seam) using a whipstitch; also to hem or join (e g ribbon or lace) by whipping 5 to beat (e g eggs or cream) into a froth with a whisk, fork, etc 6 to overcome decisively; defeat – infml 7 to snatch suddenly; esp to steal – slang

²**whip** n 1 an instrument consisting usu of a lash attached to a handle, used for driving and controlling animals and for punishment 2 a dessert made by whipping some of the ingredients 3 a light hoisting apparatus consisting of a single pulley, a block, and a rope 4a a member of Parliament or other legislative body appointed by a political party to enforce discipline and to secure the attendance and votes of party members b often cap an instruction (e g a three-line whip or a two-line whip) to each member of a political party in Parliament to be in attendance for voting c (the privileges and duties of) membership of the official parliamentary representation of a political party

¹**whirl** /wɜːl/ v 1 to move along a curving or circling course, esp with force or speed 2 to turn abruptly or rapidly round (and round) on an axis; rotate, wheel 3 to pass, move, or go quickly 4 to become giddy or dizzy; reel

²**whirl** n 1 (sth undergoing or having a form suggestive of) a rapid rotating or circling movement 2a a confused tumult; a bustle b a confused or disturbed mental state; a turmoil 3 an experimental or brief attempt; a try – infml

whirlpool /ˈwɜːlpuːl/ n (sth resembling, esp in attracting or engulfing power) a circular eddy of rapidly moving water with a central depression into which floating objects may be drawn

whirlwind /ˈwɜːlwɪnd/ n 1 a small rapidly rotating windstorm of limited extent marked by an inward and upward spiral motion of the lower air round a core of low pressure 2 a confused rush; a whirl

¹**whisk** /wɪsk/ n 1 a quick light brushing or whipping motion 2a any of various small usu hand-held kitchen utensils used for whisking food b a small bunch of flexible strands (e g twigs, feathers, or straw) attached to a handle for use as a brush

²**whisk** v 1 to convey briskly 2 to mix or fluff up (as if) by beating with a whisk 3 to brandish lightly; flick

whisker /ˈwɪskə/ n 1a a hair of the beard or sideboards b a hair's breadth 2 any of the long projecting hairs or bristles growing near the mouth of an animal (e g a cat)

whisky /ˈwɪski/ n a spirit distilled from fermented mash of rye, corn, wheat, or esp barley

¹**whisper** /ˈwɪspə/ v 1 to speak softly

with little or no vibration of the vocal cords 2 to make a hissing or rustling sound like whispered speech 3 to report or suggest confidentially – ~er n

²**whisper** n 1a whispering; esp speech without vibration of the vocal cords b a hissing or rustling sound like whispered speech 2 a rumour b a hint, trace

¹**whistle** /'wɪsəl/ n 1 a device (e g a small wind instrument) in which the forcible passage of air, steam, the breath, etc through a slit or against a thin edge in a short tube produces a loud sound 2 (a sound like) a shrill clear sound produced by whistling or by a whistle

²**whistle** v 1 to utter a (sound like a) whistle (by blowing or drawing air through the puckered lips) 2 to make a whistle by rapid movement; also to move rapidly (as if) with such a sound 3 to blow or sound a whistle

¹**white** /waɪt/ adj 1a free from colour b of the colour white c light or pallid in colour d of wine light yellow or amber in colour e Br, of coffee served with milk or cream 2 of a group or race characterized by reduced pigmentation 3 of magic not intended to cause harm 4a dressed in white b accompanied by snow 5 reactionary, counterrevolutionary – ~ness n

²**white** n 1 the neutral colour that belongs to objects that reflect diffusely nearly all incident light 2 a white or light-coloured part of sthg: e g a the mass of albumin-containing material surrounding the yolk of an egg b the white part of the ball of the eye c (the player playing) the light-coloured pieces in a two-handed board game 3a pl white (sports) clothing b a white animal (e g a butterfly or pig) 4 sby belonging to a light-skinned race

white-collar adj of or being the class of nonmanual employees whose duties do not call for the wearing of work clothes or protective clothing

white elephant n 1 a property requiring much care and expense and yielding little profit 2 sthg that is no longer of value (to its owner)

¹**whitewash** /'waɪtwɒʃ/ v 1 to apply whitewash to 2a to gloss over or cover up (e g vices or crimes) b to exonerate by concealment or through biased presentation of data 3 to defeat overwhelmingly in a contest or game – infml

²**whitewash** n 1 a liquid mixture (e g of lime and water or whiting, size, and water) for whitening outside walls or similar surfaces 2 a whitewashing

Whitsun /'wɪtsən/ adj or n (of, being, or observed on or at) Whitsunday or Whitsuntide (the 7th Sunday after Easter)

whiz, whizz /wɪz/ v 1 to move (through the air) with a buzz or whirr 2 to move swiftly

who /huː/ pron, pl **who** 1 what or which person or people? 2 – used to introduce relative clause (e g my father who was a lawyer) USE often used as

object of a verb or of a following preposition though still disapproved of by some

whoever /huː'evə/ pron 1 whatever person 2 no matter who 3 who in the world? – chiefly infml USE (1&2) used in any grammatical relation except that of a possessive

¹**whole** /həʊl/ adj 1a free of wound, injury, defect, or impairment; intact, unhurt, or healthy b restored 2 having all its proper constituents; unmodified 3 each or all of; entire 4a constituting an undivided unit; unbroken b directed to (the accomplishment of) 1 end or aim 5 very great – in a whole lot

²**whole** n 1 a complete amount or sum; sthg lacking no part, member, or element 2 sthg constituting a complex unity; a coherent system or organization of parts

wholehearted /,həʊl'hɑːtɪd/ adj earnestly committed or devoted; free from all reserve or hesitation

¹**wholesale** /'həʊlseɪl/ n the sale of commodities in large quantities usu for resale (by a retailer) – ~r n

²**wholesale** adj or adv 1 (sold or selling) at wholesale 2 (performed) on a large scale, esp without discrimination

wholesome /'həʊlsəm/ adj 1 promoting health or well-being of mind or spirit 2 promoting health of body; also healthy – ~ness n

wholly /'həʊl-li/ adv 1 to the full or entire extent; completely 2 to the exclusion of other things; solely

whom /huːm/ pron, objective case of **who** – used as an interrogative or relative; used as object of a preceding preposition (e g for whom the bell tolls); or less frequently as object of a verb or of a following preposition (e g the man whom you wrote to)

¹**whose** /huːz/ adj of whom or which, esp as possessor agent or object of an action (e g whose hat is this; the factory in whose construction they were involved)

²**whose** pron, pl **whose** that which belongs to whom – used without a following noun as a pronoun equivalent in meaning to the adjective whose (e g tell me whose it was)

¹**why** /waɪ/ adv for what cause, reason, or purpose?

²**why** conj 1 the cause, reason, or purpose for which 2 on which grounds

³**why** n, pl **whys** a reason, cause – chiefly in the whys and wherefores

⁴**why** interj – used to express mild surprise, hesitation, approval, disapproval, or impatience

wick /wɪk/ n a cord, strip, or cylinder of loosely woven material through which a liquid (e g paraffin, oil, or melted wax) is drawn by capillary action to the top in a candle, lamp, oil stove, etc for burning

wicked /'wɪkɪd/ adj 1 morally bad; evil 2 disposed to mischief; roguish 3 very unpleasant, vicious, or dangerous – infml – ~ly – ~ness n

wicket /'wɪkɪt/ n 1 a small gate or

door; *esp* one forming part of or placed near a larger one **2a** either of the 2 sets of stumps set 22yd (20.12m) apart, at which the ball is bowled and which the batsman defends in cricket **b** the area 12ft (3.66m) wide bounded by these wickets **c** a partnership between 2 batsmen who are in at the same time

¹**wide** /waɪd/ *adj* **1a** having great horizontal extent; vast **b** embracing much; comprehensive **2a** having a specified width **b** having much extent between the sides; broad **3a** extending or fluctuating over a considerable range **b** distant or deviating from sthg specified **4** *Br* shrewd, astute – *slang* – ~**ly** *adv*

²**wide** *adv* **1** over a great distance or extent; widely **2a** so as to leave much space or distance between **b** so as to miss or clear a point by a considerable distance **3** to the fullest extent; completely – often as an intensive + *open*

³**wide** *n* a ball bowled in cricket that is out of reach of the batsman in his normal position and counts as 1 run to his side

widespread /ˈwaɪdspred/ *adj* **1** widely extended or spread out **2** widely diffused or prevalent

¹**widow** /ˈwɪdəʊ/ *n* **1** a woman whose husband has died (and who has not remarried) **2** a woman whose husband spends much time away from her pursuing a specified (sporting) activity

²**widow** *v* **1** to cause to become a widow **2** to deprive of sthg greatly valued or needed

widower /ˈwɪdəʊə/ *n* a man whose wife has died (and who has not remarried)

width /wɪdθ/ *n* **1** the measurement taken at right angles to the length **2** largeness of extent or scope

wield /wiːld/ *v* **1** to handle (e g a tool) effectively **2** to exert, exercise – ~**er** *n*

wife /waɪf/ *n, pl* **wives** a married woman, *esp* in relation to her husband

wig /wɪg/ *n* a manufactured covering of natural or synthetic hair for the (bald part of a) head

wigwam /ˈwɪgwæm/ *n* a N American Indian hut having a framework of poles covered with bark, rush mats, or hides

¹**wild** /waɪld/ *adj* **1a** (of organisms) living in a natural state and not (ordinarily) tame, domesticated, or cultivated **b** growing or produced without the aid and care of humans **2** not (amenable to being) inhabited or cultivated **3a(1)** free from restraint or regulation; uncontrolled **(2)** emotionally overcome; *also* passionately eager or enthusiastic **(3)** very angry; infuriated **b** marked by great agitation; *also* stormy **c** going beyond reasonable or conventional bounds; fantastic **4** uncivilized, barbaric **5a** deviating from the intended or regular course **b** having no logical basis; random **6** *of a playing card* able to represent any card designated by the holder – ~**ly** *adv* – ~**ness** *n*

²**wild** *n* **1** the wilderness **2** a wild, free, or natural state or existence

³**wild** *adv* in a wild manner: e g **a** without regulation or control **b** off an intended or expected course

wilderness /ˈwɪldən‹s/ *n* **1a** a (barren) region or area that is (essentially) uncultivated and uninhabited by human beings **b** an empty or pathless area or region **c** a part of a garden or nature reserve devoted to wild growth **2** a confusing multitude or mass **3** *the* state of exclusion from office or power

wild-goose chase *n* a hopeless pursuit after sthg unattainable

wildlife /ˈwaɪldlaɪf/ *n* wild animals

wilful /ˈwɪlfəl/ *adj* **1** obstinately and often perversely self-willed **2** done deliberately; intentional – ~**ly** *adv* – ~**ness** *n*

¹**will** /wɪl/ *v, pres sing & pl* **will**; *pres neg* **won't** /wohnt/; *past* **would** /wəd; *strong* wood/ **1** – used to express choice, willingness, or consent or in negative constructions refusal (can find no one who *will* take the job); used in the question form with the force of a request or of an offer or suggestion (e g *will* you have some tea) **2** – used to express custom or inevitable tendency (accidents *will* happen); used with emphatic stress to express exasperation (e g he *will* drink his tea from a saucer) **3** – used to express futurity (e g tomorrow I will get up early) **4** can (e g the back seat will hold 3 passengers) **5** – used to express logical probability (e g that *will* be the milkman) **6** – used to express determination or to command or urge (e g you *will* do as I say at once) **7** to wish, desire (e g whether we *will* or no)

²**will** *n* **1** a desire, wish: e g **a** a resolute intention **b** an inclination **c** a choice, wish **2** what is wished or ordained by the specified agent **3a** a mental power by which one (apparently) controls one's wishes, intentions, etc **b** an inclination to act according to principles or ends **c** a specified attitude towards others **4** willpower, self-control **5** a (written) legal declaration of the manner in which sby would have his/her property disposed of after his/her death

³**will** *v* **1** to bequeath **2a** to determine deliberately; purpose **b** to (attempt to) cause by exercise of the will

¹**willing** /ˈwɪlɪŋ/ *adj* **1** inclined or favourably disposed in mind; ready **2** prompt to act or respond **3** done, borne, or given without reluctance – ~**ly** *adv* – ~**ness** *n*

²**willing** *n* cheerful alacrity – in **show willing**

willow /ˈwɪləʊ/ *n* **1** any of a genus of trees and shrubs bearing catkins of petal-less flowers **2** an object made of willow wood; *esp* a cricket bat – *infml*

willpower /ˈwɪl‚paʊə/ *n* self-control, resoluteness

willy-nilly /ˌwɪli ˈnɪli/ adv or adj **1** by compulsion; without choice **2** (carried out or occurring) in a haphazard or random manner

¹wilt /wɪlt/ archaic pres 2 sing of **will**

²wilt v **1** of a plant to lose freshness and become flaccid; droop **2** to grow weak or faint; languish

³wilt n a disease of plants marked by wilting

wily /ˈwaɪli/ adj full of wiles; crafty

¹win /wɪn/ v **won 1a** to gain the victory in a contest; succeed **b** to be right in an argument, dispute, etc; also to have one's way **2a** to get possession of by qualities or fortune **b** to obtain by effort; earn **3a** to solicit and gain the favour of; also to persuade – usu + over or round **b** to induce (a woman) to accept oneself in marriage **4** to reach by expenditure of effort

²win n **1** a victory or success, esp in a game or sporting contest **2** first place at the finish, esp of a horse race

¹wind /wɪnd/ n **1a** a (natural) movement of air, esp horizontally **2** a force or agency that carries along or influences; a trend **3** breath **4** gas generated in the stomach or the intestines **5a** wind instruments collectively, esp as distinguished from stringed and percussion instruments **b** sing or pl in constr the group of players of such instruments

²wind /wɪnd/ v **1** to make short of breath **2** to rest (e g a horse) in order to allow the breath to be recovered

³wind /waɪnd/ v **winded, wound** to sound (e g a call or note) on a horn

⁴wind v **wound 1** to have a curving course; extend or proceed in curves **2** to coil, twine **3a** to surround or wrap with sthg pliable **b** to tighten the spring of **4** to raise to a high level (e g of excitement or tension) – usu + up

⁵wind n a coil, turn

windfall /ˈwɪndfɔːl/ n **1** sthg, esp a fruit, blown down by the wind **2** an unexpected gain or advantage; esp a legacy

windmill /ˈwɪndˌmɪl/ n **1** a mill operated by vanes that are turned by the wind **2** a toy consisting of lightweight vanes that revolve at the end of a stick

window /ˈwɪndəʊ/ n **1** an opening, esp in the wall of a building, for admission of light and air that is usu fitted with a frame containing glass and capable of being opened and shut **2** a pane (e g of glass) in a window **3** an interval of time within which a rocket or spacecraft must be launched to accomplish a particular mission

windpipe /ˈwɪndpaɪp/ n the trachea – not used technically

windscreen /ˈwɪndskriːn/ n, Br a transparent screen, esp of glass, at the front of a (motor) vehicle

wind up v **1** to bring to a conclusion; specif to bring (a business) to an end by liquidation **2** to put in order; settle

windy /ˈwɪndi/ adj **1a** windswept **b** marked by strong or stormy wind **2** chiefly Br frightened, nervous – infml – **windily** adv – **windiness** n

¹wine /waɪn/ n **1** fermented grape juice containing varying percentages of alcohol together with ethers and esters that give it bouquet and flavour **2** the usu fermented juice of a plant or fruit used as a drink **3** the colour of red wine

²wine v to entertain with or drink wine – usu in wine and dine

¹wing /wɪŋ/ n **1a** (a part of a nonflying bird or insect corresponding to) any of the movable feathered or membranous paired appendages by means of which a bird, bat, or insect flies **b** any of various body parts (e g of a flying fish or flying lemur) providing means of limited flight **2** an appendage or part resembling a wing in shape, appearance, or position: e g **a** a sidepiece at the top of a high-backed armchair **b** any of the aerofoils that develop a major part of the lift which supports a heavier-than-air aircraft **c** Br a mud-guard, esp when forming an integral part of the body of a motor vehicle **3** a means of flight – usu pl with sing. meaning **4** a part of a building projecting from the main or central part **5** pl the area at the side of the stage out of sight of the audience **6a** a left or right flank of an army or fleet **b** any of the attacking positions or players on either side of a centre position in certain team sports **7** sing or pl in constr a group or faction holding distinct opinions or policies within an organized body (e g a political party) **8** an operational and administrative unit of an air force – **~less** adj

²wing v **1** to (enable to) fly or move swiftly **2** to wound (e g with a bullet) without killing

¹wink /wɪŋk/ v **1** to shut 1 eye briefly as a signal or in teasing; also, of an eye to shut briefly **2** to avoid seeing or noting sthg – usu + at **3** to gleam or flash intermittently; twinkle

²wink n **1** a brief period of sleep; a nap **2** an act of winking **3** the time of a wink; an instant **4** a hint or sign given by winking

winner /ˈwɪnə/ n sthg (expected to be) successful – infml

¹winter /ˈwɪntə/ n **1** the season between autumn and spring comprising in the N hemisphere the months December, January, and February **2** the colder part of the year **3** a year – usu pl **4** a period of inactivity or decay – **-try, ~y** adj

²winter adj **1** of, during, or suitable for winter **2** sown in autumn and harvested the following spring or summer

³winter v to keep or feed (e g livestock) during the winter

¹wipe /waɪp/ v **1a** to clean or dry by rubbing, esp with or on sthg soft **b** to draw or pass for rubbing or cleaning **2a** to remove (as if) by rubbing **b** to erase completely; obliterate **3** to spread (as if) by wiping

²wipe n **1** an act or instance of wiping **2** power or capacity to wipe

wipeout /'waɪpaʊt/ *n* a fall from a surfboard caused usu by loss of control

wipe out *v* to destroy completely; annihilate

¹wire /waɪə/ *n* **1** metal in the form of a usu very flexible thread or slender rod **2a** a line of wire for conducting electrical current **b** a telephone or telegraph wire or system **c** a telegram, cablegram **3** a barrier or fence of usu barbed wire

²wire *v* to send or send word to by telegraph

¹wireless /'waɪəll̩s/ *adj, chiefly Br* of radiotelegraphy, radiotelephony, or radio

²wireless *n, chiefly Br* (a) radio

wiry /'waɪəri/ *adj* **1** resembling wire, esp in form and flexibility **2** lean and vigorous; sinewy – **wiriness** *n*

wisdom /'wɪzdəm/ *n* **1a** accumulated learning; knowledge **b** the thoughtful application of learning; insight **2** good sense; judgment

¹wise /waɪz/ *n* manner, way

²wise *adj* **1a** characterized by or showing wisdom; marked by understanding, discernment, and a capacity for sound judgment **b** judicious, prudent **2** well-informed **3** possessing inside knowledge; shrewdly cognizant – often + *to*

¹wish /wɪʃ/ *v* **1** to express the hope that sby will have or attain (sthg); *esp* to bid **2a** to give form to (a wish) **b** to feel or express a wish for; want **c** to request in the form of a wish; order **3** to make a wish

²wish *n* **1a** an act or instance of wishing or desire; a want **b** an object of desire; a goal **2a** an expressed will or desire **b** an expressed greeting – usu pl **3** a ritual act of wishing

wit /wɪt/ *n* **1** reasoning power; intelligence **2a** mental soundness; sanity **b** mental resourcefulness; ingenuity **3a** the ability to relate seemingly disparate things so as to illuminate or amuse **b** a talent for banter or raillery **4** a witty individual **5** *pl* senses

witch /wɪtʃ/ *n* **1** one who is credited with supernatural powers; *esp* a woman practising witchcraft **2** an ugly old woman; a hag – **~ery** *n*

with /wɪð, wɪθ/ *prep* **1a** in opposition to; against (e g had a fight *with* his brother) **b** so as to be separated or detached from (e g I disagree *with* you) **2a** in relation to (e g the frontier *with* Yugoslavia) **b** – used to indicate the object of attention, behaviour, or feeling (e g in love *with* her) **c** in respect to; so far as concerns (e g the trouble *with* this machine) – sometimes used redundantly (e g get it finished *with*) **3a** – used to indicate accompaniment or association **b** – used to indicate one to whom a usu reciprocal communication is made (e g talking *with* a friend) **c** – used to express agreement or sympathy (e g forced to conclude *with* him that it is a forgery) **d** able to follow the reasoning of **4a** on the side of; for **b** employed by **5a** – used to indicate the object of a statement of comparison, equality, or harmony (e g dress doesn't go *with* her shoes) **b** as well as **c** in addition to – used to indicate combination **d** inclusive of (e g costs £5 *with* tax) **6a** by means of; using **b** through the effect of (e g pale *with* anger) **7a** – used to indicate an attendant or contributory circumstance (e g stood there *with* his hat on) **b** in the possession or care of (e g the decision rests *with* you) **8a** – used to indicate a close association in time e g *with* the outbreak of war, they went home) **b** in proportion to (e g the pressure varies *with* the depth) **9a** notwithstanding; in spite of (e g love her *with* all her faults) **b** except for (e g similar, *with* 1 important difference)

withdraw /wɪð'drɔː, wɪθ-/ *v* **1a** to go back or away; retire from participation **b** to retreat **c** to remove money from a place of deposit **2** to become socially or emotionally detached **3** to retract – **~al** *n*

wither /'wɪðə/ *v* **1** to become dry and shrivel (as if) from loss of bodily moisture **2** to lose vitality, force, or freshness **3** to make speechless or incapable of action; stun – **~ing** *adj* – **~ingly** *adv*

withhold /wɪð'həʊld, wɪθ-/ *v* **1** to hold back from action; check **2** to refrain from granting or giving

¹within /wɪ'ðɪn/ *adv* **1** in or into the interior; inside **2** in one's inner thought, mood, or character

²within *prep* **1** inside – used to indicate enclosure or containment, esp in sthg large **2** – used to indicate situation or circumstance in the limits or compass of: e g **a**(1) before the end of (e g gone *within* a week) (2) since the beginning of (e g been there *within* the last week) **b**(1) not beyond the quantity, degree, or limitations of (e g was *within* his income) (2) in or into the scope or sphere of (e g *within* his rights) (3) in or into the range of (e g *within* reach) (4) – used to indicate a specific difference or margin (e g *within* a mile of the town) **3** to the inside of; into

³within *n* an inner place or area

¹without /wɪ'ðaʊt/ *prep* **1** – used to indicate the absence or lack of or freedom from sthg **2** outside – now chiefly poetic

²without *adv* **1** with sthg lacking or absent **2** on or to the exterior; outside – now chiefly poetic

³without *conj, chiefly dial* unless

⁴without *n* an outer place or area

withstand /wɪð'stænd, wɪθ-/ *v* **1** to resist with determination; *esp* to stand up against successfully **2** to be proof against

¹witness /'wɪtnl̩s/ *n* **1** sby who gives evidence, specif before a tribunal **2** sby asked to be present at a transaction so as to be able to testify to its having taken place **3** sby who personally sees or hears an event take place **4** public affirmation by word or example of usu religious faith or conviction

²witness *v* **1** to testify to **2** to act as

legal witness of (e g by signing one's name) **3** to give proof of; betoken – often in the subjunctive **4** to observe personally or directly; see for oneself **5** to be the scene or time of

¹wizard /'wizəd/ n **1** a man skilled in magic **2** one who is very clever or skilful, esp in a specified field – infml

²wizard adj, chiefly Br great, excellent – infml

¹wobble /'wobl/ v **1a** to proceed with an irregular swerving or staggering motion **b** to rock unsteadily from side to side **2** to waver, vacillate

²wobble n **1** an unequal rocking motion **2** an act or instance of vacillating or fluctuating – **wobbly** adj

woeful /'wəʊfəl/ also **woful** adj **1** feeling or expressing woe **2** inspiring woe; grievous – ~**ly** adv

woke /wəʊk/ past of **wake**

woken /'wəʊkən/ past part of **wake**

¹wolf /wʊlf/ n **1** (the fur of) any of various large predatory flesh-eating mammals that resemble the related dogs, prey on livestock, and usu hunt in packs **2** a fiercely rapacious person **3** a man who pursues women in an aggressive way – infml – ~**ish** adj

²wolf v to eat greedily; devour – often + down

woman /'wʊmən/ n, pl **women 1a** an adult female human as distinguished from a man or child **b** a woman belonging to a particular category (e g by birth, residence, membership, or occupation) – usu in combination **2** womankind **3** distinctively feminine nature; womanliness **4** a personal maid, esp in former times – ~**ly**

womb /wuːm/ n **1** the uterus **2** a place where sthg is generated

won /wʌn/ past of **win**

¹wonder /'wʌndə/ n **1a** a cause of astonishment or admiration; a marvel **b** a miracle **2** rapt attention or astonishment at sthg unexpected, strange, new to one's experience, etc

²wonder adj noted for outstanding success or achievement – ~**ingly** adv

³wonder v **1** to be in a state of wonder; marvel at **b** to feel surprise **2** to feel curiosity or doubt; speculate

wonderful /'wʌndəfəl/ adj **1** exciting wonder; astonishing **2** unusually good; admirable – ~**ly** adv

¹wood /wʊd/ n **1** a dense growth of trees, usu greater in extent than a copse and smaller than a forest – often pl with sing. meaning **2a** a hard fibrous plant tissue that makes up the greater part of the stems and branches of trees or shrubs beneath the bark **b** wood suitable or prepared for some use (e g burning or building) **3a** a golf club with a wooden head **b** a wooden cask **c** any of the large wooden bowls used in the sport of bowling

²wood adj **1** wooden **2** suitable for cutting, storing, or carrying wood

wooden /'wʊdən/ adj **1** made or consisting of or derived from wood **2** lacking ease or flexibility; awkwardly stiff

woodland /'wʊdlənd, -lænd/ n land

covered with trees, scrub, etc – often pl with sing. meaning

woodwind /'wʊd,wɪnd/ n **1** any of a group of wind instruments (e g a clarinet, flute, or saxophone) that is characterized by a cylindrical or conical tube of wood or metal, usu with finger holes or keys, that produces notes by the vibration of a single or double reed or by the passing of air over a mouth hole **2** sing or pl in constr the woodwind section of a band or orchestra – often pl with sing. meaning

woodwork /'wʊdwɜːk/ n **1** wooden interior fittings (e g mouldings or stairways) **2** the craft of constructing things from wood

wool /wʊl/ n **1** the soft wavy coat of various hairy mammals, esp the sheep **2** a dense felted hairy covering, esp on a plant **3** a wiry or fibrous mass (e g of steel or glass) – usu in combination – ~**len** adj

¹woolly /'wʊli/ NAm also **wooly** adj **1** (made) of or resembling wool; also bearing (sthg like) wool **2a** lacking in clearness or sharpness of outline **b** marked by mental vagueness or confusion **3** boisterously rough – chiefly in wild and woolly – **-liness** n

²woolly, woolie, NAm also **wooly** n, chiefly Br a woollen jumper or cardigan

¹word /wɜːd/ n **1a** sthg that is said **b** pl talk, discourse **c** a short remark, statement, or conversation **2** a meaningful unit of spoken language that can stand alone as an utterance and is not divisible into similar units; also a written or printed representation of a spoken word that is usu set off by spaces on either side **3** an order, command **4** the expressed or manifested mind and will of God; esp a Gospel **5a** news, information **b** rumour **6** the act of speaking or of making verbal communication **7** a promise **8** pl a quarrelsome utterance or conversation **9** a verbal signal; a password **10** the most appropriate description – ~**less** adj – ~**lessly** adv – ~**lessness** n

²word v to express in words; phrase

wording /'wɜːdɪŋ/ n the act or manner of expressing in words

wore /wɔː/ past of **wear**

¹work /wɜːk/ n **1a** sustained physical or mental effort to achieve a result **b** the activities that afford one's accustomed means of livelihood (e g a specific task, duty, function, or assignment **2a** (the result of) expenditure of energy by natural phenomena **b** the transference of energy that is produced by the motion of the point of application of a force and is measured by the product of the force and the distance moved along the line of action **3a** (the result of) a specified method of working – often in combination **b** sthg made from a specified material – often in combination **4b** pl structures in engineering (e g docks, bridges, or embankments) or mining (e g shafts or tunnels) **5** pl but sing or pl in constr a place where industrial activity is carried out; a factory – often in combination **6** *pl* the working or moving parts of a mechanism **7** an artistic production or creation **8a** effective operation; an effect, result **b** activity, behaviour, or experience of the specified kind **9** *pl* everything possessed, available, or belonging – *infml*; + *the* **b** subjection to all possible abuse – *infml*; usu + *get or give*

²**work** *adj* **1** suitable for wear while working **2** used for work

³**work** *v* **worked, wrought** **1** to bring to pass; effect **2a** to fashion or create sthg by expending labour on; forge, shape **b** to make or decorate with needlework; embroider **c** to prepare or form into a desired state for use by kneading, hammering, etc **3** to operate **4** to solve (a problem) by reasoning or calculation – usu + *out* **6** to carry on an operation in (a place or area) **7a** to manoeuvre (oneself or an object) gradually or with difficulty into or out of a specified condition or position **b** to contrive, arrange

worker /'wɜːkə/ *n* **1a** one who works, esp at manual or industrial work or with a particular material – often in combination **b** a member of the working class **2** any of the sexually underdeveloped usu sterile members of a colony of ants, bees, etc that perform most of the labour and protective duties of the colony

working class *n sing or pl in constr* the class of people who work (manually) for wages – often *pl* with sing. meaning

workman /'wɜːkmən/ *n* an artisan

workout /'wɜːkaut/ *n* a practice or exercise to test or improve fitness, ability, or performance, esp for sporting competition

work out *v* **1a** to find out by calculation **b** to amount to a total or calculated figure – often + *at or to* **2** to devise by resolving difficulties **3** to elaborate in detail

works /wɜːks/ *adj* of a place of industrial labour

workshop /'wɜːkʃɒp/ *n* **1** a room or place (e g in a factory) in which manufacture or repair work is carried out **2** a brief intensive educational programme for a relatively small group of people in a given field that emphasizes participation

¹**world** /wɜːld/ *n* **1** the earth with its inhabitants and all things on it **2** the course of human affairs **3** the human race **4** the concerns of earthly existence or secular affairs as distinguished from heaven and the life to come or religious and ecclesiastical matters **5** the system of created things; the universe **6** a distinctive class of people or their sphere of interest **7a** human society as a whole; *also* the public **b** fashionable or respectable people; public opinion **8** a part or section of the earth that is a separate independent unit **9a** one's personal environment in the sphere of one's life or work **b** a particular aspect of one's life **10** an indefinite multitude or a great

quantity or amount **11** a planet; *esp* one that is inhabited **USE** (*except* 10 & 11) + *the*

²**world** *adj* **1** of the whole world **2** extending or found throughout the world; worldwide

worldwide /,wɜːld'waɪd/ *adj* extended throughout or involving the entire world

¹**worm** /wɜːm/ *n* **1a** an earthworm **b** any of numerous relatively small elongated soft-bodied invertebrate animals **2** a human being who is an object of contempt, loathing, or pity; a wretch **3** infestation with or disease caused by parasitic worms – usu *pl* with sing. meaning but sing. or *pl* in constr **4** the thread of a screw

²**worm** *v* **1a** to cause to move or proceed (as if) in the manner of a worm **b** to insinuate or introduce (oneself) by devious or subtle means **2** to obtain or extract by artful or insidious questioning or by pleading, asking, or persuading – usu + *out of*

worn /wɔːn/ *past part of* **wear**

worn-out *adj* exhausted or used up (as if) by wear

¹**worry** /'wʌri/ *v* **1** to shake or pull at with the teeth **2** to work at sthg difficult **3a** to feel or experience concern or anxiety; fret **b** to subject to persistent or nagging attention or effort **4** to afflict with mental distress or agitation; make anxious – ~**ingly** *adv*

²**worry** *n* **1** mental distress or agitation resulting from concern, usu for sthg impending or anticipated; anxiety **2** a cause of worry; a trouble, difficulty – -**ried** *adj* – -**riedly** *adv*

¹**worse** /wɜːs/ *adj, comparative of* **bad** *or* **ill** **1** of lower quality **2** in poorer health

²**worse** *n, pl* **worse** sthg worse

³**worse** *adv, comparative of* **bad, badly,** *or* **ill** in a worse manner; to a worse extent or degree

¹**worship** /'wɜːʃɪp/ *n* **1** (an act of) reverence offered to a divine being or supernatural power **2** a form of religious practice with its creed and ritual **3** extravagant admiration for or devotion to an object of esteem **4** *chiefly Br* a person of importance – used as a title for various officials (e g magistrates and some mayors)

²**worship** *v* **1** to honour or reverence as a divine being or supernatural power **2** to regard with great, even extravagant respect, honour, or devotion – ~**per** *n*

¹**worst** /wɜːst/ *adj, superlative of* **bad** *or* **ill** **1** most productive of evil **2** most wanting in quality

²**worst** *n, pl* **worst** **1** the worst state or part **2** sby or sthg that is worst **3** the utmost harm of which one is capable (e g do your *worst*)

³**worst** *adv, superlative of* **bad, badly,** *or* **ill** in the worst manner; to the worst extent or degree

⁴**worst** *v* to get the better of; defeat

¹**worth** *prep* **1a** equal in value to **b** having property equal to (e h he's *worth*

£1,000,000) **2** deserving of – **~less** *adj*
– **~lessly** *adj* – **~lessness** *adv*

²**worth** *n* **1a** (money) value **b** the equivalent of a specified amount or figure (e g 3 quids*worth* of petrol) **2** moral or personal merit, esp high merit

worthwhile /,wɜːð'waɪl/ *adj* worth the time or effort spent

¹**worthy** /'wɜːðɪ/ *adj* **1a** having moral worth or value **b** honourable, meritorious **2** important enough; deserving – **-thily** *adv* – **-thiness** *n*

²**worthy** *n* a worthy or prominent person – often humor

would /wod/ *past of* **will 1a** to desire, wish **b** – used in auxiliary function with *rather* or *soon*, *sooner* to express preference **2a** – used in auxiliary function to express wish, desire, or intent (e g those who *would* forbid gambling); used in the question form with the force of a polite request or of an offer or suggestion (e g *would* you like some tea?) **b** – used in auxiliary function in reported speech or writing to represent *shall* or *will* (e g said he *would* come) **3a** used to (e g we *would* meet often for lunch) – used with emphatic stress to express exasperation **b** – used in auxiliary function with emphatic stress as a comment on the annoyingly typical (e g you *would* say that) **4** – used in auxiliary function to introduce a contingent fact, possibility, or presumption (e g it *would* break if you dropped it) or after a verb expressing desire, request, or advice (e g wish he *would* go) **5** could (e g door *wouldn't* open) **6** – used in auxiliary function to soften direct statement (e g that *would* be the milkman)

¹**wound** /wuːnd/ *n* **1** an injury to the body or to a plant (e g from violence or accident) that involves tearing or breaking of a membrane (e g the skin) and usu damage to underlying tissues **2** a mental or emotional hurt or blow

²**wound** /wuːnd/ *v* to cause a wound to or in

³**wound** /waʊnd/ *past of* **wind**

wove /wəʊv/ *past of* **weave**

²**wove** *n* paper made in such a way that no fine lines run across the grain

woven /'wəʊvən/ *past part of* **weave**

¹**wrap** /ræp/ *v* **1a** to envelope, pack, or enfold in sthg flexible **b** to fold round sthg specified **2** to involve completely; engross – usu + *up*

²**wrap** *n* **1** a wrapping; *specif* a waterproof wrapping placed round food to be frozen, esp in a domestic freezer **2** an article of clothing that may be wrapped round a person; *esp* an outer garment (e g a shawl)

wreath /riːθ/ *n* **1** sthg intertwined into a circular shape; *esp* a garland **2** a drifting and coiling whorl

¹**wreck** /rek/ *n* **1** sthg cast up on the land by the sea, esp after a shipwreck **2a** (a) shipwreck **b** destruction **3a** the broken remains of sthg (e g a building or vehicle) wrecked or ruined **b** a person or animal of broken constitution, health, or spirits

²**wreck** *v* **1** to cast ashore **2a** to reduce to a ruinous state by violence **b** to cause (a vessel) to be shipwrecked **c** to involve in disaster or ruin

wreckage /'rekɪdʒ/ *n* **1** wrecking or being wrecked **2** broken and disordered parts or material from a wrecked structure

¹**wrench** /rentʃ/ *v* **1** to pull or twist violently **2** to injure or disable by a violent twisting or straining **3** to distort, pervert **4** to snatch forcibly; wrest

²**wrench** *n* **1a** a violent twisting or a sideways pull **b** (a sharp twist or sudden jerk causing) a strain to a muscle, ligament, etc (e g of a joint) **2** a spanner with jaws adjustable for holding nuts of different sizes

wrestle /'resəl/ *v* **1** to fight hand-to-hand without hitting with the aim of throwing or immobilizing an apponent **2** to push, pull, or manhandle by force – **-tling** *n*

wretch /retʃ/ *n* **1** a profoundly unhappy or unfortunate person **2** a base, despicable, or vile person or animal – **~ed** *adj* – **~edly** *adv* – **~edness** *n*

¹**wriggle** /'rɪgəl/ *v* **1** to move the body or a bodily part to and fro with short writhing motions; squirm **2** to move or advance by twisting and turning **3** to extricate or insinuate oneself by manoeuvring, equivocation, evasion, etc

²**wriggle** *n* a short or quick writhing motion or contortion

wring /rɪŋ/ *v* **wrung 1** to twist or compress, esp so as to extract liquid **2** to exact or extort by coercion or with difficulty **3** to twist together (one's clasped hands) as a sign of anguish **4** to distress, torment **5** to shake (sby's hand) vigorously in greeting

¹**wrinkle** /'rɪŋkəl/ *n* **1** a small ridge, crease, or furrow formed esp in the skin due to aging or stress or on a previously smooth surface (e g by shrinkage or contraction) **2** a valuable trick or dodge for effecting a result – infml – **-kly** *adj*

²**wrinkle** *v* to contract into wrinkles

wrist /rɪst/ *n* **1** (a part of a lower animal corresponding to) the (region of the) joint between the human hand and the arm **2** the part of a garment or glove covering the wrist

wristwatch /'rɪstwɒtʃ/ *n* a small watch attached to a bracelet or strap and worn round the wrist

write /raɪt/ *v* **wrote 1a** to form (legible characters, symbols, or words) on a surface, esp with an instrument **b** to spell in writing **c** to cover, fill, or fill in by writing **2** to set down in writing: e g **a** to be the author of; compose **b** to use (a specific script or language) in writing

write-off *n* sthg written off as a total loss

write off *v* **1** to cancel **2** to concede to be irreparably lost, useless, or dead

writer /'raɪtə/ *n* one who writes as an occupation; an author

writing /'raɪtɪŋ/ n **1** the act, practice, or occupation of literary composition **2a** written letters or words; esp handwriting **b** a written composition

¹**wrong** /rɒŋ/ n **1** an injurious, unfair, or unjust act; action or conduct inflicting harm without due provocation or just cause **2** what is wrong, immoral, or unethical **3a** the state of being mistaken or incorrect **b** the state of being or appearing to be the offender

²**wrong** adj **1** against moral standards; evil **2** not right or proper according to a code, standard, or convention; improper **3** not according to truth or facts; incorrect; also in error; mistaken **4** not satisfactory (e g in condition, results, health, or temper) **5** not in accordance with one's needs, intent, or expectations **6** of or being the side of sthg not meant to be used or exposed or thought the less desirable – ~**ly** adv

³**wrong** adv **1** without accuracy; incorrectly **2** without regard for what is proper **3** on a mistaken course; astray **4** out of proper working order

⁴**wrong** v **1** to do wrong to; injure, harm **2** to mistakenly impute a base motive to; misrepresent

wrote /rəʊt/ past of **write**

wrung /rʌŋ/ past of **wring**

wry /raɪ/ adj **1** bent or twisted, esp to one side **2** ironically or grimly humorous – ~**ly** adv

X

xerox /'zɪərɒks, 'ze-/ v, often cap to photocopy

Xmas /'krɪsməs, 'eksməs/ n Christmas

x-ray /'eks reɪ/ v, often cap x to examine, treat, or photograph with X rays

X ray n **1** an electromagnetic radiation of extremely short wavelength that has the properties of ionizing a gas when passing through it and of penetrating various thicknesses of all solids **2** an examination or photograph made by means of X rays

Y

¹**yacht** /jɒt/ n any of various relatively small sailing or powered vessels that characteristically have a sharp prow and graceful lines and are used for pleasure cruising or racing

²**yacht** v to race or cruise in a yacht

¹**yard** /jɑːd/ n **1a** a unit of length equal to 3ft (about 0.914m) **b** a unit of volume equal to 1yd³ (about 0.765m³) **2** a long spar tapered towards the ends to support and spread a sail

²**yard** n **1a** a small usu walled and often paved area open to the sky and adjacent to a building; a courtyard **b** the grounds of a specified building or group of buildings – in combination **2a** an area with its buildings and facilities set aside for a specified business or activity – often in combination **b** a system of tracks for the storage and maintenance of railway carriages and wagons and the making up of trains **3** cap, Br Scotland Yard – + the **4** NAm a garden of a house

³**yard** v to drive into or confine in a restricted area; herd, pen

¹**yarn** /jɑːn/ n **1** thread; esp a spun thread (e g of wool, cotton, or hemp) as prepared and used for weaving, knitting, and rope-making **2a** a narrative of adventures; esp a tall tale **b** a conversation, chat USE (2) infml

²**yarn** v to tell a yarn; also to chat garrulously – infml

¹**yawn** /jɔːn/ v **1** to open wide; gape **2** to open the mouth wide and inhale, usu in reaction to fatigue or boredom

²**yawn** n **1** a deep usu involuntary intake of breath through the wide open mouth **2** a boring thing or person – slang

year /jɪəʳ, jɜːʳ/ n **1a** the period of about 365¼ solar days required for 1 revolution of the earth round the sun **b** the time required for the apparent sun to return to an arbitrary fixed or moving reference point in the sky **2a** a cycle in the Gregorian calendar of 365 or 366 days divided into 12 months beginning with January and ending with December **b** a period of time equal to 1 year of the Gregorian calendar but beginning at a different time **3** a calendar year specified usu by a number **4** pl age; also old age

yearly /'jɪəli, 'jɜː-/ adj **1** reckoned by the year **2** done or occurring once every year; annual

yearn /jɜːn/ v **1** to long persistently, wistfully, or sadly **2** to feel tenderness or compassion – ~**ing** n

yeast /jiːst/ n **1** a (commercial preparation of) yellowish surface froth or sediment that consists largely of fungal cells, occurs esp in sweet liquids in which it promotes alcoholic fermentation, and is used esp in making alcoholic drinks and as a leaven in baking **2** a minute fungus that is present and functionally active in yeast, usu has little or no mycelium, and reproduces by budding

¹**yell** /jel/ v to utter a sharp loud cry, scream, or shout

²**yell** n a scream, shout

¹**yellow** /'jeləʊ/ adj **1a** of the colour yellow **b** yellowish through age, disease, or discoloration; sallow **2a** featuring sensational or scandalous items or ordinary news sensationally distorted **b** dishonourable, cowardly – infml

²**yellow** v to make or become yellow – ~**ish** adj

³**yellow** n **1** a colour whose hue resembles that of ripe lemons or dandelions and lies between green and orange in the spectrum **2** sthg yellow: esp the yolk of an egg

¹yes /jes/ *adv* **1** – used in answers expressing affirmation, agreement, or willingness; contrasted with *no* **2** – used in answers correcting or contradicting a negative assertion or direction

²yes *n* an affirmative reply or vote; an aye

¹yesterday /'jestədi, -deɪ/ *adv* on the day before today

²yesterday *n* **1** the day before today **2** recent time; time not long past

¹yet /jet/ *adv* **1a** again; in addition **b** (e g a *yet* higher speed) **2a** up to this or that time; so far – not in affirmative statements **b** still (e g while it was *yet* dark) **c** at some future time and despite present appearances (e g we may win *yet*) **3** nevertheless (e g strange and *yet* true)

²yet *conj* but nevertheless

¹yield /jiːld/ *v* **1** to give or render as fitting, rightfully owed, or required **2** to give up possession of on claim or demand: e g **a** to surrender or submit (oneself) to another **b** to give (oneself) up to an inclination, temptation, or habit **3a** to bear or bring forth as a natural product **b** to give as a return or in result of expended effort **c** to produce as revenue **4** to give way under physical force (e g by bending, stretching, or breaking) **5** to give place or precedence; acknowledge the superiority of another

²yield *n* the capacity of yielding produce; *also* the produce yielded

yoga /'jəʊgə/ *n* **1** *cap* a Hindu philosophy teaching the suppression of all activity of body, mind, and will so that the self may attain liberation from them **2** a system of exercises for attaining bodily or mental control and well-being

¹yoke /jəʊk/ *n* **1a** a bar or frame by which 2 draught animals (e g oxen) are joined at the heads or necks for working together **b** a frame fitted to sby's shoulders to carry a load in 2 equal portions **2** *sing or pl in constr* 2 animals yoked or worked together **3a** an oppressive agency **b** a tie, link; *esp* marriage **4** a fitted or shaped piece at the top of a garment from which the rest hangs

²yoke *v* **1** to attach (a draught animal) to (sthg) **2** to join (as if) by a yoke

yolk /jəʊk/ *also* **yoke** *n* the usu yellow round mass of stored food that forms the inner portion of the egg of a bird or reptile and is surrounded by the white

you /jə, jʊ; *strong* juː/ *pron, pl* **you 1** the one being addressed – used as subject or object; **2** a person; one

¹young /jʌŋ/ *adj* **1** in the first or an early stage of life, growth, or development **2** recently come into being; new **3** of or having the characteristics (e g vigour or gaiety) of young people – ~ish *adj*

²young *n pl* **1** young people; youth **2** immature offspring, esp of an animal

youngster /'jʌŋstə/ *n* **1** a young person or creature **2** a child, baby

your /jə; *strong* jɔː/ *adj* **1** of you or yourself or yourselves, esp as possessor,

agent or object of an action – used with certain titles in the vocative (e g *your* Eminence) **2** of one or oneself (e g when you face north, east is on *your* right) **3** – used for indicating sthg well-known and characteristic; *infml* (e g *your* typical commuter) *USE* used attributively

yours /jɔːz/ *pron, pl* **yours** that which or the one who belongs to you – used without a following noun as a pronoun equivalent in meaning to the adjective *your* in the

yourself /jɔː'self/ *pron, pl* **yourselves 1a** that identical person or creature that is you – used reflexively, for emphasis, or in absolute constructions (e g *yourself* a man of learning, you will know what I mean) **b** your normal self (e g you'll soon be *yourself* again) **2** oneself

youth /juːð/ *n* **1** the time of life when one is young; *esp* adolescence **2a** a young male adolescent **b** young people – often *pl* in constr **3** the quality of being youthful – ~ful *adj* – ~fully *adv* – ~fulness *n*

Z

zeal /ziːl/ *n* eagerness and ardent interest in pursuit of sthg; keenness

zebra /'ziːbrə, 'ze-/ *n* any of several black and white striped fast-running African mammals related to the horse

zebra crossing *n* a crossing in Britain marked by a series of broad white stripes to indicate that pedestrians have the right of way across a road

¹zero /'zɪərəʊ/ *n, pl* **zeros** *also* **zeroes 1** the arithmetical symbol 0 or denoting the absence of all magnitude or quantity **2** the number 0 **3** the point of departure in reckoning; *specif* the point from which the graduation of a scale begins **4a** nothing **b** the lowest point

²zero *adj* having no magnitude or quantity

³zero *v* to move near to or to focus attention as if on a target; close – usu + *in on*

¹zigzag /'zɪgzæg/ *n* a line, course, or pattern consisting of a series of sharp alternate turns or angles

²zigzag *adj* forming or going in a zigzag; consisting of zigzags

³zigzag *v* to proceed along or consist of a zigzag course

zinc /zɪŋk/ *n* a bluish white bivalent metallic element that occurs abundantly in minerals and is used esp as a protective coating for iron and steel

¹zip /zɪp/ *v* **1** to move with speed and vigour **2** to become open, closed, or attached by means of a zip **3** to travel (as if) with a sharp hissing or humming sound **4** to add zest or life to – often + *up*

²zip *n* **1** a light sharp hissing sound **2** energy, liveliness **3** *chiefly Br* a fastener that joins 2 edges of fabric by means of 2 flexible spirals or rows of teeth brought together by a sliding clip

zodiac /'zəʊdiæk/ *n* an imaginary belt in the heavens that encompasses the apparent paths of all the principal planets except Pluto, has the ecliptic as its central line, and is divided into 12 constellations or signs each taken for astrological purposes to extend 30 degrees of longitude – ~**al** *adj*

Zombie /'zɒmbi/ *n* **1** a human in W Indies voodooism who is held to have died and have been reanimated **2** a person resembling the walking dead; a shambling automaton

¹zone /zəʊn/ *n* **1** any of 5 great divisions of the earth's surface with respect to latitude and temperature **2** a distinctive layer of rock or other earth materials **3** an area distinct from adjoining parts **4** any of the sections into which an area is divided for a particular purpose – -**nal** *adj*

²zone *v* **1** to arrange in, mark off, or partition into zones **2** to assign to a zone

zoo /zuː/ *n, pl* **zoos** a collection of living animals usu open to the public

¹zoom /zuːm/ *v* **1** to move with a loud low hum or buzz **2** to rise sharply

²zoom *n* **1** an act or process of zooming **2** a photographic lens that can be used to move quickly from a distant shot into close-up